This is an authoritative and valuable contribution to the discussion surrounding the way in which the criminal law deals with homicide offences. It should be read by anyone researching this increasingly complex area of law.

Christopher J. Newman, University of Sunderland, UK

Homicide in Criminal law is a sophisticated account of a range of conceptual problems in the law of homicide. The text, both intellectually challenging yet immensely readable, provides a feast of ethical, philosophical and practical reflection for serious students of criminal law. An admirable addition to Bohlander and Reed's collaborative series on substantive criminal law.

Warren Brookbanks, Auckland University of Technology, New Zealand

Homicide in Criminal Law

This volume presents a leading contribution to the substantive arena relating to homicide in the criminal law. In broad terms, the ambit of homicide standardisations in extant law is contestable and opaque. This book provides a logical template to focus the debate. The overall concept addresses three specific elements within this arena, embracing an overarching synergy between them. This edifice engages in an examination of UK provisions, and in contrasting these provisions against alternative domestic jurisdictions as well as comparative contributions addressing a particularised research grid for content. The comparative chapters provide a wider background of how other legal systems treat a variety of specialised issues relating to homicide in the context of the criminal law.

The debate in relation to homicide continues apace for academics, practitioners and within the criminal justice system. Having expert descriptions of the wider issues surrounding the particular discussion and of other legal systems' approaches serves to stimulate and inform that debate. This collection will be a major source of reference for future discussion.

Alan Reed is Associate Pro Vice Chancellor (Research and Innovation) in the Faculty of Business and Law at the University of Northumbria. He is a Professor of Criminal and Private International Law, and Editor of *The Journal of Criminal Law*.

Michael Bohlander is the International Co-Investigating Judge at the Extraordinary Chambers in the Courts of Cambodia. He holds the Chair of Comparative and International Criminal Law at Durham Law School.

Nicola Wake is Associate Professor in Law and Deputy Director for Northumbria Centre for Evidence and Criminal Justice Studies.

Emma Engleby is a Senior Lecturer in Law at Northumbria University. Her research interests are in Criminal Evidence, specifically in the use and admissibility of character evidence.

Verity Adams is a barrister at Trinity Chambers currently completing a PhD at the University of Durham. Her research interests are in Criminal Law and Evidence, Immigration and Public International Law.

Substantive Issues in Criminal Law

Substantive Issues in Criminal Law presents a series of volumes that systematically address areas of the criminal law that are in need of reform or which belong to the core areas of law where doctrinal abstraction or greater analysis is required. One part of each book is dedicated to an in-depth look at the situation in the UK, with individual chapters analysing points of current interest. A second feature of each volume is a major comparative section of other domestic jurisdictions. These international contributions are written to a uniform research grid provided by the editors in order to ensure a maximum degree of ease of comparison. The key purpose of the series is to produce a major library of reference works to which all actors in the wider criminal justice and policy community in the UK and elsewhere will have recourse for academic, judicial and policy purposes.

Series Editors:
Alan Reed and Michael Bohlander

Other titles in this series:

Participation in Crime
Domestic and Comparative Perspectives
Edited by Alan Reed and Michael Bohlander

General Defences in Criminal Law
Domestic and Comparative Perspectives
Edited by Alan Reed and Michael Bohlander with Nicola Wake and Emma Smith

Consent: Domestic and Comparative Perspectives
Edited by Alan Reed and Michael Bohlander with Nicola Wake and Emma Smith

Homicide in Criminal Law
A Research Companion
Edited by Alan Reed and Michael Bohlander with Nicola Wake, Emma Engleby and Verity Adams

For more information about this series, please visit: www.routledge.com/Substantive-Issues-in-Criminal-Law/book-series/ASHSER1396

Homicide in Criminal Law

A Research Companion

Edited by
Alan Reed and Michael Bohlander with
Nicola Wake, Emma Engleby and Verity Adams

Routledge
Taylor & Francis Group
LONDON AND NEW YORK

First published 2019
by Routledge
2 Park Square, Milton Park, Abingdon, Oxon OX14 4RN

and by Routledge
52 Vanderbilt Avenue, New York, NY 10017

First issued in paperback 2020

Routledge is an imprint of the Taylor & Francis Group, an informa business

British Library Cataloguing in Publication Data
A catalogue record for this book is available from the British Library

Library of Congress Cataloging in Publication Data
Names: Reed, Alan (Matthew Alan), editor. | Bohlander, Michael, 1962-, editor. | Wake, Nicola, editor.
Title: Homicide in criminal law : a research companion / edited by Alan Reed, Michael Bohlander, Nicola Wake.
Description: New York : Routledge, 2018. | Series: Substantive issues in criminal law | Includes bibliographical references and index.
Identifiers: LCCN 2018019283 | ISBN 9781138498419 (hardback)
Subjects: LCSH: Homicide--Great Britain. | Criminal law--Great Britain.
Classification: LCC KD7963 .H66 2018 | DDC 345.4/10252--dc23
LC record available at https://lccn.loc.gov/2018019283

ISBN 13: 978-0-367-58657-7 (pbk)
ISBN 13: 978-1-138-49841-9 (hbk)

Typeset in Galliard
by Taylor & Francis Books

Contents

List of contributors ix
Preface xiv

Introduction 1

Part 1 5

1 The mandatory sentence and the case for second degree murder 7
JEREMY HORDER

2 Killings short of murder: Examining culpable homicide in Scots law 21
CLAIRE MCDIARMID

3 Reforming English homicide law: Fair labelling questions and comparative answers 37
MATTHEW GIBSON AND ALAN REED

4 The current state of murder in English law: A critique, wrong turns and all 62
J.J. CHILD AND G.R. SULLIVAN

5 'Loss of self-control': The cultural lag of sexual infidelity and the transformative promise of the fear defence 82
SUSAN S.M. EDWARDS

6 Diminished responsibility: A limited partial defence to murder 102
RUDI FORTSON QC

7 Causing death 119
SALLY KYD

8 The termination of pregnancy and the criminal law 136
JONATHAN HERRING

9 Homicide and the vulnerable subject of criminal law 153
CLAIRE DE THAN AND JESSE ELVIN

10 Recording murder: videos depicting homicide and the law 174
ALISDAIR A. GILLESPIE

Part 2 193

11 South Africa 195
GERHARD KEMP

12 United States of America 216
VERA BERGELSON

13 Germany 245
KAI AMBOS AND STEFANIE BOCK

14 New Zealand 264
JULIA TOLMIE

15 The Netherlands 284
ERIK GRITTER

16 Turkey 300
MURAT ÖNOK

17 Islamic law 322
MOHAMMAD HEDAYATI-KAKHKI

18 Sweden 347
MAGNUS ULVÄNG

Index 361

Contributors

Kai Ambos: Kai Ambos is since May 2003 the holder of the Chair of Criminal Law, Criminal Procedure, Comparative Law and International Criminal Law at the Georg-August-University Göttingen, Germany. He is also Head of the Department of Foreign and International Criminal Law, Institute of Criminal Law and Justice at the Georg-August-University Göttingen and also since December 2013 Director of the Centro de Estudios de Derecho Penal y Procesal Penal Latinoamericano (CEDPAL) of Georg-August-Universität Göttingen. He served as a Judge at the Provincial Court (Landgericht) of Lower Saxony in Göttingen from 24 March 2006 to 7 February 2017 (from January 2015 to 30 September 2015 delegated to the Appeals Court (Oberlandesgericht) Braunschweig); with his appointment as Judge at the Kosovo Specialist Chambers (KSC), The Hague, on 7 February 2017 he took leave from this judicial position. On 6 December 2017 he has been selected as Advisor (Amicus Curiae) to the Colombian Special Jurisdiction for Peace.

Vera Bergelson: Vera Bergelson is a Professor of Law and Robert E. Knowlton Scholar at Rutgers University School of Law, USA. She specialises in criminal law theory. She has written widely about consent, provocation, self-defense, necessity, duress, strict liability and victimless crime. Her book *Victims' Rights and Victims' Wrongs: A Theory of Comparative Criminal Liability* (SUP 2009) raises questions about comparative liability in criminal law. She has also served as a chair of the Association of American Law Schools' Section on Jurisprudence. She is on the editorial boards of *BdeF* and *Edisofer* (Buenos Aires and Madrid) and *Law and Philosophy*.

Stefanie Bock: Professor for Criminal Law, Criminal Procedure, International Criminal Law and Comparative Law at the Philipps-Universität Marburg, Germany, and the Executive Director of the International Research and Documentation Centre for War Crimes Trials. Her main fields of research are international criminal law, European criminal law and comparative criminal law.

J.J. Child: Dr John Child is a Senior Lecturer in Law at the University of Birmingham, and co-founding Director of the Sussex Crime Research Centre and the Criminal Law Reform Now Network. Prior to this John held positions at Oxford Brookes University (Senior Lecturer in Law) and the Law Commission of England and Wales (Research Assistant). John's research interests focus on criminal law, both doctrine and theory. Within this field John has published widely, including within the *Cambridge Law Journal, Legal Studies*, the *Criminal Law Review*, etc. John also co-authors the textbook Smith, Hogan and Ormerod's *Essentials of Criminal Law* (Oxford University Press 2017) currently in its second edition.

Claire De Than: Professor Claire de Than is the author of over 80 academic publications, including over 20 books or book contributions and many articles in leading international journals. She is Professor and Director of Studies of the Institute of Law, Jersey, a fractional Professor elsewhere (University of London) and a Law Commissioner (Jersey). She has been an Expert for the Law Commission of England and Wales on two recent criminal law projects. A regular keynote speaker at legal and medical conferences, she has advised several governments and many organisations on criminal law, human rights law, disability rights and law reform issues, and made many media appearances. Her research specialisms include comparative criminal law, comparative human rights law and the law of consent. She is Chair of SHADA, the Sexual Health and Disability Alliance, Chair of The Outsiders Trust and a member of the Board of Enable Jersey.

Susan S.M. Edwards: BA., MA., Ph.D, LLM., is a barrister and Professor of Law and Dean at the University of Buckingham. She is an activist and campaigner for human rights of women, LGBTI, ethnic minority and marginalised voices. She is a member variously of Stop the War Coalition, Amnesty International, Peace and Progress and the Bar Human Rights Committee. For the Bar Human Rights Committee she wrote an expert report on Witchcraft Accusation in Nepal with the Witchcraft and Human Rights Information Network (WHRIN). She has acted as NGO with a several international organisations. She has practiced in criminal and civil cases in England and Wales and is also a member of the Expert Witness Institute and has given expert opinion in criminal cases involving domestic violence cases where battered women have killed and where they have been victims of assault and with regard to duress in the criminal courts and also acted in a Criminal Cases Compensation Tribunal hearing and in family cases. She has also provided expert opinion on wearing the *niqab* in court in a criminal case. Her books include *Female Sexuality and the Law* (Martin Robertson 1981), *Women on Trial* (MUP 1984), *Policing Domestic Violence: Women, the Law and the State* (SAGE Publications 1989), and *Sex and Gender in the Legal Process* (Blackstone Press 1996). She is also a regular contributor to the Criminal Law Review, the Journal of Criminal Law, and the Journal of Family Law. Her most recent media appearances have included taking part in the Sky news debate on rape anonymity (December 2017). Previously, she has spoken as a contributor on women's issues where she was a panellist at the Battle of Ideas 2015 'Rape Culture Myth or Menace' (YouTube), the Sky debate on International Women's Day 2016, and the BBC Radio 4 'Unreliable Evidence' with Clive Anderson (September 2016).

Jesse Elvin: Graduated from the University of London in 1994 with a BA in Law and Anthropology. He obtained a LLM in Law from the University of London in 1995, and a PhD from the same institution in 2005. Before joining City, University of London, he taught at the London School of Economics and University College London. He has published a number of journals, including the *Cambridge Law Journal* and the *Modern Law Review*, and is a regular conference speaker. His research and teaching interests include criminal law, tort law and contract law.

Rudi Fortson QC: Rudi Fortson QC, LLB (Lond.), barrister, has been a criminal practitioner for over 30 years at 25 Bedford Row, London, and a visiting Professor of Law at Queen Mary, University of London. He has written and lectured extensively on criminal law issues. He was a member of the Police Foundation Independent Inquiry into the Misuse of Drugs Act 1971 and a member of the Criminal Justice Forum for the Institute of Public Policy Research (IPPR). He is a member of the Criminal Bar Association of

England and Wales, the Proceeds of Crime Lawyers Association, the Forensic Science Society and the British Academy for Forensic Science.

Matthew Gibson: Dr Matthew Gibson is a Senior Lecturer in Law at Liverpool Law School, University of Liverpool, and Co-Director of Liverpool's International Criminological Research Unit. He predominantly researches criminal law doctrine and theory. In particular, his work focusses on the creation and structure of criminal offences, including processes of criminalisation, offence definition and defendant 'fair' labelling. More broadly, he is also interested in the role of law reform and criminal justice policy in the framing of offences. Separately, he researches the interaction between criminal law and religion. Here, he investigates the creation/scope of criminal laws, their impact on religiously-motivated conduct and the extent to which – if at all – such conduct can/should be accommodated in criminal law.

Alisdair A. Gillespie: Professor Alisdair A. Gillespie is Professor of Criminal Law and Justice and Head of Lancaster University Law School. After reading for the Bar (Middle Temple), he entered academia and has taught at a number of UK universities, culminating in his appointment to a chair at Lancaster University. Alisdair's research relates primarily to cybercrime and, in particular, legal responses to the sexual exploitation or abuse of children. He has published widely in this field and has also acted as an expert advisor to, amongst others, the EU, Council of Europe and UN.

Erik Gritter: Erik Gritter, LLM, is a Senior Lecturer in Criminal Law and Criminal Procedure at the University of Groningen, the Netherlands. He has a broad experience in teaching substantive criminal law and criminal procedure. The focus of his research is mainly on substantive criminal law. In this field of law, he has published several papers and book contributions. His PhD thesis (Groningen 2003) concerns a comparative analysis of the impact of considerations of effectiveness on the enforcement of regulatory law and on the origins and development of certain aspects of criminal liability (e.g., the fault principle and criminal liability of corporations).

Mohammad Hedayati-Kakhki: Dr Mohammad Hedayati-Kakhki is a Senior Lecturer and an Honorary Fellow at Durham Law School and Greenwich School of Management in London. He was the Co-Founder and the Associate Director of the Islam, Law & Modernity (ILM) research group at Durham University and continues to act as a Special Advisor on matters pertaining to Islamic law and associated jurisprudence. He is also a Special Advisor to the Centre for Criminal Law and Criminal Justice at Durham University. He qualified from Shahid Beheshti University in Tehran with a law degree, before moving on to complete a Master's in International Law at the University of Shiraz. He holds a PhD in Middle Eastern Politics and Law from Durham University and has continued to teach at this university since 2009. Alongside teaching BSc, LLB and LLM modules he works as a Director of PhD studies. Before moving to the UK, he practiced as a First Class Attorney at Law at the Iranian Bar and still continues his legal practice by acting as a Legal Consultant on Islamic law and jurisprudence.

Jonathan Herring: Jonathan Herring is the Vice Dean and Professor of Law at the Law Faculty, Oxford University and DM Wolfe-Clarendon Fellow in Law at Exeter College, Oxford University. He has written on medical law and ethics, family law, criminal law and legal issues surrounding vulnerability, care and old age. His books include: *Criminal Law* (Oxford University Press 2018); *Medical Law and Ethics* (Oxford University Press 2018);

Vulnerable Adults and the Law (Oxford University Press 2016), *Caring and the Law* (Hart 2014) *Older People in Law and Society* (Oxford University Press 2009); *European Human Rights and Family Law* (Hart 2010) (with Shazia Choudhry); *Family Law* (Pearson 2017) and *The Woman Who Tickled Too Much* (Pearson 2009).

Jeremy Horder: Jeremy Horder is a Professor of Criminal Law at the London School of Economics, and a Fellow of the British Academy. He was a Law Commissioner for England and Wales from 2005–2010, and Porjes Foundation Fellow of Worcester College, Oxford from 1989–2010.

Gerhard Kemp: Gerhard Kemp is Professor of Criminal Law and International Criminal Law at Stellenbosch University, South Africa, and holds an Alexander von Humboldt Stiftung research fellowship in Germany. He is an advocate of the High Court of South Africa and serves on the board of directors of the Institute for Justice and Reconciliation, Cape Town. He also serves on the editorial boards of various scientific journals, including *Criminal Law Forum*, the *South African Journal of Criminal Justice* and *Zeitschrift für Internationale Strafrechtsdogmatik*.

Sally Kyd: Sally Kyd (formerly Cunningham) has been a Professor of Law at the University of Leicester since 2013. Prior to this she was a lecturer and senior lecturer, also at Leicester, having completed her PhD there. Her research interests relate to criminal law and criminal justice, and she has particular expertise in homicide and driving offences. She is co-author of a leading textbook: *Clarkson and Keating: Criminal Law: Text and Materials* (6th, 7th, 8th and 9th editions, Sweet & Maxwell), and author of a monograph entitled *Driving Offences: Law, Policy and Practice* (Ashgate 2008). Sally held an AHRC Early Career Fellowship in 2011–2012 in order to conduct a project related to causing death by driving offences and has been involved with research projects for the Ministry of Justice and Sentencing Council relating to sexual offences, non-fatal offences and robbery.

Claire McDiarmid: Dr Claire McDiarmid is a Reader at the University of Strathclyde, Glasgow, specialising in criminal law. Her main research interest is in legal responses to children who offend and she has written extensively on the age of criminal responsibility and on the Scottish children's hearings system (having also been a (lay) children's panel member). She is currently working on a project funded by the Carnegie Trust looking at decision-making in relation to certain children who commit grave offences in Scotland. She also works in the area of Scots criminal law more generally. She is co-author (with Professor Pamela Ferguson) of *Scots Criminal Law: A Critical Analysis*, now in its second edition (EUP 2014) and she has a research interest in homicide particularly provocation and the *mens rea* of murder.

Murat Önok: Dr R. Murat Önok is an Assistant Professor in the Law School at Koç University, Istanbul. His fields of research are criminal law, human rights law and international criminal law. He has also taught public international law. He has authored or co-authored various books on criminal law in Turkish, and written various book chapters published abroad. Dr Önok has also been serving as Vice-President of the Turkish Press Council since 2013. He also serves as executive board member of the national chapter of Transparency International, and was previously a board member of Turkish Penal Law Association. He is an instructor for the Turkish Union of Bar Associations (TBB), training lawyers in the fields of human rights law and criminal procedure law, and a member of TBB's Human Rights Center Scientific Advisory Board.

Alan Reed: Alan Reed is Associate Pro Vice Chancellor (Research and Innovation) in the Faculty of Business and Law at the University of Northumbria. He is a Professor of Criminal and Private International Law, and Editor of *The Journal of Criminal Law*.

G.R. Sullivan: G.R. Sullivan is Emeritus Professor of Law, University College London. His research interests are in the fields of substantive criminal law theory. He is co-author of *Simester and Sullivan's Criminal Law: Theory and Doctrine* (6th edn, Hart 2016) (with Simester, Spencer, Stark and Virgo). He has published widely in the general and specialist journals.

Julia Tolmie: Professor Julia Tolmie teaches Criminal Law and Women and the Law at The University of Auckland. She served as chair of the New Zealand Family Violence Death Review Committee from December 2011–2016, and as a member of the New Zealand Government's Expert Advisory Group on Family Violence in 2013.

Magnus Ulväng: Magnus Ulväng is Professor of Criminal Law at Uppsala University (Sweden) where he also got his legal education, LLM (1997) LL.D (2005). He has written extensively on topics within Criminal Law and Sentencing theory and is author and co-author of several books. He has also been an expert in numerous legislative committees.

Preface

We are pleased to present the fifth volume of our joint cooperation in areas of substantive criminal law, following on from previous collections on Consent, Diminished Responsibility, Participation in Crime and General Defences. This monograph forms part of a series which will continue to systemically address areas of the criminal law in the UK that are in need of reform or which belong to the core areas of the law where doctrinal abstraction or greater analysis is required.

The ambit of homicide standardisations in extant law is contestable and opaque. Homicide is the death of a human being in circumstances where the death can be attributed to the conduct of one or more human beings, or exceptionally to a corporation or other organisation. A homicide may be lawful or unlawful. Moreover, where a defendant is found to be causally responsible for the victim's death, significant penal consequences can follow that are unchartered elsewhere in substantive criminal law, and substantive variations in culpability may apply across a spectrum of differential killings. As this monograph will demonstrate, causing death may involve morally debatable forms of liability and risk exposure to excessive punishment. Concerns are also prevalent related to the equipoise between individual autonomy and state paternalism which are often in conflict. Individual rights engender a perspective that the autonomy of the other person is involved, and that if that person accedes to harm via the conduct there should be no offence. However, we can also identify an attitude of paternalism that is primordial in a number of leading judgments. The proposition that the criminal law should be used to protect persons from themselves. Legal moralism can also be adduced in that where conduct *per se* is viewed as immoral then the stigmatisation of legal censure is presumptively justified; wholly outwith the participatory nature of the act itself. Homicide precepts have developed in the UK in this regard in a solipsistic ad-hoc manner, and haphazardly rather than in a coherent structure.

Extant law in the UK reveals significant problems in adoption of consistent approaches to doctrinal and theoretical underpinnings of homicide liability and culpability thresholds. This has been exemplified by a plethora of recent jurisprudential authorities revealing varying degrees of confusion and vacillation. A variety of Law Commission proposals, although emboldening the debate, have yet to be adopted in any logical template. The first part of this monograph shall engage in an examination of UK provisions, with specialist contributions on Scottish law, and in contrasting these provisions against alternative domestic jurisdictions as well as comparative contributions addressing a particularised research grid for content. The comparative and international chapters will provide a wider background of how other legal systems treat a variety of specialised issues relating to homicide in the context of the criminal law. The aim is production of an edited monograph which serves as a leading point of reference in the substantive arena relating to homicide.

As with previous volumes, we thank our contributing authors for their willingness to commit to such a time-consuming and demanding project, and for putting up with the manifold of requests from the editors in the process of putting their manuscripts together into a coherent volume. We owe a gratitude of debt to Nicola Wake, Emma Engleby and Verity Adams who provided cheerful and overall meticulous and sterling editorial support in the collation. We could not have done it without them, nor without the outstanding assistance of Sean Mennim who has worked tirelessly with the team on the proof reading and formatting of the final manuscript.

We have endeavoured to state the law as in force in each jurisdiction on March 2018.

Micheal Bohlander
Alan Reed

Introduction

The English Law Commission in 2006 made radical proposals for a newly reformulated hierarchical structure for homicide offences, predicated upon fair labelling and appropriate standardisation of culpability thresholds. These new pathways were rejected in terms of stratification of liability, and only minor reforms instead were trammelled within the limited arena of partial defences with new conceptualisation of loss of self-control and diminished responsibility. It is submitted that the time is ripe again for a fundamental review of the ambit and parameters of homicide reform, and domestic chapters herein address bespoke and particularised issues that prevail within doctrinal and theoretical precepts. This focus is complemented by consideration and evaluation of alternative templates that exist within other legal jurisdictions to unlawful killings.

The proposed chapter breakdowns and detailed abstracts of relevant content are set out sequentially below. This edifice engages in an examination of UK provisions, with specialist contributions on Scottish law, and in contrasting these provisions against alternative domestic jurisdictions as well as comparative contributions addressing a particularised research grid for content.

The comparative chapters will provide a wider background of how other legal systems treat a variety of specialised issues relating to homicide in the context of the criminal law.

The debate in the UK in relation to homicide principles continues apace for academics, practitioners and within the criminal justice system. Having expert descriptions of the wider issues surrounding the particular discussion and of other legal systems' approaches will serve to stimulate and inform that debate.

In chapter one, entitled 'The mandatory sentence and the case for second degree murder', Professor Jeremy Horder reviews the case for having a category of second degree murder in English law. The author compares the merits of introducing a second degree murder category with alternative ways of reducing the applicable scope of the mandatory life sentence, through an examination of the English historical background to the issues. The author also considers an important source somewhat neglected by criminal lawyers, the Report of the Commission on Capital Punishment of 1866.

Chapter two is entitled 'Killings short of murder: examining culpable homicide in Scots law' by Dr Claire McDiarmid. The author explores how Scots law recognises two distinct crimes of homicide (murder and culpable homicide) each with its own separate mental elements, though sharing a common *actus reus*, that is the destruction of the life of another. The dividing line between these crimes is, therefore primarily, the question of whether the accused possessed the *mens rea* for murder (though in some cases the nature of the act as murderous is determinative). The *mens rea* of murder can be constituted by wicked intention to kill or by wicked recklessness, demonstrating the requirement of the, potentially nebulous, concept of wickedness. Involuntary lawful act culpable homicide requires only recklessness; involuntary unlawful act type takes the *mens rea* of the underlying crime and voluntary culpable homicide is perhaps most easily categorised as murder reduced. Through an examination of case law, the author considers the categorisation of individual acts of killing by application of this murder / culpable homicide binary looking at the judgments made on blameworthiness as a consequence. Particular attention will be paid to cases of culpable homicide since the lesser homicide offence is rather less illuminated in academic analyses. The author also considers whether the current criteria embedded in the criminal law provide a rational, defensible basis for such decisions.

Chapter three is entitled 'Reforming English homicide law: fair labelling questions and comparative answers', by Professor Alan Reed and Dr Matthew Gibson. The chapter focuses on the principle of 'fair labelling', which has become common currency in debates about homicide law reform. In particular, it is regularly invoked to support normative claims about how best to define murder and involuntary manslaughter – the offences which form the focus of this chapter. Accordingly, fair labelling represents the starting point in reviewing the existing crimes of murder and involuntary manslaughter in English law, along with potential reform options. The chapter begins by analysing how far current domestic murder and involuntary manslaughter provisions cohere with fair labelling. Next, it assesses the Law Commission's proposed homicide ladder to determine the extent to which this would improve fair labelling of these offences. Subsequently, the authors undertake a comparative analysis of murder and involuntary manslaughter in South Africa, the United States, Australia and Canada. Finally, based on their findings, they conclude by offering some suggested future reform options for these crimes in England and Wales.

In chapter four, 'The current state of murder in English law: a critique, wrong turns and all', Dr J.J. Child and Professor G.R. Sullivan explore the offence of murder in the context of its uniquely draconian mandatory sentence. The chapter highlights the normative restraints that such a sentence imposes; criticising the current law for its failure to maintain a narrow definition. In Part 1, the authors discuss the primary route to murder liability, where a defendant (D1) acts as a principal agent, highlighting the inappropriate breadth of current *mens rea* requirements in particular. In Part 2, discussion switches to the secondary route to murder liability, where D2 commits murder as the accomplice of D1. Focusing upon the recent landmark Supreme Court case of Jogee [2016] UKSC 8, the authors discuss and generally welcome the court's ambition to narrow accomplice liability in murder to require something approaching a parity of culpability between D1 and D2. However, they also highlight conflicts and uncertainties within the judgment that threaten to undermine its potential in narrowing liability, including (a) uncertainty as to whether D2 must intend D1 to commit murder; (b) the use of conditional intention; and (c) assumptions around manslaughter as an alternative or back-up to murder. Across these alternative routes to murder liability, the chapter contends that liability should be interpreted narrowly and consistently and offers some guidance on associated reform.

In chapter five, entitled '"Loss of self-control" – the cultural lag of sexual infidelity and the transformative promise of the fear defence', Professor Susan Edwards explores The Coroners and Justice Act 2009 (C and JA 2009) s.55(3); 'loss of self-control' manslaughter, acknowledges that 'fear of serious violence' is now a 'qualifying trigger' which may 'cause' a defendant to lose self-control and kill another. However, the retention of loss of self-control is problematic as in everyday and legal contemplation it remains conjoined with anger such that requiring the emotion of fear to trigger a loss of self-control fails to capture the specific effect of violence on the abused partner which is not realised in an eruptive moment as with an angered response, but is very differently a cumulative and chronic state and contemplation of future violence. Notwithstanding, the evolving social and legal consciousness and the developing legal discourse acknowledges fear in loss of self-control manslaughter, in self-defence and no intent / involuntary manslaughter. But so embedded in language, and in social, cultural and legal constructs of meaning is the conjoining of loss of self-control with anger that the legal requirement of loss of self-control when in fear is misconceived. The generic statistical evidence available indicates that there have been few cases since the introduction of the C and JA where s.55 (3), has been applied. For the period April 2011–March 2015, 39 female defendants were convicted of 'other manslaughter' including loss of control manslaughter' killings s.54 (1), loss of control, fear manslaughter s.55 (3), a combination of both s.54 (1) and s.55 (3); involuntary or constructive manslaughter no intent, and killings where there was no intention to kill including accident and gross negligence regardless of relationship of victim to suspect. This gives some indication of the likely little use of the fear / manslaughter defence since its enactment. However, the very advent of the fear triggers s.55(3), and the symbolic importance of this recognition of the role of fear in understanding what drives an abused partner to kill is significant.

Rudi Fortson QC, in chapter six entitled 'Diminished responsibility: a limited partial defence to murder', will argue that the definition of 'diminished responsibility' as originally enacted in s.2 of the Homicide Act 1957, not only lacked clinical and legal precision, but that it also required an examination of whether a defendant's 'mental responsibility' for his acts and omissions had been 'substantially impaired'. Although still styled 'diminished responsibility', the revised wording of s.2 of the 1957 Act, by the Coroners and Justice Act 2009, no longer contains the element of 'responsibility'. Instead, the emphasis is now placed on a medical evaluation of the defendant's mental condition (at the time of the killing) and the causative impairment of any of the mental functions specified in s.2 (1A) HA 1957. The author will discuss the structural differences in the original and revised definitions of 'diminished responsibility' whether the differences are more theoretical than practical in their effect, the role of experts and the courts, and whether further reform is warranted.

Chapter seven by Professor Sally Kyd is entitled 'Causing death'. In this chapter the author suggests that under English law the importance of causation bares an inverse relationship to the *mens rea* requirement of any homicide offence. That is to say, because murder requires an intention to kill or cause grievous bodily harm and it is this *mens rea* requirement that separates it from lesser forms of homicide, causation has less of a role to play in determining liability where such *mens rea* can be proved. Where constructive homicide offences are concerned, however, particularly those involving offences requiring minimal if any *mens rea*, establishing causation becomes essential to establishing sufficient blameworthiness on the part of D to be held liable for the death. In this chapter the legal rules and principles relating to causation are discussed in relation to the offences of murder, manslaughter and causing death by driving. It is seen that the context in which a death is caused, and the *mens rea* requirements of the alleged offence, unavoidably affect judgments of whether D has caused the death of V. The law is currently lacking in providing clear limitations as to when a death can be attributed to a particular act, and the chapter ends with a suggestion as to how this might be rectified.

In chapter eight, 'The termination of pregnancy and the criminal law', Professor Jonathan Herring considers how the criminal law should respond to cases which have resulted in the death of a foetus. This topic is commonly presented as a highly problematic one for criminal law in that it either strongly protects the rights of the foetus and this severely restricts access to abortion or the law fails to adequately acknowledge the wrong done when a foetus is killed outside the context of a medical termination (e.g., by virtue of an attack on a pregnant woman). This chapter proposes a solution to this dilemma. It identifies the value in foetal life, indeed of life generally, as resting in relationships. This means that a wanted pregnancy should be regarded as a valuable relationship to be protected by the criminal law, with a grave wrong being committed when it is terminated. However, in the case of an unwanted relationship, the relationship has no value and the law's responsibility is to facilitate its ending. This can justify the law promoting a liberal approach to abortion, while offering a severe punishment to non-consensual terminations of pregnancy.

Chapter nine, 'Homicide and the vulnerable subject of criminal law' by Professor Claire De Than and Dr Jesse Elvin, examines the law on homicide as it relates to cases where V is in the actual custody, charge or care of D and V is a person who is vulnerable or has a special dependence on D. Examples of such situations are where young children are in the custody or charge of their parents or a school, where prisoners are under the control of prison officers, where a worker is under the control of a manager, and where residents are in a care home. In civil law, D will owe V a non-delegable duty of care in such a case (*Woodland v Swimming Teachers Association* [2013] UKSC 66). Similarly, in criminal law, D will typically owe V a duty of care in criminal law, breach of which could give rise to liability for murder or manslaughter. In this chapter, the authors will consider in which circumstances D should be criminally liable for causing V's death in such situations. The chapter will then go on to consider 'hard cases', such as the potential liability of: (a) parents, head teachers, prison governors and care home managers in relation to the provision of inappropriate diets to those under their authority; (b) parents in relation to the potential medical treatment for religious or pseudoscientific reasons; (c) managers for deaths arising from workplace stress; and (d) prison officers and governors for the suicide of prisoners.

Chapter ten by Professor Alisdair Gillespie is entitled 'Recording murder: videos depicting homicide and the law'. In this chapter the author explores the legalities of recording a homicide. 'Recording' in this instance means a written, audio or visual depiction of the killing of another. Should this be regulated and, if so, as what? The first part of the chapter will consider those who video-record (via a smartphone or camera) the real-life killing of an individual. What is their liability? If they are seen to be doing this, could they be considered an accomplice? What if they are not seen and instead record the material for some other purpose? What is the liability of those who distribute the footage? It will be remembered that so-called Islamic State and other terrorist groups have filmed the 'execution' / murder of hostages and there is some evidence that gangs have done similar. What should be of those who distribute footage? Similarly, what of those who 'consume' it? The second part of the chapter will consider a different form of recording: that of textual recording. What happens if someone describes the death of another, should this be criminalised? What if the person is not dead? It may be the product of fantasy, but if it involves a real person does that mean that there is a justification for criminalising it? What if it is the plan for a killing? At one point does this become inchoate liability? All of these issues will be discussed, together with a discussion about how this interacts with the freedom of expression.

Part 1

1 The mandatory sentence and the case for second degree murder

Jeremy Horder[1]

Introduction

This chapter will review the case for having a category of second degree murder in English law. The introduction of a 'homicide ladder' was recommended by the Law Commission in 2006.[2] The ladder involved reform dividing the general offences of homicide into three rungs or categories: first degree murder, second degree murder and manslaughter. Although generally welcomed by consultees, the proposal for the ladder system did not find favour with Government and is not currently on the law reform agenda.[3] Should reformers accept the current two-tier framework consisting of murder and manslaughter, and concentrate their efforts on working to improve the definitions of these two offences? The arguments for and against an affirmative answer are quite evenly balanced, but I believe that the case for a three-tier law of homicide is still strong. Here I will compare the merits of introducing a second degree murder category with alternative ways of reducing the scope to apply the mandatory life sentence, through an examination of the English historical background to the issues. In particular, I consider an important source somewhat neglected by criminal lawyers, the Report of the Commission on Capital Punishment of 1866.

Overview: how problems may arise

English law, in common with many other jurisdictions, seeks to bolster the moral power of the message it conveys through the law of homicide by the appropriation of moral categories or labels (such as 'murder') to describe forbidden kinds of wrongdoing. This is an example of law's dependence on morality. Conversely, morality may be dependent on law in this context.[4] The law's ability to provide clear and authoritative definitions of wrongdoing is an example of this. That the *law* of murder settles what murder is, in a way that (*ex hypothesi*) commands or has the potential to command wide acceptance, may itself provide indirect support for the moral obligation not to kill. It may, for example, prevent the vagueness of the moral concept undermining people's confidence in it as a source of distinct and special

1 I am very grateful to John Child and Nicola Wake for comments on previous drafts; the responsibility for the final produce is mine.
2 Law Commission, *Murder, Manslaughter and Infanticide* (Law Com No 304, 2006).
3 This was confirmed in October 2016 by the Justice Minister, Oliver Heald MP. See text at n 48 below.
4 The classic argument is to be found in A.M. Honoré, 'The Dependence of Morality on Law' (1993) 13(1) Oxford Journal of Legal Studies.

obligations.[5] The law of murder also performs important bureaucratic functions, functions connected to the state's duty to uphold and promote certain virtues, such as justice. These functions include the making of provision for trial and conviction, and the conferral of sentencing powers on judges. How might a category of second degree murder fit into this picture? As a legal category, second degree 'murder' relies in part on the moral understanding of murder for its legitimacy. So, what falls within the category should, notwithstanding the existence of a category of first degree murder lying above it, also reflect in the right measure what Feinberg calls, 'the nontechnical sense [of murder] – "the most heinous kind of unjustified killing generally (wanton, barbarous, etc.) whether lawful or not"'.[6] In that regard, there is bound to be disagreement over what should fall within the category of second degree murder.[7] However, few doubt that such a category is in principle capable of meeting this demand. As we will see in the next section, it does so perfectly satisfactorily in many jurisdictions.

The real difficulty with a category of second degree murder lies in the way that it may help, or hinder, the state's duty to secure justice in homicide cases. On the one hand, it appears to provide a means by which the law's bureaucratic functions – the provision of trial and punishment – could be performed in a more fine-grained way, in a legal system in which the mandatory life penalty remained for 'first degree' murder. There is the potential for greater moral sophistication in a jury verdict that reflects a choice between three different grades of homicide offence. A related point, at the sentencing stage, is that an over-inclusive law of manslaughter may leave judges with no secure factual basis for sentencing.[8] A judge may have no very obvious way of settling the question whether, for example, the defendant was convicted of manslaughter on the basis that there was no intent to cause serious harm, or whether the conviction reflected the jury's view that the defendant, in intentionally killing, lost self-control in exceptional circumstances or was suffering from diminished responsibility.[9] Whilst the introduction of a category of second degree murder would not rid the law of such difficulties – far from it – it might reduce them in number.

However, such a gain, in point of the ability to do justice, must be weighed against a potential loss. More choice is not necessarily better than less. The greater the number of possible verdicts, the greater the scope for jury disagreement over the right outcome, and hence the greater the scope for inconclusive trials.[10] This problem is liable to be aggravated in trials involving multiple defendants, where the defendants are making different and perhaps incompatible claims, on different bases, about the nature of their liability (if any liability is conceded at all). Consider this hypothetical example, as it might arise under a law of homicide shaped by the Law Commission's recommendations for reform:[11]

5 See, more generally, J. Feinberg, 'On Being "Morally Speaking" a Murderer' (1963) 61(5) Journal of Philosophy 158, 162–63.
6 Ibid. 161–62.
7 For thoughtful discussions, see V. Tadros, 'The Homicide Ladder' (2006) 69(4) Modern Law Review 601; J. Rogers, 'The Law Commission's Proposed Restructuring of Homicide' (2006) 70 Journal of Criminal Law 223.
8 See, now, the guidelines for sentencing issued by the Sentencing Council: <www.sentencingcouncil.org.uk/news/item/new-sentencing-guidelines-proposed-for-manslaughter-offences/> accessed 29 March 2018.
9 M. Wasik, 'Sentencing in Homicide' in A. Ashworth and B. Mitchell (eds), *Rethinking English Homicide Law* (Oxford University Press 2000) 171–72.
10 Rogers (n 7); R. Taylor, 'Jury Unanimity in Homicide' (2001) Criminal Law Review 283.
11 Law Commission (n 2).

> D1, D2 and D3 are charged with first degree murder, arising out of the stabbing of V through the heart in the course of a melée. D1 claims that V caused him to lose self-control and encourage D2 to stab V, which D1 says D2 did, but that he (D1) did not intend D2 to do serious harm to V. D2 claims it was D3 who stabbed V, that D1 cold-bloodedly encouraged D3 to kill V, that D1 is blaming him (D2) for the stabbing out of spite, and that he (D2) had no idea that an attack of any kind on V was planned. D3 claims to have driven D1 and D2 to the scene with no knowledge of their plans, beyond an intention to fight.

On such facts, even with no more than verdicts of murder, manslaughter and outright acquittal to consider, the route to verdict might not be an easy one for the jury without independent evidence bearing on who played which role in the offence, or showing the defendants were all in it together. It might be hard to see what benefit is to be derived from adding a further possible verdict into the mix, a verdict of second degree murder. Such a possibility might even make a difficult situation worse, in point of justice.

The situation is aggravated, as a result of the highly regrettable decision of the House of Lords in *Coutts*.[12] In that case, a decision of a strong Court of Appeal led by the Lord Chief Justice was overturned by the House of Lords. The House of Lords held that the public interest in the administration of justice requires the trial judge, irrespective of the wishes of Counsel, to leave to the jury, 'any obvious alternative [verdict] which there is evidence to support'.[13] So, in a case charged as first degree murder with facts such as those in the example just given, it would not be open to the trial judge to acquiesce in an agreement between prosecution and defence to run the trial on the simple basis that one or more of the defendants was guilty (other than in relation to D2's plea of loss of self-control[14]) either of first degree murder or of manslaughter, or was not guilty of a homicide offence. The trial judge would be obliged to introduce the possibility of a second degree murder verdict, in relation to each and every defendant, alongside possible verdicts of first degree murder, manslaughter and outright acquittal.

In spite of these formidable difficulties, it is still possible to justify the introduction of the new two-tier murder structure, comprised of first degree and second degree murder. However, it would probably be undesirable to do so exactly in accordance with the Law Commission's recommendations, for fear of aggravating the problem of jury disagreement on the factual basis for verdict. That issue will be addressed in the concluding section of this chapter. If the mandatory life penalty for murder is to remain, the introduction of a second degree murder category is generally to be preferred, as a way of ameliorating or finessing the law, to a form of individualised 'discretionary assessment' in which the judge and the jury can decide in a particular case that, in the circumstances, the life penalty should not apply.[15]

12 [2006] UKHL 39.

13 Ibid. [24] (Lord Bingham). For criticism, see J. Horder, *Homicide and the Politics of Law Reform* (Oxford University Press 2012) 245–49.

14 In relation to which, a verdict of second degree murder would be appropriate, rather than one of manslaughter, in accordance with the Law Commission's recommendations for reform of the offence: see Law Commission (n 2).

15 Although, as we will see, that does not rule out the possibility that other restrictions on or ameliorations of the life sentence could usefully be introduced. Later, I consider, for example, abolishing custody for life for offenders under 21, and introducing a review of the 'life' element to a life sentence, when the offender has complied with his or her licence provisions over a period of time: see text following n 49 below.

What has not been appreciated by would-be reformers is that we have been here before. The Law Commission's Consultation Paper on homicide contained a good deal of historical background on the law.[16] Regrettably, though, it did not cover previous attempts to introduce a category of second degree murder into English Law, or examine older proposals for forms of individualised discretionary assessment. There is much to learn from these historic debates.

Second degree murder and law reform in Victorian England

The Victorian period saw lively debate over the future of the criminal law, through Parliamentary reform. As early as 1843, law reformer Charles HB Ker had expressed the view that, '9/10th of the Criminal Law is already Statute Law'.[17] However, the scattered nature of the statutory material meant that it was commonly held at that time, even by those opposed to codification generally, that the criminal law was best suited to codification.[18] Full codification of the criminal law was, though, decisively opposed by the judges. This meant that the consolidations of 1861 were in large measure all the reformers had to show for their efforts. The failure of codification has overshadowed the vigour and range of the debate over reform at that time, perhaps especially in the case of murder.[19]

The principal issue was the possible abolition of the death penalty, a subject voted on in the House of Commons no less than eight times between 1840 and 1869.[20] Abolition in the case of murder (as well as for other offences) was strongly advocated by many influential Parliamentarians and others, from at least the 1840s onwards, but reform efforts in the case of murder were successful only in ending public executions in 1868.[21] The death penalty for murder remained. What is more, the sharpening of the issues through debate meant that the link between the death penalty and the crime of murder became firmly underpinned by the honing of a two-pronged argument, an argument that would sustain the link for another hundred years. This argument involved an appeal to the uniqueness of the crime as an attack on the sanctity of an innocent life, combined with the (supposed) potential of the existence of the death penalty to impress upon certain demonised classes of society the awful power and majesty of the law. As Liberal Home Secretary, Henry Bruce put it, in 1869:

> We ha[ve] in all our large cities a certain number of degraded and lawless individuals. It was a fact to be mentioned with shame; but the fact itself was beyond all question, that the tendencies of this class were only kept in check by fear of the most severe punishments.[22]

Three times Home Secretary, Sir George Grey, was of a similar view, offering the opinion that the prospect of hanging taught any hardened criminal inclined to commit murder that there was:

16 Law Commission, *A New Homicide Act for England and Wales?* (Law Com No 177, 2005).

17 Brougham MS 11610 (11 September 1843), cited by M. Lobban, 'How Benthamic was the Criminal Law Commission?' (2000) 18(2) Law and History Review <www.historycooperative.org/journals/lhr/18.2/lobban.html.> accessed 29 March 2018. See further (n 28).

18 Lobban (n 17), para 9.

19 See, more generally, K.J.M. Smith, *Lawyers, Legislators and Theorists* (Oxford University Press 1998); Horder (n 13) 3–53.

20 R. McGowan, 'History, Culture and the Death Penalty: The British Debates 1840–70' (2003) 29(2) Historical Reflections 229.

21 Ibid. 229–30.

22 Ibid. 242

> A barrier set up against the indulgence of his bloody and brutal instincts beyond which he might not pass without becoming, in all probability, a similar spectacle.[23]

In seeking to meet and overcome such arguments, reformers faced a difficult tactical decision, not unlike those currently opposed to the mandatory sentence of life imprisonment. Should they concentrate on promoting complete abolition, thus opening themselves to attack for failing adequately to address the concerns just mentioned, and hence allegedly cheapening the offence and weakening the deterrent effect of the law? Or, should they pursue a 'halfway house' solution, in the form of an argument either that the death penalty should be reserved for the worst kind of murders, or that the judge or jury should be given a discretion to find grounds for clemency in individual cases ('discretionary assessment')? The weakness of the halfway house strategy might prove to be that it fell between two stools, neither securing the abolition of the death penalty, nor providing an acceptable basis for deciding in which cases that penalty should continue to apply. The halfway house course was, in effect, the course perforce pursued by the Law Commission in 2006. With the continuance of the life sentence for murder outside its terms of remit, the Law Commission recommended that the penalty should be restricted to the narrower category of first degree murder.[24] We should note, though, that it was not the only halfway house recommendation to be considered, and rejected, following the Commission's Report in 2006. At a late stage in the Parliamentary debates on what was to become the Coroners and Justice Act 2009,[25] an attempt was made in the House of Lords to replace the provisions of the Act dealing with specific defences to murder, with a more loose-limbed 'extenuating circumstances' provision:

> In a trial for murder the trial judge may in the course of his summing up direct the jury that if they are satisfied that the defendant is guilty of murder, but are of the opinion that there were extenuating circumstances, they may on returning their verdict add a rider to that effect.[26]

In a case where the jury found 'extenuating circumstances', the judge would be freed from the obligation to pass the life sentence, and could pass such sentence as he or she thought appropriate. The provision is based on a similar one introduced into the French Penal Code in 1832, which was much discussed by English jurists in the Victorian period and after.[27] Their criticisms are considered shortly.

Under the influence of the writings of Montesquieu and Beccaria,[28] the category of second degree murder was first introduced in Pennsylvania in 1794, building on a definition of murder that had already been restricted in 1706 to wilful and premeditated killing:[29]

> Section I … [N]o crime whatsoever, hereafter committed (except murder of the first degree) shall be punished with death in the state of Pennsylvania … Section II. [A]ll murder, which shall be perpetrated by means of poison, or by lying in wait, or by any

23 Ibid.
24 Law Commission (n 2).
25 HL Deb 26 Oct 2009, vol. 713, col 1013.
26 For critical discussion, see Horder (n 13) 52–3.
27 See J.W. Garner, 'Criminal Procedure in France' (1916) 25(4) Yale Law Journal 255, 277–80.
28 See e.g., C. Beccaria, *Crimes and Punishments* (1764) xiii, 17 (Philip H Nicklin, 1819).
29 E.R. Keedy, 'History of the Pennsylvania Statute Creating Degrees of Murder' (1949) 97(6) University of Pennsylvania Law Review 759, 762.

other kind of wilful, deliberate and premeditated killing, or which shall be committed in the perpetration or attempt to perpetrate any arson, rape, robbery, or burglary, shall be deemed murder of the first degree; and all other kinds of murder shall be deemed murder in the second degree.

Of the reforms, a contemporary French commentator on criminal law (and French Revolutionary leader) remarked:

> [T]he Americans indeed guard themselves against consulting the incoherent and barbarous laws of Europe ... they listen to the philosophers; they follow a second time the profound Locke; they read and correct Montesquieu and Rousseau; they are especially careful against following England too closely.[30]

Second degree murder was punishable by imprisonment with hard labour, or in solitude, or both together, for any time not exceeding 21 years. In the debates leading up to the reforms, one Justice of the Pennsylvania Supreme Court, drawing inspiration from Montesquieu, had expressed the view that the death penalty was appropriate only for cases of 'deliberate assassination'.[31] This was, of course, the language in which the highest category of homicide came to be expressed in the French Penal Code of 1810:

> 295 HOMICIDE, committed wilfully, is denominated *murder*.
> 296 Every murder, committed with premeditation, or with lying in wait, is denominated *assassination*.
> 297 Premeditation consists in a design formed, before the action, of attacking the person of any particular individual, or even of any one who shall be found or met with, even though such design may be dependent upon some circumstance or condition.[32]

Today, nearly every state in America distinguishes different degrees of murder, and most states treat premeditation as the focal point in defining the highest grade of murder.[33] In France, though, as indicated above, from 1832 it was possible for the jury to determine that the death penalty would not be imposed, through a finding that the killing was accompanied by extenuating circumstances ('circonstances atténuantes').[34] The provision was designed to counter the previous tendency of juries to acquit altogether where such circumstances existed.[35]

30 B. de Warville, cited in J.P. Selsam, 'Brissot de Warville on the Pennsylvania Constitution of 1776' (1948) 72(1) Pennsylvania Magazine of History and Biography 25, 40. See also Keedy (n 29) 767. Nonetheless, following the contemporary English approach (see e.g., the opinion of Holt CJ in *R v Mawgridge* (1707) Kel 119), some Pennsylvania courts broadened first degree murder to include any intentional killing, whether or not literally premeditated: see the discussion in Keedy (n 29) 773–75.

31 W. Bradford, 'An Enquiry How Far the Punishment of Death is Necessary in Pennsylvania' (T. Dobson 1793).

32 For a discussion of the modern law, see J.R. Spencer, 'Intentional Killings in French Law', in J. Horder (ed.) *Homicide Law in Comparative Perspective* (Hart Publishing 2007) 39–55.

33 See C. Finkelstein, 'Two Models of Murder: Patterns of Criminalisation in the United States' in J. Horder (n 32) 83–107.

34 Garner (n 27). See also H.E. Boyle, 'Extenuating Circumstances in French Law' (1906–07) 18 Juridical Review 341.

35 In introducing the provision, the Minister of Justice said, 'With the new power afforded to the jury, justice will not henceforth have to groan under acquittals pronounced contrary to the

How were these developments regarded in Victorian England? Would-be reformers latched on to both second degree murder and 'extenuating circumstances' as ways in which to implement a halfway house strategy, narrowing the scope of but not (at least not immediately) abolishing the death penalty for murder. In supporting a motion for the establishment of a Select Committee on the death penalty, Quaker and Liberal radical, John Bright said:

> There can be no doubt whatever that if capital punishment be retained, and if it be absolutely necessary that there should be a crime called murder to which capital punishment attaches, it is no less necessary that there should be, as there are in some other countries, three or four degrees of manslaughter, and that for the highest degree of manslaughter there should be the highest kind of secondary punishment, and that the power should be placed in the hands of the jury of determining what should be the particular class in which the criminal should be placed.[36]

In the course of the same debate, William Ewart, a noted reformer,[37] said:

> Another objection to the punishment of death is, that it admits of no gradations. There are different shades of criminality even in murder; yet the punishment is sternly, uniformly one … Our proceedings, our interest in this subject, are not peculiar to this nation. In other countries there is the same shrinking from the punishment of death. In France, we are told, the juries persist in returning verdicts of murder, "with extenuating circumstances," which exempts the accused from execution.[38]

When the Capital Punishment Commission reported in 1866, both Bright and Ewart found themselves in a minority of four out of twelve Commissioners who supported the complete abolition of capital punishment. However, having debated the matter extensively, the Commission recommended the introduction of a three tier general law of homicide.[39] The definitions of murder and manslaughter were to remain untouched, but the death penalty (no longer to be carried out in public) was to be confined to (a) 'murders deliberately committed with express malice aforethought, such malice to be found as a fact by the jury', and (b) murder (whether committed with express or implied malice) committed in the course of arson, rape, burglary, robbery or piracy.[40] In all other murder cases, the sentence was to be penal servitude for life, or such a period of imprisonment (not to be less than seven years in length) as the trial judge should decide.

The Commissioners also unanimously agreed that the judicial power (taken away in 1861) to record, but not pass, a death sentence should be restored. It had up to that point

evidence …where the enormity of the punishment formerly served as a pretext for the acquittal', cited by Boyle (n 34) 350.

36 HC Deb 3 May 1864, vol. 174, col 2094.

37 In 1834 he successfully carried a bill to abolish hanging in chains. See further, McGowan (n 20) 234.

38 See (n 36) 2060–63. See also the opinion of C. Neate, at 2081–82, 'He (Mr Neate) thought it would be right to consider whether a distinction could not be established by law between aggravated cases of murder and other cases which were not of so deep a die. In other countries the juries were allowed to declare, if they so thought fit, that "extenuating circumstances" existed, and, in his opinion, that practice might be introduced into this country.'

39 Capital Punishment Commission, *Report of the Capital Punishment Commission* (Eyre and Spottiswoode 1866) para 12.

40 Ibid.

been the practice for the judge to record but not formally to pass the death sentence, and make a written note of the sentence he or she thought appropriate, in cases where it seemed that the matter of sentence should be immediately referred to the Home Secretary.[41] Content with that recommendation, the Commissioners could see no case for the introduction of a Court of Appeal especially for capital cases. However, the evidence given to the Commission showed how sharply opinion was divided on the issues as a whole, with one commentator remarking of the recommendations:

> It needs the close perusal of such a book … to make the public understand the vast difficulties which the legislature has to face, and the curiously equal balance of opinions on the great question of the death penalty.[42]

The result, on the back of 670 pages of analysis and evidence, was solely the abolition of public executions,[43] although that was no mean achievement. Between 1 January 1860 and 26 May 1868 (the very last occasion), 115 men and 5 women were executed in public.[44]

It is understandable, but certainly regrettable, that neither the Law Commission in recommending a three-tier general law of homicide, nor those members of the House of Lords who thereafter so enthusiastically endorsed the introduction of an 'extenuating circumstances' provision,[45] considered the extensive debates about these very issues in the 1866 report. A complete account of these debates cannot be given here, but some of the key points are still well worth considering.

The Committee of 1866: extenuating circumstances and beyond

Let us start with the possibility that the jury be given a power to find 'extenuating circumstances', with the result that the death penalty would no longer be applicable. The proposal did garner some support within the Committee. Sergeant Perry was of the opinion that the 'whole discrimination' as to a murderer's guilt should be a matter for the jury, because there was more public trust in juries than in judges (2548[46]). Sir Fitzroy Kelly MP agreed with Perry, but thought that it would be inadvisable to ask juries to give reasons for their findings, because that would lead to, 'danger, difficulty, inconvenience and mischief' (1044–45): still, today, largely the explanation for not questioning the jury about the basis for manslaughter verdicts. I return to this point shortly.

However, the majority of witnesses were against the proposal (other than in infanticide cases), principally on the grounds that it would be used too much, leaving capital murder as a largely redundant category. Lord Cranworth, the Lord Chancellor, said:

> I think that juries often wish to get out of the responsibility of finding a man guilty when he is to suffer death as a result of their verdict and that they would almost always say that there were extenuating circumstances (23).[47]

41 Ibid. para 16.
42 Anon, 'Anecdotes from a Blue Book' (1866) 17 Temple Bar 47, cited by McGowan (n 20) 246.
43 Capital Punishment (Amendment) Act 1868.
44 <www.capitalpunishmentuk.org/endpublic.html> accessed 29 March 2018.
45 See (n 25).
46 As here, references to individual views in the Report (n 39) will be given by paragraph number in the text.
47 See, similarly, the remarks of Baron Bramwell in the Capital Punishment Commission Report (n 39) para. 192.

This point relates to a view underlying not only past but also present objections to the reform of murder. This is the view that where there is a unique penalty for the crime – be it death or life imprisonment – the message sent by the imposition of that unique penalty is weakened, or may even be lost entirely, if it is not conveyed sufficiently often, in virtue of discretion being exercised in the killer's favour too frequently. The same argument applies in murder cases, if the unique penalty is not imposed often enough because the definition of murder is perceived to be too narrow. Baron Bramwell offered his opinion that, 'where a jury have an option of finding a man guilty of one or the other of two offences, they will almost invariably find the minor offence' (192). If sound, that objection obviously applies to the introduction of a category of second degree murder. 130 year later, in rejecting a move towards a three-tier structure including second degree murder, Minister of State for Justice, Sir Oliver Heald QC MP argued (in similar terms) that:

> There would ... undoubtedly be some public concern about any proposed changes to the categories of homicide which could appear to dilute the seriousness of, or affect the sentence in, any particular case.[48]

By contrast, of course, as for their Victorian predecessors, for modern supporters of an extenuating circumstances provision (or of a new category of second degree murder), a jury inclination towards a lesser offence, or towards a finding of extenuating circumstances, may well be seen as a positive advantage. It increases the number of cases in which the trial judge is free to determine a sentence that fits the circumstances of the case; and reformers were then, and are now, much more comfortable than Parliament with a greater role for judge and jury on matters of sentence in murder cases. In that regard, of course, by way of contrast with the position in 1866, we now have empirical evidence about the attitudes of the public in murder cases. Contrary to the view expressed by Sir Oliver Heald, it is only in the 'worst' kinds of murder case that members of the public support the imposition of the life sentence.[49]

So, let us turn to a different kind of objection to extenuating circumstances provisions. Emile Chédieu, an experienced French barrister gave evidence to the Commission (3183–3258), explaining the extenuating circumstances provision, as it worked at that time.[50] It was considered separate from provocation, as a basis for mitigation (3183), although a verdict based on both provocation and extenuating circumstances could be given. Whereas provocation was regarded as changing the 'character of the crime', extenuating circumstances focused on a feature of the defendant (such as immaturity), even when the crime he or she had committed was inexcusable (3185). It would thus have been possible to find extenuating circumstances even in a case of parricide or of 'assassination' (premeditated murder), the highest degree of homicide in France.[51] The effect of a finding of extenuating

48 Letter from Sir Oliver Heald to Bob Neill (Chairman of the Justice Committee), dated 24 October 2016. See also Home Office, *Murder, Manslaughter and Infanticide: Proposals for Reform of the Law: Summary of Responses and Government Position; Response to Consultation* CP (R) 19/08 14 January 2009 (Home Office, 2009), para 121.

49 See B. Mitchell and J.V. Roberts, *Public Opinion and Sentencing for Murder: An Empirical Investigation of Public Knowledge and Attitudes in England and Wales* (Nuffield Foundation & Coventry University 2010) 6.

50 It was applicable to all crimes, not just those carrying the death penalty.

51 Even when a jury found no extenuating circumstances, the penalty might still be remitted by the Sovereign through the *droit de grâce* (3200).

circumstances in such a case would be to put in place of the death penalty, hard labour for life, or possibly a fixed term between five and twenty years.

For Sir George Grey MP such a provision was objectionable on the grounds of uncertainty:

> One jury would adopt one rule and another jury would adopt another rule, and I think it would thus lead to the greatest possible uncertainty in the administration of the law (1495).

Although he does not elaborate on this claim, it is in fact an objection of very considerable substance, and something not considered by the House of Lords when it more recently supported the introduction of such a provision.[52] Take the issue of inconsistencies that would arise in the treatment of the same factor by different juries. Currently, for example, somewhat arbitrary though they may be, there are clear guidelines on the effect that relative youth is to have on the judge's starting point, when setting the minimum term to be spent in prison by someone convicted of murder. So, even in the worst kinds of murder case, that starting point will not be a whole life order if the offender was aged under 21 at the time of the offence.[53] The public and accessible nature of that rule means that it is fully open to scrutiny, criticism and change in the light of experience. By contrast, even in the interests of showing mercy, it is not desirable that juries should be entitled to (in effect) have an impact on sentence, in accordance with a perhaps wholly erroneous theory of maturation, when that theory will remain unarticulated and beyond challenge. If a softer line is justified on the grounds of relative immaturity, far better simply to abandon custody-for-life sentences for offenders under the age of 21 at the time of their contribution to the offence. Other kinds of anomaly would be bound to arise, For example, given that juries are not obliged to disclose their route to verdict, it would be possible for a jury to apply extenuating circumstances to an offender, on the basis that he or she only assisted or encouraged the offence in a minor way, when in fact the judge finds at the sentencing hearing that this offender was the highly culpable perpetrator. It would not be hard to imagine other problems arising. Suppose a jury could not agree on whether there were extenuating circumstances: would that justify a re-trial?

Sir James Stephen described the introduction of an extenuating circumstances provision as a, 'great blot' on the French system.[54] In general, in 1866, a number of witnesses thought the provision to be inferior to restoration of the power (mentioned earlier[55]) abolished only in 1861, that a judge previously possessed to 'record' (as opposed to pass) a death sentence. Normally, Baron Martin claimed, the Home Secretary would act on the judge's recommendation (253–54). At that time, judicial views on penal questions were held in much higher esteem by politicians, from whom they were far less independent than they are today.[56] Even putting aside the political-legal role of the Lord Chancellor, the Recorder of London, for example, was also an MP at the time of the 1872–74 Homicide Bill.[57] Modern insistence on the role of independent tribunals in determining questions of liberty has, of

52 See (n 24).

53 Criminal Justice Act 2003, schedule 21, s 4(1).

54 Sir J.F. Stephen, *History of the Criminal Law of England* (Vol. 1, Macmillan & Co 1883) 560.

55 See text at (n 41). To similar effect, see further, Sir J.F. Stephen, (n 54) above, at 561–62, who points out that the jury could itself recommend mercy to the judge; J. Garner, 'Criminal Procedure in France' (1916) 25(4) Yale Law Journal 255, 280.

56 Horder (n 13) 6.

57 Smith (n 19) 146.

course, now closed off this convenient way of shifting responsibility to the political sphere for the ultimate determination of murder sentences.[58] Might there be some other way in which to introduce a further discretionary element into the life sentence process, whilst avoiding the intrusion of politics?

Let us leave aside the current system for determining how long someone convicted of murder must spend in prison, and concentrate on an offender's liability, following release, to be recalled from licence at any point during his or her life. Could a mechanism be introduced for relieving an offender of this liability, after he or she has ceased to pose any significant threat? One analogy is provided by what was, before its repeal in 2011, Canada's so-called 'faint hope' clause. Someone convicted of first degree murder, and hence sentenced under Canadian law to a minimum of 25 years' imprisonment without parole eligibility, could nonetheless be granted a judicial review of the sentence after 15 years' imprisonment (other than in cases of multiple murder).[59] If the review was granted, because the judge believed the offender had a reasonable chance of success before the jury, the case would go to a jury to decide.[60] The political will to introduce such a system is always likely to be lacking, but there is a respectable case for saying that such a system should be introduced for cases where an offender has been abiding by the terms of his or her licence for (say) five, or perhaps ten years.

The Committee of 1866 and second degree murder

> I think the less the jury have to say the better ... I cannot help thinking that anything which multiplies distinctions, and the chances of escape to a criminal, is much to be deprecated.[61]

As indicated above, the 1866 Committee recommended that, whilst the definition of murder should remain unchanged, a two-tier structure, involving the categories of first and second degree murder, should be superimposed on the law. Under this structure, a key element in first degree murder would be played by 'express' malice (literal premeditation). This basis for dividing murder was probably always doomed to failure. There was even resistance to it in Pennsylvania, where courts expanded first degree murder to include unpremeditated (but intentional) killings.[62] Influential witnesses giving evidence to the 1866 Committee doubted the wisdom of seeking to draw the line between premeditated and other killings. Mr Justice Willes professed himself unable, 'to draw the line where express malice ends and implied malice begins' (2068). For Baron Bramwell, a callous disposition revealed by an unprovoked albeit spontaneous killing was as much in need of 'checking' – by the threat of the death penalty – as premeditated killing (198).[63] Perhaps surprisingly, though, very few witnesses reached the logical conclusion that this was simply not the place to draw the line. Lord Wensleydale, a judge, was one of the few to suggest

58 *R v Secretary of State for the Home Department Ex Parte Anderson* [2002] UKHL 46.

59 Canadian Criminal Code, s.745.4.

60 Ibid., s745.61(5). Evidence showed that those released by virtue of the 'faint hope' clause did better, in terms of rehabilitation, than offenders who did not benefit from it: see D. Beeby, 'Ottawa study praising "faint hope" clause for murderers never released' *The Globe and Mail* (Canada, 8 May 2011) <www.theglobeandmail.com/news/politics/ottawa-study-praising-faint-hope-clause-for-murderers-never-released/article1322268/> accessed 23 November 2017.

61 Capital Punishment Commission (n 39) (Baron Bramwell) 196.

62 Keedy (n 29). A similar development was noted by, in relation to the courts' understanding of malice in Massachusetts: Wasik (n 9) 259.

63 To similar effect, see the opinion of Wasik (n 9) 258.

that it would be better to draw the line in such a way as to divide all intentional killings (first degree murder) from other serious cases (second degree murder) above manslaughter (370). He accordingly rejected the suggestion that it should be capital murder in a case where a robber intentionally rendered the victim unconscious in the course of the robbery (but did not intend to kill), as a result of which the victim died (375).

Quite apart from the definitional controversies that might arise with a focus on express malice, witnesses worried about procedural difficulties with any new categorisations. Mr Justice Willes appeared to suggest that he thought that juries might not only find second degree murder when they ought to have found first degree murder, but that they might also find second degree murder when they ought to have found manslaughter or perhaps acquitted altogether (2063). Baron Bramwell objected both to an extenuating circumstances provision, and to a two-tier law of murder, on the grounds (suggested to him by the Under Secretary of state for the Home Department, Horatio Waddington) that, 'with country juries, the difficulty of their stating clearly upon what the extenuating circumstances are, might in many cases be very great' (198). Put aside the possibility that what is being spoken of here is the difficulty of a requirement that the jury articulate the reasons for or route to a verdict. What Baron Bramwell clearly had in mind was the unwelcome possibility of jury disagreement about verdict, if gradations of murder were introduced, just as there might well be disagreement about the presence or absence of extenuating circumstances: the problem posed by more choice as opposed to less.[64]

One hundred and forty years later, Richard Taylor made similar criticisms of the Law Commission's recommendations in respect of a division of murder into first and second degree categories.[65] The Law Commission initially consulted on a simple scheme in which first degree murder would be confined to cases of intentional killing, with killings through reckless indifference being treated as second degree murder.[66] Following criticism that this would make the scope of first degree murder too narrow, and the scope of second degree murder too uncertain, a more sophisticated but also more complex scheme was finally recommended.[67] Under this scheme, following a line of argument vigorously pursued by Fitzjames Stephen,[68] the fault element of first degree murder was to be expanded beyond intent to kill, to include an intention to do serious injury where there was also an awareness of a serious risk of causing death. The fault element in second degree murder was to be clarified by being given a definition based on cognitive states, in place of the affective state of mind constituted by 'reckless indifference'. It would include an intention to do serious injury, but also an intention to cause injury, or to cause fear or risk of injury, where the killer was aware that his or her conduct involved a serious risk of causing death. The substantive arguments for and against this scheme will not be rehearsed here.[69] Taylor's key arguments against the recommended scheme were, like Baron Bramwell's, procedural rather than substantive. He said:

> Suppose that six jurors think that D intended serious injury with no awareness of a serious risk of causing death but the other six jurors think that there was only an intent to

64 See Ashworth and Mitchell (n 9).

65 R. Taylor, 'The Nature of Partial Defences and the Coherence of (Second Degree) Murder' (2007) Criminal Law Review, May, 345.

66 Law Commission (n 16).

67 Law Commission (n 2).

68 Sir J.F. Stephen, *History of the Criminal Law of England* (Vol. 3, Macmillan & Co 1883) 92.

69 Horder (n 32) 19–39.

> cause injury but these second six consider that there was awareness of a risk of death … [T]here can be no conviction since although both sets of jurors are convinced of facts which independently amount legally to second degree murder, they do not all (or a majority of them) agree that any single one of the relevant facts (intention to cause serious injury or awareness of a serious risk of death) is proven. This problem is likely to occur not simply in relation to alternative verdicts but also where the prosecution case from the outset is second degree murder on one or other of these alternatives.[70]

Taylor's remedy is not to dispense with the distinction between first and second degree murder. Instead, he thought the procedural problem outlined above could be resolved by (a) sticking to the Law Commission's revised definition of first degree murder, (b) confining the fault element of second degree murder to the case where D intended to injure, or to cause fear or risk of injury, in the awareness that this would involve a serious risk of causing death, and (c) reducing to manslaughter cases where D killed through an intention to cause serious harm (without more).[71] It is hard to imagine that the latter suggestion – (c) – would find favour with any Government. It is worth noting that the procedural problem would also have been avoided, had the Law Commission retained its original Consultation Paper proposals. It will be recalled that these involved first degree murder confined to cases where there was an intent to kill, and second degree murder confined to cases of reckless indifference to causing death in the absence of such an intent (along with cases in which a partial defence to murder was successfully pleaded).

Conclusion

The procedural context against which the 1866 Committee deliberations were conducted was in significant ways different from the background to the Law Commission's recommendations. In the nineteenth century, even contested trials were very short (commonly lasting only a few minutes[72]), even though sitting days could be very long. Sometimes judges would sit from 9.00 am to 9.00 pm at the Old Bailey (following dinner at 5.00 pm[73]), even after the formal discontinuation of evening sittings in 1844.[74] Late sittings – favoured by Fitzjames Stephen himself – flourished in part as a means not only of dealing with a heavy list, but also as a way to avoid keeping a jury incommunicado – as was then the practice – overnight or (even worse) over the weekend, in part heard cases.[75] The relevance of this is that awareness of such a procedural background might have militated strongly against the view that an extra layer of legal complexity should be added to murder trials by the introduction of degrees of murder alongside manslaughter, perhaps thereby lengthening the trials themselves.

Clearly, these conditions no longer obtain. However, in 1866, judges summed up largely as they saw fit, and there was no right to appeal. Still less was there a prospect of re-trial.[76]

70 Taylor (n 65) 357–58.

71 For criticism of this proposal, see Horder (n 13) 102–03.

72 Homicide trials might well have lasted a little longer <www.oldbaileyonline.org/static/Trial-procedures.jsp> accessed 24 November 2017.

73 Allegations that judges appeared drunk when sitting after dinner were not uncommon.

74 D. Bentley, *English Criminal Justice in the Nineteenth Century* (Hambledon Press 1998) 55, 63.

75 Ibid. 63–4. In one notorious instance in 1834, Baron Smith tried 14 cases – some capital cases – between 6.00 pm and 6.00 am at the Armagh Assizes.

76 Bentley (n 74) 74.

So, the burden on judges to get the law right was not a heavy one. By contrast, a concern about a multi-layered law of homicide may now be not simply the prospect of jury disagreement and slightly longer trials. The worry may now pertain to increasing numbers of judicial errors in explaining the law, and the proper route to verdict, in the face of conflicting or complex claims in the alternative by (perhaps) a number of co-defendants.[77] That prospect might, in turn, lead to increased willingness on the part of prosecutors to accept a plea of guilty to second degree murder on a charge of first degree murder, something that may not necessarily be a welcome development to those who continue to be concerned about any 'dilution of murder'.[78] Nonetheless, the fact remains that there was, 'strong and widespread support' for the Law Commission's recommended division of murder into two degrees, including the support of the Old Bailey judges (amongst other judicial groups), victims' groups, the Police Federation and even the Ministry of Defence.[79] Morality relies on the law to provide a means of expressing in terms what Feinberg called, 'the most heinous kind of unjustified killing generally (wanton, barbarous, etc.).' A category of second degree murder permits the law to do this in a morally more sophisticated manner in the case of homicide, yet also in a way readily understood by jurors, whatever the procedural concerns may be. As a path to reform, perhaps following the Law Commission's proposals in its Consultation Paper,[80] it is also submitted that it is much to be preferred to the introduction of an 'extenuating circumstances' provision, for the reasons given earlier.

77 See the example given by the Law Commission in the text at (n 2) above.
78 See (n 48).
79 Law Commission (n 2) para 2.2.
80 Law Commission (n 16).

2 Killings short of murder

Examining culpable homicide in Scots law

Claire McDiarmid

Introduction

In a society which gives legal recognition to the right to life,[1] the state is required to have laws which ensure that, as a right, this is respected.[2] Thus, causing the death of another is, generally, absolutely proscribed and murder, one part of the recognition of this principle in criminal law, is, on occasion, described as the most serious crime[3] – though even murder can be aggravated.[4] Indeed, protection for the sanctity of life has been a part of Scots law throughout its history.[5] In 1827, for example, Lord Mackenzie was able to state that '[t]he law of Scotland is peculiarly tender of human life'.[6]

Murder is not, however, the only crime which can be charged where the accused has caused death. Scots law also encompasses the lesser offence of culpable homicide demonstrating that it is not merely the taking of life which murder censures (because culpable homicide sends this message too) but the particularly seriously wrong way in which, and/or (wicked) mindset with which, this is done. While identifying the relative seriousness of (even broadly similar) crimes in relation to each other is not straightforward,[7] a murder conviction signals that the killing was grave and the perpetrator was conspicuously blameworthy. Given, however, that the mechanisms by which one person may be the agent of the destruction of the life of another are myriad, from a relatively minor act which activates a pre-existing

1 For example, Art 2 of the European Convention on Human Rights (1950) states 'Everyone's right to life shall be protected by law. No one shall be deprived of his life intentionally save in the execution of a sentence of a court following his conviction of a crime for which this penalty is provided by law.'

2 *A v UK* (1999) 27 EHRR 611. See also *McCann v UK* (1996) 21 EHRR 97.

3 See, e.g., B. Mitchell and J. Roberts, 'Public Attitudes Towards the Mandatory Life Sentence for Murder: Putting Received Wisdom to the Empirical Test' (2011) 6 Criminal Law Review 456; D. Ormerod, 'Worth the Wait?' (2012) Criminal Law Review 79, 80; I. Grant, 'The Boundaries of the Criminal Law: The Criminalization of the Non-Disclosure of HIV' (2008) 31(1) Dalhousie Law Journal 123, 125; F. Stewart and A. Freiburg, 'Provocation in Sentencing: A Culpability-Based Framework' (2008) 19(3) Current Issues in Criminal Justice 283, 302.

4 For example, the Preamble to the Rome Statute of the International Criminal Court (1998) makes reference to 'the most serious crimes of concern to the international community as a whole' defining these (in Art 5(1)) as genocide, crimes against humanity, war crimes and the crime of aggression.

5 Sir George Mackenzie of Rosehaugh, *The Laws and Customs of Scotland in Matters Criminal* (James Glen 1678) 109; Baron David Hume, *Commentaries on the Law of Scotland Respecting Crimes* (Vol 1, 4th edn, Benjamin R Brown Bell & Bradfute 1844) Chap VI.

6 *Spring-Gun Case* 1827 Syme 209, 214.

7 See, for example, M. Gibson, 'Getting Their "Act" Together? Implementing Statutory Reform of Offences Against the Person' (2016) 9 Criminal Law Review 597–617.

condition[8] to an entirely intentional attack using extreme violence which is inflicted in order to kill,[9] there are advantages in relation to quantifying seriousness in having these two separate offences.

This chapter examines the crime of culpable homicide, looking, in particular, at the way in which it navigates the broad range of behaviours which may be brought within its own ambit of lesser seriousness in killing. Criminalisation is generally only regarded as necessary or justified at all for seriously harmful behaviours. Killing is perhaps the clearest example of such a behaviour – few would dispute the need to criminalise murder – and culpable homicide also reflects society's absolute repugnance towards killing by ensuring that the criminal sanction is still imposed even where the destruction of life was not deliberate but the by-product of some other reprehensible behaviour.

In fulfilling this function, culpable homicide occupies potentially more difficult, and certainly rather broader, terrain than murder, extending from killing which is so serious as to sit on the borderline with it to that which, for any of a wide variety of reasons, renders the agent of the death so unblameworthy that the question may be whether to prosecute for a homicide offence at all.

This paper will first of all provide an overview of the way in which culpable homicide is defined in Scots law. It will then consider its operation on the borderline with murder – where the accused has killed in a manner which bears possible hallmarks of the more serious crime but the lesser offence is, in fact, indicated. Next, it will move to consider culpable homicide in its own right where this is the crime to be charged from the outset. The law recognises two forms of this 'involuntary' type: lawful act and unlawful act. Finally, it will draw on these discussions to evaluate the efficacy of the offence as it operates in Scots criminal law currently.

Defining culpable homicide in Scots law

Culpable homicide occupies the borderlands of killing less than murder – concerned with the reasons for deeming (otherwise serious) killings 'not murder' at one end of the spectrum and with the reasons for convicting of an offence of homicide at all at the other, whilst also accommodating any killing which is *clearly* culpable homicide (rather than murder) from the outset. This highlights the broad range of the crime from killings which are relatively grave (not quite murder) to those which only just qualify as criminally blameworthy at all.

Unlike other areas of homicide law,[10] and perhaps surprisingly, there is no time-honoured definition to which all cases initially make reference. Instead, the crime tends to be described rather than defined. Thus, in *Drury v HM Advocate*[11] it was stated that 'the crime of culpable homicide covers the killing of human beings in all circumstances, short of murder, where the criminal law attaches a relevant measure of blame to the person who kills'.[12]

8 See, for example, *Bird v HM Advocate* 1952 JC 23; 1952 S.L.T. 446.

9 *Walker v HM Advocate* 2003 SLT 130. The varying forms of killing which can constitute culpable homicide are noted in *Gordon v HM Advocate* [2018] HCJAC 21; 2018 SLT 278 [53] (Lord Brodie).

10 For example, the definition of: murder – originally stated in J.H.A. Macdonald, *A Practical Treatise on the Criminal Law of Scotland* (5th edn, James Walker and D. J. Stevenson 1948) 89 and see *HM Advocate v Purcell* [2007] HCJ 13, 2008 JC 131, [9] (Lord Eassie); provocation – Macdonald, 94; diminished responsibility – Criminal Procedure (Scotland) Act 1995, s.51B.

11 2001 SLT 1013.

12 Ibid. [13] (LJ-G Rodger). This dictum has been cited with approval in subsequent cases including *Transco plc v HM Advocate (No 1)* 2004 JC 29 [4] (Lord Osborne); and *Lilburn v HM Advocate* [2011] HCJAC 41, 2012 JC 150 [4] (LJ-G Hamilton).

On this basis, then, culpable homicide incorporates any killing which is not murder but which is still criminally blameworthy. By, effectively, identifying the crime as 'not murder' this description draws murder's own definition into the equation:

> Murder is constituted by any wilful act causing the destruction of life, whether [wickedly] intended to kill, or displaying such wicked recklessness as to imply a disposition depraved enough to be regardless of consequences.[13]

Culpable homicide shares with murder the *actus reus* (the destruction of life). Macdonald writes of the 'death of a person [being] caused, or materially accelerated by the improper conduct of another'.[14] In general, then, since both murder and culpable homicide arise through the killing of another person, this first dividing line between them is drawn by whether one or other of murder's two alternative *mentes reae* (wicked intention to kill or wicked recklessness) can be established. The proximity between the two forms of homicide, at this level of seriousness, can be seen in this description, from *Ross v Lord Advocate*,[15] a case concerning the Lord Advocate's policy on the prosecution of assisted suicide. Lord Justice-Clerk Carloway stated:

> ... if a person does something which he knows will cause the death of another person, he will be guilty of *homicide* if his act is the immediate and direct cause of the person's death[16] ... Depending upon the nature of the act, the crime may be murder or culpable homicide. Exactly where the line of causation falls to be drawn is a matter of fact and circumstance for determination in each individual case. That does not, however, produce any uncertainty in the law.[17]

The question of whether the law is certain may be debatable – indeed the view has been expressed elsewhere that 'the mental element in murder and culpable homicide in contemporary Scots law ... is in need of a thorough re-examination'[18] What is clear, however, is that descriptions such as these from *Drury* and *Ross* alone would leave culpable homicide as rather an amorphous category, lacking even a clear definition of *actus reus* and *mens rea*. In practice, then, it is divided into voluntary and involuntary forms, with the latter being subdivided into lawful act and unlawful act types. While these divisions have existed since historical times,[19] conviction will always be of the generic offence of culpable homicide without necessarily much discussion of the form. These forms do, however, have slightly clearer definition.

Voluntary culpable homicide arises where the accused has killed in a way which would, in principle, satisfy the definition of murder but a partial defence (of provocation or of diminished responsibility) operates to 'reduce' the crime to the lesser form.[20] These defences are

13 Macdonald (n 10) 89 (as amended by *Drury* (n 11) [11] (LJ-G Rodger).

14 Macdonald (n 10) (1st edn 1867) 150.

15 [2016] CSIH 12, 2016 S.C. 502.

16 Referencing *MacAngus v HM Advocate* [2009] HCJAC 8, 2009 SLT 137 [42] (LJ-G Hamilton).

17 *Ross* (n 15) [29] (LJ-C Carloway) (emphasis added).

18 *Petto v HM Advocate* [2011] HCJAC 80, 2012 JC 105 [20] (LJ-C Gill).

19 Hume (n 5) identified 'Culpable homicide by doing a lawful act without due caution' 233, 'Culpable homicide where death ensues on a purpose to do some slight injury' 235 and 'Culpable homicide where there is a mortal purpose, but taken up on gross provocation' 239.

20 See, for example, discussion in *Lieser v HM Advocate* 2008 SCL 1050 [11] (Lord Kingarth). The terminology of 'reducing' is not accepted in *Drury* (n 11) where LJ-G Rodger described it as

discussed elsewhere in this series[21] and voluntary culpable homicide will not, therefore, be considered in detail in this chapter. Involuntary culpable homicide generally arises where the death of the deceased was not within the accused's actual or deemed contemplation but s/he is nonetheless considered to be sufficiently blameworthy for it that criminal liability is entailed. The unlawful act type arises where the accused is involved in committing another crime (in modern times this is almost invariably the crime of assault) and death ensues. Macdonald explains this category as 'the doing of any unlawful act … where death could not reasonably be foreseen as the consequences of the act.'[22] The *mens rea* is that for the underlying crime. Involuntary lawful act culpable homicide,[23] by contrast, occurs where the accused's act is (for these purposes) lawful but nonetheless causes the victim's death. The *mens rea* is recklessness.[24]

The way in which culpable homicide operates at the top end of seriousness (where the issue is the division with murder) will be considered first.

Murder or culpable homicide: policy decisions

It is fair to say that one of the functions of culpable homicide is to make it possible for the law to be seen to acknowledge the inherent wrongfulness of killing, without the 'baggage' (stigma and mandatory life sentence[25]) of murder. This being the case, on occasion, it may seem that the decision as to category (murder or culpable homicide) is taken for policy reasons without clearly engaging legal principle. Such killings, then, though named culpable homicide, may be particularly difficult to classify in terms of seriousness. Precisely for that reason of the difficulty of fitting them into the homicide binary however, they clearly sit on the line with murder. In other words, there are perhaps equally good reasons to classify as one as the other.

Prior to trial, such decisions are entirely the Crown's. 'In Scotland the master of the instance in all prosecutions for the public interest is the Lord Advocate. It is for him to decide when and against whom to launch prosecution and upon what charges.'[26] Given the range of ways in which, and reasons for which, death may be caused, the public interest encompasses a wide variety of considerations. The concept of 'mercy killing' may illustrate these points. In *HM Advocate v Brady*,[27] the accused had, at least *prima facie*, met the (then) requirements of murder by destroying the life of the victim (his terminally ill brother) with intention to kill. Whilst the original charge was murder, the Crown accepted a plea of guilty to culpable homicide. The other members of the family (who, given the nature of the killing were the family of both the deceased and the accused) supported the accused's

'essentially misleading' [17] however it has continued to be used. See J. Chalmers and F. Leverick, *Criminal Defences and Pleas in Bar of Trial* (W Green 2006) para 1.02 n 6.

21 A. Reed and M. Bohlander (eds), *Loss of Control and Diminished Responsibility: Domestic, Comparative and International Perspectives* (Routledge 2011). For a discussion of provocation in Scots law, see C. McDiarmid, 'Don't Look Back in Anger: the Partial Defence of Provocation in Scots Criminal Law' in J. Chalmers, F. Leverick and L. Farmer (eds) *Essays in Criminal Law in Honour of Sir Gerald Gordon* (Edinburgh University Press 2010).

22 Macdonald (n 10) 96.

23 See *Transco* (n 12) [35] – [38] (Lord Hamilton).

24 Ibid.

25 Criminal Procedure (Scotland) Act 1995, s.205.

26 *Boyle v HM Advocate* 1976 JC 32, 37 (Lord Cameron).

27 1997 GWD 1–18.

actions and were relieved that the deceased's suffering (from Huntingdon's disease) was at an end.[28] The trial judge imposed the most lenient sentence available (admonishment).

Here, the existence of culpable homicide allowed the Crown leeway to balance the competing public interests in respecting the very particular wishes and interests of the deceased's family for clemency against the fact of the, entirely deliberate, taking of the life of another.[29] The structure of homicide allows this to be accomplished at conviction rather than merely through sentencing. It also raises that question of the way in which the law mediates its own principles. The Crown's decision to accept the plea of guilty to culpable homicide may meet the justice of the case (though, for example, church leaders were not in agreement with it, considering that it failed to uphold the importance of the sanctity of life).[30] Nonetheless, it allocates the issue wholly to the Crown's discretion thereby bypassing the *law* on the distinction from murder. It does not assist in understanding, or developing, the legal principles of that distinction.

The more recent case of *Ross*[31] concerned the related issue of assisted suicide, where a seriously ill petitioner sought further guidance from the Lord Advocate as to the circumstances in which anyone helping him to bring his own life to an end would be prosecuted. As noted above, the Inner House of the Court of Session simply accepted that the law of *homicide* would apply,[32] again failing to differentiate murder from culpable homicide at the level of principle in such circumstances. While clearly the so-called right to die raises particularly fraught issues of law, ethics, morality and compassion it is precisely in such cases, and because of the intense anxiety which attends them, that clearer legal principle is particularly valuable and necessary. Without bespoke legislation in relation to assisted suicide, the common law on homicide is required to do this work.

The line with murder

Such policy decisions are, then, concerned with the usefulness of having a lesser form of homicide available rather more than with the legal principles. Where the matter is not determined at a preliminary stage on policy grounds but is tested in court, legal reasons for the outcome become available for scrutiny. Thus, to be convicted of culpable homicide, such a reason must be identified. Is there, however, any remaining scope to apply the binary question of murder / not murder rather than clearly to cast the determination in terms of culpable homicide's own mental and behavioural elements?

Because murder and culpable homicide share the *actus reus* of the destruction of life,[33] in principle, the question for a court to determine is whether or not the accused has the *mens rea* of murder.[34] For murder, both possible mental elements incorporate wickedness (wicked

28 Editorial, 'Family declare support for brother's mercy killing' *The Herald* (Glasgow, 1 October 1996) <www.heraldscotland.com/news/12024044.Family_declare_support_for_brother_apos_s_mercy_killer/> accessed 24 July 2018.

29 Having given the deceased increased quantities of his standard medication and some alcohol, the accused then smothered the deceased with a pillow.

30 Editorial (n 28).

31 *Ross* (n 15).

32 See text accompanying (n 17).

33 J. Chalmers and F. Leverick (eds), Gerald H Gordon, *The Criminal Law of Scotland* (Vol. 2, 4th edn, W Green 2017) para 30.01. See also *Gordon v HM Advocate* [2018] HCJAC 21; 2018 SLT 278 where an accused person was initially charged with murder but ultimately a plea of guilty of culpable homicide on the grounds of diminished responsibility was accepted.

34 See, for example, *Scott v HM Advocate* [2011] HCJAC 110, 2012 SCCR 45 [10], [16] (Lord Bonomy).

recklessness or wicked intention to kill) and both require some attitude on the part of the accused towards the death of the victim.[35] The accused must either have (wickedly) intended to kill the victim or else have had (in addition to an intention to cause physical injury)[36] an indifference as to whether the victim lived or died.[37] It is possible for the matter to be determined by reference to the (tautologically) murderous quality of the act itself.[38]

The fact that conviction of the lesser offence is always for the generic crime of culpable homicide creates possible scope for the argument, not necessarily that the accused's crime conforms to the principles of culpable homicide in either its voluntary or involuntary form but rather that the accused is, simply, insufficiently blameworthy to be convicted of murder. In other words, the argument is that the crime committed is 'not murder' rather than that it *is* (on its own terms) culpable homicide. Where such an argument is led in an appeal, the fact that the jury at first instance has returned a murder conviction supports the seriousness of such cases and indicates that, even if they *could* constitute culpable homicide, they still occupy this liminal territory right on the line with murder.

In such cases, the accused's claim is likely to be that the scope for a culpable homicide verdict (and hence a more favourable outcome for him/her) was not fully exploited thereby resulting in detriment. Following *Ferguson v HM Advocate*,[39] the (murder) trial judge has a responsibility to put the possibility of a culpable homicide verdict (indeed any alternative verdict reasonably available on the evidence) to the jury unless there is no basis at all on which such a verdict could be returned. In principle, then, this is an issue of procedure however it requires an assessment of the principles of the substantive law on homicide by the trial judge to determine whether a culpable homicide instruction needs to be given.

In *Ferguson*, and the subsequent case of *Anderson v HM Advocate*, [40] such an instruction had been omitted. Both appeals are concerned with the nature of the act bringing about death. In *Ferguson* a single stab wound to the back, just below the shoulder blade was considered still to leave open the possibility of a culpable homicide verdict[41] because only the one wound was inflicted (rather than 'multiple injuries')[42] and this was not regarded as a 'particularly vulnerable area[…] of the body'.[43] By contrast, in *Anderson*, a single stab wound to the abdomen, directed upwards so that it injured the heart was considered to preclude any such option because this was a 'vulnerable part of the deceased's body and in particular [because it was] in the direction of his heart.'[44] It can be seen, then, that the *actus reus* of murder is not entirely separate from the *mens rea*. Certain acts – here, a stab wound to a vulnerable part of the body – allow at least wicked recklessness to be inferred. Culpable

35 For a full discussion, see C. McDiarmid '"Something Wicked This Way Comes": The *Mens Rea* of Murder in Scots Law' (2012) 4 Juridical Review 283–304.
36 See *Purcell* (n 10).
37 See, for example, *Cowie v HM Advocate* [2009] HCJAC 76, 2010 JC 51 [21] (LJ-C Gill).
38 See *Meikle v HM Advocate* [2014] HCJAC 116, 2014 S.L.T. 1062 [15] (Lord Drummond Young); *Humphrey v HM Advocate* [2016] HCJAC 5, 2016 SCL 275 [32] (LJ-C Carloway).
39 [2008] HCJAC 71, 2009 SLT 67. See also *Woodside v HM Advocate* [2010] HCJAC 94, 2011 JC 100.
40 [2010] HCJAC 9, 2010 SCCR 270.
41 Ferguson was re-tried following the success of his appeal and was again convicted of murder: Editorial, 'Evil Airdrie thug convicted for teenager's playground murder' *Daily Record* (Glasgow 12 August 2009) <www.dailyrecord.co.uk/news/local-news/evil-airdrie-thug-convicted-teenagers-2831954> accessed 24 July 2018.
42 *Ferguson* (n 39) [37] (Lord Osborne).
43 Ibid.
44 *Anderson* (n 40) [17] (Lord Mackay of Drumadoon).

homicide is mobilised to sweep up any possibility of lesser blameworthiness (even where this is ultimately rejected).

Such appeals are, of course, concerned with the review of the matter undertaken by the trial judge, who, in determining how to frame the charge to the jury, is likely to have considered whether, and why, culpable homicide (on its own principles) was or was not an option. At the appeal stage, the issue is cast more in terms of whether or not murder is unequivocally indicated. The argument here is not that the *principles* of culpable homicide have no relevance. It is rather that they tend to be subsumed in the more general, higher level question of whether the crime *must* be characterised as murder.

Another area in which the resort to a culpable homicide verdict on a murder charge sits a little outside the voluntary / involuntary formulations is in relation to art and part killing.

Art and part killings

The particularities of Scots law on killing on an art and part basis are such that, in some circumstances, individual co-accused can seek to argue that grounds exist for a conviction of culpable homicide even where others are convicted of murder.[45] The distinction between murder and culpable homicide *is* generally underpinned by principle in that a distinction exists between killing where there is pre-concert and killing which arises spontaneously,[46] though this distinction has been described as 'nonsensical'.[47]

Where a crime is pre-arranged and there is a common plan to commit it then all co-accused who are parties to that plan must be convicted of the same offence.[48] Again, the key issue is whether or not the accused has the *mens rea* for murder which, in such cases, relates to analysis of the plan. Thus:

> … an accused is guilty of murder art and part where, first, by his conduct, for example his words or actions, he actively associates himself with a common criminal purpose which is or includes the taking of human life or carries the obvious risk that human life will be taken, and, secondly, in the carrying out of that purpose murder is committed by someone else.[49]

Rather than wicked intention or wicked recklessness, this active association with such a risk (where life is in fact taken) constitutes the *mens rea* for murder on an art and part basis.[50] The rule can have serious consequences. In the leading case of *McKinnon*[51] for example, there was a common plan to commit robbery using chef's knives as a weapon. The forensic evidence indicated that the fatal stab wounds had most likely been inflicted by only one co-accused but four of the co-accused were convicted of murder on the art and part basis. Since the purpose of art and part is to ensure that responsibility is brought home to those who are

45 See, for example, *Sim v HM Advocate* [2016] HCJAC 48, 2016 JC 174, 2016 SCL 612; *Carey v HM Advocate* [2016] HCJAC 10, 2016 SLT 377.
46 See, for example, *Parfinowski v HM Advocate* [2013] HCJAC 123, 2014 SCCR 30, [24] (Lady Dorrian).
47 F. Leverick, 'The (Art and) Parting of the Ways: Joint Criminal Liability for Homicide' (2012) 37 Scots Law Times 227, 231.
48 *McKinnon v HM Advocate* 2003 JC 29; 2003 SLT 281.
49 Ibid. [32] (LJ-G Cullen).
50 *Poole v HM Advocate* [2009] HCJAC 42, 2009 SCCR 577 [11] (Lord Kingarth).
51 *McKinnon* (n 48).

associated with a crime but who may not actually have carried it out,[52] it is at least logical that all should be convicted of the same crime.

Nonetheless, and somewhat less logically, where the conduct with fatal consequences arises spontaneously, there is scope for each accused to be judged on his or her own actions, yet still under the ambit of art and part liability. The issue is whether the co-accused shared a common murderous purpose:[53]

> Where [a co-accused] is not proved to have associated himself [sic] with that [common murderous] purpose [ie carrying the obvious risk that human life will be taken] or is proved to have participated in some less serious common criminal purpose in the course of which the victim dies, [that] accused may be guilty art and part of culpable homicide, whether or not any other person is proved guilty of murder.[54]

The art and part principle is thus operating to make the co-accused guilty of a homicide offence – to draw him/her into taking responsibility (albeit at a lower level) for the death – whilst deeming the offence itself, potentially at least, one of murder. Given that the essence of art and part liability is that the co-accused shared *the same* criminal purpose, this may be problematic.

In *Carey v HM Advocate*[55] the death arose from a fracas in a flat in Saltcoats during which the deceased was punched, kicked and, ultimately, stabbed in the chest. The co-accused Carey was charged and convicted of culpable homicide and this was upheld on appeal but his conviction stood on an art and part basis with the other co-accused, McCulloch, who inflicted the fatal wound and was charged with, and convicted of, murder. Lord Justice-Clerk Carloway stated '[t]here appears to be an illogicality in this approach; that a person can be art and part guilty of culpable homicide when the victim is found to have been murdered, but this is the law as it presently stands'[56]

It is, presumably, always better for an accused person to be convicted of culpable homicide than of murder and this 'illogicality' does allow such an outcome. This potential benefit to a co-accused can be seen in a case such as *Parfinowski v HM Advocate*,[57] where there is clear evidence of the accused's participation in a fatal attack but insufficient evidence that his or her own purpose was, during that attack, murderous. In *Parfinowski*, the deceased was killed by a (spontaneous) attack with a baseball bat accompanied by punching, kicking and stamping. The fatal blow was delivered by a co-accused named Robertson. Parfinowski had apparently, prior to the attack with the bat, punched the deceased and, subsequent to it, he had kicked him. Parfinowski was, however, wearing light canvas shoes and the forensic evidence was that his kicks could not have caused the fatal injuries. Also, it could not be stated with confidence that he had shared the murderous purpose. A conviction of culpable homicide was substituted for the murder conviction[58] because the jury had not been instructed that this was possible when the evidence, did, in fact support such a conclusion.

52 See, for example, Lord Patrick's charge to the jury in *HM Advocate v Lappen* [1956] SLT 109.
53 *Parfinowski* (n 46) [24] (Lady Dorrian),
54 *McKinnon* (n 48) [32] (LJ-G Cullen),
55 *Carey* (n 45).
56 Ibid. [29] (LJ-C Carloway).
57 *Parfinowski* (n 46).
58 Editorial, 'Andrew Parfinowski Brett Lodge murder conviction quashed' *BBC News* (Scotland, 19 November 2013) < www.bbc.co.uk/news/uk-scotland-edinburgh-east-fife-25001625> accessed 24 July 2018.

Lady Dorrian explained that '[o]n the evidence, it could be said that there was scope for a finding that there were striking differences between the actions of the first accused and the appellant.'[59]

In such circumstances, then, the ability to return different verdicts even though the conviction for homicide at all still depends on the existence of art and part liability *may* be viewed by the accused as an advantage. Nonetheless, it does not resolve the logical problem outlined above which, as Lord Carloway also noted, 'opens up the prospect of a conviction for homicide where the co-accused has not associated himself with a lethal attack.'[60]

At the heart of art and part liability is the issue of the common criminal purpose to which the accused signed up. If this question is addressed, as in *Parfinowski*, from the perspective of 'saving' the accused from a murder conviction then the issue will be whether there is scope to say that the s/he did *not* share the murderous purpose. In *Carey*, by contrast, it was eventually determined that the fatal blow had been inflicted by the co-accused (McCulloch). If Carey had been judged on his own actions, then, he had not carried out the *actus reus* of homicide so he could only have been convicted of assault. He was only able to be convicted of culpable homicide by being tied into the homicide element art and part.

It is not quite clear how the common criminal purpose is being defined for these purposes, however. The 'obvious risk of life being taken' test applies to the common plan – that is to cases involving pre-concert. The *mens rea* of murder on an individual basis is, of course, wicked intention to kill or wicked recklessness. As will be discussed in more detail in the next section, the *mens rea* for involuntary culpable homicide is not directed towards the bringing about of death. How then can it be determined that the criminal purpose to which an individual co-accused signed up falls somewhere between assault only and murderousness? It is (involuntary unlawful act) culpable homicide where an assault causes death but, almost by definition, in those circumstances, the criminal purpose is not towards death. Involuntary means that the death was not contemplated. It is hard to think of a common criminal purpose to commit culpable homicide *per se*. In such cases, the accused is getting the benefit of the decision that his/her crime is not murder – but if s/he only joined into an assault and is horrified that another co-accused caused death a culpable homicide verdict may be cold comfort.

Given that the incidents from which the relevant deaths occur are often fast-moving and, by definition, involve a number of people, it is not always easy to impose the legal framework on the facts. It is also fair to say that these cases frequently involve relatively extreme violence. Culpable homicide allows the law to recognise, in spite of this, that such acts, even those that cause death, should still be legally graduated. They also illustrate the crime's close proximity to murder in such cases.

In addition, it is clear that where the art and part concept arises spontaneously, the definition of involuntary culpable homicide on an individual basis can come into play and attention will now be turned to this.

Involuntary culpable homicide

Where culpable homicide is the crime charged from the outset it is trite to say that the accused's fault or the circumstances attending the death are of a lesser order of seriousness

59 *Parfinowski* (n 46) [24].

60 *Carey* (n 45) [27], discussing *Brown v HM Advocate* 1993 S.C.C.R. 382.

than for murder. In terms of fair labelling,[61] this seems helpful, but it is worth bearing in mind that the accused is still being labelled a killer. It is unclear to what extent this favourable distinction from 'murderer' is recognised in the popular consciousness. It is therefore important to look at the operation of involuntary culpable homicide and to see to what it attaches blameworthiness.

Unlawful act type

As noted above, different rules apply depending on whether the death arises from a lawful or an unlawful act on the part of the accused – though the category of *un*lawful act is narrow. This form of the crime is found where the accused carries out an unlawful act and (unanticipated) death results. In general, the unlawful act will be an assault on the victim, following from the historical position recognised by both Hume[62] and Archibald Alison where one category of culpable homicide was constituted 'By the unintentional deprivation of life, in pursuance of an intention not to kill, but to do some inferior bodily injury, from which it was not probable that death would follow'.[63]

It is not the case that, where an accused is engaged in any criminal act whatsoever and death results, this constitutes unlawful act type. Indeed, assault is probably the only crime which is accepted without question as the basis for it.[64] Scots law is then somewhat more restricted in the underlying crimes which can constitute this form of culpable homicide than are those other jurisdictions which require only criminality and dangerousness.[65]

The criterion for relevant unlawful acts is affirmed in *MacAngus v HM Advocate* [66] where it is stated that 'there appears to be no support for the view that unlawful act culpable homicide can be made out except where, as in assault or analogous cases, the conduct is directed in some way against the victim.'[67]

As a crime, assault, in Scots law, requires an attack on the person of another[68] carried out with evil intent which is defined as intent to cause immediate bodily harm or the fear of immediate bodily harm.[69] The *mens rea* for culpable homicide arising from an unlawful act is simply that for that underlying offence. The usual rules of causation apply so that the accused must take the victim as s/he finds him/her. Thus if, even very slight, violence, activates a pre-

61 See J. Chalmers and F. Leverick, 'Fair Labelling in Criminal Law' (2008) 71(2) Modern Law Review, 217–246.
62 (n 19) (second category) Culpable homicide where death ensues on a purpose to do some slight injury.
63 A. Alison, *Principles of the Criminal Law of Scotland* (William Blackwood 1832) 92
64 The view has also been expressed that death arising from fire-raising might constitute unlawful act type culpable homicide because fire is so volatile that a particular duty to take care arises. See Gordon (n 33) para 31–27 n 167 referring to *Mathieson v HM Advocate* 1981 SCCR 196. By contrast, the case of *Sutherland v HM Advocate* 1994 JC 62 found that death arising from fire-raising (to defraud insurers) had to be treated as lawful act type.
65 See T. Storey, 'Unlawful and Dangerous: A Comparative Analysis of Unlawful Act Manslaughter in English, Australian and Canadian Law' (2017) 81(2) Journal of Criminal Law, 143–60.
66 *MacAngus* (n 16).
67 Ibid. [29] (LJ-G Hamilton).
68 Macdonald (n 10) 115.
69 *Smart v HM Advocate* 1975 JC 30, 33 (LJ-C Wheatley).

existing condition and the victim dies, culpable homicide is a possible outcome.[70] In charging the jury in *HM Advocate v Hartley*, [71] Lord Sutherland gave this example:

> So, to take an example, if you are having an argument with somebody and give him a punch on the chin, not a very hard one, but a punch on the chin, and he is taken aback and stumbles backwards, catches his heel on the kerb of the pavement, falls over, cracks his skull and dies, you would be guilty of culpable homicide because you have committed an unlawful act, an assault by punching him, and as a direct consequence of that act he sustained injuries from which he died.[72]

In *Gay v HM Advocate* [73] the accused inflicted a single punch on the victim who died subsequently in hospital. He had sustained injury to his chin and to the back of his head as well as a fractured jaw and was found to have had a cardiac arrest. He suffered from underlying health issues including heart disease.[74] The jury convicted Gay of assault to the severe injury on a charge of culpable homicide. The case is reported only as an appeal against sentence so there is no discussion of the principles of the substantive law. While juries are always free to return any verdict open to them, and evidence in relation to causation is not recorded in the case report, this does at least suggest that there is scope for criminal culpability to be tailored to the accused's perceived blameworthiness so that it is not always necessary to label him/her a killer simply because death ensued following his/her initial act. Culpable homicide then also occupies this territory at the opposite end of the seriousness spectrum from murder where death has resulted but, for whatever reason, it is not ultimately deemed appropriate to attach the stigma of a homicide conviction, only that of assault

Lawful act type

In *Sutherland v HM Advocate* [75] fire-raising to defraud insurers was not accepted as a relevant unlawful act[76] because it is not a crime against the person.[77] To convict of culpable homicide, therefore, recklessness[78] on the accused's part was required. In other words, because the underlying act was not directed against the victim in the necessary way, lawful act type was deemed the appropriate form. Because any conviction will always be simply for

70 As in *Bird* (n 8) where the accused had caused the victim considerable fear but had used very little actual violence against her. By contrast in *Gay v HM Advocate* [2017] HCJAC 62, 2017 SCL 913, the accused punched the deceased in the face and he died very shortly afterwards having suffered from a number of underlying conditions. Gay was convicted by the jury only of assault to the severe injury.

71 1989 SLT 135

72 Ibid. 136. Issues arising in relation to so-called 'one punch assaults' including dangerousness, are discussed in J. Schreiber, A. Williams and D. Ranson, 'Kings to Cowards: One-Punch Assaults' (2016) 44(2) Journal of Law, Medicine and Ethics 332.

73 *Gay* (n 70).

74 Editorial, 'Kirkcaldy football coach acquitted of culpable homicide' *Fife Today* (Scotland, 8 March 2017) <www.fifetoday.co.uk/news/crime/kirkcaldy-football-coach-acquitted-of-culpable-homicide-1-4386743> accessed 24 July 2018.

75 *Sutherland* (n 64)

76 Ibid. 68 (LJ-G Hope setting out ground of appeal).

77 Ibid. 65 (LJ-G Hope explaining trial judge's directions).

78 Ibid. 67 variously described as fire-raising 'done in the face of obvious risks which were or should have been guarded against or in circumstances which showed a complete disregard for any potential dangers which might result' and, more simply 'criminal negligence' (LJ-G Hope).

culpable homicide, this potential overlap, or slippage between lawful and unlawful act is not likely to be problematic in practice. The complexity is that certain acts which *do*, in fact, constitute criminal offences (like fire-raising to defraud insurers) need to follow the rules of *lawful* act type (i.e., *actus reus* of the destruction of life; *mens rea* of recklessness) for a culpable homicide conviction to ensue.

The category of crimes which can be unequivocally seen to be directed against the victim (i.e., assault alone) is, thus, pretty narrow. Behaviour constituting other criminal offences will be placed in the lawful act category for culpable homicide purposes. This may be confusing semantically – but possibly only at that level. The issue arises particularly in cases where the accused supplied drugs to the victim with his/her consent (or even at his/her request) and s/he ultimately died from ingesting these.[79] While, clearly, supply of a controlled drug is an offence in terms of s.4(3)(a) of the Misuse of Drugs Act 1971, the law is that 'a charge libelling culpable homicide in the context of the supplying (or the administration of) a controlled drug is relevant only if the Crown offers to prove that the supplying (or the administration) of the drug was in the circumstances reckless.'[80] Scots law recognises two relevant crimes of recklessness – causing real injury as in *Khaliq v HM Advocate* [81] and causing reckless injury from *HM Advocate v Harris*.[82] Either of these crimes might be appropriately directed against the victim (Khaliq was selling glue-sniffing kits to children in the knowledge that this was the (harmful) purpose for which they would be used; Harris was a bouncer who ejected a woman from a nightclub by pushing her in such a way that she fell down a flight of stairs and out onto the road where she was run over by a passing car.) Where either of these crimes is committed and death results it will not be clear whether lawful or unlawful act type culpable homicide has been committed since both have the *mens rea* of recklessness. Conviction for the overarching generic offence allows access to the full gamut of sentencing options from admonishment[83] through community service[84] to a (discretionary) life sentence[85] so that there is scope for a nuanced approach to overall blameworthiness. The lawful / unlawful act dichotomy in such a case is therefore of limited significance. It does however matter considerably to an accused who has committed another type of crime from which death resulted. The need to establish recklessness protects him/her from conviction of a homicide offence where this was completely outwith his / her contemplation.

The development of lawful act type recognises the need for the law to identify sufficient fault on the accused's part that conviction of a criminal offence is warranted. *Paton v HM Advocate*, [86] which has been influential in defining recklessness more generally, noted this fault requirement whilst not wholeheartedly welcoming it. Lord Justice-Clerk Aitchison said:

> There is evidence in the case that the appellant was driving his car at a fairly high speed, and there is also evidence in the case that there was, perhaps, a want of care. The difficulty that the case presents is whether there was evidence that the appellant was guilty of criminal negligence in the sense in which we use that expression. At one time the rule of

79 See *Lord Advocate's Reference* (*No 1 of 1994*) 1996 JC 76; *MacAngus* (n 16).
80 *MacAngus* (n 16) [30] (LJ-G Hamilton).
81 1984 JC 23.
82 1993 JC 150.
83 *Brady* (n 27).
84 *Docherty v HM Advocate* 2000 SCCR 106 (300 hours community service)
85 *K (A Child) v HM Advocate* 1993 SLT 237 (detention without limit of time for a child-accused aged 12); *Kirkwood v HM Advocate* 1939 JC 36 (penal servitude for life)
86 1936 JC 19

> law was that any blame was sufficient, where death resulted, to justify a verdict of guilty of culpable homicide. Unfortunately, this law has to some extent been modified by decisions of the Court, and it is now necessary to show gross, or wicked, or criminal negligence, something amounting, or at any rate analogous, to a criminal indifference to consequences, before a jury can find culpable homicide proved.[87]

While in *Paton* the accused was charged with culpable homicide (though ultimately convicted of a lesser motoring offence) it is interesting that this concept of recklessness, used as the fault element, is disconnected completely from the issue of the destruction of life. Thus, the concept has developed in both lawful act culpable homicide cases and cases of other, non-fatal, crimes of recklessness. *Paton*'s definition of recklessness was quoted with approval in *Quinn v Cunningham*,[88] a case relating to riding a bicycle recklessly (though without causing death). Lord Clyde offered the further definition of 'an utter disregard of what the consequences of the act in question may be so far as the public are concerned'[89] and 'a recklessness so high as to involve an indifference to the consequences for the public generally'.[90] Finally *Transco plc v HM Advocate*,[91] – an (unsuccessful) attempt to prosecute a company for bringing about the deaths of a family of four in a gas explosion – whilst broadly accepting the concept, took issue with the circularity of the *Paton* definition. Lord Hamilton stated 'There may be some difficulty in regarding Lord Justice-Clerk Aitchison's observation as a comprehensive definition — not least because of the circularity which arises from the use (twice) of the adjective "criminal" in the definition of the crime. But it does at least point … to a degree of want of care which is grave.'[92]

There are two issues here. The first is the rather unsatisfactory way in which this central concept of recklessness is defined. The other is the disconnect between the *mentes reae* of lawful and unlawful act culpable homicide and the victim's death.

Absence of reference to homicidal attitude

Considering, first, the latter point – murder arises where the accused causes death either intending to do so (wicked intention to kill) or intending to cause (only) physical injury together with an indifference as to whether the victim lived or died (wicked recklessness). Both of these formulations encapsulate blameworthiness arising from the accused's aim, or, at least, acceptance of causing the death of the victim. The *mens rea* components of culpable homicide (which are that of the underlying (non-fatal) offence for unlawful act type and recklessness for lawful act type) by contrast, make no reference to death whatsoever. Culpable homicide is a serious offence. It is, for example, sometimes charged in road traffic cases on the basis that 'the degree of culpability required to prove that charge is greater than that required for the statutory offences and in particular is greater than that required for s 1 of the Road Traffic Act, causing death by dangerous driving'.[93] Its *mens rea* elements however

87 Ibid. 22
88 1956 JC 22
89 Ibid. 24
90 Ibid. 25
91 *Drury* (n 12)
92 Ibid. [37]
93 *HM Advocate v McDowall* 1999 SLT 243, 245 (Lord Abernethy's charge to the jury). In *Purcell* (n 10), the driving was considered so dangerous that the Crown initially tried to charge the accused with murder. This was unsuccessful

are the same as for non-fatal offences and, in recklessness, even for the crime of reckless endangerment[94] which requires only the creation of a foreseeable risk without any actual adverse consequences. How, then, is its seriousness to be gauged alongside these other crimes of recklessness? The principle of *actus non facit reum nisi mens sit rea* [95] is generally applied in Scots law meaning that the act cannot be reprehensible unless the mind is also guilty. If it is accepted that the mental element is deemed to confer blameworthiness in this way, then it is noticeable that involuntary culpable homicide's *mens rea* elements are the same as those of the non-fatal offences of assault (unlawful act type) and various crimes of recklessness (lawful act type). This, therefore, brings the behavioural component (the destruction of life) into focus in terms of allocating culpability. Since the mental element equates to that of non-fatal offences, presumably it must be the fact of causing death – of violating the value placed on the sanctity of life or breaching the victim's right to life – which supplies culpable homicide's seriousness. Thus, if it is accepted that it is the *mental* element which *generally* imputes blameworthiness (and, potentially, degrees of blameworthiness)[96] then it becomes necessary to accept that the act of destroying the life of another is, in itself, so wholly unacceptable that it is given a leading role not necessarily accorded to the behavioural element in other crimes in determining culpability within culpable homicide. Nonetheless, killing on its own is far from sufficient and the concept of recklessness used as the mental element in lawful act type is worthy of some scrutiny

Recklessness

Findlay Stark has undertaken an exhaustive and meticulous critical analysis of the (many) concepts of recklessness applied in Scots law[97] concluding, in part, that culpable homicide's recklessness is not, and should not be, different to that employed in non-fatal crimes against the person.[98] It is not entirely clear whether, for this purpose, it has to denote a state of mind[99] so that the accused recognised, in his/her own mind, a risk and chose to ignore it, or whether it can simply be inferred from the quality of the behaviour.[100]*MacAngus v HM Advocate* [101] insisted on the need for recklessness in cases of death resulting from the supply of a controlled drug but it may also illustrate the vagaries of identifying the existence of the concept. The appeal court heard the conjoined appeals of Kevin MacAngus and of Michael Kane in relation to entirely separate incidents. MacAngus had supplied ketamine to a number of people known to him at their request and the deceased had selected how much to ingest (or 'snort' herself). Kane, on the other hand, administered heroin (by injection) to the deceased who was unable to do this for herself and, having seen her slump to the ground and having been informed that the other (assault) victim (who did not die) had never taken heroin before, he proceeded to inject him also. Are both equally reckless? The

94 See *Cameron v Maguire* 1999 JC 63; *Robson v Spiers* 1999 SLT 1141

95 See also J. Horder, 'Two Histories and Four Hidden Principles of *Mens Rea*' (1997) 113(Jan) Law Quarterly Review, 95–119.

96 See, for example, M.D. Bayles, 'Character, Purpose, and Criminal Responsibility' (1982) 1(1) Law and Philosophy 5.

97 F. Stark, 'Rethinking Recklessness' (2011) 3 Juridical Review, 163–203.

98 Ibid. 180

99 *Transco* (n 12)

100 Stark (n 97) 184

101 *MacAngus* (n 16)

case was brought as a preliminary plea to the relevance of the charges so the outcome is not reported.

A further key point is that, unlike in English law, the deceased's voluntary intervention does not necessarily break the chain of causation between the supply and the death[102] and the appeal court linked the causal question directly to the existence of recklessness. Lord Hamilton said:

> Moreover, while causation is distinct from the *mens rea* of the accused, the foundation in Scots law of the charge of culpable homicide in cases of this kind (namely, recklessness) is not, in our view, wholly irrelevant. The law can with justification more readily treat the reckless, as against the merely unlawful, actor as responsible for the consequences of his actions, including consequences in the form of actings by those to whom he directs such recklessness. Reckless conduct, judged in the context of any vulnerability of the victim, may of its nature have a compelling force. … Subject always to questions of immediacy and directness, the law may properly attribute responsibility for ingestion, and so for death, to the reckless offender.[103]

Such a formulation effectively removes the agency of the victim in deciding to ingest a potentially harmful substance[104] and relies heavily on the accused's recklessness as a justification. English law has taken a different course and has determined that the voluntary act of the deceased, certainly in freely administering controlled drugs supplied by a defendant, negates any criminal liability on that defendant's part.[105] Here, again, then, is a possible example of culpable homicide's liminal quality, occupying a space in relation to the destruction of the life of another which in another jurisdiction has been regarded as not criminally blameworthy.

Conclusion

Culpable homicide serves an important function in Scots criminal law. It offers two certainties: (1) it cannot be charged unless the accused's behaviour has brought about the death of someone else; and (2) it is always less serious than murder. As such, it covers a broad range of terrain sweeping up killings the seriousness of which places them on the borderline with murder at one edge and crossing a range of its own territory, through clear examples of its involuntary and voluntary forms, to reach fatal behaviours which might almost escape criminal liability altogether or at least the stigma carried by a homicide conviction in any form. Culpable homicide facilitates fair labelling within the homicide category, censures violations of the principle of the sanctity of life and recognises the gravity and the distress caused by taking life, even where this is not done intentionally or wickedly.

When approached on a murder / not murder binary, as an attempt to argue that the Crown has not proved the more serious crime, its own principles may be a little subsumed in the attempt to establish that those of murder have not been made out. Taken on its own terms, however, it offers a relatively reasoned set of formulations for determining when a

102 Ibid.

103 Ibid. [45]

104 For a fuller discussion see A. Reed, 'Culpable Homicide and Drug Administration' (2009) 73(3) Journal of Criminal Law 207–11; and L. Farmer, 'MacAngus (Kevin) v HM Advocate: "Practical But Nonetheless Principled"?' (2009) 13(3) Edinburgh Law Review 502–07

105 *R v Kennedy* [2007] UKHL 38; [2008] 1 AC 269.

killing is, as its name suggests, criminally culpable. In its involuntary forms, the absence of any reference to a mental attitude specifically encompassing killing demonstrates again the significance which it attaches to the act of ending another's life. Overall, it offers an interesting perspective on mechanisms for criminalising a generally abhorrent behaviour (killing) where this takes place in circumstances which the accused did not necessarily orchestrate for the purpose.

3 Reforming English homicide law

Fair labelling questions and comparative answers

Matthew Gibson and Alan Reed

1. Introduction

Domestic criminal lawyers have become accustomed to the often slow pace of reform in their discipline. In the context of English homicide law, this pace has stalled completely following the Law Commission's 2006 publication of recommendations for a new 'ladder' of homicide offences.[1] The Government has rejected that proposed scheme,[2] despite making separate changes to the partial defences to murder of diminished responsibility and provocation (updating the former and replacing the latter with loss of control).[3]

Against this backdrop, debates persist about the merits of the Law Commission's ladder, especially in respect of its proposed amendments to murder and involuntary manslaughter, the offences which form the focus of this chapter.[4] Frequently those debates concentrate on the levels of fault that should be required for these crimes so as to differentiate *culpability* between types of killing.[5] The preoccupation with fault is understandable given how English law links all homicide offences to a *single* conduct element: causing death. These analyses suggest that the current murder / involuntary manslaughter structure obscures the sheer *breadth* of ways in which a defendant may be at fault – and thereby *differently* culpable for killing the victim. Of course, not all commentators locate the difference between murder and involuntary manslaughter in point of culpability. Some argue that the Law Commission's ladder would do better to frame the distinction between these offences as one of attack vs. endangerment, respectively.[6] Here, killing by intentional attack is conceptually a different *species* of wrong from that of killing by reckless endangerment. Other scholars highlight further factors that might be taken into account in determining the wrongfulness of such killings. Those factors might include the defendant's motive and mode of

1 Law Commission, *Murder, Manslaughter and Infanticide* (Law Com No 304, 2006).

2 See the Law Commission website: <www.lawcom.gov.uk/project/murder/> accessed 11 February 2018.

3 In relation to the former, see s.2(1) of the Homicide Act 1957, as amended by s.52 of the Coroners and Justice Act 2009 (the 2009 Act). Regarding the latter, see ss.54–56 of the 2009 Act.

4 The existing murder and involuntary manslaughter offences, together with the Law Commission's proposed replacements, are outlined below: see 'Murder and involuntary manslaughter: fair labelling priorities'.

5 On this point, see A. Cornford, 'The Architecture of Homicide' (2014) 34(4) Oxford Journal of Legal Studies 819, 826–30. As Cornford notes, the Law Commission recommended that equivalently *culpable* killings receive equivalent treatment (n 1): paras 2.24 and 2.45–2.49.

6 See the views of W. Wilson in: 'Murder and the Structure of Homicide' in A. Ashworth and B. Mitchell (eds) *Rethinking English Homicide Law* (Oxford University Press 2000); 'The Structure of Criminal Homicide' (2006) Criminal Law Review 471; and 'What's Wrong with Murder?' (2007) 1(2) Criminal Law and Philosophy 157.

responsibility for the killing ('mode' pertaining to the *way* in which the defendant caused death), along with the victim's age and vulnerability.[7]

Clearly, these debates reveal disagreements as to how the Law Commission's ladder should distinguish between murder and involuntary manslaughter. They also reveal one notable area of *agreement*: the scope of these crimes should be driven by a concern for *fair labelling* of offences. In homicide literature, the expression 'fair labelling' has become a familiar rhetorical device – it is regularly invoked to support normative claims regarding how best to define murder and involuntary manslaughter.[8] Accordingly, fair labelling seems an appropriate starting point from which to scope the murder / involuntary manslaughter terrain.

As Ashworth identifies, the principle of fair labelling reflects a need to ensure that 'widely felt distinctions between kinds of offences and degrees of wrongdoing are respected and signalled by the law, and that offences are subdivided and labelled so as to represent fairly the nature and magnitude of the law-breaking'.[9] This means that crimes should be labelled in proportion to their *seriousness*. Horder interprets such seriousness as being taken up with 'a combination of the gravity of the wrong or of the harm done or risked, together with the culpability of the offender in causing – or posing a risk of – the harm'.[10] Given the various consequences of being charged with, and potentially convicted of, a murder or involuntary manslaughter offence, it is unsurprising that fair labelling features prominently in discourse on homicide reform. For this reason, section two begins by assessing the labelling implications of the current murder / involuntary manslaughter framework, before considering how satisfactorily these are addressed by the Law Commission's homicide ladder. That process reveals a range of labelling priorities across these offences. Section three undertakes a comparative study of murder and involuntary manslaughter provisions in South Africa, Australia, Canada and the United States of America. This exercise contextualises the domestic fair labelling priorities already considered and points to possible improvements in labelling strategy. Finally, in light of the domestic and comparative findings, section four considers alternative options in the quest for fair labelling of murder and involuntary manslaughter in English law.

2. Murder and involuntary manslaughter: fair labelling priorities

There are a number of perceived fair labelling problems with murder and involuntary manslaughter, as identified in the relevant literature. Those problems are the focus of this section, along with the Law Commission's proposed replacement crimes and their utility in addressing these problems. Ultimately, the ensuing analysis unveils a series of fair labelling priorities which apply to these offences. Undeniably, the labelling stakes here are high: empirical evidence suggests that, unsurprisingly, citizens across jurisdictions generally rate homicides amongst the most serious crimes that can be committed.[11] In the absence of

7 V. Tadros, 'The Homicide Ladder' (2006) 69(4) Modern Law Review 601, 602.

8 There are many examples. For a selection, see: J. Horder, *Homicide and the Politics of Law Reform* (Oxford University Press 2012), chapters three and five; Law Commission, *A New Homicide Act for England and Wales?* (CP No 177, 2005), paras 1.45–1.46; Wilson (n 6), 'Murder and the Structure of Homicide' 21, 22, and 'The Structure of Criminal Homicide', 475; and C. Clarkson, 'Context and Culpability in Involuntary Manslaughter: Principle or Instinct?' in Ashworth and Mitchell (n 6), 133, 141–42.

9 A. Ashworth, *Principles of Criminal Law* (6th edn, Oxford University Press 2009) 78.

10 J. Horder, *Ashworth's Principles of Criminal Law* (8th edn, Oxford University Press 2016) 22.

11 For example, see the findings documented in P.H. Robinson, *Intuitions of Justice and the Utility of Desert* (Oxford University Press 2013) 362–69.

further empirical research, it is *suspected* – at least in the domestic sphere – that these offences attract a notable amount of stigma. This is seemingly true of murder, which is one reason it has not been merged with manslaughter into a single offence.[12] It is probably also true of manslaughter: a key reason for introducing specific crimes of causing death on the roads[13] was supposed jury reluctance to convict of 'manslaughter' in such cases because of a 'distaste' for the label – leading to unmerited acquittals.[14]

Murder and involuntary manslaughter: perceived fair labelling problems

As noted previously[15] the key difference between murder and involuntary manslaughter in English law is *culpability* (these offences are united by a single conduct element – causing death). Yet there is widespread scholarly dissatisfaction with the fault requirements for these crimes, often for reasons of fair labelling.

Murder

The *mens rea* of murder is an intention to kill or cause grievous bodily harm (GBH).[16] 'Intention' comprises two modes: 'direct' and 'indirect'. Applying this to murder, it must be asked, respectively: did the defendant *aim* to kill or cause GBH; or did the defendant undertake conduct from which death or GBH was *virtually certain* to occur, and was this foreseen by the defendant?[17] Liability for murder thus exists where death or GBH was either the defendant's objective, or – in the course of other behaviour – foreseen to a *very* high degree. It might be wondered whether foreseeing the occurrence of death or GBH as virtually certain – a form of reckless endangerment – is sufficiently similar to *wanting* to bring about that level of harm via an intentional attack. Are these separate wrongs? If so, should homicide law distinguish between them for fair labelling purposes? Certainly, indirectly intending to kill may warrant the 'murder' label – alongside directly intending to kill – because death is foreseen as *inevitable*. However, that is not the case with the GBH rule. Whilst indirectly intending GBH may, likewise, be broadly as bad as directly intending GBH, there is a problem here: a murder conviction is permitted where the defendant caused death without intending or foreseeing death *at all*. This presents its own challenge: constructive liability.

Ashworth submits that constructive liability contravenes what he calls the 'correspondence principle': each part of the *mens rea* of an offence should directly relate ('correspond') to each part of the *actus reus*.[18] The correspondence principle ascribes great significance to individual autonomy (with its emphasis on subjective choice and control) and the rule of law (allowing individuals to plan their conduct).[19] Constructive liability neglects these interests

12 See comments by the Criminal Law Revision Committee, *Twelfth Report: Penalty for Murder* (Cmnd 5184, 1973), para 6; and Criminal Law Revision Committee, *Fourteenth Report: Offences against the Person* (Cmnd 7844, 1980) para 15. See also similar comments by the Law Commission (n 2) para 2.19 and (n 8) para 2.31.
13 See offences in the Road Traffic Act 1988, ss. 1, 2B, 3A and 3ZB.
14 Horder (n 8) 80–1. See also S. Cunningham, 'Vehicular Homicide: Need for a Special Offence?' in C. Clarkson and S. Cunningham (eds), *Criminal Liability for Non-Aggressive Death* (Ashgate 2008) 115.
15 See 'Introduction' of this chapter.
16 *R v Cunningham* [1982] AC 566.
17 Indirect intention is defined in *R v Woollin* [1999] AC 82.
18 Ashworth (n 9) 76–8.
19 Ibid., 76.

by penalising someone for a result which was brought about but *not* intended or foreseen. Some argue that constructive liability is acceptable because an individual causes a prohibited result from initial criminal conduct. Assuming there was choice exercised over that conduct, it changes the individual's 'normative position' with regard to any consequences (serious or otherwise) flowing from it.[20] This rationale may be a defence of *proximate* constructive liability (where there is little moral distance between the intended or foreseen outcome and that which actually occurred);[21] but it struggles to explain why a defendant's original behaviour should be accorded such *far-reaching* moral and legal significance in establishing liability for events *outside* his or her contemplation.[22]

In this way, the *mens rea* of murder creates a fair labelling dilemma: it bundles together two kinds of wrong (intention to kill; intention to do GBH) which are not necessarily morally equivalent. Killing with an intention to cause GBH is evidently reprehensible, but is it sufficiently morally close to killing with an intention to kill so as to warrant coming within the same offence? An intention to kill is the paradigmatic culpability standard in murder. If an intention to do the *next worst* type of harm (short of killing) – GBH – is to sit alongside it, perhaps it should require the defendant to advert to the risk of death to *some* degree so as to maintain a sense of moral equivalence via correspondence. For this reason, many scholars contend that the present GBH rule labels as murderers those whose blameworthiness falls far short of the murder paradigm.[23] This is because some instances of GBH (such as breaking a limb) clearly do not render death a foreseeable consequence. Of course, where an intention to do GBH has resulted in the victim's death, it may be rare that the defendant had *no* awareness of the risk of causing death. Nevertheless, because that awareness may sometimes be absent (due to the nature of the intended injury), this points to the need for more labelling nuance than the current 'murder' tag can offer.

Involuntary manslaughter

The main crimes under involuntary manslaughter are unlawful act manslaughter (UAM), gross negligence manslaughter (GNM) and reckless manslaughter (RM). Problems of correspondence emerge immediately in UAM. This crime is completed upon proof of *any* dangerous criminal act which causes death.[24] The only *mens rea* element in UAM is that which attaches to the 'base' offence which resulted in the killing. There is *no* fault stipulation as to the victim's death. Consequently, as with the 'intention to do GBH' provision in murder, UAM breaks with the correspondence principle – it sanctions constructive liability

20 J. Gardner, 'Rationality and the Rule of Law in Offences against the Person' (1994) 53(3) Cambridge Law Journal 502, 508–09.

21 Generally, see J. Horder, 'A Critique of the Correspondence Principle in Criminal Law' (1995) Criminal Law Review 759.

22 A. Ashworth, 'A Change of Normative Position: Determining the Contours of Culpability in Criminal Law' (2008) 11(2) New Criminal Law Review 232, 255–56.

23 For discussion, see: A. Ashworth, 'Principles, Pragmatism and the Law Commission's Recommendations on Homicide Law Reform' (2007) Criminal Law Review 333, 334, 337; J. Rogers, 'The Law Commission's Proposed Restructuring of Homicide' (2006) 70(3) Journal of Criminal Law 223, 226; and Wilson, 'Murder and the Structure of Homicide' (n 6) 22. See also judicial comments to this effect by Lord Steyn in *R v Powell* [1998] 1 Cr App R that 'GBH-murder' results in 'defendants being classified as murderers who are not in truth murderers'.

24 There is uncertainty as to whether this must be an 'intrinsic' criminal act (one going beyond regulatory / strict liability or negligence), or whether it includes *any* offence. Note that UAM can only be committed by an act, not an omission: *R v Lowe* [1973] QB 702.

where the defendant foresees no risk of death. Once again, this creates fair labelling difficulties: there may be a large gap between the culpable wrongdoing which constituted the initial crime and the eventual killing. For example, in *DPP v Newbury and Jones* [25] the base act was one of criminal damage to property as opposed to an offence against the person (so as at least to come within the same family of crimes, those concerned with bodily integrity, as homicide offences).

Assuming the original act *is* an offence against the person,[26] it may be that this only amounted to minor harm (for example, battery[27]). Culpability for causing that level of harm, which may amount to no more than a shove, causing someone to fall awkwardly, bang their head and die, is too far removed from the ensuing death to be labelled 'manslaughter'.[28] Conversely, there may be greater proximity between the defendant's initial crime and the resulting death where that crime represented a greater interference with the victim's bodily integrity, such as, an assault occasioning actual bodily harm (ABH),[29] or wounding / causing GBH (with or without intent to cause GBH).[30] Nonetheless, this still raises fair labelling matters. There remains a blurred line between *how* extreme the base offence must be and appropriate liability for causing death.[31] To be sure, ABH does not include especially life-threatening injuries: anything more than 'transient or trifling' counts,[32] including bruising and temporary loss of consciousness. Culpably causing these types of injuries may *still* be too remote from the death which followed to be labelled 'manslaughter'. For this reason, where the initial crime posed minimal threat of injury, or was not an offence against the person, Mitchell has proposed a lesser offence of 'unlawful and dangerous act resulting in death'. That crime would sit beneath UAM in any homicide hierarchy and require a recognisable (albeit unlikely) risk of death.[33] However, none of this is to deny that where the original offence was wounding/causing GBH with intent to do GBH – unaccompanied by foresight of a risk of death – a conviction for UAM may be proportionate.

The next major head of involuntary manslaughter is GNM – a crime which operates at the lower limits of manslaughter. It comprises a duty of care (or duty to act for omissions, which doubles as a duty of care), a breach of that duty, reasonable foreseeability that the breach gave rise to an obvious and serious risk of death, a breach that causes death and a finding that the breach was 'grossly' negligent (the negligence must be 'bad' enough to amount to a crime, not a civil wrong).[34] Predictably, fair labelling issues arise in the *mens rea* test of 'gross negligence'. As the jury has to interpret 'grossness' for itself (there is no specific guidance on that threshold), this means that conviction or acquittal – and thereby appropriate labelling – is something of a lottery. Different juries could return different verdicts on similar facts. There is more guidance on the meaning of 'negligence'. At its lowest, and

25 [1977] AC 500.
26 Empirical research indicates that these are the most common base crimes: see B. Mitchell and R. Mackay, 'Investigating Involuntary Manslaughter: An Empirical Study of 127 Cases' (2011) 31 (1) Oxford Journal of Legal Studies 165, 186.
27 Both contained in the Criminal Justice Act 1988, s.39 – although still defined at common law.
28 See *R v Williams* [1996] 2 Cr App R (S) 72 and *R v Mitchell* [1983] 76 Cr App R 293.
29 Offences against the Person Act 1861, s.47.
30 Ibid., ss.18 and 20, respectively.
31 Cornford (n 5) 830.
32 *R v Donovan* [1936] 25 Cr. App. R. 1.
33 B. Mitchell, 'More Thoughts about Unlawful and Dangerous Act Manslaughter and the One-Punch Killer' (2009) Criminal Law Review 502, 510–11.
34 *R v Adomako* [1995] 1 AC 171.

exceptionally for such a serious crime, this will be satisfied by *in*advertent killings: would a reasonable person (or, if the defendant holds a special skill, a reasonable professional) have foreseen a serious and obvious risk of death?[35] That foresight standard is 'objective': the defendant need not have foreseen any such risk. Problematically, advertent killings will be accepted as *evidence* of gross negligence: where a defendant does foresee a risk of death (a 'subjective' foresight standard) this will be potent proof of such negligence. That possibility permits a spectrum of culpability to sit within GNM, meaning that – like UAM – the GNM label obscures an offender's true blameworthiness for causing death. It positively *misrepresents* blameworthiness in subjective foresight cases. Foresight amounts to recklessness – not (gross) negligence. As Stark argues, '[i]t is problematic, from a labelling perspective, that this distinction in relative culpability is not reflected more explicitly in English criminal law's offence of involuntary manslaughter, particularly where the comparison is between inadvertence and advertence regarding a risk of death'.[36]

This suggests the need for an overhaul of involuntary manslaughter crimes to mark more emphatically the difference between 'subjectively' and 'objectively' foreseeing a risk of death. That would capture the moral dissonance between the former (choice-based) and latter (non-choice-based) types of wrongdoing, with the former including reckless and potentially heinous homicides falling just short of murder. Such separation in labelling is not overt in involuntary manslaughter, as represented by continuing confusion regarding the existence of RM as an independent head of involuntary manslaughter alongside GNM.[37] To make matters worse, the recent decision in *R v Rose* [38] now makes the application of GNM uncertain even in instances of *objective* foresight. *Rose* has diluted the objectivity inherent in the gross negligence test: it stipulates that the question is whether a reasonable person (or professional) *with the defendant's knowledge at the time of breach* would have foreseen a serious and obvious risk of death?[39] Laird highlights that this imbues that notional person / professional with the defendant's shortcomings, perversely making it *easier* for grossly negligent individuals to escape liability.[40] These developments prompt wider questions about how homicide law should tackle the threshold between grossly negligent and accidental killings. Nevertheless, *Rose* may sanction overly generous acquittals in egregious GNM cases, allowing for less personal criminal accountability (which would otherwise be communicated via conviction and censure). Victims' families may experience this as unfair labelling.[41]

The Law Commission's homicide ladder: fairer labelling of culpability?

In 2006, the Law Commission published its report on *Murder, Manslaughter and Infanticide.* [42] Whilst its proposals for reform were rejected by Government, they were generally

35 Ibid. See also *R v Gurphal Singh* [1999] Crim LR 582 and *R v Misra* [2004] EWCA Crim 2375.

36 F. Stark, 'Reckless Manslaughter' (2017) Criminal Law Review 763, 780.

37 Stark submits that there is no doctrinal basis for RM in English criminal law. He claims that the judgment in the 'leading' (and only) RM decision – *R v Lidar* [2000] 4 Archbold News 3 – indicates that it is a simple case of GNM: Ibid, 772–80. It is also difficult to identify use of RM in practice: Mitchell and Mackay (n 26) 190.

38 [2017] 2 Cr App R 28.

39 Ibid. (Sir Brian Leveson P) [84]

40 K. Laird, 'Manslaughter: R. v Rose' [2018] Criminal Law Review 76, 78–81.

41 See comments of the victim's family in *Rose*, cited in D. Lamming, 'Letter' (2018) Criminal Law Review 241.

42 See above (n 1).

welcomed by commentators for their more subtle approach to differentiating shades of culpability, and thereby labelling, than the existing offences.

Central to the Law Commission's changes was its replacement of the present two-tier homicide structure with a three-tier structure, or 'homicide ladder', tracking more refined gradations in fault. For present purposes, that structure includes:

First degree murder – intentional killing; killing with an intention to cause serious injury in the awareness that there is a serious risk of causing death.
Second degree murder – killing with an intention to cause serious injury; killing with the intention to cause injury or fear or risk of injury, in the awareness that there is a serious risk of causing death.
Manslaughter – causing death by gross negligence; causing death through a criminal act intended to cause injury, or in the awareness of a serious risk that injury may be caused.

This hierarchy better *groups* killings of comparable culpability. It also better *ranks* killings of different culpability. In Horder's words:

> [a] 'three-layer cake' structure makes it possible to distinguish between wrongs, and hence to respect the principles of fair labelling, in a more sophisticated way. To achieve this, each of the three tiers within the recommended structure has two morally equivalent wrongs [or a principal wrong and subsidiary wrong], each (with first degree murder at the top) being in principle lower down in the scale of severity than the wrongs in the tier above.[43]

First degree murder

The identification of 'morally equivalent' wrongs in the Law Commission's framework is not without controversy. In its 2005 consultation paper on homicide reform,[44] the Commission recommended that first degree murder be restricted to an intention to kill, the murder 'paradigm'. The subsequent inclusion in that offence of an intention to cause serious injury, with an awareness of a serious risk of causing death (a form of reckless killing) weakens that paradigm by association, although it still upholds the correspondence principle.

However, the change can perhaps be seen as a pragmatic attempt to acknowledge that many killings where serious injury is intended are *likely* to involve foresight of death. It is defensible that such cases of reckless killing – where intention as to causing that level of harm is accompanied by foresight of a *serious* risk of death – are labelled *as if* the defendant had intended to kill. The totality of the culpability elements for this lesser form of first degree murder is of a sufficiently similar level to the culpability present in the paradigm example of murder. Admittedly, this envisages a high threshold of 'serious risk', and one that may be set too low by the Commission's contention that 'a risk is to be regarded as serious if it is more than insignificant or remote'.[45] Such a threshold would be too far removed from the other mode of reckless killing caught by first degree murder – where death is foreseen as a virtually certain consequence of other conduct (satisfying an 'indirect' intention to kill). As a result, the definition of 'serious risk' ought to be more stringent.

43 Horder (n 8) 95 and fn 12.
44 See above (n 8).
45 Above (n 1) para 3.40.

Second degree murder and manslaughter

Reckless killings are also caught by second degree murder. Here, once again, the defendant must have an awareness of a serious risk of causing death – with all the uncertainty this engenders about the meaning of 'serious risk'. Nonetheless, unlike first degree murder, that awareness must stem from intentional conduct which is more distant to the prospect of causing death. There is no requirement of an intention to cause serious injury: rather, awareness of a serious risk of causing death need only flow from an intention to cause (a) any level of injury, or (b) fear or (c) risk of any such level of injury.

The effect is to upgrade to second degree murder various killings which, at present, fall under manslaughter. Given that foresight of a serious risk of death is mandated by second degree murder, many of these killings will be those that, through advertence, currently fit within GNM or RM. Horder claims an example of (a) would be where an individual injects the victim (an intended injury) with an illegal drug, realising that the drug may amount to an overdose or contain potentially lethal impurities (an awareness of a serious risk of causing death). The drug is an overdose and does contain such impurities, and the victim dies.[46] In light of the recklessness as to death, and by analogy to previous drug death cases, this could be GNM under existing homicide law.[47] Meanwhile, the facts of *Arobieke* help illustrate (b).[48] The defendant had intended to frighten the victim (an assault) by following him to a railway station and hunting for him on a train. The victim disembarked the train and climbed onto the live railway track to escape. He was electrocuted, causing his death. The defendant was prosecuted for UAM, although had he realised *how* the victim might flee, he would have satisfied second degree murder. Finally, Ashworth highlights an instance of (c) whereby a driver overtakes on a blind bend and causes the death of someone in an oncoming vehicle.[49] Considering the clear existence of a duty to other road users, GNM would be the obvious charge here under the present homicide framework.

The idea that heads of conduct (a), (b) and (c) *should* be re-classified from murder to second degree murder is not completely obvious. On this point, Ashworth comments that:

> [s]uggestions of a different label for the middle tier, such as grave or culpable homicide, have not moved the Commission. One may grant the Commission its argument that the current law is too generous to some reckless killings, and that such cases should be placed one tier below the highest category; but the argument put forward is that the culpability in these cases is so high that manslaughter is an inadequate label, not that they justify classification as "murder".[50]

However, one of the obstacles to a different second-tier label is that second degree murder also comprises killings committed with an intention to do serious injury – killings which at the moment come within murder. This amounts to a downgrading of liability, which is appropriate given the lack of correspondence between the *actus reus* (causing death) and the *mens rea* (which stipulates no advertence as to death). The placing of killings of broadly

46 Horder (n 8) 98.
47 See the facts of *R v Evans* [2009] EWCA Crim 650. Theoretically, RM would be an alternative offence.
48 [1988] Crim L.R. 314.
49 Ashworth (n 22) 339.
50 Ibid.

similar culpability in the same homicide tier is always going to result in awkward labelling trade-offs. As Horder observes, '[t]here are no easy or perfect solutions to be found in this hinterland between murder and lesser homicide offences … the labelling issue will continue to divide commentators'.[51]

Arguably, one less contested aspect of the Law Commission's ladder is its regulation of manslaughter on the third 'rung' of the ladder. To be sure, it continues to label as manslaughter those inadvertent killings which currently constitute GNM. This suggests a more principled labelling split between advertence and inadvertence as to death – respectively, 'murder' (in the first or second degree), or 'manslaughter'. The replacement offence for UAM, causing death through a criminal act intended to cause *injury*, or in the *awareness* of a serious risk that injury may be caused, still breaches the correspondence principle. That proposed offence is divided into two alternative forms, according to the nature of the base crime. This introduces (some) greater labelling precision. It is recognised that the base crime will either be an offence against the person, or any *other* criminal conduct. In relation to the former, 'injury' presumably means *more* than an assault or battery since there need be no advertence as to the risk of causing death. Regarding the latter, because there is no offence against the person, it is appropriate that it be coupled with an awareness of a serious risk of causing injury.

3. Murder and involuntary manslaughter

Comparative fair labelling priorities

It is now important to contextualise the prevailing fair labelling views on murder and involuntary manslaughter at the domestic level with comparative analysis of these crimes. Such an exercise affords a fuller appreciation of the fair labelling priorities underpinning those offences in *different* jurisdictions – priorities which may prompt further reflection in England and Wales on the best labelling routes to follow for these various crimes.

South African homicide law: A revisitation of **dolus eventualis**, *recklessness*, **luxuria** *and the* **versari** *doctrine*

An examination of South African homicide precepts is instructive in terms of fair labelling determinations, and construction of alternative reform pathways. A bifurcated hegemony has been engendered wherein culpability is predicated upon *dolus* (intention), or alternatively negligence (*luxuria*), but since 1965 the doctrine of *versari in res illicita* (constructive manslaughter – UAM) has been abolished.[52] It was perceived, as in a number of other comparative legal systems, as contradictory to a foundational cornerstone, that a defendant ought not to be punished without specific and individuated fault for homicide, and

51 Horder (n 8) 101. See also R. Taylor, 'The Nature of "Partial Defences" and the Coherence of (Second Degree) Murder' (2007) Criminal Law Review 345, 355–57.

52 See generally, P. Carstens, 'Revisiting the Relationship between *Dolus Eventualis* and *Luxuria* in the Context of Vehicular Collisions Causing the Death of Fellow Passengers and/or Pedestrians: *S v Humphreys*' (2012) 26(1) South African Journal of Criminal Justice 67; A. St. Q. Skeen, 'Two Differing Views as to Whether Intentional Killing May Sometimes but Considered as Culpable Homicide' (1982) 99 South African Law Journal 524; and G. Kemp, 'South Africa' in A. Reed and M. Bohlander (eds) *Homicide in Criminal Law: A Research Companion* (Routledge 2018).

consequently that constructivist liability of this nature should be eradicated as, 'a primitive relic from canon law.'[53] The crime of murder is not graded *per se*, and unlike the United States, there are no formal degrees of murder in South African jurisprudence.[54] Bespoke sentencing legislation is in place to reflect harm (culpability gradation thresholds). Significantly, European settlers brought different legal systems to South Africa with the introduction of English and Roman-Dutch laws. These traditions, and Dyadic polarities, remain today, centred around the development of customary and common law.[55]

Murder: dolus directus *and* dolus eventualis

The offence of murder is standardised and iterated as the intentional and unlawful killing of a person. In terms of offence-definitional construction, the fault element of intention is mandated: the concept of *dolus directus* applies where the defendant foresees the possibility of the circumstance or consequence existing, and proceeds with his conduct; alternatively, culpability may be predicated upon *dolus eventualis*, the form of intention which does not reflect the aim and object of the accused.[56] As in English law, this latter conceptualisation of fault for murder has provoked judicial arguments which, on occasion, appear to have blurred pragmatic reality, and arguably, to have facilitated injudicious semantic pugilism.[57] A transposition of words has, at times, occasioned confusion and extensive debate.[58] The relationship between *dolus eventualis* and *luxuria* has been revisited in more recent times by the Supreme Court of Appeal in *S v Humphreys.* [59] Culpable homicide has been formulated as the unlawful and negligent causation of the death of another person. It is negligence alone that is supererogatory within the realm of involuntary manslaughter.[60]

Indirect intention for murder within South African law has been embodied in a dual test that involves a cognitive part, and a conative (or volitional) element. The cognitive component engages foresight of the possibility of harm (death) and is entirely subjective in nature.

53 *S v Bernardus* 1965 (3) SA 287, 298 A-B; and see O.C.M. Davis, 'Constructive Homicide' [1938] 2 Journal of Criminal Law 451.

54 See J.H. Hugo, 'Can Murder and Culpable Homicide Overlap – Another Penny in the Old Man's Hat' (1973) 90 South African Law Journal 334; J. Burchell, *Principles of Criminal Law* (5th edn, Juta 2016); and G. Kemp *et al., Criminal Law in South Africa* (2nd edn, Oxford University Press 2015).

55 P. Lenta, 'The Tikoloshe and the Reasonable Man: Transgressing South African Legal Fictions' (2004) 16(3) Law and Literature 353; and see M. Nathan, 'The Roman-Dutch Law of Homicide' (1902) 19 South African Law Journal 15.

56 See S. Hoctor, 'Death on the Roads and *Dolus Eventualis: S v Humphreys*' (2013) 26(1) South African Journal of Criminal Justice 75.

57 For alternative perspectives on the meaning of *dolus* in South African law see C.R. Snyman, *Criminal Law* (16th edn, Lexis Nexis 2014): J.M.T. Labuschagne and J.A. Van Den Heever, 'Liability Arising from the Killing of a Fellow Human Being in South African Indigenous Law' (1995) 28(3) The Comparative and International Law Journal of South Africa 442; and W. Bertelsmann, 'What Happened to Luxuria? Some Observations on Criminal Negligence, Recklessness and *Dolus Eventualis*' (1975) 92 South African Law Journal 59.

58 The true meaning of oblique intent in English criminal law has, of course, also provoked considerable evaluation and critique by leading academics: see generally, G. Williams, 'Oblique Intention' (1987) 46(3) Cambridge Law Journal 417; A. Norrie, 'After *Woollin*' (1999) Criminal Law Review 532; and A. Simester, 'Moral Certainty and the Boundaries of Intention' (1996) 16 Oxford Journal of Legal Studies 445.

59 2013 (2) SACR 1 (SCA)

60 R. Whiting, 'Negligence, Fault and Criminal Liability' (1991) 108 South African Law Journal 431.

The impact is that the only assessment that is initially relevant is whether the defendant actually foresaw the possibility of death.[61] The court should warn against conflating the tests for intention and negligence via a flawed process of deductive reasoning, that because the defendant ought to have foreseen the consequence of death, it can be concluded that he did.[62] Inferential reasoning applies to prove the construction of subjective foresight:

> [C]ommon sense dictates that the process of inferential reasoning may start out from the premise that in accordance with common human experience, the possibility of the consequences that ensued would have been obvious to a person of normal intelligence. The next logical step would be to ask whether in the light of all the facts and circumstances of this case, there is any reason to think that the appellant would not have shared this foresight, derived from common human experience, with other members of the general population.[63]

The second part of the indirect intention formulation in *Humphreys* (discussed further later in this chapter) is conative, invoking a *reconciliation doctrine*, asking if the defendant reconciled himself to the possibility that an unlawful result (death), which he had foreseen as a possibility, may follow.[64] A significant concomitant of this duality standardisation is that it will be the reconciliation to the foreseeability of harm, or otherwise, on the part of the accused that demarcates liability for murder or culpable homicide.[65] Lack of reconciliation by a defendant will preclude fault for murder, but may be indicative of *luxuria* (negligence) through the legal prism that a reasonable person would have reconciled himself to the fatal consequences which the defendant in the circumstances failed to advert to in terms of relational volitional comportation.[66] Inculpation for culpable homicide may follow.

What is particularly striking is the blurred distinction, and conflation of intention and recklessness as part of the *dolus eventualis* reconceptualisation under South African homicide precepts. Subjective recklessness under English law, and the fault element ingredients for RM as a type of involuntary manslaughter, arguably established in the domestic precedent of *Lidar*,[67] are traduced in South Africa as a variety of intention. The corollary is that in contemporary South African criminal law progenitation of subjective recklessness has occurred, and developed, under the second part of the test of indirect intention embodied as *dolus eventualis*.[68] This may have been the labelling dichotomy that might have developed under English law on indirect intention if the majority perspective advanced over 40 years ago in *Hyam*[69] had taken root to ascertain oblique intent for murder.

It should be recalled that in *Hyam* the House of Lords, by a majority, determined that a high degree of subjective recklessness, configured around foreseeability of the probability of death (or GBH) equiparated with the fault element for murder.[70] This standardisation was

61 Carstens (n 52) 78–80.
62 Ibid. 80–2.
63 *Humphreys* (n 59) [13].
64 See Hoctor (n 56) 80–2
65 Ibid.
66 Ibid., 82–3
67 See fn 36
68 See Carstens (n 52) 72–4.
69 [1925] AC 55, and see Simester (n 58); and C. Kaveny, 'Inferring Intention from Foresight' (2004) 120 Law Quarterly Review 81.
70 Ibid.

effectually abrogated in *Moloney*[71], where it was highlighted that the culpability threshold for murder was stricter and more straitened, and nothing less than an intention to kill or cause GBH was satisfactory. Residually, there was an assumption in the dissenting judgments in *Hyam* that where a defendant is subjectively reckless, and foresees that he may kill or seriously injure another person, this culpability gradation would suffice to support a verdict of RM.[72] This category of manslaughter has been rarely prosecuted with the determination in *Lidar* a rare exception, and indictments instead have been trammelled within the ambit of either UAM, or GNM.[73] Although the Law Commission made no proposals in their final report on homicide law reform[74] for a new statutory offence of reckless *Cunningham*-type manslaughter, nonetheless we suggest herein that it ought to be beneficially promulgated. A critique of the South African Supreme Court of Appeal decision in *Humphreys*, comparatively reviewed against the optionality of RM, and set against a background of principled abolition of the *versari* doctrine, suggest newly formulated epistemic panoply of culpability thresholds predicated on fair(er) labelling for homicide.

Humphreys: the blurring of dolus eventualis *and recklessness*

The interface between *dolus eventualis* and RM, and conflation of culpability thresholds, were self-evident in *Humphreys*. The accused, a minibus taxi-driver, drove his taxi over a railway crossing near Blackheath, Cape Town. Tragically, the vehicle, which was transporting children to school, was hit by a train, and consequentially ten of the fourteen passengers in the vehicle were fatally wounded, whilst the remaining four children were seriously injured. The defendant, convicted on ten counts of murder and four counts of attempted murder, appealed on the predicate that the State had failed to prove the element of murder categorised as *dolus eventualis*. The issue, *ab initio*, focused on the parameters of the second leg of the doctrine, notably reconciliation on the part of the accused with the foreseen possibility (death).[75]

The Supreme Court of Appeal determined that the reconciliation element of *dolus eventualis* had not been established, but convictions for *luxuria* (culpable homicide by negligence) were justifiable.[76] As Carstens[77] and Kemp[78] highlight, there was advancement of two rationales for this outcome. The court iterated that 'common sense' meant that if Humphreys had foreseen the possibility of fatal injury, then counter-intuitively, it followed that he would have foreseen fatal injury to himself – he foresaw the possibility of a collision, but believed it would not happen: in essence, a non-materialisation risk. The proven evidence identified that the defendant had successfully performed this crossing manoeuvre many times when the boon had partially lowered, and, this past practice had led him to a misplaced sense of confidence over repetition.[79] This misplaced confidence, in the eyes of

71 [1985] AC 905; and see generally, A. Simester and B. Sullivan *et al., Simester and Sullivan's Criminal Law* (Hart Publishing 2016) 408–25.
72 Ibid.
73 See A. Ashworth; 'Manslaughter: Generic or Nominate Offences?' in Clarkson and Cunningham (n 14) chapter 11.
74 See Law Commission, *Partial Defences to Murder* (Law Com CP No 173, 2003); Law Commission, *Partial Defences to Murder* (Law Com No 290, 2004).
75 *Humphreys* (n 59) [5]
76 Ibid. [7]
77 See Carstens (n 52)
78 See Kemp (n 52)
79 *Humphreys* (n 59) [14]

the court, did not detract from a manifest lacuna herein precluding liability for murder: 'the absence of reconciliation with the consequences he subjectively foresaw'.[80] The cognitive component of *dolus eventualis* was established, the same could not be said for the conative component.

The 'true enquiry' on the conative prong of *dolus eventualis,* within South African criminal law, as Hoctor states,[81] is whether D took the consequences that he foresaw into the bargain. The posited issue is whether it can be inferred that it was immaterial to the accused whether these consequences would flow from their actions. Anglo-American separate identification of intention and recklessness fault components are merged together in *Humphreys* as part of *dolus eventualis*:

> Conscious negligence is not to be equated with *dolus eventualis.* The distinguishing feature of *dolus eventualis* is the volitional component: the agent (the perpetrator) "consents" to the consequence foreseen as a possibility, he "reconciles himself" to it, he "takes it into the bargain" ... [O]ur cases often speak of the agent being "reckless" of that consequence, but in this context it means consenting, reconciling or taking into the bargain ... [It] is the particular, subjective, volitional mental state in relation to the foreseen possibility which characterises *dolus eventualis* and which is absent in *luxuria.*[82]

South African homicide precepts and fair labelling: abolition of the versari *doctrine*

Beyond the blurring of intention / recklessness fault components for murder in South Africa, it is significant that since 1965 the *versari* doctrine of constructive liability for manslaughter has been abolished.[83] Deleteriously, the equivalent common law offence of UAM still applies in English law, akin to, and a counterpart of the eradicated felony murder rule, whereby if the unlawful act causative of death was not a felony, but volitionally engaged another 'dangerous' criminal act, the perpetrator of the unlawful act was stigmatised as a manslaughterer.[84] The breadth of liability is extraordinary and it is contended that the dissonance between fair labelling of unlawful conduct / culpability is egregious. It is an unpredictable ground of liability that is ripe for reform, and preferably abrogation as engineered by the South African Supreme Court of Appeal in *S v Bernardus,*[85] where, in a seminal decision, the *coup de grace* was delivered to the *versari* doctrine.

It is instructive to analyse the import and wider policy-sensitive choices adopted in ending constructive manslaughter liability. In *Bernardus,* the accused participated in an unlawful attack, throwing a knobkerrie at the victim to scare them, without possibly foreseeing the victim's death. Liability applied for *luxuria* (culpable negligence); constructive (unlawful act manslaughter) was pejoratively delineated as an 'excrescence on the law'[86] in positing homicide culpability on causality rather than identifying that an accused cannot be punished without particularised fault. In the hegemony of homicide liability it was charted that liability only existed for murder (*dolus* – intention) or culpable homicide (*luxuria* – negligence):

80 Ibid. [17].
81 Hoctor (n 56) 79–80.
82 *Humphreys* (n 59) [5].
83 See Kemp (n 52); and Hugo (n 54).
84 See R. Buxton, 'By Any Unlawful Act' (1966) 82 Law Quarterly Review 174.
85 1965 (3) SA 287 (A); and see generally St. Q. Skeen (n 52); and B.V.D. Van Niekerk, '*Versari* Resuscitated – Some Points on Culpable Homicide' (1971) 88 South African Law Journal 145.
86 Van Niekerk (n 85) 147.

'all negligent killing is unlawful killing and it covers a large part of the field of unlawful killings. But the converse is not true, and not all unlawful killings are negligent'.

Abolition of constructive manslaughter liability in South Africa should invoke renewed cognisance and heightened scrutiny domestically. As Van Niekerk[87] and Whiting[88] have cogently asserted, a court focused on handing down a verdict inspired by a sense of justice and of appropriate culpability equiparation, should not baulk at opting for a conviction for the lesser offence (the actual unlawful act itself), that takes no account of the fact of death. In specified circumstances, the fact death transpired may for social and deterrent reasons be reflected in an alternative punishment.[89] It is regarded in such terms that the sentence accurately reflects the quantum of moral and legal turpitude of which the unlawful actor made himself guilty.

The beneficial abrogation of *versari* doctrine ought to be conjoined with a more nuanced bifurcation of *dolus eventualis* principles within South African criminal law. This should engage a separation of intent for murder and reckless subjective manslaughter liability to avoid post-*Humphreys* confusion engendered by beguiling applications of the reconciliation doctrine. A separate category of involuntary manslaughter based upon *Cunningham*-type recklessness should be supererogatory, reflective of our appellate determination in *Lidar*.

Lidar involved a dispute between two groups of young men in a public house, which continued in the care park after they had been thrown out of the premises. The accused positioned himself in the driving seat of his Land Rover with his brother in the front passenger seat. The victim then went over to the front passenger window, which was open, and leaned in so that half of his body was in the car. A fight then ensued, and Lidar drove off at speed with the victim still half in the window. The car reached over 30 mph when V's feet caught the rear wheel and he fell to the ground, suffering several crush injuries to his chest from which he died. The appellate court, upholding a conviction, stated that the trial judge had been correct to treat this case as one of RM, and that the judge had not been required to give the jury a direction on GNM which would have been 'superfluous' and 'unnecessary'.[90] The key issue was whether Lidar, the driver of the motor vehicle, was aware of the necessary degree of risk of serious injury to the victim and nevertheless chose to disregard it.

Inculpation for reckless manslaughter has been affirmed where the individual actor is subjectively reckless in consciously adverting to the risk of serious injury.[91] Fair labelling is adventitiously deployed in that for culpability the defendant must foresee the risk of serious injury as highly probable and take an unjustified risk of it occurring. The trial judge needs to specify that there has to be a high probability of serious physical injury, and not just of 'some injury to health' or 'some physical harm', however slight.[92]

As previously adumbrated, binary divide applies in South African criminal law between intention (*dolus* – murder) and negligence (*luxuria*). There is no middle ground in terms of reckless or constructive manslaughter. A conviction for murder or culpable homicide focuses exclusively on *dolus eventualis*, and more particularly *reconciliation doctrine* under the

87 Ibid. 149.

88 Whiting (n 60) 435.

89 Van Niekerk (n 85) 149–50.

90 See generally, A. Reed and B. Fitzpatrick, *Criminal Law* (4th edn, Sweet and Maxwell 2009).

91 In *R v Stone and Dobinson* [1977] QB 354, the appellate court held as sufficient *mens rea* for manslaughter, that the accused had unconsciously taken the risk of causing injury to health and welfare.

92 Reed and Fitzpatrick (n 90); and see generally, G. Virgo, 'Reconstructing Manslaughter on Defective Foundations' (1995) 54(1) Cambridge Law Journal 14.

purview of the second limb of the test. The absence of volitional reconciliation to foresight of harm on the part of the individual actor will preclude culpability for murder. Instead, it may indicate that presence of *luxuria* in the corollary that a reasonable person would have reconciled himself to the fatal consequences which the accused in the circumstances failed to do.

Culpable homicide and medical negligence: Anglo-South African standardisations

As a final point of comparison it is significant, as Carstens identifies,[93] that South African precepts applicable to prosecution of medical negligence as culpable homicide draw extensively from extant English law and GNM liability. It is policy-driven and sensitive to avoidance of defensive medicine in severely curtailing the causative factorisation of medical misadventure as a *novus actus interveniens* that may otherwise insulate the original assailant from culpability for homicide. A foreseeability and preventability standardisation is engendered, equiparated with the normative yardstick of the reasonable and competent health care professional in the same circumstances.[94] For culpable homicide liability it has to be established that the medical evidence as a new intervening event caused the death of the victim. It has been established by a series of precedential authorities in South Africa that only if the medical negligence was 'overwhelming' can it be said to be a *novus actus interveniens*: if at the time of death the original wound inflicted by the defendant is still an operating and substantial cause of death then the death could properly be construed as part of the wound.[95] In essence, for societal policy reasons, it is deontologically prescribed that it is inappropriate to prosecute doctors who act with anything less than conscious advertence to the risk of harm.

South African courts have, in this substantive arena, relied almost exclusively on English precedential authorities.[96] As such, the important recent determination of our appellate court in *Rose*[97] has wider international ramifications for inculpation of medical practitioners.[98] The defendant, a registered optometrist, based at a branch of Boots opticians in Ipswich, was engaged to conduct a routine eye test and examination on a boy, aged seven. Rose failed to use an ophthalmoscope, or to inspect retinal images obtained by another of her colleagues, which would have revealed acute hydrocephalus, and that the obstruction of the brain had been a longstanding chronic problem, from which the boy died some five months later. The appellate court, however quashing Rose's conviction for manslaughter, determined that in assessing the reasonable forseeability of risk of death in cases of gross negligence manslaughter under English law the court was not entitled to take into account information which would only have been available to a defendant following the actual

93 See P. Carstens, 'Medical Negligence as a Causative Factor in South African Criminal Law: Novus Actus Interveniens or Mere Misadventure' (2006) South African Journal of Criminal Justice 19(2).

94 Ibid.

95 See generally *S v Tembani* 1999 (1) SACR 192 (w); *S v Counter* 2003 (1) SACR 143 (SCA); and *S v Ramosunya* 2002 (2) SACR 257 (7).

96 See Carstens (n 93) 209–10.

97 See fn 95.

98 The appellate court clearly delineated that in cases of gross negligence manslaughter there are five offence-definitional elements that need to be proven by the Crown for inculpation: (1) a duty of care (or duty to act for omissions, which doubles as a duty of care); (2) a breach of that duty; (3) reasonable foreseeability that the breach gave rise to an obvious and serious risk of death; (4) that death was caused by the breach; and (5) gross negligence – Ibid., at para [77].

breach of duty in question.[99] There remained the possibility that signs of potentially life-threatening disease or abnormality might be missed by failing to properly conduct the eye examination. This was insufficient to establish culpability; there had to be a serious and obvious risk of death at the time of the breach, and retrospective normative awareness was inapplicable for liability.[100]

What is palpable from the outcome in *Rose* is that the parameters of GNM have been recast again in terms of culpability. The objective reasonable person in the defendant's situation does not have any knowledge which the defendant would have had but for the breach: 'hindsight is irrelevant'.[101] The contours of liability, or otherwise, have been significantly skewed against successful prosecution. South African/English law may have adopted a blended approach to *luxuria,* that is reflective of societal policy-sensitive inculcations *vis-a-vis* fair labelling, but a fundamental dissonance applies to *dolus* and intentional homicide revisitations.

Stratification of the homicide ladder: lessons from the United States, Australia and Canada

As noted above,[102] the English Law Commission in their final report on homicide law reform recommended the adoption of a three-tier structure of general homicide offences to replace the extant bifurcation of 'murder' and 'manslaughter'.[103] It was submitted that broader stratification ought to occur to allow fair labelling of culpability / fault gradations: the offences should be 'first degree murder', 'second degree murder' and 'manslaughter'.[104] Notably, this hierarchical optionality structure has derivations in both U.S. common law, and in the Model Penal Code (MPC) that systemically reclassified homicide law in 1962, and has been adopted with variegation by a number of states.[105] A single tripartite offence of criminal homicide applies, delineated by dissonant fault thresholds that are constitutive of inculpation determination and step changes in culpability levels.[106] In accordance with MPC s. 210.1 (1):

> A person is guilty of criminal homicide if he purposely, knowingly, recklessly or negligently causes the death of another human being. Liability can be established for murder; manslaughter, or negligent homicide depending on the individual actor's mental state, and the three tiers of offences are not divided into degrees.[107]

99 Ibid. [86].
100 Ibid.
101 See T. Storey, 'Whether Obvious and Serious Risk of Death in Cases of Gross Negligence Manslaughter to be Determined Both Objectively and Prospectively' (2017) 81(5) Journal of Criminal Law 343.
102 See 'The Law Commission's homicide ladder: fairer labelling of culpability?'
103 In its 2006 report: see above (n 1).
104 Ibid., para 1.67; and see generally, Wilson, 'The Structure of Criminal Homicide' (n 6); and A. Norrie, 'Between Orthodox and Moral Contextualism' (2006) Criminal Law Review 486.
105 P.W. Low, 'The Model Penal Code, The Common Law and Mistakes of Fact: Recklessness, Negligence or Strict Liability' (1988) 19 Rutgers Law Journal 539; and see generally, P.H. Robinson and M.D. Dubber, 'The American Penal Code: A Brief Overview' (2007) 10 New Criminal Law Review 319; and S.H. Kadish, S.J. Schulhofer and R.E. Barkow, *Criminal Law and It's Processes: Cases and Materials* (10th edn, Walters Kluwer, 2016).
106 MPC and Commentaries (1980) (hereinafter MPC) s.210.
107 V. Bergelson, 'United States of America' in Reed and Bohlander (n 52); and see K. Kessler Ferzan, 'Plotting Premeditation's Demise' (2012) 75(2) Law and Contemporary Problems 83;

As Robinson[108] has stated, there is a single paradigm that governs homicide grading statutes in the US: 'grading corresponds to the offender's state of mind at the time that he causes the death of his victim'.[109] The jury, as normative arbiters, are required to determinatively examine the actor's state of mind as to causing the victim's death.[110] Stratification transpires in that an offender who purposefully or knowingly causes death is typically inculpated for murder, underneath this presupposition a defendant who recklessly causes death commits the lesser offence of manslaughter, and an individual who negligently brings about death will be stigmatised within the lower hierarchical offence of negligent homicide. Consequentially, we have four MPC culpability standardisations – purposeful, knowing, reckless and negligent – that are the foundational cornerstones of homicide grading, and are defined with precision in many American criminal codes.[111] It is contended that this structure provides a morally defensible boundary between murder and manslaughter. There are advantages to this more nuanced approach in terms of labelling offenders more accurately, especially when conjoined together with a bespoke division in state statutes of murder into degrees, constitutively related to culpability. The prosecution must establish that the defendant engaged in conduct with the conscious objective of causing death of another or at least with awareness that death of another was practically certain to result from his act.[112]

A binary classification system for murder itself was adopted by Pennsylvanian legislation in 1794, initiating a premeditation or deliberation formula, delineating 'wilful, deliberate, and premeditated killings' as first degree murder.[113] The stratification of murder into degrees, with the deliberation/premeditation formula serving as the crucial determinant of liability, was an attempt to limit the death penalty to only the most heinous of killings.[114] It has proved extremely influential, and many states have followed Pennsylvania's lead over deliberation / premeditation offence-definitional elements for first degree murder:[115] 'the true test is not the duration of time as it is the extent of the reflection',[116] straddling culpability standardisations.

and K.W. Simons, 'Should the Model Penal Code's *Mens Rea* Provisions be Amended?' (2003) 1 (1) Ohio State Journal of Criminal Law 179.

108 P.H. Robinson, 'Abnormal Mental State Mitigation of Murder: The U.S. Perspective' in A. Reed and M. Bohlander (eds), *Loss of Control and Diminished Responsibility: Domestic and Comparative Perspectives* (Ashgate 2011).

109 Ibid.

110 Ibid.; and see generally, J.G. Murphy, 'The State's Interest in Retribution' (1994) 5 Journal of Contemporary Legal Issues 283; and L. Alexander, 'Crime and Culpability' (1994) 5 Journal of Contemporary Legal Issues 1.

111 In most jurisdictions, this broad scheme is drawn from Model Penal Code, Art. 210.

112 See A.C. Michaels, 'Rationales of Criminal Law Then and Now: Towards a Judgemental Descriptivism' (2000) 100(1) Columbia Law Review 54.

113 E.R. Keedy, 'History of the Pennsylvania Statute Creating Degrees of Murder' (1949) 97(6) University of Pennsylvania Law Review 759; and see Ferzan (n 107) 87–8.

114 J. Dressler, *Understanding Criminal Law* (5th edn, Lexis Nexis 2009) 511; and see M.J. Zydney Mannheimer, 'Not the Crime but the Cover Up: A Deterrence Based Rationale for the Premeditation – Deliberation Formula' (2011) 86(3) Indiana Law Journal 879.

115 See Ferzan (n 107) 83–4 who has iterated that 29 states in addition to the District of Columbia, and the federal Government which currently adopt a premeditation or deliberation template.

116 *State v Solomon*, 254 P. 3d, 501, 518 (Cal. 2010); and see S. Mounts, 'Premeditation and Deliberation in California: Returning to a Distinction Without a Difference' (2002) 36(2) University of San Francisco Law Review 261.

The Canadian Criminal Code has replicated extant U.S. jurisprudence in hierarchically categorising first and second degree murder for sentencing purposes.[117] Contemporaneously, first degree murder requires a planning and deliberation concurrence. There is a necessity for both planning as well as the intention to carry out the killing. Second degree murder engages intention to cause harm that will likely result in death, but for which death was not planned.[118] Unlawful act manslaughter is distinguished from murder in that the latter demands, at the very least, subjective foreseeability of death on the part of the accused.[119] The Supreme Court, however, in *R v Creighton* [120] unanimously held that for unlawful act manslaughter an objective, rather than a subjective, standard of fault applied. For inculpation there is a requirement for an objective foreseeability of bodily harm which is neither trivial nor transitory in the context of a dangerous act. Lack of collinearity with fair labelling in this regard is considered subsequently, in that substantial social stigma applies to a culpable homicide conviction, but the breadth of what constitutes foreseeable 'bodily harm' can include all but the most trivial injuries.

Fair labelling prioritisations and contemporaneity in U.S. homicide culpability gradations

Bergelson has cogently reviewed the adaptation of the determination / premeditation culpability formula that has been adopted in a majority of U.S. state criminal codes to define the most serious type of killings.[121] A preponderance of these codes do not mandate additional time between conscious formulation of the criminal engagement and act, and so constitutively the requisite fault for first degree murder may be formed whilst the defendant, 'is pressing the trigger that fired the fatal shot'.[122] A growing number of alternative state jurisdictions, however, mandate more meaningful reflection, predicating a determination to kill reached calmly and some appreciable time prior to the homicide:[123] 'deliberation requires a cool mind that is capable of reflection and premeditation requires that the one with the cool mind did in fact reflect, at least for a short period of time, before killing.'[124]

The determination / premeditation formula, that has enhanced significance in the U.S., may be comparatively reviewed against the conceptualisation of *dolus* (intention) that applies within Anglo/South African criminal law precepts. It is significantly narrower than the *dolus eventualis* adaptation threshold for murder inculpation, a form of indirect intention which does not reflect the aim and object of the accused. The doctrinal clarity of each may be

117 Canadian Criminal Code R.S.C. 1985, as amended 2012, s. 231. Note that first degree murder includes killings committed whilst in the course of carrying out another crime, or in association with a criminal organisation.

118 See s.231(7).

119 See generally, L.C. Wilson, 'Too Many Manslaughters' (2007) 52 Criminal Law Quarterly 433.

120 [1993] 3 SCR 3, 105 DLR (4th) 632; and see A. Khoday, '*R v Creighton* Twenty Years Later: Harm Versus Death Revisited' (2013) 37 Manitoba Law Journal 167. Creighton, an experienced drug dealer and user, injected another user with heroin resulting in her death. Liability for unlawful act manslaughter was predicated on objective foreseeability of bodily harm, rather than death.

121 See Bergelson (n 107).

122 See *Young v State*, 428 50 2d. 155, 158 (Ala. Crim. App. 1982); and see Ferzan (n 107) 88.

123 W.R. LaFave, *Substantive Criminal Law* (2nd edn, West Pub. Co. 2003) s.14–7.

124 *State v Bowser*, 199 S.E. 31 (N.C. 1938); *Byford v State*, 994 P. 2d. 700 (Nev. 2000); and see Bergelson (n 107).

reflected against the contours of culpability gradations, that Ferzan[125] in the United States has identified may involve at least six factorisations: the analysis of risks imposed; the reasons why they were imposed; the defendant's thoughts about the killing – either identifying with the wrong or displaying utter indifference to it; the quality of the defendant's reasoning process; the number of choices the defendant made in killing; and the defendant's responsibility for prior choices that may lead to degradation of his later reasoning.[126] Viewed through such a prism it is contended that the determination / premeditation formula appropriately stratifies and iterates the most heinous killings in a justifiable and logically compelling way – a morally defensible boundary applies for murder in a contextualisation of an aggressive and deliberately hostile act directed at another after conscious formulation of an 'objective' to cause death that succeeds in completion.[127]

Within U.S. state statutes, second degree murder is usually defined as intentional killing of another, but where the higher offence-definitional element of premeditation/ deliberation are absent; moreover, the fault element of intent to commit serious bodily harm (transmogrified in English law as the *mens rea* for murder) is reconceptualised as second degree murder in the U.S.[128] A further striking difference is that whilst the felony murder rule was abolished in England back in 1957, it still thrives today in the vast majority of U.S. states, as concomitantly does misdemeanour – manslaughter constructive form of liability in about one-quarter of U.S. states.[129] The felony-murder doctrine imports liability if a death results from conduct during the commission or attempted commission of a felony.[130]

It is contended on our part that this form of *ex-post facto* reconstructive liability remains capricious, ought to be abrogated, and fails to satisfy appropriate culpability gradations. The actor ought to be liable for the individual felony (unlawful act) committed with corresponding fault. The reasons for doctrinal rejection remain as cogent today as back in 1957, as the Law Commission have postulated.[131] The list of offences that are relationally relevant, in the comportational sense that they form a panoply of offences in the course of which it

125 Ferzan (n 107) 86–7; and see D.M. Kahan and M.C. Nussbaum, 'Two Conceptions of Emotion in Criminal Law' (1996) 96 Columbia Law Review 269.

126 Ibid.; and see Mounts (n 116) 265–67, who articulates that a rationale why the distinction between first and second degree murder in the U.S. may be deteriorating is that some murders that are not premeditated are still particularly 'gruesome': consequently, this presents societal public pressure to 'level up' and standardise all murders within the most serious categorisation.

127 See Kahan and Nussbaum (n 125).

128 See Bergelson (n 107). Note that there has been continual doubts expressed by some that the premeditation / deliberation formula truly stigmatises murders deserving greater punishment, and such concerns are reflected in the MPC Commentaries: 'Prior reflection may reveal the uncertainties of a tortured conscience rather than exceptional depravity. The very fact of a long internal struggle may be evidence that the homicide impulse was deeply aberrational land far more the product of extraordinary circumstances than a true reflection of the actor's normal character … [I]t also seems clear, moreover, that some purely impulsive murders will present no extenuating circumstances. The suddenness of the killing may simply reveal callousness so complete and depravity so extreme that no hesitation is required'; see MPC s. 210.6 Cmt. 4(b) 127–28.

129 See G. Binder, 'The Origins of American Felony Murder Rules' (2004) 57 Stanford Law Review 59.

130 See W.R. LaFave, *Substantive Criminal Law* (2nd edn, West Pub. Co. 2003) 2, 15.5.

131 See above (n 1) para 2.112–2.114; and see C. Finkelstein, 'Merger and Felony Murder' in S. Green and A. Duff (eds) *Defining Crimes* (Oxford University Press 2005) 218; and K.K. Ferzan, 'Murder After The Merger: A Commentary on Finkelstein' (2006) 9(2) Buffalo Criminal Law Review 561.

would be murder to kill by reckless indifference, are inevitably arbitrary in scope. In many situations it is extremely problematic to demarcate the offence in the course of which the killing transpired, and the conduct imbued as establishing reckless indifference. Dilemmatic issues prevail as to whether the killing itself was committed in the course of, or arose from, the effectuation of another offence.[132] The MPC limits the felony-murder rule in such circumstances to participation in a 'dangerous' felony (as defined)[133] which creates a rebuttable presumption of recklessness with extreme indifference to the value of human life, supporting a murder conviction. Otherwise the MPC posits the abandonment of the doctrine with drafters opposed to constructive culpability precepts:

> [U]nder the Model Code, as at common law, murder occurs if a person kills purposely, knowingly, or with extreme recklessness. Lower culpability yields lesser liability, and a person who inadvertently kills another under circumstances not amounting to negligence is guilty of no crime at all. The felony murder rule contradicts this scheme. It bases conviction of murder not on any proven culpability with respect to homicide but on liability for another crime.[134]

There is a contemporaneity to U.S. state grading statutes that underscore liability for tier 2 (reckless manslaughter) and tier 3 culpable (negligent) homicide that are outwith the higher level gradation of murder.[135] Reckless manslaughter engages the conscious disregard of a substantial and unjustifiable risk of causing death with death resulting.[136] It is contended that the criminal actor consciously chooses to engage in risky behaviour, and pre-consciously recognises why the behaviour is risky.[137] In contrast, the negligent defendant needs only to disregard a risk of which he 'should be aware.'[138] A conviction for culpable (negligent) homicide requires the normative judgment that the actor's failure to perceive the risk involves a gross deviation from the standard of care that a reasonable person would observe in the actor's situation.[139] The 'gross-deviation' externality requirement, as in English law post-*Adomako* [140] for gross negligence manslaughter, reflects criterion standardisation on the boundaries of civil and criminal liabilities. It is reflective of a gross disregard for the societal interests and claims of impacted individuals, and a typical definition of the parameters of culpability was provided in *State v Barnett*:

> [T]he negligence of the accused must be "culpable", "gross" or "reckless", that is, the conduct of the accused must be such a departure from what would be the conduct of an

132 Ibid.
133 A 'dangerous' felony is categorised as where D participates in robbery, rape or deviate sexual intercourse by force or threat of force, arson, burglary, kidnapping, or felonious escape.; see MPC s. 210.2 (1) (b).
134 MPC s.210.2, cmt 6, 36; and see Finkelstein (n 130).
135 See Bergelson (n 107).
136 Ibid.; and see MPC s.210.2(1)(b).
137 K.K. Ferzan, 'Opaque Recklessness' (2001) 91(3) Journal of Criminal Law and Criminology 579, 631.
138 Ibid.
139 MPC s. 2.02 (2)(d); and see Dressler (n 114) 511.
140 [1995] 1 AC 171; and see A. Simester, 'Can Negligence be Culpable?' in J. Horder (ed.) *Oxford Essays in Jurisprudence* (4th series, Oxford University Press 2000) 85.

ordinarily prudent or careful man under the circumstances as to be incompatible with a proper regard for life, or conduct amounting to an indifference to consequences.[141]

A particular challenge for courts on both sides of the Atlantic, and indeed in recent common law determinations within Australia,[142] has been the significance of defendant capacity, or otherwise, within the amorphous 'reasonable person' standardisation for involuntary / culpable homicide, as set out above.[143] Can, or should, an individual defendant be fairly judged against an awareness of risk of harm standardisation that is ineffectual to them, and may abrogate equitable culpability inculcations? The matter has arisen in the arena of involuntary manslaughter by omission.

The seminal U.S. case is *State v Williams* [144] has provoked significant debate. The defendants, who were clearly loving parents, were convicted of involuntary (negligence) manslaughter for letting their 14-month-old son die of pneumonia, although it was not proven that they had any realisation at all of life endangerment.[145] A legitimate question is raised of the import of retributive punishment herein, especially in light of reduced capacity limitations. Walter Williams was categorised as, 'a 24 year old full-blooded Sheshont Indian with a sixth grade education':[146] his wife Bernice was referred to in court, as, 'a 20-year old part Indian with an 11th grade education'.[147] Believing that their son was only suffering from an infection of the mouth and cheek, and with a justifiable fear at the time that state welfare authorities might remove the child from them to be placed with non-native American families, they failed to seek medical help. Medical testimony established that their son would have survived had he received adequate medical care at least one week prior to his death.[148]

The involuntary manslaughter determination in *Williams* has provoked a range of responses across a continuum:[149]

i the Williamses had no good reason to risk life endangerment of their son and were guilty of reckless manslaughter not simply involuntary (negligence) manslaughter;
ii they were 'justified' in not seeking medical assistance given they risked losing their child to welfare authorities;

141 63 S.E. 2d 57, 58–59 (S.C. 1951). Note that for unlawful act manslaughter (misdemeanour-manslaughter) the U.S. state statutes that have adopted such constructive liability demand that the unlawful act be: (1) the proximate cause of the resulting death; (2) *malum in se* (a serious type of offence), not merely *malum prohibitum* (of a more regulatory quasi-criminal nature); and (3) 'dangerous' to the point of evincing a marked disregard for the safety of others, see Bergelson (n 107).

142 Australia does not have a uniform criminal law. Each of the six states (New South Wales, Queensland, South Australia, Tasmania, Victoria and Western Australia), the two territories (the Australian Capital Territory and Northern Territory) and the federal jurisdiction has its own criminal law.

143 See generally, S. Yeo, 'The Fault Elements for Involuntary Manslaughter: Some Lessons from Downunder' (2000) 43(1) Criminal Law Quarterly 291; and Ashworth (n 22).

144 484 P. 2d. 1167 (Wash. App. 1971); and see, S.P. Garvey, 'What's Wrong with Involuntary Manslaughter?' (2006) 85 Texas Law Review.

145 Ibid., 1169.

146 Ibid.

147 Ibid., 1170.

148 Ibid., 1173–74.

149 See P.H. Robinson, *Would You Convict? Seventeen Cases That Changed the Law* (New York University Press 1999) 142.

iii the outcome was correct as the Williamses should have seen the risk as a reasonable person in their situation would have seen it; or
iv the Williamses lacked capacity to realise the risk of life endangerment and should have been acquitted.[150]

The arguments presented are central to our discussion of fair labelling and appropriate societal culpability gradation, and invoke choice retribution theory where choice is the touchstone of desert.[151] The punishment that actors' deserve depends on the choices that they make with relational capacity to make those choices.[152]

It is submitted on our part that the Williamses ought to have been acquitted of involuntary manslaughter. The fundamental imposition is to desist from imposing on others an unjustified risk of causing death or serious harm, and imperatively an actor who sees no risk in what he is doing, lacking cognitive or conative capacity, cannot be said to have volitionally chosen to have taken such a risk. It is insufficient that he 'ought' to have foreseen the risk as it would have been palpable to the amorphous reasonable person: the individual actor has not 'chosen' to act (or omit to act) in a way the law demands he refrain from acting and punishment is 'illegitimate'.[153] There are parallels herein with the much discussed outcome in *Stone and Dobinson*, [154] where the English appellate court inculpated respective parties for involuntary manslaughter (gross negligence) on the predicates of indifference to a risk of harm to the health and welfare of the victim. Stone and his mistress (Dobinson) had apparently assumed responsibility to the victim (Stone's sister), and precluded others from helping, by allowing her to lodge with them, and making some limited efforts to assist her whilst she stayed with them. The sister died from anorexia nervosa, and both were convicted of manslaughter, irrespective of the fact that the defendants were described in the judgment as of 'very limited intelligence' 'educationally backward' and 'weak' and 'ineffectual'.[155] Their inculpation for manslaughter stands as the high water mark in English law of manslaughter by omission, predicated only on risk of harm to 'health and welfare' (not even death or serious injury), and contradicts fair labelling, retributive choice theory and the excusatory inculcations appurtenant to lack of capacity.[156]

Interestingly, the recent lessons from Australian jurisprudence reveal alternative perspectives to capacity and choice theory, aligned also with a higher foresight of risk of harm culpability standardisation.[157] An individual actor is guilty of involuntary manslaughter at

150 Ibid., 140–41, highlighting reports of a survey based on facts of the *Williams* case determining that, '17% of the people would impose no punishment, but 45% would impose a substantial punishment of a year or more in person'; and see Garvey (n 144).

151 See L. Alexander, 'Insufficient Concern: A Unified Conception of Criminal Culpability' (2000) 88 California Law Review 931.

152 See Garvey (n 144).

153 See Ferzan (n 131); and D.M. Treiman, 'Recklessness and the Model Penal Code' (1981) 9 American Journal of Criminal Law 281.

154 [1977] QB 354; and see A. Ashworth, 'The Scope of Criminal Liability for Omissions' (1989) 105 Law Quarterly Review 434; and G. Williams, 'Criminal Omissions – The Conventional View' (1991) 107(86) Law Quarterly Review 86.

155 Ibid.

156 See Williams (n 154), but contrast the perspectives advanced by Ashworth (n 22); and see further A. Ashworth, 'Public Duties and Criminal Omissions: Some Unresolved Questions' (2011) Journal of Commonwealth Criminal Law 1.

157 See generally, G. Roberts, 'Unlawful and Dangerous Act Manslaughter: *R v Wills*' (1984) 10(4) Monash University Law Review 228; M. O'Reilly, 'The Law of Involuntary Manslaughter: *Wilson v R*' (1993) 15 Sydney Law Review 357; and Yeo (n 143).

common law if he kills by an unlawful and dangerous act.[158] A majority of the High Court in *Wilson v R*, [159] advocating a closer connection between moral culpability and legal foresight, raised the 'dangerous' conceptualisation in declaring, contrary to English law, and Canadian precepts established in *Creighton*, that the Crown must prove that all sober and reasonable people would have foreseen the risk of '*serious*' harm, as opposed to '*some*' harm, arising from the unlawful criminal act.[160] The normative template, assessing the definitional element of 'dangerousness' against parameters of the 'sober and reasonable' bystander standardisation, has been attenuated to allow relational characteristics and capacity of the defendant to be considered by the jurors as moral arbiters.[161] This comports with legitimate arguments that Mitchell has provided that one of the major functions of a criminal justice system is to provide a proportionate response to crime and criminality.[162] Moreover, liability for involuntary manslaughter ought therefore, to arise only where there is a foreseeable or foreseen risk of killing or at least serious harm – as propounded in *Wilson*, distinguishing *Creighton* and extant English law.

There has been a rapprochement in subjective choice retributive theory, and primordial capacity invocation, by the Supreme Court of New South Wales in *R v Thomas*. [163] It was not in issue that the defendant had unlawfully killed his adoptive mother, but at issue was whether the normative reasonable person standardisation could be attenuated to be invested with the actor's psychiatric condition. Thomas had been assessed by a forensic psychologist, and a clinical neuropsychologist after the killing, who established that he had a 'moderate intellectual disability', elements of which included extremely limited attention, extremely poor information processing speed and impaired conceptual reasoning abilities. The court determined that 'objectively ascertainable' attributes that affect an accused's ability to appreciate the consequences of these actions were comportationally relevant. Learning difficulties as part of individual capacity impacted upon choices linked to appreciation of consequences provided there were 'nothing transient or ephemeral' about the characteristic[164] and age also, as *DPP v TY* [165] before the Supreme Court of Victoria, was of significance in dilution of the objective categorisation:

> [D's] intellectual capacity is so far removed from that of the vast majority of people in the community that it strikes me as patently unfair to require him and his actions to be judged by standards that he could never hope to emulate … To my mind to judge the actions of a person who has an intellectual capacity in the bottom 0.1% of the population to the standards of the vast majority of citizens is to widen the gap between moral culpability and legal responsibility to a point that is simply unacceptable.[166]

158 See Yeo (n 143).
159 [1992] HCA 31; (1992) 174 CLR 313, High Court of Australia.
160 Ibid., M.C.J. Toohey, Gaudron and McHugh JJ at [49].
161 See O'Reilly (n 157) 362, who cogently asserts that the more progressive majority judgment is to be preferred as it recognises a moral obligation to deal justly with the accused, whereas the conservative minority judgment is, 'an outdated and blinkered moral vision'; Ibid.
162 B. Mitchell, 'Minding the Gap in Unlawful and Dangerous Act Manslaughter: A Moral Defence of One Punch Killers' (2008) 72 Journal of Criminal Law 537.
163 [2015] NSWSC 537, Supreme Court of New South Wales.
164 Ibid. at [69].
165 [2006] VSC 494, (2006) 167. A Crim. R. 596, Supreme Court of Victoria.
166 *TY* (n 163) [70].

It is unfair to punish an actor who lacks capacity at the time of the commission of the unlawful act (T2 stage) and, lacked any awareness of the risk he was imposing, and may not be said to have chosen to take that risk. Individual temporal time-framing occurs, however, and as Garvey highlights,[167] he can fairly be punished in terms of just desserts, if he culpably chose to impose a risk of causing death at some earlier point in time (T1). Prevening fault may apply, unlike in *Williams*, and the fair labelling paradigm is treated in a fundamentally different, manner, in a similar vein to prior fault invocation that applies to basic intent crimes and voluntary intoxication under English precepts.[168] The individual actor is constitutively 'reckless' at T1 temporal individuation via volitional choice.[169] *Ex ante* the MPC treats the prior choice to risk intoxication as the predicate upon which he 'forfeits' that defence: his failure to be aware of the risk is 'immaterial' if related to intoxication.[170] The intervening retributive choice and capacity paradigms are illustrated by the off-cited New York Court of Appeals review in *People v Decina* [171] as an iteration of 'narrow' prior choice theory. Decina, an epileptic suffered a seizure whilst driving his car. The car veered out of control and tragically four children were killed. The defendant asserted that a valid defence applied to the crime charged, and sought to dismiss the indictment on the predicate that whilst in the midst of the seizure he lacked the capacity to control his car. Decina, in essence, contended that, as a non-insane automation,[172] he could not have avoided creating the lethal risk. The Court of Appeals, however, upheld liability, and addressed prevening fault and choice culpability as the accused knew he suffered from epilepsy and might at any moment have a seizure. Nonetheless, he chose to get into his car and drive. Although he did not choose to let his car go out of control at T2 individuation, he did choose to create a lethal risk at T1. Fault attached to the volitional choice with capacity at T1 to drive – culpably attached to that choice which ultimately caused the victims' deaths.[173]

4. Conclusion

English law, as Stark has recently highlighted, does not meaningfully delineate in terms of fair labelling between different types of culpability in respect of the causing of death. There is no stratification of liability within murder to reflect the heinousness of the killing, and for involuntary manslaughter the common law offences of unlawful act (constructive) manslaughter and the gross negligence variegation are grouped together with no articulation of fault gradation in terms of societal expectations. Reckless manslaughter, if it exists as a separate category for inculpation at all, is wrongly graded equally and contemporaneously

167 Garvey (n 144).

168 See *DPP v Majewski* [1977] A.C. 443 (HL); and A. Simester, 'Intoxication is Never a Defence' (2009) Criminal Law Review 3.

169 See A. Reed and N. Wake, 'Reconceptualising the Contours of Self-Defence in the Context of Vulnerable Offenders: A Response to the New Zealand Law Commission?' (2016) 3(2) Journal of International and Comparative Law 195.

170 See MPC s.2.08. Prior choice to risk intoxication results in D's forfeiture of any opportunity to substantiate the defence. The Code treats an actor as suffering from 'self-induced intoxication' when he knowingly introduces substances into his body, the tendency of which to cause intoxication … he ought to know. See MPC s.2.08(5)(b).

171 138 NE 2d. 799 (NY 1956).

172 See generally: J. Child and A. Reed, 'Automatism is Never a Defence' (2014) 65(2) Northern Ireland Legal Quarterly 167.

173 See generally: J. Rumbold and M. Wasik, 'Diabetic Drivers, Hypoglycaemia, Unawareness and Automatism' (2011) Criminal Law Review 863.

with liability for inadvertent risk-taking in terms of sentencing or offence stigmatisation. As intimated herein, a choice-based model of culpability, reflective of defined elements of U.S./ Australian/Canadian precepts, is particularly attractive within a delineated hierarchical template for homicide liability. The lessons from our comparative review suggest an optimised reform pathway: a dichotomy within murder itself in terms of a modified premediation / deliberation formula to reflect and stigmatise the most serious criminal actor; a binary threshold divide between reckless- and negligence-based homicide in terms of advertent / inadvertent risk-taking; abrogation of the *versari* doctrine and constructive manslaughter as in South Africa, or at the very least a raised foreseeability of harm threshold comporting with serious harm individual awareness; and a broader appreciation of capacity inculcations within prior choice deliberations that reflect conscionable fair labelling.

4 The current state of murder in English law

A critique, wrong turns and all

J.J. Child and G.R. Sullivan

Introduction

The term 'murder', derived from the Germanic *morth,* originally denoted a secret killing. In the immediate post-Conquest period the term was used to denote any secret killing of a Norman, entailing hefty fines on the hundred where the body was found.[1] By the thirteenth century, murder was the term used for any unpardonable killing.[2] The seventeenth century gave us Coke's classic formulation which, to paraphrase, required an unlawful killing of a human being under the king's peace carried out with malice aforethought, express or implied, death to occur within a year and a day from the infliction of the wound or hurt.[3]

Remarkably, Coke's defining elements of murder are still reiterated in modern murder cases and modern texts, save for the absence of the year and a day limitation, which has been removed by statute.[4] This puts us on notice that there is no statutory definition of murder; it is still a common law offence. But the invocation of Coke is now a matter of ritual rather than substance. The common law of murder has changed since his time. Though it remains, we will contend, unacceptably wide and undiscriminating in its catchment, both as it applies to principal offenders as well as to accomplices.

Our primary focus in each case is the culpability standards required for murder liability. It is now well established that murder is not confined to persons who kill with intent to kill, but encompasses persons who kill without intending to kill yet intend to cause serious injury.[5] Serious injury need not be life-threatening injury, and the victim's self-neglect,[6] or even deliberate refusal of treatment,[7] will not necessarily sever the causal link between D's intentional infliction of serious injury and the subsequent death of V.[8] What intent means in the context of intending to kill or seriously injure has also been a matter of dispute, still not fully resolved. What is clear is that a spontaneous killing may be an intentional killing for the

1 J. Stephen, *A History of the Criminal Law of England* (Vol. 3, MacMillan & Co. 1883) 40.
2 Sir Frederick Pollock and F. Maitland, *The History of English Law* (Vol. 2, 2nd edn, Cambridge University Press 1898) 478–84.
3 *Coke's Institutes* (Vol. 3) 47.
4 Law Reform (Year and a Day Rule) 1996.
5 *Cunningham* [1982] AC 566.
6 *Governor Wall's Case,* 28 State Trials, 53.
7 *Blaue* [1975] 3 All ER 446.
8 Importantly, medical interventions, however ill-advised or inept, will not sever in law the causal linkage between D's injurious conduct and V's death, even in cases where the treatment supervenes over the injury, unless the circumstances are truly exceptional. The leading case on medical interventions is *Cheshire* [1991] 3 All ER 670.

purposes of a murder conviction just as much as a premeditated killing.[9] Hence the expression 'malice aforethought' can be safely set to one side. From this basis, complicity in murder extends liability still further for those associated with D's crime, and despite recent attempts to narrow its impact, liability remains highly problematic. We consider these problems at length in the sections that follow.

The wide catchment of murder would not matter as much if liability could be tempered at the sentencing stage. But the sentence for murder is implacable: the sentence is always a sentence of life imprisonment.[10] To be sure, that does not always mean incarceration for life. But it does mean that persons found guilty of murder spend a considerably longer time in prison than persons found guilty of manslaughter and other homicide offences.[11] And this arises despite often fine line distinctions between murder and manslaughter.[12] Fine lines are inevitable in any rule-based system of adjudication, but the mandatory life sentence for murder places an obligation to confine murder convictions to the very worst kinds of killings. It will be argued that the current law of murder in England and Wales does not meet that obligation.

Although there is not space to discuss the issue in detail here, it should also be highlighted that the current law of murder has contributed to problems and inconsistencies in associated areas of law as courts have sought to mitigate its application. English law allows a very large latitude to killings done in self-defence and the prevention of crime.[13] Some narrowing of the legal definition of intent is to be found in cases of bona fide medical treatment,[14] together with some fudging of the distinction between acts and omissions.[15] Partial

9 For instance, the partial defence of loss of self-control which reduces what would otherwise be murder to manslaughter is based on the assumption that a killing induced by a loss of self-control is compatible with a finding that D killed V, intending to kill or cause serious injury: Coroners and Justice Act 2009, ss 54–6.

10 The death penalty for murder was suspended by the Murder (Abolition of Death Penalty) Act 1965. Abolition became permanent following affirmative resolutions of both houses of Parliament on 16 and 18 December 1969. The 1965 Act imposes a mandatory penalty of life imprisonment for all cases of murder.

11 Most instances of homicide are either murder or manslaughter. There are also some vehicular homicides (e.g., causing death by dangerous driving) and infanticide. Manslaughter can be punished with life imprisonment but such a sentence is discretionary. The usual sentence is a determinate term of years and in such cases, subject to good behaviour, only half of the term of years will be spent in prison. By contrast, each murderer will receive a minimum term (almost invariably not less than 15 years), which must be served in full. See further (n 26) and associated text.

12 Particularly, for example, where we are unsure whether D foresaw killing or seriously harming V as a virtual certainty (providing the intent required for murder) or just short of this.

13 Private persons and also officials such as police officers and soldiers are permitted to use 'such force as is reasonable in the circumstances', by way of self-defence or when preventing crime. What constitutes reasonable force is evaluated on the basis of the facts that D believed to be the case, allowing force to be condoned when force in fact was not necessary: Criminal Justice and Immigration Act, s 76(3). When D is using defensive force against an intruder in his home, the force used is taken to be proportionate unless it was 'grossly disproportionate': s 76(5)(a). This provision was found to be compatible with Article 2 of the European Convention on Human Rights in *Denby Collins* [2016] EWHC 33 (Admin) following a minimalist interpretation of the provision.

14 See A. Ashworth, 'Criminal Liability in a Medical Context: The Treatment of Good Intentions' in Andrew P. Simester and A.T.H. Smith (eds) *Harm and Culpability* (Oxford University Press 1996) 173.

15 In *Bland* [1993] AC 789 there was a wide consensus amongst members of the appellate committee that medical procedures such as terminating induced respiration in what was considered the best interests of the patient was an omission to treat further, rather than a positive act ending the patient's life.

defences of loss of self-control,[16] diminished responsibility arising from a recognised medical condition,[17] and provisions relating to suicide pacts[18] can reduce murder to manslaughter, allowing a large discretion in the sentencing outcome.[19] The offence of infanticide,[20] which is broadly interpreted, and punishable on the same terms as manslaughter, avoids charging with murder mothers who kill their infant children of under 12 months when psychologically disturbed.[21] Taken together, these provisions and interpretations make for a significant diminution in the incidence of murder convictions. On the other hand, the defence of duress which requires nothing less than an immediate threat of death or serious injury is categorically disallowed for murder.[22] No leeway at all is given to the direct causing of death for reasons of compassion, even compelling reasons.[23]

The penal consequences of murder

In *Redfern*, [24] D and two others attacked V, a 40-year-old man who had offered no provocation. V was punched to the ground and then subjected to a sustained kicking about the head and body, resulting in an extensive and fatal brain haemorrhage. The prosecution accepted pleas of guilty to manslaughter. Each defendant received a sentence of five years, and six months imprisonment. If a prison sentence is not a life sentence, nor a special measure for public protection, subject to good behaviour, the prisoner will serve half of the fixed term in prison, with the rest of the sentence served on licence in the community. Consequently, the three prisoners left prison after serving two years, six months in custody.

16 Coroners and Justice Act 2009, ss 52–54. (hereafter, the 'CJA 2009').
17 Homicide Act 1957, s 2 (as amended by CJA 2009, s52).
18 Ibid. s 4.
19 Descending from life imprisonment to an absolute discharge.
20 Infanticide Act 1938, s 1.
21 For an instructive account of the law and sentencing practice of infanticide, see R.D. Mackay, *Infanticide and Related Diminished Responsibility Manslaughters: An Empirical Study* in Law Commission, *Murder Manslaughter and Infanticide* (Law Com No 304, 2006).
22 On the theory that the killing of a non-threatening person cannot be excused or justified even if the death of D would have ensued: *Dudley and Stephens* [1884] 14 QBD 273. In *Hasan* [2005] UKHL 22, Lord Bingham considered that there was no principled basis for excluding murder from the scope of the defence but considered the exclusion was of such long-standing that only Parliament could change the law. The Law Commission of England and Wales recommended making duress an applicable defence to murder (Law Commission, *Murder, Manslaughter and Infanticide* (Law Com 304, 2006), Part 6) but no legislative change has been made or is likely to be made. It may be that, very exceptionally, ending the life of an innocent person may be justified where the person whose life was ended was, however blamelessly and inadvertently, a lethal threat to another innocent person: *Re A (Children)* [2001] Fam 147.
23 In *Cox* [1992] 12 BMLR 38, D, a doctor, administered a fatal injection to V, his patient, at her request. She suffered from a very painful and terminal condition for which there was no effective pain relieving treatment. The Court of Appeal had no doubt that D's conduct would, but for some evidential uncertainty, (causing the charge to be one of attempted murder) have amounted to murder, drawing a distinction between palliative measures which incidentally shorten life (permissible) and the deliberate causing of death. In *Nicklinson* [2014] UKSC 38, the Supreme Court emphatically re-asserted that all forms of euthanasia, voluntary or otherwise, amounted to murder. The United Kingdom Parliament has consistently rejected legislative proposals which supported changing, in a more permissive direction, the proscriptions of euthanasia and assisting suicide.
24 [2001] 2 Cr App Rep 33.

The culpability for murder will be discussed in detail below. Yet no schooling in that topic is necessary to perceive from the facts of *Redfern* clear evidence against each of the defendants of an intention to inflict serious injury on V. If the prosecution had not accepted pleas of guilty to manslaughter[25] and had brought successful charges of murder, the fate of the defendants would have been radically different. Each defendant would have spent at least 15 years in prison. Release would not necessarily have been forthcoming after 15 years. Release would require a favourable decision by the Parole Board that the release of the prisoners would not unduly threaten public safety.[26]

The punishment regime for murder was made significantly harsher by the Criminal Justice Act 2003.[27] With the suspension and then the abolition of the death penalty, a mandatory sentence of life imprisonment became the only sentencing option. Prior to the 2003 Act,[28] the trial judge would recommend the minimum time to be spent in prison having given consideration to retribution, deterrence and public safety. The judge's papers would then be sent to the Lord Chief Justice for scrutiny, and then delivered to the Home Secretary, the person who ultimately decided when the prisoner could be released. Unsurprisingly, this administrative rather than judicial process was found to be non-compliant with the right to a fair trial guaranteed by Article 6 of the European Convention on Human Rights.[29] Under these superseded arrangements, the average time a 'lifer' would spend in prison before release on licence was approximately 12 years.

Under the Criminal Justice Act 2003, determination of the minimum term is entirely in judicial hands, subject to strong statutory presumptions as to the appropriate minimum term. The minimum term for any murder is 15 years, although it may well be greater and, very exceptionally, lesser.[30] The minimum term must be greater if the murder is a 'serious murder' as identified by the guidelines, such as murders of police or prison officers, use of firearms, sexual or sadistic killings, or killings motivated by racial or sexual prejudice. For such killings, the minimum term is 30 years. If the killing is 'exceptionally serious' – premeditated killing of two or more people, sexually or sadistically motivated killing of children, politically motivated killings – the appropriate term is a whole life term.[31] Since the guidelines were set, a 25 year-minimum term has been introduced for any person over the age of

25 One can only speculate on why murder charges were not brought. It may have been because the defendants had taken drink and drugs: evidence of intoxication can be used to throw doubt on whether there is proof of intent: *Majewski* [1977] AC 443.

26 For full discussion of the law and practice relating to life sentences for murder, see B. Mitchell and J. Roberts, *Exploring the Mandatory Life Sentence for Murder* (Hart 2012).

27 Criminal Justice Act 2003, s 269 and schedule 21.

28 For the law and practice of life sentences prior to the 2003 Act see S. Shute, 'Punishing Murders: Release Procedures and the "Tariff"' (2004) Criminal Law Review 873.

29 *Home Secretary, ex Dl Anderson* [2002] UKHL 46.

30 In *Sullivan* [2005] 1 Cr App R 308 the Court of Appeal ruled that the schedule 21 guidelines were presumptive, though strongly presumptive rather than mandatory. Accordingly, a 12-year minimum term was set for the circumstances of the instant case.

31 Whole life terms were found to contravene Article 3 of the European Convention on Human Rights in *Vinter* v *the UK* [2014] Criminal Law Review 81. In *A-G's Reference (No 69 of 2013)* [2014] EWCA Crim 188, the Court of Appeal considered that *Vinter* had overstated the rigidity of the whole life sentence regime and had not appreciated the degree of latitude it allowed to react appropriately to any exceptional circumstances which might arise. The European Court of Human Rights agreed with this criticism of *Vinter* in *Hutchinson v the UK* (2015, App No 57592/08).

18 who takes a knife or other weapon to commit murder.[32] The impact over the years of these presumptions as to minimum terms for murder has been profound.[33] Final release by the Parole Board is unlikely to coincide with the expiry of the minimum term. There is a backlog of cases awaiting scrutiny.[34] The outcome of the scrutiny will be far from certain.

For such a draconian regime, it is essential that the facts which determine the length of the minimum term should be securely established. That will not always be possible, particularly in complicity cases. For instance, the Reds and the Blues, two opposing groups of young men, meet and fight, first with fists and boots, whereupon a Red, who cannot be identified, stabs and kills a Blue. There was until very recently in English law an extension of secondary liability known as parasitic accessory liability (PAL) based on a finding of a joint enterprise,[35] which would have imposed liability for murder on any member of the Red faction if it could be proved against any individual Red defendant that he must either have been the unidentified principal or, alternatively, involved in the general fighting, or at least present in support of the fighting. With one of those alternatives established against a particular defendant, liability for murder would follow in his case on proof of foresight that the fighting might escalate and that a Blue might be seriously injured by a Red acting with intent to cause serious injury.[36] Where two or more of the defendants were found guilty by a jury on these terms, the only practicable minimum term is the same minimum term for each defendant.[37] Ostensibly, joint enterprise liability was recently abolished by the Supreme Court in *Jogee and Ruddock*. [38] However, as will be argued later in this chapter, much of its substance remains, still permitting murder verdicts where the material contribution and precise state of mind of the defendant may be far from clear, but almost certainly a state of mind of a lesser order than required of an identified principal.

A further example of uncertainty as to the factual basis of D's involvement in a murder may arise when V, a child or vulnerable adult, dies in circumstances amounting to murder, in a household of which D is a member. It may not be clear whether D, or other members of the household, may have been a principal or accomplice in the murder or uninvolved in

32 Criminal Justice Act 2003 (Mandatory Life Sentence: Determination of Minimum Term) Order 2010.

33 As well as raising punishment levels for murder, the Court of Appeal found it to be anomalous if there were not to be a corresponding rise in the terms of imprisonment served by persons convicted of manslaughter. See F. Gibb, '"One punch" killers to get longer jail sentences' *The Times* (19 December 2009).

34 In January 2015, there were 3,163 prisoners whose minimum terms of imprisonment had expired left waiting to receive a decision concerning their release date or notification of further detention from the Parole Board. In *Osborn v the Parole Board* [2013] UKSC 61, the Supreme Court tightened the criteria, requiring an oral hearing attended by the prisoner rather than a committee decision, thereby increasing by 70% the number of oral hearings. Attempts are being made to address this backlog, a work in progress: National Audit Office, *Report on Parole Backlog*, Comptroller General and Auditor General, HC, 1013, Session 2016–17, 28 February 2017.

35 A term never precisely defined, but would certainly have covered two opposed fighting groups. The expression was originally coined by J.C. Smith, 'Criminal Liability of Accessories: Law and Law Reform' (1997) 113 Law Quarterly Review 453, 455 cf. G. Virgo, 'Joint Enterprise is Dead: Long Live Accessorial Liability' (2012) Criminal Law Review 850, 855–56.

36 The modern statement of this long-established basis of liability for murder and other offences was given in the Privy Council in *Chan Wing-Sui* [1985] AC 168, and was fully endorsed by the House of Lords in *Powell v English* [1999] 1 AC 1 and *Rahman* [2008] UKHL 45.

37 As the killing involved use of a knife the presumptive minimum term would be 25 years for each convicted defendant. As it is unclear in respect of each convicted defendant whether he was a principal or an accessory, the default is to punish all those convicted as principals.

38 [2016] UKSC 8.

the murder. All members of the household can be charged with a specific statutory offence of failing to take adequate steps to protect the child or vulnerable adult.[39] That charge can be joined to a charge of murder.[40] Should D fail to give any explanation for his or her failure to protect V, and the evidence establishes that V was murdered by some member of the household, the jury are empowered to return a verdict of murder against D, even if the evidence falls short of raising a case for D to answer on the charge of murdering V.[41]

There are thousands of prisoners serving life sentences.[42] Among that population there will be a significant cohort of dangerous offenders who would pose considerable risk to the public if released, but to move from that generalisation to identifying dangerous individuals is difficult.[43] A less difficult question is to query whether life prisoners as a whole have in large degree committed or associated themselves with acts sufficiently heinous to warrant imprisonment of these degrees of magnitude. To that question we now turn.

The conditions of liability for murder

There are two ways of becoming a murderer and subject to life imprisonment: as a principal offender (D1) or as a secondary offender (D2). A secondary offender is fully liable for the crime of murder alongside the principal. Accordingly, D1 should only satisfy the elements of murder where his conduct and *mens rea* is sufficiently culpable to be deserving of the penal consequences discussed above, and D2's liability should require a 'parity of culpability' between accomplices and principals. As we explore now, within the current law, both of these are far from being the case.

(a) Murder as a principal offender

In English law, the principal offender must make, by his unmediated conduct, some form of direct and more than minimal input to the *actus reus* of the offence. In the case of murder and for most other 'result crimes' too, the conduct of an agent who is not coerced, deceived or performing a legal duty is to be regarded as an autonomous agent, not subject to the causal influence of other human agents.[44] So, if D2 pays money to D1 to kill V, should D1 kill V as paid for, he and he alone is the principal offender.

39 Domestic Violence, Crimes and Victims Act, 2004, s 5, as amended by Domestic Violence, Crimes and Victims Act, 2012.

40 Ibid. s 6.

41 Section 6 leaves it open to the jury to find that D was the principal or the accessory to V's murder if he or she fails to give evidence suggestive of non-involvement in the death of V and fails to give evidence of any effort to protect V. If these conditions obtain, the jury is permitted to reach a verdict of murder against D, even if the evidence does not establish a case for him to answer on the murder charge. It is questionable whether this is compatible with the right to a fair trial, guaranteed by Article 6 of the European Convention on Human Rights. In *Quinn and Casterton* [2017] EWCA Crim 1071 the Court of Appeal accepted without critical comment that murder verdicts could be reached on this basis. On the facts, there was sufficient evidence that the appellants were involved in V's murder as accomplices.

42 In March 2016 there were 7,468 prisoners serving life sentences in England and Wales and 1,010 in Scotland. In Germany, there were 1,953 prisoners serving life sentences, 1,599 in Italy and 466 in France: See A. Travis, 'UK prison population is biggest in western Europe' *The Guardian* (8 March 2016).

43 P. Ramsey, 'Imprisonment for Public Protection' in G.R. Sullivan and Ian Dennis, *Seeking Security: Pre-empting the Commission of Criminal Harms* (Hart, 2012) 195.

44 *Kennedy (No 2)* [2007] UKHL 38. A broader view of causation may be taken in regulatory contexts such as pollution control as in *Empress Car company v National Rivers Authority* [1999] 2 AC 22.

It is now firmly established that the principal must act with intent to kill V *or to cause V serious injury.* [45] That a *mens rea* relating to serious injury rather than death suffices for a conviction for murder and its mandatory penalty is crucial to the understanding of the offence. At one time in the recent past there was a chance that an intent to cause serious injury would not suffice for a murder conviction, but that chance has now gone[46] and this alternative and lesser form of culpability is set to stay. Not only does this enlarge the scope of murder, it makes the offence much easier to prove. In the case of inchoate offending where murder is posited as the substantive offence, there must be proof of an intent to kill in the cases of conspiracy[47] and attempt,[48] and at least foresight of death for the offences of encouraging or assisting crime.[49] We contend that for murder too, the culpability should relate to death and nothing less.

It is important to recognise the role of 'intention'. In the typical case of murder involving an attack, particularly an armed attack, the jury can be safely left to decide for themselves whether D intended to kill or seriously hurt V.[50] But where D's conduct is *not* motivated by a purpose to kill or to seriously injure V (as when striking miners drop from a motorway bridge a paving stone intended to fall close to a taxi carrying strike-breaking miners)[51] direction is required. In such circumstances, an intent to kill or seriously injure may be found if D's conduct gave rise to a virtual certainty that V would be killed or seriously hurt and D was aware that it was virtually certain that V would be killed or seriously injured.[52]

Even if we put aside morally freighted cases such as D killing V at V's request to end unbearable suffering, it is obvious that even among the class of persons who are acting

45 Resolving the culpability required for murder involved six appeals to the House of Lords during the second half of the last century, but it's commonly agreed that the last case in this cycle, *Woollin* [1999] 1 AC 82 has finally resolved the form of words to be spoken to the jury for those cases where the facts require the jury to be given guidance on the meaning of intent.

46 In *Hyam* [1975] AC 55 the House of Lords was divided 2:2 on whether an intent to cause serious harm was doctrinally supportable. The swing vote, Lord Cross, found himself unable to decide doctrinally between the two camps but nonetheless threw in his lot with the view that an intent to cause serious harm sufficed. The House of Lords in *Cunningham* (n 5) decided on a majority that an intent to cause serious harm did suffice.

47 Criminal Law Act 1977, s 1. Conspiracy requires an agreement, which if carried out will *necessarily* bring about the commission of the substantive offence. That would not be the case where the agreement is to cause serious injury rather than death.

48 Criminal Attempts Act 1981, s 1. See also *Pearman* [1984] 80 Cr App R 259.

49 Serious Crime Act 2007, ss 44–46.

50 Something emphasised by Lord Bridge in *Moloney* [1985] AC 905, 926. For him not directing the jury on the meaning of intent in plain cases was a 'golden rule' only rarely to be departed from.

51 The facts of *Hancock* [1986] AC 455, a case where direction was required but given in terms now superseded by *Woollin* (n 45).

52 *Woollin* (n 45) 90. There is still some controversy over whether the House of Lords was setting down a rule of law as to the meaning of intent in non-attack cases or merely delineating the evidential base for permissible findings of intent at the jury's discretion. The latter is the more common view although for practical purposes it is a distinction without significance in the main run of cases. For instance, in *Mathews and Alleyne* [2003] Cr App R 30 D and others threw V into a river after robbing him, aware that he could not swim. Questionably, this was regarded as a case where a direction was needed and the Court of Appeal ruled that the trial judge had misdirected the jury when instructing them that a verdict of murder was required if the defendants were aware that V would almost certainly drown, rather than instructing them that they were entitled to record a verdict of murder if they chose to do so. The murder verdict was upheld on the basis that on a proper direction a murder verdict would have been returned because the defendants were aware that V would almost certainly drown.

without legal justification or excuse or any claim to moral vindication, a broad range of conduct is accommodated within murder. As already noted, D's conduct need not be intrinsically life-threatening. The defence of duress is categorically excluded. The defence of self-defence either succeeds or fails: an entitlement to use some degree of force will not reduce the killing to manslaughter if the bounds of the entitlement are exceeded.[53] The partial defences of diminished responsibility and loss of control may narrowly fail on particular facts yet the facts may nonetheless support some degree of mitigation; mitigation which cannot be expressed within the constraints of the mandatory sentence.[54]

(b) Murder as a secondary party

Where D2 commits murder as a secondary party, his role will always be fundamentally different from that of D1. D1 directly causes V's death; whereas D2's involvement is indirect, merely influencing or communicating approval of D1's crime before or at the time of its commission.[55] Yet despite such differences, both D2 and D1 are labelled and punished as murderers.[56] That D1 and D2 are each guilty of the same offence is essential to maintain the forensic advantage of complicity liability: the ability to charge D2 and D1 with murder without having to identify which party was the principal and which was the accomplice (as long as it is proven that D was one or the other).[57] All being equal we may prefer to conceive of complicity in murder as a separate wrong from principal liability, with a distinct label and punishment, but such an approach would deprive us of a powerful prosecutorial weapon and risk significant injustice.[58] It is therefore correct for complicity to remain a well-trodden path to murder liability.

In recognising complicity as a route to murder liability, however, a number of normative restrictions arise. Most importantly, although D2's conduct as accomplice will always be different from D1's as principal, if the two are to be labelled and punished for the same offence, it is clear that the law should require (as far as is possible) a parity of culpability between the two. Indeed, this uncontroversial logic explicitly underpinned the Law Commission's most recent recommendations on complicity.[59] In many cases, parity of culpability can be straightforwardly demonstrated: we see this where D2 has significant control over D1's actions, where, for example, D1 is a hitman or gang underling, and D2 orders D1 to commit murder with intent that he should do so. However, the minimum requirements for complicity in English law have become over-inclusive in their catchment.

Prior to 2016, cases demonstrating a lack of parity in culpability had become common across all forms of complicity liability. This was clearest in relation to so-called joint enterprise (or PAL) cases: D2 joins a criminal venture to commit a particular offence, Crime A (e.g., burglary), foreseeing that in the course of this offence D1 may commit a further

53 *Clegg* [1995] 1 AC 482.
54 Given the strong presumption that 15 years should be the minimum term for all murders, the scope for mitigation is limited.
55 For what remains an excellent framework analysis, see S. Kadish, 'Complicity, Cause and Blame: A Study in the Interpretation of Doctrine' (1985) 73 California Law Review 324.
56 Accessories and Abettors Act 1861, s 8.
57 *Giannetto* [1997] 1 Cr App R 1.
58 This can be especially important in the context of gang violence, where it may be impossible to know which member of the gang struck a fatal blow, but clear that all members were encouraging such violence (as in our Reds and Blues example above).
59 Law Commission, *Participating in Crime* (Law Com No 305, 2007) [3.1–3.167].

offence, Crime B (e.g., murder).[60] In such cases, where D1 went on to commit murder, D2 was jointly liable despite not necessarily assisting or encouraging murder, and despite only foreseeing murder by D1 as a possibility. When compared to D1's actions in directly causing V's death, and doing so with the required intention for murder, the lack of parity in culpability between the parties becomes clear.[61] And even beyond joint enterprise, similar differences between the culpability of D1 and D2 became evident with standard aiding and abetting routes to complicity liability as well. Although the courts consistently required some basic connection between D2's conduct and D1's offence (understood in terms of communicated encouragement, or material assistance[62]), it has never been necessary to prove that D2's assistance or encouragement had any causal impact.[63] *Mens rea* requirements to be proved against D2, *both* as to the assisting or encouraging effects of D2's own conduct as well as to D1 committing the principal offence, have also softened and diminished over time, with more recent cases applying a foresight standard,[64] or simply displaying legal uncertainty as to the *mens rea* for accomplices.[65] Procuring, the final species of complicity, whilst retaining a more robust causal conduct requirement, has also seen similar problems with clarifying a minimum *mens rea*.[66]

Against this unsatisfactory background, 2016 marked a significant change in the rules of complicity. This arose in the Supreme Court and Privy Council, with the combined cases of *Jogee and Ruddock* (hereafter *Jogee*), mentioned previously on page 66,[67] both of which involved appeals from findings of complicity in murder. The facts of these cases are largely unremarkable, but they provided the platform for the Supreme Court to fundamentally change the law on complicity on the basis of what they identified as a legal 'wrong turn' some 30 years previous.[68] First, and perhaps most significantly, the Supreme Court confirmed dicta from previous cases to the effect that joint enterprise liability no longer represents a separate species of complicity, meaning that D2 may only be complicit in D1's offence though aiding, abetting, counselling or procuring.[69] In doing so, the court has arguably removed a core element of the law that has given rise to perceived injustice through over-inclusivity. Second, the

60 B. Krebs, 'Joint Criminal Enterprise' (2010) 73 Modern Law Review 578.

61 G.R. Sullivan, 'First Degree Murder and Complicity—Conditions For Parity of Culpability Between Principal and Accomplice' (2007) 1(2) Criminal Law & Philosophy 271. Simester has well defended joint enterprise as a legitimate basis for criminalisation, A.P. Simester, 'The Mental Element in Complicity' (2006) 122 Law Quarterly Review 578, but the essential case for joint enterprise as an *equivalent* to principal liability remains weak.

62 Discussed in *Stringer* [2011] EWCA Crim 1396.

63 For example, it would be sufficient for D2 to respond 'Oh goody' to D1 upon hearing the latter's plan to kill his wife. This is a much quoted example from *Giannetto* (n 57).

64 See, for example, *Rook* [1993] 1 WLR 1005; *Bryce* [2004] EWCA Crim 1231; *Webster* [2006] 2 Cr App R 6; M. Dyson, 'Might Alone Does Not Make Right: Justifying Secondary Liability' (2015) Criminal Law Review 967.

65 *Gnango* [2011] UKSC 59. The range and diversity of approaches discussed in this case provides striking illustration of apparent legal uncertainty. See G.R. Sullivan, 'Accessories and Principals after *Gnango*' in A. Reed and M. Bohlander, *Participation in Crime: Domestic and Comparative Perspectives* (Ashgate 2013) 25.

66 *AG's Reference (No 1 of 1975)* [1975] QB 773.

67 *Jogee* (n 38).

68 The court in *Jogee* identified this 'wrong turn' as the case of *Chan Wing-Siu* [1985] AC 168, where the Privy Council explicitly identified joint enterprise as a separate form of complicity liability, as well as a foresight standard of *mens rea*. They did so despite multiple Court of Appeal, House of Lords and Supreme Court decisions endorsing this approach.

69 *Jogee* (n 38) [61–87].

Supreme Court also took aim at standard routes to complicity liability. The court did not revisit issues within the *actus reus*,[70] but the judgment is dominated by discussion of *mens rea*, and the reassertion of 'intention' as the core required standard.[71]

In line with our focus on the importance of parity of culpability between a principal and secondary party in murder, the headlines from *Jogee* should be roundly welcomed. In abolishing joint enterprise and narrowing the *mens rea* of complicity to an intention standard, the court was clearly convinced of the need to adjust the law of complicity to ensure a greater degree of parity. Indeed, they explicitly criticised the previous law for creating 'the striking anomaly of requiring a lower mental threshold for guilt in the case of the accessory than in the case of the principal.'[72] However, despite the clarity of the headlines in *Jogee*, and despite the explicit break from the last 30 years of jurisprudence, sections of the judgment seeking to clarify the law moving forward are much more problematic, and seem hesitant in their application of the new intention standard. This should not be a surprise. It must be remembered that complicity has become a major route to murder liability, and so despite the court's willingness to accept principled arguments in favour of an intention standard, they were also inevitably and sensibly conscious of what the impacts of narrowing the law might be: impacts in terms of appeals from previous convictions (from those convicted following the legal wrong turn),[73] as well as impacts in blunting what had become a popular and powerful prosecutorial weapon.[74]

There is a clear policy conflict throughout *Jogee*, with the court headlining the narrowing of complicity liability to achieve parity of culpability between D2 and D1, whilst simultaneously attempting to maintain as far as possible its prosecutorial advantages. Unfortunately, it is a conflict that is not resolved within *Jogee* itself, but instead leads the court to significant legal error and uncertainty within core aspects of its judgment. In the following sub-sections, we highlight the three most important areas of uncertainty or error apparent post-*Jogee*: (i) uncertainty as to what D2 must intend for complicity liability; (ii) misuse of conditional intention; and (iii) misunderstanding of complicity in manslaughter. In each case, it is clear that the policy conflict just described has in some sense forced the court into locating a compromise position. However, it is contended here that such a position is not logically or legally available without sacrificing the core messages from *Jogee* – abolition of joint enterprise liability and intention as the *mens rea* for complicity. It is to be hoped that courts will do what they can to interpret *Jogee* in a manner that is compatible with these core messages, particularly in murder cases. But as will be seen below, considerable optimism is required to believe that this will turn out to be the case.

Uncertain mens rea

Following a long line of appellate judgments straining for consistent identification and application of *mens rea* on complicity, it was vital for the Supreme Court in *Jogee* to provide

70 More could be done in this area to focus the law on 'substantial' assistance or encouragement only, or to explore the German law approach which focuses on the level of control or dominance D has over V. See T. Hörnle, 'Commentary to "Complicity and Causality"' (2007) 1(2) Criminal Law & Philosophy 143, 147; M. Dubber and T. Hörnle, *Criminal Law: A Comparative Approach* (Oxford University Press 2014) 304–28.

71 *Jogee* (n 38) [88–9].

72 Ibid. [84].

73 Ibid. [100].

74 We explore this further in the sections below.

clarity moving forward.[75] In this vein, the court was explicit in its rejection of previous jurisprudence as a wrong turn, requiring the correction to joint enterprise (i.e., its effective abolition), as well as confirming an intention requirement within core complicity cases. However, despite clarity in the approach rejected, there is a conspicuous and damaging lack of clarity in the court's restatement of the law, particularly on the core aspects of *mens rea* that became the focus of the case. It is not sufficient for the court to simply state they are correcting a 30 year old wrong-turn, or restabilising old principles, when the precise elements of complicity liability have never been entirely settled.[76]

There are two limbs to the *mens rea* of complicity, the first is D2's *mens rea* as to the effects of his own conduct, and the second is D2's *mens rea* as to D1's future offence (including D1's *mens rea*). On the first of these, *Jogee* is clear that D2 must *intend* his conduct to assist or encourage D1's offence.[77] This provides useful confirmation following some inconsistency in previous case law,[78] and brings complicity into line with inchoate assisting or encouraging.[79] So far so good, perhaps, but subject to the court's understanding of intention discussed in the next sub-section.

Despite relative clarity on the first limb, however, the court provided little guidance on what *mens rea* is required of D2 as to D1's future offence. This omission is surprising, as it was this second limb that was the central point of debate within previous cases and reviews,[80] and indeed it was confusion on this topic within the previous law (culminating in the identification of a foresight standard) that led the court in *Jogee* to identify a wrong turn to begin with.[81] At this point we might accuse the Supreme Court of having conflated the two limbs of *mens rea* in a manner that is not at all uncommon among both courts and commentators, but this was not strictly the case. Rather, the court in *Jogee* provided a few fleeting references to *mens rea* as to D1's offence – stating that D2 must intend D1 to act with *mens rea*, [82] and at other points that D2 must know the elements of D1's offence[83] – but such references are not fully worked through, and are anyway inconsistent with examples of complicity provided elsewhere in the judgment.[84] The result, of course, is continued debate and uncertainty, and vulnerability as to arguably the core requirement of ensuring,

75 This is particularly true given that the court in *Jogee* did not apply the 1966 Practice Statement, and so (in theory at least) the judgment simply stands alongside previous conflicting precedent rather than overruling it.

76 Even the role and definition of foresight has been challenged in its historical setting. See, F. Stark, 'The Demise of "Parasitic Accessorial Liability": Substantive Judicial Law Reform, Not Common Law Housekeeping' (2016) 75(3) Cambridge Law Journal 550. See also, K.J.M. Smith, *A Modern Treaties on the Law of Criminal Complicity* (Clarendon 1991).

77 *Jogee* (n 38) [90].

78 See Law Com No 305 (n 59) B.69-B.76.

79 Inchoate assisting or encouraging offences are contained within the Serious Crime Act 2007, ss 44–46, with the section 44 offence requiring D2 to intend to assist or encourage D1's future offence. It would be highly anomalous for complicity liability to be more widely drawn than the inchoate offences.

80 The Law Commission's review of complicity, for example, focus their reform recommendations exclusively on this limb of the *mens rea*, highlighting this as the limb that has most exercised the courts. See Law Com No 305 (n 59) B.75-B.78 and (n 99).

81 This is clear in the court's discussion of the cases leading to and following the 'wrong turn', with most of the quoted passages focusing on D2's *mens rea* as to D1's offence (as opposed to D2's *mens rea* as to his own conduct). See *Jogee* (n 38) [36–59].

82 Ibid. [10].

83 Ibid. [9].

84 E.g., the weapon supplier example at [90]. We discuss these examples below.

doctrinally, parity of culpability between D2 and D1. And with this in mind, it is useful to set out the main alternatives within that debate.

One potential interpretation of *Jogee* would limit D2's liability to cases in which he *intends* all elements of D1's future offence. This interpretation highlights clear statements in *Jogee* that D2 must intend D1 to act with any required *mens rea*, and extrapolates from this (in line with the court's headlines of narrowing liability) that this must mean that D2 must also intend D1's future *actus reus* elements as well.[85] Several academics have adopted this full-offence intention interpretation;[86] and it is clearly an attractive one in terms of narrowing D2's liability to ensure parity in culpability between principal and accomplice.

However, a full-offence intention interpretation also raises several problems. First, there are theoretical problems with the definition of 'intention' as it applies to the actions of another. If we accept standard interpretations of intention as a motivation for causal action (i.e., D intends x if he acts because he believes that this action might cause x) or when he recognises x to be a virtually certain consequence of his conduct,[87] then D2 can only intend something that he believes he can causally influence with his conduct. Thus, to claim that D2 must intend the actions of D1 is to claim that D2 can (in some sense at least) *cause* the voluntary actions of D1, a point of intense philosophical debate,[88] and a point standardly rejected in law.[89] It is partly on this basis, therefore, that commentators such as Simester have rejected the full-offence intention interpretation of *Jogee*.[90] Second, in addition to problems of legal theory, interpreting *Jogee* to require D2 to intend D1's full offence would represent a significant narrowing of liability that does not seem to have been accepted by the court in their judgment. For example, the court in *Jogee* present the following as an example where complicity liability should result:

> D2 supplies a weapon to D1, who has no lawful purpose in having it, intending to help D1 by giving him the means to commit a crime ..., but *having no further interest in what he does, or indeed whether he uses it at all.*[91]

85 Note that in the context of murder and other constructive liability offences, intention as to the *actus reus* does not include the constructive elements. Thus, for example, D2 would have to intend D1 to cause GBH, but not necessarily to cause death. See *Bristow* [2013] EWCA Crim 1540.

86 See, for example, David Ormerod and Karl Laird, '*Jogee* – Not the End of a Legal Saga but the Start of a New One?' (2016) Criminal Law Review 543; Sir Richard Buxton, '*Jogee*: Upheaval in Secondary Liability for Murder' (2016) Criminal Law Review 324. This interpretation is also favoured by B. Krebs, but with an alternative view of 'authorised' intention: 'Accessory Liability: Persisting in Error' (2017) 76(1) Cambridge Law Journal 7 and *The Scope of the Enterprise: Liability for 'Joint Enterprise' Murder and Manslaughter after Jogee* (Hart 2018).

87 See *Woollin* (n 45), *Hyam* (n 46); A. Duff, *Intention, Agency and Criminal Liability* (Blackwell 1990); Gideon Yaffe, *Attempts* (Oxford University Press 2011).

88 See, for example, S. Kadish, 'Complicity, Cause and Blame: A Study in the Interpretation of Doctrine' (1985) 73 *California Law Review* 324; John Gardner, 'Complicity and Causality' 1(2) (2007) Criminal Law & Philosophy 127; M. Moore, 'Causing, Aiding and the Superfluity of Accomplice Liability' (2008) 156 Pennsylvania Law Review 395; J. Gardner, 'Moore on Complicity and Causation' (2008) 156 Pennsylvania Law Review 432. For discussion of an alternative form of 'participatory intention', see C. Kutz, 'The Philosophical Foundations of Complicity Law' in J. Deigh and D. Dolinko (eds) *Philosophy of Criminal Law* (Oxford University Press 2011) 147.

89 *Kennedy* (n 44).

90 A.P. Simester, 'Accessory Liability and Common Unlawful Purposes' (2017) 133(1) Law Quarterly Review 73.

91 *Jogee* (n 38) [90] (emphasis added).

This example, confirmed elsewhere in the judgment,[92] is entirely incompatible with a full-offence intention interpretation of *Jogee*: D2 neither acts in order that D1 will commit the principal offence, nor foresees that offence as a virtual certainty.

Moving away from the full-offence intention interpretation, an alternative interpretation of *Jogee* would substitute intention with *knowledge*. Thus, D2 must act with an intention to assist or encourage D1 to commit the future principal offence (first limb of *mens rea*), and have knowledge as to the *actus reus* and *mens rea* elements of that principal offence (second limb of *mens rea*). What may be described as a full-offence knowledge interpretation has strong foundations in older case law (although the requirement was later read down to mean foresight only),[93] and although fleeting, the judgment in *Jogee* makes an explicit reference to 'knowledge of ... existing facts' that can be read in support of this view.[94] As with the full-offence intention interpretation, the full-offence knowledge interpretation has received academic support.[95]

However, again, this interpretation remains problematic. On a practical policy level, as with the intention-based interpretation, requiring knowledge as to D1's future offence is incompatible with examples given in *Jogee* that imply a much wider criminal net: if we want to criminalise D2 who provides D1 with a weapon, uncertain what D1 will do next, and not caring what D1 will do next, then we cannot maintain a knowledge requirement.[96] Knowledge in this context is also theoretically problematic. There is a convincing argument that D2 can know future events (as opposed to simply believe them), and so knowledge is not categorically excluded: for example, it is logical to say that D2 knows the sun will rise tomorrow in New York.[97] However, knowledge in this context relies on a level of near absolute certainty which is logically absent from the context of human interaction and practical agency. Within a complicity case we can know what D1 has done *after* the principal offence is completed, but whether this can be known when D2 assists or encourages may be doubted, and this is the crucial point for coincidence of *mens rea* within the offence.[98]

In this manner, *Jogee* takes one step forward but risks two steps backwards: clarifying an intention standard for D2's assistance or encouragement, but creating uncertainty for *mens rea* as to D1's offence. The danger, of course, is that without an established requirement that D2 must *intend* D1's offence, or have *knowledge* of D1's offence, the courts will be encouraged to interpret the law (as previously) to require wider standards of *mens rea* such as belief,[99] or even simple foresight. Despite the headlines of intention within *Jogee* therefore, and despite the apparent aim of requiring a parity of culpability between D2 and D1, uncertainty remains.

92 *Jogee* (n 38) 10.
93 *Johnson v Youden* [1950] 1 KB 544.
94 *Jogee* (n 38).
95 The leading advocate of this interpretation is A.P. Simester. See Simester (n 90) and (n 61). See also Simester *et al.*, *Simester and Sullivan's Criminal Law* (6th edn, Hart 2016) 237.
96 See discussion in previous paragraph, and *Jogee* (n 38) [10, 90].
97 See, G.R. Sullivan, 'Knowledge, Belief and Culpability'; and S. Shute, 'Knowledge and Belief in the Criminal Law' in S. Shute and A.P. Simester (eds) *Criminal Law Theory* (Oxford University Press 2002) 207 and 171 respectively.
98 cf. Simester (n 61) 587.
99 Dyson, for example, has continued to advocate a belief standard. See M. Dyson, 'Shorn-Off Complicity' (2016) 75(2) Cambridge Law Journal 196 (comment) and 'Ever Working in Practice, but Never in Theory? The New English Law of Criminal Complicity' (2017) 129(1) Zeitschrift für die gesamte Strafrechtswissenschaft 232.

Misuse of conditional intention

Arguably the most troubling aspect of the judgment in *Jogee* arises from the court's interpretation of conditional intention, skewed again by attempts to maintain an intention standard whilst resisting the narrowing of liability such a standard entails. Conditional intention is a problematic concept that has tested courts and commentators for many years, and its exact definition remains contested.[100] However, as contended elsewhere in greater detail,[101] it is possible to give meaning to conditional intention in such a way that allows for its consistent application as a valid form of criminal intention, and coherence with other *mens rea* terms. To do so, conditional intention should be defined as synonymous with future conduct intention, with D's decision at t1 to perform certain conduct at t2. Therefore, where D1 decides to commit a certain offence in the future, whether he considers explicit conditions to this future conduct or not, we can conclude in law that he intends (conditionally) to commit the offence. This definition is central to our application of all offences where D1 must intend future conduct, including, for example, incomplete attempts, section 9(1)(a) burglaries, certain conspiracies, and so on. However, crucially, this interpretation will never apply within complicity: within complicity D2's intention to assist or encourage relates to *present* conduct, and D2's intention as to the principal offence relates to the conduct of *another*.[102] For complicity, it is important to apply standard definitions of intention, asking whether D2 acted because he believed that this action might cause x, or if he recognised x to be a virtually certain consequence. Yet, despite this, for the court in *Jogee*, 'it will … often be necessary to draw the jury's attention to the fact that the intention to assist, and indeed the intention that the crime should be committed, may be conditional.'[103]

In order to understand the court's misuse of conditional intention within *Jogee*, two groups of cases / hypotheticals should be distinguished. In the first, D2 intends to assist or encourage D1 to commit Crime A, and Crime B if necessary. For example:

> The group of young men which faces down a rival group may hope that the rivals will slink away, but it may well be a perfectly proper inference that all were intending that if resistance were to be met, grievous bodily harm at least should be done.[104]

We agree with the court here that intention may be properly inferred, but not conditional intention. In this example, we are assuming that D2 has acted to assist and encourage other members of the gang, and has done so in order to influence those other members *both* to confront the other gang *and* to cause serious harm if necessary. In this manner, both parts of D2's foresight are motivating his present conduct, and both parts are therefore directly intended. D2 is not conditioning his current conduct (i.e., it is being performed), and he is not conditioning his future conduct (i.e., his future conduct is irrelevant to his complicity

100 See, for example, G. Yaffe, 'Conditional Intent and Mens Rea' (2004) 10 Legal Theory 273; J.P. W. Cartwright, 'Conditional Intention' (1990) 60(3) Philosophical Studies 233; K. Campbell, 'Conditional Intention' (1982) 2(1) Legal Studies 77.

101 J.J. Child, 'Understanding Ulterior Mens Rea: Future Conduct Intention is Conditional Intention' (2017) 76(2) Cambridge Law Journal 311.

102 See also Simester (n 90). Note that we could label D2's intention as a form of 'shared conditional intention', but this would mark a linguistic alternative only, and standard legal definitions of 'intention' would still need to apply.

103 *Jogee* (n 38) [92].

104 Ibid.

liability[105]), and so although intention should be found, talk of conditional intention is misconceived.

Although the first group of cases/hypotheticals present a mislabelling of intention, the second group is considerably more dangerous. In this group, conditional intention is identified where D2 intends to assist or encourage Crime A, foreseeing that D1 will or may perform an unwanted Crime B if necessary. This approach is not *explicitly* endorsed within *Jogee*, but it is arguably implied from the court's examples involving escalating violence, and certainly left open from the use of vague language such as 'scope of the venture' and 'tacit agreement'.[106] Indeed, the potential for conditional intention to apply to Crime B in this kind of example has been endorsed in case law post-*Jogee*, including *Johnson* [107] and *Anwar*, [108] as well as some academic commentary.[109] The reason this is dangerous is because the potential assistance or encouragement of Crime B, and D1 potentially committing Crime B, are not motivating factors in D2's conduct, and are not foreseen as a virtually certain consequence either. Therefore, simply put, the courts are wrong to label D2's mental state as a form of intention (conditional or otherwise), and in doing so they are collapsing the concept of intention into recklessness.[110]

The discussion of conditional intention given in *Jogee* is provided in obiter statements, and so it may be easily corrected by the common law. This must happen soon, however, to prevent its entrenchment within subsequent cases. The view of conditional intention set out in *Jogee*, encompassing a recklessness standard, will preserve the prosecutorial reach of the pre-*Jogee* law of complicity. This may be seen as an advantage for prosecutors, but it undermines the headline changes promised within the judgment, and undermines the search for parity in culpability between D2 and D1. It is for this reason that courts and commentators have begun to present complicity post-*Jogee* as business as usual.[111] Indeed, for the court in *Anwar*,

> ... the same facts which would have been used to support the inference of mens rea before the decision in *Jogee* will equally be used now.[112]

But this is not the end of our current concerns. Not only does the *Jogee* interpretation of conditional intention reintroduce a mere foresight standard into extended complicity cases

105 Although it may be relevant to a potential defence of withdrawal.

106 *Jogee* (n 38) [90–5].

107 *Johnson and Others* [2016] EWCA Crim 1613: combined cases involving appeals against pre-*Jogee* convictions. See F. Stark, 'The Taming of Jogee' (2017) 76(1) Cambridge Law Journal 4 (comment).

108 *Anwar* [2016] EWCA Crim 551: case successfully challenging an earlier narrow interpretation of *Jogee*. See G.R. Sullivan, 'Law Reform in the Supreme Court: The Abolition of Joint Enterprise Liability?' (Forthcoming).

109 See, for example, D. Baker, 'Lesser Included Offences, Alternative Offences and Accessorial Liability' (2016) 80(6) Journal of Criminal Law 446, 448; 'Jogee: Jury Directions and the Manslaughter Alternative' (2017) Criminal Law Review 51 (letter).

110 D2's choice to assist or encourage Crime A even though he foresees the chance that Crime B will also be assisted or encouraged, and even though Crime B might be committed as a result, demonstrates recklessness only.

111 See, for example, Stark (n 107); Krebs, (n 86); Dyson (n 99); and Sullivan (n 108). See also criticism in the High Court of Australia *Miller v The Queen* [2016] HCA 30, [21, 38] and the Hong Kong Court of Final Appeal *HKSAR v Chan Kam Shing* [2016] HKCFA 87.

112 *Anwar* (n 108) [22].

(i.e., those traditionally analysed as joint enterprise),[113] but as a *mens rea* term of general application, the effects of this judgment may be felt within core complicity cases, as well as more widely across the criminal law. To give just one example, for many years courts and commentators have discussed the application of conditional intention to cases of attempt and conspiracy where D intends to act 'even if' a certain unknown circumstance might be present, for example, to make sexual contact with V *even if* she might not consent (i.e., conditionally intending to touch V with consent and without consent).[114] Importantly, this approach has been rejected, with D's conduct correctly described as making sexual contact reckless as to consent;[115] an approach also applied in other contexts.[116] However, the interpretation of conditional intention in *Jogee* would allow intention to be found in all such cases, significantly expanding the boundaries of criminal liability.

It is concluded that the concept of conditional intention has no appropriate role to play when analysing intention for complicity liability, either as to the effects of D2's conduct, or as to the potential conduct of D1. Rather, within both limbs of D2's *mens rea*, we must only inquire whether the result motivated D2's present conduct or whether D2 foresaw it as a virtually certain consequence of that conduct. This approach will significantly narrow the law of complicity, but this is the inevitable outcome of applying a genuine intention standard. To the extent that such narrowing is *not* desired, then a different standard of men rea should be explicitly applied, for example the full-offence knowledge interpretation discussed in the previous section.

Misunderstanding of complicity in manslaughter

The final of our three post-*Jogee* concerns relates to the asserted availability of complicity in manslaughter as a safety-net for cases where murder liability can no longer be found. The Supreme Court are very clear on their view of the law.

> If a person is a party to a violent attack on another, without an intent to assist in the causing of death or really serious harm, but the violence escalates and results in death, he will not be guilty of murder but guilty of manslaughter. So also if he participates … in any other unlawful act which all sober and reasonable people would realise carried the risk of some harm (not necessarily serious) …[117]

The court's statements here do not relate to murder liability, and so our analysis will be brief. However, we believe that complicity in manslaughter should not be logically available in many cases of this kind, with only complicity in the lesser intended offence (e.g., non-fatal offence against the person) or potential inchoate liability resulting. If this view is correct, then it becomes clear *again* that the court in *Jogee* cannot rely on an artificial compromise position within complicity liability, but must rather recognise and embrace the full implications of narrowing this route to murder.

113 It is notable that these are the cases the court in *Jogee* focus on when discussing conditional intention. *Jogee* (n 38) [92–4].
114 G. Williams, 'Intents In the Alternative' (1991) 50(1) Cambridge Law Journal 120.
115 Child (n 101).
116 See, for example, *Saik* [2006] UKHL 18: rejecting the application of conditional intention where D was reckless as to the circumstantial origin of currency.
117 *Jogee* (n 38) [96].

In order to understand our objections to the position asserted in *Jogee*, four factual variations should be distinguished, in which only the first two are consistent with the quotation above. In the first case, D2 intentionally assists D1 to seriously harm V (e.g., shooting in the stomach), D1 does so in the manner intended, and V dies from the attack. Here, due to the constructive nature of murder liability, both D2 and D1 will be liable for murder despite neither intending V to be killed. Both take the risk that causing serious harm may result in death, and the law treats them equally where that risk materialises. In the second case, D2 intentionally assists D1 to harm V in a relatively non-serious manner (e.g., punching in the face), D1 does so in the manner intended, and V dies from the attack. Here, again, due to the constructive nature of unlawful act manslaughter, both D2 and D1 will be liable for manslaughter despite neither intending to kill V or even to cause serious non-fatal harm. Constructive liability may be rightly criticised for overcriminalising the actions of both parties, but they are treated equally.

It is in the third case that major problems arise. Here D2 intentionally assists D1 to harm V in a relatively non-serious manner (e.g., punching in the face), but amid escalating violence D1 intentionally kills V (e.g., shooting in the chest), and V dies from the attack. For the Supreme Court in *Jogee*, D1 should be liable for murder, and D2 for manslaughter. However, we do not believe this can be correct.[118] V has not died as a result of intentional action endorsed by both D2 and D1, with both taking the risk together, but rather from the intentional conduct of D1 alone. To hold D2 liable for the death, through manslaughter or any other offence, is either to claim that D2 has intentionally assisted the actions of D1 in shooting V in the chest (which is factually inaccurate), or to guess that the attack D2 did intend to assist would have resulted in death. The latter option seems the only one logically available for the court, but it is also clearly inappropriate. The application of constructive liability can be harsh enough without it also being applied on the basis of a predictive fiction, and even worse, on the basis of a predictive fiction that is not undermined by D2's (often valid) claims that death was very unlikely to have resulted from the conduct he intended to assist. We may describe this scenario in terms of a 'fundamental departure', or as an 'overwhelming supervening act',[119] but what should be clear is that the action D2 assisted has not been performed by D1, and so deriving liability from an unforeseen potential outcome of that conduct is incoherent.

In the fourth and final case, D2 intentionally assists D1 to seriously harm V (e.g., shooting in the stomach), but amid escalating violence D1 intentionally kills V (e.g., shooting in the chest), and V dies from the attack. Following *Jogee*, it is clear that both D1 and D2 will be liable for murder: D1 acted with the intention to kill, and although D2 only intended to assist the causing of non-fatal serious harm, such *mens rea* is sufficient for murder as a constructive crime. However, it is our view that the same arguments that should undermine D2's complicity liability in case three apply equally here as well: D1 has not performed the attack that D2 assisted, and so there is no basis upon which to derive liability for the resulting death from a different attack. Rather, again, D2's liability should be limited to complicity in the lesser included non-fatal offence,[120] or the inchoate alternative.

118 See also, Simester (n 90), Baker (n 109).

119 The Supreme Court in Jogee state that these rules will be narrower in their application, but the point is not fully explored or clarified. *Jogee* (n 38) [97–8]. See also J. Horder, *Homicide and the Politics of Law Reform* (Oxford University Press 2012) 159–69, who refers to a form of 'moral remoteness'.

120 Although D1 has attacked V in a different way from that intended by D2, a simple change in method should not undermine liability for the non-fatal offence, if that offence is a lesser included

The problem cases discussed here are not entirely novel to post-*Jogee* complicity, and have featured in previous case law.[121] However, if complicity in murder is to require a *genuine* intention to assist or encourage, and intention or knowledge that D1 commits murder,[122] then many standard cases of escalating violence (e.g., common within group scenarios) will be shifted for consideration within manslaughter complicity. It is our view that liability for manslaughter in such cases must be considered carefully, and not simply assumed. Where D1 performs an action intentionally assisted by D2 then both may have to accept the unexpected constructive consequences of their crime; but where D1 intentionally performs a more dangerous or damaging action, then there is no basis for constructing upon the intentions of D2. D2 should not be liable for the consequences of actions which he did not intend to assist or encourage.

Reform

Unfortunately, this section need only be brief, at least as it relates to statutory reform, as in the current climate within England and Wales any proposals are likely to fall on deaf ears.[123] In 2006, the Law Commission made detailed proposals for a more nuanced and limited law of murder, including an offence of first degree murder.[124] If enacted, only first degree murder would have been punished with a mandatory penalty of life imprisonment, which likely would have resulted in some decrease in the number of life sentences imposed.[125] The Labour Government of that time showed no interest. Only the Commission's proposals for reforming the partial defences of provocation and diminished responsibility influenced subsequent legislation, legislation which narrowed their scope.[126] Later governments have shown no inclination to change this state of affairs. Indeed, similar political inertia has been apparent in relation to complicity liability as well.

within D1's crime. For example, whether D1 uses a knife or a bat, and whether he goes further than D2 foresaw, D1 is still *also* causing harm as D2 intended. The problem cases only arise because of the application of constructive principles to D2's liability, as now D1's escalation makes it impossible for us to know what might have happed if only the lesser offence had been committed, and the application of constructive liability relies on guess work.

121 See, for example, *Yemoh and Others* [2009] EWCA Crim 930 (commentary by D. Ormerod [2009] *Criminal Law Review* 888) and *Carpenter* [2011] EWCA Crim 2568 (commentary by D. Ormerod [2012] *Criminal Law Review* 269).

122 I.e., subject to our discussion in the previous two subsections.

123 The only political parties likely to form a government or be the dominant parties in a coalition government, namely Labour and the Conservatives, have not showed any recent interest in the reform of murder, nor is any private member bill for the reform of murder likely to be introduced to Parliament and supported. This state of affairs is unlikely to change any time soon, particularly when the process of leaving the European Union will dominate proceedings in Parliament for at least the next two years.

124 Law Commission, *Murder, Manslaughter and Infanticide* (Law Com 304, 2006).

125 First degree murder was defined as an intentional killing or a killing with intent to cause serious injury coupled with awareness of a serious risk of causing death: Law Com No 304, [2.69]. We would prefer a simpler reform, with murder confined to intentional killings for the purposes of labelling what are *prima facie* the worst kind of killings. But as even intentional killings can vary greatly in terms of moral wrongdoing, there would be no mandatory penalty, a life term would be just a sentencing option. Although such a reform is most unlikely, there is evidence that the public by and large conceive of murder as an intentional killing and favour giving judges sentencing discretion in murder cases: Mitchell and Roberts (n 26).

126 CJA 2009, ss 52–6. See O. Quick and C. Wells, 'Getting Tough with Defences' (2006) Criminal Law Review 154.

Accordingly, there is limited utility in working up detailed proposals. But certain things must still be said and repeatedly said, if only for the record. First and foremost, the mandatory sentence should be abolished. Expert opinion has consistently and convincingly concluded that murder is too varied in its particular instances to attract a life sentence in each case.[127] Recall that the strong default position for any murder falling outside the aggravated circumstances presumptions is 15 years, a sentence to be served in full and with no unconditional right to release on licence at the expiry of that period. This is simply too punitive in a significant number of cases.[128] The policy of earmarking murder as an exceptionally heinous offence should not come at the cost of punishment disproportionate to the circumstances of the offence. Moving to discretionary life sentences would also lead to significant gains in simplicity and efficiency. The partial defences to murder of loss of self-control and diminished responsibility could be abolished. Provocation, (now in England and Wales, the partial defence of loss of self-control) has proved particularly problematic in common law jurisdictions. Matters which can be suitably accommodated in the sentencing process can be intractable when made the subject of rules. Loss of self-control inducing serious violence is something that must be deterred. For D to say 'I lost it' as his explanation for causing the death of V is not even the beginning point of an excuse. Yet sometimes the story of why D lost it may arouse a degree of sympathy, even though his killing of V was perpetrated with an intent to kill or cause serious harm and lacked justification or excuse. But attempts to cast rules pinpointing when sympathy should require a verdict of manslaughter rather than murder is no easy task.[129]

The route to murder liability, as a principal and as an accomplice, are also in need of clarification and reform. Defining murder has not proved easy in England and Wales. That said, the *mens rea* for murder by a principal offender is now reasonably clear. Ideally an intent to cause serious bodily harm should not suffice; murderers should be confined to persons who kill with intent to kill. This reform is particularly important in view of the mandatory life sentence, but even if this were to be abolished, narrowing of this kind would still be warranted as a matter of fair-labelling. For complicity, post-*Jogee*, clarification and reform is required across the three areas highlighted in discussion in the latter parts of this chapter, whether this is done through Parliament or the considerably more likely route of the courts. It remains vital to ensure parity of culpability between principal and accomplice, labelled and punished in the same way, and this can only be achieved through embracing

127 Most notably the Select Committee of the House of Lords (The Nathan Committee) HL Paper 78–1. The Committee's conclusion with only one dissentient is also shared by lay persons, see (n 26) above. However, there is no political will to depart from mandatory life sentences. Two Home Affairs Committee Reports allowed that the question of the mandatory sentence was 'exceptionally finely balanced' but recommended retention: Home Affairs Committee, *Murder: The Mandatory Life Sentence* First Report (Session 1995–96), Paper 111; Second Report (Session 1995–96), Paper 412. The terms of reference for the Law Commission review of murder (n 124) precluded consideration of the mandatory sentence.

128 Most notably in cases of consensual killings to end suffering but also for example cases of young, impressionable persons caught up in a joint enterprise who played no direct part in the killing and also persons who inflicted serious but non- life threatening harm where the victim died from self-neglect or because of medical negligence.

129 The revamped version of provocation – loss of self-control – has not stemmed the need for appellate clarifications and adjustments: e.g., *Clinton* [2013] QB 1. The same applies to a lesser extent to the revamped defence of diminished responsibility although whether particular symptoms arising from recognised medical conditions reduce responsibility is more amenable to rule-based decisions.

some of the positive headlines within *Jogee* and avoiding future uncertainties: clarifying *mens rea* requirements, defining conditional intention to avoid collapse into recklessness and not overstating the reach of constructive crimes. Significant reform in this area may seem unlikely at the time of writing, but many of us thought the same before *Jogee*.

5 'Loss of self-control'

The cultural lag of sexual infidelity and the transformative promise of the fear defence

Susan S.M. Edwards

Introduction

The Coroners and Justice Act 2009 (C and JA 2009) s.55(3), 'loss of self-control' manslaughter, acknowledges 'fear of serious violence' as a 'qualifying trigger' which may 'cause'[1] a defendant to lose self-control and kill another. This new provision is the result of both public and legal recognition that the former defence of manslaughter-provocation,[2] in relying on the presence of anger to precipitate loss of self-control, and in requiring an immediate response to provocation, excluded the delayed and chronic 'passion' of fear of further violence so often experienced by women victims of intimate partner violence which could 'cause'[3] them to kill the violent partner. The law also recognises that fear, which includes heightened anxiety and anticipation of future violence, may cause women victims[4] of domestic abuse to kill the abusive partner in circumstances where their 'reaction' to the deceased's last act is delayed.[5] Notwithstanding the introduction of fear as a qualifying trigger,[6] the legal and everyday construction of loss of self-control continues to contemplate and interpret this behaviour within an anger template.[7]

In this chapter, I argue that the construction of loss of self-control is bound together with anger in its interpretation (ontology) and by the corroborative manifestations deemed demonstrative of its proof. Furthermore, in so far as anger / loss of self-control remains a lawful exoneration for killing conduct and sexual infidelity continues as a primary excuse granting permission for such action in learnt behaviour (notwithstanding its express exclusion as a trigger in s.55(6)(c)) it will continue to be pleaded in some form. I argue that retention of loss of self-control as an excuse for killing cannot subvert the ideological fixity of language[8] which at the level of meaning permits sexual infidelity at least in some form to continue as an excuse for conduct.

1 This article draws a distinction between 'cause' and 'allow' or 'permit' as the basis for human action and is a distinction developed later.
2 Homicide Act 1957 (HA 1957), s.3.
3 Teleological survival in the future is the primary goal.
4 Whilst the new law is premised on an understanding of women's fear of violence in heterosexual relationships, it also applies to same-sex relationships.
5 Provided for in C and JA 2009, s.54 (2)(c).
6 C and JA 2009, s.55 (3).
7 J. Horder, 'Reshaping the Subjective Element in the Provocation Defence' (2005) 25(1) Oxford Journal of Legal Studies123–40, calls this the 'loss of self-control dilemma.'
8 R. Barthes, *Elements of Semiology* (Hill and Wang 1968). See also S. Tiefenbrun, *Decoding International Law: Semiotics and the Humanities* (Oxford University Press 2010).

I argue that the new fear defence as currently constructed fails adequately to accommodate the very different manifestations of fear and that the overarching requirement of loss of self-control with its fixed and historical features of angered reaction obtrudes into this possibility of an alternative template. There is no commensurability between anger / loss of self-control and fear of serious violence / loss of self-control. Loss of self-control provides a perfect example of what Goodrich coins (albeit in another context) the 'scientific status of legal dogmatics'[9] in so far as the signification of loss of self-control is found, almost if not exclusively, in its allegiance to anger.

Counsel will need to employ new understandings and new descriptors in communicating how fear might result in a particular but different configuration of loss of self-control. Jurors too will need direction. Experts will be needed to elaborate on the fluidity and polysemicity of the signs and manifestations of fear. Loss of self-control in its traditional form will need to be uncoupled from anger. Without such assistance in interpreting the law and making sense of the enactments as intended, signs of anger will remain 'the' arrogated instantiated evidence of loss of self-control whilst manifestations of fear will likely fail to satisfy a manslaughter fear / loss of self-control defence.

Relevances – women who kill

The irrelevance of a history of male violence.

Of course whilst there have been some gains, the exegesis of this dual problem of construction of loss of self-control around anger and sexual infidelity and the exclusion of fear is rooted in the history of the law on provocation from which the current law needs to be cleaved.

The former defence of provocation[10] was hopelessly unsuited to providing a defence for circumstances where an abused partner out of fear and self-defence killed the abuser. Whilst the defence of provocation authorised 'male' anger (within the statute) and recognised 'male' reasons for lethal violence (largely sexual infidelity as indicated in the case law) the abused partners fear of further violence and necessity for self-preservation were all excluded as evidentially irrelevant. Significantly the new law has reversed that position. Devlin J., had stated in *Duffy*:[11]

> A long course of cruel conduct may be more blameworthy than a sudden act provoking retaliation, but you are not concerned with blame here – the blame attaching to the dead man. You are not standing in judgment on him. He has not been heard in this court. He cannot now ever be heard. He has no defender here to argue for him. It does not matter how cruel he was, how much or how little he was to blame, except in so far as it resulted in the final act of the accused.[12]

Mrs. Duffy, it was never doubted, was the victim of repeated violence from the deceased, recorded both in her own police statements and those of witnesses.[13] Devlin J's direction on

9 P. Goodrich, 'Law and Language: An Historical and Critical Introduction' (1984) 12 Journal of Law & Society 173, 180.
10 HA 1957, s.3.
11 *Duffy* [1949] 1 All ER 932.
12 Ibid. [933]. See also 'Girl sentenced to death for murder of husband' *The Guardian* (Manchester, 18 March 1949).
13 S. Edwards, 'Justice Devlin's Legacy: Duffy – a Battered Woman "Caught" in Time' (2009) 12 Criminal Law Review 851–69.

the law on provocation, upheld by the Court of Appeal, excluded the deceased's previous violent conduct and instead, in determining the defendant's loss of self-control, focused exclusively on the proximity in time of the provocative act of the deceased to the defendant's response. Devlin J., said:

> Provocation is some act, or series of acts, done by the dead man to the accused which would cause in a reasonable person, and actually causes in the accused, a sudden and temporary loss of self-control, rendering the accused so subject to passion as to make him or her for the moment not master of his mind … Severe nervous exasperation or a long course of conduct causing suffering and anxiety are not by themselves sufficient to constitute provocation in law.[14]

Lord Goddard C.J., though not without sympathy for Mrs. Duffy's suffering, approved Devlin J's direction stating that it would still be 'a classic direction' for cases 'in which the sympathy of everyone would be with the accused and against the dead man.'[15]

In the post-*Duffy* era, judges at the sentencing stage in passing lenient sentences tempered the *Duffy* ruling especially where sons killed fathers who had been violent to mothers.[16] But judges little understood the entrapment of the battered woman and seemed influenced by legal principles guiding the law on self-defence[17] which resulted in judges remarking upon what they considered were alternatives to staying in an abusive relationship and killing an abusive partner. In *Grieg*, [18] where the applicant killed her violent husband following years of his repeated abuse, Lord Dunpark withdrew the defence of self-defence from the jury and also foreclosed the possibility of the jury returning a provocation verdict.

> Now ….there is evidence before you … that he assaulted his wife from time to time … But, hundreds indeed thousands of wives in this country unfortunately suffer this fate. The remedy of divorce or judicial separation or factual separation is available to end this torment … If you can find some evidence, which frankly I cannot, that the accused was provoked …[19]

14 *Duffy* (n 11) [932e].

15 Ibid.

16 In *Jones* (1972) *Daily Telegraph*, 18 July 1972, where a son killed a violent and bullying father, Everleigh J., took into account the father's violent course of conduct. In *Bell* (1974) *The Guardian*, 29 October 1974, where a son killed a violent father, Chapman J., said, 'I find it impossible to regard you as a criminal. Your father was appallingly ruthless, brutal, and violent.'

17 This particular requirement to consider alternative courses of action forms the bedrock of the common law on self-defence and whilst retreat is not a requirement it is a factor to be taken into consideration. See *Regina v Bird* [1985] 1 WLR 816.

18 *HM Advocate v Grieg*, May 1979, *unreported*. June Grieg killed her violent husband by stabbing him while he sat dozing in a chair. Lord Dunpark allowed the provocation to go to the jury but stated that he did not believe that the grounds for the defence of provocation had been established – See J. Chalmers, F. Leverick, L. Farmer (eds) *Essays in Criminal Law* (Edinburgh University Press 2010) 214. The case of *Greig*, is also cited in S. Edwards and A. Halpern, 'Protection For the Victim of Domestic Violence: Time for Radical Revision?' (1991) 13(2) Journal of Social Welfare and Family Law, 96. See also C. Gane and C. Stoddart, *A Casebook on Scottish Criminal Law* (Sweet and Maxwell 1984) 444; C. Connelly, 'Women who Kill Violent Men' (1996) 108(3) Juridical Review 215.

19 Ibid.

The appeal court agreed. Lord Wheatley LJC., Lord Kissen and Lord Robertson, elaborated:[20]

> There are various expedients open to a woman subjected to rough treatment by her husband, but a licence to kill is not one of them. There is no doubt that this was a deliberate and intentional killing, and provocation in law was at most minimal. Even at the last moment when she was given an opportunity to leave the house, she rejected the offer and opted for the fatal course.[21]

The judicial perception that retreat was a realistic option persisted. Judge J., (as he then was) in *Thornton* [22] (where a battered wife killed an abusive husband and pleaded diminished responsibility) in leaving provocation to the jury in the alternative, said:

> There are ... many unhappy, indeed miserable, husbands and wives. It is a fact of life. It has to be faced, members of the jury. But on the whole it is hardly reasonable, you may think, to stab them fatally when there are other alternatives available, like walking out or going upstairs.[23]

Judges in Anglo-American jurisdictions have displayed a similar lack of understanding.[24] Countervailing such assumptions, Lenore Walker[25] an American clinical psychologist, was raising awareness in legal and clinical circles of the role of psychosocial factors,[26] economic dependency, lack of support, fear, trepidation, paralysis to act effectively and sheer physical vulnerability, all of which incapacitated and bound the abused woman to her violent partner contributing to her inability, as Judge J., had so phrased it 'to walk out' or 'go upstairs.'[27] Walker formulated the concept 'learned helplessness'[28] to capture and describe the abused woman's state of mind, apparent inertia and inability to leave the relationship.[29] This contrapuntal narrative gradually permeated into legal argument informing defence submissions, galvanising the movement for reform, which focused on challenging two recalcitrant problems.

The first, focused on the concern that angered lethal male violence was too readily exonerated in provocation especially where women were about to leave men, pursued other relationships, or merely declared that the relationship with the abused was over. The second concern focused on lethal female defensive violence and the need to recognise in law as in fact that women's motive was one of self-preservation and survival, little understood within the criminal law except within a mental illness related defence of diminished responsibility.

20 Ibid.
21 See *The Herald* (Glasgow, 31 March 1992). See also M. Maynard and J. Hanmer (eds) *Women, Violence and Social Control* (Macmillan Press 1987) 116.
22 [1992] 1 ALL ER 306.
23 Ibid., 312h. *R v Thornton* (No 2) – [1996] 2 All ER 1023, [1028j].
24 *R v Wang* (1991) LRC (Crim) 469.
25 L. E. Walker, *The Battered Woman* (Harper Row 1979).
26 Ibid., xvi.
27 *Thornton* (n 22).
28 Drawing on the work of Martin Seligman. See M.E. Seligman and G. Beagley, 'Learned Helplessness in the Rat' (1975) 88(2) Journal of Comparative and Physiological Psychology 534.
29 A. Browne, *When Battered Women Kill* (Free Press 1989) 109, 267.

Permissible male maelstrom of anger

Horder, as did others, conceded that the accepted excuses and dominant narrative of the provocation defence 'seemed to privilege men,'[30] and 'indulge predominantly male anger'.[31] Of course (C and JA 2009) s. 55(6)(c), by establishing that, 'a thing done or said constitu[ting] sexual infidelity is to be disregarded'[32] partly addresses male privilege in the loss of self-control defence. However, case law has interpreted this exclusion to operate only in those circumstances where sexual infidelity stands alone as the sole reason to trigger loss of self-control. Additionally, the reform seems somewhat unfinished as the law has stopped short of addressing a central and problematic feature since the construction of, and instantiated evidence for, a loss of self-control continues to be articulated and cognised as being triggered by and conjoined with anger. Anger is the typological behavioural indicator of loss of self-control in manslaughter and together with the discourse within and outside the law continues to be privileged as 'the' excusable emotional state. This symbiotic synergy between loss of self-control and anger is so elided in common sense and legal understanding that legal arguments presenting loss of self-control resulting from fear will be less persuasive when considered by fact finders. The process by which the emotion of fear and its corollaries result in a loss of self-control, which the proof of a manslaughter defence requires, is yet to be clearly and convincingly articulated.

This task will in part rest with the judge who is required to form a view as to whether the defendant lost his or her self-control. Section 54(6) provides 'For the purposes of subsection (5), sufficient evidence is adduced to raise an issue with respect to the defence if evidence is adduced on which, in the opinion of the trial judge, a jury, properly directed, could reasonably conclude that the defence might apply' and if so found, it is then for the jury to determine whether self-control was lost or not. As stated in *Gurpinar, Kojo-Smith*, a trial judge must undertake a much more rigorous evaluation of the evidence before the defence could be left to the jury than was required under the former law of provocation.[33]

Rooted in the legal discourse on male anger, loss of self-control is excused under certain defined and agreed circumstances and is justified by prescribed excuses and reasons for indignation, whilst sexual infidelity is precluded, this particular excuse persists in the public mind as of relevance and remains interlocked with the emotion of anger. The new legislation (C and JA 2009) s. 55(6)(c), through its retention of particular words which are carriers of signification, continues to perpetuate some of the earlier problems it seeks to address and remedy.

Let us explore these carriers of signification including language and ideology which through interpellation are embraced by the acting subject.[34] First, in assessing the qualifying trigger for loss of self-control, the circumstances (things done or said) must be of 'extremely grave character'.[35] What constitutes extremely grave circumstances is an objective matter for the jury but is also derived from their own intersubjective understanding. The statute sets a high threshold and also narrows the circumstances the defendant might claim are relevant. However 'extremely grave character' must be read together with an assessment of whether the defendant has a 'justifiable sense of being seriously wronged'.[36] 'Justifiable', it is

30 Horder (n 7) 123.
31 *Blackstone's Criminal Practice 2016*, B1.25. 196.
32 C and JA 2009, s.55(6)(c).
33 *Gurpinar, Kojo-Smith and another* [2015] EWCA Crim 178 [12]-[14].
34 Derived from L. Althusser, '"Lenin and Philosophy" and Other Essays. Ideology and Ideological State Apparatuses (Notes towards an Investigation)' (New York Monthly Review Press, 1970).
35 C and JA 2009, s.55(4)(a).
36 Ibid. s.55(4)(b).

contended, was no doubt intended by those drafting the legislation to connote whether a thing is 'reasonable' but it is a word which carries moral overtones, overlayed with meaning, invoking a sense of a right to behave in a certain way when particular circumstances prevail. This is not the same as reasonable. Significantly, it was precisely the objection to the notion that men regarded their fatal actions as 'justifiable' in circumstances of sexual infidelity or 'unreasonable' female partners[37] that propelled the move for reform of the law on provocation, as Horder noted (on p.4). Typical contributory past conduct articulated by defendants included: she was about to or already had left, suspected or actual sexual infidelity or departure from the stereotypical female gender role, such that the actions of the male defendant was 'justifiable'.[38] Such conduct of the female deceased was frequently considered sufficient to 'justify' male anger and consequent lethal violence even if not expressly stated as such. Diplock J., in *Simpson*,[39] (where the husband had strangled a wife) told the jury to take into account her persistent nagging, her threats to leave him taking their child, her demands for a divorce and for child maintenance.[40] In *Wright*,[41] where a husband killed a wife with a hammer, the judge said he had to put up with her 'Saturday night and Sunday morning activities'. In *Fantle*,[42] where the accused had shot and killed his wife's paramour whom he said had taunted him, Salmon J., in instructing the jury to consider the previous bad character of the deceased, asserted:

> The serious provocation you received from the dead man has reduced your crime from murder to manslaughter ... Well, I do not suppose you will have any doubt about [it] that he was provoked to lose his self-control.[43]

Lord Hoffman in *Smith*,[44] contributed significantly to the movement which challenged such justifications: '[m]ale possessiveness and jealousy should not today be an acceptable reason for loss of self- control leading to homicide, whether inflicted upon the woman herself or her new lover.'[45] Persisting with the use of the word 'justifiable'[46] will only muddy the waters by perpetuating a motif of male privilege in how 'a justifiable sense of being seriously wronged' is intended to be read. Justifiable to whom exactly? To the defendant (subjective)? To the jury (objective)? Sexual infidelity and its corollary or flip side of male sexual possessiveness is so rooted in a linguistic and psychical linkage to anger / loss of self-control,[47] that s.55(6)(c) which precludes sexual infidelity has been grudgingly received and

37 S. Lees, 'Naggers, Whores and Libbers: Provoking Men to Kill' in J. Radford and D. Russell (eds) *Femicide* (Twayne Publishers 1992) 267–89.
38 Ibid., 267. See also J. Radford 'Woman Slaughter A License to Kill: The Killing of Jane Asher' in *Femicide,* ibid. 253.
39 *Simpson* [1957] Criminal Law Review 815.
40 See also *Elliot* [1960] Criminal Law Review 10, where the court in referring to Simpson, referred to the deceased as 'an endlessly nagging wife'.
41 *The Times*, 24 October 1975.
42 *Fantle* [1959] Criminal Law Review 584. See also *Batson, The Times*, 6 December 1980.
43 J.P. Eddy 'The New Law of Provocation' (1958) Criminal Law Review 778, commenting on *Fantle* cited the defendant's account of his provocation and said 'The defendant said, "... he treated me like dirt ... shrugging his shoulders ... he stood up and showed me the door"' 784.
44 *Smith* [1999] 1 AC 146.
45 In Australia, since *Stingel v The Queen* (1990) 171 CLR 312, where such reasons allegedly resulted in killing, provocation has been withdrawn from the jury.
46 C and JA 2009, s.55(4)(b).
47 Jacques Lacan argues that the unconscious is structured as a language and that language precedes the unconscious mind. See J. Lacan, *Ecrits* (W.W. Norton and Co 2002).

other avenues for its continuing inclusion imaginatively crafted.[48] Furthermore, defence strategies have also sought to adduce such evidence within a plea of diminished responsibility manslaughter which requires an abnormality of mental functioning[49] which 'provides an explanation for D's acts and omissions in doing or being a party to the killing'.[50]

The second problem lies with the insistence of the word 'tolerance.' Section 54(3) provides:

> In subsection (1)(c) the reference to "the circumstances of D" is a reference to all of D's circumstances other than those whose only relevance to D's conduct is that they bear on D's general capacity for tolerance or self-restraint.

Whilst 'tolerance' is a highly intersubjective concept, fluid and its meaning unsettled, the new provision whilst inserting a requirement for 'tolerance' intends limiting the range of excuses for loss of self-control by being read alongside the 'extremely grave circumstances' requirement. That of course may appear to be positive in setting down a requirement for a 'normal degree' of tolerance and expectation that the defendant cannot rely on his own bigotedness to justify conduct.[51] The Court of Appeal in *Dawes* [52] laid down some boundary markers:

> For the individual with normal capacity of self-restraint and tolerance, unless the circumstances are extremely grave, normal irritation, and even serious anger do not often cross the threshold into loss of control.[53]

However, retention of the term 'tolerance' also communicates a set of behaviours which men have not been expected to endure, these contemplated behaviours are conjoined to women's conduct and thus the retention of the concept presents challenges to the current law and the very conduct it wishes to exclude. Of course it would be incorrect to argue that since much of the past language of provocation is so linked to a set of excuses, reasons, and rhymes for male conduct then it should be abandoned. But the problem of determining the

48 Lord Bladen thought its exclusion 'absurd' HL Deb 26 October 2009, 1061 (Lord Neill of Bladen). See for discussion A. Reed and N. Wake, 'Sexual Infidelity Killings: Contemporary Standardisation and Comparative Stereotypes' in A. Reed and M. Bohlander (eds), *Loss of Control and Diminished Responsibility: Domestic, Comparative and International Perspectives* (Routledge 2011) 115.

49 C and JA 2009, s.52(c).

50 V. Allen, 'Husband who stabbed his wife 30 times is cleared of her murder' *Daily Mail* (London, 30 October 2009) < www.dailymail.co.uk/news/article-1224150/Alisdair-Sinclair-Nine-years-jealous-husband-knifed-Vodafone-executive-wife-death-frenzied-attack.html> accessed 21 November 2017. Historically there have been references to 'Othello syndrome' and 'pathological jealousy'. See also Delusional Disorder DSM-5 297.1 (F22). The defendant Alasdair Sinclair used evidence of his wife seeking a divorce and a relationship with another man as well as his own mental illness in a successful diminished responsibility defence. He had stabbed her 30 times with a serrated knife and nearly cut her head off. He was sentenced to nine years' imprisonment.

51 The Judicial College, Crown Court Compendium (2017) <www.judiciary.gov.uk/wp-content/uploads/2016/06/crown-court-compendium-pt1-jury-and-trial-management-and-summing-up-nov-2017-v2.pdf> accessed 13 December 2017. The reference to 'tolerance' excludes the person with unacceptable attitudes as well as those with an unacceptable temper. See 19–11, para 13, 19–15 para 22–23.

52 [2013] EWCA Crim 322.

53 Ibid.

boundaries of what one is expected to tolerate, what conduct invokes a justifiable sense of being seriously wronged and what can be included in extremely grave circumstances, are social constructs welded to exonerations which law reform cannot necessarily address.

Permission for anger – learnt behaviourism

Since the law now expects a defendant to exercise control, no longer presume male proprietorialness and tolerate circumstances of sexual infidelity hitherto considered intolerable,[54] it implicitly seeks to engineer male conduct. By deleting sexual infidelity from the range of circumstances sufficiently grave to excuse anger and contribute to loss of self-control, it is suggested that the law recognises that loss of self-control is no longer simply reducible to a pathological and hermetically sealed physiological or parasympathetic response over which an individual has no control but is in fact constructed in the material condition and is learnt behaviour. Exploring this ontological question further, whilst rising to anger once initiated may well indeed be predominantly physiological it is the social context or the material condition which in fact releases the moral bind facilitating the permission for anger and loss of self-control and its emotional and physical expression.

This theorising is a challenge to the common sense understanding which assumes (incorrectly) that some personalities, cultures and genders are more pathologically prone to rise to anger. Such understandings incline to a deterministic construction of groups, cultures and genders and essentialist narrations of angry personalities, angry cultures and angry men. Such generic stereotypes are learnt and construct who is permitted to lose self-control and when loss of self-control is excusable. In turn personalities, cultures and genders (men) exploit these stereotypes inverting them, giving themselves special privilege and permission to behave without restraint (*ad libitum*). So, 'I am very passionate and lose self-control because I have Latin blood' is an example of where special permission is sought to excuse intemperate conduct. Precisely this kind of cultural stereotyping arguing for recognition of a lower level for tolerance and self-restraint has also been exploited in defence and prosecution argument in homicide cases.[55] In South East Asia[56] it continues to be the case that male defendants advance a defence that killing a wife is an acceptable way of dealing with marital difference or desire for divorce.[57]

54 C and JA 2009 s.55(6)(c).

55 So for example the judge's instruction to the jury on the reasonable man standard in C. Howard, 'What Colour is the "Reasonable Man"'(1961) Criminal Law Review [43] in reviewing the cases of *Patipatu* 1951 NTJ 18; *Patipatu* (unreported) May 15 1951; *MacDonald* (1961) Criminal Law Review 41; *Macdonald* (unreported) July 21 1953 44 in which the judge directed the jury that a 'native aborigine' required less provocation than a white man such that a defence of provocation should be open to him. In *Nelson* (1961) Criminal Law Review (1961) 41; *Nelson* (*unreported*) March 21 1956 46, the judge said it would take a longer time for the blood of a man of the Pitjantjatjara tribe to cool than that of a white Australian. See also C. Morris and C. Howard *Studies in Criminal Law* (Clarendon Press 1964).

56 See A. Renteln, 'The Use and Abuse of the Cultural Defence' (2005) 20(1) Canadian Journal of Law and Society / Revue Canadienne Droit et Société 47. See also A. Phillips, 'When Culture Means Gender: Issues of Cultural Defence in the English Courts' (2003) 66(4) Modern Law Review 510.

57 A. Gill, 'Reconfiguring "Honour"-Based Violence as a Form of Gendered Violence' in M. M. Idriss and T. Abbas (eds) *Honour, Violence, Women and Islam* (Routledge 2011) 218–232. See also *R v Shabir Hussain* [1997] EWCA Crim 2876; A. Clough, 'Honour Killings, Partial Defences and the Exclusionary Conduct Model' Journal of Criminal Law (2016) 80(3) 177.

In Anglo-American jurisprudence, in recent years such attempts at advancing a 'cultural defence' have been rejected, for example, see *Masciantonio* [58] and *Karimi*'s[59] defence in a murder trial, the latter alleging that he had been provoked by a friend who had spoken the words 'you have no honour' (*Bisharaf*). Such examples suggest that the aetiology of anger which prompts a loss of self-control provides further evidence that such materialisations of emotion are less to be found in some essentialistic pathology of peoples, cultures and men, and instead are learnt, tempered and mediated by social convention changing through time and across cultures. The case for the temporal nature of the circumstances adjoined to this conduct and considered to prompt anger is substantiated and reflected in society and in law's fluidity over time in what conditions are considered to excuse it.[60]

This understanding that self-control and toleration is learnt and configured in social interaction and not simply reducible to intrinsic individual and social group factors and crude stereotypes has been long recognised, such that attempting to change conduct overnight through legal exclusion will inevitably fail. Such considerations have been developed by critical legal theorists. Uniacke[61] considers the notion of permission regarding the development of the law on self-defence. Raz writing in more general terms asserts:[62]

> … My suggestion is that we can think of people who perform normally expressive actions as people who let themselves express their emotions, feelings, or moods in action. They permit themselves to do so … In the case of purely expressive actions we … allow the emotion to express itself, the will acting as a non-interfering gatekeeper.

Horder takes up this notion of 'permission' in his discussion of loss of self-control within the criminal law.[63] David Matza's[64] work on 'neutralization' is particularly instructive. He identifies those excuses in society and shows how they are used by offenders to mitigate and neutralise their conduct in an interactive process in which the law breaker becomes deviant.

58 *Masciantonio v The Queen* [1995] 183 CLR 58 [66].
59 *James, Karimi* [2006] EWCA Crim 14.
60 Within the criminal law these 'neutralisation techniques' for conduct are relational and change over time. See the Homosexual advance defence (HAD). See *R v Cavanagh R v Shaw* [1972] 2 All ER 704. See also Australian cases of *Green v The Queen* [1997] HCA 50; *Lindsay v The Queen* [2015] HCA 16. See also R.B. Mison, 'Homophobia in Manslaughter: The Homosexual Advance as Insufficient Provocation' (1992) 80(1) California Law Review 133; A. Kent, Comments 'A Matter of Law: The Non-Violent Homosexual Advance Defense Is Insufficient Evidence of Provocation' (2009) 44 University Of San Francisco Law Review 155; R. McGeary and K. Fitz-Gibbon, 'The Homosexual Advance Defence in Australia: An Examination of Sentencing Practices and Provocation Law Reform' (2018) The Australian & New Zealand Journal of Criminology Research Article <https://doi.org/10.1177/0004865817749261> accessed 6 June 2018. See also Review of the 'Homosexual Advance Defence' Attorney Generals Department New South Wales (August 1996) <http://www.gaylawnet.com/ezine/crime/panic.html> accessed 6 June 2018.
61 S. Uniacke, *Permissible Killing* (Cambridge University Press 1996) 143.
62 See J. Raz, *Engaging Reason* (Oxford University Press 1999) 44.
63 J. Horder, *Excusing Crime* (Oxford University Press 2004) 128. See also J. Dancy, and C. Sandis (eds) *Philosophy of Action: An Anthology* (Wiley Blackwell 2015) 242. See also S. Gough, 'Taking the Heat out of Provocation' (1999) 19(3) Oxford Journal of Legal Studies 487, where he says 'Anger … modifies perspective, directing focus towards (existing) reasons to confront and fight at the expense of reasons to bite one's tongue, walk away or otherwise act sensibly.'
64 D. Matza, *Delinquency and Drift* (John Wiley 1964) 61. D. Matza, *Becoming Deviant* (Prentice Hall 1969) 47. See also G. Sykes and D. Matza 'Techniques of Neutralisation' (1957) American Sociological Review 667.

This 'becoming deviant', as Matza describes it, evolves over time in a process of learning the permissions which release the law breaker from the normative bind. Significantly the law has adopted some of these techniques of neutralisation which have been elevated to the level of partial defences whilst others function in mitigation of sentence.

Within the framework of permissions, language is central to the learnt material context. De Saussure's[65] contribution to structural linguistics with his concept of signs which include signifiers and signified is instructive. Considering the loss of self-control and its relation to anger, the language of anger is scripted and performed mimetically by anger's subjects who talk in a recognised and commonly shared idiom. Such that 'seeing red,' does not mean the night sky, 'something coming over me,' does not mean evening fog or morning mist and 'being out of control' does not mean indecision or cognitive dissonance, but an emotional and physical loss of self-control. All of these expressions are part of a learnt symbolic language for arranging emotional expression in performing[66] hurt and insult, indignation and anger. Legal discourse builds this nomenclature in what Foucault[67] would describe as a wider regime of understanding or episteme. But as Gough recognises there is a 'danger of utilizing metaphors within legal definitions.'[68] It is the case that the language or metaphor of loss of self-control continues to privilege anger's stereotypical reaction constructing a *leitmotif* of the angry man and an angry man permitted to act. One of those significant permissions arising in social understanding and anchored in social learning and in language is a prevailing attitude legitimating male sexual proprietorialness.

The question is whether it is possible for a loss of self-control without anger, and anger without sexual infidelity, both within the law and within everyday lay and common sense reasons for action. Gough writes perceptively: 'It is because scholars have largely ignored angers' impact upon reasoning, presenting it instead as a fundamentally irrational force, that modern interpretations of the defence obscure so much of its moral detail.'[69] Certainly, s.55(6)(c) is intended to foreclose sexual infidelity as a technique of neutralisation for killing conduct, to exclude it from the episteme of loss of self-control and to uncouple it from anger.

Unsurprisingly some defendants, continue to present such narrations as reasons and excuses for conduct. The law has made a structural system change but it will take time for intimate partner abusers (largely men) who kill to unlearn those former social permissions which have hitherto shaped their learnt behaviour.[70] Andrew Edis QC, prosecuting in

65 F. De Saussure, *Course in General Linguistics* (10th edn, Open Court Publishing 2000).

66 See 'performative expression' in Raz (n 62), and 'performative utterances' in J. L. Austin, *Philosophical Papers* (3rd edn Clarendon Press 1989) 233.

67 M. Foucault, *POWER/KNOWLEDGE Selected Interviews and Other Writings 1972–1977*, Colin Gordon (ed.) (Pantheon Books: New York, 1980) See <www.monoskop.org/images/5/5d/Foucault_Michel_Power_Knowledge_Selected_Interviews_and_Other_Writings_1972-1977.pdf> accessed 13 December 2017.

68 See Gough (n 63).

69 Ibid. 481.

70 By contrast, in cases where women killed male partners courts were rarely, if ever, presented with the sexual infidelity of the deceased as a reason for her lethal conduct. Certainly jurors would be unlikely to consider this as adequate grounds for provocation because of the ideological biased and gender specific social constructions of what behaviour women are expected to tolerate without complaint. It is likely that even if such reasons were articulated that they would be filtered out by defence counsel in crafting submissions and legal argument as they would be likely to undermine a defence or be considered irrelevant.

Clinton; Parker; Evans [71] described s.55(6)(c) as a 'formidably difficult provision'[72]. What exactly he meant is unclear. The appellant's grounds in these appeals certainly suggested there was an appetite for muting the impact of what many assumed was intended to be a blanket exclusion of sexual infidelity. The Court of Appeal ruling adds to future uncertainty regarding the interpretation of this section:

> ... sexual infidelity is not subject to a blanket exclusion when the loss of control defence is under consideration. .... events cannot be isolated from their context. ... to seek to compartmentalise sexual infidelity and exclude it when it is integral to the facts as a whole is not only much more difficult, but is unrealistic and carries with it the potential for injustice. ..., where sexual infidelity is integral to and forms an essential part of the context in which to make a just evaluation whether a qualifying trigger properly falls within the ambit of subsections 55(3) and (4), the prohibition in section 55(6)(c) does not operate to exclude it.[73]

That said, the Court of Appeal's ruling that sexual infidelity remained relevant (permissible) to loss of self-control where it was part of a wider context of circumstances or on the 'margins of sexual infidelity'[74] is both unconvincingly and problematically nebulous.

> ... experience over many generations has shown that, however it may become apparent, when it does, sexual infidelity has the potential to create a highly emotional situation or to exacerbate a fraught situation, and to produce a completely unpredictable, and sometimes violent response. This may have nothing to do with any notional "rights" that the one may believe that he or she has over the other, and often stems from a sense of betrayal and heartbreak, and crushed dreams.[75]

Appellant No 1, Parker, stabbed his wife 53 times. The jury rejected his loss of self-control defence. Convicted of murder, his appeal against conviction was dismissed. Appellant No 2, Evans, stabbed his wife after she told him that she was going to leave him. The jury rejected the loss of self-control defence. His appeal against a murder conviction was also dismissed. Appellant No 3, Clinton, killed his wife and was convicted of murder, having beaten her about the head with a wooden baton, strangled her with a belt and a piece of rope.[76] Pictures of her dead body were sent to her paramour, which the Crown contended was evidence of his desire for revenge.[77] The trial judge ruled that there was insufficient evidence of loss of self-control for the issue to be considered by the jury and withdrew it from their consideration. Clinton appealed. One of the grounds related to the fact that the judge had withdrawn the defence of loss of self-control. The Court of Appeal concluded:

> For the reasons we have endeavoured to explain in this judgment, we have concluded that she misdirected herself about the possible relevance of the wife's infidelity. We have

71 [2012] EWCA Crim 2.
72 See A. Reed and N. Wake (n 48) who assert that the section is opaque and will be impossible to disentangle.
73 *Clinton* (n 71) [37].
74 *Blackstone's Criminal Practice 2016*, B.125
75 *Clinton* (n 71) [16].
76 Ibid. [54].
77 Ibid. [64].

> reflected whether the totality of the matters relied on as a qualifying trigger, evaluated in the context of the evidence relating to the wife's sexual infidelity, and examined as a cohesive whole, were of sufficient weight to leave to the jury.[78]

The conviction was quashed and a retrial ordered,[79] on the basis that since sexual infidelity formed part of a broader context which included other arguable 'triggers' the defence should have been left to the jury.[80] Section 54(6) of the C and JA 2009 provides:

> For the purposes of subsection (5), sufficient evidence is adduced to raise an issue with respect to the defence if evidence is adduced on which, in the opinion of the trial judge, a jury, properly directed, could reasonably conclude that the defence might apply.[81]

Clinton at retrial pleaded guilty to murder such that the jury were never to consider the point raised on appeal or the arguments presumably of the weight of the evidence on the broader context of sexual infidelity, or its admissibility, or its relevance to loss of self-control. So what does that say about the weight of the evidence and the likely persuasibility of a jury on this point? One possibility is that counsel for the appellant at trial[82] (unlike Birnbaum QC who successfully argued this point on appeal) may not have considered that the facts were sufficient to persuade a jury that the references to the broader context of sexual infidelity were relevant and thus advised his client accordingly.[83]

Following *Clinton*, several murder convictions have been appealed (albeit excepting *Wilcocks* (*Callum Paul*)[84] unsuccessfully) on the ground that where evidence of sexual infidelity is not compartmentalised and, for example, had been the subject of taunts it had been wrongly withheld from the jury. The Lord Chief Justice in *Dawes* stated (see p.7) that the fact of the breakup of a relationship, of itself, will not normally constitute circumstances of an extremely grave character and entitle the aggrieved party to feel a justifiable sense of being seriously wronged.[85] Guidance to judges however adds little.[86] In *Wilcocks (Callum Paul)* [87], the applicant strangled his female partner who died from a heart attack brought on by asphyxiation. Convicted of murder, there were eight grounds of appeal, one of which related to the judge's direction to the jury to disregard sexual infidelity which had amounted to the deceased saying to the defendant that C was not his child. This constituted one of the

78 Ibid. [77].

79 See Editorial, 'Jon-Jaques Clinton jailed for murder of wife Dawn' *BBC News* (London, 4 September 2012) <http://www.bbc.co.uk/news/uk-england-berkshire-19480076> accessed 21 November 2017.

80 Compare with reasoning in *Moffa v The Queen* [1977] 138 CLR 601, where court recognised cumulative nature of 'wholesale promiscuity' of the wife.

81 In *Dawes* (n 52) [761], the Lord Chief Justice observed that the section requires a judgment, not the exercise of a discretion. See also Crown Court Compendium (n 51) 19–2, 19.9.

82 Editorial (n 79). See also B. Barnes, 'Jon Clinton's sentence slashed at murder re-trial' *GetReading* (London, 4 September 2012) reduced by six years from 26 to 20 years. <www.getreading.co.uk/news/local-news/jon-clintons-sentence-slashed-murder-4196454> accessed 21 November 2012.

83 *R. v McDonald (James Luke)* [2016] EWCA Crim 1529 [31]. Clinton did in fact receive a reduction in sentence of six years from that handed down at the original trial. So indeed if sentencing reduction was the strategy prompting the appeal, the goal was achieved.

84 [2014] EWCA Crim 2217.

85 *Dawes* (n 52).

86 Crown Court Compendium (n 51) Para(s) 24–30.

87 *Wilcocks* (n 84).

grounds upon which he was granted leave. At retrial, Wilcocks was convicted of murder.[88] In *Otunga (Richard Nyawanda)*,[89] the appellant stabbed his wife 32 times. Convicted of murder, on appeal it was argued that the sexual infidelity of the wife had been improperly excluded. This was rejected by the Court of Appeal both at the point of conviction and sentence. In *McDonald (James Luke)*,[90] the appellant killed his former wife by strangling her with an electric flex. He pleaded her sexual infidelity as a wider part of his defence case. The judge at trial found that there was insufficient evidence of at least two of the requirements of the section to leave the defence to the jury. The Court of Appeal agreed and dismissed his appeal.[91] However it may be the case that where sexual infidelity has been argued as part of a wider loss of self-control, trial judges[92] in the Crown Courts are permitting the loss of self-control defence to be put before a jury.[93] It is also to be noted that research by Horder and FitzGibbon[94] discovered that sexual infidelity remains a significant factor in mitigation at the sentencing stage.[95] For all the reasons discussed, loss of self-control will continue to be understood and articulated as 'the' expression of anger and whilst excluding sexual infidelity from the loss of self-control defence, this feature continues to inhabit the public mind as part of an episteme of learnt permissions for anger / loss of self-control.

The problem of loss of control triggered by fear

This raises the interesting question of the prospect for defendants (women victims of violence in heterosexual relationships, and men and women in same-sex partner relationships) who wish to construct a loss of control defence on the grounds of fear.[96] The Crown Court Compendium Part I in acknowledging the complexity of the situation for the abused intimate partner advises, 'The relationship between this defence and self-defence under s.76 of the Criminal Justice and Immigration Act 2008 (CJIA 2008) needs to be approached with care.'[97]

88 [2016] EWCA Crim 2043 a further appeal against sentence dismissed. See also J. Humphries, 'Callum Wilcocks found guilty of murdering teenager Kelsey Shaw after re-trial' *Liverpool Echo* (Liverpool, 1 December 2015) <www.liverpoolecho.co.uk/news/liverpool-news/callum-wilcocks-found-guilty-murdering-10531145> accessed 21 November 2017.

89 [2015] EWCA Crim 2517.

90 *McDonald (James Luke)* (n 83).

91 J. Horder, and K. FitzGibbon, 'When Sexual Infidelity Triggers Murder: Examining the Impact of Homicide Law Reform on Judicial Attitudes in Sentencing' (2015) 74(2) Criminal Law Journal 307.

92 Crown Court Bench Book, Part I (February 2017 19–2) para 24–29. See also Ministry of Justice Circular, 'Partial Defences to Murder: Loss of Control and Diminished Responsibility; and infanticide: Implementation of Sections 52, and 54 to 57 of the Coroners and Justice Act 2009' (MoJ/C, 2010/13).

93 Minta Addido, stabbed his wife several times to her arms, chest and abdomen and pleaded loss of self-control due to anger and jealousy because she had another relationship, and was convicted of murder. See H. Gye, 'Jealous husband stabbed his wife 15 times, ran her over then sent her a Christmas card as she lay dying in hospital' *Daily Mail* (London, 16 December 2013) <www.dailymail.co.uk/news/article-2524723/Jealous-husband-stabbed-wife-15-times-ran-sent-Christmas-card-lay-dying-hospital.html> accessed 21 November 2017.

94 Horder & FitzGibbon (n 91).

95 *Haywood* [2011] 2 Cr App R (S) 71, 410. In Attorney General's Reference (No 23 of 2011), Lord Judge LCJ said: 'Even if not amounting to a defence of provocation, provocation may provide relevant mitigation to murder'.

96 C and JA 2009, s.55(3).

97 Crown Court Bench Book (n 92) para 17.

This final section explores whether there truly is a performative place for the defence of fear / loss of self-control and also considers the interface between fear and self-defence for the abused intimate partner who kills. To repeat, the C and JA 2009 is engaged when '... D's loss of self-control was attributable to D's fear of serious violence from V against D or another identified person.'[98] Returning to the discussion at the outset of this chapter, this new provision reflects a moral and conceptual shift and retreat from *Duffy* in that the past violent conduct of the deceased becomes foregrounded as a centrifugal aspect of the relevant factual and evidential narrative in evaluating whether there exists evidence of a claim of fear of serious violence. Assessment of the past to establish the basis of the claim of present and future fear is pivotal. Further, the abused woman's (or, where relevant, man's) psychological reaction to past and future violence now becomes a relevant factor in assessing *mens rea*. In respect of the first reform Ashworth[99] in 1975, in his research on sentencing in provocation cases, uncovered the harbinger of a judicial retreat from the legal and moral bind of Devlin J's ruling in *Duffy*, 'it does not matter how cruel he was ...'. Ashworth[100] pointed out 'Now those last few words beg the very question: surely the final act of the accused can only be interpreted properly if the whole course of conduct is taken into account and weighed cumulatively?'[101] Wasik[102] also found evidence that '... judges have ... chafed at the strictness of the *Duffy* view.' By 1991, Jack Ashley introduced the Crimes [Homicide] Amendment Bill[103] where he said of Sara Thornton:

> When he died [Malcolm Thornton], she was arrested and taken to court. The court found that she was not provoked, because the law says that she had no provocation for killing her husband. The years of brutality were brushed aside. My Bill would simply remove the word "sudden". It includes the requirement that cumulative violence be taken into account.

The Law Commission also recommended that, '... the jury should continue to take into consideration previous provocation before the one which produced the fatal reaction'.[104] So, for example, Josephine Smith convicted of murder in 2002[105] had suffered emotional and physical abuse from her husband; the appeal court in quashing the conviction for murder and substituting manslaughter without seeking a new trial said that the trial judge had, 'wrongly restricted the jury's attention to the events surrounding the killing and did not ask them to consider a whole history of potentially provocative behaviour that had occurred prior to that.'[106] For the appellant, the defence expert found that she was suffering from 'learned helplessness' arising from Battered Woman Syndrome (BWS) with which the Crown's expert agreed. And so the background of violence became an increasingly important aspect of the defence.

The understanding of the impact of fear on human action and inaction has had significant impact on the development of the law in this area. The history is well-known. When a

98 C and JA 2009, s.55(3).
99 A. J. Ashworth, 'Sentencing in Provocation Cases' (1975) Criminal Law Review 553.
100 Ibid.
101 Ibid, 557.
102 M. Wasik, 'Cumulative Provocation and Domestic Killing' (1982) Criminal Law Review 29.
103 HC Deb 18 December 1991, vol 201, cols 273–4.
104 Law Commission, *Partial Defences to Murder* (Law Com No 290, 2004).
105 *Smith (Josephine)* [2002] EWCA Crim 2671.
106 Ibid., 84.

battered woman killed an abusive partner she would talk of fear, survival, self-preservation and self-defence. Ann Jones had said in 1980 'what lawyers omit or trial judges exclude is precisely what a woman has to say in her own defence'[107] such that lawyers representing women were forced to intercalate these descriptive accounts as best they could into existing defences by which they were tethered. Nicholson and Sanghvi,[108] recognised that the law was 'based upon male standards of behaviour as to cause considerable injustice to battered women who kill' such that much of women's experiences were silenced by being excluded or maladroitly framed. In the early days fear, survival and self-preservation became maleated into the existing provocation defence, and the very best that lawyers could do was to stretch the time between the last act of provocation and the killing (the immediacy requirement) and hone a new concept of 'cumulative provocation' which recognised the past history of violence.[109] Horder alluded to the monumental misfit women's reaction presented to this legal fixity when he said:

> ... women are far less likely to 'permit themselves' to lose self-control in the face of provocation ... It is obvious that when a defendant is taunted by a victim who is known or believed to be physically more powerful and aggressive than the defendant, the defendants anger at the taunt is liable to be tempered by fear of the provoking victim's own reaction to any expressive display by the defendant of annoyance at the taunt.[110]

To be more precise, he argued that the defendant's reaction was more likely one of mixed emotions, both fear and anger.[111] Significantly, from a psychological perspective, Walker in her experience of counselling and acting and providing expert opinion found that battered women lived in a denial of their anger.[112] Women's own linguistic accounts shortly after the killing reflected both fear and moral indignation: 'I didn't mean to kill but he deserved it'. Reilly[113] notes, 'Fear might be associated with external signs which are not easily detectable; perhaps being characterized more typically by paralysis and submission ...'. Fear is not referable to a loss of self-control and therefore it is easy to understand why a state of disintegration and collapse in despair and anxiety failed then, and possibly to a lesser extent at the present time, to satisfy the outward emotional state of anger cognised and demanded as 'the' privileged and accepted evidential base of loss of self-control.[114]

To assist in bolstering the defence of provocation and diminished responsibility prior to the C and JA 2009, the defendant's experience of fear in perceiving the possibility of future

107 A. Jones, *Women Who Kill* (The Feminist Press 2009) 361.

108 D. Nicholson and R. Sanghvi, 'Battered Women and Provocation: The Implications of R v Ahluwalia' (1993) Criminal Law Review 728 (note). See also J. Horder, 'Sex, Violence, and Sentencing in Domestic Provocation Cases' (1989) Criminal Law Review 546. Horder recognised the need to correct the law's apparent bias in favour of stereotypically 'male violent reactions to provocation.'

109 Ibid., Horder (n 108), Ashworth (n 99) 547. See also M. Wasik, 'Cumulative Provocation and Domestic Killing' (1982) 29 Criminal Law Review 32–3.

110 J. Horder, *Homicide and the Politics of Law Reform* (Oxford University Press 2012).

111 See Horder (n 7) 128.

112 L. E. Walker, *Terrifying Love: Why Battered Women Kill and How Society Responds* (Harper and Row 1989) 203.

113 A. Reilly, 'Loss of Self-Control in Provocation' (1997) 21 Criminal Law Journal 320, 323.

114 See S. Edwards, 'Loss of Self-Control: When His Anger is Worth More than Her Fear' in D. Bohlander and A. Reed (eds) *Loss of Self-control and Diminished Responsibility* (Ashgate 2011) 79–97.

violence and her reaction to that possibility was assisted by expert opinion. However, since rules of evidence dictate and constrain what can be admitted in the courtroom, and by whom, fear of violence was constructed as part of a 'syndrome'. Caught by the admissibility hurdle, expert evidence could not be adduced unless women's fear of abuse was a recognised medical condition such that her fear and its corollaries required medical veneering to meet the admissibility threshold.[115] BWS served this purpose in setting out a medical symptomatology. 'BWS has severely limited the effects of violence on women to a pathological condition such that it resembles more of a disease thereby essentialising the woman and seeing it as her problem[116] rather than a set of responses to fear and anticipated future violence.'[117] Its limitations created a 'pathological cul-de-sac for women'[118] and shifted the emphasis from the reasonableness of the defendant's action onto her personality, such that women relying on the effects of battering might be required to be passive and without agency lest the case for victimhood be undermined.[119] The additional problem presenting defence counsel was that it was not certain that jurors would accept fear as a sufficient reason to kill in the face of the absence of the imminency or immediate threat of violence and where a defendant failed to meet the traditional (explosive) and outward manifestation of loss of self-control making pleading provocation a high risk.[120]

But new defence strategies developed, appeals were based on fresh evidence which included BWS, and more significantly the prosecution at the trial stage demonstrated a willingness to accept defence pleas of provocation without insisting on a full trial, such that the fear experienced by abused women came to be recognised as a pivotal component of their defensive response to intimate partner violence. Where provocation had been pleaded at trial and failed counsel then appealed, submitting fresh evidence under the limb of diminished responsibility. So, for example, in *Sangha* [121], an appeal against a conviction for murder on the grounds of diminished responsibility was successful where the wife was the victim of long-term mental and physical cruelty over a period of more than 20 years of marriage including, 'being punched, kicked, almost strangled, struck with a walking stick and with a pan, beaten whilst she was pregnant and beaten in front of her parents'.

Similarly, Kiranjit Ahluwalia[122] convicted of the murder of a violent husband, had unsuccessfully pleaded no intent manslaughter, and provocation in the alternative. On appeal, fresh evidence was submitted regarding a plea of diminished responsibility. Judgment

115 See L. E. Walker (n 112) 75. From 1977 onwards Walker acted as expert in U.S. cases where battered women killed. Walker points out for example that it took six years for the court to rule that her expert testimony in the case of Ibn Tamas court be admitted. See also *Beverly Ibn-Tamas, Appellant, v United States*, Appellee. No. 12614. District of Columbia Court of Appeals. Argued 30 June 1978. 407 A.2d 626 (1979).

116 See A. Shalleck, 'Theory and Experience in Constructing the Relationship between Lawyer and Client: Representing Women Who Have Been Abused' (1997) 64 Tennessee Law Review 1019, reprinted in C. Dalton and E. M. Schneider, *Battered Women and the Law* (Foundation Press 2001) 1063.

117 S. Edwards, 'Expert Witnesses for the Prosecution in Domestic Violence "Prosecuting Domestic Violence – Using Expert Evidence and Expert Witnesses"' Report prepared for the CPS and Standing Together (2001) 34. See also, H. Kennedy, *Eve Was Framed* (Vintage 1992) 734.

118 Ibid. Kennedy, 93–4.

119 *R. v Butler* (Diana Helen) [1999] Criminal Law Review 835

120 Nicholson and Sanghvi (n 108) 734.

121 [1997] 1 Cr.App.R. (S) 202.

122 *R v Ahluwalia* [1992] 4 All ER 889.

was reserved,[123] a retrial ordered, and in September 1992, the Crown accepted the fresh evidence of BWS and her plea to diminished responsibility.[124] Kathleen Hobson killed a violent husband and a plea of provocation and self-defence failed. She called the police on 30 previous occasions, making formal complaints on four occasions. On appeal, she pleaded that the effects of violence including BWS were relevant to a defence of diminished responsibility. This fresh evidence was admitted and the conviction quashed.[125] A retrial was ordered where the Crown accepted the evidence of diminished responsibility.[126] Diana Butler[127] stabbed her partner in the course of an hour-long assault in which he dragged her down the stairs by her hair, kicked her against walls and began smashing up the house. Her defence was no intent manslaughter, which was not accepted by the jury. The prosecution had adduced evidence of her previous violence. On appeal, her murder conviction was quashed; at retrial, her pleas of guilty to diminished responsibility manslaughter were accepted by the Crown.[128]

The decisions of the trial courts are much more difficult to track, but there is some evidence of change. For example, during the trial of Alisa Brookes the Crown indicated that it would accept a plea of guilty to manslaughter on grounds of provocation following a successful submission by the defence of 'no case to answer'.[129] Diane Clark[130] stabbed her violent husband, and her plea to provocation was accepted by the prosecution. Judge Gerald Gordon spoke of a 'smoking fuse of provocation'.[131]

However, in developing a fear discourse and raising awareness of the effects of fear on her emotional state and *mens rea*, the new provision continues to misframe the battered woman holding, seeing her reaction often as an overreaction.[132] This cognitive cliché has been

123 H. Mills, 'Brutalised wife appeals against murder verdict' *The Independent* (London, 19 July 1992) <www.independent.co.uk/news/uk/brutalised-wife-appeals-against-murder-verdict-kiranjit-ahluwalia-given-a-life-sentence-for-killing-1534433.html> accessed 23 November 2017

124 G. Robertson, *The Justice Game* (Vintage 1992). Sara Thornton killed a violent husband and was convicted of murder following an unsuccessful plea of involuntary manslaughter and diminished responsibility. On appeal a retrial was ordered. On retrial a jury found her not guilty of murder but guilty of manslaughter diminished responsibility and provocation. See W. Bennett, 'Sara Thornton is cleared of murder' *The Independent* (London, 30 May 1996) <www.independent.co.uk/news/sara-thornton-is-cleared-of-murder-1349913.html> accessed 22 November 2017. See also S. Edwards and C. Walsh, 'The Justice of Retrial' (1996) 146 National Law Journal 857.

125 *R v Hobson* [1998] 43 B.M.L.R. 181. See also K. O'Hanlon, 'Battered woman's conviction overturned' *The Independent* (London, 5 June 1997) <www.independent.co.uk/news/people/law-report-v-6-june-1997-battered-womans-conviction-overturned-1254390.html > accessed 22 November 2017

126 *The Guardian,* 16 December 1997.

127 *Butler* (n 119); *The Independent,* October 3 1999.

128 Editorial, 'Woman who killed violent partner gets probation' *The Guardian* (London, 2 October 1999) <www.theguardian.com/uk/1999/oct/02/4> accessed 23 November 2017. Not all successful see *R v Williams* [2007] EWCA Crim 2264, who killed her partner and on appeal adduced evidence of BWS was not successful and her appeal was dismissed.

129 Y. Roberts, 'A woman in fear for her life is not a murderer' *The Independent* (London, 21 September 1999) <www.independent.co.uk/arts-entertainment/a-woman-in-fear-for-her-life-is-not-a-murderer-1120984.html> accessed 23 November 2017

130 *The Evening Standard,* 7 July 1998.

131 See C. Comerford, 'Woman "driven" to kill husband' *The Independent* (London, 10 August 1998) <www.independent.co.uk/news/woman-driven-to-kill-husband-1170893.html > accessed 23 November 2017.

132 S. Edwards, 'Abolishing Provocation and Reframing Self-Defence—the Law Commission's Options for Reform' (2004) Criminal Law Review 181.

embedded in the psyche of courts and within the legal critique[133]such that the current legislative requirement of 'fear' must meet the standard or threshold of 'fear of serious violence'.[134] This suggests that there still exists some misunderstanding of the abused partner's fear of intimate partner violence. Yet whilst the law requires evidence of fear of significant violence (serious violence) before the defence can be triggered, with regard to self-defence the fear of a householder of a trespasser's violence is more readily understood and not requiring of so high a threshold.[135]

So whilst fear of 'serious violence' need not be of imminent violence, it must be serious nonetheless. What fear means, and what is required to prove 'fear of serious violence', is left to be determined. In relation to the 'fear of serious violence', the test is subjective. What constitutes 'serious violence', rather like what constitutes 'grave circumstances', is undetermined. Will it be aligned to grievous bodily harm or will chronic long-term violence be accepted as 'serious violence' because of its habituated and cumulative impact?

In developing a fear defence, the considerable body of earlier research and writing on BWS is material, especially with regard to the understanding of a cumulative and prospective fear of violence. For example, in *Longsworth*, [136] 'the appellant threw an accelerant on her common law husband, set him on fire with a candle and then tried to extinguish the fire by throwing water over him', her defence on appeal centered around fresh evidence with regard to BWS. In submissions, counsel said that:

> (4) the appellant's loss of self-control was a result of buildup of anger over the years. It appeared that her capacity to absorb such violence was finally exhausted and she threw the petrol and candle described this response as "slow burn" to cumulative provocation, which is observed in women who have experienced repeated abuse.[137]

The appeal court said:

> She explained that the appellant had reached her psychological "breaking point". This type of response, she stated, had also been described as a "slow burn" response to cumulative provocation, particularly observed in women who have experienced repeat abuse and which may occur in response to what objectively appears to be a relatively minor or trivial provocation, often after an apparent time delay between the last provocative act and the apparent loss of control … The court considered Dr Mezey's opinion where she stated at para 15.31 of her report that the appellant's cognitive, emotional and behavioral deficits associated with PTSD and BWS would have affected her perception of the severity of the provocation.[138]

133 S. Edwards, 'Loss of Self-Control: When His Anger is Worth More Than Her Fear' in M. Bohlander and A. Reed (eds) *Loss of Control and Diminished Responsibility: Domestic, Comparative and International Perspectives* (Routledge 2011) 93. See also, Law Com CP No 173 (n 104) para 1.62, and Law Commission, *Murder, Manslaughter and Infanticide* (Law Com No 304, 2006) para 5.1, fear of serious violence is recognised fear but nonetheless in anticipating future violence whilst the Law Commission was willing to expand the definition of provocation to include 'fear driven killings' it still considered that fear leading to killing another was an 'overreaction'.

134 C and JA 2009, s.55 (3)

135 See, for example, where D has killed when attacking a trespasser in a dwelling s 76 of the CJIA 2008 as amended by the Crime and Courts Act 2013.

136 [2015] 3 LRC 580.

137 Ibid. [607].

138 Ibid. [611].

The appellant's conviction for murder was quashed, substituted with a manslaughter verdict based on diminished responsibility, and a sentence of eight years' was imposed.

As was expected and anticipated, violent men have also tried to take advantage of the defence and such cases have been the subject of appeal. In these circumstances, trial judges have withdrawn the defence of loss of control.[139] The withdrawal of the defence was successfully challenged on appeal in *Clinton.* [140]

Most problematically for the abused partner, the fear limb of the loss of control defence[141] has not removed the incongruency problem wherein the abused partner who kills out of fear is required to satisfy the loss of self-control requirement. Given the construction of loss of self-control in thought, language, outward emotional and physical expression, its fixity as a signifier, the way it is conjoined conceptually, linguistically and cognitively to anger, articulated in symbolic descriptions of red mist, losing it, becoming wild and deranged etc., fear, so different in every way can never ever earn its place in the framework of the loss of self-control defence.

So what of the possibility that self-defence might be mounted? Undoubtedly, it is the case that the evolving consciousness in society and in legal discourse regarding the predicament of the battered woman and the new fear limb in loss of self-control manslaughter has influenced legal argument in cases of murder, self-defence and no intent/involuntary manslaughter. The Crown Court Compendium states:

> (5) Self-defence and this s.54 defence may both be pleaded. Care is needed. Unlike self-defence, D has lost control. Unlike self-defence, D can rely on fear of future non-imminent attack. If D has intentionally killed V, pleads self-defence but is alleged to have used excessive force, the complete defence of self-defence might fail, but D may still be able to rely on the new partial defence, the excessive amount of force being explicable by reference to the "loss of self-control". Section 54(5) requires only that sufficient evidence is adduced to raise an issue under s 54(1). Thereafter, the prosecution shoulders the legal burden of proving, to the criminal standard of proof, that the defence is not satisfied.[142]

The case of Elizabeth Hart-Browne is a case in point. On 27 April 2017, she pleaded not guilty to murder and pleaded self-defence stating that she picked up a knife and stabbed her partner accidentally in the course of a struggle. The defence presented argument of his continual violence towards her over a period of time and her fear of serious violence from him such that she took out a life insurance policy so that her children would be provided for if she was killed. She was acquitted of murder and all charges, including manslaughter, following 15 hours of deliberation.[143]

However, an investigation of the generic statistical evidence indicates that there have been few cases since the enactment of C and JA where fear has provided a basis for loss of control.

139 *Dawes* (n 52), *McDonald (James Luke)* (n 83), *Khan* (Jamshaid) [2016] EWCA Crim 1786, *Gurpinar* [2015] EWCA Crim 178.
140 *Clinton* (n 71).
141 C and JA 2009, 55(3).
142 Crown Court Compendium (n 51) 19-13 para 18(5).
143 A. Ross, 'West London jeweller cleared of murdering abusive boyfriend' *The Guardian* (London, 27 April 2017) < www.theguardian.com/society/2017/apr/27/west-london-jeweller-cleared-of-murdering-abusive-boyfriend> accessed 22 November 2017. See also *Van Den Hoek v R* [1986] 161 CLR 158; *Ivanovic* [2005] VSCA 238; *Osland* [1998] 2 VR 636.

For the period when the C and JA 2009 was in force (April 2011–March 2015, latest figures available), 39 female defendants were convicted of 'other manslaughter'[144] irrespective of the relationship of victim to suspect. This gives some indication of the likely little use of the fear limb of the manslaughter defence. However, the very advent of the fear trigger and the symbolic importance of this recognition of the role of fear in understanding what drives an abused partner to kill is significant.

Conclusion – What is to be done now?

One is left considering whether the 'loss of self-control' defence be removed altogether. Should anger continue to be privileged? Should the fear limb of the defence be restructured since, as it exists in law and in public discourse, the battered woman in fear can never neatly be interpellated to meet the loss of self-control requirement.

Should legal reform look to ensure that the abused partner's fear is also explicitly accommodated elsewhere within the criminal law? Certainly there seems to be little logic or fair play in recognising that a householder in fear[145] may not react with measure but a victim of domestic violence is nonetheless required to do so. Further refining is required. The wording of the modern fear manslaughter defence is ill-equipped to accommodate the fear of the abused partner trapped within a domestic context who reacts emotionally, linguistically and physically in accordance with the effects of fear of violence, whilst the requirement of loss of self-control continues to privilege anger and, through both interpellation and instantiation, continues even if unintended to perpetuate the gendered exonerations of male abusers as the normative template.

144 'Other manslaughter' includes 'loss of control manslaughter' killings (s.54(1), loss of control, fear manslaughter (s.55(3), a combination of both (s.54(1) and s.55(3)); and involuntary or constructive manslaughter no intent, and killings where there was no intention to kill including accident and gross negligence.

145 CJIA 2008, s.76.

6 Diminished responsibility

A limited partial defence to murder

Rudi Fortson QC

Overview

Section 52(1) of the Coroners and Justice Act 2009 (C and JA 2009) replaced the definition of 'diminished responsibility' as originally enacted in s.2(1) of the Homicide Act 1957 (HA 1957),[1] and it added subsections (1), (1A) and (1B) to that Act.[2] The revised definition of diminished responsibility includes the following requirements, namely, that the defendant (D):

a suffered from an 'abnormality of mental functioning'[3]
b which arose from a 'recognised medical condition'[4]
c that 'substantially impaired D's ability'[5] to:

 i 'understand the nature of D's conduct,'[6] and/or,
 ii 'form a rational judgment,'[7] and/or
 iii 'exercise self-control,'[8] and

d 'provides an explanation for D's acts and omissions in doing or being a party to the killing'.[9]

An abnormality of mental functioning will provide an explanation for the defendant's conduct 'only if it causes, or is a significant contributing factor in causing D to carry out that conduct'.[10]

1 'Where a person kills or is a party to the killing of another, he shall not be convicted of murder if he was suffering from such abnormality of mind (whether arising from a condition of arrested or retarded development of mind or any inherent causes or induced by disease or injury) as substantially impaired his mental responsibility for his acts and omissions in doing or being a party to the killing'.
2 '(1) A person ("D") who kills or is a party to the killing of another is not to be convicted of murder if D was suffering from an abnormality of mental functioning which - (a) arose from a recognised medical condition, (b) substantially impaired D's ability to do one or more of the things mentioned in subsection (1A), and (c) provides an explanation for D's acts and omissions in doing or being a party to the killing. (1A) Those things are – (a) to understand the nature of D's conduct; (b) to form a rational judgment; (c) to exercise self-control. (1B) For the purposes of subsection (1)(c), an abnormality of mental functioning provides an explanation for D's conduct if it causes, or is a significant contributory factor in causing, D to carry out that conduct.'
3 HA 1957, s.2(1).
4 Ibid., s.2(1)(a).
5 Ibid., s.2(1)(b).
6 Ibid., s 2(1A)(a).
7 Ibid., s.2(1A)(b).
8 Ibid., s.2(1A)(c). See *Byrne* [1960] 2 QB 396; and *Khan* [2009] EWCA Crim 1569.
9 ibid, s.2(1)(c).
10 Ibid., s.2(1B).

Where the defendant proves (on a balance of probabilities) that, by virtue of s.2(1) HA 1957, his responsibility for the killing was diminished, he is not to be convicted of murder[11] but he will be convicted of manslaughter.[12]

If a section 2 defence is to succeed, medical evidence to support it is a practical necessity: see *R v Bunch*, [13] applying *Byrne* [14] and *Dix*. [15]

The partial defence of diminished responsibility is not available to a defendant who is 'unfit to plead' within the meaning of section 4 of the Criminal Procedure (Insanity and Unfitness to Plead) Act 1964.[16]

In cases where the defence succeeds, the Court has discretion to sentence in a flexible way having regard to the circumstances of the case in question.

History

The revised section 2 of the HA 1957 introduced major structural changes to the partial defence of diminished responsibility that go beyond mere 'clarification of the way in which that defence works'.[17] As Professor Mackay has pointed out,[18] little of original section 2 of the HA 1957 has been retained save for the expressions 'substantially impaired'[19] and 'abnormality'.

The concept of 'diminished responsibility' has a long history in Scotland, summarised by the Lord Justice General (Rodger) in *Galbraith v HM Advocate*.[20] The concept can be traced back to 1873,[21] which has been variously described by Scottish judges as 'diminished responsibility',[22] 'full responsibility to partial responsibility',[23] 'partial responsibility',[24] 'lessened responsibility'[25] and 'partial insanity'.[26]

11 Ibid., s.2(2).
12 Ibid., s.2(3).
13 [2013] EWCA Crim 2498.
14 [1960] 2 Q.B. 396.
15 [1982] 74 Cr. App. R. 306.
16 *Regina v Antoine* [2001] 1AC 340.
17 See Coroners and Justice Bill Deb 3 February 2009, cols 8–9.
18 Conference with Professor Alan Reed (Durham Castle, 30 September 2010); and see R. Mackay and B. Mitchell, 'The New Diminished Responsibility Plea' (2017) Criminal Law Review, 1, 18–35.
19 See *R v Golds* [2016] UKSC 61 for the meaning of 'substantial'.
20 [2001] S.C.C.R 551. See also Scottish Law Commission, *Report on Insanity and Diminished Responsibility* (Scot Law Com No 195, 2004) 80–81 <www.scotlawcom.gov.uk/files/3612/7989/6586/rep195.pdf> accessed 6 January 2018.
21 In the preface to the third edition of Francis Wharton's, *Treatise on Mental Unsoundness Embracing a General View of Psychological Law* (4th edn, Kay and Brother 1882) xiv: *Galbraith* (n 20) [24].
22 *Kirkwood v HM Advocate* [1939] J.C. 36 [37] (Lord Justice General Normand); and see Transcript of the proceedings in Edinburgh High Court on 8 November 1938, 58, 1939 Justiciary Papers no 5, Advocates Library; and similarly by Lord Justice Clerk Cooper in *HM Advocate v Braithwaite*, at 1945 J.C, 57; 1945 SLT, 210, but, a year later, he referred to 'reduced responsibility': *Russell v HM Advocate*, 1946 JC 37; 1946 SLT 93. Similarly, Lord Russell at trial, and Lord Normand on appeal, used the expression 'diminished responsibility': *Carraher v HM Advocate*, 1946 JC 108; 1946 SLT 225. Lord Normand used that expression again in *Caldwell v HM Advocate* [1946] SLT (Notes) 9.
23 *HM Advocate v Edmonstone* [1909] 2 S.L.T 223 [224] (Lord Guthrie).
24 *HM Advocate v Savage* [1923] J.C 49; 1923 S.L.T 659 (Lord Alness).
25 *Muir v HM Advocate* [1933] J.C 47; 1933 S.L.T 403 [404] (Lord Justice General Clyde).
26 Lord Justice Clerk, Dumfries High Court, 13 April 1933, 200, 1933 Justiciary Papers no 8, Advocates Library; and Lord Sands, P 50 (405).

In *Galbraith*,[27] the Appeal Court (High Court of Justiciary) said that, following *Caldwell v HM Advocate*,[28] the expression 'diminished responsibility' seems to have taken root and it observed that '[even] in England the phrase "diminished responsibility" does not actually appear in the body of s.2 of the Homicide Act 1957 but finds a toe-hold in the side-note.'[29] From 25 June 2012 (in relation to criminal proceedings commenced on or after that date, and irrespective of the date the offence was committed)[30] s.168 of the Criminal Justice and Licensing (Scotland) Act 2010 came into force and adds s.51A and s.51B to the Criminal Procedure (Scotland) Act 1995 (CP(S)A 1995). The former states that a person is not 'criminally responsible for conduct constituting an offence, and is to be acquitted of the offence, if the person was at the time of the conduct unable by reason of mental disorder to appreciate the nature or wrongfulness of the conduct.' (see *Mackay v HM Advocate* [2017] HCJAC 44). The new s.51B of the CP(S)A 1995 puts 'diminished responsibility' on a statutory footing in Scotland.[31] It builds (with some modification) on the decision in *Galbraith*.[32] The provision retains the expression 'abnormality of mind'.[33]

As for England and Wales, in 1956, the then Home Secretary introduced a clause in the Homicide Bill (that became s.2 HA 1957) to provide a new defence in respect of persons who 'although not insane in [the] legal sense, are regarded in the light of modern knowledge as insane in the medical sense and those who, not insane in either sense, are seriously abnormal, whether through mental deficiency, inherent causes, disease or injury'.[34] The decision of the legislator to use the expression 'mental deficiency' was perhaps influenced by the wording of the Mental Deficiency Acts of 1913 and 1927 – wording which would be wholly unacceptable today.[35] The latter Acts applied to 'idiots', 'imbeciles', 'feeble minded persons' and 'moral imbeciles' ('moral defectives'[36]) who were 'defective in mind from birth or from an early age.' The Act of 1927, amended s.1 of the 1913 Act by adding s.1(2) which provided that 'mental defectiveness' meant 'a condition of *arrested or incomplete development of mind* existing before the age of eighteen years, whether arising from inherent causes or induced by disease or injury' [emphasis added]. Original s.2(1) HA 1957 spoke of 'arrested or *retarded* development of mind' rather than '*incomplete* development'.[37]

27 *Galbraith* (n 20).
28 *Caldwell* (n 22).
29 *Galbraith* (n 20) [26].
30 SSI 2012 No. 160, art.3.
31 Section 51B of the CP(S)A 1995 reads: '(1) A person who would otherwise be convicted of murder is instead to be convicted of culpable homicide on grounds of diminished responsibility if the person's ability to determine or control conduct for which the person would otherwise be convicted of murder was, at the time of the conduct, substantially impaired by reason of abnormality of mind. (2) For the avoidance of doubt, the reference in subsection (1) to abnormality of mind includes mental disorder. (3) The fact that a person was under the influence of alcohol, drugs or any other substance at the time of the conduct in question does not of itself – (a) constitute abnormality of mind for the purposes of subsection (1), or (b) prevent such abnormality from being established for those purposes. (4) It is for the person charged with murder to establish, on the balance of probabilities, that the condition set out in subsection (1) is satisfied. (5) In this section, "conduct" includes acts and omissions.'
32 *Galbraith* (n 20).
33 CP(S)A 1995, s.51B(1).
34 HC Deb, 15 November 1956, vol. 560, col 1154; and see Law Commission, *Partial Defences to Murder* (Law Com No 173, 2003) paras 7.1–7.9.
35 The Acts of 1913 and 1927 were repealed by the Mental Health Act 1959.
36 Mental Deficiency Act 1927 s.1(1)(d).
37 Law Com No 173, 2003 (n 34) paras 7.49–52.

In 2004, the Law Commission of England and Wales recommended that there 'be no change to section 2 of the 1957 Act.'[38] The Commission was 'not persuaded that the acknowledged infelicities of the current formulation presently cause injustice in practice'.[39] A year earlier, it noted that the Appellate Committee of the House of Lords had occasion to visit the s.2(1) HA 1957 on only one occasion in almost 50 years,[40] and that the provision appeared to have worked in practice largely as Parliament had intended.[41] On the whole, psychiatrists did not 'have difficulty in forming and explaining to the jury their reasons for an opinion whether the defendant was suffering from an abnormality of mind within section 2'.[42]

However, following mounting criticisms of the original formulation of 'diminished responsibility' a revised formulation was substituted by s.52 of the C and JA 2009.

The former aetiologies of diminished responsibility

Under the old s.2(1) HA 1957, the focus of fact-finders was on whether, at the time of the killing, the defendant suffered an abnormality of the 'mind' – an open-textured descriptor that was not, in any event, a scientifically recognised psychiatric condition.[43] Furthermore, as Professor Mackay has pointed out, the aetiologies embodied in the bracketed words in original s.2 HA 1957 were not recognised medical terms.[44] Notwithstanding the assessment made by the Law Commission in 2004, it is submitted that the original wording of s.2 HA 1957 did result in a significant number of psychiatrists being left uncertain of whether or not their diagnosis and assessment of an accused's mental state (at the moment of killing) satisfied the definition of 'diminished responsibility'.

The original wording of s.2(1) HA 1957 might suggest that the abnormality had to arise from one (or more) of four aetiologies specified in that subsection. Such a construction is arguably supported by the often applied decision in *Byrne* [45] when Lord Parker CJ said that:

> To satisfy the requirements of the subsection the accused must show: (a) that he was suffering from an abnormality of mind; and (b) that such abnormality of mind (i) arose from a condition of arrested or retarded development of mind or any inherent causes or was induced by disease or injury; and (ii) was such as substantially impaired his mental responsibility for his acts in doing or being a party to the killing.

However, in *Robinson v The State (Trinidad and Tobago)*[16] the Privy Council said that the purpose of the legislation in naming the possible sources of 'abnormality of mind'[47] was '*to*

38 Law Commission, *Partial Defences to Murder* (Law Com No 290, 2004) para. 1.16.
39 Ibid. para. 1.17.
40 Law Com No 173, 2003 (n 34) para 7.91. See also Law Com No 290, 2004 (n 38) para 5.84.
41 Ibid.
42 Law Com No 173, 2003 (n 34) para 5.50.
43 See Law Commission, *Murder, Slaughter and Infanticide* (Law Com No 304, 2006) para 5.111. See also Law Commission Consultation Paper, *A New Homicide Act for England and Wales?* (Law Com No 177, 2005) para.6.4
44 R.D. Mackay 'The Coroners and Justice Act 2009 – Partial Defences to Murder (2) The New Diminished Responsibility Plea' (2010) 4 Criminal Law Review 290. For the wording of s.2(1) HA 1957 as originally worded, see n 1.
45 *Byrne* (n 8) [403].
46 [2015] UKPC 34.
47 As the words 'abnormality of the mind' appeared in s 4A(1) of the Offences Against the Person Act 1925 (Trinidad and Tobago) – the wording of which mirrored the original wording of s.2(1) HA 1957.

extend rather than to restrict the scope of the expression'.[48] It is understandable that a court would wish to construe a provision in terms that give it current relevance and meaning, but it is submitted that the bracketed words in old s.2(1) HA 1957 were usually taken to be descriptive of all forms of abnormality of the mind (consider *Dix* [49]). Professor Mackay similarly appears to have been of that understanding, pointing out that the abnormality of mind 'had to fall within one or more of these bracketed causes, thus restricting the plea's availability'.[50] In *Robinson,* [51] it was common ground that R's underlying condition was chronic schizophrenia which 'is a plain abnormality of mind. It may derive at least in part from inherent causes, but if it does not it is properly described as a disease of the mind; indeed it may be that it can be both'.[52] There was thus 'no point whatever in spending time on discussing which of those two is its technical classification, and no psychiatrist can properly be criticised for not adverting to the question'.[53] The Law Commission found that there had been 'very little systematic analysis of the aetiological components by the English courts'.[54]

Developmental immaturity

The Law Commission pointed out[55] that immaturity and the effect of traumatic events, other than those involving injury, were not included within the range of aetiologies specified in old s.2(1) HA.[56] The omission had been the subject of strong criticism by leading psychiatrists and psychologists (for example, by Dr Eileen Vizard[57]).[58] The Law Commission proposed that it should be possible to bring in a verdict of diminished responsibility on the grounds of the developmental immaturity of an offender who was under 18[59] at the time that he or she played his or her part in the killing.[60] It observed that experts might find it impossible to distinguish between the impact of developmental immaturity on the defendant's functioning and the impact of a mental abnormality on that functioning process. It therefore concluded that it was 'wholly unrealistic and unfair' to expect medical experts to assess the impact of mental abnormality whilst disregarding developmental immaturity.[61]

However, the Government was not convinced that the issue of developmental immaturity created significant practical problems and that there was a risk that to widen the partial defence to include developmental immaturity would catch inappropriate cases.[62] Given the revised wording of s.2(1) HA 1957, it is conceivable that there may be cases where an

48 *Robinson* (n 46) [11(e)].
49 *Dix* (n 15).
50 Mackay (n 44).
51 *Robinson* (n 46).
52 Ibid. [11(e)] (Lord Hughes).
53 Ibid.
54 Law Com No 173, 2003 (n 34) para.7.45.
55 Law Com Com No 177, 2005 (n 43).
56 Ibid. para 6.34, (n 43).
57 A child and adolescent psychiatrist.
58 See Law Com No 290, 2004 (n 38) paras 5.102–103.
59 The Royal College of Psychiatrists recommended that the age be 21 years. See Law Com No 304, 2006 (n 43) paras.5.125, and 5.129.
60 Ibid. Law Com No 304, 2006 (n 43) para. 5.125.
61 Ibid. para. 5.128.
62 Ministry of Justice, 'Murder, Manslaughter and Infanticide: Proposals for Reform of the Law' (Law Com CP No. 19/08, 2008) para. 53.

accused would be able to bring his/her developmental immaturity within the expression 'recognised medical condition' for the purposes of revised s.2(1). However, an unintended consequence of the abolition of the *doli incapax* defence for children aged between 10 to 14 years,[63] is that it may be difficult to contend that, notwithstanding a young person's developmental immaturity (but whose mental age corresponds to his chronological age), s.2 HA 1957 permits the separation of the psychological cause of a killing that he carried out, from his legal responsibility for it.[64] As Professor Sir John Spencer QC has pointed out,[65] where a person's mental age 'was significantly below his physical age', there would be 'developmental immaturity', which would constitute a 'recognized medical condition'. Such a set of circumstances is 'already catered for' under the terms of revised s.2 HA 1957. But, Professor Spencer QC described as 'grossly unfair' rules that allow a man aged 40, with a mental age of 10, a partial defence of diminished responsibility on the grounds that his developmental immaturity amounts to a 'recognized medical condition', whereas a child, who is actually aged 10, will not be able to avail himself of this defence *unless* (apart from his age) he has some other recognised medical condition that brings him within the scope of new s.2(1) HA 1957. Even if a person's developmental immaturity constituted a 'recognised medical condition', the remaining elements of diminished responsibility must be made out including that the abnormality of mental functioning 'provides an *explanation*' of the defendant's acts and omissions (s.2(1)(c) HA) *and* – by s.2(1B) HA 1957 – the condition '*causes* or is a significant contributory factor in *causing*' that person to act as he did [emphasis added].

Does the partial defence embody 'moral responsibility'?

In *R v Conroy*,[66] the Court of Appeal (Criminal Division) considered revised s.2 HA 1957, and remarked that the section is so worded to reflect *some* of the general observations of Lord Parker CJ in *Byrne*[67] that an 'abnormality of mind' was wide enough to cover:

> … the mind's activities in all its aspects, not only the perception of physical acts and matters, and the *ability to form a rational judgement* whether an act is *right or wrong*, but also the ability to exercise willpower to control physical acts in accordance with that rational judgment [author emphasis added].

However, the Court emphasised that the revised section has 'distinct differences'.[68] In *Conroy*, various psychiatrists, who had examined the appellant, considered whether he knew, (a) what he was doing and, (b) that it was 'wrong'. Counsel for the prosecution had contended[69] that the words in s.2 HA 1957 concerning the ability 'to form a rational judgment' meant an ability to form a rational judgment as to whether an act is right or wrong.[70] The Court was clearly correct (it is submitted) to have held that the 1957 Act, as amended, 'is

63 *T* [2009] UKHL 20.
64 Consider G. Sullivan, 'Intoxicants and Diminished Responsibility' (1994) Criminal Law Review 156
65 Law Com CP No. 19/08, 2008 (n 62).
66 [2017] EWCA Crim 81.
67 *Byrne* (n 8).
68 *Conroy* (n 66) [5] (Davis LJ).
69 In counsel's written arguments, but not orally, and basing himself on the decision in *Byrne* (n 8).
70 *Conroy* (n 66) [33] (Davis LJ).

not in terms confined to such a scenario. The wording is altogether more open-ended'.[71] Furthermore, the concept of 'diminished responsibility' ought not to be seen as something akin to rules relating to insanity as expressed in *R v McNaughten*. [72] In that case, Maule J said [emphasis added]:

> To render a person *irresponsible* for crime on account of unsoundness of mind, the unsoundness should, according to the law as it has long been understood and held, be such as rendered him *incapable of knowing right from wrong*.

In *Conroy*, the Court had 'little doubt that in a usual case' the defendant's ability to form a rational judgment as to whether an act is *right or wrong* 'will be one element and potentially an important element on which a jury's appraisal may be directed as part of the overall circumstances'.[73] In this connection, see s 2(1A)(a) HA 1957 (substantial impairment to 'understand the nature of D's conduct' (see later in the chapter)).

Thus, to the extent that it is relevant for a court/jury to consider (for the purposes of s.2 HA 1957) whether the accused knew that his acts were 'right or wrong', the issue of diminished responsibility includes a question of morality. However, this is a different issue (it is submitted) from that of 'moral responsibility' which has been said to be a feature of old s.2(1) HA 1957. Old s.2(1) HA referred to a defendant's impairment of 'mental responsibility' (revised s.2(1) does not). The reason for the inclusion of 'mental responsibility' was explained by the Attorney General, speaking for the Government in the House of Commons in 1956, when clause 2 of the Homicide Bill 1956 was debated:

> ... [regarding] the word "mental" as it appears before "responsibility" [it] is put there by design, because one is there considering mental responsibility with a view to determining whether legal responsibility would be reduced. It would not read very well to say: ... such abnormality of mind as substantially impaired his legal responsibility. It is either one or the other and the word "mental" is inserted to remove the doubt. If his mental responsibility has been impaired, then his legal responsibility is reduced. That follows from the operation of subsection (1).

As Glanville Williams pointed out, the draftsman of original s.2, HA 1957, 'avoided the words "*moral* responsibility" because he did not want to bring moral questions into the criminal law'.[74] However, in another renowned textbook (Smith and Hogan, *Criminal Law*) it was said that the impairment of the defendant's 'mental responsibility' had been 'a *moral question* of degree and essentially one for the jury'.[75] In a later edition,[76] the authors comment by way of a footnote:[77]

71 Ibid.
72 [1843] 8 ER 718.
73 *Conroy* (n 66) [33] (Davis LJ).
74 G. Williams, *Textbook of Criminal Law* (2nd edn, Stevens and Sons 1983) 624; Stevens (author emphasis added).
75 D. Ormerod, *Smith and Hogan's Criminal Law* (12th edn, Oxford University Press 2011) 511.
76 D. Ormerod and K. Laird, *Smith and Hogan's Criminal Law* (14th edn, Oxford University Press 2015) 612.
77 Footnote 254.

> A person whose impulse is irresistible bears no moral responsibility for his act, for he has no choice; a person whose impulse is much more difficult to resist than that of an ordinary person bears a diminished responsibility of moral responsibility for his act.

However, the moral question here is not whether the defendant's actions were morally 'right or wrong', but whether the *jury* can regard *itself* as being morally justified in reducing a defendant's legal responsibility for the killing from murder to manslaughter. Some members of the judiciary expressed their dislike of directions to the jury which 'give an undue normative role to their decisions' (Pitchers J), and Mr Justice Stanley Burnton (as he then was) stated that he disliked definitions that 'involves the jury in a value judgment'.[78] Professor Griew regarded the wording of original s.2 HA 1957 as 'improperly elliptical' and that the word 'responsibility' served a 'double function' that was suggestive of the defendant's capacity to comprehend and to conform to the requirements of the law as well as an assessment of culpability for the killing that flowed from his condition.[79] It is not apparent from the decided cases that, in practice, juries had been directed to determine the issue of an accused's 'mental responsibility' as a moral question or that a jury should act as a moral barometer of a defendant's responsibility for the killing. Instead, the jury had to approach diminished responsibility from the perspective of 'essentially seeking to ascertain ...whether at the time of the killing the accused was suffering from a state of mind bordering on but not amounting to insanity. That task is to be approached in a broad common sense way'.[80] In *Walton v The Queen*, [81] the Privy Council remarked that, on the issue of diminished responsibility,

> ... the jury are entitled and indeed bound to consider not only the medical evidence but the evidence upon the whole facts and circumstances of the case. These include the nature of the killing, the conduct of the defendant before, at the time of and after it and any history of mental abnormality.

The above approach had the virtue of requiring juries to make an objective assessment of the defendant's mental condition having regard to all relevant circumstances.

Although revised s.2 HA 1957 retains the heading 'persons suffering from diminished responsibility', the word 'responsibility' does not feature in the body of the section.[82] It is therefore entirely appropriate that the Crown Court Compendium states[83] that 'the use of the words "diminished responsibility", depending on the circumstances, may not be helpful when directing the jury'.

Recognised medical condition

Revised s.2(1)(a) ensures that the defence of diminished responsibility is founded on a 'recognised medical condition'. Although this can be the subject of expert testimony, the

78 Law Com No 290, 2004 (n 38) para 5.55 [fn. 61]
79 Edward Griew, 'The Future of Diminished Responsibility' (1998) Criminal Law Review, 75.
80 *Byrne* (n 8) [404]. See also *Walton v. R* [1977] 3 W.L.R. 902.
81 Ibid. *Walton* [791] (Lord Keith of Kinkel).
82 This is in marked contrast to s 51B of the CP(S)A 1995.
83 The Judicial College, Crown Court Compendium (2017) <www.judiciary.gov.uk/wp-content/uploads/2016/06/crown-court-compendium-pt1-jury-and-trial-management-and-summing-up-nov-2017-v2.pdf> accessed 13 December 2017.

issue is not exclusively a medical one and it will be for the courts to decide whether a particular condition is capable of being a 'recognised medical condition' in law (see, for example, *R v Lindo* [2016] EWCA Crim 1940). Thus, in *Dowds,* [84] the Court of Appeal re-affirmed the principle that simple voluntary drunkenness was incapable of founding a plea of diminished responsibility (see *R v Dietschmann,* [85] *R v Wood,* [86] *R v James Stewart* [87]) and this could not be overridden merely because voluntary 'acute intoxication' is a medical condition specified in the two accepted international classificatory systems of mental conditions, namely, the *World Health Organisation: International Classification of Diseases* (ICD-10), and the *American Psychiatric Association: Diagnostic and Statistical Manual of Mental Disorders* (DSM-1V).[88]

However, it is submitted that the case of *Dowds* needs to be seen in the context of the general principle that operated in that case concerning voluntary intoxication. There can be cases where voluntary intoxication ***triggers*** a 'recognised medical condition' such as psychosis that brings the defendant within s.2(1) HA 1957. Thus, it was said in *R v Joyce and Kay*:[89]

> ... The law does not debar someone suffering from schizophrenia from relying on the partial defence of diminished responsibility where voluntary intoxication has triggered the psychotic state, but he must meet the criteria in section 2(1). He must establish, on the balance of probabilities, that his abnormality of mental functioning (in this case psychotic state) arose from a recognised medical condition that substantially impaired his responsibility. The recognised medical condition may be schizophrenia of such severity that, absent intoxication, it substantially impaired his responsibility (as in the case of *Jenkin* [90]); the recognised medical condition may be schizophrenia coupled with drink/drugs dependency syndrome which together substantially impair responsibility. However, if an abnormality of mental functioning arose from voluntary intoxication and not from a recognised medical condition an accused cannot avail himself of the partial defence. This is for good reason. The law is clear and well established: as a general rule voluntary intoxication cannot relieve an offender of responsibility for murder, save where it may bear on the question of intent.

Those two classificatory systems of medical diagnoses will be of assistance in terms of identifying a 'recognised medical condition'. It may avoid individual doctors offering idiosyncratic 'diagnoses' as the basis for a defence of diminished responsibility.[91] However, the Government accepted that it is important that s.2 HA 1957 must be sufficiently flexible to cater for emerging medical conditions. It opined that it would be open to the defence to call a 'recognized specialist who has had their work peer-reviewed, although it has not quite got on the list' and that it would be for the jury to decide whether the evidence met the partial defence requirements.[92] In-court experience of the revised formulation of diminished

84 [2012] EWCA Crim 281.
85 [2003] UKHL 10.
86 [2008] EWCA Crim 1305 [23] (Sir Igor Judge).
87 [2009] EWCA Crim 593.
88 Law Com No 304, 2006 (n 43) para 5.114.
89 [2017] EWCA Crim 647 [16] (Hallett LJ).
90 [2014] EWCA Crim 1394.
91 Law Com No 304, 2006 (n 43) para. 5.114.
92 Coroners and Justice Bill Deb 3 March 2009 (n 17) col 414.

responsibility has not manifested instances of medical disorders that have been unjustly excluded from a jury's consideration.

The defendant's ability to understand the 'nature of D's conduct': section 2(1A)(a)

Section 2(1A)(a) HA 1957 is confined to the defendant's understanding of his own conduct and not that of (for example) the victim.[93] If the defendant's impairment at the time of the killing was such that he / she lacked the ability to form a rational judgment with regards to the victim's conduct (that is to say, that the defendant misjudged it, for example, on a deluded basis) then – arguably – his / her case may fall within s.2(1A)(b) HA 1957.

It will be incumbent on a trial judge (it is submitted) to explain to a jury what the expression 'nature of his conduct' means, and to identify those aspects of the defendant's conduct that bear on the 'nature' of it. Unfortunately, amended s.2 HA 1957offers no guidance on this issue. Law Com No 304 states[94] that the wording (as it now appears in s.2 (1A)(a)) replaces the words 'understanding events' (at the suggestion of the Criminal Cases Review Commission and Professor Mackay) with the aim of ensuring that the accused's lack of understanding of, say, global political events, is not relevant to his or her plea. The example given by the Law Commission is that of a 10-year-old boy who, having played very violent video games, killed the victim believing that he would be able to revive the victim as had happened in the games that he had been playing continually.[95]

It is arguable that the language of s.2(1A)(a) is wide enough to include cases where, for example, the defendant, by reason of his disability, did not appreciate the nature or quality of his act (for example its lethality). But, if the defendant did not know that the act of killing was 'wrong', is that sufficient for the purposes of s.2(1A)(a)? The defendant's ability to judge whether an act is right or wrong has been a recognised basis for a plea of diminished responsibility under Scottish law.[96] However, in English criminal law, this basis for a plea of diminished responsibility has not featured prominently in appellate decisions.[97] It is tentatively submitted that a defendant who genuinely does not understand that his / her act is 'wrong' by reason of an 'abnormality of mental functioning', falls within s.2(1A)(a). His impaired ability to *form* a rational judgment as to whether or not his actions are right or wrong arguably falls within s.2(1A)(b).

93 The wording of s 2(1A)(a) closely follows the wording proposed by the Law Commission: see Law Com No 304, 2006 (n 43) para 5.112. See also G. R. Sullivan (n 64).

94 Ibid. Law Com No 304, 2006 (n 43). [fn 84].

95 Law Com No 304, 2006 (n 43) para. 5.121.

96 *Galbraith* (n 21) [51], 'The abnormality may mean, for example, that the individual perceives physical acts and matters differently from a normal person. In some cases he may suffer from delusions. Or else it may affect his ability to form a rational judgment as to whether a particular act is right or wrong or to decide whether to perform it. In a given case any or all of these effects may be operating and may impair the accused's ability to determine and control his acts and omissions. The cases of diminished responsibility recognised by the law in the past do indeed involve abnormality of mind of this kind and, therefore, fall within this general description.' Note now s 51B of the CP(S)A 1995, inserted by s 168 of the Criminal Justice and Licensing (Scotland) Act 2010.

97 Consider *Khan* (n 8); and, of less relevance, see *R v Walker* [2009] EWCA Crim 1829; and consider the discussion in *R v Conroy* [2017] EWCA Crim 81.

Ability to form a rational judgment: section 2(1A)(b)

The Law Commission preferred the wording of what is now s.2(1A)(b) to the words 'to judge whether his or her actions were right or wrong'.[98] The example given by the Law Commission to illustrate the application of this provision is where the defendant believes himself to be the reincarnation of Napoleon. Although he might realise that it is morally and legally wrong to take the law into his own hands by killing V, he does so by reason of his substantially impaired capacity to form a rational judgment.[99] In *Conroy*, [100] the Court of Appeal rejected the argument that the 'ability to form a rational judgment' requires some rationality to the *final* judgment. The Court remarked that one cannot always neatly separate the 'decision making process' from the actual ultimate decision, but a jury may need, as part of its overall consideration, to consider how it was that, in the particular defendant's mind, the decision was arrived at:

> ... There may be cases where an entirely "irrational" decision may be taken: for example, to kill one's neighbour because of a fixed belief that he is an alien from Mars intent on blowing up innocent people in the village. But that decision and the motivation for it may then be accompanied, in terms of giving effect to the decision, by ostensibly logical and rational decisions with a view to carrying out the intended killing: for example by buying a knife, by waiting for the neighbour to be at home alone and so on.[101]

Ability to exercise self-control: section 2(1A)(c)

For the purposes of original s.2 HA 1957, the Court of Criminal Appeal held, in *Byrne*, that the provision was wide enough to cover the defendant's ability to exercise will power to control physical acts 'in accordance with ... rational judgment'. One might question whether a loss of self-control can ever be 'rational' but modern s.2 HA 1957 does not expressly link a defendant's inability to exercise self-control [s.2(1A)(c)] with irrational judgments or irrational thought processes [s.2(1A)(b)]. The Law Commission gave the example of the person who believes that he is possessed by the devil and this implants in him a desire to kill.[102] But rather more commonplace scenarios may also bring the defendant within s.2(1A)(c) HA 1957, for example, where organic brain damage causes the defendant to lash out violently. The problem for fact-finders will be distinguishing between cases of actual impairment of a defendant's ability to exercise self-control and cases where the defendant *chooses* not to control his or her conduct. However, by s.2(2) HA 1957, the burden of proving diminished responsibility is on the defendant (to the civil standard of proof).

Impairment must be 'substantial'

An abnormality of mental functioning, which arose from a recognised medical condition, must *substantially* impair the defendant's ability to do one or more of the things mentioned in s.2(1A).

98 Law Com No 304, 2006 (n 43) para 5.112 [fn 85].
99 ibid. [fn 85].
100 *Conroy* (n 66).
101 Ibid. [30] (Davis LJ).
102 Law Com No 304, 2006 (n 43) para 5.121.

In *Byrne* [103] Lord Parker CJ said that substantial impairment (in the context of old s.2) was a question of degree and essentially one for the jury. However, in the light of subsequent decisions, it had been thought that 'substantially impaired' meant that impairment need not be total but must be more than trivial or minimal.[104] But, in *R v Golds*, [105] the UKSC reviewed the authorities and held that 'substantial' meant 'important or weighty'[106] and that it is not synonymous with 'anything more than merely trivial impairment'.[107] It is neither necessary nor wise to attempt a re-definition of 'substantially' for the jury.[108] The jury should normally be given to understand that the expression is an ordinary English word, that it imports a question of degree, and that whether (in the case before it) the impairment can properly be described as substantial is for it to resolve. If the question of degree arises, the judge should explain that whilst the impairment must be more than "merely trivial" before it need be considered, it is not the law that *any* impairment beyond the trivial will suffice.[109] One commentator has argued that the Supreme Court's assertion that 'substantial' can be applied by juries in this way without difficulty is 'undermined by the sheer volume of case law that has considered how this word ought to be understood'.[110]

The defendant's abnormality as an 'explanation' and 'cause' of the killing

As part of its ninth programme of law reform (homicide), the Law Commission contemplated shifting the focus from 'whether there was "substantial impairment of mental responsibility"' to 'whether the defendant's "abnormality of mind" was a significant cause of his acts or omissions in doing or being a party to the killing'.[111] However, the Commission took note of leading experts who advised against the introduction of a strict causation requirement.[112] It decided that, although the final choice of words was a matter for the legislator, an abnormality of mental functioning that was shown to be 'an *explanation*' for the defendant's conduct ensures that there is an 'appropriate connection' between the abnormality and the killing. It would leave open the possibility that other causes or explanations (e.g., loss of self-control) may have operated 'without prejudicing the case for

103 *Byrne* (n 8).
104 See *Lloyd* [1967] 1QB 175. In *Egan* [1992] 95 Cr App R 278, it was said in the context of original s2 of the Homicide Act 1957: Guidance as to the meaning of 'substantial' should be explicitly provided for the jury by using one or other of the two meanings in *Lloyd* (1966) 50 Cr. App.R. 61, [1967] 1 Q.B. 175, i.e., (1) the jury should approach the word in a broad common-sense way, or (2) that the word meant 'more than some trivial degree of impairment which does not make any appreciable difference to a person's ability to control himself, but it means less than total impairment'. In *R v Ramchurch* [2010] EWCA Crim 194 the Court said that the jury had to decide for itself whether the defendant's mental responsibility was impaired and whether that impairment was substantial. See also N. Wake, 'Substantial Confusion Within Diminished Responsibility?' (2011) 75(1) Journal of Criminal Law 12–16.
105 *Golds* (n 19).
106 Ibid. [28].
107 Ibid. [39].
108 Ibid. [40].
109 Ibid. [43]; see also *R v Squelch* [2017] EWCA Crim 204.
110 K. Laird 'Determining the Proper Function of Judge and Jury' (2018) 134 Law Quarterly Review 10–15.
111 Law Com No 173, 2003 (n 34) para 7.92.
112 Law Com No 304, 2006 (n 43) para 5.124.

mitigation'.[113] The Government, however, felt that there must be 'some connection between the condition and the killing in order for the partial defence to be justified'.[114] It therefore enacted s.2(1B) with the result that it is not merely sufficient to show that the abnormality of mental functioning provides 'an explanation' for the defendant's conduct in respect of the killing, but that the abnormality was also a *cause* of (or it was 'a significant contributory factor in *causing*') the conduct. This provision has been the subject of strong criticism.[115] Jo Miles has suggested that, 'from a psychiatric perspective proving even a contributory causal link can be extremely difficult, if not impossible, to do in practice'.[116] There may be cases where proving a causal connection is problematic.

However, it is submitted that there are reasons why concerns about the existence of the causation requirement in s.2(1)(c) ought not to be overstated. First, there will be cases where the causal link between the abnormality of mental functioning and the defendant's act of killing, or being a party to the killing, will be evident. Second, regard must be paid to the combined effect of s.2(1)(c) and (1B) of the 1957 Act. The abnormality need not be the sole cause or explanation for the defendant's conduct. Thus, it is arguable that the causation requirement does no more than give legislative effect to the decision and reasoning of the House of Lords in *Dietschmann*, [117] in which their Lordships held that original s.2(1) of the 1957 Act did not require the existence of an abnormality of mind to be the *sole cause* of the defendant killing or being a party to the killing.[118] The issue has frequently arisen in cases where a defendant (D) killed at a time when D had suffered from an abnormality of mind, and D had taken alcohol before the killing (consider *R v Lindo* [2016] EWCA Crim 1940 where L was a habitual drug user). Lord Hutton opined that 'even if the defendant would not have killed if he had not taken drink, the causative effect of the drink does not necessarily prevent an abnormality of mind suffered by the defendant from substantially impairing his mental responsibility for his fatal acts'.[119] HO Circular 2010/13 states that 'The aim is that the defence should not be able to succeed where the defendant's mental condition made no difference to their behaviour, i.e., when they would have killed regardless of their medical condition.'[120] Similarly, in Scotland, s.51B(3)(b) of the CP(S)A 1995 provides that the fact that a person was 'under the influence of alcohol, drugs or any other substance at the time of the conduct in question does not of itself prevent an abnormality of mind from being established' for the purpose of mounting a partial defence of diminished responsibility within the meaning of s.51B.

Each case will therefore turn on its own facts. As Lord Hutton remarked in *Dietschmann*, 'no doubt in many cases (as in *Fenton* [121]) if the jury concluded that the defendant would not have killed if he had not taken drink they will also find that his abnormality of mind had not substantially impaired his mental responsibility for his fatal acts'.[122] *Dietschmann* was not a case where the evidence was capable of establishing 'alcohol dependence syndrome', and

113 Ibid.
114 Law Com CP No. 19/08, 2008 (n 62) para 51; and see Coroners and Justice Bill Deb 3 February 2009 (n 17) (Maria Eagle).
115 Mackay (n 44).
116 J. Miles, 'A "Dog's Breakfast" of Homicide Reform' Archbold News, 2009, Issue 6. See also the speech of Baroness Murphy, HL Deb 30 June 2009, vol. 712, cols 178–81.
117 *Dietschmann* (n 85). See also *R v Hendy* [2006] Cr.App.R. 33.
118 Ibid. *Dietschmann* [18].
119 Ibid. [33].
120 MOJ Circ No 13, 2010 [8]. See also, HC Deb, 3 March 2009, 410.
121 (1975) 61 Cr App R 261.
122 *Dietschmann* (n 85) [34] (Lord Hutton).

the distinction between the aetiology of the abnormality of the mind (or an abnormality of mental functioning arising from a recognised medical condition), and a transient state of intoxication, needs to be kept in mind.[123]

Finally, the Advice of the Judicial Committee given by Lord Keith of Kinkel in *Walton*, [124] remains relevant, namely, that 'upon an issue of diminished responsibility the jury are entitled and indeed bound to consider not only the medical evidence but the evidence upon the whole facts and circumstances of the case'.[125]

Diminished responsibility, discretion and the 'benign conspiracy'

Concern has been expressed that the revised, tighter definition of diminished responsibility may reduce the potential usefulness of the defence as a way of giving judges discretion when sentencing persons who have killed, but who ought not to be stigmatised as 'murderers'.[126] The Law Commission referred to cases where a conviction for the murder could only be avoided by a 'benign conspiracy' between psychiatrists, the defence, the prosecution and the Court, to bring cases within the limits of diminished responsibility.[127]

The existing construction of the offences of murder and manslaughter remain untouched by the C and J Act 2009. The Act does not treat as an exception to the mandatory requirement to impose a sentence of life imprisonment for murder, those killings that occurred in extenuating circumstances. It is thus unlikely that the revised definition of diminished responsibility will see the end of the 'benign' practice that has (it is submitted) worked satisfactorily. The burden of proving the partial defence of diminished responsibility remains on the accused, and decisions by prosecutors to accept such a plea are not taken lightly.

The existence and exercise of discretion, within the criminal justice process, has much to commend it.[128] The use of discretion, exercised judiciously, is also apt to deal with borderline cases (for example, some 'mercy killing' cases, or where a jury is likely to be sympathetic to a defendant in any event, for example, the battered spouse who was suffering from post-traumatic stress disorder, or depression). The so-called 'benign conspiracy' is capable of bringing about a just and sensible conclusion to cases that warrant neither the label 'murder' nor a mandatory life sentence of imprisonment. The simplest way to end the 'benign conspiracy' is to end the mandatory sentence of life imprisonment in cases of murder.

Expert testimony on a plea of diminished responsibility

Although it is for the jury to decide whether the defendant's ability to do one or more of the things mentioned in new s.2(1A) HA 1957 was substantially impaired, it seems likely (as anticipated by the Law Commission in CP 173) that the medical expert will be expected to testify to the nature of the abnormality of mental functioning and 'from the medical viewpoint, whether it caused or materially contributed to the killing'.[129]

123 See, for example, *Tandy* [1989] 1 All ER 267; *Wood* (n 86); *Stewart* (n 87); and Sullivan (n 64).
124 [1978] AC 788, 793[F].
125 And see *Khan* (n 8), noting, in particular, the observations of the Court at para.18 of the judgment.
126 See, for example, Miles (n 116).
127 Law Com No 290, 2004 (n 38) para 2–34.
128 And see the debate of David Howarth MP, *Hansard*, March 3 2009, col. 412, HC.
129 Law Com No 173, 2003 (n 34) para.7.92; and see, Maria Eagle, Coroners and Justice Bill Deb (n 17) 415.

In response to the Law Commission's consultation on homicide, the Royal College of Psychiatrists said that 'Although it is common for the courts to accept, or even encourage a psychiatric expert to comment upon whether the defendant should be seen as "substantially impaired", the College believes that this should be resisted'.[130] However, it is submitted that, in practice, it will often be difficult in cases where diminished responsibility is raised, for psychiatrists not to express an opinion on the ultimate issue (as they often do). In any event, as the Court of Appeal pointed out in *R v Squelch*, [131] it was decided in *R v Brennan* (see below) that an expert psychiatrist may not only express an opinion on all four elements of the offence as set out in section 2 but also, if willing to do so, may express an opinion on the ultimate issue.

What is the position where the medical evidence is agreed or unchallenged that the defendant's responsibility for the killing was 'diminished' within the meaning of s.2 HA 1957? In *R v Brennan*, [132] B was convicted of murder. The jury rejected diminished responsibility. A consultant psychiatrist testified that, in her opinion, B suffered from schizotypal disorder and emotionally unstable personality disorder which would have substantially impaired his ability to form a rational judgment and to exercise self-control at the relevant time; and would have been a significant contributory factor in causing him to act in the way he did at the time. There was no expert evidence called by the Crown and the psychiatrist's evidence was not challenged although she was asked about features of B's behaviour indicative of a significant degree of pre-planning which the expert said might have appeared to be controlled but were the product of an abnormal mind. The Court allowed the appeal substituting a verdict of manslaughter. The case disclosed two relevant but potentially conflicting principles. The first is that in criminal trials, cases are decided by juries, not by experts. The second principle is that juries must base their conclusions on the evidence. No difficulty normally arises where there is a dispute as to the expert evidence: the jury decides. But, where there is 'no rational or proper basis for departing from uncontradicted and unchallenged expert evidence *then juries may not do so*'.[133] The issue was further considered by the UK Supreme Court in *Golds*, that said [correctly it is submitted; emphasis added]:

> 49. Given the answers of the psychiatrist in *Brennan* and the state of the evidence, it is clear that the Crown could not properly ask the jury to convict of murder unless it was to reject one or more parts of the expert evidence. *Certainly a jury is not bound by the expert …*
>
> *However, as the Court of Appeal rightly held, if the jury is to be invited to reject the expert opinion, some rational basis for doing so must at least be suggested, and none had been at trial nor was on appeal. It is not open to the Crown in this kind of situation simply to invite the jury to convict of murder without suggesting why the expert evidence ought not to be accepted. In particular, it would not have been a proper basis for rejecting diminished responsibility that the circumstances of the killing had been particularly violent or sadistic.* It is a well-known factor in such cases that such brutality may (understandably) be taken by a jury to point away from the partial defence; sometimes it may truly do so, but not infrequently it is the product of the mental disorder.

130 See Law Com No 304, 2006 (n 43) paras 5.118–120; and see *Khan* (n 8).
131 [2017] EWCA Crim 2004, at [53].
132 [2014] EWCA Crim 2387.
133 Ibid. [44] (Davis LJ).

50. It may be agreed that the ordinary principles of *R v Galbraith* are capable of being applied in a trial where the sole issue is diminished responsibility. A court ought, however, to be cautious about doing so, and for several reasons … That the judge may entertain little doubt about what he thinks the right verdict ought to be is not sufficient reason in this context, any more than in any other, for withdrawing from the jury issues which are properly theirs to decide.

51. Where, however, in a diminished responsibility trial the medical evidence supports the plea and is uncontradicted, the judge needs to ensure that the Crown explains the basis on which it is inviting the jury to reject that evidence … While he needs to make it clear to the jury that, if there is a proper basis for rejecting the expert evidence, the decision is theirs – that trial is by jury and not by expert – it will also ordinarily be wise to advise the jury against attempting to make themselves amateur psychiatrists, and that *if there is undisputed expert evidence the jury will probably wish to accept it, unless there is some identified reason for not doing so. To this extent, the approach of the court in Brennan is to be endorsed.*

In *R v Blackman*,[134] Lord Thomas CJ said [emphasis added]:

> It is important to note the emphasis in the *Golds* judgment not only on the prosecution's right (if not duty) to assess the medical evidence and to challenge it, where there is a rational basis for so doing, but also on the primacy of the jury in determining the issue. It is clear that a judge should exercise caution before accepting the defence of diminished responsibility and removing the case from the jury (see paragraph 50). The fact that the prosecution calls no evidence to contradict a psychiatrist called by the defence is not in itself sufficient justification for doing so. In the light of the judgment in *Golds*, we see no reason not to follow the broad approach of this court in *R v Khan (Dawood)* [2009] EWCA Crim 1569, [2010] 1 Cr App R 4, to which reference was made in *Brennan*, which we would express as follows: *it will be a rare case where a judge will exercise the power to withdraw a charge of murder from the jury when the prosecution do not accept that the evidence gives rise to the defence of diminished responsibility.*

Cited in *Brennan*, but not discussed in *Golds* or *Blackman*, is the decision of the Court of Appeal in *R v Bailey*[135] (cited in *Walton*[136]) where the Court of Criminal Appeal substituted a verdict of manslaughter for the jury's verdict of murder. Lord Parker C.J., delivering the judgment of the Court, said:

> This court has said on many occasions that of course juries are not bound by what the medical witnesses say, but at the same time they must act on evidence, and if there is nothing before them, no facts and no circumstances shown before them which throw doubt on the medical evidence, then that is all that they are left with, and the jury, in those circumstances, must accept it.

The current stance of policy-makers is to be more trusting of juries to reach the correct result on the evidence, and that trial judges should exercise caution before withdrawing a

134 [2017] EWCA Crim 190 [43].
135 [1961] Crim. L.R. 828
136 *Walton* (n 80).

case from the jury even if the judge entertains little doubt about what he thinks the right verdict should be. There is force in the point made by Karl Laird that judges may be reluctant to pre-empt the jury's evaluation of the final element of the partial defence of diminished responsibility, namely, whether the defendant's abnormality of mental functioning provides an explanation for his or her acts or omissions in respect of the killing.[137] However, the balance to be struck is the same now as it was in 1981 when *Galbraith* was decided by the Court of Appeal,[138] namely, 'on the one hand, a usurpation by the judge of the jury's functions and on the other, the danger of an unjust conviction.' Neither consideration must be lost sight of: in particular, the latter. Neither in *Golds*, nor in *Blackman*, was it said or suggested that the outcome of the appeal in *Brennan* (substituting a verdict of manslaughter for murder) was erroneous.

Concluding remarks

The reforms introduced by the C and JA 2009 in respect of the two partial defences to murder (diminished responsibility and loss of control) have given rise to complex legal arguments requiring guidance from the appellate courts. Ultimately, the purpose of those two partial defences is to provide flexibility of sentencing for a killing that might otherwise attract a mandatory life sentence of imprisonment for murder. Despite the reluctance shown by successive governments to reform and to codify rules relating to homicide, the case for a coherent and comprehensive code remains valid.

137 Laird (n 110) 14.
138 (1981) 73 Cr.App.R. 124.

7 Causing death

Sally Kyd

Introduction

> In cases of homicide, it is rarely necessary to give the jury any direction on causation as such. Of course, a necessary ingredient of the crimes of murder and manslaughter is that the accused has by his act caused the victim's death. But how the victim came by his death is usually not in dispute. What is in dispute is more likely to be some other matter: for example, the identity of the person who committed the act which indisputably caused the victim's death; or whether the accused had the necessary intent; or whether the accused acted in self-defence, or was provoked. Even where it is necessary to direct the jury's minds to the question of causation, it is usually enough to direct them simply that in law the accused's act need not be the sole cause, or even the main cause, of the victim's death, it being enough that his act contributed significantly to that result.[1]

The very essence of a homicide offence is that it involves the *causing* of death of a human being, usually by another human being.[2] In Coke's classic description of murder, this is signified by the use of the word *killeth*. Much could be said about the differences between 'killing' and 'causing death', but that will not be the focus of this chapter.[3] The importance of an unambiguous meaning of causation in cases of homicide leads to the question of whether a sufficiently clear understanding of the legal requirements of the doctrine can be identified. The further one strays from the paradigmatic offence of murder, the more knotted the issues become.[4] Where an alleged offender (D) is proven to have the intention to kill, this in itself will mean that the law will rarely operate to prevent the finding of liability based on lack of causation. However, without such *mens rea* corresponding to the *actus reus* and the final result of death required for homicide, there is more work to be done by causation in ensuring that D is sufficiently blameworthy to be attributed with the label of a killer. It might be suggested that the importance of causation bares an inverse relationship to the *mens rea* requirement of any homicide offence. That is to say, because murder requires an intention to kill or cause grievous bodily harm and it is this *mens rea* requirement that separates it from lesser forms of homicide, causation has less of a role to play in determining

1 *R. v Pagett* [1983] 76 Cr. App. R. 279 [288] (Goff LJ).
2 The one exception being corporate manslaughter.
3 For a discussion of the distinction, see G. Fletcher, *Rethinking Criminal Law* (Oxford University Press 2000) 235 and M. Moore, *Causation and Responsibility: An Essay in Law, Morals and Metaphysics* (Oxford University Press 2009) 5–16.
4 For an exploration of the role of causation in criminal law generally, in comparison to tort law, see S. Steel, 'Causation in Tort Law and Criminal Law: Unity or Divergence?' in M. Dyson (ed.), *Unravelling Tort and Crime* (Cambridge University Press 2014) 239–73.

liability where such *mens rea* can be proved. Where constructive crimes are concerned, however, particularly those involving offences requiring minimal if any *mens rea*, establishing causation becomes essential to establishing sufficient blameworthiness on the part of D to be held liable for the death.

This chapter starts with a discussion of the law and theory of causation in relation to murder as the paradigmatic homicide offence, before moving on to consider the law in relation to constructive homicide offences, where the lack of *mens rea* relating to the causing of death causes problems of attribution. Lastly, gross negligence manslaughter and matters relating to causation are examined, with particular attention paid to issues arising from liability based on omission. The chapter is limited to the offences of murder, involuntary manslaughter and statutory causing death by driving offences committed by a principal offender. What is not covered are the requirements, if any, of causation in relation to other statutory 'homicide' offences such as causing or allowing the death of a child or vulnerable adult[5] or corporate manslaughter,[6] or murder or manslaughter committed by a secondary party.[7] That said, causation has traditionally formed part of what is considered the 'general part' of the criminal law, and the attempts of commentators to draw out rational principles of causation have largely related to result crimes in general, rather than being restricted to homicide. In some respects, there is little reason to limit what is said here to the homicide offences under discussion, but in recent years the universal nature of principles of causation has been questioned: 'causation is not a single, unvarying concept to be mechanically applied without regard to the context in which the question arises'.[8] The context in which a death is caused, and the *mens rea* requirements of the alleged offence, unavoidably affect judgments of whether D has caused the death of V.[9] The law is currently lacking in providing clear limitations as to when a death can be attributed to a particular act, and the chapter ends with a suggestion as how this might be rectified.

Murder

As noted by Lord Justice Goff in the quotation at the start of this chapter, causation is rarely the element of a case on which liability for homicide turns and is not often an aspect taking up much of the court's time, particularly where the case is one of murder. Denial of liability is more likely to be based on lack of *mens rea*, or a defence such as self-defence.[10] Where

5 The 'Offence' under Domestic Violence, Crime and Victims Act 2004, s.5.
6 Corporate Manslaughter and Corporate Homicide Act 2007.
7 See chapter 4 by J.J. Child and G.R. Sullivan in this volume.
8 *Kennedy (No.2)* [2008] 1 A.C. 269 [15] (Lord Bingham).
9 Simester argues, however, that whether D's intentions are relevant to causation will depend on whether causation is direct or indirect. Direct causation, where we can trace a series of physical reactions from cause to effect, is non-normative. Where causation is indirect, on the other hand, we must bridge the gaps between D's act and the end result in order to attribute causation and, in doing so, we are involved in a normative exercise in which D's *mens rea* may be relevant: A.P. Simester, 'Causation in (Criminal) Law' (2017) 133 Law Quarterly Review 416–41.
10 See B. Mitchell and S. Cunningham, 'Defences to Murder' in Law Commission, *Murder, Manslaughter and Infanticide* (Law Com No 304, 2006) Appendix C. The claim that lack of causation is rarely argued is difficult to substantiate and is not empirically proven, but in Mitchell and Cunningham's study of 93 cases of murder and manslaughter dealt with by the courts in 1995–1996, denial of responsibility due to lack of causation was rarely argued. However, any case where such argument was successful would by its very nature not have fallen within the sample of cases examined.

mens rea is admitted or can be proved, it is likely that causation can similarly be made out. In the leading text on causation, Hart and Honoré quote with approval a commentary on an American case: 'As the seriousness of the defendant's act increases, not only in the danger to life which it creates but also in the viciousness of the intent with which it is committed, the legal eye follows its consequences farther and farther'.[11] They later cite (albeit with a certain degree of disapproval) Turner, who said, 'Under the modern concept of *mens rea* no hardship can result from any fine drawn investigation of causes, since the more remote the cause the greater the difficulty of proving that the accused person intended or realised what the effect of it would be'.[12] Thus, those who have not caused death are unlikely to be held liable for murder as the case against them is likely to fail due to lack of proof of *mens rea*.

Hart and Honoré note, however, that the idea that principles of causation are not needed in criminal law due to the requirement of *mens rea* does not apply for all offences, particularly statutory offences, which do not require the *mens rea* of intention or recklessness.[13] This is even truer today, as exemplified in the following section relating to causing death by driving offences. The cases on causation do provide some support, however, for Turner's proposition, given that in cases where the *mens rea* for murder has been found, it is rare for an appeal against conviction to be allowed on the basis that D did not *cause* the victim's death. This might occur in rare cases reflecting the examples provided by Hart and Honoré, involving V being struck by a falling tree on his way to hospital, or a nurse who 'takes pity' on V and euthanises him,[14] but what is suggested is that where *mens rea* is present and but-for causation is found, causation will be established in the absence of any *novus actus interveniens* breaking the chain of causation.

This can be seen in cases well-known to law undergraduates from lectures on causation in criminal law, starting with those on the question of whether the act of a third party will be seen to have broken the chain of causation. Cases such as *Smith*, [15]*Cheshire* [16] and *Mellor* [17] show that where D attacks V with intent to do at least grievous bodily harm, D will be liable for murder even where the most immediate cause of death appears to be the negligence of medical practitioners, with the one exception being the arguably anomalous case of *Jordan*.[18] The reasons for this are clear: a violent and blameworthy D should not escape liability due to V receiving sub-standard medical treatment, particularly in current times where the National Health Service is stretched to breaking point.

To suggest otherwise would have the knock-on effect of casting doubt on another principle of causation: the thin-skull rule. As confirmed in cases such as *Dear* [19] and *Blaue*, [20] D must take V as D finds V, both in mind and body. D will therefore be liable for murder where D attacks V with malice aforethought and V dies in circumstances in which some other victim might have survived. This is to focus on D's blameworthiness. D should not escape liability where V suffers from a rare condition increasing the chances of death in the

11 H.L.A. Hart and T. Honoré, *Causation in the Law* (2nd edn, Oxford University Press 1985) 99–100 citing an extended comment on *Stephenson v. the State* by G.C.T. in (1933) 31 Mich. L.R. 675–76.

12 J.W.C. Turner, *Kenny's Outlines of Criminal Law* (16th edn, Cambridge University Press 1952) 20–1, cited in Hart and Honoré (n 11) 390.

13 ibid

14 Hart and Honoré (n 11) 391.

15 [1959] 2 Q.B. 35.

16 [1991] 93 Cr. App. R. 251.

17 [1996] 2 Cr. App. R. 245.

18 [1956] 40 Cr. App. R. 152

19 [1996] Crim. L.R. 595.

20 [1975] 61 Cr. App. R. 271

same way as D should not escape liability where V could have been saved were it not for the incompetence of those treating V. D does not have control over these matters, just as D does not have control over e.g., whether V, whom D has left for dead in remote woodland, will be found by a local dog-walker and rushed to hospital. Where V is fortunate enough to be discovered in this way, receiving appropriate care allowing for V's survival, D clearly cannot be held liable for murder as D has not caused death. But where V is left without medical treatment for whatever reason, or receives treatment to no avail due to an underlying condition leading to complications in V's care, or receives negligent medical treatment, D's intention to cause at least grievous bodily harm will ensure D's conviction for murder.[21]

This approach to causation might be more palatable if it were not for the 'GBH rule', however. The weight given to the presence of *mens rea* in determining causation can justifiably be heavier where D intended to cause the harm which actually resulted. It is far more difficult to justify causation being determined by the presence of *mens rea* where that *mens rea* breaches the principle of correspondence and does not relate to the harm actually suffered. This is the present position in the law of murder, whereby malice aforethought has been confirmed to include an intention to cause grievous bodily harm (GBH), as well as an intention to kill.[22] If murder required intention to kill, then where it was obvious that D did in fact intend to kill and where death had resulted, it would be far easier to justify conviction for murder even where there were other competing contributions to death, such as the act of a third party or a pre-existing medical condition. But to convict for murder a defendant who intended serious harm less than death in circumstances where, were it not for extreme bad luck, V would have survived, appears harsh.

Before the confirmation of the validity of the GBH rule in *Cunningham*, Lord Diplock had in *Hyam* [23] examined the rationale behind the continued application of the rule, noting that at the time the GBH rule was established:

> Medical and surgical science were in a very primitive state. Any bodily injury, particularly if it involved risk of sepsis through an open wound, might well prove mortal although today the likelihood of its resulting in death would be insignificant. It was not until the last quarter of the 19th century that antiseptics came into general use.[24]

The relevance of this point was questioned by Lord Hailsham in *Cunningham*, where he doubted whether the influence of advances in medical care would be sufficient to prompt a change in the law. It is the case, however, that such medical advances have since been acknowledged by a change in the law in the form of the Law Reform (Year and A Day Rule) Act 1996 which abolished the year and a day rule. This rule had been in existence since at least the Middle Ages,[25] preventing a prosecution for murder in cases where V's death occurred more than a year and a day after D's act.

21 The conviction in *Blaue* (n 20) was for manslaughter rather than murder, but this was on the basis of diminished responsibility rather than lack of malice aforethought. Simester argues that causation is established in *Blaue* not because of D's intention but simply due to mechanical causation being present, stating that omissions cannot break the causal chain. See Simester (n 9) 439–40.

22 *R v Cunningham* [1982] AC 566.

23 [1975] A.C. 55.

24 Ibid. [90] (Lord Diplock).

25 Law Commission *Legislating the Criminal Code: The Year and a Day Rule in Homicide* (Law Com. No. 230, 1995) para.2.4 <https://s3-eu-west-2.amazonaws.com/lawcom-prod-storage-11jsxou24uy7q/uploads/2015/06/lc230.pdf> accessed 25 December 2017

The year and a day rule was not confined to murder, but extended to other homicide offences, and its purpose was to ensure that causation was established between D's act and V's death. This can be seen in the case of *Dyson*:[26]

> ... it is still undoubtedly the law of the land that no person can be convicted of manslaughter where the death does not occur within a year and a day after the injury was inflicted, for in that event it must be attributed to some other cause. [27]

The Law Commission notes that in *Dyson* the Court of Appeal appeared to turn what was probably a question of fact for the jury into an irrebuttable presumption that where death occurred more than 366 days after D's act, D did not cause the death.[28] Having posed the question of whether problems with proving causation should prevent the removal of the rule, the Law Commission received no responses suggesting it should, and decided that the rule could be abolished, concluding that:

> With the advance of modern medical science it is normally possible to ascertain the cause of a death, and in particular to point to a specific cause which may have arisen some years earlier.
>
> ... In consequence, the rule operates to prevent convictions when the cause of death could otherwise be shown, to the required standard of proof, to be a wrongful act which occurred more than a year and a day before the death. In cases where the prosecution cannot satisfy the burden of proving causation, the abolition of the rule would not lead to injustice because a verdict of not guilty would have to be entered.[29]

The change in the law resulting from the Law Reform (Year and a Day Rule) Act 1996 does not appear to have proved problematic in terms of causation. An example of how the change in law has allowed for successful prosecutions relying on ordinary principles of causation can be seen in the case of *Clift.* [30] D caused a catastrophic brain injury to V in 2000, when he attacked V and plunged a screwdriver into V's head. V initially survived the attack and in 2002 D was convicted for an offence of causing grievous bodily harm with intent under s.18 of the Offences Against the Person Act 1861. He was sentenced to ten years' imprisonment, and was released in 2007. Until 2009 V was fed through a tube and was reliant on carers, but that year he died after complications developed following a medical procedure to reinsert the feeding tube. The post-mortem concluded that the original attack and the death were connected, providing evidence of causation sufficient to see D convicted of murder. This was the only additional factor to be proven, given that the Court of Appeal confirmed that D's conviction under s.18 could be adduced to provide evidence that D intended to cause GBH and thus had the necessary *mens rea* for murder. D's minimum term was set at six years, given that D had already been sentenced to ten years for GBH. The case was conjoined with that of *Harrison*, a case with similar facts of V dying some time after suffering a brain injury at the hands of D, with D already having been imprisoned for an offence under s.18. Harrison's conviction for murder was similarly upheld.

26 [1908] 2 K.B. 454.
27 Ibid. [456].
28 Law Com (n 25) para.2.7.
29 Ibid., para. 4.20.
30 [2013] 1 Cr. App. R. 15.

Another case is that of *Keane* [31] where D again caused a brain injury, this time without a weapon other than a shod foot, and V developed post-traumatic epilepsy as a result. The assault took place in 2011, leading to D's conviction under s.18 in 2012. V subsequently died in 2013, having suffered an epileptic seizure, and D was convicted of murder in 2015. At the murder trial, it was accepted that D had caused the brain injury leading to the post-traumatic epilepsy but the defence case was that the prosecution could not prove that the post-traumatic epilepsy had caused death. Having heard evidence from medical experts including a neuropathologist, who concluded that in view of the history of epilepsy and the deceased's failure to self-medicate properly, and of the circumstances in which he died, the diagnosis of death from epilepsy was sound, the jury rejected the defence case and convicted D of murder. The time he had served for the s.18 offence was taken into account by the judge when setting the minimum term of imprisonment as part of his life sentence, and his appeal against conviction was dismissed by the Court of Appeal.

Some might not feel any opposition to the convictions for murder in these cases. It was perhaps lucky that the deceased in both cases had survived the initial assault; lucky that the deceased in *Keane* had not died from the first epileptic seizure he suffered; lucky that advancements in medical treatment had been able to keep the deceased in *Clift* alive for nearly a decade. Why should D benefit from that luck by avoiding conviction for murder once the true extent of the consequences of the assault arose?[32] There appears little doubt in these cases that the defendants' acts were both operating and substantial causes of the victims' deaths, and were not merely part of the history of the cases. The sentences clearly took into account the time already served for the earlier convictions for GBH.[33] Had the appellants intended to kill there would be little to object to. The cases serve primarily to underline the degree to which the GBH rule relies on luck to establish liability for murder in general.[34]

Constructive homicide: manslaughter and causing death by driving

Beyond murder, which at least requires D to have *mens rea* in relation to causing a serious degree of physical harm, constructive homicide offences arguably place greater reliance on the doctrine of causation in order to establish sufficient blameworthiness on the part of D to be attributed with V's death. As argued by Hart and Honoré, if the law enabling conviction based on constructive liability is to be retained, 'some relationship between act and harm sufficient for responsibility is required which does not depend on accused's knowledge or belief'.[35] The development of new statutory driving offences causing death has in recent

31 [2016] EWCA Crim 2018.

32 It is beyond the scope of this chapter to answer this question which is, arguably, a matter of instinct. For opposing views on the role of moral luck in criminal liability see e.g., J. Horder, 'A Critique of the Correspondence Principle in Criminal Law' (1995) Criminal Law Review, 759–70 and A. Ashworth, 'Change of Normative Position: Determining the Contours of Culpability in Criminal Law' (2008) 11 New Criminal Law Review 232–56.

33 Simester acknowledges that mechanical causation is the primary vehicle for allocating moral luck, leading him to suggest that this effect on culpability should be reflected in sentencing: Simester (n 9) 423–24.

34 For criticisms of the GBH rule see: Law Commission, *A New Homicide Act for England and Wales?* (Law Com CP Paper No 177, 2005) paras.3.29–3.39 < https://s3-eu-west-2.amazonaws.com/lawcom-prod-storage-11jsxou24uy7q/uploads/2015/03/cp177_Murder_Manslaughter_and_Infanticide_consultation_overview_.pdf> accessed 25 December 2017

35 Hart and Honoré (n 11) 393.

years raised questions as to the existence of such a relationship in some cases. Before turning to these statutory offences we will first examine the role of causation in establishing liability for common law constructive manslaughter.

Constructive manslaughter

One of the leading cases on causation in criminal law, *Kennedy (No.2),* [36] is, of course, a case of constructive manslaughter. This was the case in which the House of Lords finally clarified whether the act of a drug-user, in taking drugs supplied to them by the defendant, broke the chain of causation between the supply of drugs and their own death by self-injecting the drugs. Full endorsement was given to Hart and Honoré's maxim that:

> The free, deliberate, and informed intervention of a second person, who intends to exploit the situation created by the first, but is not acting in concert with him, is normally held to relieve the first actor of criminal responsibility.[37]

The decision in *Kennedy (No.2)* operates to limit the liability of those who supply drugs, requiring them to be involved in a joint administration of the drug before they can be said to have caused death. Whatever the desirability of creating a special homicide offence for suppliers of drugs,[38] the decision does at least bring some clarity to the law and helps, to some degree, to limit the extent to which D can be held liable for manslaughter based on an unlawful and dangerous act subsequent to which D has exerted little control over the consequences. It rejected the approach to causation taken by the House of Lords in the case of *Environment Agency v Empress Car Co (Abertillery) Ltd,* [39] a case involving a strict liability offence of pollution, where it was held that only an extraordinary event would break the chain of causation. In comparison to this, in cases of manslaughter involving joint administration, D's *mens rea* for the underlying offence of administering a noxious substance under s.23 of the Offences Against the Person Act 1861 does at least require subjective foresight of physical harm. This is in turn a step closer to the result of death compared to the alternative of supplying a class A drug, an offence which requires no *mens rea* pertaining to the causing of harm. Although it can be argued that the ultimate harm prevented by the offence of supplying controlled drugs is death, such an act is not proximate enough for any ensuing death to be attributable to the individual supplier, however objectionable such an individual's moral outlook might be. The law on causation as set out in *Kennedy (No.2)* enables those on the periphery of the arc of liability for homicide, who have minimal, if any, control over events that follow on from their unlawful act, to be excluded from liability.

That is not to say that a defendant cannot be held liable for manslaughter having committed an unlawful and dangerous act with little control over the consequences. So long as the unlawful and dangerous act causes death, D will face liability for such consequences. The thin-skull rule, discussed above, can have the effect of transforming what might otherwise be

36 *Kennedy (No.2)* (n 8).
37 Hart and Honoré (n 11) 326.
38 See, for example, W. Wilson, 'Dealing with Drug Induced Homicide' in C. Clarkson and S. Cunningham (eds) *Criminal Liability for Non-Aggressive Death* (Ashgate 2008); C. Elliott and C. de Than, 'Prosecuting the Drug Dealer When a Drug User Dies' (2006) 69 Modern Law Review 986–95; T. Jones, 'Causation, Homicide and the Supply of Drugs' (2006) 26 Legal Studies 139.
39 [1999] 2 A.C. 22.

a minor assault (or affray) into an offence of homicide. This can be seen in cases such as *R v M*, [40] where V, a doorman, suffered an aneurysm as a result of dealing with an affray. In *Carey* [41] on the other hand, D's conviction for manslaughter was quashed where it was found that D's unlawful act of affray was not dangerous in the sense required by the test in *Church*. [42] What is puzzling about this case, however, is that the Court of Appeal also claimed that although D had assaulted V, the assault could not be said to be a cause of death. V, a young girl, suffered a heart attack after running away from an altercation. As noted by Ormerod, there seems no reason why the thin-skull rule would not apply to convict D of manslaughter. One explanation that might be offered is that factual causation could be difficult to prove; after being confronted by D, V may have run away, causing her heart attack, even if she had not been punched. This was the reasoning in the case of *R v DJ* [43] where the Ds committed battery against V by throwing stones at him, but it may have been that V would have suffered a heart attack as a result of the incident, which involved verbal abuse and spitting, even in the absence of stone-throwing. These last two cases act to soften somewhat the harshness of the law of unlawful act manslaughter, highlighting the need for prosecutors to ensure that the elements of *actus reus* of an identifiable unlawful act, which is objectively dangerous in creating an obvious risk of physical harm, and which is also both a factual and legal cause of death, all coincide to enable conviction.

The law remains harsh though in other circumstances, allowing for conviction for manslaughter as a result of the most minor of offences. Where but-for causation can be shown, V's own act will only break the chain of causation where it is free, deliberate and informed, as per Hart and Honoré. Where V increases the risk of D's dangerous act by reacting in a way that exacerbates the situation, D may be liable for manslaughter on the grounds of what might otherwise have been a minor assault, so long as V's response to D's act was reasonably foreseeable. Thus, in *Lewis* [44] an incident of road rage resulted in a manslaughter conviction where D had remonstrated with a group of inebriated students who had impeded his progress in his car. Having got out of his car it appears that he may have pushed a female student, whose brother, V, retaliated by pushing or punching D (although even here the witness evidence was inconsistent). V then ran away into the road, chased by D, and V was struck by an oncoming car and died. It was alleged by the prosecution that D had committed at least one of two unlawful acts by giving chase: either a technical assault or, if V was unaware that D was chasing him when he ran off, attempted battery.[45]

The Court of Appeal upheld D's conviction for manslaughter, relying on the decision in *Williams and Davis* [46] which deals with the issue of V's own act possibly breaking the chain

40 [2013] 1 Cr. App. R. 10.
41 [2006] EWCA Crim 17.
42 [1966] 1 Q.B. 59.
43 [2007] EWCA Crim 3133.
44 [2010] EWCA Crim 151.
45 It was argued on the appellant's behalf that the attempted battery should not have been left to the jury, on the basis that it opened up the possibility of the jury convicting of manslaughter in the absence of causation. If V was not aware of D chasing him (the reason for attempted battery being argued) then surely it could not be the case that D had caused V to run into the car, and so could not have caused his death. This argument was rejected by the Court of Appeal on the basis that the trial judge had made it clear that the jury could only convict if they found that D had chased V and in doing so had committed an unlawful act that caused death. It seems though, that the attempted battery argument had no place in this case since if D had committed only an attempted battery and not an assault, causation was not present.
46 *R v Williams and Davis* [1992] 1 WLR 380.

of causation between D's unlawful act and V's death in the case of manslaughter.[47] In that case V had jumped out of a moving car in order to escape some sort of attack on the part of the defendants, and had suffered fatal head injuries. Stuart-Smith L.J. stated:

> … the nature of the threat is of importance in considering both the foreseeability of harm to the victim from the threat and the question whether the deceased's conduct was proportionate to the threat; that is to say that it was within the ambit of reasonableness and not so daft as to make it his own voluntary act which amounted to a novus actus interveniens and consequently broke the chain of causation. It should of course be borne in mind that a victim may in the agony of the moment do the wrong thing.[48]

This was applied in *Lewis* by the court identifying two issues to be addressed in establishing causation in a case of constructive manslaughter. The first is but-for causation, expressed by Pitchford L.J. as requiring 'cause and effect'. The second is that 'the nature of the flight or escape proved must be a foreseeable consequence of the unlawful act; in more familiar language, it was not so daft as to make it the deceased's own voluntary act which intervened to break the chain of causation'.[49] Despite V's drunken state (V was found to have a blood alcohol concentration of 168mg per 100ml blood), which the jury were told to factor in to their considerations, the jury found that his response was within the range to be expected, and returned a verdict of guilty.

Causing death by driving

Other constructive homicide offences rely equally on causation as an essential element in establishing liability, and in such cases where *mens rea* is not required as to the causing of any physical harm, let alone death, the courts can be seen to be taking a policy approach to questions of causation. It was seen in the section above on murder (pp.120–124) that where D has the *mens rea* of an offence then causation is likely to be established unless the chain of causation is broken. But what of offences of strict liability not requiring any *mens rea*? Constructive manslaughter at least requires D to have the *mens rea* of the underlying offence, which is likely to involve some form of cognitive *mens rea* given that the unlawful act cannot be one which is lawful unless negligently performed, according to *Andrews v DPP*. [50] It was as a result of this, and the suggestion that juries were reluctant to convict drivers of gross negligence manslaughter due to a mentality of 'there but for the grace of God go I', that Parliament created the constructive offence of causing death by dangerous driving.[51] This offence has given rise to a number of cases dealing with the issue of causation, establishing that D's driving must be more than a trifling or *de minimis* cause of death.[52]

The Court of Appeal in *Girdler* held that a test akin to that applied in cases of negligence in tort law ought to be imported in the application of causing death by driving, which 'places an outside limit on the culpability of a driver in circumstances where there is more than a trifling link between the dangerous (or careless) driving and a death. It seeks to

47 Applying *Roberts* [1972] 56 Cr App R 95.
48 *Williams and Davis* (n 46) 388–89.
49 *Lewis* (n 44) [25].
50 [1937] AC 576.
51 See S. Cunningham, *Driving Offences: Law, Policy and Practice* (Ashgate 2008) 97.
52 *Hennigan* [1971] 55 Cr. App. R. 262.

exclude consequences which are simply "too remote" from the driver's culpable conduct'.[53] In that case, the defendant's car collided with a taxi on a three-lane dual carriageway. The taxi was propelled into the fast lane where it came to rest broadside on to approaching traffic. Some cars avoided the taxi, but one collided with it, killing both its driver and the taxi driver. It was clear that the defendant's driving had set off a chain of events which resulted in a fatal collision, but the question was whether the deceased driver's own bad driving broke the chain of causation. In seeking an appropriate test, Hooper L.J. distinguished the offence under consideration from that in *Empress*, arguing that although Lord Hoffmann had rejected a test of reasonable foreseeability in that case due to it being too favourable to the defendant, causing death by dangerous driving is not an offence of strict liability and such a test was appropriate. However, he was clear that the decision should be confined to cases of causing death by driving: 'We bear in mind that Lord Bingham, in *R. v Kennedy* [2008] 1 A.C. 269, said ... (at [33]...) that, "The House was not in [*Empress*] purporting to lay down general rules governing causation in criminal law".'[54]

Causing death by dangerous driving does not require cognitive *mens rea*, but it does at least require normative *mens rea* in the form of negligence – dangerous driving – and is not an offence of strict liability. One of the effects of *Kennedy (No.2)* was to restrict the effect of *Empress*, which seemingly allows for an offence to be proved based on but-for causation alone, to offences of strict liability. Many strict liability offences are regulatory in nature, often applying to corporate bodies and resulting in a fine rather than some harsher punishment. It would defeat their object if fault was needed to be proved, and as such it is commonly accepted that only an extraordinary act should break the chain of causation between an act of the defendant and the prohibited harm. But what of a homicide offence constructed from a regulatory offence? Should a driver be liable for killing where the death resulted from commission of a strict liability offence not requiring even negligence on the part of D?

The answer came with the Supreme Court decision in *Hughes*, [55] in which the court was tasked with analysing the offence of causing death by driving whilst unlicensed, uninsured or disqualified under s.3ZB Road Traffic Act 1988 (RTA 1988), created by Parliament in 2006.[56] The underlying documentary offences upon which this homicide offence is constructed are all offences of strict liability: it need not be proved that D knew D was driving without insurance, other than in accordance with a licence, or was disqualified. The Home Office, in proposing creation of the offence, suggested that some degree of causation would be needed to be proved, but implied that this need be no more than but-for causation:

> The offence will apply where "but for" the defendant's car being on the road the person would not have been killed. For example, if the defendant caused a ten car pile up then he could be charged in relation to the death of a person in the tenth car, even though he might not have made contact with that car. Conversely, if he was unavoidably involved in the pile up but it would have occurred even if he had not been present, then he could not be held responsible for any deaths.[57]

53 *Girdler* [2010] RTR 28 [37].
54 Ibid. [42].
55 [2013] UKSC 56.
56 Road Safety Act 2006, s.21.
57 Home Office, *A Summary and Next Steps: The Review of Road Traffic Offences Involving Bad Driving*, (2005) 8.

The question is what it means for D to have 'caused' a ten car pile-up in this scenario? Fatal road traffic collisions are often the result of a number of factors converging to create a tragic outcome, as can be seen in *Girdler*. In other cases the fault for a collision can easily be attributed to one particular driver, but what if that driver is the person killed?

In *Hughes*, in which the Supreme Court was faced with determining the meaning of causation in relation to the s.3ZB offence, it was clear that responsibility for the crash lay squarely with the deceased, in the sense that he had been driving whilst under the influence of drugs and whilst fatigued, and had swerved onto the wrong side of the road. D, driving his camper van in the opposite direction, could not have avoided the collision at that moment, and his driving could not be criticised. Consequently, the trial judge ruled that D could not be liable on the facts of the case; the Crown then appealed against this decision to the Court of Appeal. The Court of Appeal ordered that D's trial resume,[58] applying the outcome of *Williams* [59] which had been decided shortly before, and which held that an unlicensed and uninsured driver could be liable for death under s.3ZB on the basis that he could have avoided the collision by not being on the road when he should not have been. This was pure *sine qua non* or but-for causation, coming under heavy criticism from Simester and Sullivan.[60]

The Supreme Court agreed with such criticisms[61] and rejected the approach of the Court of Appeal, and the argument of the Crown that D could be said to have caused another's death whenever he is on the road at the wheel and a fatal incident involving his vehicle occurs:

> To give effect to the words "causes … death … by driving" there must be something more than "but for" causation. If causing death by driving cannot be constituted simply by being involved in a fatal collision, it would be contrary to the common law's common sense approach to agony of the moment situations for it to be constituted by (for example) a desperate last-millisecond attempt to swerve out of the way of the oncoming vehicle of such as [the deceased]. Once this is accepted, there is no stopping point short of some act or omission in the driving which is open to criticism, i.e. which involves some element of fault. [The appellant's] concession in the present case proves, on close inspection, to go further than it should. The statutory expression cannot, we conclude, be given effect unless there is something properly to be criticised in the driving of the defendant, which contributed in some more than minimal way to the death.[62]

Thus, whilst it has been thought that in offences such as murder, the fault demonstrated by D in harbouring *mens rea* of the offence enables the finding of causation, in the absence of any *mens rea* requirement for an offence the courts have had to inject a requirement of fault into the test for causation itself. Causation is a general principle of criminal law, usually understood to fall under the *actus reus* requirements of an offence: D must *cause death* to be liable for homicide. Additionally, for D to be liable for a serious offence it has traditionally

58 *H* [2011] EWCA Crim 1508.
59 [2010] EWCA Crim 2552.
60 G.R. Sullivan and A.P. Simester, 'Causation Without Limits: Causing Death While Driving Without a Licence, While Disqualified, or Without Insurance' (2012) 10 Criminal Law Review 753–76; A.P. Simester and G.R. Sullivan, 'Being There' (2012) 71(1) Criminal Law Journal 29–32.
61 *Hughes* (n 55) [29].
62 Ibid. [32].

been required that the prosecution prove *mens rea* and lack of defence where one is raised, in order to establish fault. But here, in the case of a strict liability homicide offence created by Parliament, the Supreme Court is saying that the *actus reus* of causing death in and of itself requires proof of fault.

The way in which the executive branch of government envisaged the offence under s.3ZB, as set out in the quotation from the Home Office above, has been frustrated by the judiciary. There seems little doubt that when the offence was proposed it was on the basis that but-for causation would be sufficient to establish liability. Given that the offence was unique in its construction, in that it creates a homicide offence out of one of three strict liability regulatory offences, there was arguably no way of knowing how the courts might interpret the requirement of causation in such an offence. However, in order to give effect to its desire to see illicit drivers held liable for their involvement in fatal collisions Parliament could, as noted by the Supreme Court, have used language already in operation in relation to other offences where causation is not required. One example given is the offence under s.170 of the RTA 1988, which is committed where D fails to stop following an accident which occurs 'owing to the presence' of D's vehicle. Prior to the Supreme Court decision in *Hughes* it had been suggested by Crown prosecutors that the wording 'owing to the presence' would have been far less ambiguous if used in s.3ZB and would have made their lives easier in knowing when it was appropriate to charge under s.3ZB.[63] They are now faced with the challenge of understanding how best to make use of a statutory offence which overlaps considerably with the offence of causing death by careless driving, in that it requires proof of driving which was open to criticism, although not to the extent that it fell below the standard of a competent and careful driver (the definition of careless driving).[64]

Since *Hughes* was decided, two developments have occurred relevant to this last point. First, the offence of causing death by driving whilst disqualified has been separated from s.3ZB, giving rise to a maximum penalty of ten years' imprisonment under s.3ZC RTA 1988.[65] This may affect charging practice given that the maximum penalty for causing death by careless driving is half that, meaning that prosecutors may see a benefit to charging s.3ZC even where careless driving can be proved, since it is, in punishment terms, a more serious offence. Second, the suggestion that the wording 'owing to the presence of a vehicle' would have been more effective in achieving the government's aims in creating the offence has been undermined by the case of *Taylor*.[66] This case applied the reasoning in *Hughes* to the offence under s.12A(2)(b) of the Theft Act 1968,[67] according to which a person is guilty of aggravated vehicle-taking if, owing to the driving of the relevant vehicle, an accident occurred by which injury or death was caused to any person. In *Taylor* there was no fault found in the manner of D's driving of the stolen vehicle,[68] and the Supreme Court quashed D's conviction, ruling that there must be something properly to be criticised in the manner of the defendant's driving in order for him to commit the offence. This came despite the

63 See S. Kyd Cunningham, 'Has Law Reform Policy Been Driven in the Right Direction? How the New Causing Death by Driving Offences are Operating in Practice' (2013) 9 Criminal Law Review 711–28, 722.

64 Road Traffic Act 1988, s.3ZA.

65 Inserted by Criminal Justice and Courts Act 2015, s.29.

66 *R v Taylor* [2016] UKSC 5.

67 Inserted by Aggravated Vehicle Taking Act 1992, s.1.

68 Although the defendant was drink-driving, the court focused narrowly on the manner of his driving and found that there was no fault.

Court of Appeal decision of *Marsh* [69] having been followed for almost two decades, establishing that no requirement of fault in D's driving was required to prove the offence. In *Hughes* the Supreme Court had stated:

> Whilst there might be some force in the contention that the expression "owing to the driving of the vehicle" imports an element of causation similar to that involved in "causing … death … by driving", the point was not argued before us and should be left open. It does not assist the construction of the present statute to compare it with different words of a different statute creating a different type of offence.[70]

That point is now closed, following *Taylor*. However, the Supreme Court's judgment is rather perplexing, in that it appears to conflate two separate issues: whether D had caused V's death and whether the offence was one of strict liability or not.[71] The issue of causation is dealt with in *Hughes* by importing a requirement of fault into the test for causation; this is then dealt with in *Taylor* as a question of whether the offence is one of strict liability or not. Whilst the effects of both decisions are widely welcomed for injecting some general principles of criminal law into draconian statutory offences, the way in which the courts have been forced into doing so, as a result of legislation being passed that on the face of it ignores such principles, has not helped in cementing clear and unambiguous legal rules of causation.

Gross negligence manslaughter

If the statutory causing death by driving offences did not exist, bad driving causing death would have to be prosecuted under the common law of gross negligence manslaughter (GNM), where at least gross negligence as to death is required to be proved as a form of normative *mens rea*. The leading case on GNM, *Adomako*, [72] requires firstly that D owes V a duty of care; second that D breached that duty; third that the breach *caused* death; and finally that D's breach of duty is to be categorised as gross negligence and therefore a crime. The breach of duty could take the form of a positive act, or of an omission. Particular issues arise with proof of causation in the case of a failure to act. In many cases it may not be particularly easy to characterise D's contribution as either an act or an omission, and a breach of duty can often be framed as both.[73] In fact, Leavens posits that '[t]he better approach is to eschew the doctrinal distinction between acts and omissions and instead simply inquire whether the actor's conduct caused the harm proscribed'.[74] However, English law has not eschewed this distinction and a duty to act must be established before D can be held liable for having caused death by failure to act.

Where it is clear that D has failed to act and owed a duty to act, how can it be said that D has caused V's death by doing nothing, or by not doing enough? Commentators trying to

69 [1997] 1 Cr. App. R. 67.
70 *Hughes* (n 55) [34].
71 S. Kyd, T. Elliott and M. Walters, *Clarkson and Keating: Criminal Law: Text and Materials* (9th edn, Sweet and Maxwell 2017) para. 3–005.
72 [1995] 1 A.C. 171.
73 See the discussion of the Californian case of *Barber* (*Barber v. Superior Court* 147 Cal. App. 3d 1006, 195 Cal. Rptr. 484 [1983]) in A. Leavens, 'A Causation Approach to Criminal Omissions' (1988) 76 Californian Law Review 547, 584–87, which shares many similarities with the English case of *Airedale NHS Trust v Bland* [1993] A.C. 789.
74 Ibid., 591.

tackle this from a philosophical perspective have suggested the following rationalisation for omissions being a *cause* of a result (in this case death). Leavens argues that omissions conceived of as a departure from the status quo can constitute a cause because:

> … the status quo is taken to include expected patterns of conduct, including actions designed to avert certain unwanted results. … Once we realize that a particular undesirable state of affairs can be avoided by taking certain precautions, we usually incorporate these precautions into what we see as the normal or at rest state of affairs. A failure to engage in the preventive conduct in these cases can thus be seen as an intervention that disturbs the status quo. When such a failure to act is a necessary condition (a "but for" cause) of a particular harm, then that failure fairly can be said to cause that harm.[75]

Leavens is here building upon the work of Hart and Honoré, who had already argued that causes of a result are those things or events that are a deviation from normal or required behaviour, and that customary techniques, procedures and routines have been developed to counteract harmful consequences of nature unless we intervene: 'when such man-made normal conditions are established, deviation from them will be regarded as exceptional and so rank as the cause of harm'.[76] This can be used to explain why a parent, who owes a duty of care to their child, would be liable for letting that child die in a shallow pool of water but a stranger would not be.[77]

Once we are able to explain causation through omission in a theoretical sense, there remains the practical task of proving causation in any given case of breach of duty. Statistics on medical manslaughter (MM) and reasons given by the CPS not to prosecute were analysed by Griffiths and Sanders.[78] In their examination of 75 CPS files which had been reviewed for a charging decision on MM, 33 (44%) were not prosecuted on the basis that causation could not be proved. As they note, it is particularly difficult to prove causation in MM cases:

> This is because, by definition, they involve cases where the victims are already ill or injured and so at greater risk of death than "normal" people. Even when someone has a non-life-threatening condition, the administration of an anaesthetic or drug to which they have an undisclosed allergy, or their exposure to hospital "superbugs", can lead to unexpected death without any negligence at all, let alone gross negligence. Vulnerable patients, particularly the elderly and the terminally ill, are (by definition) more vulnerable. Not only are they more susceptible to "things that go wrong" (such as operations, allergies and exposure to superbugs), but they usually present to hospital with a series of existing ailments.[79]

Whilst it is true that a medical practitioner must take her victim as she finds him, it is still the case that factual, but-for causation needs to be established, and it is this that is presumably difficult in MM cases. Detailing these cases, Griffiths and Sanders go on to identify five

75 Ibid., 572–73.

76 Hart and Honoré (n 11) 37.

77 Leavens (n 73) 577.

78 D. Griffiths and A. Sanders, 'The Road to the Dock: Prosecution Decision-Making in Medical Manslaughter Cases', in Griffiths and Sanders (eds) *Bioethics, Medicine and the Criminal Law Vol 2: Medicine, Crime and Society* (Cambridge University Press 2013).

79 Ibid. 141.

instances in which causation was the one identifiable and independent stumbling block to prosecution. In these cases, they were clear that a minimum of gross negligence could be proven, but they conclude that the circumstances were such that the GNM tests could not be met because:

i The victims are generally at risk of death even before they get into the hands of the accused, thus often making causation impossible to prove.
ii As with corporate killings,[80] many medical deaths occur as a result of a chain of relatively small mistakes. At any point in that chain of events a good decision would have averted catastrophe. Thus the contribution of each individual is often either impossible to determine or so small that it cannot said to be a substantial cause of death.[81]

The one requirement for proving GNM in relation to medical negligence cases which is usually not problematic is the first in the above list in *Adomako*: that D must have owed a duty of care to V. But in other categories of GNM, namely cases of prohibited drugs supply, this becomes the crucial stumbling block for prosecution. As noted above, one of the few clear rules of causation in criminal law is that V's free, deliberate and informed decision will break the chain of causation between D's act and V's death.[82] And yet in *Evans* [83] the Crown successfully circumvented this obstacle to finding a drug supplier (V's half-sister) liable for manslaughter by pursuing a charge of manslaughter based on gross negligence rather than unlawful act. The Court of Appeal upheld D's conviction for GNM through an extension of the principle in *Miller* [84] on the basis that she owed a duty of care to V because she had created a dangerous situation by supplying V with drugs and the situation was such that she knew, or ought reasonably to have known, that it had become life threatening. Thus, in a case where a drug supplier would otherwise avoid liability for manslaughter due to lack of causation, the rule in *Kennedy* can be dodged so long as D was present at the time V took drugs and remained present once V lapsed into unconsciousness.

In order to reconcile these two cases (*Evans* and *Kennedy*) one must think carefully about the chain of causation and understand that in the case of GNM based on an *Evans* scenario, the chain commences once D fails to act when she is under a duty to do so. This is *after* V has taken the drugs and so V's act of drug-taking cannot break the chain of causation that has not, at that point in time, commenced. Ashworth highlights the lack of common sense such reasoning entails, however. If V's act breaks the chain of causation for the purposes of constructive manslaughter then surely it cannot be said that D (rather than V) *creates* in the

80 It is not clear whether causation is a stumbling block in charging decisions for corporate manslaughter as it is in cases of medical manslaughter; empirical research is needed to establish whether this is the case. However, as noted by Wells in the same volume as Griffiths and Sanders, unlike other elements of corporate manslaughter, the CMCHA 2006 under-defines causation: C. Wells, 'Medical Manslaughter: Organisational Liability" in Griffiths and Sanders (n 78) 204 and 209. Antrobus has suggested that when prosecuting corporate manslaughter: 'once the prosecution have been able to establish sufficient proximity and foreseeability to prove the existence of a duty of care and breach of that duty, it is not likely to be much further for the jury to go to find causation proven according to what is a very unexacting standard demanded by the criminal law' (in S. Antrobus, 'The Criminal Liability of Directors for Health and Safety Breaches and Manslaughter' (2013) 4 Criminal Law Review 309–22, 315).
81 Griffiths and Sanders (n 78) 146.
82 *Kennedy (No.2)* (n 8).
83 [2009] 2 Cr. App. R. 10.
84 [1983] 2 A.C. 161.

sense of *causes* a dangerous situation by supplying the drugs to V, suggesting that the Court of Appeal's decision is an *over*-extension of the principle in *Miller*. [85] The combined effect of *Kennedy* and *Evans* is such that forms one of several defects in the law of manslaughter which Dyson argues ought to be rectified, suggesting that: 'causation could be made the same across different forms of manslaughter, after *Kennedy* and *Evans*'.[86] It remains unclear at this juncture, however, how such sameness could be achieved.

Towards rationality in causation in homicide

As seen throughout this chapter, there is no single test of causation to be applied in order to establish liability for homicide. Steel has suggested that causation may either be a constitutive element of a crime or alternatively causation 'may simply be a requirement of the … crime'.[87] He provides the offence under s.3ZB RTA 1988 as an example of the latter. The question that arises from this distinction is: how is it that the causing of death could be seen not to be a constitutive element of an offence of causing death? Steel's answer seems to be that under s.3ZB causation does not form part of the legal wrong consisting of a breach of a legal duty, unlike the position in GNM. It is not clear, however, that this distinction is a valid one.

The basis of all homicide offences must be that D has committed a legal wrong leading to death. The government's suggestion for the offence under s.3ZB was that D has breached the legal duty of being insured / licensed / not disqualified from driving a vehicle on a road. All death by driving offences involve a breach of a duty of some kind: the duty to hold a valid driving licence; to have valid insurance; to abide by a court order disqualifying one from driving; to not have a blood-alcohol concentration above the prescribed limit; to drive to the standard of a competent and careful driver. These are all legal wrongs, but the question is how such legal wrongs must be connected to the occurrence of a fatality in order for D to be answerable for that death. More attention should perhaps be paid to the causal *salience* of a legal wrong. According to Simester and Sullivan, 'Salience is frequently in point in cases of manslaughter, whether by gross negligence or by an unlawful and dangerous act. In each case, it must be the conduct constituting the gross negligence or the unlawful and dangerous act that caused death'.[88] The lack of causal salience on the facts of *Carey* [89] provides an explanation for the lack of liability for manslaughter in that case.[90] The problem is that, under current law, there is no clear rule setting out the requirement of causal salience for the purposes of constructive homicide offences. For gross negligence, on the other hand, the cumulative requirements that D's breach of duty caused death and that the breach was sufficiently bad to be considered criminal, given the risk of *death* involved, meet this causal salience requirement.

How then, might the causal salience requirement become a more prominent requirement of the law? One answer is that, as noted by Dyson, the real problem is with the law of manslaughter itself.[91] The same is true of the causing death offences: s.3ZB is not only an

85 A. Ashworth, 'Manslaughter by Omission and the Rule of Law' (2015) 8 Criminal Law Review 563–77, 573.
86 M. Dyson, 'The Smallest Fault in Manslaughter' (2017) 6 Archbold Review 4, 6.
87 Steel (n 4) 239.
88 A.P. Simester, J.R. Spencer, F. Stark, G.R. Sullivan and G.J. Virgo, *Simester and Sullivan's Criminal Law: Theory and Doctrine* (6th edn, Hart Publishing 2016) 92.
89 *Carey* (n 41).
90 Simester and Sullivan (n 88) 93.
91 Dyson (n 86).

example of terrible draftsmanship, but is an offence that should not have been created in breach of general principles of criminal law. This provides an explanation for the Supreme Court's approach in *Hughes;* as a matter of policy the legal requirements of the offence as set out in the statute needed to be interpreted in such a way so as to require some kind of causal salience. This causal salience is extremely weak, arguably too weak, in requiring only that there could be something to be criticised in D's driving (as opposed to there being an obvious risk of death from D's driving).[92]

Here, English law could learn from the Model Penal Code (MPC) in the United States, which sets limitations on the causal relationship between conduct and result.[93] This 'harm within the risk' requirement, originating in tort law,[94] should be accepted by Parliament as a restriction on it creating offences such as that under s.3ZB, and by the courts in interpreting the requirements of the common law offence of manslaughter. Ideally, if the criminal law were ever to become truly codified, a rule similar to that in the MPC would be incorporated to this effect.[95]

Conclusion

Under the current law of homicide the boundaries of causation are tied up with questions of, and balance with, *mens rea* requirements. The uniqueness of homicide, involving as it does the most serious of harms, means that causation is a very fluid concept. Proof of cognitive *mens rea* relating to death or GBH will in all but the most knotty cases mean that causation is likely to be established for homicide (murder). Where the limits of causation have particularly been tested is in relation to those offences which do not require blameworthiness corresponding to the harm of death or at least GBH, where the lack of fault in the form of any *mens rea* requirement is in some cases compensated through a policy approach to causation by injecting some element of fault into the causation requirements, as in *Hughes.* The human need to attribute death to *someone* [96] has led to defendants displaying minimal fault relating to death being held liable for constructive offences of causing death, where causation is having to do much of the work traditionally done by *mens rea* in establishing guilt. It would be preferable if there were clear codified rules set out to help define the appropriate limits of causation, as per the U.S. Model Penal Code. In their absence, the law must rely on judicial common sense to rectify the overzealous law-making of the legislature.

92 For a suggestion on how the law of manslaughter and vehicular homicide could be reformed in such a way as to satisfy the causal salience requirement see S. Kyd, 'Done to Death? Reform of Homicide Law' in J.J. Child and R.A. Duff (eds) *Criminal Law Reform Now* (Hart 2018, forthcoming).

93 §2.03.

94 C. Stuckenberg "Causation" in M.D. Dubber and T. Hornle (eds) *The Oxford Handbook of Criminal Law* (Oxford University Press 2014) 468–89.

95 It should be noted that the drafting of §2.03 is not without its critics, however. For a suggestion on how it could be further improved, see P. Robinson, 'The Model Penal Code's Conceptual Error on the Nature of Proximate Cause, and How to Fix It' (2015) 51(6) Criminal Law Bulletin 1311–26.

96 See S. Lloyd-Bostock, 'The Ordinary Man, and the Psychology of Attributing Causes and Responsibility' (1979) 42 Medical Law Review 143.

8 The termination of pregnancy and the criminal law

Jonathan Herring

Introduction

A pregnant woman at 20 weeks' is punched in the stomach by her partner. This results in a miscarriage ('assault case').

A pregnant woman at 20 weeks' is punched in the head by her partner. She flees the relationships and decides to terminate the pregnancy. A doctor performs an abortion ('abortion case').

For many commentators, the 'assault case' should be recognised as a serious wrong, whereas in the 'abortion case' there is no legal wrong; indeed the woman has a right to act as she does. Yet it has proved difficult to capture this intuition in the law. The assault case is clearly actual bodily harm or grievous bodily harm to the woman, but most people will feel there is a more serious wrong involved here. There is a more serious wrong than the same punch of a woman who is not pregnant, because the pregnancy has ended. The most natural way to capture the extra wrong is to see it as an extra crime against foetus, feticide as it is sometimes called. Yet, if it is acknowledged that the foetus is a person or has highly significant interests which need to be protected by the law in the assault case, then that poses a challenge for the abortion case. If termination of a pregnancy is a major wrong to the foetus justifying criminal sanction, then in the context of abortion, there needs to be a strong enough justification to commit that wrong. I am confident such arguments can be found, but there is no doubt that the justification for an abortion becomes much harder if the foetus is given significant moral status.

This is why those seeking a liberal approach to abortion law typically claim that the foetus lacks personhood.[1] As Porter puts it:

1 Foetuses are non-persons.
2 Killing non-persons is morally permissible. Therefore,
3 Killing foetuses is morally permissible. Therefore,
4 Abortion is morally permissible.[2]

That line of argument makes it harder to identify any wrong, beyond the physical injury to the woman in the assault case. The third of Porter's arguments seem to deny any wrongdoing in relation to the foetus by the assailant.

1 For a sustained argument that such a claim is required to justify abortion see K. Greasley, *Arguments About Abortion* (Oxford University Press 2017).
2 L. Porter, 'Miscarriage and Person-Denying' (2015) 46 Journal of Social Philosophy 59, 61.

This issue has come to a head given the growing calls to de-criminalise abortion.[3] The argument in favour of decriminalisation of abortion has both a practical and theoretical aspect. The practical point is that 'the current threat and stigma of criminal sanctions may deny some women access to services, where healthcare professionals are reticent, or are not permitted, to be involved in all aspects of the provision of a safe abortion service.'[4] The theoretical point is that:

> Criminalisation of abortion reflects a deep mistrust of women (and doctors) being able to make moral choices. It denies women fundamental rights to make decisions about their own bodies. Abortion should be treated in the same way as other medical decisions.[5]

Sheldon,[6] leading advocate for the decriminalisation of abortion, explains:

> The guiding principle of such reform would be that where self-induced or requested by the pregnant woman, the destruction of an embryo or foetus would no longer form an independent ground for criminal sanction. This would not, of course, leave abortion in a legal vacuum. Rather, it would be treated as any other area of medical practice, remaining subject to the same range of criminal, civil, administrative and disciplinary regulations that apply to all clinical procedures. Specifically, this should mean that criminal sanction remains available where terminations involve a serious harm to the woman concerned, most obviously, where they are non-consensual.

The argument made by Sheldon seems to be that termination in a medical setting should be seen as involving no wrong (as distinct from being a justified wrong). There are very good reasons for that, but the question arises how the same thing can be a legal wrong in another setting. Sheldon clearly imagines that the assault case should be a crime, but notably puts the assault case as a wrong to the woman. She is right in saying that, but we need to explain what the serious harm is (over and above just the injuries to herself).

It seems if you are a liberal-minded and/or feminist-minded academic you are on the horns of dilemma. If you say the foetus is 'nothing' or just part of the woman's body, you can have a liberal abortion law, but do not recognise the additional 'fetal wrong' in the assault case. Nor do you have a legal description of pregnancy which matches the experience of many women in wanted pregnancies. But, if you recognise the foetus has some important interests and that in the assault case a serious wrong is committed, it becomes harder to justify a liberal abortion law. This chapter seeks to present a way to jump off the horns. The aim is to show how one can support a very liberal abortion law, and recognise that if a pregnancy is ended without the woman's consent a serious wrong involving the foetus is done.

3 S. Sheldon, 'The Decriminalisation of Abortion: An Argument for Modernisation' (2016) 36 Oxford Journal of Legal Studies 334.

4 British Medical Association, *Decriminalisation of Abortion: Discussion Paper* (BMA 2017) available at <www.bma.org.uk/advice/employment/ethics/ethics-a-to-z/abortion > accessed 20 December 2017.

5 Ibid.

6 Ibid.

The legal status of the foetus in criminal law

The moment of birth has a dramatic impact on the legal status of the foetus. Prior to the birth, the foetus holds a somewhat ambiguous position but afterwards it is a legal person with the full protection of the law. Lord Mustill in *Attorney-General's Reference (No 3 of 1994)* [7] explained the foetus was 'a unique organism' and 'protected by the law in a number of different ways'. He went on:

> [T]he foetus does not (for the purposes of the law of homicide and violent crime) have any relevant type of personality but is an organism sui generis lacking at this stage the entire range of characteristics both of the mother to which it is physically linked and of the complete human being which it will later become ... I would, therefore, reject the reasoning which assumes that since (in the eyes of English law) the foetus does not have the attributes which make it a 'person' it must be an adjunct of the mother. Eschewing all religious and political debate I would say that the foetus is neither. It is a unique organism.[8]

He rejected an argument that the foetus should be regarded as equivalent to a limb of the mother, and the claim the foetus was nothing. Lord Mustill struggled to articulate what the foetus was. In *St George's Healthcare NHS Trust v S*, [9] Judge LJ stated that a 36-week-old foetus is 'not nothing: it is not lifeless and is certainly human'.[10] It seems, therefore, that the foetus has some kind of interests in the law. It certainly does not have the legal status of being a person,[11] nor can it claim rights under the European Convention on Human Rights.[12]

This approach to the status of the foetus is reflected in the criminal law. The foetus cannot be the victim of offences against the person. Killing a foetus cannot be the offence of murder because the *actus reus* of murder involves causing the death of a person and a foetus is not a person.[13] If, however, the child is injured in utero, is born alive and dies sometime later of those injuries, a conviction for murder or manslaughter is possible.[14]

A foetus cannot be victim of offences under the Offences Against the Person Act 1861 (OAPA 1861). A threat 'I am going to kill your baby' uttered to a pregnant woman was not the offence of threat to kill[15] according to *Tait.* [16] In *CP (a child) v First-tier Tribunal (Criminal Injuries Compensation)* [17] a mother who drank alcohol to excess pre-birth could not be said to be guilty of administration of a noxious thing to a person.[18] The simple point being the foetus was not, at the time of the administration, a person.

7 [1998] AC 245 [256].
8 Ibid. [256–7].
9 [1998] 44 BMLR 160 [163].
10 For discussion and criticism of this comment, see S. Fovargue and J. Miola, 'Policing Pregnancy: Implications of the Attorney-General's Reference (No.3 of 1994)' (1998) 6(3) Medical Law Review 265.
11 J.K. Mason, 'A Lord's Eye View of Fetal Status' (1999) 3(2) Edinburgh Law Review 246.
12 *Vo v France* [2004] 2 FCR 577.
13 *A-G Ref (No.3 of 1994)* (n 7) 245.
14 Ibid.
15 Offences Against the Person Act 1861 (OAPA 1861), s.16.
16 *R v Tait* [1990] 1 QB 290.
17 [2014] EWCA Civ 1554.
18 OAPA 1861 s.23.

Although the foetus cannot be a person, this does not mean the foetus is unprotected in the criminal law. The foetus is protected by the offences of unlawfully procuring a miscarriage under s.58 OAPA 1861, and the offence of child destruction under the Infant Life (Preservation) Act 1929. These are treated as very serious offences and carry a potential life sentence. In respect of both statutes, no offence is committed if the procedure is rendered lawful by the Abortion Act 1967. It might be questioned whether these offences were created to protect the foetus or the woman. The *mens rea* of child destruction appears to relate clearly to the foetus: 'with intent to destroy the life of a child capable of being born alive.' In *CP*, the Court of Appeal referred to the three offences as legislation 'in the interests of the unborn child'.[19] Indeed that terminology (rather than a reference to the foetus) may be revealing in itself. A clearer picture of the law may be obtained by looking at the use of these offences in practice, which will be undertaken in the next section.

The use of criminal law in relation to termination

A clearer picture of the use of the criminal law in this area is given by analysis of the cases where charges have been brought in relation to termination. These can be separated into four categories.

First, there are cases of people providing abortion services outside the terms of the Abortion Act 1967. For example in *Kaur* [20] a woman, who was not medically qualified, was supplying Mifepristone in unauthorised circumstances contrary to s.59 OAPA 1861. The issue came to the attention of the authorities after some women became ill following ingesting her medication. She was sentenced to 27 months' imprisonment. In *Mills,* [21] a 'back street abortion' was performed by a defendant with no medical qualifications and not in an authorised place. An 18 months' sentence of imprisonment was imposed. In *Spicer,* [22] a man offered to 'help' a woman who was pregnant. He inserted his fingers into her vagina out of curiosity. She subsequently suffered a miscarriage, but not as a result of what the defendant had done. He was sentenced to a six months' imprisonment. A surprisingly light sentence on what was, on one reading of the facts, a serious sexual assault.

One of the very few cases involving a medical qualified doctor was *Smith* [23] when a prosecution was bought under s.58 OAPA 1861. A doctor was said to have performed an abortion without being satisfied that one of the grounds under the Abortion Act 1967 was present. The claim was, in essence, that the doctor had taken a pregnant woman at her word that she wished to have an abortion and made no further enquiries concerning the Abortion Act 1967 grounds. Notably, he was sentenced to 12 months in prison, suspended for two years and had a £5,000 fine. That might indicate it was not regarded as a very serious offence. In *R (Hubert) v Manchester Crown Court,* [24] a private prosecution for what was said to be a sex-based abortion failed.

Three things are particularly notable about the prosecutions in these unauthorised abortion cases. First, there are few of them. Second, the sentences are relatively low. Third, there

19 *CP* (n 17) [47] (Treacy LJ).
20 HM Government, 'Woman sentenced to 27 months for selling abortion pills illegally' <www.gov.uk/government/news/woman-sentenced-to-27-months-for-selling-abortion-pills-illegally> accessed 16 November 2017.
21 [1963] 47 Cr App R 49.
22 [1955] 39 Cr App R 189.
23 [1974] 58 Cr App R 106.
24 [2015] EWHC 3734 (Admin).

is no reference in the cases to the harms being done to the foetus. It seems these cases are punished as being professional misconduct, harmful to women or socially undesirable activities, rather than anything like murder (or attempted murder) of the foetus.

The second category of cases are those where defendants have sought to procure abortions or miscarriages without a woman's consent. In *Ahmed*, [25] the defendant took his wife, who spoke no English, to an abortion clinic for an appointment he and his family had made. He purported to act as an interpreter for his wife and told the clinic she wanted a termination. It was only because an Urdu speaking nurse was able to talk to the wife shortly before the abortion was due to take place that it became clear that the wife did not want an abortion. The husband was charged under s.59 of the 1861 Act. He was convicted, but successfully appealed on the basis that the evidence did not show that the defendant had supplied or procured anything. The *actus reus* of the offence was not satisfied, as the 'thing' in s.59 had to relate to an object or article, and not a procedure. Although the court accepted that 'On any view the defendant's behaviour was appalling,'[26] he was not guilty of the offence charged, nor had any suggestion been made to the court as to what would be the correct charge.

In *Magira*, [27] the husband was very unhappy when his wife became pregnant, and sought to persuade her to have an abortion. The husband gave the wife abortion pills disguised in food, which caused her stomach cramps and bleeding, but no miscarriage. He was sentenced by the judge to three years and nine months' imprisonment. The Court of Appeal, in upholding the sentence, mentioned the foetus but the main emphasis was on the impact of the conduct on the woman:

> The court can imagine what the effect on her must have been from that and from the fear that she was about to miscarry. ... As we have observed, it is inconceivable that he could not have known the risk that he was running, not only to the foetus but also to the mother. He could not have thought that procuring an abortion at home, in all the circumstances here, was without any significant risk.[28]

There is notably a reference to the foetus, but the primary focus of the sentencing discussion seems to have been on the mother. The sentence was upheld.

In *Fletcher*, [29] the defendant was charged under s.58 OAPA 1861. He was a corporal in the Royal Artillery and was unhappy when his partner became pregnant. She was happy with the pregnancy. He obtained various tablets from India, designed to produce an abortion. He was sentenced to two years' imprisonment. This was suspended for a year on appeal as an act of mercy and in recognition of his usefulness to the military. There was no mention of the nature of the wrong. Similarly, in *Erin* [30], a doctor ground up medication in his lover's drink without her knowledge in an attempt to produce a miscarriage. He was sentenced to six years' imprisonment. The fact he was a doctor was regarded as aggravating the offence.

These cases carry higher sentences, because the act is done without the consent of the woman. It certainly suggests the court see the offence as primarily against the woman, and there are only fleeting references to the interests of the foetus.

25 [2010] EWCA Crim 1949.
26 Ibid. [16].
27 [2008] EWCA Crim 1939.
28 Ibid. [29]
29 [2014] EWCA Crim 1876.
30 *Decriminalisation of Abortion: Discussion Paper* (n 4)

Third, there have been cases where women have terminated their own pregnancies. In *Catt* [31], a 35-year-old woman obtained misoprostol over the internet and used it to procure her own termination, when around 40 weeks' pregnant. She buried the baby on her own. She was convicted under s.58 OAPA 1861 and initially sentenced to 8 years' imprisonment. That was reduced to three and a half years on appeal. The case is striking as the court, having summarised her personal history, commented it was 'a history which throws out the potential for disturbance, personal misery and entrenched problems'. She had made some unsuccessful attempts to obtain a lawful abortion. Given the case appears to be one involving a deeply troubled woman, the prosecution and high sentence is surprising. Notably, however, the trial judge referred to the 'the extinguishing of a life about to begin.'[32] And that 'she ended the life of a child presumptively capable of being born alive by inducing birth or miscarriage.'[33] It was said by the Court of Appeal, 'Mrs Catt waited until term before premeditatedly she destroyed her child—the archaic language of an old Act of Parliament.'[34] The British Medical Association report[35] also refers to a case involving Natalie Towers, a 24-year-old woman, who procured her own miscarriage when around 32 weeks' pregnant, using medication purchased online. Her sentence was two and a half years. However, prosecution in these kinds of cases appear very rare.[36]

Finally, there are cases where a pregnant woman is attacked and a miscarriage results. Sheldon, in her study found that often the defendant is simply charged in relation to the assault.[37] For example, Gallacher[38] was convicted of racially aggravated assault occasioning actual bodily harm after attacking a pregnant Muslim woman. The judge, in sentencing, noted that the attack had been followed by a miscarriage. In cases of this kind it may be that there is the difficulty in proving the attack caused the miscarriage (a point alluded to in the judge's reported comments in the newspaper) or the *mens rea*, if it cannot be established the assailant knew the victim was pregnant.[39]

The most sustained discussion of these kinds of offences is found in *Wilson*.[40] The defendant and his friend attacked the mother of his child who was 32 weeks' pregnant, after he had unsuccessfully sought to persuade her to have an abortion. They deliberately stamped on her stomach. He and his friend were both charged with intentional infliction of grievous bodily harm and child destruction under the Infant Life Preservation Act 1929. In sentencing him to 14 years' imprisonment, the trial judge listed various factors as justifying the sentence including.

31 [2013] EWCA Crim 1187.
32 Ibid. [23].
33 Ibid. [12].
34 Ibid. [18].
35 *Decriminalisation of Abortion: Discussion Paper* (n 4).
36 Sheldon (n 3) 345.
37 Ibid.
38 W. Worley, '"Shabby racist" jailed after kicking pregnant Muslim woman in stomach "causing her to lose baby"' *The Independent* (London, 24 May 2017) <www.independent.co.uk/news/uk/crime/muslim-pregnant-woman-kick-david-gallacher-racist-stomach-lose-baby-samsam-haji-a li-bletchley-a7753591.html> accessed 16 November 2017.
39 In another horrific case, Michael Gray was charged with sexual offences, but not specifically in relation to the loss of pregnancy that resulted. See T. Mann, 'Pregnant woman raped with pool cue describes horror of losing baby' *Metro* (London, 20 October 2017) <www.metro.co.uk/2017/10/20/pregnant-woman-raped-with-pool-cue-describes-horror-of-losing-baby-7013761/> accessed 16 November 2017.
40 [2016] EWCA Crim 1555.

> (cthere were two vulnerable victims of the attack, a young pregnant woman and an unborn child;
>
> (dW, as the father of the unborn child, had a responsibility to ensure the continued well-being of mother and baby ...[41]

The Court of Appeal commented:

> ...We cannot lose sight of the fact that the unborn child here was 32 weeks' old, and only two months away from birth. The bond between mother and unborn child was extremely strong. This was a deliberate, calculated and successful attempt to end the prospect of the foetus being born a living, healthy child. It was an unspeakably wicked act committed, as the judge said, in a cowardly, vile and callous attack. We consider that the judge was fully entitled to conclude that individually the offences would have merited determinate sentences of 18 years, and in the case of the child destruction, possibly longer.[42]

It is notable that the language of 'unborn child', rather than the more common foetus was used. The final sentence implies that child destruction was seen as more serious than grievous bodily harm to the woman.

The case law generally seems to recognise what I described as the intuition earlier; that in cases where the woman is consenting to the abortion, the wrong done is low level. Where the woman is attacked and a pregnancy ended, a serious wrong is done. Sheldon,[43] in her survey, suggested that 'the great majority' of prosecutions under ss.58–60 of the OAPA 1861 are the result of assaults on pregnant women. Sheldon found no convictions of clinicians acting in their professional role, and only two of women procuring their own (very late term) miscarriages. Yet, the standard approaches to the moral status of the foetus fails to capture these distinctions.

The traditional approach to moral status

At the heart of the law's approach to termination of pregnancy is the issue of what ethicists call personhood. The terminology is problematic because it became easily confused with a biological concept, such as human being. In the literature, personhood is used to refer to a moral status, the highest moral status known to us. As Warren[44] explains:

> To have moral status is to be morally considerable, or to have moral standing. It is to be an entity towards which moral agents have, or can have, moral obligations. If an entity has moral status, then we may not treat it in just any way we please.

In more colloquial terms, it might be taken to capture why, if faced with a fire in a building, you could choose to save a person or a non-person, you would be making a profound moral mistake to choose the non-person. There is nothing in the building that could be of more

41 Ibid. [18].
42 Ibid. [35].
43 S. Sheldon, 'The Decriminalisation of Abortion: An Argument for Modernisation' (2016) 36 Oxford Journal of Legal Studies 334, 340.
44 Mary Warren, *Moral Status* (Oxford University Press 1993) 3.

moral value than a fellow person, not even your iPhone! For lawyers, this is commonly aligned with the idea of human rights which, typically, people take to apply to persons but not non-persons. Persons are thereby given privileged legal rights.

The question turns to what generates moral status and whether the foetus does or does not have the attributes that generate those protections. There is an extensive literature on the issue of personhood; it is not the aim of this chapter to explore these in depth.[45] In broad terms, it is possible to identify two primary schools of thought on the question. I will briefly summarise these, before outlining in more detail a third proposal, which is the one I advocate.

Personhood at or close to birth and beyond

Under this approach, commentators list particular characteristics of personhood in order to ascertain whether or not the foetus has the status of being a person. Typical examples would be those listed by Fletcher:[46]

(1) Minimal intelligence
(2) Self-awareness
(3) Self-control
(4) A sense of time
(5) A sense of futurity
(6) A sense of the past
(7) The capability to relate to others
(8) Concern for others
(9) Communication
(10) Control of Existence
(11) Curiosity
(12) Balance of rationality/feeling
(13) Idiosyncrasy
(14) Change/changeability
(15) Neo-cortical function.

Normally on the basis of such an approach it is said that because the foetus lacks such features, or only has them to a limited extent, it cannot claim the moral or legal status of personhood. There is little agreement as to when these characteristics are acquired. For some it will be in the very later stages of pregnancy, at birth, or some time after birth.[47] For others, there is no precise moment when these criteria are achieved as the foetus gradually moves into personhood over time.

Others reach a similar conclusion, but based on the approach that personhood is acquired by virtue of being accepted as a member of the community of the human species.[48] That might be said to be at birth, when the foetus can interact with fellow humans; only then does the foetus acquire personhood.

45 A helpful overview of the arguments in found in K. Greasley and C. Kaczor, *Abortion Rights: For and Against* (Cambridge University Press 2017).
46 J. Fletcher, *Humanhood: Essays in Biomedical Ethics* (Prometheus Books 1979) 15.
47 P. Singer, *Practical Ethics* (Cambridge University Press 1979).
48 B. Williams, 'The Human Prejudice' in Bernard Williams (ed.), *Philosophy as a Humanistic Discipline* (Princeton University Press 2006).

For those for whom human personhood begins at birth or some time after birth, the abortion question is relatively straightforward. As the foetus lacks personhood, its interests will be insufficient to trump the claims of the woman to bodily autonomy. It also means they are unlikely to see an attack on a pregnant woman as only an attack on the body of the woman and the termination of something of minimal significance.

Personhood at conception

For others, the foetus is a person from the moment of conception:

> The adult human being that is now you or me is the same being who, at an earlier stage, was an adolescent and, before that, a child, an infant, a foetus, and an embryo. Even in the embryonic stage, you and I were undeniably whole living members of the species Homo sapiens. We were then, as we are now, distinct and complete – though, in the beginning, developmentally immature – human organisms. We were not mere parts of other organisms.[49]

As the foetus contains the entire genetic material of the adult it will become it has the hallmark of humanity and is a person.

Under such a view, the question of abortion becomes much more problematic. The killing of the foetus is the killing of a person and requires a very strong moral justification. The wrong is equivalent to (or is in fact) murder.

As mentioned earlier, much has been written about these standard accounts of foetal status and there are many more understandings than those presented.[50] I will not enter that fevered debate here because I want to present an alternative understanding.

Developing a new approach

The traditional approaches see the individual as the primary focus of legal and other obligations. Nussbaum[51] explains why she believes the individual should be the basic unit for political thought:

> It means, first of all, that liberalism responds sharply to the basic fact that each person has a course from birth to death that is not precisely the same as that of any other person; that each person is one and not more than one, that each feels pain in his or her own body, that the food given to A does not arrive in the stomach of B.

Whatever one thinks of this argument generally, it is immediately clear that what she is saying is not true of the foetus. The pain of the mother affects the foetus and the food given to the mother can arrive in the stomach of the foetus. The biological reality is that pregnancy is one of profound interconnection. There is no clear point at which foetal tissue ends and the woman's tissue begins. They share fluids and space. The health and well-being of the woman profoundly affect the foetus and vice versa.[52] As Young explains:

49 R. George, 'Embryo Ethics' (2008) 137 Daedalus 23, 23.
50 J. Herring, *Medical Law and Ethics* (Oxford University Press 2016) 368–430.
51 M. Nussbaum, *Sex and Social Justice* (Oxford University Press 1999) 62.
52 See J. Herring and P-L Chau, 'My Body. Your Body. Our Bodies' (2007) 15(1) Medical Law Review 34 for a discussion of the biology.

> [p]regnancy challenges the integration of my body experience by rendering fluid the boundary between what is within, myself, and what is outside, separate. I experience my insides as the space of another, yet my own body.[53]

The interconnection between the two shows that the standard individualised approach is particularly inappropriate in relation to the foetal status.

The relational approach argues that rather than asking what rights or responsibilities are owed to an individual in response to their status, we ask what responsibilities and rights are owed in relation to a relationship. In terms of the personhood debate, this means the question is not whether the foetus has moral value individually, nor the pregnant woman on her own, but rather to ask of the moral status of the relationship between woman and foetus, and what legal response is appropriate to a relationship of that kind.[54] In short, where a relationship is marked by care, I would advocate the law should allocate rights and responsibilities to ensure that relationship is upheld and maintained.[55] Where, however, that relationship is not marked by care, then it does not have moral value and the law should enable parties to find other caring relationships. The relational approach to personhood differs from the standard approach as not focusing on the capacity or attribute of an individual and giving them status, but rather focusing on relationships and considering whether there is moral value there.

The relational approach understands rights in a different way from the standard approach as they attach to and through relationships, rather than individuals. It is not as strange an idea as it may sound at first. Many of our rights and responsibilities flow from our relationship with others, rather than our own status. If you want to know your legal rights and responsibilities towards someone else, you cannot say much without knowing your relationship to them. Your responsibilities to a child are completely different if you are a parent than if you are a stranger. If you are the other person's doctor, the legal responsibilities are transformed. Contractual claims can change the responsibilities one person owes to another. Even tort duties require a duty of care emerging typically from the nature of the relationship and carry depending on that relationship. Much more could be said about the broader implications of this relational approach. I will not peruse them here, as for this chapter my focus is on pregnancy.

The standard approach seeks to determine the status of the foetus so that it can be balanced against the interests of the mother. That is why the status of the foetus plays such a big role in these debates. But that leads to the presentation of pregnancy as conflict between the rights of the foetus and the rights of the mother. Mair writes that the notion of the maternal / foetal conflict:

> is a violent image which disrupts the coexistence of mother and foetus. It is an emotive phrase which suggests unmotherly feelings and a grotesque perception of the struggling foetus[56]

53 I.M. Young, *On Female Body Experience* (Oxford University Press 2005) 49.

54 This argument is developed more fully in C. Foster and J. Herring, *Personhood, Identity and the Law* (Springer 2017).

55 J. Herring, *Caring and the Law* (Hart 2013), chapter 2 offers a full definition of care, including that it involves meeting needs in a relationship marked by mutuality and respect.

56 J. Mair, 'Maternal / Foetal Conflict: Defined or Defused?' in S.A.M. McLean (ed.) *Contemporary Issues in Law, Medicine, and Ethics* (Dartmouth Publishing 1996) 79.

Very quickly, and all too easily under this model, the rights of the woman are pitted against those of the foetus. That is the essence of problem identified at the start of this chapter: it presents a false choice – you must choose between protecting the rights of the woman to abortion or protecting the foetus from termination.

This conflict model reflects what Morris has called 'an ignorance of what it means to be pregnant'.[57] As she argues, 'the issues involved are much more complex than the easy label of maternal/foetal conflict suggests … instead of seeking to resolve maternal/foetal conflicts by defining more clearly the individual legal rights of the pregnant woman and the foetus, should we not question the construction of these so-called conflicts?'[58] We need instead, as Rothman suggests, an acknowledgement that '[m]otherhood is an experience of interpersonal connection. The isolated, atomistic individual is an absurdity when one is pregnant: one is two, two are one.'

The heart of the relational approach is this interconnection. This is a highly physical interconnection. Little[59] emphasises the significance of the intercorporality involved in pregnancy:

> To be pregnant is to be *inhabited*. It is to be *occupied*. It is to be in a state of physical *intimacy* of a particularly thorough-going nature. The foetus intrudes on the body massively; whatever medical risks one faces or avoids, the brute fact remains that the foetus shifts and alters the very physical boundaries of the woman's self. To mandate continuation of gestation is, quite simply, to force continuation of such occupation.

Conceiving of the foetus on its own terms fails to capture the fact that the foetus is integrated into the woman. It presents some kind of fairy tale image that the woman provides a cosy sitting room for the foetus to live in, awaiting birth. But, the woman is not simply a 'fetal container'.[60] Rothman[61] writes of:

> the reigning medical model of pregnancy, as an essentially parasitic and vaguely pathological relationship, [which] encourages the physician to view the foetus and mother as two separate patients, and to see pregnancy as inherently a conflict of interests between the two. Where the foetus is highly valued, the effect is to reduce the woman to what current obstetrical language calls the "maternal environment".

The reality is that all interaction and dealings with the foetus must be mediated through and with the woman. Dworkin[62] puts it this way:

> her foetus in not merely "in her" as an inanimate object might be, or something live but alien that has been transplanted into her body. It is "of her and is hers more than

57 A. Morris, 'Once Upon a Time in a Hospital … the Cautionary Tale of *St George's NHS Trust v S., R. v Collins and Others ex parte S.* [1998] 3 All ER 673' (1999) 7 Feminist Legal Studies 79, 84.

58 Mair (n 56) 93.

59 M. Little, 'Abortion, Intimacy and the Duty to Gestate' (1999) 2 Ethical Theory and Moral Practice 295.

60 G. Annas, 'Pregnant Women as Fetal Containers' (1986) 16 Hastings Centre Report 13, 14.

61 B.K. Rothman, *Recreating Motherhood: Ideology and Technology in a Patriarchal Society* (Rutgers University Press 1989) 89.

62 R. Dworkin, *Life's Dominion* (Alfred Knopf 1993) 203.

anyone's" because it is, more than anyone else's, her creation and her responsibility; it is alive because she has made it come alive.

The experience of pregnancy profoundly impacts on the body and identity of the woman. As Elvey[63] explains:

> ... the pregnant body ... calls into question these assumptions of separateness and sameness. When I am pregnant, "my" body is both "I" and "not I", mine and not mine. The boundaries of the body shift as the pregnant body creates its own expanding space. While the skin stretches the boundary between the body and its outside is continually renegotiated, until in birth the inside enters the outside. The pregnant body is, moreover, two or more under the influence of a third, the placenta, through the agency of which self and other are interconnected.

Of course, not every woman will perceive pregnancy in this way, but we need a model and discourse which recognises the profound impact that pregnancy can have on identities and bodies.[64] The traditional approaches, whether seeing a foetus as a person or a non-person, fail to capture these experiences. A relational view does.[65] As Rothman[66] puts it:

> A holistic view of pregnancy understands that pregnancy is a unique relational existential reality that simultaneously represents physiological, existential, and social duality and oneness. This view is consistent with both physiological and maternal understandings of pregnancy. It is reflective of both intended and unintended pregnancies. It is honest. And, it is woman-centered.

Applying a relational approach to termination of pregnancies

As should already be clear, the relational approach opens up the possibility for a different weighting and understanding of wanted and unwanted pregnancies. Wanted pregnancies are caring and therefore of highest moral value. We need to protect them through the criminal law from unwanted termination and to recognise the value of them. By contrast, unwanted pregnancies lack moral value as there is coerced care, which may well impede other wanted caring relationships. As Stoyles[67] puts it:

> Relational accounts of fetal value allow that pregnancies have whatever meaning and value they are given by the pregnant woman. Thus, relational accounts allow that pregnancy can have little or no positive value and also that pregnancy can have great value.

63 A. Elvey, 'The Material Given: Bodies, Pregnant Bodies and Earth' (2003) 18 Australian Feminist Studies 199–209.
64 S. Matambanadzo, 'Reconstructing Pregnancy' (2016) 69 Southern Methodist Law Review 187, 189.
65 C. Pickles, *Pregnancy Law in South Africa* (Juta 2017).
66 Rothman (n 61).
67 B. Stoyles, 'The Value of Pregnancy and the Meaning of Pregnancy Loss' (2015) 46 Journal of Social Philosophy 91.

The relational approach provides a meaningful way to respond to all pregnancies. As Pickles argues:

> Female autonomy must also recognise women's vested interests in their unborn. Therefore, female autonomy must be understood as including the decision to continue with a pregnancy, as well as decisions on *how* to progress through pregnancy. This manifestation of autonomy must be protected in law in order for it to have any meaningful effect for women who want children. Consequently, the single-entity approach only speaks to one side of female autonomy and fails to assist those women who plan to continue with their pregnancies and to adequately protect such decisions.[68]

Those who do experience unwanted termination find the law's approach that the foetus is not of moral status problematic. As Roberts[69], a lecturer in Law whose eight months' pregnancy was terminated through a car accident, writes:

> The current law's attempt to answer this riddle is a clumsy one. It characterises our daughter's death as one of my "injuries", because she died in utero, and was not a legal "person" with a separate existence from me at the time she died. Calling our loss an "injury" fails to acknowledge the depth of sorrow involved in grieving a child.

Significantly, for this chapter, she is then reluctant to claim that the foetus is a legal person:

> Once the foetus is defined as a legal person, the law has a direct relationship with it, and the mother's consent becomes irrelevant. She becomes invisible in the eyes of the law, despite the physical realities of pregnancy meaning that any interaction with the foetus necessarily involves her.

The relational approach offers a solution for these concerns. Through her care and love for the foetus in a wanted relationship it accepts this relationship is deserving of especial moral status.[70] But, where the relationship is unwanted, it has a different moral status and the legal response can be completely different.

A major problem for the current approach is that it offers no effective response to unwanted miscarriage. Women's experience of unwanted miscarriage is not captured by the 'foetus as non-person' response. Browne[71] argues that miscarriage is 'disenfranchised grief'. There is a concern:

> … if one were to acknowledge that there was something of value lost, something worth grieving in a miscarriage, one would be conceding ground to antiabortion or "pro-life" arguments.

68 C. Pickles, 'Approaches to Pregnancy Under the Law: A Relational Response to the Current South African Position and Recent Academic Trends' (2015) 47(1) De Jure Law Review 2, 16.

69 H. Robert, 'Responding to unwanted termination, Why losing my daughter means I don't support Zoe's law' *The Conversation* (London, 17 November 2013) <www.theconversation.com/why-losing-my-daughter-means-i-dont-support-zoes-law-19985> accessed 20 December 2017.

70 L. Tonkin, 'Haunted by a "Present Absence"' (2012) 4 Studies in the Maternal 1.

71 V. Browne, 'Feminist Philosophy and Prenatal Death: Relationality and the Ethics of Intimacy' (2016) 41 Signs 485.

However, as she goes on to argue, the relational approach offers a way to better capture the experience of miscarriage.[72] Rogers[73] in her heart-breaking account writes to her miscarried twins:

> I'm writing a letter to you both as our departure and our "relationship" over the past nine months comes to an end. All I do know is that as I say goodbye to our future together I am no longer full of emptiness. It has taken some time to make peace, but we are getting there, wherever there is. I do know that whatever happens in the future, wherever the path of life takes us, you will always be a part of that. Your tiny tiny bodies might have gone, but your spirits live on. Not in any real sense but in the fact that your short lives where you grew inside of me will live with me and impact on my life forever.

This account is profoundly relational and captures the experience of many women who experience miscarriage. The relational approach regards unwanted miscarriage as a serious loss and where this is the result of a criminal offence a serious wrong.

A relational approach can also be helpful when thinking about abortion.[74] The relational approach focuses the question on what obligations flow from the pregnancy given it is unwanted. The familiar arguments based on bodily integrity, the lack of duty on people to rescue those in peril, and personal autonomy come into play. Given a parent is not obliged by the law to give organs or even suffer the prick of needle to give some blood in order to save the life of their child, it is inconceivable the law could require a woman to go through pregnancy and birth for a foetus. The law is not in the business of coercing relationships through threat of legal sanction as that undermines the very goodness of a mutually respectful caring relationship. As Manninen[75] argues, even if one accepts foetal personhood, there are major limits to the responsibilities that can be imposed on others:

> As much as we can feel for the life of patients in need of organ transplants, we cannot force otherwise healthy persons to donate non-vital organs to save the sick. This does not mean that the lives of these patients have no value; rather what it means is that no matter how valuable they are, this value cannot be used as grounds to infringe upon the rights of other persons. Similarly, we can argue that being prochoice need not entail a wanton disregard of fetal life, but, rather, an acknowledgment that, like all persons, pregnant women have a right to decide if they want to use their bodies to sustain another.

Lindemann argues:

> … anti-abortion legislation holds pregnant women—who are innocent of any wrongdoing—to a punitive standard of specific performance, sentencing them against their will to the many kinds of hard work, physical discomfort, and outright danger that my

72 Porter (n 2).
73 C. Rogers, 'Hope as a Mechanism in Emotional Survival: Documenting Miscarriage' (2017) 2 Open Access Journal of Gynaecology 10, 13.
74 For an extended discussion see Pickles (n 65).
75 B. Manninen, 'The Value of Choice and the Choice to Value: Expanding the Discussion about Fetal Life within Prochoice Advocacy' (2003) 28 Hypatia 664, 679.

> daughter willingly undertook to bring her child into the world. No other class of people is held to this standard in peacetime. No woman should be held to it either.[76]

Given this is a relationship not marked by care, indeed it is hindering the woman from entering other caring relationships, the law's response should be to facilitate the parties to escape from that relationship and to be free to form other relationships if they are able to do so.

This relational approach better captures the kind of thinking that women use in abortion decisions. The argument that the foetus has no interests and so the woman is entitled to remove it fails to appreciate the complex responses of woman who undertake abortions. While abortion may be seen by some women as equivalent to the cutting of hair or removal of a growth, in fact the evidence suggests that for most women the abortion decision is not viewed that way, but is viewed as a decision made about the relationship.

Mackenzie[77] has written of the way that academic discussions on abortion:

> ... have focused philosophical and moral reflection away from the contexts in which deliberations about abortion are usually made and away from the concerns and experiences which motivate those involved in the processes of deliberation. The result is that philosophical analyses of abortion often seem beside the point, if not completely irrelevant, to the lives of the countless women who daily not only have to make moral decisions about abortion but, more importantly, who often face serious risks to their lives in contexts where abortion is not a safe and readily accessible procedure.

If we turn to look at the reasons women actually give for abortions, the academic discussion looks, as Mackenzie suggests, disconnected from reality. The decision is made on the basis of what is appropriate for both the mother and the foetus.[78] Consider, for example, these comments from three women who had abortions, provided to the 'My Body, My Life' project:

> I was 22 when I found out I was pregnant. I had just qualified as a teacher but was yet to find my first teaching position. My partner had a decent job but he was recovering from a prolonged period of severe depression and while he lived with his elderly mother, I was caring for my grandmother who had been diagnosed with a degenerative illness. Although we were very much in love and hoped to have children one day, our finances and living arrangements meant we were not equipped to raise a child. We would want to give our children the very best possible start in life and, at that time, we didn't have the opportunity to do so.[79]
>
> I had made my decision even before it had happened. I got pregnant at 23 and knew I could not have it. I wasn't ready to give the baby the life it deserved.[80]
>
> I fell pregnant again shortly after my son turned a year old. I have a long term health condition that means pregnancy can be dangerous for both myself and foetus. I had to

76 H. Lindemann, '"But I Could Never Have One": The Abortion Intuition and Moral Luck' (2009) 21 Hypatia 41, 57.

77 C. Mackenzie, 'Abortion and Embodiment' (1992) 70 Australian Journal of Philosophy 136, 142.

78 J. Ludlow, 'Sometimes, it's a Child *and* a Choice: Toward an Embodied Abortion Praxis' (2008) 20 National Women Studies Association Journal 26–50.

79 Taken from <www.mybody-mylife.org/user-submitted-post-15/ > accessed 17 November 2017.

80 Taken from <www.mybody-mylife.org/user-submitted-post-9/> accessed 17 November 2017.

> consider my son's welfare and was the risk of having another child worth making myself very unwell?[81]

A review of women's abortion decision-making found that reasons for termination of a pregnancy were often based on a desire to be a good parent to a child when born.[82] They are influenced by women's responsibilities to other people and to themselves. Sherwin reports explanations involve '... her feelings about her foetus, her relationship with her partner, other children she may have, and her various obligations to herself and others — contextually defined considerations that reflect her commitments to the needs and interests of everyone concerned'.[83]

As these comments demonstrate, abortion is not regarded as simply disposing of a 'nothing' and abortion is not made on 'selfish' grounds. Rather, the abortion decision is taken in the context of their relationship with their foetus and those around them. These perspectives can be captured by the relationship-based approach in a way the status-based approach cannot.

The relational model also requires a consideration of the emotional issues raised. Hadfield[84] writes of those who focus on choice in the abortion decision:

> Who are these people who populate the economist's ... imaginatio[n], who calmly assess the alternatives available according to a stable set of internally consistent preferences and proceed to select the obvious choice, who apparently feel no passion or emotion, who do not worry about whether they are choosing well, who never feel trapped by their choices, and who never discover over time more about themselves and their understanding of their choices? Where is love, duty, fear, self-doubt, and power?

An approach which seeks to understand the obligations and rights that flow from relationships can be better nuanced in considering the emotions that govern such a decision and what rights and responsibilities can be expected as a result. A relational approach can recognise that pregnancy can create responsibilities for pregnant woman. It enables the decisions about pregnancy and parenthood to be placed in the real mucky world of relationships where sometimes things go wrong and sometimes they go right. The world of family life where being a parent is sometimes about survival, rather than reaching the highest ideals of being a parent. Where weighing up nicely the competing moral interests makes no sense when everything is going crazy and control over life is a long-lost fiction. Abortion decisions are complex and not reducible to straightforward analysis of my rights against the non-person. That is a parody of the complexity of women's abortion decisions.

Conclusion

This chapter has argued against the common approach towards discussions of the law on termination, which focus on determining the status of the foetus and weighing these against

81 Taken from <www.mybody-mylife.org/user-submitted-post-16/> accessed 17 November 2017.

82 M. Kirkman, H. Rowe, A. Hardiman, S. Mallett and D. Rosenthal 'Reasons Women Give for Abortion: A Review of the Literature' (2009) 12 Archives of Women's Mental Health 365; J. Hainsberg, 'Homologizing Pregnancy and Motherhood: A Consideration of Abortion' (1985) 94 Michigan Law Review 371.

83 S. Sherwin, *No Longer Patient* (Temple University Press 1992) 102.

84 G. Hadfield, 'An Expressive Theory of Contract' (1998) 146 University of Pennsylvania Law Review 1235.

the rights of women. It has argued instead that we should focus on the relational context of pregnancy which puts caring relationships as the marker of moral value. Doing this, I suggest, leads to a very different legal response to wanted and unwanted pregnancies.

In relation to unwanted pregnancies, the relationship is not marked by mutual care and so it lacks moral value. The law has no interest in enabling these relationships to continue and indeed cannot compel people to continue in them when they involve the kind of bodily interference involved in pregnancy and birth. In no other context does the law compel one party to give up bodily integrity to save another even to the slightest degree, let alone the extent required in pregnancy. The law must enable the termination of unwanted pregnancies so that caring responsibilities and be fulfilled. This account better matches a moral justification but also the reasons women give for seeking an abortion.

In relation to wanted pregnancies, these are wanted caring relationships of the highest moral value. The law should do all it can to maintain, uphold and respect these. That includes, among many other things, ensuring there are effective criminal sanctions imposed on those who terminate wanted pregnancies without the consent of the woman.

9 Homicide and the vulnerable subject of criminal law

Claire de Than and Jesse Elvin

Introduction

This chapter examines the law on homicide as it relates to cases where V is in the actual custody, charge or care of D and V is a person who is vulnerable or has a special dependence on D. Examples of such situations are where young children are in the custody or charge of their parents or a school, where prisoners are under the control of prison or police officers, where a worker is under the control of a manager, and where residents are in a care home. In civil law, D will owe V a non-delegable duty of care in such a case.[1] Similarly, D will owe V a duty of care in criminal law, breach of which could give rise to liability for murder or manslaughter.[2] There will also be human rights implications under the right to life and freedom from inhuman and degrading treatment or punishment.[3] In this chapter, we will consider in which circumstances D should be criminally liable for causing V's death in such situations. We will be focusing on 'hard cases', considering the potential liability of: (a) parents, head teachers, prison governors and care home managers in relation to the provision of inappropriate diets to those under their authority; (b) parents in relation to the rejection of medical treatment for religious or pseudoscientific reasons; (c) managers for deaths arising from workplace stress; and (d) prison officers and governors for the suicide of prisoners. Drawing upon notions of vulnerability, autonomy and discrimination, we aim to advance theory in this area and to provide greater clarity on the appropriate legal approach to the important situations at hand.

The concept of vulnerability

Focusing upon the duty of care concept in tort law, Carl Stychin argues that 'vulnerability could provide both some doctrinal order to a confused legal state, and it gives us a means by which to enrich our understanding of how we conceive of our ethical and legal obligations'.[4] More specifically, he claims that 'Duties arise from the demand upon us to be attentive to

1 *Woodland v Swimming Teachers Association* [2013] UKSC 66. As Lord Sumption JSC put it in this case: 'The expression "non-delegable duty" has become the conventional way of describing those cases in which the ordinary principle [of a duty to take reasonable care of another] is displaced and the duty extends beyond being careful, to procuring the careful performance of work delegated to others' (ibid [6]).

2 However, unlike in tort law, the duty will not extend beyond being careful, to procuring the careful performance of work delegated to others.

3 Articles 2 and 3 of the European Convention on Human Rights (ECHR) respectively.

4 C. Stychin, 'The Vulnerable Subject of Negligence Law' (2012) 8 International Journal of Law in Context 337.

the vulnerability of others'[5] and that 'Vulnerability provides a discursive means by which to articulate demands for the legal responsibility of those in positions of privilege who otherwise can claim that they have not assumed responsibility and that they are not responsible'.[6] Stychin rightly points out that 'vulnerability theory' has a rich tradition, both in tort law and elsewhere.[7] It is connected to an ethic of care, which is 'hospitable to the relatedness of persons'[8] and 'sees many of our responsibilities as not freely entered into but presented to us by the accidents of our embeddedness in familial and social and historical contexts'.[9] The rich tradition in question stems back to the work of Carol Gilligan[10] and Nel Noddings:[11] in unequal power relationships, there is a responsibility to protect the more vulnerable person and to respond in a manner which takes context into account. This idea that many of our responsibilities are not freely entered into is relevant in relation to the cases involving parents that we will consider later. Jonathan Herring claims that 'the obligations attached to parenthood … arise not from a specific choice of an individual, but from the relationship that exists'.[12] However, the issue is more complicated than this. People are not forced to become parents or to retain parental responsibilities, except in extreme situations or in a limited financial sense, and so it is possible to argue that parenthood is also a choice – even an unplanned pregnancy carried to full-term against the wishes of the parents would not necessarily mean enforced parenthood, since a child may be surrendered for adoption or fostering. It is true that 'a relational life is inevitable … We all at some points in our lives have been dependent on others for our survival and many people … are dependent on us'.[13]However, many of the cases that we will look at in this chapter, such as those involving prison governors and the suicide of prisoners, involve responsibilities that are clearly freely entered into. For example, our decisions are often reached as a result of economic pressures and most of us are effectively compelled to enter into an employment relationship, but we are not economically forced to enter into the types of employment where we have custody, charge or care of a person who is vulnerable or who has a special dependence upon us. Each of the situations we will examine involves an imbalance of power in a relationship, where the stronger party has important sanctions, although the nature and impact of the sanctions will vary. Some of the situations involve multiple inequalities and vulnerabilities: for example, where a prisoner has a mental health condition or is threatened by other prisoners. Our view is that the law has to respect the right of V to make an unwise decision where V has mental capacity, and that this means that D should not necessarily be expected to override V's wishes. However, liability for homicide may nonetheless be appropriate in some cases where V is in the actual custody, charge or care of D and V is a person who is vulnerable or has a special dependence on D. It is instructive to consider the approach of the House of Lords in

5 Ibid. 346.
6 Ibid. 350.
7 Ibid. 347, citing R. Goodin, *Protecting the Vulnerable* (University of Chicago Press 1985); M. Fineman, 'The Vulnerable Subject: Anchoring Equality in the Human Condition' (2008–09) 20 Yale Journal of Law and Feminism, 1–23; and J. Conaghan, 'Tort Law and Feminist Critique' (2003) 56 Current Legal Problems 175.
8 V. Held, *The Ethics of Care* (Oxford University Press 2006) 14.
9 Ibid.
10 C. Gilligan, *In a Different Voice: Psychological Theory and Women's Development* (Harvard University Press 1982).
11 N. Noddings, *Caring: A Feminine Approach to Ethics and Moral Education* (University of California Press 1984).
12 J. Herring, *Relational Autonomy and Family Law* (Springer 2014) 16.
13 Ibid. 11.

R v Kennedy (No 2).[14] Here, the House decided that D is not liable for homicide when V makes a free, voluntary and informed choice to take a drug supplied by D and subsequently dies. This is because 'generally speaking, informed adults of sound mind are treated as autonomous beings able to make their own decisions how they will act'.[15] In many of the situations that we will examine, this ability to make a free, voluntary and informed choice is either lacking or impeded to some extent and thus the law should not necessarily treat V as an autonomous being able to make decisions. As the House put it in *Kennedy (No 2)*: 'The law recognises certain exceptions [to the assumption of the existence of free will], in the case of the young, those who for any reason are not fully responsible for their actions, and the vulnerable and it acknowledges situations of duress and necessity, as also of deception and mistake'.[16] This approach is similar to the one taken by Munby J in *Re S.A. (Vulnerable Adult with Capacity: Marriage)*, where he made a helpful exploration of the scope of the Court of Protection's inherent jurisdiction to help vulnerable persons, stating that, although an attempt at a definition was inadvisable, there are at least three categories of vulnerability where a court might be required to protect a person or their interests:

> ... the inherent jurisdiction can be exercised in relation to a vulnerable adult who, even if not incapacitated by mental disorder or mental illness, is, or is reasonably believed to be, either (i) under constraint or (ii) subject to coercion or undue influence or (iii) for some other reason deprived of a capacity to make the relevant decision, or disabled from making a free choice, or incapacitated or disabled from giving or expressing a real and genuine consent.[17]

'Hard cases'

(a) Parents, head teachers, prison governors and care home managers, in relation to the provision of inappropriate diets

This is an area where it is settled that D owes a duty of care to V in criminal law. The concept of vulnerability is relevant in relation to parents and children, since a parental duty arises through a combination of a blood or other close relationship and the fact 'that V's well-being can be said to be dependent on action by D'.[18] Parents, and others who assume parental responsibilities, owe a duty of care to children who are in their care and dependent upon them.[19] Furthermore, prison governors, care home managers and head teachers owe a duty of care to those in their charge for two reasons under the current law. First, if D 'takes it upon himself to look after a person unable to care for themselves, whether by reason of age or infirmity, then he will be under a duty to continue to act'.[20] Second, a contractual obligation to care for V, or members of a class to whom V belongs, can create an equivalent

14 *R v Kennedy (No 2)* [2007] UKHL 38.
15 Ibid. [14].
16 Ibid.
17 [2005] EWHC 2942 [77].
18 C. de Than and R. Heaton, *Criminal Law* (4th edn, Oxford University Press 2013) 24.
19 See *Gibbins and Proctor* [1918] 13 Cr App R 134, where a father was liable for murdering his child by deliberately starving her to death.
20 De Than and Heaton (n 18) 25. See *Nicholls* [1874] 13 Cox CC 75, *Instan* 1 QB 450, and *Stone and Dobinson* [1977] 2 All ER 341.

criminal law duty.[21] The difficult question in this area is determining when D has breached his or her duty of care. Cases have generally involved neglect and failing to feed,[22] where it is straightforward to show breach under existing case law, and deliberate but misguided feeding with an inappropriate diet. In *R v Gay* the conviction was on the basis that the child had been fed a massive dose of salt,[23] but a retrial was ordered on appeal because the medical evidence was contradictory about the cause of death and the couple were subsequently acquitted. *R v Williams* led to an acquittal,[24] again after contradictory medical evidence about the cause of a child's abnormally high salt levels at time of death. We are not aware of any cases concerning bad diet which have led to convictions in England; the death of three-month-old Leroy Elders in 1999 was due to his parents feeding him adult food in ignorance that it contains salt levels which can kill a baby, but the coroner's verdict was accidental death.[25]

Tracey Elliott has debated whether overfeeding a child, or failing to heed medical advice about an obese child, could lead to criminal liability for parents.[26] Her view is that 'parents must bear some responsibility if they do nothing to prevent their child becoming obese'[27] but that 'it does not follow that we should criminalise this failure'.[28] Whilst we would agree with this, there is no reason in principle why parents should not be liable for manslaughter by gross negligence where there was a serious breach of duty causing V's death and V lacked the ability to make a free, voluntary and informed decision because of youth. The difficult issue is where the law should find a gross breach of duty. In other jurisdictions, parents' imposition of strict and unsuitable dietary regimes upon babies has led to highly-publicised homicide convictions and much media debate, with parents' veganism often highlighted as a cause. However, babies and young children can of course be perfectly healthy on a balanced and appropriate vegan diet – breast milk is vegan – so the issue here is actually one of neglect via inadequate feeding and poor nutritional knowledge. Examples of convictions in such cases include Peter S and Sandrine V in Belgium in 2017, who fed their baby son on plant milk after self-diagnosing him with allergies;[29] and Jade Sanders and Lamont Thomas in the US, who were sentenced to life for murder and manslaughter in 2007 for feeding their infant son only soya milk and apple juice until he died of malnutrition.[30] The suffering and slow death in such cases, in front of parents who do nothing to seek help, arguably justifies a gross negligence manslaughter conviction under English law, since there is no real distinction from other forms of neglect. Parents should have a certain degree of autonomy to raise their children as they see fit: for example, according to their cultural beliefs.

21 See e.g., *Pittwood* [1902] 19 TLR 37.

22 As in *Gibbins and Proctor* (n 19) and, for example, *R v Sabrina H* [2009] EWCA Crim 397.

23 [2006] EWCA Crim 820.

24 Winchester Crown Court, 27 October 2006.

25 See Editorial, 'Warning after salt kills baby' *BBC News* (London, 27 July 1999) <www.news.bbc.co.uk/1/hi/uk/404667.stm> accessed 24 January 2018.

26 T. Elliott, 'Pursued by the Fat Police? Prosecuting the Parents of Obese Children' in A.M. Viens, J. Coggon and A. Kessel (eds) *Criminal Law, Philosophy and Public Health Practice* (Cambridge University Press 2013) 102.

27 T. Elliott, 'No Need for the Fat Police' (2007) 157 New Law Journal 427.

28 Ibid.

29 See T. Mann, 'Baby given gluten-free diet dies weighing just 9lbs' *Metro* (London, 16 May 2017).

30 See D. Glaister, 'Parents jailed for death of underfed baby' *The Guardian* (London, 10 May 2007) <www.theguardian.com/world/2007/may/10/usa.danglaister> accessed 29 January 2018.

'Freedom of religion and the general freedom to choose a lifestyle of one's own are considered not simply personal and individual freedoms, but freedoms which extend to the way in which one rears one's children'.[31] However, there must be limits to these freedoms,[32] as we shall explain in more detail below. It is important for a court to understand D's culture in order to determine whether or not the *mens rea* for murder was present,[33] but liability for gross negligence manslaughter does not require a particular state of mind. (The offences under the Domestic Violence, Crime and Victims Act 2004 both require an unlawful act rather than an omission, and the existence of a 'household', and so would be very difficult to apply to the harms under discussion here without multiple amendments.) A similar approach should apply in relation to the liability of head teachers in relation to deaths caused by the provision of inappropriate diets: for example, where V is a child at a boarding school, and the head teacher thus has particularly extensive control over V's diet. Head teachers should have a degree of autonomy to run their schools as they see fit, but this autonomy should not extend to practices that threaten permanent serious harm or death.

In relation to prisoners, an inadequate diet may be an aspect of inhuman punishment[34] and could, in a suitable case, lead to a violation of the right to life and to liability for murder or gross negligence manslaughter. Insufficient food has been held to be inhuman treatment in *Moisejevs v Latvia*.[35] However, it is important to recognise that prisoners are usually adults, and thus generally likely to be able to make an informed decision when offered with a choice and provided with relevant information. Although we do not take the position that the criminal law should always respect an individual's autonomy,[36] there are no valid moral reasons for extending criminal liability in this context if V, a prisoner, makes a free, voluntary and informed decision. Thus, prison governors should generally not be held liable for the consequences where prisoners choose an inadequate diet, if suitable balanced options are available to them.

The same can be said about care home residents where they make a free, voluntary and informed decision. As the British Medical Association points out, generalisation is difficult in relation to care home residents.[37] Such homes cater 'for people with a very wide range of needs including older people with dementia, the learning disabled and those with long-term mental health conditions'.[38] However, many care home residents will be able to make informed decisions, since they will not suffer from these conditions or in any case be able to understand the consequences of their decisions with appropriate support and education. This might not sound like a controversial view, but it does not seem to be universally shared by those who run care homes. For example, one set of care homes apparently takes the view

31 E-L. Marcus, C. Wasserstein Fassberg, J. Namestnik, D. Guedj and Y.Caine, 'Strict Vegan, Low-Calorie Diet Administered by Caregiving Daughter to Elderly Mother – Is this Elder Abuse?' (2005) 24 Medical Law 279, 290.

32 Thus, Article 8(2) allows restrictions on the right to respect for private and family life: e.g., for the protection of the rights and freedoms of others.

33 See A. Rentelyn, *The Cultural Defense* (Oxford University Press 2004) 72.

34 *Testa v Croatia* App no 20877/04 (ECHR, 12 July 2007); the applicant had hepatitis C and required a low fat diet for that condition.

35 App no 64846/01 (ECHR, 15 June 2006).

36 See e.g., J. Elvin and C. de Than, 'Consent to Death' in A. Reed, C. Ashford and N. Wake (eds) *Legal Perspectives on State Power: Consent and Control* (Cambridge Scholars Publishing 2016) 50.

37 British Medical Association, 'Deprivation of Liberty in Care Homes' <www.bma.org.uk/advice/employment/ethics/mental-capacity/deprivation-of-liberty-safeguards/deprivation-of-liberty-in-care-homes> accessed 24 January 2018.

38 Ibid

that 'Making sure that residents eat smaller portions of nutrient-rich food throughout the day is essential',[39] that care homes should 'Use only high-quality, nutritious ingredients',[40] and that 'raw foods should be avoided'.[41] If taken literally, this would seem to deny all care home residents the ability to choose to eat an uncooked apple or any 'junk food' on the basis of a paternalistic presumption of vulnerability. This would be unacceptable, since care home residents are not necessarily 'deprived of a capacity to make the relevant decision, or disabled from making a free choice, or incapacitated or disabled from giving or expressing a real and genuine consent'.[42] Indeed, the Mental Capacity Act 2005 starts with presumptions that adults have capacity and should be allowed to make as many decisions for themselves as possible, and states that unwise decisions do not in themselves show lack of capacity. Thus, in sum, there is a duty on care home managers and staff to ensure that adequate and nutritious food, and accessible dietary information, are available, but only to intervene if a vulnerable adult is at risk of serious harm or death due to the food they actually eat.

(b) Parents in relation to the rejection of medical treatment for religious or pseudoscientific reasons

As previously stated,[43] there is no doubt that parents owe a duty of care to dependent children in their care. However, there is debate about how the law should deal with parents who reject medical treatment for religious or pseudoscientific reasons. In the U.S., the majority of states have at least some religious exemptions to criminal child abuse and neglect statutes.[44] Nonetheless, there are also many convictions of U.S. parents for failing to provide medical treatment for their children, including 'faith-healing' cases, since it only appears to be a small minority of states which allow the religious exemptions to apply to manslaughter charges.[45] The controversial religious exemptions have been met with strong criticism from the medical profession: 'The opinion of the American Academy of Pediatrics (AAP) Committee on Bioethics is that the basic moral principle of justice requires that children be protected uniformly by laws and regulations. Parents and others who deny a child necessary medical care on religious grounds should not be exempt from civil or criminal action that otherwise would be appropriate'.[46] Given that the parents and child are clearly in an unequal power relationship in this situation, that there are medical professionals able and willing to 'rescue' the vulnerable child by providing care and that English law allows a *Gillick*-competent child to consent to treatment against the wishes of the parents,[47] there are strong arguments here for the appropriate response to the vulnerability of the child to be a homicide charge when death is caused by parental refusal of lifesaving treatment for a child. However, should this extend to death from preventable disease, for example where the children of 'anti-vaxers' die from a condition

39 S. Murray, 'Care home residents need tailored nutrition – here are some guidelines' *The Guardian* (London, 5 August 2016) <www.theguardian.com/social-care-network/2016/aug/05/care-home-residents-need-tailored-nutrition-guidelines> accessed 29 January 2018
40 Ibid.
41 Ibid.
42 *Re S.A.* (*Vulnerable Adult with Capacity: Marriage*) (n 17).
43 See (n 19).
44 A. Sandrom, 'Most states allow religious exemptions from child abuse and neglect laws' *Pew Research* <www.pewresearch.org/fact-tank/2016/08/12/most-states-allow-religious-exemptions-from-child-abuse-and-neglect-laws/> accessed 24 January 2018.
45 Ibid. (there were seven such states at the time of writing of this chapter).
46 E-L. Marcus *et al.* (n 31) 293.
47 *Gillick v West Norfolk and Wisbech AHA* [1985] UKHL 7.

which could have been eradicated if universal vaccination were achievable? Parents have been convicted of manslaughter by providing ineffective 'treatment' rather than allowing medical care: for example, in the Canadian case of David and Collet Stephan, whose son Ezekiel died of meningitis after they had chosen to give him hot peppers, garlic, onions and horseradish rather than vaccinations and medicine.[48] Their sentencing caused a public outcry for its perceived leniency and has led to a Crown sentencing appeal – David received four months' imprisonment, Collet three months of strict house arrest, and both additionally received probation and community service.[49] In England, there has been a string of convictions of parents whose strict religious beliefs led to them failing to provide medical treatment for their children. Mr and Mrs Kunene were convicted of manslaughter in 2014 after failing to seek medical help for their son, who died of rickets.[50] On sentencing, Mr Justice Singh used the language of vulnerability and care: '… the right to manifest one's religion is not absolute. It is limited in particular by the rights of others. The state has a particularly important duty to protect the right to life, especially when a young child is concerned'.[51] Mr and Mrs Kandare were also convicted of manslaughter in 2015 when their baby daughter was given prayer rather than food or medical treatment and died of pneumonia.[52]

Our view is that parents should have a legal right to make important decisions about their children unless and until the latter are legally competent to make their own decisions, but that there should be limits to this right and that gross negligence manslaughter convictions may be appropriate where parents reject conventional medical treatment for religious or pseudoscientific reasons. Stephen Lyons argues that 'When spiritual healing as an expression of religious conscience is compared with the less-than-perfect record of its secular counterpart, there is no compelling state interest that would warrant prohibiting its use on children'.[53] However, the issue at hand is not whether there is a compelling state interest in prohibiting alternative medicine such as spiritual healing but whether there should be criminal liability for homicide where parents reject orthodox treatment because they do not believe in it. Our view is that this should be a possibility where parents fail to provide any treatment at all for religious reasons (e.g., because they trust in God's will to determine the outcome) and they were, or should have been, aware that potentially effective treatment was available. '[B]oth religious and secular parents should be required to provide responsible care. There is no reason for treating religious parents differently'.[54] Whilst 'responsible care does not always mean conventional medical intervention',[55] we also believe that liability for

48 See M. Grant, 'Parents' convictions in son's meningitis death upheld by Alberta Appeal Court' *CBC News* (Canada, 14 November 2017) <www.cbc.ca/news/canada/calgary/david-collet-stephan-meningitis-death-son-failure-provide-necessaries-appeal-1.4402665> accessed 24 January 2018.

49 Ibid.

50 L. Haddou, 'Parents jailed for manslaughter of baby who had rickets' *The Guardian* (London, 28 February 2014) <www.theguardian.com/uk-news/2014/feb/28/parents-jailed-manslaughter-baby-rickets> accessed 29 January 2018.

51 Ibid.

52 Editorial, 'Rebecca Kandare death: parents jailed for malnourished baby killing' *BBC News* (London, 10 November 2015) <www.bbc.co.uk/news/uk-england-birmingham-34781044> accessed 24 January 2018.

53 D. Tate and S. Lyons, 'First Amendment: Should Parents be Punished for Using Prayer to Treat a Fatally Ill Child?' (1992) 78 American Bar Association 38, 39.

54 J. Thomas, 'Prosecuting Religious Parents for Homicide: Compounding a Tragedy?' (1994) Virginia Journal of Social Policy and the Law 409, 428.

55 Ibid. 418.

gross negligence manslaughter should be a possibility where the parents used 'alternative' rather than conventional medical treatment and they should have realised that pursuing this course of treatment significantly increased the risk of death. Such parents could be concerned and loving, but they could also be grossly negligent, which is the central issue in terms of culpability here.[56] If so, some of the sentences imposed are startlingly low in comparison to those for parents whose children die from comparable levels of neglect but with other causes, such as malnutrition.

(c) Managers in relation to deaths arising from workplace stress

Despite the view of Sarah Waters, an expert on workplace suicides, that employers 'have been able to turn a blind eye' to deaths arising from workplace stress,[57] the situation is not so simple. Unlike Japan, which recognises death by overwork ('karoshi') as a specific legal concept for which there is compensation,[58] the UK has no specific laws to address such deaths. Nonetheless, workplace stress claims are a major source of litigation in tort law,[59] and there are various corporate offences that are relevant in this context.[60] In addition, managers could in principle also be convicted for any deaths caused by such stress, whether these deaths arise through suicide[61] or by a medical condition such as a heart attack or a stroke.[62] Although there are no leading English criminal law cases on this issue, it is clear that managers owe a duty of care to employees in criminal law and that leaders can thus be liable for gross negligence manslaughter in this context:[63] e.g., because they have a contractual obligation to care for employees. This is appropriate because, as Stychin says in the context of tort law, 'Duties arise from the demand upon us to be attentive to the vulnerability of others'.[64] Managers are in control of employees; it is this control and the 'the

56 *R v Adomako* [1995] 1 AC 171.

57 S. Waters, 'Suicidal Work: Work-Related Suicides are Uncounted' <www.hazards.org/suicide/suicidalwork.htm> accessed 24 January 2018.

58 See T. Kobayashi and S. Middlemiss, 'Employers' Liability for Occupational Stress and Death from Overwork (Karoshi) of Workers in Japan' (2008) 1 International Journal of Private Law 256.

59 D Christie, 'Stress and Employers' Liability – Where are We Now?' (2004) Employment Law Bulletin 2, 4.

60 These include the Corporate Manslaughter and Corporate Homicide Act 2007.

61 There are no official UK workplace suicide statistics, but 'Workplace suicides are sharply on the rise internationally, with increasing numbers of employees choosing to take their own lives in the face of extreme pressures at work' and there is no reason to believe that the UK is any exception (S. Waters and J. Chan, 'How work can lead to suicide in a globalised economy' *The Conversation* (London, August 16 2016) <www.theconversation.com/how-work-can-lead-to-suicide-in-a-globalised-economy-62847> accessed 24 January 2018). As the Health and Safety Executive (HSE) puts it, 'The latest estimates from the [UK] Labour Force Survey … show … [t]he total number of cases of work related stress, depression or anxiety in 2015/16 was 488,000 cases, a prevalence rate of 1510 per 100,000 workers' (HSE, 'Work Related Stress, Anxiety and Depression Statistics in Great Britain 2016' <www.hse.gov.uk/statistics/causdis/stress/> accessed 24 January 2018).

62 Research indicates that workplace stress 'has been linked to an increased risk of coronary heart disease' and that '[j]ob strain may be associated with an increased risk of ischemic stroke' (E. Fransson, S.T. Nyberg, K. Heikkilä, *et al.*, 'Job Strain and the Risk of Stroke: An Individual-Participant Data Meta-Analysis' (2015) 46 Stroke 557).

63 See e.g., CPS, 'Failed Company and its Manager Convicted of Corporate and Gross Negligence Manslaughter' <www.cps.gov.uk/news/latest_news/failed_company_and_its_manager_convicted/> accessed 24 January 2018.

64 Stychin (n 4) 346.

relative power of the parties that helps us to understand the relationship, and the ethical and legal responsibilities that flow from it'.[65] It is true that in many cases – e.g., concerning death caused by a heart attack – it may be impossible to prove that the fault of a specific manager caused the death.[66] However, in some cases, employees leave letters or notes blaming work for their decision to commit suicide and evoking 'experiences of working life that has been disrupted by chaotic restructuring, forced redeployment, increased production targets or management bullying'.[67] In these cases, it may be appropriate to convict D for causing another person to commit suicide, although as the law stands there would also be a need for extreme carelessness rather than mere negligence.[68]

Until very recently, there had been few cases in which a vulnerable person's suicide had led to liability for a homicide offence. This has begun to change in both English law and elsewhere. Most of the earlier cases concerned physical injuries which were still the operating and substantial cause of death, regardless of whether V took their own life. Thus, in the U.S. case of *People v Lewis*, [69] D was liable for manslaughter where V cut his own throat while dying slowly from a gunshot wound inflicted by D. In the English case of *Dear* [70] the Court of Appeal left open the possibility that V had reopened the wounds inflicted by D, or had failed to staunch the blood flow in order to die, hence upholding a conviction which may have been on the basis of causing suicide. *Blaue* and the other self-neglect cases are also, on one view, victim suicides in similar situations.[71] In cases like *Blaue*, it can be argued that V has a 'moral thin skull'; that is, ' "a personal vulnerability that must be taken account of" in a particular way in calculating D's liability'.[72] There are a few relevant historical trials,[73] and while suicide was still a crime, counselling it could attract liability (see for example the conviction of George Bowen in 1815 in Northampton, Massachusetts for persuading a fellow prisoner to kill himself before the hangman could).[74] However, it is only in recent years that driving a person to commit suicide through psychological abuse has become a greater concern for the courts, and the first such convictions are occurring in several legal systems at the time of writing. In July 2017, Nicholas Allen was sentenced to 15 years' imprisonment for manslaughter by an English court, having pleaded guilty on the basis that his stalking and threats had led his former partner to commit suicide.[75] In June 2017, a Massachusetts court found Michelle Carter guilty of involuntary manslaughter by urging her friend to commit

65 Ibid., 345, discussing the duty of care concept in tort law, but also making a broader point.
66 A similar point could be made in relation to potential criminal liability for a non-fatal offence: e. g., where D must have caused a recognised psychiatric illness or physical injury.
67 Waters (n 57).
68 *Adomako* (n 56).
69 [1899] 124 Cal 551.
70 [1996] Crim LR 595.
71 [1975] 1 WLR 1411.
72 J. Elvin, 'Causation and Legal Responsibility: "Take Your Victim as You Find Him?"' (2017) 1 Journal of the Institute of Law 45, 49, quoting M. Ramsay, 'The Religious Beliefs of Tort Victims: Religious Thin Skulls or Failures of Mitigation?' (2007) 20 Canadian Journal of Law and Equality 399. See too D. Klimchuk, 'Causation, Thin Skulls and Equality' (1998) 11 Canadian Journal of Law and Jurisprudence 115.
73 *Vaux's case* [1592] 4 Co. Rep. 44, under the logic of which a person who deliberately causes another to commit suicide would be guilty of murder as principal, not merely as an accomplice, see East, 1 *Pleas of the Crown* 228; *R v Gaylor* [1857] D and B 288.
74 See J. Tager, '"Murder by Counseling": The 1816 Case of George Bowen (Northampton)' (2010) 38 Historical Journal of Massachusetts 103.
75 See D. Connett, 'Stalker jailed for manslaughter of former partner who killed herself' *The Guardian* (London, 28 July 2017) < https://www.theguardian.com/uk-news/2017/jul/28/sta

suicide in text messages.[76] He got out of his truck when it was filling with exhaust fumes, but obeyed a text from her telling him to get back in. The most relevant leading English case in this area, *R v Dhaliwal*, states that 'subject to evidence and argument on the critical issue of causation, unlawful violence on an individual with a fragile and vulnerable personality, which is proved to be a material cause of death (even if the result of suicide) would at least arguably, be capable of amounting to manslaughter'.[77] This does not necessarily require V to suffer from a recognisable psychiatric illness caused by D's abuse, but it is arguable that V's action would break the chain of causation if such a psychiatric condition were not present.[78] The problem with allowing such a break in the chain of causation is that there would be an element of illogicality in the requirements here: V would need to suffer sufficient psychiatric injury for it to be possible for her suicide to be regarded as caused by D's abuse or violence, but still have the presence of mind to seek medical treatment and a diagnosis before taking a desperate step. As one of us has argued elsewhere in conjunction with Catherine Elliott, the 'gap between theoretical legal liability and actual effective justice for suicide victims driven to suicide by domestic abuse, requires a change in legal culture which can only be achieved through a new statutory offence giving official recognition that homicide liability should be pursued in such cases'.[79] Such a statutory offence could equally cover workplace abuse as well as domestic abuse, would create a straightforward means of prosecution and avoid the complexities and uncertainties under the current law. We will propose the offence at the end of this chapter.

Under the existing law, there is no reason why a manslaughter conviction should not be brought in relation to causing suicide, although a charge of unlawful act manslaughter imposes particularly high hurdles in relation to causation, the unlawful act and psychiatric harm. The basis of Nicholas Allen's conviction remains unclear due to the guilty plea, although there was evidence of psychiatric harm to the victim, and the judge's sentencing remarks include a statement that 'it is not suggested that you intended at any time that she should die but clearly you intended that she should suffer serious psychological harm'.[80] The most appropriate charge in such cases is rather a moot point at present, but Jeremy Horder and Laura McGowan have argued in relation to violent domestic abuse that a charge of gross negligence manslaughter would be more suitable.[81] We would agree with this, since it avoids the complexities identified in *Dhaliwal*, and indeed suicide may be a 'natural' or foreseeable reaction to a history of abuse or neglect; but we will take the argument further to encompass cases of deaths arising from workplace stress in our proposed new statutory offence. As Horder and McGowan put it, 'The destructive effect domestic abuse has on the victim's autonomy can be regarded as rendering the defendant criminally responsible for the

lker-jailed-manslaughter-former-partner-killed-herself-nicholas-allen-justene-reece> accessed 29 January 2018.

76 See Editorial, 'Michelle Carter guilty over texts urging boyfriend's suicide' *BBC News* (BBC US & Canada, 16 June 2017) <www.bbc.co.uk/news/world-us-canada-40304433> accessed 22 January 2018.

77 *R v Dhaliwal* [2006] EWCA Crim 1139 [8].

78 This is a different issue from the requirement of a recognised psychiatric condition on the facts in *Dhaliwal*, where the basis of an unlawful act manslaughter charge would have been s.20 OAPA 1861 via psychiatric injury.

79 C. Elliott and C. de Than, 'Restructuring the Homicide Offences to Tackle the Problems of Violence, Discrimination and Drugs in Modern Society' (2009) 20 King's Law Journal 69, 83.

80 See Connett (n 75).

81 J. Horder and L. McGowan, 'Manslaughter by Causing Another's Suicide' (2006) Criminal Law Review, 1035.

victim's suicide'.[82] It might seem strange to develop Elliott and de Than's, and Horder and McGowan's, arguments in this way. However, there are parallels between workplace abuse, which involves a manager and a subordinate, and domestic abuse. In both cases, there is 'a relation of controlling influence'[83] that may be 'established and maintained over a long period'[84] through coercion and threats. Furthermore, Horder and McGowan correctly state that 'When a relationship is characterised by persistent domestic abuse, the experience of living with the abuse is liable to affect the victim's decision-making processes',[85] and a similar point can be made in relation to workplace abuse.[86] Abuse in the workplace may be less likely to involve actual or threatened physical violence, but this does not mean that it cannot be physically or psychologically devastating. As Jesse Berdinka, who worked for the notorious film producer Harvey Weinstein, put it about this experience: 'You see stories of domestic abuse on the news and think, how can people keep subjecting themselves to that? And then I would walk into the office the next day … For me at least it was the drip, day after day, of never knowing if you are good enough'.[87] In many professions, employees spend more waking hours at work than at home, so abuse of workplace power dynamics may justify liability in the same way as domestic abuse. A new offence of causing suicide, which would apply in the workplace context and elsewhere, could run parallel to a domestic abuse homicide offence, and the evidence to support its introduction is arguably as strong. We are not aware of any English cases where managers have been convicted for gross negligence manslaughter because of workplace abuse. Evidence points 'to a steep rise in suicides in the context of a generalised deterioration in working conditions',[88] yet it seems that 'company bosses are rarely held to account [in criminal law] for inflicting … misery on their employees'.[89]

Where would criminal liability be appropriate in this context? It would be impossible to provide a comprehensive consideration of all relevant issues here, but we would like to consider some basic matters, such as the significance of an employee's agreement to undertake work. Our starting point is that adopted by Hugh Collins:

> [W]orkers are people, not things. As such, they deserve to be treated with respect. By agreeing to work for another, employees do not consent to be treated like chattels or slaves. They expect to be treated fairly and with reasonable care for their safety.[90]

82 Ibid. 1042

83 Ibid. 1041, discussing domestic abuse.

84 Ibid. 1043, again discussing domestic abuse.

85 Ibid. 1042.

86 See e.g., N. Tehrani, stating that 'people exposed to [workplace] bullying can develop symptoms of post-traumatic stress' (N. Tehrani, 'Counselling and Rehabilitating Employees Involved with Bullying' in S. Einarsen, H. Hoel, D. Zapf and C. Cooper (eds), *Bullying and Emotional Abuse in the Workplace: International Perspectives in Research and Practice* (Taylor and Francis 2003) 270, 271).

87 J. Berdinka, quoted by S. Kirchgaessner and H. Ellis-Peterson, '"The Cult of Harvey": Weinstein's staff at Miramax describe bullying and abuse' *The Guardian* (London, 25 October 2017) <www.theguardian.com/film/2017/oct/25/the-cult-of-harvey-weinsteins-staff-at-miramax-describe-bullying-and-abuse> accessed 29 January 2018.

88 Waters and Chan (n 61).

89 Ibid. As one of us put it when writing about liability for suicide linked to domestic abuse, 'Thus, while in theory it may well be possible to fit this type of homicide into the existing common law, in practice this has not been happening'. Elliott and de Than (n 79).

90 H. Collins, *Employment Law* (2nd edn, Oxford University Press 2009) 3.

Managers should be criminally liable in some workplace stress or bullying cases not because the law should protect competent adult employees, 'against their will, from the harmful consequences even of their fully voluntary choices and undertakings',[91] but because there may be no meaningful consent both in relation to the workplace conditions and to a death caused by these conditions.[92] 'Employers may in reality be in a position to dictate the terms of the employment contract, and … enforcing the contract may therefore amount to a form of illegitimate interpersonal exploitation'.[93] Such exploitation can occur where the employee has no practical alternative (or thinks that this is the case) but to remain in the current employment and the manager seriously jeopardises the employee's health by insisting upon the performance of the employment contract[94] or more than is required by it. (It is important to bear in mind that learned helplessness can be a factor here, as with 'battered woman syndrome': 'workplace bullying … entails negative events that may be perceived as uncontrollable'.[95]) Whilst we accept that consent is morally transformative because it 'can make an action right when it would otherwise be wrong',[96] employees in such a situation do not meaningfully accept their treatment if they do not approve of it and merely submit to it, having been 'disabled from making a free choice'.[97] Furthermore, there is no reason in principle why D should not be liable where this situation results in the employee's death: e.g., because of a heart attack, a stroke, or a suicide. A decision to commit suicide may not be a meaningful exercise of autonomy because there may have been no other practical alternative to avoiding the abuse or V may have felt that this was the case because of a mental disorder caused by the workplace stress. This is parallel to the cases of *People v Lewis, Dear* and *Nicholas Allen* discussed earlier in the chapter. As Jerome Hall puts it, it is potentially 'criminal homicide to cause a normal adult to commit suicide by creating a situation so cruel and revolting that death is preferred to unavoidable continued submission'.[98]

Industry standards are relevant here, but not necessarily as a factor in D's favour. As Mustill LJ put it in the context of tort law, the case law shows that 'one employer is [not] exonerated simply by proving that other employers are just as negligent, but … the standard of what is negligent is influenced, although not decisively, by the practice in the industry as a whole'.[99] Evidence that other managers behave similarly might show that D's behaviour is reasonable. On the other hand, where there is a serious risk of injury to the health of employees, it might instead suggest that there is a problem across the industry, that the other managers are also negligent and that employees have no real choice but to submit to

91 See J. Feinberg, *Harm to Self: The Moral Limits of the Criminal Law* (Oxford University Press 1986) 12, characterising this as the basis for what he calls 'hard' paternalism and drawing a distinction between this and 'soft' paternalism. According to Feinberg, ibid., the latter type of paternalism in contrast holds that 'the state has the right to prevent self-regarding harmful conduct … when but only when that conduct is substantially non-voluntary, or when temporary intervention is necessary to establish whether it is voluntary or not'.

92 We have written elsewhere that enthusiastic consent should be required as a defence to the infliction of serious injury or death: see e,g., Elvin and de Than (n 36).

93 J. Elvin, 'How Should the Law Respond to Stress-Related Claims?' (2010) 21 King's Law Journal 43, 55.

94 Ibid.

95 A-K Samnani, 'The Early Stages of Workplace Bullying and How It Becomes Prolonged: The Role of Culture in Predicting Target Responses' (2013) 113 Journal of Business Ethics 119.

96 H. Hurd, 'The Moral Magic of Consent' (1996) 2 Legal Theory 121, 123.

97 *Re S.A. (Vulnerable Adult with Capacity: Marriage)* (n 17).

98 J. Hall, *General Principles of Criminal Law* (2nd edn, The Bobbs Merrill Company 1960) 274.

99 *Thompson v Smith Shiprepairers* [1994] QB 405, 416.

the practice. Whilst a court must be slow to blame a manager 'for not ploughing a lone furrow',[100] behaviour is not acceptable simply because it is common. Managers have responsibilities to those who are dependent upon them and thus vulnerable, and this responsibility is not necessarily fulfilled by copying the behaviour of others in a position of privilege.

It might seem harsh to suggest that managers should be liable for certain deaths arising from workplace stress, since it is legitimate for them to place employees under a degree of stress to meet certain institutional goals. However, those who undertake management duties have an ethical as well as a legal duty to consider more than institutional goals: employees in such cases 'find themselves vulnerable to the defendant in a manner that is outside their control and to a degree that sets them apart from the world at large'.[101] Moreover, it is important to remember that there is a business case for managing stress in the workplace. Stress does not improve decision-making and can lead to errors which may cause significant problems for employers, including but not limited to legal liability to third parties. It 'has serious implications for organisational performance .... in terms of increased employee absence, staff turnover and reduced productivity. In addition, stress is a major cause of conflict at work, undermines positive employee relations, and can also lead to reputational damage'.[102] As Tamie Kobayashi and Sam Middlemiss argue, especially in the present economic conditions in the UK, there is a danger of short-termism, where employers attach undue importance to short-term financial or other performance indicators at the expense of the 'welfare and health of their staff'.[103] In sum, the inequality of the employment relationship, in combination with employers' possession of information and observations which indicate to them that particular employees are vulnerable, justify legal as well as moral responsibility for the well-being of staff.

The last issue we would like to consider in relation to liability for a death caused by workplace stress is to what extent, if at all, it should be relevant whether a manager was following orders from a superior. This is not necessarily a relevant matter in relation to each case: there will be cases where a manager was not acting 'under orders' or even acting contrary to them. However, it may be relevant in some instances. As the law stands, whether D was grossly negligent 'will depend on the seriousness of the breach of duty committed by the defendant in all the circumstances in which the defendant was placed when it occurred'.[104] Although case law has also made it clear that there must have a '"serious and obvious risk of death" at the time of breach',[105] the vagueness of the law effectively leaves the matter to the jury to determine. There is a need for clarity here. English criminal law does not currently recognise a defence of superior orders per se. As Shlomit Wallerstein puts it, 'English criminal law is based on the notion of individual liability and the recognition of all people, including subordinates, as rational agents. As such, presumably, they are required to obey only legal orders. If they obey an illegal order they may be held liable for their choices'.[106] However, as she adds, this does not mean that superior orders cannot, and

100 Ibid., discussing tort law.

101 D. Manderson, *Proximity, Levinas, and the Soul of Law* (McGill-Queen's University Press 2006) 124, discussing the ethics of proximity rather than the specific issue at hand here.

102 Chartered Institute of Personnel and Development, *Building the Business Case for Managing Stress in the Workplace* (2008) 5.

103 Kobayashi and Middlemiss (n 58) 156.

104 *Adomako* (n 56) 187.

105 *R v Rose (Honey Maria)* [2017] EWCA Crim 1168

106 S. Wallerstein, 'Why English Law Should Not Incorporate the Defence of Superior Orders' (2010) Criminal Law Review 109, 120.

should not, be relevant in determining liability: for example, duress may be a relevant defence where D, a soldier, feared being killed by a superior for disobeying an order.[107] Are there any good reasons for taking superior orders into account in D's favour when considering whether D was grossly negligent in relation to a death caused by workplace stress? Let us suppose that D, a manager, has a reasonable fear that his superior will try to sack him for disobedience to an order, but there is an obvious and serious risk that obeying this order will lead to V's suicide. There is no reason why a threat to D's economic well-being should take priority over a serious and obvious threat to V's life; thus, there is no reason why this economic threat should count in D's favour in determining whether there was a gross breach of duty, although it is arguable that the matter of superior orders should be relevant at the stage of sentencing. (To say this is not to reject the argument that 'a threat to cause the defendant economic harm, to damage his reputation or to harm his property might constitute overwhelming pressure in some circumstances,'[108] and that this pressure should count as a defence in certain circumstances in criminal law generally.) We will return in another publication to the case for new statutory crimes related to non-fatal ill-treatment of employees.

(d) Prison officers and governors in relation to the suicide of prisoners

As Lord Rodger put it in *R L (a Patient) v Secretary of State for Justice:*

> Whenever a prisoner kills himself, it is at least *possible*, that the prison authorities, who are responsible for the prisoner, have failed, either in their obligation to take general measures to diminish the opportunities for prisoners to harm themselves, or in their operational obligation to try to prevent the particular prisoner from committing suicide. Given the closed nature of the prison world, without an independent investigation you might never know. So there must be an investigation of that kind to find out whether something did indeed go wrong.[109]

There were 119 self-inflicted deaths in prisons in England and Wales in 2016, more than double the number in 2010,[110] and these figures have been noted with great concern.[111] The trend is in stark contrast to the dramatic decrease in suicides in police custody in the same period.[112] There is a difficult balance to be drawn between paternalism and autonomy

107 Ibid. 124.

108 A. Reed, 'Duress and False Imprisonment: The Constituent Elements of the Threat' (2012) 76 (5) Journal of Criminal Law 377, 379.

109 [2009] 1 AC 588, [90].

110 Ministry of Justice, 'Deaths in Prison Custody 1978–2016', Table 1.1 < https://data.gov.uk/dataset/safety-in-custody/resource/10042783-7328-40f6-903d-38de1ace70fb> accessed 24 January 2018.

111 Joint Committee on Human Rights, *Mental Health and Deaths in Prison: Interim Report* (HL Paper 167, HC 893, 2017) 3. See also N. Padfield, 'What's Going on in Prisons?' (2015) Criminal Law Review 751 and R. Epstein, 'Deaths in Detention' (2015) 179(10) Criminal Law and Justice Weekly <www.criminallawandjustice.co.uk/features/Deaths-Detention> accessed 24 January 2018.

112 See the Dame Angiolini Report, *Report of the Independent Review of Deaths and Serious Incidents in Police Custody* (2017) para 6.3 <www.gov.uk/government/uploads/system/uploads/attachment_data/file/655401/Report_of_Angiolini_Review_ISBN_Accessible.pdf> accessed 24 January 2018.

in this situation, since although there is no general right to die under English law where assistance in causing death would be required[113] there is in essence a human right to commit suicide as an exercise of self-determination.[114] This has been seen mainly in cases relating to indirect means of killing oneself such as refusal of medical treatment, e.g., force-feeding,[115] or choices to refuse lifesaving surgery, even by persons who lack mental capacity,[116] and to end-of-life decisions.[117] There is a lack of clarity as to the extent to which autonomy overrides paternalism here, since recent English cases have prioritised autonomy[118] but the European Court of Human Rights (ECtHR) has spoken in terms which appear to assume capacity is required before autonomy can be exercised, stating: 'the imposition of medical treatment, without the consent of a mentally competent adult patient, would interfere with a person's physical integrity in a manner capable of engaging the rights protected under art.8(1) of the Convention'.[119] More recently, the ECtHR has held:

> ... an individual's right to decide by what means and at what point his or her life will end, provided he or she is capable of freely reaching a decision on this question and acting in consequence, is one of the aspects of the right to respect for private life within the meaning of Article 8 of the Convention.[120]

A further application of this issue has been seen in the context of a hunger strike: in *Governor of X Prison v P McD*, [121] Ms. Justice Baker stated in the Irish High Court:

> I am satisfied that Mr. McD has freely made a choice to continue his hunger strike and to refuse treatment should he become incapacitated as a result and fall into coma. I am also satisfied that the State may properly respect the personal autonomy and right of self-determination of Mr. McD by giving effect to his stated wish and direction not to

113 *Nicklinson v Ministry of Justice* [2014] UKSC 38; detailed consideration of that case is beyond the scope of this chapter, but one of the clearest messages it gave is that judges regard this as a matter for Parliament rather than the courts, although the Supreme Court repeatedly reaffirmed that an autonomous wish to die should be respected by the law – see for example [108], [186], [300] and [326]. Noel Conway is, at the time of writing, awaiting a date for his Court of Appeal hearing regarding a right to die via assisted suicide for those with mental capacity but physical incapacity which prevents them from committing suicide unaided. See further our discussion of these issues (n 36).

114 In spite of assertions to the contrary by Humphries J in the Irish High Court in *A.B. v C.D.* [2016] IEHC 541 [13]: 'An order sentencing a person to life imprisonment, or to any other period, is a court order which must be obeyed like any other order ... A person ordered to be imprisoned cannot lawfully frustrate the court's order by destroying himself'. Humphreys J did not cite any cases on Article 8 of the ECHR, focusing only on Articles 2 and 3, which can be seen as a flaw in the judgment.

115 *A NHS Foundation Trust v Ms X* [2014] EWCOP 35.

116 *Wye Valley NHS Trust v B (Rev 1)* [2015] EWCOP 60.

117 *Pretty v UK* [2002] 35 EHRR 1 [63].

118 As Jackson J put it in *Wye Valley* (n 116) [11]: 'As the [Mental Capacity] Act and the European Convention make clear, a conclusion that a person lacks decision-making capacity is not an *"off-switch"* for his rights and freedoms. To state the obvious, the wishes and feelings, beliefs and values of people with a mental disability are as important to them as they are to anyone else, and may even be more important. It would therefore be wrong in principle to apply any automatic discount to their point of view'.

119 Ibid.

120 *Gross v Switzerland* [2014] 58 EHRR 7 [79].

121 [2015] IEHC 259.

> be treated. I consider he has fully and freely expressed a decision that treatment not be afforded to him.[122]

In contrast to this, where suicide by a prisoner or other person deprived of their liberty is not an autonomous exercise of self-determination, but rather the product of the manner in which they have been treated, there is a clear set of duties upon authorities under Articles 2 and 3 of the European Convention on Human Rights (ECHR).[123] In summary, Article 2 imposes duties to take appropriate measures to ensure that a prisoner does not commit suicide when authorities know, or should have known, of that risk.[124] Importantly for the purposes of this chapter, it also imposes a duty to make an effective investigation capable of leading to the identification and punishment of any person responsible for any death in custody;[125] this extends to deaths which are not caused intentionally, but which result from e.g., medical negligence.[126] However, there is a broad range of effective responses to deaths of prisoners, depending on the circumstances:

> … if the infringement of the right to life or to personal integrity is not caused intentionally, the positive obligation imposed by Article 2 to set up an effective judicial system does not necessarily require the provision of a criminal-law remedy in every case. In the specific sphere of medical negligence the obligation may for instance also be satisfied if the legal system affords victims a remedy in the civil courts, either alone or in conjunction with a remedy in the criminal courts, enabling any liability of the doctors concerned to be established and any appropriate civil redress, such as an order for damages and for the publication of the decision, to be obtained. Disciplinary measures may also be envisaged.[127]

Human rights law has long imposed a duty to take particular care of vulnerable prisoners; the case law on such duties is now detailed and makes explicit reference to concepts of vulnerability, inequality and care, albeit not from an overt theoretical perspective. In the contexts of both the right to life under Article 2 and freedom from torture and inhuman and degrading treatment and punishment under Article 3, the ECtHR has repeatedly stressed that prisoners as a class are vulnerable and may be unable to make effective complaints about their treatment or may face sanctions for doing so,[128] and that states always have an obligation to provide appropriate medical care for detainees who have health problems,[129] regardless of their crime.[130] Indeed, prisoners who have displayed suicidal tendencies, or

122 Ibid. [129]–[130].
123 As discussed by Lang J in *Daniel v St George's Healthcare NHS Trust* [2016] EWHC 23.
124 *Keenan v UK* [2001] 33 EHRR 38; applied in e.g., *Orange v Chief Constable of West Yorkshire* [2001] EWCA Civ 611.
125 *Salman v Turkey* [2002] 34 EHRR 17; although a criminal prosecution is not a necessity in every case – see *Armani Da Silva v UK* [2016] 63 EHRR 12 (the Jean Charles de Menezes shooting, where no prosecutions were made due to honest belief in an imminent threat) and *Tyrrell v HM Senior Coroner County Durham and Darlington* [2016] EWHC 1892.
126 *Calvelli v Italy* App no 32967/96 (ECHR, 17 January 2002) [39].
127 Ibid. [51].
128 See for example C. de Than, 'Positive Obligations Under the European Convention On Human Rights: Towards The Human Rights Of Victims and Vulnerable Witnesses' (2003) 67 Journal of Criminal Law 165.
129 *Murray v The Netherlands* [2017] 64 EHRR 3.
130 *Rooman v Belgium* App no 18052/11 (ECHR, 18 July 2017).

have a psychiatric condition which involves such tendencies, require special measures to be taken which are dictated by their condition, regardless of the seriousness of the offence of which they may have been convicted.[131] However, the ECtHR has recognised that not all prisoners are equally vulnerable, and that when the state is aware of a particular vulnerability of an inmate then it must tailor a response which is appropriate for the latter's specific needs and rights:[132] this is an ethic of care theory without such a label. Sometimes a specific vulnerability will appear to allow the state to override autonomy, as in *Gennadiy Naumenko v Ukraine*, where the ECtHR found insufficient evidence that requiring a suicidal prisoner to take medication was inhuman or degrading treatment, even though it was unclear whether he had consented.[133] Indeed the Recommendation No. R (98) 7 of the Committee of Ministers of the Council of Europe concerning the ethical and organisational aspects of health care in prison, states: 'The risk of suicide should be constantly assessed both by medical and custodial staff. Physical methods designed to avoid self-harm, close and constant observation, dialogue and reassurance, as appropriate, should be used in moments of crisis …'. Once there is a real risk of self-harm by a prisoner in circumstances of which the authorities know or ought to know, the latter must do all that could reasonably be expected of them to prevent that risk from materialising.[134] A disability may require more care to be taken, but this must not be the basis of discriminatory treatment.[135]

The approach taken by the ECtHR is contextual and situational, as is the theory of ethic and care: for example, in relation to whether a prisoner's treatment violates Article 3, all the circumstances must be taken into account, including 'the nature and context of the treatment, the manner and method of its execution, its duration, its physical or mental effects and, in some instances, the sex, age and state of health of the victim.'[136] The state has particularly strong responsibilities for the lives and safety of prisoners where they have multiple inequalities of power or vulnerabilities, such as where a prisoner has a mental health condition or a physical disability; the care must be specialised.[137] In essence there is a duty to provide a safe environment both as part of the positive obligation to protect life and of that to protect against torture and inhuman and degrading treatment and punishment. But where there is no evidence that the authorities were aware of information which could have

131 *Riviere v France* App no 33834/03 (ECHR, 11 July 2006), reported in French only. There is an analogy with the law on liability for deaths caused by workplace stress here, since special measures are likely to be required in relation to employees who have displayed special vulnerability to workplace stress (see *Walker v Northumberland County Council* [1995] 1 All ER 737, a civil law decision endorsing this position).

132 See e.g., *Dybeku v Albania* App no 41153/06 (ECHR, 18 December 2007). States must ensure appropriate conditions of detention, and in particular adequate medical treatment, for prisoners who require special care due to their (lack of) health; *Rupa v Romania* [2010] 50 EHRR 12, where one of the factors in finding a violation of Article 3 was failure to react appropriately to the prisoner's vulnerable psychiatric state.

133 App no 42023/98 (ECHR, 10 February 2004).

134 *Keenan* (n 124); *Younger v UK* App no 57420/00 (ECHR, 7 January 2003); *Trubnikov v Russia* App no 49790/99 (ECHR, 5 July 2005).

135 See C. de Than and J. Elvin, 'How Should Criminal Law Deal with People who have "Partial Capacity"?' in A. Reed, N. Wake and B. Livings (eds) *Mental Condition Defences and the Criminal Justice System: Perspectives from Law and Medicine* (Cambridge Scholars Publishing 2015) 295, 313–15.

136 *Kudla v Poland* [2000] 35 EHRR 198 [91].

137 See e.g., *Raffray Taddei v France* App no 36435/07 (ECHR, 21 March 2007) and *ZH v Hungary* App no 28973/11 (ECHR, 8 November 2012).

alerted them to the prisoner's specific vulnerability, they owe only the usual duties as to care of detainees.[138]

Even where a prisoner's behaviour in custody merits disciplinary punishment, the severity of such punishment must be tailored to their mental health, since excessive disciplinary punishment may violate the positive obligation to protect life; it may break the prisoner's 'physical and moral resistance'.[139] Further, human rights principles seem not to be judgmental here: even where a prisoner's disability is due to their own actions, indeed by the crime which lost them their freedom, the authorities must tailor their medical care to their vulnerabilities.[140]

The ECtHR does impose a duty to intervene where a prisoner has a psychiatric illness. It is not sufficient for medical treatment to be prescribed; there is also a duty to supervise and monitor treatment and the taking of medicines.[141] In *Kudla v Poland*,[142] although no violation of Article 3 was found on the facts, the ECtHR outlined the duties on the state in relation to inmates:

> the State must ensure that a person is detained in conditions which are compatible with respect for his human dignity, that the manner and method of the execution of the measure [of detention] do not subject him to distress or hardship of an intensity exceeding the unavoidable level of suffering inherent in detention and that, given the practical demands of imprisonment, his health and well-being are adequately secured by, among other things, providing him with the requisite medical assistance.[143]

Since the applicant had displayed suicidal tendencies and the authorities knew about that fact, 'the very nature of the applicant's psychological condition made him more vulnerable than the average detainee and …his detention may have exacerbated to a certain extent his feelings of distress, anguish and fear'.[144] Where the detainee's physical or mental condition deteriorates, there is a duty to consider release, transfer to a more suitable prison or other forms of response.[145] Sometimes the state's liability for a prison suicide will fall under Article 3 rather than Article 2, as in *Keenan v UK*, [146] since there was not sufficient evidence of a reasonable step which ought to have been taken in order to protect the inmate's life, but the lack of effective monitoring of his condition and the lack of informed input from a psychiatrist into his treatment was inhuman treatment given that he was mentally ill and known to be a suicide risk. Yet another layer of vulnerability enhances the state's duties where a detainee has a psychiatric condition and is young, as in *Guvec v Turkey* [147] and *Coselav v Turkey*;[148] in the latter, the ECtHR emphasised the authorities' indifference to the young person's condition, and hence displayed a clear expectation of 'care' in both senses.

138 *Marro and others v Italy* App no 29100/07 (ECHR, 30 April 2014). As stated previously, this appears analogous to the position in the employment context: see (n 131).
139 *Renolde v France* [2009] 48 EHRR 42.
140 E.g., *Xiros v Greece* App no 1033/07 (ECHR, 9 September 2010).
141 *Jasinska v Poland* App no 28326/05 (ECHR, 1 September 2010).
142 (n 136).
143 Ibid. [94].
144 Ibid. [97].
145 *Mouisel v France* App no 67263/01 (ECHR, 14 November 2002).
146 *Keenan* (n 124).
147 App no 70337/01 (ECHR, 20 January 2009).
148 App no 1413/07 (ECHR, 9 October 2012).

Similarly to the aforementioned cases on vulnerability to suicide, the ECtHR has held that the authorities owe duties to take all reasonable measures to prevent prisoners from being killed by other inmates or by guards.[149] In *Premininy v Russia*, the ECtHR pointed out that 'it has been the Court's constant approach that Article 3 imposes on States a duty to protect the physical well-being of persons who find themselves in a vulnerable position by virtue of being within the control of the authorities, such as, for instance, detainees or conscripted servicemen'.[150] There are practical constraints beyond the mere fact of detention which worsen a prisoner's vulnerability: he cannot run from danger or make free decisions about his day-to-day life. What is required depends upon the circumstances, bearing in mind that some prisoners may be particularly vulnerable. Advanced age may enhance the necessary response.[151]

A recent English case, *R. (on the application of Scarfe) v Governor of Woodhill Prison*,[152] found that there is no remedy in public law for prison suicides unless there is evidence of a systemic failure rather than a series of individual failures by particular members of staff to identify the relevant risk factors in individual prisoners; given the strict requirements of human rights law in relation to prison suicides, might the criminal law of homicide actually be a better way of ensuring care for the vulnerable?

The Corporate Manslaughter and Homicide Act 2007 (CMHA 2007) extends to deaths in custody, imposing criminal liability on the prison service 'if the way in which its activities are managed or organised (a) causes a person's death, and (b) amounts to a gross breach of a relevant duty of care owed by the organisation to the deceased'.[153] However, this Act is of questionable value in ensuring appropriate care. First, as previously stated,[154] the number of suicides in prisons has increased in recent years, yet 'the CMHA 2007 has not yet been invoked for a single death in prison custody, or, for that matter, a fatality in any other complex large-scale organisation in the public or private sector'.[155] Second, judicial interpretation of the relevant provisions could prove problematic for the prosecution.[156] Third, 'A custodial institution can hardly be imprisoned, moderate fines can be swallowed up as operational costs, and severe fines may result in further reductions in the number of prison officers which would inevitably have deleterious effects on the safety and welfare of inmates'.[157] Given the second and third factors in particular, individual criminal liability may be more effective in securing protection for the vulnerable. The 2007 Act does not replace individual liability; thus, individual prisoner officers and governors could be liable for

149 *Premininy v Russia* App no. 44973/04 (ECHR, 10 February 2011); *Stasi v France* App. no 25001/07 (ECHR, 20 October 2011); *Yuriy Illarionovich Shchokin* v *Ukraine* App no 4299/03 (ECHR, 3 October 2013); *D.F. v Latvia* App No 11160/07 (ECHR, 29 October 2013).

150 Ibid. [73].

151 E.g., *Farbtuhs v Latvia* App no 4672/02 (ECHR, 2 December 2004), where the applicant was a seriously ill 84-year-old convicted of genocide and crimes against humanity; *Contrada (no. 2) v Italy* App no 7509/08 (ECHR, 11 February 2014).

152 [2017] EWHC 1194.

153 CMHA 2007, s. 1(1). As far as deaths in custody are concerned, the relevant duty came into force in 2011 as a result of a commencement order (the Corporate Manslaughter and Corporate Homicide Act 2007 (Commencement No. 3) Order 2011/1867).

154 Ministry of Justice, 'Deaths in Prison Custody 1978–2016' (n110).

155 D. Doyle and S. Scott. 'Criminal Liability for Deaths in Prison Custody: The Corporate Manslaughter and Corporate Homicide Act 2007' (2016) 55 Howard Journal of Crime and Justice 295, 308.

156 Ibid.

157 Ibid. 307.

common law manslaughter if they are careless. The problem here seems to be that the available law is not being used in this context. In 2012, the High Court noted in the context of a case concerning a prisoner who was found hanging dead from the bars in his cell:

> Whilst there appeared to be no authority in the criminal courts for the proposition that gross negligence causing suicide could amount to gross negligence manslaughter, nor any examples from the coronial courts in which a verdict of unlawful killing had been returned on that basis, S [the Secretary of State] accepted that gross negligence causing someone to take his own life could, in theory, amount to unlawful killing provided all relevant elements of the offence were present and proved.[158]

As with employment law and domestic abuse, it is arguable that the 'gap between theoretical legal liability and actual effective justice for suicide victims driven to suicide … requires a change in legal culture which can only be achieved through a new statutory offence giving official recognition that homicide liability should be pursued in such cases'.[159] There is ample evidence that individual members of the prison service are at fault here: a 'major challenge is [the] negative attitudes of prison officers and health-care staff'.[160] Thus, it is surprising that there does not appear to have been a single relevant prosecution for homicide.

Concluding remarks and reform[161]

If the minimum obligation on the state in relation to people who have broken the law is to ensure that they are kept safe from reasonably foreseeable risks to their lives and in conditions which respect their human dignity, that they are not subjected to distress or hardship of an intensity exceeding the unavoidable level of suffering inherent in detention and that their health is not compromised,[162] surely a similar minimum level of care should apply to the other categories of unequal relationship discussed in this chapter? In the categories which we have examined, English criminal law at least theoretically acknowledges that, in unequal power relationships, there is a responsibility to protect the more vulnerable person. However, this does not mean that the implementation of the relevant legal principles is beyond criticism. In the areas which we have examined, criminal liability is justifiable in some cases, yet convictions for homicide are not necessarily occurring in this jurisdiction. Indeed, there do not appear to have been any English prosecutions for homicide in relation to what are arguably the two areas of greatest concern in practice here: deaths due to workplace stress and suicides in custody. It is for this reason that we believe that there may be a need for the introduction of a specific new offence to address these matters. A change in law and legal culture is required to vindicate the rights of the vulnerable. Hence we propose an offence of causing suicide, formulated as a general offence but which can be

158 *R (on the application of Secretary of State for Justice) v HM Deputy Coroner for the Eastern District of West Yorkshire* [2012] EWHC 1634, H11.

159 Elliott and de Than (n79).

160 K. Hawton, L. Linsell, T. Adeniji, A. Sariaslan and S. Fazel 'Self-Harm in Prisons in England and Wales: An Epidemiological Study of Prevalence, Risk Factors, Clustering, and Subsequent Suicide' (2014) 383 The Lancet 1147.

161 We have drawn various conclusions in each of the sections above.

162 See for example *Florea v Romania* App no 37186/03 (ECHR, 14 October 2010).

committed in different ways, and with a maximum sentence of life imprisonment. It could be drafted as follows:

> A person may be convicted of this offence if he causes another person's suicide (i) by committing a gross breach of duty owed to V in an existing relationship; or (ii) intending or being reckless as to causing serious harm or death to V; or (iii) by an offence contrary to s.2 or 2A of the Protection from Harassment Act 1997.[163]

Detailed guidance would explain that the normal criminal law approach to causation, intention and recklessness applies; that the existence of this offence does not preclude other charges where appropriate on the facts; would give examples of situations where a gross breach of duty could lead to liability, including the workplace and prisons; and further explain that factors relevant to whether a breach of duty is gross include any imbalance of power in the relationship and any vulnerability of V.

163 (iii) is intended to include situations where there is no existing relationship between D and V, who may not actually know each other, and where there could be difficulties in imposing liability under existing law.

10 Recording murder: videos depicting homicide and the law

Alisdair A. Gillespie

Introduction

This chapter does not look at the substantive law of homicide but instead focuses on what the legal liability should be in respect of those who record or disseminate footage of a homicide. The chapter will consider the legal liability of all those within the chain of production (i.e., producer, distributor and possessor). It will consider whether the existing law tackles such videos, whether there is a need for the law to tackle such videos and ultimately whether the law is in need of reform.

The recording of homicides is a controversial issue. For many years, there has been a folklore of the so-called 'snuff video', which was the recording of a real killing, supposedly produced for the purposes of sexual gratification.[1] Parliament ultimately criminalised the possession of such videos,[2] although little evidence was adduced about their existence. Indeed, no credible evidence has ever been adduced to prove their existence.

The Internet has arguably changed this. Whilst there remains scepticism about whether 'snuff' videos exist, there are undoubtedly videos that do show the killing of a person. The most notable of these are perhaps the videos that have been posted by terrorists, such as Daesh,[3] particularly at the turn of the decade when hostages were shown being executed.

There are also videos that are not related to terrorism. Whilst few in number, there are some that are particularly notable. One of the most well-known concerned Steve Stephens, who posted a video on Facebook that showed him killing Robert Godwin in Cleveland, Ohio.[4] The reason behind posting this video is unclear, but nonetheless it showed him killing his victim. It was almost two hours before Facebook eventually removed the video.[5]

1 E. Jonson and E. Schaefer 'Soft Core/Hard Gore: Snuff as a Crisis in Meaning' (1993) 45 Journal of Film and Video 40–59.

2 Criminal Justice and Immigration Act 2008 (CJIA 2008), s.63.

3 For a commentary on the impact of this see S.M Friis '"Beyond Anything We Have Ever Seen": Beheading Videos and the Visibility of Violence in the War Against ISIS' (2015) 91 International Affairs 725–46.

4 See, for example, Editorial, 'Cleveland shooting: Race to track down Ohio's "Facebook shooter" before he can kill again' *The Independent* (London, 17 April 2017) <www.independent.co.uk/news/world/americas/cleveland-ohio-facebook-killer-shooter-steve-stephens-robert-godwin-a7686771.html> accessed 19 November 2017

5 See, for example, N. Dillon, 'Video of Robert Godwin's murder prompts Facebook to examine policies' *New York Daily News* (New York, 17 April 2017) <www.nydailynews.com/news/national/facebook-examining-policy-video-robert-godwin-murder-article-1.3066572> accessed 19 November 2017

Perhaps the most infamous is that entitled '1 Lunatic 1 Icepick'. This showed the torture and ultimate killing of Jun Lin by Luka Magnotta. The video has gained notoriety because it was picked up by so-called 'gore' websites.[6] These are websites that host extreme material. Often described as 'real news' or 'uncensored news', they host videos that show life and death in an unfiltered way.

This chapter will consider the issue in three parts. The first two will consider whether the law currently criminalises the production, distribution or possession of videos of murder. In doing so, it will draw a distinction between non-terrorist and terrorist-related killings. The reason for doing so is that it is widely acknowledged that (most) terrorism is dealt with by distinct laws, and that these laws tend to be more intrusive than traditional criminal laws.[7] The justification for this distinction is sometimes contested, but it is commonly thought that the state has the right to protect itself and its citizens from attacks for political or ideological reasons.[8] The third part will consider why some seek to criminalise these videos and whether this should be the subject of the criminal law.

Non-terrorist killings

There is scant evidence that there are UK-based homicide videos in circulation, although that is partly due to luck rather than intention. In *Skeggs and Field,* [9] the appellants were two of a group of four men who attacked a man sleeping in a bus shelter. The Court of Appeal concluded that the attack 'was simply for the pleasure of inflicting injury, coupled with the decision to film what was to be done'.[10] The victim did not die, but the Court of Appeal noted 'it was a matter of chance whether or not he died'.[11] Whilst therefore, this did not lead to a homicide video, it is clear that the defendants did not care whether the victim died or not, and therefore it was a matter of pure luck that they did not record a homicide. It serves as an exemplar, however, that people are prepared to record attacks that could lead to death.

Recording homicide

The first issue is the creation of a recording of a killing. Is making such a recording illegal? If so, under what law? The difficulty with this question is that there are lots of different reasons why a murder could be recorded. For our purposes, let us consider three situations:

> **Scenario A**
> S is walking along with a group of friends. They spot V, someone they intensely dislike and they all chase after him. X and Y grab V and start to punch him. S records this, and records X pulling a knife and stabbing V 20 times. V dies.
> **Scenario B**
> S is out for a walk and recording the walk when he comes across a fight. He watches X and Y fighting. He sees X grab a knife and stab V to death. He keeps the footage.

6 M. Alverez 'Online Spectatorship of Death and Dying: Pleasure, Purpose and Community in Bestgore.com' (2017) 14 Participations: Journal of Audience & Reception Studies 1–21.
7 See the first chapter of C. Walker, *Blackstone's Guide to the Anti-Terrorism Legislation* (3rd edn, Oxford University Press 2014)
8 Ibid. 1–4.
9 [2009] EWCA Crim 439.
10 Ibid. [5].
11 Ibid. [6].

Scenario C

S hears a noise outside his house. He looks out of the window and sees X and Y fighting. He starts to record the footage. He realises that X has a knife in his hand and he records Y being stabbed to death. He keeps the footage.

For these purposes, let us assume that in none of these instances does S either telephone the police or alert them to the fact that he has the footage. Is there any liability?

Arguably the easiest scenario to deal with is A. As S is part of a group that has led to a killing, the question is whether S could be guilty of murder through joint enterprise. Following *Jogee*,[12] there is now only one form of joint enterprise and that is that the parties engage in a common enterprise, with the secondary party intending to assist or encourage the principal. If we assume in Scenario A that S was aware that X and Y were going to attack V, and S's inclusion in the chase and subsequent recording was part of the plan, then S is culpable for murder, in the same way that X and Y are. Indeed, Scenario A is akin to *Skeggs and Field*[13] discussed previously. It does not matter that X and Y were the ones who committed the *actus reus* of the murder, it suffices that S was aware, participated in, and encouraged the homicide.

What of Scenario B? Here, it can be assumed that S, X and Y do not know each other, and therefore it is unlikely that there could be a common purpose, ruling out joint enterprise. It is not necessarily possible to rule out complicity immediately. Section 8, Accessories and Abettors Act 1861 criminalises the aiding, abetting, counselling or procuring of an offence. 'Abet' means, *inter alia*, to encourage the commission of the offence.[14] In Scenario B, there is no evidence that S has directly encouraged the commission of the offence (e.g., by urging X and Y to attack V), but the more interesting question is whether there can be implicit encouragement through presence and the recording?

In *Coney*,[15] the courts held that mere presence does not demonstrate encouragement:

> Where presence may be entirely accidental, it is not even evidence of aiding and abetting. Where presence is *prima facie* not accidental it is evidence, but no more than evidence, for the jury.[16]

Secondary liability requires actual encouragement. A jury must be sure that the principal was encouraged and, indeed, that S intended to encourage. Coney indicates that where S's presence is non-accidental, the jury should consider the circumstances as to how S was present, and decide whether that makes it more likely that there was encouragement. This was taken further in *Wilcox v Jeffrey*. [17] The Aliens Order 1920 permitted restrictions to be placed on foreign citizens coming to the UK. In this case, Hawkins, a famous saxophonist, came to the country but his visa did not permit him to work. Hawkins entered the UK with the intention of playing a show. The defendant (Wilcox) was the proprietor of a jazz periodical and so knew of this and attended the show.

Wilcox paid an entrance fee and later wrote a review. The latter is, to an extent, something of a red-herring because encouragement must be at the time of the act and not

12 [2017] AC 387.
13 *Skeggs & Field* (n 9).
14 See *Attorney-General's Reference* No 1 of 1975 [1975] QB 773.
15 [1884] 8 QBD 534.
16 Ibid. [540] (Cave J).
17 [1951] 1 All ER 464.

afterwards. The fact that Wilcox knew of the show meant that he undoubtedly fell within the second limb of the dictum in *Coney*. Lord Goddard CJ upheld Wilcox's conviction for aiding and abetting the breach of the Order, noting that because of Wilcox's knowledge of the show, an intention to encourage Hawkins to play and to produce 'copy' for his periodical was present.[18] Clearly the presence of an individual would provide actual encouragement, and both elements were satisfied.

Perhaps the most definitive statement was put forward in *Clarkson*. [19] Clarkson and two others were members of the Army, based in Germany. Upon returning to their barracks, they heard a noise in a room. They entered the room and watched as a teenage girl was raped by a number of soldiers. They were charged[20] with aiding and abetting the rapes. The Court held that there was no evidence[21] that Clarkson had undertaken any positive act to assist or encourage. The prosecution sought to argue that his presence encouraged the principals to commit rape.

The court conceded that the presence of people observing the rape could act as encouragement, but the Court emphasised the *mens rea* requirement:

> In a case such as the present… it was essential that that element should be stressed; for there was here at least the possibility that a drunken man with his self-discipline loosened by drink, being aware that a woman was being raped, might be attracted to the scene and might stay on the scene in the capacity of what is known as a voyeur; and, while his presence and the presence of others might in fact encourage the rapers or discourage the victim, he himself, enjoying the scene or at least standing by assenting, might not intend that his presence should offer encouragement to rapers and would-be rapers or discouragement to the victim …[22]

This quote is directly relevant to the issue of murder videos where S comes across the killing of another. The question that has to be asked is whether S *intended* to encourage P to commit the crime; in many instances, this presumably would be difficult to prove or demonstrate. The recording may be for some other reason; including the fascination of S or the desire to share the footage (akin to the voyeur in *Clarkson*). It is not enough for S to realise that recording it *might* constitute encouragement: that would be recklessness and the law is clear that it is intent. For that reason, save for situations such as Scenario A, it is unlikely that secondary liability could apply.

In the absence of secondary participation, the most likely alternative offence would be the common-law offence of outraging public decency. In its modern guise, this is an offence that is most commonly used in respect of sexual conduct, but it has been used more broadly in the past,[23] and indeed in recent history.[24]

18 Ibid. [466].
19 [1971] 1 WLR 1402.
20 As they were on a military base, English law applied even though the base was on German soil.
21 *Clarkson* (n 19) [1404] although interestingly Megaw LJ, giving the judgment of the Court, expressly qualifies this by saying 'no admissible evidence'.
22 Ibid. (n 19) [1406] (Megaw LJ).
23 See Law Commission, *Simplification of Criminal Law: Public Nuisance and Outraging Public Decency* (Law Com CP No 193, 2010) para 3.2 for examples of conduct beyond sexual activity.
24 Philip Laing, a 19-year-old student pleaded guilty to outraging public decency when he urinated on a war memorial. See Editorial, 'Jail threat for urinating student' *BBC News* (London, 4 November 2009) <http://news.bbc.co.uk/1/hi/england/south_yorkshire/8342191.stm> accessed 31 October 2017

The contemporary definition of the offence was set out in *Hamilton* [25] as requiring two elements:

> (1) The act was of such a lewd character as to outrage public decency; this element constituted the nature of the act which had to be proved before the offence could be established;
> (2) That it took place in a public place and must have been capable of being seen by two or more persons who were actually presented … This constituted the public element of the offence which had to be proved.[26]

The first point to note is the offence requires an act and not an omission. The recording of a murder must be an 'act' even if the failure to summon help is an omission. The question will become whether stopping to watch and record a murder could constitute an act that could cause outrage. Depending on the circumstances, this might be possible. It was noted earlier (n 24) that urinating on a war memorial was deemed to cause public outrage, presumably because people expect greater respect for the fallen. Perhaps the same could be true of recording a murder. People may be outraged by the fact that someone consciously stopped to record the killing of another.[27] Let us take an example:

> **Scenario D**
> D is walking and notices that a man is strangling his wife in a local park. D records the footage, intending to host this online on a 'gore website'.

Would such actions outrage public decency? In *Lynn*, [28] it was held that the benchmark was 'common decency',[29] with the test being whether:

> such an act of a lewd obscene or disgusting nature … constitutes an outrage to public decency involving great disgust and annoyance of divers of Her Majesty's subjects.[30]

It will be remembered that it is not the murder that must be lewd, obscene or disgusting, it is the act that would constitute outraging public decency, i.e., recording the killing. That said, it is submitted that in situations such as Scenario D, it is quite likely that the public would be outraged by somebody who simply stands and records a murder. What then is the test for outrage? The Law Commission stated that 'the offence caused must be strong enough to amount to shock or disgust: mere distaste or embarrassment would not seem to be enough'.[31] Whilst it will differ depending on the context of the video, it is easy to conceive of situations (such as in Scenario D) where shock or disgust would be caused by a person recording a homicide. To that extent, the 'outraging' aspect of the offence may be satisfied.

25 [2008] QB 224.
26 Ibid. [235].
27 On this see M.G. Antony and R.J. Thomas '"This is Citizen Journalism at its Finest": YouTube and the Public Sphere in the Oscar Grant Shooting Incident' (2010) 12 New Media & Society 1280–296 who recount the outrage that appeared online when footage of the killing of a person by law enforcement agents was uploaded by bystanders.
28 100 ER 394 [1788].
29 Ibid. [395].
30 *R v Mayling* [1963] 2 QB 717 [726] (Ashworth J).
31 Law Com CP No 193 (n 23) para 3.21.

The second aspect that must be satisfied is the so-called 'public' element of the offence. It is not enough that something is done which would outrage the public, it must be done in such a way that it can be witnessed. In *Knuller (Publishing, Printing and Promotions) Ltd v DPP*, [32] the House of Lords made clear that the act must take place in a public space. This does perhaps act as a significant limiting factor since it means that an act that took place away from a public space (e.g., in a house, hotel or private car[33]) would not suffice. That said, it is clear that so long as the public can see the area then it can be considered a public space.[34] Woodland, for example, may be considered a public space even if few members of the public actually visit. It has been suggested that a private dwelling could be the subject of an offence if it took place in front of the window,[35] although presumably not if the curtains were shut.

The second part of the public element is that it must be capable of being witnessed by more than one person. As the Law Commission notes, 'the requirement is not that two persons saw the act, but that two persons could have seen it'.[36] Again, we must be clear by what 'the act' means. It is not the murder, it is the recording of the murder. In *Rose v DPP* [37] it was made clear that the viewing must take place at the time of the act. The defendant in that case was involved in an act of oral sex in the foyer of a bank, to which members of the public would be able to gain access through swiping their bank cards. The area was monitored by (recorded) CCTV. Whilst there was little doubt that had someone come into the foyer that the act could have been seen, there was no evidence that anybody was in the foyer at the time of the act. The bank staff saw the footage the next day, but the High Court ruled that this did not constitute an offence because the 'offence was committed when it is committed',[38] meaning that the observation would have to take place at the time the act took place, not later.

In *Hamilton* [39] the Court of Appeal stated:

> The public element in the offence is satisfied if the act is done where persons are present and the nature of what is being done is capable of being seen; the principle is that the public are to be protected from lewd, obscene or disgusting acts which are of a nature that outrages public decency and which are capable of being seen in public.[40]

People must be present and not merely *capable* of being present.[41] It is necessary to show that more than one person was present at a location close to the murder who would be capable of seeing that D was recording the murder. In some instances this will simply not be

32 [1973] AC 435.
33 Whilst a bus has been considered a public place for these purposes (*R v Holmes* [1853] 1 Dears CC 207) a private car is probably not considered to be a public place unless it is deliberately placed somewhere where the public have access. Some support for this statement can probably be found in the Regulation of Investigatory Powers Act 2000 which considers a private vehicle to be akin to residential premises for the purposes of state surveillance (Regulation of Investigatory Powers Act 2000, s.26(5)(a)).
34 Law Com CP No 193 (n 23) para 3.25.
35 Ibid.
36 Ibid. para 2.50.
37 [2006] 1 WLR 2626.
38 Ibid. [2632].
39 [2008] QB 224.
40 Ibid. [242] (Thomas LJ).
41 *R v F* [2010] EWCA Crim 2243.

satisfied, although it is conceded that it may in others. This brings about an inconsistency in criminalisation. The same action (recording a murder) will result in two different outcomes in terms of criminal liability depending on who was present at the scene. This problem is made worse by the inconsistency of public space. Accordingly, whilst some recordings would be caught by this offence, many would not.

Distributing videos

The next stage in the cycle is distribution. Digital communication technologies mean that uploading camera footage to the Internet, or sending it to others, is simple. This poses further challenges to the law, particularly in deciding whether such dissemination should be permissible.

The most obvious relevant legislation is the Obscene Publications Act 1959 (OPA 1959). Whilst commonly thought to apply only to sexualised materials, the OPA 1959 has a much broader reach. Section 2(1), OPA 1959 criminalises, *inter alia*, '... any person who, whether for gain or not, publishes an obscene article'. The test for obscenity for the purposes of the Act is:

> ... an article shall be deemed to be obscene if its effect ... is, if taken as a whole, such as to tend to deprave and corrupt persons who are likely, having regard to all relevant circumstances, to read, see or hear the matter contained or embodied in it.[42]

The test for the OPA 1959 differs from the common-law definition of obscenity.[43] That the definition of obscenity is not restricted exclusively to sexual matters is demonstrated by some of the cases that have been tried under the Act. In *Calder & Boyars Ltd* [44], a publishing company was convicted for publishing *Last Exit to Brooklyn*, a book that focuses on drug use and violence, and which is now considered a literary classic.[45] Whilst this decision was reversed on appeal, it was not because the content was not considered capable of constituting obscenity, but rather that the judge had not properly directed the jury as to whether it was possible for the defence of artistic merit to be raised in this case.[46] Similarly, in *John Calder (Publications) Ltd v Powell* [47] a book that glorified drug taking was considered capable of being obscene, and in *DPP v A and B. C. Chewing Gum Ltd* [48] a set of 'chewing gum' cards that depicted scenes of battles were considered capable of being obscene.[49]

In *Calder & Boyers*, the Court of Appeal stated that the essence of 'deprave and corrupt' was whether a person was morally corrupted by the article.[50] It was also noted that the test

42 OPA 1959, s. 1(1).
43 That is best thought of as offending contemporary standards of propriety: see *R v Stanley* [1965] 2 QB 327.
44 [1969] 1 QB 151.
45 At the time of the appeal, it was noted that the book had received literary praise from critics: see [1969] 1 QB 151 [165] (Salmon LJ).
46 Ibid. [172].
47 [1965] 1 QB 509.
48 [1968] 1 QB 159.
49 The appeal in that case concerned whether expert evidence could be tendered by the prosecution to show the psychological effect the cards could have on children. That evidence was only relevant if the cards were, at the very least, capable of being obscene.
50 *Calder & Boyars Ltd* (n 45) [167].

relates to the likely reader and not every conceivable reader.[51] This can be important. The book in *Calder & Boyers* was an expensive publication, meaning only serious (interested) readers were likely to purchase the book.

Accessibility has become a key battleground in respect of the Internet. Whilst the World Wide Web is considered to be an open resource, this is not always the case, and sometimes material can be hidden in such a way that only few can access it. The first-instance decision in *Darryn Walker*[52] is illustrative. D was charged under the OPA 1959 for publishing an article that imagined the kidnap, rape and murder of the members of 'Girls Aloud', a popular female singing band. Central to the prosecution case was that 'Girls Aloud' was popular with teenagers, and therefore there was a risk that they would find this material and be depraved or corrupted by it. The defence commissioned expert evidence to show that it was difficult to find the piece without knowing where to look, meaning it would only appeal to a select audience. The prosecution offered no evidence and Walker was acquitted. Similar logic can be found in *Perrin*.[53] A website provided access to pornographic content focusing on, *inter alia*, coprophilia and coprophagia. Two counts were proffered at first-instance. The first related to material on the 'preview' page (i.e., to which anyone had access). The second count related to content that was to be found behind a 'pay-wall', meaning that people would have to pay to view the footage. The jury returned a guilty verdict for count one but an acquittal for count two. The logic must be that those who paid for the footage were not being corrupted.

Whilst the courts have stated that it is possible for corrupted people to continue to be corrupted,[54] presumably because a failure to do so would lead to the position whereby once a person had been corrupted they could be freely supplied with material that would otherwise be considered illegal, they have also noted that if material is so obscene as to repel people rather than tempt them, then there can be no corruption.[55] This is subject to a limitation. It was made clear in *DPP v Whyte*[56] that corruption is not all or nothing. Lord Wilberforce stated that the OPA 1959 'equally protects the less innocent from further corruption'.[57] Whilst many would perhaps take issue with the suggestion that the OPA 1959 is a preventative piece of legislation, the argument is probably sound. Corruption is not a switch: you are not either corrupted or not corrupted. It must be accepted that some people who view material would not be further corrupted and, if they are the likely viewers, then an acquittal must follow.[58] This returns us to the point in previously mentioned *Walker* and *Perrin*. Culpability is likely to depend on where footage is hosted, how it is described and the likely audience.

If the OPA 1959 does not apply, then the only other alternative would be to rely on the Communications Act 2003. Section 127 of this Act creates the (summary) offence of, *inter alia*, sending by means of a public electronic communications network a message that is

51 Ibid. [168].

52 (2009) Newcastle Crown Court, unreported.

53 [2002] EWCA Crim 747.

54 *DPP v Whyte* [1972] AC 849 [863] (Lord Wilberforce).

55 This is known as the aversion argument and is perhaps best articulated by Lord Widgery CJ in *R v Anderson* [1972] 1 QB 304 [315].

56 *Whyte* (n 54).

57 Ibid. [863].

58 In *R v Commissioner of the Police of the Metropolis, ex parte Blackburn and Another (No 3)* [1973] QB 241 [250] (*Blackburn and Another*) Lord Denning MR suggested that this had taken the form of trickery where its skilful advancement would lead to an acquittal. His Lordship suggested that the definition of 'obscene' needed amending although this has not happened.

'grossly offensive, or of an indecent, obscene or menacing character'.[59] It would be difficult to argue that posting or otherwise distributing a video that depicted a murder would not be grossly offensive or obscene,[60] and thus culpability is likely.

Possession of murder videos

The final stage of the cycle of production is possession. This is perhaps a relatively easy issue to deal with. The general rule of obscenity is that personal possession is not criminalised. Child pornography was the first illicit material where simple possession was criminalised,[61] but this is thought to be justified on the basis that possession harms a child, partly through secondary victimisation.[62]

There is no current statute that criminalises the simple possession of murder videos in their own right. The only piece of legislation that could criminalise certain videos of homicide would be the Criminal Justice and Immigration Act 2008 (CJIA 2008) which criminalises the possession of extreme pornography.[63] Illicit material for these purposes bears a very particular definition. To come within the offence, it must be both pornographic and extreme.[64] 'Extreme' includes 'an act which threatens a person's life'.[65] Whilst it refers to 'threatening', the wording must also include actual killings. The principal difficulty will be the requirement that the footage is pornographic. This means 'it is of such a nature that it must reasonably be assumed to have been produced solely or principally for the purpose of sexual arousal'.[66] It will be remembered that there is considerable doubt as to whether snuff videos exist, but, in any event, the kind of footage that would be obtained in scenarios A–D would simply not meet this criterion. Accordingly, simple possession is not currently illegal.

Terrorist killings

The second part of this chapter will look at the same stages, but in the context of terrorism killings. Terrorism is defined as:

The use or threat of action where:

(1) It:

(a) involves serious violence against a person;
(b) involves serious damage to property;
(c) endangers a person's life (other than the person committing the act);
(d) creates a serious risk to the health or safety of the public, or a section of the public; or
(e) is designed to seriously interfere with or seriously to disrupt an electronic system.

59 Communications Act 2003, s. 127(1)(a).
60 The latter does not bear the OPA 1959 definition of obscenity but rather the common-law definition that it offends against recognised standards of propriety.
61 Criminal Justice Act 1988, s.160.
62 See S. Ost 'Children at Risk: Legal and Societal Perceptions of the Potential Threat that the Possession of Child Pornography Poses to Society' (2002) 29 Journal of Law & Society 436–40.
63 CJIA 2008, s.63.
64 Ibid. s.63(2).
65 Ibid. s.63(7)(a).
66 Ibid. s.63(3).

(2) The use of threat is designed to influence the government or international governmental organisation, or to intimidate the public or a section of the public, and
(3) the use or threat is made for the purpose of advancing a political, religious, racial or ideological cause.[67]

For our purposes, we need not critique this definition[68] as we are simply examining the current law. As with the previous section, let us use an example to assist our examination:

> **Scenario E**
> S, A and B travel to a shopping centre. They grab a victim (V) and decapitate her in the presence of everyone, making clear whilst doing so that this is in support of their cause. A held V down whilst B killed her. S recorded the entire incident.

Assuming 'the cause' is political, religious, racial or ideological (and it would be difficult to think of many causes that would not fit within this definition), then this would clearly meet the definition of terrorism.

Recording a killing

Unlike the discussion that took place in the first part of this chapter, it is unlikely that complicity would be particularly difficult to prove in respect of Scenario E. Quite clearly, S is aware of what is going to happen and this would appear to be a classic example of joint enterprise. S clearly intends to encourage the killing, and both A and B are encouraged by S's actions.

What would the position be if S was arrested en route to where the murder was to take place? Section 1(4), Criminal Attempts Act 1981 precludes an attempt to aid, abet, counsel or procure an offence. Given S would not be the person who would kill V, then even if proximity could be shown,[69] she could not commit the offence of attempted murder. A more relevant offence would be s.5, Terrorism Act 2006 (TA 2006) which criminalises the preparation of terrorist acts. This states:

> A person commits an offence, if with the intention of- (a) committing acts of terrorism, or (b) assisting another to commit such acts, he engages in any conduct in preparation for giving effect to his intention.[70]

The offence is punishable by a maximum sentence of life imprisonment,[71] and it is clearly a serious crime. It has been noted that the offence is deliberately broad[72] and almost any act will suffice. There is the requirement that the act is done with the intention of furthering terrorism, and in light of the fact that acts could include otherwise innocuous actions this is perhaps the most important part of the offence. In many instances this will not be

67 Terrorism Act 2000, s.1(1) when read in conjunction with s.1(2).
68 Although others have. Most notably, David Anderson QC, when serving as the Independent Reviewer of Terrorism Legislation (D. Anderson, The Terrorism Acts in 2012 (2013, HMSO: London)). For academic critiques see, most notably, Walker (n 7) 7–19.
69 An attempt requires more than 'merely preparatory steps' (Criminal Attempts Act 1981, s.1(1)).
70 TA 2006, s.5(1).
71 Ibid. s.5(3).
72 Walker (n 7) 227.

problematic to prove as terrorists tend to leave plenty of evidence as to their motives.[73] Returning to Scenario E, if S were to be arrested before she went to the shopping centre then, subject to proof of intent, there would be no difficulty in showing breach of section 5 as the act of travelling (and carrying the equipment to record the attack) would suffice.

Distribution of the footage

The next stage in the production cycle is the distribution. In respect of Scenario E, what would the position be if S passed the footage onto T, who then uploaded it onto the Internet?

The OPA 1959 does not seem an appropriate vehicle for criminalising the mischief of what S and T have done. It is not that they have decided to post something obscene: they have posted something that they believe will either terrorise the public or encourage people to take up their cause, therefore terrorism legislation becomes relevant.

The most likely offence would be dissemination of terrorist publications contrary to s.2, TA 2006. The basics of this offence are as follows:

> A person commits an offence if he engages in conduct falling within subsection (2) and, at the time he does so:
>
> (a) he intends an effect of his conduct to be a direct or indirect encouragement or other inducement to the commission, preparation or instigation of acts of terrorism;
>
> (b) he intends an effect of his conduct to be the provision of assistance in the commission or preparation of such acts; or
>
> (c) he is reckless as to whether his conduct has an effect mentioned in (a) or (b).[74]

The relevant conduct in subsection (2) is:

> (a) distributes or circulates a terrorist publication;
> (b) gives, sells or lends such a publication;
> (c) offers such a publication for sale or loan;
> (d) provides a service to others that enables them to obtain, read, listen or look at such a publication, or to acquire it by means of a gift, sale or loan;
> (e) transmits the contents of such a publication electronically; or
> (f) has such a publication in his possession with a view to its becoming the subject of conduct falling within any of paragraphs (a) to (e).

For our purposes, realistically paragraphs (a), (e) and (f) will be most suitable. It is interesting that any subsequent paragraphs are required since 'distributes' within paragraph (a) would presumably cover everything other than (f). This might simply be an example of ensuring that there are no loopholes, and that all forms of dissemination are considered culpable.

What then is a 'terrorist publication'? It is a publication that contains matter that is likely:

> (a) to be understood, by some or all of the persons to whom it is or may become available as a consequence of that conduct, as a direct or indirect encouragement or

73 For example, notes, recordings or other postings explaining the reasoning behind the attack.
74 TA 2006, s.2(1).

other inducement to them to the commission, preparation or instigation of acts of terrorism; or
(b) to be useful in the commission or preparation of such acts and to be understood, by some or all of those persons, as contained in the publication, or made available to them, wholly or mainly for the purpose of being so useful to them.[75]

Realistically it is paragraph (a) that would be most relevant. Encouragement and inducement includes glorifying the commission or preparation of the terrorist conduct.[76] Whether the conduct is terrorism must be determined at the time of the conduct, and having regard both to the contents of the publication and the circumstances in which the conduct occurs.[77] It is submitted that the recording in Scenario E is unlikely to be problematic, and the posting of such footage is likely to be considered the glorification of the original act of terrorism. 'Publication' is defined as including any 'matter to be looked at or watched',[78] and therefore the video itself would suffice.

The *mens rea* for section 2 is that the dissemination takes place either with the intent, *inter alia*, to directly or indirectly encourage others to commit acts of terrorism, or being reckless as to whether this happens. In Scenario E, proving intent is unlikely to be problematic. What of the situation where somebody sees the footage online in a niche area and reposts it to a gore site? It is unlikely that the intent to encourage terrorism would be present. That person may not be reckless either given where it is posted. Is a person consciously taking an unjustified risk that another person may be encouraged, directly or indirectly, to commit terrorism? If it is posted to a gore site, then perhaps not.[79] Where it is posted elsewhere, including in more mainstream areas of the Internet, it may be reckless. There is a defence for a person to prove that the publication was not his views or had his endorsement, and that it was clear in all the circumstances that this did not have his endorsement.[80]

Withholding the footage

An interesting issue arises about the position if a person simply records the footage by chance. For example, S in Scenario B and Scenario C outlined in the first part of this chapter. English law famously does not have a Good Samaritan rule,[81] and S would be under no obligation to pass the recorded footage onto the police. The same is not true, however, where the killing is a result of terrorist action. Section 38B of the Terrorism Act 2000 (TA 2000) criminalises a person who 'has information which he knows or believes might be of material assistance' in 'securing the apprehension, prosecution or conviction of another person' where it relates to the commission or instigation of an act of terrorism.[82]

75 Ibid. s.2(3).
76 Ibid. s.2(4).
77 Ibid. s.2(5).
78 Ibid. s.2(13)(c).
79 On this see *R v Roddis* [2009] EWCA Crim 585 where it was noted that possession of a video may be for 'morbid curiosity', meaning no offence would take place (at [13]). The same logic can be applied to s.2 because it would mean that where someone posts a video to those who seek out murder videos, then the purpose would not be terrorism but rather morbid curiosity, meaning the TA 2006 should not apply.
80 TA 2006, s.2(9).
81 See, for example, A. Ashworth 'The scope of Criminal Liability for Omissions' (1989) 105 Law Quarterly Review 424.
82 TA 2006, s.38B(1): paragraph (b) being the most pertinent for these purposes.

Footage of a murder would unquestionably be material information that *might* be of assistance in the apprehension or prosecution of the suspects, and S can be asked to surrender this footage to the police. Failure to do so is an either-way offence, punishable by up to five years' imprisonment.[83] A defence exists for the defendant to prove that he had a reasonable excuse as to why the information was withheld,[84] but it is unlikely that in most instances this would be relevant for those who simply remain quiet about the fact that they have recorded footage.

Possession

What of the simple possession of these videos? It will be remembered that for non-terrorist killings there is no specific offence that would criminalise those who possess the footage. For terrorism, the most likely offence would be s.58, TA 2000 which, *inter alia*, criminalises those who possess a 'document or record' of a kind likely to be useful to a person committing or preparing an act of terrorism.[85] A recording is undoubtedly a 'document or record',[86] but the question is whether it would be likely to be useful to a person committing or preparing an act of terrorism?

At first sight, it would seem difficult to argue that recorded footage of a killing could meet this test. Whilst the press have stated that the downloading of extremist videos can constitute an offence,[87] the courts have been more cautious. In *R v K*[88] the then Lord Chief Justice rejected a suggestion that propaganda is within this offence. Lord Philips stated:

> A document or record will only fall within section 58 if it is of a kind that is likely to provide practical assistance to a person committing or preparing an act of terrorist. A document that simply encourages the commission of acts of terrorism does not fall within section 58.[89]

Whilst *K* was later doubted by the House of Lords,[90] this was on different grounds,[91] and the comment remains good law. A video such as that envisaged in Scenario E, would not provide assistance in the commission or preparation of an act of terrorism, and accordingly would not fall within s.58, meaning that its simple possession would not be an offence. Where the video goes further – for example, stating 'this is how you behead someone with a knife' or 'this is the best way to stab someone' – then this would undoubtedly come within the scope of s.58 and simple possession would be prohibited. That is a different type of video from that discussed in this chapter.

83 Ibid. s. 38B(5).
84 Ibid. s. 38B(4).
85 Ibid. 58(1)(b).
86 Defined as including an electronic record (see TA 2000, s.58(2)).
87 See, for example, J. Watts, 'Watching terrorist propaganda online to become a criminal offence, says Tory Home Secretary Amber Rudd' *The Independent* (London, 3 October 2017) <www.independent.co.uk/news/uk/politics/terrorist-propaganda-criminal-offence-new-law-amber-rudd-streaming-watching-extremist-material-isis-a7979986.html> accessed 19 November 2017
88 [2008] QB 827.
89 Ibid. [834].
90 See *R v G* [2010] 1 AC 43.
91 The meaning of the statutory defence contained within TA 2000, s.58(3).

Should murder videos be the subject of criminal law?

The preceding sections have identified that the recording of a murder and the dissemination or possession of the footage, is not necessarily illegal. Whilst it may be in some instances, it cannot be said that it is always illegal. Some of the distinctions are difficult to justify. For example, take the offence of outraging public decency, it would be odd to say that X should be culpable for recording a murder within the front room of a house, but Y should not, because it took place behind the curtains. In both situations, a murder occurred, and footage was recorded. Either both should be illegal or neither should. Similarly, it would seem odd that the culpability of the dissemination of murder videos should be primarily based on its location on the web rather than its distribution, and the reason behind this.

If it were decided that murder footage should be prohibited, then on what basis should the law act? It is commonly accepted that harm is the most appropriate justification for the criminal law,[92] but who is harmed here? It would seem unlikely that the dead person can be harmed, since harm would suggest damage to an individual; the dead are no longer individuals, they are former individuals. Do the dead have rights? From a practical perspective, the European Court of Human Rights held that an action need not be struck out because the claimant died.[93] That, however, is a very different proposition to initiating action on behalf of the dead. The Court has accepted the notion of 'indirect victims',[94] which are those who are indirectly affected by the alleged breach. Whilst that makes sense in the context of Article 2,[95] it does not follow that this applies to all rights. Any restriction on the footage of a murder would need to be based on Article 8,[96] and yet this is the paradigm of an individual right, excluding indirect victims.[97]

Rosenblatt notes that the dead have certain rights, principally concerned with protecting the remains from interference,[98] but he notes that is very different to granting them universal human rights. He argues that 'living people have responsibilities to the dead, but these are ultimately based on the rules and rights that are best for the living community … the dead body itself has no rights, makes no claims over the future'.[99] What of the concept of dignity, which is often associated with death? Dias has suggested that there should be legally recognised dignity after death,[100] although that was restricted to the remains of the dead. It is notable, however, that there is controversy over that. Rosenblatt notes that prescribing rights to the dead based on dignity would require the diversity of humanity to be taken into account;[101] as each culture and religion differs about what the status of the dead are, and

92 Most famously articulated by J.S. Mill, *On Liberty* (J.W. Parker & Son 1859).
93 D.J. Harris *et al. Harris, O'Boyle & Warbrick: Law of the European Convention on Human Rights* (3rd edn, Oxford University Press 2014) 94.
94 Ibid. 91.
95 The Right to Life. This includes various procedural rights. If an indirect victim could not initiate action under Article 2 then death through excessive force could never be litigated.
96 Right to respect for private life. This has included, *inter alia*, a right to privacy, confidence and autonomy: see Harris *et al.* (n 93) 541–43 (moral, physical and psychological integrity) and 551–57 (privacy).
97 Harris *et al.* (n 93) 93.
98 A. Rosenblatt 'International Forensic Investigations and the Human Rights of the Dead' (2010) 32 Human Rights Quarterly 921, 927.
99 Ibid. 931.
100 M. Dias 'Dignity after Death and Protecting the Sanctity of Human Remains' (2015) *Voices in Bioethics* (21 May 2015) <www.voicesinbioethics.net/newswire/2015/05/21/dignity-after-death ≥ accessed 12 November 2017.
101 Rosenblatt (n 98) 940.

what the status of the body is, whose approach is adopted as being determinative? Rosenblatt argues, 'the dead are often treated with respect and consideration, but they do not have inherent dignity'.[102] Without inherent dignity then it would be difficult to see how one could encapsulate a right that respected the victim. Whilst a living person has the right not to be degraded,[103] this is premised on the dignity inherent in any individual, the very thing it is said that the dead do not possess.

If the dead cannot be harmed, what of harm to others? Farmand suggests that the existence of murder videos 'provide new incentive for people to kill'[104] although little evidence is adduced to substantiate this point. It would seem unlikely that many people commit murder because there is an off-chance that someone will record it and they will become famous. Where a person records themselves killing, which will be culpable as homicide, the recording should be an aggravating factor in sentencing.[105] This does not justify a new offence. The same is true of those who assist a killer by recording the death. As noted in the first section, this would be treated as secondary participation, and S would be sentenced accordingly. Farmand's belief does not justify either recordings or the distribution of the footage.

What of the rights of the families of the deceased? Farmand notes that the families of the murder victim can suffer, due to the knowledge that people are using the footage of the death for their own gratification.[106] This is an interesting point. In respect of child pornography, the impact that is caused by a victim knowing that others are using the footage of their sexual assault for sexual gratification is recognised as harm.[107] However, this is a different proposition. First, this secondary victimisation is considered to amplify the primary victimisation that they suffer from the (original) sexual abuse.[108] For obvious reasons, the victim of a homicide cannot suffer secondary (psychological) victimisation. Whilst parents may conceivably be distressed by the knowledge of the footage, mere distress is not often considered to be harm for the purposes of the law.[109]

If criminalising on the basis of harm is not possible, then perhaps we need to look towards offence. Feinberg states:

> To be forced to suffer an offense, be it an affront to the senses, disgust, shock, shame, annoyance, or humiliation, is an unpleasant inconvenience, and hence an evil, even when it is by no means harmful … it is morally legitimate for the criminal law to be concerned with their regulation.[110]

102 Ibid. 941.

103 Perhaps most famously encapsulated in Article 3, *European Convention of Human Rights* but which is also encapsulated under Article 8 where it is less severe: see, for example, Harris *et al.* (n 94) 271.

104 M.K. Farmand 'Who Watches This Stuff: Videos Depicting Actual Murder and the Need for a Federal Criminal Murder-Video Statute' (2016) 68 Florida Law Review 1915–942, 1918.

105 In the same way that this is now accepted for non-fatal offences and sexual offences (see, for example, Sentencing Council, *Sexual Offences: Definitive Guideline* (2013) pg. 10 <www.sentencingcouncil.org.uk/wp-content/uploads/Final_Sexual_Offences_Definitive_Guideline_content_web1.pdf> accessed 18 December 2017.)

106 Farmand (n 104) 1918.

107 *R v Beaney* [2004] EWCA Crim 449. See also A.A. Gillespie, *Child Pornography: Law and Policy* (Routledge 2011) 38–9.

108 Ibid.

109 See, for example, *R v Dhaliwal* [2006] EWCA Crim 1139 [20] et seq.

110 J. Feinberg, *Offense to Others: The Moral Limits of the Criminal Law* (Oxford University Press 1985) 49.

Not all offence should lead to criminal sanction. Feinberg refers to 'wrongful offense', which he suggests is rights-violating.[111] Whilst not a harm, he is drawing an analogy to harm and suggesting that it is not merely about regulating morality. 'Wrongful' offence requires a causal link between the actions of the offender and the offence caused, including a requirement that the victim feels resentful that it has happened.[112] It is not all offence that should be criminalised, it must be serious offence (which he refers to as profound offence[113]), but it is also about balance, with Feinberg arguing that the law must 'weigh … the seriousness of the offense caused by to unwilling witnesses against the reasonableness of the conduct'.[114]

Does the offence principle apply to murder videos? Certainly, the recording and dissemination of footage of a murder could be considered offensive depending on what it portrays. Feinberg noted that the dead arouse strong feelings of sympathy because they resonate with our lives.[115] He argues that any offence must go beyond the individual family to be actionable under the criminal law.[116] This perhaps returns us to the question of how the public would react if a person simply stands by and records footage, rather than trying to seek help or provide assistance. Whilst the rule of omissions does not require them to seek help, the *act* of recording is separate from the omission to summon help. As discussed previously, it is quite possible that some will be disgusted by the fact that S simply recorded the footage, although that is likely to depend on the context and what S intended to do with the footage.[117]

What of distributing the footage? It will be remembered that Feinberg thought the justification was the offence caused to *unwilling* witnesses, and he accepts that some will deliberately seek out the act that could lead to offence, either because they are curious or because they seek pleasure from it.[118] This perhaps returns us to the discussion about the current rules on obscenity. Where material is stored in locations that are difficult to find, then it would seem unreasonable to object to that which people have deliberately sought out. That does not assist in ensuring certainty as to conduct. Distributing the same video could be culpable depending on who sees it (or has the potential to see it). That would seem odd, but it is perhaps justified by Feinberg's insistence that personal offence is insufficient. The next of kin of the victim portrayed in the footage is unlikely to be impressed by people looking at the murder for entertainment or gratification purposes, even if hidden from public view. As that is neither harmful or a matter of (public) offence, it would seem difficult to justify criminalisation.

What of morality? Whether morality can justify criminal action has been discussed for many years, with the classic protagonists being Devlin and Hart. Ashworth and Horder note that a difficulty with Devlin's argument was that it was based on a dubious definition of

111 Ibid. 2.
112 Ibid. 3.
113 Ibid. 51 et seq.
114 Ibid. 26.
115 Ibid. 57.
116 Feinberg believed that where the offence was individual then it would be left to the civil law. He provides the example of a scientist who procures a corpse to perform an experiment that disfigures the face of the deceased. He notes that this will be profoundly distressing to the next of kin, but suggests that as a personal feeling, this is best left to the civil law. However, as more learn about the experiment, there may be public distress, justifying the imposition of criminal penalties. See Feinberg (n 110) 70.
117 If S recorded the footage because she believed that it would assist the police in identifying the perpetrator, it is likely that this would be considered differently to someone who records it because they wish to profit from it (for example, by selling the footage) or who posts it to the internet for the purposes of entertainment.
118 Feinberg (n 110) 26.

'morals'.[119] The central issue with morality is identifying whose moral judgment the law should be based on. Ashworth and Horder note that leaving it to individuals carries with it the risk that it is based not on morality but on prejudice.[120] A community standard is similarly problematic as it will shift, but more than this, individuals need not conform to a homogenous standard. Freedom of speech to conform to the consensus is not worth having. Ashworth and Horder also note that paternalism, which must be a moral concept irrespective of whether it purports to act on the basis of harm, can only be justified for the vulnerable.[121] It is difficult to argue that the dead are vulnerable. The physical corpse may be,[122] but the deceased, that is to say the embodiment of who that person was, is not. If it is the risk that the vulnerable may see the footage, then that raises different issues. First, it would not by itself justify the recording of the footage, nor its simple possession.[123] Second, it would, once again, mean that criminalising the dissemination of footage is not focused on what the footage shows, but rather who sees it. That is unlikely to appease the next of kin of the person portrayed who wishes to prevent the death from being exploited.

It would seem difficult to encapsulate a justification for criminalising murder videos. That said, it must be acknowledged that our legislators do not seem worried about the philosophical underpinning of criminal offences, and are happy to act on the basis of the 'common good' or 'morality'.[124] That being the case, legislation could conceivably seek to tackle such issues. However, in doing so, the law would need to identify how it draws a distinction between 'bad' murder videos and 'newsworthy' murder videos. The assassination of President John F. Kennedy was captured on film, and has been shown on television.[125] This must be one of the most famous murders captured on film and it is freely accessible on mainstream internet sites. How does the law draw a distinction between this and '1 Lunatic 1 Icepick'? Is it the status of the victim? What of footage of those who perished in the 9/11 attacks in New York? Again, there is footage that clearly shows victims dying. Again, this must be murder, but we do not seek to control such footage. Perhaps the argument is to include a defence of 'public good' but such a defence has not worked particularly well for the OPA 1959,[126]

119 A. Ashworth and J. Horder, *Principles of Criminal Law* (7th edn, Oxford University Press 2013) 35.

120 Ibid. 36.

121 Ibid.

122 In that it cannot defend itself from attack, being disinterred or experimented on.

123 Just because footage is recorded does not mean that it has to be disseminated. Thus if X, who is not vulnerable, records footage then there is no danger that a vulnerable person will see the footage unless X distributes it, but that is a separate act.

124 Contemporary examples of this would include the prohibition of the possession of extreme pornography (CJIA 2008, s.63) which would seem to be based on morality. C. McGlynn and E. Rackley 'Criminalising Extreme Pornography: A Lost Opportunity' (2009) Criminal Law Review 245–60. Note McGlynn and Rackley believe that potential societal harm was missed (at 256 et seq.), and also the prohibition of possession of so-called virtual child pornography (more properly known as 'prohibited images of children' (Coroners and Justice Act 2009, s.62)) which again appears to be based on morality (see S. Ost 'Criminalising Fabricated Images of Child Pornography: A Matter of Harm or Morality? (2010) 30 Legal Studies 230–56.)

125 Admittedly, it was not shown on U.S. networks until 1975. See T. Sneed, 'How John F. Kennedy's assassination changed television forever' *U.S. News* (United States of America, 14 November 2013) <www.usnews.com/news/articles/2013/11/14/how-john-f-kennedy-assassination-changed-television-forever > accessed 19 November 2017.

126 Perhaps best summarised by the Court of Appeal in *Blackburn and Another* (n 58) where Lord Denning MR concluded that the 'defence of public good … has got out of hand' [254] and in which Phillimore LJ said, 'section 4 has been the source of much confusion and difficulty' [257] before suggesting that s.4 needed amending [258].

and the same would probably prove true here. Is the solution based on exploitation? That we seek to tackle those images that exploit the death of the individual? That may be more certain as a test but it raises interesting questions about who is being protected from exploitation if the dead have no rights.

Conclusion

Unlike the myth of the 'snuff video', there is clear evidence that videos depicting homicide are now appearing on the Internet. This raises interesting questions for the law as to how such footage should be dealt with by the law. Most footage of homicides is gruesome and horrifying. Is that sufficient justification to warrant prohibition? There is a long history of death being captured on film, including violent deaths, and this has not previously been criminalised.

There is perhaps a stronger justification for criminalising the distribution of the material. The offence principle permits people to go about their business without being caused undue offence. The footage that is being discussed in this chapter is such that it is likely to cause disgust and distress to many who see it. However, does that justify a blanket ban? Probably not. It would seem more likely that any law would need to tackle dissemination that poses the risk that the community could be offended. Where, however, there can be no offence, because, for example, people realise what they are looking at, then it may be more difficult to justify criminalisation. In essence this is the existing law of obscenity, but this law is considered to be ineffective and arbitrary.

Ultimately the difficulty with the law is that whilst morally we believe that there should be dignity in death, we have never identified how such a concept could be translated into law. As the dead do not have human rights, it is difficult to justify the use of the criminal law to protect their representation (as distinct from their remains).

Part 2

11 South Africa

Gerhard Kemp

Overview and historical development of homicide offences and offence structure

Historical development of homicide offences

Indigenous legal systems in South Africa recognised homicide as a wrong, but the differentiation between what would be considered a criminal and a civil wrong (tort or delict) was not always as pronounced as one would find in the legal systems that were introduced by the European settlers.[1] Anthropologists and legal historians have identified instances of what could be described as criminal liability for the deliberate or negligent killing of another person. For instance, deliberate or negligent killing of another person (*palao*) was punishable by death under the law of the Northern Sotho people of South Africa.[2] The Tembu people, for their part, did not differentiate between murder and culpable homicide, but the killing of another person was nevertheless treated as a crime. However, it was not regarded as a crime against the victim but rather as a crime against the tribal chief, to whom all his subjects 'belonged'.[3] The Ndebele people differentiated between deliberate homicide (*ukubulala ngabomu*) and negligent homicide (*ukubulala ngokunganaki*). Both forms were regarded as crimes and were punishable with death in the case of deliberate homicide and more lenient forms of punishment (such as fines or corporal punishments) for negligent homicide.[4] Although it is difficult to draw general conclusions about the legal principles and structure of homicide in the indigenous legal systems of South Africa, one prevalent view is that more often than not homicide crimes or delicts were primarily viewed as offences against the collective or the tribal chief, rather than as against individual victims / human life. The legal anthropologists Labuschagne and Van den Heever conclude that the protected interests in indigenous homicide law appears to have 'a bio-arithmetical (loss in human numbers), socio-psychological (loss of social and emotional support and interaction), and an economic (loss of labour and/or *lobolo* [5] value) dimension.'[6]

1 J.M.T. Labuschagne and J.A. van den Heever, 'Die oorsprong van en die onderskeid tussen die fenomene misdaad en delik in primigene regstelsels' (1991) Obiter 80.
2 J.M.T. Labuschagne and J.A. van den Heever, 'Liability Arising From the Killing of a Fellow Human Being in South African Indigenous Law' (1995) 28 The Comparative and International Law Journal of Southern Africa 422, 423.
3 Ibid. 426.
4 Ibid. 427.
5 A traditional form of dowry payable to the family of the bride-to-be.
6 J.M.T. Labuschagne and J.A van den Heever (n 2) 430.

The European settlers brought to South Africa two legal traditions – Roman-Dutch law and English law, both of which formed the historical foundations of what is today known as the 'common law', as opposed to 'customary law', which is the collective term for the indigenous legal systems of South Africa. During colonial and apartheid rule, customary law was not considered to be on equal footing with the common law. Courts were entitled to take judicial notice of customary law, provided it did not clash with public policy and natural justice (the so-called 'repugnancy' provision).[7] The post-apartheid, democratic constitutional order gives new status to customary law. It is now on equal footing with the common law.[8] The constitutional protection of customary law, alongside the common law of South Africa, presents an opportunity for harmonisation of the two systems within the framework of a democratic constitutional system. The processes of adaptation and harmonisation are more evident in private law (especially family law)[9] and not so much in the sphere of criminal law. However, aspects like African customary law values and the emphasis on restorative justice in traditional African criminal law is gaining traction in academic debate[10] and in jurisprudence.[11]

The main homicide offences in modern South African criminal law have their historical roots in Roman-Dutch and English law.[12] Murder, suicide, infanticide and culpable homicide were crimes under Roman-Dutch and / or English law. However, it should be noted that the Roman-Dutch and English law influences on the development of the various forms of homicide offences vary quite significantly.

Murder (intentional homicide) was punishable under Roman law, Roman-Dutch law and under English law.[13] The Roman-Dutch authorities[14] viewed murder as the intentional causation of the death of a human being. They also differentiated between various forms of intentional killing, with reference to the victim (for instance, ordinary murder as opposed to the killing of a father, or '*vadermoord*'); and with reference to the means of killing, for instance murder with the bare hands, with weapons, with poison, and so forth. The old authorities also referred to motive as a distinguishing factor, for instance murder with the motive to rob.[15] Unlike the Roman-Dutch authorities' categorisation of different forms of murder, South African law, probably under influence of English law, adopted a more general definition of murder. English law required the murder to be committed with 'malice of forethought'. In modern South African common law, the crime of murder is: the intentional and unlawful killing of a person.[16] 'Malice of forethought' ('*voorbedagte rade*' in Afrikaans)

7 Law of Evidence Amendment Act 45 of 1988, s.1.

8 *Alexkor Ltd v Richtersveld Community* [2004] (5) SA 460 (CC).

9 See generally, G. van Niekerk, 'Reflections on the Interplay of African Customary Law and State Law in South Africa' (2012) 5 SUBB Jurisprudentia 5–20.

10 See, for instance, A. Skelton, 'Tapping Indigenous Knowledge: Traditional Conflict Resolution, Restorative Justice and the Denunciation of Crime in South Africa' (2007) Acta Juridica 228–46.

11 *S v Makwanyane* [1995] (3) SA 391 (CC).

12 J. Burchell, *Principles of Criminal Law* (5th edn, Juta 2016) 577–78; G. Kemp *et al.*, *Criminal Law in South Africa* (2nd edn, Oxford University Press 2015) 297; C.R. Snyman, *Criminal Law* (6th edn, LexisNexis 2014) 437–38.

13 Burchell (n 12).

14 Professor J.C. de Wet, arguably the foremost authority on the work of the Roman-Dutch authors and their influence on the development of South African law, noted the works of Damhouder, Matthaeus, Van Leeuwen, Voet, Moorman, Van der Linden and Postma as particularly relevant in terms of the historical development of the crime of murder in South Africa. See J.C de Wet, *Strafreg* (4th edn, Butterworth 1985) 225.

15 Ibid.

16 Burchell (n 12) 578.

is no longer an element of the crime. Intent in the general sense (including *dolus eventualis*) is now required.[17]

There is some indication[18] that (attempted) suicide was punishable as a crime during the reign of the Dutch East India Company[19] at the Cape.[20] There is no indication that (attempted) suicide was punished as a crime in the rest of what is now South Africa. Indeed, case law (including a decision by the Supreme Court of Appeal) confirmed that suicide is not a crime under South African law.[21] However, assisting another person to commit suicide was historically treated as murder.[22] Contemporary developments regarding voluntary active euthanasia will be considered later in the chapter.

In terms of the main historical foundations of South African common law it is worth pointing out that negligent killing of another person was not punishable under Roman law. It was instead treated as a misfortune (*casus*).[23] Germanic law, on the other hand, punished homicide in all its forms, including negligent killing of another person.[24] Most of the Roman-Dutch authorities distinguished between intentional and negligent forms of homicide, despite the fact that they did not use terms that would be the equivalents of 'murder' and 'culpable homicide' in modern South African law.[25] Under influence of English law the clear distinction between the intentional and negligent forms of homicide became somewhat murkier.[26] The notion of culpable homicide initially included not only the element of negligence, but also the possibility of culpability based on the unintended death of another person arising from an illegal activity (thus, an application of the *versari in re illicita* doctrine) and even intentional homicide which was accompanied by a partial excuse.[27] Intentional homicide, which would today be regarded as murder, could be treated as culpable homicide in cases where mitigating circumstances could be found. Since the decisions by the Supreme Court of Appeal in *S v Bernardus* [28] and later in *S v Thenkwa* [29] it is clear that there is no such thing as culpable homicide without fault in the form of negligence. The

17 de Wet (n 14) 225.

18 Sources and Roman-Dutch authorities cited in *R v Peverett* [1940] AD 213 [214–215]. The Court cited a letter from the Chief Archivist, Cape Town, in which he made reference to a case of attempted suicide which served before the Judicial Council (*Raad van Justisie*) in Cape Town on 2 August 1781. A man named Jan was convicted of the crime of attempted suicide. There are no further convictions for attempted suicide mentioned in the records of the *Raad van Justisie* (*Peverett* [215]).

19 The Dutch East India Company was effectively in control of the Cape of Good Hope from 1652 until 1795. R. Davenport and C. Saunders, *South Africa – A Modern History* (5th edn, Macmillan 2000) 21–2.

20 Burchell (n 12) 582.

21 *S v Gordon* [1962] (4) SA 727 (N) [729]; *Ex parte Die Minister van Justisie: In re S v Grotjohn* [1970] (2) SA 355 (A) [363D], [366].

22 Burchell (n 12) 582.

23 Burchell (n 12) 583; de Wet (n 14) 230.

24 Burchell (n 12) 583.

25 de Wet (n 14) 230. See also the author's critique of early South African cases like *R v Hercules* (3) SA 826 (A) where the courts muddied the waters and failed to appreciate the fact that the Roman-Dutch authorities did not simply regard culpable homicide as a lesser form of intentional homicide. De Wet referred to the old authorities Matthaeus and Voet to illustrate the fact that these Roman-Dutch authorities clearly differentiated between intentional and negligent forms of homicide as two distinct forms.

26 de Wet (n 14) 231.

27 Burchell (n 12) 584.

28 1965 (3) SA 287 (A).

29 1970 (3) SA 529 (A).

versari and partial excuse doctrines were also abandoned.[30] Culpable homicide in modern South African criminal law is thus: the unlawful, negligent causation of the death of another person.[31]

Although the elements of murder and infanticide are essentially the same (intentional killing of another person), the killing of a new-born child is classified as a separate form of murder in South Africa.[32] Under Roman-Dutch law a crime known as *crimen expositionis infantis* (abandoning a child with the expectation that it would die) was punishable by death.[33] Commentators and the courts seem to agree that *crimen expositionis infantis* (which causes death) has been retained as a separate homicide offence in South Africa.[34] Prosecutions for the common law crime of *crimen expositionis* are extremely rare.[35] The pragmatic reason is that prosecutors seem to prefer to charge the accused with murder if the child died as a result of abandonment and exposure.[36]

Under common law, and following the writings of the Roman-Dutch authorities (notably Van der Linden) there appears to have been some overlap between the crimes of infanticide and abortion. Where actions were taken to cause the death of a foetus which was still in the mother's womb, it was treated as infanticide. Abortion, on the other hand, was the unlawful expulsion of the foetus from the womb, thereby causing the death of the foetus.[37] The crime of abortion was nevertheless a separate crime under common law and was not regarded as murder.[38] A mother who consented to the abortion was liable as a *socius* to the crime of abortion.[39] The common law authorities held that an abortion could legally be performed in order to save the life of the mother.[40] The Abortion and Sterilization Act 2 of 1975 aimed to bring some procedural and doctrinal order regarding abortion in South Africa. The common law pertaining to abortion was indeed described as a 'mine-field' in one of the reported pre-statutory court cases.[41] The 1975 Act liberalised the abortion dispensation somewhat, although the conditions under which legal abortions could be performed were still rather stringent.[42] Following the entry into force of South Africa's post-apartheid Constitution, 1996, the Choice on Termination of Pregnancy Act 92 of 1996 ('CTPA 1996') was promulgated. It repealed the 1975 Abortion Act insofar as it relates to abortion. The 1996 Act aims to liberalise and largely decriminalise the abortion dispensation in South Africa. The Act provides for three offences, namely: it is an offence for any person who is not authorised under the Act to perform the termination of a pregnancy; any person who prevents the lawful termination of a pregnancy commits an offence; and any person who obstructs access to a facility for the termination of pregnancies commits an offence.[43]

30 Burchell (n 12) 584.
31 *S v Burger* [1975] (4) SA 877 (A); de Wet (n 14) 231; Burchell (n 12) 584.
32 Burchell (n 12) 582; Kemp (n 12) 303;
33 Kemp (n 12) 303.
34 Burchell (n 12) 582.
35 Snyman (n 12) 444.
36 Ibid. 445.
37 J. Sarkin, 'Patriarchy and Discrimination in Apartheid South Africa's Abortion Law' (1998) 4 Buffalo Human Rights Law Review 141, 143.
38 Ibid. 144.
39 *R v Thielke* [1918] AD 373; *R v P* 1948 (4) SA 103 (C); *R v Voges* [1958] (1) SA 412 (C); Sarkin (n 37) 145.
40 Sarkin (n 37) 145.
41 *S v King* [1971] (2) PH H103 (T), cited in Sarkin (n 37) 146.
42 Sarkin (n 37) 156.
43 Burchell (n 12) 573, 576.

Intentional homicide

Snyman noted that, since there 'are many different ways in which a person can cause another's death unlawfully and intentionally, the crime of murder in South African law covers a wide field'.[44] Murder is defined as the 'unlawful and intentional killing of another person'[45] (some authors use the term another 'human being' instead of 'person').[46]

At the outset it is necessary to point out that there are no formal degrees of murder in South African law. Premeditated murder (on the one end of the extreme), assisted suicide, killing in the heat of the moment and everything in between are all regarded as homicide in the form of murder. The crime is not graded.[47] Punishment will, of course, vary according to the facts and the applicability of minimum sentencing legislation, which will be discussed later in this chapter.

Reckless homicide

Reckless, for present purposes, means 'consciously accepts a risk.'[48] The question is whether recklessness is a distinct basis for liability for homicide offences, alongside intent and negligence. Professor J.C. Smith, the well-known scholar of English criminal law, observed that what would be called 'recklessness' in English law is in South Africa 'simply a variety of intention'.[49] It is the case that recklessness and the form of intent known as *dolus eventualis* were historically often used as interchangeable concepts, or at least as conceptually very close, even indistinguishable.[50] In 1958 the Supreme Court of Appeal observed:

> It is clear that in the case of *dolus eventualis* intent to kill will be present where the wrong-doer pursued the act with recklessness as to whether or not his act is fulfilled in death. The natural concomitant of this recklessness is that the wrong-doer must in fact have (not ought to have) preconceived death as a result; for it would be impossible for him to be reckless as to whether death ensues or not if he never actually appreciated that death was a possible result. The appreciation of death as a possible result is a fact which cannot be proved by an objective test. However difficult it may be for the Crown, this must be proved as an actual fact by inference from all the circumstances.[51]

The imprecise use of the term 'recklessness'[52] in the context of the fault element should be avoided. Indeed, in 1975 Bertelsmann proposed that 'the unhelpful concept of recklessness' should be eliminated. The proposition was that *dolus eventualis*, as a form of intent, should

44 Snyman (n 12) 437.
45 Burchell (n 12) 577.
46 Kemp (n 12) 297; Snyman (n 12) 437.
47 Snyman (n 12) 437–438.
48 Ibid. 181.
49 J.C. Smith, 'The Element of Chance in Criminal Liability' (1972) 1 Natal University Law Review 4, 11, quoted in W. Bertelsmann, 'What Happened to *luxuria*? Some Observations on Criminal Negligence, Recklessness and *dolus eventualis*' (1975) 92 South African Law Journal 59, 74.
50 Bertelsmann (n 49) 72.
51 *R v Horn* [1958] (3) SA 457 (A) [466F]-[466G].
52 The problem is that, historically, the courts, including the Supreme Court of Appeal, had used the term 'reckless' occasionally to describe 'gross negligence'; and on other occasions to determine the lower limit of *dolus eventualis*. See Bertelsmann (n 49) 71, and the case law cited.

be clearly distinguished from negligence, with 'recklessness' not retained as a free-standing concept and basis for culpability alongside intent and negligence.[53]

In contemporary South African criminal law 'recklessness' simply refers to the second leg of the test for intent in the form of *dolus eventualis*. The courts now follow the view that the test for *dolus eventualis* always consists of two parts, namely the cognitive part and the conative (or, volitional) part. Thus, the accused acted with intent in the form of *dolus eventualis* if he had reconciled himself to the possibility that an unlawful result (which he had foreseen as a possibility) may follow.[54]

Negligent homicide

A controversial decision by the Supreme Court of Appeal illustrates the thin conceptual line between intent in the form of *dolus eventualis* and negligence. In *S v Humphreys*[55] the appellant was convicted in the High Court of ten counts of murder and four counts of attempted murder. The offences were committed when the appellant drove his minibus taxi containing 14 schoolchildren through a boom-controlled level crossing and collided with a train. Ten of the children were killed; four of them survived. The appellant had been a shunter for most of his life but when he retired neighbours employed him to transport their children to school in a different suburb. He had been doing this for almost ten years when the fateful incident occurred, and had always used the same route to get the children to school. The route involved him crossing the level crossing at a time in the morning when there was heavy traffic. On the fateful morning the traffic before him at the level crossing had stopped because the boom, which covered only half the road in either direction, was down, and the lights were flashing, indicating that a train was approaching the level crossing. Despite these warning signals, the appellant overtook the line of cars on their right, and proceeded into the level crossing on the wrong side[56] of the road. Evidence at the hearing established that it took a few seconds for the booms to come down after the lights started flashing, and then one minute elapsed before the train entered the crossing. When the minibus entered the crossing on this particular morning, it was struck by a train on its left side. The trial court held that the appellant did not have the direct intent to cause the death of ten of his passengers, but he did have intent in the form of *dolus eventualis*, in that he had both foreseen the possibility of fatal injuries to his passengers, and reconciled himself with that possibility. The Supreme Court of Appeal disagreed with this finding. It held that the appellant did not reconcile himself to the possibility of the collision, because such an inference would necessarily entail that he had reconciled himself with his own death. The Appeal Court's inferential reasoning led them to conclude that the conative part of the test for *dolus eventualis* was not satisfied. Since there was no intent, the appeals court considered the possibility that the accused acted with negligence, and concluded that he was indeed negligent when he caused the death of the ten children. The convictions of murder were therefore set aside and replaced with ten convictions of culpable homicide.[57]

53 Bertelsmann (n 49) 75.
54 Snyman (n 12) 181.
55 2013 (2) SACR 1 (SCA).
56 In South Africa, like in the United Kingdom, drivers drive on the left-hand side of the road, and motor vehicles are normally right-hand drive vehicles.
57 *Humphreys* (n 55).

Culpable homicide is defined as 'the unlawful, negligent causing of the death of another human being.'[58] The difference between culpable homicide and murder centres on the form of culpability. It is, of course, not possible to be convicted of attempted culpable homicide. This is so because one cannot intend to be negligent.[59] However, it is necessary to briefly consider the concept of 'conscious negligence' (*luxuria*) which still plays a role in South African criminal law.

Negligence in the form of *luxuria* is where a person foresaw a particular result, but 'unreasonably came to the conclusion that it would not materialise'.[60] This is different from unconscious negligence, where a person is unaware of the possibility of a particular result's materialisation (while he *should* have been aware of it).[61] *Luxuria* is a form of negligence; not of intention.[62] While it is relatively easy to recognise the conceptual difference between (unconscious) negligence and intent, the same cannot be said of the difference between intent and *luxuria*. Carstens noted that 'the main difference between *dolus eventualis* and *luxuria* is not to be found in the presence or absence of the *foresight* of the result (the so-called cognitive element), but whether or not the accused reconciled himself/herself to the foreseen possibility (result) (the so called volitional element)'.[63]

The decision in *Humphreys* above illustrates not only the difference between intent in the form of *dolus eventualis* and negligence generally; it also concerns *luxuria*. [64] With reference to the facts, the Supreme Court of Appeal concluded:

> I believe common sense dictates that if the appellant foresaw the possibility of fatal injury to one or more of his passengers — as I found he did — he must by the same token have foreseen fatal injury to himself. An inference that the appellant took the death of his passengers into the bargain when he proceeded with his action would unavoidably require the further necessary inference that the appellant also took his own death into the bargain. Put differently, the appellant must have been indifferent as to whether he would live or die. But there is no indication on the evidence that the appellant valued his own life any less than the average person or that it was immaterial to him whether or not he would lose his life. In consequence I do not think it can be said that the appellant had reconciled himself with the possibility of his own death. What must follow from this is that he had not reconciled himself with the occurrence of the collision or the death of his passengers either. In short, he foresaw the possibility of the collision, but he thought it would not happen; he took a risk which he thought would not materialise.[65]

The Court thus distinguished clearly between intent in the form of *dolus eventualis* and negligence in the form of *luxuria*. The difference between *dolus eventualis* and *luxuria* also

58 Snyman (n 12) 442.
59 Ibid. 443. One cannot intend to be negligent.
60 Ibid. 183.
61 Ibid.
62 P. Carstens, 'Revisiting the Relationship Between *dolus eventualis* and *luxuria* in Context of Vehicular Collisions Causing the Death of Fellow Passengers and/or Pedestrians: *S v Humphreys* 2013 (2) SACR 1 (SCA)' (2013) 26 South African Journal of Criminal Justice 67, 68.
63 Ibid. 68.
64 *Humphreys* (n 55) [15].
65 Ibid. [18].

serves as clear delineation between the crimes of murder and culpable homicide. Regarding the impact of the decision in *Humphreys* on future homicide cases, Carstens reckons that

> when courts in future, in these kind of cases, grapple to determine whether an accused should be convicted of murder or culpable homicide, more often than not, it will be the *absence* of the second leg of *dolus eventualis* that will indicate the *presence* of *luxuria* (in the sense that a reasonable person would have reconciled himself/herself to the fatal consequence, which the accused, in the circumstances, failed to do) to justify a conviction of culpable homicide.[66]

Result-qualified / constructive / versari in re illicita */ felony homicide offences*

Constructive crimes 'are committed by persons who, having engaged in certain acts bring about results which in the ordinary sense of the word they did not intend.'[67] Related to this is the *versari*-doctrine. Burchell notes that both Roman-Dutch and English law recognised the *versari in re illicita* doctrine, which serves as the basis for the felony-murder rule in English homicide law. In terms of this rule an accused who, while committing a felony, '*accidentally*' caused the death of the deceased, could be guilty of murder.[68] The *versari*-doctrine was applied in South Africa until 1965, when it was abolished by the Supreme Court of Appeal.

The decision in *R v Hillebrand* [69] illustrates the pre-1965 application of the *versari in re illicita*-doctrine in South African criminal law. In this case the accused and the deceased engaged in what the Court described as 'a rough game'[70] in terms of which the accused, without intent to harm the deceased, injected a stream of compressed air via the deceased's rectum into his intestines. This led to the rupture of one of the intestines, with fatal consequences for the deceased. The Court was not concerned with the commission of a lawful act performed in a negligent manner; indeed, the Court noted that negligence was not under consideration because the accused *intended* to do what he did and his act was a deliberate one.[71] The question was whether the act was a lawful act or not. Regarding the act performed by the deceased, the Court held that the direction of a stream of compressed air by one person upon another is an assault, which is an unlawful act.[72] Applying the *versari*-doctrine, the Court held as follows:

> The accused was guilty of an assault upon the dead man and therefore guilty of an unlawful act which was the cause of the death of the deceased, and he is therefore guilty of the crime of culpable homicide as laid to his charge.[73]

The *versari*-doctrine was abolished in South Africa in 1965 by the Supreme Court of Appeal.[74] The accused in *Bernardus* was accused in the trial court of murder. He was

66 Carstens (n 62) 73.
67 O.C.M. Davis, 'Constructive Homicide' (1938) 2 Journal of Criminal Law 451, 453.
68 Burchell (n 12) 446.
69 1959 (3) SA 22 (T).
70 *Ruwe spel*, translated from the original Afrikaans.
71 *Hillebrand* (n 69) [23C-D].
72 Ibid. [23F].
73 Ibid. [23G-H].
74 *Bernardus* (n 28).

convicted of culpable homicide and sentenced to two years' imprisonment. The accused in this case admitted to the fact that he had thrown a *knopkierie* (a wooden stick with a thick, round head) at the deceased. He denied that he could reasonably have foreseen that it would hit the deceased with fatal consequences. He thus denied any negligence on his part. The trial court, however, found that the throwing of the *knopkierie* constituted an unlawful assault, which caused the death of the deceased. The trial court, clearly applying the *versari*-doctrine, thus found the accused guilty of culpable homicide. The Supreme Court of Appeal considered the historical foundations of the *versari*-doctrine in Roman-Dutch[75] and canon law, and concluded that the *versari*-doctrine, with its roots in canon law, was not strongly supported by the Roman-Dutch authors. The Appeal Court noted, however, that since its inception in South African criminal law, the *versari*-doctrine seemed to have received ever growing support in South African legal practice. The Appeal Court found this to be troublesome, since the *versari*-doctrine, as applied by the courts in South Africa, is in conflict with one of the foundational principles of South African and a number of comparative legal systems, namely that an accused cannot be punished without fault, or, *actus non facit reum nisi mens sit rea*.[76] The Supreme Court of Appeal thus abolished the *versari*-doctrine, a 'primitive relic from canon law', from South African criminal law.[77]

General elements

Beginning of life

The South African common law was not very clear about the beginning of life (that is, the moment when a pregnancy and birth results in independent human life). De Wet suggests this is so because the common law authorities were not very clear about the distinction between murder of a child, on the one hand, and abortion of a developed foetus, on the other hand.[78] The question about live birth for purposes of homicide offences is now governed by s.239 of the Criminal Procedure Act 51 of 1977 ('CPA 1977'). Under the heading 'Evidence on charge of infanticide or concealment of birth' subsection (1) provides as follows:

> At criminal proceedings at which an accused is charged with the killing of a newly-born child, such child shall be deemed to have been born alive if the child is proved to have breathed, whether or not the child had an independent circulation, and it shall not be necessary to prove that such child was, at the time of its death, entirely separated from the body of its mother.

Since the homicide offences of murder and culpable homicide are committed in respect of living human beings, and not unborn foetuses, it is crucial to determine whether a child was born alive. Le Roux-Kemp and Wilkinson noted that the evidentiary issue contained in s.239(1) is a statutory confirmation that the 'appropriate manner in which to determine whether a foetus was born alive is to determine whether the foetus had breathed'. However, the authors also noted that, from a medical perspective, 'the first breath drawn by the foetus is not necessarily a conclusive

75 Notably the authors Grotius, Matthaeus, Voet, Moorman and Van der Linde. See *Bernardus* (n 28) [294D].
76 *Bernardus* (n 28) [296E-F].
77 Ibid. [298A-B].
78 de Wet (n 12) 228.

sign of life.'[79] Having said that, it is clear that the hydrostatic test, first developed by Wilhelm Gottfried Ploucquet in the seventeenth century, is still widely used to determine whether a new-born child had breathed. Le Roux-Kemp and Wilkinson described the test as follows:

> The lungs of a recently born foetus are cut into pieces and then placed in water. If the lung tissue floats, it is accepted that the foetus had inhaled air and that it was absorbed into the lungs just before death. The lungs of a still-born child (a child that has not breathed) will, however, sink in water.[80]

The authors pointed out that the relatively simplistic hydrostatic test is the subject of criticism, since it does not adequately account for other factors that could cause lung tissue to float or sink in water.[81] Regardless, it is still applied today, also in South Africa.[82]

End of life

The end of life, or, moment of death, was not defined under common law.[83] In the case of *S v Williams* [84] the Supreme Court of Appeal suggested *obiter dicta* that brainstem death, or somatic death, was not the only factor in determining end of life. It was suggested that 'end of life' is a more complex notion which also needs to consider the legal, moral and religious beliefs of the community.[85] The moment of death is now defined in the National Health Act 61 of 2003 as 'brain death'.[86] Trauma can lead to a situation where no brain activity can be detected in a patient, which makes it easier to declare the patient 'brain dead'. However, as pointed out by commentators, brain death, as a moment of death, is of 'no assistance in cases where a patient is very much biologically alive (the brain and brainstem are intact), but the patient is in a persistent vegetative state and has no cognition or conation.'[87] Since the patient can still be viewed as biologically 'alive', but with no quality of life, many would say that such an individual is 'dead' in a social sense.[88] This is the grey area of end-of-life decisions.

Pre-birth causes with post-birth effect

A prosecutorial attempt to expand the crime of murder to include pre-birth causation of death of a fully developed foetus was considered in *S v Mshumpa.* [89] A woman, in the 38th

79 A. Le Roux-Kemp and J. Wilkinson, 'A Novel Application of the Hydrostatic Test in Determining Live (Non)-Birth' (2012) 25(2) South African Journal of Criminal Justice 271, 273.
80 Ibid. 274.
81 Ibid. 275.
82 Ibid. 276.
83 P. Carstens and D. Pearmain, *Foundational Principles of South African Medical Law* (LexisNexis 2007) 204.
84 1986 (4) SA 1188 (A). The deceased was shot in the neck by the accused. The jugular vein and carotid artery were severed. Her brain and brain stem were dead as a result, however, she was kept alive for a further 48 hours by means of artificial respiration. She was declared dead when the artificial respirator was disconnected.
85 Ibid. [1194]. See also comments by A. Le Roux-Kemp, 'A Question of Life and Death' (2013) 46(1) Comparative and International Law Journal of Southern Africa 74, 83.
86 National Health Act 61 of 2003, s.1: '"death" means brain death'.
87 Carstens and Pearmain (n 83) 205.
88 For more on the moral, social, cultural and religious views on the moment of death, see Le Roux-Kemp (n 85) 81–89.
89 2008 (1) SACR 126 (E).

week of gestation of her pregnancy, was hijacked together with her partner, who was also the father of the child. All indications were that a birth without any complications could be expected. In fact, the couple received this confirmation from their gynaecologist on the day of the fateful hijacking. One of the central issues in *Mshumpa* was the parameters of the crime of murder. The facts relating to the murder charge were as follows: Mshumpa not only kidnapped both the pregnant woman and her partner, but also shot and wounded them in what later transpired to be a staged hijacking, devised by the woman's partner and the accused, Mr Mshumpa. The real motive all along was not to hijack a vehicle but rather to provide a pretext in order to shoot the woman and to ensure the killing of the foetus. That aim was achieved. Both the woman and her partner survived; however, the foetus was injured to such an extent that it died in the womb. At the trial expert medical evidence was led to the effect that a foetus in the 38th week of gestation is normally viable and, given the health of the foetus in this particular case, a living birth was an almost certainty.[90] The neo-natal medical expert further testified that the unborn foetus in this case reacted to the pain caused by the bullets, and there were forensic signs of distress before its death, including amniotic fluid and red blood cells in the lungs of the foetus. It was submitted that, from a medical point of view, 'the unborn foetus's life and death inside the womb did not differ in its very nature from the life and death of a normal person living outside the womb.'[91]

The presiding judge was asked by the prosecution to extend the common law definition of murder in order to make provision for the type of situation where pre-birth conduct causes the death of an otherwise healthy and viable foetus. The judge declined and stated that 'such a development of the common law of crimes must be done incrementally and cautiously in accordance with the dictates of the Constitution'.[92]

We can thus conclude that pre-birth causes which result in the death of the foetus in the mother's womb is not homicide with respect to the foetus; it is of course an attack on the mother's body and can as such be the basis for criminal liability for assault or attempted murder (if the mother lives) or homicide (if the mother dies). The nature of the assault on the mother, including the killing of an otherwise healthy foetus, may be taken into account for sentencing purposes.[93] If the foetus in the *Mshumpa*-type scenario lives for long enough to be born alive, and dies shortly after birth, it could potentially be treated as homicide in the form of infanticide, which is a form of common law murder.[94] The *Mshumpa*-type scenario does not qualify as an unlawful abortion. The latter is the unlawful termination of a pregnancy after 20 weeks of gestation, meaning the separation and expulsion, by medical or surgical means, of the contents of the pregnant uterus.[95]

Medical treatment scenarios

The doctrine of double effect holds that 'all intended bad ends and all bad means chosen to achieve ends are morally wrong. By contrast, unintended but foreseen consequences are

90 Ibid. [48].
91 See Le Roux-Kemp and Wilkinson (n 79) 278 and 277–78 for more detail and discussion of the medico-legal and forensic aspects of the case of *Mshumpa* (n 89) para 47–8.
92 *Mshumpa* (n 89) [60]. For more commentary on the case, see G.A. du Plessis, 'Feticide: Creating a Statutory Crime in South African Law' (2013) 24(1) Stellenbosch Law Review 73.
93 Kemp (n 12) 304.
94 For a discussion of infanticide, see Burchell (n 12) 582–83; *S v Jokasi* [1987] (1) SA 431 (ZS).
95 CTPA 1996, s.2(1)(c)(i) and (ii); Burchell (n 12) 575.

side-effects, which may be justified according to the totality of the circumstances.'[96] The doctrine involves both legal and ethical issues. In a medical context, the doctrine is seen as a justification for medical treatment or relief which may be life-shortening, but justified on moral and legal grounds. The state of mind of the medical practitioner is not the only determining factor. Objective factors, for instance the question of whether the treatment or pain relief administered is for a patient who is suffering from a terminal illness, and the life expectancy of the patient, will be taken into account.[97] Although double effect is occasionally cited in the context of abortion, it is at present mostly referenced in the context of medical treatment and euthanasia.[98]

In 1999 the South African Law Reform Commission submitted its Report on Euthanasia and the Artificial Preservation of Life[99] to the Minister of Justice. A number of recommendations and options informed a draft bill on euthanasia which was also contained in the Report. One of the Commission's recommendations read as follows:

> A medical practitioner or, under specified circumstances, a nurse may relieve the suffering of a terminally ill patient by prescribing sufficient drugs to control the pain of the patient adequately even though the secondary effect of this conduct may be the shortening of the patient's life.[100]

Although the above recommendation does not explicitly mention the double effect doctrine, it is clearly comparable to the doctrine as briefly described above by way of introduction. It should be noted that, although the draft bill on euthanasia was published more than 15 years ago, there still is no real parliamentary movement in this regard. There has, however, been case law which illustrates the complexity of the euthanasia debate, and which also underscores the urgent need for the legislature to consider and to act on the many legal and ethical uncertainties surrounding the question of euthanasia.

In *Minister of Justice v Estate Stransham-Ford* [101] the Supreme Court of Appeal considered the order granted by a division of the High Court. The applicant, Stransham-Ford, who was terminally ill, was granted an order (a) that a medical practitioner could either end his life by administering a lethal substance, or (b) provide him with the lethal substance to enable him to administer it himself. In order for the order to be lawful the applicant sought a declaration that the common law of homicide (the crimes of murder and culpable homicide) be developed in terms of section 39 of the Constitution, 1996, which enjoins courts, when developing the common law, to promote the spirit, purport and objects of the Bill of Rights. The order was granted by the High Court two hours after the applicant's death. The Court was unaware of his death. Nevertheless, the order granted by the High Court specified that the medical doctor who administered the lethal substance upon request of the applicant would not be acting unlawfully. The doctor could therefore not be prosecuted for any offence related to the administering of the lethal substance to Stransham-Ford, and he could also not be disciplined by the medical profession. The far-reaching order by the High

96 D. Price, 'Euthanasia, Pain Relief and Double Effect' (1997) 17(2) Legal Studies 323.
97 Ibid. 324.
98 Ibid. 326.
99 South Africa Law Commission (1998) *Project 86 RP 186/1999 Report submitted to the Minister of Justice on 25 May 1999* <http://salawreform.justice.gov.za/reports/r_prj86_euthen_1998nov.pdf> accessed 5 April 2018.
100 Law Commission Report on Euthanasia at xi.
101 *Minister of Justice v Estate Stransham-Ford* [2017] (3) SA 152 (SCA).

Court was set aside by the Supreme Court of Appeal. The Supreme Court of Appeal was alarmed by the precedential effect of the High Court order and the reasoning that underscored it. It was therefore necessary for the Supreme Court of Appeal to address the merits of the High Court order, despite the fact that the applicant in that case had died. The question of euthanasia is complex, in South Africa and elsewhere. Not all of the aspects and nuances of the debate will be explored here. Some of the relevant parts of the Supreme Court of Appeal's decision are noted, specifically those aspects related to medical treatment, the double effect doctrine and end-of-life decisions.

The Appeals Court examined the current state of South African law and legal doctrine relating to the question of euthanasia.[102] The Court stated that it is a matter of personal autonomy and constitutional principle (notably the right to dignity and bodily integrity) for any individual to refuse medical treatment that would otherwise prolong life. Such a refusal can only be made by a patient with the necessary mental and legal capacity. Medical practitioners who would adhere to such a refusal by the patient do not commit an offence 'by ceasing treatment or other forms of medical intervention that serve neither a therapeutic nor a palliative purpose'.[103] Furthermore, a medical practitioner 'commits no offence by prescribing drugs by way of palliative treatment for pain that the doctor knows will have the effect of hastening the patient's death.'[104] The latter aspect refers to the 'double effect' doctrine, as described above.

The Supreme Court of Appeal confirmed that 'mercy killing' constitutes the crime of murder under South African law, and consent is not a defence.[105] While the Court acknowledged that law reform is needed, the Court also stated that the notion of a dignified death had to be 'informed by a rounded view of society, not confined to a restricted section of it.'[106] In the absence of legislative reform the courts will probably have to grapple with the lawful boundaries of physician-assisted euthanasia and related matters for the foreseeable future.

Homicide by omission

In terms of the general principles of criminal liability an individual can only be held criminally accountable for an omission if there exists a legal duty on that individual to act. And a legal duty is not the same as a moral duty.[107] Legal duties can be created expressly, typically through legislation, or more generally based on the legal convictions of the community. The latter must be viewed and considered through the prism of the Bill of Rights.[108]

The existence or creation of risks – especially potential dangerous situations – can also create legal duties which are potentially relevant for purposes of homicide law. For instance, in *S v Fernandez*[109] a private citizen was convicted of culpable homicide because he failed to secure the cage of a pet baboon, which escaped from the cage and fatally attacked a small child.

102 Ibid. [29].
103 Ibid. [33].
104 Ibid. [35].
105 Ibid. [36]. See also the older cases of *S v Hartmann* [1975] (3) SA 532 (C); *S v De Bellocq* [1975] (3) SA 538 (T), and *S v Marengo* [1991] (2) SACR 43 (W).
106 Ibid. [100].
107 Snyman (n 12) 58.
108 *Carmichele v Minister of Safety and Security* [2002] (91) SACR 79 (CC); Snyman (n 12) 59.
109 1966 (2) SA 259 (A).

Protective relationships, notably that of parent / child or guardian / child, may also give rise to a legal duty to protect against harm. Previous positive acts, where an individual has created a potentially dangerous situation, for instance starting a fire and then failing to put it out or to control it, may cause criminal liability for harm caused by the fire.[110] Persons in positions of responsibility or authority, such as police officers, may also be required to take positive actions in order to prevent harm to others.[111]

Omitting to effect an easy rescue

In South Africa there is no duty of general rescue, nor a duty to effect an easy rescue.[112] The exceptions to this general rule are governed by the principles pertaining to the existence of a legal duty, as discussed in the previous section. While it is tempting to use the somewhat amorphous concept of 'legal convictions of the community' to create new duties (including duties to rescue), commentators like Burchell warn that this should be done with due regard for the fundamental principle of legality.[113] One should be careful not to insidiously convert the exception into the general rule.

Intentional homicide offences

In South Africa there are two forms of intentional homicide, namely murder and infanticide under common law. Attempted murder is a separate crime.[114] Although the killing of newly born children is often referred to as 'infanticide', it is generally prosecuted as the crime of murder, since it also involves the intentional killing of another human being, albeit a newly born human being.[115]

Actus reus

The *actus reus* for the crime of murder is very broad. Any unlawful method which causes the death of another human being is covered under this element. Direct forms of violence are certainly the most common forms of killing, but indirect forms, for instance where the victim was frightened into a fatal heart attack, are also covered.[116] The crucial question is whether the particular act or omission *caused* the death of the victim.[117]

Mens rea

Intent, at least in the form of *dolus eventualis*, is required.[118]

110 Snyman (n 12) 60.
111 *Minister van Polisie v Ewels* [1975] (3) SA 590 (A). In this case a police officer on duty witnessed an assault, but failed to come to the rescue of the assault victim. The police officer was held to have failed to fulfil a legal duty to come to the rescue of the assault victim. On that basis one can assume that, had the victim died, the police officer could probably have been held liable for culpable homicide.
112 Burchell (n 12) 80.
113 Burchell (n 12) 81.
114 *S v Ndlovu* [1984] (3) SA 23 (A).
115 *S v Jokasi* (n 94).
116 Burchell (n 12) 578.
117 *R v Makali* [1950] (1) SA 340 (N). The fact that someone was going to die anyway as result of an illness is irrelevant as long as the perpetrator hastens, even in the slightest way, the death of the victim.
118 Burchell (n 12) 581.

Reckless homicide offences

It was noted above under the heading 'Reckless homicide' that there is no longer in South Africa a separate form of homicide known as 'reckless homicide'. Homicide offences are either based on intent (murder) or negligence (culpable homicide). Recklessness forms part of the second leg of intent in the form of *dolus eventualis.*

Negligent homicide offences

In South Africa there is one negligent crime of homicide, namely culpable homicide.

Actus reus

By the numbers, the most common instances of culpable homicide in South Africa are traffic-related and the negligent handling of firearms.[119] Regardless of the act, the test is whether the conduct of the accused was the 'factual and legal cause of the death of the deceased.'[120]

Mens rea

Fault in the form of negligence is required for the crime of culpable homicide. The usual form of negligence, or inadvertent negligence, as well as so-called conscious negligence (*luxuria*) can form the basis for liability for the crime of culpable homicide.[121]

Result-qualified / constructive / *versari in re illicita* / felony homicide offences

As pointed out on page 202, the *versari*-doctrine was abolished in South Africa. There is also no separate category of homicide offences under the heading 'felony homicide offences'.

Abortion and homicide

Abortion

Abortion has largely been decriminalised in South Africa. In terms of the CTPA 1996, women have a great deal of freedom to end pregnancies. A pregnant woman's informed consent forms the basis for a legal abortion.[122]

Relationship to homicide

Unlawful abortion is not a homicide offence. The CTPA 1996 provides for the different requirements of a lawful abortion, linked to three distinct stages in the pregnancy.[123] An

119 Ibid. 584–85.
120 Ibid.
121 See also the discussion above.
122 For more detail, see G. Kemp 'South Africa' in A. Reed and M. Bohlander (eds) *Consent* (Routledge 2017) 235.
123 Kemp (n 12) 305–7.

attack on the mother's body, which causes an abortion of the foetus, is treated as an offence against the mother (for instance assault, or attempted murder). See also the discussion above, under 'Pre-birth causes with post-birth effects'.

Defences to homicide

Consent

Consent, in the context of assisted suicide and euthanasia, is still not regarded as a defence to homicide charges (murder or culpable homicide). The recent decision by the Supreme Court of Appeal in *Minister of Justice v Estate Stransham-Ford* confirmed this position.[124]

Self-defence

Self-defence, or private defence, is a complete defence to a homicide charge. The Constitutional Court[125] also stated that killing in self-defence is permissible under the Constitution, thus confirming the general position under common law.

Duress

The defence of duress is available even in situations where the killing of an innocent third person is made necessary. However, the courts will not lightly accept the defence.[126]

Necessity

Since the test for the defence of necessity is rather strict, it is doubtful that the courts will easily allow this defence for homicide acts. Other defences and grounds of justification, including self-defence, duress and public authority, will conceivably be more appropriate potential defences.[127]

Insanity

Mental illness and intellectual disability can form the basis of a defence in South African criminal law. The position is governed by s.78 CPA 1977.[128]

Diminished responsibility

Section 78(7) of the CPA 1977, as amended by Act 4 of 2017, provides that if a court finds that an accused at the time of the commission of the act in question was criminally responsible for the act but that his or her capacity to appreciate the wrongfulness of the act or to act in accordance with an appreciation of the wrongfulness of the act was diminished by

124 See discussion above, under 'Medical treatment scenarios'. See also Kemp in Reed and Bohlander (n 122) 231–34.
125 *S v Makwanyane* (n 11) [138]. See also G. Kemp, 'South Africa' in A. Reed and M. Bohlander (eds) *General Defences in Criminal Law* (Ashgate 2014) 291–92.
126 Reed and Bohlander (n 125) 293.
127 Ibid.
128 Ibid. 293–96 for a more detailed discussion.

reason of mental illness or intellectual disability, the Court may take the fact of such diminished responsibility into account when sentencing the accused.

Loss of control / provocation – including battered woman syndrome

In *S v Eadie* [129] the accused battered the victim to death in a fit of apparent road rage. The Supreme Court of Appeal rejected the accused's defence of non-pathological incapacity due to loss of self-control. The Court thus curtailed the defence of provocation in South African criminal law to such an extent that it is now probably[130] only available as a defence under circumstances where the provocation led to involuntary conduct (automatism), or where the provocation affected the accused's capacity to appreciate wrongfulness.[131]

The restrictive approach to provocation and loss of self-control as (potential) defences in South African criminal law, as espoused by the Supreme Court of Appeal in the *Eadie* case, means that so-called 'battered woman syndrome' is probably not available as a complete defence to a criminal charge, including murder. In *S v Ferreira* [132] the Supreme Court of Appeal allowed evidence of spousal abuse and battered woman syndrome as mitigating factors for sentencing purposes.

Superior orders

There is no general defence of superior orders under South African criminal law. The defence of obedience to superior orders is limited to the military and police contexts. The essential elements of the defence are as follows:

- The order must emanate from a person lawfully placed in authority over the subordinate;
- The subordinate must have been under a duty to obey the order; and
- The subordinate must have done no more than was necessary to carry out the order.[133]

The defence of obedience to superior orders is not unqualified. It is required that the orders which are relied on are not 'manifestly and palpably' unlawful.[134]

Official authority

The Constitutional Court has laid down the legal requirements for the lawful use of force, including deadly force, by the police when effecting an arrest. All the requirements are not repeated here. It is sufficing to note the Court's observations regarding the use of (potentially) lethal force in the context of an arrest:

129 2002 (3) SA 719 (SCA).
130 The judgment was rightly criticised for its ambiguity. See S. Hoctor, 'A peregrination through the law of provocation' in J.J. Joubert (ed.), *Essays in Honour of CR Snyman* (Jakaranda 2008) 153–60.
131 Burchell (n 12) 329.
132 2004 (2) SACR 454 (SCA).
133 Burchell (n 12) 192.
134 *S v Banda* [1990] (3) SA 466 (B) [485B-C].

- Shooting a suspect solely in order to carry out an arrest is permitted in very limited circumstances only.
- Ordinarily such shooting is not permitted unless the suspect poses a threat of violence to the arrester or others or is suspected on reasonable grounds of having committed a crime involving the infliction or threatened infliction of serious bodily harm and there are no other reasonable means of carrying out the arrest, whether at that time or later.
- These limitations in no way detract from the rights of an arrester attempting to carry out an arrest to kill a suspect in self-defence or in defence of any other person.[135]

The legal principles as set out by the Constitutional Court are now reflected in s.49 of the CPA 1977. This section was amended in 2012 in order to bring police powers and practice in line with the Constitutional Court decision.[136]

Honour killings

'Honour killings' as a phenomenon is not widespread, pervasive or even that well-known in South Africa. To the extent that 'honour killings' as a phenomenon has traditionally been associated with (conservative) Muslim communities, it should be noted that South Africa has a relatively small Muslim community, and the South African Muslim community is traditionally also relatively liberal compared to more traditional communities elsewhere. Of course, the notion of honour killing is not confined to Muslim societies, but it is clear that the term is associated with the practice which has its roots in Muslim societies in Asia, and in Pakistan in particular.[137]

More relevant in a South African context are other cultural motivations in homicide cases, notably 'witch burning', *muti*-killings[138] and violence against LGBTQ persons. Violence against sexual minorities is not always in the form of homicidal violence, and include practices such as so-called 'corrective rape' of lesbian women.[139] The practice of witch burning, on the other hand, is almost always homicidal. The practice was so pervasive in some of South Africa's provinces that it prompted the government to appoint a commission of inquiry to investigate the circumstances and motivations which underscore the phenomenon.[140] In South African law it is illegal to accuse another person of witchcraft or sorcery, or to name a person as a witch or wizard or to injure or damage any person or thing on the advice of any witchdoctor, witch-finder or similar person.[141] Although a belief in the existence of witches or sorcerers does not constitute a defence in South African criminal law, a 'truly-held belief' in witches and sorcerers was historically acknowledged as a mitigating

135 *Ex Parte: Minister of Safety and Security: In Re S v Walters* [2002] (4) SA 613 (CC) [643].
136 Act 9 of 2012, amending CPA 1977, s.49.
137 For a discussion, see N.A. Shah, 'Honour Killings: Islamic and Human Rights Perspectives' (2004) 55(1) Northern Ireland Legal Quarterly 78–89.
138 The killing of another person in order to harvest his or her body parts, usually for witchcraft-related practices. For a discussion, see J. Mihálik and Y. Cassim, 'Ritual Murder and Witchcraft: A Political Weapon?' (1993) 110 South African Law Journal 127–140.
139 Johanna Bond noted the practice whereby South African black lesbians are often perceived as deviants. They suffer 'curative rapes' intended to 'erase their desires to be male'. See J. Bond, 'Gender and Non-Normative Sex in Sub-Saharan Africa' (2016) 23 Michigan Journal of Gender & Law 65, 85.
140 For a discussion, see Pieter Carstens, 'The cultural defence in criminal law: South African perspectives' [2004] 37 De Jure 312, 314–322.
141 Witchcraft Suppression Act 3 of 1957.

factor by the courts in cases of witch-killing. This is no longer the case. Discretionary minimum sentences of life imprisonment in cases of witch killing are now applicable.[142]

Sentencing framework

South Africa has high levels of violent crime.[143] In the 2015/2016 financial year (the latest available report) 18,673 murders were recorded by the police; an increase of 4.9% from the previous year.[144] During the same period a total number of 18,127 attempted murders were recorded by the police, an increase of 3.4% compared to the previous year.[145] The police report does not mention the number of culpable homicide cases recorded. The most recent statistics for culpable homicide appear from other sources and are from the year 2015. According to these reports 11,185 cases of culpable homicide were reported or were detected as a result of police action.[146] Unfortunately neither of the latest available annual reports of the National Prosecuting Authority[147] and the Department of Correctional Services[148] contain any breakdown of specific numbers for homicide convictions and sentences.

Mandatory sentencing regimes

Prior to the democratic constitutional dispensation, the crime of murder, together with crimes like rape and treason, were punishable by death. The death penalty was declared unconstitutional by the Constitutional Court in *S v Makwanyane.* [149] It was held to be a cruel, inhuman and degrading punishment. Subsequent to the decision in *Makwanyane* Parliament enacted a *mandatory* minimum sentencing regime in 1997.[150] This regime was amended in 2007[151] in order to give effect to judicial interpretation of the 1997 sentencing regime and to provide for statutory *discretionary* minimum sentences.

Discretionary sentencing regimes

It was held by the Supreme Court of Appeal that the discretionary minimum sentences for certain serious crimes, including murder, limits, but has not eliminated, the Court's discretion in imposing sentence.[152] Sentencing courts must consider the applicable minimum

142 See also the discussion under 'Sentencing framework'.
143 The report on mortality and causes of death in South Africa, released by Statistics South Africa in February 2017, also notes the high levels of violence and deaths attributed to accidents. See Statistical Release P0309.3 (28 February 2017) <www.statssa.gov.za> accessed 5 April 2018.
144 South African Police Service Annual Crime Report to the Minister of Police (31 August 2016) <www.saps.gov.za/services/c_thumbnail.php?id=282> accessed 5 April 2018, 11.
145 Ibid. 18.
146 Crime Stats South Africa < www.crimestatssa.com/national.php> accessed 5 April 2018.
147 National Prosecuting Authority, 'Annual Report 2016/2017' <www.npa.gov.za/sites/default/files/annual-reports/NDPP-Annual%20Report-2016-17.pdf> accessed 5 April 2018.
148 Department of Correctional Services Annual Report 2015–16 <www.dcs.gov.za/Publications/Annual%20Reports/DCS%20Annual%20Report%202015-16.pdf> accessed 5 April 2018
149 *S v Makwanyane* (n 11).
150 Criminal Law Amendment Act 105 of 1997.
151 Criminal Law (Sentencing) Amendment Act 38 of 2007.
152 *S v Malgas* [2001] (1) SACR 469 (SCA).

sentence and can deviate from the prescribed minimum sentence if the Court is satisfied that there are 'substantial and compelling circumstances'[153] justifying a lesser sentence.[154]

The discretionary minimum sentence regime does not apply to persons who were under the age of 18 years at the time of the commission of the crime.[155] Although South African criminal law does not distinguish between different 'categories' of murder, the discretionary minimum sentence regime does provide for differentiation for purposes of sentencing. Life imprisonment is prescribed for the following categories:

- Murder, when (a) it was planned or premeditated; (b) the victim was (i) a law enforcement officer performing his or her functions as such, whether on duty or not; or (ii) a person who has given or was likely to give material evidence with reference to any of the serious offences referred to in Schedule 1 to the CPA 1977, at criminal proceedings in any court.
- Life imprisonment is prescribed in cases where the death of the victim was caused by the accused in committing or attempting to commit one of the following offences:
    - Rape or compelled rape
    - Robbery with aggravating circumstances
- Life imprisonment is also applicable to murder cases where the offence was committed by a person, group of persons or syndicate acting in the execution or furtherance of a common purpose or conspiracy.
- Two further categories of murder for purposes of discretionary minimum sentence of life imprisonment were added, namely where the victim was killed in order to unlawfully remove any body part of the victim, or as a result of such unlawful removal of a body part of the victim; and, where the death of the victim resulted from, or is directly related to, any offence contemplated in the relevant provisions of the Witchcraft Suppression Act 3 of 1957.

'Premeditated' and 'planned' murders for purposes of the above described sentencing regime are not defined by statute. In *S v PM*[156] the Court noted that 'premeditated' and 'planned' are two different concepts:

> "Premeditated" refers to something done deliberately after rationally considering the timing or method of so doing, calculated to increase the likelihood of success, or to evade detection or apprehension. On the other hand, "planned" refers to a scheme, design or method of acting, doing, proceeding or making, which is developed in advance as a process, calculated to optimally achieve a goal. Such process has general features which include:
>
> (1) The identification of the goal to be achieved;
> (2) the allocation of time to be spent;
> (3) the establishment of relationships necessary to execute;
> (4) the formulation of strategies to achieve the goal;

153 'Substantial and compelling circumstances' means 'truly convincing reasons'. 'There must not be marginal differences in personal circumstances or degrees of involvement.' See *S v Mahlangu* [2012] (2) SACR 373 (GSJ) [377g-h].
154 *S v Mcoseli* [2012] (2) SACR 82 (ECG).
155 Judicial Matters Amendment Act 42 of 2014, s. 26.
156 2014 (2) SACR 481 (GP).

(5) arrangement or creation of the means or resources required to achieve the goal; and
(6) directing, implementing and monitoring the process.[157]

Sentencing for murder in circumstances other than those already referred to (planned, premeditated and other aggravated forms of murder), is governed by a different discretionary sentencing regime. The following regime applies:[158]

- A first offender: imprisonment for a period not less than 15 years;
- A second offender: imprisonment for a period not less than 20 years; and
- A third or subsequent offender: imprisonment for a period of not less than 25 years.

In cases of culpable homicide sentencing courts enjoy the traditional unfettered discretion to impose punishment (including imprisonment). A sentence which is deemed just and appropriate according to the general principles of sentencing as developed by the courts, will be imposed in each case.[159]

157 Ibid. [36].
158 Criminal Law Amendment Act 105 of 1997, s.51(2).
159 For more detail, see E. Du Toit *et al.*, *Commentary on the Criminal Procedure Act* (Juta 2017) 28–18T - 28–20E.

12 United States of America

Vera Bergelson[1]

Overview and historical development of homicide offences and offence structure

Historical development of homicide offences

The law of homicide in the United States is codified in 52 criminal codes – the federal criminal code and the codes of each of the 50 states and the District of Columbia. It is, thus, difficult to state 'the' American rule on any particular issue. However, there are numerous similarities and trends that stem from the common history, influences and developments.[2]

The American homicide law has inherited the English common law distinctions between murder, manslaughter and non-culpable – justifiable or excusable – homicide. The principal function of these distinctions was to differentiate criminal from noncriminal homicides, and criminal homicides that, in the absence of royal clemency, were capital from those that were not. The American law sought to go further in (1) narrowing the category of capital homicides and (2) prescribing and varying the penalties for non-capital ones.[3]

The most significant departure from the common law classifications was the division of murder into degrees, a change initiated by the Pennsylvania legislation of 1794. The new statute provided that

> all murder, which shall be perpetrated by means of poison, or by lying in wait, or by any other kind of wilful, deliberate or premeditated killing, or which shall be committed in the perpetration, or attempt to perpetrate any arson, rape, robbery or burglary shall be deemed murder in the first degree; and all other kinds of murder shall be deemed murder in the second degree.[4]

The purpose of this reform was to limit the death penalty, which was then mandatory on conviction of any common law murder, to particularly heinous homicides. Many states

1 Professor of Law, Robert E. Knowlton Scholar, Rutgers School of Law. I am grateful to my research assistants Christa McLeod and Chris Byrnes for their excellent research and help in preparing this chapter for publication.

2 P.H. Robinson and M.D. Dubber, 'An Introduction to the Model Penal Code' (12 May 1999) <www.legis.iowa.gov/docs/publications/IH/6753.pdf> accessed 12 February 2018.

3 H.L. Wechsler and J. Michael, 'A Rationale of the Law of Homicide' (1937) 37 Columbia Law Review 701.

4 American Law Institute, *The Model Penal Code and Commentaries* (1980 American Law Institute) [MPC] s 210, cmt 2, 16.

followed the Pennsylvania practice until at one time the vast majority of American jurisdictions differentiated degrees of murder and the term 'first-degree murder' passed into common parlance.[5] In later decades, some states also divided other forms of homicide (primarily manslaughter) into degrees.[6]

Another dramatic reform of American homicide laws was brought about by the Model Penal Code. Promulgated in 1962, the MPC prompted a wave of state penal code reforms in the 1960s and 1970s. In the area of homicide, those reforms were needed, in part, to deal systemically with a wide range of distinct and largely unrelated offences. Consider one example: prior to the reform, New York had distinct statutes for

> homicides resulting from duels outside the state, negligent use of machinery, leaving mischievous animalsat large, overloading passenger vessels, bursting of steamboat vessels, bursting of steam boilers, acts of physicians while intoxicated, making or keeping explosives contrary to law, and criminal negligence while operating a motor vehicle.[7]

The MPC, as well as the jurisdictions that followed its lead, replaced numerous homicide statutes with a single tripartite offence of criminal homicide: 'A person is guilty of criminal homicide if he purposely, knowingly, recklessly or negligently causes the death of another human being'.[8] That offence can be murder, manslaughter or negligent homicide depending on the perpetrator's mental state. The MPC does not divide those offences into degrees.

Intentional homicide

In accordance with the common law tradition, American criminal codes divide intentional homicide into murder and manslaughter. Historically, American courts viewed murder as the unlawful killing of another human being with 'malice aforethought' and manslaughter as intentional killing 'without malice aforethought'.

In the jurisdictions that divided murder into degrees, premeditated and deliberate homicide was first degree murder; other homicide 'which would have been murder at common law' was second degree murder.[9]

With time, the 'deliberation premeditation' formula has developed into a term of art to the exclusion of 'the two elements which the words normally signify: a determination to kill reached (1) calmly and (2) some appreciable time prior to the homicide'.[10] As a result, the meaning of 'deliberation-premeditation' became increasingly unclear. The lack of clarity was one reason for the MPC to reject the 'deliberation-premeditation' formula. Another reason was the doubt that premeditation and deliberation identify the murders deserving the greatest punishment. That doubt is reflected in the MPC Commentaries:

> Prior reflection may reveal the uncertainties of a tortured conscience rather than exceptional depravity. The very fact of a long internal struggle may be evidence that the homicidal impulse was deeply aberrational and far more the product of extraordinary circumstances than a true reflection of the actor's normal character … It also seems

5 Ibid.
6 Ibid. 46–7.
7 Ibid. 6.
8 MPC s 210.1(1).
9 Wechsler and Michael (n 3) 705.
10 Ibid. 707.

> clear, moreover, that some purely impulsive murders will present no extenuating circumstance. The suddenness of the killing may simply reveal callousness so complete and depravity so extreme that no hesitation is required.[11]

More than half of U.S. jurisdictions, however, still retain the criteria of premeditation or deliberation or both to identify the most severe instances of homicide.[12]

Traditionally, intentional homicide was considered to be without malice, and hence manslaughter (or voluntary manslaughter) rather than murder, if it was committed 'in the heat of passion upon adequate provocation'.[13] By the time of the MPC reform, virtually every American state recognised the crime of manslaughter. However, most states lacked an explicit definition of the crime and determined its meaning by reference to the common law. Under the common law, murder could be reduced to manslaughter when provocation was such as likely to deprive a reasonable man of self-control. To be such, the provocation had to fall into one of the specifically delineated categories. A Commentary to the MPC gives details:

> First and foremost, physical attack might constitute provocation, though not every technical battery could suffice … Mutual combat became another established category of provocation. Less clearly, a threat of physical attack might constitute provocation, at least in extreme cases. Unlawful arrest would sometimes suffice, and the law frequently recognized witnessing adultery as provocation for intentional homicide of either the unfaithful spouse or the paramour. Certain other acts – chiefly violent or sexual assault on a close relative – might also constitute adequate provocation.[14]

The MPC rejected the common law categories and provided an alternative theory of provocation based on the 'influence of extreme mental or emotional disturbance for which there is reasonable explanation or excuse'.[15] Today, roughly 20 states follow some version of the MPC definition.[16]

Reckless homicide

Just like intentional homicide, reckless killing could constitute murder or manslaughter depending on the presence or lack of malice aforethought. Such malice was implied when the killing resulted from an intentional act which 'was deliberately performed by a person who kn[ew] that his conduct endanger[ed] the life of another and who act[ed] with conscious disregard for life.'.[17] To define malice, courts often used colourful formulas like 'the dictate of a wicked, depraved and malignant heart' or 'an abandoned and malignant heart'.[18]

11 MPC (n 4) s 210.6, cmt 4(b), 127–28.
12 K.K. Ferzan, 'Plotting Premeditation's Demise' (2012) 75(2) Law & Contemporary Problems 83, 84 (identifying 29 states, in addition to the District of Columbia and the federal government, which currently use criterion of premeditation or deliberation).
13 MPC (n 4) s 210.3, cmt 1, 44.
14 Ibid., cmt 5(a), 57–8
15 Ibid., s 210.3.1(b).
16 C. Forell, 'Homicide and the Unreasonable Man' (2004) 72 George Washington Law Review 597, 603 (usually, limited to the 'extreme emotional disturbance').
17 *People v Dellinger*, 783 P.2d 200, 201 [Cal. 1989].
18 S.H. Kadish, S.J. Schulhofer and R.E. Barkow, *Criminal Law and its Processes: Cases and Materials* (10th edn, 2016 Wolters Kluwer) 511.

Classic examples of such an abandoned and malignant heart included: playing the game of Russian roulette; throwing a heavy object down upon a busy street; shooting into an occupied building; and beating a person so severely that the person is unintentionally killed.[19]

In the absence of malice, unintentional killing constituted manslaughter (or involuntary manslaughter) if the perpetrator acted with the subjective awareness of substantial unjustifiable risk to human life. Today, many states use the MPC terms to draw similar lines: ordinary recklessness supports conviction of manslaughter only; murder conviction requires a finding of recklessness 'under circumstances manifesting extreme indifference to the value of human life'.[20]

Negligent homicide

Traditionally, homicide that resulted from an act that was unduly dangerous to life or limb or from an act that was otherwise unlawful was labelled as manslaughter (or involuntary manslaughter). Involuntary manslaughter did not explicitly distinguish between recklessness and negligence. Inadvertence as to risk sufficed for conviction of manslaughter but the degree of negligence had to be great.[21]

Prior to the MPC, American penal codes did not define negligent homicide. Most of them punished manslaughter without specifying the required culpability. Some defined involuntary manslaughter as homicide 'in the commission in an unlawful manner, or without due caution and circumspection, of a lawful act which might produce death'. Still others punished 'culpable' or 'criminal' negligence without explaining the meanings of those terms.[22]

The MPC distinguished between reckless and negligent homicide by underscoring that the reckless actor must consciously disregard a substantial and unjustifiable homicidal risk created by his conduct, whereas the negligent actor needs only to disregard a risk of which he 'should be aware'. Conviction of negligent homicide requires the judgment that the actor's failure to perceive the risk involves a 'gross deviation from the standard of care that a reasonable person would observe in the actor's situation'.[23]

Felony-murder

> The classic formulation of the felony-murder doctrine declares that one is guilty of murder if a death results from conduct during the commission or attempted commission of any felony.[24]

It has been believed that the harsh felony-murder rule, which essentially made the defendant strictly liable for any death caused by him during the commission or attempted commission of any offence, came to the United States from the common law.[25] An important recent study, however, challenges this account and insists that there was no common law felony-murder rule in England at the time of the American Revolution.[26] Professor Guyora Binder argues that the 'first felony murder rules were enacted not in medieval England, but in

19 Ibid.
20 MPC s 210.2.
21 Ibid., cmt 1, 81.
22 Ibid. 82.
23 Ibid. 81.
24 Ibid.
25 W.R. LaFave, *Criminal Law* (3rd edn, 2000 West Group) 671.
26 G. Binder, 'The Origins of American Felony Murder Rules' (2004) 57 Stanford Law Review 59, 63.

nineteenth-century America. They were developed not by common law adjudication but by means of legislation and statutory construction'.[27]

The MPC drafters were highly critical of the rule, stating:

> [U]nder the Model Code, as at common law, murder occurs if a person kills purposely, knowingly, or with extreme recklessness. Lesser culpability yields lesser liability, and a person who inadvertently kills another under circumstances not amounting to negligence is guilty of no crime at all. The felony-murder rule contradicts this scheme. It bases conviction of murder not on any proven culpability with respect to homicide but on liability for another crime.[28]

Having pointed out that the felony-murder rule has either been unknown in other countries or had long fallen into disfavour, the MPC drafters conceded that, in the United States, the attack on the rule had not proven so successful.[29]

The MPC did not completely eliminate the felony-murder rule but offered a compromise: one's participation in a dangerous felony (robbery, rape or deviate sexual intercourse by force or threat of force, arson, burglary, kidnapping or felonious escape) creates a rebuttable presumption of recklessness with extreme indifference to the value of human life which can support a murder conviction.[30] Beyond the operation of this presumption, the MPC position is that the felony-murder rule should be abandoned as an independent basis for establishing the criminality of homicide.[31] That position has not been influential in the post-MPC statutory reforms. The felony-murder rule today 'still thrives',[32] at least in a limited form, in the absolute majority of American states.[33]

Just as a felony resulting in death can provide a basis for a murder conviction without the proof of malice, in many states a misdemeanour resulting in death can provide a basis for an involuntary manslaughter conviction without the proof of recklessness or negligence. Under the misdemeanour-manslaughter rule, also known as the unlawful-act doctrine, if a defendant, after driving through a red light, has killed a pedestrian, the prosecution needs only to show that the defendant's unlawful act caused the death; no proof of criminal *mens rea* is necessary.[34] The unlawful-act doctrine is rejected by the MPC and the majority of the states; it is still followed in about one-quarter of U.S. jurisdictions.[35]

General elements

Beginning of life

Up until recently, the majority of American states followed the common law 'born-alive' rule to mark the beginning of human life.[36] To determine whether the infant was ever

27 Ibid. 64.
28 MPC (n 3) s 210.2, cmt 6, 36.
29 *ibid* 40.
30 MPC s 210.2(1)(b).
31 MPC (n 4) s 210.2, cmt 6, 30.
32 *State v Maldonado*, 645 A.2d 1165, 1171 (N.J. 1994).
33 J. Dressler, *Understanding Criminal Law* (6th edn, 2012 LexisNexis) 510–11.
34 Kadish *et al.* (n 18) 527; *State v. Hupf*, 101 A.2d 355 (1953).
35 W.R. LaFave, *Substantive Criminal Law* (2nd edn, 2003 West Publishing Company) s 15.5.
36 *Keeler v Superior Court*, 2 Cal.3d 619, 627 (1970) ('As early as 1797 it was held that proof the child was born alive is necessary to support an indictment for murder.').

'alive', courts considered various factors – whether the child was 'wholly born', possessed 'independent circulation';[37] could breathe, etc.[38] Yet, regardless of the specific factor required to prove live birth, unless it was present, there was no 'human being' for the purposes of criminal law.[39] The MPC held the same view.[40]

As late as 1970, the born-alive rule dominated American statutes and court decisions. That year, the California Supreme Court, in the oft-cited decision *Keeler v Superior Court*, [41] held that the defendant who beat and kicked his estranged pregnant wife with the purpose of killing the foetus was not guilty of homicide of the baby later delivered stillborn, its head fractured. As a result of that decision, a number of states, including California, amended their homicide statutes to include some form of criminal liability for killing a foetus.[42]

Today, some states retain the born-alive rule but it has largely lost its significance.[43] At least 38 states have foetal homicide laws.[44] The vast majority have adopted them by statute,[45] while a few have done so judicially.[46] The standards as to when the criminal liability attaches vary widely, ranging from conception to quickening to viability.[47]

End of life

The end of life has received far less legislative and judicial attention than the beginning of life. Determining the exact moment of death has only become a pressing legal issue in the last few decades, mainly in connection with the medical advances in organ transplantation.[48] Until then, death has been conceptualised by the law as, simply, the absence of life: 'Death is the opposite of life; it is the termination of life'.[49] The MPC homicide article has no definition of death.

Courts have held death to occur, for purposes of homicide prosecutions, where, due to the defendant's criminal act, the victim has suffered irretrievable brain damage,[50] brain death[51] or irreversible cessation of circulatory and respiratory functions.[52]

37 *Rex v Crutchley* [1837] 173 ER 355, 356; *Rex v Brain*, [1834] 172 ER 1272, 1272.
38 *Regina v Reeves* [1839] 173 ER 724, 725; *Rex v Poulton* [1832] 172 ER 997, 997.
39 *Keeler* (n 36) 627.
40 MPC s 210.1 (defining human being as 'a person who has been born and is alive').
41 *Keeler* (n 36) 624.
42 Cal. Penal Code § 187(a) (Deering 2008); Ind. Code § 35–42–1-1(4), 157 (supp, 2004).
43 A.S. Murphy, 'A Survey of State Fetal Homicide Laws and Their Potential Applicability to Pregnant Women Who Harm Their Own Fetuses' (2014) 89(2) Indiana Law Journal 847, 864.
44 NCSL, 'Fetal Homicide State Laws' (*National Conference of State Legislatures*, 16 November 2017) <www.ncsl.org/research/health/fetal-homicide-state-laws.aspx> accessed 30 May 2018.
45 Ala. Code § 13A-6–1 (supp 2008); Mich. Comp. Laws Ann. § 750.322 (West 2004); Wis. Stat. § 940.01(1)(b) (2008).
46 *Com. v Cass*, 467 N.E.2d 1324, 1325 (Mass. 1984).
47 LaFave (n 35) s 14.1(c), 422–23. At least 23 states have fetal homicide laws that apply to the earliest stages of pregnancy ('any state of gestation,' 'conception,' 'fertilization' or 'post-fertilization'). 'Fetal Homicide State Laws' (n 44).
48 S.K. Shah and F.G. Miller, 'Can We Handle the Truth? Legal Fictions in the Determination of Death' (2010) 36(4) American Journal of Law and Medicine 540, 543.
49 *People v Eulo*, 63 N.Y.2d 341 (1984) (quoting *Evans v People*, 49 N.Y. 86, 90) (1872)).
50 *Com. v Golston*, 366 N.E.2d 744 (Mass. 1977).
51 *State v Meints*, 322 N.W.2d 809 (Neb. 1982).
52 *People v Lara*, 289 Ill. App. 3d 675, 681 (1st Cir. 1997) (When circulatory and respiratory functions are mechanically maintained, the irreversible cessation of brain functions or brain death standard may be used to determine death.)

Under the Uniform Determination of Death Act adopted in 39 U.S. jurisdictions,[53] an individual who has sustained either (1) irreversible cessation of circulatory and respiratory functions, or (2) irreversible cessation of all functions of the entire brain, including the brain stem, is dead.[54] This definition has been approved by the American Medical Association and the American Bar Association.[55]

Pre-birth causes with post-birth effect

Under the traditional rule as it survives today, 'If the child is born alive, despite an attack upon it and an injury to the mother while it was in the mother's womb, and the child thereafter dies as a result of the prenatal injury, a homicide has been committed'.[56] Accordingly, a baby who was born alive through caesarean birth but died from injuries inflicted in utero when the pregnant mother was stabbed has been held to be a 'person' under a murder statute, and thus the defendant could be charged with murder for the death of the baby.[57]

In 2002, Congress enacted the Born-Alive Infants Protection Act which extends legal protection to an infant born alive after a failed attempt at induced abortion.[58] In addition, in 2004, Congress enacted the Unborn Victims of Violence Act (UVVA) which is directed at 'protect[ing] unborn children from assault and murder'.[59] Under the UVVA, a person is guilty if he 'engages in conduct that violates [certain federal statutes] and thereby causes the death of, or bodily injury ... to, a child, who is in utero at the time the conduct takes place'.[60] Importantly, the UVVA has excluded from prosecution the mothers of the unborn children,[61] thus making it clear that the legislative purpose is protecting foetuses from crimes of violence against pregnant women, not protecting foetuses against those who carry them.[62]

The majority of the states that have passed statutes recognising embryos and foetuses as potential victims of violent crimes also exempt pregnant women from prosecution for the harm done to their unborn children. Some statutes, however, provide only limited protection to pregnant women. For example, Arkansas exempts pregnant women from prosecution for the homicide, but not the battery, of their foetuses.[63] A number of states are silent on the issue of whether pregnant women may be prosecuted for crimes of violence against their foetuses and a few states expressly authorise such prosecutions.[64]

53 'Legislative Fact Sheet – Determination of Death Act' (*Uniform Law Commission*, 2017) <www.uniformlaws.org/LegislativeFactSheet.aspx?title=Determination%20of%20Death%20Act> accessed 30 May 2018.
54 Uniform Determination of Death Act s 1.
55 President's Commission for the Study of Ethical Problems in Medicine and Biomedical and Behavioral Research, *Defining Death: A Report on the Medical, Legal and Ethical Issues in the Determination of Death* (1981 Government Printing Office) 73.
56 C.E. Torcia, *Wharton's Criminal Law* (15th edn, 1994 Clark Boardman Callaghan) s 116, 140.
57 *State v Courchesne*, 757 A.2d 699 (Conn. Super. Ct. 1999).
58 Pub. L. 107–207, 116 Stat. 926, enacted August 5, 2002, 1 U.S.C. § 8.
59 Unborn Victims of Violence Act of 2004; 18 U.S.C. § 1841, 10 U.S.C. § 919a (2012).
60 18 U.S.C. § 1841(a)(1) (defining 'child in utero' as 'a member of the species *Homo sapiens*, at any stage of development, who is carried in the womb').
61 *ibid* § 1841(c)(3) ('Nothing in [the Act] shall be construed to permit the prosecution ... of any woman with respect to her unborn child').
62 Murphy (n 43) 853.
63 Ark. Code Ann. §§ 5-1-102(13) and 5–13–201.
64 Murphy (n 43) 865.

In addition, a number of states authorise prosecution for child abuse, child endangerment and other crimes of women who use illegal drugs during pregnancy.[65] In 2014, Tennessee became the first state to permit criminal prosecution for assault of a woman who used illegal drugs during pregnancy 'if her child is born addicted to or harmed' by the drug.[66] In response to widespread concerns about the impact of the law on maternal, foetal and child health, the legislature included a two years' sunset provision. After studies indicated such negative impact, Tennessee General Assembly voted not to extend the law. The law is no longer in effect.[67]

Medical treatment scenarios

Medical decisions often involve difficult choices. Sometimes, it is impossible to do good to a patient without also causing him harm due to the inevitable *side effects*. [68] Other times, harm is the direct *means* of achieving a benevolent outcome. It is generally morally and legally acceptable to cause harmful side effects in the course of achieving a benevolent goal; it is less acceptable to use harmful means. The most dramatic circumstances when harmful means may be involved include the end-of-life and the termination of a viable pregnancy decisions. The law approaches these decisions cautiously, usually aiming to balance the harms and benefits to the affected individuals and public at large.

Physician-assisted suicide

No state authorises a physician to purposefully cause a patient's death. However, terminating a patient's life support is permissible despite the resulting death.[69] It is also permissible to prescribe a terminally-ill patient an aggressive palliative medication with the intent of alleviating pain even though the painkiller may hasten the patient's death.[70]

There is no constitutionally protected right to assisted suicide and states may ban physician-assisted suicide if they can show legitimate reasons for doing so.[71] Seven states – six by

65 L. Miranda, V. Dixon and C. Reyes, 'How States Handle Drug Use During Pregnancy' (Pro Publica 2015) <https://projects.propublica.org/graphics/maternity-drug-policies-by-state> accessed 30 May 2018; V. Reid Soderberg, 'RECENT DEVELOPMENT. More Than Receptacles: An International Human Rights Analysis of Criminalizing Pregnancy in the United States' (2016) 31 Berkeley Journal of Gender, Law & Justice 299.

66 'Tennessee's Fetal Assault Law Sunsets July 1, 2016' (*ACLU*) <www.aclu-tn.org/wp-content/uploads/2016/09/Fetal-Assault-Legal.pdf> accessed 30 May 2018.

67 Ibid.

68 A.B. Shaw, 'Two Challenges to the Double Effect Doctrine: Euthanasia and Abortion' (2002) 28 (2) Journal of Medicine and Ethics 102.

69 *Barber v Superior Court*, 147 Cal.App.3d 1006 (1983).

70 *Vacco v Quill*, 521 U.S. 793, 802, n.11 (1997) (citing a New York Task Force report that the medical community has widely recognised this practice as ethical and professionally acceptable).

71 *Washington v Glucksberg*, 521 U. S. 702, 728–35 (1997) (among such reasons are: prohibiting intentional killing and preserving human life; preventing the serious public-health problem of suicide, especially among the young, the elderly and those suffering from untreated pain or from depression or other mental disorders; protecting the medical profession's integrity and ethics and maintaining physicians' role as their patients' healers; protecting the poor, the elderly, disabled persons, the terminally ill and persons in other vulnerable groups from indifference, prejudice and psychological and financial pressure to end their lives; and avoiding a possible slide toward voluntary and perhaps even involuntary euthanasia).

legislation[72] and one by judicial ruling[73] – have legalised a limited form of physician-assisted death. Under the laws of those states, physicians may prescribe an 'aid-in-dying drug' to qualifying patients.[74] To qualify, the patient must satisfy the strict requirements of the law. For example, under the Oregon Death With Dignity Act, the patient who seeks such a prescription must: (1) be terminally ill and have six months or less to live; (2) make two oral and one written requests for assistance in dying; (3) convince two physicians that he is sincere and not acting on a whim, under depression, and that the decision is voluntary; (4) be informed of 'the feasible alternatives', including, but not limited to, comfort care, hospice care and pain control; and (5) wait for 15 days.[75]

Abortion[76]

The U.S. Supreme Court has held that a woman's right to an abortion is not absolute and states may restrict or ban abortions after the foetal viability, provided that:

- states may not prohibit abortions 'necessary to preserve the life or health' of the woman;[77]
- 'health' in this context includes physical and mental health;[78]
- only the physician, in the course of evaluating the specific circumstances of an individual case, can define what constitutes 'health' and when a foetus is viable; and
- states may not require additional physicians to confirm the attending physician's judgment that the woman's life or health is at risk in cases of medical emergency.[79]

Homicide by omission

The omission of a duty of care owed by one individual to another, where such omission results in the death of the one to whom the duty is owed, may constitute culpable homicide.[80] As summarised by a court, the duty of care may come from different sources:

> One can be held criminally liable: first, where a statute imposes a duty to care for another; second, where one stands in a certain status relationship to another;[81] third,

72 California, Colorado, Hawaii, Oregon, Vermont and Washington, 'State-by-State Guide to Physician-Assisted Suicide' (*ProCon.org*, 21 December 2017) <http://euthanasia.procon.org/view.resource.php?resourceID=000132> accessed 30 May 2018.
73 *Baxter v Montana*, 224 P.3d 1211 (Mt. 2009).
74 End of Life Option Act (defining aid-in-dying drug as 'a drug determined and prescribed by a physician for a qualified individual, which the qualified individual may choose to self-administer to bring about his or her death due to a terminal disease').
75 The Oregon Death with Dignity Act, Or. Rev. Stat. § 127.800 et seq (1994).
76 For more detailed discussion of abortion, see section 'Abortion and homicide' below.
77 *Roe v Wade*, 410 U.S. 113 (1973); *Planned Parenthood v Casey*, 505 U.S. 833 (1992).
78 *Doe v Bolton*, 410 U.S. 179 (1973).
79 'State Policies on Later Abortions' (*Guttmacher Institute*, 20 March 2018) <www.guttmacher.org/state-policy/explore/state-policies-later-abortions> accessed 30 May 2018.
80 *United States v Hatatley*, 130 F.3d 1399 [10th Cir. 1997]; *State v Batson*, 831 P.2d 924 [Haw. 1992]; *People v. Banks*, 641 N.E.2d 331 (Ill. 1994); *Com. v Pestinikas*, 617 A.2d 1339 (Pa. 1992).
81 For example, parents to minor children; spouses to each other; ship crew to passengers; and employer to employees. W.R. LaFave and A.W. Scott, Jr., *Criminal Law* (2nd edn, West Publishing Co 1986) s 6.2.

> where one has assumed a contractual duty to care for another; and fourth, where one has voluntarily assumed the care of another and so secluded the helpless person as to prevent others from rendering aid.[82]

In addition, one may acquire a duty of care by virtue of creating the peril.[83] Many American courts hold that this duty arises even when the peril has been created non-culpably, as long as the perpetrator is aware of the peril. In *Commonwealth v Levesque*, the defendants accidentally started a fire and then, despite their awareness of the danger, failed to report it. The blaze went out of control and six firefighters died attempting to put it out. The court upheld the defendants' conviction of involuntary manslaughter.[84]

Most cases of homicide premised on the defendant's failure to act are cases of involuntary manslaughter. However, such cases may constitute murder too – if the defendant refused to provide care with the intention of causing death or with the awareness of a significant risk that the victim would die. For example, in *Commonwealth v Pestinikas*, the defendant allowed a 92-year-old man to die of starvation after agreeing to feed him, knowing that the old man had no one else to provide him with food. The defendant was convicted of a third degree murder.[85]

Omitting to effect an easy rescue

There is no general legal duty to aid a person in peril, even when that aid can be rendered without danger or inconvenience to the rescuer. For example, in *State v Ulvinen*, the court held that the defendant was not criminally liable for the death of her daughter-in-law whom she had failed to warn that the defendant's son was planning to kill her.[86] The court observed: 'However morally reprehensible it may be to fail to warn someone of their impending death, our statutes do not make such an omission a criminal offense'.[87]

Only a handful of states impose on individuals some, usually quite limited, criminally enforceable duty to rescue. For example, Vermont statute provides:

> A person who knows that another is exposed to grave physical harm shall, to the extent that the same can be rendered without danger or peril to himself or without interference with important duties owed to others, give reasonable assistance to the exposed person unless that assistance or care is being provided by others.[88]

In all those states, violation of that duty is merely a misdemeanour or petty misdemeanour and prosecutions are extremely rare.[89]

82 *Jones v United States*, 308 F.2d 307, 310 (C.A.D.C. 1962).
83 *Jones v State*, 43 N.E.2d 1017, 1018 (Ind. 1942) ('one who by his overpowering criminal act has put another in danger of drowning has a duty to preserve her life').
84 766 N.E.2d 50 (Mass. 2007).
85 617 A.2d 1339 (Pa. Super. Ct. 1992).
86 313 N.W.2d 425 (Minn. 1981).
87 Ibid. 428.
88 Vt. Stat. Ann. 2016, tit. 12, § 519.
89 D.A. Hyman, 'Rescue Without Law: An Empirical Perspective on the Duty to Rescue' (2006) 84 (3) Texas Law Review 653, 685.

Intentional homicide offences

Actus reus

Intentional homicide includes murder and voluntary manslaughter. The *actus reus* of both offences is the same – the *act* of killing or injuring (if the injury results in death) or the *omission* (provided there is a duty to act) resulting in the death of the victim. As 'result' crimes, homicide offences are usually defined without reference to the specific conduct. Instead, a typical definition of criminal homicide is phrased in terms of causation.[90] For example, under the MPC, a person is guilty of criminal homicide if he culpably 'causes the death of another human being'.[91]

Some jurisdictions, however, consider the manner in which homicide has been committed for distinguishing between the degrees of murder. For example, the crime is ordinarily first degree murder where the death is brought about by lying in wait, torture or poisoning.[92]

Mens rea

Murder

Under the MPC and the laws of the jurisdictions that follow it, in the absence of mitigation, criminal homicide committed purposely or knowingly is murder.[93] The MPC rejects the 'presumption' favoured by some courts that a person intends the natural and probable consequences of his acts. Liability for murder may not rest merely on a finding that the defendant purposely or knowingly did something that had the death of another as its natural and probable consequence:[94]

> Rather, the prosecution must establish that the defendant engaged in conduct with the conscious objective of causing death of another or at least with awareness that death of another was practically certain to result from his act.[95]

Jurisdictions that divide murder into degrees often use the criterion of 'premeditation and/or deliberation' to identify first degree murders.[96] The majority of those jurisdictions hold that premeditation and deliberation do not require any additional time and 'may be formed while the killer is 'pressing the trigger that fired the fatal shot'.[97] A significant minority of jurisdictions, however, require more meaningful reflection, and this view is growing in

90 *Auman v People*, 109 P.3d 647 (Colo. 2005) (opining that, for a defendant to be held liable for a homicide offense, the death must be a natural and probable consequence of the defendant's unlawful act).
91 MPC s 210(1).
92 40 Am Jur 2d Homicide § 40. Other circumstances that may qualify homicide for first degree murder include: the status of the victim (e.g., police officer) or the fact that the murder was committed for pay, involved the killing of more than one person, or was committed by a person with a prior murder conviction or a person in prison. LaFave (n 35) s 14.7.
93 MPC s 210.2(1)(a).
94 MPC (n 4) s 210.2, cmt 3, 21.
95 Ibid.
96 See section 'Intentional homicide' above; K.K. Ferzan, 'Plotting Premeditation's Demise' (2012) 75 Law and Contemporary Problems 83, 84.
97 *Young v State*, 428 So. 2d 155, 158 [Ala. Crim. App. 1982]; Ferzan (n 96) 88.

popularity.[98] Pursuant to it, 'deliberation' requires a cool mind that is capable of reflection, and 'premeditation' requires that the one with the cool mind did in fact reflect, at least for a short period of time, before killing.[99]

Second degree murder is usually defined as intentional killing without the added ingredients of premeditation and deliberation. In addition, intent-to-do-serious-bodily-injury murder (whether this intent is premeditated and deliberated or not) is often conceptualised as second degree murder.

Manslaughter

Homicide that otherwise would be murder may be reduced to manslaughter if committed in the heat of passion upon adequate provocation (the majority view) or under extreme mental or emotional distress (the MPC view).[100]

Reckless homicide offences

Actus reus

Reckless homicide may be murder or manslaughter. For both crimes, *actus reus* involves creation of a high degree of risk of death or serious bodily injury of another. For murder, the degree of risk must be higher – there has to be a probability, rather than a mere possibility that death will result.[101] A reckless omission satisfies the *actus reus* requirement where there is a duty to act.[102]

Mens rea

Murder

Some penal codes use the old 'abandoned and malignant heart'[103] language or refer more generally to the conduct evincing either a 'depraved mind'[104] or 'depraved heart,'[105] while other penal codes offer no definition at all.[106]

The depraved mind murder is usually classified as the second degree murder. In a very small group of states, it can also be first degree murder.[107] First degree depraved mind murder may be imposed where the defendant acts with conscious disregard for the welfare of others by engaging in mortal danger. In *State v Dowling*, the defendant

98 LaFave (n 35) s 14.7.
99 *State v Bowser*, 199 S.E. 31 (N.C. 1938); *Byford v. State*, 994 P.2d 700 (Nev. 2000).
100 For detailed discussion, see Section 'Intentional homicide' above.
101 *State v Radziwil*, 563 A.2d 856 (N.J. App. 1989), aff'd. 582 A.2d 1003 (N.J. 1990).
102 LaFave (n 35) s 14.4.
103 Ga. Code Ann. § 16–5-1.
104 Fla. Stat. Ann. § 782.04; Minn. Stat. Ann. § 609.195; Okla. Stat. Ann. Tit. 21, § 22–16–7; S.D. Cod. Laws § 22–16–4
105 Miss. Code Ann. § 97-3-19.
106 Cal. Penal Code § 189; Idaho Code § 18–4001; Iowa Code Ann. § 707.3. A significant minority of American jurisdictions do not recognise this type of murder at all. See Neb. Rev. Stat. § 28–304; N.J. Stat. Ann. § 2C:11–3; Ohio Rev. Code Ann. § 2903.02; Or. Rev. Stat. § 163.115.
107 New Mexico, Washington, and Colorado, *State v Dowling*, 2011-NMSC-016, 257 P.3d 930 (N. M. 2011) 934.

was driving 80 mph on a suburban street when he struck and injured a jogger and failed to brake as he attempted to flee. He then drove onto the sidewalk and killed a pedestrian. He did not stop to aid either victim. The court found this conduct indicative of recklessness characterised by a depraved mind and worthy of a first degree murder conviction.[108]

Under the MPC, reckless homicide is murder only if committed 'under circumstances manifesting extreme indifference to the value of human life'.[109] This language has been substantially followed in several states' penal codes.[110]

Manslaughter

Under the MPC and the majority of the penal codes recodified since its promulgation, homicide is manslaughter if the actor was 'reckless,' that is, if he 'consciously disregarded a substantial and unjustifiable risk that his conduct would cause the death of another'; and if the risk was

> of such a nature and degree that, considering the nature and purpose of his conduct and the circumstances known to him, its disregard involves a gross deviation from the standard of conduct that a law-abiding person would observe in the actor's situation.[111]

Negligent homicide offences

Actus reus

Homicide caused by negligence may constitute manslaughter or a lesser offence of negligent homicide. In addition, some jurisdictions have enacted more specific offences designated to address particular risks caused by negligence – vehicular homicide is a typical example.

Under the MPC, inadvertent killing committed negligently constitutes negligent homicide. Negligent homicide has the same *actus reus* as manslaughter but constitutes a crime of a lesser degree. A commentary to the MPC describes the current state of the law:

> The great majority of jurisdictions have closely followed the MPC's definition of negligence. There are, however, several different types of statutes. Most modern revisions cover negligent homicide in a separate negligent or vehicular homicide statute, though some do so with specific attention to the types of situations that are regarded as justifying penal treatment. Finally, some of the newly revised codes reach negligent homicide as a form of manslaughter. Despite this variety in statutory form, however, the general proposition that negligent homicide should be treated less severely than reckless homicide or its common-law equivalent has found widespread acceptance.[112]

108 Ibid. 932.
109 MPC s 210.2(1)(b).
110 Ariz. Rev. Stat. Ann. § 13–1104; N.H. Rev. Stat. Ann. § 630:1-b; Wash. Rev. Code. § 9A.32.050; LaFave (n 34) s 14.4.
111 MPC ss 210.3(1)(a) and 2.02(2)(c).
112 MPC (n 4) s 210.4, cmt 3, 87–8.

Degree of negligence

It has been often declared by legislatures and courts alike that criminal negligence requires higher culpability than ordinary, civil negligence sufficient for tort liability. However, it is not entirely clear what that standard means. Statutes routinely use such terms as 'gross negligence' or 'culpable negligence' or 'criminal negligence,' without further definition of these terms.[113] Courts have been striving to fill in this gap. Quoting *State v Barnett*,

> [T]he negligence of the accused must be "culpable," "gross," or "reckless," that is, the conduct of the accused must be such a departure from what would be the conduct of an ordinarily prudent or careful man under the same circumstances as to be incompatible with a proper regard for human life, or conduct amounting to an indifference to consequences.[114]

The MPC punishes negligent conduct if the actor should have been aware of a substantial and unjustifiable risk

> of such a nature and degree that the actor's failure to perceive it, considering the nature and purpose of his conduct and the circumstances known to him, involves a gross deviation from the standard of care that a reasonable person would observe in the actor's situation.[115]

An MPC commentary to the negligent homicide provision explains that the quoted definition ensures that the liability for inadvertent risk creation is limited to cases where the actor is grossly insensitive to the interests and claims of other persons in society.[116]

Result-qualified / constructive / *versari in re illicata* / felony homicide offences

Actus reus

Most penal codes provide that a death that results from the commission of or attempt to commit a specifically listed felony (such as arson, rape, robbery or burglary) constitutes first degree murder, and a death that results from the commission of an unspecified felony is second degree murder.[117] In addition, about one-half of all states provide that a death that results from the commission of a misdemeanour or other unlawful act is manslaughter.[118]

Both the felony-murder and the misdemeanour-manslaughter rules are consistently disfavoured by courts and commentators as being irrational and unduly harsh. In an attempt to limit the reach of those rules, courts have imposed significant restrictions on their application. For felony-murder, those restrictions usually are the following: (1) for the unspecified

113 LaFave (n 35) s 5.4.
114 *State v Barnett*, 63 S.E.2d 57 58–59 (S.C. 1951).
115 MPC s 2.02(2)(d).
116 MPC (n 4) s 210.4, cmt 3, 87.
117 Dressler (n 33) 511.
118 LaFave (n 35) s 15.5.

felonies, the triggering felony has to be 'inherently dangerous'; (2) the triggering felony may not be assaultive in nature; if it is, it 'merges' with the death and cannot be used for the purposes of the felony-murder rule; and (3) the killing has to be 'in furtherance of the felonious objective'.[119]

For the misdemeanour-manslaughter, many courts require that the unlawful act be: (1) the proximate cause of the resulting death;[120] (2) *malum in se*, not merely *malum prohibitum*;[121] and (3) dangerous to the point of 'evinc[ing] a marked disregard for the safety of others'.[122]

Mens rea *and negligence combinations*

Both the felony-murder and the misdemeanour-manslaughter rules apply whether the perpetrator kills the victim intentionally, recklessly, negligently or accidentally. Thus, both rules potentially authorise strict liability for a death that has resulted from the commission of an offence or unlawful act, as the case may be.[123]

The MPC rejects both rules but retains the felony-murder doctrine as a presumption of recklessness with extreme indifference to the value of human life. If unrebutted, that evidence can warrant conviction of murder.[124]

Infanticide / child destruction

There is no crime of infanticide in the United States. Killing an infant or a child is treated the same as killing any other human being.[125]

In 2009, Texas legislature considered a bill that would define infanticide as a distinct and lesser crime than homicide. Under the terms of the bill, if jurors concluded that a mother's 'judgment was impaired as a result of the effects of giving birth or the effects of lactation following the birth', they would be allowed to convict her of the crime of infanticide rather than murder.[126] The maximum penalty for infanticide would be two years in prison. The bill has not been enacted.

Abortion and homicide

Abortion

Abortion has been defined in different ways. Some courts define it as 'the expulsion of the fetus at so early a period of uterogestation that it has not acquired the power of sustaining

119 Kadish (n 18) 530–52.
120 *Commonwealth v Williams*, 1 A.2d 812 (Pa.Super. 1938) (holding that expiration of a driver's license had no causal connection to the deadly car accident resulting from the carelessness of another driver).
121 *People v Holtschlag*, 684 N.W.2d 730, 740. (Mich. 2004).
122 *State v Lingman* (1939) 91 P.2d 457 (Utah); Kadish (n 18) 526–27.
123 Dressler (n 33) 511. Some courts limit the application of misdemeanour-manslaughter rule to the misdemeanours that rise to the level of criminal negligence. *State v. Green* (2007) 647S.W.2d 736 (W. Va.) 746.
124 MPC s 210.2.
125 *People v Chavez* (1947) 77 Cal.App.2d 621, 625–26.
126 J. Farrar, 'H.B. No. 3318'. <www.legis.state.tx.us/tlodocs/81R/billtext/pdf/HB03318I.pdf#navpanes=0> accessed 30 May 2018.

an independent life'.[127] For other courts, an '"abortion" occurs at any time that a pregnancy ends without a viable baby being born'.[128]

Today, following the Supreme Court's 1973 landmark decision in *Roe v Wade* [129] and subsequent decisions, particularly *Planned Parenthood v Casey,* [130] which has affirmed but largely reconceptualised *Roe v Wade*, abortion is legal in the United States but states may regulate and restrict it to promote legitimate state goals (including protecting the potentiality of human life)[131] as long as those regulations do not pose an 'undue burden' on women's fundamental right to an abortion[132] and provide sufficient protection for women's life and health.[133]

A legal restriction poses an 'undue burden' if it has 'the purpose or effect of placing a substantial obstacle in the path of a woman seeking an abortion of a nonviable fetus'.[134] A recent Supreme Court decision once again addressed the meaning of the 'undue burden,' saying that courts must consider 'the burdens a law imposes on abortion access together with the benefits those laws confer'.[135]

Relationship to homicide

In recent years, two-thirds of the states have passed laws providing greater protection for foetuses in gestation. Those laws have either (1) amended the existing homicide statutes to include an unborn child as a possible victim; (2) redefined the homicide victim (e.g., person, human being, individual) to include an unborn child; or (iii) created new crimes directed exclusively at protection of the unborn child (e.g., feticide). The great majority of these provisions cover an unborn child at 'any stage of development' (or from 'fertilisation' or 'conception'); a few apply only to an unborn child after 'quickening' or 'viability;' a few more refer to a 'foetus' without further definition.[136]

These statutes are directed at third parties and not at the pregnant woman even if the harmful act is done with her knowledge and consent.[137] Nevertheless, recent years have seen numerous arrests, prosecutions and even convictions that have been later overturned of pregnant women who, usually through neglect or drug use, caused the death of their unborn babies.[138]

127 *State v Grissom*, 298 P. 666 [N.M. 1930]; *Coffmanv. Com.*, 50 S.E.2d 431 (Va. 1948).

128 *Rhode Island Medical Soc. v Whitehouse*, 66 F. Supp. 2d 288 (D.R.I. 1999), aff'd 239 F.3d 104 (1st Cir. 2001); G.K. Harnad, *Abortion* (2nd edn, 1962 American Jurisprudence) s 1.

129 410 U.S. 113 (1973).

130 505 U.S. 833 (1992).

131 For example, 43 states prohibit abortions, except when necessary to protect the woman's life or health, after a specified point in pregnancy. Nineteen states have laws in effect that prohibit 'partial-birth' abortion. Three of these laws apply only to post viability abortions. 'State Policies on Later Abortions' (n 79).

132 *Casey* (n 77) 877.

133 See section 'Medical treatment scenarios' above.

134 *Casey* (n 77) 877.

135 *Whole Woman's Health v Hellerstedt*, 136 S. Ct. 2292, 2324 (2016).

136 LaFave (n 35) s 14.1.

137 1 Am Jur 2d Abortion and Birth Control § 121. The MPC still holds the opposite view: '[a] woman whose pregnancy has continued beyond the twenty-sixth week commits a felony of the third degree if she purposely terminates her own pregnancy otherwise than live birth, or if she uses instruments, drugs or violence upon herself for that purpose', MPC s 230.3(4).

138 E. Bazelon, 'Purvi Patel could be just the beginning' (*The New York Times Magazine*, 1 April 2015) <www.nytimes.com/2015/04/01/magazine/purvi-patel-could-be-just-the-beginning.html?_r=0> accessed 30 May 2018.

Defences to homicide

Consent

Consent is not a defence to homicide in any U.S. jurisdiction or under the MPC.[139] In most jurisdictions, mercy killing or any other killing on request of the victim is considered murder.

The victim's consent may be taken into account at the sentencing stage of a criminal trial. Presently, approximately half of all states and the federal government recognise the victim's consent to the criminal conduct as a mitigating factor.[140] The victim's consent to homicide is also a mitigating factor for capital sentencing purposes in the absolute majority of death penalty jurisdictions that list statutory mitigating factors.[141] The MPC comments that in the situation of a mercy killing, 'the defendant's homicidal act may not have occurred had the victim not consented to it. [In that case], the conduct of the victim in bringing about his own death deserves consideration as a mitigating factor in assigning a death sentence'.[142]

Self-defence

Self-defence is a complete justification in prosecution for homicide if certain requirements are satisfied. In most U.S. jurisdictions, it is such a defence if

> at the time of the killing it appeared to the defendant and she *believed* it to be *necessary* to kill the decedent to save herself from *imminent death or great bodily harm.* That belief must be *reasonable*, however, in that the circumstances as they appeared to the defendant would create such a belief in the mind of a person of ordinary fitness. Further, the defendant must not have been the *initial aggressor* provoking the fatal confrontation.[143]

In addition, many jurisdictions require the actor to retreat (unless he is at home) before using deadly force if he can do so with safety.[144]

If the actor cannot meet all the required elements of self-defence, in most states, he loses the defence entirely and thus is guilty of murder.[145] Some jurisdictions, however, recognise 'imperfect' self-defence that does not completely exculpate the defendant but mitigates his liability from murder to voluntary manslaughter. The imperfect self-defence may be granted in two sets of circumstances: one, when the defendant, 'although without murderous intent, was the aggressor in bringing on the affray or used excessive force';[146] and two, when the

139 MPC ss 210.5 and 2.11.

140 V. Bergelson, 'Victims and Perpetrators: An Argument for Comparative Liability in Criminal Law' (2005) 8 Buffalo Criminal Law Review 385, 436.

141 J.R. Acker and C.S. Lanier, 'In Fairness and Mercy: Statutory Mitigating Factors in Capital Punishment Laws' (1994) 30 Criminal Law Bulletin 299, 320–21.

142 MPC (n 4) s 210.6, cmt 6(b).

143 *State v Norman*, 324 N.C. 253, 258–59 (1989) (citing *State v Gappins*, 320 N.C. 64, 71 (1987)) (emphasis added).

144 For more detailed discussion of the U.S. self-defence law, see L.E. Chiesa, 'United States of America' in A. Reed and M. Bohlander (eds) *General Defences in Criminal Law: Domestic and Comparative Perspectives* (Ashgate 2014) 335.

145 *Ross v State*, 211 N.W. 2d 274, 282–84 (Conn. 2006) (explaining the all-or-nothing rule).

146 *State v McAvoy*, 417 S.E.2d 489, 497 (N.C. 1992).

defendant honestly but unreasonably believed that the factual circumstances justified his use of deadly force.[147]

The MPC approach differs from the majority rules in two important ways. One, the MPC does not ban the defence to the actor who was honestly but unreasonably mistaken about the need to kill in self-protection; instead, the actor is guilty of a crime at the level of his culpability: manslaughter if he was reckless, and negligent homicide if he was negligent.[148] And two, the MPC replaces the requirement of the 'imminence of harm' with a less rigid standard which allows use of force when 'immediately necessary' to protect oneself on the present occasion.[149] Other noteworthy features of the MPC self-defence provisions are that the initial aggressor does not lose the right to use deadly force in self-protection, unless he has provoked that encounter with the purpose of causing the opponent's death or serious bodily harm;[150] and that the MPC endorses the 'retreat' rule as a prerequisite for the use of deadly force.[151]

Duress

Duress is a complete defence of excuse.[152] Traditional elements of duress include: (1) a threat of death or great bodily harm to the actor or close relative; (2) the threat being 'present, imminent, and impending'; (3) the actor's reasonable belief that the threat was genuine; (4) the lack of escape from the threat other than through compliance with the unlawful request; and (5) the actor not being at fault in exposing himself to the threat.[153]

The majority of the U.S. jurisdictions follow the common law rule that duress is not a defence to murder.[154] In addition, some courts have held that duress is not available as a defence in prosecution for reckless homicide either.[155] On the other hand, a few jurisdictions allow duress to serve as a mitigator from murder to manslaughter.[156]

There is a division in law regarding whether duress should be allowed as a defence to felony-murder. Some states follow the general rule by disallowing the defence to any form of murder while other states recognise duress as a defence if it negatives the underlying felony.[157] Under the latter theory, if one is not guilty of the underlying felony (say, robbery) due to duress, one cannot be guilty of felony murder based on that felony.[158]

The MPC version of duress is broader than the traditional rule in several respects: the threats of bodily harm do not have to be grave or imminent nor do they have to be directed

147 Dressler (n 33) 232–33.
148 ss 3.04(1), 3.09(2)–(3).
149 Ibid. s 3.04(1).
150 Ibid. s 3.04(2)(b)(i).
151 Ibid. s 3.04 (2)(b)(ii) (the use of deadly force is not justifiable if the actor knows that he can avoid the necessity of using such force with complete safety by retreating).
152 Chiesa (n 144) 339 (discussing the United State duress law in detail).
153 Ibid.
154 40 Am. Jur. 2d Homicide § 115; *People v Sims*, 869 N.E.2d 1115 (Ill. 1st Dist. 2007), appeal denied, 879 N.E.2d 937 (Ill. 2007).
155 40 Am. Jur. 2d Homicide § 115; *Carrigg v. State*, 696 N.E.2d 392 (Ind. Ct. App. 1998).
156 N.J. Rev. Stat. § 2C:2–9 (2013); Minn. Stat. § 609.20930 (2011).
157 *Moore v State*, 697 N.E.2d 1268 (Ind. Ct. App. 1998); *State v. Ng*, 750 P.2d 632 (Wash. 1988).
158 40 Am. Jur. 2d Homicide § 115; *People v Wilson*, 114 P.3d 758 (Cal. 2005), cert. denied (Cal. 2006).

only at the actor or a close relative. As a defence of general applicability, duress may be raised in prosecution for murder. Even if the facts do not support the complete defence of duress, the compulsion may be relevant as a mitigator from murder to manslaughter under the MPC 'extreme mental or emotional distress' provision.[159]

Necessity

Engaging in conduct that otherwise would constitute a crime is justifiable when such conduct is necessary to avert a more serious harm or evil than the harm or evil brought about by that conduct; the actor engages in such conduct with the purpose of averting the greater harm; and the greater harm is in fact averted.[160]

Today, 19 states codify this defence; some define it in broad general terms while others use more specific definitions. Common requirements include: the imminence of harm averted by the actor; the actor not being at fault in creating the need to break the law; and the absence of the legislative solution to the choice between the two evils.[161]

The defence is not available in prosecution for intentional homicide. Three states explicitly provide so by statute, one state allows the defence as a mitigator from first degree murder to second degree murder, but most state statutes do not address the issue. At the same time, no American court has ever concluded that the killing of an innocent human being amounts to a lesser evil and may be justified pursuant to necessity.[162]

The MPC, on the other hand, holds the opposite view. In a commentary to the necessity provision, the drafters opined:

> [R]ecognizing that the sanctity of life has a supreme place in the hierarchy of values, [nonetheless] conduct that results in taking life may promote the very value sought to be protected by the law of homicide. Suppose, for example, that the actor makes a breach in a dike, knowing that this will inundate a farm, but taking the only course available to save a whole town. If he is charged with homicide of the inhabitants of the farm house, he can rightly point out that the object of the law of homicide is to save life, and that by his conduct he has effected a net saving of innocent lives. The life of every individual must be taken in such a case to be of equal value and the numerical preponderance in the lives saved compared to those sacrificed surely should establish legal justification for the act.[163]

This position, as the MPC version of necessity defence in general, has not proven to be influential. In fact, it has been suggested that the MPC 'necessity defense is bad law that should not be cited without significant qualification as the basis for legal advice in any American jurisdiction'.[164]

159 Dressler (n 33) 313 n.87.
160 Chiesa (n 144) 337–38 (discussing the United States necessity law in detail).
161 For example, the defendant may not use the defence to justify his illegal use of marijuana for medical purposes if the legislature has refused to decriminalise medical marijuana. *State v Tate*, 505 A2d. 941, 946 [N.J. 1986].
162 Chiesa (n 144) 337–38.
163 MPC (n 4) s 3.02 cmt 3, 14–15.
164 M.H. Hoffheimer, 'Codifying Necessity: Legislative Resistance to Enacting Choice-of-Evils Defenses to Criminal Liability' (2007) 82 Tulsa Law Review 191, 243.

Insanity

A person who is legally insane at the time of the commission of a crime is excused.[165] Standard requirements of the defence include the following:

> First, the defendant must suffer from a mental disease or defect at the time of the commission of the offense. Second, the mental disease or defect must prevent the defendant from understanding the nature of his act or from distinguishing right from wrong. In some jurisdictions, insanity also applies if the mental disease or defect prevents the defendant from conforming his conduct to the mandates of the law.[166]

The defence is available in the absolute majority of the U.S. jurisdictions. However, some states have abolished it,[167] and it has been held that since a defendant has no fundamental right under the U.S. Constitution to put on an insanity defence, its abolition is not violative of the U.S. Constitution.[168]

Insanity is a complete defence; however, a person found not guilty by reason of insanity may be committed to a mental institution until he is no longer a threat to society.[169] Courts usually hold that a claim of insanity cannot be used for mitigating first degree murder to second degree murder or from murder to manslaughter,[170] nor can partial insanity be used to diminish the full measure of criminal responsibility for an act of homicide.[171] However, under some state statutes, the fact that the person who committed a homicide was temporarily insane when he formed and executed the design to kill may be taken into consideration in determining the degree of the murder and in fixing the penalty for the offence.[172]

Diminished responsibility

Under the doctrine of diminished responsibility,[173] the defendant's mental inadequacies or defects not amounting to legal insanity may be introduced in a homicide prosecution for the

165 40 Am. Jur. 2d. Criminal Law § 103; Chiesa (n 144) 340 (discussing the United States insanity law in detail).
166 Chiesa (n 144) 340. This last, volitional, prong was promulgated by the MPC along the cognitive prong modelled after the M'Naghten rule. Initially, both prongs were adopted with some variations by the majority of the United States jurisdictions. In more recent years, however, most of those jurisdictions have dropped the volitional prong and reverted to the more stringent M'Naghten rule. ibid 340–41.
167 Idaho Code § 18–207 (2005).
168 40 Am. Jur. 2d, Criminal Law § 46; *State v Korell*, 690 P.2d 992, 998 (Mont. 1984). The Supreme Court has not directly answered the question of constitutionality but, in *Clark v Arizona*, it indicated that the states maintain the capacity to define crimes and defences. 1 Subst. Crim. L. § 7–1 (2d ed.) (citing *Clark v Arizona*, 548 U.S. 735 (2006)); 1B-31 Criminal Defense Techniques § 31.01, 2.
169 Chiesa (n 144) 340.
170 *State v Baacke*, 932 P.2d 396 (Kan. 1997]; *People v Klumbach*, 202 A.D.2d 1009 [1994].
171 *Jones v Com.*, 117 S.E.2d 67 [Va. 1960].
172 40 Am. Jur. 2d Criminal Law § 103; *Evers v State*, 20 S.W. 744 (Tex. 1892).
173 This doctrine is different from diminished capacity with which it is often confused. Diminished capacity is a failure-of-proof defence. 'That is, evidence of mental abnormality is *not* offered by the defendant to partially or fully *excuse* his conduct, but rather as evidence to negate an element of the crime charged, almost always the *mens rea* element'. Dressler (n 33) 361 (citations omitted).

purpose of showing the defendant's inability or reduced ability to form a specific mental state, such as malice aforethought, deliberation or premeditation.[174] Only a few jurisdictions today follow this doctrine.[175]

While one state has held that a diminished mental capacity negates the mental element of murder and provides a complete defence,[176] in most jurisdictions, a diminished mental capacity short of insanity reduces criminality but does not completely excuse or justify the homicide.[177] Diminished responsibility is often considered a defence only for specific intent crimes like first degree murder;[178] under this view, it may not be used in cases of second degree murder where that crime is defined as a general intent crime.[179]

The MPC provides that a homicide that would otherwise be murder is manslaughter if committed under the 'extreme mental or emotional disturbance for which there is a reasonable explanation or excuse'.[180] A commentary to the MPC explains how the 'extreme mental or emotional disturbance' (EMED) provision applies to cases of diminished responsibility:

> It looks into the actor's mind to see whether he should be judged by a lesser standard than that applicable to ordinary men. It recognizes the defendant's own mental disorder or emotional instability as a basis for partially excusing his conduct. This position undoubtedly achieves a closer relation between criminal liability and moral guilt.[181]

This defence is not without controversy though, and the drafters of the MPC have recognised that: 'By restricting the extreme condemnation of liability for murder to cases where it is fully warranted in a relativistic sense, diminished responsibility undercuts the social purpose of condemnation'.[182]

It is unclear how many states with the codified EMED provision allow its use for the defence of diminished responsibility but, in at least two states, courts have explicitly done so.[183]

Loss of control and / or provocation

An intentional homicide committed without malice aforethought, in a sudden heat of passion as a result of adequate legal provocation, is manslaughter.[184] The majority of the U.S.

174 40 Am. Jur. 2d Homicide § 104. Diminished responsibility is not necessarily established by the defendant's mental retardation or low I.Q., history of psychotic disorders, or suicidal state of mind, *ibid.*
175 Dressler (n 33) 362.
176 *State v Juinta*, 541 A.2d 284 (NJ App. Div. 1988).
177 *Com. v Legg*, 711 A.2d 430 (Pa. 1998); *State v Amazeen*, 526 A.2d 1268 (R.I. 1987).
178 *Veverka v Cash*, 318 N.W.2d 447 [Iowa 1982] (not defence to felony murder); *State v Hill*, 744 P.2d 1228 [Kan. 1987]; *Amazeen*, 526 A.2d.
179 *People v Gallegos*, 628 P.2d 999 [Colo. 1981]; *People v Biggs*, 509 N.W.2d 803 (Mich. 1993); *State v Page*, 488 S.E.2d 225 (N.C. 1997).
180 MPC s 210.3(1)(b).
181 MPC s 210.3, 71.
182 Ibid.
183 Dressler (n 33) 369; *State v Perez*, 976 P.2d 379 [Haw. 1999]; *State v Counts*, 816 P.2d 1157 [Or. 1991].
184 *State v Ruffner*, 911 A.2d 680 (R.I. 2006).

jurisdictions recognise, in some form, the doctrine of provocation or heat of passion (the two terms are often used interchangeably) as a partial defence to homicide.[185]

The criteria for the defence vary by jurisdiction. Under the more traditional version, the elements of heat-of-passion manslaughter are: (1) adequate provocation (i.e., such that would cause a reasonable person to lose his self-control);[186] (2) a passion such as fear, terror, anger, rage or resentment; (3) the homicide occurred while the passion still existed and before a reasonable opportunity for the passion to cool; and (4) a causal connection between the provocation, passion and homicide.[187]

Jurisdictions that still follow the common law rule of provocation consider it legally adequate only if it stems from one of the following scenarios: (1) an aggravated assault or battery; (2) mutual combat; (3) commission of a serious crime (chiefly, violent or sexual assault) against a close relative of the defendant; (4) illegal arrest; and (5) sudden discovery of an adultery.[188] However, most states today do not follow the rule so strictly and allow the jury to decide whether the circumstances of the case constitute adequate provocation.[189]

More modern state statutes, modelled after the MPC, use the broader EMED language: murder is mitigated to manslaughter if the homicide is 'committed under the influence of extreme mental or emotional disturbance for which there is reasonable explanation or excuse'.[190] Under the MPC, the reasonableness of such explanation or excuse is to be determined 'from the viewpoint of a person in the actor's situation under the circumstances as he believes them to be'.[191] About 20 states today employ some version of EMED but most of them have adopted it with considerable alterations – for example, requiring a provocative act and rejecting the 'actor's situation' language in favour of a more general 'reasonableness' standard.[192]

The law of provocation is far from settled. Professor Victoria Nourse has observed:

> Although most jurisdictions have adopted what appears to be a ... "reasonable man" standard, that standard has been applied in dramatically different ways, with jurisdictions borrowing from both liberal and traditional theories. Some states require a "sudden" passion, others allow emotion to build up over time; some reject claims based on "mere words," others embrace them. Today, we are only safe in saying that in the law of passion, there lie two poles – one exemplified by the most liberal MPC reforms and the other by the most traditional categorical view of the common law. In between these poles, a majority of states borrow liberally from both traditions.[193]

One of the most contentious issues in the law of provocation is whether the reasonableness of the defendant's loss of control should be considered from the entirely objective perspective, and if not – if some features of the actual defendant are to be included in that

185 R.G. Fontaine, 'Adequate (Non)Provocation and Heat of Passionas Excuse Not Justification' (2009) 43 University of Michigan Journal of Law Reform 27.

186 MPC s 210.3 cmt. 5(a), 56.

187 40 Am Jur 2d Homicide § 48; *Eizember v State*, 164 P.3d 208 (Okla. Crim. App. 2007), as corrected, (Aug. 10, 2007) and cert. denied, 170 L. Ed. 2d 374 (U.S. 2008).

188 MPC (n 4) s 210.3 cmt 5(a), 57–58.

189 Dressler (n 33) 525.

190 MPC s 210.3(1)(b).

191 Ibid.

192 Kadish (n 18) 483.

193 V. Nourse, 'Passion's Progress: Modern Law Reform and the Provocation Defense' (1997)106 Yale Law Journal 1331, 1341.

consideration – what should be included and what excluded. A commentary to the MPC explains that personal handicaps and some external circumstances (such as 'blindness, shock from traumatic injury, and extreme grief')[194] should be in, while idiosyncratic moral values should be out. Should the defendant's other special circumstances (low IQ, depression, post-traumatic stress disorder, battered woman syndrome) be included in deciding whether to mitigate murder to manslaughter is not as clear and the answers may differ from one court to another.[195]

A number of courts have allowed provocation and heat-of-passion manslaughter instructions in prosecutions of battered victims who kill their batterers. For example, In *State v Vigilante*, the court held that a battered child prosecuted for killing his father was entitled to a heat-of-passion manslaughter instruction.[196] The court concluded that the child's past abuse and his contemplation of future abuse, combined with the father's threat to kill the child, presented grounds for a provocation and heat-of-passion manslaughter charge.[197] In *State v Guido*, a mistreated wife killed her husband.[198] The court observed that, with respect to physical abuse, the jury could find that although there were only a few incidents of actual injury, there was a constant threat of it.[199] The court concluded that the jury should have been instructed on manslaughter. It opined:

> It seems to us that a course of ill treatment which can induce a homicidal response in a person of ordinary firmness and which the accused reasonably believes is likely to continue, should permit a finding of provocation. In taking this view, we merely acknowledge the undoubted capacity of events to accumulate a detonating force, no different from that of a single blow or injury. The question is simply one of fact, whether the accused did, because of such prolonged oppression and the prospect of its continuance, experience a sudden episode of emotional distress which overwhelmed her reason, and whether, if she did, she killed because of it and before there had passed time reasonably sufficient for her emotions to yield to reason.[200]

At least in some jurisdictions, continuous abuse may constitute adequate provocation.[201]

Superior orders

Superior orders is a plea in a court of law that a person – whether a member of the military, law enforcement, a firefighting force or the civilian population – not be held guilty for actions that were ordered by a superior officer or an official.[202]

The United States follows the 'manifest illegality principle', according to which a soldier who obeyed an order issued by a superior to perform an act which was later proved to have

194 MPC (n 4) s 210.3, 62.
195 Kadish (n 18) 485–88.
196 608 A.2d 425 (NJ 1992).
197 *Brooks v State*, 630 So. 2d 160 (Ala Crim. App.1993).
198 191 A.2d 45 (N.J. 1963).
199 Ibid. 48.
200 *Vigilante*, 608 A.2d at 429–30 (quoting *Guido*, 191 A.2d at 56).
201 *State v Erazo*, 594 A.2d 232 (N.J. 1991); *State v Whye*, DOCKET NO. A-3910–10T3 [N.J. Super. App. Div. Apr. 26, 2013]; *State v Pritchett*, DOCKET NO. A-2690–10T1 (N.J. Super. Apr. 25, 2012).
202 L.C. Green, *Superior Orders in National and International Law* (1976 A.W. Sijthoff International Publishing Co.).

been unlawful would have a defence in any consequent legal proceedings, if, and only if, the order was one which could credibly have appeared lawful at the time when it was received.[203]

The current United States Army Field Manual reads:

> The fact that the law of war has been violated pursuant to an order of a superior authority, whether military or civil, does not deprive the act in question of its character as a war crime, nor does it constitute a defense in the trial of an accused individual, unless he did not know and could not reasonably have been expected to know that the act ordered was unlawful … That the individual was acting pursuant to orders may be considered in mitigation of punishment.[204]

From the practical perspective, a soldier who asserts a superior order raises the defence of mistake of fact or law. For example, pursuant to his squadron commander's order, a pilot may fire his munitions at a hospital, knowing that international law protects hospitals, but mistakenly believing his commander's assurance that the enemy employs this hospital as an anti-aircraft gun position.[205] Similarly, an artilleryman may fire on a museum upon receiving orders to do so, knowing the target to be a museum, but believing it to be a lawful target. Both claims may provide successful defences.[206]

In contrast, a defendant may not claim the defence for following an order that is 'so palpably atrocious as well as illegal that one ought [to] instinctively feel that it ought not to be obeyed'.[207] Examples include a Vietnam War case involving an order to kill unarmed women and children,[208] and a Korean War case involving an order to rape and steal.[209]

Official authority

The official authority, more commonly known in the United States as the public authority, defence is available to a person acting under an official capacity (as a public servant), a court order, a duty or authority to assist, or on behalf of a public officer.[210]

In prosecution for homicide, public authority can serve as a ban to criminal prosecution (e.g., in the case of an executioner giving the prisoner a lethal injection in accordance with the execution order) or an affirmative defence of justification (e.g., in the case of a police officer shooting and killing a fleeing suspect). Versions of the public authority justification are contained in the codes of nearly every state in the United States.[211]

203 H. Takemura, *International Human Right to Conscientious Objection to Military Service and Individual Duties to Disobey Manifestly Illegal Orders* (2009 Springer) 157.
204 Department of the United States Army, *The Law of Land Warfare* (1956 Department of the Army) para 509 (a).
205 G.D. Solis, 'Obedience of Orders and the Law of War: Judicial Application in American Forums' (1999) 15(2) American University. International Law Review 481, 522.
206 Ibid.
207 *McCall v McDowell*, 15 F. Cas. 1235, 1241 (C.C.D. Cal. 1867) (No.8, 673).
208 Solis (n 205) 521.
209 Ibid.; *U.S. v Kinder*, 14 C.M.R. 742, 775 (A.C.M. 1953).
210 Modern penal codes provide general justification for conduct that is 'required or authorized by law'. Some statutes specifically require that the actor be a public servant. Actors may include members of the military, police officers and other law enforcement personnel. LaFave (n 25) 534–36, 558–59, 565–66 (4th edn 2003).
211 P. Robinson, *Criminal Law Defenses: Volume 2* (1984 West) § 142.

The defence is available to a law enforcement officer who uses deadly force to make an arrest if it is used (i) in the course of a felony that involves the use or threatened use of deadly force, or (ii) when there is a substantial risk that the arrestee will cause death or serious bodily injury if his apprehension is delayed.[212] In the absence of those circumstances, use of deadly force violates the Fourth Amendment's prohibition against unreasonable seizures.[213]

Some statutes bar deadly force in effecting arrests for misdemeanours but permit its use for all felonies. Other statutes permit the use of deadly force in arresting only for certain specified felonies or only for forcible felonies or dangerous felonies.[214]

Deadly force provisions are also found in the law enforcement authority to prevent escape from custody. Deadly force to prevent escape prior to confinement in a penal facility is typically permitted if deadly force would be permissible to make the arrest. After detention, however, deadly force is often permitted regardless of the seriousness of the offence, although a few jurisdictions continue to distinguish felons and misdemeanants. Still another approach conditions the use of deadly force in preventing an escape on the degree of security of the place of confinement – i.e., maximum *versus* minimum security.[215]

A dozen state codes also provide justification for the conduct authorised by the law governing armed forces or the lawful conduct of war. In addition, as a matter of federal law, no state may deny a defence to a soldier acting in obedience to a lawful order of his superior because such obedience is a legal duty.[216] The defence is also specifically provided for in the U.S. military's Manual for Courts-Martial, which states that a 'death, injury, or other act caused or done in the proper performance of a legal duty is justified and not unlawful'.[217]

Honour killings

Honour killings are a practice existing in certain traditional communities by which family members kill a relative for bringing dishonour to the family or clan. The perceived dishonour often stems from the violation of a sexual taboo, such as engaging in premarital sex or extramarital relations, elopement or romantic involvement with someone disapproved by the family.[218] There is very limited data regarding honour killings in the United States.

212 Ibid. Similarly, the MPC stipulates that deadly force can be used to prevent a crime or effect an arrest only when 'the crime for which the arrest is made involved conduct including the use or threatened use of deadly force; or … there is a substantial risk that the person to be arrested will cause death or serious bodily harm if his apprehension is delayed'. MPC ss 3.07(2)(b)(iv), 3.07 (5)(a)(i) and (ii).

213 *Tennessee v Garner*, 471 U.S. 1, 11–12 (1985) (rejecting police officer's claim to justifiable use of deadly force against a fleeing suspected burglar).

214 Robinson (n 211).

215 Ibid.

216 P. Robinson, M. Kussmaul, C. Stoddard, I. Rudyak and A. Kuersten, 'The American Criminal Code: General Defenses' (2015) 7 Journal of Law Analysis 317; 10 U.S.C. § 892(1); *Arce v State*, 202 S.W. 951, 953 (Tex. Crim. App. 1918) (releasing Mexican soldiers from liability for killing an American officer during the Mexican–American War because they were directed to fight according to lawful orders).

217 *Manual for Courts-Martial United States* (2012 edn) 916(C). See also Colonel G. P. Corn, 'Should the Best Offense Ever Be a Good Defense? The Public Authority to Use Force in Military Operations' (2016) 49(1) Vanderbilt Journal of Transnational Law 1 (discussing in detail public authority to use force in military operations).

218 J.A. Cohan, 'Honor Killings and the Cultural Defense' (2010) 40(2) California Western International Law Journal 177, 192.

According to the 2014 Justice Department reports, such killings make up about 23 to 27 of the approximately 15,000 murders reported to the FBI annually.[219]

There is no special defence available in any U.S. jurisdiction for honour killings. However, in a number of cases, defendants have presented a 'cultural defence' arguing that they acted without malice or in the heat of passion produced by a cultural norm prevalent in their community. Even though the 'cultural defence' has long been rejected,[220] sometimes, provocation and diminished responsibility arguments stemming from a different cultural norm have been allowed and, when successful, led to the defendants' conviction of lesser offences or more lenient sentences.[221]

For example, in *People v Wu*, an appellate court held that the trial judge committed a reversible error by refusing to instruct the jury on the effect the defendant's cultural background might have had on the issue of premeditation, malice aforethought, deliberation or the existence of heat of passion at the time of the killing.[222] The defendant killed her son and attempted to kill herself. At her trial, she argued that her actions would have been acceptable in China as a reaction to the information about her husband's infidelity and mistreatment of their son.[223]

Sentencing framework

Mandatory sentencing regimes

Mandatory sentencing statutes limit the discretion of a sentencing court by requiring it to impose a certain kind or amount of punishment. The most common forms are mandatory minimum statutes that demand that offenders be sentenced to imprisonment for 'not less than' a designated term. Some mandatory minimums are triggered by the nature of the offence, others by the criminal record of the offender.[224]

Pursuant to the current interpretation of 'cruel and unusual punishment',[225] the U.S. Constitution forbids mandatory death penalty for any crime.[226] It also forbids a mandatory sentence of life imprisonment without the possibility of parole ('LWP') for a homicide

219 K. Winston, 'Activists: Trump call for honor killings report targets Muslims' (*USA Today*, 7 March 2017) <www.usatoday.com/story/news/2017/03/07/activists-trump-call-honor-killings-report-targets-muslims/98861230/> accessed 30 May 2018.

220 *Carlisle v U.S.*, 83 U.S. 147 (1872).

221 *People v Chen*, No. 87–7774 (N.Y. Sup. Ct. Mar. 21,1989) (defendant who killed his wife upon learning of her infidelity argued 'diminished capacity' as a result of Chinese cultural pressures regarding infidelity; he was convicted of second degree manslaughter and sentenced to five years' probation); N.S. Kim, 'The Cultural Defense and the Problem of Cultural Preemption: A Framework for Analysis' (1997) 27 New Mexico Law Review 101, 119–21.

222 *People v Wu*, 286 Cal. Rptr. 868 (Cal. Ct. App. 1991).

223 Cohan (n 218) 177, 238.

224 C. Doyle, *Federal Mandatory Minimum Sentencing Statutes* 1–2 (Congressional Research Service 2013).

225 U.S Const. Amend. VIII ('Excessive bail shall not be required, nor excessive fines imposed, nor cruel and unusual punishments inflicted').

226 *Woodson v North Carolina*, 428 U.S. 280 (1976); *Louisiana v Roberts*, 428 U.S. 325 (1976). In subsequent cases, the Court confirmed that no form of mandatory death penalty could be Constitutional. *Sumner v Shuman*, 483 U.S. 66 (1987) (invalidating a mandatory death penalty statute for life-term inmates convicted of murder).

committed by a juvenile offender.[227] Other mandatory sentences, including life sentences, are endorsed by the laws of the majority of the U.S. jurisdictions[228] and have withstood federal and state challenges of proportionality, double jeopardy, *ex post facto*, due process, separation of powers and equal protection.[229] For example, state courts have upheld statutes providing for mandatory sentence of LWP for 50 years upon conviction of capital murder where death penalty was not imposed.[230]

Among the federal mandatory provisions are sentences for first degree murder;[231] murder committed in the course of a sexual crime while in federal custody or within the special maritime or territorial jurisdiction of the United States;[232] and homicides resulting from the commission of various federal offences, including sex trafficking[233] and production of child pornography.[234]

Habitual offender (commonly known as 'three strikes') laws adopted in most U.S. jurisdictions to impose harsher punishments for repeat offenders often produce similar results for lesser homicide offences. For example, the defendant's mandatory sentence of LWP following his third strike conviction for second degree murder was upheld under the state constitution.[235]

Until relatively recently, the Sentencing Reform Act[236] required federal judges to follow the narrowly designed sentencing guidelines whenever the case fell within the heartland of typical or ordinary cases on which the guidelines were based.[237] In *United States v Booker*, decided in 2005, the U.S. Supreme Court held that that constraint interfered with the constitutional guarantee of a jury trial.[238] The remedy adopted by the Court was making the federal guidelines 'advisory' and allowing an appellate court to set aside the decision of the sentencing judge, whether within the guideline range or not, only when the sentence was 'unreasonable'.[239] A few years later, the Supreme Court held that any factual finding that increases a mandatory minimum sentence must be admitted by the defendant or proved to the jury beyond a reasonable doubt.[240] As of 2016, almost one-half of all federal sentences were within the advisory federal guidelines, with the departures being predominantly downward.[241]

There has been evidence that mandatory minimum laws have had a significant discriminatory effect on minorities. According to the Statistical Overview of Mandatory Minimum Penalties presented in October 2011, of all offenders convicted of an offence carrying

227 *Miller v Alabama*, 567 U.S. 460 (2012).
228 Ibid. (J. Roberts, dissent).
229 Doyle (n 224).
230 *State v Borden*, 605 SW2d 88 (Mo. 1980); *State v Olinghouse* 605 SW2d 58 (Mo. 1980).
231 18 U.S.C. § 1111 (first degree murder punishable by death or life imprisonment).
232 Ibid. (murder within the special maritime and territorial jurisdiction of the United States), s 1118 (murder by federal prisoners) (both providing for mandatory life imprisonment).
233 Ibid. s 1591.
234 Ibid. s 2251(e) (establishing a 30-year mandatory minimum).
235 West's RCWA Const. Art. 1, Ibid. § 14; West's RCWA 9.94A.570; *State v Hart*, 353 P.3d 253 (Wash. Ct. App. Div. 3 2015]; 18 U.S.C. § 3559(c) (a defendant convicted of a federal 'serious violent felony' must be sentenced to life imprisonment if he has two prior state or federal violent felony convictions or one such conviction and a serious drug offense conviction).
236 H.R. 9z3713, 114th Cong. (2016).
237 *Koon v U.S.*, 518 U.S. 81, 92–94 (1996).
238 543 U.S. 220, 232 (2005).
239 Ibid.; *Kimbrough v. United States*, 552 U.S. 85 (2007).
240 *Alleyne v United States*, 133 S. Ct. 2151 (2013).
241 U.S. Sentencing Commission, 2016 Datafile, USSCFY16.

a mandatory minimum punishment, 38.3% were Hispanic, 31.5% were Black and 27.4% were White.[242]

Discretionary sentencing regimes

More than a half of American jurisdictions authorise broad discretionary sentencing.[243] After the defendant has been convicted, the judge conducts a separate sentencing hearing at which he imposes a sentence based on his assessment of the offender and the circumstances under which the crime was committed.[244]

The imposed sentence has to be within the boundaries of the statutory range. In selecting a sentence within that range, judges often consider such factors as: the defendant's criminal record, employment history, family ties, educational level, military service, charitable activities and age; the harm caused by the criminal act; and the defendant's motive.[245] Whether to consider any of these factors and what weight to accord each of them are decisions left almost entirely to the discretion of individual judges[246] (except that judges are forbidden from using in their decision-making false information or improper factors such as the defendant's race, gender or religion).[247] Many states today have advisory or voluntary guidelines, some with less appellate review than the post-*Booker* federal guidelines or even no appellate review at all.[248]

The sentencing factors must be found by the judge by the preponderance of the evidence whereas the offence elements must be found by the jury beyond the reasonable doubt: 'Other than the fact of a prior conviction, any fact that increases the penalty for a crime beyond the prescribed statutory maximum must be submitted to a jury, and proved beyond a reasonable doubt'.[249]

In death penalty cases, the sentencing decision is typically made by the jury during a separate hearing. Jurors are asked to weigh the aggravating factors presented by the prosecution against the mitigating factors presented by the defence. Every state except Alaska provides LWP as a sentencing option to death penalty.[250]

Punishment for an attempt and, in most jurisdictions, other inchoate crimes is usually a reduced factor of the punishment for the completed crime.[251] The MPC makes attempt, solicitation and conspiracy felonies of the same grade and degree as the underlying completed offence, except for the felonies of the first degree, for which the corresponding

242 United States Sentencing Commission, *2011 Report to the Congress: Mandatory Minimum Penalties in the Federal (Criminal Justice System)* <www.ussc.gov/research/congressional-reports/2011-report-congress-mandatory-minimum-penalties-federal-criminal-justice-system> accessed 30 May 2018.

243 R.E. Barkow, 'Administering Crime' (2005) 52 UCLA Law Review 715, 741 n.74.

244 C.B. Hessick and F. A. Hessick, 'Recognizing Constitutional Rights at Sentencing' (2011) 99 California Law Review 47, 52.

245 C.B. Hessick and F.A. Hessick, 'Procedural Rights at Sentencing' (2014) 90 Notre Dame Law Review 187.

246 Ibid. 190–91.

247 Hessick (n 244) 54–6 (collecting cases involving improper sentencing factors).

248 Kadish (n 18) 1252.

249 *Apprendi v. New Jersey*, 530 U.S. 466 (2000).

250 N.V. Demleitner, D. Berman, M.L. Miller, R.F. Wright, *Sentencing Law and Policy: Cases and Materials* (3rd edn, Wolters Kluwer 2013) 252, 258.

251 Kadish (n 18) 745. For example, in California, attempt carries a maximum term of not more than one-half of the maximum term authorised for the completed offense. Cal. Penal Code § 664 (2016).

inchoate offences are reduced to the second degree.[252] Many states have followed the MPC lead.[253] For example, about one-third of the states make the punishment for conspiracy the same as that authorised for the object crime, except in the case of the most serious felonies.[254]

252 MPC s 6.06. A felony of the first degree is punishable by imprisonment for a term whose minimum is between one and ten years and maximum is life. A felony of the second degree is punishable by imprisonment for a term whose minimum is between one and three years and maximum is ten years. Ibid.

253 Conn. Gen. Stat. Ann. § 53a-51 (2016) (providing for the same punishment for attempt as completed crimes, except for crimes punishable by death or life imprisonment).

254 Kadish (n 18) 745.

13 Germany

Kai Ambos and Stefanie Bock

Overview and historical development of homicide offences and offence structure

Short overview on the historical development of homicide offences

The current German criminal law is to a large extent based on the Prussian Criminal Code of 1851,[1] which distinguished between simple intentional[2] and premediated killing, i.e., killing with deliberation (murder).[3] This approach proved to be unsatisfactory though. In case of mercy killings, for example, the defendant typically struggles with his conscience over a long time, before he finally decides to act. We therefore had a killing with deliberation and the defendant had to be convicted for murder which carried a mandatory death sentence. On the other hand, killings out of sexual desire are considered to be particularly reprehensible, but are often committed in the heat of the moment and thus without premeditation.[4]

In 1941, the homicide offences were therefore fundamentally revised. Murder as the most severe offence against life was construed as a particularly heinous or dangerous form of killing. The phrasing of the new sec. 211[5] was clearly influenced by the ideology of the National Socialists which focused on the personality of the offender (*Täterstrafrecht*) and tried to classify him / her[6] according to certain types (*Tätertypen*).[7] Nevertheless and despite several reform efforts,[8]

1 W. Joecks, 'Einleitung' in B. von Heintschel-Heinegg (ed.), *Münchener Kommentar zum Strafgesetzbuch, Band 1, §§ 1–37* (3rd edn, C.H. Beck 2017) marginal number [hereinafter: mn] 82.
2 Sec. 176 Prussian Criminal Code.
3 Sec. 175 Prussian Criminal Code: 'Wer vorsätzlich und mit Überlegung einen Menschen tödtet, begeht einen Mord.'; Englisch translation by M.D. Dubber and T. Hörnle, *Criminal Law – A Comparative Approach* (Oxford University Press 2014) 537 ('Who intentionally and with deliberation kills a human being is punished by death for murder.').
4 R. Maurach, F.C. Schroeder and M. Maiwald, *Strafrecht Besonderer Teil. Teilband 1: Straftaten gegen Persönlichkeits- und Vermögenswerte* (10th edn, C.F. Müller 2009) § 2 mn 3.
5 'A murderer under this provision is …' instead of 'Whosoever kills a person … shall be convicted of murder.'
6 To improve readability we will use exclusively the male form which is understood to be gender-independent.
7 Dubber and Hörnle (n 3) 537; Maurach, Schroeder and Maiwald (n 4) § 2 mn 3; see also the contemporary analysis by R. Freisler, 'Gedanken über das Gesetz zur Änderung des Reichsstrafgesetzbuches' (1941) 103 Deutsche Justiz 929–36.
8 Overview in Expertengruppe zur Reform der Tötungsdelikte, *Abschlussbericht* (June 2015) <www.bmjv.de/DE/Ministerium/ForschungUndWissenschaft/ReformToetungsdelikte/ReformToetungsdelikte_node.html> accessed 11 June 2018.

this provision is still valid today. In May 2014, the Federal Ministry of Justice and Consumer Protection set up an expert committee for the reform of homicide offences. It remains to be seen whether and how its rather modest modification proposals will be implemented.[9]

Forms of homicide

The basic homicide offence in modern German criminal law is *Totschlag* ('voluntary manslaughter')[10] which is defined as the intentional killing of another person (sec. 212 *Strafgesetzbuch* [StGB]).[11] In certain aggravating circumstances, voluntary manslaughter turns into murder. According to sec. 211 StGB, a murderer is a person who kills a person 'for pleasure, for sexual gratification, out of greed or otherwise base motives, by stealth or cruelly or by means that pose a danger to the public or in order to facilitate or to cover up another offence.' On the other side of the 'scale of wrongfulness' is sec. 216 StGB on killing on request of the victim – a special form of lesser manslaughter. In addition, sec. 213 StGB recognises the partial defence[12] of provocation and other mitigating circumstances. The sentence is reduced if the defendant 'was provoked to rage by maltreatment inflicted on him or a relative, or was seriously insulted by the victim and immediately lost self-control and committed the offence, or in the event of an otherwise less serious case'. Notably, this provision applies only to voluntary manslaughter, not to murder.[13]

Although it is clear that these three forms of intentional homicide – killing on request, voluntary manslaughter and murder – represent different degrees of wrongfulness and culpability, their systematic relationship is subject to debate. The Supreme Court (*Bundesgerichtshof* [BGH]) traditionally argues that the underlying acts (killing, killing out of base motives or by particular reprehensible means[14], mercy killing) are so different in nature and substance that sec. 211, 212 and 216 StGB must be treated as separated offences.[15] The prevailing literature, to the contrary, stresses that all three offences share one common element: the intentional killing of another person. Therefore, it is more convincing to understand voluntary manslaughter as the basic offence, and sec. 211, 216 as aggravated

9 Ibid. The majority proposed to maintain the basic structure of the homicide offences, to extend sec. 211 StGB by further qualifying factors (e.g., killing on racial, ethnic or religious ground) and to restrict some of the requirements for murder (killing by stealth or cruelly).

10 Terminology based on A. Du Bois-Pedain, 'Intentional Killings: The German Law' in J. Horder (ed.) *Homicide Law in Comparative Perspective* (Hart Publishing 2007) 55 (65); cf. also Law Commission, *A New Homicide Act for England and Wales? An Overview* (Law Com CP No 177, 2005) D. 21; T. Weigend, 'Germany' in K.J. Heller and M.D. Dubber (eds) *The Handbook of Comparative Criminal Law* (Stanford University Press 2011) 252–77.

11 An English translation of the German Criminal Code (StGB) is available at <https://www.gesetze-im-internet.de/englisch_stgb/> accessed 11 June 2018.

12 German legal doctrine does not consider sec. 213 StGB as a distinct homicide offence, but as a sentencing provision in relation to voluntary manslaughter (sec. 212 StGB), M. Bohlander, *Principles of German Criminal Law* (Hart Publishing 2009) 181; H. Schneider, '§ 213 – Minder schwerer Fall des Totschlags' in G.M. Sander (ed.) *Münchener Kommentar zum Strafgesetzbuch, Band 4, §§ 185–262 StGB* (3rd edn, C.H. Beck 2017) mn 1; U. Murmann, *Grundkurs Strafrecht* (4th edn, C.H. Beck 2017) § 21 mn 5; for a different view, see Maurach, Schroeder and Maiwald (n 4) § 2 mn 55.

13 Bohlander (n 12) 181; Schneider (n 12) mn 2; Murmann (n 12) § 21 mn 5.

14 cf. Weigend (n 10) 277.

15 See e.g., BGHSt [Entscheidungen des Bundesgerichtshofes in Strafsachen – Official Journal of Reportable Federal Supreme Court Decisions] 1, 368 (370–71); BGHSt 2, 258; BGHSt 36, 231 (233); BGH Neue Juristische Wochenschrift [hereinafter: NJW] 2005 996, 998.

respective privileged forms of homicide.[16] This controversy is relevant for the liability of co-perpetrators and secondary parties.[17]

Germany has no felony-murder rule,[18] that is, all offences treated so far require the intention[19] to kill. Sec. 222 StGB, however, establishes the separate offence of negligent homicide. Moreover, German Criminal Law has several result-qualified homicide offences (*erfolgsqualifizierte Delikte*) in which death is the (non-intended) result of the commission of a basic offence, e.g., rape causing death (sec. 178), infliction of bodily harm causing death (sec. 227), stalking causing death (sec. 238(3)), robbery causing death (sec. 251) and arson causing death (sec. 306c).

General elements

Beginning and end of life / pre-birth causes with post-birth effect

All homicide offences presuppose the killing of another person, which means they must be directed against a living human being. For the purpose of criminal law offences,[20] life begins with the first stage of labour / the first stage pains[21] or – in case of a caesarean section – with the opening of the uterus.[22] Whether or not the new-born is capable of surviving is irrelevant. It is sufficient that it is alive at the time of the respective conduct and lives inde-

16 See, e.g., Murmann (n 12) § 21 mn 8; R. Rengier, *Strafrecht Besonderer Teil II* (19th edn, C.H. Beck 2018) § 4 mn 1, § 6 mn 3; J. Wessels, M. Hettinger and A. Engländer, *Strafrecht Besonderer Teil 1: Straftaten gegen Persönlichkeits- und Gemeinschaftswerte* (41st edn, C. F. Müller 2017) § 2 mn 84; H. Schneider, 'Vorbemerkung zu den §§ 211 ff.' in G. M. Sander (ed.) *Münchener Kommentar zum Strafgesetzbuch, Band 4, §§ 185–262 StGB* (3rd edn, C.H. Beck Verlag 2017) mn 184, 189–90 and the sources cited there; differentiating A. Eser and D. Sternberg-Lieben, 'Vorbemerkungen zu den §§ 211 ff.' in A. Schönke and H. Schröder (eds) *Strafgesetzbuch – Kommentar* (29th edn, C.H. Beck 2014) mn 3–7.

17 In view of the BGH, the qualifying factors of sec. 211 StGB establish the liability of the principal. If they are absent in the person of the secondary participant, they receive a mandatory statutory discount on sentencing (sec. 28(1) StGB). According to the literature, the qualifying factors of sec. 211 StGB aggravate punishment. If they are absent in the person of the secondary participant, he will be liable only for instigating or aiding and abetting voluntary manslaughter (and not for participation in murder, sec. 28 (2)); cf. Bohlander (n 12) 180; Rengier (n 16) § 5 Rn. 3 ff.; Wessels, Hettinger and Engländer (n 16) § 2 mn 159 ff.

18 Under the US-American felony murder rule, a defendant can be held liable for murder, only because he caused the death of another person in the course of committing a felony, i.e., an especially serious offence. His culpability level / *mens rea* as to causing the death is irrelevant, see P.H. Robinson and T.S. Williams, *Mapping American Criminal Law: Variations Across the Fifty States – Ch. 5 Felony-Murder Rule* (May 17, 2017). University of Pennsylvania Law School, Public Law Research Paper N0. 17–3, available < https://papers.ssrn.com/sol3/papers.cfm?abstract_id=2895017> accessed 11 June 2018.

19 On the meaning of intention *infra* text accompanying n 56.

20 The private law takes a more restrictive approach. According to sec. 1 of the German Civil Code (*Bürgerliches Gesetzbuch – BGB*), the legal capacity of a human being begins on the *completion* of birth. English translation of the BGB available at <www.gesetze-im-internet.de/englisch_bgb/englisch_bgb.html#p0025> accessed 11 June 2018.

21 BGHSt 32, 194; Bohlander (n 12) 181; Schneider (n 16) mn 11; Murmann (n 12) § 21 mn 14; Maurach, Schroeder and Maiwald (n 4) § 1 mn 8.

22 Bohlander (n 12) 182; Murmann (n 12) § 21 mn 14; Maurach, Schroeder and Maiwald (n 4) § 1 mn 8; for a different view see Schneider (n 16) mn 12 (opening of the abdominal wall).

pendently from the mother.[23] Sec. 211 ff. StGB thus offer an absolute protection of life regardless of the victim's expectation of life, the quality of his life or his (assumed) value for the society.[24]

At the pre-natal stage, the embryo is protected by sec. 216 StGB which penalises the termination of a pregnancy. For a delimitation between abortion and homicide, the time when the effects of the act begin to manifest themselves is crucial. The point of death is irrelevant.[25] Thus, if D intentionally induces pre-term labour, he is guilty of abortion regardless of whether the embryo dies in the mother's womb or shortly after birth as a result of D's pre-birth action.[26] If, to the contrary, the abortion fails, the child is born alive and D decides to stifle it with a pillow, this qualifies as voluntary manslaughter.[27]

According to the prevailing view, life as protected by sec. 211 ff. StGB ends at brain death.[28] This corresponds with the German Transplantation Statute which allows for the taking of organs only after the complete, definite and irreversible loss of brain function.[29]

Medical treatment scenarios

It follows from sec. 216 StGB that victim's consent does not exempt the perpetrator from criminal responsibility for that victim's killing[30] Even the victim's 'express and earnest request' does not relieve the defendant from criminal responsibility, but only results in a mitigation of punishment (sec. 216 StGB).[31] Consequently, voluntary active euthanasia, that is, a direct act of killing, done with the consent of the victim and intended to end his

23 BGHSt 10, 291 (292); Bohlander (n 12) 182; Rengier (n 16) § 3 mn 6; Maurach, Schroeder and Maiwald (n 4) § 1 mn 10.

24 Wessels, Hettinger and Engländer (n 16) § 1 mn 2; see, also, Eser and Sternberg-Lieben (n 16) mn 14. German law thus unequivocally opposes the idea of 'life unworthy of life', Rengier (n 16) § 3 mn 6, which laid the foundation for the NS-euthanasia program, that is, the systemic killing of mentally and physically disabled persons.

25 BGHSt 10, 5; BGHSt 31, 348 (351); BGH Neue Zeitschrift für Strafrecht [hereinafter: NStZ] 2008, 393 394; Bohlander (n 12) 182; Wessels, Hettinger and Engländer (n 16) § 1 mn 12; Schneider (n 16) 13; Eser and Sternberg-Lieben (n 16) 15; U. Neumann 'Vorbemerkungen zu § 211' in U. Kindhäuser, U. Neumann and H.-U. Paeffgen (eds) *Nomos Kommentar – Strafgesetzbuch* (5th edn, Nomos 2017) 14–15.

26 Schneider (n 16) mn 13; Neumann (n 25) mn 14; Wessels, Hettinger and Engländer (n 16) § 1 mn 13; cf., also, BGH NStZ 2008, 393 394.

27 BGHSt 10, 291 (293); BGHSt 13, 21 (24); Schneider (n 16) mn 13; Murmann (n 12) § 21 mn 15a; Neumann (n 25) mn 14.

28 Maurach, Schroeder and Maiwald (n 4) § 1 mn 12; Wessels, Hettinger and Engländer (n 16) § 1 mn 21; Rengier (n 16) § 3 mn 7. In more detail on the discussion with a particular view on alternative concepts (cardiac death / cortical death) Neumann (n 25) mn 17 ff.

29 § 3(2) No. 2 des Gesetzes über die Spende, Entnahme und Übertragung von Organen und Geweben (Transplantationsgesetz – Transplantation Statute).

30 The following section is based on K. Ambos and S. Bock, 'Germany' in A. Reed and M. Bohlander (eds) *Consent – Domestic and Comparative Perspectives* (Routledge 2017) 262, 270–71.

31 A rather innovative approach to take into account the particularities of interfamilial mercy killings was adopted by the Amtsgericht [*Municipal Court*] Köln, Strafverteidiger 2015, 572. The Court argued that the defendant who was found guilty of killing his beloved, but fatally ill, father on his request, suffered so severely from the consequences of his action, that the imposition of a penalty would be clearly inappropriate and ordered a discharge based on sec. 60 StGB, see, also, Ambos and Bock (n 30) 271.

suffering, is a criminal offence.[32] Assistance in an autonomous act of suicide, to the contrary, does not entail criminal liability.[33]

Given the advances in intensive-care medicine and life-prolonging measures, however, the general prohibition on euthanasia is subject to several exceptions: palliative care, in particular medical treatment to reduce pain, which has the side effect of speeding the patient's death (indirect euthanasia), is considered permissible, because the primary intention of the defendant is not to kill, but to comfort the patient.[34] Moreover, the Federal Supreme Court held in a fundamental ruling, that under certain circumstances even passive euthanasia by omission or active withdrawal of medical treatment can be justified.[35] The Court's reasoning is based on the notion that medical treatment against the victim's will constitutes physical assault in terms of sec. 223 StGB.[36] The patient therefore has the right to refuse medical treatment in the first place, which implies that he also has the right to insist on the withdrawal of life-prolonging measures. Whether his wish for non-treatment is implemented by mere omission or a positive act like switching off a life-support machine or disconnecting a feeding tube is deemed irrelevant.[37] In both cases, the defendant is relieved from criminal responsibility if the following three requirements are fulfilled:

- The patient suffers from a life-threating disease, which, if untreated, results in death;
- The defendant withholds, withdraws or restricts medical treatment associated with this disease;
- The defendant acts with the (presumed) will of the victim.[38]

The case law's approach towards passive and indirect euthanasia is convincing insofar as it respects the patient's right to self-determination at the end of his life. From a doctrinal perspective this approach is however hard to reconcile with sec. 216 StGB and its underlying principle that consent is not a full defence to homicide offences.[39]

Homicide by omission / omission to effect an easy rescue

As a rule,[40] all homicide offences can be committed by omission. According to sec. 13 StGB, whosoever 'fails to avert a result which is an element of a criminal provision shall only be liable under this law if he is responsible under law to ensure that the result does not

32 Schneider (n 16) mn 100; Wessels, Hettinger and Engländer (n 16) § 1 mn 28; Eser and Sternberg-Lieben (n 16) mn 24; see also BGH NJW 1987, 1092; BGHSt 55, 191.

33 See for more detail Ambos and Bock (n 30) 270 and the sources cited there. Note, however, that sec. 217 StGB penalises the commercial promotion of suicide. In more detail on this very controversial provision: T. Weigend and E. Köln, '§ 217 StGB – Bemerkungen zur Auslegung eines zweifelhaften Tatbestandes' *Zeitschrift für Internationale Strafrechtsdogmatik* 2017, 682.

34 See BGHSt 42, 301 (305); BGHSt 46, 279 (284–285); Bohlander (n 12) 183; Wessels, Hettinger and Engländer (n 16) § 1 mn 31–33; Murmann (n 12) § 21 mn 77, 78.

35 BGHSt 55, 191.

36 See Ambos and Bock (n 30) 274–75 and the sources cited there.

37 BGHSt 55, 191 (202).

38 Summary based on Rengier (n 16) § 7 mn 7b. In practice, the determination of the hypothetical will of the patient can be very difficult, in particular, if he has not made a formal living will, see in detail Eser and Sternberg-Lieben (n 16) mn 28b-28h.

39 In more detail: Schneider (n 16) mn 106–30; see also Eser and Sternberg-Lieben (n 16) mn 28a; Rengier (n 16) § 7 mn 8; Murmann (n 12) § 21 mn 78–79.

40 It is, however, controversial if all qualifying elements of sec. 211 StGB can be committed by omission. According to the BGH, killing by means that pose a danger to the public, for example,

occur, and if the omission is equivalent to the realisation of the statutory elements of the offence through a positive act'. The core element of this constructive[41] or derivative[42] omission liability (*unechte Unterlassungdelikte*) is the existence of a duty to act. German doctrine refers to two different sets of obligations as a basis for such a duty:[43] on the one hand, it is imposed upon persons with a special responsibility over certain sources of danger, for example, dangerous products or industrial plants, which entails a duty to secure *and* supervise them (*Überwachungs- / Sicherungspflicht*); they are 'supervisor guarantors'. On the other hand, it is imposed on persons who, because of their special protective position with regard to certain legal interests, for example, parents with regard to their children, have a protective duty towards them (*Schutz- / Obhutspflicht*); they are 'protector guarantors'.[44] The details are very controversial.[45]

If the defendant was under no special obligation to prevent the death of the victim in terms of sec. 13 StGB, his inaction may still give rise to liability for a failure to rescue (*unterlassene Hilfeleistung*). German law recognises a general duty to aid[46] and failure to render necessary assistance is a punishable offence.[47] Notably, the relevant sec. 323c StGB applies to all kind of accidents or common dangers that threaten the personal rights of one or more persons or important property values.[48] It is not limited to the prevention of death or in any other way linked to homicide offences. Nevertheless, the Supreme Court argues that even an autonomous suicide attempt qualifies as accident in terms of sec. 323c StGB[49] and thus turns the non-prevention of suicide into a punishable offence.[50] Yet, this view is hardly compatible with the suicidal person's right to self-determination.[51]

requires a positive act. It is not sufficient if the defendant merely takes advantage of an already existing, dangerous situation, BGH NStZ 2010, 87.

41 Dubber and Hörnle (n 3) 207.

42 Bohlander (n 12) 40.

43 This twofold approach goes back to A. Kaufmann, *Die Dogmatik der Unterlassungsdelikte* (1959 Schwartz) 283.

44 For an overview on the main categories of duties to act see Bohlander (n 12) 42 ff.

45 Cf. C. Roxin, *Strafrecht Allgemeiner Teil, Band 2: Besondere Erscheinungsformen der Straftat* (C. H. Beck 2003) § 32 mn. 17 ff.; G. Freund, '§ 13 – Begehung durch Unterlassen' in B. von Heintschel-Heinegg (ed.) *Münchener Kommentar zum Strafgesetzbuch, Band 1, §§ 1–37* (3rd edn, C.H. Beck Verlag 2017) mn 105 ff.; K. Gaede '§ 13 – Begehung durch Unterlassen' in U. Kindhäuser, U. Neumann and H.-U. Paeffgen (eds) *Nomos Kommentar – Strafgesetzbuch* (5th edn, Nomos 2017) mn 38 ff. and the sources cited therein.

46 Dubber and Hörnle (n 3) 207; R. Maurach, F.C. Schroeder and M. Maiwald, *Strafrecht Besonderer Teil. Teilband 2: Straftaten gegen Gemeinschaftswerte* (10th edn, C.F. Müller 2012) § 55 mn. 2, 14; G. Freund, '§ 323c – Unterlassene Hilfeleistung' in R. Hefendehl and O. Hohmann (eds) *Münchener Kommentar zum Strafgesetzbuch, Band 5, §§ 263–358* (2nd edn, C.H. Beck Verlag 2014) mn 1.

47 Sec. 323c(1) StGB provides: 'Whosoever does not render assistance during accidents or a common danger or emergency although it is necessary and can be expected of him under the circumstances, particularly if it is possible without substantial danger to himself and without violation of other important duties shall be liable to imprisonment not exceeding one year or a fine.'

48 Maurach, Schroeder and Maiwald (n 46) § 55 mn 14; Freund (n 46) § 323c mn 18.

49 BGHSt 6, 147; BGHSt 13, 162; BGHSt 32, 367 (375).

50 On the non-criminalisation of assistance in suicide see text accompanying n 33.

51 cf. Maurach, Schroeder and Maiwald (n 46) § 55 mn 15; Freund (n 46) § 323c mn 18; D. Sternberg-Lieben and B. Hecker, '§ 323c – Unterlassene Hilfeleistung' in A. Schönke and H. Schröder (eds) *Strafgesetzbuch – Kommentar* (29th edn, C.H. Beck 2014) mn 8.

Intentional homicide offences

Voluntary manslaughter

The *actus reus* of voluntary manslaughter is the killing of a human being. Sec. 212 StGB thus refers to any act that causes the death of another person. Determining causality requires, first, the establishing of a naturalistic connection between the result of a crime and a wilful action.[52] In this vein, an action A is considered to be causal for result R, when R would not have occurred without A (A as a *conditio sine qua non*).[53] On a second level, the broadness of this approach must be adjusted by normative considerations. According to the prevailing theory of objective imputation (*Lehre von der objektiven Zurechung)*, a result can only be attributed to the defendant, if his conduct has created a wrongful risk and this risk has found its realisation in the harmful result.[54]

The *mens rea* of sec. 212 StGB requires proof of the defendant's intention to kill (cf. sec. 15 StGB). The prevailing view defines intention as the will to fulfil all objective elements of an offence definition in the knowledge of these elements.[55] For all homicide offences, *dolus eventualis* is sufficient.[56] In its established case law, the Supreme Court holds that the defendant acts intentionally:

> … when he recognizes the occurrence of the result in the definition of the crime as possible and not entirely unlikely, and therefore agrees with it in such a way that he accepts and condones the realization of the definition or at least comes to terms with it for the sake of the objective which he seeks, even if the occurrence of the result is in itself not desired by him.[57]

The necessary volitional element (acceptance) is missing, if the defendant is aware of the risk he has created but is confident that it will not materialise.[58] In practice, the demarcation line between *dolus eventualis* and such a 'conscious'[59] or 'advertent'[60] negligence is often hard to draw. The courts tend to put a particular emphasis on the objective dangerousness of the

52 cf. C. Roxin, *Strafrecht Allgemeiner Teil. Band I: Grundlagen. Der Aufbau der Verbrechenslehre* (4th edn, C.H. Beck 2006) § 11 mn. 3–4, 7; J. Eisele, 'Vorbemerkungen zu den §§ 13 ff.' in A. Schönke and H. Schröder (eds) *Strafgesetzbuch – Kommentar* (29th edn, C.H. Beck 2014) mn 71–2.

53 BGHSt 1, 332; BGHSt 7, 112 (114); BGHSt 31, 96 (98); Eisele (n 52) mn 73a; K. Kühl, *Strafrecht Allgemeiner Teil* (8th edn, 2017 Verlag Franz Vahlen) § 4 mn 9.

54 Dubber and Hörnle (n 3) 301. The details are very controversial, cf. Roxin (n 52) § 11 mn 20 ff., 46 ff.; Eisele (n 52) mn 77 ff., 93 ff.; Kühl (n 53) § 4 mn 43 ff. and the sources cited there. Overview on core problems in Bohlander (n 12) 48 ff.

55 See Weigend (n 10) 361; Murmann (n 12) § 24 mn 7; Kühl (n 53) § 5 mn 6.

56 The general *mens rea* of homicide offences (intent) must not be confused with the specific intent required by some variants of sec. 211 StGB (e.g., killing in order to cover up another offence), see text accompanying n 101.

57 BGHSt 36, 1 (9), English translation by Dubber and Hörnle (n 3) 569; see also BGHSt 7, 363, English translation by Dubber and Hörnle (n 3) 229; BGH NStZ 1994, 584; BGH NStZ 2015, 266; for more details on the controversial discussion see Roxin (n 52) § 12 mn 21 ff. and the sources cited therein.

58 BGHSt 36, 1 (9–10), English translation by Dubber and Hörnle (n 3) 569; BGH NStZ 2009, 91; Murmann (n 12) § 24 mn 19; Kühl (n 53) § 4 mn 75 ff.

59 Weigend (n 10) 262; Dubber and Hörnle (n 3) 368.

60 Bohlander (n 12) 67.

conduct.[61] In homicide cases, however, the Supreme Court assumes that there is a special threshold to kill[62] and demands a particular thorough proof of the defendant's *mens rea.* [63]

Murder

Sec. 211 StGB contains two different types of qualifying factors that turn a killing from voluntary manslaughter into murder: objective, deed-focused circumstances which describe killings by particular reprehensible means (killing by stealth, cruelly or by means that pose a danger to the public) and subjective, perpetrator-focused circumstances which refer to killings out of base motives (killing for pleasure or sexual gratification, out of greed or otherwise base motives, in order to facilitate or to cover up another offence).[64]

Objective qualifying factors

A person is killed by stealth, if the offender intentionally exploits the victim's absence of suspicion and his consequent defencelessness.[65] It is required, first, that the victim is not expecting an attack by the defendant on his life.[66] If V is unsuspecting when he falls asleep, i.e., if he goes to sleep in the confidence that nothing will harm him, he takes this state of mind with him into the sleep.[67] Thus, the killing of a sleeping and therefore particularly defenceless victim is the prime example for murder by stealth.[68] Arguably, the case is different for unconscious victims. Unconsciousness is an unnatural condition which unexpectedly overcomes the victim without him being able to prevent it; he thus cannot take his unexpecting state with him.[69] Second, the victim must be defenceless, that is, he must be unable to defend himself, or, at least, his readiness and ability to defend himself must be considerably reduced.[70] The defencelessness must result from the absence of suspicion.

61 cf. BGH NStZ 2002, 314; BGH NStZ 2009, 91; BGH NStZ 2012, 443 444; BGH Neue Zeitschrift für Strafrecht – Rechtsprechungsreport [hereinafter: NStZ-RR] 2014, 371, 372.

62 BGH NStZ 2002, 314, 315; BGH NStZ 2009, 91; BGH NStZ 2010, 571, 572.

63 BGHSt 57, 183, 189.

64 Du Bois-Pedain (n 10) 67; Weigend (n 10) 277; Dubber and Hörnle (n 3) 539; Murmann (n 12) § 21 mn 22; Rengier (n 16) § 4 mn 6–7.

65 BGHSt 23, 119 (120), English translation by Dubber and Hörnle (n 3) 535; BGH NStZ 1984, 261; BGH NStZ 2008, 273, 274; Bohlander (n 12) 190; H. Schneider, '§ 211 – Mord' in G.M. Sander (ed.) *Münchener Kommentar zum Strafgesetzbuch, Band 4, §§ 185–262 StGB* (3rd edn, C. H. Beck 2017) mn 150; Maurach, Schroeder and Maiwald (n 4) § 2 mn 43.

66 BGHSt 23, 119 (120), English translation by Dubber and Hörnle (n 3) 536; BGH NStZ 2005, 688; BGH NStZ 2006, 338, 339; A. Eser and D. Sternberg-Lieben, '§ 211 – Mord' in A. Schönke and H. Schröder (eds) *Strafgesetzbuch – Kommentar* (29th edn, C.H. Beck Verlag 2014) mn 24; Murmann (n 12) § 21 mn 34. On the contested question whether small children can be 'unsuspecting' see text accompanying n 127.

67 BGHSt 23, 119, 120, English translation by Dubber and Hörnle (n 3) 536; BGH NStZ 2007, 523 524; BGH NStZ 2006, 338, 339; Wessels, Hettinger and Engländer (n 16) § 2 mn 139; Rengier (n 16) § 4 mn 29.

68 BGHSt 23, 119, 120, English translation by Dubber and Hörnle (n 3) 536; cf., also, Eser and Sternberg-Lieben (n 66) mn 24; Schneider (n 65) mn 144; Murmann (n 12) § 21 mn 39; for a different view see U. Neumann and F. Saliger '§ 211 StGB – Mord' in U. Kindhäuser, U. Neumann and H.U. Paeffgen (eds) *Nomos Kommentar – Strafgesetzbuch* (5th edn, Nomos 2017) mn 57.

69 BGHSt 23, 119, 121, English translation by Dubber and Hörnle (n 3) 536; Rengier (n 16) § 4 mn 29a; Maurach, Schroeder and Maiwald (n 4) § 2 mn 44; differentiating Neumann and Saliger (n 68) mn 57.

70 BGH *Goltdammer's Archiv für Strafrecht* 1971, 113; BGH NStZ 1999, 506, 507; Schneider (n 65) mn 175; Wessels, Hettinger and Engländer (n 16) § 2 mn 131.

The killing of a person, who is defenceless (e.g., because she is tied to a chair) but not unexpecting, is not sufficient.[71] In subjective terms, the Supreme Court requires that the offender has a hostile intention.[72] Murder by stealth thus is excluded if D kills V for V's (alleged) own good.[73] This can be the case if D wants to end the suffering of the terminally ill V[74] or to spare him from poverty and disgrace.[75]

The perpetrator acts cruelly, if he – out of an unempathetic and merciless attitude – causes the victim more physical or mental suffering than necessary to kill him.[76] Take the case of a mother letting her baby starve to death[77] or that of a man who burns his pregnant girlfriend alive to escape the responsibilities of fatherhood.[78] Moreover, the Supreme Court is of the view that the cruelty-element must not necessarily be in the act of killing, but can also be satisfied in the preparation stage. Imagine that D announces to V that he is going to kill him and forces V to watch him preparing the execution before he finally shoots him in the head. Although the actual method of killing is painless, D caused great emotional suffering to V by striking fear and terror into him and thus killed him cruelly.[79]

'Means that pose a danger to the public' are means that when used are 'no longer controllable and pose[s] a danger to a larger, indeterminate group of people apart from the intended victim'.[80] In the classical textbook examples, D kills V by setting an apartment building on fire[81] or by launching a bomb in a popular restaurant.[82]

Subjective qualifying factors

A person kills out of pleasure, if his purpose is 'killing for killing's sake'[83], that is, his main motivation is to see another person die. This is in particular the case if the perpetrator enjoys the destruction of a human life.[84] Killing out of pleasure requires direct intent to cause the death of the victim; *dolus eventualis* is not sufficient.[85]

71 Rengier (n 16) § 4 mn 31; Wessels, Hettinger and Engländer (n 16) § 2 mn 137; Eser and Sternberg-Lieben (n 66) mn 24b.
72 BGHSt 9, 385; BGHSt 11, 139, 143; BGH NStZ 2008, 93, 94; for a critic see Schneider (n 65) mn 194.
73 BGHSt 9, 385; Eser and Sternberg-Lieben (n 66) mn 25b; see, also, Schneider (n 65) mn 191.
74 cf. BGHSt 37, 376, 377; BGH NStZ 2008, 93, 94; Bohlander (n 12) 190; Maurach, Schroeder and Maiwald (n 4) § 2 mn 45.
75 BGHSt 9, 385 (in a case of 'murder-suicide'); Eser and Sternberg-Lieben (n 66) mn 25b; Murmann (n 12) § 21 mn 44.
76 BGH NStZ 2008, 29, translation based on Bohlander (n 12) 190; Murmann (n 12) § 21 mn 31; Eser and Sternberg-Lieben (n 66) mn 27.
77 BGH NStZ-RR 2009, 173; Maurach, Schroeder and Maiwald (n 4) § 2 mn 47; Schneider (n 65) mn 131; see, also, BGH NStZ 2007, 402.
78 BGH NStZ 2017, 218; cf., also, Rengier (n 16) § 4 mn 44a; Neumann and Saliger (n 68) mn 75.
79 BGH NJW 1951, 666, 667; concurring Bohlander (n 12) 191; Eser and Sternberg-Lieben (n 66) mn 27; a different view take Murmann (n 12) § 21 mn 32 and Schneider (n 65) mn 137.
80 BGHSt 38, 353, 354; BGH NStZ 2006, 167, 168, translation according to Bohlander (n 12) 191; see also, Wessels, Hettinger and Engländer (n 16) § 2 mn 121; Schneider (n 65) 121.
81 BGH NJW 1985, 1477; Eser and Sternberg-Lieben (n 66) mn 29; Rengier (n 16) § 4 mn. 46a.
82 cf. Bohlander (n 12) 191; Murmann (n 12) § 21 mn 28; Wessels, Hettinger and Engländer (n 16) § 2 mn 121.
83 Bohlander (n 12) 190.
84 BGHSt 34, 59, 61; BGHSt 47, 128, 133; BGH NStZ 2007, 522, 533; Schneider (n 65) mn 49; Rengier (n 16) § 4 mn 11.
85 BGHSt 47, 128, 133; BGH NStZ 2007, 522, 523; Eser and Sternberg-Lieben (n 66) mn 15; Neumann and Saliger (n 68) mn 9.

A 'killing for sexual gratification' exists if the act of killing as such gives the perpetrator sexual gratification, if the defendant kills the victim in order to commit necrophiliac acts on the corpus or if during the commission of a rape the perpetrator accepts and condones that the victim dies (*dolus eventualis* with regard to V's death).[86] In any case, the defendant must kill the object of his sexual desire. If D kills V because he wants to rape V's wife, he does not kill V for sexual gratification but in order to facilitate another offence (rape).[87]

Greed means 'a striving for material goods or advantages which in its lack of restraint and consideration far exceeds the extent that is tolerable and which as a rule is driven by uninhibited compulsive selfishness.'[88] Classical examples are the hired contract killer who kills for money[89] or the hold-up murderer who wants to take away a valuable object belonging to the victim.[90] According to the jurisprudence, the greed-element is also fulfilled if the defendant kills to free himself from a debt or a duty of maintenance.[91]

Murder 'out of otherwise base motives' is a kind of catch-all-provision[92] to cover all instances in which the motivation of the perpetrator, 'according to the moral views of society, is an expression of deepest moral depravity and utterly deplorable'.[93] As sec. 211 StGB provides for a mandatory life sentence[94], this clause must be interpreted restrictively. It is not fulfilled if the offender's motivation is understandable in some way.[95] Jealousy, for example, is a base motive, if the defendant kills his former girlfriend in the belief that if he cannot have her, than no one will.[96] Imagine, to the contrary, that D caught his wife *in flagrante* with his best friend, immediately lost self-control and killed them both. His reaction is (albeit legally condemnable) emotionally comprehensible und thus not *utterly* reproachable.[97] It would be disproportionate to hold him liable for murder. Clear examples of base motives are racism[98] or unstrained selfishness.[99]

The last variant requires the specific intent (*dolus directus* of first degree / *Absicht*) to facilitate[100] or cover up a crime. With regard to the actual killing, however, *dolus eventualis*

86 BGHSt 19, 101, 105, translation based on Bohlander (n 12) 190; Schneider (n 65) mn 55; Maurach, Schroeder and Maiwald (n 4) § 2 mn 32.
87 Rengier (n 16) § 4 mn 12; Murmann (n 12) § 21 mn 56; Eser and Sternberg-Lieben (n 66) mn 16; cf., also, BGHSt 50, 80, 87.
88 BGH NJW 1993, 1164, English translation according to Dubber and Hörnle (n 3) 535; Maurach, Schroeder and Maiwald (n 4) § 2 mn 33; Schneider (n 65) mn 59.
89 BGH NStZ 2006, 34, 35; Eser and Sternberg-Lieben (n 66) mn 17; Neumann and Saliger (n 68) mn 13; Bohlander (n 12) 190.
90 BGH NJW 1993, 1664, 1665; BGH NStZ 2001, 194, 195; Schneider (n 65) mn 62; Maurach, Schroeder and Maiwald (n 4) § 2 mn 33.
91 BGH NJW 1993, 1164, English translation by Dubber and Hörnle (n 3) 534; in more detail on the discussion Eser and Sternberg-Lieben (n 66) mn 17.
92 Schneider (n 65) mn 70; Maurach, Schroeder and Maiwald (n 4) § 2 mn 37.
93 BGHSt 47, 128, 130, translation according to Bohlander (n 12) 190; Wessels, Hettinger and Engländer (n 16) § 2 mn 112; Eser and Sternberg-Lieben (n 66) mn 18.
94 See, also, text accompanying n 166.
95 BGH NStZ 2015, 690, 692; Rengier (n 16) § 4 mn 17; Neumann and Saliger (n 68) mn 27; cf., also, BGH NStZ 2002, 368.
96 BGHSt 3, 180.
97 cf. Rengier (n 16) § 4 mn 21; also BGH NStZ 1984, 261.
98 BGHSt 18, 37; BGH NStZ 1994, 124; BGH NStZ 2004, 89; Wessels, Hettinger and Engländer (n 16) § 2 mn 114.
99 cf. BGHSt 2, 60 (D killed V because she had refused to have sexual intercourse with him); BGHSt 3, 133 (killing one's spouse to start a new life with a new partner); BGH NStZ 1985, 454 (killing a person to fake one's own dead).
100 See the example above at n 87.

is sufficient.[101] In a prominent case, D killed X. To cover his tracks D set X's flat on fire. He knew that V was sleeping in the upper floor, foresaw the risk that V might die in the fire, but decided nevertheless to act as described. V indeed died and D was convicted for murder because he acted with the aim of covering up that he has killed X. That V's death was only a (accepted) by-product and not D's main purpose was considered irrelevant.[102] Nor is it necessary that D is motivated by avoiding punitive sanctions. Sec. 211 is also fulfilled if D kills V out of fear for social sanctions like being fired from work, getting divorced, etc.[103]

Killing on request of the victim

Although consent of the victim is not a full defence to homicide offences,[104] the defendant receives a considerably lesser punishment,[105] if he is induced to kill by the express and earnest request of the victim. The respective sec. 216 requires:[106]

- The victim requests to die. A request is more than mere consent.[107] The victim must exert psychological influence on the defendant and induce him to kill.[108]
- The request is express, that is unambiguous. An unequivocal gesture can be sufficient.[109]
- The request is earnest, which presupposes a free, fully informed and reflected decision.[110]
- The defendant is induced by the request. The victim's wish to die must be his guiding motive, the driving force behind his action.[111]

Negligent homicide offences

Where the defendant (D) lacks intention to kill,[112] he can be held liable for negligent manslaughter in terms of sec. 222 StGB under the following conditions:[113]

- D caused the death of another person.[114]

101 Schneider (n 65) mn 237 240; Neumann and Saliger (n 68) mn 101; Rengier (n 16) § 4 mn 57.
102 BGHSt 41, 358.
103 cf. BGHSt 41, 8; BGH NStZ 1999, 615; Wessels, Hettinger and Engländer (n 16) § 2 mn 145; a different view take Schneider (n 65) mn 105 and Rengier (n 16) § 4 mn 55 f.
104 See text accompanying n 30.
105 See text accompanying n 177.
106 cf. also Ambos and Bock (n 30) 272.
107 On consent see Ambos and Bock (n 30) 263 ff.
108 BGH NJW 2005, 1876, 1879; A. Eser and D. Sternberg-Lieben, '§ 216 – Tötung auf Verlangen' in A. Schönke and H. Schröder (eds) *Strafgesetzbuch – Kommentar* (29th edn, C.H. Beck Verlag 2014) mn 5.
109 Eser and Sternberg-Lieben (n 108) mn 7; Murmann (n 12) § 21 mn 84; Wessels, Hettinger and Engländer (n 16) § 2 mn 176; see also BGH NJW 1987, 1092.
110 BGH NStZ 2011, 340; BGH NStZ 2012, 85.
111 BGH 2005, 1876 (1879); Eser and Sternberg-Lieben (n 108) mn 9; Murmann (n 12) § 21 mn 84.
112 On the demarcation between intent and negligence see text accompanying n 57 ff.
113 Overview on the general requirements of negligence liability in Roxin (n 52) § 24 mn 3; R. Rengier, *Strafrecht Allgemeiner Teil* (9th edn, C.H. Beck 2017) § 52 mn 11 ff.; Kühl (n 53) § 17 mn 11 ff.
114 On causality and normative attribution see text accompanying n 52.

- D violated a duty of care. The details are very controversial, but it is commonly accepted that the respective standard of care is closely linked to the concept of foreseeability. If it is foreseeable that a certain conduct results in harm, the actor must do everything necessary to avoid the actual occurrence of harm.[115] In line with the – already mentioned – theory of objective imputation[116], however, a person cannot be held liable if he has merely created a socially adequate or accepted risk. Thus, the mere fact that car driving has immanent risks, including the one of fatal accidents is as such not sufficient to establish negligence.[117]
- Given his individual capacities, D could have foreseen and avoided that his action results in the death of V.[118]

Sec. 222 is mainly applied in the area of traffic accidents and medical treatments with fatal outcome.[119]

Result-qualified homicide offences

All result-qualified homicide offences presuppose that the death of the victim is immediately or directly caused by the commission of the basic offence (e.g., infliction of bodily harm, rape, stalking etc.).[120] The latter must be committed intentionally; with regard to the ulterior result of death negligence is – as a rule – a minimum requirement (sec. 18 StGB). In some instances (e.g., robbery causing death, sec. 251 StGB) the law requires gross negligence with regard to the deadly result, that is, a severe violation of a duty to care that shows disregard of or indifference towards the rights of others.[121]

Generally speaking, the nexus-requirement is fulfilled, if the death is the result of the particular risk inherent to the basic offence conduct.[122] The details, however, are far from clear. In a prominent case, D hit V with a gun. Accidently, a shot went off and killed V. The Supreme Court upheld the conviction for infliction of bodily harm causing death arguing that V's death was the direct consequence of D's dangerous conduct.[123] Parts of the literature, to the contrary, take the view that sec. 227 StGB should be limited to instances where the victim dies as a result of the injuries intentionally caused by the defendant, i.e., the underlying acts have been per se lethal (so-called '*Letalitätstheorie*').[124] Likewise problematic

115 Weigend (n 10) 263; G. Duttge, '§ 15 StGB – vorsätzliches und fahrlässiges Handeln' in B. von Heintschel-Heinegg (ed.) *Münchener Kommentar zum Strafgesetzbuch, Band 1, §§ 1–37* (3rd edn, C.H. Beck Verlag 2017) mn 107 ff.; see, also, Bohlander (n 12) 56; Kühl (n 53) § 17 mn 19; Maurach, Schroeder and Maiwald (n 4) § 3 mn 2.

116 See text accompanying n 54.

117 cf. Bohlander (n 12) 56; Murmann (n 12) § 30 mn 17; in more detail Duttge (n 115) mn 135 ff.

118 cf. Weigend (n 10) 263; Rengier (n 113) § 52 mn 83; Kühl (n 53) § 17 mn 89 ff.

119 cf. Maurach, Schroeder and Maiwald (n 4) § 3 mn 9; D. Sternberg-Lieben and F. Schuster, '§ 15 StGB – Vorsätzliches und fahrlässiges Handeln' in A. Schönke and H. Schröder (eds) *Strafgesetzbuch – Kommentar* (29th edn, C.H. Beck 2014) mn 208 ff. and the sources cited there.

120 cf. BGHSt 31, 96 (98); BGH NStZ 1997, 341; BGH NStZ 2008, 686, 687.

121 Rengier (n 113) § 52 mn 9; Sternberg-Lieben and Schuster (n 119) mn 205.

122 cf., e.g., BGHSt 31, 96; B. Hardtung, '§ 227 StGB – Körperverletzung mit Todesfolge' in W. Joecks and K. Miebach (eds) *Münchener Kommentar zum Strafgesetzbuch Band 4, §§ 185–262 StGB* (3rd edn C.H. Beck 2017) mn 9 f.; Rengier (n 16) § 16 mn 5 ff.; Bohlander (n 12) 33.

123 BGHSt 14, 110.

124 W. Stree and D. Sternberg-Lieben, '§ 227 StGB – Körperverletzung mit Todesfolge' in A. Schönke and H. Schröder (eds) *Strafgesetzbuch – Kommentar* (29th edn, C.H. Beck 2014) mn 5; Roxin (n 52) § 10 mn 115 f.; in more detail on the discussion Hardtung (n 122) mn 16.

are cases where the victim dies when fleeing from mistreatment. In recent decisions, the Supreme Court tends to argue that the victim's intervention does not break the chain between the basic offence and the deadly result, if it is an understandable and foreseeable reaction to the defendant's conduct.[125]

Infanticide / child destruction

Until 1998, sec. 217 StGB provided for a sentencing mitigation for mothers killing their children within or shortly after the act of birth. Under the current law, the emotional stress situation of giving birth may justify a conviction for a less serious case of voluntary manslaughter in terms of sec. 213 StGB.[126]

As there are no special rules, the general homicide offences also apply to infanticide. Notably, the prevailing view holds that children under the age of three – as a rule – cannot be killed by stealth.[127] As they have not yet developed the ability to distrust others, they cannot be 'unsuspecting' or deceived in an expectation that nobody will harm them.[128] However, it is sufficient if the defendant exploits the absence of suspicion of a third person willing to protect the young child.[129] In a controversial case, the sickly new-born V is monitored 24/7 by his parents. When his father F went to bed, his mother D took over the night watch during which she killed the crying V out of exhaustion. D was convicted for murder by stealth because she was said to have exploited F's absence of suspicion who had not expected that D would attack V.[130] Critics argue that this interpretation goes too far and ignores that D has merely taken advantage of F's absence.[131]

Abortion and homicide

In a fundamental judgment, the Constitutional Court held that the German Basic Law[132] requires the legislator to protect unborn children by means of criminal law. As a matter of principle, every pregnant woman is obliged to carry her child to birth and abortion must be marked as legal wrong. Only under very exceptional circumstances can the rights and interests of the pregnant women outweigh the right to life of the unborn and allow for a decriminalisation of abortion.[133]

The implementation of these constitutional guidelines has led to a quite complex set of criminal provisions. According to sec. 218(1) StGB, a person who terminates a pregnancy is liable to imprisonment of not more than three years or a fine. The offence can be committed

125 BGHSt 48, 34, 38–39; BGH NJW 1992, 1709; BGH NStZ 2008, 278; a different view was taken in BGH NJW 1971, 152; in more detail on the discussion Rengier (n 16) § 16 mn 17 ff.
126 See text accompanying n 163.
127 On the meaning of 'killing by stealth' see text accompanying n 65.
128 BGHSt 4, 11, 12; BGH NStZ 2006, 338, 339; BGH NStZ 2013, 158 (159); Eser and Sternberg-Lieben (n 66) mn 25c; Maurach, Schroeder and Maiwald (n 4) § 2 mn 44.
129 BGH NStZ 2006, 338, 339; BGH NStZ 2013, 158, 159; Wessels, Hettinger and Engländer (n 16) § 2 mn 140; Eser and Sternberg-Lieben (n 66) mn 25c.
130 BGH NStZ 2013, 158.
131 cf. Rengier (n 16) § 4 mn 30c and the sources cited therein.
132 The Court based its ruling on Art. 2(2) of the German Basic Law (*Grundgesetz*) which grants every person the right to life and physical integrity. English translation of the German Basic Law available at <www.gesetze-im-internet.de/englisch_gg/englisch_gg.html#p0025> accessed 11 June 2018.
133 BVerfG NJW 1993, 1751.

by the physician, who performs the abortion, other third persons and the pregnant woman[134] herself.[135] The latter, however, is privileged insofar as she benefits from a reduced sentencing range[136] and is exempted from attempt liability.[137] Notably, acts with effects preceding the conclusion of the nidation do not qualify as abortion. Sec. 218(1) StGB thus does not cover the taking of the 'morning-after pill' or the use of intrauterine devices.[138]

In balancing the child's right to life against the mother's right to self-determination, sec. 218a(1) StGB provides that the offence of abortion is not fulfilled, if:

1 the pregnant women requests the termination of the pregnancy and demonstrates to the physician that the she has received a special counselling for pregnant women in a situation of emergency or conflict;[139]
2 the termination of the pregnancy is performed by a physician; and
3 not more than twelve weeks have elapsed since conception.

In addition, a termination of pregnancy is justified, if it is necessary to avert a danger to the life or the physical or mental health of the pregnant women (medical indication) or if there are strong reasons to believe that the pregnancy was caused by rape or another sexual offence (criminological indication).[140] In any case, the physician performing the intervention must act with the consent of the pregnant women.[141]

As already explained, for delimiting abortion from homicide offences German doctrine focuses on the time when the effects of the act begin to manifest themselves.[142] If a person intentionally kills a pregnant woman and approvingly takes into account that this may result in the death of the unborn, he is guilty of voluntary manslaughter *and* abortion.[143] In case an improper abortion leads to the death of both, the embryo and the mother, the

134 As the abortion offence aims at the protection of the unborn child, consent of the pregnant women is – as a rule – no valid defence, see Ambos and Bock (n 30) 272 and the sources cited there.

135 A. Eser, '§ 218 StGB - Schwangerschaftsabbruch' in A. Schönke and H. Schröder (eds) *Strafgesetzbuch – Kommentar* (29th edn, C.H. Beck 2014) mn 28–32; W. Gropp, '§ 218 - Schwangerschaftsabbruch' in W. Joecks and K. Miebach (eds.) *Münchener Kommentar zum Strafgesetzbuch Band 4, §§ 185–262 StGB* (3rd edn, C.H. Beck 2017) mn 37–41; Ambos and Bock (n 30) 272.

136 Sec. 218 (3) StGB: imprisonment of not more than one year or a fine.

137 Sec. 218 (4) StGB.

138 Eser (n 135) mn 34; Ambos and Bock (n 30) 272.

139 The details of the counselling are laid down in sec. 219 StGB. In particular, it must 'be guided by effort to encourage the women to continue the pregnancy and to open her to the prospects of a life with the child'.

140 cf. in more detail W. Gropp, '§ 218a – Straflosigkeit des Schwangerschaftsabbruchs' in W. Joecks and K. Miebach (eds), *Münchener Kommentar zum Strafgesetzbuch Band 4, §§ 185–262 StGB* (3rd edn, C.H. Beck 2017) mn 41 ff; A. Eser, '§ 218a StGB – Straflosigkeit des Schwangerschaftsabbruchs' in A. Schönke and H. Schröder (eds) *Strafgesetzbuch – Kommentar* (29th edn, C.H. Beck 2014) mn 20 ff.

141 Eser (n 140) mn 61; cf. also Gropp (n 140) mn 20. Consent of the father of the unborn child is not required, Eser (n 140) mn 62. Terminating pregnancy against the will of the pregnant women is an especially serious case of abortion punishable by imprisonment from six month to five years, sec. 218 (2) StGB.

142 See text accompanying n 25.

143 BGH NStZ 1996, 276; Eser (n 135) mn 68; Gropp (n 135) mn 58.

defendant – depending on the circumstances of the case – can be held liable for intentional abortion and infliction of bodily harm causing death (sec. 227 StGB).[144]

Defences to homicide

Consent

Consent of the victim is not a full defence to homicide offences but will only mitigate punishment.[145]

Self-defence

The intentional killing of another person, however, is justified by self-defence if it is necessary to avert an imminent unlawful attack on oneself or another. Notably, the relevant sec. 32 StGB does not require the defensive action to be proportional, so that a balancing of the conflicting interests between the defender and the aggressor is not necessary. This means in particular, that sec. 32 StGB even allows for the use of deadly force for the protection of property if no other less intrusive defensive means are available.[146]

Necessity / duress

The case is different for necessity (sec. 34 StGB), the classical lesser evil defence which is essentially based on a proportionality test. The commission of the counter-act is only justified if the thereby protected interest substantially outweighs the violated interest. According to a fundamental principle of the German legal order, all lives are of equal value and no life prevails over another. A balancing of life against life is not possible – be it in quantitative (one life against hundreds) or qualitative (the life of an old man against the life of a newborn child) terms. Therefore, the prevailing view in German legal doctrine and jurisprudence assumes that necessity can never be a valid defence to homicide offences.[147] But if the person acts in order to avert an imminent danger to life, limb or freedom on himself, a relative or a person close to him, he is excused[148] under sec. 35 StGB on duress.[149]

Psychological disorders

Persons who suffer from psychological disorders[150] which make them unable to appreciate the wrongfulness of their conduct or to act accordingly cannot be blamed for having violated the law and are thus excused if they, for example, commit the crime of murder (sec. 20

144 BGH NJW 1978, 2040, 2042; Gropp (n 135) mn 58.
145 See text accompanying n 104.
146 For further details see K. Ambos and S. Bock, 'Germany' in A. Reed and M. Bohlander (eds) *General Defences in Criminal Law – Domestic and Comparative Perspectives* (Routledge 2014) 227–31 and the sources cited there.
147 Ambos and Bock (n 146) 234–35 with a particular view on battered women cases.
148 On the differentiation between justification (the act is lawful because the actor acted on the basis of a permissive norm) and excuses (the actor is not blamed for committing a wrong) Ambos and Bock (n 146) 227.
149 Ambos and Bock (n 146) 235–36.
150 Note, that alcohol intoxication is under certain circumstances regarded as a temporary mental disease, Ambos and Bock (n 146) 237.

StGB). Mental disorders that do not completely remove the cognitive or volitional capacities of a person may result in a mitigation of punishment (sec. 21 StGB).[151]

Provocation and otherwise less serious cases of voluntary manslaughter

Sec. 213 StGB recognises provocation as a partial defence to voluntary manslaughter.[152] The standard sentencing range of imprisonment of not less than five years is reduced to imprisonment from one to ten years if the defendant kills the victim out of justified anger.[153] This presupposes that the defendant was provoked to rage by a physical[154] or psychological[155] mistreatment or a (objectively)[156] serious insult. The provoking act can be directed against the defendant himself or a relative, e.g., the spouse or the same sex partner.[157] It must have been committed by the later victim; provocations by third persons do not suffice.[158] Moreover, there must be a motivational nexus between the provocation and the offence, that is, the killing must be committed because of and under the effect of the provocation.[159] Notably, sec. 213 StGB is excluded if the defendant has culpably caused the provocation in such a way that the provocation can be regarded as a proportional reaction to his previous behaviour.[160] This is for example the case, if the defendant had stalked his ex-girlfriend over a longer period, ignored her frequently expressed wish to be left alone and finally killed her in rage when she told him that he does not deserve her and that her new boyfriend is a better lover than he ever was.[161]

Sec. 213 StGB with its reduced sentencing range also applies to 'otherwise less serious cases of voluntary manslaughter'. This catch-all provision covers all cases in which a minimum sentence of five years (pursuant to sec. 212 StGB) would be overly harsh given the concrete circumstances of the offence and the diminished blameworthiness of the defendant.[162] Typical examples are the killing of a child within or shortly after birth in a situation of emotional stress[163] or killings in situations close to self-defence.[164] In some older

151 Ambos and Bock (n 146) 236.

152 See text accompanying n 12.

153 Wessels, Hettinger and Engländer (n 16) § 2 mn 194; Rengier (n 16) § 3 mn 14.

154 Schneider (n 12) mn 11.

155 BGH NJW 1995, 1910, 1911; A. Eser and D. Sternberg-Lieben, '§ 213 – Minder schwerer Fall des Totschlags' in A. Schönke and H. Schröder (eds) *Strafgesetzbuch – Kommentar* (29th edn, C. H. Beck Verlag 2014) mn 5.

156 BGH NStZ 1985, 216; BGH NStZ 1996, 33; BGH NStZ 2011, 339; Eser and Sternberg-Lieben (n 155) mn 5.

157 For a legal definition of 'relative' see sec. 11(1) No. 1 StGB.

158 Eser and Sternberg-Lieben (n 155) mn 6; Schneider (n 12) mn 24.

159 BGH NStZ 1995, 83; BGH NStZ-RR 2007, 200; BGH NStZ 2012, 691, 693; Maurach, Schroeder and Maiwald (n 4) § 2 mn 56; for a more restrictive reading of sec. 213 StGB Schneider (n 12) mn 33 (requiring a close temporal relation between the provocation and the killing).

160 See Schneider (n 12) mn 35 ff. and the sources cited there. See, also, BGH NStZ 1983, 554; BGH NStZ 1992, 588; BGH NStZ 2012, 691, 693.

161 BGH NStZ 2012, 691, 693.

162 BGH NStZ 1984, 118; Schneider (n 12) mn 45; Eser and Sternberg-Lieben (n 155) mn 13; Wessels, Hettinger and Engländer (n 16) § 2 mn 196.

163 cf. BGH NStZ-RR 2004, 80; Schneider (n 12) mn 46; Eser and Sternberg-Lieben (n 155) mn 15 ff; Wessels, Hettinger and Engländer (n 16) § 2 mn 196.

164 BGH NStZ-RR 2007, 194; BGH NStZ-RR 2013, 305, 306; Wessels, Hettinger and Engländer (n 16) § 2 mn 196; Eser and Sternberg-Lieben (n 155) mn 13a.

decisions, the courts tended to resort to sec. 213 StGB when the perpetrator acted in accordance with foreign cultural values and, e.g., killed his unfaithful wife to restore his honour.[165] Meanwhile, the prevailing view evaluates motives on the basis of the German value system.[166] Honour killings are characterised by a blatant disparity between felt provocation (violation of honour and reputation) and reaction (denying the victim the right to life). As a rule, they are treated as an aggravated form of homicide: murder out of base motives[167] in terms of sec. 211 StGB.[168]

Official authority – police/armed forces

If and under which circumstances police officers may resort to deadly force is regulated in the respective federal and state Police Laws. One of the broadest provisions can be found in sec. 54(2) of the Police Law of Baden-Württemberg (PolG-BW) which allows for (final) fatal shooting if this is necessary to avert an imminent danger of death or serious injury. If, however, a police officer oversteps his competences under public law, he may – according to the jurisprudence – still rely on criminal law defences.[169] Thus, even in absence of a provision like the one quoted, the killing of a hostage-taker by a police officer may be justified by defence-of-others.[170]

Superior orders

In (quasi-)military contexts, acting on superior orders might excuse the otherwise punishable[171] killing of other persons. According to sec. 5 of the Military Criminal Law (*Wehrstrafgesetzbuch*) a subordinate who commits a criminal offence pursuant to a superior order can be found guilty only if he realises that his conduct is unlawful or if it is manifestly unlawful. In a similar vein, sec. 3 of the German Code of Crimes against International Law (*Völkerstrafgesetzbuch – VStGB*) provides that a person who commits a war crime[172], e.g., the war crime of killing a person protected under international humanitarian law (sec. 8(1)

165 BGH NStZ 1982, 115; see also Maurach, Schroeder and Maiwald (n 4) § 2 mn 57.

166 BGH NStZ 1995, 79; BGH NStZ 2002, 369; BGH NStZ 2006, 284; overview on the discussion in Rengier (n 16) § 4 mn 22.

167 See text accompanying n 93.

168 cf. BGH NStZ 1995, 79; BGH NStZ-RR 2004, 361; Bohlander (n 12) 190; Maurach, Schroeder and Maiwald (n 4) § 2 mn 37. In more detail E. Pohlreich, *"Ehrenmorde" im Wandel des Strafrechts* (Duncker & Humblot 2009) 212 ff. and the sources cited there.

169 cf. BGHSt 27, 260, 262; BGH NJW 1958, 1405; in more detail on the controversial discussion V. Erb, '§ 32 – Notwehr' in B. von Heintschel-Heinegg (ed.) *Münchener Kommentar zum Strafgesetzbuch, Band 1, §§ 1–37* (3rd edn, C.H. Beck Verlag 2017) mn 186 ff.

170 cf. Erb (n 169) mn 189. Depending on the circumstances of the case, the officer will have to face disciplinary measures.

171 As a rule, a person acting under superior orders is justified, if the order itself is lawful, cf. T. Lenckner and D. Sternberg-Lieben, 'Vorbemerkungen zu den §§ 32 ff.' in A. Schönke and H. Schröder (eds) *Strafgesetzbuch – Kommentar* (29th edn, C.H. Beck Verlag 2014) mn 87; Bohlander (n 12) 93.

172 The exclusion of the superior order offence for genocide (sec. 6 VStGB) and crimes against humanity (sec. 7 VStGB) goes back to Art. 33(2) of the Rome Statute of the International Criminal Court, which establishes the unrebuttable presumption that orders to commit genocide or crimes against humanity are always manifestly unlawful, cf. O. Triffterer and S. Bock, 'Article 33 – Superior Orders and Prescription of Law' in O. Triffterer and K. Ambos (eds) *Rome Statute of the International Criminal Law* (3rd edn, C.H. Beck 2016) mn 30.

No. 1 VStGB), 'in execution of a military order or of an order comparable in its actual binding effect shall have acted without guilt so far as the perpetrator does not realise that the order is unlawful and so far as it is also not manifestly unlawful.'[173]

Sentencing framework

Murder (sec. 211 StGB) carries with it a mandatory life sentence and thus leaves no room to adapt the sanction to the individual circumstances of the case. This might conflict with the constitutional principle that a sentence must adequately reflect the wrong caused by the criminal conduct, and the culpability of the perpetrator.[174] In a famous case, D's wife W was raped by his uncle V, became depressed and made several suicide attempts, whilst V boasted about having had sex with W. Out of despair, D finally killed V by stealth.[175] The Supreme Court took the view that in light of V's humiliating behaviour a life sentence would be entirely inappropriate and overturned the Trial Court's decision imposing an imprisonment from three to 15 years.[176]

The standard sentencing range for voluntary manslaughter is imprisonment of not less than five years (sec. 212 StGB), the maximum sentence being 15 years (sec. 38(2) StGB). In especially serious cases, e.g., if the perpetrator killed several persons[177] or tortured his victim before he eventually decided to kill her,[178] the penalty is imprisonment for life (sec. 212(2) StGB). Killing at the request of the victim (sec. 216) is punishable by imprisonment from six months to five years, negligent manslaughter (sec. 222) by imprisonment not exceeding five years or a fine. The sentencing ranges for result-qualified offences vary from imprisonment from one to ten years (stalking causing death) up to imprisonment for life or not less than ten years (robbery or rape causing death). In cases of attempt or diminished responsibility the law allows for a mitigation of punishment.[179]

As to the concrete sentencing process, sec. 46(1) StGB states that the guilt of the offender is the basis for sentencing which in turn is determined by the gravity of the crime, its overall significance for the legal order and the personal blameworthiness of the offender.[180] In 2015,[181] 123 persons have been convicted of murder, 85 of them received life imprisonment. The others were sentenced to fix-termed imprisonment ranging from three to 15 years. The average sentence length for voluntary manslaughter was imprisonment between

173 English translation by G. Werle and F. Jeßberger 'International Law is Coming Home: The New German Code of Crimes Against International Law' (2002) 13 Criminal Law Forum 191–215.

174 The seminal judgment is BVerfGE [Entscheidungen des Bundesverfassungsgerichts – Official Journal of Reportable Constitutional Court Decisions] 45, 187.

175 See text accompanying n 65.

176 BGHSt 30, 105. This ruling is based on an analogous application of sec. 49(1) StGB on special mitigating circumstances established by law (e.g., attempt or diminished responsibility); in more detail Schneider (n 65) mn 23 ff.

177 BGH NStZ 2006, 166, 167.

178 BGH NJW 1986, 265, 266.

179 cf. sec. 49(1) StGB. In case of attempted voluntary manslaughter, for example, the reduced sentencing range is from two to 11 years and three months.

180 The seminal case is BGHSt 20, 264, 266.

181 Statistisches Bundesamt, *Rechtspflege – Strafverfolgung 2015*, Fachserie 10, Reihe 3 (9 February 2017) available at <www.destatis.de/DE/Publikationen/Thematisch/Rechtspflege/StrafverfolgungVollzug/Strafverfolgung2100300157004.pdf?__blob=publicationFile> accessed 11 June 2018.

five and ten years (164 convictions out of 280). One perpetrator was sentenced to life; in 11 cases, the sentence was suspended on probation.[182] Negligent manslaughter is in most cases punished with a fine (210 convictions out of 279); only two perpetrators received prison sentences without being placed on parole.

182 According to sec. 56 StGB, a suspension on probation is only possible, if the term of imprisonment does not exceed two years.

14 New Zealand

Julia Tolmie

Overview and historical development of homicide offences and offence structure

The Criminal Code Act 1893 was the first codification of the criminal law in New Zealand.[1] The homicide provisions in that Act were borrowed, almost word for word, from The Draft Code of the UK Royal Commission on the Law Relating to Indictable Offences in 1879. Ironically the draft code was not enacted in England.

The homicide offences in New Zealand are currently codified in the Crimes Act 1961 ('CA 1961').[2] With three exceptions these offences have not substantially changed since they were first enacted in 1893. These exceptions are: the defence of provocation has been abolished; sentencing for murder has changed (with, first the abolition of the death penalty and then the replacement of mandatory life imprisonment with a presumption of life); and the offence of infanticide has been enacted. These developments are discussed later in the chapter.

There are three types of homicide offences in New Zealand: Murder,[3] manslaughter[4] and infanticide.[5] All require, as a first step, proof of a 'homicide' that is 'culpable'.[6] In most instances this will mean a death that is caused by an unlawful and dangerous act or the breach of a duty to act. If no *mens rea* for murder is established then a finding of culpable homicide will automatically result in a conviction for manslaughter.

There are no *degrees* of murder in New Zealand, but there are different *types* of murder: intentional murder,[7] reckless murder[8] and felony murder.[9] The latter is a form of constructive murder, which does not require proof that the defendant had intention or recklessness as to death but does require that they were pursuing a serious offence when they caused death.

Whilst infanticide is technically a third form of homicide, in effect it operates as a partial defence to either murder or manslaughter in a very specific set of circumstances - when a

1 A. Lintock, *An Encyclopedia of New Zealand* (New Zealand Government 1966).
2 Section 9 of the CA 1961 provides that there are no common law offences.
3 Ibid., ss.167, 168.
4 Ibid., s.171.
5 Ibid., s.178.
6 Ibid., s.160(2).
7 Ibid., s.167(a).
8 Ibid., s.167(b), (d).
9 Ibid., s.168.

mother who has given birth or is breastfeeding develops a mental disorder as a consequence and kills one of her children who is under ten.

There are a number of offences in the Land Transport Act 1998 ('LTA 1998') that exacerbate the criminal justice response to various driving offences in the event of death. These are not homicide offences and it is always possible that a driving offence could, instead, form the foundation of a manslaughter charge on the basis of an unlawful and dangerous act that causes death.[10]

General elements

Beginning of life – definition

Section 159(1) of the CA 1961 states that a child becomes a human being when it 'has completely proceeded in a living state from the body of its mother, whether it has breathed or not, whether it has an independent circulation or not, and whether the naval string is severed or not'. Under this definition the child does not have to be capable of independent existence.

End of life – definition

New Zealand does not have a statutory definition of death. The common law originally defined death as the 'the permanent cessation of heart beat, blood circulation and breathing'.[11] Such a definition has become less helpful as advances in medicine and technology have made it possible to maintain a person's vital functions indefinitely by mechanical means.

In *Auckland Area Health Board v AG*[12] Justice Thomas defined death as the irreversible cessation of the functions of the entire brain, including the brain stem. However, he raised the possibility that the loss of higher brain function, without the loss of brain stem function, could also amount to death.

Pre-birth causes with post-birth effect

Once a child becomes a 'human being' only then are they able to be the victim of a homicide.[13] Section 159(2) provides that this is so whether the injuries that cause their death were inflicted before, during or after they became a human being.

If the child is not yet a human being when death occurs, the offences of killing of an unborn child or procuring an abortion are applicable instead.[14]

Medical treatment scenarios

Given that death is inevitable for everyone, to cause death is simply to accelerate death. This is so even when the victim is already dying.[15] It follows that actions that accelerate death, accompanied by intention or recklessness as to death, will amount to murder regardless of

10 Ibid., s.160(2)(a).
11 *Auckland Area Health Board v AG* [1993] 1 NZLR 235, 246.
12 Ibid.
13 CA 1961, s.158.
14 Ibid., ss.182, 183.
15 Ibid., s.164.

how worthy the person's motivations were (for example, to relieve unbearable pain during the process of dying).

An exception is the 'principle of double effect' which permits doctors to deliberately provide proper medical treatment that has the effect of hastening death without being liable for homicide.[16] For example, doctors may administer morphine in doses that will ultimately be lethal, provided that the primary intention is to alleviate pain in the context of palliative care and the dose is only what is proper for that purpose.

Homicide by omission

As already noted, establishing a 'culpable homicide' is an essential first step for all types of homicide. There are several types of culpable homicide, including an omission that causes death.[17] A failure to act can only register as a criminal omission for these purposes if it is in breach of a duty to act.

There are two types of statutory duties in the CA 1961 – duties based on a particular relationship with the victim (ss.151–52) and duties based on a particular relationship with the harm (ss.155–57). The first category requires those who have the care of vulnerable adults or children to provide the necessaries of life or protection from injury. The second are duties to take reasonable care that lie on those who have the charge of something or are doing something which, in the absence of reasonable care, might be dangerous to life.

Duties are created by other legislative instruments.[18] For example, in *R v Paenga* [19] the judge considered that regulation 17(1) of the Traffic Regulations 1976 (which prohibits permitting a person to ride in a vehicle in a manner that may be liable to cause injury) creates a legal duty not to drive a vehicle if someone proposes to ride in it in such a manner.

The statutory duties are complemented by common law duties.[20] For example, there may be a duty to take reasonable steps to address a danger that you have created[21] (although there has yet to be an application of this duty in New Zealand).

The duties based on a special relationship with the victim were expanded in 2011 to include the duty to take reasonable steps to safeguard against the risk of 'injury' (meaning physical harm that is more than minimal).[22] Whilst parents and caregivers in New Zealand have always been prosecuted for failing to protect a child from another violent adult,[23] the reforms opened a wider range of negligent parenting practices up to the scrutiny of the criminal law. For example, since the reform parents (predominantly mothers) have been prosecuted for unsafe sleeping practices[24] and not using proper child restraints in a car.[25] When death cannot be established to have been caused by the omission, criminal nuisance is charged instead.[26]

16 *R v Martin* [2004] 3 NZLR 69; *Auckland Area Health Board v AG* (n 11); *Seales v AG* [2015] 3 NZLR 556.
17 CA 1961, s.160(2)(b).
18 Section 157 of the CA 1961 suggests that a duty cannot be based on a private contractual undertaking unless that undertaking is to do something that may prevent someone from dying.
19 (HC, 10 February 2006).
20 *R v Lunt* [2004] 1 NZLR 498.
21 *R v Miller* [1983] 2 AC 161; *R v Evans* [2009] EWCA Crim 650.
22 CA 1961, s.2.
23 *R v Witika* [1993] 2 NZLR 424; *R v Kuka* [2009] NZCA 572.
24 *R v Tukiwaho* [HC, 31 May 2012]; *R v Tuheke* [HC, 3 Feb 2014].
25 *JF v Police* [2013] NZHC 2729; [2014] NZHC 547.
26 CA 1961, s.145.

As noted previously,[27] whilst deliberately *acting* to accelerate death will amount to a culpable homicide (except for those actions that fall within the principle of 'double effect'), a number of cases have held that doctors are entitled to allow a person to die by *doing nothing*, so long as doing nothing does not constitute a breach of their duty to provide the necessaries of life to patients who are vulnerable adults in their care.

In *Auckland Area Health Board v AG* [28] the issue was whether doctors could withdraw life support from a person with Guillain-Barré syndrome who was permanently unable to communicate or move, and who, without artificial breathing, would immediately die. Justice Thomas said that the first issue was whether ventilation was a 'necessity of life' in the circumstances of the case. He concluded that it would be if required to prevent, cure or alleviate a disease that endangered the life or health of the patient. However, because in this case the patient was beyond recovery and was effectively a 'ventilated corpse', it was not.[29] Thomas J went on to hold that even if he was wrong there was a 'lawful excuse' under s.151 for discontinuance of ventilation on the basis of good medical practice. Such practice:

> ... must begin with a bona fide decision on the part of the attending doctors as to what, in their judgment, is in the best interests of the patient. Equally, it must encompass the prevailing medical standards, practices, procedures and traditions which command general approval within the medical profession. All relevant tests would need to be carried out ... Consultation with the medical profession's recognised ethical body is also critical. It must approve the doctors' decision. Finally, the patient's family or guardian must be fully informed and freely concur in what is proposed.[30]

Omitting to effect an easy rescue

As noted on page 266,[31] the duties to act in New Zealand depend on having either a particular relationship with the victim or with the activity or thing that causes the harm. There is no duty to rescue someone in the absence of either type of relationship, even in circumstances where rescue would be easy and incur no cost to the rescuer.

Intentional homicide offences

Actus reus

All forms of homicide in New Zealand have the same core *actus reus* requirements. There must be a 'culpable homicide,' defined as the killing of a person by any one of the five means set out in s.160(2) of the CA 1961:

- An unlawful act;
- An omission without lawful excuse to perform any legal duty;[32]
- Both combined;

27 Text to n 15.
28 *Auckland Area Health Board v AG* (n 11).
29 Ibid. [250].
30 Ibid.
31 Text to nn 17–26.
32 These are discussed above (text to nn 17–25) and will not be revisited here.

- Causing that person by threats or fear of violence, or by deception, to do an act which is both reasonably foreseeable[33] and causes their death; or
- Wilfully frightening a child under the age of 16 years or a sick person.

An 'unlawful act' is defined in s.2 to mean 'a breach of any Act, regulation, rule or bylaw'. This is a broad definition because it is not confined to criminal offences. It has included, for example, a breach of the Fencing of Swimming Pools Act 1987.[34]

The last type of culpable homicide listed above (wilfully frightening a child or sick person)[35] does not appear to have been used in practice. It could cover situations where the accused deliberately engenders fear in the mind of someone who is vulnerable without threatening violence (for example, telling horror stories or threatening negative consequences other than violence), causing stress or illness that results in that person's death.[36]

Did the defendant's acts or omissions cause death?

The primary test used in New Zealand to determine whether the defendant's act or omission caused the victim's death is the 'substantial and operative cause' test.[37] The test requires fact finders to make a normative judgment about when the accused's actions have ceased to be current or have become so insignificant as a causal factor in the victim's death that they should no longer be considered, as an objective question of fact, to be making a contribution to it. Whilst the Court of Appeal in *Kirikiri* [38] said it would not decide if the operating cause had to be 'substantial', there is a significant amount of dicta suggesting that something lesser might be sufficient. For example, 'substantial' was described by Justice Fisher in *The Queen v Gedson* as being 'more than … trifling'.[39] Some courts have used an alternative formulation, asking whether the suggested intervening cause of death 'is or is not so overwhelming as to make the original wound merely part of the history or the setting in which the death occurred'.[40]

Omissions present a distinct set of challenges in deciding causation because there is an element of speculation involved in determining what might have happened had the accused acted, as opposed to failing to act. In *R v Kuka* [41] the Court of Appeal said the test for causation is whether 'but for an accused's omission the victim "would or would probably" not have died'. It is not enough to show that 'life might have been prolonged'.[42]

The accused does not have to be the *main* or *sole* cause of death, so long as they satisfy the legal test for causation. It follows that there can be multiple causal factors that register as legally significant in relation to one death. This is not problematic when multiple defendants are held accountable for their role in respect of one death. However, in *Kuka* [43] the accused

33 *R v Tomars* [1978] 2 NZLR 505.
34 *R v Turton* [HC, 31 October 1989].
35 Section 160(2)(e).
36 See also s.163, CA 1961.
37 *R v Myatt* [1991] 1 NZLR 674.
38 [1982] 2 NZLR 648.
39 (HC, 4 December 1997).
40 *R v Stubbings* [HC, 26 February 1987].
41 *Kuka* (n 23).
42 Ibid. [33].
43 Ibid. Extending a line of authority that originated in *Clark* [1982] 1 NZLR 654.

was convicted of manslaughter twice in relation to the death of her one child because her failure to protect her child from another person's violence and her failure to get her medical treatment once she was injured each satisfied the legal test for causation and therefore caused the child's death. This has troubling ramifications.[44] The obvious impression is that a person who has been convicted of multiple manslaughter offences has killed multiple victims.

Section 166 deals with intervening medical treatment. It provides that:

> Everyone who causes to another person any bodily injury, in itself of a dangerous nature, from which death results, kills that person, although the immediate cause of death be treatment, proper or improper, applied in good faith.

In *Kirikiri*[45] the court said that s.166 was declaratory of the common law. This means that, because the law does not require death to be attributed to a single cause both the accused's original act and any subsequent medical treatment (negligent or otherwise), depending on the facts, can be a substantial and operative cause of the victim's death.

In the UK in *R v Kennedy (No 2)*[46] the House of Lords said that it was a 'fundamental and non-controversial' principle of criminal law that the 'free, deliberate and informed intervention of a second person, who intends to exploit the situation created by the first, but is not acting in concert with him' will normally 'relieve the first actor of criminal responsibility'.[47] In this case the appellant prepared a syringe with heroin for the deceased who knowingly injected himself with it. It followed that, whilst the appellant had supplied the drug, he had not 'caused' the drug to be administered to the deceased and therefore had not caused his death.

In *R v Leaitua*[48] Justice Katz in the New Zealand High Court applied *Kennedy (No 2)*, finding that a person who supplied packages of drugs to an adult who was to act as a courier did not cause her death when she voluntarily ingested those packages and one ruptured inside her. However, in *R v Tema*[49] the court used the distinctive offence structure in New Zealand to convict the defendant of manslaughter on a similar set of facts. Because the consumption of a controlled substance is an offence in New Zealand,[50] unlike in England, the accused, by supplying drugs to the victim, was a party[51] to *her* offence of consumption when she voluntarily ingested those drugs. This, in turn, directly caused her death.

The year and a day rule

Under s.162 the victim's death must occur within a year and a day of the defendant's acts or omissions that cause their death. The period of a year and a day is calculated inclusive of the day on which the last unlawful act (or omission) contributing to the death took place (or ceased).

44 See *Paenga* (n 19); *King v R* [2011] NZCA 664, [47].
45 *Kirikiri* (n 38).
46 [2007] UKHL 38.
47 Ibid. [14].
48 [2013] NZHC 702.
49 (HC, 30 April 2010).
50 Misuse of Drugs Act 1975 ('MDA 1975'), s.7(1)(a).
51 Under s.66(1) of the CA 1961.

Mens rea

A culpable homicide that is accompanied by an intention to kill is murder under s. 167(a) of the CA 1961. An intention to kill means that death was either the defendant's purpose or desire in acting (direct intention) or they knew that death would be a virtually certain outcome (oblique intention).[52]

Reckless homicide offences

In New Zealand there are two forms of reckless homicide – both variants of murder.

Actus reus

The *actus reus* for both forms of reckless murder is the same as that outlined for intentional homicide.[53]

Mens rea

Section 167 provides that if a culpable homicide is accompanied by one of the following forms of *mens rea* it will be reckless murder:

- An intention to cause bodily injury *and* recklessness as to death (subs (b)); or
- An intention to pursue an unlawful object *and* recklessness as to death (subs (d)).[54]

Both forms of *mens rea* require a nexus between the intention to cause bodily injury or pursue an unlawful object *and* recklessness as to death. For example, in *R v Pira* [55] it was held that recklessness as to death must be established in relation to the bodily injury that was intentionally inflicted under s.167(b). In *Shadrock v R* [56] the Court of Appeal required under s.167(d) an unlawful object that is a crime[57] *and* a separate act performed in *furtherance* of that crime which is known to the offender to be likely to cause death and does, in fact, cause death.

In *Shadrock* the accused and his associates snatched a handbag in a car park. His car then hit and killed the owner whilst they were trying to flee. The issue was whether the act causing death (the assault), which occurred *after* the accused had satisfied the elements of theft, was nevertheless done for the object of carrying out the crime (the theft). The court thought that acts committed after the accused had left the scene would not qualify because the crime is already completed. On the other hand, the offence could not be regarded as

52 *R v Wentworth* [1993] 2 NZLR 450. Note that s.167(a) uses the phrase 'means to cause' rather than 'intends' and some have argued that this may not include 'knowledge of a virtual certainty'. However, this point has not yet been resolved: *R v Matthews and Alleyne* [2003] Crim LR 553; *R v Aramakutu* [1991] 3 NZLR 429, 432.

53 Text to nn 30–48.

54 The words of the provision are: 'If the offender for any unlawful object does an act that he knows to be likely to cause death, and thereby kills any person, though he may have desired that his object should be effected without hurting anyone.'

55 [1991] 7 CRNZ 650.

56 [2011] 3 NZLR 573.

57 This is stricter than the requirement in s.160(2)(a) for culpable homicide, where an 'unlawful act' rather than a crime is sufficient.

concluded, 'merely … when the legal elements of the offence are complete'.[58] On this set of facts because the victim had immediately tried to recover the bag after it was taken from her, it was open to the jury to find that the offending was still continuing at the time of the assault that caused her death – the accused was persisting in his attempt to alienate the bag from the victim in order to commit a theft.

Recklessness is a subjective form of *mens rea*. It requires proof that the accused consciously chose to run the risk of 'likely' death.[59] It does not include failing to give any thought to a serious and obvious risk.[60] In *R v Piri* [61] the court, said that 'likely' meant a 'real or substantial' risk of death.[62] This does not require proof that the accused thought that the result was 'more likely than not'. A fine calculation that the odds are against it, although the risk was plainly there, is no defence:

> If the risk of the death of the victim was truly no more than negligible or remote in the offender's eyes, the stigma of murder should be withheld. To be distinguished from that however are cases where the risk is so appreciable that to indulge in the conduct is seen by society as the virtual equivalent of intentional killing.[63]

Many people who commit crimes of violence have had exposure to serious violence themselves as victims. In *R v Makoare* [64] the court refused to allow expert psychiatric opinion evidence to the effect that the 15-year-old accused lived in a subcultural context where violence was the norm, with the result that he underestimated the dangers involved in beating people up and / or sticking knives in them. The court thought, given the accused was mentally normal, that such testimony may unduly influence juries on the central question they needed to decide and was likely to be unnecessary.

In *R v Paton* [65] expert testimony was not introduced. In this case the defendant stabbed her violent partner with a kitchen knife after he had attacked her in the hallway of their house and then pursued her into the kitchen. The jury rejected self-defence but, instead of convicting her of murder, she was convicted of manslaughter. This verdict meant that the jury accepted that she did not know that stabbing her partner in the neck with a large knife was likely to cause his death. The sentencing judge commented that:

> I treat the jury analysis as recognising that the view as to the risk of death from a stab wound of this kind, by a woman in your position, would not be analysed as it would be by most of us. The prolonged history of beatings conditioned you to downplay the risks and consequences of violent attacks, so that a woman in your position would not appreciate the risk of causing death when others, who had not experienced the sad domestic history you had, could reasonably be expected to recognise that risk.[66]

58 (n 56) [74].
59 *R v Dixon* [1979] 1 NZLR 641; *R v Curtis* [2009] NZCA 521.
60 *R v Harney* [1987] 2 NZLR 576.
61 [1987] 1 NZLR 66.
62 See also *R v Wickliffe* [1987] NZLR 55.
63 *Piri* (n 61) [79].
64 [2001] 1 NZLR 318.
65 [2013] NZHC 21.
66 Ibid. [11].

In other words, despite the absence of expert evidence to that effect, the jury was taken to have accepted that her chronic exposure to violent victimisation had diminished her ability to realistically estimate the dangers of using violence.

Negligent homicide offences

Manslaughter is the form of homicide that is negligence based. Since the abolition of provocation in 2009, New Zealand has no partial defences to murder. It is thus not possible to commit a reckless or intentional murder that results in a manslaughter conviction because of the application of a partial defence.

Actus reus

Manslaughter is a culpable homicide where the accused does not have the additional *mens rea* for murder.[67] This means that the *actus reus* for manslaughter is identical to that set out in relation to intentional homicide.[68]

Degree of negligence

Four of the five types of culpable homicide set out in section 160(2) on pages 267–268 (death by an unlawful act, an omission, both combined or the fright response of the victim) have a negligence element.

Only the last (causing death by wilfully frightening a child or sick person) is not negligence-based.[69] Because there is no public record of this provision ever being used, it is discussed no further here.

Omissions: a major departure from the standard of care expected of a reasonable person

As already noted,[70] ss.151–152 of the CA 1961 create a duty on those who have a care-giving relationship with a vulnerable adult or a parental relationship with a child to provide necessities and take reasonable steps to protect them from physical injury. Sections 155–157 create a duty to use reasonable care for those who have in their charge a dangerous thing or undertake dangerous activities. If the breach of a duty results in death this will constitute a culpable homicide under s.160(2)(b).

Early case law held that, because the duty provisions in the CA 1961 did not expressly specify a criminal or elevated standard of negligence, simple civil negligence on the part of the accused was sufficient to mean that a duty had been breached.[71] Thus in *R v Yogasakaran*[72] a doctor was convicted of manslaughter for a mistake that had tragic consequences but was understandable in the circumstances.[73]

67 CA 1961, s.171.
68 Text to nn 30–48.
69 Section 160(2)(e) of the CA 1961 requires intentional actions in relation to a vulnerable victim, knowing that victim to be vulnerable.
70 Text to nn 17–18.
71 *R v Storey* [1931] NZLR 417.
72 [1990] 1 NZLR 399.
73 He was an anaesthetist who, during an emergency in the course of a surgery, injected a drug which was correctly labelled but in the wrong drawer. Had the drawer been stocked correctly he would have injected the correct drug.

Section 150A was introduced in response to this case. This section now requires proof of a 'major departure' from the standard of care expected of a reasonable person for the purposes of establishing an omission under one of the duty provisions set out in the CA 1961.[74]

The unlawful act must be dangerous

The New Zealand courts have required that the unlawful act that causes death for the purposes of s.160(2)(a) be 'dangerous'. In *R v Lee*[75] it was said that the test is whether the act was 'likely to do at least some (more than trivial) harm'.[76] This formulation suggests that there is no need to prove a risk of 'serious harm'. It also suggests that dangerousness is established even if a reasonable person would have foreseen risk to a class of persons that does not include the ultimate victim, so long as they foresaw the risk of harm to *someone*.

Because dangerousness is a negligence based test, the fact that the accused did not personally appreciate that they were running the risk of harming someone is not relevant. Dangerousness does, however, have to be assessed:

> ... within the framework of the circumstances as they appeared to the defendant at the time. So here the reasonable person must be placed in the shoes of the accused facing the situation as it then appeared to the accused.[77]

This knowledge is confined to facts – the reasonable person will not necessarily form the same opinions as the accused from those facts (for example, the opinion that on these facts it is safe to proceed).

In *R v Myatt*[78] it was held that the unlawful act did not have to be the breach of a provision which was concerned with public safety, so long as the *actions* of the accused which breached the provision met the objective test of dangerousness.

Putting aside the issue of dangerousness, s.150A(1)(a) was amended in 2011 to provide that where the unlawful act that causes death under s.160(2)(a) 'requires proof of negligence or is a strict or absolute liability offence,' the relevant standard of negligence 'is a major departure from the standard of care expected of a reasonable person who performs that act'. This avoids different standards of negligence being applied to the defendant on the same set of facts depending on whether the prosecution has chosen to charge them with a negligence-based driving offence (an unlawful act) causing death under s.160(2)(a) or a failure to use reasonable care in operating a motor vehicle under s.160(2)(b), based on the s.156 duty on persons who are in charge of dangerous things to use reasonable care. Whether one is charged with an unlawful act employing a negligence standard or the failure to comply with a duty, the standard of negligence is the elevated criminal standard set out in s.150A.[79]

74 Note that the provision says that this elevated standard applies 'for the purposes of this Part' of the CA 1961. The provision is contained in Part 8 which deals with crimes against the person. It is thought to be unclear, therefore, whether it applies to criminal offences not contained in Part 8, such as criminal nuisance (s.145) set out in Part 7 of the 1961 Act.
75 [2006] 22 CRNZ 568.
76 Ibid. [138].
77 *Gedson* (n 39).
78 *Myatt* (n 37).
79 This gives statutory expression to the position taken in *R v Powell* [2002] 1 NZLR 666.

The victim's fright response must be reasonably foreseeable

Causing the victim by threats or fear of violence or by deception to do an act which causes his own death is a form of culpable homicide under s.160(2)(d). It must also be established, as a common law gloss on the legislation, that the victim's actions were:

> ... the kind of action on his part which could reasonably have been foreseen by reasonable and responsible persons in the accused's shoes? This question must be asked by reference to the likely actions of someone in the circumstances of the deceased; in other words someone subjected to whatever course of conduct is proved against the accused.[80]

In this instance the negligence based requirement is exculpatory rather than inculpatory. In other words, the accused is only held responsible for actions on the part of the victim that they should have foreseen. They are not responsible for unpredictable over-reactions by the victim.

Result-qualified / constructive/ *versari in res illicata* / felony homicide offences

Felony homicide offence

New Zealand has one form of felony murder, which is set out in s.168 of the CA 1961.[81] If the legal requirements are satisfied, s.168(1) makes it clear that culpable homicide will be murder 'whether the offender means or does not mean death to ensue, or knows or does not know that death is likely to ensue'. In other words, intention or recklessness as to death does not have to be proven. The purpose of the doctrine is to penalise those who deliberately engage in highly dangerous actions in the pursuit of serious crime when death results.

Actus reus

The *actus reus* for felony murder is a culpable homicide[82] when the unlawful act that causes death (and constitutes the culpable homicide) consists of either:

- the infliction of grievous bodily harm;
- the administration of a stupefying or overpowering thing; or
- the stopping of a person's breath.

Mens rea

The *mens rea* for felony murder is twofold. First, the infliction of grievous bodily harm, administration of a stupefying thing or stopping of a person's breath (resulting in death) must be intentional.[83]

80 *Tomars* (n 33) [510].
81 Although note that reckless murder in s.167(d) (discussed on page 270) also has its origins in the felony murder rule, as should be apparent from the offence structure.
82 CA 1961, s.160(2).
83 *R v Waikato and Tawera* [HC, 28 March 2001].

Second, the act or omission that causes death (and constitutes the culpable homicide) must have been committed for one of following purposes:

- resisting lawful apprehension[84] in respect of any offence whatsoever;
- facilitating the commission of any of the offences mentioned in s. 168(2); or
- facilitating the escape afterwards or avoidance of detection upon the commission or attempted commission of one of the offences mentioned in s. 168(2).

Section 168(2) lists the following offences: treason;[85] communicating secrets;[86] sabotage;[87] piracy;[88] piratical acts;[89] escape or rescue from penal institution or lawful custody or detention;[90] sexual violation;[91] murder;[92] abduction;[93] kidnapping;[94] robbery;[95] burglary;[96] arson.[97] The offences listed include aggravated versions of those offences.[98]

Driving offences

The LTA 1998 creates a series of aggravated driving offences, where the penalty for a particular driving offence is increased because death was caused by the offence. For example, reckless or dangerous driving (s.7) carries a maximum penalty of three months' imprisonment or a fine of $4,500. When death results s.36AA increases the maximum penalty to ten years or $20,000.[99] Driving carelessly or without reasonable consideration for others (s.8) has a maximum penalty of $3,000 or three months' imprisonment. The maximum potential fine is elevated to $4,500 under s.38 when the offending causes injury or death.[100] The basic driving offences can, however, form the basis of a culpable homicide under s.160(2)(a) (an unlawful act that causes death). A manslaughter conviction carries a maximum penalty of life imprisonment.

Section 61 of the LTA 1998 creates a series of offences where death results from the operation of a motor vehicle whilst over the legal limit for alcohol, under the influence of a controlled drug, or under the influence of drugs or alcohol to the extent that the driver is incapable of proper control.[101] Causing death by careless driving whilst under the influence of drink and / or drugs is also an offence under s.62.

84 In *Shadrock* (n 56) it was held that a 'lawful apprehension' includes a citizen's arrest under CA 1961, s.35.
85 CA 1961, s.73.
86 Ibid., s.78.
87 Ibid., s.79.
88 Ibid., s.92.
89 Ibid., s.93.
90 Ibid., ss.119 to 122.
91 Ibid., s.128.
92 Ibid., s.167.
93 Ibid., s.208.
94 Ibid., s.209.
95 Ibid., s.234.
96 Ibid., s.241.
97 Ibid., s.294.
98 *R v Kaukasi* [HC, 22 July 2002].
99 See also engaging in unauthorised drag or street racing (s.22A), causing the death of another person (s.36A).
100 See also careless use of a motor vehicle in excess of the speed limit, or in breach of the rules regarding overtaking, resulting in death (s.39).
101 Specified in Schedule 1 of the MDA 1975 (n 50).

Infanticide / child destruction

The third type of culpable homicide – infanticide – is always available as an alternative conviction on homicide charges.[102] Because it carries a maximum penalty of three years' imprisonment, in effect infanticide operates as a specialised form of the diminished responsibility defence in a narrow set of circumstances.

Section 178(1) of the CA 1961 provides that a culpable homicide will result in an infanticide verdict when the following criteria are satisfied:

- the defendant is a woman;
- she causes the death of a 'child of hers';
- the child is under ten;
- at the time 'the balance of her mind was disturbed';
- the disturbance was a result of her 'not having fully recovered from the effect of giving birth to that or any other child, or by reason of the effect of lactation, or by reason of any disorder consequent upon childbirth or lactation'; and
- her mind was disturbed 'to such an extent that she should not be held fully responsible'.

Infanticide has been applied in cases involving diagnosed mental disorder, such as post-partum depression, and where there is no proof of a psychiatric illness or disorder.[103] Section 178 has rarely been applied in cases of post-partum psychosis because the defence of insanity is generally thought more appropriate in such instances and an insanity verdict is always available on homicide charges.[104]

The phrase 'any child of hers' is not confined to biological children. It includes 'all children who can, in fact and law and common sense, be said to be hers,'[105] including foster children. As is apparent from the wording of the section, the defence of infanticide is available even though the child who is killed is not the one whose birth or feeding has triggered the relevant disturbance of mind.

Section 181 creates the offence of concealing the dead body of a child 'with intent to conceal the fact of its birth, whether the child died before, or during, or after birth'. It carries a maximum penalty of two years and tends to be charged where a newborn's body is discovered and it is not clear whether they were born alive and killed afterwards or whether they were still-born or died after birth without fault on the part of the mother.

Abortion and homicide

Abortion

There are two offences in the CA 1961 that criminalise killing an unborn person who is not yet a human being and who therefore cannot be the victim of a homicide: Section 182 creates the offence of 'killing a child that has not become a human being'[106] and s.183

102 Section 178(2).

103 P. Dean, 'Child Homicide and Infanticide in New Zealand' (2004) 24 International Journal of Law and Psychiatry 339–48.

104 Ibid. See CA 1961, s.178(3), (7).

105 *R v P* [1991] 2 NZLR 116.

106 Causing death 'in such a manner that he would have been guilty of murder if the child had become a human being'.

creates the offence of 'procuring a miscarriage,' which applies to the destruction of an embryo or foetus.[107]

Whilst the provisions have the same maximum penalty they have a different defence structure. The offence of killing an unborn child has one defence for those who cause the death of such a child, 'by means employed in good faith for the preservation of the life of the mother'.[108]

By way of contrast two different defences are available in respect of procuring the destruction of a foetus, depending on whether the pregnancy is of more than 20 weeks' gestation or not. If the pregnancy is of more than 20 weeks' gestation then s.187A(3) provides a defence if; 'the person doing the act believes that the miscarriage is necessary to save the life of the woman or girl or to prevent serious permanent injury to her physical or mental health'. This is a broader defence than that offered in relation to s.182 as it covers permanent injury, and not just danger to life.

The defence that is available if the pregnancy is less than 20 weeks' gestation is broader again – covering not just situations of clear necessity but also where there is merely a potential risk. The defence is available if the person destroying the foetus believes;

> ... that the continuance of the pregnancy would result in serious danger (not being danger normally attendant upon childbirth) to the life, or to the physical or mental health, of the woman or girl.[109]

Matters which can be considered in deciding whether the continuance of the pregnancy would result in serious danger to the women's life or physical or mental health include the fact that her age is near the beginning or the end of the usual child-bearing years or that there are reasonable grounds for believing that the pregnancy is the result of sexual violation.[110]

At face value ss.183 and 182 have considerable overlap – although one deals with an 'unborn child' and the other a 'foetus'. It was originally thought that s.182 only applied where a child was killed while it was in the process of being born, but before it was completely born and had become a human being. However, it was held in *R v Henderson* [111] that the section could not be limited in that way. The court also held that there was no justification for reading a requirement into s.182 that the child was 'capable of being born alive'.

On the other hand, in *R v Woolnough* [112] Justice Richmond said that s.182 had no application to abortions carried out in the first trimester of pregnancy. Although he did not indicate at what point a foetus becomes an unborn child, he suggested it was at the later stages of pregnancy. In *Henderson* [113] a 26-week foetus was held to be an unborn child for the purposes of s.182 but the court said it was not prepared to decide at what stage the foetus had become an unborn child before the 26 weeks.

The degree of overlap between ss.182 and 183 makes the differences in the defences available in respect of two provisions problematic. Where a foetus is also an unborn child then whether the accused has the broader defence applicable to s.183 or is required to meet the more stringent defence applicable to s.182 would depend on which provision the

107 A miscarriage is defined in s.182A of the CA 1961 as the destruction of an embryo or foetus.
108 CA 1961, s.182(2).
109 Ibid., s.187A.
110 Ibid., s 187A(2).
111 [1990] 3 NZLR 174.
112 [1977] 2 NZLR 508.
113 *Henderson* (n 111).

prosecution chose to charge them under. Accordingly, in *Henderson* [114] the court held that the defences applicable to s 183, although not expressed to apply to s.182, impliedly must.

Defences to homicide

Consent – incl. mercy killings

Section 63 of the CA 1961 provides that no one has the right to consent to their own death and such consent 'is not a defence in law'. The court in *Seales v Attorney-General* [115] made the point that s.63 removes the defence of consent only in respect of the intentional infliction of death. People are still legally permitted to consent to activities that *risk* death – for example, a risky operation or unsafe sex.

When the accused deliberately accelerates someone's death it is no defence to murder that the killing was a mercy killing. For example, that the person was terminally ill, in unbearable suffering and wanted to die. Whilst historically the defence of provocation was sometimes available in these circumstances to reduce a murder charge to manslaughter,[116] in 2009 this defence was abolished.

Although attempting suicide is no longer a criminal offence, s.179 creates the offence of aiding, abetting, inciting, counselling or procuring (essentially encouraging or helping) another person's suicide. Whilst the offence carries a maximum penalty of 14 years, in recent years convictions for mercy killings under this provision have resulted in very light sentences. For example, in 2011 Sean Davison was given 5 months home detention for assisting his terminally ill mother to kill herself[117] and in 2012 Evans Mott received a discharge without conviction for assisting his terminally ill wife to kill herself.[118]

In 2015 Lucretia Seales sought declarations that a doctor who administered, or assisted her to self-administer, a fatal drug dose would not be committing murder, manslaughter or assisting a suicide in circumstances where she was a competent and consenting adult with a terminal illness causing intolerable suffering.[119] The court declined to make these declarations.

The court also refused to make declarations that the homicide laws were inconsistent in the unique circumstances of the case, with s.8 (the right not to be deprived of life) and s.9 (the right not to be subject to torture or cruel treatment) of the New Zealand Bill of Rights Act 1990. The argument under s.8 was that, in the absence of lawful assistance to die, she would be forced to take her life earlier than she wanted for fear that she would be incapable of doing so when her condition deteriorated. Following *Carter v Canada (Attorney-General)* [120] the court held that Ms Seales did have her right to life engaged in the circumstances of the case – however, the State's interference with this right was on 'grounds

114 Ibid.

115 [2015] NZHC 1239.

116 See J. Corbett, 'Simpson case: bizarre night when "normal" ended' *NZ Herald* (New Zealand, 16 September 2001) <www.nzherald.co.nz/nz/news/article.cfm?c_id=1&objectid=217492> accessed 5 April 2018.

117 See M. Van Beynen, 'Son sentenced for helping mum die' *Stuff* (New Zealand, 24 November 2011) <www.stuff.co.nz/national/crime/6025813/Son-sentenced-for-helping-mum-die> accessed 5 April 2018.

118 See I. Steward, 'Husband discharged over wife's suicide' *Stuff* (New Zealand, 13 September 2012) <www.stuff.co.nz/auckland/local-news/7669500/Husband-discharged-over-wifes-suicide> accessed 6 April 2018.

119 *Seales* (n 16).

120 (2015) SCC 5; [2015] 1 SCR 331.

established by law' (namely, the offence provisions in the CA 1961) and consistent with the principles of fundamental justice.

The argument under s.9 was that by depriving her of the opportunity to bring her suffering to an end the State, through the offence provisions in the CA 1961, was subjecting her to cruel, degrading or disproportionately severe treatment. The court held that her distressing circumstances were the consequence of her tumour not her treatment, and that a failure to allow her to end her life was not 'treatment'. It followed that her right under s 9 was not engaged.

In June 2017 the End of Life Choice Bill was introduced into Parliament as a private members bill. If passed into legislation it would give a person with a terminal illness or irremedial medical condition the option of requesting assisted dying.

Self-defence

Self-defence is a general and complete defence. It is available in respect of all forms of homicide and, if successfully raised, provides a complete acquittal. The defence is set out in s.48 of the CA 1961, which provides that 'Everyone is justified in using, in the defence of himself or another, such force as, in the circumstances as he believes them to be, it is reasonable to use'. The defence has been discussed in detail in an earlier volume in this series.[121]

A little under 50% of all homicides that take place in New Zealand are family violence homicides and half of these are homicides involving intimate partners.[122] In the majority of these the offender in the death event is the predominant aggressor in the prior recorded abuse history. In a small number of cases the primary victim in the abuse history is the offender in the death event.[123] Killings by primary victims have strong defensive features[124] in that the offender (invariably female) tends to be responding to a situation of escalating threat or is under attack from a man who past experience would suggest is capable of hurting her very badly. Typically she spontaneously picks up a weapon readily at hand (usually a kitchen knife) and inflicts one injury in an attempt to frighten him. Despite this, very few defendants who are primary victims are successful in raising self-defence in response to murder charges.[125]

Expert testimony on battered woman syndrome has been accepted by the New Zealand courts in such cases.[126] However, whilst such testimony was developed in order to explain why it is reasonable to believe that defensive self-help might be necessary in an abusive relationship, it has been taken as explaining why primary victims develop the mistaken belief that they are unable to leave the relationship and / or otherwise achieve safety.[127] The New Zealand Family Violence Death Review Committee has suggested that understanding

121 A. Reed and M. Bohlander (with N. Wake and E. Smith), *General Defences in Criminal Law: Domestic and Comparative Perspectives* (Ashgate 2014) 277–79.

122 New Zealand Family Violence Death Review Committee, *Fifth Report Data: January 2009 to December 2015* (HQSC, 2017) 18 <www.hqsc.govt.nz/assets/FVDRC/Publications/FVDRC-FifthReportData-2017.pdf> accessed 5 April 2018.

123 Ibid. 32.

124 Ibid. 54–56.

125 Ibid. 56.

126 Expert testimony on battered woman syndrome traditionally posited that battering typically cycles through three stages (tension building, battering and loving contrition), escalating with repetition. Having survived at least two cycles the victim was thought to develop 'learned helplessness' in which she believes the batterer is all powerful and that she is unable to escape the abuse. Such testimony was accepted in New Zealand in *R v Oakes* [1995] 2 NZLR 673.

127 Ibid.

intimate partner violence as a form of social entrapment would be a more accurate lens through which to interpret the facts of these cases.[128]

Recently the New Zealand Law Commission made a number of recommendations to attempt to make self-defence more accessible to primary victims, including abolishing the common law requirement that a person must be responding to an imminent threat to be acting in self-defence.[129]

Duress

The defence of duress, referred to as 'compulsion' in the New Zealand context, is not available for murder, attempted murder or wounding or injuring with intent under ss.188 and 189 of the CA 1961 (which may be the unlawful act that forms the foundation of a culpable homicide constituting manslaughter).[130] It is available, however, in respect of lesser forms of assault or driving offences that may cause death and result in a manslaughter conviction. It is therefore only available as a defence to manslaughter in these limited circumstances.

Compulsion is set out in s.24(1) of the CA 1961. The defendant must have been ordered to commit the crime under threat of immediate death or grievous bodily harm from a person who was present whilst the crime was committed. The defence has been discussed in detail in an earlier volume in this series.[131]

Necessity

Necessity is a common law defence that is preserved by s.20 of the CA 1961. Recent case law suggests that it has two manifestations: Duress of circumstances and necessity 'proper'.[132] The first is an excuse based defence, covering situations where the defendant is compelled to act as they do because they are in emergency circumstances that mean that the alternative to offending is grievous bodily harm or death. The latter is a justification, covering situations where a person is faced with two evils and the offending is, on balance, the right thing to do because it avoids a greater harm.[133] It is likely that the latter but not the former is available in respect of murder charges.[134] Necessity is discussed in an earlier volume in this series.[135]

Insanity

The defence of insanity is available in respect of all offences, including murder and manslaughter, and results in a verdict of not guilty by reason of insanity. There are a range of

128 New Zealand Family Violence Death Review Committee, *Fifth Report: January 2014 to December 2015* (HQSC 2016) 39–47 <www.hqsc.govt.nz/assets/FVDRC/Publications/FVDRC-5th-report-Feb-2016.pdf> accessed 5 April 2018.

129 Law Commission (New Zealand), *Understanding Family Violence: Reforming the Criminal Law Relating to Homicide* (Report 139, 2016) <www.lawcom.govt.nz/sites/default/files/projectAvailableFormats/R139%20Understanding%20Family%20Violence%20-%20Reforming%20the%20Criminal%20Law%20Relating%20to%20Homicide.pdf> accessed 5 April 2018.

130 CA 1961, s.24(2).

131 Reed and Bohlander (n 121) 279–81.

132 *AG v Leason, Murnane and Land* [HC 31 August 2011].

133 See Lord Brooke in *Re A (Conjoined Twins)* [2001] 2 WLR 480.

134 Ibid.

135 Reed and Bohlander (n 121) 281–83.

potential disposition options that follow on from such a verdict, including compulsory indefinite detention in a secure mental health facility.

The defence is set out in s.23 of the CA 1961 and requires that the defendant was labouring under a natural imbecility or disease of the mind at the time of offending that rendered them incapable of understanding the nature and quality of the act or omission or knowing that it was morally wrong. The defence is discussed in an earlier volume in this series.[136]

Diminished responsibility

New Zealand has never had the partial defence of diminished responsibility. However, as noted on page 276, the offence of infanticide currently operates as a diminished responsibility defence in very limited circumstances.

Loss of control and / or provocation

The defence of provocation was a partial defence, available in relation to murder and resulting in a conviction for manslaughter. In order to raise the defence the defendant had to have killed during a loss of emotional control in response to provocation that could have caused an ordinary person to have similarly lost self-control.[137]

The defence was abolished in December 2009 in response to the *Weatherston* case.[138] Clayton Weatherston took a knife to his ex-girlfriend's house and stabbed her 216 times, unsuccessfully raising the defence of provocation afterwards. Weatherston had narcissistic personality disorder and the New Zealand public was revolted by his attempt over the course of days in the stand to excuse his actions by dissecting the character and behaviour of the deceased (Sophie Elliot).

Some felt that provocation should be modified rather than abolished, so that it could not be used to justify lethal intimate partner or homophobic violence but was still available to primary victims who killed their abusive partner in circumstances where self-defence was not available.[139] Ironically, since the defence has been abolished half of the primary victims who kill their abusive partners continue to be convicted of manslaughter on the basis that they lacked the *mens rea* for murder but nonetheless committed an unlawful and dangerous act that resulted in death.[140] This is so even in cases where it is difficult to see how the defendant could have lacked the *mens rea* for murder, prompting the Law Commission to raise the possibility that this is an example of jury nullification.[141]

Superior orders

Every member of the armed forces is provided with a justificatory defence if they obey the command of their superior officer given for the suppression of a riot, unless that

136 Reed and Bohlander (n 121) 283–84.
137 Formerly s.169 of the CA 1961.
138 The Crimes (Provocation Repeal) Amendment Act 2009.
139 For example, *R v Rihia* [2012] NZHC 2720.
140 See J. Tolmie, 'Defending Battered Defendants on Homicide Charges in New Zealand: The Impact of Abolishing the Partial Defences to Murder' (2015) 4(4) New Zealand Law Review 649.
141 Law Com (n 129) 129–32.

command is manifestly unlawful.[142] Every person who obeys the order of the senior member of the police acting at the place of a riot, including where they reasonably use necessary force to carry those orders in effect, is justified at law unless those orders are manifestly unlawful.

The master or officer in command of a ship on a voyage or the pilot in command of an aircraft in flight is justified in using reasonable and necessary force 'to maintain good order and discipline' on board. Everyone acting in good faith is justified in using force in obedience to their order 'if the force used is reasonable in the circumstances'.[143]

Official authority

The police are justified in using necessary and reasonable force to execute a sentence, warrant or process or make a justified arrest, including any overcoming resistance,[144] or prevent a person who is justifiably arrested or imprisoned from avoiding arrest, escaping or remaining at large.[145] If the force used is necessary and reasonable then it is justified even if it is intended or likely to cause death or grievous bodily harm.[146] The police are also given powers to use necessary and proportionate force to suppress a riot.[147]

Everyone, including the police and the armed forces, are justified in using such force as is reasonably necessary to prevent the commission of suicide or the commission of an offence which would be likely to cause immediate and serious injury to a person or property.[148]

Honour killings

Provocation is a defence that, prior to its repeal in 2009, provided a potential excuse for culturally condoned violence against women.[149]

Sentencing framework

The sentencing consequences that follow on from the three different forms of homicide are significantly different. Murder once carried mandatory life, but now has a presumption of life imprisonment. The presumption can only be overturned where, 'given the circumstances of the offence and the offender, a sentence of imprisonment for life would be manifestly unjust'.[150] This phrase has been interpreted very restrictively by the courts.[151] The two circumstances where it is commonly acknowledged to be appropriate to overturn the presumption are mercy killings in terminal situations and where battered defendants have killed

142 CA 1961, s.47.
143 Ibid., s.60.
144 Ibid., s.39.
145 Ibid., s.40.
146 For those other than the police or a person called upon by the police to assist, the use of force intended or likely to cause death or grievous bodily harm is not justified by this provision.
147 CA 1961, s.44. Note that members of the public are also given the power to use necessary and proportionate force to suppress a riot under s.43.
148 Ibid., s.41.
149 Ibid., s.169 (now repealed). See *R v Dincer* [1983] 1 VR 461.
150 Sentencing Act 2002, s.102(1)
151 *R v O'Brien* [2003] 20 CRNZ 572; *R v Mayes* [2004] 1 NZLR 71; *R v Rapira* [2003] 3 NZLR 794.

their abusive partners.[152] Even then sentences are likely to be in the 10–12 year range for primary victims of intimate partner violence.[153]

Where the presumption of life is not overturned, the court must decide on a minimum non-parole period, which can be no less than ten years.[154] If certain factors are present the court *must* impose a minimum non-parole period of 17 years unless 'it would be manifestly unjust to do so'.[155] These include where the murder was committed in an attempt to get away with a crime, in the course of another serious offence, or as part of a terrorist act; involved calculated or lengthy planning (including the exchange of money), or unlawful entry into a dwelling house; was committed with a high level of brutality, cruelty, depravity or callousness; if the deceased was a police officer or prison officer or particularly vulnerable; where the offender was convicted of two or more counts of murder, or where there were other exceptional circumstances.

The court can, if it is not satisfied that any minimum term would serve the purposes of accountability, denunciation, deterrence and protection of the community, order the offender to serve their sentence without parole.[156] Under New Zealand's 'three strikes' regime, there is a presumption in favour of life imprisonment without parole if a conviction for murder is a second or third stage offence, unless such a sentence would be 'manifestly unjust'.[157]

Section 177 of the CA 1961, by way of contrast, prescribes life imprisonment as the maximum sentence for manslaughter – meaning that there is a genuine sentencing discretion for this offence. Typically the starting point for manslaughter will be considerably lower than life imprisonment. Sentences handed out for manslaughter have included discharges without conviction.[158]

When the core offending that results in death and a manslaughter conviction involves the infliction of grievous bodily harm, the guideline judgment of *R v Taueki* [159] is used. This sets out three bands for the starting point sentence. Band One covers violence at the lower end of the spectrum and will attract a starting point sentence of 3–6 years. The judgment sets out a list of aggravating factors. The presence of one or two of these factors will attract a starting point sentence in Band Two (5–10 years), whilst three or more will attract a starting point sentence in Band Three (9–14 years). This starting point sentence is then adjusted up and down to accommodate mitigating and aggravating factors personal to the accused.

For infanticide, the maximum penalty is three years' imprisonment.[160] However, there is no record of an infanticide conviction attracting a custodial sentence in recent years.[161]

152 NZP Deb 14 August 2001, 594, 10910–11; Justice and Electoral Committee, *Sentencing and Parole Reform Bill* (148–2) 8.
153 *R v Wihongi* [2011] NZCA 592; [2012] NZSC 12; *Rihia* (n 139)
154 Sentencing Act 2002, s.103(2).
155 Ibid., s.104(a)–(i).
156 Ibid., s.103(2A).
157 Ibid., s.86E.
158 *R v M* [2014] NZHC 1848; *R v Q* [2014] NZHC 550.
159 [2005] 3 NZLR 372.
160 CA 1961, s.178(3).
161 *R v Wright* [2001] 3 NZLR 22; P. Dean, 'Child Homicide and Infanticide in New Zealand' (2004) 27(4) International Journal of Law and Psychiatry 339.

15 The Netherlands

Erik Gritter

Overview and historical development of homicide offences and offence structure

Overview and offence structure

Dutch homicide law draws a sharp line between offences in which the death of another person is the intended result of certain conduct and offences in which death is an unintended result.[1] Within the first group, ***doodslag*** (art. 287 DPC) is the core offence. The offence description is fulfilled, if someone 'intentionally causes the death of another person'. All other 'voluntary homicide' offences can be seen as variations: ***doodslag*** committed in either aggravating circumstances (e.g., ***moord***, art. 289 DPC) or mitigating circumstances (e.g., assisted suicide, art. 294 DPC). The second group of homicide offences shows a wide variation. It encompasses, for instance, causing death by gross negligence (art. 307 DPC, with a maximum of two years' imprisonment in case of 'plain negligence'[2] or four years in case of 'recklessness') and result qualified offences like art. 302 s.2 DPC (inflicting serious bodily harm, with the death of the victim as a – not intended – result). Another important offence in this group is art. 6 of the Dutch Road Traffic Act 1994 (RTA 1994), which penalises gross negligent conduct in traffic that causes the death of another person. Such conduct may be punished by up to three years' imprisonment. If the negligence consists of 'recklessness' (***roekeloosheid***), then the causing of death of another person may be punished by up to six or nine years, depending on the existence of aggravating factors such as driving under the influence of alcohol.[3]

Dutch criminal law accepts a threefold offence structure.[4] In the assessment of criminal liability, first the ***actus reus*** and ***mens rea*** (as defined by the offence description) will be examined. If one or more essential elements cannot be proven, an acquittal will follow. The

1 C.P.M. Cleiren, *T&C Strafrecht* (online version Kluwer Navigator), Introduction, Title XIX, comment 2 (updated 1 September 2017). Dutch criminal law recognises two 'ground forms' of *mens rea*: intention ('*opzet*') and gross negligence (*schuld* or *culpa*). Normally, one of these subjective elements is part of the offence description of felonies, such as the Dutch homicide offences.

2 H. Wolswijk, 'Serious Traffic Offences: The Dutch Perspective' in A. van Dijk and H. Wolswijk (eds), *Criminal Liability for Serious Traffic Offences: Essays on Causing Death, Injury and Danger in Traffic* (Eleven International Publishing 2015) 17.

3 In Dutch criminal law, as will be explained further on in this chapter, *roekeloosheid* (which linguistically resembles 'recklessness') is seen as the most severe form of negligence.

4 E. Gritter, 'The Netherlands' in A. Reed and M. Bohlander (eds) *General Defences in Criminal Law – Domestic and Comparative Perspectives* (Ashgate 2014) 255.

next steps in the examination of the offence concern the lawfulness of the conduct and the blameworthiness of the defendant, depending on the existence of a ground for justification (such as self-defence) or disculpation (such as duress). If a defence applies, the defendant will be discharged. With offences of negligence, the structure is essentially the same, but the different steps are much more intertwined. The result is that an accepted defence will always lead to an acquittal (not a discharge) because gross negligence cannot be established.

Historical development of homicide offences

The current Dutch system of homicide offences is mainly the result of choices made by the Dutch legislator at the end of the nineteenth century. Before the Dutch Penal Code came into force (1886), the core source of Dutch substantive criminal law had been the French *Code Pénal.* This law book had been introduced in The Netherlands in 1811 by Napoleon Bonaparte, and continued in force after the end of the French occupation in 1813. The new Dutch code broke explicitly with the (old) French system of homicide law, in which intended conduct that resulted in the unintended ('unwanted') death of another person could also be punished as intentional homicide (*meurte*, art. 295 CP) through the doctrine of *dolus indirectus* (in the way this concept is understood in The Netherlands).[5] Instead, as already has been mentioned, only the intended (wanted) death of another person can mount up to intentional homicide, albeit that conditional intent (*dolus eventualis*) in any case suffices.

General elements

Beginning of life

In Dutch criminal law, the protection of life through the homicide offences starts at a certain pregnancy period. According to art. 82a DPC, 'taking another person's life' or 'taking the life of a child during or shortly after birth' (which is part of the offence description of 'voluntary child homicide' and 'murder of a child', arts. 290 and 291 DPC) includes the killing of a foetus (*vrucht*) that can reasonably be expected to stay alive outside the body of the mother. Although art. 82a DPC isn't more specific than that, it is commonly understood that a period of 24 weeks of pregnancy or more invokes the protection of the criminal law.[6]

End of life

At the other end of the spectrum, the state of death can be said to have been entered if the heart and the lungs no longer function, and pupillary responses are absent.[7] So in a state of

5 In Dutch criminal law, *dolus indirectus* is to be distinguished from *dolus eventualis* or any other (accepted) form of intention. See explicitly on the denial of the doctrine of *dolus indirectus* in the Dutch Penal Code: D. Simons, *Leerboek van het Nederlandsche Strafrecht* (4th edn, P. Noordhof 1921) 205; J. Remmelink, *Mr. D. Hazewinkel-Suringa's Inleiding tot de Studie van het Nederlandse Strafrecht* (15th edn, Gouda Quint 1996) 222 (Remmelink calls this 'indirect intent' (as it is understood in The Netherlands) a 'misconception' (*wanbegrip*)).

6 The period is the same as the period wherein an abortion may legally be performed. See <www.rijksoverheid.nl/onderwerpen/abortus/vraag-en-antwoord/abortus-hoeveel-weken> accessed 4 April 2018; M.A.H. van der Woude, *T&C Strafrecht* (online version Kluwer Navigator), art. 82a DPC, comment 2 (updated 22 April 2018).

7 See the guideline on autopsies for medical doctors: Dutch Society for General Practitioners et al., *Richtlijn Lijkschouw voor Behandelend Artsen. Werkwijze en Samenwerking met Gemeentelijk*

coma, there is still life; the intentional killing of a person in coma will, in principle, amount to voluntary homicide.[8]

Medical treatment scenarios

Medical end-of-life decisions may in Dutch criminal law be treated in different ways, depending on the circumstances. They can arise in the sphere of an abortion after 24 or more weeks of pregnancy, in the sphere of (il)legal euthanasia or under the heading of defences (especially the defence of necessity). Any relevant issues will be discussed in the concerning paragraphs that follow.

Homicide by omission

Dutch criminal law accepts the concept of homicide by omission.[9] This is relevant for negligent homicide – which core is usually an omission – but also for intentional homicide. If a causal relationship can be established between intentionally omitting to act (where the defendant was under a legal duty to act), and the result (the death of another person), then the defendant may be held criminally liable for voluntary homicide. An example from Dutch case law concerns a case of complicity by omission.[10] The defendant in this case had inflicted extremely grievous bodily harm to the victim, who was later again brutally harmed by another person, after which the victim died. According to the Dutch Supreme Court, the extreme violence – which had made the victim helpless – had vested upon the defendant a duty to seek help and protect the victim for further harm. By not acting upon this duty, which accommodated the commission of the homicide offence, the defendant was liable for 'aiding and abetting by omission'.

Omitting to rescue or help another person

The Dutch Penal Code knows several offences that deal with – in broad terms – liability for abandoning helpless people, or not ensuring that help is called in. Art. 255 DPC for instance (a felony), makes it an offence for a person whose duty it is (by law or agreement) to care for another person (or to nurse this person or support him or her) to intentionally 'bring' or 'leave' that person in a helpless position. If the death of that person is the result, the defendant may be punished with up to nine years' imprisonment (art. 257 s.2 DPC). Art. 450 DPC (a misdemeanour) makes it an offence for anyone who witnesses acute life-threatening danger for another person to omit helping this person or to omit that help is called in. Liability will only arise, according to the offence description, if help may be supplied without danger for the witness or others, and if the death of the other person has followed.

Lijkschouwers en Politie (June 2016) <www.nhg.org/sites/default/files/content/nhg_org/uploads/final_mdr_lijkschouw_2016_sk_web_bookmarks_0.pdf> accessed 4 April 2018. See for a (seemingly) slightly different view Cleiren (n 1) comment 3b.

8 Example derived from Cleiren (n 1) comment 3b.

9 G. Knigge and H.D. Wolswijk, *Ons Strafrecht 1. Het Materiële Recht* (15th edn., Wolters Kluwer 2015) 75; J. de Hullu, *Materieel Strafrecht: Over Algemene Leerstukken van Strafrechtelijke Aansprakelijkheid naar Nederlands Recht* (7th edn., Wolters Kluwer 2018) 77ff.

10 HR 12 December 2000, NJ 2002/516.

Intentional homicide offences

The Dutch concept of intention

Acting with intention in Dutch criminal law means acting wilfully and knowingly. Under this heading, four gradations of intention are recognised.[11] Applied to voluntary homicide, an 'intention to kill' can either mean (1) the purpose to kill; (2) being certain that the death of another person will follow as a consequence (although it was not the perpetrator's purpose to kill); (3) acting in the awareness that the result is highly probable or virtually certain; or (4) conditional intent (*dolus eventualis*).

Dolus eventualis is as such not a concept with a universal definition or meaning. In Dutch criminal law *dolus eventualis* means, in relation to intentional homicide offences, that the perpetrator *consciously accepted the severe risk* (or *substantial chance*) that death would follow from his actions. Mere conscious acceptance of the *possibility* that death would follow from his actions is never enough. According to the Dutch Supreme Court, the question whether certain conduct has created a *severe* risk that a certain result would follow needs to be answered upon the specific circumstances of the case, among which are the nature of the conduct and the circumstances under which that conduct was performed. In any case, so the Supreme Court ruled, it should concern a risk or chance that is 'severe' (or 'substantial') according to 'rules of general experience'.[12] This comes down to a more or less objective approach.[13] It must be established in the end that the defendant had been aware of this severe risk (he acted 'knowingly') *and* had consciously accepted this risk (he acted 'wilfully').

An interesting illustration of the Dutch concept of conditional intent can be found in a case wherein an elderly man of almost 74-years-old was visited by two men in his flat.[14] The two men demanded payment for work they had done for the man's son in setting up a cannabis plantation. The man was being threatened. He managed to grab a gun and pointed it at the two men. After the elderly man was told that he would now definitely end up in hospital, he pulled the trigger and shot one of the men in the breast area.[15] While the men tried to flee, the other man was shot in a leg.

With regard to the second victim, the Court of Appeal convicted the man for attempted voluntary homicide. In response to a plea in which proof of the (conditional) intent was denied, the Court ruled that the defendant had wilfully and knowingly accepted the severe risk that vital body parts would have been hit from which the second victim could have died. The Court ruled that the defendant had wilfully and knowingly accepted that severe risk, by targeting the victim at a low angle in a small room, while the defendant had been an unexperienced shooter because he had never before used a gun. The Supreme Court stressed in its ruling that from the mere fact that the defendant had been aware of the substantial risk of death, it cannot be derived that the defendant had *thus* accepted the severe risk.[16] The Court of Appeal had come to this conclusion, according to the Supreme Court, since its reasoning implied that the defendant's conduct, as it appeared, had been so clearly aimed at

11 Knigge and Wolswijk (n 9) 111ff.
12 HR 25 March 2003, NJ 2003/552.
13 See e.g., De Hullu (n 9) 243.
14 HR 30 May 2017, ECLI:NL:HR:2017:973.
15 The case is also of interest with regard to the assessment of the (proportionality) of self-defence.
16 Conditional intent can come close to the concept of 'conscious negligence' in Dutch criminal law, in which cases the defendant was aware of the (severe) risk that a certain result would follow, but did not accept this.

killing the second victim, that the defendant must be said to have consciously accepted the severe risk. This reasoning, however, was incomprehensible, according to the Supreme Court, since the Court of Appeal had also established upon statements made by the defendant that he had shot only once and that he had targeted and shot at a low angle. The ruling shows that establishing conditional intent is a very precise matter, in which the elements of this concept (severity of the risk, consciousness of this risk and the (conscious) acceptance of this risk) must be assessed thoroughly. In this case, the severity of the risk of death (small room, inexperienced shooter) seems clear. The conscious *acceptance* of this severe risk, however, raised questions in the light of the established facts.

Doodslag *(art. 287 DPC)*

The offence description of *doodslag* (voluntary homicide; art. 287 DPC) is, as already has been shown, quite straightforward. It merely states that the intentional killing of another person is an offence. A conviction may lead to imprisonment up to a maximum of 15 years. The offence description does not specify any particular conduct; as a consequence, *any* intentional conduct (including omissions) that has caused the result (the death of another person) can lead to punishment. In Dutch criminal law, causation is established (or denied) with the help of a central 'criterion'. The question that needs to be answered is whether the result can 'reasonably be attributed' to the defendant or the defendant's conduct.[17] Within this criterion, more classic ways of approaching causation (such as the *causa proxima* theory) can be used to provide arguments pro or contra the reasonableness of the attribution, alongside other aspects such as the intentionality of the conduct (intention with regard to the result).[18] In the end, the 'reasonable attribution test' is a normative, juridical test (in which the outcome may differ from a more empirical approach of causation).[19]

Murder (art. 289 DPC)

The Dutch offence description of murder is essentially the same as the description of voluntary homicide (art. 287 DPC), but with the added (aggravating) element of *premeditation* (*met voorbedachte raad*). So, murder in Dutch criminal law is characterised by the intentional *and* premeditated killing of another person. Murder may be punished with life imprisonment or temporary imprisonment up to a maximum of 30 years.

Premeditation can be seen as a certain 'quality' of intention as such[20], but – probably more accurate – as a 'process' in which the intention was formed, with the effect of giving this intention (that may be conditional) a certain quality.[21] The substantive law definition of premeditation has not changed over the years, but the approach to prove this element has. The (substantive) meaning of premeditation consists of several elements: (1) the defendant could have considered his decision (or the taking of the decision) during a certain time; (2)

17 The Dutch Supreme Court developed this rule in HR 12 September 1978, NJ 1979/60. See on this rule e.g., De Hullu (n 9) 185ff; Knigge and Wolswijk (n 9) 85ff. See for a more elaborate treatise E.M. Witjens, *Strafrechtelijke Causaliteit. De Redelijke Toerekening Vergeleken met het Privaatrecht* (Kluwer 2011).
18 Knigge and Wolswijk (n 9) 87, 89ff.
19 Witjens (n 17) 212ff.
20 According to De Hullu (n 9) 261.
21 G.A. van Hamel, *Inleiding tot de Studie van het Nederlandsche Strafrecht*, J.V. van Dijck (ed.) (4th edn, De Erven F. Bohn/Gebr. Belinfante 1927) 310; Remmelink (n 5) 224.

while he did not act on impulse (e.g., due to a sudden emotional upwelling); (3) so he had been in a position (had the opportunity) to think about the meaning and the consequences of the intended act, and to appreciate (understand) these.[22] Although the Dutch legislator had probably wanted proof of actual, subjective consideration in murder cases, the Dutch Supreme Court had gradually accepted a more objective test in which the mere passing of time and the non-existence of a situation of sudden anger or rage could easily lead to proof of premeditation.[23] Since 2012, however, the Supreme Court has changed its course (for which actual consequences are, at the time of writing, still in discussion).[24] The Supreme Court ruled that proof of premeditation requires specific attention. The Court seems to require proof of *actual* consideration.[25] But given the fact that delivering proof for this can be very difficult, it can be reasonable to establish premeditation if the defendant has had time and opportunity to consider his decision. On the other hand, according to the Supreme Court, the Court may find contra-indications that may deny the existence of a situation of premeditation: sudden rage during planning and commission, the fact that the time between decision and commission had been short or that there had only been opportunity to consider during the execution of the decision. The fact that proof of premeditation needs 'specific attention' seems to imply that courts should in any case take a factual, concrete approach of the relevant factors. An example is a case in which the defendant and the victim had a row, after which the defendant left.[26] Later he returned with a knife, went after the victim and stabbed the victim without hesitation and without warning. The Court of Appeal ruled that premeditation could be proved; it argued that there had been enough time to consider the decision to stab the victim with the knife, while none of the contra-indications applied. The Supreme Court however found the Court's reasoning incomprehensible. It argued that the Court had only stated *in general terms* that there had been time for the defendant to consider his decision; the Court had not established *when* the defendant had taken his decision, nor how much time had been available to him to decide. The mere fact that the defendant had gone away at first, and returned later with the knife, did not change this according to the Supreme Court.

Other homicide offences committed in aggravating circumstances

Besides murder, Dutch criminal law knows two other homicide offences that come down to *doodslag* committed in aggravating circumstances. The maximum sentences for these offences are the same as for murder. The first can be found in art. 288 DPC, which is usually called 'qualified voluntary homicide':

> Voluntary homicide, followed, accompanied or preceded by a criminal offence and committed with the purpose of preparing the commission of that offence or to make the commission of that offence more easy, or, in case the offence was discovered while committed[27], to ensure, either for himself or other participants, impunity or the

22 In (not very modern) Dutch: '*zich daarvan rekenschap geven*'. See for this description of premeditation e.g., HR 12 October 2013, NJ 2014/156; De Hullu (n 9) 262.

23 See e.g., Remmelink (n 5) 224; Knigge/Wolswijk (n 9) 132.

24 HR 28 February 2012, NJ 2012/518, clarified in HR 12 October 2013, NJ 2014/156.

25 HR 12 October 2013, NJ 2014/156, at 3.4. See further De Hullu (n 9) 262.

26 HR 5 July 2016, ECLI:NL:HR:2016:1411.

27 According to art. 128 Code of Criminal Procedure, *flagrante delicto* (*ontdekking op heterdaad*) not only means the discovery of the offence *while* it is committed, but it also covers a short time

possession of what has been unlawfully obtained, will be punished with life imprisonment or temporary imprisonment not exceeding thirty years or a fine of the fifth category.

The offence of art. 288 DPC covers for instance the intentional killing of a shop keeper, with the purpose of making it easier to rob him from his money. In that case, the voluntary homicide is *followed* by the offence of theft.[28] If in such a case, for whatever reason, the intention to kill cannot be proved, the defendant may under circumstances be charged with a 'qualified theft offence' (art. 312 s.1 and s.3). This offence covers, for instance, situations wherein a theft was preceded by violence or a threat of violence, to make the theft easier. If this leads to the death of the victim, the defendant may be punished with temporary imprisonment up to 15 years. With such a result-qualified offence, *mens rea* with regard to the result need not be proved. The court then only has to establish that such a theft has caused the death of the victim. The main question is then, whether the death of the victim can reasonably be attributed to the defendant.

Art. 288a DPC also covers a form of voluntary homicide, committed with a specific purpose (*oogmerk*): 'voluntary homicide committed with a terroristic purpose'. This offence is the implementation of the EU Council Framework Decision 2002/475/JHA on combatting terrorism.

Homicide offences committed in mitigating circumstances

Dutch criminal law describes several homicide offences that can be labelled as *doodslag* or 'murder' committed in mitigating circumstances. Art. 290 DPC deals with 'voluntary child homicide'. In such a case, a child has been killed by its mother, during or shortly after birth, while the mother acted under the fear for discovery of the birth (maximum sentence six years imprisonment). Art. 291 DPC describes the offence of 'child murder', which may be punished by up to nine years' imprisonment. The offence penalises the intentional killing of the child by the mother during or shortly after birth, while this killing is the execution of the mother's decision to do so, which decision was taken under the fear for discovering the coming birth. According to literature, the two offences should be appreciated in their historical context, stemming from a time in which having a baby as an unmarried woman had been very shameful, or in situations where there had not been good opportunities for such mothers to raise the child.[29]

Art. 293 DPC deals with cases of euthanasia. Section 1 contains the offence description for the intentional killing (committed by 'anyone') of another person on the victim's express and severe desire. Such conduct may be punished by up to a maximum of 12 years' imprisonment. Art. 294 s.1 DPC makes it an offence to intentionally encourage another person to commit suicide, where the suicide actually followed. Section 2 of art. 294 DPC deals with assisted suicide: intentionally helping another person to commit suicide, or giving him the

after it was committed (of relevance for the use of police powers such as arrest). Art. 288 DPC however only refers to the situation wherein the offence was discovered *at the time* it was committed: in case of *betrapping op heterdaad*.

28 In the example, the other offence is a felony. The other criminal offence than homicide, however, does not *have* to be a felony; it may also be a misdemeanour. See for a recent example of a case of art. 288 DPC HR 14 February 2017, ECLI:NL:HR:2017:223.

29 J.M. van Bemmelen, *Ons Strafrecht deel 3. Het Materiële Strafrecht (Bijzondere Delicten)*, Th. W. van Veen (ed.) (Samsom/H.D. Tjeenk Willink 1990) 23.

means to do so. All offences mentioned in s.294 DPC may be punished by up to three years' imprisonment.

Section 2 of art. 293 DPC gives a special provision regarding *legal euthanasia*, which is also applicable in cases of assisted suicide. According to art. 293 s.2 DPC (in conjunction with art. 294 s.2 DPC), the offences of art. 293 s.1 and 294 s.2 DPC are 'not punishable', if they have been committed by a medical doctor who has met the relevant standard of care (as laid down in separate legislation) and who has notified the coroner in accordance with the relevant legislation.[30] The practical effect is, that if the relevant requirements have been met, the medical doctor who carries out the act of euthanasia or is helpful in suicide will not be prosecuted.

Article 293 s. 2 DPC states that the medical doctor who has performed euthanasia should inform the coroner. As soon as the coroner has been notified, the act of euthanasia is subject to review by a Regional Review Commission on Euthanasia. This commission will, in hindsight, review whether the doctor has met the standard of care. Whether or not euthanasia or assisted suicide was legally performed, depends on whether the standard of care as laid down in art. 2 s.1 (a–f) of the Act on the Review of Euthanasia and Assisted Suicide has been met.

With regard to that standard, the first mentioned rule of conduct is that the medical doctor who agrees to perform euthanasia must be convinced that the patient's request is done freely and was well considered.[31] Second, the medical doctor must be convinced that there is a situation of hopeless and unbearable suffering for the patient. The 'hopelessness' of the patient's suffering is for the greater part a medical matter.[32] It concerns, for instance, the question of whether a disease from which the patient suffers knows any curative and / or palliative options.[33] The 'unbearableness' of the suffering is harder to assess, due to its subjective nature.[34] The commission will review, whether or not the medical doctor has experienced 'emotional empathy' with the patient's suffering.[35]

The third standard of care is that the doctor must have informed the patient of his medical situation, and of his prospects. Fourth, together with the patient, the doctor must be convinced that there is no other reasonable solution for the situation of the patient. Fifth,

30 In Dutch criminal law, evoking art. 293 s.2 DPC or art. 294 s.2 DPC must not be seen as a defence that – if accepted – will deny the unlawfulness of the offence of euthanasia within the tripartite offence structure. In Dutch criminal law, the assessment of a plea based on section 2 of art. 293 DPC will be treated *after* the decision that the charge is proved, but in any case *before* the assessment of any 'real' defences that focus on the wrongfulness and/or the blameworthiness of the act. If the plea succeeds, the defendant will be discharged because no criminal offence has been committed.

31 It is worth mentioning that legal euthanasia is not restricted to somatic diseases, but may also concern psychiatric diseases such as dementia (See the Chabot case, HR 21 June 1994, NJ 1994/656). It will be clear that euthanasia cases concerning psychiatric diseases can be very complex in relation to the quality of the request (freely done and well considered). The Dutch Supreme Court requires in any case a medically classified disease. The *Brongersma* case shows that euthanasia or assisted suicide (by a medical doctor) can never be allowed in cases of (mere) 'life fatigue' or a 'completed life' without a medical context (HR 24 December 2001, ECLI:NL:HR:2002:AE8772).

32 W.L.J.M. Duijst, *T&C Strafrecht* (online version Kluwer Navigator), art. 2 Euthanasiewet, comment 4b (updated 1 March 2018).

33 See the website of the Regional Review Commissions on Euthanasia <www.euthanasiecommissie.nl/zorgvuldigheidseisen/uitzichtloos-en-ondraaglijkInfo toetsingscommissie> accessed 4 April 2018.

34 Duijst (n 32) comment 4c.

35 Ibid.

the doctor must have consulted at least one other independent medical doctor, who has seen the patient and who has expressed (in writing) his view on the first four requirements. Lastly, the euthanasia or assistance in suicide must be performed according to the medical standards of care.

If aspects of the process need to be clarified, the medical doctor may be asked questions by the Review Commission. If the medical doctor has met the standard of care according to the Review Commission, the procedure will be terminated. If the Commission is of the opinion that the standard of care has not been met, then the Health Care Inspection is notified, as well as the prosecuting authorities. In the end, a prosecution for illegal euthanasia (art. 293 s.1 DPC) may be possible.[36] In a case wherein the standard of care has not been met, the medical doctor may try to rely on the defence of necessity, although the standard for such a defence probably lies very high.[37] The Supreme Court has ruled that the defence of necessity is also available if the defendant has performed euthanasia or assisted suicide without being a medical doctor. There, the mere fact that the legislator has created a special provision only for *medical doctors* to perform legal euthanasia has the effect that the standard for acceptance lies very high.[38]

Gross negligence and reckless homicide

The Dutch concept of gross negligence and recklessness

Gross negligence, in Dutch criminal law usually expressed by the words *schuld* (in legislation) or *culpa* (in literature), is usually defined as a severe degree of blameworthy carelessness that is followed by a result. Another way of expressing this concept of negligence is 'a blameworthy, gross (or substantial) deviation from the required standard of care that has caused a certain unwanted result'.[39] This concept of negligence is of a complex nature, in which the main aspects of carelessness, blameworthiness and unlawfulness are closely interlinked. Carelessness in principle means not foreseeing what ought to have been foreseen, which can come down to 'not noticing', 'inconsiderateness' or 'not knowing' where the perpetrator ought to have noticed, ought to have considered or ought to have known. The finding that the perpetrator acted carelessly implies that he was under a duty to act in a different manner. Not all cases wherein the fatal result could have been foreseen will amount to careless conduct, however. Dutch doctrine implies that, as the case may be, a *permissible risk* may be taken.[40] In that case, a duty to act otherwise must be denied; there was no 'careless' conduct. The element of permissible risk assures that not *every* risk (such as mere participating in traffic) should be avoided. A duty to act otherwise must also be denied if a ground for justification applies, such as necessity. Where a certain activity is regulated by

36 See for a recent (but rare) case (at the time of writing in the phase of criminal investigations) Editorial, 'Public prosecutor investigates euthanasia of woman with dementia' *DutchNews.nl* (Netherlands, 28 September 2017) <www.dutchnews.nl/news/archives/2017/09/public-prosecutor-investigates-euthanasia-of-woman-with-dementia/> accessed 4 April 2018.

37 See for an example HR 9 November 2004, NJ 2005/217.

38 See the *Heringa* case, HR 14 March 2017, ECLI:NL:HR:2017:418, at 4.2.2. The Supreme Court found the Court of Appeal's acceptance of the defence of necessity (raised by a defendant who wasn't a medical doctor) incomprehensible, because the Court had not taken into account the fact that the defendant had not been a medical doctor, and moreover had not met (all of) the rules of conduct that are written for medical doctors.

39 Wolswijk (n 2) 19.

40 Ibid. 20.

(written) standards of care, breach of such a standard that causes the fatal result will normally be regarded as careless.[41] In normal cases the blameworthiness of the carelessness can be established, but in exceptional cases – where a ground for disculpation applies, for instance mistake of fact[42] – this element must be denied with a full acquittal as a procedural consequence.

In 2006, the Dutch legislator introduced 'recklessness' (*roekeloosheid*) as an explicit form of negligence that works as an aggravating factor within the category of certain gross negligence offences.[43] In Dutch criminal law, recklessness is seen as the most severe form of gross negligence.[44] As such, it borders on conditional intent.[45] The guideline the Dutch Supreme Court has developed concentrates on the existence of 'exceptional careless conduct which has led to a very severe danger', while the defendant had been or ought to have been aware of such danger.[46] Whether the application of this guideline will lead to proof of recklessness is highly factual; the nature and the severity of the conduct of the defendant needs to be assessed, as well as all other relevant factors.[47]

Case law shows, that cases of recklessness within the realm of gross negligence offences are exceptional and rare, due to the high standard of proof. This can be illustrated by a case in which the defendant – who did not have and never had a driver's license – had driven a car under the influence of alcohol, had swayed the car over roads, had driven at different speeds, had driven too close to other cars, and at one point had hit a traffic island, whereafter he landed on the opposite road and collided with another car, which resulted in serious bodily harm for the other car's driver.[48] The Court of Appeal had found that the serious bodily harm had been the result of reckless conduct. The Supreme Court, however, found the Court of Appeal's reasoning incomprehensible. The established facts as such did not justify the labelling of the defendant's conduct as 'reckless', according to the Supreme Court.

Article 307 DPC

Article 307 s.1 DPC gives the offence description for (general) gross negligence homicide. The description merely requires proof of the fact that the death of another person can be 'ascribed to' the gross negligence of the defendant. If the gross negligence consists of recklessness, so s.2 of art. 307 DPC states, the prison sentence may be doubled to a maximum of four years.

Article 6 Road Traffic Act 1994

Article 6 of the RTA 1994 contains an important provision on gross negligence homicide in traffic situations. The article reads as follows[49]:

41 Knigge and Wolswijk (n 9) 147.
42 Gritter (n 4) 269.
43 Knigge and Wolswijk (n 9) 154ff.
44 Ibid. 147ff; Wolswijk (n 2) 27ff.
45 De Hullu (n 9) 277.
46 See e.g., HR 4 March 2014, ECLI:NL:HR:2014:470.
47 Ibid. See also De Hullu (n 9) 278.
48 HR 4 March 2014 (n 46).
49 The article also penalises the causing of serious bodily harm in traffic or 'such physical injury that it results in temporary illness or impediment of the performance of daily routines' (see Wolswijk (n 2) 18).

> Anyone who participates in traffic is forbidden to behave in such a way that a traffic accident which may be attributed to his negligence takes place which causes another person to be killed (…).[50]

Gross negligence homicide in traffic may be punished by up to three years' imprisonment.[51] If the negligence consists of recklessness, the maximum sentence is six years' imprisonment.[52] Art. 175 s.3 RTA 1994 sums up several aggravating circumstances that will increase the maximum penalties with a half; recklessness may in those cases be punished with up to nine years' imprisonment. The aggravating circumstances concern, among others, being under the influence of alcohol or another substance, a serious exceedance of the maximum speed or not having given right of way.

The Dutch concept of recklessness has already been discussed earlier in the chapter. It was shown there, that the Dutch Supreme Court has set a high standard of proof for recklessness. It is worth mentioning with respect to reckless homicide in traffic that the Supreme Court has ruled – which fact illustrates that high standard – that recklessness may not be based on the mere presence of the mentioned aggravating circumstances as such. It is the Supreme Court's opinion, that it would otherwise mount up to 'double accounting'.[53]

Result-qualified offences

Dutch criminal law knows several 'result-qualified offences', in which the death of another person is an aggravating circumstance if such death can – in law – be seen as a result of the offence in question. Examples can be found (among many more) in art. 300 s.3 DPC (inflicting bodily harm), art. 302 s.2 DPC (grievous bodily harm), art. 312 s. 3 DPC (qualified theft), art. 157 under 3 DPC (arson) and art. 282 s.3 DPC (the unlawful deprivation of liberty). In case of a result-qualified offence, causation is assessed in two steps. With the offence of art. 300 s.3 DPC in mind as an example, first a causal relationship has to be established between the defendant's conduct and the victim's bodily harm. The second step is whether there is causation between the bodily harm and the victim's death. It should be noted that Dutch criminal law does not require proof of negligence in this second step.

Cases like these can give a good insight into the way causation is established in Dutch criminal law. An example is a case in which the Court of Appeal could prove that the defendant had caused bodily harm (art. 300 DPC), but could not find evidence that showed that the victim had died as a result of the harm.[54] In carrying out a theft, the defendant had suddenly clasped an arm around the neck of the victim and he had also bitten him. The victim died shortly after. According to the Court of Appeal, no causal relationship could be established between the inflicted bodily harm and the death that followed. The Court of Appeal reasoned that the victim had been 46 or 49 years, and had suffered from heart diseases, while at the time of the commission of the offence, the victim had used cocaine. The violent conduct *in itself* could not have caused the death of the

50 Ibid., see for the basis of this translation – which has been slightly altered.
51 Art. 6 RTA 1994 in conjunction with art. 175 s.1 under a RTA 1994.
52 Ibid. in conjunction with art. 175, s.2 under a RTA 1994.
53 See for this term Wolswijk (n 2) 30.
54 HR 14 October 2014, NJ 2015/5.

victim, or have increased the chance of dying, according to the Court of Appeal; the Court of Appeal concluded that there had been a real opportunity that the victim would have died without the bodily harm. The Supreme Court, however, ruled that Court's reasoning of its decision that the death could not reasonably be attributed to the defendant had been incomprehensible, with regard to the Court of Appeal's findings concerning the victim's predisposition. The victim's predisposition seemingly did not put a bar to the attribution of the result of the victim's conduct to the defendant.

Abortion and homicide

The Dutch law on (il)legal abortion has a complex, layered structure. As a start, art. 296 s. 1 DPC describes the offence of aborting pregnancy: 'to give a woman a treatment', knowing or reasonably suspecting that this treatment will abort pregnancy. The offence may be punished with imprisonment up to a maximum of four years. This offence is not part of Title XIX (Book 2) within the DPC that contains the homicide offences; the offence of aborting pregnancy is the sole offence of Title XIXA on abortion. Sections 2–4 of the article describe several aggravating circumstances in relation to the offence: the situation that the woman had died as a result of the offence (sentencing maximum of six years), the situation that the offence is committed without the consent of the woman (sentencing maximum 12 years) and the situation in which the woman did not consent and died as a result of the offence (sentencing maximum 15 years).

Art. 296 s.5 DPC deals with *legal* abortion: if the treatment aimed at abortion was carried out by a medical doctor in a hospital or clinic wherein such a treatment is allowed in accordance with the Act on Aborting Pregnancy, the offence of abortion is 'not punishable'.[55] Besides rules regarding recognition of hospitals or clinics in which abortion is allowed through a system of permits, The Act on Aborting Pregnancy contains several standards of care. Impunity can for instance only be granted if the woman requesting abortion is in a state of 'emergency' (which is not further defined as such in the Act).

In cases wherein the pregnancy lasted 24 weeks or more, an abortion that leads to the death of the child will in principle also fall under the protection of the homicide offences (art. 82a DPC). Whether or not a conviction for a homicide offence is possible, will depend on the factual circumstances. Abortions that are committed as a medical necessity after a pregnancy duration of 24 weeks may be treated in the sphere of necessity (art. 40 DPC) or the (unwritten ground of the) 'medical exception'. In its decision in a particular case whether or not to prosecute, the prosecutor will take into account the decision of a special committee on late pregnancy abortions, where the committee may investigate whether or not the medical doctor acted carefully.[56] Apart from the execution of the abortion according to medical standards, the committee may investigate whether an accepted ground of medical necessity applies (such as, for instance, foreseeable hopeless suffering for the child if the pregnancy is carried out and the child is born in a natural way).

55 See for the meaning of 'not punishable' (n 30).

56 See the 'Regeling beoordelingscommissie late zwangerschapsafbreking en levensbeëindiging bij pasgeborenen' Stc. 2016/3145 <www.rijksoverheid.nl/onderwerpen/levenseinde-en-euthanasie/late-zwangerschapsafbreking-en-levensbeeindiging-bij-pasgeborenen> accessed 4 April 2018.

General defences to homicide

Full defences

In Dutch criminal law, the general defences apply to any offence.[57] If accepted, a defence always work as full defence. So, in for instance a case of voluntary homicide (art. 287 DPC), an accepted defence of self-defence will always lead to a full discharge. A 'fallback' in such cases to a lesser charge is unknown in Dutch criminal law. Another question is of course the level of acceptance of defences, in relation to the nature of the offence that was committed.

Self-defence

The commission of a homicide offence may be lawful, if the commission of that offence by the defendant was 'required for the necessary defence of his person or the person of another, or his or another person's integrity or property, against an immediate, unlawful attack' (defence of self-defence, art. 41 s.1 DPC).[58] As is shown, several factors need to be examined in order to assess the lawfulness of the committed offence in a situation of possible self-defence. Besides the existence of an immediate, unlawful attack on one of the mentioned legal interests (which includes an immediate threat of an attack), the self-defence must be 'necessary'. If effective alternative actions could have been taken that would have caused less harm to the victim, the defence will be denied. A strict duty to flee from an attack, whenever this is possible, is however not accepted in Dutch criminal law. The courts need to examine in this respect also whether the defendant *should have* fled. Another important aspect is whether the commission of the offence was 'required'. Under this heading, courts will examine the proportionality of the defence. Some leeway is offered on this point, since a reasonable balance has to be struck between the interest at stake and the means and the intensity of the defence. If the way the defendant defended himself was found to be disproportionate, he may rely under circumstances on the defence of excessive self-defence (a ground for disculpation). It must then be established that the excessive nature of the defence 'directly resulted from a strong emotion brought about by the attack' (art. 41 s.2 DPC).

Duress

Defences of duress are also seldom accepted. This can for instance be seen in battered woman cases.[59] Originally, a case of duress required a situation of acute, compelling pressure at the time of the commission of the offence.[60] This would provide hardly any room in situations where the commission of an offence originated from long-term, permanent pressure. Nowadays, the acuteness requirement doesn't play a very strict role anymore. Due to

57 See for a more elaborate treatment of the Dutch system of general defences: Gritter (n 4) 255ff. 'Mercy killings' are not treated under the heading of General Defences, since – as has been explained – euthanasia has its own offence description, and legal euthanasia makes the offence as such 'not punishable', which in Dutch legal doctrine cannot be related to the wrongfulness of the offence within the tripartite offence structure (n 30).

58 See for a more extensive treatise of self-defence in Dutch criminal law Gritter (n 4) 260ff.

59 Gritter (n 4) 265ff.

60 Ibid.

that, a duress defence may be accepted in cases of long-term threats. The acceptance of long-term situations of pressure, however, has another side: the examination of a case of duress requires the court also to examine whether the defendant should have resisted the pressure.[61] If the defendant had been able to seek help in escaping the pressure situation, the defence will be denied. An example is a Dutch case in which the defendant, who was prosecuted for voluntary homicide, claimed that she had killed her partner in a situation of duress.[62] She had been threatened and humiliated by her partner for a long time. One night she was raped by him, and he threatened to do the same to her daughter and said that he would kill the woman the next day. That night, after he had fallen asleep, the woman killed her partner. The Court of Appeal sentenced the defendant to two years' imprisonment. Although the Court acknowledged that she had acted under strong emotions, it had not found that she acted under a pressure that she could not have resisted. Other options had been available to her to escape the situation, according to the Court. The offence with which she was charged played an important role; the Court considered the fact that there had not been a moment in which she had to choose between preserving her own life and taking that of the victim. Elements of subsidiarity and proportionality will of course be of importance in assessing any defence; the very nature of homicide offences (especially the ones that are committed intentionally) will have the effect that only in very extreme situations a defence will be accepted.[63]

Duress might also be the framework for assessing cases in which a homicide has been committed with cultural motives, such as honour killings.[64] The defendant may plead that he acted under the unbearable pressure of his family to save family honour. Dutch case law does not show any accepted defences of duress in relation to honour killings. As with battered woman cases, Dutch courts use a very high standard of acceptance, due to the nature of the offence, with the effect that the defendant can be said to have had some freedom left to act otherwise. Case law shows, that a more or less objective test, grounded on Dutch morals, is used to assess whether the defendant could have reasonably acted otherwise. In a case concerning the murder of a young girl by her Hindustani mother, the mother claimed that she acted in duress.[65] The child, she pleaded, had been bewitched or was under the influence of a 'bad ghost', and she had been under an enormous pressure do to something about it. She and others inflicted serious bodily harm to the child, the child was seriously neglected and eventually the child died. According to the District Court, the mother had not done enough to escape the pressure situation. In examining her claim of duress, the District Court explicitly used what it called 'Dutch standards', knowing that the woman was born in India and had lived, in the Netherlands, in an environment that was for the most part Indian. Using 'Dutch standards' brought the District Court to the conclusion that the mother should have acted in the interest of protecting the health and the life of the small child. CSE-She ought not to have acted (or omitted action) out of fear for social exclusion. In other words: the defendant should have resisted family pressure.

61 Ibid.
62 HR 26 May 1992, NJ 1992/681, discussed by De Hullu (n 9) 306 and Gritter (n 4) 265ff.
63 See also De Hullu (n 9) 307.
64 See on this subject H.D. Wolswijk, 'De Nederlandse Strafrechter en Culturele Delicten' (2010) 16 Ontmoetingen: Voordrachtenreeks van het Lutje Psychiatrisch-Juridisch Gezelschap 21 ff.
65 District Courts-Gravenhage 14 December 2007, ECLI:NL:RBSGR:2007:BC0775. This case is also discussed by Wolswijk (n 64) 26ff.

Necessity

Before legal euthanasia was enacted, the Dutch Supreme Court had accepted legal euthanasia, performed by a medical doctor, under the doctrine of necessity.[66] In those cases, the medical doctor could plead that he had been confronted with the necessity to choose between his duty to preserve the life of his patient on the one hand, and his duty to relieve his patient of unbearable and hopeless suffering on the other hand. Necessity might still have a function today in relation to legal euthanasia, if – as has already been discussed earlier in the chapter – euthanasia was performed while the standard of care has not been met. Otherwise the defence of necessity might play an important role in end-of-life decisions in extreme medical situations, in which euthanasia cannot be performed because the patient could not have expressed his strong desire to end life.[67]

Insanity

In extreme cases, an accepted defence of insanity may lead to a full acquittal in homicide cases because intention cannot be proved. This will only happen, however, if the defendant lacked *any* insight at all into the effects and consequences of his conduct.[68] Apart from this, if some (conditional) intent can be found or constructed, a defence of insanity rarely leads to a discharge in the sphere of defences. The situation is thus, that courts can usually find *some* blameworthiness left to justify conviction and punishment. Due to the mental disorder, the defendant may in such cases also be sentenced to a hospital order.

Sentencing framework

Legal aspects

A characteristic of Dutch criminal law is the absence of (substantial) minimum terms of sentencing. This is also the case with homicide offences; only the maximum terms are of relevance.[69] The maximum temporary prison sentence in the DPC is generally set at 18 years (art. 10 s.2), but the maximum may be set at 30 years if an offence may be punished with either life imprisonment or a temporary prison sentence (art. 10 s.3 DPC). This is the case, as already has been mentioned, with murder. In case of conjuncture of offences, the prison sentence may also climb up to a maximum of 30 years (art. 10 s.3 and s.4 DPC).[70]

In case of murder (art. 289 DPC), it is for the courts to decide whether life imprisonment is appropriate or rather a temporary sentence should be imposed with a maximum of 30 years. Mandatory sentences are unknown in Dutch criminal law. Once the court has ruled that life imprisonment should be imposed, the execution of this sentence is strict; 'life is life'. Only a pardon by the King, in exceptional circumstances, may lead to an early release. Due

66 Knigge and Wolswijk (n 9) 182; Gritter (n 4) 264.

67 See for an example HR 9 November 2004 (n 37). The so called 'medical exception', an unwritten ground for justification, will probably not come into play with regard to end-of-life decisions, because this defence seems to be reserved for committing offences – such as causing the death of a patient – in the course of normal medical (careful) treatment, such as surgery.

68 Gritter (n 4) 267.

69 According to art. 10(2) DPC, the minimum term of a temporary prison sentence is one day. The minimum amount of a fine is € 3 (see art. 23(2) DPC).

70 When a conjuncture of (separate) felonies is concerned, the court will impose only *one* prison term (art. 57 DPC).

to case law of the European Court of Human Rights on the realistic existence (or not) of possibilities for early release, however, the execution of life sentences is nowadays much in discussion. In 2016, the Supreme Court ruled that the Dutch criminal law is in breach of art. 3 of the European Convention on Human Rights as far as the execution of life imprisonment is concerned.[71] On the outset, Dutch criminal law should ensure, according to the SC, that there is a 'real possibility' of revision of a life sentence after (not more than) 25 years. The review should face the question whether there have been such changes in the convicted person and such progress in his resocialisation, that life imprisonment is no longer justified.

Since 2017 Dutch criminal law has an Advisory Commission on life imprisonment that gives advice on possible (requested) pardons and re-integration, on the basis of a review of life imprisonment after 25 years.[72] The Dutch Supreme Court has ruled, that this solution is sufficient in the light of art. 3 of the European Convention on Human Rights. [73]

Statistics

Dutch criminal law shows a gradual decline in homicide cases brought to court.[74] The years 2001 up to and including 2010 respectively shows 1460, 1510, 1730, 1640, 1615, 1325, 1145, 1270, 1055 and 1045 decided cases each year. After 2010, the amount of decided cases has dropped further: from 980 cases in 2011 to 605 cases in 2016.[75] From 2011 up to and including 2016, each year shows 25 cases in which the defendant was discharged.

Since 1981, 35 people have been convicted in the Netherlands for life imprisonment.[76] On 1 November 2015, 33 definitive convictions to life imprisonment were being executed in the Netherlands as such.[77]

71 HR 5 July 2016, ECLI:NL:HR:2016 (n 26):1325. The imposition of life imprisonment as such raises no questions in the light of art. 3 of the Convention, according to the Supreme Court. See, in the aftermath, District Court The Hague 10 August 2016, ECLI:NL:RBDHA:2016:9397, for a case in which a court – upon the case law of the European Court and the Dutch Supreme Court – ordered the State of The Netherlands to draw up a resocialisation plan for a person convicted for life, in order to make a review possible in the future.

72 Besluit Adviescommissie Levenslanggestraften, Stc. 2017/32577.

73 HR 19 December 2017, ECLI:NL:HR:2017:3185.

74 The figures are based on the statistics by the Dutch Central Bureau of Statistics (CBS), drawn up for so called '*levensmisdrijven*'. According to the Bureau's definition, the term covers the (intentional) homicide offences of art. 287 up to and including art. 291 DPC, art. 293 DPC, art. 294 and art. 296 DPC. So, gross negligence homicide offences and result qualified offences do not fall under this definition. See <www.cbs.nl/nl-nl/onze-diensten/methoden/begrippen?tab=m#id=misdrijf-tegen-het-leven> accessed 4 April 2018. Data of the CBS can be accessed through their website <www.cbs.nl> accessed 4 April 2018.

75 The figures for 2016 are still open for change, according to the Central Bureau of Statistics.

76 See Forum Levenslang (Forum Life Imprisonment), Statistiek Mei 2016 (part of the May 2016 Newsletter) to be found at <www.forumlevenslang.nl/publicaties/nieuwsbrieven/> accessed 4 April 2018.

77 Ibid. The numbers differ, e.g., due to the death of some convicted persons, life sentences imposed in foreign countries but converted to Dutch life sentences, a conviction *in absentia*, etc.

16 Turkey

Murat Önok

Overview and historical development of homicide offences and offence structure

Historical development of homicide offences

The first penal code of the Republic of Turkey was Law no. 765 (adopted on 1 March 1926). Intentional homicide was regulated under art. 448, and required a term of imprisonment of 24 to 30 years. Aggravating circumstances were laid down in arts. 449 and 450, requiring –respectively – life-time imprisonment and capital punishment. Art. 451 provided for a special provision on causal link: where death was a result of the combination of the act of the perpetrator and other (pre-existing or subsequent) factors, the punishment would be mitigated. Art. 452 regulated intentional acts of 'wounding' which caused death – the perpetrator would be held responsible for the death on the mere basis of causality. Art. 453 provided for a mitigating circumstance where murder was committed by the mother against the new-born under the motive of 'saving (her) honour'. Finally, art. 455 regulated unintentional homicide.

The second (and current) Turkish Penal Code (hereinafter 'TPC') is Law no. 5237 (adopted on 26 September 2004, entry into force on 1 June 2005). Intentional homicide is regulated under art. 81 and requires life-time imprisonment. Aggravating circumstances are laid down in art. 82. Art. 83 concerns intentional homicide committed through omission. Although this is a novel provision, there was no doubt in the practice of the previous code that homicide could have been committed through omission. There is no counterpart of former art. 451; where the existence of a causal link between the act of the perpetrator and the death of the victim is determined, the fact that other factors entered into play in bringing about this result will not have any effect on the applicable tariff of punishment. There is also no counterpart of the heavily criticised former art. 453.

Art. 462 of the former PC provided that where murder or wounding is committed against a person who is caught in the act of, or immediately after committing, or when about to commit adultery or unlawful sexual intercourse, the punishment would be decreased *to* one-eighth. The perpetrator had to be the spouse, or ascendant, or brother or sister. The victim had to be a spouse, or sister (not brother!), or descendent or the sexual partner (or both). This provision was abolished in 2003, and does not reappear in the new code.

In addition, art. 463 of the former PC – applicable to both homicide and wounding – provided for reduced punishment where the act was committed together by two or more persons and the actual perpetrator could not be determined. There is no counterpart for this provision either since the understanding of the new PC is that where two persons act in a concerted way to commit a crime together they shall be treated as 'joint principals': both shall be subject to full punishment regardless of whom dealt the decisive blow provided that they decided to commit the crime together.

Intentional homicide – degrees / aggravated forms, etc.

Art. 81 simply states that 'whoever shall intentionally kill a person shall be punished to life-time imprisonment'.

Art. 82 provides for 'qualified circumstances requiring an increase in the punishment' if killing is perpetrated:

- With premeditation;
- With monstrous sentiments or through 'tormenting';
- By causing fire, flood, destruction, sinking, bombing or by using nuclear, biological or chemical weapons;
- Against a direct ascendant, direct descendant, spouse or sibling;
- Against a child or against a person who cannot protect himself physically or mentally;
- Against a woman who is known to be pregnant;
- On account of a public service the victim performed;
- In order to conceal an offence or destroy evidence thereof or facilitate its' commission, or for the purpose of escaping apprehension;
- Out of frustration for not being able to commit an offence;
- With the motive of a blood feud;
- With the motive of traditions.

Where one (or more) of the above exists, the penalty is 'aggravated' life-time imprisonment. The difference with 'normal' imprisonment is that conditions of enforcement are harsher and the time to serve in prison to be eligible for conditional (early) release is longer (30 years instead of 24).

Art. 83 regulates intentional homicide by omission, and provides that the punishment *may* be mitigated.

Finally, where the offences laid down in arts. 82–83 TPC are committed in the framework of the activities of a terrorist organisation, and for terrorist purposes, this is considered a 'terrorist crime' by virtue of art. 4 of the Law on the Fight Against Terror (Law no. 3713, entry into force 12 April 1991), as a result of which the punishment is increased (art. 5 of the same Law).

Reckless homicide

Recklessness does not exist as a term of art under Turkish penal law. Instances of recklessness can be treated under intentional homicide since this crime may be committed through both direct intent and indirect intent (*dolus eventualis*). However, in the latter case, art. 21 (2) TPC provides for a mandatory reduction of the punishment: life-time in lieu of 'aggravated' life-time imprisonment, 20–25 years in lieu of life-time imprisonment, and a reduction of one-third to one-half in other cases.

Where the existence of intent, even in the indirect form, cannot be conclusively determined, the provision on negligent homicide will apply. In this case, the general provision of

TPC art. 22 on advertent / conscious negligence (*bilinçli taksir*) may apply. According to art. 22 (2) TCP negligence exists where an act is committed without foreseeing the results as stated in the legal definition of the offence, due to a failure to discharge a duty of care and attention. Negligence may be inadvertent (*bilinçsiz taksir*) or advertent / conscious (*bilinçli taksir*). The latter is the case where the perpetrator has foreseen the result without, however, intending to bring it about. In this case the punishment for the offence shall be increased by one-third to one-half (art. 22 (3)). In case of advertent negligence the perpetrator is aware of the fact that his action may cause a certain result, but he or she thinks or believes or trusts that it will not.

Negligent homicide

According to art. 85 (1) TPC, 'Any person who causes the death of another through negligence shall be sentenced to a term of imprisonment of two to six years.'

According to art. 85 (2), the sentence shall be a term of imprisonment of two to 15 years where the act has caused the death of more than one person, or injury to one or more person together with the death of one or more person.

Result-qualified / constructive / **versari in re illicita** */ felony homicide offences*

With regard to many crimes, the emergence of death as an unintended result of the criminal act constitutes an aggravating factor. The previous penal code adopted strict liability based on the understanding of '*versari in re illicita*'. Hence, the perpetrator was held responsible for the consequences of his or her own conduct based solely on the existence of a causal nexus.[1] For example, in the case of death resulting from an act aimed at causing injury it sufficed that the result had a causal link with the act for the perpetrator to be held responsible. According to the new TPC, unless a person has been found to have acted intentionally or negligently in a specific case, he or she cannot be held criminally responsible for such act (Arts. 21–23). This is expressly stated in art. 23: 'Where an act causes a more serious result, or a result other than that intended, a person will only be held responsible if he has acted, at least, with negligence in respect of such result'. This means that, as a minimum, the unintended result must be foreseeable for liability to arise. Crimes falling under the provision of art. 23 are known in Turkish academic writings as 'result-aggravated offences' (*Netice Sebebiyle Ağırlaşan Suçlar*).[2]

According to art. 90 (5) TPC on human experimentation, where the victim is injured or killed as a result of this crime, the perpetrator shall be held responsible under the provisions on *intentional* wounding and homicide. The same rule applies in case of preventing the nourishment of convicts and detainees – but only where the victim suffers one of the grave injuries under art. 87 or is killed (art. 298 (3)). Where the victim is killed, the provisions on intentional homicide shall apply in case of trafficking of organs or tissues (art. 91 (8)). art. 87 (4) covers cases where an intentional act of wounding leads to the victim's death (see further on pages 311–312).

1 M. Özen, *Ceza Hukukunda Objektif Sorumluluk* (Ankara 1998) 123 *et seq.*
2 *Erfolgsqualifizierte Delikte* in German, *Delitti aggravati dall'evento* in Italian.

General elements

Beginning of life

The TPC has left to academic writings the determination of the moment life begins. There are different views on the matter:

- According to one view life begins the moment birth has begun.[3] To be more precise, that is when labour pains have started in case of normal birth,[4] and when the uterus is opened in caesarean delivery.[5]
- Another view argues that, in line with art. 28 (1) of the Turkish Civil Code, 'full birth' is required, thus total separation of the baby from the mother's body is required.[6] In a rather recent case, the Court of Cassation has adopted this view.[7]
- A final view argues that a *partial* separation of the baby from the uterus suffices.[8]

On the other hand, as long as the child is 'born' (in the sense described previously) alive, it does not matter if he or she is capable of sustaining life.[9] Where it cannot be conclusively determined that the baby was born alive, he or she cannot be the material object of homicide offences.[10] Therefore, an embryo or foetus cannot be the object of these crimes.[11] Where there is the requisite intent, a person who causes a pregnancy to terminate can be held responsible under art. 99 TPC on abortion. In the alternative, where a pregnant woman is wounded and the act results in a miscarriage, the perpetrator may be held responsible for the result-qualified (aggravated) version of the crime of wounding (art. 87 (2) (e)) provided that he or she acted with negligence as regards this result.

3 S. Dönmezer, *Kişilere ve Mala Karşı Cürümler* (14th edn, Beta: İstanbul 1995) 10.
4 T. Demirbaş, *Yeni Doğmuş Çocuğu Öldürme Suçu* (Ankara 1992) 84; V.Ö. Özbek, K.Doğan, P. Bacaksız and İ.Tepe, *Türk Ceza Hukuku Özel Hükümler* (12th edn, Ankara 2017) 103.
5 D. Tezcan, M.R. Erdem and R.M. Önok, *Teorik ve Pratik Ceza Özel Hukuku* (15th edn, Ankara 2017) 132.
6 S. Erman, in *Erman/Özek Ceza Hukuku Özel Bölüm – Kişilere Karşı İşlenen Suçlar* (Dünya Yayıncılık: İstanbul, 1994), no. 9; N. Toroslu, *Ceza Hukuku Özel Kısım* (9th edn, Ankara 2018) 24; N. Centel, H. Zafer and Ö. Çakmut, *Kişilere Karşı İşlenen Suçlar* – Cilt I (4th edn, Beta: Istanbul 2017) 28; M. Koca and İ. Üzülmez, *Türk Ceza Hukuku Özel Hükümler* (4th edn, Ankara 2017) 28; Z. Hafizoğulları and M. Özen, *Türk Ceza Hukuku Özel Hükümler Kişilere Karşı Suçlar* (5th edn, Ankara, 2016) 34–5; K. Bayraktar, 'Kasten Öldürme' in *Özel Ceza Hukuku Cilt II - Kişilere Karşı Suçlar* (On İki Levha: İstanbul 2017) 16.
7 Court of Cassation (hereinafter 'CC') 9th Criminal Chamber, judgment of 24 December 2008 (no. 16443/14064).
8 Dönmezer (n 3) 12; A. Önder, *Şahıslara ve Mala Karşı Cürümler ve Bilişim Alanında Suçlar* (Filiz Kitabevi: İstanbul, 1994) 4; A. Gökcen and M. Balcı, *Kasten Öldürme Suçları (TCK m. 81–83)* (Adalet: Ankara 2013) 33; M.E. Artuk, A. Gökcen, M.E. Alşahin and K. Çakır, *Artuk & Gökcen Ceza Hukuku Özel Hükümler* (16th edn, Adalet: Ankara 2017) 55; D. Soyaslan, *Ceza Hukuku Özel Hükümler* (11th edn, Yetkin: Ankara 2016) 125.
9 Önder (n 8) 4; Erman (n 6) 10; Toroslu (n 6) 25; Soyaslan (n 8) 125; Centel, Zafer and Çakmut (n 6) 28; Özbek *et al.* (n 4) 104; Gökcen and Balcı (n 8) 34; Artuk *et al.* (n 8) 55; Hafizoğulları and Özen (n 6) 35; Bayraktar (n 6) 17.
10 CC Grand Criminal Chamber, judgment of (no. 1–101/107). In the same direction Artuk *et al.* (n 8) 55.
11 CC 9th Cr.Ch., judgment of 25.12.2008 (no. 18229/13979). Also see H. Hakeri, *Kasten Öldürme Suçları TCK 81–82–83* (2nd edn, Seçkin: Ankara 2007) 21.

End of life

There is no general definition on the issue in statutory law. Art. 11 of the Law on the Transplantation of Organs and Tissues provides that the realisation of 'medical death' shall be ascertained by a unanimous decision taken in accordance with evidence based on medical rules by a body composed of two doctors, one being a neurologist or neurosurgeon, and the other being an anaesthesiology and reanimation or intensive care expert.

It is unclear whether the term 'medical death' refers to 'cerebral death', however a reading of art. 27 of the By-Law on Organ and Tissue Transplant Services leads to that result. However, the above-mentioned Law and By-Law provide for a definition that is only applicable for their own purpose.

The prevailing view in academic writings is that life ends with cerebral death – which refers to the irreversible loss of cerebral functions.[12]

Pre-birth causes with post-birth effect

One view argues that unless life has begun, an act committed against the foetus or embryo cannot fall under homicide offences because one of the material elements of the offence cannot be fulfilled.[13] Another view argues that where birth has been given to a baby who has later died because of an act committed during pregnancy, the provisions on homicide can be applied.[14] There is no case law on the issue.

Furthermore, there are also those who argue that where birth has been given but the new-born has later died because of damage sustained during pregnancy, the provisions of the TPC on abortion (art. 99) may apply.[15] This view can be questioned vis-à-vis the principle of legality: the wording of this provision requires pregnancy to be 'terminated' in order for the provision to be applicable. Again, there is no case law on the issue.

Medical treatment scenarios

Where the side-effect of medication provided to a pregnant woman is the termination of pregnancy, a distinction shall be made: where the termination of the pregnancy is intended (in the form of direct or indirect intent), the provision of TPC art. 25 (2) on state of necessity *may* apply where the aim was to protect the mother's well-being. Where there is no intent, there shall be no liability for the 'death' of the 'child': the provisions on homicide do not apply to the foetus, and the crime of abortion laid down in art. 99 can only be committed through intent.

12 Önder (n 8) 6; Erman (n 6) 10; Toroslu (n 6) 26; Centel, Zafer and Çakmut (n 6) 27; Gökcen and Balcı (n 8) 24; Artuk *et al.* (n 8) 50; H. Hakeri, *Tıp Hukuku* (12th edn, Seçkin: Ankara 2017) 439; Özbek *et al.* (n 4) 105; Koca and Üzülmez (n 6) 29; Hafizoğulları and Özen (n 6) 35; Bayraktar (n 6) 28. Compare Soyaslan (n 8) 126.

13 Tezcan, Erdem and Önok (n 5) 134; Toroslu (n 6) 24.

14 Gökcen and Balcı (n 8) 34; Artuk *et al.* (n 8) 55; Koca and Üzülmez (n 6) 29 (the writers provide a condition: that the effect of the pre-birth act has begun to manifest itself after birth).

15 B. Dönmez, 'TCK'da Çocuk Düşürtme Suçu – Mukayeseli Hukuk ve AİHM'nin Bakış Açısıyla Ceninin Yaşam Hakkının Sınırlandırılması' (2007) 9(2) DEÜHFD Law Journal of Eylül University Law School 99, 113; M. Aydın, 'Çocuk Düşürtme Fiilleri ve Ceza Sorumluluğu' (2011) 19(2) Selçuk Üniversitesi Hukuk Fakültesi Dergisi Law Journal 77; S. Keskin-Kiziroğlu, 'Çocuk Düşürtme ve Düşürme Suçları' in K. Bayraktar *et al.* (eds) *Özel Ceza Hukuku, c. II, Kişilere Karşı Suçlar* (On İki Levha, Istanbul 2017) 434.

In case of conjoined twins, where it is a medical necessity to 'sacrifice' the life of either twin in order to be able to save the life of the other, the provision of TPC Art (25) 2 shall also apply.[16]

A more difficult scenario is where it is necessary to terminate the pregnancy in order to protect the life of the mother, who does not however consent to such an operation. In this case, it is argued that a physician shall not incur liability under TPC art. 99 since this provision does not seek the consent of the mother, but only the presence of 'medical necessity' to perform an act of abortion.[17] In this vein, according to art. 5 (2) of the Law on Population Planning, abortion may be performed where the life of the mother is under threat.[18] According to a similar view, a balance of interests is required between the rights of the mother and those of the foetus: where failure to perform the medical operation will result in a serious threat to the life or physical integrity of the mother, her rights shall prevail over any interest belonging to the child, and medical treatment will be excused in the absence of consent.[19] Finally, according to the opposite view, where it is possible to resort to the will of the mother, such an operation will always be in breach of art. 99 unless her consent is obtained.[20]

Finally, there may be cases where the pregnant woman's cerebral death has occurred but the foetus still displays vitality. In this case, would it fall under art. 99 to 'turn off' the machines attached to the mother? There is no reason to depart from the general rule:[21] where the various biological functions of the body are still being performed and the foetus is 'alive', any action that causes a termination of the pregnancy will fall under art. 99.

Homicide by omission

Art. 83 regulates this crime. The first paragraph requires 'the omission of the duty which causes the formation of [death] to be equivalent to an active conduct'. The second paragraph then explains that this is the case where:

- There is a duty incumbent on the perpetrator to perform certain positive acts arising from law or a contract;
- The perpetrator has previously caused a risk towards the life of other persons through a prior behaviour.

In these cases the perpetrator is considered to be in a 'position of guarantorship' and is thus obliged to refrain from failing to act. Where art. 83 applies, the punishment may be decreased to 20–25 years in lieu of aggravated life imprisonment, 15–20 years in lieu of life imprisonment, and 10–15 years in other cases.

Where the perpetrator (e.g., a doctor) is under a legal obligation to administer treatment which would extend the life-span of the victim, a failure to act will result in the application of this provision. However, to establish the causal link between this omission and the result,

16 Hakeri (n 12) 453.
17 Tezcan, Erdem and Önok (n 5) 341; Keskin-Kiziro⊠lu (n 15) 436.
18 Dönmez (n 15) 120.
19 Özbek *et al.* (n 4) 302. For a similar view see Keskin-Kiziro⊠lu (n 15) 425.
20 Aydın (n 15) 90–1.
21 Hakeri (n 12) 499–500.

it must be proved that timely action would have been very likely to succeed in prolonging the life of the victim.[22]

As explained previously, where the crime is committed through omission, the perpetrator may benefit from a reduced punishment. Sometimes the conduct of the perpetrator may include acts which entail both an active and an omissive aspect (e.g., giving the key of one's car to a drunk friend and not preventing him from driving, a doctor 'pulling off' the plug of the support unit keeping the patient alive, giving a patient an ineffective medication instead of the proper one and so forth). In this case, the 'point of weight' which carries importance from a normative criminal law perspective and the 'social importance' of the act must be taken into account in determining whether there is active conduct or an omission.[23]

The extent of the obligation to prevent the result will be determined on a case-by-case basis and on a subjective basis by taking into account the perpetrator at hand. Therefore, the perpetrator must be in a position to prevent the result,[24] if he or she is unable to do so, the death cannot be imputed on him or her. This necessitates an individual assessment on whether the required action could have been expected of the perpetrator.[25]

In addition, causality must be determined.[26] It is no longer possible to apply the '*conditio sine qua non*' test in omissive crimes – it must be determined that had the required action be taken, the same result would *almost certainly* not have occurred.[27]

Omitting to effect an easy rescue

Unless a person is under a *legal* obligation to intervene, failure to effect a rescue, no matter how easy or uncostly it is, cannot result in liability for homicide offences.[28] Mere actual possibility to prevent the result or any ethical expectation to do so cannot result in criminal law liability.[29]

However, art. 98 TPC lays down a separate crime concerning the omission of the duty to assist or notify. According to the first paragraph of this provision, any person who comes across an individual who is incapable of caring for himself on account of age, illness, injury or any other reason, shall either assist this person or immediately notify the relevant authorities of the situation. Failure to do so will result in a term of imprisonment of up to one year, or a judicial fine. According to the second paragraph, where a failure to act results in the death of the victim, the perpetrator shall be sentenced to a term of imprisonment of one to three years.

On the other hand, where there is a legal obligation to prevent harm to the person in danger, the provisions on homicide or wounding may apply.

22 Tezcan, Erdem and Önok (n 5) 142. Also see Hakeri (n 12) 152.
23 Ibid., Tezcan, Erdem and Önok (n 5) 140.
24 Özbek *et al.* (n 4) 162; Bayraktar (n 6) 25; Hakeri (n 12) 134.
25 Tezcan, Erdem and Önok (n 5), 142. Refer to Hakeri (n 12) 159–65 for extensive debate.
26 CC 9th Criminal Chamber, judgment of 20.2.2006 (no. 6627/939).
27 Tezcan, Erdem and Önok (n 5) 142; cfr Centel, Zafer and Çakmut (n 6) 109 (it should be established that the result would have likely or probably not occurred).
28 R.M. Önok, 'TCK'da Koruma, Gözetim, Yardım veya Bildirim Yükümlülüğünün İhlali Suretiyle İşlenen Suçlar' (2012) Jan (1) İKÜHFD Law Journal of Istanbul Kultur University Law School 31 *et seq.*
29 Tezcan, Erdem and Önok (n 5) 140.

Intentional homicide offences

Actus reus

Any act directed at ending the life of another person may constitute the *actus reus* of this crime.[30] The methods and means used in bringing about the intended result are irrelevant. However, the use of certain methods and means (e.g., killing by inflicting torment) may lead to the application of an aggravating circumstance under TPC art. 82.

The existence of a causal link between the act and the result must be established in accordance with the '*conditio sine qua non*' theory. In addition, the 'objective imputability' of the result to the perpetrator must then be determined. As a result, an 'atypical' run of events which leads to an unpredictable result will mean that the resulting death may no longer be imputed on the perpetrator – in this case responsibility will only arise for attempted murder.[31] However, unless extraordinary circumstances are present, the mere fact that medical intervention was delayed or not applied properly, or that it did not provide positive results will not diminish the liability of the initial perpetrator.[32]

It suffices for the perpetrator to shorten the life of the victim: liability may not be eschewed by arguing that the victim would have died anyway ('irrelevance of the reserve cause').[33]

Mens rea

Under Arts. 81–82 the perpetrator may act with either direct or indirect intent, but in the latter case there is a statutory decrease (art. 21 (2)) of the punishment.

The Court of Cassation considers the behaviour of the perpetrator before, during and after the crime, and employs the following criteria in determining whether the intent of the perpetrator was directed towards the death of the victim or merely at causing injury to him or her:[34]

- The existence or not of any animosity between the parties, and the reason and extent of any such animosity;
- The number, location and character of the wounds inflicted;[35]
- The lethal potential of the weapon employed, and the way it was utilised;
- Whether or not vital organs were targeted;
- Whether or not the perpetrator had the opportunity to aim where to inflict those injuries;
- The run of events and the causes leading to it;

30 Dönmezer (n 3) 12; Toroslu (n 6) 26; Soyaslan (n 8) 126; Centel, Zafer and Çakmut (n 6) 28; Koca and Üzülmez (n 6) 30; Özbek *et al.* (n 4) 106; Hafizoğulları and Özen (n 6) 36; Gökcen and Balcı (n 8) 21; Artuk *et al.* (n 8) 48.

31 Centel, Zafer and Çakmut (n 6) 29; Koca and Üzülmez (n 6) 40; Özbek *et al.* (n 4) 112.

32 CC Grand Criminal Chamber, judgment of 7.11.1995 (no. 1–280/326); CC 1st Criminal Chamber, judgment of 14.4.1992 (no. 594/786).

33 Özbek *et al.* (n 4) 111.

34 CC Grand Criminal Chamber, judgments of 2.5.2006 (no. 1–97/132) and 8.7.2008 (no. 1–88/184).

35 In an interesting case where the victim of an attempted rape assault had stabbed the aggressor 28 times, the court concluded that there was no intent to kill the aggressor since the knife had not been stabbed with strength and violence despite the lack of any obstacle to do so (CC Grand Criminal Chamber, judgment of 24.3.1986, no. 364/140).

- Whether or not there was an external factor which prevented the perpetrator from bringing about the death of the victim;
- The conduct towards the victim after the event.

These factors have to be weighed on a case-by-case basis to determine the intent of the perpetrator. Where it cannot be proved beyond reasonable doubt that the perpetrator intended to kill the victim, he or she shall be treated as having acted with intent to cause bodily injury by virtue of the principle known as '*in dubio pro reo*'.[36]

On the other hand, the *motive* of the perpetrator is not relevant in determining whether intent exists or not. Where it can be proved that the perpetrator knew that his conduct would bring about the death of the victim, this is sufficient to prove the existence of *direct* intent.[37] However, the motive may lead to the application of the aggravating circumstances in art. 82 TPC.

Finally, '*error in persona*' (mistake as to the identity of the victim) does not negate intent, and the perpetrator will be held responsible as if the intended victim had been killed.[38] However, aggravating circumstances attached to the person of the intended victim will not apply.

Reckless homicide offences

Recklessness does not exist as a term in Turkish criminal law. The closest category would be 'indirect intent' (*dolus eventualis* – named 'probable intent' in the PC), and advertent negligence (*bilinçli taksir*) would come close to it.

As explained on pages 301–302 the crime would have to be categorised as either negligent homicide (art. 85) or intentional homicide (arts. 81–83).

Death caused by drivers not complying with traffic safety rules often leads to dispute as to the chacterisation of the perpetrator's *mens rea*. In judicial practice, even in the case of the most egregious violations, the Court of Cassation regards the crimes to have been committed through negligence, and not indirect intent.[39]

Negligent homicide offences

Actus reus

Any negligent act (in the sense of TPC art. 22) which has causal value in bringing about the death of the victim can constitute the *actus reus* of the crime under TPC art. 85. Where the combination of negligent acts by multiple actors leads to the result, the link of causality is

36 CC Grand Criminal Chamber, judgment of 2.5.2006 (no. 1–97/132).

37 See, for instance, CC 1st Criminal Chamber, judgment of 6.5.2015, 6430/2929.

38 CC Grand Criminal Chamber, judgment of 27.10.2015 (no. 1–1336/352).

39 Examples: an unlicensed driver who was also drunk (CC 9th Criminal Chamber, judgment of 20.11.2006 (no.4050/6231)), a drunk driver who speeded, and did not slow down at a crossroad hence hitting a bike from behind (CC 9th Criminal Chamber, judgment of 12.11.2007 (no. 4840/8117)), a driver eight times over the allowed alcohol limit, speeding and hitting a car from behind (CC 9th Criminal Chamber, judgment of 28.6.2007 (no. 9159/5712)), an underage (and, obviously, unlicensed) drunk driver, disregarding a police warning and speeding in the wrong lane (CC 9th Criminal Chamber, judgment of 19.6.2006 (no. 1680/3456)).

not affected and each perpetrator shall be sentenced according to his or her own culpability (art. 22 (5)).

This crime may be committed through both active and omissive conduct. As opposed to intentional homicide, no statutory reducement is attached to omissive conduct.

The existence of a causal link is determined in the same way as in intentional crimes – i.e., through the application of the *conditio sine qua non* theory. Again, in case of omissive conduct, it must be determined that had the perpetrator acted as required, the result would have *almost certainly* not occurred.[40]

In addition, the result must be objectively imputable to the perpetrator. Hence, death must be a direct result of the failure to discharge the expected duty. For example, where the driver is slightly speeding, and a pedestrian suddenly jumps in front of his car, it cannot be argued that the ensuing incident is a result of the failure to respect the speed limit. Similarly, it cannot be argued that had the driver respected speed limits, he would not have been at that point of the road – the purpose of speed limits is not to delay a driver's arrival to, or passage from, one spatial point.

When a person is killed as a result of a negligent act, and another person is wounded, the aggravating circumstance laid down in art. 85 (2) will apply regardless of the gravity of the injury suffered. However, as a general rule, the prosecution of negligent wounding is subject to the complaint of the victim.[41] In this case, where there is no complaint, the basic version of the crime (art. 85 (1)) shall apply.[42]

Degree of negligence

In order to be able to speak of negligent liability for manslaughter, three basic elements are required: (i) A failure to discharge an objective duty of care and attention; (ii) Foreseeability of the result; (iii) Preventability of the result

(i) A failure to discharge an objective duty of care and attention

The scope and extent of this duty varies in time according to the measure and process of societal development. The content of this duty shall be determined objectively by taking into account the type of behaviour that would be expected by an average and reasonable third person. On the other hand, it may also be argued that a mixed (objective and subjective) approach shall be employed in making this determination. In any case, the special status and knowledge of the perpetrator (e.g, that he is a specialised doctor) shall be taken into account. The Court of Cassation seems to prefer a rather subjective approach as it considers factors such as the personal level of education and culture of the perpetrator as well as the place where he or she lives, his or her lifestyle and social surroundings.[43]

40 Tezcan, Erdem and Önok (n 5) 207.

41 Except when there is advertent negligence and the injury inflicted on the victim exceeds the threshold established under Art. 89 (1).

42 CC 9th Criminal Chamber, judgments of 1.5.2006 (no. 964/2486) and 6.4.2009 (no. 6740/3960).

43 CC 9th Criminal Chamber, judgment of 5.10.2004 (no. 4154/5043); CC 2nd Criminal Chamber, judgment of 14.11.2001 (no. 26765/20208).

The existence of a duty of care and attention may be derived from legal norms, contractual obligations, professional rules, previous behaviour of the perpetrator causing a risk, but also by rules of general life experience.[44]

(ii) Foreseeability of the result

Unless the result was objectively foreseeable, no criminal liability will arise. Again, there are diverging views as to the test to be employed: an objective one, a subjective one, or a mixed one? It may be argued that, as with the above element, a predominantly objective test shall be employed but the special level of knowledge and skill of the perpetrator shall also be weighed in.

Where the perpetrator has actually foreseen the eventuality of the result occurring and has acted nonetheless in the belief that it would not occur, advertent negligence exists. In this case, art. 22 (3) TPC provides for a mandatory increase in the punishment. Where the perpetrator has foreseen the possible result and has acted nonetheless by accepting, or consenting to, that eventuality; in other words, where he assumed the risk that the result would occur by remaining indifferent to that probability, 'probable' (indirect) intent (TPC art. 21 (2)) exists. In this case, the perpetrator shall be sentenced for intentional homicide but with a mandatory reduction in punishment.

In the practice of the Court of Cassation, the following cases of road accidents are treated under the provision of advertent negligence: driving under the influence of alcohol where the concentration of alcohol in the blood exceeds 50mg/100ml,[45] running the red light[46] and improperly overtaking other vehicles.[47] In cases of speeding violations[48] or driving without a driver's license,[49] normally, the rules on advertent negligence do not automatically apply.

(iii) Preventability of the result

According to the academic position adopted on the characteristic of negligence within the structure of the criminal offence, this element may be seen as part of the 'typical elements of the crime' or as part of the assessment on the 'culpability' of the perpetrator (or both). Without dealing with the details of this debate, it must be noted that the preventability of the result must be determined *in casu* and according to a subjective evaluation based on the individual perpetrator. The result of this determination is also particularly relevant in determining the severity of the punishment to be imposed on the perpetrator since art. 85 provides for great flexibility to the judge in leaving a large gap between the minimum and maximum punishment in the tariff. Where the eventual result was easily foreseeable (and thus, preventable) the culpability of the perpetrator is greater and the rule of proportionality requires the judge to weigh the appropriate punishment accordingly.[50] Indeed, art. 22 (4)

44 Tezcan, Erdem and Önok (n 5) 210–11.
45 CC 12th Criminal Chamber, judgment of 29.4.2013 (no. 28691/11610).
46 CC 12th Criminal Chamber, judgment of 30.10.2013 (no. 4357/23737).
47 CC 12th Criminal Chamber, judgment of 06.05.2013 (no. 18913/12397).
48 CC 9th Criminal Chamber, judgment of 09.04.2009 (no. 14600/4142).
49 CC 12th Criminal Chamber, judgment of 19.03.2012 (no. 12696/7562).
50 CC Grand Criminal Chamber, judgments of 10.3.2015 (no. 701/36) and 31.3.2015 (no. 767/79).

states that in negligent crimes the punishment to be imposed shall be determined in accordance with the culpability of the perpetrator.

Result-qualified / constructive / *versari in re illicita* / felony homicide offences

Actus reus

Causing death as a result of an act of wounding

According to art. 87 (4) TPC, where an intentional act aimed at wounding the victim results in his or her death, the offender shall be sentenced to a penalty of imprisonment for a term of eight to 16 years depending on the nature of the injury initially inflicted.

In principle, any act which intended to cause 'wounding' in the sense of art. 86 (1) (that is, causing physical pain to the victim or impairing his or her health or ability to perceive) may trigger the application of art. 87 (4).[51] The act may also be omissive provided that the perpetrator is in a position of guarantorship.[52]

However, because of the way art. 87 (4) is formulated, academic writings[53] and case law[54] concur that an act which causes an injury so light that it's effect 'can be cured by a simple medical treatment' (art. 86 (2)), cannot lead to the application of art. 87 (4). This is because art. 87 (4) does not make reference to instances of wounding which fall under art. 86 (2). In this case, the perpetrator may be held responsible for negligent homicide (art. 85) if the result was foreseeable.

A major practical problem is when the victim has a pre-existing medical condition which combines with an act of wounding the effect of which could normally have been eliminated through a simple medical treatment. In this case, the Court of Cassation makes the following distinction: (i) If the perpetrator knew of this condition, he or she must be held responsible for negligent homicide caused with advertent negligence; (ii) If the perpetrator did not know of this condition, he or she must be held responsible for negligent homicide.[55]

This approach has led to two major criticisms:[56] (i) Where the medical condition of the victim is not known to the perpetrator, it is not possible to hold him responsible for the death since this result would be unforeseeable. In this case, the perpetrator should only be held responsible for the crime of intentional wounding;[57] (ii) Where the medical condition is known, the judge should further investigate into whether the perpetrator might have acted with *dolus eventualis.* [58]

51 Koca and Üzülmez (n 6) 192; S. Kaymaz and H.T. Gökcan, *5237 Sayılı Türk Ceza Kanununda Taksirle Adam Öldürme ve Yaralama Suçları* (Seçkin: Ankara 2006) 253.
52 Koca and Üzülmez (n 6) 192.
53 Centel, Zafer and Çakmut (n 6) 173; Kaymaz and Gökcan (n 51) 248; Özbek *et al.* (n 4) 219; Hafizo⊠ulları and Özen (n 6) 91; Koca annd Üzülmez (n 6) 193; S. Keskin Kiziro⊠lu, 'Kasten Yaralama Suçu' in *Prof. Dr.Nevzat Toroslu'ya Arma⊠an* (Ankara 2015) 679.
54 CC 1st Criminal Chamber, judgments of 17.4.2007 (no. 4671/2883), 22.5.2007 (no. 5796/3947) and 2.2.2016 (no. 5759/351).
55 CC 1st Criminal Chamber, judgments of 12.2.2007 (no. 5/323), 2.4.2008 (no. 9444/2549) and 04.07.2008 (no. 4815/5662.)
56 Tezcan, Erdem and Önok (n 5) 252.
57 Kaymaz and Gökcan (n 51) 250. See also Keskin Kiziro⊠lu (n 53) 679; Özbek *et al.* (n 4) 221.
58 Ibid. See also Gökcen and Balcı (n 8) 30.

In order to apply art. 87 (4), the deadly consequence should be a direct result of the wound inflicted, and not merely a result of the act directed at the victim.[59] To give an example, where the perpetrator throws a stone at the victim who, in trying to eschew the blow, tumbles and falls in a well, and is killed by banging his head, death is not the direct result of the wound inflicted – hence art. 87 (4) will not apply. The adoption of this position will also mean that attempted acts cannot lead to the application of art. 87 (4) since there would be no wound in the first place.[60]

Other crimes which lead to the death of the victim

An increased punishment shall be applied when the victim is killed as a result of:

- A failure to discharge the duty of assistance or notification (art. 98 (2));
- Torture (art. 95 (4)) – in this case the punishment is aggravated life-time imprisonment;
- Abortion (art. 99 (3) and (4) – obviously, the victim in question here is the pregnant woman);
- Sexual assault (art. 102 (5)) or sexual exploitation of minors (art. 103 (6)).

The result must be objectively imputable to the perpetrator (e.g., where the victim of abortion later commits suicide, this is a result of the wilful act of the victim and due to the principle of responsibility the person who carried out abortion can no longer be imputed this result).

Mens rea / *negligence combinations*

Causing death as a result of an act of wounding

In case of art. 87 (4) the criminal act must be intentional, an unintended result of death must arise from this act, and this result must be foreseeable. Hence, where the initial act was negligent, only the provisions on negligent homicide can apply, and where there exists indirect intent with regard to the death of the victim, the provisions on intentional homicide shall apply.

Other crimes which lead to the death of the victim

The deadly result must be foreseeable since no responsibility can arise unless the perpetrator has acted (at least) negligently with respect to such result (art. 23).

Where the perpetrator has intended – through either direct or indirect intent – to bring about the death of the victim, the perpetrator will be held directly responsible under the provisions on intentional homicide.

Infanticide / child destruction

Art. 453 of the former PC provided for a mitigating circumstance where murder was committed by the mother against the new-born under the motive of 'saving (her) honour'. This provision

59 Ibid. 253. See also Koca and Üzülmez (n 6) 194; Tezcan, Erdem and Önok (n 5) 254.
60 Ibid. 252. See also Tezcan, Erdem and Önok (n 5) 254–55.

no longer exists. On the contrary, homicide committed against a direct descendant constitutes an aggravating circumstance under art. 82. Therefore, the only 'saving' provision for the mother in this case may be to resort to art. 34 (1) on so-called 'transitory reasons'[61]: where the perpetrator is unable to comprehend the legal meaning and consequences of an act he or she has committed, or where his or her ability to control his or her behaviour regarding such act is significantly diminished, the perpetrator is deemed not to be culpable and cannot be punished.

Abortion and homicide

Abortion performed by a third person (i.e., someone else than the pregnant woman) is regulated under art. 99 TPC. Abortion performed under the consent of the woman is allowed for the first ten weeks of pregnancy. After the first ten weeks, only 'medical necessity' may excuse the performance of abortion (art. 99 (2)). However, according to art. 99 (6), the time-limit is extended to 20 weeks where the pregnancy is the result of a crime suffered by the mother, provided that the pregnancy is terminated by specialist physicians in a hospital environment. Abortion which falls outside this framework is punished under art. 99, even if the mother has consented. Where the pregnant woman auto-performs abortion after the first ten weeks of pregnancy, she shall be punished under art. 100 (which provides for a more lenient punishment).

Defences to homicide

Consent

There is no specific regulation on euthanasia or mercy killings or killing on request of the victim.

According to the unanimous academic view, since an individual is not granted a right to dispose of his or her own life, such consent would be irrelevant, and the perpetrator would be held responsible for intentional homicide (art. 81).[62] The motive of the perpetrator may be taken into account by virtue of art. 61 (1) (g) concerning the individualisation of the penalty. However, this would have no practical effect since the punishment for art. 81 is lifetime imprisonment, and art. 61 (1) bears on the determination of the punishment when there is a lower and upper limit prescribed by law.

Euthanasia has led to particular debates. The Draft Penal Codes of 1989 and 1997 incorporated a provision on euthanasia which required, *inter alia*, the 'insistent request' of an incurable patient, and provided for a lenient sentence (1–3 years). This provision was later dropped.

Academic writings draw a distinction between active, passive and indirect euthanasia.[63] It is unanimously accepted that active euthanasia amounts to intentional homicide, and that indirect euthanasia does not constitute a crime.[64] There is debate as to whether passive

61 These are temporary conditions that cannot be considered mental disorder in the sense of art. 32.

62 Tezcan, Erdem and Önok (n 5) 184–185.

63 Active euthanasia refers to conduct which is aimed at ending the life of a terminal patient. Passive euthanasia refers to all omissive conduct that encompasses a failure to provide medical treatment, thus leading to a patient's death. Indirect euthanasia refers to medical treatment aimed at decreasing suffering, but which has the collateral effect of shortening a patient's life.

64 Refer to Tezcan, Erdem and Önok (n 5) 187–88 for references. In fact, in most cases, this will constitute 'premeditated' murder, which carries a punishment of 'aggravated life-time imprisonment'.

euthanasia shall be treated as intentional homicide. The majority opines in the negative,[65] while some authors,[66] usually based on the doctor's position of guarantorship which imposes a legal obligation to prevent the patient's death, consider such inaction to also amount to intentional killing by omission (art. 83).

Self-defence

TPC art. 25 (1) provides that an act committed in self-defence shall not be punished subject to certain conditions. As explained in detail in an early volume of this series,[67] the following conditions are required:

- i There must be unlawful attack;
- ii The attack must be directed against a right to which the person acting in self-defence or a third person was entitled;
- iii The attack must be ongoing (if an attack that has not yet been launched is certain to be carried out, or an attack which has terminated is certain to be repeated, this requirement is satisfied);
- iv Resort to the action which constitutes self-defence must be indispensable / inevitable;
- v The act of self-defence must be proportionate to the assault;
- vi The act in self-defence must be directed at the aggressor.

In light of the above-conditions, it is possible to rely on self-defence in case of homicide, provided that it was 'proportionate' to the legal interest sought to be protected. There must be a proportion, and not necessarily 'equivalence' between the right sought to be protected, and the legal interest harmed by the act in self-defence. Similarly, the third condition above has been interpreted in a rather relaxed manner. The same may be said about conditions (iv) and (v).

In case of excessive self-defence, when the permissible limits of self-defence are unintentionally exceeded, the perpetrator may be punished for negligent homicide, and the punishment imposed for the crime shall be further reduced by one-sixth to one-third (art. 27 TPC). This provision regulates exceeding the permissible limits of a justification as regards its material conditions, e.g., an agent acting under self-defence exceeds the limits of the requirement of proportionality, and causes the death of the attacker.

Exceptionally, if the limits were exceeded as a result of excitement, fear or agitation that can be regarded as excusable, the offender shall not be subject to any punishment (TPC art. 27 (2)). This provision concerns culpability – if the excessive response is deemed as excusable under the circumstances of the case, no punishment shall be inflicted.

65 Refer to Meral Ekici Şahin, *Ceza Hukukunda Rıza* (On İki Levha: Istanbul 2012) 276–82 for extensive debate and references.

66 Refer to Tezcan, Erdem and Önok (n 5) 88 for references. Further see Centel, Zafer and Çakmut (n 6) 36; Artuk *et al.* (n 8) 67; and Soyaslan (n 8) 148 (the writers draw no distinction between different types of euthanasia in concluding that it does not constitute a justification under Turkish Law).

67 R.M. Önok, 'Turkey' in A. Reed and M. Bohlander, N. Wake and E. Smith (eds) *General Defences in Criminal Law: Domestic, Comparative and International Perspectives* (Ashgate 2014) 315 *et seq.*

Duress

According to art. 28 TPC, no punishment shall be imposed upon a person who commits a criminal offence as a result of an irresistible or inevitable use of force or violence, or an imminent and grave menace or threat against himself.

According to art. 223(3)(b) of the Penal Procedure Code, the judge shall decide that the person acting under such influence is not culpable, and that there is no need to inflict punishment upon him. In such cases, the person using material or moral compulsion to force another to commit the crime shall be deemed to be the offender (indirect perpetration).

It is generally accepted that, when thinking in terms of the legal values at stake, the harm sought to be avoided is at least equal to the harm inflicted, the perpetrator may rely on art. 28.[68] There has not been much academic debate as to whether homicide may be excused under duress. However, a minority defends that homicide falls outside the acceptable limits.[69] Since it is unanimously accepted that necessity may constitute a defence to homicide, there is no reason to think that duress by threats may also excuse homicide.[70] In my opinion, the important point here would be to determine whether the threat was imminent and grave, and there was no other option to escape the damage but to perform the criminal act.

Necessity

This ground is regulated under TPC art. 25(2), and it prevents any punishment from being imposed upon the offender. The legal character of this provision (whether it constitutes a justification or an excuse) had been debated in an earlier volume of this series.[71] The following conditions are required:

- i There must be a serious and certain danger;
- ii The danger must be directed at a right to which the perpetrator, or a third person, is entitled;
- iii The danger must not have been knowingly caused by the perpetrator himself;
- iv The perpetrator should not be under a legal obligation to confront the danger;
- v There should be no other means of protection;
- vi The means used must be proportionate to the gravity and object of the danger.

With regard to the last requirement, the legal value protected through the commission of homicide must be at least equal to the harmed legal value belonging to a third person. Therefore, in Turkish academic writings and case law, necessity is admitted as a defence to homicide provided that the interest sought to be protected is also the right to life of oneself or a third person.

Insanity

When it comes to mental disorder (or infirmity or insanity), TPC art. 32 makes a three-fold distinction with regard to mental disorders:

68 B. Akbulut, *Ceza Hukuku Genel Hükümler* (4th edn, Adalet: Ankara 2017) 523.
69 H. Hakeri, *Ceza Hukuku Genel Hükümler* (21st edn, Adalet: Ankara 2017) 438.
70 For the view, couched in general terms, that art. 28 is applicable to intentional homicide see Gökcen and Balcı (n 8) 105–106.
71 R.M. Önok (n 67) 315–28.

i If the perpetrator cannot comprehend the legal meaning and consequences of the act he has committed, no punishment shall be imposed.

ii If, in respect of such act, the perpetrator's ability to control his or her own behaviour was significantly diminished, no punishment shall be imposed.

iii If the perpetrator's ability to control his or her own behaviour in respect of the impugned act is diminished, but not to the extent defined above, the sentence shall be reduced.[72]

Contrary to some Common Law systems, the charge against the perpetrator cannot be reduced to a minor or lesser version of the crime on account of mental disorder. If the perpetrator falls under category (iii), he or she will be held responsible as if the crime was committed by a mentally sane person but the punishment will be reduced as provided for art. 32.

Diminished responsibility

Minors who had not reached the age of 12 at the time of commission of the criminal act cannot be held criminally responsible but so-called 'security measures' of a preventive and rehabilitative nature may be imposed on them (termed 'protective and supportive measures' in the Children Protection Law (Law no. 5395, Arts. 5, 11)).

With regard to minors older than 12 but younger than 15 years of age at the time of commission of the crime, a distinction has to be made. If, at the time of an offence,

i They are incapable of appreciating the legal meaning and consequences of the act or the capability to control their behaviour is not sufficiently developed, they shall be exempt from criminal liability. However, such minors shall be subject to security measures specific to children. Their mental capacity has to be assessed by an expert in order to determine the applicable regime, and this determination has to be made in light of the specific crime in question.

ii Where the minor has the capability to comprehend the legal meaning and result of the act, and to control his behaviours in respect of such act, he or she shall be convicted but the sentence has to be reduced (art. 31 (2)).[73]

Minors older than 15 but younger than 18 years at the time of the offence are deemed by law to possess criminal capacity however their sentence shall be reduced (art. 31 (3)).[74]

72 25 years where the offence committed requires a punishment of aggravated life imprisonment; 20 years for crimes that require a punishment of life imprisonment; other penalties to be imposed shall be reduced by no more than one-sixth. In this case, the punishment to be imposed may be enforced partially or completely as a security measure specific to mentally disordered persons (art. 57), provided the length of the punishment remains the same.

73 For offences requiring a punishment of aggravated life imprisonment, a term of 12 to 15 years of imprisonment shall be imposed; for offences that require a punishment of life imprisonment, a term of nine to 11 years imprisonment shall be imposed. Otherwise the punishment to be imposed shall be reduced by half, and, in any case, for each act such punishment shall not exceed seven years.

74 18–24 years of imprisonment instead of aggravated life imprisonment; 12–15 years of imprisonment instead of life imprisonment; other penalties to be imposed shall be reduced by one-third, and, in any case, the punishment for each act shall not exceed 12 years.

The provisions which relate to minors under 12 years of age apply to deaf and mute persons under the age of 15. The provisions which relate to minors who are over 12 years of age but under 15 apply to deaf and mute persons who are over 15 years of age but under 18 years of age. The provisions which relate to minors over 15 years of age but under 18 years of age apply to deaf and mute persons who are over 18 years of age but under 21 years of age (TPC art. 33).

Loss of control / provocation

Turkish statutory law or case law does not recognise a 'battered women syndrome' or similar defence. Having committed a crime under the influence of a psychological anomaly may only fall under the general provisions on mental infirmity (art. 32) or transitory reasons (art. 34).[75]

However, case law has been ready to accommodate cases that might have fallen under this heading in regards to the rules on self-defence by accepting that past attacks or potential future attacks may be treated as an 'ongoing' assault.[76]

Superior orders

According to art. 24(2) TPC, a person who carries out an order the execution of which is compulsory as part of his duty shall not be punished. However, Art. 24 (3) provides that:

> [A]n order constituting an offence shall never be executed in any circumstances. Otherwise, the person who carried out the order and the person who gave the order shall be liable.

This provision mirrors art. 137 (2) of the Constitution which determines that:

[A]n order which in itself constitutes an offence shall under no circumstances be executed; the person who executes such an order shall not evade responsibility.

Therefore, where an order that constitutes an offence is carried out, both the superior who made the order, and the subordinate who complied with it, will incur criminal responsibility. As a result, the commission of homicide under superior orders can only be justifiable or excusable if such act falls under one or more of the other provisions precluding criminal liability.

Official authority

According to TPC art. 24(1), a person who carries out the provisions of a statute shall not be subject to punishment. This provision constitutes a justification. Similarly, according to art. 26 (1), 'A person who exercises his right shall not be subject to punishment'.

There are a variety of statutory provisions which grant law enforcement (and even other) officials a right to use force, including firearms. Examples are the law on the Duties and

75 See above under 'Infanticide / child destruction'.

76 A telling example is a judgment by the 1st Criminal Chamber (CC, dated 13.7.2011): the perpetrator, a victim of repeated sexual attacks by her father, had killed the father in his sleep the morning after another attack. The CC considered that, in light of threats to repeat similar acts, the assault on the woman was 'certain to be repeated', and hence 'ongoing'.

Competences of the Police, The Internal Service Law of Turkish Armed Forces, the Law on Martial Law, The Law on the Organization, Duties and Competences of the Gendermrie.

It should be borne in mind that Turkey is a party to both the European Convention on Human Rights and the 1966 United Nations International Covenant on Civil and Political Rights. According to art. 90 / last para. of the Turkish Constitution: 'In case of conflict between international agreements in the area of fundamental rights and freedoms duly put into effect and the domestic laws due to differences in provisions on the same matter, the provisions of international agreements shall prevail'. Thus, the statutory rules on the use of force and firearms must be interpreted under the guidance of the provisions on the right to life of these international treaties, and of the related case law.

In that light, the use of potentially lethal force may only be justified under the circumstances laid down in the case law of the European Court of Human Rights, and the Human Rights Committee. Even so, case law has often appeared to be rather too permissive on instances of seemingly excessive use of force.[77] In any case, acting under the colour of law does not constitute an aggravating or mitigating circumstance in case of homicide.

Honour killings

Honour killings may be treated under art. 82(1)(k) which provides for an aggravating circumstance in case of acting under the motive of traditions (*töre saiki*). However, the Court of Cassation has interpreted this provision in a rather restrictive manner. While the Court initially treated all honour killings under this provision,[78] it more recently determined that only certain instances of honour killing will fall under the provision.[79] In particular, where the perpetrator has acted under his or her personal understanding of honour or morals, the provision shall not apply.[80] The provision will only apply where:[81]

- A given form of conduct or way of living is considered by traditions to require that person's murder;
- This tradition arises from value judgments generally adopted by a given community;
- The perpetrator *solely* acts with the purpose of fulfilling a duty of conforming to this tradition in the belief that he or she will be 'rewarded' with esteem in doing so, and will be condemned in case of failure to do so.

Therefore, where a person is murdered not on account of tradition, but under the psychological effect caused on the perpetrator by his or her own unlawful act, this provision will not apply and the perpetrator of murder may further benefit from the reduction provided by the provision on 'unjust provocation' (TPC art. 29). This is also confirmed by the official

77 Refer to D. Tezcan, M.R. Erdem, O. Sancakdar and R.M. Önok, *İnsan Hakları El Kitabı* (6th edn, Seçkin: Ankara 2016) 116–30 for examples from case law and academic analysis. Also see the booklet entitled *Kolluğun Silah Kullanma Yetkisi*, published by the Turkish Penal Law Association (Istanbul 2005).

78 CC 1st Criminal Chamber, judgments of 15.4.2009 (no. 7373/2154) and 8.4.2009 (2339/1937).

79 CC Grand Criminal Chamber, judgments of 14.6.2011 (no. 1–138/130) and 3.7.2012 (no. 1–76/258).

80 Tezcan, Erdem and Önok (n 5) 168; Koca and Üzülmez (n 6) 79–80.

81 CC 1st Criminal Chamber, judgment of 29.4.2014 (no. 1719/2733).

explanation of the provision. On the other hand, where the murder does fall under art. 82 (1)(k), the provision on unjust provocation will be inapplicable.[82]

Sentencing framework – including statistics

Mandatory sentencing regimes

Attempt

In cases of attempt, the sentence is determined according to the scale laid down in art. 35 (2), and by taking into account the seriousness of the damage or danger that was caused by the conduct. There is a mandatory reduction imposed by law: a term of 13–20 years of imprisonment where the offence committed requires a punishment of aggravated life imprisonment, a term of 9–15 years of imprisonment where the offence committed requires a punishment of life imprisonment; other penalties shall be reduced by one-quarter to three- quarters.

Participation in crime

The PC adopts the system which is known as 'duality' with regard to the punishment of participants. Their punishment is determined in view of the importance of their role in the commission of the crime. Participation may be technically divided into two types: perpetration and complicity. Perpetration includes 'direct or individual perpetration', 'joint perpetration' and 'indirect' perpetration. 'Complicity' includes instigation and assistance. In the PC, assistance refers to providing both material assistance, and moral assistance.

Categories that are subject to full punishment for the act (principals) are: perpetrators and instigators. So-called moral and material accessories are subject to a mandatory reduction in their punishment.

Art. 22 (6) on negligent crimes

According to art. 22 (6), a punishment shall not be imposed if, as the result of a negligent act, the offender is victimised, by reference to his personal and family circumstances only, to such a degree that imposing a punishment becomes unnecessary. Where the offence is committed with conscious negligence the punishment to be imposed may be reduced by one-sixth to one-half.

This provision is applicable to negligent homicide. Three points are contentious:

(I)MUST THERE BE A KINSHIP BETWEEN THE PERPETRATOR AND THE VICTIM?

According to the prevailing academic opinion[83] and the Court of Cassation,[84] the answer is affirmative. Another possible interpretation is that what matters in not the existence of

82 CC 1st Criminal Chamber, judgment of 15.4.2009 (no. 7373/2154). See in the same direction Gökcen and Balcı (n 8) 231.

83 Refer to Tezcan, Erdem and Önok (n 5) 218 *et seq.* for detailed debate and academic references.

84 CC Grand Criminal Chamber, judgment of 29.4.2014 (no. 9–104/216), CC 9th Criminal Chamber, judgment of 26.11.2007 (no. 4584/8621).

kinship but whether the perpetrator has already been harmed – personally and in the familial sense – by the crime to a degree that renders any punishment unnecessary.[85] There is one decision where the existence of religious marriage was deemed sufficient,[86] and one decision where the provision was applied with regard to killing caused against a friend.[87] The existence of engagement was deemed insufficient.[88] In all other publicly available decisions, there was a relationship of kin.

(II)WHO CAN BE THE VICTIM?

According to the majority academic opinion[89] and the Court of Cassation,[90] the provision is applicable only where the victim is *exclusively* a relative. Where third persons have been harmed, even if in the shape of minor bodily injury, the provision becomes inapplicable *in toto*. There is only one case where the provision was applied despite the existence of harm to a third person.[91]

(III)VICTIMISATION SUFFERED BY THE PERPETRATOR

The judge must ascertain the extent and degree of victimisation personally incurred by the perpetrator as a result of the criminal act. This shall be done by taking into account the relationship between the perpetrator and the victim, and their social circumstances.[92] Hence, mere existence of kinship does not suffice.[93]

Indirect intent and advertent negligence

As explained earlier in the chapter, there is a mandatory statutory decrease in punishment where intent is found to be indirect, and a mandatory statutory increase where negligence is found to be advertent.

Unjust provocation

If a person commits an offence in a state of anger or severe distress caused by an unjust act, the sentence shall be reduced in the following way: 18–24 years instead of aggravated life-

85 İ. Özgenç, *Türk Ceza Hukuku Genel Hükümler* (13th ed., Seçkin: Ankara 2017) 274.
86 CC 12th Criminal Chamber, judgment of 12.12.2012 (no. 5297/27023) cited from C. Şahin, 'Yargıtay Kararları Işığında Taksirli Suçlarda Şahsi Cezasızlık Nedeni veya Cezayı Hafifleten Neden' in TAAD, Review of Turkish Justice Academy, No. 2013/14, 847.
87 CC 12th Criminal Chamber, judgment of 29.9.2011 (no.1881/2020) cited from Şahin (n 86) 853–55.
88 CC 12th Criminal Chamber, judgment of 21.12.2011 (no.3953/9139) cited from Şahin (n 86) 849.
89 Refer to Tezcan, Erdem and Önok (n 5) 219 for references.
90 CC 9th Criminal Chamber, judgments of 15.5.2007 (no.8401/4178) and 19.4.2007 (no.7496/3466); CC Grand Criminal Chamber, judgment of 29.4.2014 (no.9–104/216).
91 CC 12th Criminal Chamber, judgment of 8.11.2012 (no.8619/23372) cited by Şahin (n 86) 862.
92 CC 9th Criminal Chamber, judgment of 30.12.2008 (no.18994/14573).
93 CC 9th Criminal Chamber, judgments of 19.4.2007 (no.1998/3479) and 01.06.2009 (no.1001/6550).

time imprisonment, 12–18 years instead of life-time imprisonment, reduction by one-quarter to three-quarters in all other cases (TPC art. 29).

Discretionary sentencing regimes

As explained on page 305, where intentional homicide is committed through omission, the judge may decrease the punishment within the limits prescribed in art. 83.

In addition, Art. 62 provides for 'discretionary mitigating circumstances'. This provision is applicable to all crimes defined under the PC or any other law laying down crimes. Where there are grounds for discretionary mitigation, the punishment to be imposed shall be reduced by up to one-sixth. In the evaluation of discretionary mitigation the following matters shall be taken into account: the background, social relations, behaviour after the commission of the offence and during trial, and the potential effects of the punishment on the future of the offender. This is not a closed list. In any case, these are criteria regarding the character of the offender. Therefore, the way the crime was committed cannot be a reason by itself for not applying art. 62.

According to official statistics,[94] in 2016, 11,774 cases have ended in convictions under art. 81, whereas 2,774 have ended in acquittal. With regard to intentional homicide by omission, the numbers are very low: 14 convictions and 47 acquittals. With regard to art. 82, the highest numbers concern murder through premeditation (either as the only aggravating circumstance or in conjunction with other(s) aggravating circumstance(s)): 2,161 convictions to 516 acquittals. With regard to unintentional homicide (art. 85), the numbers are as follows: 4,711 convictions to 1,989 acquittals for the basic version of the offence (para. 1), 2,530 convictions to 367 acquittals as regards the aggravated version (para. 2). With regard to demographics[95], those tried under art. 81 were of the following age: 262 defendants were under 16, a further 651 defendants were under 18; of these, only 18 were female. Only 263 defendants were foreigners.

94 <www.adlisicil.adalet.gov.tr/Istatistikler/1996/2016karartck.pdf> accessed 11 June 2018.
95 <http://www.adlisicil.adalet.gov.tr/Istatistikler/1996/2016acilantck.pdf> accessed 11 June 2018.

17 Islamic law

Mohammad Hedayati-Kakhki

Introduction

In Islam, human life is the most valuable gift from Allah.[1] The right to life is considered by the Quran to be sacrosanct and it is consequently deeply entrenched in all primary sources of Islamic law. Any unlawful interference with this right will constitute *qatl* (homicide) and is deemed to be a severe breach of Islamic law. For example, the unlawful killing of another is treated by the Quran to be tantamount to the '[killing] of all people'.[2]

Islamic law sets out strong substantive protection of the right to life and clear procedural guidelines as to how a defendant ought to be treated. This chapter seeks to elucidate the fundamental principles and classification of homicide and its related offences in Islam as well as explaining the sentencing process.

Historical development of homicide offences

Despite the unequivocal sanctity of human life, there is no uniform formulation of the law of homicide across Islamic jurisdictions. The constituent elements of the offence and the corresponding punishment evolved organically, resulting in a prohibition across all Islamic jurisdictions, but with specific elements that differ from region to region.

Evolution from pre-Islamic Arabia

The backdrop to this historical evolution is a structure of systematic retaliation in specie. In pre-Islamic Arabia, a system of tribal retaliation (*thár*) was the ultimate response to homicide. The appropriate retaliation was considered to be a killing in response, often of more than one of the opposing tribesmen. This led to a state of 'blood-feud'[3] where the constituent elements of the offence were not formulated with any clarity or consistency and where the punishment was often disproportionate to the offence committed.

The offence of homicide was given structure by the primary sources of Islam which introduced three key elements. In terms of the constituent elements of the offence, it became necessary that the killing be wrongful; with reference to the punishment, only the guilty party (the killer) could be killed in retaliation; and in terms of procedure, the offence would only be satisfied where the facts were proven before an Islamic judge. These

1 S.S. Shah, 'Homicide in Islam: Major Legal Themes' (1999) 14(2) Arab Law Quarterly 159–68.

2 Al-Quran, Surah al-Ma'iidah: 32.

3 J.N.D. Anderson, 'Homicide in Islamic Law' (1951) 13 Bulletin of the School of Oriental and African Studies 811–28, 812.

elements, whilst interpreted differently by different Islamic schools of thought, undoubtedly tempered the state of 'blood-feud' and introduced a degree of consistency into the Islamic law of homicide. However, it would be wrong to dismiss the pre-Islamic position as merely historical; undoubtedly, elements of the historical position can be traced into the practice of modern Islamic jurisdictions.

A particularly clear example of the impact of the pre-Islamic state of affairs on current law and practice is the retention of the notion of personal vengeance. The Shafi'is and Hanbalis propose universal election between retaliation and compensation for the heirs of the victim. Other orthodox schools of Islamic thought go even further in their retention of the notion of personal vengeance and deny the availability of compensation where retaliation is expressly available.[4] This results in modern legal systems which incorporate *qisas* (capital punishment) and *diyat* (compensation) into their sentencing for offences.

Qisas punishment differs from the pre-Islamic notion of *thár* in two important ways. First, the availability of *qisas* is now limited to the offence of murder.[5] This differs from the pre-Islamic state of affairs where the intention behind the killing was immaterial to the legitimacy of retaliation. Second, the killing is administered by the State in modern Islamic practice,[6] rather than in the informal manner by which *thár* was tribally or personally exercised.

Private tort or public wrong?

The differing interpretations of the constituent elements and sentencing will be examined in detail below. In terms of the evolution of the offence, there is an interesting development in the legal taxonomy that can be mapped from pre-Islamic Arabia into modern Islamic jurisdictions. Broadly speaking, there has been a development from treating homicide as a private tort to treating homicide as a hybrid offence to both the public and private spheres.

A number of factors illustrate this private conception of the offence in its historical context. Traditionally, offences under Islamic law can be subdivided into a tripartite classification based on the holder of the right violated. This can be a right of God, a right of the individual or a hybrid of the two. Historically, jurists viewed homicide as a violation purely of the right of the individual.[7] One particular manifestation of this categorisation is the relevance of the victim's or the victim's heirs' election to bring the matter before the judge. The fact that the State would only judge a case brought before it and that it was open to the victim's heirs to pardon the defendant or claim compensation instead demonstrates the tortious nature of the offence pre-Islam.[8]

Conversely, a clear evolution towards classifying homicide as a *public* wrong can be seen across all Islamic jurisdictions. An example of this is the relevance afforded to compensation

4 This is the Maliki view.

5 Quranic *ayah*, al-Baqarah: 178.

6 Although note a potential exception to this in practice stemming from the liberal application of the defence of provocation.

7 Anderson (n 3).

8 This stands in notable contrast to the approach taken to criminal wrongs in the United Kingdom where the will of the victim (or the victim's heirs where appropriate) as to the fate of the defendant is necessarily immaterial. The position in the United Kingdom is encapsulated by Lord Templeman's decision in the landmark case of *R v Brown* [1994] 1 A.C. 212 [237] where he held that 'society is entitled and *bound* to protect itself against ... violence'. In other words, there is no room for the pardon of the victim, the wrong committed is deemed to be one against society and society is legally obliged to punish the defendant.

in Pakistan. Article 311 of the Pakistan Penal Code, as pointed out by Pascoe and Miao,[9] treats the compensation and the criminal sanction as distinct matters. The payment of compensation has no impact on the sentencing discretion of the Pakistani courts which retain the capacity to impose a death sentence. This seems to bring the taxonomy of the offence into closer alignment with its classification as a public wrong where the law is obliged to criminalise it regardless of the wishes of the victim's heirs.

Some jurisdictions do, however, retain a connection between the payment of compensation or the presence of a pardon and the sentence imposed. For example, in Yemen, acceptance of compensation by the victim's heirs or a pardon (*afw*) gives rise to a discretionary judicial sentence of up to 15 years imprisonment[10] in lieu of the death sentence that would otherwise be available. That a pardon or compensatory payment can negate the imposition of a death sentence in some jurisdictions, illustrates that homicide is not within the exclusive domain of the public law in certain Islamic jurisdictions.

Structure of homicide offences

As with criminal offences in most legal systems, a discriminating taxonomy of the offence is required so as to attribute an appropriate level of culpability to the defendant for his actions. There is no consensus amongst the schools of Islamic thought as to the classifications of homicide. There is even disagreement *within* the schools as to the appropriate classification to use.[11] There are five possible forms of the offence:[12] (a) intentional murder (*qatl-i-amd*), (b) quasi-intentional murder (*qatl-i-sibhi-amd*), (c) accidental murder (*qatl-i-khata*), (d) involuntary murder (*qatl-i-Jari majra al-Khata*) and (e) indirect murder (*qatl-i-bit-tasabbur*). The extent to which each of these is accepted as a separate form of homicide will be assessed below.

In terms of the distinction between intentional and quasi-intentional murder, the intention as to the result (death) is crucial. In the case of intentional murder the defendant must intend to kill; whereas, an intention to harm will suffice for quasi-intentional murder. In his analysis, Pervin argues that the weapon used is a second way of distinguishing between these offences.[13] He submits that intentional murder requires use of a *mortal* weapon, whereas quasi-intentional murder requires use of an instrument generally not considered to endanger life. This distinction is echoed in Nigerian criminal law where the use of a lethal instrument will be conclusive evidence that there was an intention to kill. However, these elements can prove contradictory; if the test is one of intention then the weapon will be no more than indicative of that intention; if the test is one of the weapon used, then the intention as to the result caused by that weapon is immaterial. One has to choose between these two possible tests, they cannot run concurrently. Other analyses seem to focus purely on the intention rather than the instrument used.[14] Furthermore, the Nigerian express acceptance of the

9 This is the classification system proposed by the Hanafi school of thought. See A. ibn Ali Jassas, *Ahkam al-Quran* (Dar al-Fikr 1916).

10 Yemen Law 12/1994, article 55.

11 F.B. Hakeem *et al., Policing Muslim Communities: Comparative International Context* (Springer 2012) 7–23.

12 This covers all proposals, although some schools argue for conflation of or disregard for some classifications.

13 M. Pervin, 'Law of Murder under Islamic Criminal Law: An Analysis' (2016) 53 Journal of Law, Policy and Globalization 143, 144.

14 An example of such a position is that taken by Shah (n 1) 163.

relevance of the weapon can be explained as a concession to the evidential difficulties of establishing an intention to kill. Such an analysis seems more consistent with the primary texts which distinguish based on the intention of result.[15]

Accidental murder requires an even further removed intention from the result. The defendant will be guilty of accidental murder where the victim is killed as a result of the defendant's actions, but where the defendant neither intended to cause harm nor death.

There is disagreement over whether involuntary murder really can be distinguished from accidental murder.[16] In fact, it is only the Hanafi school that accepts this as an individual head of homicide. Pervin explains the distinction as being based on the lack of a deliberate act. It is important to note that accidental murder, whilst requiring a lack of intention as to the result, does require a deliberate act. For example, if A kills B thinking that B is a wild beast, there is no intention to kill B but there is nevertheless a deliberate act of killing. It would be hard to say that the action is in any sense involuntary. On that basis, a distinction between such forms of homicide seems plausible.

The final form of homicide is that by an intermediate cause. Few schools of thought accept this as a separate head of homicide. The individualised classification of indirect homicide is rejected by the Shafei, Hanbali, Zaydi, Maliki and Zahiri schools. Generally, it is the Hanafi school of thought alone that considers it to be a distinct form of homicide. The distinction from all other forms of homicide appears to be based on the manner in which the death is caused. For example, Pervin gives the example of a well being dug on a road by the defendant and the victim then falling in the well and being killed as a result.[17] The issue with such a classification seems to be that it undermines the purpose of having a classificatory system in the first place. If the aim of classifying forms of homicide is to accurately attribute an appropriate level of culpability to the defendant, then whether or not the manner of killing is direct or not ought to be immaterial. Taking Pervin's example, the level of culpability of the defendant must depend on whether he intended danger, foresaw danger, shut his eyes to the danger, or had no way of predicting the danger. In other words, there is no correlation between culpability and directness of harm.

With the exception of the Hanafis, indirect murder as a distinct head of homicide is rejected. Furthermore, the Hanafi school is unique in its distinction between accidental and involuntary murder. As already argued, this distinction has a sound conceptual foundation, although whether the two forms of homicide are deserving of differing levels of culpability is doubted. For that reason, a classification that distinguishes between them may well be superfluous. The disregard for the materiality of the directness of the killing and the conflation of accidental and involuntary murder effectively summarise the Shafeii, Hanbali and Zayidi tripartite distinction between intentional murder, quasi-intentional murder and accidental murder. It is this tripartite taxonomy that is most prevalent in Islamic jurisdictions. For example, it is adopted in Iran,[18] Nigeria[19] and Pakistan,[20] as well as many other Islamic jurisdictions.

15 See, for example, Al-Quran, al-Nisa: 93.

16 Notably, Imam Malik, Imam Shafie and Imam Ahmed include involuntary murder as a form of accidental murder. See also Pervin (n 13) 148.

17 Pervin (n 13) 148.

18 For example, article 204 of the 1991 Islamic Penal Code sets out that homicide has three possible classifications: 'wilful murder, quasi-intentional homicide and unintentional homicide'.

19 Nigerian Penal Code, articles 206 et seq.

20 Pakistan Penal Code, articles 300 et seq.

The final possible system of classification is that proposed by the Maliki and Zahiri schools. Within these schools, a simple distinction between intentional and accidental murder can be drawn;[21] an act falls into the first category where there is general intent of aggression.[22]

General elements

Certain elements of the offence of homicide will transcend any classificatory system. By definition, the offence will require causation of the death of another human being. It is to these general elements that we now turn our attention.

Beginning of life

Clearly, the offence of homicide requires the victim to be alive. The exact point at which human life begins is controversial; the fundamental issue is that the primary Islamic sources can be interpreted in varying ways. The key text is a hadith of the Prophet Muhammad that states everyone is 'collected in the womb of his mother for 40 days, becomes a clot for 40 days, and a piece of flesh for 40 days. Then Allah sends an angel to breath the soul into his body.'[23] The key factor in the commencement of life for theological purposes is the point at which the foetus gains a soul. The issue with the hadith is that these phases of development could be interpreted as occurring consecutively (120 days total) or concurrently (40 days total). It is the former of these two interpretations that appears to prevail in Islamic juristic thought.[24] In a positivist sense, consensus has recently been reached in Iran that an exception to the general illegality of abortions ought to be available where the abortion is carried out within four months of conception.[25] This suggests that the 120-day period is the one deemed to most accurately define the beginning of human life in modern Islamic jurisdictions.

Further evidence for this finding is the Islamic laws of testate which state that an embryo has a right to a share of its father's estate upon the father's death. Whilst the right to distribution is deemed to exist from the point of conception, such an assumption requires the death of the father to post-date the gestation period of 120 days. This too suggests that it is 120 days from conception when human life begins.[26]

Additionally, the appropriate ceremonial funeral procedure of a miscarried foetus depends on whether a period of four months has elapsed since conception. If so, Islamic law requires that it undergo ceremonial washing and embalmment before burial.[27] This further suggests the significance Islam attaches to the expiration of the 120-day period.

21 T. Wasti, *The Application of Islamic Criminal Law in Pakistan* (Brill 2009) 68.
22 M.E. Badar, *The Concept of Mens Rea in International Criminal Law* (Hart 2013) 213.
23 Sahih Bukhari 4:54:430.
24 See, for example, M.N. Yaseen, 'The Inception of Human Life in the Light of Statements of the Holy Quran and Sunnah' (1990) 22 Journal of the Islamic Medical Association of North America 159–67.
25 K. Aramesh, 'A Closer Look at the Abortion Debate in Iran' (2009) 9(8) American Journal of Bioethics 57.
26 M.A. Albar, 'Ethical Considerations in the Prevention and Management of Genetic Disorders with Special Emphasis on Religious Considerations' (2002) 23(6) Saudi Medical Journal 627, 628.
27 A. Shaw, 'Rituals of Infant Death: Defining Life and Islamic Personhood' (2013) 28(2) Bioethics 84–95.

End of life

The requirement of death is deceptively complex. Whilst determining whether a victim has died will be clear in certain cases, the array of possible barometers by which the presence of life can be assessed will make other cases more difficult. Death can be defined in terms of legal, ethical, medical or spiritual parameters. Primary Islamic sources state that death occurs when the body and soul are separated.[28] Clearly, however, these spiritual parameters are far too imprecise for any legal analysis to be workable or of practical applicability.

Scientifically, cessation of breathing alone cannot be the determinative factor given that this would class those on artificial breathing support machines as dead. Furthermore, the absence of a heartbeat cannot be conclusive as modern medical procedures may result in the temporary termination of a heartbeat for periods of up to several hours.[29]

Scientific anomalies aside, the Islamic notion of death, whilst too imprecise to be of legal help, maps neatly into the general medical understanding of death. It is arguable that in both of the aforementioned scenarios the soul has not split from the body. A difficult issue for this analysis is whether being brain-dead is tantamount to death. Under Islamic law, the components of a human are the self (*nafs*), the spirit (*rooh*) and spiritual mind (*qalb*). As Khan argues, all of these elements relate to cranial functions. The absence of a functioning brain therefore vitiates the existence of these elements. On that basis, Khan is right to assert that classifying the brain-dead as deceased is in no way a violation of principles of Islamic law.[30]

Pre-birth causes with post-birth effects

Another issue that all jurisdictions must confront is the way in which eventually fatal defects caused by mistreatment whilst in the womb are dealt with. Essentially, this is an issue of causation and a question of whether the defendant who commits an offence against the mother can be held responsible for the consequences of the offence for the child. There are two scenarios to distinguish in this analysis: infliction of harm by another on the mother and self-infliction of harm by the mother herself.

With reference to the first example, it is worth noting that Islamic criminal law generally accepts the doctrine of transferred defences. So, where A has a defence to the killing of B and in attempting to kill B, kills C instead, the defence to the offence of homicide will remain operative. Furthermore, there can be no doubt that an act intended to harm the unborn child will be treated in the same way as any other homicide so long as the foetus is at least 120 days old and has, for the purposes of Islam, begun its human life. So, if A deliberately kicks B (the mother) with the intention of harming C (the unborn child) with the result that C dies, there is no principled reason why A has not committed the offence of homicide against C.

There is also the situation to consider in which the mother is harmed by a legally defenceless defendant, who unintentionally causes the consequential death of the unborn child. Essentially, this is a question of the extent to which transferred malice applies in Islamic law. There is no uniform formulation or absolute consensus on this issue, however, the general rule seems to be that an intention to cause harm can be transferred to an unforeseen or

28 Quranic Sura 23, Verse 100.

29 F.A. Khan, 'The Definition of Death in Islam: Can Brain Death be used as a Criteria of Death in Islam?' (1986) 18 Journal of the Islamic Medical Association of North America 18.

30 Ibid.

unintended victim where the *intended* victim is a human being.[31] So, a lack of foresight regarding the injury to the unborn child will be immaterial and the defendant will be criminally responsible for the homicide of the child.

The more difficult of the two cases is where the mother harms herself with the unintended consequence that the unborn child is killed. There is little authority on the point, presumably due to the complexity of factual matrix that such litigation would require; however, the general principles of mistaken homicide would appear to cover such a case. Whilst the general Islamic approach is that human error is not punishable, a lack of due care and caution will give rise to criminal responsibility for the consequential results.[32] A mother who harms herself whilst pregnant undoubtedly exercises insufficient care towards the unborn child and will be responsible for the accidental homicide of the unborn child.[33] Furthermore, given the unlawfulness of suicide in Islamic law, the doctrine of transferred malice could apply so as to find the mother liable for the consequences that the criminal offence of suicide has for the unborn child.

Medical treatment scenarios: double effect doctrine and end of life decisions

The doctrine of double effect is often invoked by doctors to justify the prescription of drugs that undoubtedly, and to the knowledge of the doctor, will shorten the life of the patient. The permissibility of this doctrine is most poignant in the case of euthanasia where the killing of a patient is carried out to eradicate their pain, in the knowledge that death will be almost immediate. We must distinguish between active and passive euthanasia in our analysis.

Euthanasia: active euthanasia

Given the Quran's uncompromising position regarding the sanctity of life, it is unsurprising that euthanasia is strictly forbidden in Islam. There is no distinction between the Sunni and Shi'a schools on this matter. Death is controlled by Allah alone and for humans to intervene, except in the course of justice, is strictly forbidden (*haram*). The counterbalancing concepts of autonomy and free will simply are a consideration, life belongs to Allah and only He can possibly have autonomy to determine its end. Active euthanasia can in no way be permitted under Islamic law.

Much academic commentary, however, advocates the treating of active euthanasia as something other than murder. For example, the Hanafis regard *qisas* as unavailable as the addition of consent would characterise the offence as less culpable than murder. The Shafis and Hanbalis go even further and consider the presence of consent to make the killing lawful.

Conversely, this simply is not reflected in the posited law of modern Islamic jurisdictions. For example, s.309 of the Penal Code of Singapore states that attempted suicide is a criminal offence. Read alongside s.107 of the Code, abetting an attempted suicide must also be an offence punishable with imprisonment of up to ten years.

31 M.H. Kakhki, 'Islamic Law' in A. Reed and M. Bohlander *Participation in Crime: Domestic Comparative Perspectives* (Routledge 2013) 354–55.

32 Shah (n 1) 163.

33 Quran, 17:31: 'Kill not your children for fear of want: We shall provide sustenance for them as well as for you. Verily the killing of them is a great sin'.

The saving grace for a doctor engaging in such activities is that a mitigating factor may exist so as to render the punishment more lenient than that which might otherwise be available (e.g., *qisas*). For example, under Article 612 of the Iranian Penal Code, such a killing would result in imprisonment of up to ten years rather than *qisas*; or under Article 268 of the same Code, the possibility of *qisas* is eliminated where the victim forgives the defendant before the victim's death. This is not to say that the assisted suicide isn't regarded with abhorrence, but rather that a more general mitigating factor is available in such circumstances.

Euthanasia: passive euthanasia

Passive euthanasia entails a failure to medically intervene. An example of this would be omitting to resuscitate the terminally ill. On a question of causation, it is the doctor's decision that has resulted in the death of the patient; unlike active euthanasia though, the course of nature is not altered.

The general Islamic position on this is explained by the Egyptian scholar Sheikh Yusuf al-Qaradawi in a recent religious ruling (*fatwa*). He explains that euthanasia is tantamount to murder unless the possible treatment is useless. In other words, where no material change is made to the patient's life, the doctor can legitimately omit to intervene. This ties in with the basic idea that life belongs to Allah. If it is He that determines when life is to end, allowing a patient to die naturally despite the medical possibility of salvation must be legitimate.[34]

Life-shortening, pain-reducing medication

The final issue to consider with regards to the doctrine of double effect concerns pain medication under Islamic law in the context of palliative care. Given that this will shorten the life of the patient, albeit in a much more indirect manner than euthanasia as mentioned in the previous sections, it merits discussion in this section.

One of the key aims of Shari'a law is the protection of the medical and physical integrity of the individual. On that basis, medication that reduces pain generally is dealt with in a positive light under the primary sources of Islamic law. Traditional Islamic discourse advocates a tripartite distinction of such medication based on its intended effect. Medication is obligatory (*wajib*) if its absence would cause death, loss of functioning of organs or development of a communicable disease. Medication is recommended (*mandub*) if its absence would cause a weakening of the body. Medication is reprehensible (*makruh*) if the medication would cause more harm than it cured.[35]

A contemporary issue relates to pain-reducing medication that inevitably shortens the life of a patient. Such medication is a relatively recent scientific phenomenon. For that reason, traditional Islamic discourse does not give us a response to the issue. We must instead look to more recent *fatwas* for guidance. The issue with this more recent guidance is that it attempts to extrapolate from the reasoning of early Islamic thought into a challenge outside of its contemplation. This has led to jurists placing emphasis on differing maxims to reach diametrically opposed positions on the issue.

34 Yusuf al-Qaradawi, 'Details of Fatwa' <https://efenem.files.wordpress.com/2009/06/qaradawis-4.doc> (2005) accessed 22 November 2017.

35 M.M. Malik, 'Islamic Bioethics of Pain Medication: An Effective Response to Mercy Argument' (2012) 3(2) Bangladesh Journal of Bioethics 4.

The first response is to focus on the encouragement of patience and perseverance. An example of this is a statement from the Prophet that 'no fatigue, nor disease, nor sorrow, nor sadness, nor hurt, nor distress befalls a Muslim, even if it were the prick he receives from a thorn, but that Allah expiates some of his sins for that'.[36] In other words, there is a purpose to the pain and suffering and persevering through the pain will be rewarded later. On that basis, pain-reducing medication that hastens death ought to be impermissible.

However, other jurists focus on the concept that 'Allah does not want to place you in difficulty'.[37] On that basis, it could be argued that Islam promotes the avoidance of pain and suffering and encourages the use of medication to that end.

Malik argues that the former interpretation of the primary sources is unrealistic and doesn't adequately understand the level of pain that some patients endure.[38] However, this criticism is misplaced; expecting the primary sources to provide a ready-made answer to this modern problem misunderstands the whole extrapolative process. His dismissal of the former interpretation on the basis that the primary extracts do not fit the situation as neatly cannot be considered as an argument in favour of the second interpretation. It is instead merely evidence of the fact that traditional Islamic discourse did not consider the specific issue in question. Simply put, the Islamic primary sources provide no conclusive guidance about the issue.

Homicide by omission

It is important to recognise the difficulty in distinguishing between acts and omissions. Causing another's death through an action instinctively seems to be more culpable than causing death through an omission. Such a position appears correct in the paradigm. For example, stabbing another man appears to be a more culpable act than failing to save another man who has already been stabbed. However, it may be difficult to classify a series of facts using this binary distinction. An example of this difficulty is the case in which a life support machine is switched off. Is this to be considered as an action, the salient detail being that a switch is actively pressed? Or would it better be classified as an omission, the salient detail being that life support is being omitted? As Ashworth writes, 'there are many ambiguous cases in which the act/omission distinction should not be used as a cloak for avoiding the moral issues'.[39]

The extent to which homicide by omission may be criminally condemned depends on the specific enunciation of the offence for which the defendant is potentially liable, or more accurately, the potential punishment for such an offence. In general, schools of Islam distinguish between homicide offences for which the punishment is retaliation (*qisas*) and those for which the punishment is something else.

Retaliation

In terms of crimes for which the punishment is retaliation, there are three different positions taken amongst the schools of Islamic thought. To the Hanafis, in order for homicide to be punished with *qisas*, it must be wilful and that requires a positive and direct act that causes

36 Al-Bukhari. Sahih al-Bukhari. Book: 70, Hadith: 545.
37 The Quran, 5:6.
38 Malik (n 35) 13.
39 A. Ashworth, *Principles of Criminal Law* (Oxford University Press 2006) 112.

the victim's death. Within the Hanafi school of thought, there is no scope for retaliation in response to a homicide by omission.

A more moderate position is taken by the Malikis, to whom an omission is punishable with retaliation where there is an obligation to act. The Maliki position is reflected in the Nigerian Penal Code. Under Article 305 therein,

> when a person undertakes to do any act the omission to do which is or may be dangerous to human life or health, it is his duty to do that act; and he is held to have caused any consequences which result to the life ...of any person by reason of any omission to perform that duty.

Furthermore, Article 314 states that a person is deemed to have killed another where 'the cause of death is an omission to observe or perform a duty' and the death consequently occurs within a year of such an omission. Article 316 makes it clear that murder can be constituted by an omission if one of the six conditions is met and the punishment of *qisas* then applies. So, murder can be committed through an omission under the Nigerian Penal Code where a duty to act has arisen. This example demonstrates the availability of *qisas* in response to a killing by omission.

A similar position is adopted by the Shafis and Hanbalis, to whom an omission is punishable with retaliation where it is linked to a positive act.[40]

It is perhaps unsurprising that a stricter requirement is in place in cases where the defendant's life is at stake given the emphasis that Islam places on the sanctity of life. Where the punishment does not endanger the life of the defendant, the lost life of the victim must take precedence in the legal analysis, leading to a broader *actus reus* of the homicide offence. Where there is a tension between the loss of the victim's life and the possible loss of the defendant's life, a stricter test needs to be in place to adequately strike the balance between the two.

Other punishments

In terms of other classifications of homicide offence, for which the punishment is *diya*, a more convoluted chain of causation is permissible.[41] Peters gives an example of the witness who gives false testimony. He explains that where that testimony leads to the death of a defendant and is consequently withdrawn, the witness is liable to pay *diya* to the heirs of the wrongly killed defendant. This example, whilst demonstrating the protracted chain of causation that can possibly lead to the punishment of *diya*, uses a particularly borderline example of an omission. It is possible that a false testimony would better be characterised as an act (the telling of a falsity) rather than an omission (omitting to tell the truth).[42]

Better examples can be found in the posited law of Islamic jurisdictions. For instance, Article 75 of the Sudanese Penal Code 1991 states that 'whoever, having it in his power to assist any injured person ... intentionally omits to perform such assistance ... [may] be punished [*inter alia*] with a fine'. Another example can be found in the Pakistan Penal Code's definition of accidental homicide in Article 321. Any 'unlawful act which becomes a cause for the death of another person' is sufficient for such an offence. The reference to an 'act' is misleading though given that Article 32 states that 'words which refer to acts done

40 R. Peters, *Crime and Punishment in Islamic Law* (Cambridge University Press 2005) 42.
41 Ibid.
42 A.S. Mehdi, 'Perjury and Its Effects in the View of Jurisprudence and Criminal Law' (2016) 9(9) Journal of Politics and Law 22–30.

extend also to omissions'. On that basis, it is clear that the offence of accidental homicide can be committed equally through act or omission; offences punishable with *diya* do not discriminate between the two.

Omitting to effect an easy rescue

The Sudanese example in the previous section demonstrates that Islamic jurisdictions often impose a duty to effect a rescue. This is also seen in the Tunisian Penal Code and the Penal Code of Tajikistan which states under Article 136 that

> failure to render aid which is necessary and clearly not suffering of postponement to a person in danger of his life, if the offender knew that such aid could be given without serious danger to himself or other persons, or failure to inform the proper authorities or persons about the necessity to render aid, is [a criminal offence].

Admittedly, these codes rarely treat such an omission as tantamount to murder. For example, the punishment in Tajikistan is corrective labour for six months, and the maximum sentence in Sudan is three months imprisonment. Nonetheless, the codification of the offence demonstrates the Islamic discouragement of such behaviour.[43]

The primary sources of Islamic law positively encourage rendering life-saving assistance; for example, the Quran states that 'whoever saves a life is as though he had saved the lives of all mankind'.[44] Given the emphasis placed on the sanctity of life in Islam, those who effect a rescue are looked upon favourably and those who shy away from a non-self-endangering rescue are scorned. It is unsurprising that many Islamic jurisdictions reflect this attitude in their penal codes with the imposition of a duty to effect an easy rescue.

Elements of homicide offences

For the purposes of this explanation, it is the Hanafi five-part classification of homicide offences that will be used. Furthermore, as Shah points out, it is merely the *mens rea* that distinguishes these offences from each other[45], the *actus reus* remains constant. There is minor disagreement on this point regarding the intentional and quasi-intentional murder distinction, with a few jurists arguing that the weapon used (part of the *actus reus*) is determinative.[46] Nevertheless, as is argued earlier in the chapter, this element is better characterised as indicative of the *mens rea* rather than a conclusive *actus reus* requirement *per se*. For that reason, the *actus reus* of all homicide offences can be explained in tandem before moving onto a detailed explanation of the requisite *mens rea* of the individual classifications.

Actus reus *of homicide*

The *actus reus* of homicide can be simply defined as the killing of another person. This definition can be split into four elements. First, the victim must be a human being. In other

43 M. Kakhki, 'Islamic Law' in A. Reed and M. Bohlander *General Defences in Criminal Law: Domestic and Comparative Perspectives* (Routledge 2003) 254.
44 Al-Ma'idah: 32.
45 Shah (n 1) 162.
46 See, for example, Pervin (n 13)

words, the victim must be a human whose life has begun and not yet ended as defined above. Second, the victim must die as discussed above. Third, the defendant must cause the death of the victim. Fourth, the killing must be unlawful. The fourth element simply requires that the killing occur outside the course of justice.

Mens rea *of intentional murder (*qatl-i-amd*)*

A finding of the offence of murder requires an intention to kill on the part of the defendant. Some jurists believe that this can only be demonstrated by the use of a fatal weapon, however, others go further and suggest that such an intention could even be present where the defendant hits another with his hands or gives a false testimony against a defendant in a murder trial.[47]

This is reflected in the Penal Code of Iran under which Article 206(a) states that murder is committed where 'where a murderer … decides to kill'. In other words, it is the intention as to the result that is crucial.

Mens rea *of quasi-intentional murder (*qatl-i-sibhi-amd*)*

This second form of homicide requires an intention to harm, but the absence of an intention to kill. This offence would be committed, for example, where A throws a stone at B, intending to frighten B, but accidentally hitting B in such a way that causes B's death. Given the difficulty in determining the true intention of a defendant[48], this is often said to require a mode of killing that sometimes, but not always, is fatal.[49] This test, whilst used to cut through the difficulty of ascertaining the inner workings of the defendant's mind, it is submitted, is particularly unhelpful. Where any death is caused by an instrument, it can be said that the instrument used is *sometimes* fatal. By definition that must be the case. So, the question then becomes whether there is a way of using the instrument in question in a way that isn't fatal. It is submitted that this is always possible. Even the most fatal of weapons, a gun, can be used in such a manner that death is not caused (for example, if someone is beaten with a gun but not shot).

Whilst a test that pertains to intention alone will be imprecise and difficult to administer, any alternative based on material facts will not work either. The test for such an offence should remain whether the defendant intended to harm and not kill. The associated evidential difficulties are the inevitable price for a workable definition of the offence.

Mens rea *of accidental murder (*al-qatl-al-khata*)*

The Quran makes it clear that killing by mistake leads to liability to pay compensation. For example, it states that 'he who has slain a believer by mistake … [must, *inter alia*,] pay blood money to the heirs'.[50] In other words, killing of another will be a punishable offence

47 E. Ghodsi, *Murder in the Criminal Law of Iran and Islam* (2004) 68 The Journal of Criminal Law 160, 167.

48 This is a problem that pervades all legal systems. See, for example, Bowen LJ's comments in the contractual sphere in the case of *Edington v Fitzmaurice* [1885] 29 Ch. D. 459 [483] that 'the state of a man's mind is as much a fact as the state of his digestion'.

49 J.R. Munshi, 'Homicide in Islamic Law and Conventional Law as Applied in Bangladesh' (2015) 4(1) Manarat International University Studies 95, 98.

50 Quran 4:92.

even if accidental. The Quran, however, gives little guidance in what killing by mistake entails. The Pakistan Penal Code helpfully explains that the offence requires a lack of intention to cause death or harm.[51] Furthermore, it sets out that the mistake can be one of act or one of fact. An example of the former would be aiming to shoot a deer but shooting the victim instead. An example of the latter would be shooting at an object that is believed to be a deer but turns out to in fact be a human being.

From these illustrations, it is clear that the mental state required for the offence of accidental murder is a genuine and honest intention to perform a lawful act. Neither the primary sources of Islamic law nor its specific enunciations in the Penal Codes of modern Islamic jurisdictions give concrete guidance on whether this belief is to be judged objectively or subjectively; it is unclear whether the belief needs to be one that it is objectively reasonable to hold. It is submitted that the sparse guidance in the Quran points towards a subjective intention. The only indication is that the killing needs to be 'by mistake', the reasonableness of the mistake appears to be immaterial. Such a conclusion would also tie in with the broader theme of judging a defendant's intention from a subjective point of view prevalent in Islamic thought.

This offence forms an exception to the general rule that there is a defence to criminal prosecution where the unlawful act is mistaken and there is no intention to commit a criminal act. That general rule is overridden by any specific enunciation of a punishment for a mistaken offence by application of the general legal principle that *lex specialis derogat lex generalis*. As the Quran expressly sets out a punishment for this offence, the general availability of the defence of mistake does not apply in these circumstances.

Infanticide and child destruction

As noted on pages 326–328, it is very possible that the offences of infanticide and child destruction can be made out through general principles of homicide in Islamic law on the basis of transferred malice.

A number of jurisdictions clarify this position with specific offences 'without prejudice to any greater penalty'.[52] Under the Penal Code of Iraq, the offences of child destruction and infanticide bear a penalty of imprisonment, however, such a penalty is unlikely to be necessary in consideration of the general principles of homicide in Islamic law.

Abortion and homicide

Before 120 days from conception has elapsed, abortion (*fiqh*) cannot be classified as homicide because a key element of homicide is that the victim is a human being. Prior to this point, a free-standing offence of procuring abortion is available depending on the laws of the state in question. For example, paragraph 417(1) of the Iraqi Penal Code states that 'any woman who wilfully procures her own miscarriage … is punishable by a period of detention not exceeding 1 year'. In other words, there is a free-standing offence of abortion, the punishment of which is far less severe than homicide itself.[53]

51 Pakistan Penal Code, Article 318.
52 Iraqi Penal Code, paragraph 419.
53 R. J. Simon, *Abortion: Statutes, Policies, and Public Attitudes the World Over* (Praeger 2007) 25–6.

The issue of abortion has already been touched upon with regards to when life is deemed to have begun in Islamic thought. As explained on page 326, there is ambiguity in the primary texts, but general consensus is that the foetus becomes a human being after 120 days, when it is given a soul by Allah. From this point onwards there is consensus that abortion is prohibited. Before that point in time, there is disagreement over the legitimacy of abortion.

The Hanafis permit abortion up to 120 days from conception. A similar position is taken by the majority of Shafis and Hanbalis, but this is certainly not a unanimous position within the school. On the contrary, the Malikis prohibit abortion from the point of conception onwards.

It is worth noting that the distinction between the schools of thought is not particularly useful in predicting how a country's posited law will deal with the issue. The Maliki school, for example, is the predominant Sunni school in North Africa. Tunisia, however, was the first Muslim country to liberalise its abortion law in 1965. To this day, their Penal Code legalises abortion up to 120 days and allows abortion after that date where there is a risk of harm for the mother or a risk of the child being seriously disabled.

Islamic jurisdictions are responding to the requirement for a more nuanced approach that balances the rights of the mother against those of the child. Abortion for social or economic reasons is still generally prohibited,[54] with one exception found in the Sunnah where the mother is breastfeeding another child and giving birth to the foetus would compromise the health of the existing child.[55] Abortion is generally permitted where the life of the mother is at risk[56], where the physical or mental health of the mother is at risk,[57] and increasingly where the pregnancy is the result of rape or incest.[58]

Defences to homicide

Justice is central to Islamic criminal law.[59] Guilt cannot be proven until the absence of defences has been established. Defences can be complete, absolving the defendant of any criminal responsibility, or partial, mitigating the sentence imposed on the defendant. Before moving onto the specific defences and their availability, three general points ought to be made regarding defences under Islamic law.

First, there is a general acceptance of transferred defences. In other words, where the defendant has a defence to his intended actions, that defence will vitiate guilt for any unintended consequences. So, if A attacks B and B, in attempting to defend himself, accidentally kills C, B will have a defence of self-defence to the killing of C. Islamic law is unique in its acceptance of this general rule.[60]

54 O. Asman, 'Abortion in Islamic Countries—Legal and Religious Aspects' (2004) 23(1) Medicine and Law 73–89.
55 G.K. Shapiro, 'Abortion Law in Muslim-Majority Countries: An Overview of the Islamic Discourse with Policy Implications' (2013) 29(4) Health Policy Plan 483, 488.
56 Ibid.
57 D.L. Bowen, 'Abortion, Islam, and the 1994 Cairo Population Conference' (1997) 29(2) International Journal of Middle East Studies 161–84
58 See *fatwa* of Algerian Islamic Supreme Council in 1998 and that of Egyptian Grand Sheikh of al-Azhar, Muhammed Sayed Tantawi in 1998.
59 See, for example, Quran, 5:8 which encourages its followers to 'be just'.
60 See, for example, Article 296 of the Iranian Penal Code which reads as follows: 'In cases where a person intends to shoot an object or an animal or another person but the bullet hits another person, his/her actions will be considered to be a simple mistake'.

The second point to note is that Islamic law places great emphasis on the subjective mindset of the defendant. One result of this emphasis is that defences are available not just where the necessary factual conditions are met, but where the defendant subjectively believes the necessary factual conditions to be met. This is seen in the Singaporean Penal Code which states that 'nothing is an offence which is done by any person ... [who] in good faith believes himself to be justified by law.'[61]

Third, all defences are subject to an exception that they will not be available where the defendant contributed to the chain of causation leading to its *prima facie* availability. The Quran and primary sources provide little guidance on what constitutes provocation of the defence; individual jurisdictions determine the extent themselves. An unequivocal example of this type of provocation would be hitting another person causing them to fight back and giving rise, *prima facie*, to a defence of self-defence. Under Islamic law, such a defence is not available as the act that ultimately gives rise to the claimed defence would be 'in the course of justice'.[62]

Consent

As explained earlier in the chapter, with reference to euthanasia, the legislation of modern Islamic states tends not to allow consent to vitiate liability for homicide. It ought to be noted though that the discussion here relates to homicide outside of the end-of-life decisions in the context of euthanasia referred to on page 327–328.

The rejection of a general defence of consent to homicide reflects the Zufar and Maliki schools' approach which both maintain that consent will not change the nature of the offence committed.

Certain schools, however, do believe that the offence substantially changes where the victim has consented. For example, the Hanafi school believes that an intentional killing with the victim's consent is better regarded as simply manslaughter, thereby waiving *qisas.* The Shafi'i and Hanbali schools go even further and claim that the killing is lawful, thereby rendering *diya* unavailable too on the basis that to insist otherwise would undermine the victim's personal autonomy.[63]

As explained on page 323, a mitigating factor may exist so as to render the punishment more lenient than that which might otherwise be available. This type of mitigation is embodied in Articles 612 and 268 of the Iranian Penal Code[64], which provide for a waiver of retaliation punishment and a lighter prison sentence where a killer has been forgiven and

61 Singaporean Penal Code, s.79.

62 Quran, 17:33.

63 I.A.K. Nyazee, *General Principles of Criminal Law: (Islamic and Western)* (Sharia'h Academy, International Islamic University 2007) 156.

64 Article 612 – Anyone who commits a murder and where there is no complainant, or there is a complainant but he has forgiven and withdrawn his application for *qisas*, or if *qisas* is not executed for any reason, if his act disrupts the public order and safety of the society or it is thought that it emboldens the offender or others [to commit murder again], the court shall sentence the offender to three to ten years' imprisonment. Article 268 – Theft shall be punishable by *hadd* punishment provided that all the following conditions are met... (i) The theft was not committed in a time of famine; (ii) The owner of the property makes a complaint against the thief before judicial bodies (iii) The owner of the property has not forgiven the thief prior to the proof of the theft; (iv) The stolen property is not returned to the owner prior to the proof of the theft; (v) The stolen property is not entered into the thief's ownership prior to the proof of offense; (vi) The stolen property has not been gained through theft or usurpation.

mitigating factors for theft offences respectively.[65] It would be wrong to label this as a defence though. It is, at most, a mitigating factor in terms of the penalty imposed.

Whilst the law of Islamic states may not reflect this divergence of opinions, there are sound policy reasons for insisting on the irrelevance of consent. Often in these cases, the only person alive to testify to the consent is the defendant himself. The rejection of a defence of consent may be considered as a concession to the evidential difficulties that it would otherwise occur.

With the exception of certain inevitable end-of-life decisions, mercy killings are treated with similar disdain under the modern law of Islamic jurisdictions.

Self-defence

The sanctity of self-defence in Islam stems from a Quranic verse, stating 'and make not your hands contribute to (your) destruction'.[66] This has been given a rather strained meaning and is now commonly cited as the Islamic source of the obligation to save oneself from harm where it is possible to do so. This is also reflected in the Quranic verse which reads: 'when an oppressive wrong is inflicted on them (are not cowed) but help and defend themselves'.[67]

With the exception of the Hanbali school, Islamic jurists are agreed that there is an obligation to defend yourself on the basis that life is sacred and to disregard it would undermine the wishes of Allah.

Whilst there is disagreement over the obligation to defend oneself, there is more Islamic authority to suggest that there is a *right* to defend oneself. An example of this is a well-known story of the Prophet Muhammad. The question was whether a man, who damages another's teeth in attempting to pull his finger from the clamp of that other man's biting teeth, has committed a wrong; the Prophet held that there was no blame relating to the damage to the other's teeth.[68]

Certain hadiths indicate that self-defence can extend to situations where it is another's integrity that is at risk and needs defending. It is thought that this stems from the general obligation to be a 'good Muslim' and help others rather than being an inevitable development of the defence of self-defence.

There does not appear to be any strict limit on the acts that can give rise to a defence of self defence. The above discussion has proceeded with reference to threats to physical integrity, however, this extends to protection of honour[69] and protection of property[70] too.[71] There is even authority to suggest that the defence can operate where the victim of the self-defence was not responsible for giving rise to the need for self-defence. Peters alludes to the availability of the defence in such a situation, stating that 'defence of one's life is also a valid defence if a person, while being on the point of starvation, kills the owner of food necessary to save his life, after the latter's refusal to give it to him; for in that case the

65 M. Pirahji and M. Shekarchizadeh, 'Self-Inflicted Death in Criminal Law of Iran' (2015) 6(6) Mediterranean Journal of Social Sciences 194–200.

66 Quran, 2:195

67 Quran, 42:39.

68 Awdah Abdul Qadir cited in S.O. Rabi'u, 'Defence Mechanism in Criminal Liability under Islamic Law' (2016) 4(4) International Journal of Innovative Legal & Political Studies 19–29, 27.

69 Quran, 49:11

70 Quran, 2:188;

71 'Violation of a Muslim's life, property and dignity are forbidden for another Muslim' (Narrated by Muslim, no. 6487).

victim acted unlawfully against the killer'.[72] In such a case, it would be wrong to say that the victim's behaviour was a sufficient and necessary cause of the risk to the defendant's life.

It ought to be noted, however, that such availability of the defence is tempered by strict rules regarding its operation. The defence, generally, must be necessary and proportionate. This is seen, for example, in Article 99 of the Pakistan Penal Code which restricts the defence to acts that do not 'inflict more harm than it is necessary to inflict for the purpose of defence'. Such a limit is also seen, *inter alia*, in Article 60 of the Afghan Penal Code, Article 61 of the Iranian Penal Code and Article 49 of the Indonesian Penal Code.[73]

Whilst the ambit of the availability of the defence is wide, the restrictions on its operation mean that, in reality, there will be no defence to killing another for their food when starving on the basis that there would inevitably be food available from another source too, thus vitiating the necessity requirement of the defence.

Duress

Compelling duress, as opposed to non-compelling duress, is generally permitted as a defence in Islamic law. This is to say, where a threat nullifies consent *and* vitiates any free choice, there will *prima facie* be a defence to the crime available.[74]

According to Abdul Qadir Audah, operation of the defence requires four requirements to be met: (i) a serious threat of harm; (ii) the threat is of an immediate nature; (iii) the threatener is capable of carrying out the threat; and (iv) the person under duress believes that the threat will be carried out.[75]

Where these requirements are met, the effect of the defence depends on the offence in question. Murder is considered to be of such a severity that duress cannot vitiate criminal responsibility.[76] This is seen in various authorities that insist upon the sanctity of life and the unacceptability of killing another simply to save your life.

Whilst the Malikis, Hanbalis and Zahiris believe that no mitigation of the punishment should be made (i.e., *qisas* is still available), there is some authority to suggest that a lesser punishment ought to be imposed. A minority of Shafis followers believe that the punishment should be capped at *diya*, whilst Abu Hanifa and Iman Muhammad believe that it should be capped at *ta'zir.* [77]

In terms of the posited law in Islamic states, there are two approaches. The most prevalent approach is to punish the coercer and the coerced. This approach is based on the

72 Peters (n 40) 25.

73 The Afghan Penal Code provides as follows, '2– Defence should be proportionate to the danger of threat; 3– Defence should be the only way of removing the danger; 4– Defence should be concurrent with the attack of the opposite side'. The relevant provisions of the Iranian Penal Code are very similar to the Afghan Penal Code in terms of proportionality and lack of alternative options: '1– The defence is proportionate to the aggression and danger. 2– The action is not excessive. 3– Resorting to governmental forces is not practicable in a reasonable time, or the intervention of such forces is not effective in repelling the aggression and danger'.

74 K.A. El Fadl, 'Law of Duress in Islamic Law and Common Law: A Comparative Study' (1991) 30(3) Islamic Studies 303, 310.

75 A.Q.A. Shaheed, *Criminal Law of Islam* (Vol. 2, International Islamic Publishers 1999) 295.

76 K.A. El Fadl, 'Law of Duress in Islamic Law and Common Law: A Comparative Study' (1991) 30(3) Islamic Studies 303, 326.

77 B. Mustafa, B.M. Yusob, B. Awang and M.H. Badrulzaman, 'Defence of Duress in Criminal Law: A Comparative Analysis Between Malaysian and Islamic Law Approach' (2014) 10(1) Journal of Islamic Law Review 183,194.

disdain for preferring your life to that of another. This is reflected in Article 94 of the Pakistan Penal Code which states that 'except murder … nothing is an offence which is done by a person who is compelled to do it by threats …'. The fact that duress is not a defence to murder is also reflected in the Shi'a jurisdictions; for example, Article 375 (formerly Article 211) of the Iranian Penal Code states that

> [c]omitting murder under duress or on the order of another person is not a licence to commit murder. Hence if someone is forced to commit murder or the order for committing murder is given, the murderer will be retaliated and the person who has ordered the murder or who has forced the murder to be committed will be sentenced to life imprisonment.

The alternative approach is to consider the coerced as an agent to the coercer and consequently not personally liable. To the supporters of this school, *diya* should still be available against the coerced on the basis that the coerced was an essential part of the causative mechanism.[78]

It is worth noting that it is almost always the former approach that is favoured in modern Islamic jurisdictions. Perhaps this can be attributed to the rarity with which the argument against such an approach would succeed.

Necessity

The defence of necessity overlaps significantly with the defences of self-defence and duress. The latter two could be described as specific enunciations of the first. All of these defences stem from the principle whereby 'if one is forced by necessity, without wilful obedience, nor transgressing due limits, then one is guiltless'.[79]

As explained by Heller and Dubber, there is a requirement of proportionality within this defence.[80] The result of the need for proportionality is that necessity cannot be a defence to homicide; if all lives are worth the same, taking a life to save a life cannot be a proportionate response. The potential factual difficulties with such a conclusion discussed in the context of self-defence are again of interest, but again currently ignored in the Islamic law discussion.

Insanity

Islamic law places firm emphasis on the *mens rea* of the offence. As seen on page 333 it is this element of the offence that distinguishes between the different levels of culpability for homicide.

Islam distinguishes between three levels of insanity: absolute, intermittent and partial.[81] The former cannot be held criminally responsible under Islamic law. The general rule is that a defendant will be liable for acts unless it is shown that the mental disorder was active at the time. For the purposes of absolute insanity, this will always be the case.[82] This position is

78 El Fadl (n 76).
79 Quran 2:173.
80 K.J. Heller and M. Dubber, *The Handbook of Comparative Criminal Law* (Stanford University Press 2010) 333.
81 G.A. Tzeferakos and A.I. Douzenis, 'Islam, Mental Health and Law: A General Overview' (2017) 16(28) Annals of General Psychiatry (2017) < www.ncbi.nlm.nih.gov/pmc/articles/PMC5498891/> accessed 4 April 2018.
82 B.G. Weiss, *Studies in Islamic Legal Theory* (Brill 2002).

reflected in the Egyptian Penal Code which states at Article 62 that 'no penalty shall be imposed on one losing … the faculty of choice in his work at the time of committing the deed: either due to insanity or mental disability'.[83] The same sentiment is seen in s.84 of the Malaysian Penal Code which states 'nothing is an offence which is done by a person who, at the time of doing it … is incapable of knowing the nature of the act'.[84]

The defence of insanity is a rare exception to the burden of proof falling on the defendant to establish a defence. Once insanity is alleged and supported by some evidence, the burden shifts to the prosecution to establish that there was no insanity.[85]

The result of insanity is not subject to general consensus. It is agreed that the homicide cannot be classed as intentional and *qisas* will not be available.[86] Some schools believe that the effect of insanity is to make the offence one of accidental homicide instead for which *diya* is payable to the heirs of the victim. This is the view of Imam Abu Hanifa, Imam Malik and Hanbali Schools of law. The Shafi'i school, in contrast, still regards the homicide as intentional but regards the insanity as a mitigating factor to the civil liability to the heirs of the victim.[87]

The former position is reflected, for example, in the Pakistan Penal Code which states at Article 308(1) that 'where the offender is a minor or insane, *diya* shall be payable as may be determined by the court'.[88] The latter position is seen, for example, in the Somaliland Penal Code which provides for complete exculpation at Article 50 ('whoever, at the moment when he committed an act, was by reason of infirmity, in a state of mind such as to preclude capacity of understanding and of volition, shall not be liable').[89]

Diminished responsibility

As is the case under the law of England and Wales, the result of diminished responsibility is not a total exculpation, but instead a mitigation of the punishment. Generally, *qisas* will be made unavailable and the punishment will be limited to *diya*. [90]

The availability of the defence will depend on the defendant establishing a mental abnormality stemming from a recognised medical condition on the facts. Whilst this seems

83 Article 62 of the Egyptian Penal Code in its entirety reads as follows: 'No penalty shall be imposed on one losing consciousness or the faculty of choice in his work at the time of committing the deed: either due to insanity or mental disability, or to unconsciousness resulting from drugs whatever their kind if he takes them forcibly or unknowingly'.

84 Laws of Malaysia, Act 574 (Penal Code), article 84 in full reads as follows: 'Nothing is an offence which is done by a person who, at the time of doing it, by reason of unsoundness of mind, is incapable of knowing the nature of the act, or that he is doing what is either wrong or contrary to law'.

85 H.M.M. Sedeghi, 'The Effect of Insanity on Criminal Liability: In Islamic and English Law' (2012) 1(1) Iranian Journal of Medical Law 32, 35.

86 See, for example, article 306(a) of the Pakistan Penal Code.

87 A.S. El Awa, *Punishment in Islamic Law* (American Trust Publications 1982) 22.

88 Article 308(1) of the Pakistan Penal Code reads as follows: 'Where an offender guilty of qatl-i-amd is not liable to qisas under s.306 or the qisas is not enforceable under clause (c) of s.307, he shall be liable to diya: provided that, where the offender is minor or insane, diya shall be payable either from his property or, by such person as may be determined by the Court'.

89 Somaliland Legislative Decree Number 5 of 16 December 1962 (Penal Code), article 50. This translation of the Penal Code available at <www.somalilandlaw.com/Penal_Code_English.pdf> accessed 4 April 2018.

90 M.I. Dien, *Islamic Law: From Historical Foundations to Contemporary Practice* (Edinburgh University Press 2004) 102.

to be the most appropriate defence within which an abused wife could have some defence to the homicide of her abusive husband, as indeed would be the case in English law, the primary sources of Islamic law make supporting such an argument difficult.

Verse 4:34 of the Quran unequivocally sets out the dominance of men and the legitimacy of abusing a wife. It states:

> Men are in charge of women, because Allah hath made the one of them to excel the other, and because they spend of their property (for the support of women). So good women are the obedient, guarding in secret that which Allah hath guarded. As for those from whom ye fear rebellion, admonish them and banish them to beds apart, and beat them.

It ought to be noted that there is disagreement over the true translation of this verse. Some scholars advocate reading 'separate from them' instead of 'beat them'. On that interpretive basis, this would not be regarded as indicative of the legitimacy of domestic abuse; however, this interpretation strays further from the literal Arabic-English translation.

Whilst there is little direct authority on the point, it seems difficult to reconcile this view with the possibility of a defence for a woman who commits homicide against her abusive husband.

Loss of control

Unlike diminished responsibility, loss of control is a partial defence that relates not to the subjective mind-set of the defendant, but instead the acts of the victim that provoked the defendant to act as they did. The Quran states 'you shall not kill any person – for God has made life sacred – except in the course of justice'.[91] In other words, there will be a defence to homicide where the killing is 'justified'.

The primary sources of Islamic law do not set out precise boundaries; it is for the individual jurisdictions to determine what will constitute a justification. Inconsistency not only arises between jurisdictions, but within jurisdictions given the imprecise drafting that this defence is often given. For example, under s.222(1) of the Nigerian Penal Code, 'capable homicide is not punished with death if the offender whilst deprived of the power of self-control by grave and sudden provocation causes the death of the person who gave the provocation'. The idea that a loss of control can justify homicide is transposed from the primary sources, but without further elucidation as to what can justifiably cause a loss of control.

Given this difficulty of definition, concrete examples of the defence are of little utility; however, it ought to be noted that Islamic cultural values are of significant importance in determining what constitutes provocation. This is seen in circumstances where the accused was punishing another for their breaches of Islamic law. The issue of honour killings provides a topical example of the operation of this defence and merits further individual discussion.

In terms of honour killings generally, some jurisdictions accept the availability of a defence to homicide where the defendant is punishing the victim for severe infringements of the Islamic moral code. There is disagreement amongst jurists as to what constitutes a severe breach of Islamic law, and there is also disagreement over whether it is just relatives of the victim who can seek this defence or whether it is available more widely.

91 Quran 17:33.

The operation of the defence is morally questionable and staggeringly open to abuse. In terms of morality, the availability of this defence can be understood where there is indeed a provocation such that the defendant cannot control his actions. Defining the defence in objective terms, however, (in terms of whether the provoking act was a severe enough infringement of Islamic morality) effectively allows the role of the State in determining what infringements merit the punishment of *qisas* to be determined by individuals. Such a position seems morally and jurisprudentially indefensible and indistinguishable from pure vigilante justice.

There are also numerous evidential difficulties with such a defence. The ease with which such a defence can be adduced to cover up for a homicide committed for other reasons is astounding. Coupled with the moral difficulties set out on page 339, the wide ambit of this defence sits uneasily with the wider values of modern society.

Superior orders

The notion of superior orders as a defence is that the acts of the defendant are excused where someone in a position of authority has ordered them. This doctrine is known as *amr al-sultan* in Islamic law; and 'Islam confers on every citizen the right to refuse to commit a crime, should any government or administrator order him to do so'.[92] In practice, therefore, the general position is that the agent will be liable (along with the commander) for the acts where he knows of the illegality of the orders.[93] El Fadl notes that such knowledge ought to be assumed where the superior official 'is well-known for his injustice'.[94]

The absence of this defence in the posited laws of modern Islamic jurisdictions can be attributed to both the absolute sanctity of life in Islam as well as the reluctance to permit a mistake of law to justify a wrongful act on the basis that this would otherwise be promoting a lack of consequences for being a bad Muslim. The Quran states, 'We decreed upon the Children of Israel that whoever kills a soul unless for a soul or for corruption [done] in the land – it is as if he had slain mankind entirely. And whoever saves one – it is as if he had saved mankind entirely'.[95] Adding to the sanctity of life detailed in the Quran and more directly relatable to the defence of superior orders, Prophet Muhammad is recorded as saying 'there is no obedience in transgression; obedience is in lawful conduct only'.[96]

Official authority

The availability of a defence to homicide for police and armed forces stems from the same general starting point as many of the defences. The Quran states that 'you shall not kill any person – for God has made life sacred – except in the course of justice'.[97] The question then returns to what constitutes the course of justice.

Occupation of a political office does not grant immunity from criminal responsibility *per se.* [98] What constitutes the course of justice will differ from state to state, but it is worth noting that the enquiry is a subjective one. So, the question is whether the official believed

92 A.A. Mawdudi, *Human Rights in Islam* (Islamic Foundation 1980) 33.
93 Hashiyah, vol. 5, 11.
94 El Fadl (n 76) 328.
95 Quran 5:32
96 Sahih Bukhari (n 23).
97 Quran 17:33.
98 M.U. Syed, *Coerced Harm Jurisprudence in Hanafism and Shafi'ism* 210.

that what they were doing was in the course of justice. This is reflected in the Penal Code of Singapore which states that 'nothing is an offence which is done by any person … [who] in good faith believes himself to be justified by law'.[99] The same sentiment is reflected in the Pakistan Penal Code which sets out a defence of legal authority or perceived legal authority in very similar terms to Singapore's Penal Code.

Honour killings

Closely related to the loss of control defence – where based on another's immorality – is the issue of honour killings. In essence, this is a defence based on the victim's defiance of honour. The paradigmatic example of the defence is a male killing a female relative for her relationship with a man from a rival tribe or clan.

The defence is distinct in that there need not necessarily be a breach of higher Islamic norms, defiance of the family honour will suffice. The consequence of this is that it will only be those whose honour has been adversely affected who have recourse to the defence. The distinction is potentially academic though. If the situations in which the loss of control defence is available are vaguely defined, there may well be a sufficient breach of Islamic morality on the facts regardless. For example, sexual deviancy may well be regarded as sufficient moral infringement to give anyone a defence under loss of control.

Sentencing framework

The punishment imposed corresponds to the specific offence committed. The primary sources of Islamic law do give some guidance in this sphere, however, a margin of appreciation is left for Islamic states to legislate as they see fit. For the purposes of this analysis, it is the tripartite distinction between intentional, quasi-intentional and accidental homicide that will be adopted.

The sentencing process can be thought of in two phases. The first relates to the wishes of the victim's heirs; the second relates to the State and its protection of public security; these phases cannot be completely separated, because often the election at phase one will impact on the result in phase two.

Intentional homicide

It is made clear in the Quran that the appropriate punishment for someone who intentionally kills another is *qisas* (capital punishment). For example, the Quran explains that the legal retribution ought to be 'the free for the free, the slave for the slave, and the female for the female'.[100] In other words, the defendant must suffer in the way that the victim has suffered. As explained on pages 338–339, this stems from the historical roots of pre-Islamic Arabian societies, although it does differ in two important ways.[101]

The consistent availability of this punishment is demonstrated by the Iranian Penal Code, which states at Article 209 that 'if a Muslim man commits first-degree murder … the penalty of retribution shall apply' and the Pakistan Penal Code which states at Article 302(a) that 'whoever commits [intentional homicide] shall be … punished with death as *qisas*'.

99 Singaporean Penal Code, s. 79.
100 Quranic *ayah*, al-Baqarah: 178.
101 See discussion of in section on 'Evolution from pre-Islamic Arabia'.

What exactly *qisas* entails is the subject of debate between the schools of Islamic thought. The Hanafis and Hanbalis believe that the death penalty should be inflicted with a sword. This is reflected in the Saudi Arabian approach, under which the death penalty is carried out through a public death by sword. To the Maliki, Zahiri and Shafei schools, the defendant should be killed in the same way that the victim was killed. So, if the defendant suffocates the victim to death, the defendant ought to be suffocated. Whilst this latter interpretation corresponds more accurately to the wording of the Quran and the idea of retribution *in specie*, such an approach is impractical. This impracticality is reflected in the Penal Code of Pakistan that requires the death sentence to invariably be carried out by hanging[102] and the Somaliland Penal Code which requires the death to be carried out by shooting inside a penitentiary.[103]

Victim's heirs' election

The availability of choice for the victim's heirs in the case of an intentional homicide is the subject of debate between the schools of Islam. It is common ground that the penalty must always be available and must be inflicted where demanded by the heirs of the victim (*wali*) [104]; however, there is disagreement over the possibility of the heirs demanding compensation (*diya*) instead. The Shafis and Hanbalis believe that the family can always elect *diya* in lieu of *qisas*, whereas the Hanafis and Malikis believe that this is not possible in the case of intentional homicide. Under this second interpretation, the only way for the offender to avoid *qisas* is for the heirs of the victim to pardon him.[105]

Punishment by the State

Public security is protected by the killing of the defendant where that is demanded by the heirs of the victim. This, however, raises the question of the appropriate punishment where the heirs of the victim do not insist upon the killing of the defendant and instead demand blood money in lieu or even forgive the defendant.

Whilst the Quran insists on following the wishes of the heirs of the victim where they demand the strictest of penalties (*qisas*), it would be contrary to common sense and public order if the punishment consisted simply of the wishes of the victim's heirs. Additionally, the State can impose *ta'zir*, a punishment determined in accordance with justice and the public interest.[106] So, the death penalty remains a possibility as a punishment imposed by the State even where the family of the victim do not demand the death of the defendant. The penalty imposed in such a case is left to the discretion of the judge within the framework of the specific legislative system in question. This system of punishment is reflected in the Pakistan Penal Code which states, at Article 302(b) that 'whoever commits [intentional homicide] can be punished with death or imprisonment for life as *ta'zir*'.

Whilst this can often be thought of as independent from the wishes of the victim and his heirs, it is not an entirely accurate analysis. The manifestation of the wishes of these parties will occasionally be reflected in the legislative sentencing guidelines. For example, Article

102 Pakistan Code of Criminal Procedure, article 368.

103 Somaliland Penal Code, article 94.

104 Al-Quran, al-Isra: 33.

105 R. Postawko, 'Towards an Islamic Critique of Capital Punishment' (2001) 1 UCLA Islamic and Near Eastern Law 269–85.

106 Anwarullah, *The Criminal Law of Islam* (3rd edn, A.S Noordeen 2008) 74.

268 of the Iranian Penal Code disallows *qisas* where the victim himself forgives the defendant before death. Moreover, in Yemen, acceptance of compensation by the victim's heirs or a pardon (*afw*) gives rise to a discretionary judicial sentence of up to 15 years imprisonment[107] in lieu of the death sentence that would otherwise be imposed.

Quasi-intentional homicide

Victim's heirs' election

In response to quasi-intentional homicide, the victim's heirs have the option of claiming *diya* (compensation) or forgiving the defendant. There is no possibility of requesting the death of the defendant. This rule stems from a hadith of Prophet.

The value of *diya* is the same for all cases of quasi-intentional and intentional homicide. The value, as stated by the Quran, is one hundred camels;[108] however, there is almost universal acceptance that an equivalent amount of money, gold or silver will suffice.[109] As calculated by Peters, this amounts to roughly 4.25 kilograms of gold or 35 kilograms of silver.[110]

Punishment by the State

In terms of the *ta'zir* punishment, judicial discretion will determine the sanctions imposed in accordance with legislative guidelines; however, it is likely that imprisonment of some term will be imposed. For example, under the Pakistan Penal Code, Article 316, the *ta'zir* punishment can be imprisonment of up to 25 years.

Accidental homicide

Victim's heirs' election

As mandated by the Quran, if another believer is killed by mistake, compensation is due.[111] As above, two options are open to the victim's heirs. *Diya* can be claimed or that right can be relinquished and the defendant forgiven.

Punishment by the State

It is then for the State to impose any residual *ta'zir* punishment in accordance with justice and public order. Sentencing provisions in Pakistan for accidental homicide permit the imprisonment of the defendant for a maximum term of five years[112]; which increases to a maximum term of ten years where the offence occurs due to negligent driving.[113]

107 Yemen Law 12/1994, article 55.
108 D. Pascoe, 'Is Diya a Form of Clemency?' (2016) 34(1) Boston University International Law Journal 149, 156.
109 Ibid.
110 Peters (n 40) 51.
111 Al Quran, 4:92.
112 Pakistan Penal Code, article 319.
113 Pakistan Penal Code, article 320.

Conclusion

Our exploration of the Islamic law of homicide has attempted to look into both the primary sources of Islamic law as well as their implementation and interpretation in modern Islamic jurisdictions. Whilst certain principles prevail throughout the Muslim world, there is also significant divergence based on cultural values or historic interpretations of convoluted and controversial primary sources. The lack of unanimity regarding the taxonomy of the offence is particularly telling in this regard.

From a comparative perspective, the way in which homicide straddles the public and private spheres is intriguing. An evolution towards treating the offence as a public issue is evident in most jurisdictions, however, its predominantly private law roots are still traceable in modern society. Another striking element of the Islamic law of homicide is its approach towards sentencing. Not only is the relevance of private law considerations such as compensation to the sentencing approach unique, but the potential severity of the punishments for homicide is also distinctive. Non-Islamic lawyers must be careful of making comparative judgments of sentencing structures without first understanding the evolution of the offence under Islamic law.

18 Sweden

Magnus Ulväng

Overview and historical development of homicide offences and offence structure

Historical development of homicide offences

Homicide, understood as the intentional causing of death of a human being, has been criminalised in Swedish law as long as there has been a Criminal Code. From the Middle Ages, a distinction was recognised between killing with some form of intent, deliberation or will (murder / voluntary manslaughter) and reckless or negligent killing (causing another's death, often termed involuntary manslaughter). Throughout history, the distinction between murder and manslaughter has been made in different ways. It was of importance whether the killing was done in secret (i.e., if the killing was carried out in secret or the corpse was hidden after the killing). Causing of death by poisoning, on the other hand, was considered witchcraft, which was punished separately.

What distinguished murder from manslaughter according to the Criminal Code of 1864 was that the former was carried out with deliberation (in cold blood) whilst the latter was done 'in haste', 'hastily' or in 'hot anger'. There has always been a difference in the blameworthiness attached to the labelling of the killing. Murder was thought of as a qualified, aggravated form of manslaughter, the latter thus being the basic form of homicide. If no aggravated circumstances were actualised, the statute of manslaughter was to be applied, thus making the sentence significantly more lenient. As we shall see, this order of labelling has been reversed in modern times. Nowadays, intentional killing is murder unless special mitigating circumstances show otherwise.

Since Swedish law separates guilt in the forms of *dolus* and *culpa*, the distinction between murder / manslaughter and causing another's death is drawn accordingly to the prerequisites of what suffices as intentional (in a broad sense). Consequently, the doctrine of fault does not require a homicidal act to be carried out with intent (to kill) or with knowledge of the outcome (death). A certain awareness of the risks involved (foresight of consequences) combined with a certain attitude towards the result (in terms of indifference, acceptance of the outcome, etc.) is sufficient for intent in the form of *mens rea* (*dolus eventualis*). This is present when the perpetrator objectively foresees the possibility of his act causing death and persists regardless of the consequences. Accordingly, some forms of reckless killing are rendered as murder / voluntary manslaughter. Other forms of carelessness, where the perpetrator who brings about death lacks the necessary hostile or indifferent attitude to the result, are labelled differently (causing another's death). The law makes no difference between reckless or negligent homicide when it comes to what is punishable, although recklessness is an aggravated form of fault which can affect sentencing as well as labelling (gross offence).

According to the principles of correspondence and fair labelling, *mens rea* assumes that every form of required guilt – *dolus* or *culpa* – must cover or include all the prerequisites of an unlawful act (*actus reus*), i.e., the act, the result and all relevant circumstances that surround the deed. It is not enough for murder that the perpetrator acted (only) with intent to cause grievous bodily harm and that the victim subsequently dies. For example:

(i) A person who intentionally shoots at an object, but lacks knowledge that the object in question is a human being, does not fulfil the *mens rea* requirement for e.g., assault, murder, etc.
A person who intentionally assaults another, intending only to cause bodily harm but where the outcome is deadly, lacks *mens rea* to homicide. In this sense, the fault-requirement is absolute.

The culprit can, of course, be sentenced for reckless causing of death (in example (i)) or intentional assault (in example (ii)), but in terms of homicide, responsibility is excluded in such cases. Hence, liability does not generally extend to consequences that accidently follow as a result of a prohibited conduct. However, liability may well be considered in cases of deviating events, e.g., when the perpetrator shoots at victim A but misses and instead kills victim B (*aberratio ictus*) or in cases of mistaken identity (*error in personam*). As long as the victim in either case is a human being and the act suffices the definition of murder, the killing might be rendered intentional. This is not, however, a question of any doctrine of transferred malice, but instead the result of an interpretation of what *mens rea* state is required and how deviant a causal chain of events can be for it still to be considered immaterial to the offence description. Mistakes regarding who the victim is or the flight a bullet will take are, as a rule, immaterial to the definition of homicide.

The doctrine of *versari in re illicita* does not apply to Swedish law.

General elements

Definitions

Life presupposes a living person. Life is considered to occur at the beginning of birth, i.e., when labour starts or an operative intervention commences (caesarean section). Normally, a child is found to be living by observing signs of life (e.g., respiration, heartbeat or clear spontaneous movements of the skeletal muscle). However, a child born brain-dead may also show some signs of life.

After 28 weeks (200 days), foetal development is usually such that the child, following his or her birth, can live an independent life. A child born after this date should be considered a crime object for e.g., murder or assault, whether it is viable or not. If, for any reason, the child is born earlier than 28 weeks of foetal development (e.g., through an operative procedure in the event of the mother's death or a legal abortion) and it is not ready to be born, the child must be viable in order to be considered a crime object. The fact that the child has shown living signs gives a presumption that it is viable.[1]

A person dies when all mental functions cease and cannot return. Normally, this is determined by finding that the heart and lungs have ceased to function for a certain period

1 Regarding abortions, see 'Abortion and homicide' section later in the chapter.

of time. The human brain is irreversibly destroyed after about five minutes without delivery of oxygen (for children and persons suffering from severe hypothermia, this time is slightly longer). The lungs can withstand a circulation stop of 15–20 minutes and the heart a circulation stop of about half an hour. If a resuscitation attempt is successful (through cardiac massage, artificial respiration, etc.), the person is considered alive all the time. Cooling and poisoning may cause apparent discontinued respiration and circulation. Death is thus an ongoing process and the cells in the body die at different times (for example skin cells can stay alive for days).

However, insofar as a person's death has legal consequences, special provisions apply to criteria for determining human death. A person is considered dead when all of the brain's functions have been completely and irretrievably lost. This is normally determined by finding that breathing and blood circulation have ceased. This concerns cases where these functions are maintained artificially.

Medical treatment scenarios

Medical procedures of various kinds – especially operations – often involve interventions that in themselves meet the offence definition of (gross) assault. Special rules exist for special interventions. This applies in particular to abortion, sterilisation, castration, transplantation and determination of gender identity. In other respects, it is largely unclear to what extent healthcare professionals are entitled to carry out an otherwise unauthorised act. The need for regulation is apparent.

In many ways, criminal responsibility for actions undertaken as a medical treatment is avoided, either by reference to special legislation or unwritten exceptions within the general doctrines of criminal responsibility. The most significant (unwritten) rule is that all acts healthcare professionals may consider represent a form of permitted risk-taking. Hence, the *actus reus* requirement is not fulfilled. What counts as acceptable risk-taking often follows from provisions forwarded by authoritative standards and instructions issued by, for example, the National Board of Health and Welfare or general doctrines of medicine. Treatment undertaken 'in accordance with science and proven experience' (*lex artis medici*) can never be considered an unauthorised risk-taking. This applies even if the controlled act itself is criminalised, e.g., assault.

If the treatment (including its consequences) is the result of a controlled action, the situation is more complex. Since the causing of e.g., bodily harm or death is controlled, it becomes conceptually impossible to refer to (permitted) 'risk-taking'.

In many cases, the provision on necessity (Swedish Criminal Code, chapter 24, section 4) may apply. The emergency situation may be so severe that is defensible to do an operation without having access to all equipment that should normally be used; i.e., it is not necessary for the act to be conducted in accordance with science and proven experience. In other situations, the provision of consent may apply.[2] In contrast to what is normally rendered as justifiable violence, etc. carried out with consent, any medically justified intervention should be considered not punishable. Hence, a rule of consent also covers acts that in other contexts would be considered as gross assault or homicide.

The problem is that what has been said about rules or principles regarding permitted risk-taking, consent, necessity etc. in no way is sufficient to explain the admissibility of interventions as generally accepted. This is mainly because valid consent requires insight into the

2 Swedish Criminal Code, chapter 24, sec. 7

relevant circumstances and risks.[3] In other words, it is assumed that certain procedures, which cannot be considered as permitted under chapter 24, sections 4 or 7 of the Swedish Criminal Code may be undertaken. This implies that rules on social adequacy must be formulated for some cases where no valid consent has been given. This applies to at least some situations where the patient has consented to an operation, etc. without having a clear idea of its consequences and risks. It may be appropriate to withhold certain information from the patient. A prerequisite for an acquittal is of course that the operation is conducted in accordance with science and proven experience. It is likely that this only applies to actions undertaken by qualified healthcare professionals

It is unclear on a number of points when a doctor can legitimately shorten a person's life, but it is clear that sometimes this is allowed. The National Board of Health's regulations and general advice on life-sustaining treatment is of value to a criminal law assessment, although it is neither legally binding nor sufficiently detailed to provide unambiguous guidance. In Swedish law, brain death is accepted as a criterion for end of life. The basic principles in this context are partly that an action whose sole purpose is to cause a patient's death is never allowed (not even at the request of the patient), and that a procedure that cannot cure or alleviate symptoms should not be undertaken in the absence of additional grounds for consideration by the patient or his or her next of kin. It is justified to consider that a patient's life may be shortened by a doctor in a legal manner in the following cases:

i when life-support measures do not serve a reasonable purpose, a doctor should be considered entitled to refrain from acting (i.e., forgoing life-sustaining treatment). Freedom from liability for failure to act can in this case also often be justified by the fact that the failure does not involve unauthorised risk-taking as the prevailing level of risk is unchanged.

ii when there is no other way of achieving a significant care goal (usually pain relief), a doctor should be entitled to undertake a procedure which, as an adverse event, accelerates death. Here again, in many cases, there is no question of a controlled killing, but only a permitted risk-taking in relation to an uncontrolled death.

iii when life is shortened by the fact that an initiated treatment is not completed when the patient will not regain consciousness. Often there is a question of seriously brain-injured patients whose condition is 'chronically vegetative'. The fact that a doctor orders the removal of nutrient droplets or cessation of blood donation is considered legal. There is less clarity when the act consists of turning off a ventilator. Even in such a case, however, the point of view is that it is meaningless to artificially extend life when all treatment has been found useless. The law therefore takes the view that the act in question must be considered socially adequate and thus permitted. It is also clear that a patient is entitled to choose to terminate an initial treatment (if it has to be terminated by a doctor).

Other forms of euthanasia and assisted dying than those mentioned under (ii) and (iii) are prohibited. Responsibility applies to the doctor, not the patient's relatives, etc. (their consent is neither necessary nor sufficient to exclude responsibility). It is also irrelevant if the patient has declared himself in a will as unwilling to be subject to life-sustaining treatment.

3 See third volume in this series, P. Asp and M. Ulväng, 'Sweden' in A. Reed, M. Bohlander, N. Wake and E. Smith (eds) *Consent: Domestic and Comparative Perspectives* (2017 Routledge).

Homicide by omission

Homicide, in any form, is not defined as a crime that requires a specific act from the perpetrator. The offence description only requires that a human being has been deprived of life. Consequently, it is possible to interpret someone's omission as the cause of a specific result (in this case death).

Responsibility for omissions differs from act-oriented crimes in that, as a main rule, it presupposes that the omitting person has a certain standing and thus a responsibility to act. Unless the offence description defines the crime as an omission to do something (in itself), it is required that the culprit has a special position as guarantor. The function behind this limiting doctrine is to restrict the circle of persons who can commit a crime. What is needed is a description of which categories are held liable for physically causing something by omission. According to the general principles of criminal law, two sub-categories can be distinguished:

i *Supervisors*, i.e., those in a supervising guarantor position who are responsible for certain sources of danger (e.g., a machine, a building site, an infant, a mental patient or dangerous situations / risks that are created by one's previous actions) and, hence, have to avert risks arising therefrom.
ii *Protectors*, i.e., those who are responsible for certain persons or property and have to avert all kinds of risks threatening these (parents, caretakers, guardians, teachers, wardens, etc.).

If a person belonging to either of the above categories omits to avert a certain danger with the result that the offence description for homicide is fulfilled, responsibility may be conferred. A paradigm case is when A omits to give his child food and thereby causes its death by starvation. Another example is when A removes the well cover from a deep well for which he is responsible, thereby resulting in another person falling into the well and dying. Whether such omission is to be classified as murder / manslaughter or causing of another's death depends on the *mens rea* requirement.

Intentional homicide offences

Murder (chapter 3, section 1 of the Criminal Code)

Murder is the basic offence of homicide and means to deliberately deprive another person of their life. In principle, any cause – by act or omission – of somebody's death is relevant to the definition. Thus, one can commit murder in a very large number of ways, for example by stabbing or shooting someone, or by starving a person to death for whom the offender is responsible (e.g., an infant), or through a combination of an act and an omission, e.g., by organising a shooting party without taking necessary precautions.

However, responsibility for homicide is limited through a number of general principles and exceptions. Already in the phrase, 'depriving life' lies a linguistic hint that more distant acts – on a causal line ending with another's death – cannot reasonably be regarded as murder. This is primarily relevant to the boundaries between the perpetration and complicity. Furthermore, when applying the statutes on homicide, it is usually not difficult to determine whether the prerequisite is fulfilled. Instead, the complex and difficult questions concern whether the result was caused intentionally, whether the act involved unjustified risk-taking, or if the outcome caused is regarded as relevant to the specific risks involved, etc.

Because a human being is mortal, a murder can be characterised as shortening someone's life. The length of lifetime lost is insignificant. To kill an already dying person is murder. Thus, after finding that a causal chain leads to someone's death, making a hypothetical assessment of when the deceased would otherwise have died is irrelevant. The crucial thing is what actually happened. Another issue is that sometimes it is difficult to determine why a death occurred at a particular time.

Since the offence description requires the causing of death of *another* human being, suicide – or attempted suicide – is not punished. Consequently, neither is the participation in such acts punishable. However, an act that appears to be a sort of complicity to suicide may sometimes constitute murder. A prerequisite is, of course, that the act falls under the offence description, i.e., that it may be called 'depriving another life'. The boundary between helping someone to deprive himself of life and committing murder is very subtle. Consider the following examples:

i A supplies a deadly dose of arsenic for B to swallow (thereby committing suicide);
ii A places arsenic tablets into B's mouth, which B swallows himself;
iii A helps B to swallow the arsenic tablets since B is incapable of swallowing them himself;
iv A injects B with a lethal dose of arsenic.

In example (i), and perhaps example (ii), A is likely to have participated in B's suicide and is thus innocent of homicide. In example (iv), A is seen as responsible for the intentional killing of B. Whether responsibility for homicide is actualised in example (iii) is an open question.

The *mens rea* requirement for murder is *dolus*, i.e., intention, knowledge or suspicion of the outcome of the act combined with an indifferent attitude to the result (death).

Manslaughter (chapter 3, section 2 of the Criminal Code)

Manslaughter is homicide considered less serious than murder, including taking into account the circumstances that caused the act. Incorrect errors of judgments in emergency situations – e.g., when the perpetrator cannot avoid committing homicide however he acts – is usually seen as a mitigating circumstance, thus affecting the labelling of the crime (if a crime is committed at all). Killing that has been provoked by abuse, insults, etc. or which otherwise originates in misfortunes, jealousy, conflicts, etc. is often judged as a manslaughter. In such cases, the perpetrator has often found himself in an uncontrolled mental state. If the perpetrator attempts to take his own life after he has killed someone, such action implies that his mood at the time of the crime is such that it can be judged as manslaughter.

Further examples of cases where mitigating circumstances surround the crime are:

- A and B jointly decide – under pressure of financial or other difficulties – that A should first kill B and then himself (collective suicide). During the course of the event, A is prevented from attempting suicide after killing B.
- A has been exposed to severe psychological or physical abuse for a long period of time and decides, after premeditation, to kills his adversary.
- A kills B out of mercy or compassion in order to save B from further suffering. This is true for all comprehensible forms of euthanasia, whether it involves seriously ill people who wish to die, but are unable to perform the act themselves, or physically or mentally malformed children whom the parents kill to save them from further physical or emotional suffering.

Corresponding examples of when a crime is not surrounded by mitigating circumstances (and, hence, is to be regarded as murder) are as follows:

- The killing has been preceded by careful planning or has been characterised by (particular) proposition or planning.
- The act has been especially ruthless because it caused severe suffering for the victim (e.g., severe violence, severe pain, unnecessary suffering or otherwise expressing unusual cruelty).
- The killing has occurred after sexual exploitation or if the act has the characteristic of an execution.
- The causation has developed a strong death toll with the victim.
- The position and standing of the victim also affects the assessment. If the crime is directed against a family member, this is an aggravating circumstance. Likewise, it is of relevance whether the offence has been carried out in the victim's home or if the crime has been carried out in front of close relatives of the victim (such as children). That the offence has been directed against someone discharging his or her duties (e.g., police officers) is correspondingly an aggravating factor.

Whether the act has been committed after consideration ('courage') or 'in haste' may have some significance for the judgment but is not decisive. A clear example of when killing in rushed courage should be considered as murder, is when the perpetrator is surprised while committing (another) crime and deliberately kills the witness.

The *mens rea* requirement for manslaughter is the same as for murder, i.e., *dolus.* Since the seriousness of the offence is also affected by the guilt element, killing with intent (direct intent/*dolus directus*) is normally not subject to mitigation or a more lenient judgment. Motives also come into consideration. Homicide is considered aggravated if:

- A kills B in order to avenge or spread horror, because of a pure desire to kill or has racist motives.
- A kills B with the underlying motive that the crime is aimed at promoting or concealing other crime; the same is true if the killing was committed in connection with another crime for profit purposes.
- A kills B and the act induces general danger, e.g., by using explosives or firearms.
- The killing is directed against a child, another defenceless person or an unknown person.

Reckless and negligent homicide offences

Causing another person's death (chapter 3, section 7 of the Criminal Code)

The offence description is to cause another person's death by recklessness or negligence. The crime has a very simple conceptual structure. It is about causing a virtually unambiguous consequence, i.e., another person's death. The actual crime definition therefore does not present any significant legal problems.

Causing another person's death is a particular crime type. No guidelines for the delimitation have been provided in legal texts or preparatory works or practice. The assessment shall take into account all factors that may be considered relevant.

Assessing acts that theoretically can meet the requirements for the current type of crime, however, involve several problems. First, there are always difficulties associated with proving causation. Second, the general principles of criminal responsibility present a number of problems regarding ascription of harm, e.g., minimum standards for act-requirements, judgments of unlawful risk-taking, limiting the scope of responsibility in cases of remote harm, setting standards for what a reasonable person is expected to do, etc. Likewise, subjective standards must be assessed concerning recklessness or negligence.

Swedish law has three degrees of reckless or negligent killing. Chapter 3, section 7 of the Criminal Code, second paragraph, defines gross crime as a special crime type, thus offering some circumstances that are to be taken into account in the assessment of the severity of the crime. As a particularly important factor, it is first mentioned that the act included a conscious risk-taking of a serious nature. This means that the perpetrator is doubtless deliberately negligent in relation to the death. The preparatory work mentions, as an example, the use of fatal violence (without intent to cause death), shooting, and even aiming for someone with a firearm (where a shot is accidentally discharged). Furthermore, two circumstances of particular importance are mentioned regarding situations where special attention or skill is required when performing a task, e.g., good ability to react, good judgment, taking of security measures (e.g., driving cars, boats, aircraft), or handling of dangerous items or subjects (e.g., police or military operations, healthcare or industry). One circumstance is where the perpetrator was under the influence of alcohol or other substances. The intoxication must have been a contributing factor to the death. The second is that the negligence in question is of a serious nature, i.e., the failure to carry out or perform prescribed or otherwise obviously necessary checks or safety measures in hazardous activities. The stated aggravated circumstances are sufficient but not necessary conditions for responsibility. A crime can be judged gross for a reason other than that stated in the law.[4]

It is not uncommon for an offence to lead to death, e.g., assault. If the offender's intentions do not include this consequence, but he is negligent in relation to it, he shall be sentenced for both assault and for the death of another person (possibly gross offence). Foresight of the danger of death can sometimes also cause the assault to be placed at a higher level of severity.

As stated above, the *mens rea* requirement is sufficed with either recklessness or negligence. Recklessness towards the result is more blameworthy than negligence, and thus more likely to affect the labelling of the crime (gross offence).

Infanticide/child killing

Infanticide (chapter 3, section 3 of the Criminal Code)

Infanticide is a privileged form of manslaughter. Even though the perpetrator is guilty of deliberately killing another human being, she is judged more leniently than other cases of intentional killing. This applies both in terms of classification and sentence.

Historically, the more lenient assessment was dependent on the woman being harmed by 'illegal coupling', i.e., when she became pregnant she was not married to the child's father and for this reason, in connection with giving birth, chose to kill the child. Such a shame-related approach has been completely abandoned today. The reason for the regulation is that biologically 'normal' physical and mental causes can cause mothers who have just given birth to harm their children. Sometimes there are compulsive beliefs that can constitute a

4 See e.g., Swedish Supreme Court Case NJA 1992 s. 85. The reason to regard the act as gross negligence was that the assaulted victim was an infant.

serious mental disorder. Given the current provisions on sentencing, it can be argued that the regulation is superfluous.

The privilege applies solely to the child's mother. A father who deliberately kills his child can only be sentenced for murder or manslaughter. When the mother in the privileged situation contributes to someone else killing her child, she should be convicted of incitement to infanticide. The person performing the act shall be convicted of murder or manslaughter. It is irrelevant whether the act has been preceded by planning or because the pregnancy or childbirth has been kept secret.

When the child is killed at birth – i.e., at the beginning of a child's birth or shortly after delivery – the mother is not required to be in a state of mind other than that caused by the birth itself. Applying the same requirements as apply for causing death after birth would be meaningless because of investigative and probative difficulties.

If the child is killed after birth, the woman must be in a distressed state of mind, and this state of mind or urge must have been caused by childbirth. Post-natal difficulties that are unrelated to this cannot be taken into account. However, the death of the child is not required to be caused by the state of mind or urge. Such a requirement would in practice mean that the woman had to make it probable that such a causal relationship had occurred. It is enough that the act has been committed for a certain, indefinite period of time, and that the woman during it was in the state of mind or acting on an urge induced by giving birth. A mentally disturbed state of mind usually occurs for about one month after birth but may sometimes persist throughout the breastfeeding period (up to seven months or more).

Financial distress should only in extraordinary circumstances be regarded as relevant under current legislation.

Abortion and homicide

Abortion is defined as the termination of a pregnancy by removing a foetus or an embryo before it can survive outside the uterus. In Sweden, abortion is freely available and the person who is pregnant decides, *a priori*, whether to terminate her pregnancy. If a woman asks for her pregnancy to be terminated, abortion may be legally executed if the action is taken before the end of the eighteenth week of pregnancy and cannot be assumed to present a serious danger to her life or health. The abortion procedure should be performed at a general hospital or other healthcare institution approved by the National Board of Health and Welfare. Only authorised medical practitioners may abort or interrupt a pregnancy.

After the end of the eighteenth week of pregnancy, abortion may only be performed if the National Board of Health and Welfare grants special permission for the measure. Such permission may only be granted in exceptional circumstances. Permission cannot be given if there is reason to assume that the foetus is viable. In cases where it can be assumed that the pregnancy, due to illness or bodily injury, poses a serious danger to the pregnant mother's life or health, the National Board of Health and Welfare may grant permission for an abortion after the end of the eighteenth week of pregnancy, regardless of how far the pregnancy has progressed.

Should a doctor intentionally breach the National Board of Health and Welfare's regulations, he shall be sentenced to a fine or imprisonment for a maximum of six months under the Abortion Act. A person who, without being an approved medical practitioner, intentionally carries out an abortion, shall be convicted for the crime of illegal abortion and not murder or manslaughter . The sentence is a fine or imprisonment for a maximum of one year. If the circumstances are aggravated, imprisonment for at least six months and no more than four years may be invoked. In assessing whether the offence is gross, particular attention should be paid to whether the act was carried out for reasons of profit or for the benefit of the woman's life or health. Attempting an illegal abortion is also criminally punishable.

In view of what has been said above about the beginning of life (see page 348), a non-viable foetus cannot be the object for a criminal offence. Instead, it is the mother who represents the protected interest behind the Abortion Act and is thus the person protected from unauthorised intervention. Once an unborn child has reached a time when it can be fairly considered viable (which occurs when the foetus is at about 28 weeks), it can be regarded as an independent criminal object. Murder or manslaughter may be invoked against termination of the pregnancy in such case.

Defences for homicide

All general defences and excuses apply to homicide (in any form), although to varying degree and always depending on the circumstances surrounding the individual case. What is rendered defensible, justified, understandable, etc. is judged on the merits of the case at hand.

Consent

Consent to murder is not accepted as a defence. In fact, any consent regarding bodily harm superseding minor assault is generally deemed irrelevant. Thus, mercy killings are punished. Although, as mentioned previously, true compassionate motives mitigate the judgment and sentence, the act itself is nevertheless, *a priori*, a crime usually labelled as manslaughter. Likewise, as already explained, some kinds of termination of life on medical grounds are not treated as homicide at all. A killing that occurs as a result of medical treatment might be regarded as lawful either because it is carried out in order to relieve the patient of further suffering (as means to an end), or the patient voluntarily rejects further treatment, or the risks of any treatment are considered in accordance with science and proven experience (and thus rendered lawful or justified).

Self-defence and necessity

Self-defence and necessity are general justifications that can render an otherwise criminal behaviour legal. Hence, killing a person in a situation of self-defence or necessity may be acceptable if the circumstances are such that the violence (causing the death of another) is deemed justifiable. In principle, the self-defence or necessity-act must be called upon by an interest of much greater importance than what is sacrificed. Thus, a person may intrude on or violate someone else's property to eliminate danger of life or severe bodily injury, but it is unclear to what extent one can interfere with someone else's property to prevent a slight bodily injury. Although the threshold for what is justified is somewhat higher for acts committed in self-defence (i.e., 'manifestly unjustifiable') than under circumstances that constitute necessity (i.e., 'justified'), there must not be a clear imbalance between the defensive act and the danger threatened through the attack. The Supreme Court has stated that the intentional use of a knife or other weaponry which causes risk for life may only be accepted in exceptional cases.[5] Killing someone in self-defence or with reference to necessity requires extraordinary circumstances and is usually never tolerated. As said previously, the rule of

5 See Swedish Supreme Court Case NJA 1994 s. 48.

necessity as a defence does not even cover all cases of medical treatment that lead to bodily harm and ending another person's life would be deemed even less justifiable. Another issue to consider is that extreme situations might provide reasons for excuse, mitigation or other forms of exoneration (e.g., excessive use of self-defence, etc.).

Insanity and diminished responsibility

Sweden takes a unique view on the relationship between insanity and criminal responsibility since the law does not contain a requirement that the actor has to have a sufficient mental capacity in order to be able to commit a crime. Hence, insanity, insane automatism, etc. is not a defence.

Diminished responsibility in terms of loss of control over physical actions (spasms, somnambulism, convulsions, etc.) could affect the assessment of the act-requirement. If the perpetrator lacks the necessary control and awareness of his actions, the result may well be that the positive fault requirements (*actus reus*) are not met. However, a mental abnormality does not automatically correspond with absence of body control. Under Swedish law, mentally ill people are often judged fit to commit rational acts. However, special consideration is given in sentencing. As a main rule (and a legal presumption), persons suffering from a serious mental disturbance may not be sentenced to imprisonment. Instead, they are to be committed for forensic psychiatric care.

Thus, persons suffering from mental illness are judged according to the general rules and principles of criminal law. Insufficient mental capacity to understand the true meaning of an action can lead to a lack of intent. To an even greater extent, mental illness should be viewed as grounds for responsibility for reckless or negligent crimes. It can hardly be claimed that a person who lacks the mental capacity to understand what he 'ought to have done' ought to have behaved in such a manner. Although there is no insanity defence in Swedish law, and courts are obliged to judge each case on its own merits (including all positive and negative fault-requirements), there are, sadly, a number of examples in case law where individuals with mental illness have been considered responsible (and sentenced) for crimes, such as e.g., murder. The reason for this is that it otherwise could become difficult to commit the culprit to forensic psychiatric care; iI.e., the mentally ill individual is treated as if he was a sane person in order to sentence him to special compulsory psychiatric care. The Swedish approach has, rightly, been subject to hard criticism

Diminished responsibility, however, is a matter of degree. Not all mentally disturbed persons that commit homicide fulfil the insanity requirements. Less serious disturbances mitigate the sentence and can lead to psychiatric treatment within the framework of punishment. Thus, it can affect both the penal value (assessed based on the severity of the crime) and the labelling of the crime (from murder to manslaughter). The same is true for provoked killings which are generally thought to be less heinous than unprovoked killings. Consequently, such crime is often labelled as manslaughter. There is no special requirement that the provoked agent actually lost his self-control (and, thus, killed as a causal explanation), but from a practical point of view this is usually the case. Provocation, nevertheless, works as a mitigating circumstance if the reasons for responding are objectively reasonable.

Superior orders or official authority

Acting on superior order or special official authority (e.g., police or armed forces) gives certain categories of person the right to use violence in special circumstances. However, this can never, as a rule, justify homicide. According to section 10 of the Police Act (1984:387), police officers are given discretion to use violence in order to enforce the law. The rule is structured in a way which resembles the structure of the general defences, in that it requires:

i that the police officer acts in a situation which allows for the use of force (these situations are listed in the section), and
ii that the violence used is defensible.

The general principles of policing, often referred to as the principles of proportionality and necessity (any intrusion should be proportionate to the aim pursued and necessary for the purpose of achieving the aim), must also be taken into account when applying this provision.

Honour killing

Honour killings do not belong to any special category of homicide. Whether the actor has killed another person for reasons of protecting the honour of 'the family', tradition, religious convictions, etc., has no relevance for either labelling the crime or the sentence. If any relevance were to be applied, citing 'honour' as a reason for ending a person's life would be viewed as an aggravating circumstance.

Sentencing framework – including statistics

As explained on page 351–353, there are (at least) three degrees of homicide – murder, manslaughter and causing another person's death (the latter differentiated in three sub-degrees). Murder is, as already explained, the basic offence of intentional homicide (the sentencing regime for reckless or negligent killing is described below). Hence, the penalty scale for murder (section 1 of the Criminal Code) sets the framework for the sentence for homicide. The offence description for murder is the following:

> A person who takes the life of another shall be sentenced for murder to imprisonment for a certain period of time, at least ten and at most eighteen years, or, if circumstances are aggravating, for life.[6]

Consequently, the minimum sentence for murder is a limited sentence of imprisonment of ten to 18 years. Lifetime imprisonment is, according to the statute, only to be used if the circumstances are aggravated. A sentence of imprisonment for life is, in effect, never imposed (unless the convict dies while serving time for the crime). In practice, a convicted murderer can beg for pardon or (after serving at least ten years of his sentence) ask the Court to change his sentence and make it limited in time. Considerations of public protection, the relative severity of the crime, as well as behaviour during the period already served will be of relevance for this.

Imprisonment for manslaughter shall be imposed for at least six and at most ten years. This means there is a certain logic to the penalty scale for intentional killings, with a minimum imprisonment of six years continuing up to imprisonment for life. However, as we shall see, the sentencing regime is neither as simple nor as clear as it sounds.

6 Criminal Code, s1.

Problems arise partly because there are no distinct features of aggravated circumstances. Murder is, in itself, an aggravated form of homicide (see above section 'Manslaughter'), but the penalty scale for murder reveals that there are aggravated forms of murder that are to be punished with imprisonment for life. There is ambiguity as to what they are. Although, there is scope for allocating general aggravated (as well as mitigating) circumstances when it comes to the labelling of a crime (murder, voluntary manslaughter, etc.), there is little guidance to what specific circumstances are determinate. Furthermore, since the penalty scale is so wide (i.e., imprisonment from six years to life), there is little guidance in how the aggravating / mitigating circumstances ought to be weighed against each other in sentencing. What is needed is an anchor point or fulcrum, i.e., knowledge of what a 'normal' case of murder is, from which it is possible to argue for a differentiated sentence (in either direction). Unfortunately, the standard case of 'normal' murder is in dispute. The Supreme Court and the legislator have different standpoints. The first takes its grounding in earlier precedents and a frugal attitude that imprisonment for life ought only to be engaged in extraordinary situations, where 18 years of imprisonment is not sufficient. This corresponds with the view taken earlier by the Swedish Parliament, in wanting to restrict the use of the most extreme punishment for the most heinous crimes (e.g., premeditated killing; multiple murders; sexual or sadistic (ritual) killings; homicide that involves causing special agony, anxiety or pain to the victim; child murders or murders which are targeted at persons holding public office such as politicians, police officers, etc.).

The legislator has, however, in the past decade shown a willingness to take a much stricter view on sentencing for murder. This follows a political ambition to make the sentencing regime generally harsher and courts less reluctant to impose lifetime imprisonment. In 2014, the Parliament passed a bill to make lifetime-imprisonment the standard sentence for murder, thus inverting the previous sentencing regime. The Supreme Court, nevertheless, quashed the new formulation proposed by Parliament with reference to the principle of legality.[7] According to the Supreme Court, the wording in the statute was not – in light of the formulations in the preparatory works to the bill – compatible with a general assumption of imprisonment for life in murder cases.

The current position is that a 'normal' case of murder – exhibiting neither prominent aggravating or mitigating circumstances – would amount to 14 years of imprisonment. Imprisonment for 16 years or more requires the circumstances to clearly indicate a higher sentence.

Involuntary manslaughter, or causing another person's death (chapter 3, section 7 of the Criminal Code), covers a wide range of varied cases where a person's actions have caused death through recklessness or negligence. For understandable reasons, the penalty scale is wide in order to cover everything from negligence in following minimum standards of "carefulness", "lawful risk-taking" or violation of standards for "a reasonable person" to various forms of recklessness, demonstrated in the form of conscious risk-taking where the only thing separating it from intentional killing is the attitude to the outcome (i.e., death). The minimum sentence for causing another person's death is a fine; the maximum sentence is imprisonment for six years.

Since the statute divides the offence of involuntary manslaughter into three levels (of severity) – minor crime / reckless or negligent killing / gross crime – for which each is given a specific penalty scale, the discretion of the Court is limited. Minor crimes can only amount to a fine. Standard cases of negligent or reckless killings are sentenced with imprisonment for a minimum of 14 days and a maximum of two years. This does not

7 See Swedish Supreme Court case NJA 2016 s. 3.

imply that the actual sanction will be a custodial sentence. Before imposing imprisonment, the Court must be satisfied that the crime was so serious that a non-custodial sentence cannot be justified. Apart from the seriousness, the Court may also take previous convictions and the 'character' of the crime into consideration. In particular, homicide committed as a result of drunk driving is considered to have such character that alternatives to a custodial sentence are excluded.

Index

abnormality of mind 105–8; as 'explanation' and 'cause' of killing 113–15
accidental murder 325, 333–4
accomplice liability, English law 2, 69–79
actual bodily harm (ABH) 41, 136
actus reus: art and part killings, Scots law 29; causation of death/homicide 119, 130; culpable homicide 1, 23, 25; homicide (Islamic law) 332–3; intentional homicide 208, 226, 267–8, 307; Islamic law 332, 332–3; murder 1, 23, 25, 26, 27, 138; negligent homicide 209, 272, 308–9; Netherlands 284; New Zealand 267–8, 270, 274; reckless homicide 227, 228, 270; result-qualified/constructive/*versari in re illicita*/felony homicide offences 229–30, 274, 311–12; South Africa 208, 209; Turkey 307, 308–9, 311–12; United States 226–30
Ahluwalia, Kiranjit 97–8
Aitchison, Craigie Mason 32–3
Alison, Archibald 30
Allen, Nicholas 161, 162
anger 2; permissible male maelstrom of 86–9; permission for 89–94
art and part killings, Scots law 27–9
Ashley, Jack 95
Ashworth, A. 38, 39, 44, 95, 189–90, 330
assassination 15
assisted suicide 23, 25, 223–4
Audah, Abdul Qadir 338
Australian law 2, 57–60

Battered Woman Syndrome (BSW) 95, 97, 98, 99, 211
Beccaria, C. 11
beginning of life: Germany 247–8; Islamic law 326; Netherlands 285; New Zealand 265; South Africa 203–4; Turkey 303; United States 220–1
behaviourism, learnt 89–94
Berdinka, Jesse 163
Binder, Guyora 219–20
blameworthiness: causation of death/homicide 121, 124; culpable homicide, Scots law 21, 23, 30, 32, 34; gross negligence manslaughter (GNM) 42; murder and involuntary manslaughter, English law 40
Bowen, George 161
Bramwell, George William Wilshere (Baron) 15, 17, 18
Bright, John 13
Brookes, Alisa 98
Browne, V. 148
Bruce, Henry 10
Burnton, Stanley 109

Canada 2; Criminal Code 54; 'faint hope' clause 17; parental refusal of lifesaving treatment for a child 159
capital punishment *see* death penalty
care home managers, inappropriate diets, provision of 155, 157–8
Carstens, P. 48
Carter, Michelle 161–2
causation of death/homicide 3, 119–35; act of wounding, death resulting from 312; acts or omissions 268–9; brain injuries 123, 124; breaking chain of causation 121, 127, 128, 133–4, 162; but-for causation 128, 129; constructive homicide 3, 124–5; by driving 124–5, 127–31; fault requirement 131; foreseeability of probability 47; as general principle of criminal law 129; gross negligence manslaughter (GNM) 131–4; murder 120–4; omission, homicide by 268–9; principles of causation 121; rationality in 134–5; serious risk 43, 44, 45, 122; Sweden 353–4; thin-skull rule 121–2, 125; wounding, act of 311–12; year and a day rule 122–3
Chédieu, Emile 14
Child, J.J. 2
Clark, Diane 98
Collins, Hugh 163

Commission on Capital Punishment 13, 17–19; Committee of 1866 14–19; Report (1866) 1, 7; *see also* pregnancy termination
Committee of 1866: extenuating circumstances 11, 14–17, 18; and second degree murder 17–19
complicity liability 69; *Jogee* judgment 70–8; *mens rea* 71, 72; misunderstanding of complicity in manslaughter 77–9
consent defence: Islamic law 336–7; New Zealand 278–9; South Africa 210; Sweden 356; Turkey 313–14; United States 232
constructive homicide 3, 124–5
constructive liability: involuntary manslaughter 40–1; murder 39–40; proximate 40
constructive manslaughter 125–7
correspondence principle: breach of 45; causation of death/homicide 122; involuntary manslaughter 40–1; *mens rea* 348; murder 39
Cranworth, Lord Robert Monsey Rolfe 14
crimen expositionis infantis (abandoning a child with expectation of death) 198
Criminal Cases Review Commission 111
criminal law: causation as a general principle of 129; codification 10; legal status of foetus 138–9; murder videos as subject of 187–91; and pregnancy termination 136–52; use of in relation to termination 139–42
Crown Court Compendium: diminished responsibility 109; self-control, loss of 94, 100
culpable homicide, Scots law 1–2, 21–36; *actus reus* 1, 23, 25; art and part killings 27–9; blameworthiness 21, 23, 30, 32, 34; co-accused, art and part killings 28; common criminal purpose 29; Crown decisions 24–5, 35; defining 22–9; involuntary culpable homicide 29–35; line with murder 25–7; *mens rea* 1, 24, 29, 30, 33; murder, or 24–7; 'obvious risk of life being taken' test 29; policy decisions 24–5; recklessness 23, 25–7, 29, 31–5; voluntary 2, 23–4
culpable homicide, South African law 51–2, 201

death penalty 10–11, 65; Islamic law 323, 330, 331, 340
defences to homicide: Battered Woman Syndrome (BSW) 95, 97–9, 211; consent 210, 232, 259, 278–9, 313–14, 336–7, 356; diminished responsibility *see* diminished responsibility; duress 210, 233–4, 259, 280, 296–7, 315, 338–9; extreme mental or emotional disturbance (EMED) 236, 237; full 296; Germany 259–62; honour killings 212–13, 282, 318–19, 343, 358; insanity 210, 235, 280–1, 298, 357; Islamic law 335–43; less serious cases of voluntary manslaughter 260–1; loss of control/ provocation 211, 236–8; necessity 210, 234, 259, 280, 298, 315, 339; Netherlands 296–8; New Zealand 278–82; official authority 211–12, 261, 282, 317–18, 342–3, 357–8; provocation 260–1; psychological disorders 259–60; self-control, loss of 341–2; self-defence 210, 232–3, 259, 279–80, 296, 314, 337–8; South Africa 210–13; superior orders 211, 238–9, 261–2, 281–2, 317, 342, 357–8; Sweden 356–8; United States 232–41
De Saussure, F. 91
De Than, Claire 4, 162, 163
Devlin, Patrick (Lord) 83–4, 95, 189–90
Dias, M. 187
diets, inappropriate 155–8; failure to heed medical advice 156; gross breach of duty 156; inadequate feeding and poor nutritional knowledge 156; inhuman punishment 157; overfeeding 156
dignity concept and death 187
diminished responsibility 64–4, 102–18; abnormality of mind 105–8, 113–15; alcohol dependence 114; Crown Court Compendium 109; defendant's ability to understand nature of conduct 111; defendant's abnormality as 'explanation' and 'cause' of the killing 113–15; definitions 3; developmental immaturity 106–7; discretion and 'benign conspiracy' 115; *doli incapax* defence 107; expert testimony on a plea of 115–18; former aetiologies 105–6; history 103–5; impairment 'substantial' 112–13; Islamic law 340–1; manslaughter 88; mental condition at time of killing 3; New Zealand 281; partial defence, embodying 'moral responsibility' 107–9; rational judgment, ability to form 112; recognised medical condition 109–11; revised definition 102; self-control, ability to exercise 112; South Africa 210–11; standard of proof 112; Sweden 357; Turkey 316–17; United States 235–6
discretionary sentencing regimes: South Africa 213–15; Turkey 321; United States 243–4
distribution: of footage 184–5; of videos 180–2
dolus directus (firm intention to commit a specific unlawful act) 46
dolus eventualis (intention not reflecting aim/ object of accused) 50, 54; and negligence 201–2; Netherlands 285, 287; and recklessness 48–9, 199–200, 209; South Africa 46–7, 48–9, 50, 54, 199–202, 209; Turkey 301, 308
doodslag (voluntary homicide) 284, 288, 289
double effect doctrine: Islamic law 328–30; New Zealand 266; South Africa 205, 207
driving offences: careless driving 130; constructive homicide 124–5; constructive

manslaughter 127–31; dangerous driving 33, 127, 128; driving whilst disqualified 130; result-qualified/constructive/*versari in re illicita*/felony homicide offences 275
Dubber, M. 339
duress: Islamic law 338–9; Netherlands 296–7; New Zealand 280; South Africa 210; Turkey 315; United States 233–4
Dworkin, R. 146–7

Edis, Andrew 91–2
Edwards, Susan 2–3
Egyptian Penal Code 340
Elliott, Catherine 162, 163
Elliott, Tracey 156
Elvey, A. 147
Elvin, Jesse 4
end of life: brain death 204; double effect doctrine and end of life decisions 328–30; Germany 247–8; Islamic law 327, 328–30; Netherlands 285–6; New Zealand 265; South Africa 204; Turkey 304; United States 221–2
English homicide law, reforming 2, 37–61, 79–81; fair labelling priorities 38–45; involuntary manslaughter and murder 38–60
English law and current state of murder 2, 62–81; complicity liability 69, 70, 77–9; conditions of liability for murder 67–79; full-offence intention interpretation 73–4; inchoate offending 68, 78; joint enterprise liability, abolition 66; knowledge 74; misunderstanding of complicity in manslaughter 77–9; misuse of conditional intention 75–7; parasitic accessory liability (PAL) 66, 69; penal consequences of murder 64–7; principal offender, murder as 2, 67–9, 80; reform 79–81; secondary party 2, 67, 69–79; uncertain *mens rea* 71–4; 'wrong turn' 70
European Convention on Human Rights: fair trial 65; freedom from torture and inhuman/degrading treatment 168; right to life 21, 34, 157, 168; and status of foetus 138; Turkey a party to 318
euthanasia: active 313, 328–9; passive 313, 329; Sweden 350; *see also* assisted suicide; mercy killings
Ewart, William 13
expert testimony, diminished responsibility 115–18
extenuating circumstances provision 11, 14–17, 18

fair labelling principle 2; comparative 45; and contemporaneity, in US homicide 54–6; culpability, English law 42–5; culpable homicide, Scots law 30; English homicide law 38–45; Law Commission homicide ladder 42–5; murder and involuntary manslaughter 38–45; perceived problems 39; and South African homicide precepts 49–51; Sweden 348
Farmand, M.K. 188
fault element: causation of death/homicide 131; *dolus* and *culpa* 347; murder 47, 55; reckless manslaughter (RM) 47; Sweden 347
Feinberg, J. 8, 188, 189
felony murder rule: abolition in England (1957) 55; United States 55, 219–20
female killers 83–5, 94–101
feticide 136
first degree murder 7–9, 11, 43; Canada 54; defining 43, 79; express malice 17, 18; homicide ladder 43; intention to kill 43; Law Commission on 19, 43, 79; United States 53; *see also* intentional homicide
Fletcher, J. 143
Fortson, Rudi 3
Foucault, Michel 91
France: assassination 15; Penal Code (1810) 12; Penal Code (1832) 11

Germany: Basic Law 257; beginning of life 247–8; Code of Crimes against International Law 261; defences to homicide 259–62; end of life 247–8; forms of homicide 246–7; general elements 247–50; historical development of homicide offences 245–6; infanticide/child destruction 257; intentional homicide 251–5; killing on request of the victim 246, 255; medical treatment 248–9; Military Criminal Law 261; murder 246, 252; negligent homicide 255–6; objective qualifying factors, intentional homicide 252–3; omission, homicide by 249–50; pre-birth causes with post-birth effect 247–8; Prussian Criminal Code (1851) 245; result-qualified homicide offences 256–7; revision of homicide offences (1941 and 2014) 245–6; sentencing framework 262–3; subjective qualifying factors, intentional homicide 253–5; voluntary manslaughter 246, 251–2, 260–1
Gibson, Matthew 2
Gillespie, Alisdair 4
Gilligan, Carol 154
Godwin, Robert 174
Goff, Robert Lionel Archibald (Lord Justice) 119, 120
Gough, S. 91
governors, inappropriate diets, provision of 155
Grey, George 10, 16
grievous bodily harm (GBH), intention to cause 3, 39, 40; death, causing 119, 122, 124; termination of pregnancy 136, 141; *see also* intention to kill

Griffiths, D. 132–3
gross negligence manslaughter (GNM) 120, 131–4; English homicide law, reforming 40, 41–2, 44, 45; inadequate diet 157; parental rejection of medical treatment 159–60; South Africa 48

Hall, Jerome 164
Hamilton, Arthur Campbell (Lord Justice-General) 35
Hart, H.L.A. 121, 124, 125, 132
Hart-Browne, Elizabeth 100
head teachers, inappropriate diets, provision of 157
Heald, Oliver 15
Heller, K.J. 339
Herring, Jonathan 3–4, 154
Hobson, Kathleen 98
Hoctor, S. 49
homicide: *actus reus* 332–3; constructive 3, 124–5; defences to *see* defences to homicide; deliberate vs. negligent 195; English law, reforming 37–61; highest category 12; indirect 325; and infanticide/child destruction 209–10, 231; intentional *see* intentional homicide; intention to kill; intermediate cause 325; involuntary culpable 29–35; legal wrong leading to death 119, 134; negligent *see* negligence/negligent homicide; by omission *see* omission, homicide by; parental refusal of lifesaving treatment for a child 158; reckless *see* recklessness/reckless homicide; recording of *see* recording of murder; three-tier structure, proposed 7, 8, 13, 13–15, 43, 52; voluntary 288; *see also* culpable homicide, Scots law
homicide ladder, proposed 2, 7, 8, 37, 38, 42–5; stratification 52–60
Honoré, T. 121, 124, 125, 132
honour killings: Islamic law 343; New Zealand 282; South Africa 212–13; Sweden 358; Turkey 318–19; United States 240–1
Horder, Jeremy 1, 43, 44, 45, 86, 87, 90, 96, 162–3, 189–90
Hume, David 21, 23, 30

infanticide/child destruction: England 64; Germany 257; and homicide 209–10, 231; Islamic law 334; New Zealand 264–5, 276; South Africa 198; Sweden 354–5; Turkey 312–13; United States 230; *see also* pregnancy termination
insanity defence: Islamic law 339–40; Netherlands 298; New Zealand 280–1; South Africa 210; Sweden 357; Turkey 315–16; United States 235
intentional homicide 199; *actus reus* 208, 226, 267–8, 307; Germany 251–5; homicide offences committed in aggravating circumstances 289–90; homicide offences committed in mitigating circumstances 290–2; indirect intent 46–7, 320; Islamic law 324, 343–5; manslaughter 352–3; *mens rea* 1–2, 39, 121, 208, 270, 307–8, 333; mortal weapon, use of 324; murder 351–2; Netherlands 287–92; New Zealand 267–70; objective qualifying factors 252–3; punishment by the state 344–5; sentencing framework 343–5; South Africa 46–8, 199, 208; subjective qualifying factors 253–5; Sweden 351–3; Turkey 301, 307–8; United States 217–18, 226–7; victim's heirs' election 344, 345; *see also dolus directus* (firm intention to commit a specific unlawful act); *dolus eventualis* (intention not reflecting aim/object of accused); first degree murder; intention to kill
intention to kill 43, 48, 78, 122, 251, 270, 287, 290, 324, 325, 333; direct and indirect intention 39, 301, 325; Dutch concept 287–8; misuse of conditional intention 75–7; as murder 23, 25, 29, 33, 40, 43, 80, 119, 122; premeditated killing 63; vs. reckless killing 37; Scotland 24; and serious injury 62; spontaneous killing 62–3; wicked 1, 23, 25, 29, 33; *see also* grievous bodily harm (GBH), intention to cause; intentional homicide; murder
involuntary culpable homicide 29–35; absence of reference to homicidal attitude 33–4; lawful act type 23, 31–3, 33; recklessness 34–5; unlawful act type 23, 30–1, 33
involuntary manslaughter: correspondence principle 40–1; gross negligence manslaughter (GNM) 40, 41–2, 44, 45, 48, 131–4, 292–4; and murder 38–60; perceived fair labelling problems 40–2; 'reasonable person' standardisation 57; reckless manslaughter (RM) 40, 42, 44, 47, 56, 60–1; suicide of vulnerable 161–2; United States case law 57–8, 60; unlawful act manslaughter (UAM) 40–1, 42, 44, 45, 48, 49, 54; *see also* murder and involuntary manslaughter
Iranian Penal Code 329, 333, 336, 339, 343, 345
Iraqi Penal Code 334
Islamic law 322–46; accidental homicide 325, 333–4; *actus reus* 332, 332–3; beginning of life 326; defences to homicide 335–43; *diyat* (compensation) 323, 340; double effect doctrine and end of life decisions 328–30; elements of homicide offences 332–4; end of life 327; euthanasia 328–9; evolution from pre-Islamic Arabia 322–3; general elements 326–32; Habali school 323, 325, 336, 338, 344; Hanafi school 325, 330–1, 332, 344; historical development of homicide offences

322–6; infanticide/child destruction 334; intentional homicide 324, 343–5; intermediate cause, homicide by 325; life, right to 322; life imprisonment 339; life-shortening, pain-reducing medication 329–30; Maliki school 326, 331, 335, 336, 338, 344; medical treatment 328–30; *mens rea* 332; omission, homicide by 330–2; pre-birth causes with post-birth effect 327–8; pregnancy termination 334–5; private tort or public wrong 323–4; *qisas* (capital punishment) 323, 330, 331, 340, 343, 344; quasi-intentional murder 324–5, 333; Quran 322, 332, 333, 334, 341, 342, 343; retaliation 330–1; sentencing framework 343–5; Shafi'i school 323, 325, 336, 340; structure of homicide offences 324–6; Zahiri school 325, 326, 338; Zaydi school 325; Zufar school 336
Islamic State (IS) 4

joint enterprise liability 66, 176
Jones, Ann 96
juries, second degree murder, case for 8, 9, 16, 18, 20

Kelly, Fitzroy 14
Kemp, G. 48
Kennedy, John F. 190
Ker, Charles HB 10
Kobayashi, Tamie 165
Kyd, Sally 3

Labuschagne, J.M.T. 195
Laird, K. 42
Law Commission, England: on complicity 72; Consultation Paper on homicide 10, 20, 116; on diminished responsibility 106, 112, 115; fair labelling of culpability 2, 42–5; first degree murder, revised definition 19, 43, 79; *Murder, Manslaughter and Infanticide* (2006) 37, 42; *Partial Defences to Murder* 48; proposed homicide ladder 2, 7, 8, 37, 38, 42–5; on recording of murder 178, 179; replacement crimes, proposed 38; three-tier homicide structure, proposed 7, 8, 13, 13–15, 43, 52; on year and a day rule 123
Law Reform Commission, South Africa, Report on Euthanasia and the Artificial Preservation of Life 206
learned helplessness 85, 95, 164
Leavens, A. 131, 132
Le Roux-Kemp, A. 204
life, right to 21, 34, 157, 168, 322
life imprisonment: aggravated 316, 319; diminished responsibility 115; discretionary sentences 80; English law and current state of murder 63, 65–6, 67, 79; Islamic law 339; minimum term 65–6; Netherlands 288, 290, 298, 299; New Zealand 264, 275, 282, 283; and recording of murder 183; and second degree murder 11, 13, 15; South Africa 213, 214; Turkey 305, 316, 319; United States 241–2; vulnerable persons, duty of care in relation to 173
Lin, Jun 175
Lindemann, H. 149–50
Little, M. 146
Lyons, Stephen 159

Macdonald, J.H.A. 23, 24
McGowan, L. 162–3
Mackenzie, C. 150
Mackenzie, Sir George 21
Mair, J. 145
malice: express 17, 18; malice aforethought 121, 122, 196–7, 217; transferred 334
Malik, M.M. 329, 330
managers, liability in relation to deaths arising from workplace stress 160–6
mandatory sentencing regimes: South Africa 213; Turkey 319–21; United States 241–4
manifest illegality principle 238–9
Manninen, B. 149
manslaughter 7; complicity in, misunderstanding 77–9; constructive 125–7; defining 43; diminished responsibility 88; driving, causing death by 124–5, 127–31; gross negligence manslaughter (GNM) 40, 131–4; homicide ladder 43; involuntary *see* involuntary manslaughter; manslaughter-provocation 82; *mens rea* 227, 228, 353; New Zealand 264; parental refusal of lifesaving treatment for a child 159; reckless manslaughter (RM) 40, 42, 44, 47, 56, 60–1; and second degree murder 44–5; Sweden 352–3; unlawful act manslaughter (UAM) 40–1; voluntary 251–2
Martin, Lord Michael 16
Matza, David 90–1
McDiarmid, Claire 1
medical manslaughter (MM) 132
medical treatment: double effect doctrine 205, 207; Germany 248–9; gross negligence manslaughter (GNM) for parental refusal 159, 160; Islamic law 328–30; medical negligence and culpable homicide, South Africa 51–2; Netherlands 286; New Zealand 265–6; palliative care 329–30; physician-assisted suicide 223–4; rejection for religious or pseudoscientific reasons 158–60; South Africa 51–2, 205–7; Sweden 349–50; Turkey 304–5; United States 223–4
mens rea: accidental murder 333–4; any homicide offence 3; causation 119, 122, 127;

child destruction 139; complicity liability 71, 72; correspondence principle 348; culpable homicide, Scots law 1, 24, 29, 30, 33; gross negligence manslaughter (GNM) 41; intention to kill/intentional homicide 1–2, 39, 121, 208, 270, 307–8, 333; involuntary culpable homicide 29; Islamic law 332, 339; manslaughter 227, 228, 353; murder 1–2, 25, 29, 39, 40, 55, 80, 120–1, 123, 226–8, 333, 352; negligence/negligent homicide 209; Netherlands 284; New Zealand 270–2, 274–5; normative, dangerous driving 128; quasi-intentional murder 333; rape 177; recklessness/reckless homicide 1–2, 32, 227–8, 270–2; result-qualified/constructive/*versari in re illicita*/felony homicide offences 230, 274–5; serious injury 68; South Africa 208, 209; terrorist killings 185; Turkey 307–8, 312; uncertain, in English law 71–4; United States 226–8, 230; wickedness 1–2, 25

mercy killings 24, 207, 278–9; *see also* assisted suicide; euthanasia

Middlemiss, Sam 165

Miles, Jo 114

minors, *doli incapax* defence 107

Mitchell, B. 41

Model Penal Code (MPC), US 52, 53, 56, 135, 217–19, 220, 230, 232, 233–4, 236, 237

Montesquieu, Charles-Louis de Secondat, Baron 11

morality and law 7, 8, 20, 189–90

Morris, A. 146

murder: accidental 325, 333–4; *actus reus* 1, 23, 25, 26, 27, 138; causation 120–4; classic definition (Coke) 62, 119; comparative fair labelling priorities 45; correspondence principle 39; culpability 48, 62–3, 65; culpable homicide, or 24–7; current state in English law 62–81; death penalty for, proposed abolition in Victorian England 10–11; depraved mind 227; English law, current state in 62–81; fault element 47, 55; first degree 7–9, 11, 17, 43; Germany 246, 252; grievous bodily harm (GBH), intention to cause 39; inadequate diet 157; indirect 325; intentional 3, 333, 351–2; intention to kill as 23, 25, 29, 33, 40, 43, 80, 119, 122; law of 7–8; line with 25–7; mandatory life penalty 9, 80; *mens rea* 1–2, 25, 29, 39, 40, 55, 80, 120–1, 123, 226–8, 333, 352; Netherlands 288–9; New Zealand 264; paradigmatic offence 43, 119, 120; penal consequences 64–7; perceived fair labelling problems 39–40; principal offender 2, 67–9, 80; punishment regime 65; quasi-intentional 324–5, 333; recording 174–91; secondary party 2, 69–79; second degree *see* second degree murder; South Africa 2, 46–8; United States 2, 53, 226–7; as wilful and premeditated killing 11–12

murder and involuntary manslaughter: comparative fair labelling priorities 45; constructive liability 39–40, 40–1; correspondence principle 39, 40–1; culpability 2, 39, 40, 41, 42–5; English law 38–60; fair labelling priorities 38–45; offence against the person 41; perceived fair labelling problems 39–42; South Africa 45–52

necessity defence: Islamic law 339; Netherlands 298; New Zealand 280; South Africa 210; Turkey 315; United States 234

negligence/negligent homicide: *actus reus* 209, 272, 308–9; advertent 320; conscious negligence 201, 209; dangerous driving 33, 127, 128; degree of negligence 229, 272–4, 309–11; vs. deliberate homicide 195; failure to discharge an objective duty of care and attention 309–10; foreseeability of the result 310; Germany 255–6; gross negligence manslaughter (GNM) *see* gross negligence manslaughter (GNM); inadvertent killings 42; kinship between perpetrator and victim 319–20; medical negligence and culpable homicide 51–2; *mens rea* 209; New Zealand 272–4; preventability of the result 310–11; South Africa 45–52, 200–2, 209; Sweden 353–4; Turkey 302, 308–11, 319–20; United States 218–19, 228–9, 230; unlawful act must be dangerous (New Zealand) 273; victim's fright response must be reasonable foreseeable 274; *see also* negligent homicide

Netherlands 284–99; Article 6 Road Traffic Act 1994 293–4; Article 307 DPC 293; beginning of life 285; defences to homicide 296–8; *doodslag* (voluntary homicide) 284, 288, 289; Dutch concept of gross negligence and recklessness 292–3; Dutch concept of intention 287–8; Dutch Penal Code 285, 286; end of life 285–6; general elements 285–6; gross negligence and reckless homicide 292–4; historical development of homicide offences 285; homicide offences committed in aggravating circumstances 289–90; homicide offences committed in mitigating circumstances 290–2; intentional homicide 287–92; legal aspects of sentencing 298–9; life imprisonment 288, 290, 298, 299; medical treatment 286; murder 288–9; offence structure 284–5; omission, homicide by 286; pregnancy termination 295; premeditation 288; qualified voluntary homicide 289–90; result-qualified offences 294–5; Review Commission 292; sentencing framework 298–9; statistics, sentencing 299

New Zealand: *actus reus* 267–8, 270, 274; beginning of life 265; defences to homicide 278–82; defendant's acts or omissions causing death 268–9; driving offences 275; end of life 265; Family Violence Death Review Committee 279–80; felony homicide offence 274; general elements 265–7; historical development of homicide offences 264–5; infanticide/child destruction 264–5, 276; intentional homicide 267–70; Law Commission 280; life imprisonment 264, 275, 282, 283; manslaughter 264; medical treatment 265–6; *mens rea* 270–2; murder 264; negligent homicide 272–4; omission, homicide by 266–7; pre-birth causes with post-birth effect 265; reckless homicide 270–2; result-qualified/constructive/*versari in re illicita*/felony homicide offences 274–5; sentencing framework 282–3; 'three strikes' regime 283; unlawful act must be dangerous 273; victim's fright response must be reasonable foreseeable 274; year and a day rule 269
Nicholson, D. 96
Nigeria 324–5, 331, 341
Noddings, Nel 154
non-terrorist killings: distribution of videos 180–2; possession of murder videos 182, recording of homicide 175–80; secondary participation 177
Nourse, Victoria 237
novus actus interveniens 51, 121, 127
Nussbaum, M. 144

obscenity 180
official authority defence: Germany 261; Islamic law 342–3; New Zealand 282; South Africa 211–12; Sweden 357–8; Turkey 317–18; United States 239–40
omission, homicide by: death, causing 268–9; distinguishing between acts and omissions 330; Germany 249–50; major departure from standard of care expected of a reasonable person 272–3; Netherlands 286; New Zealand 266–7, 268–9; omitting to effect an easy rescue 267; protectors 351; retaliation 330–1; South Africa 207–8; supervisors 351; Sweden 351; Turkey 305–6, 330–2; United States 224–5
omitting to effect an easy rescue: Germany 249–50; Islamic law 332; Netherlands 286; New Zealand 267; Turkey 306; United States 225
overwork, death by 160

Pakistan Penal Code 324, 331, 334, 338, 343, 344, 345
palliative care 329–30
parents: inappropriate diets, provision of 155–7; rejection of medical treatment for religious/pseudoscientific reasons 158–60
paternalism: vs. autonomy xii, 166–7; 'hard' and 'soft' 164; and morality 190
Perry, Sergeant 14
personhood: at/close to birth and beyond 143–4; at conception 144; foetus lacking 136; relational approach to 145, 147–9; *see also* pregnancy termination
Pervin, M. 324, 325
Peters, R. 331
Pickles, C. 148
Porter, L. 136
pre-birth causes with post-birth effect: Germany 247–8; Islamic law 327–8; New Zealand 265; South Africa 204–5; Turkey 304; United States 222–3; *see also* pregnancy termination
pregnancy termination 136–52; abortion case 136, 137; abortion services outside terms of Abortion Act 1967 139; assault case 136, 137, 141; consent by woman, lack of 140; de-criminalising of abortion 137; developing a new approach 144–7; Germany 257–9; Islamic law 334–5; legal status of foetus 4, 136, 138–9, 145, 148, 151; moral status, traditional approach 142–3; Netherlands 295; New Zealand 276–8; offence of unlawfully procuring a miscarriage 139; outside context of medical termination 4; relational approach, applying 145, 147–51; rights to abortion vs. protection of foetus 146; South Africa 209–10; standard individualised approach, shortcomings 145; Sweden 355–6; Turkey 313; unauthorised abortions 139–40; United States 224, 230–1; unwanted miscarriage 148, 149; use of criminal law in relation to 139–42; woman, offences against 140; by women themselves 141; *see also* beginning of life; personhood
prison officers and governors, liability for suicides of prisoners 166–72
provocation defence: abused partner, killing by 83; cumulative provocation 96; manslaughter-provocation 82; New Zealand 281; problematic in common law jurisdictions 80; South Africa 211; Turkey 320–1; United States 236–8; unjust provocation 320–1; *see also* self-control, loss of

al-Qaradawi, Sheikh Yusuf 329
quasi-intentional murder 333

rape 177
rationality, in causation 134–5
Raz, J. 90
reasonableness, standard of care 272–3

recklessness/reckless homicide: *actus reus* 227, 228, 270; culpable homicide, Scots law 23, 25–7, 29, 31–5; and *dolus eventualis* (intention not reflecting aim/object of accused), South Africa 48–9, 199–200, 209; involuntary culpable homicide 34–5; *mens rea* 1–2, 32, 227–8, 270–2; Netherlands 292–4; New Zealand 270–2; reckless indifference 18; reckless manslaughter (RM) 40, 42, 44, 47, 56, 60–1; second degree murder 18, 44; South Africa 48–9, 199–200, 209; subjective recklessness, English law 47; Sweden 353–4; Turkey 301–2, 308; United States 218–19, 227–8; wicked recklessness 1–2, 23, 25–7, 29, 33
reconciliation doctrine, South Africa 47, 50–1
reconstructive liability, *ex-post facto* 55
recording of murder 174–91; accessibility 181; 'deprave and corrupt' 180; distributing videos 180–2; distribution of footage 184–5; families of deceased, rights of 188; 'gore websites' 175, 178; homicide 175–80; indirect victims 187; and Internet 181; morality 189–90; murder videos 182, 187–91; non-terrorist killings 175–82; obscenity 180; possession of footage 186; possession of murder videos 182; secondary participation 177, 188; 'snuff video' 174; terrorist killings 4, 182–6; withholding of footage 185–6; 'wrongful offense' 189
Reed, Alan 2
reform: English homicide law 37–61; second degree murder (Victorian England) 10–14; vulnerable persons, duty of care in relation to 172–3
Report of the Commission on Capital Punishment (1866) 1, 7
result-qualified/constructive/*versari in re illicita*/felony homicide offences: *actus reus* 274, 311–12; Germany 256–7; *mens rea* 274–5; Netherlands 294–5; New Zealand 274–5; South Africa 45, 202–3, 209; Turkey 302, 311–13; United States 229–30
retaliation 330–1
road traffic accidents *see* driving offences
Roberts, H. 148
Robinson, P.H. 53
Rogers, C. 149
Rosenblatt, A. 187–8
Rothman, B.K. 146, 147

Sanders, A. 132–3, 156
Sanghvi, R. 96
Scotland: culpable homicide in *see* culpable homicide, Scots law; diminished responsibility 103
second degree murder 1; arising of problems 7–10; Canada 54; case for 7–20; Committee of 1866 1, 7, 13, 17–19; compared to individualised 'discretionary assessment' 9, 11; *Coutts* judgment (2006) 9; defining 43; gross negligence manslaughter (GNM) 44; helping or hindering state's duty to secure justice 8; homicide ladder 43; intention to cause serious injury 44; introduction of (Pennsylvania, 1794) 11–12, 53, 216–17; juries 8, 9, 16, 18, 20; and law reform in Victorian England 10–14; and manslaughter 44–5; reckless manslaughter (RM) 44; recklessness 18, 44; United States 11–12, 53, 55, 216–17, 227
self-control, loss of 2–3, 63, 82–101; and ability to exercise self-control 112; abused partner, killing by 83, 94–6, 100; Battered Woman Syndrome (BSW) 95, 97–9, 211; Crown Court Compendium 94, 100; 'cultural defence' 90; 'extremely grave character' 86; fear, triggered by 2–3, 82, 94–101; Islamic law 341–2; learned helplessness 85, 95; learnt behaviourism 89–94; male violence, irrelevance of history 83–5; neutralization 90; New Zealand 281; permissible male maelstrom of anger 86–9; permission for anger 89–94; relevances 83–5; self-defence 100; serious violence, fear of 95, 99, 100; sexual infidelity 82, 86, 87, 91, 92; South Africa 211; statistics 3; structural linguistics 91; tolerance 88; Turkey 317; United States 236–8; without anger 91; women who kill 83–5, 94–101; *see also* provocation defence
self-defence: Islamic law 337–8; Netherlands 296; New Zealand 279–80; self-control, loss of 100; South Africa 210; Sweden 356–7; Turkey 314; United States 232–3
sentencing framework: attempt 319; discretionary regimes 213–15, 243–4, 321; Germany 262–3; identity of victim 320; indirect intent and advertent negligence 320; Islamic law 343–5; mandatory regimes 213, 241–3; negligent crimes 319–20; Netherlands 298–9; New Zealand 282–3; participation in crime 319; South Africa 213–15; Sweden 358–60; Turkey 319–21; United States 241–4; unjust provocation 320–1; victimisation suffered by perpetrator 320
Shah, S.S. 332
Sheldon, S. 137, 142
Simester, A.P. 134
Singapore, Penal Code 328, 343
Smith, Josephine 95, 199
South Africa 45–52, 195–215; abolition of *versari* doctrine 45, 49–51, 209; abortion and homicide 209–10; *actus reus* 208, 209; Anglo-South African standardisations of culpable homicide and medical negligence 51–2; beginning of life 203–4; common law

196, 197, 198; culpable homicide 51–2, 201; customary law 196; defences to homicide 210–13; *dolus* (intention) 45, 49; *dolus directus* (firm intention to commit a specific unlawful act) 46; *dolus eventualis* (intention not reflecting aim/object of accused) 46–9, 50, 54, 199, 201–2, 209; easy rescue, omitting to effect 208; end of life 204; English law 196, 197; general elements 203–8; historical development of homicide offences 195–8; homicide precepts and fair labelling 49–51; *Humphreys* judgment 46, 47, 48–9; indirect intention for murder 46–7; infanticide/child destruction 198; intentional homicide 46–8, 199, 208; intention and negligence 50–1; involuntary manslaughter 2; Law Reform Commission 206; legal traditions brought to by European settlers 196; medical negligence and culpable homicide 51–2; medical treatment scenarios 205–7; *mens rea* 208, 209; mercy killings 207; murder 2, 46–8; Ndebele people 195; negligence (*luxuria*) 45–52, 200–2, 209; Northern Sotho people 195; omission, homicide by 207–8; pre-birth causes with post-birth effect 204–5; reckless homicide 199–200, 209; reconciliation doctrine 47, 50–1; result-qualified/constructive/*versari in re illicita*/felony homicide offences 45, 202–3, 209; Roman-Dutch law 196, 197, 198; sentencing framework 213–15; Tembu people 195; *versari in res illicita* (constructive manslaughter) 45, 48, 49–51, 209

Spencer, John 107
spiritual healing 159
Stark, F. 42
Stephan, Collet 159
Stephan, David 159
Stephen, Fitzjames 18, 19
Stephen, James 16
Stephens, Steve 174
Stoyles, B. 147
strict liability offences 128
Stychin, Carl 153, 154, 160
Sudanese Penal Code 331
suicide: assisted 23, 25, 223–4; physician-assisted 223–4; prison officers and governors, liability for suicides of prisoners 166–72; psychological abuse 161; workplace stress and liability of managers 160–6
Sullivan, G.R. 2, 134
superior orders, Islamic law 342
superior orders defence: Germany 261–2; New Zealand 281–2; South Africa 211; Sweden 357–8; Turkey 317; United States 238–9
Sweden: Criminal Code 350, 351–5, 358; defences to homicide 356–8; definitions 348–9; general elements 348–51; guilt 347; historical development of homicide offences 347–8; honour killings 358; infanticide/child destruction 354–5; intentional homicide 351–3; medical treatment 349–50; murder/manslaughter distinction 347; National Board of Health and Welfare 349, 350, 355; negligent homicide 353–4; omission, homicide by 351; pregnancy termination 355–6; reckless homicide 353–4; self-defence 356–7; sentencing framework 358–60

Tajikistan, Penal Code of 332
Taylor, Richard 18–19
termination of pregnancy *see* pregnancy termination
terrorist killings 4, 182–6; defining terrorism 182; distribution of footage 184–5; possession of footage 186; publications 184–5; recording a killing 174–5, 183–4; withholding of footage 185–6
thin-skull rule, causing death 121–2, 125
Thomas, Lamont 156
tort law, duty of care concept 153
tribunals, role of 16–17
Tunisian Penal Code 332
Turkey: act of wounding, death resulting from 312; *actus reus* 307, 308–9, 311–12; beginning of life 303; causing death as result of wounding 311–12; *conditio sine qua non* theory 307; Court of Cassation 307–10, 318, 320; crimes leading to the death of the victim, other 312; defences to homicide 313–19; *in dubio pro reo* principle 308; end of life 304; general elements 303–6; historical development of homicide offences 300–1; infanticide/child destruction 312–13; intentional homicide 301, 307–8; Law on the Transplantation of Organs and Tissues 304; life imprisonment 305, 316, 319; mandatory sentencing regime 319–21; medical treatment 304–5; *mens rea*/negligence combinations 312; mistake as to identity of victim 308; negligent homicide 302, 308–11, 319–20; omission, homicide by 305–6; Penal Code 300–1, 319; Penal Procedure Code 315; pre-birth causes with post-birth effect 304; pregnancy termination 313; reckless homicide 301–2, 308; result-qualified/constructive/*versari in re illicita*/felony homicide offences 302, 311–13; sentencing framework 319–21
Turner, J.W.C. 121

Unborn Victims of Violence Act (UVVA), US 222
Uniacke, S. 90

United States: *actus reus* 226–30; American Academy of Pediatrics (AAP) 158; Army Field Manual 239; beginning of life 220–1; common law 52; Constitution 235, 241; criminal homicide 52; defences to homicide 232–41; determination/premeditation formula 53, 54–5, 217; end of life 221–2; fair labelling prioritisations and contemporaneity in homicide culpability gradations 54–60; felony murder rule 219–20; general elements 220–5; grading of homicide 46, 53, 54–60; historical development of homicide offences 216–17; infanticide/child destruction 230; intentional homicide 217–18, 226–7; involuntary manslaughter 2; manslaughter 2, 227, 228; medical treatment 158, 223–4; *mens rea* 226–8, 230; Model Penal Code (MPC) 52, 53, 56, 135, 217–19, 220, 230, 232, 233–4, 236, 237; murder 2, 53, 226–8; negligence/negligent homicide 218–19, 228–9, 230; omission, homicide by 224–5; Pennsylvanian legislation (1794), second degree murder 11–12, 53, 216–17; physician-assisted suicide 223–4; pre-birth causes with post-birth effect 222–3; pregnancy termination 224, 230–1; reckless homicide 218–19, 227–8; rejection of medical treatment for religious/pseudoscientific reasons 158; result-qualified/constructive/ *versari in re illicita*/felony homicide offences 229–30; *Roe v Wade* 231; second degree murder 11–12, 53, 55, 216–17, 227; sentencing framework 241–4; Statistical Overview of Mandatory Minimum Penalties 242–3; stratification of homicide ladder 52–4; Unborn Victims of Violence Act (UVVA) 222
unlawful act manslaughter (UAM): Canada 54; English homicide law, reforming 40–1, 42, 44, 45; South Africa 48, 49

Van den Heever, J.A. 195
Van Niekerk, B.V.D. 50
versari in res illicita (constructive manslaughter), South Africa 45, 202–3
Victorian England, law reform 10–14; death penalty for murder, proposed abolition 10–11; extenuating circumstances provision 11, 14–17, 18; halfway house strategy 11; juries 16, 18
Vizard, Eileen 106
voluntary homicide, Netherlands 284, 288, 289
voluntary manslaughter, Germany 246, 251–2, 260–1
vulnerable persons, duty of care in relation to 153–73; concept of vulnerability 153–5; European Court of Human Rights 169–71; 'hard cases' 153, 155–72; inappropriate diets, provision of 155–8; managers' liability in relation to deaths arising from workplace stress 160–6, 172; parents' liability for rejection of medical treatment for religious/ pseudoscientific reasons 158–60; paternalism vs. autonomy xii, 166–7; prison officers and governors, liability for suicides of prisoners 166–72; reform 172–3; tort law, duty of care concept 153; vulnerability theory 154

Waddington, Horatio 18
Walker, Lenore 85
Wallerstein, Shlomit 165
Warren, Mary 142
Waters, Sarah 160
Weinstein, Harvey 163
Whiting, R. 50
wicked recklessness 1–2, 23, 25–7, 29, 33
Wilkinson, J. 204
Willes, James S. (Justice) 17
Willes, Justice 18
Williams, Glanville 108
workplace stress, deaths arising from (liability of managers) 160–6, 172; criminal liability, where appropriate 163–4; following orders from superiors 165–6; institutional goals, limitations of 165

year and a day rule 122–3
Young, I.M. 144–5

www.ingramcontent.com/pod-product-compliance
Ingram Content Group UK Ltd.
Pitfield, Milton Keynes, MK11 3LW, UK
UKHW050755180926
475701UK00007B/1053
* 9 7 8 0 3 6 7 5 8 6 5 7 7 *

Rigorous Numerics in Dynamics

Proceedings of Symposia in
APPLIED MATHEMATICS

Volume 74

Rigorous Numerics in Dynamics

AMS Short Course
Rigorous Numerics in Dynamics
January 4–5, 2016
Seattle, Washington

Jan Bouwe van den Berg
Jean-Philippe Lessard
Editors

AMERICAN MATHEMATICAL SOCIETY
Providence, Rhode Island

LECTURE NOTES PREPARED FOR THE AMERICAN MATHEMATICAL SOCIETY SHORT COURSE ON RIGOROUS NUMERICS IN DYNAMICS HELD IN SEATTLE, WASHINGTON, JANUARY 4–5, 2016

The AMS Short Course Series is sponsored by the Society's Program Committee for National Meetings. The series is under the direction of the Short Course Subcommittee of the Program Committee for National Meetings.

2010 *Mathematics Subject Classification.* Primary 37M99, 65G99, 37B30, 65L99, 35B32, 65N35, 34K13.

Library of Congress Cataloging-in-Publication Data

Names: Berg, Jan Bouwe van den, 1973- editor. | Lessard, Jean-Philippe, 1978, editor.
Title: Rigorous numerics in dynamics : AMS Short Course, Rigorous Numerics in Dynamics, January 4-5, 2016, Seattle, Washington / Jan Bouwe van den Berg, Jean-Philippe Lessard, editors.
Description: Providence, Rhode Island : American Mathematical Society, [2018] | Series: Proceedings of symposia in applied mathematics ; volume 74 | Includes bibliographical references and index.
Identifiers: LCCN 2017043850 | ISBN 9781470428143 (alk. paper)
Subjects: LCSH: Nonlinear mechanics. | Topological dynamics. | AMS: Dynamical systems and ergodic theory – Approximation methods and numerical treatment of dynamical systems – None of the above, but in this section. msc | Numerical analysis – Error analysis and interval analysis – None of the above, but in this section. msc | Dynamical systems and ergodic theory – Topological dynamics – Index theory, Morse-Conley indices. msc | Numerical analysis – Ordinary differential equations – None of the above, but in this section. msc | Partial differential equations – Qualitative properties of solutions – Bifurcation. msc | Numerical analysis – Partial differential equations, boundary value problems – Spectral, collocation and related methods. msc | Ordinary differential equations – Functional-differential and differential-difference equations – Periodic solutions. msc
Classification: LCC QA321.5 .R54 2018 | DDC 515/.39–dc23
LC record available at https://lccn.loc.gov/2017043850

DOI: http://dx.doi.org/10.1090/psapm/074/00645

Printed in the United States of America.

∞ The paper used in this book is acid-free and falls within the guidelines established to ensure permanence and durability.
Visit the AMS home page at http://www.ams.org/

10 9 8 7 6 5 4 3 2 1 23 22 21 20 19 18

Contents

Preface vii

Introduction to rigorous numerics in dynamics: General functional analytic setup and an example that forces chaos
JAN BOUWE VAN DEN BERG 1

Validated numerics for equilibria of analytic vector fields: Invariant manifolds and connecting orbits
J.D. MIRELES JAMES 27

Continuation of solutions and studying delay differential equations via rigorous numerics
JEAN-PHILIPPE LESSARD 81

Computer-assisted bifurcation diagram validation and applications in materials science
THOMAS WANNER 123

Dynamics and chaos for maps and the Conley index
SARAH DAY 175

Rigorous computational dynamics in the context of unknown nonlinearities
KONSTANTIN MISCHAIKOW 195

Preface

Nonlinear dynamics shape the world around us. It shapes biology, from the electrophysiological properties of neurons, via the spiralling waves in contracting heart muscles, to gene regulatory networks. It shapes physics, from the swirling motions in fluid flows, via the creation of complex patterns in materials, to the harmonious motions of celestial bodies. It shapes chemistry, from the rich reaction kinetics phenomena, via the chemical basis of morphogenesis at the origin of patterns on animals, to the complicated biochemistry in the living cell. Mathematically, these beautiful and highly complicated phenomena can be described by nonlinear dynamical systems in the form of ordinary differential equations (ODEs), partial differential equations (PDEs), delay differential equations (DDEs), finite and infinite dimensional maps. Characterizing quantitatively (or even only qualitatively) the solutions of these models presents severe complications. While some difficulties are partially explained by the presence of nonlinearities in the models, the challenges are even greater for PDEs and DDEs, which are naturally defined on infinite dimensional function spaces. The recent availability of high-performance computers and sophisticated softwares made numerical simulations the primary tool used by scientists to study the complicated dynamics arising from the equations. However, the ubiquitous presence of computational methods in modern day science naturally leads to the fundamental question of validity of the outputs. Even for finite dimensional ODEs, this question inevitably arises if the system under study is chaotic, as small differences in initial conditions (such as those due to rounding errors in numerical computations) yield widely diverging outcomes. To address this fundamental issue in the context of nonlinear dynamics, the recent field of rigorous numerics emerged at the intersection of several fields of pure and applied mathematics. This field draws inspiration from the ideas in scientific computing, nonlinear analysis, numerical analysis, algebraic topology, functional analysis and approximation theory. In a nutshell, rigorous computations are mathematical theorems formulated in such a way that the assumptions can be rigorously verified on a computer. In this book, we introduce novel and exciting techniques within the field of rigorous numerics to study finite and infinite dimensional discrete and continuous dynamical systems.

The book begins with the first introductory chapter by Jan Bouwe van den Berg entitled *Introduction to rigorous numerics in dynamics: general functional analytic setup and an example that forces chaos.* In this chapter, we introduce some basic concepts of rigorous computing in a dynamical systems context, and as first application, we demonstrate how topological braids can be combined with rigorous numerics to prove the existence of chaos in ODEs. The second chapter *Validated numerics for equilibria of analytic vector fields: invariant manifolds and connecting orbits* by J.D. Mireles James introduces a rigorous computational approach to compute rigorously stable and unstable manifolds of steady states of ODEs using the parameterization method and Taylor expansions. Once the local information from the invariants manifold is obtained, a projected boundary value problem is solved yielding computer-assisted proofs of existence of connecting orbits. The third chapter *Continuation of solutions and studying delay differential equations via rigorous numerics* by Jean-Philippe Lessard demonstrates how rigorous numerics helps studying the dynamics of delay equations. We present a rigorous continuation method for solutions of finite and infinite dimensional parameter dependent problems, which is then applied to compute branches of periodic solutions of two DDEs. In the fourth chapter *Computer-assisted bifurcation diagram validation and applications in materials science* by Thomas Wanner, it is demonstrated how rigorous computational techniques can be used to validate bifurcation diagrams, both in finite- and certain infinite-dimensional problems. We focus particularly on the verification of branches, as well as on saddle-node and symmetry-breaking pitchfork bifurcations. The method is applied to a finite dimensional discrete dynamical systems and to a PDE. In the fifth chapter *Dynamics and chaos for maps and the Conley index* by Sarah Day, we examine methods for constructing outer approximations, finite representations of discrete-time models that are amenable to computational studies and computer-assisted proofs. These methods rely heavily on Conley index theory, an algebraic topological generalization of Morse Theory. In the final and sixth chapter *Rigorous computational dynamics in the context of unknown nonlinearities* by Konstantin Mischaikow, we provide a brief introduction to a novel approach to dynamics whose aim is to provide, in a computationally tractable manner, an accurate description of the dynamics of models without precise nonlinearities. We characterize the dynamics using the language of combinatorics and algebraic topology.

This volume is the proceedings of the AMS Short Course on Rigorous Numerics in Dynamics, organized for the Joint Mathematics Meetings in Seattle on January 4–5, 2016.

Proceedings of Symposia in Applied Mathematics
Volume **74**, 2018
http://dx.doi.org/10.1090/psapm/074/00639

Introduction to rigorous numerics in dynamics: General functional analytic setup and an example that forces chaos

Jan Bouwe van den Berg

ABSTRACT. In this paper some basic concepts of rigorous computing in a dynamical systems context are outlined. We often simulate dynamics on a computer, or calculate a numerical solution to a partial differential equation. This gives very detailed, stimulating information. However, mathematical insight and impact would be much improved if we can be sure that what we see on the screen genuinely represents a solution of the problem. In particular, rigorous validation of the computations allows such objects to be used as ingredients of theorems.

The past few decades have seen enormous advances in the development of computer-assisted proofs in dynamics. One approach is based on a functional analytic setup. The goal of this paper is to introduce the ideas underlying this rigorous computational method. As the central example we use the problem of finding a particular periodic orbit in a nonlinear ordinary differential equation that describes pattern formation in fluid dynamics. This simple setting keeps technicalities to a minimum. Nevertheless, the rigorous computation of this single periodic orbit implies chaotic behavior via topological arguments (in a sense very similar to "period 3 implies chaos" for interval maps).

1. Introduction

This paper contains slightly extended lecture notes that accompanied the introductory lecture of the AMS short course on *Rigorous Numerics in Dynamics* at the Joint Mathematics Meetings 2016 in Seattle. We begin with a few sections that are meant to provide motivation and general background information, and these are therefore of a rather global nature (there is a vast amount of introductory texts on nonlinear dynamics; some examples are [**17, 26, 33**]). In §2 we turn to a precise mathematical formulation of the general analytic-computational approach. In §3 we introduce an example for which the approach is subsequently worked out in complete detail in §4.

The core of the material presented here is a synopsis of the state-of-the-art. In §1.2 we give several references to recent work which forms the foundation of the method described in this paper. However, it is by no means an exhaustive list. Additional references can be found in the papers mentioned. The main underlying

---

2010 *Mathematics Subject Classification.* 37-04.
Supported in part by NWO-VICI grant 639.033.109.

references for the detailed calculations in this paper are [**40**] and [**18**]. In particular, the bulk of §3 is summarized from [**40**, §1]. We note that in the details of the computer-assisted proof we deviate substantially from the original approach. The new estimates presented in §4.5 and §4.6 are simpler to explain and lead to a computationally cheaper proof. Furthermore, the setup in §4.3 with *two* so-called radii polynomials depending on *two* radii (which characterize a rectangle in a the product space of unknowns) is more systematic than the ad-hoc choices of weights that were used in [**40**]. We believe that this leads to improved understanding and has the potential for generalizations far beyond the relatively simple example chosen here to illustrate the method.

1.1. Background: dynamical systems. Informally, a dynamical system is a system that evolves in time according to a deterministic law. The time variable $t \in \mathcal{T}$ may be either discrete or continuous. The time may flow forward ($\mathcal{T} = \mathbb{N}$ or $\mathcal{T} = \mathbb{R}^+ = [0, \infty)$) or forward-and-backward ($\mathcal{T} = \mathbb{Z}$ or $\mathcal{T} = \mathbb{R}$). It may happen that an evolution stops after some finite time (e.g. because it reaches infinity in finite time), but we will not be considering such details of a technical nature here. Mathematically, what we need are a topological space $\mathcal{X}$, the phase space, and a continuous function, the flow, $\varphi : \mathcal{X} \times \mathcal{T} \to \mathcal{X}$ with the properties

$$\varphi(x; 0) = x \qquad \text{for all } x \in \mathcal{X}, \tag{1a}$$

$$\varphi(x; t_1 + t_2) = \varphi(\varphi(x; t_1); t_2) \qquad \text{for all } x \in \mathcal{X} \text{ and } t_1, t_2 \in \mathcal{T}. \tag{1b}$$

The interpretation is that after a time t the state x has moved to $\varphi(x; t)$. The identity (1b) expresses that flowing for some time t_1 to a point $x_1 = \varphi(x; t_1)$ and then flowing another t_2 from x_1, gives the same result as flowing for a time $t_1 + t_2$ directly.

One usually writes $x(t) = \varphi(x(0); t)$ if it is clear which flow is meant. The fundamental problem of dynamical systems is that in all but the simplest cases we do not know φ, i.e., we have no useful explicit description of the flow. However, there are many cases where a "law of motion" (for which we have an explicit description) together with initial data determine the entire future dynamics deterministically, hence we know there *is* a flow φ, i.e., it is a dynamical system.

Indeed, dynamical systems appear in all branches of sciences. To give a few examples:

- Physics: Newton's law of motion in classical mechanics
- Chemistry: the Schrödinger equation
- Fluid dynamics: the Navier-Stokes equations
- Economics: the Black-Scholes equation for option pricing
- Meteorology: coupled ocean-atmosphere models in weather forecasting
- Systems biology: reaction-diffusion equations for reaction networks
- Astronomy: planet-, star-, galaxy- and cluster-formation and their evolution
- Neuroscience: dynamic models for bursting neurons

Dynamical systems do not just occur in applications. Indeed, they are interesting from a mathematical perspective in their own right. Moreover, they appear in many branches of mathematics, such as in the Calculus of Variations (gradient flows), in differential geometry (e.g. the Ricci flow, leading, eventually, to the resolution of the

Poincaré conjecture), in evolutionary and stochastic partial differential equations, and in symplectic geometry (pseudoholomorphic curves).

The modern theory of dynamical systems dates back to Poincaré and his study of the (in)stability of the solar system and its ultimate fate. More generally, the central question in dynamical systems is the following: start at some point $x(0)$ and let it evolve under the flow φ; *now what happens?* And how do the individual orbits fit together to give a global description of the behavior of the system as a whole? Additionally, one would like to know not just how the ultimate fate depends on the initial position, but also on parameters in the system, and on the "type" of system (e.g. Hamiltonian, gradient, symmetric, network structure).

Clearly, no single method can answer all these questions, especially since there are so many types of dynamical systems (linear, nonlinear, ordinary differential equations (ODEs), partial differential equations (PDEs), delay equations, finite and infinite dimensional maps).

Linear dynamical systems can often be analyzed by hand using linear algebra, functional analysis and special functions. In this paper we are interested in *nonlinear* dynamics, for which the analytic tools are much coarser. Topological approaches (e.g. fixed point theorems, Conley index) and variational methods (e.g. Morse theory) give some information about existence of solutions for large classes of systems. However, such robust but coarse results often lack information about multiplicity of solutions for specific nonlinear dynamical systems. Moreover, they usually provide very little qualitative (let alone quantitative) information about the shape of the solutions.

In practice, a topological approach is often complemented by computer simulations. While the latter give numerical evidence for the behavior of solutions, there is unquantified uncertainty in this information due to the absence of explicit error bounds on the outcome of numerics. These errors originate from rounding errors and, more importantly, truncation and discretization errors.

The goal of the paper is to introduce a framework in which the quantitative but tentative information from computer simulations can be turned into mathematically rigorous statements (theorems). Numerical computations are naturally limited to a relatively small range of parameter values and a restricted part of phase space. In particular, our methods focus on rigorously (in the mathematical sense) finding solutions in nonlinear dynamical systems that represent *special features*. One may think of equilibria, cycles, connecting orbits (homoclinic or heteroclinic), horseshoes ("chaos"), invariant tori, etc.

What the special solutions of most interest are will depend on the dynamical system. Nevertheless, some useful global statements can be made. In particular, in dissipative systems all dynamics will evolve towards an *attractor*, and hence studying this attractor is of most interest. More generally, the fundamental theorem of dynamical systems, due to Conley [**9**], states that any flow (on a compact metric space) decomposes into a *chain recurrent* part and a *gradient-like* part. The recurrent components consist, roughly speaking, of points that come back arbitrarily close to themselves under the evolution of the flow, whereas points in the gradient part do not. The dichotomy is thus that points are either recurrent, or they run "downhill" towards a recurrent component (and if we can go back in time: they come from *another* recurrent component). It is thus interesting to study recurrent components as well as the connecting (heteroclinic) orbits between them. As an example, in a gradient flow the principle interest is in the (hyperbolic) equilibria and the heteroclinic orbits that connect equilibria with Morse index difference one.

1.2. Rigorous numerics. computer-assisted proofs have a relatively short history in mathematics. Nevertheless, the proof of the four color theorem [**1**, **27**] and of the densest sphere packing (Kepler problem) [**16**] belong to the classics in the field. Regarding the role of computers in dynamical systems, the start of the systematic study of nonlinear dynamical systems coincided with the advent of the computer (Feigenbaum diagram, Mandelbrot set). Although some qualitative properties were already sketched by Poincaré and contemporaries, only with the help of numerical simulations were people able to imagine and map the variety of dynamics exhibited by nonlinear systems. Ever since, computers have been a crucial instrument in the mathematical analysis of dynamical systems, providing both inspiration and a way to test (and reject) conjectures. Moreover, due to the very limited availability of tools for doing quantitative nonlinear analysis by hand, computers have been used as proof-assistants very early on. Prime examples are the proof of the universality of the Feigenbaum constant [**21**] and the existence of the (numerically "obvious") chaotic attractor in the Lorenz system [**36**].

By now there is a variety of computational frameworks that aid in the study of nonlinear dynamics. Each of these involves a combination of topological (or analytic-topological) arguments with (interval arithmetic) computations. Here we delve into the wealth of possibilities of one approach. Nevertheless, it is important to stress that there is a range of partly overlapping methodologies, each with their own strengths and relative weaknesses. To name a few (very briefly; we refer the reader to the references for examples and more details):

- Piotr Zgliczyński and collaborators have developed a method based on integrating the flow using rigorous enclosures and Taylor methods, combined with topological arguments (Conley index, covering relations) and derivative information (through so-called cone conditions) [**43**, **44**]. An extensive C++ package CAPD (computer-assisted Proofs in Dynamics) is available for supporting these proofs [**7**].
- Hans Koch, in collaboration with Gianni Arioli, has developed a general functional analytic approach to computer-assisted proofs in nonlinear analysis (e.g. [**3**, **4**]). That work has provided the crucial underlying ideas for the techniques discussed in this paper.
- In a spirit similar to the above method, techniques have been developed by Mitsuhiro Nakao, Michael Plum and collaborators for studying elliptic problems by combining a Newton-like fixed point map with computer-assisted computations with a variable mix of functional analytic and computational effort (e.g. [**6**, **25**]). This forms another stepping stone for the techniques discussed below.
- Konstantin Mischaikow and collaborators have developed a "database" approach to representing the global behavior of parameterised families of nonlinear dynamical systems [**2**, **20**]. The database encodes the minimal Morse-Conley graphs and their dependence on parameters. This framework focuses on global dynamics while working up to a finite resolution. It hence complements the local but "infinitesimal" results that form the core of the method discussed in the current paper.

The method described in this paper has been developed in the past decade by a large number of people, and we refer to [**8, 11, 12, 14, 23, 37, 39**] and the references therein for a limited sample of the contributions.

1.3. Forcing theorems. Forcing theorems in dynamical systems are statements of the form: if there exists a solution (orbit) of type A, then there must be orbits of types B, C and D. In the most interesting cases, the list of implied orbits is infinitely long. Such forcing theorems are strong tools in the study of nonlinear dynamics. The main obstacle to applying them in concrete situations is that it is usually very difficult to show that an orbit of type A exists, even if numerical simulations may be tentatively convincing. This is the perfect setting for showcasing the power of rigorous computations, as they may be used as a tool to prove the existence of a type A orbit in concrete problems.

Examples of forcing theorems are (roughly in increasing order of sophistication)

- In scalar autonomous ordinary differential equations: if there are two equilibria then there exists a heteroclinic orbit (non necessarily between these equilibria), or (in very degenerate situations) a continuum of equilibria.
- In a planar system of ODEs: a periodic orbit implies the existence of an equilibrium (located inside the orbit). This is a classical result, where the forcing is via index theory.
- Interval maps: "period 3 implies chaos" [**24**]. If there exists a periodic orbit of (minimal) period 3, then there are periodic orbits of arbitrary period (this generalizes to the Sharkovsky ordering [**31**]) and there is an invariant set on which the dynamics is chaotic (has positive entropy with respect to a suitably defined distance).
- Three dimensional systems of ODEs: a Shilnikov homoclinic orbit (to an equilibrium with a one-dimensional unstable manifold and a two dimensional 'spiral' stable manifold) implies chaos if the expansion rate of the unstable manifold is larger than the contraction rate in the stable manifold [**32**].
- In a system of ODEs with three or more degrees of freedom: the existence of a transversal homoclinic orbit to a cycle implies that there is a Smale horseshoe in the return map, hence chaos. Similarly, any hyperbolic periodic point of a discrete time dynamical system that has its stable and unstable manifolds intersecting transversally, implies chaos.
- Maps on two-dimensional manifolds: a periodic orbit whose associated braid (after suspension) is of pseudo-Anosov type implies chaotic dynamics for the map [**35**].
- Second order Lagrangian system: certain periodic orbits (to be made explicit in Section 3) imply chaos [**15**].
- In variational problems: the *Morse-Floer homology* encodes forcing relations between equilibria with certain (Morse-Floer) indices and connecting (heteroclinic) orbits between such equilibria [**29**].
- More generally for dynamical systems without a variational structure but with "sufficient compactness properties": as already mentioned, the *Conley index* encodes relations between invariant set and connecting orbits.

We note that in most of these examples a combination of topological arguments and rigorous computation leads to the strongest results.

2. The general setup

2.1. Motivation: Newton's method. If we numerically try to find a solution of $f(x) = 0$, where $f : \mathbb{R}^N \to \mathbb{R}^N$ is some nonlinear problem, then, starting from with some initial guess x_0, we may iterate the Newton scheme

$$x_{n+1} = \widetilde{T}(x_n) \stackrel{\text{def}}{=} x_n - Df(x_n)^{-1} \cdot f(x_n)$$

to obtain a sequence that hopefully approaches a zero of f quickly. Since

$$D\widetilde{T}(x)y = y - (D[Df(x)^{-1}]y) \cdot f(x) - Df(x)^{-1} \cdot Df(x) \cdot y$$

we find that $D\widetilde{T}(\hat{x})y = 0$ for any $\hat{x}$ such that $f(\hat{x}) = 0$, provided $Df(\hat{x})$ is invertible. This implies that if $Df(\hat{x})$ is invertible, then $\|D\widetilde{T}(x)\|$ is small near the fixed point $\hat{x}$, hence $\widetilde{T}$ is a contraction mapping with very strong contraction rate. If we merely want a (moderately strong) contraction mapping (e.g. because we rely on analytic arguments in addition to computer calculations), then there is thus quite a lot of room to alter the definition of the map $\widetilde{T}$ and still be successful. For example, one may try replacing $Df(x)^{-1}$ by $Df(x_0)^{-1}$ so that there is no need to recompute the inverse after every iteration.

2.2. Setup. Our approach starts by recasting the dynamic problem of interest as a zero finding problem $F(x) = 0$ in some *infinite* dimensional space. To fix ideas, let X and X' be Banach spaces, and $F : X \to X'$ be a (Fréchet) differentiable map (in practice: $F \in C^1(X, X')$ or $C^2(X, X')$). Assume that $\overline{x} \in X$ is an approximate zero of F, i.e. $\|F(\overline{x})\|_{X'} \approx 0$, and that we have a left inverse $DF(\overline{x})^{-1}$ of $DF(\overline{x})$. Then we can define the Newton-like map

$$\widehat{T}(x) = x - DF(\overline{x})^{-1}F(x).$$

If, as is explicitly assumed, $DF(\overline{x})$ is invertible, then fixed points of $\widehat{T}$ are in one-to-one correspondence with zeros of F. In this case we can attempt to show that $\widehat{T}$ is a contraction mapping in a neighborhood of $\overline{x}$. However, in practice inverting $DF(\overline{x})$ is "too difficult" in this infinite dimensional setting.

Thus we make use of an approximate inverse, typically obtained in part by computing a numerical inverse. We approximate $DF(\overline{x})$ by a (simpler) linear operator $A^\dagger : X \to X'$ and choose $A \in L(X', X)$ to be an approximate left inverse of $A^\dagger$.

In our computational framework the choice of the linear operator A is based on a computer calculation (a non-rigorous one). Namely, we choose (Galerkin) projections π_N and π'_N of X and X' onto N-dimensional subspaces X_N and X'_N, respectively, for some $N \in \mathbb{N}$. The natural embedding of X_N into X is denoted by ι. The finite dimensional truncated problem is given by

$$0 = F_N(x_N) \stackrel{\text{def}}{=} \pi'_N F(\iota x_N),$$

where $F_N : X_N \to X'_N$ and $x_N \in X_N$. We then seek a numerical approximation $\overline{x}_N$ of a solution to $F_N(x_N) = 0$, for example using a (finite dimensional) Newton iteration scheme. The idea is that $\overline{x} \stackrel{\text{def}}{=} \iota\overline{x}_N$ is an approximate solution of $F(x) = 0$.

Next we compute the Jacobian $DF_N(\overline{x}_N)$ and determine a numerical inverse $A_N \approx DF_N(\overline{x}_N)^{-1}$. We now need to "extend" the operator $A_N : X'_N \to X_N$ (or $\iota A_N : X'_N \to X$) to an *injective* operator $A : X' \to X$. How one goes about making this extension depends on the problem. It should be simple enough to allow for explicit analysis, while accurate enough to be an "approximate" left inverse of $DF(\iota \overline{x}_N)$ in a sense that will be made precise in §2.3.

Finally we are ready to define the Newton-like operator

$$T(x) \stackrel{\text{def}}{=} x - AF(x). \tag{2}$$

Observe that if A is injective, then fixed points of T correspond to zeros of F. Our goal is to show that T is a contraction map on a ball around $\overline{x}$. This ball should not be chosen too small (since then it won't contain a zero of F), but neither should it be chosen too large (since one cannot prove that T is a contraction on such larger balls (in fact it might not *be* a contraction there)).

REMARK 1. *The space X' has no significance. The only important requirement is that we choose a linear operator A such that $AF(x) \in X$ for all $x \in X$.*

REMARK 2. *To have correspondence between fixed points of T and zeros of F, we need that $AF(x) = 0$ implies $F(x) = 0$, i.e., A is injective on the range of F. In fact, one only needs that A is injective on the range of F when the domain of F is restricted to the fixed point space of T (e.g., one may have a priori knowledge about this due to symmetries).*

2.3. The theorem. The following theorem provides conditions under which we can guarantee the existence of a fixed point of T (and hence a zero of F provided A is injective).

Let X be a Banach space. Let $B_r(\overline{x})$ denote the *closed* ball of radius r around $\overline{x} \in X$.

THEOREM 3. *Let T be a Fréchet differentiable map from a Banach space X to itself, such that for all $r > 0$*

$$\|T(\overline{x}) - \overline{x}\|_X \leq Y \tag{3a}$$

$$\|DT(x)\|_{B(X)} \leq Z(r) \qquad \text{for all } x \in B_r(\overline{x}), \tag{3b}$$

for some $Y \in \mathbb{R}^+$ and some function $Z : \mathbb{R}^+ \to \mathbb{R}^+$. If there exists an $\hat{r} > 0$ such that

$$Y + \hat{r}Z(\hat{r}) < \hat{r}, \tag{4}$$

then T has a unique fixed point in $B_{\hat{r}}(\overline{x})$.

The proof of the theorem is given in §2.5. We note that this is an abstract theorem in the sense that does not immediately reveal the context of §2.2. However, one should keep in mind that the bounds Y and $Z(r)$ will be given by complicated but explicit formulas that depend on numerically obtained values, see §4 for a detailed example. Indeed, both A (which appears in the definition (2) of T) and $\overline{x}$ are determined (largely) numerically. The inequality (4) is then checked with the help of a computer by using interval arithmetic. In practice Z usually depends polynomially on r. We then denote the so-called *radii polynomial* by

$$p(r) \stackrel{\text{def}}{=} Y + r[Z(r) - 1],$$

and we look for an $\hat{r} > 0$ such that $p(\hat{r}) < 0$. We note that we keep r as a variable parameter at the cost of having to work with a functional form for $Z = Z(r)$, which requires careful bookkeeping. The advantage is that we have more flexibility, not just enhancing the chance of proving that a fixed point of T exists, but also allowing better bounds both on the location of the fixed point (by determining the smallest $\hat{r}$ for which $p(\hat{r})$ is negative) and on the uniqueness range (by determining the largest $\hat{r}$ for which $p(\hat{r})$ is negative).

One may interpret (3a) as an estimate of the residue (but observe that the residue is "preconditioned" with the linear operator A), while (3b) represents both a bound on how well A approximates $DF(\overline{x})^{-1}$ and an estimate of how nonlinear the problem is.

On the one hand, one may view Theorem 3 as a mathematically rigorous form of an explicit a-posteriori error analysis. On the other hand, it represents the widely used approach in analysis of setting up a fixed point problem on some ball around a guess for the solution, using a "suitable choice" of a linear operator (denoted by A in our case). In our context, the formulation is adjusted to a situation where both the (center of the) ball and the linear operator depend heavily on numerically obtained values.

Since the theorem gives uniqueness, it is clear that one can only attack problems that are formulated in such a way that they have isolated solutions (e.g. one needs to quotient out any continuous symmetries). Moreover, since the solution is obtained from a contraction argument (see §2.5), the solution is stable under small perturbations of the problem $F(x) = 0$, hence only robust solutions can be found, and only problems with robust solutions can be analyzed. Often this requirement can be achieved by carefully reformulating the problem, after understanding the sources of non-uniqueness and/or non-robustness. This robustness feature should also be viewed as an advantage, since if one finds a solution then it is automatically "in general position" (e.g. hyperbolic or transversal), a property that is often required when using it as an ingredient in a larger mathematical context, such as in forcing theorems. Moreover, the setup is perfect for performing continuation in parameters, which is of crucial importance in most applications of nonlinear dynamical systems.

2.4. Alternative formulations. Since $T(x) = x - AF(x)$, the conditions (3a) and (3b) may be reformulated in terms of F. Furthermore, in practice the estimate on DF is split into three components with the help of an operator $A^\dagger$ that approximates $DF(\overline{x})$. The conditions (3) are then replaced by

$$\|AF(\overline{x})\|_X \leq Y \tag{5a}$$

$$\|I - AA^\dagger\|_{B(X)} \leq Z^0 \tag{5b}$$

$$\|A[A^\dagger - DF(\overline{x})]\|_{B(X)} \leq Z^1 \tag{5c}$$

$$\|A[DF(x) - DF(\overline{x})]\|_{B(X)} \leq Z^2(r) \qquad \text{for all } x \in B_r(\overline{x}), \tag{5d}$$

for some Y, Z^0, $Z^1 \in \mathbb{R}^+$ and $Z^2 : \mathbb{R}^+ \to \mathbb{R}^+$, and one sets $Z(r) = Z^0 + Z^1 + Z^2(r)$. The final estimate (5d) is often replaced by a Lipschitz bound

$$\|A[DF(x) - DF(x')]\|_{B(X)} \leq \widehat{Z}^2 \|x - x'\|_X \qquad \text{for all } x, x' \in B_{r^*}(\overline{x}),$$

where $r^* > 0$ is some a priori bound on the radius, and $Z^2(r) = \widehat{Z}^2 r$. The Lipschitz bound may, in turn, be supplanted by a bound on the second derivative:

$$\|AD^2F(x)[v,w]\|_X \leq \widehat{Z}^2 \qquad \text{for all } v, w \in B_1(\overline{x}) \text{ and all } x \in B_{r^*}(\overline{x}).$$

In both cases one needs an a posteriori check that the radius $\hat{r}$ for which $p(\hat{r}) < 0$ also satisfies $\hat{r} \leq r^*$. In this notation the radii polynomial is written as

$$p(r) = Y + r[Z^0 + Z^1 - 1] + r^2 \widehat{Z}^2 \qquad \text{for } r \in [0, r^*].$$

When we find a radius $\hat{r} \leq r^*$ such that $p(\hat{r}) < 0$, and if we know that A is injective, then we conclude that F has a unique zero in $B_{\hat{r}}(\overline{x})$. As mentioned before, the smallest such $\hat{r}$ gives the best bound on where the solution is, whereas the biggest such $\hat{r}$ gives the strongest uniqueness result.

2.5. The proof of Theorem 3. The goal is to show that T is a uniform contraction on $B_{\hat{r}}(\overline{x})$. First, we check that $B_{\hat{r}}(\overline{x})$ gets mapped into itself. Let $x \in B_{\hat{r}}(\overline{x})$ and apply the Mean Value Theorem for Banach spaces to obtain

$$\begin{aligned}\|T(x) - \overline{x}\|_X &\leq \|T(x) - T(\overline{x})\|_X + \|T(\overline{x}) - \overline{x}\|_X \\ &\leq \sup_{x' \in B_{\hat{r}}(\overline{x})} \|DT(x')\|_{B(X)} \|x - \overline{x}\|_X + Y \\ &\leq Z(\hat{r})\hat{r} + Y.\end{aligned}$$

Since $Z(\hat{r})\hat{r} + Y < \hat{r}$ by assumption, it follows that that T maps $B_{\hat{r}}(\overline{x})$ into itself. Second, to see that T is a contraction on $B_{\hat{r}}(\overline{x})$, let $x_1, x_2 \in B_{\hat{r}}(\overline{x})$ be arbitrary, and use the estimate (again applying the Mean Value Theorem)

$$\|T(x_1) - T(x_2)\|_X \leq \sup_{x' \in B_{\hat{r}}(\overline{x})} \|DT(x')\|_{B(X)} \|x_1 - x_2\|_X \leq Z(\hat{r}) \|x_1 - x_2\|_X. \tag{6}$$

It follows readily from $Y + Z(\hat{r})\hat{r} < \hat{r}$ with $Y \geq 0$ that the contraction rate $Z(\hat{r})$ in (6) is less than unity. Applying the Banach contraction mapping theorem finishes the proof.

3. Example of a rigorous computation that forces chaos

To illustrate how one can apply the general setup from §2, we consider as our key example a problem from pattern formation. The following description (in §3) is a condensed version of the main result in the paper "Chaotic braided solutions via rigorous numerics: chaos in the Swift-Hohenberg equation" by Jan Bouwe van den Berg and Jean-Philippe Lessard [**40**].

We first sketch the context. The *Swift-Hohenberg* equation [**10**, **34**] is the fourth order parabolic partial differential equation (PDE)

$$\frac{\partial U}{\partial T} = -\left(\frac{\partial^2}{\partial X^2} + 1\right)^2 U + \alpha U - U^3. \tag{7}$$

It is a model equation for pattern formation due to a finite wavelength instability (e.g. in Rayleigh-Bénard convection). The onset of instability is at parameter value $\alpha = 0$. Time-independent solutions to the PDE (7) satisfy the *ODE*

$$-U'''' - 2U'' + (\alpha - 1)U - U^3 = 0. \tag{8}$$

The latter has a conserved quantity, the *energy*:

$$E = U'''U' - \frac{1}{2}U''^2 + U'^2 - \frac{\alpha - 1}{2}U^2 + \frac{1}{4}U^4 + \frac{(\alpha - 1)^2}{4}.$$

For $\alpha > 1$, the energy level $E = 0$ contains two constant solutions $U = \pm\sqrt{\alpha - 1}$. For $\alpha > \frac{3}{2}$, these are stable equilibria of the PDE (7) and saddle-foci for the ODE (8). It is well known that saddle-foci can act as organizing centers for complicated dynamics [**13**, **19**]. By combining a topological forcing result with rigorous numerics (to obtain the "seed" of the forcing), we can indeed establish chaos for a large range of parameter values, as explained below.

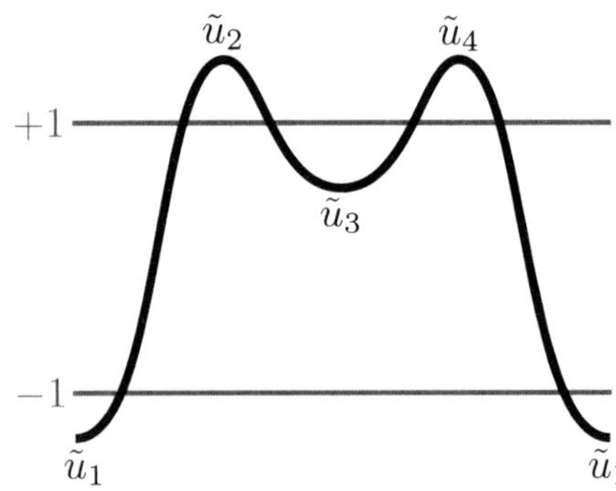

FIGURE 1. Sketch of a periodic profile $\tilde{u}$ satisfying the geometric properties $\mathcal{H}$.

PROPOSITION 4 (Proposition 1 in [**40**]). *The dynamics of the Swift-Hohenberg ODE* (8) *on the energy level $E = 0$ is chaotic for all $\alpha \geq 2$.*

We first perform a change of coordinates that compactifies the parameter range:

$$y = \frac{X}{\sqrt[4]{\alpha - 1}}, \qquad u(y) = \frac{U(X)}{\sqrt{\alpha - 1}}, \qquad \xi = \frac{2}{\sqrt{\alpha - 1}}. \tag{9}$$

The parameter range $\alpha \geq 2$ in Proposition 4 corresponds to $\xi \in (0, 2]$. The differential equation now becomes

$$-u'''' - \xi u'' + u - u^3 = 0, \tag{10}$$

with energy

$$E = u'''u' - \frac{1}{2}u''^2 + \frac{\xi}{2}u'^2 + \frac{1}{4}(u^2 - 1)^2. \tag{11}$$

Proposition 4 is proved by showing that chaos is forced by a *single* periodic solution $\tilde{u}$ with the following geometric properties (see also Figure 1):

$$\mathcal{H} \begin{cases} (H_1)\ \tilde{u} \text{ has exactly four monotone laps and extrema } \{\tilde{u}_i\}_{i=1}^4; \\ (H_2)\ \tilde{u}_1 \text{ and } \tilde{u}_3 \text{ are minima, and } \tilde{u}_2 \text{ and } \tilde{u}_4 \text{ are maxima;} \\ (H_3)\ \tilde{u}_1 < -1 < \tilde{u}_3 < 1 < \tilde{u}_2, \tilde{u}_4; \\ (H_4)\ \tilde{u} \text{ is symmetric in its minima } \tilde{u}_1 \text{ and } \tilde{u}_3. \end{cases}$$

The forcing theorem is formulated below.

THEOREM 5 (forcing; Theorem 2 in [**40**]). *Let $\xi \in [0, \sqrt{8})$, and suppose there exists a periodic solution $\tilde{u}$ of* (10) *at the energy level $E = 0$, satisfying the geometric conditions $\mathcal{H}$. Then* (10) *is chaotic on the energy level $E = 0$ in the sense that there exists a two-dimensional Poincaré return map which has a compact invariant set on which the topological entropy is positive.*

The set of solutions of (10) that implies chaotic dynamics is obtained by combining the three building blocks in Figure 2 in any order that obeys intuitive geometric restrictions. The final technical step is then to establish a semi-conjugacy to a subshift of finite type, see [**40**, §2].

The solutions to the ODE (10) thus constructed from the three building blocks, correspond to stationary profiles of the PDE (7). It turns out that all these profiles are *stable* under the evolution of the PDE, illustrating the pattern forming tendencies of the Swift-Hohenberg model.

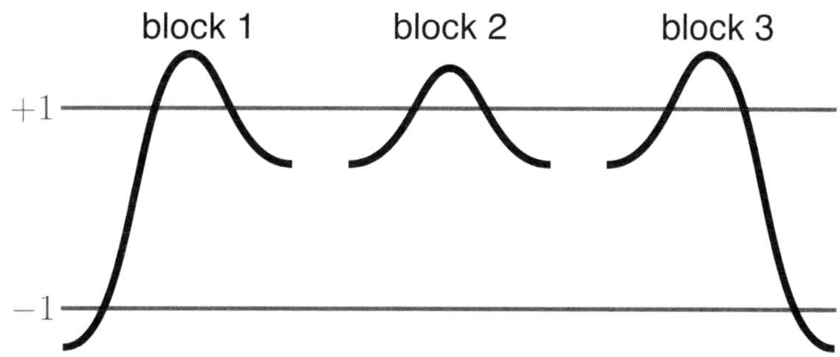

FIGURE 2. The shape of the building blocks that lead to positive entropy in Theorem 5. It should be intuitive that block 3 can be followed by block 1 only, while blocks 1 and 2 can be followed by either block 2 or block 3.

Since Theorem 5 is a forcing theorem, to establish chaos we only need to find, in our case via rigorous numerics, a *single* periodic solution $\tilde{u}$ satisfying $\mathcal{H}$.

THEOREM 6 (rigorous computation; Theorem 3 in [**40**]). *For every* $\xi \in [0,2]$ *the ODE* (10) *has a periodic solution* $\tilde{u}$ *at energy level* $E = 0$ *satisfying the geometric properties* $\mathcal{H}$.

The change of variables (9) directly converts Theorems 5 and 6 into Proposition 4.

In this paper we present a new, streamlined proof of Theorem 6. In particular, we will discuss all details of how to prove that for *fixed* parameter value ξ equation (10) has a periodic solution at energy level $E = 0$, see §4. Since the method provides a *quantitative* description of the solution with a small *explicit* error bound, it is relatively easy to check the geometric properties $\mathcal{H}$. In §4.7 we briefly discuss this issue, and we refer to [**40**, §4] for more details.

One can also prove the result for a *continuous* range of ξ-values. Indeed, in §4.7 we explain how one may use interval arithmetic computations to perform "brute force" continuation (by extending from single parameter values to small intervals of parameter values). Again we refer to [**40**] for more details. Moreover, a discussion of proper continuation techniques can be found elsewhere in this volume [**22**, **42**], as well as in [**5**, **41**].

Finally, we will not discuss the proof of the forcing Theorem 5 as it requires methods that are disjoint from the aims of the current paper; we refer the interested reader to [**40**, §2].

4. The computational proof

We will first convert the problem of finding a periodic solution to Fourier space (§4.1). Then we introduce a convenient norm on the space Fourier coefficients. The brief description in §4.2 is similar to the one in [**18**]. It diverges from [**40**] for the purpose of simplifying the exposition. The full problem consists of the ODE (10) and the energy constraint $E = 0$, with the Fourier coefficients and the frequency as variables. In §4.3 we reformulate this as a fixed point problem of the type (2), although viewed from a non-standard perspective, namely situated in a product space (of Fourier coefficients and frequency). In particular, we define finite dimensional projections and the linear operator A. The two radii polynomials for the problem are defined in §4.4. The formulation and proof of Theorem 11, which is a variation on Theorem 3 adapted to the product space setting (with two radii polynomials depending on two radii), are novel. Theorem 12 explains that injectivity of the linear operator A is automatic if one finds a pair of radii for which both radii polynomials are negative. Explicit expressions for the necessary bounds Y and Z are derived in §4.5 and §4.6, respectively. Finally, the Matlab code that clinches the proof is discussed in §4.7.

4.1. Fourier transform. We are going to restrict our attention to symmetric periodic solutions u satisfying $\mathcal{H}$, hence we expand u as a cosine series:

$$u(y) = a_0 + 2\sum_{m=1}^{\infty} a_m \cos(mqy), \tag{12}$$

with $q > 0$ an *a priori unknown* variable ($\frac{2\pi}{q}$ is the period) and $a_m \in \mathbb{R}$ for $m \geq 0$. One may also think of this as

$$u(y) = \sum_{m\in\mathbb{Z}} a_{|m|} e^{imqy}, \tag{13}$$

i.e., the Fourier transform with symmetry constraint $a_{-m} = a_m$.

Since $u'(0) = 0$, and since the energy (11) is a conserved quantity along the orbits of (10), we get that

$$\begin{aligned} E &= u'''(0)u'(0) - \frac{1}{2}u''(0)^2 + \frac{\xi}{2}u'(0)^2 + \frac{1}{4}(u(0)^2-1)^2 \\ &= -\frac{1}{2}\left[u''(0) - \frac{1}{\sqrt{2}}\left(u(0)^2-1\right)\right]\left[u''(0) + \frac{1}{\sqrt{2}}\left(u(0)^2-1\right)\right]. \end{aligned}$$

We look for u such that $E = 0$, $u(0) < -1$ and $u''(0) > 0$, hence the energy condition boils down to

$$u''(0) - \frac{1}{\sqrt{2}}[u(0)^2 - 1] = 0. \tag{14}$$

Substituting the expansion (12) for $u(y)$ in (14), we obtain

$$f_q(q,a) \stackrel{\text{def}}{=} -2q^2 \sum_{m=1}^{\infty} m^2 a_m - \frac{1}{\sqrt{2}}\left[a_0 + 2\sum_{m=1}^{\infty} a_m\right]^2 + \frac{1}{\sqrt{2}} = 0. \tag{15}$$

In Fourier space the ODE (10) converts into an infinite sequence of algebraic equations:

$$(f_a)_k(q,a) \stackrel{\text{def}}{=} -\lambda_k(q)a_k - \sum_{\substack{k_1+k_2+k_3=k \\ k_i\in\mathbb{Z}}} a_{|k_1|}a_{|k_2|}a_{|k_3|} = 0 \qquad \text{for all } k \geq 0, \tag{16}$$

where

$$\lambda_k(q) \stackrel{\text{def}}{=} k^4q^4 - \xi k^2q^2 - 1 = (k^2q^2 - \xi/2)^2 - (1+\xi^2/4).$$

Equations (15) and (16) together constitute $F = (f_q, f_a)$.

4.2. The norm on the space of Fourier coefficients. Since the differential equation is analytic, the solution is going to be analytic as well and the coefficients will decay geometrically. This motivates us to work with the norm

$$\|a\|_{\ell^1_\nu} \stackrel{\text{def}}{=} \sum_{k=0}^{\infty} |a_k|\, \omega_k(\nu),$$

where the exponential weights are

$$\omega_k(\nu) = \omega_k \stackrel{\text{def}}{=} \begin{cases} 1 & k = 0 \\ 2\nu^k & k \geq 1, \end{cases} \tag{17}$$

for some $\nu > 1$ to be chosen when doing the final computer-assisted step of the proof (we suppress the dependence on ν in the notation for ω_k). The factor 2 in (17) is related to our choice of cosine series; it facilitates the simple expression for the estimate (18) below. We denote the corresponding Banach space by ℓ^1_ν. In view of (13), this norm may also be written as

$$\|a\|_{\ell^1_\nu} = \sum_{k\in\mathbb{Z}} |a_{|k|}|\, \nu^{|k|}.$$

We endow the one-sided ℓ^1_ν with the following discrete convolution product: given $a, b \in \ell^1_\nu$ the convolution product $a * b \in \ell^1_\nu$ has components

$$(a * b)_k \stackrel{\text{def}}{=} \sum_{k'\in\mathbb{Z}} a_{|k'|} b_{|k-k'|}.$$

This product satisfies the Banach algebra property

$$\|a * b\|_{\ell^1_\nu} \leq \|a\|_{\ell^1_\nu} \|b\|_{\ell^1_\nu}, \tag{18}$$

as can be checked directly (applying the triangle inequality):

$$\begin{aligned} \|a * b\|_{\ell^1_\nu} &= \sum_{k\in\mathbb{Z}} |(a * b)_{|k|}| \nu^{|k|} = \sum_{k,k'\in\mathbb{Z}} |a_{|k'|}||b_{|k-k'|}| \nu^{|k|} \\ &\leq \sum_{k,k-k'\in\mathbb{Z}} |a_{|k'|}| \nu^{|k'|} |b_{|k-k'|}| \nu^{|k-k'|} = \|a\|_{\ell^1_\nu} \|b\|_{\ell^1_\nu}. \end{aligned}$$

In this notation the expression for $(f_a)_k$ in (16) reduces to

$$(f_a)_k = -\lambda_k(q) - (a * a * a)_k.$$

The dual of ℓ^1_ν is $(\ell^1_\nu)^* \cong \ell^\infty_{\nu^{-1}} = \{(b_m)_{m=0}^\infty : \sup_{m\in\mathbb{N}} |b_m \omega_m^{-1}| < \infty\}$. Namely, for $b \in (\ell^1_\nu)^*$ we may use linearity to write

$$b(a) = \sum_{m\in\mathbb{N}} b(\delta^m) a_m,$$

where δ is the usual Knonecker delta:

$$\delta^m_k \stackrel{\text{def}}{=} \begin{cases} 1 & k = m \\ 0 & k \neq m. \end{cases}$$

Hence, writing $b_m \stackrel{\text{def}}{=} b(\delta^m)$ we obtain

$$|b(a)| = \left| \sum_{m=0}^{\infty} b_m a_m \right| = \left| \sum_{m=0}^{\infty} (b_m \omega_m^{-1})(a_m \omega_m) \right| \leq \sup_{m\in\mathbb{N}} |b_m \omega_m^{-1}| \sum_{m\in\mathbb{N}} |a_m| \omega_m.$$

We will identify $(\ell^1_\nu)^*$ with $l^\infty_{\nu^{-1}}$ and use

$$\|b\|_{(\ell^1_\nu)^*} \stackrel{\text{def}}{=} \sup_{m\in\mathbb{N}} |b(\delta^m)|\omega_m^{-1} = \sup_{m\in\mathbb{N}} |b_m|\omega_m^{-1}$$

REMARK 7. *If $G \in B(\ell^1_\nu, \ell^1_\nu)$, then by linearity*

$$\begin{aligned}\|G(a)\|_{\ell^1_\nu} &= \sum_{k\in\mathbb{N}} |G(a)_k|\omega_k = \sum_{k,m\in\mathbb{N}} |G(\delta^m)_k a_m|\omega_k \\ &\leq \sum_{m\in\mathbb{N}} |a_m|\omega_m \sup_{m\in\mathbb{N}}\Big(\omega_m^{-1}\sum_{k\in\mathbb{N}}|G(\delta^m)_k|\omega_k\Big) = \|a\|_{\ell^1_\nu} \sup_{m\in\mathbb{N}} \omega_m^{-1}\|G(\delta^m)\|_{\ell^1_\nu}.\end{aligned}$$

Hence, writing $G_{km} \stackrel{\text{def}}{=} G(\delta^m)_k$, we obtain the explicit expression

$$\|G\|_{B(\ell^1_\nu,\ell^1_\nu)} = \sup_{m\in\mathbb{N}} \omega_m^{-1} \sum_{k\in\mathbb{N}} |G_{km}|\,\omega_k.$$

4.3. The product space. Since our unknowns are $x = (q, a)$, we use the product space $X = \mathbb{R} \times \ell^1_\nu$. We will use projections π_q and π_a onto $\mathbb{R}$ and ℓ^1_ν, respectively. The trivial embedding of $\mathbb{R}$ and ℓ^1_ν into X are both denoted by ι, since this will never cause confusion.

We fix a computational parameter $N \in \mathbb{N}$ (to be chosen when we do the final computer-assisted step of the proof, see §4.7). Given $x = (q, a) \in X$, we define the finite dimensional projection $\pi_N x = (q, a_0, \ldots, a_N) \in X_N \cong \mathbb{R} \times \mathbb{R}^{N+1} \cong \mathbb{R}^{N+2}$. We slightly abuse notation to write π_q and π_a for the projections from X_N onto $\mathbb{R}$ and $\mathbb{R}^{N+1}$, respectively: $\pi_q x_N = q$ and $\pi_a x_N = (a_k)_{k=0}^N$. The embedding of X_N into X by extending with zeros is again denoted by ι:

$$\pi_N \iota x_N = x_N \qquad \text{and} \qquad (\pi_a \iota x_N)_k = 0 \quad \text{for } k > N.$$

The truncated system, or Galerkin projection, is given by

$$F_N : X_N \to X_N, \qquad F_N(x_N) = \pi_N F(\iota x_N).$$

We solve $F_N = 0$ numerically (using a good initial guess and Newton's iteration method) to obtain an approximate zero $\overline{x}_N = (\overline{q}, \overline{a}_0, \ldots, \overline{a}_N)$ of F_N, and a corresponding approximate zero $\overline{x} = \iota\overline{x}_N$ of F. The Jacobian matrix

$$A_N^\dagger \stackrel{\text{def}}{=} DF_N(\overline{x}_N)$$

is inverted *numerically* to obtain

$$A_N \approx (A_N^\dagger)^{-1}.$$

Based on our expectation that the linear part in (16) will dominate for large k, the linear operators $A^\dagger$ and A are then built up as follows:

$$\text{(19a)} \quad \pi_N(A^\dagger x) = A_N^\dagger \pi_N x \quad \text{and} \quad (\pi_a(A^\dagger x))_k = -\lambda_k(\overline{q})(\pi_a x)_k \quad \text{for } k > N$$

$$\text{(19b)} \quad \pi_N(Ax) = A_N \pi_N x \quad \text{and} \quad (\pi_a(Ax))_k = -\lambda_k(\overline{q})^{-1}(\pi_a x)_k \quad \text{for } k > N.$$

The shape of the operator A (and $A^\dagger$) as an "infinite matrix" is illustrated in Figure 3. We are now ready to define

$$T(x) \stackrel{\text{def}}{=} x - AF(x).$$

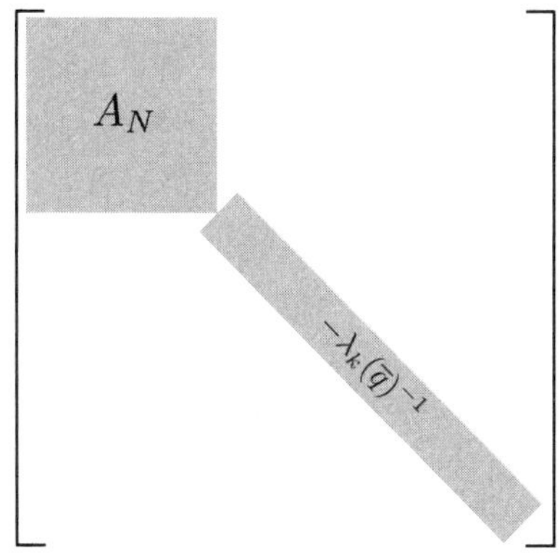

FIGURE 3. The shape of the linear operator A interpreted as an infinite matrix. The finite matrix A_N has size $(N+2) \times (N+2)$. The shape of $A^\dagger$ is identical (but of course with different values for the nonzero entries).

REMARK 8. *Let Γ be a linear operator on X, then it can be decomposed into*

$$\Gamma = \begin{bmatrix} \Gamma_{qq} & \Gamma_{qa} \\ \Gamma_{aq} & \Gamma_{aa} \end{bmatrix}$$

with $\Gamma_{qq} \in \mathbb{R}$, $\Gamma_{qa} \in (\ell^1_\nu)^*$, $\Gamma_{aq} \in \ell^1_\nu$ and $\Gamma_{aa} \in B(\ell^1_\nu, \ell^1_\nu)$. Formally:

$$\begin{aligned} \pi_q \Gamma x &= \Gamma_{qq}\pi_q x + \Gamma_{qa}\pi_a x \\ \pi_a \Gamma x &= \Gamma_{aq}\pi_q x + \Gamma_{aa}\pi_a x. \end{aligned}$$

We will use the same notation for bounded linear operators on X_N.

REMARK 9. *Moreover, suppose $\Gamma \in L(X, X)$ is of the form*

$$\pi_N \Gamma x = \Gamma_N \pi_N x \qquad \text{and} \qquad (\pi_a \Gamma x)_k = \gamma_k x_k \quad \text{for } k > N,$$

with $\sup_{k>N} |\gamma_k| = \hat{\gamma} < \infty$ given. Then $(\Gamma_{qa})_k$ and $(\Gamma_{aq})_k$ vanish for $k > N$, hence their norms are computable, and

$$\|\Gamma_{aa}\|_{B(\ell^1_\nu, \ell^1_\nu)} = \max\left\{\hat{\gamma},\ \max_{0\le m\le N} \frac{1}{\omega_m} \sum_{k=0}^{N} |(\Gamma_{aa})_{km}|\omega_k\right\}$$

is also computable.

REMARK 10. *We choose the truncation dimension $N \geq \widehat{N}(\overline{q}, \xi)$, where*

$$\widehat{N}(\overline{q}, \xi) \stackrel{\text{def}}{=} \frac{((1+\xi^2/4)^{1/2} + \xi/2)^{1/2}}{\overline{q}},$$

so that

$$0 < \lambda_{N+1}(\overline{q}) \leq \lambda_k(\overline{q}) \quad \text{for all } k \geq N+1. \tag{20}$$

This ensures both that the factor $\lambda_k(\overline{q})^{-1}$ in (19b) is well-defined for all $k > N$, and that A is of the form discussed in Remark 9 with $\hat{\gamma} = \lambda_{N+1}(\overline{q})^{-1}$.

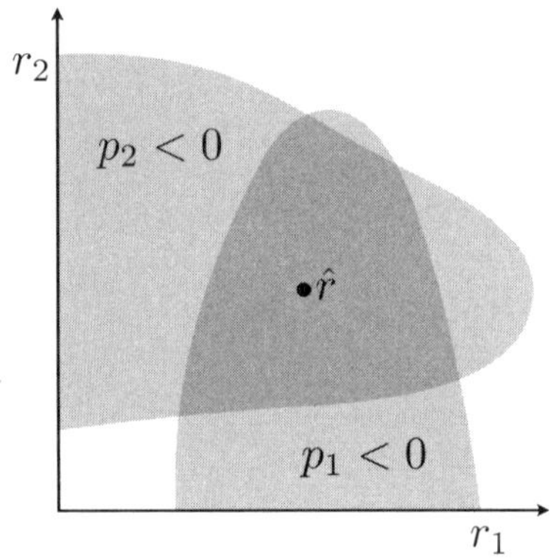

FIGURE 4. An illustration of a nonempty intersection of $\{p_1(r_1, r_2) < 0\}$ and $\{p_2(r_1, r_2) < 0\}$. Note that p_1 is monotone in r_2, while p_2 is monotone in r_1. Hence the set $\{p_1 = 0\}$ is a graph over r_1, while the set $\{p_2 = 0\}$ is a graph over r_2.

4.4. The radii polynomials. Since we (decide to) work on a product space, we are going to deviate from the setup in §2.3 and [**40**]. For $r = (r_1, r_2)$ with $r_1, r_2 > 0$ we define the *rectangle*

$$\mathcal{B}_r = \mathcal{B}_r(\overline{x}) = \{x \in X : |\pi_q(x - \overline{x})| \leq r_1, \|\pi_a(x - \overline{x})\|_{\ell^1_\nu} \leq r_2\}.$$

We will establish bounds (with D_q and D_a denoting partial derivatives)

$$|\pi_q[T(\overline{x}) - \overline{x}]| \leq Y_1 \tag{21a}$$

$$\|\pi_a[T(\overline{x}) - \overline{x}]\|_{\ell^1_\nu} \leq Y_2 \tag{21b}$$

$$\|D_q \pi_q T(x)\|_{B(\mathbb{R},\mathbb{R})} \leq Z_{11}(r) \qquad \text{for all } x \in \mathcal{B}_r, \tag{21c}$$

$$\|D_a \pi_q T(x)\|_{B(\ell^1_\nu,\mathbb{R})} \leq Z_{12}(r) \qquad \text{for all } x \in \mathcal{B}_r, \tag{21d}$$

$$\|D_q \pi_a T(x)\|_{B(\mathbb{R},\ell^1_\nu)} \leq Z_{21}(r) \qquad \text{for all } x \in \mathcal{B}_r, \tag{21e}$$

$$\|D_a \pi_a T(x)\|_{B(\ell^1_\nu,\ell^1_\nu)} \leq Z_{22}(r) \qquad \text{for all } x \in \mathcal{B}_r, \tag{21f}$$

for some Y_1, $Y_2 \in \mathbb{R}^+$ and $Z_{ij} : \mathbb{R}^+ \to \mathbb{R}^+$ for $i, j \in \{1, 2\}$. Clearly in (21c)-(21e) one should read $B(\mathbb{R}, \mathbb{R}) = \mathbb{R}$, $B(\ell^1_\nu, \mathbb{R}) = (\ell^1_\nu)^*$ and $B(\mathbb{R}, \ell^1_\nu) = \ell^1_\nu$. Then the *two radii polynomials* for our problem are

$$p_1(r_1, r_2) = Y_1 + r_1[Z_{11}(r_1, r_2) - 1] + r_2 Z_{12}(r_1, r_2) \tag{22a}$$

$$p_2(r_1, r_2) = Y_2 + r_1 Z_{21}(r_1, r_2) + r_2[Z_{22}(r_1, r_2) - 1]. \tag{22b}$$

We need to find an $\hat{r} = (\hat{r}_1, \hat{r}_2) > 0$ such that $p(\hat{r}) < 0$ component-wise, i.e.,

$$p_1(\hat{r}_1, \hat{r}_2) < 0 \qquad \text{and} \qquad p_2(\hat{r}_1, \hat{r}_2) < 0. \tag{23}$$

The geometry of these sublevel sets is illustrated in Figure 4.

THEOREM 11. *Assume that Y_i and Z_{ij} satisfy the bounds* (21) *for $i, j \in \{1, 2\}$. Let p_1 and p_2 be the radii polynomials defined in* (22). *If $\hat{r}_1, \hat{r}_2 > 0$ are such that the inequalities* (23) *are satisfied, then T has a unique fixed point in $\mathcal{B}_{\hat{r}}(\overline{x})$.*

PROOF. To show that T maps $\mathcal{B}_{\hat{r}}(\overline{x})$ into itself, we use arguments similar to the ones in §2.5. To simplify notation, define the projected balls

$$B^q \stackrel{\text{def}}{=} \{q \in \mathbb{R} : |q - \overline{q}| \leq \hat{r}_1\} \qquad \text{and} \qquad B^a \stackrel{\text{def}}{=} \{a \in \ell^1_\nu : \|a - \overline{a}\|_{\ell^1_\nu} \leq \hat{r}_2\},$$

so that $\mathcal{B}_{\hat{r}}(\overline{x}) = B^q \times B^a$. Let $x = (q,a) \in \mathcal{B}_{\hat{r}}(\overline{q},\overline{a})$. Then, by applying the triangle inequality and the intermediate value theorem, we obtain

$$\begin{aligned}\left|\pi_q T(q,a) - \overline{q}\right| &\leq \left|\pi_q[T(q,a) - T(q,\overline{a})]\right| \\ &\qquad + \left|\pi_q[T(q,\overline{a}) - T(\overline{q},\overline{a})]\right| + \left|\pi_q T(\overline{q},\overline{a}) - \overline{q}\right| \\ &\leq \sup_{a'\in B^a} \|D_a \pi_q T(q,a')\|_{(\ell^1_\nu)^*} \|a' - \overline{a}\|_{\ell^1_\nu} \\ &\qquad + \sup_{q'\in B^q} |D_q \pi_q T(q',\overline{a})|\,|q' - q| + Y_1 \\ &\leq Z_{12}(\hat{r})\hat{r}_2 + Z_{11}(\hat{r})\hat{r}_1 + Y_1.\end{aligned}$$

Since $p_1(\hat{r}) < 0$ by assumption, it follows that $|\pi_q T(q,a) - \overline{q}| < \hat{r}_1$. By an analogous argument, $\|\pi_a T(q,a) - \overline{a}\|_{\ell^1_\nu} < \hat{r}_2$. Hence T maps $\mathcal{B}_{\hat{r}}(\overline{x})$ into itself.

To show that T is a contraction mapping on $\mathcal{B}_{\hat{r}}(\overline{x})$ we need to choose a norm on the product space $X = \mathbb{R} \times \ell^1_\nu$. It turns out that T contracts with respect to the *weighted norm*

$$\|(q,a)\|_X \stackrel{\text{def}}{=} \max\{|q|/\hat{r}_1, \|a\|_{\ell^1_\nu}/\hat{r}_2\}. \tag{24}$$

Indeed, let $x_1, x_2 \in B_{\hat{r}}(\overline{x})$, then, by applying the mean value theorem and the triangle inequality,

$$\begin{aligned}|\pi_q[T(x_1) - T(x_2)]| &\leq \sup_{x'\in B_{\hat{r}}(\overline{x})} |D_q \pi_q T(x')|\,|\pi_q(x_1 - x_2)| \\ &\qquad + \sup_{x'\in B_{\hat{r}}(\overline{x})} \|D_a \pi_q T(x')\|_{(\ell^1_\nu)^*} \|\pi_a(x_1 - x_2)\|_{\ell^1_\nu} \\ &\leq [Z_{11}(\hat{r})\hat{r}_1 + Z_{12}(\hat{r})\hat{r}_2]\,\|x_1 - x_2\|_X,\end{aligned}$$

and analogously

$$\|\pi_a[T(x_1) - T(x_2)]\|_{\ell^1_\nu} < [Z_{21}(\hat{r})\hat{r}_1 + Z_{22}(\hat{r})\hat{r}_2]\,\|x_1 - x_2\|_X.$$

From the above estimates we conclude that

$$\|T(x_1) - T(x_2)\|_X \leq \max\big\{Z_{11}(\hat{r}) + Z_{12}(\hat{r})\hat{r}_2/\hat{r}_1, Z_{21}(\hat{r})\hat{r}_1/\hat{r}_2 + Z_{22}(\hat{r})\big\}\|x_1 - x_2\|_X. \tag{25}$$

It follows from the negativity of both radii polynomials (22) that the contraction rate

$$\max\big\{Z_{11}(\hat{r}) + Z_{12}(\hat{r})\hat{r}_2/\hat{r}_1, Z_{21}(\hat{r})\hat{r}_1/\hat{r}_2 + Z_{22}(\hat{r})\big\} \tag{26}$$

is less than unity. □

THEOREM 12. *Suppose the assumptions of Theorem* 11 *are met. Then the unique fixed point* $\hat{x} = (\hat{q},\hat{a})$ *obtained in Theorem* 11 *corresponds to a zero of* F, *hence* $\hat{a}$ *corresponds, via* (12), *to a* $2\pi/\hat{q}$*-periodic solution of* (10) *with energy* $E = 0$.

PROOF. The only thing left is to prove is injectivity of A, which is *automatic* from the negativity of the radii polynomials. Indeed, since $\lambda_k(\overline{q}) \neq 0$ for $k > N$ by (20), injectivity of A is equivalent to injectivity of A_N. The latter could be checked numerically, but that is not needed, since by the arguments in the proof of Theorem 11, negativity of the radii polynomials for $r = \hat{r}$ implies that $\|(I - ADF(\overline{x}))v\|_X < \|v\|_X$ for all $v \in X$, where the norm on X is given by (24). Namely, it follows from (25) that the operator norm $\|I - ADF(\overline{x})\|_{B(X,X)}$ is bounded by the expression (26), which is less than unity. Specializing to $v = \iota v_N$ one finds, for the induced finite dimensional norm $\|x_N\|_{X_N} = \|\iota x_N\|_X$, that $\|(I_N - A_N A_N^\dagger)v_N\|_{X_N} < \|v_N\|_{X_N}$ for all $v_N \in X_N$. This implies that A_N is invertible, hence A is injective. □

4.5. The estimates Y. Recalling (21a) and (21b), in this section we establish the bounds

$$|\pi_q AF(\overline{x})| \leq Y_1,$$
$$\|\pi_q AF(\overline{x})\|_{\ell^1_\nu} \leq Y_2.$$

We have

$$f_q(\overline{x}) = -2\overline{q}^2 \sum_{m=1}^{N} m^2 \overline{a}_m - \frac{1}{\sqrt{2}}\left[\overline{a}_0 + 2\sum_{m=1}^{N} \overline{a}_m\right]^2 + \frac{1}{\sqrt{2}} = 0,$$

$$(f_a)_k(\overline{x}) = \begin{cases} -\lambda_k(\overline{q})\overline{a}_k - (\overline{a} * \overline{a} * \overline{a})_k & k = 0, \dots, N \\ -(\overline{a} * \overline{a} * \overline{a})_k & k = N+1, \dots, 3N \\ 0 & k > 3N. \end{cases}$$

There are thus only finitely many non-vanishing terms. Hence we set

$$Y_1 = \left|\pi_q A_N \pi_N F(\overline{x})\right|,$$
$$Y_2 = \sum_{k=0}^{N} \left|(\pi_a A_N \pi_N F(\overline{x}))_k\right| \omega_k + \sum_{k=N+1}^{3N} \lambda_k(\overline{q})^{-1} |(\overline{a} * \overline{a} * \overline{a})_k| \omega_k,$$

computed using interval arithmetic to obtain rigorous upper bounds.

4.6. The estimates Z. In this section we construct bounds, see (21),

$$|D_q \pi_q T(x)| \leq Z_{11}(r) \quad \text{for all } x \in \mathcal{B}_r, \tag{27a}$$
$$\|D_a \pi_q T(x)\|_{(\ell^1_\nu)^*} \leq Z_{12}(r) \quad \text{for all } x \in \mathcal{B}_r, \tag{27b}$$
$$\|D_q \pi_a T(x)\|_{\ell^1_\nu} \leq Z_{21}(r) \quad \text{for all } x \in \mathcal{B}_r, \tag{27c}$$
$$\|D_a \pi_a T(x)\|_{B(\ell^1_\nu, \ell^1_\nu)} \leq Z_{22}(r) \quad \text{for all } x \in \mathcal{B}_r. \tag{27d}$$

We will write

$$\mathcal{B}_1 \stackrel{\text{def}}{=} \mathcal{B}_{(1,1)} = \{(q,a) \in X : |q - \overline{q}| \leq 1, \|a - \overline{a}\|_{\ell^1_\nu} \leq 1\}.$$

As already mentioned in §2.4, for each of the four derivatives in (27), we split $DT(\overline{x} + w)v$, where $w = (w_q, w_a) \in \mathcal{B}_r$ and $v = (v_q, v_a) \in \mathcal{B}_1$ are arbitrary, into three pieces:

$$DT(\overline{x} + w)v = [I - AA^\dagger]v - A[DF(\overline{x}) - A^\dagger]v - A[DF(\overline{x} + w) - DF(\overline{x})]v. \tag{28}$$

By bounding these three terms separately, we will find bounds $Z_{ij}(r) = Z^0_{ij} + Z^1_{ij} + Z^2_{ij}(r)$, $i, j \in \{1, 2\}$. We note that the first two terms are independent of w, hence only the third term depends on $r = (r_1, r_2)$.

4.6.1. *The bounds* Z^0. We infer from the definitions of A and $A^\dagger$ in (19) that the first term in (28) reduces to a finite dimensional operator:

$$[I - AA^\dagger]v = \iota[I_N - A_N A_N^\dagger]\pi_N v.$$

Let us write $\Gamma = I - AA^\dagger$, which is of the form discussed in Remark 9 with $\hat{\gamma} = 0$. With the notation introduced in Remark 8 it follows from Remark 9 that the computable numbers

$$\begin{aligned} Z_{11}^0 &= |\Gamma_{qq}| \\ Z_{12}^0 &= \|\Gamma_{qa}\|_{(\ell_\nu^1)^*} \\ Z_{21}^0 &= \|\Gamma_{aq}\|_{\ell_\nu^1} \\ Z_{22}^0 &= \|\Gamma_{aa}\|_{B(\ell_\nu^1,\ell_\nu^1)}, \end{aligned}$$

bound the respective components of $I - AA^\dagger$.

4.6.2. *The bounds* Z^1. For the second term in (28) we first compute, recalling that $A_N^\dagger = DF_N(\pi_N\overline{x})$,

(29a)

$$[Df_q(\overline{x}) - \pi_q A^\dagger]v = -2\overline{q}^2 \sum_{m=N+1}^{\infty} m^2 (v_a)_m - \sqrt{2}\left(\overline{a}_0 + 2\sum_{m=1}^{N} \overline{a}_m\right)\left(2\sum_{m=N+1}^{\infty}(v_a)_m\right)$$

and

$$([Df_a(\overline{x}) - \pi_a A^\dagger]v)_k = \begin{cases} -3\,(\overline{a} * \overline{a} * v_a^0)_k & \text{for } 0 \le k \le N \\ -3\,(\overline{a} * \overline{a} * v_a)_k & \text{for } k > N, \end{cases} \tag{29b}$$

where

$$(v_a^0)_k \stackrel{\text{def}}{=} \begin{cases} 0 & 0 \le k \le N \\ (v_a)_k & k > N. \end{cases}$$

Figure 5 illustrates the nonzero elements in the linear operator $Df(\overline{x}) - A^\dagger$ interpreted as an "infinite matrix". We note that both right-hand sides in (29) are independent of v_q, which implies that $D_q f(\overline{x})\pi_q - A^\dagger\iota\pi_q = 0$, hence

$$Z_{11}^1 = 0 \qquad \text{and} \qquad Z_{21}^1 = 0.$$

We then estimate for all $v \in \mathcal{B}_1$, using the characterization of $(\ell_\nu^1)^*$ in §4.2,

$$\left|\sum_{m=N+1}^{\infty}(v_a)_m\right| \le \sup_{m>N} \omega_m^{-1} \le \omega_{N+1}$$

$$\left|\sum_{m=N+1}^{\infty} m^2 (v_a)_m\right| \le \sup_{m>N} m^2\omega_m^{-1} \le \tfrac{1}{2}Q(\nu, N),$$

where

$$Q(\nu, N) \stackrel{\text{def}}{=} \begin{cases} \frac{4}{(e\ln\nu)^2} & N+1 \le 2/\ln(\nu) \\ 2(N+1)^2\omega_{N+1} & N+1 > 2/\ln(\nu). \end{cases}$$

We immediately see that ν should not be chosen too close to 1 as this would lead to a very large value for Q. We define bounds $d_N = (d_q, d_{a0}, \ldots, d_{aN})$ as follows:

$$d_q \stackrel{\text{def}}{=} \overline{q}^2 Q(\nu, N) + \sqrt{2}\,\omega_{N+1}^{-1}\left|\overline{a}_0 + 2\sum_{m=1}^{N}\overline{a}_m\right| \ge |[Df_q(\overline{x}) - \pi_q A^\dagger]v| \quad \text{for all } v \in \mathcal{B}_1,$$

$$DF(\overline{x})-A^{\dagger}=$$

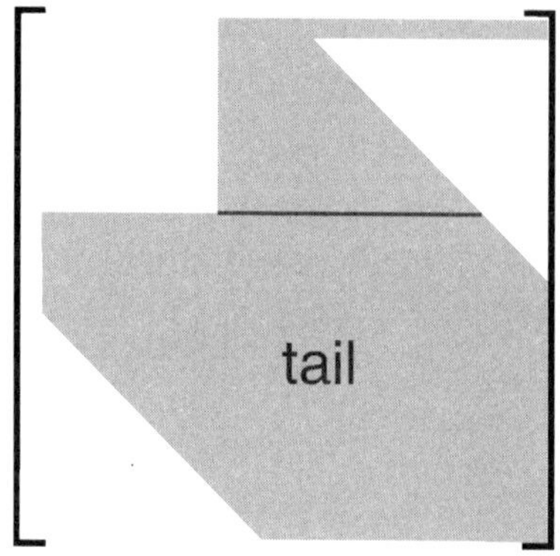

FIGURE 5. A sketch of the shape of the linear operator $DF(\overline{x})-A^{\dagger}$ interpreted as an infinite matrix. Note that the first column vanishes, whereas the top row has infinitely many nonzero elements. The size of the block of zeros at the top left is $(N+2)\times(N+2)$. The width of the infinite non-vanishing "diagonal" strip (the "tail") is $4N+1$.

and for $k=0,\ldots,N$

$$d_{ak} \stackrel{\text{def}}{=} 3(|\overline{a}*\overline{a}|*\chi)_k \geq |([Df_a(\overline{x})-\pi_a A^{\dagger}]v)_k| \quad \text{for all } v\in\mathcal{B}_1,$$

where

$$\chi_k=\begin{cases}0 & 0\leq k\leq N\\ \omega_k^{-1} & N+1\leq k\leq 3N\\ 0 & k>3N,\end{cases}$$

and where absolute values in $|\overline{a}*\overline{a}|$ are taken component-wise. For $k>N$ we note that

$$|(\pi_a A[Df(\overline{x})-A^{\dagger}]v)_k| \leq \lambda_k(\overline{q})^{-1}|3(\overline{a}*\overline{a}*v_a)_k|,$$

hence we may estimate, by using (18) and (20),

$$\sum_{k=N+1}^{\infty}|(\pi_a A[Df(\overline{x})-A^{\dagger}]v)_k|\omega_k \leq 3\lambda_{N+1}(\overline{q})^{-1}\|\overline{a}*\overline{a}\|_{\ell^1_\nu} \qquad \text{for all } v\in\mathcal{B}_1,$$

provided $N\geq\widehat{N}(\overline{q},\xi)$. We thus set

$$Z^1_{21}=\pi_q|A_N|d_N$$
$$Z^1_{22}=\|\pi_a|A_N|d_N\|_{\ell^1_\nu}+3\lambda_{N+1}(\overline{q})^{-1}\|\overline{a}*\overline{a}\|_{\ell^1_\nu},$$

where absolute values in the matrix $|A_N|$ are taken entry-wise.

4.6.3. *The bounds Z^2.* The final term in (28) is expanded in powers of r_1 and r_2 by writing $w=(r_1\widetilde{w}_q,r_2\widetilde{w}_a)$ with $\widetilde{w}\in\mathcal{B}_1$:

$$[Df_q(\overline{x}+w)-Df_q(\overline{x})]v=v_q\sum_{i,j}c_q^{ij}(\overline{x},\widetilde{w})r_1^i r_2^j+\sum_{i,j}\widetilde{c}_q^{ij}(\overline{x},v_a,\widetilde{w})r_1^i r_2^j, \tag{30a}$$

$$\big([Df_a(\overline{x}+w)-Df_a(\overline{x})]v\big)_k=v_q\sum_{i,j}c_{ak}^{ij}(\overline{x},\widetilde{w})r_1^i r_2^j+\sum_{i,j}\widetilde{c}_{ak}^{ij}(\overline{x},v_a,\widetilde{w})r_1^i r_2^j, \tag{30b}$$

c_q^{10}	$-4\widetilde{w}_q \sum_{m=1}^{N} m^2 \overline{a}_m$	$\widetilde{c}_q^{10}$	$-4\overline{q}\widetilde{w}_q \sum_{m=1}^{\infty} m^2 (v_a)_m$
c_q^{01}	$-4\overline{q} \sum_{m=1}^{\infty} m^2 (\widetilde{w}_a)_m$	$\widetilde{c}_q^{01}$	$-\sqrt{2}\left((\widetilde{w}_a)_0 + 2\sum_{m=1}^{\infty}(\widetilde{w}_a)_m\right)\left((v_a)_0 + 2\sum_{m=1}^{\infty}(v_a)_m\right)$
		$\widetilde{c}_q^{20}$	$-2\widetilde{w}_q^2 \sum_{m=1}^{\infty} m^2 (v_a)_m$
c_q^{11}	$-4\widetilde{w}_q \sum_{m=1}^{\infty} m^2 (\widetilde{w}_a)_m$		
c_{ak}^{10}	$-2k^2\widetilde{w}_q\left(6k^2\overline{q}^2 - \xi\right)\overline{a}_k$	$\widetilde{c}_{ak}^{10}$	$-2k^2\widetilde{w}_q\left(2k^2\overline{q}^3 - \xi\overline{q}\right)(v_a)_k$
c_{ak}^{01}	$-2k^2\left(2k^2\overline{q}^3 - \xi\overline{q}\right)(\widetilde{w}_a)_k$	$\widetilde{c}_{ak}^{01}$	$-6\left(\overline{a} * \widetilde{w}_a * v_a\right)_k$
c_{ak}^{20}	$-12k^4\widetilde{w}_q^2\overline{q}\overline{a}_k$	$\widetilde{c}_{ak}^{20}$	$-k^2\widetilde{w}_q^2\left(6k^2\overline{q}^2 - \xi\right)(v_a)_k$
c_{ak}^{11}	$-2k^2\widetilde{w}_q\left(6k^2\overline{q}^2 - \xi\right)(\widetilde{w}_a)_k$		
		$\widetilde{c}_{ak}^{02}$	$-3\left(\widetilde{w}_a * \widetilde{w}_a * v_a\right)_k$
c_{ak}^{30}	$-4k^4\widetilde{w}_q^3\overline{a}_k$	$\widetilde{c}_{ak}^{30}$	$-4k^4\widetilde{w}_q^3\overline{q}(v_a)_k$
c_{ak}^{21}	$-12k^4\widetilde{w}_q^2\overline{q}(\widetilde{w}_a)_k$		
		$\widetilde{c}_{ak}^{40}$	$-k^4\widetilde{w}_q^4(v_a)_k$
c_{ak}^{31}	$-4k^4\widetilde{w}_q^3(\widetilde{w}_a)_k$		

TABLE 1. The non-zero coefficients in the expansions (30).

C_q^{10}	$4\left\lvert\sum_{m=1}^{N} m^2\overline{a}_m\right\rvert$	$\widetilde{C}_q^{10}$	$2\overline{q}Q_\nu$
C_q^{01}	$2qQ_\nu$	$\widetilde{C}_q^{01}$	$\sqrt{2}$
		$\widetilde{C}_q^{20}$	Q_ν
C_q^{11}	$2Q_\nu$		
C_{ak}^{10}	$2k^2\lvert 6k^2\overline{q}^2 - \xi\rvert\lvert\overline{a}_k\rvert$	$\widetilde{C}_{ak}^{10}$	$2k^2\lvert 2k^2\overline{q}^3 - \xi\overline{q}\rvert\omega_k^{-1}$
C_{ak}^{01}	$2k^2\lvert 2k^2\overline{q}^3 - \xi\overline{q}\rvert\omega_k^{-1}$	$\widetilde{C}_{ak}^{01}$	$6\lVert\overline{a}\rVert_{\ell_\nu^1}\omega_k^{-1}$
C_{ak}^{20}	$12k^4\overline{q}\lvert\overline{a}_k\rvert$	$\widetilde{C}_{ak}^{20}$	$k^2\lvert 6k^2\overline{q}^2 - \xi\rvert\omega_k^{-1}$
C_{ak}^{11}	$2k^2\lvert 6k^2\overline{q}^2 - \xi\rvert\omega_k^{-1}$		
		$\widetilde{C}_{ak}^{02}$	$3\omega_k^{-1}$
C_{ak}^{30}	$4k^4\lvert\overline{a}_k\rvert$	$\widetilde{C}_{ak}^{30}$	$4k^4\overline{q}\omega_k^{-1}$
C_{ak}^{21}	$12k^4\overline{q}\omega_k^{-1}$		
		$\widetilde{C}_{ak}^{40}$	$k^4\omega_k^{-1}$
C_{ak}^{31}	$4k^4\omega_k^{-1}$		

TABLE 2. The uniform bounds $C(\overline{x})$ and $\widetilde{C}(\overline{x})$ on the coefficients $c(\overline{x}, \widetilde{w})$ and $\widetilde{c}(\overline{x}, v_a, \widetilde{w})$, see (31).

where we write $(c_a^{ij})_k = c_{ak}^{ij}$ for convenience. All sums are finite sums; the non-vanishing coefficients c_q^{ij} and c_{ak}^{ij} are listed in Table 1.

We now compute uniform bounds

$$C_q^{ij}(\overline{x}) \geq |c_q^{ij}(\overline{x}, \widetilde{w})| \qquad \text{for all } \widetilde{w} \in \mathcal{B}_1, \tag{31a}$$

$$\widetilde{C}_q^{ij}(\overline{x}) \geq |\widetilde{c}_q^{ij}(\overline{x}, v_a, \widetilde{w})| \qquad \text{for all } \widetilde{w} \in \mathcal{B}_1, \|v_a\|_{\ell_\nu^1} \leq 1, \tag{31b}$$

$$C_{ak}^{ij}(\overline{x}) \geq |c_{ak}^{ij}(\overline{x}, \widetilde{w})| \qquad \text{for all } \widetilde{w} \in \mathcal{B}_1, \qquad 0 \leq k \leq N, \tag{31c}$$

$$\widetilde{C}_{ak}^{ij}(\overline{x}) \geq |\widetilde{c}_{ak}^{ij}(\overline{x}, v_a, \widetilde{w})| \qquad \text{for all } \widetilde{w} \in \mathcal{B}_1, \|v_a\|_{\ell_\nu^1} \leq 1, \quad 0 \leq k \leq N. \tag{31d}$$

These are summarized in Table 2, using the notation

$$Q_\nu \stackrel{\text{def}}{=} \frac{4}{(e \ln \nu)^2} \geq 2 \sum_{m \in \mathbb{N}} m^2 |(v_a)_m| \qquad \text{for all } \|v_a\|_{\ell_\nu^1} \leq 1. \tag{32}$$

		$\widetilde{C}^{10}_{\text{tail}}$	$4\overline{q}^3\mu_{N+1}$
C^{01}_{tail}	$4\overline{q}^3\mu_{N+1}$	$\widetilde{C}^{01}_{\text{tail}}$	$6\lambda_{N+1}(\overline{q})^{-1}\|\overline{a}\|_{\ell^1_\nu}$
		$\widetilde{C}^{20}_{\text{tail}}$	$6\overline{q}^2\mu_{N+1}$
C^{11}_{tail}	$12\overline{q}^2\mu_{N+1}$		
		$\widetilde{C}^{02}_{\text{tail}}$	$3\lambda_{N+1}(\overline{q})^{-1}$
		$\widetilde{C}^{30}_{\text{tail}}$	$4\overline{q}\mu_{N+1}$
C^{21}_{tail}	$12\overline{q}\mu_{N+1}$		
		$\widetilde{C}^{40}_{\text{tail}}$	μ_{N+1}
C^{31}_{tail}	$4\mu_{N+1}$		

TABLE 3. The uniform norm bounds $C^{ij}_{\text{tail}}(\overline{x})$ and $\widetilde{C}^{ij}_{\text{tail}}(\overline{x})$ on the non-vanishing tail terms c^{ij}_{ak} and $\widetilde{c}^{ij}_{ak}$ for $k > N$, incorporating the left-multiplication by the diagonal part of A, see (33).

For $k > N$ we use that $N \geq \widehat{N}(\overline{q}, \xi)$, see Remark 10, hence we obtain the bound

$$\mu_{N+1} \stackrel{\text{def}}{=} \frac{(N+1)^4}{\lambda_{N+1}(\overline{q})} \geq \frac{k^4}{\lambda_k(\overline{q})} \qquad \text{for all } k \geq N+1.$$

This allows the uniform "tail" estimates

$$\text{(33a)} \quad C^{ij}_{\text{tail}}(\overline{x}) \geq \sum_{k>N} \left| \lambda_k(\overline{q})^{-1} c^{ij}_{ak}(\overline{x}, \widetilde{w}) \right| \omega_k \qquad \text{for all } \widetilde{w} \in \mathcal{B}_1,$$

$$\text{(33b)} \quad \widetilde{C}^{ij}_{\text{tail}}(\overline{x}) \geq \sum_{k>N} \left| \lambda_k(\overline{q})^{-1} \widetilde{c}^{ij}_{ak}(\overline{x}, v_a, \widetilde{w}) \right| \omega_k \qquad \text{for all } \widetilde{w} \in \mathcal{B}_1 \text{ and } \|v_a\|_{\ell^1_\nu} \leq 1,$$

where the non-zero C^{ij}_{tail} and $\widetilde{C}^{ij}_{\text{tail}}$ are listed in Table 3.

Finally, with the notation

$$C^{ij}_N = (C^{ij}_q, C^{ij}_{a0}, \ldots, C^{ij}_{aN}) \quad \text{and} \quad \widetilde{C}^{ij}_N = (\widetilde{C}^{ij}_q, \widetilde{C}^{ij}_{a0}, \ldots, \widetilde{C}^{ij}_{aN}),$$

we set

$$Z^2_{11}(r_1, r_2) = \sum_{i,j} \pi_q |A_N| C^{ij}_N \, r_1^i r_2^j,$$

$$Z^2_{12}(r_1, r_2) = \sum_{i,j} \pi_q |A_N| \widetilde{C}^{ij}_N \, r_1^i r_2^j,$$

$$Z^2_{21}(r_1, r_2) = \sum_{i,j} \|\pi_a |A_N| C^{ij}_N\|_{\ell^1_\nu} \, r_1^i r_2^j + \sum_{i,j} C^{ij}_{\text{tail}} \, r_1^i r_2^j,$$

$$Z^2_{22}(r_1, r_2) = \sum_{i,j} \|\pi_a |A_N| \widetilde{C}^{ij}_N\|_{\ell^1_\nu} \, r_1^i r_2^j + \sum_{i,j} \widetilde{C}^{ij}_{\text{tail}} \, r_1^i r_2^j.$$

All sums are over (a subset of) $0 \leq i \leq 4$, $0 \leq j \leq 2$.

4.7. Success. The estimates from §4.5 and §4.6, as well as the radii polynomials (23) have been implemented in the Matlab code `SHproof.m`, which uses the interval arithmetic package Intlab [**28**]. All code can be found at [**38**]. Based on Theorems 11 and 12 the script `runproofpointwise.m` successfully proves the existence aspect (as discussed at the end of §3) of Theorem 6 for $\xi = 0.01n$ where $n = 0, 1, \ldots, 203$. We use $N = 20$ and $\nu = 1.5$. These choices were made after some experimentation with the code. The run time is less than a minute on a standard Macbook Pro.

The code also verifies, by using `checkgeometry.m`, that the geometric conditions $\mathcal{H}$ are satisfied. Indeed, first we use the cosine series (12) to transform the Fourier coefficients $\overline{a}$ back to physical space to obtain the approximate solution

$$\overline{u}(y) = \overline{a}_0 + 2\sum_{m=1}^{N} \overline{a}_m \cos(m\hat{q}y).$$

Note that the value of $\hat{q}$ (which lies somewhere in the interval $[\overline{q}-\hat{r}_1, \overline{q}+\hat{r}_1]$) plays no role in the geometric conditions $\mathcal{H}$ and is thus not used in this part of the code. Denoting the true solution by

$$\hat{u}(y) = \hat{a}_0 + 2\sum_{m=1}^{\infty} \hat{a}_m \cos(m\hat{q}y),$$

the characterization of $(\ell^1_\nu)^*$ in §4.2 leads to the error estimate

$$\|\hat{u}-\overline{u}\|_\infty \le |\hat{a}_0-\overline{a}_0| + 2\sum_{m=1}^{\infty} |\hat{a}_m - \overline{a}_m| \le \hat{r}_2.$$

Adding the uncertainty interval $[-\hat{r}_2, \hat{r}_2]$ to $\overline{u}$ thus leads to a rigorous interval arithmetic description of the solution:

$$\hat{u}(y) \in \overline{u}(y) + [-\hat{r}_2, \hat{r}_2].$$

Analogous constructions lead to explicit quantitative descriptions of the first and second derivative $\hat{u}'(y)$ and $\hat{u}''(y)$, with extra factors $\hat{q}/(e\ln\nu)$ and $4\hat{q}^2/(e\ln\nu)^2$, respectively, in the uncertainty intervals for these derivatives, cf. (32). Since our interest is in the sign of these derivatives only, the value of $\hat{q}$ again plays no role (and is "scaled out" in the code). Next, we split the interval $[0,\pi/\hat{q}]$ into 50 equal pieces. We note that $\hat{u}'(0) = \hat{u}'(\pi/\hat{q}) = 0$ by construction. To verify that there are exactly two monotone laps on $[0,\pi/\hat{q}]$ and that the local minima and maxima satisfy (H_3), we check that the second derivative is nonzero on the intervals where the first derivative is potentially zero, and that the value of $\hat{u}$ on these intervals must lie in the appropriate range. See the code `checkgeometry.m` and [**40**, §4] for additional details.

Finally, the script `runproofcontinuous.m` proves Theorem 11 for all $0 \le \xi \le 2.02$, i.e., for a continuous range of parameter values. The interval $[0, 2.02]$ is split into 202000 intervals of width 0.00001, and all bounds are derived uniformly for ξ in each of these small intervals (by using interval arithmetic). We use $N = 70$ and $\nu = 1.15 + 0.15\xi$, i.e., we need more modes than for the pointwise proof and the choice of ν is a little more subtle, namely linear in ξ. These choices were made after some experimentation with the code. Again, we also verify that the geometric conditions $\mathcal{H}$ are satisfied, as described above. This brute force continuation takes several hours (see [**5, 22, 30, 41, 42**] for more sophisticated approaches).

References

[1] Kenneth Appel and Wolfgang Haken, *Every planar map is four colorable*, Contemporary Mathematics, vol. 98, American Mathematical Society, Providence, RI, 1989. With the collaboration of J. Koch. MR1025335

[2] Zin Arai, William Kalies, Hiroshi Kokubu, Konstantin Mischaikow, Hiroe Oka, and Paweł Pilarczyk, *A database schema for the analysis of global dynamics of multiparameter systems*, SIAM J. Appl. Dyn. Syst. **8** (2009), no. 3, 757–789, DOI 10.1137/080734935. MR2533624

[3] Gianni Arioli and Hans Koch, *Computer-assisted methods for the study of stationary solutions in dissipative systems, applied to the Kuramoto-Sivashinski equation*, Arch. Ration. Mech. Anal. **197** (2010), no. 3, 1033–1051, DOI 10.1007/s00205-010-0309-7. MR2679365

[4] Gianni Arioli and Hans Koch, *Integration of dissipative partial differential equations: a case study*, SIAM J. Appl. Dyn. Syst. **9** (2010), no. 3, 1119–1133, DOI 10.1137/10078298X. MR2728184

[5] Maxime Breden, Jean-Philippe Lessard, and Matthieu Vanicat, *Global bifurcation diagrams of steady states of systems of PDEs via rigorous numerics: a 3-component reaction-diffusion system*, Acta Appl. Math. **128** (2013), 113–152, DOI 10.1007/s10440-013-9823-6. MR3125637

[6] B. Breuer, J. Horák, P. J. McKenna, and M. Plum, *A computer-assisted existence and multiplicity proof for travelling waves in a nonlinearly supported beam*, J. Differential Equations **224** (2006), no. 1, 60–97, DOI 10.1016/j.jde.2005.07.016. MR2220064

[7] CAPD*: Computer Assisted Proofs in Dynamics, a Package for Rigorous Numerics*, `http://capd.ii.uj.edu.pl/`.

[8] Roberto Castelli and Jean-Philippe Lessard, *Rigorous numerics in Floquet theory: computing stable and unstable bundles of periodic orbits*, SIAM J. Appl. Dyn. Syst. **12** (2013), no. 1, 204–245, DOI 10.1137/120873960. MR3032858

[9] Charles Conley, *Isolated invariant sets and the Morse index*, CBMS Regional Conference Series in Mathematics, vol. 38, American Mathematical Society, Providence, R.I., 1978. MR511133

[10] M.C. Cross and P.C. Hohenberg, *Pattern formation outside of equilibrium*, Rev. Mod. Phys. **65** (1993), no. 3, 851–1112.

[11] Sarah Day and William D. Kalies, *Rigorous computation of the global dynamics of integrodifference equations with smooth nonlinearities*, SIAM J. Numer. Anal. **51** (2013), no. 6, 2957–2983, DOI 10.1137/120903129. MR3124898

[12] Sarah Day, Jean-Philippe Lessard, and Konstantin Mischaikow, *Validated continuation for equilibria of PDEs*, SIAM J. Numer. Anal. **45** (2007), no. 4, 1398–1424, DOI 10.1137/050645968. MR2338393

[13] Robert L. Devaney, *Homoclinic orbits in Hamiltonian systems*, J. Differential Equations **21** (1976), no. 2, 431–438, DOI 10.1016/0022-0396(76)90130-3. MR0442990

[14] Marcio Gameiro and Jean-Philippe Lessard, *Efficient rigorous numerics for higher-dimensional PDEs via one-dimensional estimates*, SIAM J. Numer. Anal. **51** (2013), no. 4, 2063–2087, DOI 10.1137/110836651. MR3077902

[15] R. W. Ghrist, J. B. Van den Berg, and R. C. Vandervorst, *Morse theory on spaces of braids and Lagrangian dynamics*, Invent. Math. **152** (2003), no. 2, 369–432, DOI 10.1007/s00222-002-0277-0. MR1974892

[16] Thomas C. Hales, *A proof of the Kepler conjecture*, Ann. of Math. (2) **162** (2005), no. 3, 1065–1185, DOI 10.4007/annals.2005.162.1065. MR2179728

[17] Morris W. Hirsch, Stephen Smale, and Robert L. Devaney, *Differential equations, dynamical systems, and an introduction to chaos*, 3rd ed., Elsevier/Academic Press, Amsterdam, 2013. MR3293130

[18] Allan Hungria, Jean-Philippe Lessard, and J. D. Mireles James, *Rigorous numerics for analytic solutions of differential equations: the radii polynomial approach*, Math. Comp. **85** (2016), no. 299, 1427–1459, DOI 10.1090/mcom/3046. MR3454370

[19] W. D. Kalies, J. Kwapisz, and R. C. A. M. VanderVorst, *Homotopy classes for stable connections between Hamiltonian saddle-focus equilibria*, Comm. Math. Phys. **193** (1998), no. 2, 337–371, DOI 10.1007/s002200050332. MR1618147

[20] William D. Kalies, Konstantin Mischaikow, and Robert C. A. M. Vandervorst, *Lattice structures for attractors I*, J. Comput. Dyn. **1** (2014), no. 2, 307–338. MR3415257

[21] Oscar E. Lanford III, *A computer-assisted proof of the Feigenbaum conjectures*, Bull. Amer. Math. Soc. (N.S.) **6** (1982), no. 3, 427–434, DOI 10.1090/S0273-0979-1982-15008-X. MR648529

[22] Jan Bouwe van den Berg and Jean-Philippe Lessard, *Chaotic braided solutions via rigorous numerics: chaos in the Swift-Hohenberg equation*, SIAM J. Appl. Dyn. Syst. **7** (2008), no. 3, 988–1031, DOI 10.1137/070709128. MR2443030

[23] Jean-Philippe Lessard and Christian Reinhardt, *Rigorous numerics for nonlinear differential equations using Chebyshev series*, SIAM J. Numer. Anal. **52** (2014), no. 1, 1–22, DOI 10.1137/13090883X. MR3148084

[24] T. Y. Li and James A. Yorke, *Period three implies chaos*, Amer. Math. Monthly **82** (1975), no. 10, 985–992, DOI 10.2307/2318254. MR0385028

[25] Mitsuhiro T. Nakao, *Numerical verification methods for solutions of ordinary and partial differential equations*, Numer. Funct. Anal. Optim. **22** (2001), no. 3-4, 321–356, DOI 10.1081/NFA-100105107. International Workshops on Numerical Methods and Verification of Solutions, and on Numerical Function Analysis (Ehime/Shimane, 1999). MR1849323

[26] Douglas E. Norton, *The fundamental theorem of dynamical systems*, Comment. Math. Univ. Carolin. **36** (1995), no. 3, 585–597. MR1364499

[27] Neil Robertson, Daniel Sanders, Paul Seymour, and Robin Thomas, *The four-colour theorem*, J. Combin. Theory Ser. B **70** (1997), no. 1, 2–44, DOI 10.1006/jctb.1997.1750. MR1441258

[28] Tibor Csendes (ed.), *Developments in reliable computing*, Kluwer Academic Publishers, Dordrecht, 1999. MR1747254

[29] Dietmar Salamon, *Morse theory, the Conley index and Floer homology*, Bull. London Math. Soc. **22** (1990), no. 2, 113–140, DOI 10.1112/blms/22.2.113. MR1045282

[30] Evelyn Sander and Thomas Wanner, *Validated saddle-node bifurcations and applications to lattice dynamical systems*, SIAM J. Appl. Dyn. Syst. **15** (2016), no. 3, 1690–1733, DOI 10.1137/16M1061011. MR3546337

[31] O. M. Šarkovs′kiĭ, *Co-existence of cycles of a continuous mapping of the line into itself* (Russian, with English summary), Ukrain. Mat. Ž. **16** (1964), 61–71. MR0159905

[32] L. P. Šil′nikov, *A case of the existence of a denumerable set of periodic motions* (Russian), Dokl. Akad. Nauk SSSR **160** (1965), 558–561. MR0173047

[33] S.H. Strogatz, *Nonlinear dynamics and chaos : with applications to physics, biology, chemistry, and engineering*, Studies in nonlinearity, Westview Press, Cambridge (Mass.), 1994.

[34] J. Swift and P. C. Hohenberg, *Hydrodynamic fluctuations at the convective instability*, Phys. Rev. A **15** (1977), no. 1, 319–328.

[35] William P. Thurston, *On the geometry and dynamics of diffeomorphisms of surfaces*, Bull. Amer. Math. Soc. (N.S.) **19** (1988), no. 2, 417–431, DOI 10.1090/S0273-0979-1988-15685-6. MR956596

[36] Warwick Tucker, *A rigorous ODE solver and Smale's 14th problem*, Found. Comput. Math. **2** (2002), no. 1, 53–117. MR1870856

[37] J. B. van den Berg, C. M. Groothedde, and J. F. Williams, *Rigorous computation of a radially symmetric localized solution in a Ginzburg-Landau problem*, SIAM J. Appl. Dyn. Syst. **14** (2015), no. 1, 423–447, DOI 10.1137/140987973. MR3323206

[38] Jan Bouwe van den Berg, *MATLAB code for "Introduction to Rigorous Numerics in Dynamics: General Functional Analytic Setup and an Example that Forces Chaos"*, 2017, `http://www.math.vu.nl/~janbouwe/code/introrignumdyn/`.

[39] Jan Bouwe van den Berg, Andréa Deschênes, Jean-Philippe Lessard, and Jason D. Mireles James, *Stationary coexistence of hexagons and rolls via rigorous computations*, SIAM J. Appl. Dyn. Syst. **14** (2015), no. 2, 942–979, DOI 10.1137/140984506. MR3353132

[40] Jan Bouwe van den Berg and Jean-Philippe Lessard, *Chaotic braided solutions via rigorous numerics: chaos in the Swift-Hohenberg equation*, SIAM J. Appl. Dyn. Syst. **7** (2008), no. 3, 988–1031, DOI 10.1137/070709128. MR2443030

[41] Jan Bouwe van den Berg, Jean-Philippe Lessard, and Konstantin Mischaikow, *Global smooth solution curves using rigorous branch following*, Math. Comp. **79** (2010), no. 271, 1565–1584, DOI 10.1090/S0025-5718-10-02325-2. MR2630003

[42] Thomas Wanner, *Computer-Assisted Bifurcation Diagram Validation and Applications in Materials Science*, 2017, To appear.

[43] Piotr Zgliczyński, *Rigorous numerics for dissipative partial differential equations. II. Periodic orbit for the Kuramoto-Sivashinsky PDE—a computer-assisted proof*, Found. Comput. Math. **4** (2004), no. 2, 157–185, DOI 10.1007/s10208-002-0080-8. MR2049869

[44] Piotr Zgliczyński, *Covering relations, cone conditions and the stable manifold theorem*, J. Differential Equations **246** (2009), no. 5, 1774–1819, DOI 10.1016/j.jde.2008.12.019. MR2494688

Department of Mathematics, Vrije Universiteit Amsterdam, de Boelelaan 1081, 1081HV Amsterdam, The Netherlands

Email address: `janbouwe.vanden.berg@vu.nl`

Proceedings of Symposia in Applied Mathematics
Volume **74**, 2018
http://dx.doi.org/10.1090/psapm/074/00642

Validated numerics for equilibria of analytic vector fields: Invariant manifolds and connecting orbits

J. D. Mireles James

ABSTRACT. This lecture describes validated numerical tools which are used for global analysis of nonlinear systems. The main focus is dynamics near and between equilibrium solutions of ordinary differential equations. The discussion focuses on Taylor methods, which are used to compute local stable/unstable manifold patches and also to compute local expansions of the flow in a neighborhood of a non-equilibrium initial condition. In both cases the first N coefficients of the series expansion are computed via recursion schemes based on power matching. Bounds on the tail of the series are obtained by a contraction mapping argument. The validated Taylor expansions are combined with the method of projected boundaries and a Newton-Kantorovich argument to prove the existence of a transverse heteroclinic connecting orbit in the Lorenz system.

1. Introduction

Equilibria, periodic orbits, and connecting orbits occupy a central place in the qualitative theory of dynamical systems. These special solutions are low dimensional invariant sets that carry global information. For example, Smale's theorem tells us that a single non degenerate orbit homoclinic to a periodic solution forces the existence of infinitely many periodic solutions of arbitrarily long period, as well as chaotic motions and mixing. Connecting orbits are fundamental in the study of nonlinear waves and for understanding pattern formation. Equilibria and connecting orbits make up the chain groups and boundary operators in Morse homology theory, allowing one to recover the homology of a compact N-dimensional manifold from zero and one dimensional data. Despite their utility, connecting orbits are difficult if not impossible to analyze by hand in applications having strong nonlinearities.

The lectures contained in the present volume describe mathematically rigorous tools in nonlinear analysis, which exploit in a fundamental way the power of the digital computer. The present lecture is a tutorial on local analysis of analytic vector fields. Suppose for example we are given a hyperbolic equilibrium point. We would like to understand the dynamics nearby– where are the local stable/unstable manifolds? Now suppose on the other hand we are given a non-equilibrium point. Then we want to understand the flow nearby – what happens to nearby points

---

2010 *Mathematics Subject Classification.* Primary 34C45, 34C37, 65G20, 65P99.

The author was partially supported by the Alfred P. Sloan Foundation grant G-2016-7320.

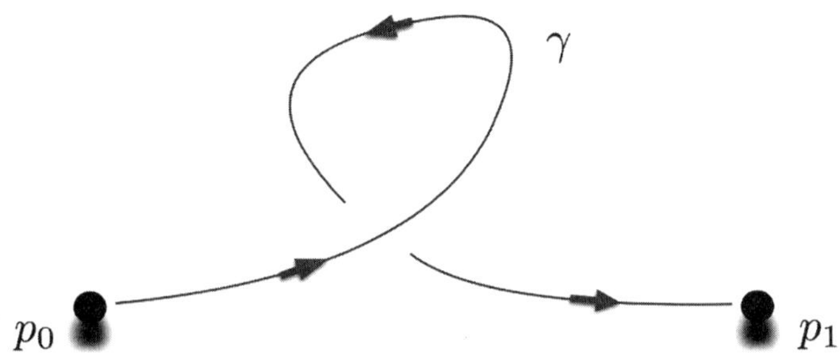

FIGURE 1. A heteroclinic connecting orbit from p_0 to p_1.

for nearby times? With enough local information a global picture of the dynamics begins to emerge. To illustrate this point we give –before the end of the lecture – a computer assisted argument which proves the existence of transverse saddle-to-saddle connecting orbits for the Lorenz system.

Our arguments are based on manipulation and analysis of Taylor series, so we first discuss a functional analytic framework for computer assisted proofs involving unknown analytic functions of several complex variables. The discussion is formulated in certain Banach spaces of infinite sequences (or infinite multi-sequences). Framing arguments in sequence space keeps us "close to the numerics," and avoids function space technicalities. The sequence space framework applies immediately to both the high order parameterization of an invariant manifold, and to the high order Taylor series solution of a initial value problem (we expand solutions of initial value problems in the spatial variables as well as in time). For both manifold and flow box computations an elementary contraction mapping argument bounds the truncation errors in the tail. For numerical applications we fix our attention on the familiar example of the Lorenz system.

Throughout the notes we make liberal use of the validated numerical algorithms discussed in [**81**], and employ the interval arithmetic library IntLab [**82**] which runs under MatLab.

1.1. Connecting orbits between equilibrium solutions of ordinary differential equations. Suppose that $f\colon \mathbb{R}^n \to \mathbb{R}^n$ is a real analytic vector field, and that $p_0, p_1 \in \mathbb{R}^n$ are equilibrium solutions of the differential equation

$$x' = f(x), \tag{1.1}$$

i.e. that p_0 and p_1 have that $f(p_0) = f(p_1) = 0$. A *heteroclinic connecting orbit* from p_0 to p_1 is a smooth curve $\gamma\colon (-\infty, \infty) \to \mathbb{R}^n$ which satisfies Equation (1.1) and which is subject to the constraints

$$\lim_{t \to -\infty} \gamma(t) = p_0, \qquad \text{and} \qquad \lim_{t \to \infty} \gamma(t) = p_1.$$

In other words γ is the solution of a boundary value problem on the unbounded domain $\mathbb{R}$ with prescribed asymptotic behavior at plus and minus infinity. The situation is illustrated in Figure 1.

A standard method for treating the boundary conditions at infinity is the *method of projected boundaries* [**12, 36–38, 44, 45**]. The idea is to look for an

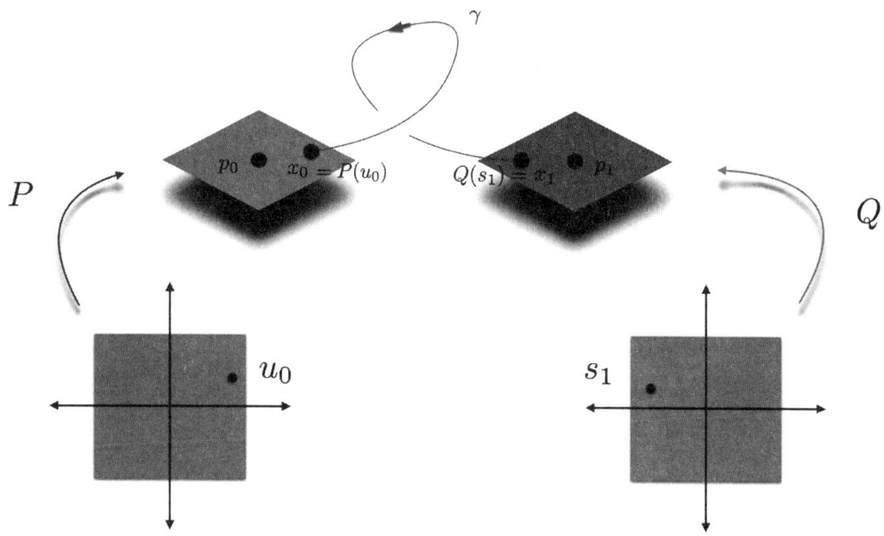

FIGURE 2. The meaning of the connecting orbit operator: Here P and Q are chart maps, or parameterizations of the local unstable and stable manifolds of p_0 and p_1 respectively. Using the charts, we are able to formulate a finite time boundary value problem for the connecting orbit. Namely we look for an orbit with initial conditions on the unstable manifold which arrives, after flowing for a time $L > 0$ on the stable manifold. The boundary conditions on the manifold are replaced with unknown coordinates u_0 and s_1 in the parameter spaces of the charts.

orbit segment $\gamma\colon [0, T] \to \mathbb{R}^n$ satisfying Equation (1.1) on $(0, T)$ and having that

$$\gamma(0) \in W^u_{\text{loc}}(p_0), \qquad \text{and} \qquad \gamma(T) \in W^s_{\text{loc}}(p_1).$$

In other words, by projecting onto local unstable/stable manifolds of the equilibria, one guaranties that the conditions at infinity are met.

Let $\mathbb{E}^u, \mathbb{E}^s$ denote the unstable and stable eigenspaces of p_0 and p_1 respectively. We write $m_0 = \dim(\mathbb{E}^u)$ and $m_1 = \dim(\mathbb{E}^s)$ and for the moment place no restrictions on m_0, m_1 (appropriate constraints will emerge momentarily). Lets postpone for the moment any discussion of approximation strategies for the local stable/unstable manifolds (though linear approximation by the stable/unstable eigenspace is a common choice) and just assume that we know some one to one maps $P\colon \mathbb{E}^u \to \mathbb{R}^n$ and $Q\colon \mathbb{E}^s \to \mathbb{R}^n$ having

$$P(0) = p_0, \qquad \text{with} \qquad \text{image}(P) \subset W^u_{\text{loc}}(p_0),$$

and

$$Q(0) = p_1, \qquad \text{with} \qquad \text{image}(Q) \subset W^s_{\text{loc}}(p_1).$$

Then the problem of locating a heteroclinic orbit from p_0 to p_1 is reformulated as follows: find $u_0 \in \mathbb{E}^u$, $s_1 \in \mathbb{E}^s$, and a smooth curve $\gamma\colon [0, T] \to \mathbb{R}^n$ so that γ solves

Equation (1.1) subject to the constraints

$$\gamma(0) = P(u_0), \qquad \text{and} \qquad \gamma(T) = Q(s_1).$$

The idea is illustrated in Figure 2.

Now, suppose that $\phi\colon \mathbb{R}^n \times \mathbb{R} \to \mathbb{R}^n$ is the flow generated by f, and define $F\colon \mathbb{E}^u \times \mathbb{E}^s \times \mathbb{R} \to \mathbb{R}^n$ by

$$F(u, s, T) = \phi(P(u), T) - Q(s). \tag{1.2}$$

If (u, s, T) is a zero of F, then

$$\gamma(t) = \phi(P(u), t),$$

is a solution of the projected boundary problem, hence a connecting orbit. We refer to F as the connecting orbit operator.

The goal of the present lecture is to deduce sufficient conditions for the existence of a zero of F in Equation (1.2). The sufficient conditions must be checkable via a finite number of operations. These will be carried out using the digital computer.

To achieve this goal it is necessary to understand P, Q, and ϕ more precisely. Typically none of them are known explicitly. Rather, they are only defined implicitly through the vector field f. This is the technical hurdle which any computer analysis of a connecting orbit must overcome. We develop algorithms for computing Taylor series expansions for $P(u)$, $Q(s)$, and $\phi(x, t)$, as well as computer assisted methods for managing the truncation errors. As we will see in Chapter 5, we also need to control derivatives of these functions if we want to obtain transversality.

REMARK 1.1 (compatibility conditions). Note that if $\gamma\colon [0, T] \to \mathbb{R}^n$ is a heteroclinic orbit segment, then for any $h \in \mathbb{R}$ the function $\hat{\gamma}_h\colon [0, T] \to \mathbb{R}^n$ defined by

$$\hat{\gamma}_h(t) = \phi(\gamma(t), h),$$

is another heteroclinic orbit segment. Similarly, if $\tilde{T} > T$ then we can extend γ to the interval $[0, \tilde{T}]$ and will have yet another heteroclinic orbit segment.

These remarks imply that if (u_0, s_1, T) is a solution of F as defined in Equation (1.2), then by the implicit function theorem $DF(u_0, s_1, T)$ has at least a two dimensional kernel. If we want to isolate a solution of F we must somehow remove two variables. This well known issue is easily managed, and we describe in detail one solution in Section 5. For the moment just note that in order to have a balanced system of equations we need that

$$\dim(\mathbb{E}^u \times \mathbb{E}^s \times \mathbb{R}) - 2 = \dim(\mathbb{R}^n),$$

and a necessary condition for an isolated solution is that $m_0 + m_1 + 1 - 2 = n$ or

$$m_0 + m_1 = n + 1.$$

1.2. A brief survey of the surrounding literature. The aim of these notes is to present a moderately concise and self contained (if technical) explanation of a computer assisted proof for a heteroclinic connecting orbit. The approach is based entirely on manipulation of power series, giving all validations a similar flavor. The note could serve as a brief introduction to computer assisted proofs with Taylor series, and after examining these notes and the supporting codes the interested reader could adapt the methods used here to any number of problems.

That being said, it should be stressed that this lecture represent the author's take on existing results and techniques. The novelty – if there is any – is the detailed presentation of this material in a single source. The interested reader will want to consult the primary literature to gain a much more complete picture of what has been done in this area. The two main topics of these notes are validated solution of initial value problems (sometimes referred to as rigorous integration) and validated computer assisted analysis of stable/unstable manifolds. These topics are by now well established pillars of the field of computer assisted proof in dynamical systems theory, and some discussion of the literature is in order.

The reader interested in interval analysis/arithmetic will want to consult the work of Moore [**73**–**75**]. The 1966 book of Moore is more or less the beginning of the subject. The work of Lanford on the computer assisted proof of the Feigenbaum conjectures is must reading for anyone interested in the computer as a tool for nonlinear analysis [**60**]. See also the Memoir of Eckmann, Koch, and Wittwer [**39**]. These proofs of the Feigenbaum conjectures make substantial use of Taylor methods. They also advanced the idea of treating an infinite dimensional problem as a fixed point problem in a sequence space of Taylor coefficients and attacking the problem with functional analytic tools based on "Newton-like" analysis.

An early example of the use of validated Taylor integrators as an ingredient in mathematically rigorous computer assisted proofs is found in the work of de la Llave and Fefferman [**40**], on the relativistic stability of matter. Modern and detailed discussion of rigorous Taylor integrators and their history, along with many supporting examples and implementation, is found in Chapter 6 of the book of Tucker [**86**]. Indeed, rigorous integrators played a critical role in Tucker's solution of Smale's 14-th problem [**84**, **85**]. See also the work of Berz and Makino [**11**].

Foundational work on general rigorous integration schemes was done by Lohner, see for example [**1**, **66**, **67**]. Building on this work, Wilczak and Zgliczynski developed efficient Taylor methods for simultaneous rigorous integration of vector fields and their variational equations [**97**, **99**] that keep track the flow and its spatial derivatives. These algorithms form the core of the CAPD library for validated numerics. More information on the CAPD library is found at

`http://capd.sourceforge.net/capdDynSys/people.php`.

These methods are extended by Zgliczynski and Cyranka to infinite dimensional semi-flows such as parabolic PDEs [**30**–**32**, **100**], and by Zgliczynski and Szczelina to semi-flows generated by delay differential equations [**101**]. Another approach to rigorous integration of parabolic PDEs is found in the work of Koch and Arioli [**6**]. The methods and the software implementations in the works mentioned in the preceding paragraphs are much more sophisticated than those discussed in the present introductory note.

Much of the community's interest in rigorous Taylor integrators is motivated by a desire to compute global dynamics. Rigorous integrators facilitate computer assisted proof of periodic orbits for ordinary differential equations [**3**–**5**, **96**] and are used to prove the existence of connecting orbits [**83**, **94**, **95**] and topological horseshoes [**3**, **8**, **9**, **46**, **47**, **71**, **72**, **96**]. Recently a computer assisted proof of chaos in the Kuramoto-Sivashinsky equation (a parabolic PDE) based on rigorous integration of the semi-flow has been announced by Wilczak and Zgliczynski [**93**].

To establish the existence of transverse connecting orbits, i.e. transverse intersections between stable/unstable manifolds, it is necessary to develop validated numerics for the local manifolds. Methods for studying local stable/unstable manifolds based on topological covering and cone conditions are developed by Zgliczynski and Capinski [**21, 24**]. These methods are used for example by Capinski, Roldan, and Wasieczko-Zajpolhk to prove the existence of center manifolds, transverse intersections of invariant manifolds in celestial mechanics problems, and to study strong stable/unstable manifolds [**22, 23, 23**]. We also mention that the Ph.D. dissertation of Alex Wittig contains a topological validation method for computer assisted analysis of stable/unstable manifolds which exploits high order polynomial enclosures of the invariant manifolds and cone conditions.

Another approach to computer assisted proof of transverse connecting orbits is based on the theory of exponential dichotomies and the notion of hyperbolic shadowing [**59, 76**]. Palmer, Coomes, and Koçak have developed validated numerical methods based on these ideas which apply to a wide variety of heteroclinic and homoclinic phenomena, including computer assisted proof of chaos [**10**]. We refer to [**28, 29**] and the references therein for more complete discussion.

Validated numerics for stable/unstable manifolds based on functional analytic tools are discussed at length below, and for the moment we only mention the work of Koch and Arioli [**2, 7**] on homoclinic connecting orbits traveling waves, and the Evans function; and also the work of the Breden, Lessard, Reinhardt, and the author on validated numerical methods for stable/unstable manifolds based on the parameterization method [**13, 88**]. Techniques based on the parameterization method lead also to validated numerics for stable/unstable manifolds of periodic orbits, as in the work of Castelli, Lessard and the author [**27**], and also to validated numerical methods for computing unstable manifolds and heteroclinic connecting orbits for parabolic PDEs [**79**]. Further discussion of the literature is found in these references.

REMARK 1.2 (Taylor remainders and fixed point problems). A validated numerical integrator involves two essential components: first, a numerical stage which produces an approximate solution of the initial value problem; and second, a validation stage which provides mathematically rigorous bounds on all truncation and round off errors. Many of the references discussed above use Taylor series methods for the initial approximation stage. Validation strategies are sometimes based on application of the Taylor remainder theorem, as for example in the works of [**1, 66, 67, 97, 99**]. Other strategies treat the Taylor remainder using fixed point methods, as in [**2, 6, 7**].

More recently Lessard and Reinhardt introduced an approach to rigorous integration based on Chebyshev series approximation [**64**]. The Chebyshev series of a real analytic function $\gamma\colon [0, T] \to \mathbb{R}^n$ converges on an ellipse in the complex plain, whose foci are at 0 and T. Because of this, the Chebyshev series is much less sensitive to poles in the complex plane than the Taylor series, and very long time steps (often much greater than one time unit) are possible. Van den Berg and Sheombarsing have studied the problem of optimal meshing for longer validated time steps [**89**]. This work uses heuristic methods based on complex pole detection. Both of the works just mentioned exploit Newton's method in a Banach space of infinite sequences for rigorous error analysis.

REMARK 1.3 (Fixed point analysis of recursion relations). Taylor series methods for local problems have the property that, via some power matching arguments, one works out explicitly the recursion describing the power series coefficients of the unknown function. This observation is elaborated on below, but briefly this is due to the lower triangular structure of the Cauchy product of two analytic functions.

Solving the recursion numerically (using interval arithmetic) leads to rigorous enclosure of as many Taylor coefficients as desired. Judiciously rescaling the problem provides control over the decay rates of the Taylor coefficients and reduces the effects of the data dependance between the lower and higher order terms.

In [**7**], Koch and Arioli develop computer assisted error bounds for analytic functions whose Taylor coefficients are defined by recursion relations. The idea is to view the recursion as a fixed point problem on a space of infinite sequences. Solving the recursion to a fixed finite order N provides a numerical approximation, which is then viewed as an approximate fixed point. A contraction mapping argument on a suitable ball in a space of "tails" provides mathematically rigorous a-posteriori bounds for the truncation error.

Similar contraction mapping arguments, formulated in analytic function spaces, have been used by other authors to study local stable/unstable manifolds in [**27, 62, 69, 90, 92**], and analysis of local stable/unstable manifolds based on Newton's method in spaces of infinite sequence spaces is developed in [**13, 88**].

The exposition in the present lecture uses the fixed point/contraction mapping approach to recursion discussed in [**7**]. The main advantage of this method is that it does not require the inversion of any matrices (large or otherwise). This is a great virtue when working with analytic functions of several complex variables.

In an attempt to make transparent the computer assisted portion of the proofs, we formulate explicit a-posteriori validation theorems for each problem we consider. These theorems are framed in Banach algebras of infinite sequences, and the style of presentation is influenced by the radii-polynomial approach of Lessard, Day, Gameiro, van den Berg, and Mischaikow (see the notes of van den Berg and Lessard in the present volume). The hypotheses of our theorems involve certain finite sums which depend only on the numerical data (the approximate solution). Implementation of the computer assisted proofs is a matter of evaluating these finite sums using interval arithmetic to manage round off errors, and then checking that some quadratic polynomial has positive roots. As one sees by inspecting the codes, our a-posteriori theorems constitute digestible pseudo-code for the computer assisted proofs.

2. Background: infinite multi-sequences

Fix $m \in \mathbb{N}$ and consider a function $a \colon \mathbb{N}^m \to \mathbb{C}$. We refer to a as an *infinite multi-sequence* of complex numbers, and write

$$a = \{a_\alpha\}_{\alpha \in \mathbb{N}^m}.$$

With $m = 1$ we recover the standard notion of an infinite sequence. It is natural then to think of a multi-sequence as an infinite m-dimensional array of complex numbers, i.e. an array whose coordinates are addressed by m-dimensional vectors of natural numbers. The m-dimensional vectors $\alpha = (\alpha_1, \ldots, \alpha_m) \in \mathbb{N}^m$ are called *multi-indices*. The order of a multi-index α is the non-negative integer $|\alpha| := \alpha_1 + \ldots + \alpha_m$.

In the next chapters we are interested in proving, with computer assistance, some theorems about analytic functions of several complex variables. Our arguments are formulated in Banach spaces and Banach algebras of infinite multi-sequences, because these spaces provide a natural framework for efficiently manipulating analytic functions of several complex variables on the digital computer.

As motivation for the more thorough discussion of multi-sequences to come, we first sketch – somewhat informally – the reduction of a nonlinear problem in functional analysis to an equivalent fixed point problem on a space of infinite multi-sequences. For the sake of simplicity we focus for a moment on the case $m = 1$.

Consider an operator equation of the form

$$\Psi(f(z)) = 0, \tag{2.1}$$

where $f(z)$ is an unknown analytic function. We think of Ψ as a mapping taking values in some space of analytic functions, and do not rule out the possibility that Ψ contains unbounded operators which are only densely defined. We look for a series solution of the form

$$f(z) = \sum_{n=0}^{\infty} a_n z^n.$$

Suppose that the power series coefficients of $\Psi \circ f$ are smooth functions of the unknown Taylor coefficients $\{a_n\}_{n=0}^{\infty}$. More precisely we assume that there are smooth, complex valued functions $\Psi_n\left(\{a_n\}_{n=0}^{\infty}\right)$ having that

$$\Psi(f(z)) = \sum_{n=0}^{\infty} \Psi_n\left(\{a_n\}_{n=0}^{\infty}\right) z^n.$$

Since an analytic function is the zero function if and only if all its Taylor coefficients are zero, the terms of the sequence $\{a_n\}_{n=0}^{\infty}$ are the Taylor coefficients of an analytic solution of Equation (2.1) if and only if

$$\Psi_n\left(\{a_n\}_{n=0}^{\infty}\right) = 0, \tag{2.2}$$

for all $n \in \mathbb{N}$. This standard "power matching scheme" reduces Equation (2.1) to a coupled system of countably many scalar equations in countably many scalar unknowns. Instead of an unknown function we now seek an unknown collection of complex numbers.

To further reduce the problem we observe that –very loosely speaking– the implicit function theorem allows us to solve Equation (2.2) for a_n in terms of the remaining variables. So for each $n \in \mathbb{N}$ we find a function T_n so that $\{a_n\}_{n=0}^{\infty}$ satisfies

$$a_n = T_n(a_0, \ldots, a_{n-1}, a_{n+1}, \ldots), \tag{2.3}$$

if and only if $\{a_n\}_{n=0}^{\infty}$ satisfies Equation (2.2).

Indeed for the applications considered in these lectures, and for many other applications whose nonlinearities involve multiplication of analytic functions or composition with elementary functions, the functions T_n in Equation (2.3) are easily derived from the Ψ_n of Equation (2.2) without any appeal to the implicit function theorem. Moreover the resulting nonlinear functionals T_n often have the form

$$a_n = T_n(a_0, \ldots, a_{n-1}), \tag{2.4}$$

for all $n \in \mathbb{N}$, where each T_n depends only on terms of order less than n.

Let $a = \{a_n\}_{n=0}^{\infty}$ denote the unknown coefficient sequence and define the map $T(a) = \{T_n(a)\}_{n=0}^{\infty}$. We now see that proving the existence of an analytic solution of Equation (2.1) is reduced to proving the existence of an infinite sequence $\{a_n\}_{n=0}^{\infty}$ solving the fixed point problem

$$T(a) = a.$$

A computer assisted solution of this problem has two major steps.

- **Step 1: Finite dimensional approximation:** We view Equation (2.4) as *recursion relations* for the unknown Taylor coefficients. Assuming that we have enough initial data to seed this recursion (a matter which must be addressed on a problem by problem basis) we compute a_n inductively from the known lower order terms $a_0, \ldots, a_{n-1}$. This recursion is repeated to any desired finite order N.
- **Step 2: Infinite dimensional validation:** Let $\bar{a}^N = (\bar{a}_0, \ldots, \bar{a}_N) \in \mathbb{C}^{N+1}$ denote the approximate solution obtained in Step 1. Since $\bar{a}^N$ is an *exact fixed point of* T *to order* N, we only have to prove the existence of a tail sequence $h = (0, \ldots, 0, h_{N+1}, h_{N+2}, \ldots)$ so that $\hat{a} = \bar{a}^N + h$ is an exact fixed point of the full operator T. In the present work this task is aided by the contraction mapping theorem. The idea is that, because Taylor coefficients of analytic functions satisfy classical growth estimates, we can choose a norm in which the tail mapping $\{T_n(\bar{a}^N + h)\}_{n=N+1}^{\infty}$ is a contraction in an appropriate ball about the known finite dimensional fixed point $\bar{a}^N$.

2.1. Banach algebras of infinite multi-sequences. Let $\mathcal{S}_m$ denote the set of all m-dimensional infinite multi-sequences of complex numbers. Note that $\mathcal{S}_m$ is a vector space, and with $\nu > 0$ define the quantity

$$\|a\|^1_{\nu,m} := \sum_{\alpha_1=0}^{\infty} \cdots \sum_{\alpha_m=0}^{\infty} |a_{\alpha_1,\ldots,\alpha_m}| \nu^{\alpha_1+\ldots+\alpha_m} = \sum_{|\alpha|=0}^{\infty} |a_\alpha| \nu^{|\alpha|},$$

The set

$$\ell^1_{\nu,m} := \left\{ a = \{a_\alpha\} \in \mathcal{S}_m : \|a\|^1_{\nu,m} < \infty \right\},$$

is a Banach space. Let $B(\ell^1_{\nu,m})$ denote the collection of all bounded linear operators from $\ell^1_{\nu,m}$ into itself, and note that $B(\ell^1_{\nu,m})$ is a Banach space.

The sequence spaces $\ell^1_{\nu,m}$ are related to Banach spaces of analytic functions. More precisely, let $z = (z_1, \ldots, z_m) \in \mathbb{C}^m$ and $r > 0$. Define the poly-disk of radius r centered at z by

$$D^m_r(z) := \left\{ w = (w_1, \ldots, w_m) \in \mathbb{C}^m : \max_{1 \le j \le m} |w_j - z_j| < r \right\},$$

where $|\cdot|$ denotes the usual complex absolute value. Endow $\mathbb{C}^m$ with the norm

$$\|z\| := \max_{1 \le j \le m} |z_j|,$$

and note that poly-disks are the balls induced by this norm. The poly-disk $D^m_r(0)$, i.e. "the ball of radius r at the origin of $\mathbb{C}^m$" is especially important in the discussion to follow and we often drop the (0) notation and write simply D^m_r.

Let $C^\omega(D^m_r)$ denote the set of all bounded analytic functions on D^m_r taking values in $\mathbb{C}$, and recall that $C^\omega(D^m_r)$ is a Banach space when endowed with the C^0 norm. Then for any $a = \{a_\alpha\}_{\alpha \in \mathbb{N}^m} \in \ell^1_{\nu,m}$, the function f defined by

$$f(z) = \sum_{|\alpha|=0}^{\infty} a_\alpha z^\alpha,$$

has $f \in C^\omega(D^m_\nu)$. A partial converse is given by the following observation: if $f \in C^\omega(D^m_r)$, then the Taylor coefficients of f are in $\ell^1_{\nu,m}$ for all $\nu < r$.

Recall also that the product of two analytic functions is again analytic, i.e. $C^\omega(D_\nu^m)$ is a Banach algebra under pointwise multiplication of functions. The sequence space $\ell^1_{\nu,m}$ inherits this Banach algebra structure, as we now discuss. Define the binary product $*\colon \ell^1_{\nu,m} \times \ell^1_{\nu,m} \to \mathcal{S}_m$ by

$$(a*b)_\alpha = \sum_{\beta_1=0}^{\alpha_1} \cdots \sum_{\beta_m=0}^{\alpha_m} a_{\alpha_1-\beta_1,\ldots,\alpha_m-\beta_m} b_{\beta_1,\ldots,\beta_m},$$

with $a, b \in \ell^1_{\nu,m}$. Note that the product is commutative. We refer to $*$ as the *Cauchy product*, and for $a, b \in \ell^1_{\nu,m}$ have

- $$\|a*b\|^1_{\nu,m} \le \|a\|^1_{\nu,m}\|b\|^1_{\nu,m},$$
  i.e. the pair $(\ell^1_{\nu,m}, *)$ is a Banach algebra.
- If $f, g \in C^\omega(D_r^m)$ have Taylor series expansions
  $$f(z) = \sum_{|\alpha|=0}^\infty a_\alpha z^\alpha, \qquad \text{and} \qquad g(z) = \sum_{|\alpha|=0}^\infty b_\alpha z^\alpha,$$
  then $f \cdot g \in C^\omega(D_r^m)$ and has power series representation
  $$(f\cdot g)(z) = \sum_{|\alpha|=0}^\infty (a*b)_\alpha z^\alpha,$$
  i.e. pointwise multiplication of functions corresponds to Cauchy products of infinite multi-sequences.

Differentiation does not define a bounded linear operator on $C^\omega(D_r^m)$, hence cannot induce a bounded linear map on $\ell^1_{\nu,m}$. But, as usual in complex analysis, we recover bounds on the derivative after giving up some portion of the domain. More precisely we have the following Lemma, whose proof is an exercise.

LEMMA 2.1 (Cauchy Bounds in Several Complex Variables). *Let $\nu > 0$, and $a = \{a_\alpha\}_{\alpha\in\mathbb{N}^m} \in \ell^1_{\nu,m}$. Define $f\colon D_\nu^m \to \mathbb{C}$*

$$f(z) := \sum_{|\alpha|=0}^\infty a_\alpha z^\alpha.$$

Let $0 < \sigma \le 1$ and

$$\tilde{\nu} = e^{-\sigma}\nu.$$

Then

$$\sup_{z\in D_{\tilde\nu}^m} \left|\frac{\partial}{\partial z_j} f(z)\right| \le \frac{1}{\nu\sigma}\|a\|^1_{\nu,m},$$

for each $1 \le j \le m$.

Recall that polynomial operations on a Banach algebra are Fréchet differentiable. For example fix $c \in \ell^1_{\nu,m}$ and define the maps $F, G\colon \ell^1_{\nu,m} \to \ell^1_{\nu,m}$ by

$$G(a) := c*a, \qquad \text{and} \qquad F(a) := a*a.$$

Then F and G are Fréchet differentiable, and the derivatives $DG(a), DF(a) \in B(\ell^1_{\nu,m})$ have action given by

$$DG(a)h = c*h, \qquad \text{and} \qquad DF(a)h = 2(a*h),$$

for $h \in \ell^1_{\nu,m}$. This is as much calculus on Banach spaces as is needed in the present note.

2.2. Projection and truncation spaces. Define the linear subspaces

$$X^N_{\nu,m} = \left\{ a = \{a_\alpha\} \in \ell^1_{\nu,m} \,|\, a_\alpha = 0 \text{ when } |\alpha| \geq N+1 \right\},$$

and

$$X^\infty_{\nu,m} = \left\{ a = \{a_\alpha\} \in \ell^1_{\nu,m} | a_\alpha = 0 \text{ when } 0 \leq |\alpha| \leq N \right\},$$

and the canonical projection operators $\pi_N \colon \ell^1_{\nu,m} \to X^N_{\nu,m}$ and $\pi_\infty \colon \ell^1_{\nu,m} \to X^\infty_{\nu,m}$ by

$$\pi_N(a)_\alpha = \begin{cases} a_\alpha & \text{if } 0 \leq |\alpha| \leq N \\ 0 & \text{if } |\alpha| \geq N+1 \end{cases},$$

and

$$\pi_\infty(a)_\alpha = \begin{cases} 0 & \text{if } 0 \leq |\alpha| \leq N \\ a_\alpha & \text{if } |\alpha| \geq N+1 \end{cases}.$$

Note that

- $X^N_{\nu,m}$, and $X^\infty_{\nu,m}$ are closed linear subspaces of $\ell^1_{\nu,m}$, hence Banach spaces in their own right (endowed with the $\ell^1_{\nu,m}$ norm).
- $\ell^1_{\nu,m} = X^N_{\nu,m} \oplus X^\infty_{\nu,m}$, i.e. each $a \in \ell^1_{\nu,m}$ has unique decomposition

  $$a = \pi_N(a) + \pi_\infty(a).$$

  Moreover, the projections are bounded linear operators.
- $X^\infty_{\nu,m}$ inherits the Banach algebra structure of $\ell^1_{\nu,m}$, i.e. if $u, v \in X^\infty_{\nu,m}$, then $u * v \in X^\infty_{\nu,m}$, and we have

  $$\|u * v\|_{X^\infty_{\nu,m}} = \|u * v\|^1_{\nu,m} \leq \|u\|^1_{\nu,m} \|v\|^1_{\nu,m} = \|u\|_{X^\infty_{\nu,m}} \|v\|_{X^\infty_{\nu,m}},$$

  as the norm on $X^\infty_{\nu,m}$ is the norm inherited from $\ell^1_{\nu,m}$. On the other hand, note that $X^N_{\nu,m}$ does not inherit the Banach algebra structure. This is because a typical pair $a, b \in X^N_{\nu,m}$ has product $a * b \in \ell^1_{\nu,m}$ with nonzero projection into $X^\infty_{\nu,m}$.

  This make sense when we view the elements of $\ell^1_{\nu,m}$ as Taylor coefficients, since the product of two polynomials of degree N is a polynomial of degree $2N$. Yet, given two analytic functions, both zero to order N, we see that there product is zero to order N as well. (In fact their product is zero to order $2N$, but this does not play an important role in the discussion to follow).
- Taking the previous remark a step further, note that if $a^N \in X^N_{\nu,m}$ and $u \in X^\infty_{\nu,m}$ then $a^N * u \in X^\infty_{\nu,m}$, as a consequence of the fact that when we multiply an analytic function by an analytic function which is zero to order N the resulting product is zero to order N.

While $X^N_{\nu,m}$ does not inherit a Banach algebra structure from the Cauchy product, there is a truncated Cauchy product on $X^N_{\nu,m}$ defined as follows. For $a^N, b^N \in X^N_{\nu,m}$ define $(\cdot * \cdot)^N \colon X^N_{\nu,m} \oplus X^N_{\nu,m} \to X^N_{\nu,m}$ by

$$(a^N * b^N)^N := \pi_N(a^N * b^N),$$

so that product $(a^N * b^N)^N$ has components

$$(a^N * b^N)^N_\alpha = \begin{cases} \sum_{\beta_1=0}^{\alpha_1} \cdots \sum_{\beta_m=0}^{\alpha_m} a_{\alpha-\beta} b_\beta & \text{if } 0 \le |\alpha| \le N \\ 0 & \text{if } |\alpha| \ge N+1 \end{cases}.$$

The pair $\left(X^N_{\nu,m}, (\cdot * \cdot)^N\right)$ is a Banach algebra.

The neglected terms define yet another a product $(\cdot * \cdot)^\infty \colon X^N_{\nu,m} \oplus X^N_{\nu,m} \to X^\infty_{\nu,m}$ by

$$(a^N * b^N)^\infty := \pi_\infty(a^N * a^N),$$

so that $(a^N * b^N)^\infty$ has components

$$(a^N * b^N)^\infty_\alpha = \begin{cases} 0 & \text{if } 0 \le |\alpha| \le N \\ \sum_{\beta_1=0}^{\alpha_1} \cdots \sum_{\beta_m=0}^{\alpha_m} a_{\alpha-\beta} b_\beta & \text{if } N+1 \le |\alpha| \le 2N \\ 0 & \text{if } |\alpha| \ge 2N+1 \end{cases}.$$

REMARK 2.2 (Derivatives of truncation errors). The projection operators commute with Fréchet derivatives. This follows from the fact that the projection operators are bounded and linear. So for example

$$D_u \pi_\infty((a^N + u) * (b^N + v))h = b^N * h + v * h,$$

and

$$D_u \pi_\infty((a^N + u) * (a^N + u))h = 2a^N * h + 2u * h,$$

for $h \in X^\infty_{\nu,m}$. Other derivatives are similar.

2.3. Error analysis for two specialized product operations. This section contains some more technical generalizations of the material above, and is used in the computer assisted analysis of invariant manifolds and Taylor integrators to follow. The two product operations defined below allow us to, in various settings, solve the recursion relations for some Taylor series problems without the use of the implicit function theorem.

2.3.1. *The "hat" product for invariant manifolds.* When analyzing invariant manifolds we encounter operator equations containing terms of the form

$$cz_j \frac{\partial}{\partial z_j} f(z_1, \ldots, z_m) = g(z_1, \ldots, z_m) f(z_1, \ldots, z_m), \tag{2.5}$$

with $c \in \mathbb{C}$, g a known and f an unknown function. Further motivation for this equation is discussed in Section 3.1, and for now we just note that the first order partial differential operator on the left hand side is the push forward of the vector field $z_j' = cz_j$ under f. Considering $1 \le j \le m$ the operators on the left hand side of Equation (2.5) form a basis for more general push forwards.

On the level of power series Equation (2.5) is

$$\sum_{|\alpha|=0}^{\infty} c\alpha_j a_\alpha z^\alpha = \sum_{|\alpha|=0}^{\infty} (a * b)_\alpha z^\alpha,$$

which, after matching like powers, is

$$c\alpha_j a_\alpha = (a * b)_\alpha = \sum_{\beta_1=0}^{\alpha_1} \cdots \sum_{\beta_m=0}^{\alpha_m} a_{\alpha_1-\beta_1,\ldots,\alpha_m-\beta_m} b_{\beta_1,\ldots,\beta_m}. \tag{2.6}$$

To solve for the coefficient a_α we remove from the sum on the right any terms whose multi-index is α. Note that a_α appears in the sum if and only if $\beta = 0$, and that b_α appears if and only if $\beta = \alpha$. So, define

$$\hat{\delta}_\beta^\alpha := \begin{cases} 0 & \text{if } \beta = 0 \\ 0 & \text{if } \beta = \alpha \\ 1 & \text{otherwise} \end{cases}, \tag{2.7}$$

and observe that

$$(a * b)_\alpha = a_\alpha b_0 + b_\alpha a_0 + \sum_{\beta_1=0}^{\alpha_1} \cdots \sum_{\beta_m=0}^{\alpha_m} \hat{\delta}_\beta^\alpha a_{\alpha_1-\beta_1,\dots,\alpha_m-\beta_m} b_{\beta_1,\dots,\beta_m}.$$

(This $\hat{\delta}$ is related to the usual *Kronecker delta* δ_β^α by $\hat{\delta}_\beta^\alpha = 1 - \delta_\beta^\alpha$).

This operation – namely extracting terms containing the multi-index α from the Cauchy product – is important enough that we define a new binary product based on the discussion above. The following discussion is somewhat tedious, but makes quite transparent the analysis of invariant manifolds in the sequel. The reader may want to skip the remainder of this section on first reading and refer back only as needed.

Let $\hat{*}\colon \ell_{\nu,m}^1 \oplus \ell_{\nu,m}^1 \to \ell_{\nu,m}^1$ have components defined by

$$(a \hat{*} b)_\alpha := \sum_{\beta_1=0}^{\alpha_1} \cdots \sum_{\beta_m=0}^{\alpha_m} \hat{\delta}_\beta^\alpha a_{\alpha-\beta} b_\beta.$$

Then

$$(a * b)_\alpha = a_0 b_\alpha + a_\alpha b_0 + (a \hat{*} b)_\alpha,$$

where $(a \hat{*} b)_\alpha$ depends only on terms of order strictly less than $|\alpha|$. Returning to Equation (2.6), we see that the power series coefficients of the solution of Equation (2.5) satisfy the recursion

$$a_\alpha = \frac{1}{c\alpha_j - b_0}\left(a_0 b_\alpha + (a \hat{*} b)_\alpha\right),$$

as long as the *non-resonance condition* $\alpha_j c \neq b_0$ for all $|\alpha| \geq 1$ is satisfied.

Define the binary operations (or products) $(\cdot \hat{*} \cdot)^N \colon X_{\nu,m}^N \oplus X_{\nu,m}^N \to X_{\nu,m}^N$ and $(\cdot \hat{*} \cdot)^\infty \colon X_{\nu,m}^N \oplus X_{\nu,m}^N \to X_{\nu,m}^\infty$ by

$$(a^N \hat{*} b^N)^N = \pi_N(a^N \hat{*} b^N) = \begin{cases} \sum_{\beta_1=0}^{\alpha_1} \cdots \sum_{\beta_m=0}^{\alpha_m} \hat{\delta}_\beta^\alpha a_{\alpha-\beta} b_\beta & \text{if } 0 \leq |\alpha| \leq N \\ 0 & \text{if } |\alpha| \geq N+1 \end{cases}$$

and

$$(a^N \hat{*} b^N)^\infty = \pi_\infty(a^N \hat{*} a^N) = \begin{cases} 0 & \text{if } 0 \leq |\alpha| \leq N \\ \sum_{\beta_1=0}^{\alpha_1} \cdots \sum_{\beta_m=0}^{\alpha_m} \hat{\delta}_\beta^\alpha a_{\alpha-\beta} b_\beta & \text{if } N+1 \leq |\alpha| \leq 2N \\ 0 & \text{if } |\alpha| \geq 2N+1 \end{cases},$$

so that

$$a \hat{*} b = \pi_N(a \hat{*} b) + \pi_\infty(a \hat{*} b)$$

where

$$\pi_N(a \hat{*} b) = (\pi_N(a) \hat{*} \pi_N(b))^N,$$

and

$$\pi_\infty(a \hat{*} b) = (\pi_N(a) \hat{*} \pi_N(b))^\infty + \pi_N(a) \hat{*} \pi_\infty(b) + \pi_N(b) \hat{*} \pi_\infty(a) + \pi_\infty(a) \hat{*} \pi_\infty(b). \tag{2.8}$$

The following estimate is used in the truncation analysis of invariant manifolds.

LEMMA 2.3. *Let $a^N, b^N \in X^N_{\nu,m}$ and $u, v \in X^\infty_{\nu,m}$. Then*

$$\|a^N \hat{*} u\|^1_{\nu,m} \leq \left(\sum_{|\alpha|=1}^{N} |a^N_\alpha| \nu^{|\alpha|} \right) \|u\|^1_{\nu,m},$$

so that

$$\begin{aligned}\|\pi_\infty((a^N + u)\hat{*}(b^N + v))\|_{X^\infty_{\nu,m}} \leq & \sum_{|\alpha|=N+1}^{2N} \left| \sum_{\beta_1=0}^{\alpha_1} \cdots \sum_{\beta_m=0}^{\alpha_m} \hat{\delta}^\alpha_\beta a^N_{\alpha-\beta} b^N_\beta \right| \nu^{|\alpha|} \\ & + \left(\sum_{|\alpha|=1}^{N} |a^N_\alpha| \nu^{|\alpha|} \right) \|v\|^1_{\nu,m} \\ & + \left(\sum_{|\alpha|=1}^{N} |b^N_\alpha| \nu^{|\alpha|} \right) \|u\|^1_{\nu,m} \\ & + \|u\|^1_{\nu,m} \|v\|^1_{\nu,m}.\end{aligned}$$

PROOF. Consider the bound on $\|a^N \hat{*} u\|^1_{\nu,m}$ and define the sequence

$$\hat{a}^N_\alpha = \begin{cases} 0 & \text{if } \alpha = 0 \\ a^N_\alpha & \text{if } 1 \leq |\alpha| \leq N \\ 0 & \text{if } |\alpha| \geq N+1 \end{cases}.$$

Note that

$$\|a^N \hat{*} u\|^1_{\nu,m} = \|\hat{a} * u\|^1_{\nu,m} \leq \|\hat{a}\|^1_{\nu,m} \|u\|^1_{\nu,m} = \left(\sum_{|\alpha|=1}^{N} |a^N_\alpha| \nu^{|\alpha|} \right) \|u\|^1_{\nu,m},$$

as desired. To complete the proof we apply the estimate above in conjunction with the Banach algebra estimate to the decomposition given in Equation (2.8). □

2.3.2. *A shift operator for initial value problems.* In our study of Taylor integrators we encounter equations of the form

$$\frac{\partial}{\partial z_j} f(z_1, \ldots, z_m) = f(z_1, \ldots, z_m) g(z_1, \ldots, z_m), \tag{2.9}$$

subject to the constraint

$$f(0, \ldots, 0) = w_0 \in \mathbb{C},$$

where, for the moment we consider g a known function. The motivation for this equation is that the right hand side provides a basis for the push forward of constant vector fields, which in turn are the foundation of the flow box theorem for initial value problems.

On the level of power series Equation (2.9) becomes

$$\sum_{|\alpha|=0}^{\infty} (\alpha_j + 1) a_{\alpha_1, \ldots, \alpha_j+1, \ldots, \alpha_m} z^\alpha = \sum_{|\alpha|=0}^{\infty} (a * b)_\alpha z^\alpha,$$

which, after matching like powers becomes

$$a_0 = w_0,$$

and

$$(\alpha_j + 1)a_{\alpha_1,\ldots,\alpha_{j+1},\ldots,\alpha_m} = (a * b)_\alpha, \qquad \text{for } |\alpha| \geq 0.$$

We prefer to write the equation indexed to order α, so that

$$a_\alpha = \frac{1}{\alpha_j}(a * b)_{\alpha_1,\ldots,\alpha_j - 1,\ldots,\alpha_m},$$

for $|\alpha_j| > 1$. Note that the expression on the right does not involve any terms of order $|\alpha|$.

The operation of lowering an index and then reindexing, which occurs any time we consider first order partial differential operators, is important enough to warrant special consideration and is formalized as follows. Again, the reader may want to skip ahead and refer back to the remainder of the section only as needed.

For $1 \leq j \leq m$ define the shift operator $S_j \colon \ell^1_{\nu,m} \to \ell^1_{\nu,m}$ by

$$S_j(a)_\alpha = \begin{cases} 0 & \text{if } \alpha_j = 0 \\ a_{\alpha_1,\ldots,\alpha_j - 1,\ldots,\alpha_m} & \text{if } \alpha_j \geq 1 \end{cases}.$$

The following lemma codifies some useful bounds.

LEMMA 2.4. *Suppose that $a^N \in X^N_{\nu,m}$ and $u \in X^\infty_{\nu,m}$. Then*

$$\left\|\pi_\infty\left(S_j(a^N + u)\right)\right\|^1_{\nu,m} \leq \nu^{N+1}\left(\sum_{|\alpha|=N}\left|a^N_{\alpha_1,\ldots,\alpha_j,\ldots,\alpha_m}\right|\right) + \nu\|u\|^1_{\nu,m}.$$

PROOF. Since S_j and π_∞ are both linear operators, we have that

$$\|\pi_\infty S_j(a^N+u)\|^1_{\nu,m} = \|\pi_\infty S_j(a^N)+\pi_\infty S_j(u)\|^1_{\nu,m} \leq \|\pi_\infty S_j(a^N)\|^1_{\nu,m} + \|\pi_\infty S_j(u)\|^1_{\nu,m}.$$

Then we will bound the pieces singly. For the first term we have that

$$\begin{aligned}
\|\pi_\infty S_j(a^N)\|^1_{\nu,m} &= \sum_{|\alpha|=0}^{\infty} \left|\left[\pi_\infty S_j\left(a^N\right)\right]_\alpha\right| \nu^{|\alpha|} \\
&= \sum_{|\alpha|=N+1}^{\infty} \left|S_j\left(a^N\right)_\alpha\right| \nu^{|\alpha|} \\
&= \sum_{|\alpha|=N+1}^{\infty} \left|a^N_{\alpha_1,\ldots,\alpha_j-1,\ldots,\alpha_m}\right| \nu^{|\alpha|} \\
&= \sum_{|\alpha|=N+1} \left|a^N_{\alpha_1,\ldots,\alpha_j-1,\ldots,\alpha_m}\right| \nu^{N+1} \\
&= \nu^{N+1}\left(\sum_{|\alpha|=N}\left|a^N_{\alpha_1,\ldots,\alpha_j,\ldots,\alpha_m}\right|\right)
\end{aligned}$$

as $a^N_\alpha = 0$ for all $\alpha \in \mathbb{N}^m$ with $|\alpha| \geq N + 1$.

For the second term we have that

$$
\begin{aligned}
\|\pi_\infty S_j(u)\|_{\nu,m}^1 &= \sum_{|\alpha|=0}^{\infty} \left|[\pi_\infty S_j(u)]_\alpha\right| \nu^{|\alpha|} \\
&= \sum_{|\alpha|=N+1}^{\infty} \left|S_j(u)_\alpha\right| \nu^{|\alpha|} \\
&= \sum_{|\alpha|=N+1}^{\infty} \left|u_{\alpha_1,\ldots,\alpha_j-1,\ldots,\alpha_m}\right| \nu^{\alpha_1+\ldots+\alpha_j+\ldots+\alpha_m} \\
&= \nu \sum_{|\alpha|=N+1}^{\infty} \left|u_{\alpha_1,\ldots,\alpha_j-1,\ldots,\alpha_m}\right| \nu^{\alpha_1+\ldots+\alpha_j-1+\ldots+\alpha_m} \\
&= \nu \sum_{|\alpha|=N}^{\infty} \left|u_{\alpha_1,\ldots,\alpha_j,\ldots,\alpha_m}\right| \nu^{\alpha_1+\ldots+\alpha_j+\ldots+\alpha_m} \\
&\leq \nu \sum_{|\alpha|=0}^{\infty} \left|u_{\alpha_1,\ldots,\alpha_j,\ldots,\alpha_m}\right| \nu^{\alpha_1+\ldots+\alpha_j+\ldots+\alpha_m} \\
&= \nu\|u\|_{\nu,m}^1,
\end{aligned}
$$

where the inequality exploits the fact that $u_\alpha = 0$ when $|\alpha| \leq N$. Combining the estimates of the first and second terms gives the result. □

Now for $1 \leq j \leq m$ consider the nonlinear operation $S_j(a * b)$. We have the following estimate.

LEMMA 2.5. *Let $a^N, b^N \in X_{\nu,m}^N$ and $u, v \in X_{\nu,m}^\infty$. Then*

$$
\begin{aligned}
\|\pi_\infty(S_j((a^N+u)*(b^N+v)))\|_{\nu,m}^1 \leq \nu^{N+1} &\left(\sum_{|\alpha|=N} \left|(a^N * b^N)_\alpha\right| \right) \\
&+ \nu \sum_{|\alpha|=N+1}^{2N} \left|(a^N * b^N)_\alpha\right| \nu^{|\alpha|} \\
&+ \nu\|a^N\|_{\nu,m}^1 \|v\|_{\nu,m}^1 \\
&+ \nu\|b^N\|_{\nu,m}^1 \|u\|_{\nu,m}^1 \\
&+ \nu\|u\|_{\nu,m}^1 \|v\|_{\nu,m}^1
\end{aligned}
$$

PROOF. First note that

$$
\begin{aligned}
\pi_\infty(S_j((a^N+u)*(b^N+v))) &= \pi_\infty(S_j(a^N * b^N + a^N * v + b^N * u + u * v)) \\
&= \pi_\infty S_j(a^N * b^N) + \pi_\infty S_j(a^N * v) + \pi_\infty S_j(b^N * u) \\
&\quad + \pi_\infty S_j(u * v).
\end{aligned}
$$

So we consider each of the four terms singly.

For the first term, recall that

$$
(a^N * b^N) = (a^N * b^N)^N + (a^N * b^N)^\infty,
$$

with $(a^N * b^N)^N \in X^1_{\nu,m}$ and $(a^N * b^N)^\infty \in X^\infty_{\nu,m}$. Then, by Lemma 2.4, we have that

$$\begin{aligned}\|\pi_\infty S_j(a^N * b^N)\|^1_{\nu,m} &= \left\|\pi_\infty S_j((a^N * b^N)^N + (a^N * b^N)^\infty)\right\|^1_{\nu,m} \\ &\leq \nu^{N+1}\left(\sum_{|\alpha|=N} \left|(a^N * b^N)^N_\alpha\right|\right) + \nu\left\|(a^N * b^N)^\infty\right\|^1_{\nu,m} \\ &= \nu^{N+1}\left(\sum_{|\alpha|=N} \left|(a^N * b^N)_\alpha\right|\right) + \nu\left(\sum_{|\alpha|=N+1}^{2N} \left|(a^N * b^N)_\alpha\right| \nu^{|\alpha|}\right).\end{aligned}$$

For the remaining terms we note that $a^N * v$, $b^N * u$, and $u * v$ are all in $X^\infty_{\nu,m}$ and hence have zero projections into $X^N_{\nu,m}$. Combining this observation with Lemma 2.4 and the Banach algebra estimate completes the proof. □

REMARK 2.6. The special products discussed above could have been defined instead as certain linear operators composed with standard Cauchy products. This results in the same bounds given above, however the analysis arguably more standard (i.e. the discussion centers on bounding the linear operators). The downside is that this approach requires carrying around a little more notation. It is a question of taste as to which approach one prefers.

2.4. Two a-posteriori existence theorems. The following theorems are sufficient for the computer assisted analysis in the remainder of the Lecture. Both theorems are "a-posteriori" in the sense that given a good enough approximate fixed point/zero of an equation they provide conditions sufficient to conclude the existence of a true solution nearby. We give the proof of the first theorem for the sake of completeness, and refer to the literature for the proof of the second. In both cases the interested reader is referred also to the works of [**39**, **60**, **61**, **77**, **78**, **91**, **98**] for more thorough discussion and historical context.

PROPOSITION 2.7. *Let X be a Banach space, $\bar{x} \in X$, and suppose that $T\colon X \to X$ is a Fréchet differentiable mapping. Suppose that Y_0, Z_1 are positive constants and that $Z_2\colon (0,\infty) \to [0,\infty)$ is a positive function, having*

$$\|T(\bar{x}) - \bar{x}\| \leq Y_0,$$

and that

$$\sup_{x \in \overline{B_r(0)}} \|DT(\bar{x} + x)\| \leq Z_1 + Z_2(r)r,$$

for all $r > 0$.

If there is an $r > 0$ so that

$$Z_2(r)r^2 - (1 - Z_1)r + Y_0 \leq 0, \tag{2.10}$$

then there is unique $\hat{x} \in \overline{B_r(\bar{x})}$ with $T(\hat{x}) = \hat{x}$.

PROOF. Note that $\overline{B_r(\bar{x})}$ is a complete metric space. Now for $x \in \overline{B_r(\bar{x})}$ consider

$$\begin{aligned} \|T(x) - \bar{x}\| &\leq \|T(x) - T(\bar{x})\| + \|T(\bar{x}) - \bar{x}\| \\ &\leq \sup_{z \in \overline{B_r(\bar{x})}} \|DT(z)\| \|x - \bar{x}\| + Y_0 \\ &\leq (Z_1 + Z_2(r)r) \|x - \bar{x}\| + Y_0 \\ &\leq Z_2(r)r^2 + Z_1 r + Y_0 \\ &\leq r, \end{aligned}$$

by the hypothesis given in Equation (2.10). Then T maps $\overline{B_r(\bar{x})}$ into itself.

Now choose $x, y \in \overline{B_r(\bar{x})}$, and consider

$$\begin{aligned} \|T(x) - T(y)\| &\leq \sup_{z \in \overline{B_r(\bar{x})}} \|DT(z)\| \|x - y\| \\ &\leq (Z_1 + Z_2(r)r) \|x - y\|. \end{aligned}$$

From Equation (2.10) we have that

$$Z_2(r)r^2 + Z_1 r + Y_0 \leq r,$$

or

$$Z_2(r)r + Z_1 + \frac{Y_0}{r} \leq 1.$$

Now since $Z_2(r), Z_1, Y_0$ and r are strictly positive, it follows that

$$Z_2(r)r + Z_1 < 1,$$

so that T is a strict contraction on $\overline{B_r(\bar{x})}$. The existence of a unique fixed point now follows from the Banach fixed point theorem. □

The following theorem provides for a-posteriori analysis of finite dimensional systems of nonlinear equations.

PROPOSITION 2.8. *Let $U \subset \mathbb{R}^n$ be an open set, $F \colon U \to \mathbb{R}^n$ be twice continuously differentiable on U, $\bar{x} \in U$, A be an $n \times n$ matrix, and $r_* > 0$ be such that $\overline{B_{r_*}(\bar{x})} \subset U$. Suppose that Y_0, Z_0, Z_2 are positive constants with*

$$\|AF(\bar{x})\| \leq Y_0,$$

$$\|Id - ADF(\bar{x})\| \leq Z_0,$$

$$\|A\| \sup_{x \in \overline{B_{r_*}(\bar{x})}} \|D^2F(x)\| \leq Z_2.$$

Define the polynomial

$$p(r) := Z_2 r^2 - (1 - Z_0)r + Y_0.$$

If $0 < r \leq r_*$ has that

$$p(r) \leq 0,$$

then A is invertible and there exists a unique $x_* \in \overline{B_r(\bar{x})}$ so that

$$F(x_*) = 0.$$

Moreover $DF(x_*)$ is invertible and

$$\|DF(x_*)^{-1}\| \leq \frac{\|A\|}{1 - Z_2 r - Z_0}.$$

A proof is found, for example in [**68**]. The interested reader can easily supply a proof by applying Theorem 2.7 to the "Newton-like" operator

$$T(x) = x - AF(x),$$

on a ball about $\bar{x}$.

2.5. A classic example: the Lorenz system. The numerical examples discussed in the remainder of this lecture focus on the familiar Lorenz system. This is the ordinary differential equation associated with the vector field $f\colon \mathbb{R}^3 \to \mathbb{R}^3$ given by

$$f(x, y, z) = \begin{pmatrix} \sigma(y - x) \\ x(\rho - z) - y \\ xy - \beta z \end{pmatrix}.$$

For $\rho > 1$ there are three real equilibrium points

$$p^0 = \begin{pmatrix} 0 \\ 0 \\ 0 \end{pmatrix}, \qquad \text{and} \qquad p^{1,2} = \begin{pmatrix} \pm\sqrt{\beta(\rho-1)} \\ \pm\sqrt{\beta(\rho-1)} \\ \rho - 1 \end{pmatrix}.$$

It is an exercise to work out the eigenvalues and eigenvectors by hand.

Remark 2.9 (Validated numerics for existence and localization of an equilibrium solution). Locating equilibrium solutions is more difficult when we study systems with more complicated nonlinearities, and it is often difficult (if not impossible) to write down explicit formulas. A typical strategy for studying equilibrium solutions is to compute a numerical zero using Newton's method, and then validate the existence of a true zero nearby using an a-posteriori Theorem such as 2.8 or one of its variants. This issue is discussed in detail in the review paper of Rump [**81**] and in the book of Tucker [**86**], and the interval arithmetic package IntLab [**82**] has a number of built-in validated nonlinear solvers.

Remark 2.10 (Validated numerics for linear stability analysis of an equilibrium solution). It is a standard exercise to work out by hand explicit formulas for the eigenvalues/eigenvectors in Lorenz. Yet for more complicated nonlinearities in higher dimensions this exercise becomes impractical. Instead this data is often obtained by a separate computer assisted proof.

Standard numerical packages are able to compute eigenvalues/eigenvectors for vector fields of up to a few thousand dimensions. Once numerics provide an approximate eigenvalue/eigenvector pair, we can study the system of (nonlinear) equations

$$Df(p)\xi - \lambda\xi = 0, \qquad \|\xi\|^2 - 1 = 0,$$

once again using Theorem 2.8 or a variant. (The constraint above works for real eigenvalue/eigenvector pair. See [**25, 81**] for more general discussion). Again, we refer to the review paper of Rump [**81**] for more thorough review of the literature and remark that IntLab [**82**] is equipped with validated eigenvalue/eigenvector solvers.

3. The local problem: equilibria, stability, and local invariant manifolds

As per the philosophy outlined in Section 2, we will formulate an operator equation whose solution is a chart map for the desired local invariant manifold. Two classical approaches to this problem are the graph transform method, and the

Lyapunov-Perron method (see Chapter 5 of [**80**] for more complete discussion of this literature) and another is found in the work of Irwin [**57**].

Our approach is based on the parameterization method of [**14–16**]. The idea of the parameterization method is to formulate a conjugacy between the invariant manifold of interest and some simpler dynamical model. The user of the method is free to choose the model system, though a poor choice may well lead to no solution. This freedom makes the method very flexible, and it applies to problems as diverse as invariant circles and their stable/unstable manifolds [**51–53**], breakdown/collisions of invariant bundles associated with quasi periodic dynamics [**17, 41**], stable/unstable manifolds of periodic orbits of differential equations and diffeomorphisms [**16, 26, 48, 50, 56**], slow stable manifolds [**14, 16**] and their invariant vector bundles [**87**], and invariant tori for differential equations [**20, 41**]. The parameterization methods leads to KAM strategies without action angle variables [**18, 19, 33, 35**], and is used to study invariant objects for PDEs [**34, 43, 79**] and DDEs [**49, 55, 65**]. Moreover the short list above is far from complete. A thorough description of the method, as well as many more examples and much more complete discussion of the literature, is found in a recent book devoted to the subject [**54**].

Since it is based on the study of conjugacy equations, the parameterization method leads naturally to a-posteriori validation and computer assisted proof. The interested reader will want to consult [**13, 58, 68, 70, 88, 92**] for more discussion of validated numerics based on the parameterization method. See also [**42**] for a modern approach to computer assisted proof for invariant tori based on the parameterization method. Again, we also refer to [**54**] for more discussion.

3.1. Representation of the local invariant manifold by a conjugating chart: the parameterization method for vector fields on $\mathbb{R}^n$. In this section we review enough parameterization method to facilitate the validated computer assisted analysis of stable/unstable manifolds in the sequel. Focusing for the moment on the stable manifold, suppose that $p \in \mathbb{R}^n$ is an equilibrium point for an analytic vector field $f\colon \mathbb{R}^n \to \mathbb{R}^n$, and that $Df(p)$ has $m \leq n$ stable eigenvalues, which we denote by $\lambda_1, \ldots, \lambda_m \in \mathbb{R}$. Assume for the present discussion that the m stable eigenvalues are real and distinct, and let $\xi_1, \ldots, \xi_m \in \mathbb{R}^n$ an associated choice of real eigenvectors. Later, when it is helpful to do so, we go a step further and assumer that $Df(p)$ is diagonalizable,

We are interested in the m-dimensional local stable manifold attached to p, and in this context the parameterization method looks for a solution of the invariance equation

$$\lambda_1 s_1 \frac{\partial}{\partial s_1} P(s_1, \ldots, s_m) + \ldots + \lambda_m s_m \frac{\partial}{\partial s_m} P(s_1, \ldots, s_m) = f(P(s_1, \ldots, s_m)). \tag{3.1}$$

Our interest in Equation (3.1) is due to the fact that a function $P\colon (-1,1)^m \to \mathbb{R}^n$ solving Equation (3.1) and subject to the first order constraints

$$P(0, \ldots, 0) = p, \qquad \text{and} \qquad \frac{\partial}{\partial s_j} P(0, \ldots, 0) = \xi_j, \qquad 1 \leq j \leq m, \tag{3.2}$$

is a chart for a local stable manifold patch at p.

This claim is made precise in Proposition 3.1 below. First let Λ denote the $m \times m$ matrix with $\lambda_1, \ldots, \lambda_m$ on the diagonal entries and zeros elsewhere. Rewriting Equation (3.1) as

$$DP(s)\Lambda s = f(P(s)),$$

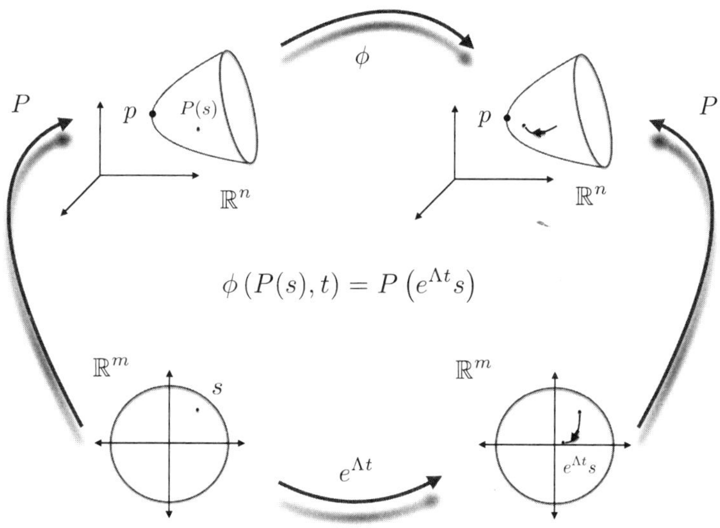

FIGURE 3. The figure illustrates the dynamical meaning of Equation (3.3). The unknown function P maps orbits of the linear flow $e^{\Lambda t}$ to orbits of the flow ϕ generated by f. Since orbits in the stable eigenspace converge to zero, and since $P(0) = p$, we have that the image of P is a local stable manifold.

makes the geometric meaning more apparent. We see that the equation now asks that the vector field f restricted to the image of P is tangent to (in fact equal to) the push forward of the linear vector field

$$\sigma' = \Lambda\sigma,$$

by the map P. Since the two vector fields are equal, they generate the same orbits, hence Equation (3.1) provides an infinitesimal conjugacy between the linear and nonlinear systems. The well understood dynamics of the linear system model the more complex dynamics of the nonlinear system restricted to the image of P. The following proposition makes this relation more precise.

PROPOSITION 3.1. *Let ϕ denote the flow generated by f, and suppose that P is a solution of Equation* (3.1) *satisfying also the linear constraints of Equation* (3.2). *Then P is a one-to-one mapping and the image of P is a local stable manifold at p. Moreover, P has*

$$\phi(P(s_1,\ldots,s_m),t) = P(e^{\lambda_1 t}s_1,\ldots,e^{\lambda_m t}s_m), \tag{3.3}$$

for all $s = (s_1,\ldots,s_m) \in (-1,1)^m$ and $t \geq 0$.

For the proof see [**87**]. The proposition says that in addition to recovering the embedding of the local stable manifold, P provides the dynamics on the manifold via this simple conjugacy given in Equation (3.3). The geometric meaning of Equation (3.3) is illustrated in Figure 3. Note also that the parameterization is not required to be the graph of a function over the stable/unstable eigenspace, hence the method can follow folds in the embedding of the manifold.

By the stable manifold theorem we actually know that if p is hyperbolic then the stable/unstable manifolds exist and are as smooth as f. So they are analytic if f is. In light of this it is reasonable to ask "Does an analytic solution of Equation (3.1) always exists?" The answer is no, and the obstruction is expressed in terms of certain algebraic conditions involving the stable eigenvalues.

DEFINITION 3.2. Let $\alpha \in \mathbb{N}^m$ have $|\alpha| \geq 2$. The eigenvalues $\lambda_1, \ldots, \lambda_m$ are said to have a *resonance* of order α if

$$\alpha_1 \lambda_1 + \ldots + \alpha_m \lambda_m = \lambda_j,$$

for some $1 \leq j \leq m$. If for all $\alpha \in \mathbb{N}^m$ with $|\alpha| \geq 2$ there are no resonances, then the eigenvalues are non-resonant.

We have the following theorem, whose proof is found in [**79**]. Much more general results are found in [**14**].

THEOREM 3.3. *Suppose that the stable eigenvalues are non-resonant. Then there is a power series* $P(s) = \sum_{|\alpha|=0}^{\infty} p_\alpha s^\alpha$ *satisfying the constraints of Equation* (3.2) *and solving Equation* (3.1) *in the sense of formal series. The solution is unique up to the choice of the scalings of the eigenvectors, and for each choice of eigenvectors there is an* $R > 0$ *so that* P *has radius of convergence* R.

The reason for this non-resonance condition will become more clear in the next two sections when we consider formal series solutions. For the moment, note that (despite first appearances) the non-resonance condition imposes only a finite number of algebraic constraints between the eigenvalues. To see this, note that there is an N so that for all $|\alpha| \geq N$ we have that $|\alpha_1 \lambda_1 + \ldots + \alpha_m \lambda_m| > |\lambda_j|$ for each $1 \leq j \leq m$. Then a resonance (if there are any) can occur only when $2 \leq |\alpha| \leq N$. So this is a finite collection of constraints, and hence non-resonance is an open condition (holds on open sets of in parameter space). Moreover, given a particular collection of stable eigenvalues $\lambda_1, \ldots, \lambda_m$, we have a finite procedure for determining if the non-resonance hypothesis holds. Note that the appearance of some obstruction to the parameterization method is not surprising, as the method provides analytic conjugacy – a stronger result than the stable manifold theorem.

The discussion above motivates our approach to solving Equation (3.1). Since we expect an analytic solution it is reasonable to make a power series *ansatz*, and try to work out the form of the unknown Taylor coefficients as discussed in the introduction of Section 2. This procedure is illustrated in detail in the next several sections.

REMARK 3.4 (Parameterization when there are resonances). In this lecture we assume diagonalizable only for the sake of convenience. Weakening this assumption introduces the usual minor complications. See for example [**88**]. The reference just cited also describes how to modify the parameterization method so that it succeeds when there is a resonance. The idea is to conjugate to a polynomial rather than a linear model system. The order of the polynomial is always the order of the resonance. It is also possible to treat complex conjugate eigenvalues, as is described in detail in [**62**]. Nearly identical comments apply to the unstable manifold, as is seen by considering the vector field $-f$. Finally, while we work exclusively with analytic vector fields in this lecture, finite differentiability is discussed in detail in [**14, 15**].

3.2. Formal series solutions: parameterized stable/unstable manifolds for the Lorenz system. Choose any one of the three fixed points of the Lorenz system and denote it by $\hat{p} \in \mathbb{R}^3$. Let λ denote an eigenvalue of $Df(\hat{p})$, and let ξ denote an associated choice of eigenvector. If λ is a stable eigenvalue, assume it is the only stable eigenvalue, so that the remaining two eigenvalues are unstable (or vice versa if λ is unstable).

In this case $m = 1$, and the invariance equation (3.1) reduces to the ordinary differential equation

$$\lambda s \frac{d}{ds} P(s) = f[P(s)].$$

We look for a power series solution

$$P(s) = \sum_{n=0}^{\infty} \begin{pmatrix} a_n \\ b_n \\ c_n \end{pmatrix} s^n.$$

Imposing the first order constraints, we have

$$\begin{pmatrix} a_0 \\ b_0 \\ c_0 \end{pmatrix} = \hat{p}, \qquad \text{and} \qquad \begin{pmatrix} a_1 \\ b_1 \\ c_1 \end{pmatrix} = \xi.$$

Proceeding formally we have that

$$\lambda s \frac{d}{ds} P(s) = \sum_{n=0}^{\infty} n\lambda \begin{pmatrix} a_n \\ b_n \\ c_n \end{pmatrix} s^n,$$

and that

$$f(P(s)) = \sum_{n=0}^{\infty} \begin{pmatrix} \sigma(b_n - a_n) \\ \rho\, a_n - b_n - \sum_{k=0}^{n} a_{n-k}\, c_k \\ -\beta\, c_n + \sum_{k=0}^{n} a_{n-k}\, b_k \end{pmatrix} s^n.$$

Matching like powers gives

$$n\lambda \begin{pmatrix} a_n \\ b_n \\ c_n \end{pmatrix} = \begin{pmatrix} \sigma(b_n - a_n) \\ \rho\, a_n - b_n - \sum_{k=0}^{n} a_{n-k}\, c_k \\ -\beta\, c_n + \sum_{k=0}^{n} a_{n-k}\, b_k \end{pmatrix},$$

for all $n \geq 2$. Extracting any terms of order n from the Cauchy products, and rearranging leads to

$$\begin{pmatrix} \sigma(b_n - a_n) - n\lambda a_n \\ \rho\, a_n - b_n - a_0 c_n - c_0 a_n - n\lambda b_n \\ -\beta\, c_n + a_0 b_n + b_0 a_n - n\lambda c_n \end{pmatrix} = \begin{bmatrix} -\sigma - n\lambda & \sigma & 0 \\ \rho - c_0 & -1 - n\lambda & -a_0 \\ b_0 & a_0 & -\beta - n\lambda \end{bmatrix} \begin{pmatrix} a_n \\ b_n \\ c_n \end{pmatrix}$$

$$= \begin{pmatrix} 0 \\ \sum_{k=1}^{n-1} a_{n-k}\, c_k \\ -\sum_{k=1}^{n-1} a_{n-k}\, b_k \end{pmatrix}.$$

But this equation, when expressed in matrix form, is

$$[Df(\hat{p}) - n\lambda \mathrm{Id}]\, p_n = R_n, \tag{3.4}$$

where we recall that $p_0 = \hat{p}$, and define $p_n = (a_n, b_n, c_n)^T$ and

$$R_n := \begin{pmatrix} 0 \\ \sum_{k=1}^{n-1} a_{n-k}\, c_k \\ -\sum_{k=1}^{n-1} a_{n-k}\, b_k \end{pmatrix}.$$

The linear equations (3.4) are referred to as the *homological equations* for the power series coefficients p_n of P with $n \geq 2$.

Observe that the left hand side of Equation (3.4) is actually the characteristic equation for $Df(\hat{p})$. Then the equation has unique solution as long as $n\lambda$ is not an eigenvalue of $Df(\hat{p})$. But we assumed that λ is the only stable eigenvalue. Then $n\lambda < \lambda < 0$ for all $n \geq 2$. Thene $n\lambda$ is never an eigenvalue, the matrix is always invertible, and the Taylor coefficients of the formal series P are uniquely defined to all orders.

Recursive solution of Equation (3.4) provides the Taylor coefficients of P to any finite order. Let

$$P^N(s) = \sum_{n=0}^{N} p_n s^n,$$

denote the N-th order approximation obtained by solving Equation (3.4) for $2 \leq n \leq N$ be our approximation of the stable/unstable manifold.

Returning to the remaining eigenvalues we proceed in a similar fashion to compute the two dimensional invariant manifold. Assume that λ_1 and λ_2 are eigenvalues of $Df(\hat{p})$ and that they have the same stability (either both stable or both unstable). We continue to enforce the assumption that the remaining eigenvalue has opposite stability (unstable or stable). Since $m = 2$ the invariance equation (3.1) is the partial differential equation

$$\lambda_1 s_1 \frac{\partial}{\partial s_1} P(s_1, s_2) + \lambda_2 s_2 \frac{\partial}{\partial s_2} P(s_1, s_2) = f[P(s_1, s_2)],$$

and we look for

$$P(s_1, s_2) = \sum_{m=0}^{\infty} \sum_{n=0}^{\infty} \begin{pmatrix} a_{mn} \\ b_{mn} \\ c_{mn} \end{pmatrix} s_1^m s_2^n.$$

Power matching as above leads to the homological equations

$$[Df(\hat{p}) - (m\lambda_1 + n\lambda_2)\mathrm{Id}]\, p_{mn} = R_{mn}, \tag{3.5}$$

where

$$p_{mn} = \begin{pmatrix} a_{mn} \\ b_{mn} \\ c_{mn} \end{pmatrix},$$

and

$$R_{mn} = \begin{pmatrix} 0 \\ \sum_{k=0}^{m} \sum_{l=0}^{n} \hat{\delta}_{kl}^{mn} a_{(m-k)(n-l)} c_{kl} \\ -\sum_{k=0}^{m} \sum_{l=0}^{n} \hat{\delta}_{kl}^{mn} a_{(m-k)(n-l)} b_{kl} \end{pmatrix}.$$

Here $\hat{\delta}_{kl}^{mn}$ is as defined in Section 2.2 (see 2.3.1 Equation (9)), and appears to remove any terms containing the multi-index (m, n) from the summation.

Now, if

$$m\lambda_1 + n\lambda_2 \neq \lambda_{1,2} \tag{3.6}$$

for all $m, n \in \mathbb{N}$ with $m + n \geq 2$, then the matrix in the left hand side of Equation (3.5) is invertible, and hence the formal series solution P is defined to all orders.

Supposing that this is the case, solving the homological equations for all $2 \leq |\alpha| \leq N$ leads to the numerical approximation

$$P^N(s_1, s_2) = \sum_{n=0}^{N} \sum_{m=0}^{n} p_{n-m,m} s_1^{n-m} s_2^m.$$

REMARK 3.5 (Resonance conditions). The conditions supposed in Equation (3.6) are the *non-resonance* conditions of Definition 3.2, and always appear in the parameterization method. As remarked above, these conditions reduce to a finite number of constraints between the eigenvalues. Nevertheless, resonances sometimes occur (for example they *will* occur if one continues along a one parameter family of equilibrium solutions), and can be treated for example using the approach discussed in [**88**]. Again, a much more general treatment of this material is found in [**14–16**].

3.3. Numerical considerations. In implementing the numerical computations outlined in Section 3.2 two important issues must be addressed.

- **Scaling:** the initial choice of scalings for the eigenvectors is free. How best to choose them?
- **Numerical domain:** the method provides a polynomial approximation, and this polynomial is defined on all of $\mathbb{R}^m$. Yet we don't expect that a Taylor series is a good approximation globally. On the other hand, we want to use the largest domain on which the polynomial is an accurate approximation. How best to restrict the domain of P^N so that we obtain meaningful results?

It turns out that these issues are intrinsically related.

To begin, lets examine the effect that rescaling the eigenvectors has on the Taylor coefficients. We have the following.

LEMMA 3.6. *Let $p \in \mathbb{R}^n$ be an equilibrium solution for a real analytic vector field $f: \mathbb{R}^n \to \mathbb{R}^n$. Suppose that $Df(p)$ is diagonalizable with m-stable eigenvalues $\lambda_1, \ldots, \lambda_m \in \mathbb{C}$. Assume that $\lambda_1, \ldots, \lambda_m$ are non-resonant, so that a formal series solution of Equation (3.1) exists for every fixed choice of eigenvectors (and is unique up to this choice).*

Let $\xi_1, \ldots, \xi_m \in \mathbb{C}^n$ be a collection of eigenvectors with

$$\|\xi_j\| = 1, \qquad 1 \leq j \leq m,$$

and suppose that $P(s) = \sum_{|\alpha|=0}^{\infty} p_\alpha s^\alpha$ is the unique formal series solution of Equation (3.1) with

$$p_{e_j} = \frac{\partial}{\partial s_j} P(0) = \xi_j.$$

For any collection of non-zero constants $\tau_1, \ldots, \tau_m \in \mathbb{R}$, define $\tilde{\xi}_1, \ldots, \tilde{\xi}_m \in \mathbb{C}^n$ by

$$\tilde{\xi}_j = \tau_j \xi_j, \qquad 1 \leq j \leq m.$$

Let $\tilde{P}(s) = \sum_{|\alpha|=0}^{\infty} \tilde{p}_\alpha s^\alpha$ denote the unique formal series solution of Equation (3.1) with

$$\tilde{p}_{e_j} = \frac{\partial}{\partial s_j} \tilde{P}(0) = \tau_j \xi_j, \qquad 1 \leq j \leq m.$$

Then

$$\tilde{p}_\alpha = \tau_1^{\alpha_1} \ldots \tau_m^{\alpha_m} p_\alpha, \tag{3.7}$$

for all $\alpha \in \mathbb{N}^m$.

PROOF. Define the $m \times m$ diagonal matrix

$$\Gamma = \begin{pmatrix} \tau_1 & \dots & 0 \\ \vdots & \ddots & \vdots \\ 0 & \dots & \tau_m \end{pmatrix},$$

and the reparameterization

$$P_\Gamma(s) = P(\Gamma s).$$

Observe that

$$\frac{\partial}{\partial s_j} P_\Gamma(s) = \frac{\partial}{\partial s_j}\left(P(\Gamma s)\right) = \frac{\partial}{\partial s_j} P(\Gamma s)\tau_j, \tag{3.8}$$

for each $1 \le j \le m$. Then

$$DP_\Gamma(s)\Lambda s = DP(\Gamma s)\Gamma\Lambda s = DP(\Gamma s)\Lambda\Gamma s = f(P(\Gamma s)) = f(P_\Gamma(s)),$$

as Γ and Λ commute and because P is a solution of Equation (3.1). This shows that P_Γ is a solution of Equation (3.1). Moreover, by evaluating at zero in Equation (3.8), we have that

$$\frac{\partial}{\partial s_j} P_\Gamma(0) = \tau_j \frac{\partial}{\partial s_j} P(0) = \tau_j \xi_j.$$

Since $\tilde{P}$ is the unique formal series solution of Equation (3.1) associated with these eigenvectors, we see that $\tilde{P} = P_\Gamma$ in the sense of formal series. Since these are equal as power series we have

$$\begin{aligned} \sum_{|\alpha|=0}^{\infty} \tilde{p}_\alpha s^\alpha &= \tilde{P}(s) \\ &= P_\Gamma(s) \\ &= P(\Gamma s) \\ &= \sum_{|\alpha|=0}^{\infty} p_\alpha (\Gamma s)^\alpha \\ &= \sum_{|\alpha|=0}^{\infty} \tau_1^{\alpha_1} \dots \tau_m^{\alpha_m} p_\alpha s^\alpha, \end{aligned}$$

and matching like powers gives the result. □

So, not only are solutions of Equation (3.1) unique up to the choice of eigenvectors, but given the Taylor series coefficients of one solution we obtain the Taylor coefficients of another solution associated with different eigenvector scalings simply applying the transformation of Equation (3.7) term by term. This fact helps us choose appropriate eigenvector scalings in numerical applications.

Example: one dimensional stable manifolds in the Lorenz system: Consider the Lorenz system with classic parameter values $\sigma = 10$, $\beta = 8/3$, $\rho = 28$, and the non-trivial equilibrium solution at

$$p \approx \begin{pmatrix} 8.485281374238570 \\ 8.485281374238570 \\ 27 \end{pmatrix}.$$

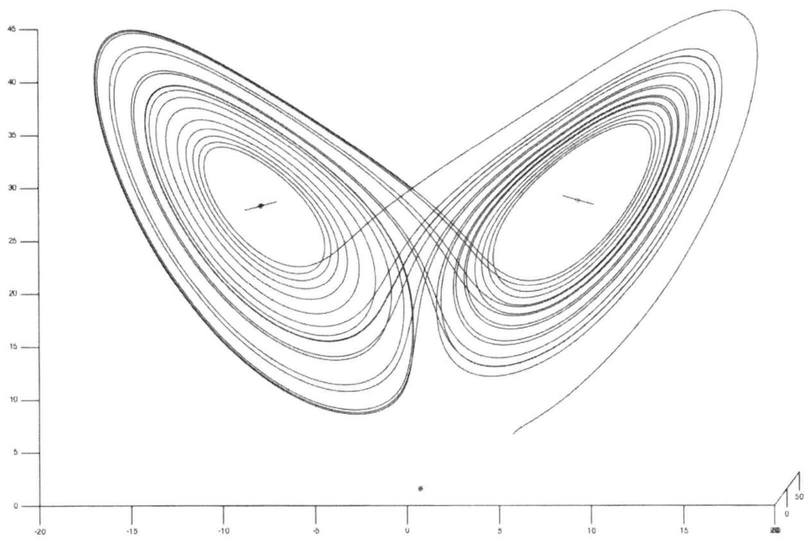

FIGURE 4. Parameterized local stable manifolds of the non-trivial equilibria in Lorenz, computed to polynomial order $N = 50$. For these parameterizations we choose an eigenvector scaled to length one, and evaluate the polynomial approximations on the unit interval $[-1, 1]$. The results illustrate that these seemingly natural choices need not lead to satisfactory results.

Then $Df(p)$ has a single stable eigenvalue

$$\lambda^s \approx -13.854577914596042.$$

We are free to choose any eigenvector we wish, and at first glance it might seem natural to take

$$\xi^s \approx \begin{pmatrix} 0.855665024602210 \\ -0.329822750612395 \\ -0.398816146677856 \end{pmatrix},$$

so that $\|\xi^s\| \approx 1$. Having made this choice, let $p_0 = p$, $p_1 = \xi^s$, and recursively solve the homological equations (3.5) to find the Taylor coefficients for $2 \leq n \leq N = 50$. Define the polynomial approximation

$$P^{50}(s) = \sum_{n=0}^{50} p_n s^n.$$

The next question is "on what domain is P^{50} a reliable approximation?" Here a natural choice is to take the unit interval $[-1, 1]$. The resulting parametric arcs are plotted in Figure 4.

The results are rather unsatisfactory, in the sense that after computing $N = 50$ terms we parameterize only a small – almost linear looking – portion of the manifold. To see better results we should either rescale the eigenvectors, or evaluate the polynomial on a larger domain. The two approaches are theoretically equivalent, so we hold the domain $[-1, 1]$ fixed and look for a better scaling of the eigenvectors.

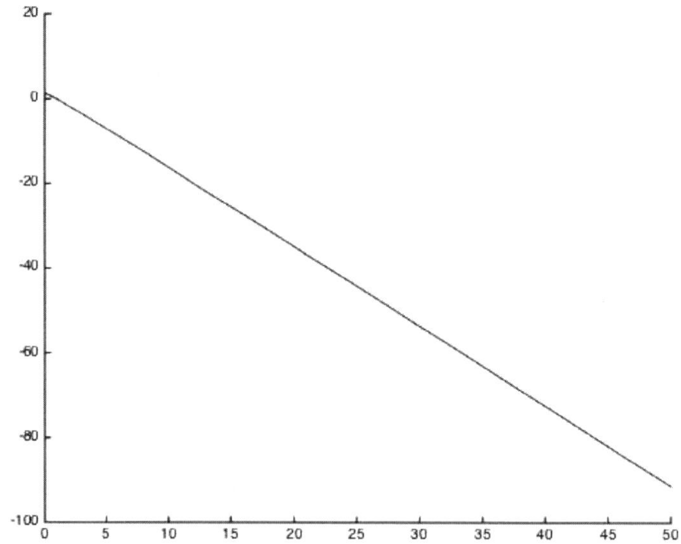

FIGURE 5. Plot of $\log_{10} \|p_n\|$ versus n for the parameterization illustrated in Figure 4. The linear appearance of the curve illustrates the exponential decay of the power series coefficients. Note that the $N = 50$ coefficient has magnitude on the order of 10^{-90}. The exponential decay rate not only suggests that we need to rescale the eigenvectors, it also suggests the correct choice for the rescaled length.

This choice is informed by the fact that numerical evaluation of a polynomial is more stable on the domain $s \in [-1, 1]$.

Question: how fast were the Taylor coefficients $\{p_n\}_{n=0}^{50}$ decaying in the previous computation? The answer is found in Figure 5, where the magnitude of the coefficients are plotted on a base ten logarithmic scale. The figure makes it clear that the coefficients have decayed below the point of numerical relevance long before the 50-th term. In fact, after about the tenth coefficient they have magnitude below double precision machine epsilon (approximately 2.2204×10^{-16}). This illustrates the problem with arbitrarily fixing the scaling of the eigvenvector to unit length: an eigenvector with length one may lead to undesirably fast exponential decay (or growth!)

To get better results we rescale the eigenvector so that the new Taylor coefficients decay much slower. For example suppose we want that the new coefficient sequence $\{\tilde{p}_n\}_{n=0}^{50}$ associated with the rescaled eigenvector has final coefficient $\|\tilde{p}_{50}\| \approx 10^{-2}$. Equation (3.7) tells us the appropriate rescaling factor τ is determined by

$$10^{-2} = \|\hat{p}_{50}\| = \|\tau^{50} p_{50}\| = \tau^{50}\|p_{50}\| = \tau^{50} 10^{-90}.$$

Solving for τ leads to $\tau = 10^{88/50} \approx 57.544$.

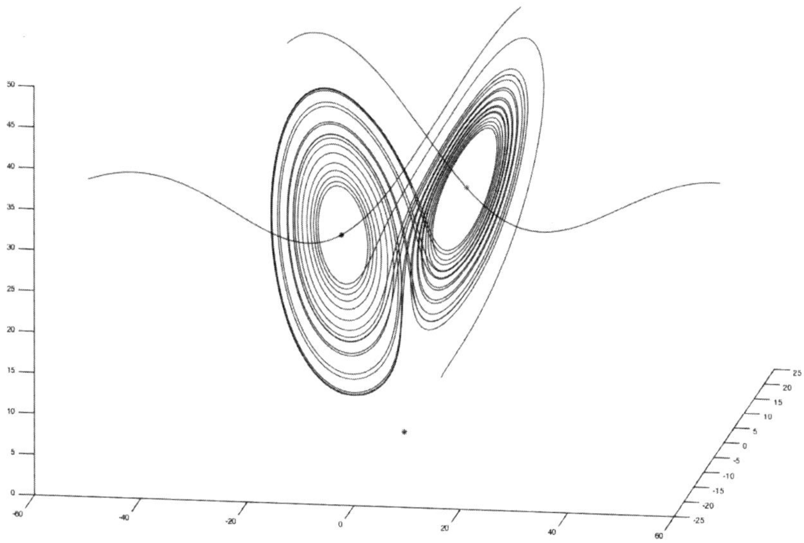

FIGURE 6. Re-parameterized local stable manifolds for the nontrivial equilibria in Lorenz, once again computed to polynomial order $N = 50$. For these computations we rescaled the eigenvector to have length 58, but still evaluate the polynomial approximations on the unit interval $[-1, 1]$. The rescaled parameterization yields a much larger embedding of the local stable manifold.

So we choose $\hat{\xi}^s = 58\xi^s$ and recompute the Taylor coefficients using the homological equations. The reason for recomputing is that, once we decide on a good scaling, it is more numerically stable to find the new coefficient $\tilde{p}_n$, $2 \leq n \leq 50$ from scratch than it is to employ the transformation given by Equation (3.7). The recomputed Taylor coefficients decay exponentially fast but at a more reasonable rate. That is, we don't let the high order coefficients get too small. The rescaled manifold is illustrated in Figure 6.

This discussion leads to the following heuristic: *rescaling the eigenvectors controls the size of the embedding of* $[-1, 1]$ *in the phase space.* Taking larger or smaller scalings we parameterize larger or smaller patches of the local stable/unstable manifolds. In general there is no reason not to fix a domain of unit size.

Example: Similar considerations apply when we compute two dimensional parameterizations of local stable/unstable manifolds. Consider first the two dimensional unstable manifold at the nontrivial equilibrium. The eigenvalues are complex conjugates with

$$\lambda_1^u \approx 0.093955623964686 - i10.194505220927850, \qquad \text{and} \qquad \lambda_2^u = \overline{\lambda_1^u}.$$

Note that the real part of the unstable eigenvalues is small, i.e. orbits move slowly away from the equilibrium even though they oscillate rather rapidly. We choose complex conjugate eigenvectors $\xi_{1,2}^u$ of length one and, since we want to absorb as much of the slow escape into the parameterization as possible, compute the manifold to order $N = 150$.

FIGURE 7. Parameterized two dimensional local unstable manifolds of the non-trivial equilibria (large, blue oval areas) in Lorenz, and two dimensional local stable manifold of the origin (red, triangular shape), computed to polynomial order $N = 150$ and $N = 50$ respectively. At the nontrivial equilibrium the unstable unit eigenvectors are rescaled by $\tau = 3.6$ and at the origin the stable unit eigenvectors are rescaled by $\tau_1 = 20$ in the slow direction and $\tau_2 = 2$ in the fast direction.

The Taylor coefficients of order $N = 150$ have magnitude on the order to 10^{-100}, i.e. they are numerically useless. We would prefer that the final coefficients had magnitude on the order of machine epsilon, and returning to Equation (3.7) we choose to rescale to

$$\hat{\xi}_1^u = \tau \xi_1^u,$$

where $\tau = 3.6$ so that $\tau^N 10^{-100} \approx 10^{-16}$. Upon recomputing the coefficients we obtain the desired decay rate (i.e. rate with coefficients of order $N = 150$ at machine precision).

At the origin the situation is a little different. There we have stable eigenvalues

$$\lambda_1^s \approx -2.667, \qquad \text{and} \qquad \lambda_2^s \approx -22.828.$$

Now, our interest is in connections from p_0 to p_1 (non-trivial to the origin) and we expect such connecting orbits to approach the origin along the slow stable manifold (sub-manifold of the stable manifold where the dynamics is analytically conjugate to the linear dynamics given by the smaller of the two stable eigenvalues. See [**87**] for more discussion). So we are more interested in the portion of the manifold tangent to the slow eigenspace. Since $\lambda_2^s \approx 10\lambda_1^s$ we scale the slow eigenvector to ten times longer than the fast eigenvector.

Choose $\|\xi_1^s\| = 1$ and $\|\xi_2^s\| = 0.1$, compute the Taylor coefficients to order $N = 50$, and find that the largest coefficients $p_\alpha \in \mathbb{R}^3$ with $|\alpha| = 50$ have magnitude approximately 10^{-80} (this time we suppress the log base 10 plot). Being conservative, we would prefer that the largest coefficients of order $|\alpha| = 50$ have magnitudes close to machine epsilon. This is achieved by taking

$$\hat{\xi}_1^s = \tau \xi_1^s, \qquad \text{and} \qquad \hat{\xi}_2^s = \tau \xi_2^s,$$

with $\tau = 20$. The results are illustrated in Figure 7.

3.4. Fixed point formulation for the truncation error. In the previous section we compute the series expansions to finite order. In this section we treat the neglected terms in the tail. Again we focus our attention on the Lorenz system.

Recall that $Df(\hat{p})$ is diagonalizable, and that the eigenvalues $\lambda_1, \lambda_2, \lambda_3 \in \mathbb{C}$, and the associated eigenvectors $\xi_1, \xi_2, \xi_3 \in \mathbb{C}^3$ are known (at least up to interval enclosures). Suppose also, using the notation of the previous section, that λ_1, λ_2 have the same stability (either both stable or both unstable). We write

$$Q = [\xi_1, \xi_2, \xi_3],$$

for the matrix whose columns are the eigenvectors. By the assumption of diagonalizability Q is invertible, and we let Q^{-1} denote its inverse. Let

$$\Lambda = \begin{pmatrix} \lambda_1 & 0 & 0 \\ 0 & \lambda_2 & 0 \\ 0 & 0 & \lambda_3 \end{pmatrix},$$

denote the diagonal matrix of eigenvalues.

Recall the linear Equation (3.5), i.e. the homological equation for the Taylor coefficients of the parameterization. Exploiting the diagonalizable assumption the homological equation becomes

$$\begin{aligned} Df(p_0) - (m\lambda_1 + n\lambda_2)\mathrm{Id} &= Q\Lambda Q^{-1} - (m\lambda_1 + n\lambda_2) Q Q^{-1} \\ &= Q\left[\Lambda - (m\lambda_1 + n\lambda_2)\mathrm{Id}\right] Q^{-1}. \end{aligned}$$

We assume that λ_1, λ_2 are non-resonant, so that

$$\left[Df(p_0) - (m\lambda_1 + n\lambda_2)\mathrm{Id}\right]^{-1} = Q\left[\Lambda - (m\lambda_1 + n\lambda_2)\mathrm{Id}\right]^{-1} Q^{-1},$$

where

$$[\Lambda - (m\lambda_1 + n\lambda_2)\mathrm{Id}]^{-1} = \begin{pmatrix} (\lambda_1 - m\lambda_1 - n\lambda_2)^{-1} & 0 & 0 \\ 0 & (\lambda_2 - m\lambda_1 - n\lambda_2)^{-1} & 0 \\ 0 & 0 & (\lambda_3 - m\lambda_1 - n\lambda_2)^{-1} \end{pmatrix}.$$

With $(m, n) \in \mathbb{N}^2$, define the matrices

$$A_{mn} = Q\left[\Lambda - (m\lambda_1 + n\lambda_2)\mathrm{Id}\right]^{-1} Q^{-1},$$

and constants

$$K_{mn} := \max\left(\frac{1}{|\lambda_1 - m\lambda_1 - n\lambda_2|}, \frac{1}{|\lambda_2 - m\lambda_1 - n\lambda_2|}, \frac{1}{|\lambda_3 - m\lambda_1 - n\lambda_2|}\right). \tag{3.9}$$

Note that $K_{mn} \to 0$ as $(m + n) \to \infty$, and that

$$\|A_{mn}\| = \|\left(Df(p_0) - (m\lambda_1 + n\lambda_2)\mathrm{Id}\right)^{-1}\| \le \|Q\| \|Q^{-1}\| K_{mn}.$$

Now, using the hat product notation of Section 2.3.1, we solve the homological equation to obtain

$$\begin{pmatrix} a_{mn} \\ b_{mn} \\ c_{mn} \end{pmatrix} = A_{mn} \begin{pmatrix} 0 \\ (a \hat{*} c)_{mn} \\ -(a \hat{*} b)_{mn} \end{pmatrix},$$

where the right hand side does not depend on coefficients of order $m+n$. (Rather, it depends only on "lower order terms"). This last equation suggests that the unknown Taylor coefficients $\{a_{mn}\}, \{b_{mn}\}, \{c_{mn}\}$ solve a fixed point problem.

To formalize this notion consider the Banach space $\left(\ell^1_{1,2}\right)^3 = \ell^1_{1,2} \oplus \ell^1_{1,2} \oplus \ell^1_{1,2}$ endowed with the product space norm

$$\|(a,b,c)\|_{\left(\ell^1_{1,2}\right)^3} := \max(\|a\|^1_{1,2}, \|b\|^1_{1,2}, \|c\|^1_{1,2}).$$

Define the operator $\Psi \colon \left(\ell^1_{1,2}\right)^3 \to \left(\ell^1_{1,2}\right)^3$ by

$$\Psi(a,b,c)_{mn} = \begin{pmatrix} \Psi(a,b,c)^1_{mn} \\ \Psi(a,b,c)^2_{mn} \\ \Psi(a,b,c)^3_{mn} \end{pmatrix} = A_{mn} \begin{pmatrix} 0 \\ (a \hat{*} c)_{mn} \\ -(a \hat{*} b)_{mn} \end{pmatrix}. \tag{3.10}$$

Note that a fixed point of Ψ solves the homological equations to all orders, i.e. if $(a,b,c) \in \left(\ell^1_{1,2}\right)^3$ is a fixed point of Ψ, then $p_{mn} = (a_{mn}, b_{mn}, c_{mn})$ are the Taylor coefficients of the desired parameterization.

To prove that such a fixed point of Ψ exists, we consider the terms of order $m+n \leq N$ and the tail terms separately. Define the subspaces $X^N_{1,2}, X^\infty_{1,2} \subset \ell^1_{1,2}$ and projections $\pi_N \colon \ell^1_{1,2} \to X^N_{1,2}$ and $\pi_\infty \colon \ell^1_{1,2} \to X^\infty_{1,2}$ as in Section 2.2. Let $\Psi^N := \pi_N \circ \Psi$ and $\Psi^\infty := \pi_\infty \circ \Psi$, so that Ψ has the decomposition

$$\Psi(a,b,c) = \Psi^N(a^N, b^N, c^N) + \Psi^\infty(u,v,w,a^N,b^N,c^N).$$

Note that $\Psi^N \colon (X^N_{1,2})^3 \to (X^N_{1,2})^3$ and $\Psi^\infty \colon (X^\infty_{1,2})^3 \oplus (X^N_{1,2})^3 \to (X^\infty_{1,2})^3$. Here the nonzero components of Ψ^N are just the homological equations for $0 \leq m+n \leq N$. So, suppose that $\bar{a}^N, \bar{b}^N, \bar{c}^N \in X^N_{1,2}$ are obtained by solving these homological equation exactly (at least in the sense of interval arithmetic). Define the map $T \colon (X^\infty_{1,2})^3 \to (X^\infty_{1,2})^3$ by

$$T(u,v,w) := \Psi^\infty(u,v,w,\bar{a}^N, \bar{b}^N, \bar{c}^N),$$

where the "barred" data is considered fixed. Since solving the recursion relations to N-th order gives the fixed point of Ψ^N, we need only prove the existence of a fixed point of the map T in order to obtain a fixed point of the full map Ψ.

The operator T is written explicitly as

$$T(u,v,w)_{mn} = \begin{pmatrix} T(u,v,w)^1_{mn} \\ T(u,v,w)^2_{mn} \\ T(u,v,w)^3_{mn} \end{pmatrix} = A_{mn} \begin{pmatrix} 0 \\ \left(\bar{a}^N + u\right) \hat{*} \left(\bar{c}^N + w\right)_{mn} \\ -\left(\bar{a}^N + u\right) \hat{*} \left(\bar{b}^N + v\right)_{mn} \end{pmatrix}, \tag{3.11}$$

for $m+n \geq N+1$.

To write the operators on a higher level, let A^{ij}_{mn} denote the i-th row and j-th column of the matrix A_{mn}, and define the bounded linear operators $A^{ij} \colon X^\infty_{1,2} \to X^\infty_{1,2}$ by

$$(A^{ij}u)_{mn} = \begin{cases} 0 & \text{if } 0 \leq m+n \leq N \\ A^{ij}_{mn} u_{mn} & \text{if } m+n \geq N+1 \end{cases}.$$

It is worth remarking that the explicit form of these operators will play no role in the analysis to follow. What is essential is that each of these operators satisfies the bound

$$\|A^{ij}\| \leq \left(\sup_{m+n\geq N+1} K_{mn}\right)\|Q\|\|Q^{-1}\|.$$

Also recall that in Section 2.2 we derived the decompositions

$$\pi_\infty\left(\bar{a}^N+u\right)\hat{*}\left(\bar{c}^N+w\right)=(\bar{a}^N\hat{*}\bar{c}^N)^\infty+(u\hat{*}\bar{c}^N)+(w\hat{*}\bar{a}^N)+(u\hat{*}w)$$

and

$$\pi_\infty\left(\bar{a}^N+u\right)\hat{*}\left(\bar{b}^N+v\right)=(\bar{a}^N\hat{*}\bar{b}^N)^\infty+(u\hat{*}\bar{b}^N)+(v\hat{*}\bar{a}^N)+(u\hat{*}v).$$

Then for $j=1,2,3$ we have

$$T(u,v,w)^j = A^{j2}\left((\bar{a}^N\hat{*}\bar{c}^N)^\infty+(u\hat{*}\bar{c}^N)+(w\hat{*}\bar{a}^N)+(u\hat{*}w)\right) \tag{3.12}$$

$$- A^{j3}\left((\bar{a}^N\hat{*}\bar{b}^N)^\infty+(u\hat{*}\bar{b}^N)+(v\hat{*}\bar{a}^N)+(u\hat{*}v)\right). \tag{3.13}$$

Note that T is Fréchet differentiable and that (suppressing for a moment the (u,v,w) arguments) $DT\colon (X^\infty_{1,2})^3\to(X^\infty_{1,2})^3$ is given by

$$DT=\begin{pmatrix} D_1T^1 & D_2T^1 & D_3T^1\\ D_1T^2 & D_2T^2 & D_3T^2\\ D_1T^3 & D_2T^3 & D_3T^3\end{pmatrix},$$

where, for $h\in X^\infty_{1,2}$ these partial derivatives have action

$$D_1T^j(u,v,w)h = A^{j2}\left(\bar{c}^N\hat{*}h+h\hat{*}w\right)-A^{j3}\left(\bar{b}^N\hat{*}h+h\hat{*}v\right)$$

$$D_2T^j(u,v,w)h=-A^{j3}\left(\bar{a}^N\hat{*}h+u\hat{*}h,\right)$$

and

$$D_3T^j(u,v,w)h = A^{j2}\left(\bar{a}^N\hat{*}h+u\hat{*}h\right),$$

for $j=1,2,3$.

3.5. A validated computation via the contraction mapping theorem. Given the data $\bar{a}^N,\bar{b}^N,\bar{c}^N\in X^N_{1,2}$, we hope to show that T is a contraction in some (hopefully small) neighborhood of the origin in $\left(X^\infty_{1,2}\right)^3$. Recalling Proposition 2.7 and the "hat star" bounds of Lemma 2.3, we have the following.

LEMMA 3.7. *Let* $\{K_{mn}\}_{(m,n)\in\mathbb{N}^2}$ *be as defined in Equation* (3.9), *and*

$$K^N := \|Q\|\|Q^{-1}\|\sup_{m+n\geq N+1} K_{mn}.$$

Define

$$Y_0 := K^N\left(\sum_{m+n=N+1}^{2N}|(\bar{a}^N\hat{*}\bar{b}^N)_{mn}|+|(\bar{a}^N\hat{*}\bar{c}^N)_{mn}|\right),$$

$$Z_1 := K^N\left(\sum_{1\leq m+n\leq N}2|\bar{a}^N_{mn}|+\sum_{1\leq m+n\leq N}\left(|\bar{b}^N_{mn}|+|\bar{c}^N_{mn}|\right)\right),$$

and

$$Z_2 := 4K^N.$$

Then

$$\|T(0,0,0)\|_{(X^\infty_{1,2})^3}\leq Y_0.$$

Moreover, for $r > 0$ let $B_r(0)$ denote the ball of radius r about the origin in $(X_{1,2}^{\infty})^3$. Then

$$\sup_{(u,v,w)\in\overline{B_r(0)}} \|DT(u,v,w)\|_{B((X_{1,2}^{\infty})^3)} \leq Z_1 + Z_2 r.$$

PROOF. Consider

$$\begin{aligned}\|T(0,0,0) - 0\|_{(X_{1,2}^{\infty})^3} &\leq \max_{1\leq j\leq 3} \|T(0,0,0)^j\|_{X_{1,2}^{\infty}} \\ &\leq \|A^{j2}\|_{B(X_{1,2}^{\infty})} \|(\bar{a}^N \hat{*} \bar{c}^N)^{\infty}\|_{1,2}^1 + \|A^{j3}\|_{B(X_{1,2}^{\infty})} \|(\bar{a}^N \hat{*} \bar{b})^{\infty}\|_{1,2}^1 \\ &\leq K^N \left(\sum_{m+n=N+1}^{2N} |(\bar{a}^N \hat{*} \bar{b}^N)_{mn}| + |(\bar{a}^N \hat{*} \bar{c}^N)_{mn}| \right) \\ &= Y_0,\end{aligned}$$

where the estimate of Lemma 2.3 provides the bound on the hat products.

Now consider $(u,v,w) \in \overline{B_r(0)} \subset \left(X_{1,2}^{\infty}\right)^3$. In light of the estimates in Lemma 2.3 one has that

$$\begin{aligned}\|DT(u,v,w)\|_{B((X_{1,2}^{\infty})^3)} &\leq \max_{1\leq j\leq 3} \sum_{k=1}^{3} \|D_k T^j(u,v,w)\|_{B(X_{1,2}^{\infty})} \\ &\leq \max_{1\leq j\leq 3} \sum_{k=1}^{3} \sup_{\|h\|_{X_{1,2}^{\infty}}=1} \|D_k T^j(u,v,w)h\|_{X_{1,2}^{\infty}}\end{aligned}$$

$$\begin{aligned}&\leq K^N \left(2 \sum_{1\leq m+n\leq N} |\bar{a}_{mn}^N| + \sum_{1\leq m+n\leq N} \left(|\bar{b}_{mn}^N| + |\bar{c}_{mn}^N|\right) \right. \\ &\qquad \left. + 2\|u\|_{X_{1,2}^{\infty}} + \|v\|_{X_{1,2}^{\infty}} + \|w\|_{X_{1,2}^{\infty}} \right) \\ &\leq K^N \left(\sum_{1\leq m+n\leq N} 2|\bar{a}_{mn}^N| + \sum_{1\leq m+n\leq N} \left(|\bar{b}_{mn}^N| + |\bar{c}_{mn}^N|\right) + 4r \right) \\ &\leq Z_1 + Z_2 r.\end{aligned}$$

□

Example: Consider the two dimensional manifold at the origin. Using interval arithmetic we check that

$$\lambda^u \in [11.82772345116345, 11.82772345116347],$$
$$\lambda_1^s \in [-2.66666666666667, -2.66666666666666],$$

and

$$\lambda_2^s \in [-22.82772345116347, -22.82772345116345].$$

Similarly, the eigenvectors satisfy the inclusions

$$\xi^u \in \begin{pmatrix} [-0.41650417819291, -0.41650417819290] \\ [-0.90913380178490, -0.90913380178489] \\ [-0.00000000000001, 0.00000000000001] \end{pmatrix},$$

$$\xi_1^s = \begin{pmatrix} 0 \\ 0 \\ 1 \end{pmatrix},$$

and

$$\xi_2^s \in \begin{pmatrix} [-0.61481678521648, -0.61481678521647] \\ [0.78866996938902, 0.78866996938903] \\ 0 \end{pmatrix}.$$

Then we recursively solve the homological equations and obtain interval enclosures of the coefficients to order $N = 50$.

The fact that the validated numerical solver succeeds in solving the the homological equations up to order $N = 50$ shows that there are no resonances up to that order. That is, validated numerical solvers have the property that they return a solution only if the system is uniquely solvable. And the homological equation is uniquely solvable if and only if the coefficient matrix is invertible. But the coefficient matrix for the homological equation is invertible at a particular order if and only if the eigenvalues are non-resonant at that order. So success to order fifty rules out lower order resonances.

To rule out resonances of order greater than 50 we argue as follows. Suppose that $(m, n) \in \mathbb{N}^2$ is a multi-index with order $n + m > 50$. Since $|\lambda_2^s| > |\lambda_1^s|$, and since the real part of $\lambda_{1,1}^s$ is opposite the real part of λ^u, we have that

$$\frac{1}{|m\lambda_1^s + n\lambda_2^s - \lambda_1^s|} \leq \frac{1}{|(m+n)\lambda_1^s - \lambda_1^s|} = \frac{1}{|m+n-1||\lambda_1^s|} \leq \frac{1}{50|\lambda_1^s|} \leq 0.0075,$$

$$\frac{1}{|m\lambda_1^s + n\lambda_2^s - \lambda_2^s|} \leq \frac{1}{|(m+n)\lambda_1^s - \lambda_2^s|} = \frac{1}{(m+n)|\lambda_1^s| - |\lambda_2^s|} \leq \frac{1}{50|\lambda_1^s| - |\lambda_2^s|} \leq 0.0089,$$

and

$$\frac{1}{|m\lambda_1^s + n\lambda_2^s - \lambda^u|} \leq \frac{1}{|(m+n)|\lambda_1^s| + |\lambda^u|} \leq \frac{1}{50|\lambda_1^s| + |\lambda^u|} \leq 0.0068.$$

Then choose

$$K^N = 0.009.$$

These estimates also show that there are no resonances when $m + n > 50$, as each of the quantities involved are unbounded at a resonance.

We scale the slow eigenvector to have length 15 and the fast eigenvector to have length 1.5 (as the difference in the magnitudes of the eigenvalues is about ten). We compute the quantities given in Lemma 3.7 and obtain a validated error bounds on the tail of the series of size 7.5×10^{-20}. This is below machine precision, however we needed roughly order $N = 50$ with this choice of scalings in order to get

$$Z_1 = 0.71 < 1.$$

Of course we could take a lower order approximation and choose smaller eigenvector scalings to validate a smaller portion of the manifold.

At "the eye" we have unstable eigenvalue enclosures

$$\lambda_1^u \in D(0.0939556239647 - 10.19450522092785\,i, 6 \times 10^{-15}),$$

and similar for the complex conjugate eigenvectors. We choose eigenvectors scaled to unit length. More importantly we check that for the complex conjugate eigenvalue, if $\lambda_1^u = a + ib$ and $\lambda_2^u = \overline{\lambda_1^u}$ then

$$\begin{aligned}\frac{1}{|m\lambda_1^u + n\lambda_2^u - \lambda_{1,2}^u|} &= \frac{1}{|m(a+ib) + n(a-ib) - (a \pm ib)|} \\ &\leq \frac{1}{|(m+n-1)a \pm ib|} \\ &\leq \frac{1}{|Na \pm ib|} \\ &\leq \frac{1}{N|\mathrm{real}(\lambda_1^u)|} \\ &\leq 0.054,\end{aligned}$$

where we take $N = 200$ the order of approximation. The contraction mapping proof succeeds and we have that the tail of the parameterization has norm less than 10^{-90}. This is fantastically small, but we need to take $N = 200$ in order to get

$$Z_1 = 0.846 < 1.$$

If we choose smaller scalings the proof is much easier, but the local manifold is smaller. Having a larger local unstable manifold is helpful for the connecting orbit proof later.

4. The flow box problem: propagating and differentiating sets of initial conditions

In the previous section we studied the dynamics near a equilibrium solution. To connect one equilibrium to another it is necessary to study the flow generated by the vector field. In this section we develop Taylor series expansions with validated error bounds for the flow map in a neighborhood of a given initial condition.

4.1. Formal series solutions: a Taylor integrator for the Lorenz system. Given a non-equilibrium point $(x_0, y_0, z_0) \in \mathbb{R}^3$, we look for a locally defined flow map of the form

$$\phi(t, x_0 + x, y_0 + y, z_0 + z) = \sum_{n=0}^{\infty}\sum_{k=0}^{\infty}\sum_{l=0}^{\infty}\sum_{m=0}^{\infty} \begin{pmatrix} a_{klmn} \\ b_{klmn} \\ c_{klmn} \end{pmatrix} x^k y^l z^m t^n, \tag{4.1}$$

having that

$$\frac{\partial}{\partial t}\phi(t, x_0 + x, y_0 + y, z_0 + z) = \tau f\left(\phi(t, x_0 + x, y_0 + y, z_0 + z)\right), \tag{4.2}$$

for all $(x, y, z, t) \in (-1, 1)^4 \subset \mathbb{R}^4$. Here we take f to be the Lorenz vector field. The parameter $\tau > 0$ simply rescales time so that we can take $t \in (-1, 1)$ and parameterize the time interval $(-\tau, \tau)$ for the differential equation. Geometrically speaking, Equation (4.2) can be seen as requiring that the push forward of the constant vector field under ϕ is tangent to f on the image of ϕ. That is, ϕ is the conjugacy guaranteed by the "flow box" theorem.

The initial conditions impose the constant constraint

$$\begin{pmatrix} a_{0,0,0,0} \\ b_{0,0,0,0} \\ c_{0,0,0,0} \end{pmatrix} = \begin{pmatrix} x_0 \\ y_0 \\ z_0 \end{pmatrix},$$

and with $c > 0$ we impose the first order constraints

$$\begin{pmatrix} a_{1,0,0,0} \\ b_{1,0,0,0} \\ c_{1,0,0,0} \end{pmatrix} = \begin{pmatrix} c \\ 0 \\ 0 \end{pmatrix}, \quad \begin{pmatrix} a_{0,1,0,0} \\ b_{0,1,0,0} \\ c_{0,1,0,0} \end{pmatrix} = \begin{pmatrix} 0 \\ c \\ 0 \end{pmatrix} \quad \begin{pmatrix} a_{0,0,1,0} \\ b_{0,0,1,0} \\ c_{0,0,1,0} \end{pmatrix} = \begin{pmatrix} 0 \\ 0 \\ c \end{pmatrix}, \tag{4.3}$$

and

$$\begin{pmatrix} a_{klm0} \\ b_{klm0} \\ c_{klm0} \end{pmatrix} = \begin{pmatrix} 0 \\ 0 \\ 0 \end{pmatrix},$$

for all $(k, l, m) \in \mathbb{N}^3$ having $k + l + m \geq 2$. These conditions give that

$$\phi((-1,1),(-1,1),(-1,1),0) = (x_0 - c, x_0 + c) \times (y_0 - c, y_0 + c) \times (z_0 - c, z_0 + c),$$

i.e. that our power series at time $t = 0$ maps the unit cube into a cube of radius c centered at the initial conditions.

Plugging the power series from Equation (4.1) into Equation (4.2) and matching like powers gives

$$\begin{pmatrix} a_{klmn} \\ b_{klmn} \\ c_{klmn} \end{pmatrix} = \frac{\tau}{n} \begin{pmatrix} \sigma(b_{klmn-1} - a_{klmn-1}) \\ \rho a_{klmn-1} - b_{klmn-1} - (a * c)_{klmn-1} \\ -\beta c_{klmn-1} + (a * b)_{klmn-1} \end{pmatrix} \tag{4.4}$$

for $n \geq 1$.

Define $\mathcal{I}_N \subset \mathbb{N}^4$ to be the set of all four dimensional multi-indices of order less than N, i.e.

$$\mathcal{I}_N := \left\{(k, l, m, n) \in \mathbb{N}^4 \,:\, 0 \leq k + l + m + n \leq N\right\}.$$

These recursion relations are solved to any desired finite order N, resulting in Taylor a coefficient $(a_{klmn}, b_{klmn}, c_{klmn}) \subset \mathbb{R}^3$ for each multi-index $(k, l, m, n) \in \mathcal{I}_N$. We approximate the flow near (x_0, y_0, z_0) using the polynomial

$$\phi^N(x_0 + x, y_0 + y, z_0 + z, t) = \sum_{(k,l,m,n) \in \mathcal{I}_N} \begin{pmatrix} a_{klmn} \\ b_{klmn} \\ c_{klmn} \end{pmatrix} x^k y^l z^m t^n,$$

taking $(x, y, z, t) \in (-1, 1)^4$.

4.2. Numerical considerations. Suppose that we are given an initial condition $(x_0, y_0, z_0) \in \mathbb{R}^3$ and that we fix a desired polynomial approximation order $N \in \mathbb{N}$. We want to choose a rescaling of time $\tau > 0$ and a re-parametrization of space $c > 0$ so that $\phi^N(x_0 + x, y_0 + y, z_0 + z, t)$ is a good approximation of the flow for all $(x, y, z, t) \in (-1, 1)^4$. These rescalings provide control over the decay rates of the Taylor coefficients of ϕ. As with the manifold computations, our strategy is to compute the coefficients once – guess the appropriate scalings – and compute a second time with the improved choice.

Example: Consider the initial condition $(-15, -15, 40) \in \mathbb{R}^3$ for the Lorenz system. The point is "near the attractor" and its behavior is fairly typical. We choose

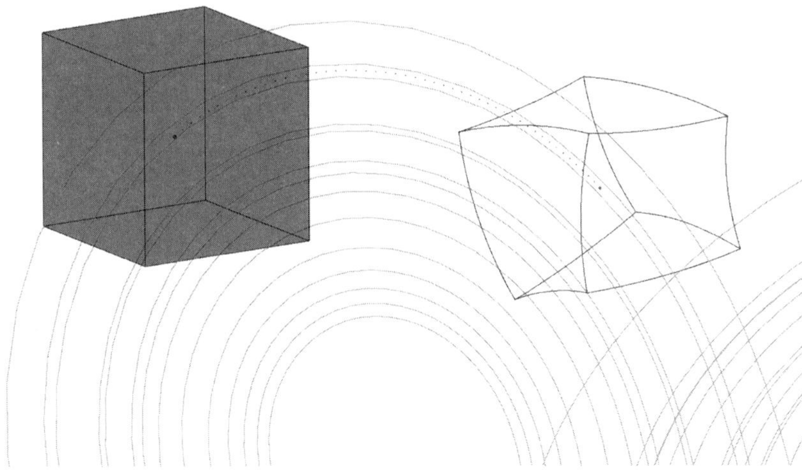

FIGURE 8. Taylor integration of a "phase box" near the attractor. The time step is $\tau = 0.1$ forward in time and the box of initial conditions has a radius $c = 4$. The advected box is illustrated as a blue wire frame and shows that the nonlinearities have time to twist and stretch the phase box.

a polynomial approximation of order $N = 30$ and recursively compute the Taylor coefficients with $\tau = c = 1$. The resulting Taylor coefficient grow exponentially fast, and the last coefficient has magnitude on the order of 10^{25}.

As is well known, rescaling time by a factor of τ has the effect of rescaling the power series coefficients by powers of τ. If we want the last coefficient on the order of 10^{-5} we take $\tau = 0.1$, so that $\tau^{30}10^{25} = 10^{-5}$ gives the desired decay. A little experimentation shows that the coefficient growth is much less sensitive to the spatial parameterization, and we can take $c = 4$ without significantly effecting the decay rates of the Taylor coefficients. We solve again the recursion from scratch, using the improved values of τ and c, and obtain a new series whose order $N = 30$ Taylor coefficients have magnitudes on the order of 10^{-5} as desired. Figure 8 illustrates the results. We see that the box, when advected for a time $\tau = 0.1$ is already distorted in a nonlinear way.

REMARK 4.1 (h-sets, and covering relations, and well aligned windows). An important technique for developing validated integrators is the choice of special, adapted coordinates for the Taylor expansion. This idea goes back to [**1**, **66**, **67**] and is used extensively in the CAPD library [**97**, **99**]. The idea, loosely speaking, is to modify the first order conditions given in Equation (4.3) so that they better represent the geometry of the flow. For example we could pre-compute the solution of the initial value problem along with the solution of the first order variational equations using a standard and inexpensive numerical integration scheme (perhaps Runge-Kutta), resulting in a good guess as to the location of the advected initial condition and also the derivative of the flow there. Computing an eigenbasis for the differential provides a frame adapted to the flow to first order.

In the references discussed above, this technique is used to minimize "wrapping effect". In the language of analytic decay rates employed in the present notes, choosing an adapted frame leads to even better decay rates for the Taylor coefficients in the spatial directions. But, in the applications to come such considerations will not play an important role. This is because, in some sense, we brute force the computations by taking higher order expansions in space. This requires more computational resources but simplifies somewhat the discussion of the integrator.

4.3. Fixed point formulation for the truncation error. Define the operator $\Psi\colon \left(\ell^1_{\nu,4}\right)^3 \to \left(\ell^1_{\nu,4}\right)^3$ by

$$\Psi(a,b,c) = \begin{pmatrix} \Psi_1(a,b,c) \\ \Psi_2(a,b,c) \\ \Psi_3(a,b,c) \end{pmatrix} \tag{4.5}$$

where the operators $\Psi_1, \Psi_2, \Psi_3\colon \left(\ell^1_{\nu,4}\right)^3 \to \left(\ell^1_{\nu,4}\right)$ are defined by

$$\Psi_1(a,b,c)_{klmn} := \begin{cases} x_0 & \text{if } k=l=m=n=0 \\ 1 & \text{if } k=1 \text{ and } l=m=n=0 \\ 0 & \text{if } l=1, \text{ and } k=m=n=0 \\ 0 & \text{if } m=1, \text{ and } k=l=n=0 \\ 0 & \text{if } n=0, \text{ and } k+l+m\geq 2 \\ \frac{\tau\sigma}{n}(b_{klm,n-1}-a_{klm,n-1}) & \text{if } n\geq 1 \end{cases}$$

$$\Psi_2(a,b,c)_{klmn} := \begin{cases} y_0 & \text{if } k=l=m=n=0 \\ 0 & \text{if } k=1 \text{ and } l=m=n=0 \\ 1 & \text{if } l=1, \text{ and } k=m=n=0 \\ 0 & \text{if } m=1, \text{ and } k=l=n=0 \\ 0 & \text{if } n=0, \text{ and } k+l+m\geq 2 \\ \frac{\tau}{n}(\rho a_{klm,n-1}-b_{klm,n-1}-(a*c)_{klm,n-1}) & \text{if } n\geq 1 \end{cases}$$

and

$$\Psi_3(a,b,c)_{klmn} := \begin{cases} z_0 & \text{if } k=l=m=n=0 \\ 0 & \text{if } k=1 \text{ and } l=m=n=0 \\ 0 & \text{if } l=1, \text{ and } k=m=n=0 \\ 1 & \text{if } m=1, \text{ and } k=l=n=0 \\ 0 & \text{if } n=0, \text{ and } k+l+m\geq 2 \\ \frac{\tau}{n}(-\beta c_{klm,n-1}+(a*b)_{klm,n-1}) & \text{if } n\geq 1 \end{cases}.$$

Consider the decomposition

$$\Psi(a,b,c) = \pi_N(\Psi(a,b,c)) + \pi_\infty(\Psi(a,b,c)),$$

and suppose that $\bar{a}^N, \bar{b}^N, \bar{c}^N \in X^N_{\nu,4}$ provide an exact fixed point of $\pi_N(\Psi)$. Note that this fixed point is given exactly by solving the recursion relations to order N. For fixed $\tau > 0$ define the operator $T\colon (X^\infty_{\nu,4})^3 \to (X^\infty_{\nu,4})^3$ by

$$T(u,v,w) := \pi_\infty(\Psi(\bar{a}^N, \bar{b}^N, \bar{c}^N, u, v, w)). \tag{4.6}$$

Let $L\colon X^\infty_{\nu,4} \to X^\infty_{\nu,4}$ be the linear operator defined by

$$L(a)_{klmn} = \begin{cases} 0 & \text{if } 0 \le k+l+m+n \le N \\ 0 & \text{if } k+l+m+n \ge N+1, \text{ and } n = 0 \\ \frac{\tau}{n} a_{klmn} & \text{if } k+l+m+n \ge N+1, \text{ and } n \ge 1 \end{cases}.$$

Then the components of T are given explicitly by

$$T_1(u,v,w) = \sigma L(\pi_\infty(S_4(\bar{b}^N + v)) - \pi_\infty(S_4(\bar{a}^N + u))),$$

$$T_2(u,v,w) = L\left(\rho\pi_\infty S_4(\bar{a}^N + u) - \pi_\infty S_4(\bar{b}^N + v) - \pi_\infty S_4((\bar{a}^N + u) * (\bar{c}^N + w))\right),$$

and

$$T_3(u,v,w) = L\left(-\beta\pi_\infty S_4(\bar{c}^N + w) + \pi_\infty S_4((\bar{a}^N + u) * (\bar{b}^N + v))\right).$$

The operator DT is given by the "three-by-three matrix" of linear operators

$$DT(u,v,w) = \begin{pmatrix} D_1T_1(u,v,w) & D_2T_1(u,v,w) & D_3T_1(u,v,w) \\ D_1T_2(u,v,w) & D_2T_2(u,v,w) & D_3T_2(u,v,w) \\ D_1T_3(u,v,w) & D_2T_3(u,v,w) & D_3T_3(u,v,w) \end{pmatrix},$$

where, for $h \in X^\infty_{\nu,4}$ the operators have act as

$$D_1T_1(u,v,w)h = -\sigma L\pi_\infty S_4(h),$$

$$D_2T_1(u,v,w)h = \sigma L\pi_\infty S_4(h),$$

$$D_3T_1(u,v,x)h = 0,$$

$$D_1T_2(u,v,w)h = \rho L\pi_\infty S_4(h) - L\pi_\infty S_4(\bar{c}^N * h) - L\pi_\infty S_4(h * w),$$

$$D_2T_2(u,v,w)h = -L\pi_\infty S_4(h),$$

$$D_3T_2(u,v,w)h = -L\pi_\infty S_4(\bar{a}^N * h) - L\pi_\infty S_4(h * u),$$

$$D_1T_3(u,v,w)h = L\pi_\infty S_4(\bar{b}^N * h) + L\pi_\infty S_4(h * v),$$

$$D_2T_3(u,v,w)h = L\pi_\infty S_4(\bar{a}^N * h) + L\pi_\infty S_4(u * h),$$

$$D_3T_3(u,v,w)h = -\beta L\pi_\infty S_4(h).$$

4.4. Validated Taylor integration of a phase box via the contraction mapping theorem. Applying the estimates of Lemmas 2.4 and 2.5 to the expressions for $T(u,v,w)$ and $DT(u,v,w)$ yields the following proposition.

PROPOSITION 4.2. *Suppose that* $\bar{a}^N, \bar{b}^N, \bar{c}^N \in X^N_{\nu,m}$ *are fixed, and that* $T\colon (X^\infty_{\nu,4})^3 \to (X^\infty_{\nu,4})^3$ *is as defined in Equation* (4.6). *Define the positive constants* Y_{01}, Y_{02}, Y_{03} *by*

$$Y_{01} = |\sigma||\tau|\nu^{N+1} \sum_{k+l+m+n=N} \frac{1}{n+1}\left(|\bar{b}^N_{klmn}| + |\bar{a}^N_{klmn}|\right)$$

$$\begin{aligned} Y_{02} = {} & |\rho||\tau|\nu^{N+1} \sum_{k+l+m+n=N} \frac{1}{n+1}|\bar{a}^N_{klmn}| \\ & + |\tau|\nu^{N+1} \sum_{k+l+m+n=N} \frac{1}{n+1}|\bar{b}^N_{klmn}| \\ & + |\tau|\nu^{N+1} \sum_{k+l+m+n=N} \frac{1}{n+1}\left|\left(\bar{a}^N * \bar{c}^N\right)_{klmn}\right| \\ & + |\tau|\nu \sum_{k+l+m+n=N+1}^{2N} \frac{1}{n+1}\left|(\bar{a}^N * \bar{c}^N)_{klmn}\right| \nu^{k+l+m+n}, \end{aligned}$$

$$\begin{aligned} Y_{03} = {} & |\beta||\tau|\nu^{N+1} \sum_{k+l+m+n=N} \frac{1}{n+1}|\bar{c}^N_{klmn}| \\ & + |\tau|\nu^{N+1} \sum_{k+l+m+n=N} \frac{1}{n+1}\left|\left(\bar{a}^N * \bar{b}^N\right)_{klmn}\right| \\ & + |\tau|\nu \sum_{k+l+m+n=N+1}^{2N} \frac{1}{n+1}\left|(\bar{a}^N * \bar{b}^N)_{klmn}\right| \nu^{k+l+m+n} \end{aligned}$$

and let

$$Y_0 := \max(Y_{01}, Y_{02}, Y_{03}).$$

Similarly, define the positive constants Z_{11}, Z_{12}, Z_{13}, Z_{21}, Z_{22}, Z_{23}, Z_{31}, Z_{32}, *and* Z_{33} *by*

$$Z_{11} = Z_{12} = |\sigma||\tau|\nu, \qquad Z_{13} = 0,$$

$$Z_{21} = |\tau|(|\rho|+1+\|\bar{c}^N\|^1_{\nu,m})\nu, \qquad Z_{22} = |\tau|\nu, \qquad \text{and} \qquad Z_{23} = |\tau|\|\bar{a}^N\|^1_{\nu,m}\nu,$$

$$Z_{31} = |\tau|\|\bar{b}^N\|^1_{\nu,m}\nu, \qquad Z_{32} = |\tau|\|\bar{a}^N\|^1_{\nu,m}\nu, \qquad \text{and} \qquad Z_{33} = |\beta||\tau|\nu$$

and let

$$Z_1 = \max_{1\le i\le 3} \sum_{j=1}^{3} Z_{ij},$$

and

$$Z_2 = 2|\tau|.$$

Then

$$\|T(0,0,0)\|_{(X^\infty_{\nu,m})^3} \le Y_0,$$

and

$$\|DT(u,v,w)\|_{B\left((X^\infty_{\nu,m})^3\right)} \le Z_1 + Z_2 r,$$

for all $u, v, w \in X^\infty_{\nu,m}$ *with* $\|u\|^1_{\nu,m}, \|v\|^1_{\nu,m}, \|w\|^1_{\nu,m} \le r$.

PROOF. Define the linear operator $A\colon \ell^1_{\nu,m} \to \ell^1_{\nu,m}$ by

$$A(a)_{kmln} = \frac{\tau}{n+1} a_{klmn}, \qquad a \in \ell^1_{\nu,m}.$$

One easily checks that

$$L\pi_\infty S_j(a) = \pi_\infty S_j A(a),$$

for all $a \in \ell^1_{\nu,m}$. Then

$$\begin{aligned}
\|T_1(0,0,0)\|_{X^\infty_{\nu,m}} &= \|\sigma L\left(\pi_\infty S_4(\bar{b}^N) - \pi_\infty S_4(\bar{a}^N)\right)\|^1_{\nu,m} \\
&= \|\sigma\left(\pi_\infty S_4 A(\bar{b}^N) - \pi_\infty S_4 A(\bar{a}^N)\right)\|^1_{\nu,m} \\
&\leq |\sigma||\tau|\nu^{N+1} \sum_{k+l+m+n=N} \frac{1}{n+1}\left(|\bar{b}^N_{klmn}| + |\bar{a}^N_{klmn}|\right) \\
&= Y_{01},
\end{aligned}$$

and similarly that

$$\begin{aligned}
\|T_2(0,0,0)\|_{X^\infty_{\nu,m}} &= \|L\left(\rho\pi_\infty S_4(\bar{a}^N) - \pi_\infty S_4(\bar{b}^N) - \pi_\infty S_4(\bar{a}^N * \bar{c}^N)\right)\|^1_{\nu,m} \\
&= \|\left(\rho\pi_\infty S_4 A(a^N) - \pi_\infty S_4 A(\bar{b}^N) - \pi_\infty S_4 A(\bar{a}^N * \bar{c}^N)\right)\|^1_{\nu,m} \\
&\leq |\rho||\tau|\nu^{N+1} \sum_{k+l+m+n=N} \frac{1}{n+1}|\bar{a}^N_{klmn}| \\
&\quad + |\tau|\nu^{N+1} \sum_{k+l+m+n=N} \frac{1}{n+1}|\bar{b}^N_{klmn}| \\
&\quad + |\tau|\nu^{N+1} \sum_{k+l+m+n=N} \frac{1}{n+1}\left|\left(\bar{a}^N * \bar{c}^N\right)_{klmn}\right| \\
&\quad + |\tau|\nu \sum_{|\alpha|=N+1}^{2N} \frac{1}{n+1}\left|(\bar{a}^N * \bar{c}^N)_\alpha\right| \nu^{|\alpha|} \\
&= Y_{02},
\end{aligned}$$

and that

$$\begin{aligned}
\|T_3(0,0,0)\|_{X^\infty_{\nu,m}} &= \|L\left(-\beta\pi_\infty S_4(\bar{c}^N) + \pi_\infty S_4(\bar{a}^N * \bar{b}^N)\right)\|^1_{\nu,m} \\
&= \|\left(-\beta\pi_\infty S_4 A(\bar{c}^N) + \pi_\infty S_4 A(\bar{a}^N * \bar{b}^N)\right)\|^1_{\nu,m} \\
&\leq |\beta||\tau|\nu^{N+1} \sum_{k+l+m+n=N} \frac{1}{n+1}|\bar{c}^N_{klmn}| \\
&\quad + |\tau|\nu^{N+1} \sum_{k+l+m+n=N} \frac{1}{n+1}\left|\left(\bar{a}^N * \bar{b}^N\right)_{klmn}\right| \\
&\quad + |\tau|\nu \sum_{k+l+m+n=N+1}^{2N} \frac{1}{n+1}\left|(\bar{a}^N * \bar{b}^N)_{klmn}\right| \nu^{k+l+m+n} \\
&= Y_{03}.
\end{aligned}$$

It follows that

$$\begin{aligned}\|T(0,0,0)\|_{(X^{\infty}_{\nu,m})^3} &= \max\left(\|T_1(0,0,0)\|_{X^{\infty}_{\nu,m}}, \|T_2(0,0,0)\|_{X^{\infty}_{\nu,m}}, \|T_3(0,0,0)\|_{X^{\infty}_{\nu,m}}\right)\\ &\leq \max(Y_{01}, Y_{02}, Y_{0,3})\\ &= Y_0.\end{aligned}$$

The estimates for the derivative are very similar. Note that the derivative can be decomposed as

$$DT(u,v,w) = \mathcal{L} + \mathcal{M}(u,v,w),$$

where for $H = (h_1,h_2,h_3) \in \left(X^1_{\nu,m}\right)^3$ the actions of $\mathcal{L}$ and $\mathcal{M}$ are given by

$$\mathcal{L}(h_1,h_2,h_3) = \begin{pmatrix} -\sigma L\pi_\infty S_4(h_1) + \sigma L\pi_\infty S_4(h_2) \\ \rho L\pi_\infty S_4(h_1) - L\pi_\infty S_4(\bar{c}^N * h_1) - L\pi_\infty S_4(h_2) - L\pi_\infty S_4(\bar{a}^N * h_3) \\ L\pi_\infty S_4(\bar{b}^N * h_1) + L\pi_\infty S_4(\bar{a}^N * h_2) - \beta L\pi_\infty S_4(h_3) \end{pmatrix}$$

and

$$\mathcal{M}(u,v,w)(h_1,h_2,h_3) = \begin{pmatrix} 0 \\ -L\pi_\infty S_4(h_1 * w) - L\pi_\infty S_4(h_3 * u) \\ L\pi_\infty S_4(h_1 * v) + L\pi_\infty S_4(h_2 * u) \end{pmatrix}$$

Then

$$\begin{aligned}\|\mathcal{L}\|_{B\left((X^1_{\nu,m})^3\right)} &= \sup_{\|H\|=1} \|\mathcal{L}H\|_{(X^1_{\nu,m})^3}\\ &\leq \sup_{\|H\|=1} \left\| \begin{pmatrix} -\sigma L\pi_\infty S_4(h_1) + \sigma L\pi_\infty S_4(h_2) \\ \rho L\pi_\infty S_4(h_1) - L\pi_\infty S_4(\bar{c}^N * h_1) - L\pi_\infty S_4(h_2) - L\pi_\infty S_4(\bar{a}^N * h_3) \\ L\pi_\infty S_4(\bar{b}^N * h_1) + L\pi_\infty S_4(\bar{a}^N * h_2) - \beta L\pi_\infty S_4(h_3) \end{pmatrix} \right\|_{(X^1_{\nu,m})^3}\\ &\leq \max_{1\leq i\leq 3} \sum_{j=1}^{3} Z_{ij}\\ &= Z_1,\end{aligned}$$

and, if $\|u\|^1_{\nu,m}, \|v\|^1_{\nu,m}, \|w\|^1_{\nu,m} \leq r$, then

$$\begin{aligned}\|\mathcal{M}(u,v,w)\|_{B\left((X^1_{\nu,m})^3\right)} &= \sup_{\|H\|=1} \|\mathcal{M}(u,v,w)H\|_{(X^1_{\nu,m})^3}\\ &\leq \sup_{\|H\|=1} \left\| \begin{pmatrix} 0 \\ -L\pi_\infty S_4(h_1 * w) - L\pi_\infty S_4(h_3 * u) \\ L\pi_\infty S_4(h_1 * v) + L\pi_\infty S_4(h_2 * u) \end{pmatrix} \right\|_{(X^1_{\nu,m})^3}\\ &\leq 2|\tau| r\\ &= Z_2 r.\end{aligned}$$

□

Example: Consider the initial conditions $x_0 = -15$, $y_0 = -15$, and $z_0 = 40$ near the attractor but otherwise arbitrary. We compute to order $N = 7$ and take a time step of size $\tau = 0.002$. Recall that the step size is controlled by rescaling the vector field by τ. We take $c = 1/4$, i.e. we reparameterize to a spatial cube of size a half. With these choices the larges coefficient of order $N = 7$ is approximately 10^{-8}.

We check that we have the bounds $Y_0 = 1.4 \times 10^{-9}$, $Z_1 = 0.44$, and $Z_2 = 0.01$. Then we obtain a validated contraction on a ball of radius $r = 2.4 \times 10^{-9}$, i.e. the order to the last coefficient computed numerically. Then, for example, the C^0 error between the exact solution and our approximation is less than or equal to r for all $x, y, z, t \leq 1$ (these are the rescaled variables).

5. The global problem: connecting one local picture to another

5.1. The method of projected boundaries (slight return). We now set up the operator used to establish the existence of a heteroclinic connection. Lets focus only on the set up actually used in the next section, and avoid the temptation to generalize. Take

$$D := \{z \in \mathbb{C} \,|\, |z| < 1\},$$

the unit disk at the origin in the complex plane and $D^2 = D \times D$ denote the unit poly-disk. Let

$$B^2 := \left\{(x, y) \in \mathbb{R}^2 \,|\, \sqrt{x^2 + y^2} < 1\right\},$$

be the unit disk at the origin in the Euclidean plane.

DEFINITION 5.1 (Focus to fast-slow saddle assumptions). Let $f\colon \mathbb{R}^3 \to \mathbb{R}^3$ be a real analytic vector field and assume that

(i) $p_0 \in \mathbb{R}^3$ is an equilibrium solution with a complex conjugate pair of unstable eigenvalues $\lambda_1^u, \lambda_2^u \in \mathbb{C}$. Let $\xi_1^u, \xi_2^u \in \mathbb{C}^3$ denote a complex conjugate pair of eigenvectors.

(ii) $p_1 \in \mathbb{R}^3$ is an equilibrium solution with two distinct, real, stable eigenvectors λ_1^s, λ_2^s having

$$\text{real}(\lambda_2^s) < \text{real}(\lambda_1^s) < 0.$$

Let $\xi_1^s, \xi_2^s \in \mathbb{R}^3$ be associated eigenvectors.

(iii) $P\colon D^2 \to \mathbb{C}^3$ is a solution of Equation (3.1) subject to the first order constraints

$$P(0,0) = p_0, \qquad \text{and} \qquad \partial_1 P(0,0) = \xi_1^u, \qquad \partial_2 P(0,0) = \xi_2^u.$$

Assume moreover that the (complex conjugate) Taylor coefficients $p \in (\ell_{1,2}^1)^3$ have $\|p\|_{(\ell_{1,2}^1)^3} \leq C_1$. Define the map $\hat{P}\colon B^2 \to \mathbb{R}^3$ by

$$\hat{P}(u, v) = P(u + iv, u - iv).$$

(iv) $Q\colon [-1, 1]^2 \to \mathbb{R}^3$ is a solution of Equation (3.1) subject to the first order constraints

$$Q(0,0) = p_1, \qquad \text{and} \qquad \partial_1 Q(0,0) = \xi_1^s, \qquad \partial_2 Q(0,0) = \xi_2^s.$$

Assume moreover that the (real) Taylor coefficients $q \in (\ell_{1,2}^1)^3$ have $\|q\|_{(\ell_{1,2}^1)^3} \leq C_2$.

PROPOSITION 5.2 (Connecting orbit operator). *Assume the existence of data as in Definition* 5.1. *For* $0 < r_u, r_s < 1$ *define the* $F\colon \mathbb{R} \times (0, \infty) \times [-1, 1] \to \mathbb{R}^3$, *by*

$$F(\theta, h, T) = \phi(\hat{P}(r_u \cos(\theta), r_u \sin(\theta)), T) - Q(h, r_s). \tag{5.1}$$

If there is a $(\hat{\theta}, \hat{h}, \hat{T}) \in \mathbb{R}^3$ *so that*

$$F(\hat{\theta}, \hat{h}, \hat{T}) = 0,$$

then $\gamma\colon \mathbb{R} \to \mathbb{R}^3$ *defined by*

$$\gamma(t) = \phi\left(\hat{P}(r_u\cos(\hat{\theta}), r_u\sin(\hat{\theta})), t\right),$$

is a heteroclinic connecting orbit from p_0 *to* p_1. *We refer to* F *as the connecting orbit operator.*

PROOF. Note that for each $t \in \mathbb{R}$, $\gamma(t)$ is a solution to the differential equation due to the fact that ϕ is the flow map.

Consider $t \geq 0$ and let $z_0 := r_u\cos(\hat{\theta}) + ir_u\sin(\hat{\theta})$. By Proposition 3.1, P conjugates the nonlinear to the linear flow so that

$$\begin{aligned}\gamma(-t) &= \phi\left(\hat{P}(r_u\cos(\hat{\theta}), r_u\sin(\hat{\theta})), -t\right)\\ &= \phi\left(P(z_0, \bar{z_0}), -t\right)\\ &= P\left(z_0 e^{-\lambda_u^1 t}, \bar{z_0} e^{-\overline{\lambda_u^1} t}\right).\end{aligned}$$

Then

$$\begin{aligned}\lim_{t\to-\infty}\gamma(t) &= \lim_{t\to\infty} P\left(z_0 e^{-\lambda_u^1 t}, \bar{z_0} e^{-\overline{\lambda_u^1} t}\right)\\ &= P(0,0)\\ &= p_0,\end{aligned}$$

as P is continuous (in fact analytic).

Similarly, suppose that $t > \hat{T}$. Then we can write $t = \hat{T} + s$ with $s > 0$, and by combining the conjugacy of Proposition 3.1 with the definition of the connecting orbit operator and the fact that $(\hat{\theta}, \hat{h}, \hat{T})$ is a zero, have that

$$\begin{aligned}\gamma(t) &= \phi\left(\hat{P}(r_u\cos(\hat{\theta}), r_u\sin(\hat{\theta})), \hat{T} + s\right)\\ &= \phi\left(\phi\left(\hat{P}(r_u\cos(\hat{\theta}), r_u\sin(\hat{\theta})), \hat{T}\right), s\right)\\ &= \phi(Q(\hat{h}, r_s), s)\\ &= Q(e^{\lambda_s^1 s}\hat{h}, e^{\lambda_s^2 s} r_s).\end{aligned}$$

Then

$$\begin{aligned}\lim_{t\to\infty}\gamma(t) &= \lim_{s\to\infty} Q(e^{\lambda_s^1 s}\hat{h}, e^{\lambda_s^2 s} r_s)\\ &= Q(0,0)\\ &= p_1,\end{aligned}$$

again by the continuity of Q. □

REMARK 5.3. This argument actually only requires that ϕ is defined in a neighborhood of the orbit segment $\gamma([0, \hat{T}])$.

In applications it is desirable to subdivide the time interval $\hat{T}$, and consider the following "multiple-shooting" scheme.

PROPOSITION 5.4 (Multiple-shooting connecting orbit operator). *Assume the existence of data as in Definition* 5.1. *For* $0 < r_u, r_s < 1$ *define the map* $F^K : \mathbb{R} \times \mathbb{R}^{3(K+1)} \times (0, \infty) \times (-1, 1) \to \mathbb{R}^{3(K+2)}$ *by*

$$F^K(\theta, x_0, x_1, x_2, \ldots, x_{K-1}, x_K, h, \tau) := \begin{pmatrix} \hat{P}(r_u \cos(\theta), r_u \sin(\theta)) - x_0 \\ \phi(x_0, \tau) - x_1 \\ \phi(x_1, \tau) - x_2 \\ \vdots \\ \phi(x_{K-1}, \tau) - x_K \\ \phi(x_K, \tau) - Q(h, r_s) \end{pmatrix}. \tag{5.2}$$

If $\hat{x} = (\hat{\theta}, \hat{x}_0, \ldots, \hat{x}_K, \hat{h}, \hat{\tau}) \in \mathbb{R}^{3(K+2)}$ *has that*

$$F^K(\hat{x}) = 0,$$

then $(\hat{\theta}, \hat{h}, (K+1)\hat{\tau})$ *is a zero of the connecting orbit operator defined in Proposition* 5.2.

We refer to F^K *as the multiple shooting connecting orbit operator.*

The proof is an elementary application of the properties of a flow. In particular if $\hat{x}$ is a zero of F^K then

$$\phi(\hat{x}_0, \hat{\tau}) = \hat{x}_1,$$

and

$$\phi(\hat{x}_1, \hat{\tau}) = \hat{x}_2,$$

which imply

$$\phi(\hat{x}_0, 2\hat{\tau}) = \hat{x}_2.$$

Repeated application of this idea gives that

$$\phi(\hat{x}_0, (K+1)\tau) = Q(\hat{h}, r_s).$$

Noting that

$$\hat{x}_0 = \hat{P}(r_u \cos(\hat{\theta}), r_u \sin(\hat{\theta})),$$

yields the result desired zero of the connecting orbit operator F of Proposition 5.2.

REMARK 5.5 (Derivatives and transversality). Observe that F^K is differentiable and that the $3(K+2) \times 3(K+2)$ Jacobian matrix of F^K is given by

$$DF^K(\theta, x_0, x_1, x_2, \ldots, x_{K-1}, x_K, h, \tau) =$$

$$\begin{pmatrix} d_P(\theta) & -\mathrm{Id}_3 & 0 & 0 & 0 & \ldots & 0 & 0 & 0 & 0 \\ 0 & D_1\phi(x_0, \tau) & -\mathrm{Id}_3 & 0 & 0 & \ldots & 0 & 0 & 0 & f(\phi(x_0, \tau)) \\ 0 & 0 & D_1\phi(x_1, \tau) & -\mathrm{Id}_3 & 0 & \ldots & 0 & 0 & 0 & f(\phi(x_1, \tau)) \\ \vdots & \vdots & \vdots & \vdots & \vdots & \ddots & \vdots & \vdots & \vdots & \vdots \\ 0 & 0 & 0 & 0 & 0 & \ldots & D_1\phi(x_{K-1}, \tau) & -\mathrm{Id}_3 & 0 & f(\phi(x_{K-1}, \tau)) \\ 0 & 0 & 0 & 0 & 0 & \ldots & 0 & D_1\phi(x_K, \tau) & d_Q(h) & f(\phi(x_K, \tau)) \end{pmatrix}$$

Here

$$d_P(\theta) := r_u \partial_1 P(z, \bar{z}) w + r_u \partial_2 P(z, \bar{z}) \bar{w},$$

where $z = \cos(\theta) + i \sin(\theta)$ and $w = -\sin(\theta) + i \cos(\theta)$, and

$$d_Q(h) := \partial_1 Q(h, r_s).$$

The explicit form of the derivative is critical for numerical calculations, but it is also useful in theoretical arguments. For example, an argument similar to that given in Section 6 of [**62**] shows that the connecting orbit $\gamma(t)$ of Proposition 5.2 is transverse if and only if the matrix $DF^K(\hat{x})$ is invertible. As we will see below, the invertibility of $DF^K(\hat{x})$ is obtained as a consequence of our computer assisted a-posteriori analysis of the multiple shooting connecting orbit operator.

REMARK 5.6 (Approximate connecting orbit). In general it is not easy to locate approximate connecting orbits, and in practice this is often the most challenging part of a computer assisted proof. For some problems it is possible to find an approximate orbit as the limit of a family of periodic orbits. Other times perturbative methods are used in conjunction with parameter continuation.

For the example at hand we perform some numerical experiments. The idea is to sample points on the boundary of the unstable manifold, and to integrate these until they pass near the stable manifold. The orbits are examined by eye until we find a reasonable candidate. Bisection is used to refine the guess. Since the boundary of the unstable manifold is one dimensional this scheme is relatively efficient, and a few minutes experimentation provide a viable guess. This initial guess is refined via Newton's method until we have defect on the order of machine precision.

REMARK 5.7 (Generalized connecting orbit operators). The discussion above assumes the connecting orbit operator has a very specific form, and the form examined above is the one used to study connections from eye to origin in the Lorenz system. That being said, the functional analytic setup introduced here generalizes to vector fields in any dimension and to hyperbolic equilibria with any stability type. Details are found for example in [**62**], and are generalized for connections between periodic orbits in [**63**].

5.2. Computer assisted proof of a transverse connecting orbit via a finite dimensional Newton like argument. Once we have an approximate connecting orbit via numerical experimentation as described above, it is a simple matter of applying Proposition 2.8 to get the computer assisted proof of existence *as long as we have the requisite bounds* $\phi(x,t)$, $P(u)$ *and* $Q(s)$. But the methods of Sections 3.5 and 4.4 provide these bounds.

For example, using the validated parameterizations discussed in Sections 3.5 and 4.4 i.e. orders $N = 150$ for the unstable and $N = 50$ for the stable manifold, and expanding ϕ to order $N = 8$ at each of the points $\bar{x}_0, \ldots, \bar{x}_K$, with $K = 8,875$, and taking $\bar{\tau} = 0.002$, we check the conditions of Proposition 2.8 for the multiple shooting connecting orbit operator and obtain a true heteroclinic connection within a ball of radius $r = 10^{-4}$ about $\bar{x} \in \mathbb{R}^{3(K+1)}$. Since the proof succeeds we have that $DF^K(\hat{x})$ is invertible, and hence the connection is transverse.

REMARK 5.8 (Second derivatives). Theorem 2.8 (which is necessary to obtain invertibility of the derivative and hence transversality) requires bounds on second derivatives near the approximate solution $\bar{x}$. But the connecting orbit operator involves derivatives of $\phi(x,\tau)$ with respect to x, as well as derivatives of $\hat{P}$ and Q. This explains the role of $r_u, r_s < 1$ in the definition of the connecting orbit operators: we need to make sure that we have some domain to "trade in" for bounds on derivatives. The necessary trade is negotiated via the Cauchy bounds of Lemma 2.1.

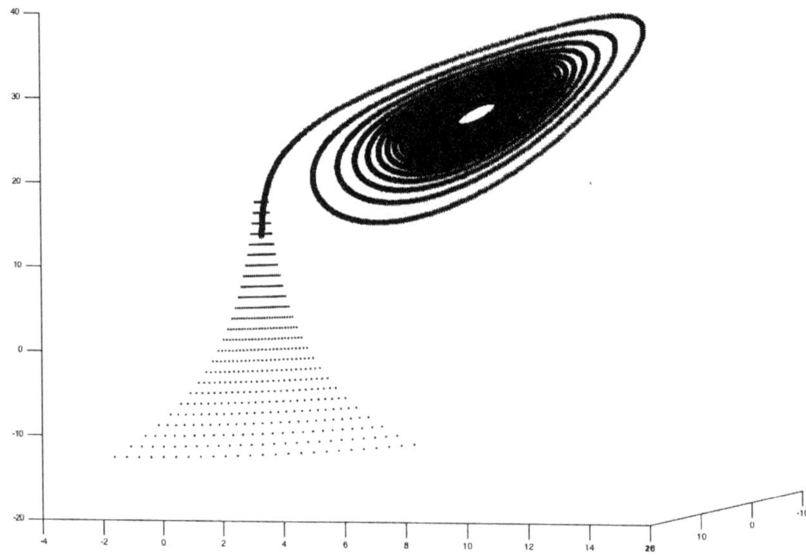

FIGURE 9. A transverse heteroclinic connecting orbit from p_0 to p_1. The existence of the orbit is validated using Theorem 2.8, in conjunction with the validated local stable/unstable manifolds and the validated Taylor integrator of Sections 3.5 and 4.4.

6. Acknowledgments

The author is deeply indebted to an anonymous referee, and also to Mengsen Zhang, Carlos Garcia Azpeitia, Jean-Philippe Lessard, and especially to Yann Ricaud for their careful reading of an earlier draft of these notes. The final version is greatly improved thanks to these efforts. Thanks also to Jean-Philippe Lessard and Jan Bouwe van den Berg for several helpful conversations which helped to shape the final content and scope of these notes. Finally, thanks to Hans Koch for helpful discussions and many valuable suggestions at the 2016 AIMS meeting in Orlando Florida.

References

[1] E. Adams, D. Cordes, and R. Lohner, *Enclosure of solutions of ordinary initial value problems and applications*, Discretization in differential equations and enclosures (Weissig, 1986), Math. Res., vol. 36, Akademie-Verlag, Berlin, 1987, pp. 9–28, DOI 10.1007/BF03322097. MR950221

[2] D. Ambrosi, G. Arioli, and H. Koch, *A homoclinic solution for excitation waves on a contractile substratum*, SIAM J. Appl. Dyn. Syst. **11** (2012), no. 4, 1533–1542, DOI 10.1137/12087654X. MR3022075

[3] Gianni Arioli, *Periodic orbits, symbolic dynamics and topological entropy for the restricted 3-body problem*, Comm. Math. Phys. **231** (2002), no. 1, 1–24, DOI 10.1007/s00220-002-0666-7. MR1947690

[4] Gianni Arioli, *Branches of periodic orbits for the planar restricted 3-body problem*, Discrete Contin. Dyn. Syst. **11** (2004), no. 4, 745–755, DOI 10.3934/dcds.2004.11.745. MR2112702

[5] Gianni Arioli, Vivina Barutello, and Susanna Terracini, *A new branch of Mountain Pass solutions for the choreographical 3-body problem*, Comm. Math. Phys. **268** (2006), no. 2, 439–463, DOI 10.1007/s00220-006-0111-4. MR2259202

[6] Gianni Arioli and Hans Koch, *Integration of dissipative partial differential equations: a case study*, SIAM J. Appl. Dyn. Syst. **9** (2010), no. 3, 1119–1133, DOI 10.1137/10078298X. MR2728184

[7] Gianni Arioli and Hans Koch, *Existence and stability of traveling pulse solutions of the FitzHugh-Nagumo equation*, Nonlinear Anal. **113** (2015), 51–70, DOI 10.1016/j.na.2014.09.023. MR3281845

[8] Gianni Arioli and Piotr Zgliczyński, *Symbolic dynamics for the Hénon-Heiles Hamiltonian on the critical level*, J. Differential Equations **171** (2001), no. 1, 173–202, DOI 10.1006/jdeq.2000.3835. MR1816799

[9] Gianni Arioli and Piotr Zgliczyński, *The Hénon-Heiles Hamiltonian near the critical energy level—some rigorous results*, Nonlinearity **16** (2003), no. 5, 1833–1852, DOI 10.1088/0951-7715/16/5/316. MR1999582

[10] Flaviano Battelli and Kenneth J. Palmer, *Chaos in the Duffing equation*, J. Differential Equations **101** (1993), no. 2, 276–301, DOI 10.1006/jdeq.1993.1013. MR1204329

[11] Martin Berz and Kyoko Makino, *Verified integration of ODEs and flows using differential algebraic methods on high-order Taylor models*, Reliab. Comput. **4** (1998), no. 4, 361–369, DOI 10.1023/A:1024467732637. MR1652147

[12] W.-J. Beyn, *The numerical computation of connecting orbits in dynamical systems*, IMA J. Numer. Anal. **10** (1990), no. 3, 379–405, DOI 10.1093/imanum/10.3.379. MR1068199

[13] Maxime Breden, Jean-Philippe Lessard, and Jason D. Mireles James, *Computation of maximal local (un)stable manifold patches by the parameterization method*, Indag. Math. (N.S.) **27** (2016), no. 1, 340–367, DOI 10.1016/j.indag.2015.11.001. MR3437754

[14] Xavier Cabré, Ernest Fontich, and Rafael de la Llave, *The parameterization method for invariant manifolds. I. Manifolds associated to non-resonant subspaces*, Indiana Univ. Math. J. **52** (2003), no. 2, 283–328, DOI 10.1512/iumj.2003.52.2245. MR1976079

[15] Xavier Cabré, Ernest Fontich, and Rafael de la Llave, *The parameterization method for invariant manifolds. II. Regularity with respect to parameters*, Indiana Univ. Math. J. **52** (2003), no. 2, 329–360, DOI 10.1512/iumj.2003.52.2407. MR1976080

[16] Xavier Cabré, Ernest Fontich, and Rafael de la Llave, *The parameterization method for invariant manifolds. III. Overview and applications*, J. Differential Equations **218** (2005), no. 2, 444–515, DOI 10.1016/j.jde.2004.12.003. MR2177465

[17] Renato Calleja and Jordi-Lluís Figueras, *Collision of invariant bundles of quasi-periodic attractors in the dissipative standard map*, Chaos **22** (2012), no. 3, 033114, 10, DOI 10.1063/1.4737205. MR3388608

[18] Renato C. Calleja, Alessandra Celletti, and Rafael de la Llave, *A KAM theory for conformally symplectic systems: efficient algorithms and their validation*, J. Differential Equations **255** (2013), no. 5, 978–1049, DOI 10.1016/j.jde.2013.05.001. MR3062760

[19] Renato C. Calleja, Alessandra Celletti, and Rafael de la Llave, *Local behavior near quasi-periodic solutions of conformally symplectic systems*, J. Dynam. Differential Equations **25** (2013), no. 3, 821–841, DOI 10.1007/s10884-013-9319-0. MR3095277

[20] Marta Canadell and Àlex Haro, *Parameterization method for computing quasi periodic reducible normally hyperbolic invariant tori*, Advances in differential equations and applications, SEMA SIMAI Springer Ser., vol. 4, Springer, Cham, 2014, pp. 85–94, DOI 10.1007/978-3-319-06953-1_9. MR3309008

[21] Maciej J. Capiński, *Covering relations and the existence of topologically normally hyperbolic invariant sets*, Discrete Contin. Dyn. Syst. **23** (2009), no. 3, 705–725, DOI 10.3934/dcds.2009.23.705. MR2461822

[22] Maciej J. Capiński, *Computer assisted existence proofs of Lyapunov orbits at L_2 and transversal intersections of invariant manifolds in the Jupiter-Sun PCR3BP*, SIAM J. Appl. Dyn. Syst. **11** (2012), no. 4, 1723–1753, DOI 10.1137/110847366. MR3032848

[23] Maciej J. Capiński and Anna Wasieczko-Zając, *Geometric proof of strong stable/unstable manifolds with application to the restricted three body problem*, Topol. Methods Nonlinear Anal. **46** (2015), no. 1, 363–399, DOI 10.12775/TMNA.2015.051. MR3443692

[24] Maciej J. Capiński and Piotr Zgliczyński, *Cone conditions and covering relations for topologically normally hyperbolic invariant manifolds*, Discrete Contin. Dyn. Syst. **30** (2011), no. 3, 641–670, DOI 10.3934/dcds.2011.30.641. MR2784613

[25] Roberto Castelli and Jean-Philippe Lessard, *A method to rigorously enclose eigenpairs of complex interval matrices*, Applications of mathematics 2013, Acad. Sci. Czech Repub. Inst. Math., Prague, 2013, pp. 21–31. MR3204427

[26] Roberto Castelli, Jean-Philippe Lessard, and J. D. Mireles James, *Parameterization of invariant manifolds for periodic orbits I: Efficient numerics via the Floquet normal form*, SIAM J. Appl. Dyn. Syst. **14** (2015), no. 1, 132–167, DOI 10.1137/140960207. MR3304254

[27] Roberto Castelli, Jean-Philippe Lessard, and J. D. Mireles James, *Parameterization of invariant manifolds for periodic orbits I: Efficient numerics via the Floquet normal form*, SIAM J. Appl. Dyn. Syst. **14** (2015), no. 1, 132–167, DOI 10.1137/140960207. MR3304254

[28] Brian A. Coomes, Hüseyin Koçak, and Kenneth J. Palmer, *Transversal connecting orbits from shadowing*, Numer. Math. **106** (2007), no. 3, 427–469, DOI 10.1007/s00211-007-0065-2. MR2302059

[29] Brian A. Coomes, Hüseyin Koçak, and Kenneth J. Palmer, *A computable criterion for the existence of connecting orbits in autonomous dynamics*, J. Dynam. Differential Equations **28** (2016), no. 3-4, 1081–1114, DOI 10.1007/s10884-015-9437-y. MR3537365

[30] Jacek Cyranka, *Efficient and generic algorithm for rigorous integration forward in time of dPDEs: Part I*, J. Sci. Comput. **59** (2014), no. 1, 28–52, DOI 10.1007/s10915-013-9749-1. MR3167726

[31] Jacek Cyranka, *Existence of globally attracting fixed points of viscous Burgers equation with constant forcing. A computer assisted proof*, Topol. Methods Nonlinear Anal. **45** (2015), no. 2, 655–697, DOI 10.12775/TMNA.2015.031. MR3408840

[32] Jacek Cyranka and Piotr Zgliczyński, *Existence of globally attracting solutions for one-dimensional viscous Burgers equation with nonautonomous forcing—a computer assisted proof*, SIAM J. Appl. Dyn. Syst. **14** (2015), no. 2, 787–821, DOI 10.1137/14096699X. MR3338669

[33] R. de la Llave, A. González, À. Jorba, and J. Villanueva, *KAM theory without action-angle variables*, Nonlinearity **18** (2005), no. 2, 855–895, DOI 10.1088/0951-7715/18/2/020. MR2122688

[34] Jordi-Lluís Figueras, Marcio Gameiro, Jean-Philippe Lessard, and Rafael de la Llave, *A framework for the numerical computation and a posteriori verification of invariant objects of evolution equations*, SIAM J. Appl. Dyn. Syst. **16** (2017), no. 2, 1070–1088, DOI 10.1137/16M1073777. MR3662023

[35] Rafael de la Llave and Jason D. Mireles James, *Parameterization of invariant manifolds by reducibility for volume preserving and symplectic maps*, Discrete Contin. Dyn. Syst. **32** (2012), no. 12, 4321–4360, DOI 10.3934/dcds.2012.32.4321. MR2966749

[36] E. J. Doedel, B. W. Kooi, G. A. K. van Voorn, and Yu. A. Kuznetsov, *Continuation of connecting orbits in 3D-ODEs. I. Point-to-cycle connections*, Internat. J. Bifur. Chaos Appl. Sci. Engrg. **18** (2008), no. 7, 1889–1903, DOI 10.1142/S0218127408021439. MR2454068

[37] E. J. Doedel, B. W. Kooi, G. A. K. Van Voorn, and Yu. A. Kuznetsov, *Continuation of connecting orbits in 3D-ODEs. II. Cycle-to-cycle connections*, Internat. J. Bifur. Chaos Appl. Sci. Engrg. **19** (2009), no. 1, 159–169, DOI 10.1142/S0218127409022804. MR2511084

[38] Eusebius J. Doedel and Mark J. Friedman, *Numerical computation of heteroclinic orbits*, J. Comput. Appl. Math. **26** (1989), no. 1-2, 155–170, DOI 10.1016/0377-0427(89)90153-2. Continuation techniques and bifurcation problems. MR1007358

[39] J.-P. Eckmann, H. Koch, and P. Wittwer, *A computer-assisted proof of universality for area-preserving maps*, Mem. Amer. Math. Soc. **47** (1984), no. 289, vi+122, DOI 10.1090/memo/0289. MR727816

[40] C. Fefferman and R. de la Llave, *Relativistic stability of matter. I*, Rev. Mat. Iberoamericana **2** (1986), no. 1-2, 119–213, DOI 10.4171/RMI/30. MR864658

[41] Jordi-Lluís Figueras and Àlex Haro, *Reliable computation of robust response tori on the verge of breakdown*, SIAM J. Appl. Dyn. Syst. **11** (2012), no. 2, 597–628, DOI 10.1137/100809222. MR2967458

[42] Jordi-Lluís Figueras, Àlex Haro, and Alejandro Luque, *Rigorous computer assisted application of kam theory: a modern approach*, (To appear in Foundations of Computational Mathematics) (2016), 1–49.

[43] Ernest Fontich, Rafael de la Llave, and Yannick Sire, *A method for the study of whiskered quasi-periodic and almost-periodic solutions in finite and infinite dimensional Hamiltonian systems*, Electron. Res. Announc. Math. Sci. **16** (2009), 9–22, DOI 10.3934/era.2009.16.9. MR2505176

[44] Mark J. Friedman and Eusebius J. Doedel, *Numerical computation and continuation of invariant manifolds connecting fixed points*, SIAM J. Numer. Anal. **28** (1991), no. 3, 789–808, DOI 10.1137/0728042. MR1098418

[45] Mark J. Friedman and Eusebius J. Doedel, *Computational methods for global analysis of homoclinic and heteroclinic orbits: a case study*, J. Dynam. Differential Equations **5** (1993), no. 1, 37–57, DOI 10.1007/BF01063734. MR1205453

[46] Z. Galias and P. Zgliczyński, *Computer assisted proof of chaos in the Lorenz equations*, Phys. D **115** (1998), no. 3-4, 165–188, DOI 10.1016/S0167-2789(97)00233-9. MR1626596

[47] Zbigniew Galias and Piotr Zgliczyński, *Chaos in the Lorenz equations for classical parameter values. A computer assisted proof*, Proceedings of the Conference "Topological Methods in Differential Equations and Dynamical Systems" (Kraków-Przegorzały, 1996), Univ. Iagel. Acta Math. **36** (1998), 209–210. MR1661345

[48] J. D. Mireles James, *Quadratic volume-preserving maps: (un)stable manifolds, hyperbolic dynamics, and vortex-bubble bifurcations*, J. Nonlinear Sci. **23** (2013), no. 4, 585–615. MR3079670

[49] Chris M. Groothedde and J. D. Mireles James, *Parameterization method for unstable manifolds of delay differential equations*, (To appear in Journal of Computational Dynamics) (2016), 1–52.

[50] Antoni Guillamon and Gemma Huguet, *A computational and geometric approach to phase resetting curves and surfaces*, SIAM J. Appl. Dyn. Syst. **8** (2009), no. 3, 1005–1042, DOI 10.1137/080737666. MR2551254

[51] À. Haro and R. de la Llave, *A parameterization method for the computation of invariant tori and their whiskers in quasi-periodic maps: numerical algorithms*, Discrete Contin. Dyn. Syst. Ser. B **6** (2006), no. 6, 1261–1300, DOI 10.3934/dcdsb.2006.6.1261. MR2240743

[52] A. Haro and R. de la Llave, *A parameterization method for the computation of invariant tori and their whiskers in quasi-periodic maps: rigorous results*, J. Differential Equations **228** (2006), no. 2, 530–579, DOI 10.1016/j.jde.2005.10.005. MR2289544

[53] A. Haro and R. de la Llave, *A parameterization method for the computation of invariant tori and their whiskers in quasi-periodic maps: explorations and mechanisms for the breakdown of hyperbolicity*, SIAM J. Appl. Dyn. Syst. **6** (2007), no. 1, 142–207, DOI 10.1137/050637327. MR2299977

[54] Àlex Haro, Marta Canadell, Jordi-Lluís Figueras, Alejandro Luque, and Josep-Maria Mondelo, *The parameterization method for invariant manifolds*, Applied Mathematical Sciences, vol. 195, Springer, [Cham], 2016. From rigorous results to effective computations. MR3467671

[55] Xiaolong He and Rafael de la Llave, *Construction of quasi-periodic solutions of state-dependent delay differential equations by the parameterization method II. Analytic case*, J. Differential Equations **261** (2016), no. 3, 2068–2108, DOI 10.1016/j.jde.2016.04.024. MR3501842

[56] Gemma Huguet and Rafael de la Llave, *Computation of limit cycles and their isochrons: fast algorithms and their convergence*, SIAM J. Appl. Dyn. Syst. **12** (2013), no. 4, 1763–1802, DOI 10.1137/120901210. MR3118249

[57] M. C. Irwin, *On the stable manifold theorem*, Bull. London Math. Soc. **2** (1970), 196–198, DOI 10.1112/blms/2.2.196. MR0271992

[58] J. B. van den Berg and J. D. Mireles James, *Parameterization of slow-stable manifolds and their invariant vector bundles: theory and numerical implementation*, Discrete Contin. Dyn. Syst. **36** (2016), no. 9, 4637–4664, DOI 10.3934/dcds.2016002. MR3541499

[59] H. Koçak, K. Palmer, and B. Coomes, *Shadowing in ordinary differential equations*, Rend. Semin. Mat. Univ. Politec. Torino **65** (2007), no. 1, 89–113. MR2339601

[60] Oscar E. Lanford III, *A computer-assisted proof of the Feigenbaum conjectures*, Bull. Amer. Math. Soc. (N.S.) **6** (1982), no. 3, 427–434, DOI 10.1090/S0273-0979-1982-15008-X. MR648529

[61] Jean-Philippe Lessard, *Recent advances about the uniqueness of the slowly oscillating periodic solutions of Wright's equation*, J. Differential Equations **248** (2010), no. 5, 992–1016, DOI 10.1016/j.jde.2009.11.008. MR2592879

[62] Jean-Philippe Lessard, Jason D. Mireles James, and Christian Reinhardt, *Computer assisted proof of transverse saddle-to-saddle connecting orbits for first order vector fields*, J. Dynam. Differential Equations **26** (2014), no. 2, 267–313, DOI 10.1007/s10884-014-9367-0. MR3207723

[63] Jean-Philippe Lessard, Maxime Murray, and J. D. Mireles James, *Computer assisted proof of transverse cycle-to-cycle connecting orbits for first order vector fields*, (In preperation) (2017), 1–40.

[64] Jean-Philippe Lessard and Christian Reinhardt, *Rigorous numerics for nonlinear differential equations using Chebyshev series*, SIAM J. Numer. Anal. **52** (2014), no. 1, 1–22, DOI 10.1137/13090883X. MR3148084

[65] Xuemei Li and Rafael de la Llave, *Construction of quasi-periodic solutions of delay differential equations via KAM techniques*, J. Differential Equations **247** (2009), no. 3, 822–865, DOI 10.1016/j.jde.2009.03.009. MR2528494

[66] Rudolf J. Lohner, *Enclosing the solutions of ordinary initial and boundary value problems*, Computerarithmetic, Teubner, Stuttgart, 1987, pp. 255–286. MR904317

[67] Rudolf J. Lohner, *Computation of guaranteed enclosures for the solutions of ordinary initial and boundary value problems*, Computational ordinary differential equations (London, 1989), Inst. Math. Appl. Conf. Ser. New Ser., vol. 39, Oxford Univ. Press, New York, 1992, pp. 425–435. MR1387154

[68] J. D. Mireles James, *Computer assisted error bounds for linear approximation of (un)stable manifolds and rigorous validation of higher dimensional transverse connecting orbits*, Commun. Nonlinear Sci. Numer. Simul. **22** (2015), no. 1-3, 1102–1133, DOI 10.1016/j.cnsns.2014.08.010. MR3282485

[69] J. D. Mireles James and Konstantin Mischaikow, *Rigorous a posteriori computation of (un)stable manifolds and connecting orbits for analytic maps*, SIAM J. Appl. Dyn. Syst. **12** (2013), no. 2, 957–1006, DOI 10.1137/12088224X. MR3068557

[70] J. D. Mireles James, *Polynomial approximation of one parameter families of (un)stable manifolds with rigorous computer assisted error bounds*, Indag. Math. (N.S.) **26** (2015), no. 1, 225–265, DOI 10.1016/j.indag.2014.10.002. MR3281703

[71] Konstantin Mischaikow and Marian Mrozek, *Chaos in the Lorenz equations: a computer-assisted proof*, Bull. Amer. Math. Soc. (N.S.) **32** (1995), no. 1, 66–72, DOI 10.1090/S0273-0979-1995-00558-6. MR1276767

[72] Konstantin Mischaikow and Marian Mrozek, *Chaos in the Lorenz equations: a computer assisted proof. II. Details*, Math. Comp. **67** (1998), no. 223, 1023–1046, DOI 10.1090/S0025-5718-98-00945-4. MR1459392

[73] R. E. Moore, *A test for existence of solutions to nonlinear systems*, SIAM J. Numer. Anal. **14** (1977), no. 4, 611–615, DOI 10.1137/0714040. MR0657002

[74] Ramon E. Moore, *Interval analysis*, Prentice-Hall, Inc., Englewood Cliffs, N.J., 1966. MR0231516

[75] Ramon E. Moore, *Interval tools for computer aided proofs in analysis*, Computer aided proofs in analysis (Cincinnati, OH, 1989), IMA Vol. Math. Appl., vol. 28, Springer, New York, 1991, pp. 211–216, DOI 10.1007/978-1-4613-9092-3_17. MR1101373

[76] Kenneth J. Palmer, *Exponential dichotomies, the shadowing lemma and transversal homoclinic points*, Dynamics reported, Vol. 1, Dynam. Report. Ser. Dynam. Systems Appl., vol. 1, Wiley, Chichester, 1988, pp. 265–306. MR945967

[77] M. Plum, *Computer-assisted existence proofs for two-point boundary value problems* (English, with German summary), Computing **46** (1991), no. 1, 19–34, DOI 10.1007/BF02239009. MR1100582

[78] Michael Plum, *Numerical existence proofs and explicit bounds for solutions of nonlinear elliptic boundary value problems* (English, with English and German summaries), Computing **49** (1992), no. 1, 25–44, DOI 10.1007/BF02238648. MR1182440

[79] Christian Reinhardt and J. D. Mireles James, *Fourier-taylor parameterization of unstable manifolds for parabolic partial differential equations: Formalism, implementation, and rigorous validation*, (Submitted) (2016), 1–54.

[80] Clark Robinson, *Dynamical systems*, 2nd ed., Studies in Advanced Mathematics, CRC Press, Boca Raton, FL, 1999. Stability, symbolic dynamics, and chaos. MR1792240

[81] Siegfried M. Rump, *Verification methods: rigorous results using floating-point arithmetic*, Acta Numer. **19** (2010), 287–449, DOI 10.1017/S096249291000005X. MR2652784

[82] Tibor Csendes (ed.), *Developments in reliable computing*, Kluwer Academic Publishers, Dordrecht, 1999. MR1747254

[83] Robert Szczelina and Piotr Zgliczyński, *A homoclinic orbit in a planar singular ODE—a computer assisted proof*, SIAM J. Appl. Dyn. Syst. **12** (2013), no. 3, 1541–1565, DOI 10.1137/120901271. MR3097025

[84] Warwick Tucker, *The Lorenz attractor exists* (English, with English and French summaries), C. R. Acad. Sci. Paris Sér. I Math. **328** (1999), no. 12, 1197–1202, DOI 10.1016/S0764-4442(99)80439-X. MR1701385

[85] Warwick Tucker, *A rigorous ODE solver and Smale's 14th problem*, Found. Comput. Math. **2** (2002), no. 1, 53–117. MR1870856

[86] ———, *Validated numerics*, Princeton University Press, Princeton, NJ, 2011, A short introduction to rigorous computations. MR2807595 (2012g:65004)

[87] J. B. van den Berg and J. D. Mireles James, *Parameterization of slow-stable manifolds and their invariant vector bundles: theory and numerical implementation*, Discrete Contin. Dyn. Syst. **36** (2016), no. 9, 4637–4664, DOI 10.3934/dcds.2016002. MR3541499

[88] Jan Bouwe van den Berg, Jason D. Mireles James, and Christian Reinhardt, *Computing (un)stable manifolds with validated error bounds: non-resonant and resonant spectra*, J. Nonlinear Sci. **26** (2016), no. 4, 1055–1095, DOI 10.1007/s00332-016-9298-5. MR3518609

[89] J. B. Van den Berg and Ray Sheombarsing, *Rigorous numerics for odes using chebyshev series and domain decomposition*, (Submitted) (2016), 1–32.

[90] Jan Bouwe van den Berg, Andréa Deschênes, Jean-Philippe Lessard, and Jason D. Mireles James, *Stationary coexistence of hexagons and rolls via rigorous computations*, SIAM J. Appl. Dyn. Syst. **14** (2015), no. 2, 942–979, DOI 10.1137/140984506. MR3353132

[91] Jan Bouwe van den Berg, Jean-Philippe Lessard, and Konstantin Mischaikow, *Global smooth solution curves using rigorous branch following*, Math. Comp. **79** (2010), no. 271, 1565–1584, DOI 10.1090/S0025-5718-10-02325-2. MR2630003

[92] Jan Bouwe van den Berg, Jason D. Mireles-James, Jean-Philippe Lessard, and Konstantin Mischaikow, *Rigorous numerics for symmetric connecting orbits: even homoclinics of the Gray-Scott equation*, SIAM J. Math. Anal. **43** (2011), no. 4, 1557–1594, DOI 10.1137/100812008. MR2821596

[93] Daniel Wilczak, *Chaos in the Kuramoto-Sivashinsky equations—a computer-assisted proof*, J. Differential Equations **194** (2003), no. 2, 433–459, DOI 10.1016/S0022-0396(03)00104-9. MR2006220

[94] Daniel Wilczak, *The existence of Shilnikov homoclinic orbits in the Michelson system: a computer assisted proof*, Found. Comput. Math. **6** (2006), no. 4, 495–535, DOI 10.1007/s10208-005-0201-2. MR2271217

[95] Daniel Wilczak, *Symmetric homoclinic solutions to the periodic orbits in the Michelson system*, Topol. Methods Nonlinear Anal. **28** (2006), no. 1, 155–170. MR2262261

[96] Daniel Wilczak and Piotr Zgliczynski, *Heteroclinic connections between periodic orbits in planar restricted circular three-body problem—a computer assisted proof*, Comm. Math. Phys. **234** (2003), no. 1, 37–75, DOI 10.1007/s00220-002-0709-0. MR1961956

[97] ———, *c^n-lohner algorithm*, Scheade Informaticae **20** (2011), 9–46.

[98] Nobito Yamamoto, *A numerical verification method for solutions of boundary value problems with local uniqueness by Banach's fixed-point theorem*, SIAM J. Numer. Anal. **35** (1998), no. 5, 2004–2013, DOI 10.1137/S0036142996304498. MR1639986

[99] Piotr Zgliczynski, *C^1 Lohner algorithm*, Found. Comput. Math. **2** (2002), no. 4, 429–465, DOI 10.1007/s102080010025. MR1930946

[100] Piotr Zgliczyński, *Rigorous numerics for dissipative PDEs III. An effective algorithm for rigorous integration of dissipative PDEs*, Topol. Methods Nonlinear Anal. **36** (2010), no. 2, 197–262. MR2788972

[101] Piotr Zgliczynski, *Attracting fixed points for the Kuramoto-Sivashinsky equation: a computer assisted proof*, SIAM J. Appl. Dyn. Syst. **1** (2002), no. 2, 215–235, DOI 10.1137/S111111110240176X. MR1968368

Department of Mathematical Sciences, Florida Atlantic University, Boca Raton, Florida 33431

Email address: jmirelesjames@fau.edu

Proceedings of Symposia in Applied Mathematics
Volume **74**, 2018
http://dx.doi.org/10.1090/psapm/074/00637

Continuation of solutions and studying delay differential equations via rigorous numerics

Jean-Philippe Lessard

Abstract. In the present work, we demonstrate how rigorous numerics helps studying the dynamics of delay equations. We present a rigorous continuation method for solutions of finite and infinite dimensional parameter dependent problems, which is applied to compute branches of periodic solutions of a delayed Van der Pol equation and of Wright's equation.

1. Introduction, Motivation and Examples

The main purpose of this paper is to demonstrate the use of rigorous numerics to study the dynamics of delay differential equations (DDEs). The main motivating example we consider is Wright's equation, essentially because it is one of the simplest looking delay equation and it is arguably the most studied equation in the broad field of DDEs. Moreover, it has been the subject of active research for more than 60 years and has been studied by many different mathematicians (e.g. see [**1**–**5**]). As will be seen later, the dynamics of this equation naturally leads to studying branches of periodic solutions. This is why a large part of the paper is dedicated to the presentation of a rigorous continuation method for solutions of finite and infinite dimensional parameter dependent problems. This part is independent from delay equations. In this section we focus on Wright's equation to introduce some concepts and ideas. Nevertheless, the method introduced is quite general and applies to a large class of DDEs and other infinite dimensional problems. Note however that the present work is not meant to provide a general introduction to the field of DDEs. The reader who is looking for a general introduction of DDEs will find very useful the book of Hale and Verduyn Lunel [**6**], the book of Diekmann, van Gils, Verduyn Lunel and Walther [**7**], and the recent survey paper of Walther [**8**].

To start the discussion, we begin by presenting a quote from R. Nussbaum taken from [**9**].

> *An intriguing feature of the global study of nonlinear functional differential equations (FDEs) is that progress in understanding even the simplest-looking FDEs has been slow and has involved*

Key words and phrases. Delay equations, continuation, rigorous numerics, periodic orbits, delayed Van der Pol equation, Wright's equation.

The author was supported an NSERC Discovery Grant.

a combination of careful analysis of the equation and heavy machinery from functional analysis and algebraic topology. A partial list of tools which have been employed includes fixed point theory and the fixed point index, global bifurcation theorems, a global Hopf bifurcation theorem, the Fuller index, ideas related to the Conley index, and equivariant degree theory. Nevertheless, even for the so-called Wright's equation,

$$y'(t) = -\alpha y(t-1)[1+y(t)], \qquad \alpha \in \mathbb{R} \tag{1.1}$$

which has been an object of serious study for more than forty-five years, many questions remain open.

Roger Nussbaum, 2002.

This comment is still true nowadays and is perhaps not surprising, as a large class of FDEs naturally give rise to infinite dimensional nonlinear dynamical systems. To understand this, let us consider an initial value problem associated to Wright's equation (1.1). More precisely, at a given time $t_0 \geq 0$, what kind of initial data guarantees the existence of a unique solution $y(t)$ for all $t > t_0$? Since $y'(t_0)$ is determined by $y(t_0)$ and $y(t_0-1)$, knowing the value of $y(t)$ for all $t > t_0$ requires knowing the value of $y(t)$ on the time interval $[t_0-1, t_0]$. In other words, the *initial condition* is a function $y_0 : [t_0-1, t_0] \to \mathbb{R}$. Shifting time to 0, the initial data is given by $y_0 : [-1, 0] \to \mathbb{R}$. Denote the space of continuous real-valued functions defined on $[-1, 0]$ by

$$C \stackrel{\text{def}}{=} C([-1,0],\mathbb{R}) = \{v : [-1,0] \to \mathbb{R} : v \text{ is continuous}\}.$$

Given $y_0 \in C$, the initial value problem

$$\begin{aligned} y'(t) &= -\alpha y(t-1)[1+y(t)], \quad t \geq 0 \\ y(t) &= y_0(t), \quad \forall\, t \in [-1,0] \end{aligned}$$

has a unique solution (e.g. see Theorem 2.3 of Chapter 2 in [**6**]), and this naturally leads to an infinite dimensional nonlinear dynamical system. Therefore a *state space* for the solutions of (1.1) is the infinite dimensional function space C. This is the reason why Wright's equation falls into the class of functional differential equations. In Figure 1, find a cartoon phase portrait of Wright's equation visualized in the function space C. Denote by $y_t \in C$ the solution at time t. As time evolves, the solution y_t of the initial value problem gain more and more regularity, somehow in a similar way that solutions of parabolic partial differential equations (PDEs) gain regularity. However, while the regularizing effect in parabolic PDEs is instantaneous in time (think for instance of the heat equation), the regularizing process in delay equations is much slower. In fact, this is a *discrete* regularizing process. As time evolves, the solution $y(t,\varphi)$ of the initial value problem with initial data $\varphi \in C$ gains more and more regularity: assuming that the solution $y(\cdot,\varphi) \in C([-1,1],\mathbb{R})$, then for $t \in (0,1]$, $y'(t) = -\alpha y(t-1)[1+y(t)]$, and so $y(\cdot,\varphi) \in C^1((0,1],\mathbb{R})$. Similarly, $y(\cdot,\varphi) \in C^2((1,2],\mathbb{R})$, and more generally $y(\cdot,\varphi) \in C^k((k-1,k],\mathbb{R})$. This is why we call this a "discrete" regularizing process. At infinity, the solution of the initial value problem is C^∞. As a consequence, this means that bounded solutions of Wright's equations are extremely regular. In fact more is true, and periodic solutions of analytic delay equations are analytic as is shown in [**10**]. This a priori knowledge about the regularity of the bounded (periodic) solutions is a

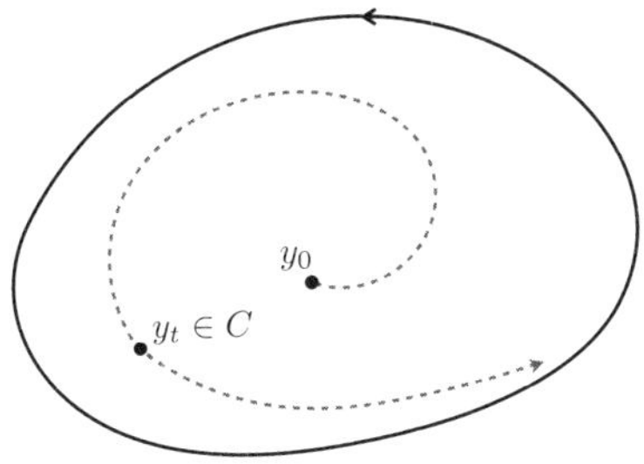

FIGURE 1. A cartoon phase portrait of Wright's equation in the function space $C = C([-1,0],\mathbb{R})$. A point $y_t \in C$ in the phase portrait is a function.

crucial ingredient in the development of the rigorous computational continuation method.

The infinite dimensional nature of the problem comes directly from the presence of the delay in the equation. Suppose for the moment that the delay is absent from the equation, that is consider the scalar ordinary differential equation (ODE)

$$y'(t) = -\alpha y(t)[1 + y(t)]. \tag{1.2}$$

Then, the phase portrait of (1.2) is simple and is portrayed in Figure 2. In particular, we get that the equilibrium solution 0 is asymptotically stable for all parameter values $\alpha > 0$.

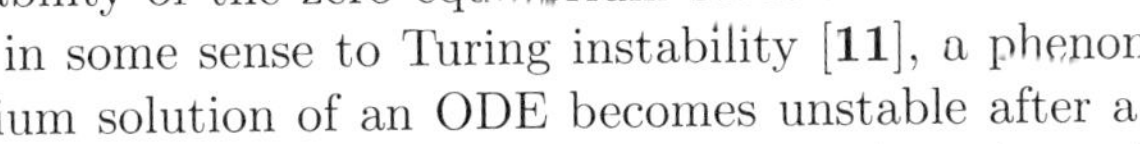

FIGURE 2. The phase portrait of (1.2) for any $\alpha > 0$.

Adding a delay severely complicates the behaviour of the solutions of the equation. In fact, we see below that the effect of the delay in Wright's equation leads to a loss of stability of the zero equilibrium solution for all $\alpha > \pi/2$. This property is similar in some sense to Turing instability [**11**], a phenomenon in which a stable equilibrium solution of an ODE becomes unstable after a diffusion term is added to the ODE. In other words, the steady state loses its stability after the finite dimensional ODE is transformed into an infinite dimensional reaction diffusion PDE.

Let us discuss the history of Wright's equation, following closely the presentation of [**12**].

At the beginning of the 1950s, the equation

$$y'(t) = -(\log 2)y(t-1)[1 + y(t)]$$

was brought to the attention of the number theorist Wright (a former Ph.D. student of Hardy at Oxford) because it arose in the application of probability methods to the theory of distribution of prime numbers. In 1955, Wright considered the more general equation (1.1) and studied the existence of bounded non trivial solutions for different values of $\alpha > 0$ [**13**]. In 1962, following the pioneer work of Wright, Jones demonstrated in [**14**] that non trivial periodic solutions of (1.1) exist for $\alpha > \frac{\pi}{2}$, and using numerical simulations, he remarked in [**15**] that a given periodic solution seemed to be globally attractive, that is seemed to attract all initial conditions. In Figure 3 and Figure 4, we reproduced some of the numerical simulations of Jones using the integrator for delay equations `dde23` in MATLAB. The periodic form he referred to is in fact a slowly oscillating periodic solution.

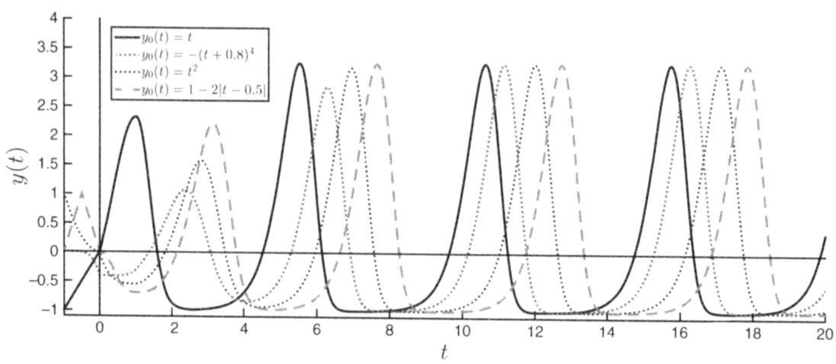

FIGURE 3. Numerical integration of Wright's equation (1.1) with $\alpha = 2.4$ with different initial conditions y_0 defined on the interval $[-1, 0]$.

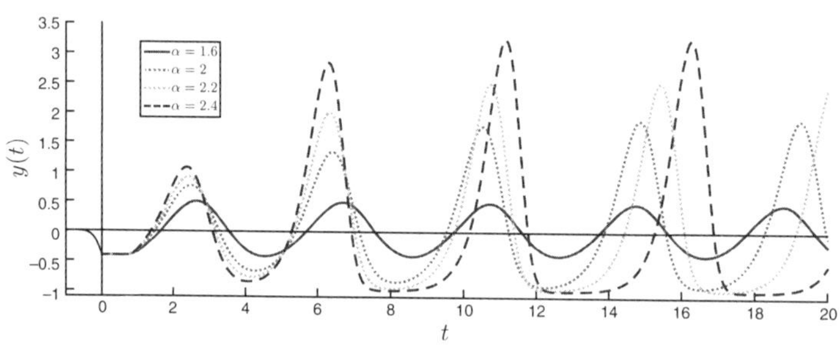

FIGURE 4. Numerical integration of Wright's equation (1.1) with the initial condition $y_0(t) = -(t + 0.8)^4$ for different parameter values of α.

DEFINITION 1.1. *A slowly oscillating periodic solution (SOPS) of (1.1) is a periodic solution $y(t)$ with the following property: there exist $q > 1$ and $p > q + 1$ such that, up to a time translation, $y(t) > 0$ on $(0, q)$, $y(t) < 0$ on (q, p), and $y(t + p) = y(t)$ for all t so that p is the minimal period of $y(t)$.*

A geometric interpretation of a SOPS is found in Figure 5.

After Jones observation in [**15**], the question of the uniqueness of SOPS in (1.1) became popular and is still under investigation after more than 50 years. The next conjecture is sometimes called *Jones Conjecture.*

CONJECTURE 1.1 (**Jones, 1962**). For every $\alpha > \frac{\pi}{2}$, (1.1) has a unique SOPS.

A result of Walther in [**16**] shows that if Jones Conjecture is true, then the unique SOPS attracts a dense and open subset of the phase space. A result from

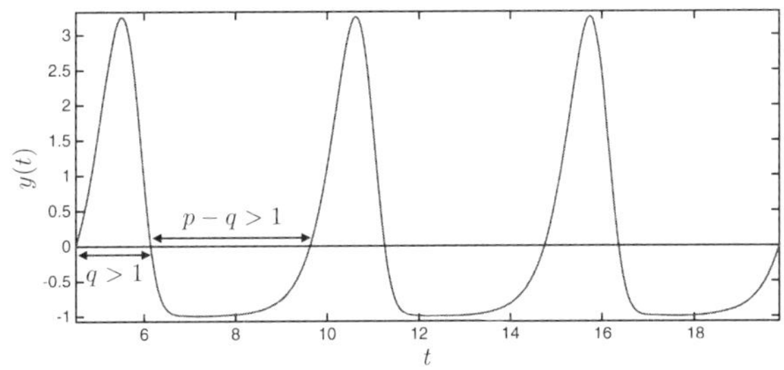

FIGURE 5. A slowly oscillating periodic solution.

Chow and Mallet-Paret from [**17**] shows that there is a supercritical Hopf bifurcation of SOPS from the trivial solution at $\alpha = \pi/2$. This branch of SOPS which bifurcates (forward in α) from 0 is denoted by $\mathcal{F}_0$. We refer to Figure 6 for a geometric interpretation of bifurcation.

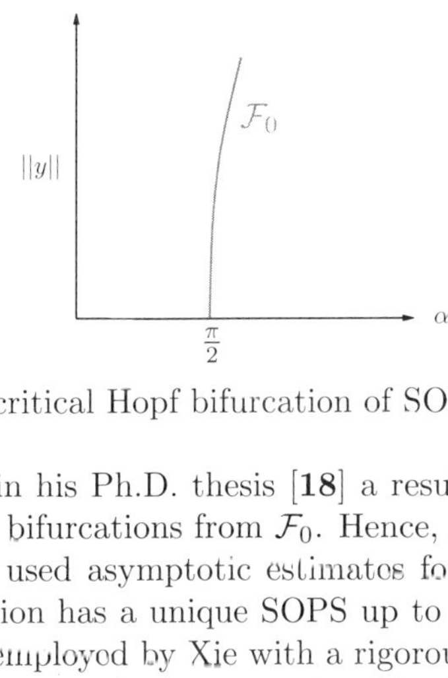

FIGURE 6. A supercritical Hopf bifurcation of SOPS from 0 at $\alpha = \pi/2$.

Regala then proved in his Ph.D. thesis [**18**] a result which implies that there cannot be any secondary bifurcations from $\mathcal{F}_0$. Hence, $\mathcal{F}_0$ is a regular curve in the (α, y) space. Later, Xie used asymptotic estimates for large α to prove that for $\alpha > 5.67$, Wright's equation has a unique SOPS up to a time translation [**19, 20**]. Combining the strategy employed by Xie with a rigorous numerical integrator, the recent work of Jaquette et al. [**21**] proves that Wright's equation has a unique SOPS for all parameter value $\alpha \in [1.9, 6.0]$. In [**12**], it was demonstrated, using the techniques that we introduce in the present paper, that the branch $\mathcal{F}_0$ does not have a fold over the parameter range $\left(\pi/2 + 7.3165 \times 10^{-4}, 2.3\right]$. The recent work [**22**] shows that the branch $\mathcal{F}_0$ does not have any fold over the parameter range $\left(\pi/2, \pi/2 + 6.83 \times 10^{-3}\right]$. Considering the work that has been done in the last 50 years, Jones Conjecture is reformulated as follows.

CONJECTURE 1.2 (**Jones Conjecture reformulated**). There are no connected components (isolas) of SOPS disjoint from $\mathcal{F}_0$ over the parameter range $(\frac{\pi}{2}, 1.9]$.

We refer to Figure 7 for a cartoon picture of a scenario which would violate Jones Conjecture.

REMARK 1.2. Another important long standing open problem, which was recently settled combining the results of [**22**] and [**23**] using the tools of rigorous

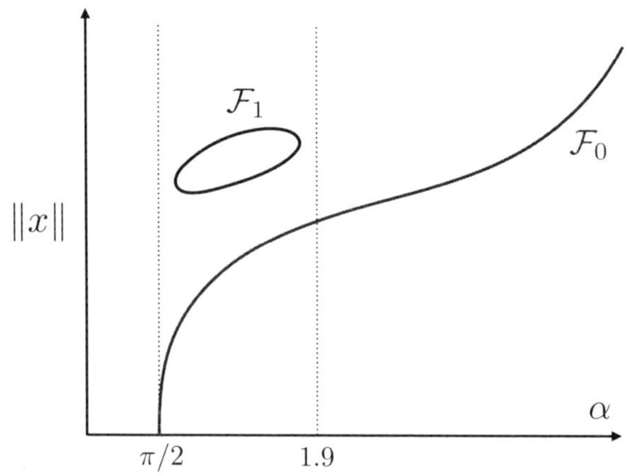

FIGURE 7. A scenario which would violate Jones Conjecture: the existence of an isola $\mathcal{F}_1$ of SOPS in the parameter range $\alpha \in (\frac{\pi}{2}, 1.9]$.

computing, is Wright's conjecture, which states that for all $\alpha \in (0, \pi/2]$ the global attractor of Wright's equation is given by the origin.

The study of Conjecture 1.2 naturally lead to study branches of periodic solutions of DDEs. This is the main topic of these notes. More precisely, we introduce a general continuation method to compute global branches of periodic solutions of DDEs using Fourier series and the ideas from rigorous computing (e.g. see [**24**]). Note that the study of periodic solutions in DDEs is rich [**25**–**32**]. Rather than focussing only on continuation of periodic solutions in DDEs, we present in Section 2 a more general approach to prove existence of branches of solutions for operator equations $F(x, \lambda) = 0$ posed on Banach spaces. In Section 2.4, we apply the general method to the context of periodic solutions of DDEs.

2. Rigorous Continuation of Solutions

Throughout this section, let $(X, \|\cdot\|_X)$ and $(Y, \|\cdot\|_Y)$ denote Banach spaces. The vectors spaces X and Y are general and are either finite or infinite dimensional.

Let $F : X \times \mathbb{R} \to Y$ a C^1 mapping (see Definition 2.2), and consider the general problem of looking for solutions of

$$F(x, \lambda) = 0, \tag{2.1}$$

where $\lambda \in \mathbb{R}$ is a parameter. The unknown variable x could represent various types of dynamical objects, e.g. a steady state of a PDE, a periodic solution of a DDE, a connecting orbit of an ODE, a minimizer of an action functional, etc. It is important to realize that the *solution set*

$$\mathcal{S} \stackrel{\text{def}}{=} \{(x, \lambda) \in X \times \mathbb{R} \mid F(x, \lambda) = 0\} \subset X \times \mathbb{R}$$

may contain different types of bifurcations and may be complicated (e.g. see Figure 8).

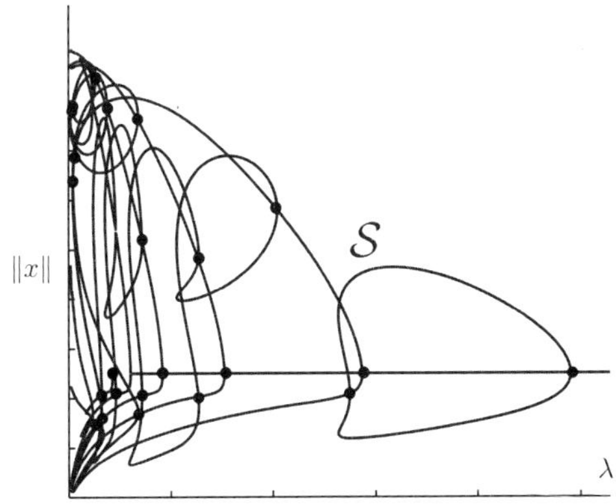

FIGURE 8. Global branches of steady states of a system of reaction-diffusion PDEs introduced in [**33**] and studied with rigorous numerics in [**34**].

There exists a vast literature on numerical continuation methods to compute solutions of (2.1). Methods to compute periodic orbits [**35, 36**], connecting orbits [**37–40**] and more generally coherent structures [**41**] are by now standard, and software packages like AUTO [**42**] and MATCONT [**43**] are accessible and well documented. We refer to [**44, 45**] for more general references on continuation methods. Next we briefly introduce two main algorithms to compute solutions of (2.1), namely the parameter continuation and the pseudo-arclength continuation. These methods fall into the class of predictor-corrector algorithms.

2.1. Predictor-Corrector Algorithms. In this section, we assume that the Banach spaces are finite dimensional and given by $X = Y = \mathbb{R}^n$ ($X = Y = \mathbb{C}^n$ is also an option), we consider a map $F : \mathbb{R}^n \times \mathbb{R} \to \mathbb{R}^n$ and we study numerically the problem $F(x, \lambda) = 0$. At this point, considering X and Y finite dimensional is natural, as any computer algorithm needs to be applied to a problem with a finite resolution. The mapping F could be a finite-dimensional projection of an infinite dimensional operator, e.g. a Galerkin approximation or a discretization scheme. The first predictor-corrector algorithm we introduce is parameter continuation.

2.1.1. *Parameter Continuation.* This method involves a predictor and a corrector step: given, within a prescribed tolerance, a solution x_0 at parameter value λ_0, the predictor step produces an approximate solution $\hat{x}_0$ at nearby parameter value $\lambda_1 = \lambda_0 + \Delta_\lambda$ (for some $\Delta_\lambda \neq 0$), and the corrector step, takes $\hat{x}_1$ as its input and produces with Newton's method, once again within the prescribed tolerance, a solution x_1 at λ_1.

The predictor is obtained by assuming that at the solution (x_0, λ_0), the jacobian matrix $D_xF(x_0, \lambda_0)$ is invertible, which in turns implies by the implicit function theorem that the solution curve is locally parametrized by λ. In this case, close to (x_0, λ_0), we have

$$\begin{aligned}\frac{\partial}{\partial\lambda}(F(x,\lambda)=0) &\iff D_xF(x,\lambda)\frac{dx}{d\lambda}(\lambda) + \frac{\partial F}{\partial\lambda}(x,\lambda) = 0\\ &\iff \frac{dx}{d\lambda}(\lambda) = -D_xF(x,\lambda)^{-1}\frac{\partial F}{\partial\lambda}(x,\lambda).\end{aligned}$$

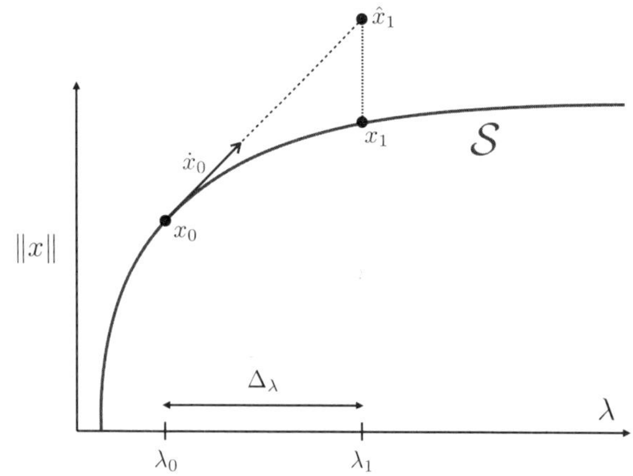

FIGURE 9. Parameter continuation.

At (x_0, λ_0), a tangent vector to the curve is $\dot{x}_0 \stackrel{\text{def}}{=} \frac{dx}{d\lambda}(\lambda_0)$ and is obtained with the formula

$$\dot{x}_0 = -D_x F(x_0, \lambda_0)^{-1} \frac{\partial F}{\partial \lambda}(x_0, \lambda_0).$$

Once the tangent vector $\dot{x}_0$ is obtained, the predictor is defined by

$$\hat{x}_1 = x_0 + \Delta_\lambda \dot{x}_0.$$

Then, fixing $\lambda_1 = \lambda_0 + \Delta_\lambda$, we *correct* the predictor $\hat{x}_1$ using Newton's method

$$x_1^{(0)} = \hat{x}_1, \qquad x_1^{(n+1)} = x_1^{(n)} - \left(D_x F(x_1^{(n)}, \lambda_1)\right)^{-1} F(x_1^{(n)}, \lambda_1), \quad n \geq 0,$$

to obtain the solution x_1 at λ_1 within the prescribed tolerance. We repeat this procedure iteratively to produce numerically a branch of solutions. We refer to Figure 9 to visualize one step of the parameter continuation algorithm.

Sometimes it may be more natural to parametrize the branches of solutions of (2.1) by arclength or *pseudo-arclength*, especially when the solution curve is not locally parametrized by λ, for instance at points where the jacobian matrix is singular. This is for instance what is happening when a saddle-node bifurcations (folds) occur. An example of such phenomenon is given by $F(x, \lambda) = x^2 - \lambda = 0$ at the point $(x_0, \lambda_0) = (0, 0)$. Pseudo-arclength continuation, as opposed to parameter continuation, allows continuing past folds.

2.1.2. *Pseudo-Arclength Continuation.* In the pseudo-arclength continuation algorithm (e.g. see Keller [**46**]), the parameter value λ is no longer fixed and instead is left as a variable. The unknown variable is now $X = (x, \lambda)$. Consider the problem $F(X) = 0$ with the map $F : \mathbb{R}^{n+1} \to \mathbb{R}^n$. As before, the process begins with a solution X_0 given within a prescribed tolerance. To produce a predictor, we compute first a unit tangent vector to the curve at X_0, that we denote $\dot{X}_0$, which is computed using the formula

$$D_X F(X_0)\dot{X}_0 = \left[D_x F(\bar{x}_0, \bar{\lambda}_0) \;\; \frac{\partial F}{\partial \lambda}(x_0, \lambda_0) \right] \dot{X}_0 = 0 \in \mathbb{R}^n.$$

We now fix a *pseudo-arclength parameter* $\Delta_s > 0$, and set the predictor to be

$$\hat{X}_1 \stackrel{\text{def}}{=} \bar{X}_0 + \Delta_s \dot{X}_0 \in \mathbb{R}^{n+1}.$$

Once the predictor is fixed, we *correct* toward the set $\mathcal{S}$ on the hyperplane perpendicular to the tangent vector $\dot{X}_0$ which contains the predictor $\hat{X}_1$. The equation of this plan is given by

$$E(X) \stackrel{\text{def}}{=} (X - \hat{X}_1) \cdot \dot{X}_0 = 0.$$

Then, we apply Newton's method to the new function

$$X \mapsto \begin{pmatrix} E(X) \\ F(X) \end{pmatrix} \tag{2.2}$$

with the initial condition $\hat{X}_1$ to obtain a new solution X_1 given again within a prescribed tolerance. See Figure 10 for a geometric interpretation of one step of the pseudo-arclength continuation algorithm. At each step of the algorithm, the function defined in (2.2) changes since the plane $E(X) = 0$ changes. With this method, it is possible to continue past folds. Repeating this procedure iteratively produces a branch of solutions.

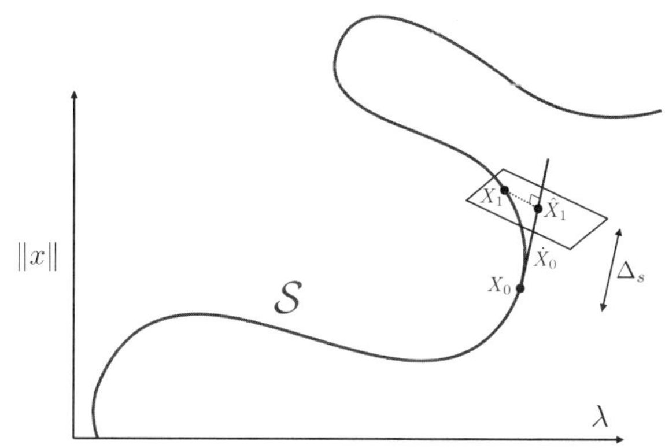

FIGURE 10. Pseudo-arclength continuation.

REMARK 2.1. The above mentioned algorithms do not cover the case of bifurcations of solutions e.g. symmetry-breaking pitchfork bifurcations, branch points, Hopf bifurcations, etc. We refer for instance to the work [**44**] for numerical continuation methods handling bifurcations.

Now that we have briefly introduced two classical algorithms to numerically compute branches of solutions of the general problem (2.1), we present an approach that combines the strength of the numerical continuation methods with the ideas of rigorous computing (e.g. see [**24**]). Before introducing the rigorous continuation method in Section 2.3, we need some background from calculus in general Banach spaces.

2.2. Background of Calculus in Banach Spaces. The space of bounded linear operators is defined by

$$B(X,Y) \stackrel{\text{def}}{=} \left\{E\colon X \to Y \mid E \text{ is linear}, \ \|E\|_{B(X,Y)} < \infty\right\},$$

where $\|\cdot\|_{B(X,Y)}$ denotes the operator norm

$$\|E\|_{B(X,Y)} \stackrel{\text{def}}{=} \sup_{\|x\|_X = 1} \|Ex\|_Y.$$

Note that $\big(B(X,Y), \|\cdot\|_{B(X,Y)}\big)$ is a Banach space.

DEFINITION 2.2. *A function* $F\colon X \to Y$ *is* Fréchet differentiable *at* $x_0 \in X$ *if there exists a bounded linear operator* $E\colon X \to Y$ *satisfying*

$$\lim_{\|h\|_X \to 0} \frac{\|F(x_0+h) - F(x_0) - Eh\|_Y}{\|h\|_X} = 0.$$

The linear operator E *is called the* derivative *of* F *at* x_0 *and denoted by* $E = D_xF(x_0)$. *We say that* $F\colon X \to Y$ *is a* C^1 mapping *if for every* $x \in X$, F *is Fréchet differentiable at* x.

Given a point $x_0 \in X$ and a radius $r > 0$, denote by $B_r(x_0) \subset X$ the closed ball of radius r centered at x_0, that is

$$B_r(x_0) \stackrel{\text{def}}{=} \{x \in X \mid \|x - x_0\|_X \le r\}.$$

The proof of the following version of the Mean Value Theorem is found in [**47**].

THEOREM 2.3 (**Mean Value Theorem**). *Let* $x_0 \in X$ *and suppose that* $F\colon B_r(x_0) \subset X \to Y$ *is a* C^1 *mapping. Let*

$$K \stackrel{\text{def}}{=} \sup_{x \in B_r(x_0)} \|D_xF(x)\|_{B(X,Y)}.$$

Then for any $x, y \in B_r(x_0)$ *we have that*

$$\|F(x) - F(y)\|_Y \le K\|x - y\|_X.$$

While the following concept could be introduced more generally in the context of metric spaces, we present it in the context of Banach spaces to best suit our needs.

DEFINITION 2.4. *Suppose that* Λ *is a set of parameters. A function* $T\colon X \times \Lambda \to X$ *is a* uniform contraction *if there exists* $\kappa \in [0,1)$ *such that, for all* $x, y \in X$ *and* $\lambda \in \Lambda$,

$$\|T(x,\lambda) - T(y,\lambda)\|_X \le \kappa\|x - y\|_X.$$

By the Contraction Mapping Theorem if $T\colon X \times \Lambda \to X$ is a uniform contraction, then for every $\lambda \in \Lambda$ there exists a unique $\tilde{x}_\lambda$ such that $T(\tilde{x}_\lambda, \lambda) = \tilde{x}_\lambda$. Thus the function $g\colon \Lambda \to X$ given by $g(\lambda) \stackrel{\text{def}}{=} \tilde{x}_\lambda$ is well defined. As the following theorem indicates this function inherits the same amount of differentiability than T. The proof is found in [**47**].

THEOREM 2.5 (**Uniform Contraction Theorem**). *Assume that the set of parameters* Λ *is a Banach space, and consider open sets* $U \subset X$ *and* $V \subset \Lambda$. *Assume that* $T\colon \overline{U} \times V \to \overline{U}$ *is a uniform contraction with contraction constant* κ. *Define* $g\colon V \to \overline{U}$ *by* $T(g(\lambda),\lambda) = g(\lambda)$. *If* $T \in C^k(\overline{U} \times V, X)$, *then* $g \in C^k(V, X)$ *for any* $k \in \{1, 2, \ldots, \infty\}$.

2.3. The Rigorous Continuation Method. Now that we have introduced some basic notions from calculus in Banach spaces, we are ready to present the general rigorous continuation method. The idea of the proposed approach is to prove the existence of true solution segments of $F(x,\lambda) = 0$ close to piecewise-linear segments of approximations by applying the Uniform Contraction Theorem (Theorem 2.5) over intervals of parameters. This approach has the advantage of being quite general and is readily generalized to problems depending of several parameters (e.g. see Remark 2.9). However, the rigorous error bounds quickly deteriorate as the width of the interval of parameters (on which the uniform contraction theorem is applied) grows. This is due to the fact that piecewise-linear approximations are coarse approximations of the solution branches of nonlinear problems. Expanding the solutions using high order Taylor approximations in the parameter could for instance increase significantly the error bounds (e.g. see [**48, 49**]), at the cost of complicating the analysis. This being said, let us mention the existence of a growing literature on rigorous numerical methods to compute branches of parameterized families of solutions [**34, 50–53**].

Assume that numerical approximations of (2.1) have been obtained at two different parameter values λ_0 and λ_1, namely there exists $(\bar{x}_0, \lambda_0)$ and $(\bar{x}_1, \lambda_1)$ such that $F(\bar{x}_0, \lambda_0) \approx 0$ and $F(\bar{x}_1, \lambda_1) \approx 0$. In other words, $(\bar{x}_0, \lambda_0)$ and $(\bar{x}_1, \lambda_1)$ are approximately in the solution set $\mathcal{S}$ (e.g. see Figure 11). The approximations are computed first by considering a finite dimensional projection of F and then by using one of the two predictor-correctors algorithms presented in Section 2.1. We refer to Section 2.5.3 for an example in the context of periodic solutions of DDEs. Define the set of *predictors* between the approximations $(\bar{x}_0, \lambda_0)$ and $(\bar{x}_1, \lambda_1)$ by

$$\{(\bar{x}_s, \lambda_s) \mid \bar{x}_s = (1-s)\bar{x}_0 + s\bar{x}_1 \quad \text{and} \quad \lambda_s = (1-s)\lambda_0 + s\lambda_1, \quad s \in [0,1]\}. \tag{2.3}$$

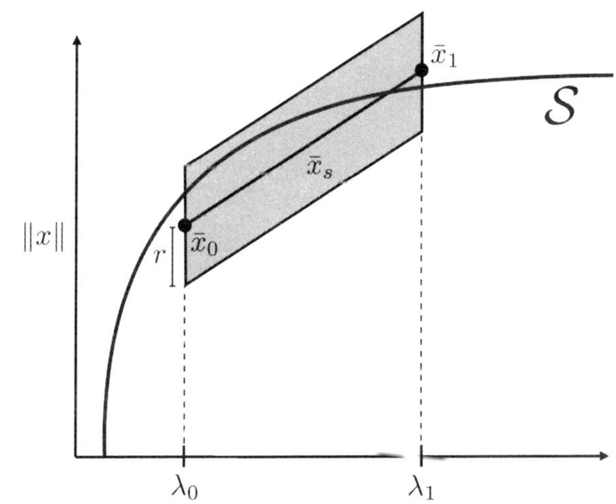

FIGURE 11. The set of predictors $\{(\bar{x}_s, \lambda_s) \mid s \in [0,1]\}$, approximating a segment of the solution set $\mathcal{S}$. The radii polynomial approach, when successful, provides a "tube" of with $r > 0$ (the shaded region) in $X \times \mathbb{R}$, where the true segment of solution curve is guaranteed to exist.

Consider bounded linear operators $A^\dagger \in B(X,Y)$ and $A \in B(Y,X)$, where $A^\dagger$ is an approximation of $D_xF(\bar{x}_0, \lambda_0)$ and A is an approximate inverse of $D_xF(\bar{x}_0, \lambda_0)$. Assume that A is injective and that

$$AF\colon X \times \mathbb{R} \to X. \tag{2.4}$$

The following theorem, often called the radii polynomial approach, is a parameter dependent Newton-Kantorovich theorem (e.g. see [**54**]) with a smoothing approximate inverse.

THEOREM 2.6 (**Radii Polynomial Approach**). *Assume that* $F \in C^k(X \times \mathbb{R}, Y)$ *with* $k \in \{1, 2, \dots, \infty\}$, *and let* $Y_0, Z_0, Z_1, Z_2 \geq 0$ *satisfying*

$$\|AF(\bar{x}_s, \lambda_s)\|_X \leq Y_0, \quad \forall\, s \in [0,1] \tag{2.5}$$

$$\|I - AA^\dagger\|_{B(X,X)} \leq Z_0 \tag{2.6}$$

$$\|A[D_x F(\bar{x}_0, \lambda_0) - A^\dagger]\|_{B(X,X)} \leq Z_1 \tag{2.7}$$

(2.8)

$$\|A[D_x F(\bar{x}_s + b, \lambda_s) - D_x F(\bar{x}_0, \lambda_0)]\|_{B(X,X)} \leq Z_2(r), \quad \forall\, b \in B_r(0) \text{ and } \forall\, s \in [0,1].$$

Define the radii polynomial

$$p(r) \stackrel{\text{def}}{=} Z_2(r) r + (Z_1 + Z_0 - 1) r + Y_0. \tag{2.9}$$

If there exists $r_0 > 0$ *such that*

$$p(r_0) < 0,$$

then there exists a C^k *function*

$$\tilde{x} : [0,1] \to \bigcup_{s \in [0,1]} B_{r_0}(\bar{x}_s)$$

such that

$$F(\tilde{x}(s), \lambda_s) = 0, \quad \forall\, s \in [0,1].$$

Furthermore, these are the only solutions in the tube $\bigcup_{s\in[0,1]} B_{r_0}(\bar{x}_s)$.

PROOF. Recalling (2.4), define the operator $T\colon X \times [0,1] \to X$ by

$$T(x,s) = x - AF(x, \lambda_s).$$

We begin by showing that for each $s \in [0,1]$, the operator $T(\cdot, s)$ is a contraction mapping from $B_{r_0}(\bar{x}_s)$ into itself. Now, given $y \in B_{r_0}(\bar{x}_s)$ and applying the bounds (2.5), (2.6), (2.7), and (2.8), we obtain

$$\begin{aligned}
\|D_x T(y,s)\|_{B(X,X)} &= \|I - AD_x F(y, \lambda_s)\|_{B(X,X)} \\
&\leq \|I - AA^\dagger\|_{B(X,X)} + \|A[D_x F(\bar{x}_0, \lambda_0) - A^\dagger]\|_{B(X,X)} \\
&\quad + \|A[D_x F(y, \lambda_s) - D_x F(\bar{x}_0, \lambda_0)]\|_{B(X,X)} \\
&\leq Z_0 + Z_1 + Z_2(r_0).
\end{aligned} \tag{2.10}$$

We now show that for each $s \in [0,1]$ the operator $T(\cdot, s)$ maps $B_{r_0}(\bar{x}_s)$ into itself. Let $y \in B_{r_0}(\bar{x}_s)$ and apply the Mean Value Theorem (Theorem 2.3) to obtain

$$\begin{aligned}
\|T(y,s) - \bar{x}_s\|_X &\leq \|T(y,s) - T(\bar{x}_s, s)\|_X + \|T(\bar{x}_s, s) - \bar{x}_s\|_X \\
&\leq \sup_{b \in B_{r_0}(\bar{x}_s)} \|D_x T(b,s)\|_{B(X,X)} \|y - \bar{x}_s\|_X + \|AF(\bar{x}_s, \lambda_s)\|_X \\
&\leq (Z_0 + Z_1 + Z_2(r_0)) r_0 + Y_0
\end{aligned}$$

where the last inequality follows from (2.10). Recalling (2.9) and using the assumption that $p(r_0) < 0$ implies that $\|T(y,s) - \bar{x}_s\|_X < r_0$ for all $s \in [0,1]$, the desired result.

Letting $a, b \in B_{r_0}(\bar{x}_s)$, apply the Mean Value Theorem and (2.10) to obtain

$$\begin{aligned}
\|T(a,s) - T(b,s)\|_X &\leq \sup_{b \in B_{r_0}(\bar{x}_s)} \|D_x T(b,s)\|_{B(X,X)} \|a - b\|_X \\
&\leq (Z_0 + Z_1 + Z_2 r_0) \|a - b\|_X.
\end{aligned} \tag{2.11}$$

Again, from the assumption that $p(r_0) < 0$, it follows from $Y_0 \geq 0$ that

$$\kappa \stackrel{\text{def}}{=} Z_0 + Z_1 + Z_2(r_0) < 1 - \frac{Y_0}{r_0} \leq 1. \tag{2.12}$$

Define the operator

$$\begin{aligned} \widetilde{T} : B_{r_0}(0) \times [0,1] &\to B_{r_0}(0) \\ (y,s) &\mapsto \widetilde{T}(y,s) \stackrel{\text{def}}{=} T(y + \bar{x}_s, s) - \bar{x}_s. \end{aligned}$$

Consider now $x, y \in B_{r_0}(0)$ and $s \in [0,1]$. Then, since $x + \bar{x}_s, y + \bar{x}_s \in B_{r_0}(\bar{x}_s)$, we use (2.11) and (2.12) to get

$$\begin{aligned} \|\widetilde{T}(x,s) - \widetilde{T}(y,s)\|_X &= \|T(x + \bar{x}_s, s) - T(y + \bar{x}_s, s)\|_X \\ &\leq \kappa \|x - y\|_X. \end{aligned}$$

Since $\kappa < 1$, we conclude that $\widetilde{T} : B_{r_0}(0) \times [0,1] \to B_{r_0}(0)$ is a uniform contraction. By the Uniform Contraction Theorem (Theorem 2.5), there exists $g\colon [0,1] \to B_{r_0}(0)$ by

$$\widetilde{T}(g(s), s) = g(s).$$

Since $F \in C^k(X \times \mathbb{R}, Y)$, then $\widetilde{T} \in C^k(B_{r_0}(0) \times [0,1], B_{r_0}(0))$, and therefore $g \in C^k([0,1], B_{r_0}(0))$. Let

$$\tilde{x}(s) \stackrel{\text{def}}{=} g(s) + \bar{x}_s$$

so that for all $s \in [0,1]$

$$T(\tilde{x}(s), s) = T(g(s) + \bar{x}_s, s) = \widetilde{T}(g(s), s) + \bar{x}_s = g(s) + \bar{x}_s = \tilde{x}(s).$$

Since $T(x,s) = x - AF(x, \lambda_s)$, we get that

$$T(\tilde{x}(s), s) = \tilde{x}(s) - AF(\tilde{x}(s), \lambda_s) = \tilde{x}(s).$$

By assumption that A is injective,

$$F(\tilde{x}(s), \lambda_s) = 0, \quad \forall\, s \in [0,1].$$

It follows from $g \in C^k([0,1], B_{r_0}(0))$ that

$$\tilde{x} : [0,1] \to \bigcup_{s \in [0,1]} B_{r_0}(\bar{x}_s)$$

is a C^k function. Furthermore, it follows from the contraction mapping theorem that these are the only solutions in the *tube* $\bigcup_{s\in[0,1]} B_{r_0}(\bar{x}_s) \times [\lambda_0, \lambda_1]$. $\square$

Theorem 2.6 provides a recipe to compute a local segment of solution curve and to obtain a uniform rigorous error bound r along the set of predictors connecting two numerical approximations $\bar{x}_0$ and $\bar{x}_1$. See Figure 11 for a representation of the region (shaded) where the true segment of solution curve is guaranteed to exist. Assume now that this argument has been repeated iteratively over the set $\{\bar{x}_0, \ldots, \bar{x}_j\}$ of approximations at the parameter values $\{\lambda_0, \ldots, \lambda_j\}$ respectively. For each $i = 0, \ldots, j-1$, this yields the existence of a unique portion of smooth solution curve $\mathcal{S}_i$ in a small *tube* centered at the segment $\{(1-s)\bar{x}_i + s\bar{x}_{i+1} \mid s \in [0,1]\}$. As the following results demonstrates, the set

$$\mathcal{S} \stackrel{\text{def}}{=} \bigcup_{i=0}^{j-1} \mathcal{S}_i$$

is a global smooth solution curve of $F(x, \lambda) = 0$.

LEMMA 2.7 (**Globalizing the C^k solution branch**). *Assume that the radii polynomial approach was successfully applied (via Theorem 2.6) to show the existence of two C^k segments S_0 and S_1 of solution curves parameterized by the parameter λ over the respective parameter intervals $[\lambda_0, \lambda_1]$ and $[\lambda_1, \lambda_2]$. Assume that the sets of predictors are defined by the three points $\bar{x}_0$, $\bar{x}_1$ and $\bar{x}_2$. Then the new segment of solution curve $S_0 \cup S_1$ is a C^k function of λ.*

PROOF. The continuity of $S_0 \cup S_1$ follows from the fact that at the parameter value $\lambda = \lambda_1$, the solution segment S_0 must connect continuously with the solution segment S_1 by the existence and uniqueness result guaranteed by the Contraction Mapping Theorem. Let $p_0(r)$ the radii polynomial built with the predictors generated by $\bar{x}_0$ and $\bar{x}_1$, and defined by the bounds Y_0, Z_0, Z_1 and Z_2. Let $r_0 > 0$ such that $p_0(r_0) < 0$. By continuity of the radii polynomial p_0, there exists $\delta_0 > 0$ and there exist bounds $\tilde{Y}_0(\delta_0)$ and $\tilde{Z}_2(r, \delta_0)$ such that

$$\|AF(\bar{x}_s, \lambda_s)\|_X \le \tilde{Y}_0(\delta_0), \quad \forall\, s \in [-\delta_0, 1+\delta_0]$$

$$\|A[D_xF(\bar{x}_s + b, \lambda_s) - D_xF(\bar{x}_0, \lambda_0)]\|_{B(X,X)} \le \tilde{Z}_2(r, \delta_0), \quad \forall\, b \in B_r(0),\ \forall\, s \in [-\delta_0, 1+\delta_0],$$

and such that

$$\tilde{p}_0(r_0) \stackrel{\text{def}}{=} \tilde{Z}_2(r_0, \delta_0) r_0 + (Z_1 + Z_0 - 1) r_0 + \tilde{Y}_0(\delta_0) < 0.$$

Then, there exists of a C^k branch of solution curve parameterized by λ over the range $\{(1-s)\lambda_0 + s\lambda_1 \mid s \in [-\delta_0, 1+\delta_0]$, extending smoothly (in fact in a C^k way) the segment S_0 on both sides. Similarly, there exists δ_1 such that the segment S_1 is extended smoothly over the parameter range $\{(1-s)\lambda_1 + s\lambda_2 \mid s \in [-\delta_0, 1+\delta_0]$. This implies that there is a C^k overlap between S_0 and S_1. □

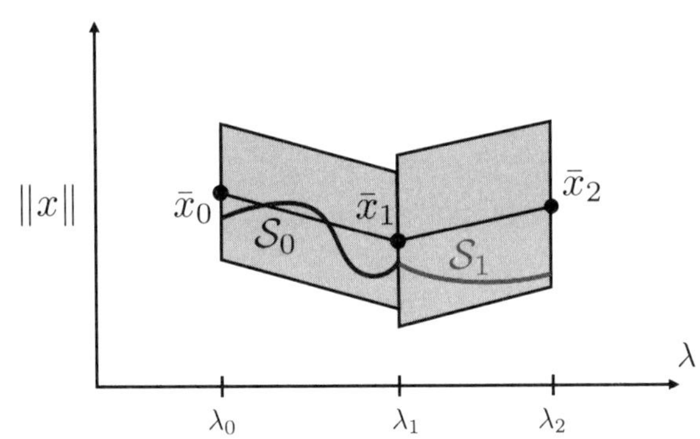

FIGURE 12. Assume that S_0 and S_1 are computed with the radii polynomial approach with predictors defined by three points $\bar{x}_0$, $\bar{x}_1$ and $\bar{x}_2$ with $\bar{x}_i \in \mathbb{C}^{2m}$ for some fixed dimension m. Then the following situation is not possible: a piecewise smooth but not globally smooth piece of solution curve.

Note that arguments using the continuity of the radii polynomials, as in the proof of Lemma 2.7, are not new and have been used previously in the works [**34, 52, 53**].

Repeating iteratively the argument of Lemma 2.7 leads to the existence of a smooth solution curve $\mathcal{S}$ of $F = 0$ near the piecewise linear curve of approximations, as portrayed in Figure 13.

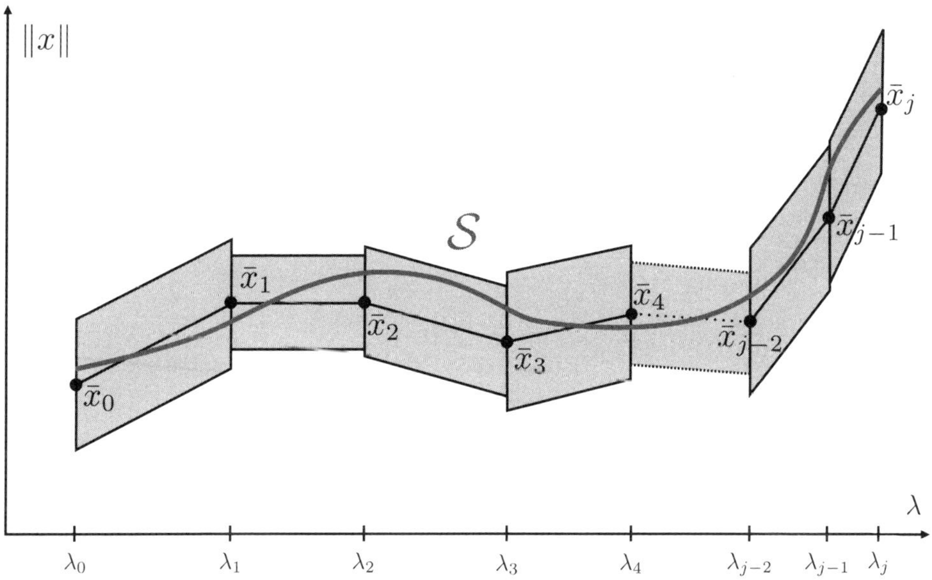

FIGURE 13. Computing rigorously a global branch of solutions.

REMARK 2.8 (**Bifurcations**). In the present work we do not discuss how to handle some type bifurcations. Instead, we refer to the paper of Thomas Wanner [**55**], where a rigorous computational method to prove existence of saddle-node bifurcations and symmetry-breaking pitchfork bifurcations is presented.

REMARK 2.9 (**Number of Parameters and Multi-parameter Continuation**). In the present work, we focus on equations depending on a single parameter $\lambda \in \mathbb{R}$. However, the radii polynomial approach (as presented below in Theorem 2.6) works also for problems depending on $p > 1$ parameters. In fact, the method may be extended to prove existence of "solution manifolds" within solutions sets of the form $\{(x, \Lambda) \in X \times \mathbb{R}^p \mid F(x, \Lambda) = 0\}$. The only difference is that the bounds which need to be computed to apply the uniform contraction theorem have to be obtained uniformly over a compact set of parameters in $\mathbb{R}^p$ instead of in $\mathbb{R}$. A more advanced approach based on a rigorous multi-parameter continuation method, generalizing the concept of pseudo-arclength continuation, is introduced in [**53**] to compute solutions manifolds and to handle higher dimensional folds.

REMARK 2.10 (**Parameter Continuation vs Pseudo-Arclength Continuation**). The method of Theorem 2.6 is based on parameter continuation: we compute branches of solutions parametrized by the parameter λ. The method is extended to pseudo-arclength continuation where solutions are parametrized by pseudo-arclength (e.g. see [**34, 52**]).

REMARK 2.11 (**Computing the bound Y_0**). To compute the Y_0 bound satisfying (2.5), denote

$$\Delta\bar{x} \stackrel{\text{def}}{=} \bar{x}_1 - \bar{x}_0 \quad \text{and} \quad \Delta\lambda \stackrel{\text{def}}{=} \lambda_1 - \lambda_0,$$

and consider the expansion

$$F(\bar{x}_s, \lambda_s) = F(\bar{x}_0, \lambda_0) + \left[D_x F(\bar{x}_0, \lambda_0) \quad \frac{\partial F}{\partial \lambda}(\bar{x}_0, \lambda_0) \right] \begin{pmatrix} \Delta\bar{x} \\ \Delta\lambda \end{pmatrix} s$$
$$+ \frac{1}{2} \left(\frac{\partial^2}{\partial s^2} F(\bar{x}_s, \lambda_s)\Big|_{s=0} \right) s^2 + h.o.t.$$

Denote

$$y_1 \stackrel{\text{def}}{=} \left[D_x F(\bar{x}_0, \lambda_0) \quad \frac{\partial F}{\partial \lambda}(\bar{x}_0, \lambda_0) \right] \begin{pmatrix} \Delta\bar{x} \\ \Delta\lambda \end{pmatrix} \tag{2.13}$$

$$y_2 \stackrel{\text{def}}{=} \frac{1}{2} \left(\frac{\partial^2}{\partial s^2} F(\bar{x}_s, \lambda_s)\Big|_{s=0} \right). \tag{2.14}$$

Hence,

$$\|AF(\bar{x}_s, \lambda_s)\|_X \leq \|AF(\bar{x}_0, \lambda_0)\|_X + \|Ay_1\|_X + \|Ay_2\|_X + \delta$$

where the extra term $\delta \geq 0$ is obtained using Taylor remainder's theorem.

2.4. A Finite Dimensional Example. In this section, we apply the radii polynomial approach (Theorem 2.6) to prove the existence of branches of solutions of the problem (2.1) with F a mapping between finite dimensional Banach spaces.

The example we consider is the problem of computing branches of steady states for the atmospheric circulation model introduced by Edward N. Lorenz in [**56**]

$$\begin{cases} x_1' = -\alpha x_1 - x_2^2 - x_3^2 + \alpha\lambda \\ x_2' = -x_2 + x_1 x_2 - \beta x_1 x_3 + \gamma \\ x_3' = -x_3 + \beta x_1 x_2 + x_1 x_3. \end{cases} \tag{2.15}$$

Let us fix $\alpha = 0.25$, $\beta = 4$ and $\gamma = 0.5$, and leave λ as a parameter. At these parameter values, equilibria of (2.15) are solutions of

$$F(x, \lambda) \stackrel{\text{def}}{=} \begin{pmatrix} -\frac{1}{4}x_1 - x_2^2 - x_3^2 + \frac{\lambda}{4} \\ -x_2 + x_1 x_2 - 4x_1 x_3 + \frac{1}{2} \\ -x_3 + 4x_1 x_2 + x_1 x_3 \end{pmatrix} = 0. \tag{2.16}$$

In this case, the Banach spaces are $X = Y = \mathbb{R}^3$ endowed with the sup-norm

$$\|x\| = \max(|x_1|, |x_2|, |x_3|).$$

At $\lambda_0 = 0.8$ and $\lambda_1 = 0.85$, we used Newton's method to compute respectively

$$\bar{x}_0 = \begin{pmatrix} -0.056551859183890 \\ 0.452495729654079 \\ -0.096879200248534 \end{pmatrix} \quad \text{and} \quad \bar{x}_1 = \begin{pmatrix} -0.043505480122129 \\ 0.466188932513298 \\ -0.077744769808933 \end{pmatrix}.$$

We wish to use Theorem 2.6 to prove the existence of a segment of solutions in the solution set $\mathcal{S} = \{(x, \lambda) \in \mathbb{R}^4 \mid F(x, \lambda) = 0\}$. For $s \in [0, 1]$, recall the set of predictors (2.3) given by $\bar{x}_s = (1-s)\bar{x}_0 + s\bar{x}_1$ and let $\lambda_s = (1-s)\lambda_0 + s\lambda_1$. Denote by

$$\Delta\bar{x} \stackrel{\text{def}}{=} \bar{x}_1 - \bar{x}_0 \quad \text{and} \quad \Delta\lambda \stackrel{\text{def}}{=} \lambda_1 - \lambda_0.$$

Recalling the Y_0 bound satisfying (2.5). Since the vector field is quadratic, recalling (2.13) and (2.14), we get the following expansion

$$F(\bar{x}_s, \lambda_s) = F(\bar{x}_0, \lambda_0) + y_1 s + y_2 s^2,$$

where

$$y_2 = \begin{pmatrix} -(\Delta\bar{x})_2^2 - (\Delta\bar{x})_3^2 \\ (\Delta\bar{x})_1(\Delta\bar{x})_2 - 4(\Delta\bar{x})_1(\Delta\bar{x})_3 \\ 4(\Delta\bar{x})_1(\Delta\bar{x})_2 + (\Delta\bar{x})_1(\Delta\bar{x})_3 \end{pmatrix}.$$

The matrix $A \approx DF(\bar{x}_0, \lambda_0)^{-1}$ is computed using MATLAB and is given by

$$A = \begin{pmatrix} -1.031444307007117 & 0.883485538811585 & 0 \\ -1.126473748855484 & 0.059891724595854 & -0.193758400497068 \\ -1.431216390563831 & 1.419669460728974 & -0.904991459308157 \end{pmatrix}.$$

Using the definition of A, y_1 and y_2, we compute $Y_0 = 0.002488451115105$. For this finite dimensional example, we set $A^\dagger = DF(\bar{x}_0, \lambda_0)$, so that $Z_1 = 0$ in (2.7). Recalling (2.6), we set $Z_0 = \|I - ADF(\bar{x}_0, \lambda_0)\|_\infty$. In this case, we computed $Z_0 = 2.27 \times 10^{-16}$. To facilitate the computation of Z_2 satisfying (2.8), consider $c \in B_1(0) \subset \mathbb{R}^3$, that is $\|c\|_\infty \le 1$, and consider $b \in B_r(0) \subset \mathbb{R}^3$, that is $\|b\|_\infty \le r$. Then,

$$[D_x F(\bar{x}_s + b, \lambda_s) - D_x F(\bar{x}_0, \lambda_0)]c = \begin{pmatrix} -2b_2c_2 - 2b_3c_3 \\ b_1c_2 - 4b_1c_3 + b_2c_1 - 4b_3c_1 \\ 4b_1c_2 + b_1c_3 + 4b_2c_1 + b_3c_1 \end{pmatrix} + s \begin{pmatrix} -2c_2(\Delta\bar{x})_2 - 2c_3(\Delta\bar{x})_3 \\ c_1(\Delta\bar{x})_2 - 4c_1(\Delta\bar{x})_3 + c_2(\Delta\bar{x})_1 - 4c_3(\Delta\bar{x})_1 \\ 4c_1(\Delta\bar{x})_2 + c_1(\Delta\bar{x})_3 + 4c_2(\Delta\bar{x})_1 + c_3(\Delta\bar{x})_1 \end{pmatrix},$$

and since $|s| \le 1$, we get the component-wise inequalities

$$|[D_x F(\bar{x}_s + b, \lambda_s) - D_x F(\bar{x}_0, \lambda_0)]c| \le \begin{pmatrix} 4 \\ 10 \\ 10 \end{pmatrix} r + \begin{pmatrix} 2|(\Delta\bar{x})_2| + 2|(\Delta\bar{x})_3| \\ |(\Delta\bar{x})_2| + 4|(\Delta\bar{x})_3| + 5|(\Delta\bar{x})_1| \\ 4|(\Delta\bar{x})_2| + |(\Delta\bar{x})_3| + 5|(\Delta\bar{x})_1| \end{pmatrix}.$$

Hence, letting

$$Z_2^{(1)} \stackrel{\text{def}}{=} \left\| |A| \begin{pmatrix} 4 \\ 10 \\ 10 \end{pmatrix} \right\|_\infty \quad \text{and} \quad Z_2^{(0)} \stackrel{\text{def}}{=} \left\| |A| \begin{pmatrix} 2|(\Delta\bar{x})_2| + 2|(\Delta\bar{x})_3| \\ |(\Delta\bar{x})_2| + 4|(\Delta\bar{x})_3| + 5|(\Delta\bar{x})_1| \\ 4|(\Delta\bar{x})_2| + |(\Delta\bar{x})_3| + 5|(\Delta\bar{x})_1| \end{pmatrix} \right\|_\infty$$

we set

$$Z_2(r) = Z_2^{(1)} r + Z_2^{(0)}.$$

Numerically, we obtain $Z_2^{(1)} = 28.971474762626638$ and $Z_2^{(0)} = 0.440592442217924$. Recalling (2.9) and that $Z_1 = 0$, the radii polynomial is given by

$$\begin{aligned} p(r) &= Z_2(r)r + (Z_0 - 1)r + Y_0 \\ &= Z_2^{(1)} r^2 + (Z_2^{(0)} + Z_0 - 1)r + Y_0 \\ &= 28.971474762626638r^2 - 0.559407557782076r + 0.002488451115105. \end{aligned}$$

Note that

$$\mathcal{I} \stackrel{\text{def}}{=} \{r > 0 \mid p(r) < 0\} \supset [0.006949765480451 \ , \ 0.012359143105166].$$

Choosing for instance $r_0 = 0.007 \in \mathcal{I}$, then by Theorem 2.6, there exists a C^∞ function

$$\tilde{x} : [0,1] \to \bigcup_{s\in[0,1]} B_{r_0}(\bar{x}_s)$$

such that $F(\tilde{x}(s), \lambda_s) = 0$ for all $s \in [0,1]$ with F given in (2.16), and these are the only solutions in the set $\bigcup_{s\in[0,1]} B_{r_0}(\bar{x}_s) \times [\lambda_0, \lambda_1]$.

Also, we applied the method on the intervals of parameters $[\lambda_1, \lambda_2]$ and $[\lambda_2, \lambda_3]$ corresponding respectively to the segments $\{(1-s)\bar{x}_1 + s\bar{x}_2 \mid s \in [0,1]\}$ and $\{(1-s)\bar{x}_2 + s\bar{x}_3 \mid s \in [0,1]\}$, with $\lambda_2 = 0.89$, $\lambda_3 = 0.925$, and

$$\bar{x}_2 = \begin{pmatrix} -0.032746172312211 \\ 0.476481288735590 \\ -0.060432810317938 \end{pmatrix} \quad \text{and} \quad \bar{x}_3 = \begin{pmatrix} -0.022963874112357 \\ 0.484866398590268 \\ -0.043537846136356 \end{pmatrix}.$$

The MATLAB program `script_proof_lorenz.m` available at [**76**] performs the above computations. It uses the interval arithmetic package INTLAB developed by Siegfried M. Rump [**57**].

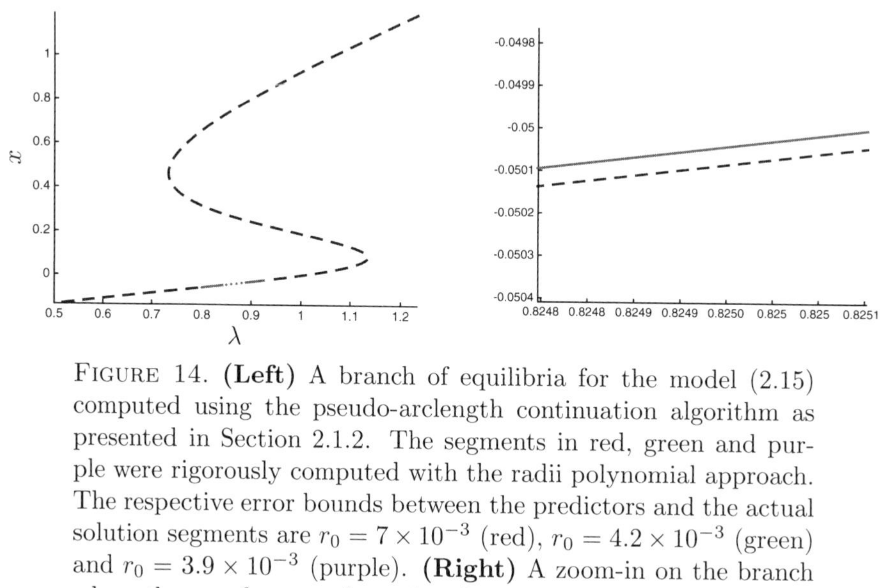

FIGURE 14. **(Left)** A branch of equilibria for the model (2.15) computed using the pseudo-arclength continuation algorithm as presented in Section 2.1.2. The segments in red, green and purple were rigorously computed with the radii polynomial approach. The respective error bounds between the predictors and the actual solution segments are $r_0 = 7 \times 10^{-3}$ (red), $r_0 = 4.2 \times 10^{-3}$ (green) and $r_0 = 3.9 \times 10^{-3}$ (purple). **(Right)** A zoom-in on the branch where the proof was performed at $\lambda = 0.825$.

REMARK 2.12 (**Proofs at fixed parameter values**). It is important to recall that the purpose of the present section is to introduce a method to compute "branches" of solutions. If however we are interested in proving the existence of a solution at a fixed parameter value, then we get dramatically better error bounds. Let us do this exercise for model (2.15) with the approximation $\bar{x}_0$. In this case, $\Delta\bar{x} = 0 \in \mathbb{R}^3$, $\Delta\lambda = 0$ and $Z_2^{(0)} = 0$, the radii polynomial is $p(r) = 28.971474762626652r^2 + (2.195852227948092 \times 10^{-15} - 1)r + 2.449129914171945 \times 10^{-16}$, and

$$\mathcal{I} \stackrel{\text{def}}{=} \{r > 0 \mid p(r) < 0\} \supset \left[2.45 \times 10^{-16} \ , \ 0.034516710253563\right].$$

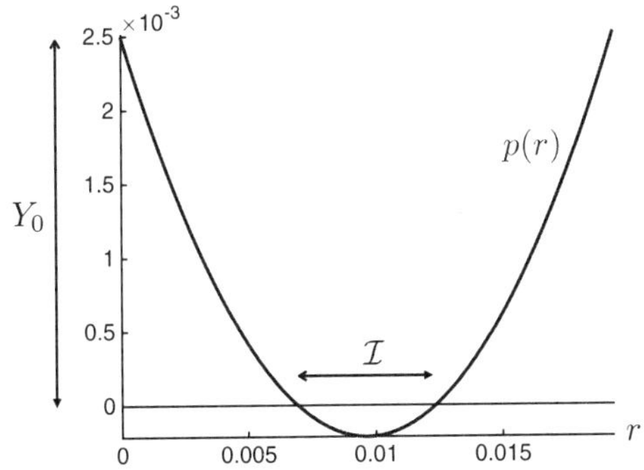

FIGURE 15. The radii polynomial $p(r) = Z_2^{(1)} r^2 + (Z_2^{(0)} + Z_0 - 1)r + Y_0$ associated to the numerical approximations $\bar{x}_0$ and $\bar{x}_1$ as defined above.

Therefore, there exists a unique $\tilde{x}_0 \in B_{2.45\times 10^{-16}}(\bar{x}_0)$ such that $F(\tilde{x}_0, \lambda_0) = 0$. In this case, the rigorous error bound is of the order of 10^{-16}, as opposed to 10^{-3} for the branch of solutions.

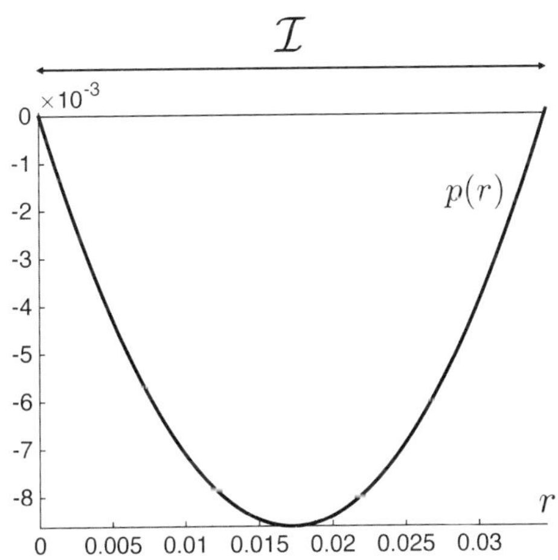

FIGURE 16. The radii polynomial $p(r) = Z_2^{(1)} r^2 + (Z_0 - 1)r + Y_0$ associated to the single numerical approximation $\bar{x}_0$.

We are now ready to present the main application of the rigorous continuation method.

In this section, we show how the radii polynomial approach (Theorem 2.6) is used to compute rigorously branches of periodic solutions of DDEs. Rather than presenting the ideas for general classes of problems, we focus on presenting the ideas for specific examples, namely for a delayed Van der Pol equation and for Wright's equation. For the delayed Van der Pol equation, we present in details in Section 2.5 all steps, bounds, necessary estimates, choices of function spaces and the explicit coefficients of the radii polynomial, whereas in the case of Wright's equation, we only briefly discuss some results in Section 2.6 and refer to [**12**] for more details. Note that the ideas presented here should be applicable to systems of N delay equations of the form

(2.17)

$$y^{(n)}(t) = \mathcal{F}\left(y(t), y(t-\tau_1), \ldots, y(t-\tau_d), \ldots, y^{(n-1)}(t-\tau_1), \ldots, y^{(n-1)}(t-\tau_d)\right),$$

where $y : \mathbb{R} \to \mathbb{R}^N$ and $\mathcal{F} : \mathbb{R}^{N(nd+1)} \to \mathbb{R}^N$ is a multivariate polynomial.

As already mentioned in Section 1 studying rigorously solutions of DDEs is a challenging problem, especially because they are naturally defined on infinite dimensional function spaces. On the other hand, as already mentioned in Section 1, for continuous dynamical systems like (2.17), individual solutions which exist globally in time are more regular than the typical functions of the natural phase space. That suggests that solving for the Fourier coefficients of the periodic solutions of (2.17) in a Banach space of fast decaying sequences is a good strategy. In fact periodic solutions of (2.17) are analytic since $\mathcal{F}$ is analytic (it is polynomial) [**10**]. We therefore apriori know that the Fourier coefficients of the periodic solutions decay geometrically by the Paley-Wiener Theorem. Before presenting the rigorous numerical method, we briefly describe different methods used to study periodic solutions of (2.17), following closely the discussion in [**58**].

Fixed point theory, the fixed point index and global bifurcation theorems are powerful tools to study the existence of solutions of infinite dimensional dynamical systems. To give a few examples in the context of DDEs, the ejective fixed point theorem of Browder [**59**] and the fixed point index are used to prove existence of nontrivial periodic solutions [**14, 60, 61**], and the global bifurcation theorem of Rabinowitz [**62**] are used to prove the existence and characterize the (non) compactness of global branches of periodic solutions [**63, 64**]. This heavy machinery from functional analysis provides powerful existence results about solutions of DDEs, but its applicability may decrease if one asks more specific questions about the solutions of a given equation. For example, it appears difficult in general to use the ejective fixed point theorem to quantify the number of periodic solutions or to use a global bifurcation theorem to conclude about existence of folds, or more generally, of secondary bifurcations. The following Figure 17 taken from [**32**] shows that global branches of periodic solutions of DDEs may be complicated, as various bifurcations may occur on the branches. These remarks further motivate the need for rigorous numerical methods for DDEs.

REMARK 2.13. Let us mention the existence of other rigorous numerical methods to study periodic orbits of DDEs. First, the work [**65**] provides a method to compute periodic solutions using a Newton-like operator and piecewise linear approximations. Second the work [**66**] presents a rigorous numerical integrator to prove existence of periodic orbits in the Mackey-Glass equation. Finally, let us mention that the work [**67**] on the parameterization method could eventually be combined with rigorous numerics to compute invariant manifolds attached to equilibria and periodic orbits.

2.5. A Delayed Van der Pol Equation. In the 1920s, the Dutch electrical engineer and physicist Van der Pol proposed his famous *Van der Pol equations* to model oscillations of some electric circuits [**68**]. Since then, variants of the so-called

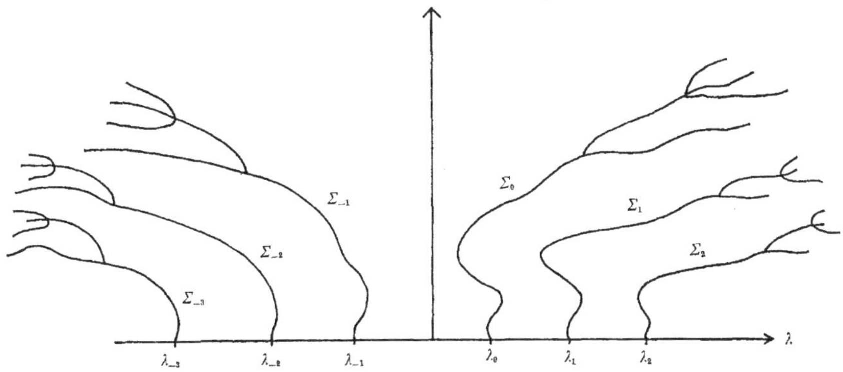

FIGURE 17. Global branches of periodic solutions of delay differential equations. The picture is taken directly from [**32**].

van der Pol oscillator have been proposed as mathematical models of various real-world processes exhibiting limit cycles when the rate of change of the state variables depend only on their current states. However, there are many processes where this relation is also influenced by past values of the system in question. To model these processes, one may want to consider the use of functional differential equations, see [**9**, **69**, **70**].

In [**71**], Grafton establishes existence of periodic solutions to

$$\ddot{y}(t) - \varepsilon\dot{y}(t)(1 - y^2(t)) + y(t - \tau) = 0, \quad \varepsilon, \tau > 0,$$

a Van der Pol equation with a retarded position variable. His results are based on his periodicity results developed in [**72**]. In [**73**], using slightly different notations, Roger Nussbaum considered the more general class of equations

$$\ddot{y}(t) - \varepsilon\dot{y}(t)(1 - y^2(t)) + y(t - \tau) - \lambda y(t) = 0, \quad \varepsilon, \tau > 0, \lambda \in \mathbb{R}, \tag{2.18}$$

and establishes existence of periodic solution of period greater than 2τ, given that $\lambda \subset (-\lambda_0, 1)$, where

$$\lambda_0 = \min\left(\frac{\varepsilon}{\tau}, \frac{2}{\tau^2}\right).$$

We refer to (2.18) as Nussbaum's equation. The techniques that Nussbaum uses are sophisticated fixed point arguments, however, as he remarks, he has to restrict the size of $|\lambda|$ to guarantee that the zeros of y are at least a distance τ apart (e.g. see p. 287 of [**73**]). Moreover, he mentions that numerical simulations suggest the existence of periodic solutions to (2.18) for a large range of $\lambda < 0$.

What we present now is an application of the rigorous continuation method introduced in Section 2, and we establish existence results for periodic solutions to (2.18) for parameter values outside of the range of parameters accessible with the above results of Nussbaum. The first step is to recast periodic solutions of (2.18) as solutions of $F(x, \lambda) = 0$.

2.5.1. *Setting up the $F(x, \lambda) = 0$ problem.* Assume that $y(t)$ is a periodic solution of (2.18) of period $p > 0$. Then

$$y(t) = \sum_{k=-\infty}^{\infty} a_k e^{ik\omega t}, \tag{2.19}$$

where $\omega = \frac{2\pi}{p}$ and the $a_k \in \mathbb{C}$ are the complex Fourier coefficients. Given a complex number $z \in \mathbb{C}$, denote by $\mathrm{conj}(z)$ the complex conjugate of z. During the rigorous continuation we verify a posteriori that the complex numbers satisfy $a_{-k} = \mathrm{conj}(a_k)$, hence y is real valued. As the frequency ω of (2.19) is not known *a-priori*, it is left as a variable. Formally, using (2.19)

$$\dot{y}(t) = \sum_{k=-\infty}^{\infty} a_k ik\omega e^{ik\omega t}, \quad \ddot{y}(t) = \sum_{k=-\infty}^{\infty} -a_k k^2 \omega^2 e^{ik\omega t}$$
$$\text{and} \quad y(t-\tau) = \sum_{k=-\infty}^{\infty} a_k e^{-ik\omega\tau} e^{ik\omega t}.$$

Thus (2.18) becomes

$$\begin{aligned}&\sum_{k=-\infty}^{\infty} \left[-k^2\omega^2 - \varepsilon ik\omega - \lambda + e^{-ik\omega\tau}\right] a_k e^{ik\omega t} \\ &\quad + \varepsilon \sum_{k_1=-\infty}^{\infty} a_{k_1} e^{ik_1\omega t} \sum_{k_2=-\infty}^{\infty} a_{k_2} e^{ik_2\omega t} \sum_{k_3=-\infty}^{\infty} a_{k_3} ik_3\omega e^{ik_3\omega t} = 0.\end{aligned} \tag{2.20}$$

The Fourier coefficients in (2.19) are obtained by taking the inner product on both sides of (2.20) with $e^{ik\omega t}$, yielding that for all $k \in \mathbb{Z}$,

$$g_k \stackrel{\text{def}}{=} \left[-k^2\omega^2 - \varepsilon ik\omega - \lambda + e^{-ik\omega\tau}\right] a_k + i\varepsilon\omega \sum_{k_1+k_2+k_3=k} a_{k_1}a_{k_2}a_{k_3}k_3 = 0.$$

Observing that

$$\begin{aligned} S_k \stackrel{\text{def}}{=} \sum_{\substack{k_1+k_2+k_3=k \\ k_j\in\mathbb{Z}}} a_{k_1}a_{k_2}a_{k_3}k_3 &= \sum_{\substack{k_1+k_2+k_3=k \\ k_j\in\mathbb{Z}}} a_{k_1}a_{k_2}a_{k_3}(k-k_1-k_2) \\ &= k \sum_{\substack{k_1+k_2+k_3=k \\ k_j\in\mathbb{Z}}} a_{k_1}a_{k_2}a_{k_3} - 2S_k \end{aligned}$$

we get that

$$S_k = \frac{k}{3} \sum_{\substack{k_1+k_2+k_3=k \\ k_j\in\mathbb{Z}}} a_{k_1}a_{k_2}a_{k_3}$$

and therefore

$$g_k = \mu_k a_k + \frac{i\varepsilon k\omega}{3}(a^3)_k, \tag{2.21}$$

where

$$\mu_k = \mu_k(\omega,\lambda) \stackrel{\text{def}}{=} -k^2\omega^2 - \varepsilon ik\omega - \lambda + e^{-ik\omega\tau} \quad \text{and} \quad (a^3)_k \stackrel{\text{def}}{=} \sum_{\substack{k_1+k_2+k_3=k \\ k_j\in\mathbb{Z}}} a_{k_1}a_{k_2}a_{k_3}.$$

Denote $a = (a_k)_{k\in\mathbb{Z}}$ and $x = (\omega, a)$ the infinite dimensional vector of unknowns. Denote $g(x,\lambda) = (g_k(x,\lambda))_{k\in\mathbb{Z}}$. To eliminate any arbitrary time shift, we append a *phase condition* given by

$$\eta(x) = \sum_{|k|<n} a_k = 0, \tag{2.22}$$

for some $n \in \mathbb{N}$, which ensures that $y(0) \approx 0$. Combining (2.22) and (2.21), we let

$$F(x,\lambda) \stackrel{\text{def}}{=} \begin{pmatrix} \eta(x) \\ g(x,\lambda) \end{pmatrix}. \tag{2.23}$$

Let us now introduce the Banach space in which we look for solutions of $F(x,\lambda) = 0$ with F given in (2.23).

Since periodic solutions of analytic delay differential equations are analytic (e.g. see [**10**]), their Fourier coefficients decay geometrically. This motivates the choice of Banach space in which we embed the Fourier coefficients. Given a weight $\nu > 1$, define the sequence space

$$\ell^1_\nu = \{a = (a_k)_{k\in\mathbb{Z}} \mid \|a\|_{1,\nu} < \infty\}, \tag{2.24}$$

where

$$\|a\|_{1,\nu} \stackrel{\text{def}}{=} \sum_{k\in\mathbb{Z}} |a_k|\nu^{|k|}. \tag{2.25}$$

Define the Banach space

$$X \stackrel{\text{def}}{=} \mathbb{C} \times \ell^1_\nu$$

endowed with the norm

$$\|x\|_X \stackrel{\text{def}}{=} \max\left(|\omega|, \|a\|_{1,\nu}\right).$$

Note that F does not map X into itself. This is because a differential operator is in general unbounded on ℓ^1_ν. To overcome this problem we look for an injective linear "smoothing" operator A such that (2.4) holds, that $AF(x,\lambda) \in X$ for all $x \in X$ and $\lambda \in \mathbb{R}$. The choice of the approximate inverse A is presented in Section 2.5.4. For now we take A as given and define the *Newton-like operator* by

$$T(x,s) = x - AF(x,\lambda_s), \tag{2.26}$$

for $s \in [0,1]$. Given $s \in [0,1]$, the injectivity of A implies that x is a solution of $F(x,\lambda_s) = 0$ if and only if it is a fixed point of $T(\cdot,s)$. Moreover $T(\cdot,s)$ now maps X back into itself.

2.5.2. *Symmetry of the fixed points of T.* We are interested in showing the existence of a real periodic solution y given by (2.19) satisfying the symmetry property

$$y(t+p/2) = -y(t), \quad \forall\, t \in \mathbb{R}.$$

In Fourier space, this means that the Fourier coefficients satisfy the relation

$$a_{2j} = 0, \ \forall\, j \in \mathbb{Z}. \tag{2.27}$$

To do this, we design the method so that fixed points of T are in the *symmetry* space

$$X_{sym} \stackrel{\text{def}}{=} \mathbb{R} \times \tilde{\ell}^1_\nu, \tag{2.28}$$

where

$$\tilde{\ell}^1_\nu \stackrel{\text{def}}{=} \left\{a \in \ell^1_\nu \,|\, a_{-k} = \text{conj}(a_k)\ \forall\, k \in \mathbb{Z}, \ \text{ and } \ a_{2j} = 0\ \forall\, j \in \mathbb{Z}\right\}. \tag{2.29}$$

REMARK 2.14. The condition $a_{-k} = \text{conj}(a_k)$ is imposed in the function space ℓ^1_ν because we want y to be a real periodic solution, that is $\text{conj}(y(t)) = y(t)$.

LEMMA 2.15. *Assume that $\bar{x}_s \in X_{sym}$ and consider the closed ball $B_r(\bar{x}_s) \subset X$. Define T as in (2.26) and assume that the approximate inverse A satisfies*

$$AF : X_{sym} \times \mathbb{R} \to X_{sym}. \tag{2.30}$$

Assume that for every $s \in [0,1]$, $T(\cdot, s) : B_r(\bar{x}_s) \to B_r(\bar{x}_s)$ is a contraction, and let $\tilde{x}_s \in X$ the unique fixed point of $T(\cdot, s)$ in $B_r(\bar{x}_s)$ which exists by the Contraction Mapping Theorem. Then, $\tilde{x}_s \in X_{sym}$ for all $s \in [0,1]$.

PROOF. By (2.30), $T : X_{sym} \times [0,1] \to X_{sym}$. Using that $\bar{x}_s \in X_{sym} \cap B_r(\bar{x}_s)$, and that X_{sym} is a closed subset of X for every $s \in [0,1]$, we obtain that

$$\tilde{x}_s = \lim_{n \to \infty} T^n(\bar{x}_s, s) \in X_{sym}. \qquad \square$$

2.5.3. *Computation of the numerical approximations.* We are ready to compute numerical approximations of $F(x, \lambda) = 0$ with F given in (2.23). Since the operator F is defined on an infinite dimensional space, this requires considering a finite dimensional projection. Given $a = (a_k)_{k \in \mathbb{Z}} \in \ell^1_\nu$ and a *projection dimension* $m \in \mathbb{N}$, denote by $a^{(m)} = (a_k)_{|k|<m} \in \mathbb{C}^{2m-1}$ a finite part of a of size $2m - 1$. Moreover, given $x = (\omega, a) \in X = \mathbb{C} \times \ell^1_\nu$, denote $x^{(m)} = (\omega, a^{(m)}) \in \mathbb{C}^{2m}$. Consider a finite dimensional projection $F^{(m)} : \mathbb{C}^{2m} \times \mathbb{R} \to \mathbb{C}^{2m}$ of (2.23) given by

$$F^{(m)}(x^{(m)}, \lambda) = \begin{pmatrix} \eta(x^{(m)}) \\ g^{(m)}(x^{(m)}, \lambda) \end{pmatrix}, \tag{2.31}$$

where $g^{(m)}(x^{(m)}, \lambda) \in \mathbb{C}^{2m-1}$ corresponds to the finite part of g of size $2m-1$, that is $g^{(m)} = \{(g^{(m)})_k\}_{|k|<m}$. More explicitly, given $|k| < m$,

$$g_k^{(m)}(x^{(m)}, \lambda) = \mu_k(\omega, \lambda) a_k + \frac{i\varepsilon k\omega}{3} \sum_{\substack{k_1+k_2+k_3=k \\ |k_i|<m}} a_{k_1} a_{k_2} a_{k_3}.$$

We apply the parameter continuation method as introduced in Section 2.1.1 to the finite dimensional problem $F^{(m)} : \mathbb{C}^{2m} \times \mathbb{R} \to \mathbb{C}^{2m}$. Assume that at the parameter value $\lambda = \lambda_0$, $\bar{x}_0 = (\bar{\omega}_0, \bar{a}_0) \in \mathbb{C} \times \mathbb{C}^{2m-1}$ is an approximate solution, that is $F^{(m)}(\bar{x}_0, \lambda_0) \approx 0$.

The next step is to introduce an approximate inverse operator A that satisfies (2.30) and the operator $A^\dagger$, required to apply the radii polynomial approach (Theorem 2.6).

2.5.4. *Definition of the operators A and $A^\dagger$.* We now define an approximate inverse A for $D_x F(\bar{x}_0, \lambda_0)$ so that (2.4) holds and the operator $A^\dagger$ which approximates $D_x F(\bar{x}_0, \lambda_0)$. Assume that $\bar{x}_0 = (\bar{\omega}_0, \bar{a}_0) \in X_{sym}$. The Fréchet derivative $D_x F(\bar{x}_0, \lambda_0)$ is visualized in block form as

$$D_x F(\bar{x}_0, \lambda_0) = \begin{pmatrix} 0 & D_a \eta(\bar{x}_0) \\ \partial_\omega g(\bar{x}_0, \lambda_0) & D_a g(\bar{x}_0, \lambda_0) \end{pmatrix},$$

since $\partial_\omega F_0(\bar{x}_0) = 0$, and where

$$\begin{cases} \partial_\omega g(\bar{x}_0, \lambda_0) : \mathbb{C} \to \ell^1_\nu, \\ D_a \eta(\bar{x}_0) : \ell^1_\nu \to \mathbb{C} \text{ is a linear functional} \\ D_a g(\bar{x}_0, \lambda_0) : \ell^1_\nu \to \ell^1_{\nu'} \text{ is a linear operator with } \nu' < \nu. \end{cases}$$

We first approximate $D_xF(\bar{x}_0,\lambda_0)$ with the operator

$$A^\dagger \stackrel{\text{def}}{=} \begin{pmatrix} 0 & A^\dagger_{a,0} \\ A^\dagger_{\omega,1} & A^\dagger_{a,1} \end{pmatrix},$$

which acts on $b=(b_0,b_1)\in X=\mathbb{C}\times\ell^1_\nu$ component-wise as

$$\begin{aligned} (A^\dagger b)_0 &= A^\dagger_{a,0}\cdot b_1 \stackrel{\text{def}}{=} D_{a^{(m)}}\eta(\bar{x}_0)\cdot b_1^{(m)} \\ (A^\dagger b)_1 &= A^\dagger_{\omega,1}b_0 + A^\dagger_{a,1}b_1 \in \ell^1_{\nu'}, \end{aligned}$$

where $A^\dagger_{\omega,1}=\partial_\omega g^{(m)}(\bar{x}_0,\lambda_0)$ and $A^\dagger_{a,1}b_1\in\ell^1_{\nu'}$ is defined component-wise by

$$\left(A^\dagger_{a,1}b_1\right)_k = \begin{cases} \left(D_{a^{(m)}}g^{(m)}(\bar{x}_0,\lambda_0)b_1^{(m)}\right)_k, & |k|<m \\ \mu_k(\bar{\omega}_0,\lambda_0)(b_1)_k, & |k|\geq m. \end{cases}$$

Let $A^{(m)}$ a finite dimensional approximate inverse of $D_xF^{(m)}(\bar{x}_0,\lambda_0)$ which is obtained numerically and which has the decomposition

$$A^{(m)} = \begin{pmatrix} A^{(m)}_{\omega,0} & A^{(m)}_{a,0} \\ A^{(m)}_{\omega,1} & A^{(m)}_{a,1} \end{pmatrix} \in \mathbb{C}^{2m\times 2m},$$

where $A^{(m)}_{\omega,0}\in\mathbb{C}$, $A^{(m)}_{a,0}\in\mathbb{C}^{1\times(2m-1)}$, $A^{(m)}_{\omega,1}\in\mathbb{C}^{(2m-1)\times 1}$ and $A^{(m)}_{a,1}\in\mathbb{C}^{(2m-1)\times(2m-1)}$. Assume moreover that $A^{(m)}$ satisfies the following *symmetry* assumptions:

$$\begin{aligned} &1.\ (A^{(m)}_{a,0})_{-j} = \operatorname{conj}\left((A^{(m)}_{a,0})_j\right),\ j=-m+1,\dots,m-1, \\ &2.\ (A^{(m)}_{\omega,1})_{-k} = \operatorname{conj}\left((A^{(m)}_{\omega,1})_k\right),\ k=-m+1,\dots,m-1, \\ &3.\ (A^{(m)}_{a,1})_{-k,-j} = \operatorname{conj}\left((A^{(m)}_{a,1})_{k,j}\right),\ k,j=-m+1,\dots,m-1, \\ &4.\ (A^{(m)}_{\omega,1})_{2k}=0,\ \forall\ 2k\in\{-m+1,\dots,m-1\}, \\ &5.\ (A^{(m)}_{a,1})_{2k,2j+1}=0,\ \forall\ 2k,2j+1\in\{-m+1,\dots,m-1\}. \end{aligned} \tag{2.32}$$

Assumption 1 of (2.32) implies that $(A^{(m)}_{a,0})_0\in\mathbb{R}$ while assumption 2 implies that $(A^{(m)}_{\omega,1})_0\in\mathbb{R}$. We define the approximate inverse A of the infinite dimensional operator $D_xF(\bar{x}_0,\lambda_0)$ by

$$A \stackrel{\text{def}}{=} \begin{pmatrix} A_{\omega,0} & A_{a,0} \\ A_{\omega,1} & A_{a,1} \end{pmatrix},$$

where A acts on $b=(b_0,b_1)\in X=\mathbb{C}\times\ell^1_\nu$ component-wise as

$$\begin{aligned} (Ab)_0 &= A^{(m)}_{\omega,0}b_0 + A^{(m)}_{a,0}b_1^{(m)} \\ (Ab)_1 &= A^{(m)}_{\omega,1}b_0 + A_{a,1}b_1, \end{aligned}$$

where $A^{(m)}_{\omega,1}\in\mathbb{C}^{(2m-1)\times 1}$ is understood to be an element of ℓ^1_ν by *padding* the tail with zeros, and $A_{a,1}b_1\in\ell^1_\nu$ is defined component-wise by

$$(A_{a,1}b_1)_k = \begin{cases} \left(A^{(m)}_{a,1}b_1^{(m)}\right)_k, & |k|<m \\ \dfrac{1}{\mu_k(\bar{\omega}_0,\lambda_0)}(b_1)_k, & |k|\geq m. \end{cases}$$

Let us now verify that (2.4) holds.

LEMMA 2.16. *Let $x \in X$ and $\lambda \in \mathbb{R}$. Then $AF(x,\lambda) \in X$.*

PROOF. Consider $x = (\omega, a) \in X$ and let $F(x,\lambda) = (\eta(x), g(x,\lambda))$, with $\eta(x)$ given in (2.22) and g given component-wise in (2.21). For sake of simplicity of the presentation, we denote $F_0 = \eta(x)$ and $F_1 = g(x,\lambda)$.

We need to show that $\|(AF(x))_1\|_\nu < \infty$. Since

$$\mu_k(\omega,\lambda) = -k^2\omega^2 - \varepsilon ik\omega - \lambda + e^{-ik\omega\tau}, \tag{2.33}$$

$$\lim_{k\to\pm\infty} \frac{|\mu_k(\omega,\lambda)|}{|\mu_k(\bar\omega_0,\lambda_0)|} = \lim_{k\to\pm\infty} \frac{|-k^2\omega^2 - \varepsilon ik\omega - \lambda + e^{-ik\omega\tau}|}{|-k^2\bar\omega_0^2 - \varepsilon ik\bar\omega_0 - \lambda_0 + e^{-ik\bar\omega_0\tau}|} = \left(\frac{\omega}{\bar\omega_0}\right)^2 < \infty,$$

there exists $C < \infty$ such that

$$\left|\frac{\mu_k(\omega)}{\mu_k(\bar\omega_0)}\right|, \left|\frac{1}{\mu_k(\bar\omega_0)} \cdot \frac{i\varepsilon k\omega}{3}\right| < C, \text{ for all } |k| \geq m.$$

Then,

$$\begin{aligned}
\|(AF(x))_1\|_\nu &= \sum_{k\in\mathbb{Z}} |((AF(x))_1)_k|\,\nu^{|k|} = \sum_{k\in\mathbb{Z}} \left|\left(A_{\omega,1}^{(m)}F_0 + A_{a,1}F_1\right)_k\right| \nu^{|k|} \\
&\leq \sum_{|k|<m} \left|\left(A_{\omega,1}^{(m)}\right)_{k,1}\right| |F_0|\nu^{|k|} + \sum_{|k|<m} \left|\left(A_{a,1}^{(m)}F_1^{(m)}\right)_k\right| \nu^{|k|} \\
&+ \sum_{|k|\geq m} \left|\frac{1}{\mu_k(\bar\omega_0,\lambda_0)}(\mu_k(\omega,\lambda)a_k + \frac{i\varepsilon k\omega}{3}(a^3)_k)\right| \nu^{|k|} \\
&\leq \sum_{|k|<m} \left|\left(A_{\omega,1}^{(m)}\right)_{k,1}\right| |F_0|\nu^{|k|} + \sum_{|k|<m} \left|\left(A_{a,1}^{(m)}F_1^{(m)}\right)_k\right| \nu^{|k|} \\
&+ C\sum_{|k|\geq m} |a_k|\,\nu^{|k|} + C\sum_{|k|\geq m} |(a^3)_k|\,\nu^{|k|} \\
&\leq \sum_{|k|<m} \left|\left(A_{\omega,1}^{(m)}\right)_{k,1}\right| |F_0|\nu^{|k|} + \sum_{|k|<m} \left|\left(A_{a,1}^{(m)}F_1^{(m)}\right)_k\right| \nu^{|k|} \\
&+ C\|a\|_{1,\nu} + C(\|a\|_{1,\nu})^3 < \infty,
\end{aligned}$$

where we used the fact that $\|a^3\|_{1,\nu} \leq (\|a\|_{1,\nu})^3$, because ℓ_ν^1 is a Banach algebra. □

Let us now show that the operator A satisfies the symmetry assumption (2.30).

LEMMA 2.17. *Let $x \in X_{sym}$ and $\lambda \in \mathbb{R}$. Then $AF(x,\lambda) \in X_{sym}$.*

PROOF. Let $x = (\omega, a) \in X_{sym} = \mathbb{R} \times \tilde\ell_\nu^1$, with $\tilde\ell_\nu^1$ as defined in (2.29). This implies that $a_{-k} = \text{conj}(a_k)$ and $a_{2k} = 0$ for all $k \in \mathbb{Z}$. Again, denote $F_0 = \eta(x)$ and $F_1 = g(x,\lambda)$.

We begin the proof by showing that the operator F preserves the symmetry conditions, that is we show that $F_0 \in \mathbb{R}$, $(F_1)_{-k} = \text{conj}((F_1)_k)$ and $(F_1)_{2k} = 0$.

Recalling the definition of the phase condition (2.22),

$$F_0 = \sum_{|k| \leq n} a_k = a_{-n} + a_{-n+1} + \cdots + a_{n-1} + a_n =$$
$$\text{conj}(a_n) + \text{conj}(a_{n-1}) + \cdots + a_{n-1} + a_n \in \mathbb{R}.$$

Also, from (2.33), we see that $\mu_{-k}(\omega, \lambda) = \text{conj}\left(\mu_k(\omega, \lambda)\right)$. Then,

$$\begin{aligned}
(F_1)_{-k} &= \mu_{-k}(\omega, \lambda) a_{-k} - \frac{i\varepsilon k\omega}{3} \sum_{k_1+k_2+k_3=-k} a_{k_1} a_{k_2} a_{k_3} \\
&= \text{conj}\left(\mu_k(\omega, \lambda) a_k\right) - \frac{i\varepsilon k\omega}{3} \sum_{k_1+k_2+k_3=k} a_{-k_1} a_{-k_2} a_{-k_3} \\
&= \text{conj}\left(\mu_k(\omega, \lambda) a_k\right) + \text{conj}\left(\frac{i\varepsilon k\omega}{3}\right) \sum_{k_1+k_2+k_3=k} \text{conj}(a_{k_1})\, \text{conj}(a_{k_2})\, \text{conj}(a_{k_3}) \\
&= \text{conj}\left((F_1)_k\right).
\end{aligned}$$

Now,

$$\begin{aligned}
(2.34) \quad (F_1)_{2k} = \mu_{2k}(\omega, \lambda) a_{2k} &+ \frac{i\varepsilon 2k\omega}{3} (a^3)_{2k} \\
&= \mu_{2k}(\omega, \lambda) 0 + \frac{i\varepsilon 2k\omega}{3} \sum_{k_1+k_2+k_3=2k} a_{k_1} a_{k_2} a_{k_3} = 0,
\end{aligned}$$

since $k_1 + k_2 + k_3 = 2k$ implies that there exists $i \in \{1, 2, 3\}$ such that k_i is even.

The second part of the proof is to show that AF preserves the symmetry conditions, that is $(AF(x))_0 \in \mathbb{R}$, $((AF(x))_1)_{-k} = \text{conj}\left(((AF(x))_1)_k\right)$ and $((AF(x))_1)_{2k} = 0$.

Combining that $A^{(m)}_{\omega,0}, F_0 \in \mathbb{R}$, $(F_1)_{-k} = \text{conj}\left((F_1)_k\right)$ and assumption 1 of (2.32),

$$\begin{aligned}
(AF(x))_0 &= A^{(m)}_{\omega,0} F_0 + A^{(m)}_{a,0} F^{(m)}_1 \\
&= A^{(m)}_{\omega,0} F_0 + \sum_{k=-m+1}^{m-1} (A^{(m)}_{a,0})_k (F_1)_k \\
&= A^{(m)}_{\omega,0} F_0 + \sum_{k=-m+1}^{-1} (A^{(m)}_{a,0})_k (F_1)_k + (A^{(m)}_{a,0})_0 (F_1)_0 + \sum_{k=1}^{m-1} (A^{(m)}_{a,0})_k (F_1)_k \\
&= A^{(m)}_{\omega,0} F_0 + (A^{(m)}_{a,0})_{1,0} (F_1)_0 + \sum_{k=1}^{m-1} \left(\text{conj}\left((A^{(m)}_{a,0})_k (F_1)_k\right) + (A^{(m)}_{a,0})_k (F_1)_k\right) \in \mathbb{R}.
\end{aligned}$$

By assumptions 2 and 3 of (2.32), for $|k| < m$,

$$
\begin{aligned}
((AF(x))_1)_{-k} &= \left(A^{(m)}_{\omega,1} F_0 + A_{a,1} F_1\right)_{-k} \\
&= \left(A^{(m)}_{\omega,1}\right)_{-k} F_0 + \left(A^{(m)}_{a,1} F_1^{(m)}\right)_{-k} \\
&= \left(A^{(m)}_{\omega,1}\right)_{-k} F_0 + \sum_{j=-m+1}^{m-1} (A^{(m)}_{a,1})_{-k,j} (F_1)_j \\
&= \left(A^{(m)}_{\omega,1}\right)_{-k} F_0 + \sum_{j=-m+1}^{m-1} (A^{(m)}_{a,1})_{-k,-j} (F_1)_{-j} \\
&= \operatorname{conj}\left(\left(A^{(m)}_{\omega,1}\right)_{k} F_0\right) + \sum_{j=-m}^{m} \overline{(A^{(m)}_{a,1})_{k,j} (F_1)_j} \\
&= \operatorname{conj}\left(((AF(x))_1)_k\right),
\end{aligned}
$$

and for $|k| \geq m$,

$$
\begin{aligned}
((AF(x))_1)_{-k} &= \left(A^{(m)}_{\omega,1} F_0 + A_{a,1} F_1\right)_{-k} \\
&= (A_{a,1} F_1)_{-k} = \frac{1}{\mu_{-k}(\bar{\omega}_0, \lambda_0)} (F_1)_{-k} = \operatorname{conj}\left(((AF(x))_1)_k\right).
\end{aligned}
$$

That shows that $((AF(x))_1)_{-k} = \operatorname{conj}\left(((AF(x))_1)_k\right)$ for all k. It remains to show that $((AF(x))_1)_{2k} = 0$.

By assumptions 4 and 5 in (2.32), and using (2.34), we get that for $|k| < m$,

$$
\begin{aligned}
((AF(x))_1)_{2k} &= \left(A^{(m)}_{\omega,1} F_0 + A_{a,1} F_1\right)_{2k} = \left(A^{(m)}_{\omega,1}\right)_{2k} F_0 + \left(A^{(m)}_{a,1} F_1^{(m)}\right)_{2k} \\
&= \sum_{j=-m+1}^{m-1} (A^{(m)}_{a,1})_{2k,j} (F_1)_j = \sum_{\substack{j=-m+1 \\ j \text{ odd}}}^{m-1} (A^{(m)}_{a,1})_{2k,j} (F_1)_j = 0,
\end{aligned}
$$

and for $|k| \geq m$,

$$
((AF(x))_1)_{2k} = \frac{1}{\mu_{2k}(\bar{\omega}_0, \lambda_0)} (F_1)_{2k} = 0. \qquad \square
$$

Having defined A satisfying (2.30) we use the radii polynomial approach to compute a branch of solutions of $F(x, \lambda) = 0$ near the set of predictors $\bar{x}_s = (1-s)\bar{x}_0 + s\bar{x}_1$, for $s \in [0,1]$. Deriving explicit bounds for the coefficients Y_0, Z_0, Z_1 and Z_2 requires a few elementary functional analytic facts.

2.5.5. *Basic functional analytic background.*

LEMMA 2.18. *The function space ℓ^1_ν defined in (2.24) is a Banach algebra under discrete convolution. More precisely, $\left(\ell^1_\nu, \|\cdot\|_{1,\nu}\right)$ is a Banach space with the norm defined in (2.25), and for any $a, b \in \ell^1_\nu$, $a * b = \{(a*b)_k\}_{k\in\mathbb{Z}}$ defined by*

$$
(a*b)_k \stackrel{\text{def}}{=} \sum_{k_1+k_2=k} a_{k_1} b_{k_2} \tag{2.35}
$$

satisfy $a * b \in \ell^1_\nu$ and $\|a*b\|_{1,\nu} \leq \|a\|_{1,\nu} \|b\|_{1,\nu}$.

PROOF. We omit the proof that ℓ_ν^1 is a Banach space. Let $a, b \in \ell_\nu^1$, that is $\|a\|_{1,\nu}, \|b\|_{1,\nu} < \infty$. Consider $a * b$ defined component-wise by (2.35). Then,

$$\begin{aligned}\|a * b\|_{1,\nu} &= \sum_{k\in\mathbb{Z}} |(a*b)_k| \nu^{|k|} = \sum_{k\in\mathbb{Z}} \left| \sum_{\substack{k_1+k_2=k \\ k_1,k_2\in\mathbb{Z}}} a_{k_1} b_{k_2} \right| \nu^{|k|} \\ &\leq \sum_{k\in\mathbb{Z}} \sum_{\substack{k_1+k_2=k \\ k_1,k_2\in\mathbb{Z}}} |a_{k_1}||b_{k_2}| \nu^{|k|} \leq \sum_{k\in\mathbb{Z}} \sum_{\substack{k_1+k_2=k \\ k_1,k_2\in\mathbb{Z}}} |a_{k_1}| \nu^{|k_1|} |b_{k_2}| \nu^{|k_2|} \\ &\leq \left(\sum_{k_1\in\mathbb{Z}} |a_{k_1}| \nu^{|k_1|} \right) \left(\sum_{k_2\in\mathbb{Z}} |b_{k_2}| \nu^{|k_2|} \right) = \|a\|_{1,\nu} \|b\|_{1,\nu}.\end{aligned}$$

That shows that ℓ_ν^1 is a Banach algebra. □

Recall the classical fact that the dual space of ℓ_1^1 is the space ℓ^∞. Similarly if $\nu > 1$ then the dual of ℓ_ν^1 is a weighted "ell-infinity" space which we define now. For a bi-infinite sequence of complex numbers $c = \{c_k\}_{k\in\mathbb{Z}}$, the ν-weighted supremum norm is defined by

$$\|c\|_{\infty,\nu^{-1}} \stackrel{\text{def}}{=} \sup_{k\in\mathbb{Z}} \frac{|c_k|}{\nu^{|k|}}. \tag{2.36}$$

Let

$$\ell_\nu^\infty = \left\{ c = \{c_k\}_{k\in\mathbb{Z}} \mid c_k \in \mathbb{C} \ \forall \ k \in \mathbb{Z}, \text{ and } \|c\|_{\infty,\nu^{-1}} < \infty \right\}. \tag{2.37}$$

LEMMA 2.19. *Suppose that $a \in \ell_\nu^1$ and $c \in \ell_\nu^\infty$. Then*

$$\left| \sum_{k\in\mathbb{Z}} c_k a_k \right| \leq \sum_{k\in\mathbb{Z}} |c_k||a_k| \leq \|c\|_\nu^\infty \|a\|_\nu.$$

The following result provides a useful and explicit bound on the norm of an "eventually diagonal" linear operator on ℓ_ν^1. The proof is omitted.

COROLLARY 2.1. Let $\mathcal{M}^{(m)}$ be an $(2m-1) \times (2m-1)$ matrix with complex valued entries, $\{\delta_k\}_{|k|\geq m}$ a bi-infinite sequence of complex numbers and $\delta_m > 0$ a real number such that

$$|\delta_k| \leq \delta_m, \text{ for all } |k| \geq m.$$

Given $a = (a_k)_{k\in\mathbb{Z}} \in \ell_\nu^1$, denote by $a^{(m)} = (a_{-m+1}, \ldots, a_{-1}, a_0, a_1, \ldots, a_{m-1}) \in \mathbb{C}^{2m-1}$. Define the map $\mathcal{M}\colon \ell_\nu^1 \to \ell_\nu^1$ by

$$[\mathcal{M}(a)]_k = \begin{cases} [\mathcal{M}^{(m)} a^{(m)}]_k, & |k| < m \\ \delta_k a_k, & |k| \geq m. \end{cases}$$

Then $\mathcal{M}$ is a bounded linear operator and

$$\|\mathcal{M}\|_{B(\ell_\nu^1, \ell_\nu^1)} \leq \max(K, \delta_m),$$

where

$$K \stackrel{\text{def}}{=} \max_{|n|<m} \frac{1}{\nu^{|n|}} \sum_{|k|<m} |\mathcal{M}_{k,n}| \nu^{|k|}. \tag{2.38}$$

The next result provides useful component-wise bounds for convolution products involving unknown elements in the unit ball in ℓ_ν^1.

LEMMA 2.20. *Given $\nu \geq 1$, $k \in \mathbb{Z}$ and $a \in \ell^1_\nu$, the function $l^k_a \colon \ell^1_\nu \to \mathbb{C}$ defined by*

$$l^k_a(h) \stackrel{\text{def}}{=} (a * h)_k = \sum_{k_1+k_2=k} a_{k_1} h_{k_2}$$

with $h \in \ell^1_\nu$, is a bounded linear functional, and

$$\|l^k_a\| = \sup_{\|h\|_{1,\nu} \leq 1} \left| l^k_a(h) \right| \leq \sup_{j \in \mathbb{Z}} \frac{|a_{k-j}|}{\nu^{|j|}} < \infty. \tag{2.39}$$

Fix a truncation mode to be m. Given $h \in \ell^1_\nu$, set

$$h^{(m)} \stackrel{\text{def}}{=} (\dots, 0, 0, h_{-m+1}, \dots, h_{m-1}, 0, 0, \dots) \in \ell^1_\nu$$
$$h^{(I)} \stackrel{\text{def}}{=} h - h^{(m)} \in \ell^1_\nu.$$

COROLLARY 2.2. Let $N \in \mathbb{N}$ and let $\bar{\alpha} = (\dots, 0, 0, \bar{\alpha}_{-N}, \dots, \bar{\alpha}_N, 0, 0, \dots) \in \ell^1_\nu$. Suppose that $|k| < m$ and define $\hat{l}^k_{\bar{\alpha}} \in (\ell^1_\nu)^*$ by

$$\hat{l}^k_{\bar{\alpha}}(h) \stackrel{\text{def}}{=} (\bar{\alpha} * h^{(I)})_k = \sum_{k_1+k_2=k} \bar{\alpha}_{k_1} h^{(I)}_{k_2}.$$

Then, for all $h \in \ell^1_\nu$ such that $\|h\|_{1,\nu} \leq 1$,

$$\left| \hat{l}^k_{\bar{\alpha}}(h) \right| \leq \Psi_k(\bar{\alpha}) \stackrel{\text{def}}{=} \max\left(\max_{k-N \leq j \leq -m} \frac{|\bar{\alpha}_{k-j}|}{\nu^{|j|}}, \max_{m \leq j \leq k+N} \frac{|\bar{\alpha}_{k-j}|}{\nu^{|j|}} \right). \tag{2.40}$$

2.5.6. *Radii polynomial to compute periodic solutions of Nussbaum's equation.* We have now derived all necessary tools to apply the radii polynomial approach (Theorem 2.6). Assume that $\bar{x}_0$ and $\bar{x}_1$ are two numerical approximation.

The Y_0 bound. We begin the computation of the coefficients of the radii polynomial with Y_0 with the help of Remark 2.11. Denote

$$\Delta\bar{x} \stackrel{\text{def}}{=} \bar{x}_1 - \bar{x}_0 \quad \text{and} \quad \Delta\lambda \stackrel{\text{def}}{=} \lambda_1 - \lambda_0,$$

and, using the mean value theorem, consider the expansion

$$F(\bar{x}_s, \lambda_s)$$
$$= F(\bar{x}_0, \lambda_0) + \begin{pmatrix} D_x F(\bar{x}_0, \lambda_0) & \frac{\partial F}{\partial \lambda}(\bar{x}_0, \lambda_0) \end{pmatrix} \begin{pmatrix} \Delta\bar{x} \\ \Delta\lambda \end{pmatrix} s + \frac{1}{2} \left(\frac{\partial^2}{\partial s^2} F(\bar{x}_s, \lambda_s)\Big|_{s=\sigma} \right) s^2,$$

for some $\sigma \in [0, 1]$. As in (2.13), denote

$$y_1 \stackrel{\text{def}}{=} \begin{pmatrix} D_x F(\bar{x}_0, \lambda_0) & \frac{\partial F}{\partial \lambda}(\bar{x}_0, \lambda_0) \end{pmatrix} \begin{pmatrix} \Delta\bar{x} \\ \Delta\lambda \end{pmatrix} \quad \text{and} \quad y_2 \stackrel{\text{def}}{=} \frac{1}{2} \left(\frac{\partial^2}{\partial s^2} F(\bar{x}_s, \lambda_s)\Big|_{s=\sigma} \right).$$

Each quantity $F(\bar{x}_0, \lambda_0)$, y_1 and y_2 is a finite sum which is evaluated using interval arithmetics. Let w_0, w_1 and w_2 such that

$$\|AF(\bar{x}_0, \lambda_0)\|_X \leq w_0$$
$$\|Ay_1\|_X \leq w_1$$
$$\|Ay_2\|_X \leq w_2.$$

Hence, set Y_0 such that

$$Y_0 \stackrel{\text{def}}{=} w_0 + w_1 + w_2 \tag{2.41}$$

so that $\|AF(\bar{x}_s, \lambda_s)\|_X \leq Y_0$ for all $s \in [0, 1]$.

The Z_0 bound. Let $B \stackrel{\text{def}}{=} I - AA^\dagger$, which we express as

$$B = \begin{pmatrix} B_{\omega,0} & B_{a,0} \\ B_{\omega,1} & B_{a,1} \end{pmatrix}.$$

Since $B \stackrel{\text{def}}{=} I - AA^\dagger$, then $[(Bc)_1]_k = 0$ for $|k| \geq m$ and $c \in X$. Define

$$Z_0^{(0)} \stackrel{\text{def}}{=} |B_{\omega,0}| + \left(\max_{|k|<m} \frac{|(B_{a,0})_k|}{\nu^{|k|}} \right) \tag{2.42}$$

$$Z_1^{(0)} \stackrel{\text{def}}{=} \sum_{|k|<m} |(B_{\omega,1})_k| \nu^{|k|} + \max_{|n|<m} \frac{1}{\nu^{|n|}} \sum_{|k|<m} |(B_{a,1})_{k,n}| \nu^{|k|}. \tag{2.43}$$

Now, recalling (2.36) and Lemma 2.19, we have that for any $c = (c_0, c_1) \in B_1(0) \subset X$,

$$|(Bc)_0| = \left| B_{\omega,0} c_0 + \sum_{k\in\mathbb{Z}} (B_{a,0})_k (c_1)_k \right| \leq |B_{\omega,0}| + \|B_{a,0}\|_{\infty,\nu^{-1}} = Z_0^{(0)}.$$

Recalling Corollary 2.1 and (2.38), we get that

$$\|(Bc)_1\|_{1,\nu} = \|B_{\omega,1}c_0 + B_{a,1}c_1\|_{1,\nu} \leq \|B_{\omega,1}\|_{1,\nu} + \|B_{a,1}\|_{B(\ell^1_\nu,\ell^1_\nu)} \leq Z_1^{(0)}.$$

Finally, setting

$$Z_0 \stackrel{\text{def}}{=} \max\left(Z_0^{(0)}, Z_1^{(0)}\right) \tag{2.44}$$

we get that

$$\|I - AA^\dagger\|_{B(X,X)} = \sup_{c\in B_1(0)} \|Bc\|_X = \sup_{c\in B_1(0)} \max\left(|(Bc)_0|, \|(Bc)_1\|_{1,\nu}\right) \leq Z_0.$$

The Z_1 bound. Recall from (2.7) that Z_1 is a bound satisfying

$$\|A[D_xF(\bar{x}_0,\lambda_0) - A^\dagger]\|_{B(X,X)} \leq Z_1$$

Let $c = (c_0, c_1) \in B_1(0)$ and set

$$z \stackrel{\text{def}}{=} (D_xF(\bar{x}_0,\lambda_0) - A^\dagger)c.$$

Denote $z = (z_0, z_1)$. Then, if $n < m$, we get that $z_0 = 0$ because the phase condition (2.22) depends only on the Fourier coefficients $(a_k)_{|k|\leq n}$. Given $k \in \mathbb{Z}$,

$$\begin{aligned}((D_xF(\bar{x}_0,\lambda_0)c)_1)_k &= \mu_k(\bar{\omega}_0,\lambda_0)(c_1)_k + \frac{\partial \mu_k}{\partial \omega}(\bar{\omega}_0,\lambda_0)c_0(\bar{a}_0)_k \\ &\quad + \frac{1}{3} i\varepsilon k(\bar{a}_0^3)_k c_0 + i\varepsilon k\bar{\omega}_0(\bar{a}_0^2 c_1)_k.\end{aligned}$$

Therefore, since $(\bar{a}_0)_k = 0$ for all $|k| \geq m$,

$$(z_1)_k = \begin{cases} i\varepsilon k(\bar{a}_0^2 c_1^{(I)})_k \bar{\omega}_0, & |k| < m \\ \frac{1}{3} i\varepsilon k(\bar{a}_0^3)_k c_0 + i\varepsilon k\bar{\omega}_0(\bar{a}_0^2 c_1)_k, & |k| \geq m \end{cases}$$

From Corollary 2.2, for all $|k| < m$

$$|(z_1)_k| \leq \zeta_k \stackrel{\text{def}}{=} \varepsilon|k|\bar{\omega}_0 \Psi_k(\bar{a}_0^2). \tag{2.45}$$

Denote $\zeta \stackrel{\text{def}}{=} (\zeta_k)_{|k|<m} \in \mathbb{C}^{2m-1}$. Hence, for $j = 0$,

$$\left|\left(A[D_xF(\bar{x}_0,\lambda_0) - A^\dagger]c\right)_0\right| = |(Az)_0| = |A_{a,0}z_1| \leq Z_0^{(1)} \stackrel{\text{def}}{=} |A_{a,0}^{(m)}|\zeta,$$

while for $j=1$,

$$\left\|\left(A[D_xF(\bar{x}_0,\lambda_0)-A^\dagger]c\right)_1\right\|_{1,\nu}=\|(Az)_1\|_{1,\nu}=\|A_{a,1}z_1\|_{1,\nu}$$
$$\le Z_1^{(1)}\stackrel{\rm def}{=}\sum_{k=-m+1}^{m-1}\left(|A_{a,1}^{(m)}|\zeta\right)_k\nu^{|k|}+\frac{\varepsilon}{3}\sum_{|k|=m}^{3m-3}\left|\frac{k}{\mu_k(\bar{\omega}_0,\lambda_0)}(\bar{a}_0^3)_k\right|\nu^{|k|}$$
$$+\frac{\varepsilon\bar{\omega}_0}{m\bar{\omega}_0^2-\frac{(|\lambda_0|+1)}{m}}(\|\bar{a}\|_{1,\nu})^2,$$

using that $\|\bar{a}_0^2c_1\|_{1,\nu}\le(\|\bar{a}_0\|_{1,\nu})^2$ and using that

$$\left|\frac{i\varepsilon k\bar{\omega}_0}{\mu_k(\bar{\omega}_0,\lambda_0)}\right|=\frac{1}{|k|}\frac{\varepsilon\bar{\omega}_0}{|-\bar{\omega}_0^2-\varepsilon i\bar{\omega}_0/k-\lambda_0/k^2+e^{-ik\bar{\omega}_0\tau}/k^2|}\le\frac{\varepsilon\bar{\omega}_0}{m\left(\bar{\omega}_0^2-\frac{(|\lambda_0|+1)}{m^2}\right)}.$$

Finally, setting

$$Z_1\stackrel{\rm def}{=}\max\left(Z_0^{(1)},Z_1^{(1)}\right)\tag{2.46}$$

$$\|A[D_xF(\bar{x}_0,\lambda_0)-A^\dagger]\|_{B(X,X)}=$$
$$\sup_{c\in B_1(0)}\max\left(|(Az)_0|,\|(Az)_1\|_{1,\nu}\right)\le\max\left(Z_0^{(1)},Z_1^{(1)}\right)=Z_1.$$

The Z_2 bound. Recall from (2.8) that the bound Z_2 satisfies

$$\|A[D_xF(\bar{x}_s+b,\lambda_s)-D_xF(\bar{x}_0,\lambda_0)]\|_{B(X,X)}\le Z_2(r),\quad\text{for all } b\in B_r(0),\ s\in[0,1].$$

REMARK 2.21. Z_2 can be computed using a bound on the second derivative on F (e.g. see Section 3.3.4 in the paper [**74**]). However, here we choose to compute Z_2 applying the mean-value theorem component-wise.

Given $c=(c_1,c_2)\in B_1(0)\subset X$ and for a fixed $k\in\mathbb{Z}$, denote $h_k(\phi)=D_xg_k(\bar{x}_{\phi s}+\tau b,\lambda_{\phi s})$. For each $k\in\mathbb{Z}$, there exists $t=t(k)\in[0,1]$ such that

$$\begin{aligned}
h_k'(t)&=h_k(1)-h_k(0)\\
&=\left(D_xg_k(\bar{x}_s+b,\lambda_s)-D_xg_k(\bar{x}_0,\lambda_0)\right)c\\
&=(-2k^2(s\Delta_\omega+b_0)c_0-k^2c_0\tau^2(s\Delta_\omega+b_0)e^{-ik(st\Delta_\omega+tb_0+\bar{\omega}_0)\tau})(st\Delta_a+tb_1+\bar{a}_0)_k\\
&+(-2k^2(st\Delta_\omega+tb_0+\bar{\omega}_0)c_0-i\varepsilon kc_0-ikc_0\tau e^{-ik(st\Delta_\omega+tb_0+\bar{\omega}_0)\tau})(s\Delta_a+b_1)_k\\
&+(-2k^2(st\Delta_\omega+tb_0+\bar{\omega}_0)(s\Delta_\omega+b_0)-i\varepsilon k(s\Delta_\omega+b_0)-s\Delta_\lambda\\
&\qquad-ik(s\Delta_\omega+b_0)\tau e^{-ik(st\Delta_\omega+tb_0+\bar{\omega}_0)\tau})(c_1)_k\\
&+i\varepsilon kc_0\left((st\Delta_a+tb_1+\bar{a}_0)^2(s\Delta_a+b_1)\right)_k\\
&+i\varepsilon k(s\Delta_\omega+b_0)\left((st\Delta_a+tb_1+\bar{a}_0)^2c_1\right)_k\\
&+(2i)\varepsilon k(st\Delta_\omega+tb_0+\bar{\omega}_0)\left((st\Delta_a+tb_1+\bar{a}_0)c_1(s\Delta_a+b_1)\right)_k.
\end{aligned}$$

Then, using that $|b_0| \leq r$ and letting $u_1 \stackrel{\text{def}}{=} \frac{1}{r} b_1 \in B_1(0)$

$$\begin{aligned}
|h_k'(t)| &\leq (2k^2(|\Delta_\omega| + r) + k^2\tau^2(|\Delta_\omega| + r))(|\Delta_a| + |u_1|r + |\bar{a}_0|)_k \\
&+ (2k^2(|\Delta_\omega| + r + \bar{\omega}_0) + \varepsilon|k| + |k|\tau)(|\Delta_a| + |u_1|r)_k \\
&+ (2k^2(|\Delta_\omega| + r + \bar{\omega}_0)(|\Delta_\omega| + r) + \varepsilon|k|(|\Delta_\omega| + r) \\
&\qquad\qquad + |\Delta_\lambda| + |k|(|\Delta_\omega| + r)\tau)|(c_1)_k| \\
&+ \varepsilon|k| \left((|\Delta_a| + |u_1|r + |\bar{a}_0|)^2(|\Delta_a| + |u_1|r)\right)_k \\
&+ \varepsilon|k|(|\Delta_\omega| + r)\left((|\Delta_a| + |u_1|r + |\bar{a}_0|)^2|c_1|\right)_k \\
&+ 2\varepsilon|k|(|\Delta_\omega| + r + \bar{\omega}_0)\left((|\Delta_a| + |u_1|r + |\bar{a}_0|)|c_1|(|\Delta_a| + |u_1|r)\right)_k \\
&= (z_2)_k^{(4)} r^3 + (z_2)_k^{(3)} r^2 + (z_2)_k^{(2)} r + (z_2)_k^{(1)},
\end{aligned}$$

where

$$\begin{aligned}
(z_2)_k^{(1)} &= k^2\left(2|\Delta_\omega| + \tau^2|\Delta_\omega|\right)(|\Delta_a| + |\bar{a}_0|)_k + \left(2k^2(|\Delta_\omega| + \bar{\omega}_0) + |k|(\varepsilon + \tau)\right)|(\Delta_a)_k| \\
&+ \left(2k^2(|\Delta_\omega| + \bar{\omega}_0)|\Delta_\omega| + \varepsilon|k||\Delta_\omega| + |\Delta_\lambda| + \tau|k||\Delta_\omega|\right)|(c_1)_k| \\
&+ \varepsilon|k| \left|\left((|\Delta_a| + |\bar{a}_0|)^2(|\Delta_a|)\right)_k\right| + \varepsilon|k||\Delta_\omega| \left|\left((|\Delta_a| + |\bar{a}_0|)^2 c_1\right)_k\right| \\
&+ 2\varepsilon|k|(|\Delta_\omega| + \bar{\omega}_0)\left((|\Delta_a| + |\bar{a}_0|)|\Delta_a||c_1|\right)_k \\
(z_2)_k^{(2)} &= 6\varepsilon|k||\Delta_\omega||(\Delta_a c_1 u_1)_k| + 4\varepsilon|k||\Delta_\omega||(\bar{a}_0 c_1 u_1)_k| + 4\varepsilon|k|\bar{\omega}_0|(\Delta_a c_1 u_1)_k| \\
&+ 2\varepsilon|k|\bar{\omega}_0|(\bar{a}_0 c_1 u_1)_k| + \tau|k||(u_1)_k| + 4k^2|\Delta_\omega||(c_1)_k| + 2|(c_1)_k|k^2\bar{\omega}_0 \\
&+ (\varepsilon + \tau)|k||(c_1)_k| + \varepsilon|k||(u_1)_k| + 4k^2|\Delta_\omega||(u_1)_k| \\
&+ k^2\tau^2(|\bar{a}_0| + |\Delta_a|)_k + 2k^2\bar{\omega}_0|(u_1)_k| + 4k^2|(\Delta_a)_k| + k^2\tau^2|\Delta_\omega||(u_1)_k| \\
&+ 3\varepsilon|k||(u_1\Delta_a^2)_k| + \varepsilon|k||(u_1\bar{a}_0^2)_k| + 3\varepsilon|k||(c_1\Delta_a^2)_k| + \varepsilon|k||(c_1\bar{a}_0^2)_k| + 2k^2|\bar{a}_0| \\
&+ 4\varepsilon|k||(\Delta_a\bar{a}_0 u_1)_k| + 4\varepsilon|k||(\Delta_a\bar{a}_0 c_1)_k| \\
(z_2)_k^{(3)} &= k^2\tau^2|(u_1)_k| + 4k^2|(u_1)_k| + 2k^2|(c_1)_k| + 3\varepsilon|k||(\Delta_a u_1^2)_k| + 2\varepsilon|k||(\bar{a}_0 u_1^2)_k| \\
&+ 3\varepsilon|k||\Delta_\omega||(c_1 u_1^2)_k| + 6\varepsilon|k||(\Delta_a c_1 u_1)_k| + 4\varepsilon|k||(\bar{a}_0 c_1 u_1)_k| \\
&+ 2\varepsilon|k|\bar{\omega}_0|(c_1 u_1^2)_k| \\
(z_2)_k^{(4)} &= \varepsilon|k|\left(3|(c_1 u_1^2)_k| + |(u_1^3)_k|\right).
\end{aligned}$$

Let us define the operators $\tilde{A}_{a,0}$, $\tilde{B}_{a,0}$, $\tilde{A}_{a,1}$ and $\tilde{B}_{a,1}$ by

$$\begin{aligned}
\tilde{A}_{a,0} &= \left\{|k||(A_{a,0}^{(m)})_k|\right\}_{|k|<m} & \tilde{B}_{a,0} &= \left\{k^2|(A_{a,0}^{(m)})_k|\right\}_{|k|<m} \\
\tilde{A}_{a,1} &= \{|j||(A_{a,1})_{k,j}|\}_{k,j\in\mathbb{Z}} & \tilde{B}_{a,1} &= \{j^2|(A_{a,1})_{k,j}|\}_{k,j\in\mathbb{Z}}.
\end{aligned}$$

Given $j = 0, 1$, denote $\|\cdot\|_j$ to be $|\cdot|$ if $j = 0$ and $\|\cdot\|_{1,\nu}$ if $j = 1$. Moreover, given $j = 0, 1$, denote $\|\cdot\|_{B(j,j)}$ to be $\|\cdot\|_{\infty,\nu^{-1}}$ if $j = 0$ and $\|\cdot\|_{B(\ell^1_\nu,\ell^1_\nu)}$ if $j = 1$.

Then, for $j = 0, 1$,

$$
\begin{aligned}
\|A_{a,j} z_2^{(1)}\|_j \le Z_2^{(1,j)} & \\
\stackrel{\text{def}}{=} & \left(2+\tau^2\right) |\Delta_\omega| \|\tilde{B}_{a,j}(|\Delta_a| + |\bar{a}_0|)\|_j + 2(|\Delta_\omega| + \bar{\omega}_0)\|\tilde{B}_{a,j}|\Delta_a|\|_j \\
& + (\varepsilon+\tau)\|\tilde{A}_{a,j}|\Delta_a|\|_j + 2(|\Delta_\omega| + \bar{\omega}_0)|\Delta_\omega|\|\tilde{B}_{a,j}\|_{B(j,j)} \\
& + (\varepsilon+\tau)|\Delta_\omega|\|\tilde{A}_{a,j}\|_{B(j,j)} + |\Delta_\lambda|\|A_{a,j}\|_{B(j,j)} + \varepsilon\|\tilde{A}_{a,j}\|_{B(j,j)}\||\Delta_a| \\
& + |\bar{a}_0|\|_{1,\nu}^2 \|\Delta_a\|_{1,\nu} + \varepsilon|\Delta_\omega|\|\tilde{A}_{a,j}\|_{B(j,j)}\||\Delta_a| + |\bar{a}_0|\|_{1,\nu}^2 \\
& + 2\varepsilon(|\Delta_\omega| + \bar{\omega}_0)\|\tilde{A}_{a,j}\|_{B(j,j)}\||\Delta_a| + |\bar{a}_0|\|_{1,\nu}\|\Delta_a\|_{1,\nu} \\
\|A_{a,j} z_2^{(2)}\|_j \le Z_2^{(2,j)} & \\
\stackrel{\text{def}}{=} & \ 6\varepsilon|\Delta_\omega|\|\tilde{A}_{a,j}\|_{B(j,j)}\|\Delta_a\|_{1,\nu} + 4\varepsilon|\Delta_\omega|\|\tilde{A}_{a,j}\|_{B(j,j)}\|\bar{a}_0\|_{1,\nu} \\
& + 4\varepsilon\bar{\omega}_0\|\tilde{A}_{a,j}\|_{B(j,j)}\|\Delta_a\|_{1,\nu} + 2\varepsilon\bar{\omega}_0\|\tilde{A}_{a,j}\|_{B(j,j)}\|\bar{a}_0\|_{1,\nu} + \tau\|\tilde{A}_{a,j}\|_{B(j,j)} \\
& + 4|\Delta_\omega|\|\tilde{B}_{a,j}\|_{B(j,j)} + 2\bar{\omega}_0\|\tilde{B}_{a,j}\|_{B(j,j)} + (\varepsilon+\tau)\|\tilde{A}_{a,j}\|_{B(j,j)} \\
& + \varepsilon\|\tilde{A}_{a,j}\|_{B(j,j)} + 4|\Delta_\omega|\|\tilde{B}_{a,j}\|_{B(j,j)} + \tau^2\|\tilde{B}_{a,j}\|_{B(j,j)}\||\Delta_a| + |\bar{a}_0|\|_{1,\nu} \\
& + 2\bar{\omega}_0\|\tilde{B}_{a,j}\|_{B(j,j)} + 4\|\tilde{B}_{a,j}\|_{B(j,j)}\||\Delta_a\|_{1,\nu} + \tau^2|\Delta_\omega|\|\tilde{B}_{a,j}\|_{B(j,j)} \\
& + 6\varepsilon\|\tilde{A}_{a,j}\|_{B(j,j)}\|\Delta_a\|_{1,\nu}^2 + 2\varepsilon\|\tilde{A}_{a,j}\|_{B(j,j)}\|\bar{a}_0\|_{1,\nu}^2 \\
& + 2\|\tilde{B}_{a,j}\|_{B(j,j)}\|\bar{a}_0\|_{1,\nu} + 4\varepsilon\|\tilde{A}_{a,j}\|_{B(j,j)}\|\Delta_a\|_{1,\nu}\|\bar{a}_0\|_{1,\nu} \\
\|A_{a,j} z_2^{(3)}\|_j \le Z_2^{(3,j)} & \\
\stackrel{\text{def}}{=} & \ \tau^2\|\tilde{B}_{a,j}\|_{B(j,j)} + 4\|\tilde{B}_{a,j}\|_{B(j,j)} + 2\|\tilde{B}_{a,j}\|_{B(j,j)} \\
& + 3\varepsilon\|\tilde{A}_{a,j}\|_{B(j,j)}\|\Delta_a\|_{1,\nu} + 2\varepsilon\|\tilde{A}_{a,j}\|_{B(j,j)}\|\bar{a}_0\|_{1,\nu} \\
& + 3\varepsilon|\Delta_\omega|\|\tilde{A}_{a,j}\|_{B(j,j)} + 6\varepsilon\|\tilde{A}_{a,j}\|_{B(j,j)}\|\Delta_a\|_{1,\nu} \\
& + 4\varepsilon\|\tilde{A}_{a,j}\|_{B(j,j)}\|\bar{a}_0\|_{1,\nu} + 2\varepsilon\bar{\omega}_0\|\tilde{A}_{a,j}\|_{B(j,j)} \\
\|A_{a,j} z_2^{(4)}\|_j \le Z_2^{(4,j)} & \\
\stackrel{\text{def}}{=} & \ 4\varepsilon\|\tilde{A}_{a,j}\|_{B(j,j)}.
\end{aligned}
$$

For $i = 1, 2, 3, 4$, set

$$
Z_2^{(j)} = \max\left(Z_2^{(j,0)}, Z_2^{(j,1)}\right)
$$

so that we define

$$
Z_2(r) \stackrel{\text{def}}{=} Z_2^{(4)} r^3 + Z_2^{(3)} r^2 + Z_2^{(2)} r + Z_2^{(1)}. \tag{2.47}
$$

From this, we conclude that

$$
\begin{aligned}
|A_{a,0}\left(D_x g(\bar{x}_s + b, \lambda_s) - D_x g(\bar{x}_0, \lambda_0)\right) c| &\le Z_2(r) \\
\|A_{a,1}\left(D_x g(\bar{x}_s + b, \lambda_s) - D_x g(\bar{x}_0, \lambda_0)\right) c\|_{1,\nu} &\le Z_2(r),
\end{aligned}
$$

and therefore

$$\begin{aligned}&\|A[D_xF(\bar{x}_s+b,\lambda_s)-D_xF(\bar{x}_0,\lambda_0)]c\|_X\\&=\left\|\begin{pmatrix}A_{\omega,0} & A_{a,0}\\ A_{\omega,1} & A_{a,1}\end{pmatrix}\begin{pmatrix}0\\(D_xg(\bar{x}_s+b,\lambda_s)-D_xg(\bar{x}_0,\lambda_0))\,c\end{pmatrix}\right\|_X\\&=\max\big(\,|A_{a,0}\,(D_xg(\bar{x}_s+b,\lambda_s)-D_xg(\bar{x}_0,\lambda_0))\,c|\,,\\&\qquad\|A_{a,1}\,(D_xg(\bar{x}_s+b,\lambda_s)-D_xg(\bar{x}_0,\lambda_0))\,c\|_{1,\nu}\,\big)\\&\le Z_2(r).\end{aligned}$$

Combining (2.41), (2.44), (2.46) and (2.47), the radii polynomial is defined by

$$p(r)\stackrel{\text{def}}{=}Z_2^{(4)}r^4+Z_2^{(3)}r^3+Z_2^{(2)}r^2+\left(Z_2^{(1)}+Z_1+Z_0-1\right)r+Y_0. \tag{2.48}$$

2.5.7. *Proof of existence of periodic solutions for Nussbaum's equation.* Using the radii polynomial approach we could prove the following two theorems.

THEOREM 2.22. *Fix $\tau=2$ and $\varepsilon=0.15$. Then there is a branch of periodic solution of Nussbaum's equation* (2.18) *parameterized by the parameter λ. Given a periodic solution $y(t)$ on the branch, letting p its period, $y(t)$ satisfies the symmetry property*

$$y(t+p/2)=-y(t),\qquad \textit{for all } t\in\mathbb{R}. \tag{2.49}$$

The continuous range of parameter for which the proof of existence is performed is $\lambda\in[-3.8521,0.65]$. The global branch is a C^∞ function of the parameter λ. The continuous range of periods of the periodic solutions over the branch contains the interval $p\in[3.7,21.5]$.

PROOF. The MATLAB program `script_proof1.m` available at [**76**] computes the coefficients of the radii polynomial $p(r)$ given by (2.48), and as a parameter continuation is performed, the code adapts the step size Δ_λ and applies successfully the radii polynomial approach (Theorem 2.6) to show the existence of a global C^∞ branch of periodic solutions. Throughout the whole continuation, the number of Fourier coefficients used for the proof is fixed to be $m=110$. Along the branch, we make sure that $\bar{x}_s\in X_{sym}$ and that the approximate inverse A satisfies the condition (2.30), that is $AF:X_{sym}\times\mathbb{R}\to X_{sym}$. By Lemma 2.15, at a given parameter value λ, the solution $\tilde{x}=(\tilde{\omega},\tilde{a})\in X_{sym}$. Hence, $\tilde{\omega}\in\mathbb{R}$ (yielding the period $\tilde{p}=\frac{2\pi}{\tilde{\omega}}\in\mathbb{R}$) and the Fourier coefficients $\tilde{a}=(\tilde{a}_k)_{k\in\mathbb{Z}}$ satisfy that $\tilde{a}_{2k}=0$ for all $k\in\mathbb{Z}$. Consider the periodic solution $\tilde{y}(t)$ associated to $(\tilde{\omega},\tilde{a})$

$$\tilde{y}(t)=\sum_{\substack{k\in\mathbb{Z}\\k\text{ odd}}}\tilde{a}_ke^{ik\frac{2\pi}{\tilde{p}}t}.$$

Hence,

$$\tilde{y}(t+\tilde{p}/2)=\sum_{\substack{k\in\mathbb{Z}\\k\text{ odd}}}\tilde{a}_ke^{ik\frac{2\pi}{\tilde{p}}(t+\tilde{p}/2)}=\sum_{\substack{k\in\mathbb{Z}\\k\text{ odd}}}\tilde{a}_k(-1)^ke^{ik\frac{2\pi}{\tilde{p}}t}=-\sum_{\substack{k\in\mathbb{Z}\\k\text{ odd}}}\tilde{a}_ke^{ik\frac{2\pi}{\tilde{p}}t}=-\tilde{y}(t).$$

The global branch of periodic solution is a C^∞ function of λ by Lemma 2.7. □

THEOREM 2.23. *Fix $\tau=5$ and $\varepsilon=0.25$. Then there is a branch of periodic solution of Nussbaum's equation* (2.18) *parameterized by the parameter λ. Given a periodic solution $y(t)$ on the branch, letting p its period, $y(t)$ satisfies the symmetry*

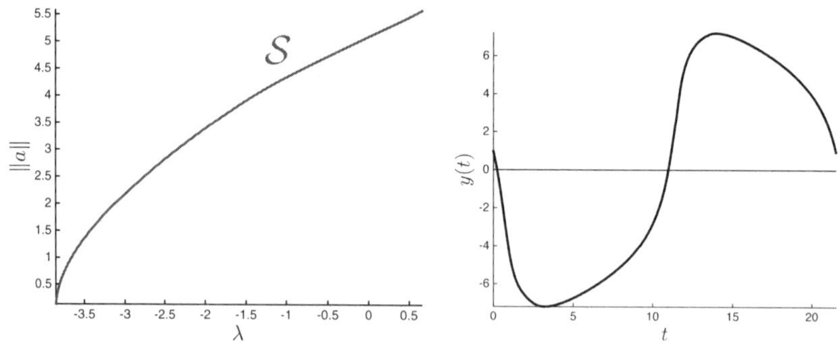

FIGURE 18. **(Left)** As proven in Theorem 2.22, a branch of periodic solutions of Nussbaum's equation (2.18) parameterized by the parameter λ. **(Right)** The graph of the most right periodic solution on the branch plotted over its period.

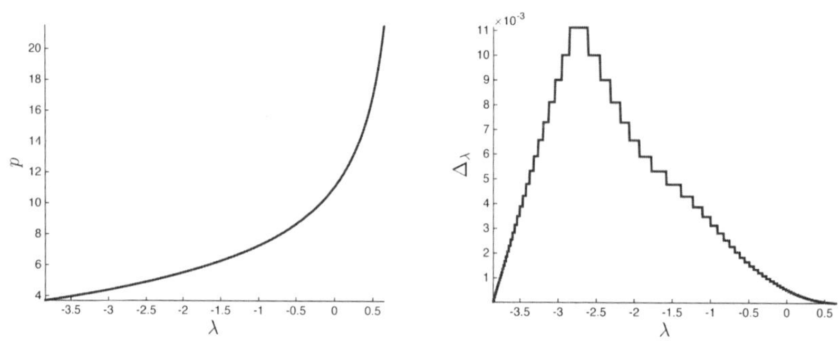

FIGURE 19. **(Left)** Continuous range of periods of the periodic solutions as a function of λ along the branch of Theorem 2.22. **(Right)** The adaptive value of Δ_λ as the parameter λ varies along the branch of Theorem 2.22.

property (2.49).*The continuous range of parameter for which the proof of existence is performed is* $\lambda \in [-4.8234, -0.476]$. *The global branch is a* C^∞ *function of the parameter* λ. *The continuous range of periods of the periodic solutions over the branch contains the interval* $p \in [3.15942, 5.253625]$.

PROOF. The proof is similar as the proof of Theorem 2.22. In this case, the number of Fourier coefficients used to perform the proof is $m = 20$. The proof is computer-assisted and terminates by executing the MATLAB program `script_proof2.m` available at [**76**]. □

In [**75**], similar results were obtained for Nussbaum's equation (2.18). The differences are that in [**75**], proofs were performed in a weighted ℓ^∞ space (as opposed to a weighted ℓ^1 here), and the proofs were obtained at discrete parameter values of λ.

2.6. Wright's Equation. As mentioned in Section 1, Jones Conjecture reformulated as in Conjecture 1.2 requires studying a global continuous branch of

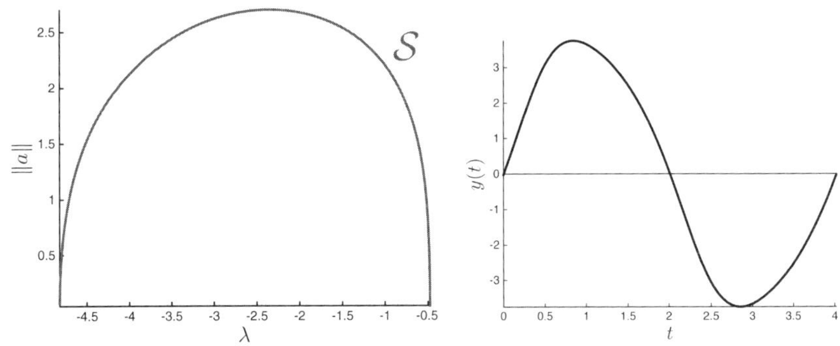

FIGURE 20. **(Left)** As proven in Theorem 2.23, a branch of symmetric periodic solutions of Nussbaum's equation (2.18) parameterized by the parameter λ. **(Right)** The graph of a periodic solution on the branch over the interval $[0, p]$ with p its period.

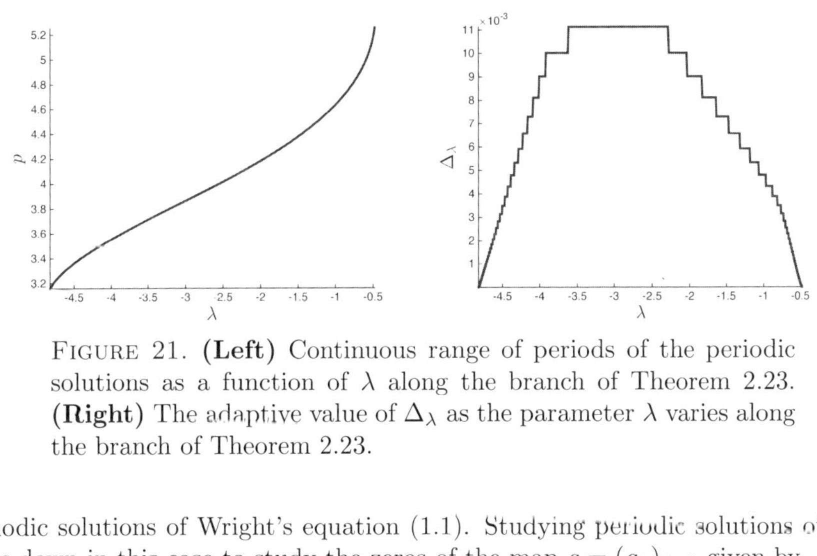

FIGURE 21. **(Left)** Continuous range of periods of the periodic solutions as a function of λ along the branch of Theorem 2.23. **(Right)** The adaptive value of Δ_λ as the parameter λ varies along the branch of Theorem 2.23.

periodic solutions of Wright's equation (1.1). Studying periodic solutions of (1.1) boils down in this case to study the zeros of the map $g = (g_k)_{k \in \mathbb{Z}}$ given by

$$g_k \stackrel{\text{def}}{=} \left(ik\omega + \alpha e^{-ik\omega}\right) a_k + \alpha \sum_{k_1+k_2=k} e^{-ik_1\omega} a_{k_1} a_{k_2}.$$

In this case the parameter is set to be $\lambda = \alpha$. Using the radii polynomial approach, a rigorous continuation method was used in [**12**] to study rigorously the behaviour of the solutions on the branch $\mathcal{F}_0$. The proofs were performed in a different Banach space, that is a weighted ℓ^∞ space. This means that the estimates are different than the one presented above in the weighted ℓ^1 space. Recall from Section 1 the notation $\mathcal{F}_0$, which denotes the branch of periodic solutions of Wright's equation (1.1) which bifurcates out of a supercritical Hopf bifurcation from the trivial solution at $\alpha = \pi/2$. Using a rigorous continuation method, as the one introduced in details for Nussbaum's equation in Section 2.5, here is the main result of [**12**].

THEOREM 2.24. *Let* $\varepsilon = 7.3165 \times 10^{-4}$. *Then* $\mathcal{F}_0$ *is a branch parameterized by* λ *over the range* $\alpha \in \left[\frac{\pi}{2} + \varepsilon, 2.3\right]$, *and so* $\mathcal{F}_0$ *does not have any fold over* $\alpha \in \left[\frac{\pi}{2} + \varepsilon, 2.3\right]$.

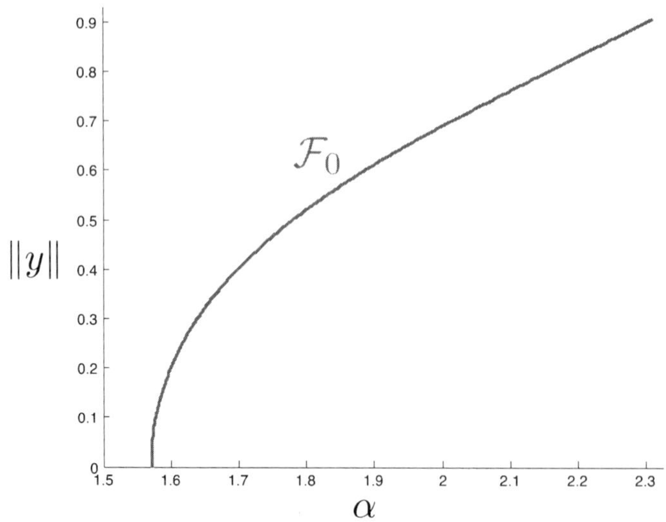

FIGURE 22. Rigorous study of a part of $\mathcal{F}_0$.

References

[1] S. Kakutani and L. Markus, *On the non-linear difference-differential equation* $y'(t) = [A - By(t-\tau)]y(t)$, Contributions to the theory of nonlinear oscillations, Vol. IV, Annals of Mathematics Studies, no. 41, Princeton University Press, Princeton, N.J., 1958, pp. 1–18. MR0101953

[2] James L. Kaplan and James A. Yorke, *On the stability of a periodic solution of a differential delay equation*, SIAM J. Math. Anal. **6** (1975), 268–282, DOI 10.1137/0506028. MR0361367

[3] James L. Kaplan and James A. Yorke, *On the nonlinear differential delay equation* $x'(t) = -f(x(t), x(t-1))$, J. Differential Equations **23** (1977), no. 2, 293–314, DOI 10.1016/0022-0396(77)90132-2. MR0427777

[4] Roger D. Nussbaum, *The range of periods of periodic solutions of* $x'(t) = -\alpha f(x(t-1))$, J. Math. Anal. Appl. **58** (1977), no. 2, 280–292, DOI 10.1016/0022-247X(77)90206-2. MR0445086

[5] Roger D. Nussbaum, *Wright's equation has no solutions of period four*, Proc. Roy. Soc. Edinburgh Sect. A **113** (1989), no. 3-4, 281–288, DOI 10.1017/S0308210500024148. MR1037733

[6] Jack K. Hale and Sjoerd M. Verduyn Lunel, *Introduction to functional-differential equations*, Applied Mathematical Sciences, vol. 99, Springer-Verlag, New York, 1993. MR1243878

[7] Odo Diekmann, Stephan A. van Gils, Sjoerd M. Verduyn Lunel, and Hans-Otto Walther, *Delay equations*, Applied Mathematical Sciences, vol. 110, Springer-Verlag, New York, 1995. Functional, complex, and nonlinear analysis. MR1345150

[8] Hans-Otto Walther, *Topics in delay differential equations*, Jahresber. Dtsch. Math.-Ver. **116** (2014), no. 2, 87–114, DOI 10.1365/s13291-014-0086-6. MR3210290

[9] Roger D. Nussbaum, *Functional differential equations*, Handbook of dynamical systems, Vol. 2, North-Holland, Amsterdam, 2002, pp. 461–499, DOI 10.1016/S1874-575X(02)80031-5. MR1901061

[10] Roger D. Nussbaum, *Periodic solutions of analytic functional differential equations are analytic*, Michigan Math. J. **20** (1973), 249–255. MR0322315

[11] A. M. Turing, *The chemical basis of morphogenesis*, Philos. Trans. Roy. Soc. London Ser. B **237** (1952), no. 641, 37–72. MR3363444

[12] Jean-Philippe Lessard, *Recent advances about the uniqueness of the slowly oscillating periodic solutions of Wright's equation*, J. Differential Equations **248** (2010), no. 5, 992–1016, DOI 10.1016/j.jde.2009.11.008. MR2592879

[13] E. M. Wright, *A non-linear difference-differential equation*, J. Reine Angew. Math. **194** (1955), 66–87, DOI 10.1515/crll.1955.194.66. MR0072363

[14] G. Stephen Jones, *The existence of periodic solutions of $f'(x) = -\alpha f(x-1)\{1+f(x)\}$*, J. Math. Anal. Appl. **5** (1962), 435–450, DOI 10.1016/0022-247X(62)90017-3. MR0141837

[15] G. Stephen Jones, *On the nonlinear differential-difference equation $f'(x) = -\alpha f(x-1)\{1+f(x)\}$*, J. Math. Anal. Appl. **4** (1962), 440–469, DOI 10.1016/0022-247X(62)90041-0. MR0151690

[16] Hans-Otto Walther, *The 2-dimensional attractor of $x'(t) = -\mu x(t) + f(x(t-1))$*, Mem. Amer. Math. Soc. **113** (1995), no. 544, vi+76. MR1230775

[17] Shui Nee Chow and John Mallet-Paret, *Integral averaging and bifurcation*, J. Differential Equations **26** (1977), no. 1, 112–159, DOI 10.1016/0022-0396(77)90101-2. MR0488151

[18] Benjamin Tolentino Regala, *Periodic solutions and stable manifolds of generic delay differential equations*, ProQuest LLC, Ann Arbor, MI, 1989. Thesis (Ph.D.)–Brown University. MR2637673

[19] Xianwen Xie, *Uniqueness and stability of slowly oscillating periodic solutions of differential delay equations*, ProQuest LLC, Ann Arbor, MI, 1991. Thesis (Ph.D.)–Rutgers The State University of New Jersey - New Brunswick. MR2687247

[20] Xianwen Xie, *Uniqueness and stability of slowly oscillating periodic solutions of delay equations with unbounded nonlinearity*, J. Differential Equations **103** (1993), no. 2, 350–374, DOI 10.1006/jdeq.1993.1054. MR1221910

[21] Jonathan Jaquette, Jean-Philippe Lessard, and Konstantin Mischaikow, *Stability and uniqueness of slowly oscillating periodic solutions to Wright's equation*, J. Differential Equations **263** (2017), no. 11, 7263–7286, DOI 10.1016/j.jde.2017.08.018. MR3705681

[22] Jan Bouwe van den Berg and Jonathan Jaquette. A proof of Wright's conjecture. To appear in J. Differential Equations, 2018.

[23] Balázs Bánhelyi, Tibor Csendes, Tibor Krisztin, and Arnold Neumaier, *Global attractivity of the zero solution for Wright's equation*, SIAM J. Appl. Dyn. Syst. **13** (2014), no. 1, 537–563, DOI 10.1137/120904226. MR3183042

[24] Jan Bouwe van den Berg and Jean-Philippe Lessard, *Rigorous numerics in dynamics*, Notices Amer. Math. Soc. **62** (2015), no. 9, 1057–1061, DOI 10.1090/noti1276. MR3444942

[25] R. D. Nussbaum, *Asymptotic analysis of functional-differential equations and solutions of long period*, Arch. Rational Mech. Anal. **81** (1983), no. 4, 373–397, DOI 10.1007/BF00250861. MR683196

[26] K. P. Hadeler, *Effective computation of periodic orbits and bifurcation diagrams in delay equations*, Numer. Math. **34** (1980), no. 4, 457–467, DOI 10.1007/BF01403681. MR577410

[27] Roger D. Nussbaum, *Periodic solutions of autonomous functional differential equations*, Bull. Amer. Math. Soc. **79** (1973), 811–814, DOI 10.1090/S0002-9904-1973-13330-0. MR0322314

[28] Shui Nee Chow, *Existence of periodic solutions of autonomous functional differential equations*, J. Differential Equations **15** (1974), 350–378, DOI 10.1016/0022-0396(74)90084-9. MR0336003

[29] J. Mawhin, *Periodic solutions of nonlinear functional differential equations*, J. Differential Equations **10** (1971), 240–261, DOI 10.1016/0022-0396(71)90049-0. MR0294823

[30] Roger D. Nussbaum, *Uniqueness and nonuniqueness for periodic solutions of $x'(t) = -g(x(t-1))$*, J. Differential Equations **34** (1979), no. 1, 25–54, DOI 10.1016/0022-0396(79)90016-0. MR549582

[31] Dietmar Saupe, *Global bifurcation of periodic solutions to some autonomous differential delay equations*, Appl. Math. Comput. **13** (1983), no. 1-2, 185–211, DOI 10.1016/0096-3003(83)90037-1. MR710357

[32] John Mallet-Paret and Roger D. Nussbaum, *Global continuation and asymptotic behaviour for periodic solutions of a differential-delay equation*, Ann. Mat. Pura Appl. (4) **145** (1986), 33–128, DOI 10.1007/BF01790539. MR886709

[33] Masato Iida, Masayasu Mimura, and Hirokazu Ninomiya, *Diffusion, cross-diffusion and competitive interaction*, J. Math. Biol. **53** (2006), no. 4, 617–641, DOI 10.1007/s00285-006-0013-2. MR2251792

[34] Maxime Breden, Jean-Philippe Lessard, and Matthieu Vanicat, *Global bifurcation diagrams of steady states of systems of PDEs via rigorous numerics: a 3-component reaction-diffusion system*, Acta Appl. Math. **128** (2013), 113–152, DOI 10.1007/s10440-013-9823-6. MR3125637

[35] E. J. Doedel, W. Govaerts, Yu. A. Kuznetsov, and A. Dhooge, *Numerical continuation of branch points of equilibria and periodic orbits*, Internat. J. Bifur. Chaos Appl. Sci. Engrg. **15** (2005), no. 3, 841–860, DOI 10.1142/S0218127405012491. MR2136749

[36] John Guckenheimer and M. Drew LaMar, *Periodic orbit continuation in multiple time scale systems*, Numerical continuation methods for dynamical systems, Underst. Complex Syst., Springer, Dordrecht, 2007, pp. 253–267, DOI 10.1007/978-1-4020-6356-5_8. MR2359334

[37] Mark J. Friedman and Eusebius J. Doedel, *Numerical computation and continuation of invariant manifolds connecting fixed points*, SIAM J. Numer. Anal. **28** (1991), no. 3, 789–808, DOI 10.1137/0728042. MR1098418

[38] Eusebius J. Doedel and Mark J. Friedman, *Numerical computation of heteroclinic orbits*, J. Comput. Appl. Math. **26** (1989), no. 1-2, 155–170, DOI 10.1016/0377-0427(89)90153-2. Continuation techniques and bifurcation problems. MR1007358

[39] E. J. Doedel, M. J. Friedman, and B. I. Kunin, *Successive continuation for locating connecting orbits*, Numer. Algorithms **14** (1997), no. 1-3, 103–124, DOI 10.1023/A:1019152611342. Dynamical numerical analysis (Atlanta, GA, 1995). MR1456497

[40] Maciej J. Capiński and J. D. Mireles James, *Validated computation of heteroclinic sets*, SIAM J. Appl. Dyn. Syst. **16** (2017), no. 1, 375–409, DOI 10.1137/16M1060674. MR3606406

[41] Alan R. Champneys and Björn Sandstede, *Numerical computation of coherent structures*, Numerical continuation methods for dynamical systems, Underst. Complex Syst., Springer, Dordrecht, 2007, pp. 331–358, DOI 10.1007/978-1-4020-6356-5_11. MR2359337

[42] Eusebius Doedel, *AUTO: a program for the automatic bifurcation analysis of autonomous systems*, Proceedings of the Tenth Manitoba Conference on Numerical Mathematics and Computing, Vol. I (Winnipeg, Man., 1980), Congr. Numer. **30** (1981), 265–284. MR635945

[43] A. Dhooge, W. Govaerts, and Yu. A. Kuznetsov, *MATCONT: a MATLAB package for numerical bifurcation analysis of ODEs*, ACM Trans. Math. Software **29** (2003), no. 2, 141–164, DOI 10.1145/779359.779362. MR2000880

[44] Wolf-Jürgen Beyn, Alan Champneys, Eusebius Doedel, Willy Govaerts, Yuri A. Kuznetsov, and Björn Sandstede, *Numerical continuation, and computation of normal forms*, Handbook of dynamical systems, Vol. 2, North-Holland, Amsterdam, 2002, pp. 149–219, DOI 10.1016/S1874-575X(02)80025-X. MR1900655

[45] Eusebius J. Doedel, *Lecture notes on numerical analysis of nonlinear equations*, Numerical continuation methods for dynamical systems, Underst. Complex Syst., Springer, Dordrecht, 2007, pp. 1–49, DOI 10.1007/978-1-4020-6356-5_1. MR2359327

[46] H. B. Keller, *Lectures on numerical methods in bifurcation problems*, Tata Institute of Fundamental Research Lectures on Mathematics and Physics, vol. 79, Published for the Tata Institute of Fundamental Research, Bombay; by Springer-Verlag, Berlin, 1987. With notes by A. K. Nandakumaran and Mythily Ramaswamy. MR910499

[47] Carmen Chicone, *Ordinary differential equations with applications*, 2nd ed., Texts in Applied Mathematics, vol. 34, Springer, New York, 2006. MR2224508

[48] J. D. Mireles James, *Polynomial approximation of one parameter families of (un)stable manifolds with rigorous computer assisted error bounds*, Indag. Math. (N.S.) **26** (2015), no. 1, 225–265, DOI 10.1016/j.indag.2014.10.002. MR3281703

[49] J. D. Mireles James, *Fourier-Taylor approximation of unstable manifolds for compact maps: numerical implementation and computer assisted error bounds*, Found. Comput. Math. **17** (2017), no. 6, 1467–1523, DOI 10.1007/s10208-016-9325-9. MR3735860

[50] Michael Plum, *Existence and enclosure results for continua of solutions of parameter-dependent nonlinear boundary value problems*, J. Comput. Appl. Math. **60** (1995), no. 1-2, 187–200, DOI 10.1016/0377-0427(94)00091-E. Linear/nonlinear iterative methods and verification of solution (Matsuyama, 1993). MR1354655

[51] Sarah Day, Jean-Philippe Lessard, and Konstantin Mischaikow, *Validated continuation for equilibria of PDEs*, SIAM J. Numer. Anal. **45** (2007), no. 4, 1398–1424, DOI 10.1137/050645968. MR2338393

[52] Jan Bouwe van den Berg, Jean-Philippe Lessard, and Konstantin Mischaikow, *Global smooth solution curves using rigorous branch following*, Math. Comp. **79** (2010), no. 271, 1565–1584, DOI 10.1090/S0025-5718-10-02325-2. MR2630003

[53] Marcio Gameiro, Jean-Philippe Lessard, and Alessandro Pugliese, *Computation of smooth manifolds via rigorous multi-parameter continuation in infinite dimensions*, Found. Comput. Math. **16** (2016), no. 2, 531–575, DOI 10.1007/s10208-015-9259-7. MR3464215

[54] James M. Ortega, *The Newton-Kantorovich theorem*, Amer. Math. Monthly **75** (1968), 658–660, DOI 10.2307/2313800. MR0231218

[55] Thomas Wanner. Computer-assisted bifurcation diagram validation and applications in materials science. To appear in the Proceedings of Symposia in Applied Mathematics, 2018.

[56] E. N. Lorenz. Irregularity: a fhndamentd property of the atmosphere. *Tellus A*, 36(2):98–110, 1984.

[57] Tibor Csendes (ed.), *Developments in reliable computing*, Kluwer Academic Publishers, Dordrecht, 1999. MR1747254

[58] Gábor Kiss and Jean-Philippe Lessard, *Computational fixed-point theory for differential delay equations with multiple time lags*, J. Differential Equations **252** (2012), no. 4, 3093–3115, DOI 10.1016/j.jde.2011.11.020. MR2871794

[59] Felix E. Browder, *A further generalization of the Schauder fixed point theorem*, Duke Math. J. **32** (1965), 575–578. MR0203719

[60] Roger D. Nussbaum, *The fixed point index and some applications*, Séminaire de Mathématiques Supérieures [Seminar on Higher Mathematics], vol. 94, Presses de l'Université de Montréal, Montreal, QC, 1985. MR791918

[61] John Mallet-Paret, Roger D. Nussbaum, and Panagiotis Paraskevopoulos, *Periodic solutions for functional-differential equations with multiple state-dependent time lags*, Topol. Methods Nonlinear Anal. **3** (1994), no. 1, 101–162, DOI 10.12775/TMNA.1994.006. MR1272890

[62] Paul H. Rabinowitz, *Some global results for nonlinear eigenvalue problems*, J. Functional Analysis **7** (1971), 487–513. MR0301587

[63] Roger D. Nussbaum, *A global bifurcation theorem with applications to functional differential equations*, J. Functional Analysis **19** (1975), no. 4, 319–338. MR0385656

[64] Roger D. Nussbaum, *A Hopf global bifurcation theorem for retarded functional differential equations*, Trans. Amer. Math. Soc. **238** (1978), 139–164, DOI 10.2307/1997801. MR482913

[65] Teruya Minamoto and Mitsuhiro T. Nakao, *A numerical verification method for a periodic solution of a delay differential equation*, J. Comput. Appl. Math. **235** (2010), no. 3, 870–878, DOI 10.1016/j.cam.2010.07.018. MR2719822

[66] Piotr Zgliczynski, *Attracting fixed points for the Kuramoto-Sivashinsky equation: a computer assisted proof*, SIAM J. Appl. Dyn. Syst. **1** (2002), no. 2, 215–235, DOI 10.1137/S111111110240176X. MR1968368

[67] C. M. Groothedde and Jason D. Mireles James. Parameterization method for unstable manifolds of delay differential equations. *Journal of Computational Dynamics*, **4** (2017), no 4, 21-70.

[68] B. Van der Pol. A theory of the amplitude of free and forced triode vibrations. *Radio Review*, 1:701–710, 1920.

[69] Thomas Erneux, *Applied delay differential equations*, Surveys and Tutorials in the Applied Mathematical Sciences, vol. 3, Springer, New York, 2009. MR2498700

[70] Jack Hale, *Theory of functional differential equations*, 2nd ed., Springer-Verlag, New York-Heidelberg, 1977. Applied Mathematical Sciences, Vol. 3. MR0508721

[71] R. B. Grafton, *Periodic solutions of certain Liénard equations with delay*, J. Differential Equations **11** (1972), 519–527, DOI 10.1016/0022-0396(72)90064-2. MR0293207

[72] R. B. Grafton, *A periodicity theorem for autonomous functional differential equations.*, J. Differential Equations **6** (1969), 87–109, DOI 10.1016/0022-0396(69)90119-3. MR0243176

[73] Roger D. Nussbaum, *Periodic solutions of some nonlinear autonomous functional differential equations*, Ann. Mat. Pura Appl. (4) **101** (1974), 263–306, DOI 10.1007/BF02417109. MR0361372

[74] Thomas Wanner, *Topological analysis of the diblock copolymer equation*, Mathematical challenges in a new phase of materials science, Springer Proc. Math. Stat., vol. 166, Springer, [Tokyo], 2016, pp. 27–51, DOI 10.1007/978-4-431-56104-0_2. MR3557602

[75] Gábor Kiss and Jean-Philippe Lessard. Rapidly and slowly oscillating periodic oscillations of a delayed van der pol oscillator. Submitted, 2015.

[76] Jean-Philippe Lessard, MATLAB codes to perform the computer-assisted proofs available at `http://archimede.mat.ulaval.ca/jplessard/AMSnotes/`

McGill University, Department of Mathematics and Statistics, 805 Sherbrooke St W, Montreal, QC H3A 0B9.

Proceedings of Symposia in Applied Mathematics
Volume **74**, 2018
http://dx.doi.org/10.1090/psapm/074/00638

Computer-assisted bifurcation diagram validation and applications in materials science

Thomas Wanner

ABSTRACT. Most differential equation models in the applied sciences involve parameters which often cannot be determined with absolute certainty. It is therefore important to study such models for whole parameter ranges, and in particular, to detect parameter values at which the system behavior changes qualitatively. A first step towards accomplishing this goal has to be the understanding of the set of equilibria or stationary solutions of the model. In this lecture, we demonstrate how rigorous computational techniques can be used to validate bifurcation diagrams, both in finite- and certain infinite-dimensional problems. We focus particularly on the verification of branches, as well as on saddle-node and symmetry-breaking pitchfork bifurcations. Throughout, our approach will be applied to two examples from materials science. On the one hand, we consider lattice dynamical systems, specifically the discrete Allen-Cahn equation. Such systems have been proposed as more realistic models due to the existing underlying discreteness, and unlike their continuum counterparts, lattice models can account for phenomena such as pinning. As our second example, we consider the diblock copolymer model, which models microphase separation.

1. Introduction

Differential equations are one of the central tools in the applied sciences. They model dynamical processes, and their study can lead to a deeper understanding of the underlying laws of nature. During the modeling process, one usually tries to incorporate all the essential dynamical variables into the final differential equation, while input quantities which are considered constant enter as parameters. In this way, most applied models can be described abstractly as a parameter-dependent differential equation of the form

$$\dot{u} = f(\lambda, u) \,, \tag{1.1}$$

where the smooth right-hand side f depends on a possibly vector-valued parameter λ, and on the vector u of dynamical variables. While in theory the study of (1.1) involves fixing the "correct" parameter value λ and then trying to understand the resulting dynamical behavior, in practice the parameter λ often cannot be determined with absolute certainty. It is therefore important to study (1.1) for

2010 *Mathematics Subject Classification.* 35B40, 35B41, 35K55, 65G20, 65G30, 65P30, 74N99.

The author was partially supported by NSF grants DMS-1114923 and DMS-1407087.

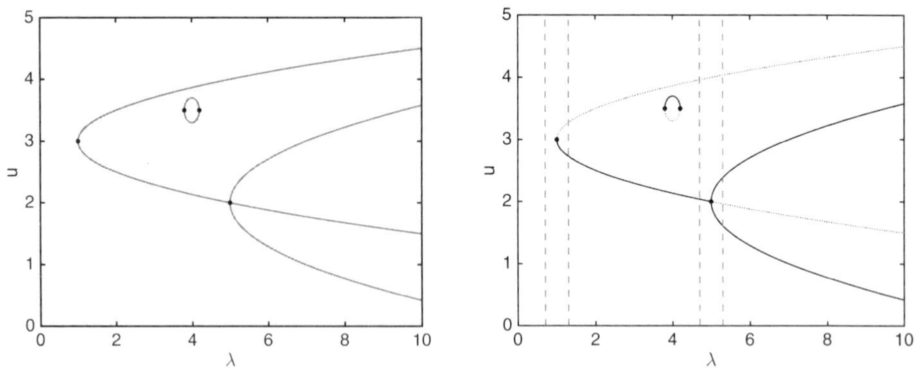

FIGURE 1. Sample bifurcation diagram for a scalar differential equation of the form (1.1). The left panel shows the set of equilibrium solutions, i.e., all solution pairs (λ, u) satisfying (1.2), with the nonlinearity given by (1.3). Black dots indicate the bifurcation points in the diagram, which from left to right correspond to three saddle-node and one pitchfork bifurcation(s). The right panel includes stability information for the associated dynamics of (1.1). Red (dotted line) equilibrium points are unstable, while blue (solid line) ones correspond to stable solutions. The vertical dashed green lines indicate parameter values that are referenced in the text.

whole parameter ranges, and in particular, to detect parameter values at which the system behavior changes significantly.

The first natural step to performing such a parameter-dependent study is of course to restrict one's attention to simpler building blocks for the dynamics, and then build more structure around them through other techniques of the qualitative theory of differential equations. The most basic building blocks are solutions of (1.1) which are constant in time, and these *equilibria*, or *stationary solutions*, satisfy the algebraic equation

$$f(\lambda, u) = 0 \,, \tag{1.2}$$

which is obtained from (1.1) by setting the left-hand side derivative equal to zero. If, for a given function f, we plot all solution pairs (λ, u) of (1.2) in a diagram, we obtain what is usually referred to as a *bifurcation diagram*. Consider for example the function $f : \mathbb{R}^2 \to \mathbb{R}$ given by

(1.3)

$$f(\lambda, u) \;=\; \left(1 + 4(u-3)^2 - \lambda\right)\left(5 + 2(u-2)^2 - \lambda\right)\left((\lambda-4)^2 + \left(u - \frac{7}{2}\right)^2 - \frac{1}{25}\right),$$

whose zero set is partially shown in the left panel of Figure 1. From this bifurcation diagram, one can readily deduce the number of equilibrium solutions for each parameter value λ^*, by intersecting the green zero set with the vertical line $\lambda = \lambda^*$. Note that in general, if (λ^*, u^*) is a point on the bifurcation diagram and if $\lambda \approx \lambda^*$, then there exists a unique value u close to u^* such that (λ, u) is also a solution of (1.2). This is no longer true if we are at an equilibrium bifurcation point, which we define informally as follows.

DEFINITION 1.1 (Bifurcation Point). A solution pair (λ^*, u^*) of (1.2) is called *(equilibrium) bifurcation point*, if as we increase the parameter λ from slightly to the left of λ^* to slightly to the right of λ^*, the number of solutions (λ, u) of (1.2) with $u \approx u^*$ changes.

One can easily see that this definition is satisfied exactly at the four black dots marked in the left panel of Figure 1. For the two solutions at $(\lambda^*, u^*) = (1,3)$ and $(\lambda^*, u^*) = (3.8, 3.5)$, the number of solutions changes from 0 over 1 to 2 with increasing λ, while for $(\lambda^*, u^*) = (4.2, 3.5)$ it changes from 2 over 1 to 0. In the following, we will call bifurcation points of this type *saddle-node bifurcation points*, and they are characterized by the creation or destruction of a pair of equilibria as λ increases. In contrast, the bifurcation point at $(\lambda^*, u^*) = (5,2)$ is called a *pitchfork bifurcation point*, since the associated jump from one to three equilibrium solutions (or vice versa) resembles the farm tool bearing the same name.

While the bifurcation diagram in the left panel of Figure 1 provides information on the structure of the equilibrium set of (1.1) with nonlinearity (1.3), it does not include information on stability properties of these stationary states. If available, such information can be incorporated into the diagram as shown in the right panel of Figure 1. In the new diagram, the branches are colored according to the stability properties of their equilibrium solutions, with blue corresponding to asymptotically stable equilibria and red to unstable ones. Such a more detailed diagram indicates for example that for $\lambda = 0.7$ all solutions of (1.1) are strictly increasing and converge to $+\infty$, while for $\lambda = 1.3$ only solutions starting at initial values larger than that of the unstable equilibrium exhibit this behavior. The remaining ones will be attracted by the second created stationary state. Similarly, while for $\lambda = 4.7$ all solutions originating for example in the interval $[0,3]$ will be attracted by the same asymptotically stable state, for $\lambda = 5.3$ there are two newly created possible stable states.

Needless to say, the sample function f given in (1.3) was conceived in such a way that its bifurcation structure can easily be inferred directly from the form of the equations, since it is defined as a product of terms which define simple geometric shapes. Note, however, that if instead of the original function f we consider the shifted nonlinearities $f \pm 1/5$, then numerical methods have to be used to determine the bifurcation structure of (1.2). The resulting bifurcation diagrams for the shifted functions $f - 1/5$ and $f + 1/5$ are shown in the left and right panels of Figure 2, respectively. It is worth noting that while these small shifts in f result in only minor changes in the overall global structure of the zero set, the observed local changes can be quite significant. For example, in both diagrams the pitchfork bifurcation is no longer present, and it breaks up in two different ways. Similarly, while the left panel still contains the zero loop close to $(4, 3.5)$, in the right diagram this loop has merged with one of the other zero branches. In all of these changes, new saddle-node bifurcations are introduced. In fact, both bifurcation diagrams in Figure 2 contain only saddle-node bifurcation points, and no other variety. We will return to this important observation later in the lecture.

From a mathematical perspective, the study of bifurcation diagrams has a long history, and many excellent introductions to the subject exist. See for example [**10**, **14**, **35**, **60**], as well as the references therein. These books contain many different results which ensure the existence of a wealth of bifurcation points (going well beyond our limited definition above), and such results can be achieved through

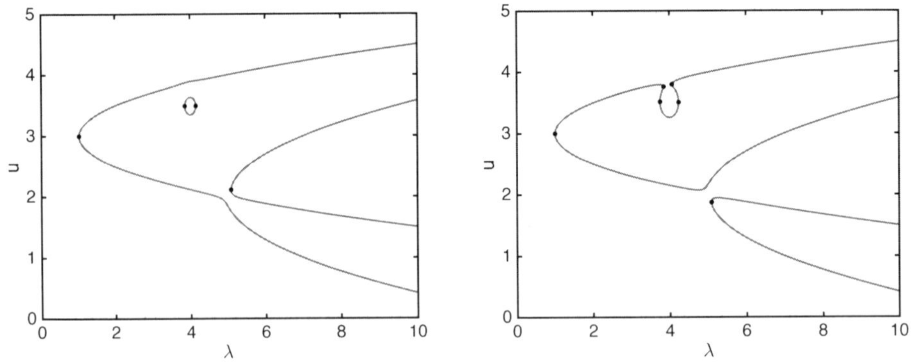

FIGURE 2. Bifurcation diagram changes under perturbations of f. The left and right panels show the equilibrium bifurcation diagrams which correspond to subtracting or adding, respectively, the constant value 1/5 to the function f defined in (1.3), which generates the left panel of Figure 1. Note that large parts of the diagram persist qualitatively, but that the pitchfork bifurcation point breaks up, and that the island close to $(4, 3.5)$ merges with a nearby branch. In both cases, new saddle-node bifurcation points are created.

both topological and analytical approaches. Of fundamental importance in this context is the implicit function theorem, which we only state in a simple finite-dimensional setting.

THEOREM 1.2 (Implicit Function Theorem). *Let $f : \mathbb{R} \times \mathbb{R}^n \to \mathbb{R}^n$ denote a smooth function, and assume that $f(\lambda^*, u^*) = 0$ for a pair $(\lambda^*, u^*) \in \mathbb{R} \times \mathbb{R}^n$. Furthermore, suppose that the Jacobian matrix $D_u f(\lambda^*, u^*) \in \mathbb{R}^{n\times n}$ of the function f with respect to u at (λ^*, u^*) is invertible. Then there exists a neighborhood $U \subset \mathbb{R}^n$ of u^*, a constant $\delta > 0$, as well as a smooth function $g : [\lambda^* - \delta, \lambda^* + \delta] \to \mathbb{R}^n$ such that the following holds:*

$$(\lambda, u) \in [\lambda^* - \delta, \lambda^* + \delta] \times U \quad \textit{satisfies} \quad f(\lambda, u) = 0 \qquad \textit{if and only if} \qquad u = g(\lambda)\ .$$

In other words, all solutions of (1.2) in the set $[\lambda^* - \delta, \lambda^* + \delta] \times U$ lie on the graph of the function g.

This result shows that as long as the Jacobian matrix $D_u f(\lambda^*, u^*)$ is invertible, small variations in the parameter λ do not lead to changes in the number of solutions (λ, u) with $u \approx u^*$, i.e., one obtains the following direct corollary.

COROLLARY 1.3 (Necessary Condition for Bifurcation). *In the situation of Theorem 1.2, if the pair (λ^*, u^*) is a solution of (1.2) with invertible Jacobian matrix $D_u f(\lambda^*, u^*) \in \mathbb{R}^{n\times n}$, then (λ^*, u^*) cannot be an equilibrium bifurcation point. In other words, a necessary condition for the point (λ^*, u^*) to be a bifurcation point is that $D_u f(\lambda^*, u^*)$ is not invertible.*

The importance of both the implicit function theorem and its simple corollary cannot be overemphasized. While Theorem 1.2 allows one in theory to establish branch segments of equilibria, Corollary 1.3 provides an algebraic criterion for where bifurcation points can occur. We would like to point out, however, that

Corollary 1.3 is usually not sufficient to ensure the actual occurrence of a bifurcation point. For this, one needs to establish additional conditions, which vary with the type of the bifurcation point.

Despite its importance, the applicability of Theorem 1.2 is limited in many practical applications. For example, the bifurcation diagrams in Figure 2 were computed numerically, and we actually do not have an explicit formula for any of the equilibrium solutions for the shifted functions $f \pm 1/5$. The goal of this lecture is to demonstrate that in such situations, rigorous computational techniques can be used to verify bifurcation diagrams through a combination of interval arithmetic and theoretical fixed point arguments. This necessarily has to address both the validation of branches, and the location and verification of bifurcation points. In order to keep the lecture as self-contained as possible, we restrict our attention to saddle-node bifurcation points and pitchfork bifurcations induced through symmetry-breaking.

In more detail, the remainder of these notes is organized as follows. In Section 2 we introduce two sample models from materials science which will serve as the main examples. While Section 2.1 is devoted to the lattice dynamical system given by the discrete Allen-Cahn equation, Section 2.2 introduces the diblock copolymer model for phase separation. These models cover the case of high-dimensional ordinary differential equations, as well as parabolic partial differential equations with gradient structure. The theoretical foundations for computer-assisted validation of bifurcation diagrams are the subject of Section 3. We begin in Section 3.1 to formulate a constructive version of the implicit function theorem, which will then be used in Section 3.2 to validate branch segments by employing a tangent-based predictor-corrector method. In the subsequent Section 3.3, it is demonstrated that the folds around saddle-node bifurcation points can be resolved using a suitable coordinate transformation. Throughout the section, the results will be applied to our two basic examples. Finally, Section 4 turns towards direct methods for verifying bifurcation points. The case of saddle-node bifurcations is the subject of Section 4.1, while symmetry breaking pitchfork bifurcations are addressed in Section 4.2. For related results we refer the reader to [**2, 18, 25, 44, 45**].

2. Two Examples from Materials Science

Throughout this lecture, we will illustrate the various results in the context of two concrete examples. The first of these is a high-dimensional ordinary differential equation, which arises as a discrete model for the motion of an interface between two phases of a binary alloy. The second example is concerned with microphase separation in diblock copolymers, and the resulting model is a parabolic partial differential equation.

2.1. The Discrete Allen-Cahn Equation. One of the fundamental models for phase separation in alloys is the Allen-Cahn equation, which is a parabolic partial differential equation of the form

$$u_t = \Delta u + \lambda f(u) \quad \text{in} \quad \Omega\,, \qquad \text{subject to} \quad \frac{\partial u}{\partial \nu} = 0 \quad \text{on } \partial\Omega\,. \tag{2.1}$$

In this equation, the domain $\Omega \subset \mathbb{R}^d$ is bounded with a suitably smooth boundary $\partial\Omega$, the strictly positive real number λ is a parameter, and the vector ν denotes the outward unit normal vector to the domain Ω at points on its boundary $\partial\Omega$.

Furthermore, the nonlinearity f is given by the cubic polynomial $f(u) = u - u^3$. For any solution u of (2.1) the value $u(t, x)$ denotes the local alloy composition at time t and spatial location $x \in \Omega$, and values of u close to ± 1 represent two different pure phases, or alloy components, of the underlying material; values between -1 and $+1$ correspond to mixtures of the phases or components, with $u = 0$ implying an equal split. One can show that if we choose an initial condition $u(0, \cdot) : \Omega \to \mathbb{R}$ which is a small random perturbation of the stationary state $u \equiv 0$, then as time increases one first observes instantaneous phase separation, followed by convergence of the solution to either the equilibrium $u \equiv +1$ or $u \equiv -1$ which is facilitated by the motion of interfaces between the two phases.

While the Allen-Cahn model does describe the interface motion fairly accurately, the above-mentioned long-term behavior is an idealization. In experiments, it is observed that interfaces can become stuck through a phenomenon called *pinning*, and this cannot be observed in (2.1). To remedy this shortcoming, discretized versions of the Allen-Cahn equation have been proposed in the literature, see for example [**11, 15–17, 24, 27–29, 31, 39**], as well as the references therein. For the purposes of this lecture, we consider the *discrete Allen-Cahn equation*

$$\dot{u}_k = u_{k+1} - 2u_k + u_{k-1} + \lambda f(u_k) \qquad \text{for all} \qquad k = 1, \ldots, n \,, \tag{2.2}$$

where we set $u_0 = u_1$ and $u_{n+1} = u_n$, and the nonlinearity is $f(u) = u - u^3$. Notice that the discrete Allen-Cahn equation is a coupled system of ordinary differential equations for the n unknown real-valued functions $u_1, \ldots, u_n$ which depend on time t. In fact, equation (2.2) can be viewed as an approximation to the Allen-Cahn model (2.1) on the one-dimensional domain $\Omega = (0, 1)$ in the following sense. Consider the spatial discretization points

$$x_k = \frac{2k - 1}{2n} \qquad \text{for} \qquad k = 1, \ldots, n \,,$$

and use the finite difference approximation of $\Delta u = u''$ given by

$$u''(x_k) \;\approx\; \frac{u(x_{k+1}) - 2u(x_k) + u(x_{k-1})}{\Delta x^2} \qquad \text{with} \qquad \Delta x = \frac{1}{n} \,.$$

Then the solution u_k of (2.2) can be interpreted as an approximation of $u(\cdot, x_k)$ if we replace λ by λ / n^2 and rescale time appropriately. Note in particular that the definition of the discretization points $u_0 = u_1$ and $u_{n+1} = u_n$ leads to the correct approximation of the boundary conditions.

Despite the above motivation via finite difference approximations, the discrete Allen-Cahn equation (2.2) has been proposed as a model in its own right, and we will consider it as such. For large values of the parameter λ one can easily see that (2.2) has an abundance of equilibrium solutions. For this, consider any vector $\bar{u} \in \mathbb{R}^n$ with $\bar{u}_k \in \{-1, 0, 1\}$ for $k = 1, \ldots, n$. Then the implicit function theorem can be used to show that for large enough $\lambda > 0$ there exists an equilibrium of the discrete Allen-Cahn equation near $\bar{u}$. In other words, if λ is sufficiently large, the system (2.2) has at least 3^n stationary states, and we call solutions arising in this way *mosaic solutions*. While some of these equilibria have counterparts in the regular Allen-Cahn model (2.1) on the domain $\Omega = (0, 1)$, the vast majority does not — and it is exactly this discrepancy that is connected to the phenomenon of pinning.

The significance of the mosaic equilibria for pinning becomes evident when we turn our attention to their stability. One can show that if the vector $\bar{u} \in \{-1, 0, 1\}^n$

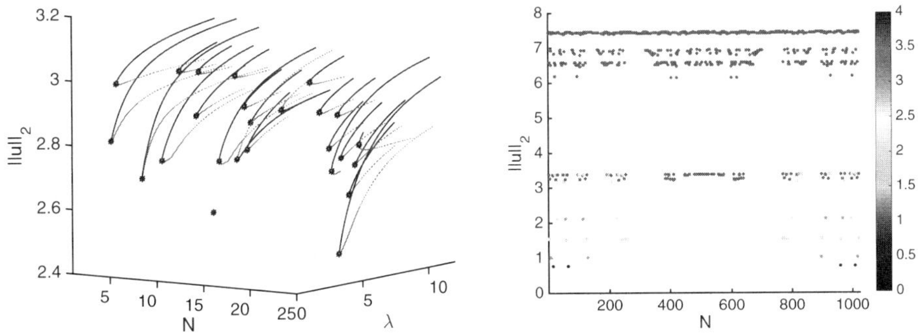

FIGURE 3. Mosaic equilibrium solutions of the discrete Allen-Cahn model (2.2) for $n = 10$. The left image shows sample branches of such stationary states, which are created through saddle-node bifurcations. Notice that in one of them, the path-following technique could only produce an extremely small piece of the branch, which therefore looks like an isolated black dot. This phenomenon is explained further in [**52**], and is related to the occurrence of secondary bifurcations on this particular branch. In the right image, we show all 2^n saddle-node bifurcation points which lead to mosaic solutions close to vectors in $\{\pm 1\}^n$. These points are color-coded by the smallest grain size in the solution, as encoded in the colorbar. The meaning of the horizontal axis in the right panel will be described in more detail in the context of Figure 11.

contains one or more zero components, then the corresponding equilibrium is unstable, while the remaining 2^n vectors $\bar{u} \in \{\pm 1\}^n$ give all rise to asymptotically stable stationary states, i.e., interface motion will get stuck upon entering the domains of attraction of these states.

But how are all of these attracting states created? We will see later that they do not exist for small λ, so it is natural to wonder at which parameter values λ they can be observed first. From a numerical point of view this question can easily be answered using the path-following software AUTO [**22**]. In the left panel of Figure 3 we plot a number of equilibrium branches which lead to mosaic solutions, and all of them seem to be created via saddle-node bifurcation points. It is worth noting that the λ-coordinates of the saddle-node points are staggered in an intriguing way, and it was conjectured in [**27**] that the precise location is correlated with the *grain size* of the mosaic solution, which is defined as the length of the smallest consecutive string of nonzero components of the same sign in the vector $\bar{u}$. We would like to point out that Grant [**27**] could partially answer this question for the special case of piece-wise linear nonlinearities f, which are qualitatively of the same form as the standard cubic polynomial $f(u) = u - u^3$. However, his methods do not seem to be applicable to this polynomial nonlinearity.

As we will demonstrate later on, rigorous computational techniques can be used to derive computer-assisted proofs linking the grain size of a mosaic solution to the specific location of the saddle-node bifurcation points. This leads to the right panel in Figure 3, which contains all 2^n saddle-node bifurcation points connected to mosaic solutions close to vectors in $\{\pm 1\}^n$. These points are color-coded by the smallest grain size in the solution, as encoded in the colorbar, and they clearly show the relation between the staggered creation of the solutions and their grain size. While the detailed results are contained in [**52**], many of the results described later in this lecture are taken from this paper.

2.2. The Diblock Copolymer Model. Our second example is concerned with diblock copolymers, which can be found in products such as upholstery foams, adhesive tapes, and asphalt additives [**4, 5**]. Their building blocks are macromolecules which are obtained by joining two chemically distinct polymer blocks, each of which is a linear chain of identical monomers. The two involved monomer types are usually thermodynamically incompatible, and this typically leads to phase separation within the material which is constrained by the covalently bonded chains — thereby resulting in a phenomenon called *microphase separation*, where the two blocks separate on a mesoscopic scale. One of the basic models for microphase separation in diblock copolymers has been described in [**3, 42, 43**]. Consider a material constrained to the bounded domain $\Omega \subset \mathbb{R}^d$. Then the model proposes a free energy functional for the relative macroscopic monomer concentration u, i.e., for the difference between the two monomer volume fractions, given by

$$E_{\lambda,\sigma}[u] = \int_\Omega \left(\frac{1}{2\lambda} |\nabla u|^2 + F(u) \right) dx + \frac{\sigma}{2} \int_\Omega \left| (-\Delta)^{-1/2} (u(x) - \mu) \right|^2 dx \,. \tag{2.3}$$

In this formula, the number $\mu = \int_\Omega u\, dx / |\Omega|$ denotes the difference of the averaged monomer masses, and the nonlinear function F is a double-well potential with global minima at ± 1. Throughout this paper, we consider the specific double-well potential $F(u) = (u^2 - 1)^2/4$. Note that the energy functional (2.3) is the standard van der Waals free energy, but with an additional nonlocal term which involves the square root of the inverse Laplacian on a space with zero total average. There are different ways in which one can associate gradient-like dynamics to (2.3), and in its standard form the diblock copolymer model considers the equation

$$\begin{aligned} u_t &= -\Delta\left(\Delta u + \lambda f(u)\right) - \lambda\sigma(u - \mu) \quad \text{in } \Omega \,, \\ \mu &= \frac{1}{|\Omega|} \int_\Omega u(x)\, dx \,, \quad \text{and} \quad \frac{\partial u}{\partial \nu} = \frac{\partial \Delta u}{\partial \nu} = 0 \quad \text{on } \partial\Omega \,, \end{aligned} \tag{2.4}$$

where $f(u) = -F'(u) = u - u^3$, and ν denotes again the unit outward normal vector to the boundary $\partial\Omega$. In this formulation, the value of u describes the local material composition in the following way, which is reminiscent of our discussion in the previous section. Values of $u(t,x)$ close to $+1$ are interpreted as only monomer A being present at point $x \in \Omega$ and at time $t \geq 0$, and the value -1 indicates that only monomer B is present; values in between correspond to mixtures of the two monomers, with zero representing an equal mixture. The parameter μ denotes the average mass of the mixture, and the two remaining parameters $\lambda > 0$ and $\sigma \geq 0$ are dimensionless interaction lengths. Informally, $\lambda > 0$ being large corresponds to short range repulsions being strong, and this induces a strong tendency to separate. On the other hand, σ being large represents strong long range chain elasticity forces, which leads to a strong tendency for holding together. We would like to point out that for $\sigma = 0$ the diblock copolymer model (2.4) reduces to the celebrated Cahn-Hilliard equation [**12**], which serves as a basic model for the phase

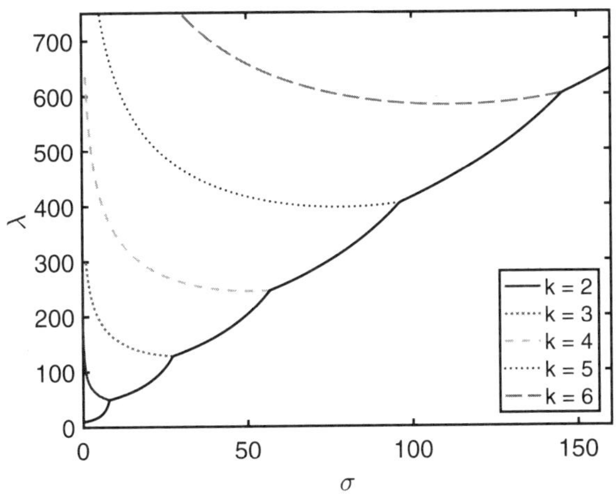

FIGURE 4. Structure of typical long-term limits for solutions of (2.4) on $\Omega = (0, 1)$ which start close to the trivial homogeneous state $\mu = 0$. The image partitions the σ-λ-parameter quadrant into regions with different behaviors of the long-term limit. Below the black lower envelope the homogeneous equilibrium is stable, i.e., no phase separation occurs and all solutions converge to the constant state. For parameter combinations in the remaining region, if the parameter point lies below the plotted curve for $k + 1$ and above the one for k, the typical long-term limit is periodic and has exactly k zeros.

separation phenomena spinodal decomposition [**20, 21, 26, 37, 38, 50, 51, 55**] and nucleation [**6–9, 19**].

The derivation of the diblock copolymer model (2.4) guarantees that along any solution u the energy $E_{\lambda,\sigma}[u]$ is strictly decreasing, unless the solution is an equilibrium. In fact, one can show that the right-hand side of (2.4) is the negative gradient of (2.3) in the H^{-1}-topology. Since the energy clearly is bounded below by zero, one would therefore expect that any solution will eventually converge to an equilibrium of the diblock copolymer model, and generically, this limit should be an (at least local) minimizer of the energy. But what can be said about this limiting stationary state? For this, we consider the question of pattern formation during the material production. In the initial polymer melt, both monomers will produce a homogeneous mixture throughout the container, i.e., the initial state $u(0, \cdot) \approx \mu$ will be a small random perturbation of the constant equilibrium μ. If the parameter λ is large enough, one can show that this stationary state is unstable, thereby triggering spontaneous phase separation.

In the recent paper [**32**], the above question was studied through a combination of numerical and rigorous bifurcation-theoretic techniques for the case $\mu = 0$ and for the one-dimensional domain $\Omega = (0, 1)$. In this paper, it was shown that while the diblock copolymer model exhibits a high level of *multistability*, i.e., the energy functional $E_{\lambda,\sigma}$ typically has many local minimizers, solutions of (2.4) which originate close to μ converge with high probability to limiting states of a characteristic shape. These limiting states seem to be periodic solutions with k zeros, whose periodicity depends only on the specific choice of the parameters λ and σ. This is illustrated further in Figure 4, which partitions the σ-λ-parameter quadrant into regions with different behaviors of the long-term limit. Below the black lower envelope one can show that the homogeneous state $\mu = 0$ is stable, i.e., no phase separation occurs. For parameter combinations in the remaining regions, the number k of zeros of the typical periodic long-term limit is one less than the value associated with the plotted curve which bounds the region from above. In other words, below the blue curve the limits have one zero, between the blue and orange curves they have two, and so on. We would like to emphasize that these results were obtained through numerical Monte Carlo type simulations, and that different long-term limits can be observed even at the same parameter combination. However, *most solutions* (by a large margin) starting close to the homogeneous state exhibit the above behavior, and the transitions between preferred limits do occur along the well-defined curves shown in Figure 4. For more details, we refer the reader to [**32**, **56**].

To explain the origin of the delineating curves in Figure 4 further, we need to turn our attention to the equilibrium solutions of the diblock copolymer model, where again we only consider the one-dimensional domain $\Omega = (0, 1)$ and total mass $\mu = 0$. Such solutions satisfy the nonlinear elliptic problem

$$-\Delta\left(\Delta u + \lambda f(u)\right) - \lambda\sigma(u - \mu) = 0 \quad \text{in } \Omega\,, \tag{2.5}$$

subject to the mass constraint $\mu = \int_\Omega u(x)\,dx/|\Omega| = 0$ and homogeneous Neumann boundary conditions for both u and Δu. One can easily see that for all $\lambda > 0$ and arbitrary $\sigma \geq 0$ this equation has the solution $u \equiv \mu = 0$, and we will call this constant equilibrium the *trivial solution* of (2.5).

For the special case $\sigma = 0$ the nonlinear problem (2.5) reduces to the stationary Cahn-Hilliard equation, whose complete equilibrium set has been derived rigorously in [**30**]. In this paper it is shown that for $\mu = 0$ and as λ increases from zero, new nontrivial solutions appear close to the trivial solution $u \equiv 0$ through an infinite series of pitchfork bifurcations. These bifurcations occur at the parameter values $\lambda = k^2\pi^2$, where $k \in \mathbb{N}$, and for every k-value, the two new nontrivial solutions qualitatively resemble the function $\varphi_k(x) = \sqrt{2}\cos k\pi x$. The nontrivial solutions grow in amplitude with increasing λ, and ultimately converge to a maximum norm close to one as $\lambda \to \infty$. This behavior is depicted in the top left bifurcation diagram of Figure 5, where the horizontal axis corresponds to the parameter λ, and the vertical axis measures the $L^2(0, 1)$-norm of an equilibrium solution u. Each colored point in the image corresponds to at least one solution of (2.5) for $\sigma = 0$ and mass $\mu = 0$. Points on the horizontal line $\|u\|_{L^2(0,1)} = 0$ are clearly the trivial solutions, while points on the emanating curves are nontrivial ones. Moreover, each point with $\|u\|_{L^2(0,1)} > 0$ gives rise to two solutions, since for the chosen parameter values, if u is a solution of (2.5), then so is $-u$. Thus, the bifurcation diagram in the top left of Figure 5 indicates that for every $k^2\pi^2 < \lambda \leq (k+1)^2\pi^2$, the Cahn-Hilliard model with mass $\mu = 0$ has exactly $2k + 1$ equilibrium solutions.

How do these rigorous results change for the diblock copolymer case $\sigma > 0$? At first glance, one would assume that any changes should be minor, since the diblock copolymer model arises from the Cahn-Hilliard model through a regular perturbation at $\sigma = 0$. Yet, nothing could be further from the truth. In the remaining images of Figure 5, we show bifurcation diagrams for increasing values of σ, all of which were computed numerically using AUTO [**22**], see also [**32**]. As in the Cahn-Hilliard case, every point on a curve corresponds to at least one equilibrium

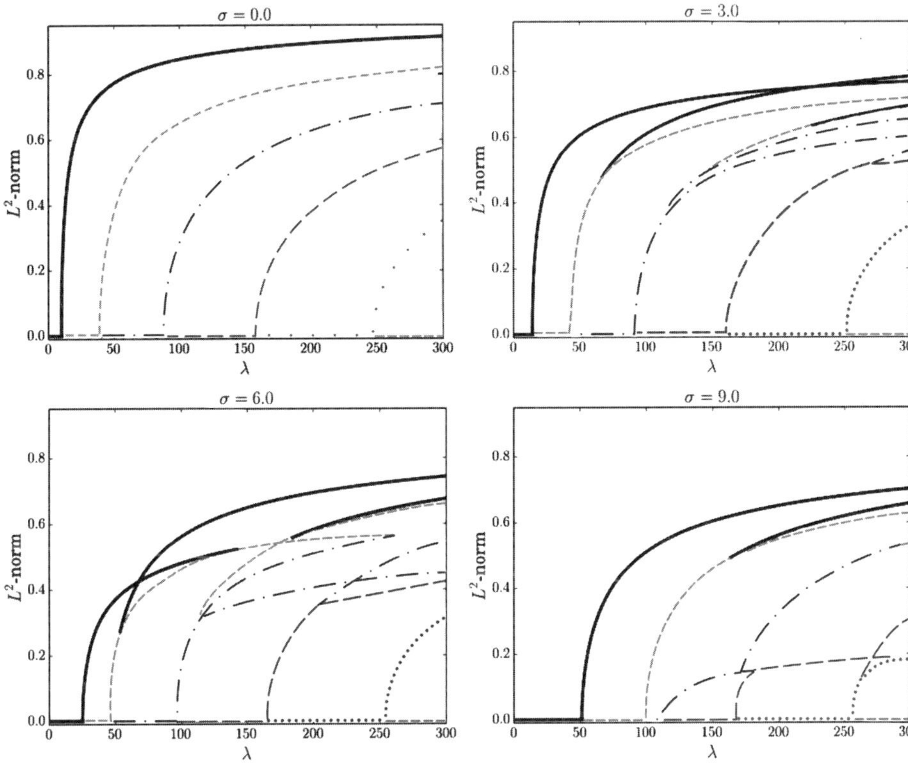

FIGURE 5. Sample equilibrium bifurcation diagrams for the diblock copolymer model given in (2.4) on the one-dimensional domain $\Omega = (0, 1)$ and for total mass $\mu = 0$. From top left to bottom right the bifurcation diagrams are for $\sigma = 0$, 3, 6, and 9, respectively. In each diagram, the vertical axis measures the $L^2(0, 1)$-norm of the solutions, and the horizontal axis uses the parameter λ. The solution branches are color-coded by the Morse index of the solutions, and black (solid), red (short dash), blue (dot-dash), green (long dash), magenta (dot), and cyan (dash) correspond to indices 0, 1, 2, 3, 4, and 5, respectively.

solution. In fact, due to symmetries in the equation, some points correspond to as many as four solutions. These diagrams indicate that the bifurcation structure of the diblock copolymer model for $\sigma > 0$ is considerably more complicated than the one in the Cahn-Hilliard setting, with many secondary bifurcations.

One of the main results in [**32**] is the insight that the basic qualitative changes in the bifurcation diagrams of (2.5) for $\mu = 0$ as σ increases from zero can be uncovered by a local bifurcation analysis. As σ increases, the branches emanating from the trivial solution line move to the right, but at varying speeds. For example, the 1-branch, i.e., the branch on which solutions have the same shape as $\varphi_1(x) = \sqrt{2} \cos \pi x$, moves quickly to the right with increasing σ, interacts with all subsequent k-branches for $k \geq 2$, and then moves off to infinity and disappears for $\sigma \geq \pi^2$. Next, the 2-branch moves to the right and interacts with the

k-branches for $k \geq 3$, before it moves off to infinity and ceases to exist for $\sigma \geq 2^2\pi^2$, and so forth. All of the local branch interactions can be analyzed rigorously using a Lyapunov-Schmidt reduction at two-dimensional kernels [**32**], and this implies that every local interaction involves a secondary bifurcation point on one of the participating branches. One of these secondary bifurcation points can be seen in the lower left image of Figure 5 for $\lambda \approx 50$. It represents a pitchfork bifurcation which creates two index one solutions, and which renders the 2-branch equilibrium asymptotically stable. In other words, the secondary bifurcation point turns an index one equilibrium into a local minimizer of the energy (2.3).

It turns out that these secondary bifurcation points lie at the heart of the long-term asymptotic behavior of solutions u of (2.4) which originate close to the homogeneous state μ. To explain this, consider again the secondary pitchfork bifurcation in the lower left diagram of Figure 5. The parameter combination $\lambda \approx 50$ and $\sigma = 6$ at which this bifurcation point can be observed lies precisely on the blue curve in Figure 4. In fact, every point on the blue curve corresponds to a parameter combination at which the 2-branch has a pitchfork bifurcation. Similarly, the remaining colored curves with labels $k \geq 3$ in Figure 5 represent the locations of pitchfork bifurcation points on the k-branch emanating from the trivial solution line. As in the case $k = 2$, all of these bifurcation points are stabilizing in the sense that they render the equilibrium on the k-branch asymptotically stable.

In view of the above numerical results it is natural to wonder whether any of these statements can be proven. Unfortunately, even the equilibrium structure of (2.4) for $\sigma > 0$ lies beyond the reach of current analytical techniques, since the ones used in [**30**] no longer apply. The situation is even more bleak in the case of the pitchfork bifurcation points. It is possible, however, to employ rigorous computational techniques to obtain computer-assisted proofs. In this way, branches of equilibrium solutions could be established in [**57**], and the location of bifurcation points can be rigorously verified using the techniques of [**36**]. Some of these results will be described in the following.

3. Branches and the Constructive Implicit Function Theorem

Beginning with this section we present the necessary theoretical foundations for validating bifurcation diagrams. Our approach for this will be somewhat different from the radii polynomial approach taken by some of the other lecturers, but is of course related. Rather than setting up explicit nonlinear systems for various problems and verifying a contraction condition, we return to the introduction of this lecture. As mentioned there, the implicit function theorem is one of the fundamental tools for understanding bifurcations, even though its applicability in the original form is somewhat limited. Based on this, we will formulate a *constructive implicit function theorem* in Section 3.1 below, which removes the assumption of a precisely known zero by the knowledge of an approximative zero. This theorem is then applied in Section 3.2 to validate branch segments of equilibrium solutions for nonlinear equations, based on a tangent-based predictor-corrector approach. Finally, Section 3.3 will explain how the constructive implicit function theorem can be used to rigorously follow branches around saddle-node bifurcation points. Much of the presentation in Section 3 reflects the one of [**52**], and we refer the reader to this paper for proofs of the involved theorems.

3.1. A Constructive Implicit Function Theorem. In its original formulation, the implicit function theorem guarantees the existence of a branch of solutions of a nonlinear parameter-dependent equation, provided we have

- an exact solution of the problem at a specific parameter value, as well as
- an invertibility condition for the linearization of the nonlinear problem at this solution.

These assumptions certainly seem reasonable, but in practice, they are usually hard to verify. Especially for high-dimensional nonlinear problems, one cannot expect to have an interesting precise solution available. Generally, the best we can hope for is a good numerical approximation. But is this enough to still conclude the existence of a nearby branch of solutions?

To answer this question, one has to take a closer look at the proof of the implicit function theorem. While there are many different approaches for doing this, see for example the excellent account in [**34**], we focus on the following technique which is based on the contraction mapping principle. To fix notation, we consider parameter-dependent problems of the form

$$\mathcal{G}(\alpha, x) = 0 \,, \tag{3.1}$$

where $\mathcal{G} : \mathcal{P} \times \mathcal{X} \to \mathcal{Y}$ is a Fréchet differentiable nonlinear mapping between two Banach spaces $\mathcal{X}$ and $\mathcal{Y}$, and the parameter α is taken from a Banach space $\mathcal{P}$. The norms on these Banach spaces are denoted by $\|\cdot\|_{\mathcal{P}}$, $\|\cdot\|_{\mathcal{X}}$, and $\|\cdot\|_{\mathcal{Y}}$, respectively.[1] Suppose further that for a pair $(\alpha^*, x^*) \in \mathcal{P}\times\mathcal{X}$ we have $\mathcal{G}(\alpha^*, x^*) = 0$, and that the Fréchet derivative $D_x\mathcal{G}(\alpha^*, x^*)$ is invertible. In order to prove the implicit function theorem, one then considers the mapping

$$\mathcal{T} : \mathcal{P} \times \mathcal{X} \to \mathcal{X} \quad \text{defined by} \quad \mathcal{T}(\alpha, x) = x - D_x\mathcal{G}(\alpha^*, x^*)^{-1}\mathcal{G}(\alpha, x) \,.$$

It can easily be seen that the fixed point equation $\mathcal{T}(\alpha, x) = x$ is equivalent to the problem (3.1), due to the assumed invertibility of $D_x\mathcal{G}(\alpha^*, x^*)$. Furthermore, one can compute the Fréchet derivative of $\mathcal{T}$ with respect to x at the pair (α^*, x^*) as

$$D_x\mathcal{T}(\alpha^*, x^*) \;=\; I - D_x\mathcal{G}(\alpha^*, x^*)^{-1}D_x\mathcal{G}(\alpha^*, x^*) \;=\; I - I \;=\; 0 \,.$$

This implies that in a small neighborhood of the pair (α^*, x^*) the operator norm of $D_x\mathcal{T}(\alpha, x)$ is bounded by a constant $c < 1$, and together with the mean value theorem and $\mathcal{G}(\alpha^*, x^*) = 0$ this shows that $\mathcal{T}$ is a uniform contraction in this neighborhood. An application of the uniform contraction mapping principle then finally furnishes the branch of solutions.

What happens in the above procedure if we only know $\mathcal{G}(\alpha^*, x^*) \approx 0$? If we are close enough to an actual solution of (3.1) at which the Fréchet derivative is invertible, then one would expect $D_x\mathcal{G}(\alpha^*, x^*)$ to be invertible as well — and this shows that the fixed point problem $\mathcal{T}(\alpha, x) = x$ is still equivalent to (3.1). Moreover, since $D_x\mathcal{T}(\alpha^*, x^*) = 0$ remains true, one can show that $\mathcal{T}$ satisfies a Lipschitz condition with constant $c < 1$ near (α^*, x^*). Thus, if we can find a neighborhood which is mapped into itself by $\mathcal{T}$, the assertion of the implicit function theorem should be valid as before.

[1] For a first reading, the reader may certainly assume that all of these spaces equal $\mathbb{R}$, and that the norm is just the regular absolute value. In this setting, Fréchet differentiability is then normal differentiability of a function $\mathcal{G} : \mathbb{R}^2 \to \mathbb{R}$, and the derivative $D_x\mathcal{G}(\alpha^*, x^*)$ is just the partial derivative of $\mathcal{G}$ with respect to x.

These heuristic arguments can be made precise, and this has been accomplished in detail in the papers [**52, 57**], which in turn are slight extensions of the approach by Plum [**46**]. To formulate the corresponding result, assume we are given a pair $(\alpha^*, x^*) \in \mathcal{P} \times \mathcal{X}$ which satisfies the following four hypotheses.

(H1) The residual of the nonlinear operator $\mathcal{G}$ at the pair (α^*, x^*) is small, i.e., there exists a constant $\varrho > 0$ such that

$$\|\mathcal{G}(\alpha^*, x^*)\|_{\mathcal{Y}} \le \varrho \,. \tag{3.2}$$

In other words, the pair (α^*, x^*) is an approximate solution of the nonlinear problem (3.1).

(H2) The Fréchet derivative $D_x\mathcal{G}(\alpha^*, x^*) \in \mathcal{L}(\mathcal{X}, \mathcal{Y})$, where $\mathcal{L}(\mathcal{X}, \mathcal{Y})$ denotes the Banach space of all bounded linear operators from $\mathcal{X}$ into $\mathcal{Y}$, is one-to-one and onto, and its inverse $D_x\mathcal{G}(\alpha^*, x^*)^{-1} : \mathcal{Y} \to \mathcal{X}$ is bounded and satisfies

$$\left\|D_x\mathcal{G}(\alpha^*, x^*)^{-1}\right\|_{\mathcal{L}(\mathcal{Y},\mathcal{X})} \le K \,, \tag{3.3}$$

where $\|\cdot\|_{\mathcal{L}(\mathcal{Y},\mathcal{X})}$ denotes the operator norm in $\mathcal{L}(\mathcal{Y}, \mathcal{X})$. In other words, the operator $D_x\mathcal{G}(\alpha^*, x^*)$ is invertible and not very close to being singular.

(H3) For (α, x) close to (α^*, x^*), the Fréchet derivative $D_x\mathcal{G}(\alpha, x)$ is locally Lipschitz continuous in the following sense. There exist positive real constants L_1, L_2, ℓ_x, and $\ell_\alpha \ge 0$ such that for all pairs $(\alpha, x) \in \mathcal{P} \times \mathcal{X}$ with $\|x - x^*\|_{\mathcal{X}} \le \ell_x$ and $\|\alpha - \alpha^*\|_{\mathcal{P}} \le \ell_\alpha$ we have

$$\|D_x\mathcal{G}(\alpha, x) - D_x\mathcal{G}(\alpha^*, x^*)\|_{\mathcal{L}(\mathcal{X},\mathcal{Y})} \le L_1 \|x - x^*\|_{\mathcal{X}} + L_2 \|\alpha - \alpha^*\|_{\mathcal{P}} \,, \tag{3.4}$$

where $\|\cdot\|_{\mathcal{L}(\mathcal{X},\mathcal{Y})}$ denotes the operator norm in $\mathcal{L}(\mathcal{X}, \mathcal{Y})$.

(H4) For α close to α^*, the Fréchet derivative $D_\alpha\mathcal{G}(\alpha, x^*)$ satisfies a Lipschitz-type bound. More precisely, there exist positive real constants L_3 and L_4, such that for all $\alpha \in \mathcal{P}$ with $\|\alpha - \alpha^*\|_{\mathcal{P}} \le \ell_\alpha$ one has

$$\|D_\alpha\mathcal{G}(\alpha, x^*)\|_{\mathcal{L}(\mathcal{P},\mathcal{Y})} \le L_3 + L_4 \|\alpha - \alpha^*\|_{\mathcal{P}} \,, \tag{3.5}$$

where ℓ_α is chosen as in (H3).

Notice that all of the constants ϱ, K, L_k, as well as both ℓ_x and ℓ_α, depend on the choice of the pair (α^*, x^*). Furthermore, in specific applications one has to be able to determine explicit values for these constants. This is usually accomplished through a combination of rigorous estimates and interval computations.

The above hypotheses specify in detail what is needed to prove the existence of a curve (in the special case $\mathcal{P} = \mathbb{R}$) of actual solutions of the nonlinear problem (3.1) if all that is available is an approximation. We would like to point out that while the first two hypotheses (H1) and (H2) put definite constraints on the admissible approximations (α^*, x^*), the remaining two hypotheses are usually satisfied and can be verified easily. The next result shows that under certain conditions on the constants ϱ, K, L_1, and ℓ_x, one can always find a "branch" of solutions parameterized by the parameter α.

THEOREM 3.1 (Constructive Implicit Function Theorem). *Let $\mathcal{P}$, $\mathcal{X}$, and $\mathcal{Y}$ be Banach spaces, suppose that the nonlinear operator $\mathcal{G} : \mathcal{P} \times \mathcal{X} \to \mathcal{Y}$ is Fréchet differentiable, and assume that $(\alpha^*, x^*) \in \mathcal{P} \times \mathcal{X}$ satisfies hypotheses (H1), (H2), (H3), and (H4). Finally, suppose that*

$$4K^2\varrho L_1 < 1 \qquad \textit{and} \qquad 2K\varrho < \ell_x \,. \tag{3.6}$$

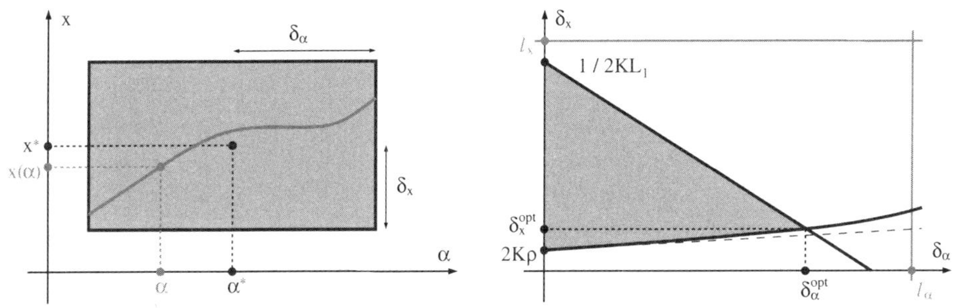

FIGURE 6. Visualization of the constructive implicit function theorem. The left image illustrates the general statement of the theorem, i.e., in a window around the approximative solution (α^*, x^*) all solutions of $\mathcal{G}(\alpha, x) = 0$ line on the curve $\alpha \mapsto x(\alpha)$. The size of the window is determined by the pair $(\delta_\alpha, \delta_x)$, and the shape of the admissible region from which these pairs can be chosen is illustrated in the right image.

Then there exist pairs of constants $(\delta_\alpha, \delta_x)$ *with* $0 \le \delta_\alpha \le \ell_\alpha$ *and* $0 < \delta_x \le \ell_x$, *as well as*

$$2KL_1\delta_x + 2KL_2\delta_\alpha \le 1 \qquad \text{and} \qquad 2K\varrho + 2KL_3\delta_\alpha + 2KL_4\delta_\alpha^2 \le \delta_x \,, \tag{3.7}$$

and for each such pair the following holds. For every $\alpha \in \mathcal{P}$ *with* $\|\alpha - \alpha^*\|_{\mathcal{P}} \le \delta_\alpha$ *there exists a uniquely determined element* $x(\alpha) \in \mathcal{X}$ *with* $\|x(\alpha) - x^*\|_{\mathcal{X}} \le \delta_x$ *such that* $\mathcal{G}(\alpha, x(\alpha)) = 0$. *In other words, if we define*

$$\mathcal{B}_{\delta_x}^{\mathcal{X}} = \{\xi \in \mathcal{X} \,:\, \|\xi - x^*\|_{\mathcal{X}} \le \delta_x\} \qquad \text{and} \qquad \mathcal{B}_{\delta_\alpha}^{\mathcal{P}} = \{p \in \mathcal{P} \,:\, \|p - \alpha^*\|_{\mathcal{P}} \le \delta_\alpha\} \,,$$

then all solutions of the nonlinear problem $\mathcal{G}(\alpha, x) = 0$ *in the set* $\mathcal{B}_{\delta_\alpha}^{\mathcal{P}} \times \mathcal{B}_{\delta_x}^{\mathcal{X}}$ *lie on the graph of the function* $\alpha \mapsto x(\alpha)$. *In addition, for all pairs* $(\alpha, x) \in \mathcal{B}_{\delta_\alpha}^{\mathcal{P}} \times \mathcal{B}_{\delta_x}^{\mathcal{X}}$ *the Fréchet derivative* $D_x\mathcal{G}(\alpha, x) \in \mathcal{L}(\mathcal{X}, \mathcal{Y})$ *is a bounded invertible linear operator, whose inverse is in* $\mathcal{L}(\mathcal{Y}, \mathcal{X})$.

The statement of the constructive implicit function theorem is visualized in the left image of Figure 6, and the right panel in this figure depicts the admissible region of all pairs $(\delta_\alpha, \delta_x)$ for which the result holds. For the proof of Theorem 3.1 we refer the reader to [**52**].

Theorem 3.1 crystallizes the main assumptions necessary for the establishment of solutions to nonlinear parameter-dependent problems in four simple hypotheses. The first of these, (H1) just states that the initial numerical approximation (α^*, x^*) has to be sufficiently accurate in the sense of having a small residual, and hypothesis (H2) ensures that the linearization of the nonlinear problem at the approximative solution is sufficiently non-singular. These are clearly the two main assumptions, and they relax the conditions of an exact solution with an invertible Fréchet derivative in the standard implicit function theorem.

Beyond (H1) and (H2), the two assumptions (H3) and (H4) are mostly technical in nature. They are always satisfied if $\mathcal{G}$ is twice continuously differentiable. Note, however, that in order to apply Theorem 3.1 we need explicit values for the constants L_1 through L_4, and they in turn depend on the choice of the constants ℓ_α and ℓ_x which determine the overall maximal "window size" for the result. Usually, these estimates can be obtained using standard mean value theorem arguments, and in many situations it is not necessary to obtain them in their sharpest form. In particular in the setting of partial differential equations this means that standard estimates involving Sobolev embeddings often suffice, and these can be formulated to hold for a wide variety of nonlinearities.

Once the constants in the above hypotheses have been established, the constructive implicit function theorem can be applied as long as (3.6) holds. While the second inequality in this assumption is usually satisfied and merely a reflection of a reasonable choice of ℓ_x, the first constraint is essential. Considering that the Lipschitz constant L_1 is what it is for a given nonlinearity, the estimate implies that as long as the residual ϱ is sufficiently small, we can always find true solutions near (α^*, x^*). In practice, of course, this is limited by the inherent accuracy limitations of specific implementations of computer arithmetic. We would like to point out, however, that of the four Lipschitz constants in (H3) and (H4) only L_1 enters the essential constraint. The role of the constants L_2, L_3, and L_4 is secondary, and merely affects the size of the solution window indicated in the left panel of Figure 6 with respect to α. This will be discussed in substantial detail in the next two sections.

As a first application of Theorem 3.1 we consider the question of verifying the existence of solutions of (3.1) at a specific parameter value α^*, or equivalently, we consider the case of a *parameter-independent nonlinear problem*, since the parameter-dependent case will be treated in considerable detail in the next two sections. Notice that if the parameter α^* is kept fixed, we can use $\ell_\alpha = 0$ in hypotheses (H3) and (H4). In fact, one can readily see that in this case (H4) is completely unnecessary, and in (H3) one only has to find a Lipschitz constant L_1 such that

$$\|D_x\mathcal{G}(\alpha^*, x) - D_x\mathcal{G}(\alpha^*, x^*)\|_{\mathcal{L}(\mathcal{X},\mathcal{Y})} \le L_1 \, \|x - x^*\|_{\mathcal{X}} \tag{3.8}$$

is satisfied whenever $\|x - x^*\|_{\mathcal{X}} \le \ell_x$. Moreover, for the verification of hypothesis (H2) one can frequently use the following important auxiliary result, whose proof can be found in [**52**], and which is a simple consequence of the Neumann series argument in [**33**, Sections I.4.4 and III.3.2].

LEMMA 3.2 (Linear Operator Norm Estimate). *Consider two Banach spaces $\mathcal{X}$ and $\mathcal{Y}$, and let $\mathcal{A} \in \mathcal{L}(\mathcal{X}, \mathcal{Y})$ denote an arbitrary bounded linear operator. In addition, let $\mathcal{B} \in \mathcal{L}(\mathcal{Y}, \mathcal{X})$ be a bounded linear operator which is one-to-one and onto, and assume that*

$$\|I - \mathcal{B}\mathcal{A}\|_{\mathcal{L}(\mathcal{X},\mathcal{X})} \le \varrho_1 < 1 \,, \qquad \textit{as well as} \qquad \|\mathcal{B}\|_{\mathcal{L}(\mathcal{Y},\mathcal{X})} \le \varrho_2 \,, \tag{3.9}$$

for two constants $0 \le \varrho_1 < 1$ and $\varrho_2 > 0$. Then the linear operator $\mathcal{A}$ is one-to-one and onto as well, and its bounded inverse $\mathcal{A}^{-1}$ satisfies

$$\|\mathcal{A}^{-1}\|_{\mathcal{L}(\mathcal{Y},\mathcal{X})} \le \frac{\varrho_2}{1 - \varrho_1} \,. \tag{3.10}$$

We now turn our attention to the existence of mosaic solutions in the discrete Allen-Cahn equation (2.2). It will be demonstrated in the following example how the parameter-independent version of the constructive implicit function theorem can be used to this effect, without any numerical assistance. More precisely, the example will show that the problem (2.2) has equilibrium solutions close to any vector $\bar{u} \in \{-1, 0, 1\}^n$ for sufficiently large $\lambda > 0$. In fact, we will obtain explicit lower bounds on λ, as well as bounds on the size of the neighborhood in which these stationary states exist.

EXAMPLE 3.3 (Mosaic Solutions for the Discrete Allen-Cahn Equation). Consider the equilibrium equation for the discrete Allen-Cahn equation (2.2), rewritten in the form

$$\mathcal{G}(u) = \frac{1}{\lambda} Au + f(u) = 0 \qquad \text{with} \qquad \lambda \in \mathbb{R}^+ \quad \text{and} \quad u \in \mathbb{R}^n ,$$

where the matrix $A \in \mathbb{R}^{n\times n}$ is given by

$$A = \begin{bmatrix} -1 & 1 & 0 & \cdots & 0 \\ 1 & -2 & 1 & \ddots & \vdots \\ 0 & \ddots & \ddots & \ddots & 0 \\ \vdots & \ddots & 1 & -2 & 1 \\ 0 & \cdots & 0 & 1 & -1 \end{bmatrix} . \tag{3.11}$$

We consider the specific nonlinearity $f(u) = u - u^3$, write $u = (u_1, \ldots, u_n)^t$ for the components of the vector u, and define $f(u) = (f(u_1), \ldots, f(u_n))^t$ componentwise. In addition, we adopt the abbreviation $\operatorname{diag}(u)$ for the diagonal matrix in $\mathbb{R}^{n\times n}$ with diagonal entries $u_1, \ldots, u_n$. Throughout these notes, we employ the maximum norm to measure the length of vectors in $\mathbb{R}^n$, as well as the induced matrix norm, i.e., for all $v \in \mathbb{R}^n$ and $B \in \mathbb{R}^{n\times n}$ we let

$$\|v\| = \max_{i=1,\ldots,n} |v_i| \qquad \text{and} \qquad \|B\| = \max_{i=1,\ldots,n} \sum_{j=1}^{n} |B_{i,j}| , \tag{3.12}$$

and drop the usual subscript ∞ for the sake of brevity.

Consider now an arbitrary vector $u^* \in \{-1, 0, 1\}^n$. Our goal is to use Theorem 3.1 to find an equilibrium solution of (2.2) for sufficiently large $\lambda > 0$, i.e., we need to to establish hypotheses (H1) and (H2), as well as (H3) in the reduced form (3.8). To begin with, notice that due to the form of f and choice of u^* one has $f(u^*) = 0 \in \mathbb{R}^n$, and together with

$$\|\mathcal{G}(u^*)\| = \left\| \frac{1}{\lambda} Au^* + f(u^*) \right\| \le \frac{\|A\|\|u^*\|}{\lambda} \le \frac{4}{\lambda}$$

we see that (H1) holds with $\varrho = 4/\lambda$. As for (H2), one can easily compute the Jacobian matrix $D_u\mathcal{G}(u^*)$ as

$$D_u\mathcal{G}(u^*) = \frac{1}{\lambda} A + \operatorname{diag} f'(u^*) ,$$

where the diagonal of the matrix $\operatorname{diag} f'(u^*)$ is a vector in $\{-2, 1\}^n$, since we have the identity $f'(u) = 1 - 3u^2$. If we let $\mathcal{B} \in \mathbb{R}^{n\times n}$ denote the inverse of $\operatorname{diag} f'(u^*)$, then one obtains with $\|\mathcal{B}\| \le 1$ the estimate

$$\|I - \mathcal{B}\, D_u\mathcal{G}(u^*)\| = \left\| I - \frac{1}{\lambda}\mathcal{B}A - \mathcal{B} \operatorname{diag} f'(u^*) \right\| = \left\| \frac{1}{\lambda}\mathcal{B}A \right\| \le \frac{\|\mathcal{B}\|\|A\|}{\lambda} \le \frac{4}{\lambda} ,$$

which together with Lemma 3.2 shows that (H2) is satisfied with $K = \lambda/(\lambda - 4)$, for $\lambda > 4$. Finally, if we let $\ell_u > 0$ be arbitrary, then an application of the standard mean value theorem furnishes for all $u \in \mathbb{R}^n$ with $\|u - u^*\| \le \ell_u$ the estimate

$$\|D_u\mathcal{G}(u) - D_u\mathcal{G}(u^*)\| \le \max_{|\xi|\le\|u^*\|+\ell_u} |f''(\xi)|\, \|u - u^*\| \le 6\,(1 + \ell_u)\, \|u - u^*\| ,$$

which establishes hypothesis (H3) with $L_1 = 6(1 + \ell_u)$.

We now restrict ourselves to finding solutions in a 0.1-neighborhood of u^*, i.e., we consider the case $\ell_u = 0.1$, which implies $L_1 = 6.6$. Then the conditions of the constructive implicit function theorem in (3.6) are equivalent to

$$\frac{105.6\,\lambda}{(\lambda-4)^2} < 1 \qquad \text{and} \qquad \frac{8}{\lambda - 4} < 0.1 \,, \qquad \text{which hold for all } \lambda > 113.459 \,.$$

Thus, Theorem 3.1 implies that for all $\lambda \ge 114$, there exists a unique equilibrium solution u_λ of (2.2) which satisfies

$$\|u_\lambda - u^*\| \le 2K\varrho = \frac{8}{\lambda - 4} \,,$$

and this solution is unique within a neighborhood of radius

$$\frac{1}{2KL_1} = \frac{\lambda - 4}{13.2\,\lambda} \to \frac{1}{13.2} \approx 0.07575 \qquad \text{for} \qquad \lambda \to \infty \,.$$

While the above estimates are clearly not best possible, they do demonstrate that the constructive implicit function theorem can be applied to obtain explicit existence proofs for equilibrium solutions. We would also like to point out that the above approach can easily be extended to show that the solutions of (2.2) for parameters $\lambda \ge 114$ do in fact form a branch of solutions, which is a continuous function of the parameter λ. $\Diamond$

Our second application of the parameter-independent version of Theorem 3.1 is not directly connected to the verification of bifurcation diagrams. It is, however, essential if we are interested in obtaining stability information for the involved equilibrium solutions. The following example demonstrates how eigenvalue/eigenvector pairs can be validated for matrices. Thus, the presented method can be used to determine the index of stationary states for the discrete Allen-Cahn equation.

EXAMPLE 3.4 (Verification of Simple Matrix Eigenvalues). Let $\mathcal{M} \in \mathbb{C}^{n\times n}$ be an arbitrary matrix, and suppose we would like to validate an eigenvalue $\eta \in \mathbb{C}$ and an associated eigenvector $v \in \mathbb{C}^n$. If one picks a fixed suitable normalization vector $\hat{v} \in \mathbb{C}^n \setminus \{0\}$, then such a pair has to solve the system

$$\mathcal{M}v - \eta v = 0 \quad \text{and} \quad \hat{v}^t v - 1 = 0 \,, \tag{3.13}$$

where the second equation is added to isolate the eigenvector. In fact, one can show that if η is a simple eigenvalue of $\mathcal{M}$, and if v is an eigenvector with $\hat{v}^t v = 1$, then the pair (v, η) is an isolated solution of (3.13). Such solutions can be validated using the constructive implicit function theorem by considering the specifically assembled nonlinear function $\mathcal{G} : \mathbb{C}^n \times \mathbb{C} \to \mathbb{C}^n \times \mathbb{C}$ defined by

$$\mathcal{G}(x) = \big(\mathcal{M}v - \eta v \,,\; \hat{v}^t v - 1\big) \,, \qquad \text{where} \qquad x = (v, \eta) \in \mathbb{C}^n \times \mathbb{C} \,,$$

whose Jacobian matrix is given by

$$D_x\mathcal{G}(x) = \left(\begin{array}{c|c} \mathcal{M} - \eta I & -v \\ \hline \hat{v}^t & 0 \end{array} \right) .$$

Now let $x^* = (v^*, \eta^*)$ denote an approximate eigenvector/eigenvalue pair. Then one can show that the estimate $\|D_x\mathcal{G}(x) - D_x\mathcal{G}(x^*)\| \le 2\|x - x^*\|$ holds with respect to the maximum norm in $\mathbb{C}^n$ and the induced matrix norm in $\mathbb{C}^{n\times n}$, i.e., hypothesis (H3) is satisfied with $L_1 = 2$ and $\ell_x = \infty$, as well as $\ell_\alpha = 0$. In order to satisfy hypotheses (H1) and (H2), assume that we have determined a suitably small constant $\varrho > 0$ such that

$$\|\mathcal{M}v^* - \eta^* v^*\| \le \varrho \qquad \text{and} \qquad \left|\hat{v}^t v^* - 1\right| \le \varrho\,, \tag{3.14}$$

as well as a constant $K > 0$ with

$$\left\| \left(\begin{array}{c|c} \mathcal{M} - \eta^* I & -v^* \\ \hline \hat{v}^t & 0 \end{array} \right)^{-1} \right\| \le K\,. \tag{3.15}$$

If we finally assume that $8K^2\varrho < 1$ holds, then for every $2K\varrho \le \delta \le 1/(4K)$ there exists a unique pair $(v, \eta) \in \mathbb{C}^n \times \mathbb{C}$ which solves the system (3.13) and which satisfies both $|\eta - \eta^*| \le \delta$ and $\|v - v^*\| \le \delta$. In other words, the maximum norm ball of radius $2K\varrho$ centered at the pair (v^*, η^*) contains a unique normalized eigenvector/eigenvalue pair for the matrix $\mathcal{M}$, and this pair is unique up to the distance $1/(4K)$.

In practical applications, the constant ϱ in (3.14) can easily be determined using interval arithmetic. As for the constant K in (3.15), one can still apply Lemma 3.2: If we denote the extended matrix in (3.15) by $\mathcal{A}$, then one can use a *numerically computed inverse* $\mathcal{B}$ of $\mathcal{A}$ as the second matrix required in the lemma. Even if $\mathcal{A}$ is an interval matrix, interval computations can be used to find rigorous bounds ϱ_1 and ϱ_2 using the numerical inverse $\mathcal{B}$ alone, and this typically leads to tight bounds K. See [**52**] for more details.

While the above procedure is easy to implement and to apply, two warnings are in order. First of all, note that the approach cannot be used to locate eigenvalues of multiplicity two and higher, since in such cases the pair (v, η) is never an isolated solution of (3.13). Secondly, while the above method proves the existence of an eigenvalue η, it does not provide an interval around η in which this eigenvalue is unique. The uniqueness assertion of the constructive implicit function theorem involves the pair (v, η), i.e., in principle there could be another eigenvalue pair $(\tilde{v}, \tilde{\eta})$ which is reasonably far away, but for which $\eta \approx \tilde{\eta}$. $\diamondsuit$

At first glance, the above method seems to be all one would need to rigorously determine the index of an equilibrium of the discrete Allen-Cahn equation, which is given by the number of positive eigenvalues of the linearization at the stationary state. Note, however, that if the dimension n in (2.2) is large and if the index of the considered equilibrium small, one would have to validate a large number of eigenvalues, most of which are negative and therefore irrelevant for determining the index. Even worse, the involved negative eigenvalues could form clusters, thereby leading to eigenvalues which are no longer simple in a numerical sense, and then the above method can easily fail to validate all n eigenvalues. In [**52**] we have described another approach based on rigorous eigenvalue exclusion and deflation which avoids these pitfalls. We refer the reader to this paper for more details.

3.2. Verification of Branch Segments. Just as in the classical case, the constructive implicit function theorem is a general result that is meant to be applied in a variety of contexts, and in this and the next section we present two of them. As a first application, we revisit the question of validating equilibrium branches. In its original form, Theorem 3.1 is ill-suited to prove the existence of branches of stationary states, since the targeted solution curve will usually not be aligned with the direction of the parameter axis.

As was already mentioned in previous lectures, efficient methods for following branches of solutions have to take the direction of the solution curve into account. This can either be accomplished by pseudo-arclength continuation, or by selecting numerical approximations of solutions at the endpoints of the considered parameter interval and then considering the line segment determined by them. The latter method can be implemented using the radii polynomial approach, which requires, however, explicit estimates along the parametrization of the line segment of approximative solutions.

In the present section, we will take a slightly different approach, which uses Theorem 3.1 as a proof-theoretic tool rather than the main continuation mechanism. In order to avoid confusion, we therefore change our notation describing the underlying parameter-dependent problems. From now on, we consider equilibrium problems of the form

$$\mathcal{F}(\lambda, u) = 0 , \tag{3.16}$$

where $\mathcal{F} : \mathbb{R} \times \mathcal{U} \to \mathcal{V}$ is a Fréchet differentiable nonlinear operator between two Banach spaces $\mathcal{U}$ and $\mathcal{V}$. The norms on these Banach spaces are denoted by $\|\cdot\|_{\mathcal{U}}$ and $\|\cdot\|_{\mathcal{V}}$, respectively. In all of the following results, we will study (3.16) in the neighborhood of a pair $(\lambda^*, u^*) \in \mathbb{R} \times \mathcal{U}$ which is an approximate solution. Our main goals will be two-fold:

- First of all, we would like to specify the line segment of approximative solutions in the form $u^* + (\lambda - \lambda^*)v^*$, for λ in an interval around λ^*, where the element $v^* \in \mathcal{U}^*$ denotes an appropriately chosen direction. Our result should explicitly state the size of the admissible λ-interval, and it should contain a criterion which measures the suitability of the "tangent" direction v^*. In this way, we do not have to provide two numerical approximations to validate the branch segment, but we can find the longest possible branch segment from a starting point and a direction alone, see also [**54**]. This is illustrated in the left panel of Figure 7.
- Secondly, we would like to avoid having to perform complicated nonlinearity estimates along the parametrized line segment of approximative solutions. Rather, we want to be able to base the result on simple standard nonlinearity results, which allow for relatively easy changes in the function $\mathcal{F}$ without the necessity for repeated involved nonlinearity estimates. See also the discussion in [**52**].

A closer look at the assumptions of the constructive implicit function theorem reveals that the main nonlinearity assumptions involve Lipschitz estimates for the first-order Fréchet derivatives. Thus, we assume that the function $\mathcal{F}$ satisfies the following.

(A) For (λ, u) close to (λ^*, u^*), the two partial Fréchet derivatives $D_u\mathcal{F}(\lambda, u)$ and $D_\lambda\mathcal{F}(\lambda, u)$ are locally Lipschitz continuous in the following sense. There exist real constants $M_k \geq 0$ for $k = 1, \ldots, 4$, as well as $d_u > 0$ and $d_\lambda > 0$, such that for all pairs $(\lambda, u) \in \mathbb{R} \times \mathcal{U}$ with $\|u - u^*\|_{\mathcal{U}} \leq d_u$ and $|\lambda - \lambda^*| \leq d_\lambda$ we have

$$\|D_u\mathcal{F}(\lambda, u) - D_u\mathcal{F}(\lambda^*, u^*)\|_{\mathcal{L}(\mathcal{U},\mathcal{V})} \leq M_1 \|u - u^*\|_{\mathcal{U}} + M_2 |\lambda - \lambda^*| , \tag{3.17}$$

$$\|D_\lambda\mathcal{F}(\lambda, u) - D_\lambda\mathcal{F}(\lambda^*, u^*)\|_{\mathcal{V}} \leq M_3 \|u - u^*\|_{\mathcal{U}} + M_4 |\lambda - \lambda^*| , \tag{3.18}$$

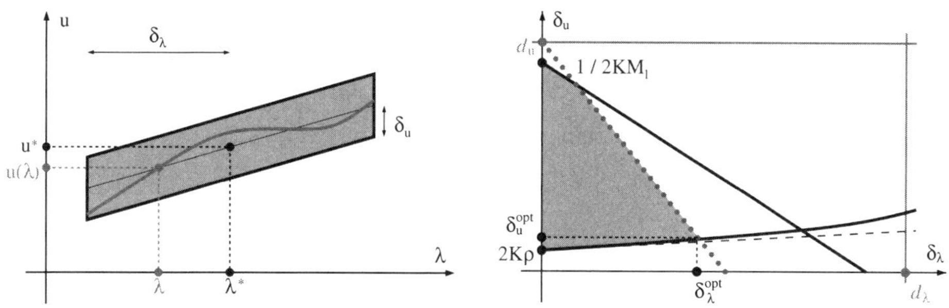

FIGURE 7. Visualization of the branch segment verification theorem. The left image illustrates the general statement of the theorem, i.e., in a slanted window around the approximative solution (λ^*, u^*) all solutions of $\mathcal{F}(\lambda, u) = 0$ lie on the curve $\lambda \mapsto u(\lambda)$. The size of the window is determined by the pair $(\delta_\lambda, \delta_u)$, and the shape of the admissible region from which these pairs can be chosen is illustrated in the right panel. Notice that if $\|v^*\|_{\mathcal{U}} \gg 0$, then the last constraint in (3.21), which is indicated in green (dotted line), might further restrict the admissible region. In practice, this usually does not happen.

where $\|\cdot\|_{\mathcal{L}(\mathcal{U},\mathcal{V})}$ denotes the operator norm in $\mathcal{L}(\mathcal{U},\mathcal{V})$, and as usual we identify $\mathcal{V}$ with $\mathcal{L}(\mathbb{R},\mathcal{V})$.

As we will see later on in the context of both the discrete Allen-Cahn equation and the diblock copolymer problem, estimates such as the ones required for (A) are usually easy to come by. Specifically in the case of partial differential equations, they can be achieved using standard Sobolev embedding techniques. Note in particular that these estimates are completely independent of the particular numerical approach which is used for finding an approximative solution pair (λ^*, u^*).

Based on the first goal stated earlier, we are trying to validate solutions (λ, u) of (3.16) close to the approximate solution $u^* + (\lambda - \lambda^*)v^*$. It is therefore natural to introduce new variables $\alpha \in \mathbb{R}$ and $x \in \mathcal{U}$ and consider the new nonlinear problem

$$\mathcal{G}(\alpha, x) = \mathcal{F}(\lambda^* + \alpha,\ u^* + \alpha v^* + x) = 0 ,$$

where $\mathcal{G} : \mathbb{R} \times \mathcal{U} \to \mathcal{V}$. Since $\mathcal{G}(0,0) = \mathcal{F}(\lambda^*, u^*)$, the new problem has an approximate zero at $(0,0)$, as long as $\mathcal{F}$ has an approximate zero at (λ^*, u^*). Moreover, the partial Fréchet derivatives of $\mathcal{G}$ with respect to x and α are given by

$$\begin{aligned} D_x\mathcal{G}(\alpha, x) &= D_u\mathcal{F}(\lambda^* + \alpha, u^* + \alpha v^* + x) , \\ D_\alpha\mathcal{G}(\alpha, x) &= D_\lambda\mathcal{F}(\lambda^* + \alpha, u^* + \alpha v^* + x) + D_u\mathcal{F}(\lambda^* + \alpha, u^* + \alpha v^* + x)[v^*] , \end{aligned}$$

and this shows that $D_x\mathcal{G}(0,0) = D_u\mathcal{F}(\lambda^*, u^*)$. This in turn implies that if we assume the existence of constants ϱ and K with

$$\|\mathcal{F}(\lambda^*, u^*)\|_{\mathcal{V}} \le \varrho \qquad \text{and} \qquad \left\|D_u\mathcal{F}(\lambda^*, u^*)^{-1}\right\|_{\mathcal{L}(\mathcal{V},\mathcal{U})} \le K ,$$

then $\mathcal{G}$ satisfies hypotheses (H1) and (H2) at the point $(\alpha^*, x^*) = (0,0)$, with the same constants. Thus, for an application of the constructive implicit function theorem we only have to establish hypotheses (H3) and (H4). For the former, one can easily see that the definition of $\mathcal{G}$ and (A) yield the estimate

$$\|D_x\mathcal{G}(\alpha, x) - D_x\mathcal{G}(0,0)\|_{\mathcal{L}(\mathcal{U},\mathcal{V})} \le M_1\|x\|_{\mathcal{U}} + (M_1 \|v^*\|_{\mathcal{U}} + M_2)\,|\alpha| \,,$$

and similarly one obtains

$$\begin{aligned}\|D_\alpha\mathcal{G}(\alpha,0)\|_{\mathcal{V}} &\le \|D_\alpha\mathcal{G}(0,0)\|_{\mathcal{V}} + \|D_\alpha\mathcal{G}(\alpha,0) - D_\alpha\mathcal{G}(0,0)\|_{\mathcal{V}} \\ &\le \|D_\lambda\mathcal{F}(\lambda^*,u^*) + D_u\mathcal{F}(\lambda^*,u^*)\,[v^*]\|_{\mathcal{V}} \\ &\qquad + |\alpha|\cdot\Big(M_1\,\|v^*\|_{\mathcal{U}}^2 + (M_2+M_3)\,\|v^*\|_{\mathcal{U}} + M_4\Big)\,.\end{aligned}$$

In other words, all the assumptions of Theorem 3.1 are satisfied, and the constants in hypotheses (H3) and (H4) can easily be computed from the constants in (A) and the choice of the continuation direction v^*. Note, however, that since (A) contains restrictions on the deviations $\|u-u^*\|_{\mathcal{U}}$ and $|\lambda-\lambda^*|$, these will lead to an additional constraint on the window sizes δ_α and δ_x in Theorem 3.1. All of this is summarized in the following result, whose detailed proof can be found in [**52**].

THEOREM 3.5 (Branch Segment Verification). *Let $\mathcal{U}$ and $\mathcal{V}$ be Banach spaces, and suppose that the nonlinear parameter-dependent operator $\mathcal{F} : \mathbb{R}\times\mathcal{U} \to \mathcal{V}$ is both Fréchet differentiable and satisfies (A). Assume that $(\lambda^*, u^*) \in \mathbb{R}\times\mathcal{U}$ satisfies the estimates*

$$\|\mathcal{F}(\lambda^*,u^*)\|_{\mathcal{V}} \le \varrho \qquad \textit{and} \qquad \left\|D_u\mathcal{F}(\lambda^*,u^*)^{-1}\right\|_{\mathcal{L}(\mathcal{V},\mathcal{U})} \le K\,, \tag{3.19}$$

for some positive constants ϱ and K, and let $v^* \in \mathcal{U}$ be given with

$$\|D_\lambda\mathcal{F}(\lambda^*,u^*) + D_u\mathcal{F}(\lambda^*,u^*)[v^*]\|_{\mathcal{V}} \le \sigma\,, \tag{3.20}$$

for some constant $\sigma \ge 0$. Finally, suppose that

$$4K^2\varrho M_1 < 1 \qquad \textit{and} \qquad 2K\varrho < d_u\,.$$

Then there exist pairs of constants $(\delta_\lambda, \delta_u)$ which satisfy

$$0 < \delta_\lambda \le d_\lambda\,, \qquad 0<\delta_u \le d_u\,, \qquad \textit{and} \qquad \delta_\lambda\,\|v^*\|_{\mathcal{U}} + \delta_u \le d_u\,, \tag{3.21}$$

as well as

$$2KM_1\delta_u + 2K\,(M_1\,\|v^*\|_{\mathcal{U}} + M_2)\,\delta_\lambda \le 1$$

and

$$2K\varrho + 2K\sigma\delta_\lambda + 2K\Big(M_1\,\|v^*\|_{\mathcal{U}}^2 + (M_2+M_3)\,\|v^*\|_{\mathcal{U}} + M_4\Big)\,\delta_\lambda^2 \le \delta_u\,,$$

and for each such pair the following holds. For every $\lambda\in\mathbb{R}$ with $|\lambda-\lambda^*| \le \delta_\lambda$ there exists a uniquely determined element $u(\lambda) \in \mathcal{U}$ with $\|u(\lambda)-(u^*+(\lambda-\lambda^*)v^*)\|_{\mathcal{U}} \le \delta_u$ for which the nonlinear equation $\mathcal{F}(\lambda,u(\lambda)) = 0$ is satisfied. In other words, all solutions of the nonlinear problem $\mathcal{F}(\lambda,u)=0$ in the slanted set

$$\{(\lambda,u)\in\mathbb{R}\times\mathcal{U} \;:\; |\lambda-\lambda^*| \le \delta_\lambda \quad \textit{and} \quad \|u-(u^*+(\lambda-\lambda^*)\,v^*)\|_{\mathcal{U}} \le \delta_u\}$$

lie on the branch $\lambda \mapsto u(\lambda)$. This statement is illustrated in the left panel of Figure 7, while the right panel depicts the admissible region of all pairs $(\delta_\lambda,\delta_u)$ for which the result holds.

Our above discussion shows that Theorem 3.5 is more or less a direct corollary of the constructive implicit function theorem. It is therefore natural to wonder why we even formulated this new result. In fact, one can easily see that for $v^*=0$ the branch segment verification theorem reduces to Theorem 3.1, albeit for the special case $\mathcal{P} = \mathbb{R}$. In this situation, the value of $L_3 = \sigma$ in (3.20) is basically given by the norm of $D_\lambda \mathcal{F}(\lambda^*, u^*)$, which in turn could be quite large. Note, however, that the value of L_3 in the constructive implicit function theorem affects the slope of the dashed blue line in the right panel of Figure 6, and large values of this slope lead to extremely small values of $\delta_\alpha^{\text{opt}}$. In other words, if L_3 is large, the parameter width of the validation window is extremely small.

Consider now the situation of Theorem 3.5, and choose the direction vector v^* close to the tangent direction of the solution branch. Then the expression on the left-hand side of (3.20) is extremely small, i.e., the slope of the dashed blue line in the right panel of Figure 7 will be close to zero, which leads to considerably larger values of $\delta_\lambda^{\text{opt}}$. This comes at the price of the additional constraint in (3.21), which is indicated in green in the right panel of Figure 7. Usually, however, this constraint does not impose any additional restriction — and even if it does, one can easily determine the new value of the optimal λ-interval. In other words, Theorem 3.5 fulfills our second goal stated at the beginning of the section. The value of σ is a means of quantifying the quality of the continuation direction: Values of σ close to zero lead to the largest window sizes in the left panel of Figure 7, larger values of σ to smaller parameter validation intervals. But in either case, the branch segment validation theorem provides explicit formulas for the size of the branch segment that can be validated.

We close this section by outlining how the branch segment verification theorem can be applied to the one-dimensional diblock copolymer model.

EXAMPLE 3.6 (Branch Segments for the Diblock Copolymer Model). We now return to the diblock copolymer equation (2.4) which was introduced in Section 2.2. To keep the presentation simple, we only consider the interval $\Omega = (0, 1)$. Moreover, we slightly rewrite the equation by incorporating the total mass value μ into the equation through the transformation $u \mapsto \mu + u$. In this way, the mass constraint for u can be kept fixed at zero, and (2.5) is equivalent to the nonlinear operator equation

$$\mathcal{F}(\lambda, u) \;=\; -\left(u_{xx} + \lambda f_\mu(u)\right)_{xx} - \lambda \sigma u \;=\; 0\,, \tag{3.22}$$

where due to the above transformation we usually choose $f_\mu(u) = (\mu + u) - (\mu + u)^3$. Note that even though both μ and σ are parameters of the model, we only emphasize the dependence on λ in the definition of F, as this is our main bifurcation parameter.

To apply Theorem 3.5, one first needs to define suitable Banach spaces for the operator $\mathcal{F}$. As usual in partial differential equations, we consider spaces which already incorporate the boundary conditions, and for the purposes of this lecture we consider function spaces related to the Sobolev spaces $H^k(0,1) = W^{k,2}(0,1)$, see for example [**1**]. Particularly important is the space $H^1(0,1)$ of all weakly differentiable $L^2(0,1)$-functions whose weak derivative u' is square-integrable, equipped with the standard norm

$$\|u\|_{H^1(0,1)} = \sqrt{\|u\|_{L^2(0,1)}^2 + \|u'\|_{L^2(0,1)}^2}\,.$$

Due to the zero mass constraint for u, we specifically consider subspaces $\mathcal{H}^k$ of the Sobolev spaces $H^k(0,1)$, which are defined as follows. Note first that the eigenvalues and eigenfunctions of the negative Laplacian $-u_{xx}$ on the interval $\Omega = (0,1)$ and subject to homogeneous Neumann boundary conditions, are given by the constant function $\varphi_0(x) = 1$ with eigenvalue $\kappa_0 = 0$, together with the sequence

$$\kappa_\ell = \ell^2\pi^2 \quad \text{and} \quad \varphi_\ell(x) = \sqrt{2}\cos \ell\pi x \quad \text{for} \quad \ell \in \mathbb{N}\, .$$

Then we define

$$\mathcal{H}^k = \left\{ u = \sum_{\ell=1}^{\infty} \alpha_\ell \varphi_\ell \; : \; \|u\|_{\mathcal{H}^k} < \infty \right\} , \qquad \text{where} \qquad \|u\|_{\mathcal{H}^k} = \sqrt{\sum_{\ell=1}^{\infty} \kappa_\ell^k \alpha_\ell^2}\, .$$

In the definition of $\mathcal{H}^k$, the constant eigenfunction φ_0 is omitted due to the zero mass constraint. For $k \geq 0$ the coefficients α_ℓ are given by $\alpha_\ell = (u, \varphi_\ell)_{L^2(0,1)}$, since the eigenfunctions φ_ℓ form a complete orthonormal set in $L^2(0,1)$. Furthermore, one can easily show that the spaces $\mathcal{H}^k$ are Hilbert spaces, see [**57**]. We would like to specifically point out that the convergence in the sum $u = \sum_{\ell=1}^{\infty} \alpha_\ell\varphi_\ell$ is measured in the $\mathcal{H}^k$-norm, i.e., it is not true in general that the series is pointwise convergent.

With the help of these spaces, we can now reformulate the nonlinear problem (3.22) in the proper functional-analytic setting. For this, let $\mu \in \mathbb{R}$ and $\sigma \in \mathbb{R}_0^+$ be arbitrary, but fixed, real constants. Then we consider the nonlinear operator $\mathcal{F}$ defined by

$$\mathcal{F} : \mathbb{R} \times \mathcal{U} \to \mathcal{V} \qquad \text{with} \qquad \mathcal{F}(\lambda, u) = -\left(u_{xx} + \lambda f_\mu(u)\right)_{xx} - \lambda\sigma u \tag{3.23}$$

$$\text{and} \qquad \mathcal{U} = \mathcal{H}^1 , \quad \mathcal{V} = \mathcal{H}^{-3} .$$

It follows from standard results that this operator is Fréchet differentiable, and straightforward partial differential equations estimates based on Sobolev's embedding theorem yield the following. Let $d_u > 0$ and $d_\lambda > 0$ be arbitrary constants, and let $(\lambda^*, u^*) \in \mathbb{R} \times \mathcal{U}$. Then for all points $(\lambda, u) \in \mathbb{R} \times \mathcal{U}$ with $\|u - u^*\|_{\mathcal{U}} \leq d_u$ and $|\lambda - \lambda^*| \leq d_\lambda$ we have

$$\begin{aligned} \|D_u\mathcal{F}(\lambda,u) - D_u\mathcal{F}(\lambda^*,u^*)\|_{\mathcal{L}(\mathcal{U},\mathcal{V})} &\leq M_1 \|u - u^*\|_{\mathcal{U}} + M_2 |\lambda - \lambda^*| , \\ \|D_\lambda\mathcal{F}(\lambda,u) - D_\lambda\mathcal{F}(\lambda^*,u^*)\|_{\mathcal{V}} &\leq M_3 \|u - u^*\|_{\mathcal{U}} . \end{aligned}$$

Using $C_a = \sqrt{(e^2+1)/(e^2-1)} \approx 1.14588$ and $C_c = \sqrt{1+\pi^2}/\pi \approx 1.04944$, see for example [**57**, Lemma 3.1], the Lipschitz constants are given by

$$\begin{aligned} M_1 &= \frac{2\sqrt{2}C_aC_c^2}{\pi^2}\left(f_{\max}^{(2)} + f_{\max}^{(3)}C_aC_cd_u + f_{\max}^{(3)}C_aC_c\|u^*\|_{\mathcal{H}^1}\right)\left(|\lambda^*| + d_\lambda\right) , \\ M_2 &= \frac{\sigma}{\pi^4} + \frac{2C_aC_c}{\pi^2}\left\|f_\mu'(u^*)\right\|_{H^1(0,1)} , \qquad \text{and} \\ M_3 &= \frac{\sigma}{\pi^4} + \frac{\sqrt{2}C_c}{\pi^2}\left(f_{\max}^{(1)} + f_{\max}^{(2)}C_aC_cd_u + f_{\max}^{(2)}C_aC_c\|u^*\|_{\mathcal{H}^1}\right) , \end{aligned}$$

where we use the abbreviations

$$f_{\max}^{(p)} = \max\left\{\left|f_\mu^{(p)}(\xi)\right| \; : \; |\xi| \leq \|u^*\|_\infty + C_aC_cd_u\right\} . \tag{3.24}$$

Thus, the nonlinear operator $\mathcal{F}$ defined in (3.23) satisfies assumption (A) with constants as above, as well as with $M_4 = 0$. We would like to point out that the above estimates hold for arbitrary nonlinearities f_μ, only the values in (3.24) have to be adjusted. For simple nonlinearities such as $f_\mu(u) = (\mu+u) - (\mu+u)^3$ this formula can easily be evaluated, and if $\|u^*\|_\infty$ is not easily available one can further use the estimate $\|u^*\|_\infty \le C_a C_c \|u^*\|_{\mathcal{H}^1}$ to extend the range for ξ in (3.24).

With the completion of the general nonlinearity estimates in (A), one is now in a position to apply the branch segment validation theorem. This can be accomplished as follows.

- Suppose we have constructed an approximation u^* of a solution of (3.22) at the parameter value λ^* in the form

$$u^* = \sum_{\ell=1}^{N} \alpha_\ell^* \varphi_\ell \quad \text{for some} \quad N \in \mathbb{N} \quad \text{and} \quad \alpha_1^*, \ldots, \alpha_N^* \in \mathbb{R} .$$

  In [**57**], for example, this was achieved by using a spectral discretization of the diblock copolymer model in combination with AUTO [**22**]. Then for polynomial nonlinearities both the first estimate in (3.19) and the one in (3.20) can be established easily using interval arithmetic.
- Finding a constant K such that the second estimate in (3.19) holds is more involved, and lies beyond the scope of this lecture. We refer the reader to [**57**] for more details, and only provide a very brief outline. The main idea is to use the eigenvalue exclusion methods developed in [**58**] to construct an interval $(-\tau, \tau)$ in which an underlying self-adjoint linear operator has no eigenvalues, and then use $K = 1/\tau$. The main difficulty in using this approach for the linearization $D_u\mathcal{F}(\lambda^*, u^*)$ is the fact that it is not self-adjoint in the space $\mathcal{H}^1$. This can, however, be addressed by showing that $(-\Delta)^{-2} D_u\mathcal{F}(\lambda^*, u^*)$ is self-adjoint in $\mathcal{H}^1$, and then considering a suitably transformed eigenvalue problem.

For a much more detailed account of the diblock copolymer case, particularly concerning the computation of the inverse operator norm bound K, we refer the reader to [**57**]. Notice that this paper only uses the constructive implicit function theorem in its original form, i.e., for the special case $v^* = 0$. This, however, can easily be extended using the estimates above. ◊

3.3. Resolving Saddle-Node Bifurcations. Through iterative applications, the branch segment validation theorem can be used to validate long pieces of solution branches. This is illustrated in the left image of Figure 8, where for each piece of the red solution curve of the equation $\mathcal{F}(\lambda, u) = 0$ one uses a possibly different direction vector v^* for the application of Theorem 3.5. For the upper half of the branch, the validation starts at the right-most box, and the black dot at its center indicates the first approximative solution. Subsequent applications move to the left, and in these cases the new solution approximations are located at the left sides of the respective previous boxes — still indicated by black dots. This leads to overlapping regions, where for the sake of clarity we only show the left halves of the later validation boxes. The lower half of the branch is also validated from right to left. Notice that in all of these applications of Theorem 3.5, the λ-extent of the validation neighborhood is automatically provided. Yet, the image also shows something else. If the solution branch contains a saddle-node bifurcation point, such as the one indicated by a dark red dot, Theorem 3.5 can in principle not be used to validate the complete branch — locally near the bifurcation point the solution curve is not a graph over λ. As will be demonstrated in the following, even though Theorem 3.5 does not apply near saddle-node bifurcation points, one can

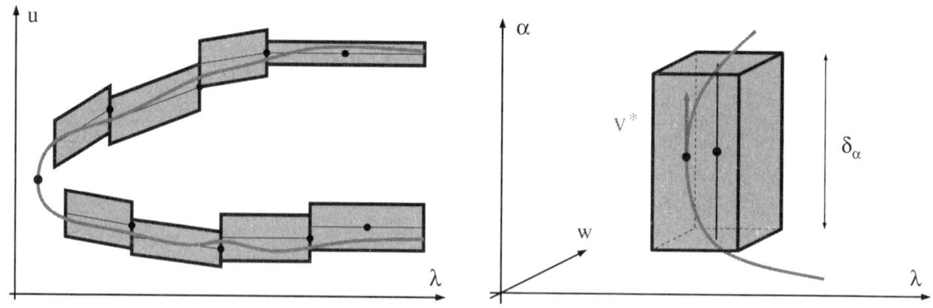

FIGURE 8. Visualization of the saddle-node branch verification theorem. The left panel illustrates how successive applications of Theorem 3.5 can be used to validate solution branches away from saddle-node bifurcation points. Notice that in the image, only the two right-most branch windows are shown in their entirety, for the remaining six windows only the left half is plotted in order to keep the image cleaner. Imagining the omitted halves indicates that the verified branch pieces do in fact overlap, which is necessary to establish the smoothness of larger branch pieces. The branch close to the bifurcation point can be validated with the help of Theorem 3.7, whose setup is illustrated in the right panel. The vector v^* is an approximation for the kernel element of the Fréchet derivative $D_u\mathcal{F}$ at the saddle-node bifurcation point. The α-axis is parallel to v^*, and the w-axis represents a complementary subspace in the Banach space $\mathcal{U}$.

still use the constructive implicit function theorem to validate the solution branch in a neighborhood of such bifurcations. This time, however, Theorem 3.1 has to be applied in combination with a suitable change of variables. We would like to point out that this type of validation can also be achieved using pseudo-arclength continuation, yet at the expense of a more involved implementation.

To motivate the change of variables used in our approach, we assume for the moment that (λ_0, u_0) is a saddle-node bifurcation point for (3.16). Then the Fréchet derivative $D_u\mathcal{F}(\lambda_0, u_0)$ has to have a nontrivial kernel — and generically one would expect that this kernel is one-dimensional and spanned by some nonzero element $v_0 \in \mathcal{U}$. In addition, at the saddle-node bifurcation point the solution curve should be parallel to the vector v_0. Now let $\mathcal{U}^\perp \subset \mathcal{U}$ denote a subspace which is complementary to the kernel of $D_u\mathcal{F}(\lambda_0, u_0)$. Based on this discussion one can expect that if we decompose $u \in \mathcal{U}$ as

$$u = u_0 + \alpha v_0 + w \quad \text{with} \quad \alpha \in \mathbb{R} \quad \text{and} \quad w \in \mathcal{U}^\perp ,$$

then locally near the assumed saddle-node bifurcation point (λ_0, u_0) the solution curve of (3.16) can be parameterized by α.

In practice, the saddle-node bifurcation point is not known exactly, i.e., one only has an approximation $(\lambda^*, u^*) \approx (\lambda_0, u_0)$ which satisfies $\mathcal{F}(\lambda^*, u^*) \approx 0$. This usually implies that the Fréchet derivative $D_u\mathcal{F}(\lambda^*, u^*)$ at the approximative bifurcation point is invertible, so at first glance there does not seem to be a natural candidate for the tangent direction v^*. Yet, one can pick any nonzero element $v^* \in \mathcal{U}$ for which $D_u\mathcal{F}(\lambda^*, u^*)[v^*] \approx 0$, and it is possible to construct the complementary space $\mathcal{U}^\perp$ in the following way. Choose a bounded linear one-to-one operator of the form $w \mapsto \mathcal{H}w$ where the range $R(\mathcal{H})$ satisfies $\mathcal{U} = \mathrm{span}[v^*] \oplus R(\mathcal{H})$. Using these preparations, the constructive implicit function theorem can then be used to validate the branch. This leads to the following theorem.

THEOREM 3.7 (Saddle-Node Branch Verification). *Let $\mathcal{U}$ and $\mathcal{V}$ be Banach spaces, and suppose that the nonlinear parameter-dependent operator $\mathcal{F} : \mathbb{R}\times\mathcal{U} \to \mathcal{V}$ is both Fréchet differentiable and satisfies (A). Assume that both $(\lambda^*, u^*) \in \mathbb{R} \times \mathcal{U}$ and $v^* \in \mathcal{U} \setminus \{0\}$ satisfy the estimates*

$$\|\mathcal{F}(\lambda^*, u^*)\|_{\mathcal{V}} \le \varrho \qquad \text{and} \qquad \|D_u\mathcal{F}(\lambda^*, u^*)[v^*]\|_{\mathcal{V}} \le \sigma\,, \tag{3.25}$$

for some nonnegative constants $\varrho \ge 0$ and $\sigma \ge 0$. In addition, let $\mathcal{W}$ denote another Banach space with norm $\|\cdot\|_{\mathcal{W}}$, and let $\mathcal{H} : \mathcal{W} \to \mathcal{U}$ be an injective bounded linear operator such that

$$R(\mathcal{H}) \ \text{is closed} \qquad \text{and} \qquad \mathcal{U} = \mathrm{span}[v^*] \oplus R(\mathcal{H})\,,$$

and assume that there exists a constant $K > 0$ such that

$$K \left\| D_\lambda\mathcal{F}(\lambda^*, u^*)\bar{\lambda} + D_u\mathcal{F}(\lambda^*, u^*)\,[\mathcal{H}\bar{w}] \right\|_{\mathcal{V}} \ge \max\left\{ |\bar{\lambda}|\,,\, \|\bar{w}\|_{\mathcal{W}} \right\} \tag{3.26}$$

for all $\bar{\lambda} \in \mathbb{R}$ and $\bar{w} \in \mathcal{W}$. Finally, define

$$L_1 = M_1 \|\mathcal{H}\|^2_{\mathcal{L}(\mathcal{W},\mathcal{U})} + (M_2 + M_3)\,\|\mathcal{H}\|_{\mathcal{L}(\mathcal{W},\mathcal{U})} + M_4$$

and suppose that

$$4K^2\varrho L_1 < 1 \qquad \text{and} \qquad 2K\varrho < \ell_x = \min\left\{ d_\lambda\,,\, \frac{d_u}{\|\mathcal{H}\|_{\mathcal{L}(\mathcal{W},\mathcal{U})}} \right\}. \tag{3.27}$$

If in addition to the definition of ℓ_x in (3.27) we also define $\ell_\alpha = d_u/\|v^*\|_{\mathcal{U}}$, then there exist pairs of constants $(\delta_\alpha, \delta_x)$ which satisfy

$$0 < \delta_\alpha \le \ell_\alpha\,, \qquad 0 < \delta_x \le \ell_x\,, \qquad \text{and} \qquad \delta_\alpha\,\|v^*\|_{\mathcal{U}} + \delta_x\,\|\mathcal{H}\|_{\mathcal{L}(\mathcal{W},\mathcal{U})} \le d_u\,, \tag{3.28}$$

as well as

$$2KL_1\delta_x + 2K\left(M_1\,\|\mathcal{H}\|_{\mathcal{L}(\mathcal{W},\mathcal{U})} + M_3 \right) \|v^*\|_{\mathcal{U}}\,\delta_\alpha \le 1 \tag{3.29}$$

and

$$2K\varrho + 2K\sigma\delta_\alpha + 2KM_1\,\|v^*\|^2_{\mathcal{U}}\,\delta_\alpha^2 \le \delta_x\,, \tag{3.30}$$

and for each such pair the following holds. For every $\alpha \in \mathbb{R}$ with $|\alpha| \le \delta_\alpha$ there exist uniquely determined elements $\lambda(\alpha) \in \mathbb{R}$ and $w(\alpha) \in \mathcal{W}$ with

$$|\lambda(\alpha) - \lambda^*| \le \delta_x \qquad \text{and} \qquad \|w(\alpha)\|_{\mathcal{W}} \le \delta_x\,,$$

for which the nonlinear equation $\mathcal{F}(\lambda(\alpha), u^* + \alpha v^* + \mathcal{H}w(\alpha)) = 0$ is satisfied. In other words, all solutions of the nonlinear problem $\mathcal{F}(\lambda, u) = 0$ in the set

$$\{(\lambda, u) \in \mathbb{R}\times\mathcal{U} \;:\; |\lambda - \lambda^*| \le \delta_x,\ u = u^* + \alpha v^* + \mathcal{H}w \ \text{with}\ |\alpha| \le \delta_\alpha,\ \|w\|_{\mathcal{W}} \le \delta_x\}$$

lie on the branch $\alpha \mapsto (\lambda(\alpha), u(\alpha))$, where we use $u(\alpha) = u^* + \alpha v^* + \mathcal{H}w(\alpha)$. This statement is illustrated in the right panel of Figure 8.

We would like to point out that the naming of Theorem 3.7 was chosen to reflect the fact that it can be used for branch validation close to a saddle-node bifurcation. However, it also does apply in situations in which there is no saddle-node bifurcation close by, but the linearization $D_u\mathcal{F}(\lambda^*, u^*)$ is close to singular.

The detailed proof of Theorem 3.7 can be found in [**52**], in the following we only present a brief sketch of the basic setup. Define $\mathcal{P} = \mathbb{R}$ and $\mathcal{Y} = \mathcal{V}$, and consider the product Banach space $\mathcal{X} = \mathbb{R} \times \mathcal{W}$ with norm $\|(\lambda, w)\|_{\mathcal{X}} = \max\{|\lambda|, \|w\|_{\mathcal{W}}\}$. Moreover, define the nonlinear operator $\mathcal{G} : \mathcal{P} \times \mathcal{X} \to \mathcal{Y}$ as

$$\mathcal{G}(\alpha, x) = \mathcal{F}(\lambda, u^* + \alpha v^* + \mathcal{H}w) , \quad \text{where} \quad x = (\lambda, w) \in \mathcal{X} = \mathbb{R} \times \mathcal{W} .$$

The goal of Theorem 3.7 is to establish the existence of a branch of solutions of $\mathcal{G}(\alpha, x) = 0$ close to the point $(\alpha^*, x^*) = (0, (\lambda^*, 0))$. Since $\mathcal{G}(\alpha^*, x^*) = \mathcal{F}(\lambda^*, u^*)$, hypothesis (H1) follows from the first estimate in (3.25). Moreover, the new mapping $\mathcal{G}$ is Fréchet differentiable at every point (α, x), where $x = (\lambda, w) \in \mathbb{R} \times \mathcal{W}$, and both

$$D_\alpha\mathcal{G}(\alpha, x) = D_u\mathcal{F}(\lambda, u^* + \alpha v^* + \mathcal{H}w)[v^*]$$

and

$$D_x\mathcal{G}(\alpha, x)\left[(\bar{\lambda}, \bar{w})\right] = D_\lambda\mathcal{F}(\lambda, u^* + \alpha v^* + \mathcal{H}w)\,\bar{\lambda} + D_u\mathcal{F}(\lambda, u^* + \alpha v^* + \mathcal{H}w)[\mathcal{H}\bar{w}]$$

are satisfied, where $\bar{x} = (\bar{\lambda}, \bar{w}) \in \mathcal{X} = \mathbb{R} \times \mathcal{W}$ is arbitrary. At the specific pair (α^*, x^*) these formulas simplify to

$$D_\alpha\mathcal{G}(\alpha^*, x^*) = D_u\mathcal{F}(\lambda^*, u^*)[v^*]$$

and

$$D_x\mathcal{G}(\alpha^*, x^*)\left[(\bar{\lambda}, \bar{w})\right] = D_\lambda\mathcal{F}(\lambda^*, u^*)\,\bar{\lambda} + D_u\mathcal{F}(\lambda^*, u^*)[\mathcal{H}\bar{w}] ,$$

and hypothesis (H2) follows readily from (3.26). The remaining two hypotheses (H3) and (H4) can easily be obtained from assumption (A), and as in the case of the branch segment validation theorem, this leads to the additional last constraint in (3.28), as well as a modified (3.29).

At first glance, the form of Theorem 3.7 might be somewhat overwhelming. However, its underlying assumptions are straightforward to verify. As before, one only needs a parameter-dependent mapping $\mathcal{F}$ satisfying (A), as well as bounds of the form

$$\|\mathcal{F}(\lambda^*, u^*)\|_{\mathcal{V}} \le \varrho \qquad \text{and} \qquad \|D_u\mathcal{F}(\lambda^*, u^*)[v^*]\|_{\mathcal{V}} \le \sigma ,$$

where usually one ensures $\|v^*\|_{\mathcal{U}} \approx 1$ and tries to make the constants ϱ and σ as small as possible. The latter should always be possible close to a saddle-node bifurcation point. Beyond these two estimates, one also needs the invertibility condition (3.26), which leads to the inverse bound K. Theorem 3.7 then applies as long as the estimate

$$4K^2\varrho\left(M_1\|\mathcal{H}\|^2_{\mathcal{L}(\mathcal{W},\mathcal{U})} + (M_2 + M_3)\|\mathcal{H}\|_{\mathcal{L}(\mathcal{W},\mathcal{U})} + M_4\right) < 1$$

holds. In other words, the above basic assumptions always guarantee the existence of a small solution branch. In practice, one would like this branch to be as large as possible, and for this one needs to be able to choose the constant δ_α as large as possible. The crucial constraint in this context is (3.30), which contains the small constant σ in the linear δ_α-term. As discussed in the last section, larger branch pieces can be obtained for smaller values of σ, and this in turn can be achieved by employing accurate approximations of the kernel function at the saddle-node bifurcation point.

We close this section by outlining how Theorems 3.5 and 3.7 can be applied to the one-dimensional discrete Allen-Cahn equation. In combination with Example 3.3, this allows us to rigorously prove the existence of global solution branches which are generated through saddle-node bifurcation points.

EXAMPLE 3.8 (Branch Validation for the Discrete Allen-Cahn Equation). Consider the discrete Allen-Cahn equation defined in (2.2), but for the specific nonlinearity $f(u) = u - u^3$. In contrast to Example 3.3, we now write the equation for equilibrium solutions of (2.2) in the form

$$\mathcal{F}(\lambda, u) = Au + \lambda f(u) = 0 \qquad \text{with} \qquad \lambda \in \mathbb{R} \quad \text{and} \quad u \in \mathbb{R}^n \, , \tag{3.31}$$

where $A \in \mathbb{R}^{n\times n}$ was defined in (3.11), we use the notation $u = (u_1, \ldots, u_n)^t$ for the components of the vector u, and define $f(u) = (f(u_1), \ldots, f(u_n))^t$ componentwise. Moreover, we consider the Banach space $\mathbb{R}^n$ equipped with the maximum norm, and on the set of matrices in $\mathbb{R}^{n\times n}$ we use the induced matrix norm, see (3.12).

In order to apply Theorems 3.5 and 3.7 to the discrete Allen-Cahn equilibrium equation, the fundamental first step is the establishment of assumption (A). Due to the simple form of the nonlinearity $f(u)$, this can easily be done using the standard mean value theorem. If we assume that $\lambda^* \in \mathbb{R}$ and $u^* \in \mathbb{R}^n$ are arbitrary, but fixed, and if $d_u > 0$ is a given constant, then for all choices of $\lambda \in \mathbb{R}$ and $u \in \mathbb{R}^n$ which satisfy $\|u - u^*\| \le d_u$ one obtains the estimates

$$\begin{aligned} \|D_u\mathcal{F}(\lambda, u) - D_u\mathcal{F}(\lambda^*, u^*)\| &\le M_1 \|u - u^*\| + M_2 |\lambda - \lambda^*| \, , \\ \|D_\lambda\mathcal{F}(\lambda, u) - D_\lambda\mathcal{F}(\lambda^*, u^*)\| &\le M_3 \|u - u^*\| + M_4 |\lambda - \lambda^*| \, , \end{aligned}$$

where

$$M_1 = |\lambda^*| \max_{|\xi|\le\|u^*\|+d_u} |f''(\xi)| \, , \quad M_2 = M_3 = \max_{|\xi|\le\|u^*\|+d_u} |f'(\xi)| \, , \quad \text{and} \quad M_4 = 0 \, . \tag{3.32}$$

In other words, the nonlinear mapping $\mathcal{F}$ defined in (3.31) satisfies (A) with d_u as above and $d_\lambda = \infty$. We would like to point out that these formulas for the constants M_k hold for arbitrary smooth nonlinearities f and can easily be evaluated for specific choices. In our situation, for example, one can choose

$$M_1 = 6\,|\lambda^*|\,(\|u^*\| + d_u) \qquad \text{and} \qquad M_2 = M_3 = 1 + 3\,(\|u^*\| + d_u)^2 \tag{3.33}$$

for the three nonzero constants by further bounding the right-hand sides in (3.32) from above using $f'(u) = 1 - 3u^2$ and $f''(u) = -6u$. Despite the fact that these new constants are not optimal, they suffice for our applications and will be used in the remainder of the example.

Applying Theorems 3.5 and 3.7 to the discrete Allen-Cahn equation is now straightforward. For this, assume we have found a numerical approximation (λ^*, u^*) to a solution of $\mathcal{F}(\lambda, u) = 0$. We only need to establish the estimates in (3.19) and (3.20), or in (3.25) and (3.26), respectively. This can be done in a computational way, by taking into account all occurring roundoff errors through the use of interval arithmetic [**41**]. For our application, we use the MATLAB toolbox INTLAB [**48**] in the following way.

- **Computing** ϱ: Using the numerical approximation (λ^*, u^*) one can use interval arithmetic to find an enclosing interval for the value of $\|\mathcal{F}(\lambda^*, u^*)\|$.

If we denote the right endpoint of this interval by ϱ, then the first estimates in both (3.19) and (3.25) hold. We would like to emphasize that if one starts with a good enough solution approximation, then the constant ϱ will be only slightly larger than machine precision.

- **Computing** σ: To establish (3.20), let v^* denote a numerical approximation of the solution v of the linear system $D_u\mathcal{F}(\lambda^*, u^*)[v] = -D_\lambda\mathcal{F}(\lambda^*, u^*)$, which in the discrete Allen-Cahn case is given by

$$Av + \lambda^* \operatorname{diag}(f'(u^*))v = -f(u^*) \; .$$

Proceeding as in the first point, one can then compute a constant σ such that (3.20) is satisfied. The same method can be used to establish the second estimate in (3.25), if the vector v^* is chosen as an approximation to the kernel function of the linearization at the saddle-node bifurcation point. This can be done by letting v^* be a normalized numerical approximation to an eigenvector of $D_u\mathcal{F}(\lambda^*, u^*)$ which corresponds to the eigenvalue closest to zero.

- **Computing** K: For the second estimate in (3.19), we need to determine a rigorous upper bound on the norm of the inverse of

$$D_u\mathcal{F}(\lambda^*, u^*) = A + \lambda^* \operatorname{diag}(f'(u^*)) \; .$$

Passing to interval enclosures for both λ^* and u^*, the software package INTLAB can be used to compute an interval matrix which contains the true linearization $D_u\mathcal{F}(\lambda^*, u^*)$. In other words, if we let Ξ denote the set of all matrices whose entries are contained in the respective interval entries of this interval matrix, then $D_u\mathcal{F}(\lambda^*, u^*) \in \Xi$. Following [**49**], let $B \in \mathbb{R}^{n\times n}$ be the numerically computed inverse of an arbitrary matrix in the set Ξ, for example the midpoint of Ξ. Then interval computations provide rigorous bounds $0 < \varrho_1 < 1$ and $\varrho_2 > 0$ with

$$\|I - BC\| \le \varrho_1 \quad \text{for all} \quad C \in \Xi \; , \quad \text{as well as} \quad \|B\| \le \varrho_2 \; ,$$

and Lemma 3.2 immediately implies that every matrix $C \in \Xi$ is in fact invertible with $\|C^{-1}\| \le \varrho_2/(1-\varrho_1)$. In other words, if we choose K as the right endpoint of the interval enclosure of $\varrho_2/(1-\varrho_1)$, then the second estimate in (3.19) holds.

Assumption (3.26) can be treated similarly, but we first have to choose the operator $\mathcal{H}$. For this, define $\mathcal{W} = \mathbb{R}^{n-1}$ and let $k \in \{1, \ldots, n\}$ denote the index for which

$$|v_k^*| \;=\; \|v^*\| \;=\; \max_{\ell=1,\ldots,n} |v_\ell^*| \;>\; 0 \; .$$

Now let $\mathcal{H} \in \mathbb{R}^{n\times(n-1)}$ denote the matrix which is obtained from the identity matrix in $\mathbb{R}^{n\times n}$ by removing the k-th column. Then the range of $\mathcal{H}$ is just the orthogonal complement of the k-th standard unit vector in $\mathbb{R}^n$, and due to $v_k^* \ne 0$ this immediately implies $\mathbb{R}^n = \operatorname{span}[v^*] \oplus R(\mathcal{H})$. Moreover, the induced matrix norm of $\mathcal{H}$ is exactly 1 and $\mathcal{H}$ has a trivial kernel. Then as above we can find a constant K such that

$$\left\| \left(\; D_\lambda\mathcal{F}(\lambda^*, u^*) \; \middle| \; D_u\mathcal{F}(\lambda^*, u^*)\mathcal{H} \; \right)^{-1} \right\| \le K \; ,$$

and this yields the inequality in (3.26).

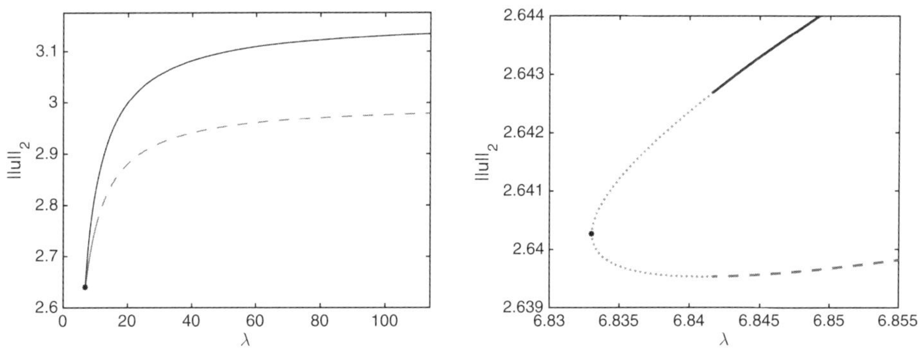

FIGURE 9. Rigorously validated branch of equilibrium solutions for the discrete Allen-Cahn equation (2.2) with $n = 10$. While the left image shows the complete validated branch, the right image depicts the neighborhood of the saddle-node bifurcation point. The numerical approximation (λ^*, u^*) of the saddle-node bifurcation point is indicated by a black dot in both images. The green(dotted) part of the branch was validated using Theorem 3.7, the red (dash) and blue parts were validated by Theorem 3.5.

As a specific application, consider the case $n = 10$ in (3.31) and the mosaic solution pattern prescribed by the vector

$$\bar{u}_m = (1, -1, 1, -1, 1, -1, -1, -1, -1, -1)^t \in \mathbb{R}^{10}. \tag{3.34}$$

It was shown in Example 3.3 that for all $\lambda \geq 114$ there exist equilibrium solutions of (2.2) close to $\bar{u}_m$, and in fact, these solutions lie on a smooth branch. How does this branch continue for smaller λ-values? Regular numerical path-following computations using AUTO [**22**] indicate the existence of a saddle-node bifurcation point close to $\lambda = 6.8330142962$, and these computations readily provide a numerical approximation $(\lambda^*, u^*) \in \mathbb{R} \times \mathbb{R}^{10}$ of the bifurcation point. At this pair, the Jacobian matrix $D_u\mathcal{F}(\lambda^*, u^*)$ has a simple eigenvalue close to zero, and we let v^* denote the approximation of an associated eigenvector with $\|v^*\| = 1$. We then applied Theorem 3.7 iteratively 25 times in the direction v^*, and 25 times in the direction of $-v^*$. In all cases, the theorem succeeded to validate branch segments, whose union is shown in green in the right image of Figure 9. Starting at each of the endpoints, we then used Theorem 3.5 iteratively to follow the two halves of the branch until the parameter λ exceeded $\lambda = 114$. Also in this case, validation succeeded in every iteration, and the resulting validated branches are shown in red and blue in the two images of Figure 9. For the validation, we needed 83 and 64 iterations, respectively. In combination with Example 3.3, these computations prove the existence of a saddle-node bifurcation point which leads to a branch of equilibrium solutions connecting the mosaic state near $\bar{u}_m$ to the mosaic equilibrium near $\bar{u} = (1, -1, 1, -1, 0, -1, -1, -1, -1, -1)^t$. In fact, the method can be used to validate almost all of the 2^n branches which involve mosaic solutions $\bar{u} \in \{\pm 1\}^n$. This is discussed further in [**52**], where in addition the stability of all involved equilibrium solutions is determined using rigorous computations. ◊

4. Direct Localization of Bifurcation Points

The results of the last section can be used to obtain computer-assisted proofs for the existence of solution branches of parameter-dependent nonlinear problems of the form $\mathcal{F}(\lambda, u) = 0$. While Theorem 3.5 can deal with branch segments which are functions of the parameter λ, Theorem 3.7 can treat branches in the neighborhood of a saddle-node bifurcation point. Combined, both results allow for the verification of a wide variety of bifurcation diagrams, namely those which only exhibit saddle-node bifurcation points. As we mentioned earlier, these are in a generic sense "almost all" bifurcation diagrams, which can be seen by means of an application of Sard's theorem [**14**, Section 2.10]. Typically, small perturbations of bifurcation diagrams such as the one shown in the left panel of Figure 1 lead to diagrams as in Figure 2, where for example all pitchfork bifurcations have been broken up into separate branch pieces involving only saddle-node bifurcations.

Based on the above discussion, one might be tempted to think that Theorems 3.5 and 3.7 suffice in the majority of all cases. This, however, is not the case. On the one hand, notice that while the two theorems can be used to detect saddle-node bifurcation points *indirectly*, one usually does not get a rigorous statement as to *where exactly* the saddle-node bifurcation point occurs. This can be seen in the right image of Figure 9. The fact that the λ-values at the endpoints of the green segment are strictly larger than the ones for other points on this segment implies that there has to be a saddle-node bifurcation point, but Theorem 3.7 provides no insight as to where it could be, or whether it has any uniqueness properties. It would therefore be nice to have a rigorous computational technique available which can locate saddle-node bifurcation points *directly*.

To complicate things further, there are quite a number of situations where one does in fact have to worry about bifurcation points other than the simple saddle-node case. As we will see later on, certain structures in a nonlinear problem can make pitchfork bifurcations robust against classes of perturbations, and one therefore has to be able to detect such bifurcations directly as well. In the following two sections, it will be demonstrated how this direct verification of bifurcation points can be achieved in a computer-assisted framework.

4.1. Saddle-Node Bifurcation Points. It was mentioned in the introduction that a pair (λ_0, u_0) cannot be a bifurcation point if it satisfies the assumptions of the implicit function theorem, as stated in Theorem 1.2. As a consequence, we obtain Corollary 1.3 which provides a *necessary* condition for bifurcation. While in the introduction these two results were only formulated in the finite-dimensional setting, they remain valid in a general Banach space framework, see for example [**14**]. Unfortunately, however, the necessary noninvertibility condition in Corollary 1.3 is in general not sufficient for bifurcation. In this, the necessary condition is comparable to the concept of a critical point in calculus, which can be used to locate potential extreme values of a function. Being a critical point is only a necessary requirement, and one needs additional conditions to actually ensure that a critical point is a local maximum or minimum. We would like to point out that in the case of extreme values, the necessary condition is formulated using the first derivative of the considered function, while the sufficient condition involves the second derivative as well. This will be similar in the case of saddle-node bifurcation points.

Before being able to use computer-assisted methods to directly locate saddle-node bifurcations, we first need to understand how they can be guaranteed, i.e., we need to recall the sufficient conditions mentioned above. For this, we return to a general nonlinear problem of the form

$$\mathcal{F}(\lambda, u) = 0 \,, \tag{4.1}$$

where $\mathcal{F} : \mathbb{R} \times \mathcal{U} \to \mathcal{V}$ is a smooth nonlinear mapping, and $\mathcal{U}$ and $\mathcal{V}$ are real Banach spaces. Throughout this section, we assume the following.

ASSUMPTION 4.1 (Fredholm Assumption for the Linearization). *Let $\mathcal{U}$ and $\mathcal{V}$ be real Banach spaces, and assume we are studying a sufficiently smooth parameter-dependent nonlinear operator $\mathcal{F} : \mathbb{R} \times \mathcal{U} \to \mathcal{V}$. Suppose that $(\lambda_0, u_0) \in \mathbb{R} \times \mathcal{U}$ is a solution of the nonlinear problem (4.1), i.e., assume that $\mathcal{F}(\lambda_0, u_0) = 0$ holds. Finally, assume that the Fréchet derivative $L = D_u\mathcal{F}(\lambda_0, u_0) \in \mathcal{L}(\mathcal{U}, \mathcal{V})$ is a Fredholm operator of index zero.*

Recall that a bounded linear operator L is a Fredholm operator if it has a finite-dimensional nullspace $N(L)$, if its range $R(L)$ has finite codimension, and if the range is closed. In this case, its index is the difference between the dimension of the nullspace and the codimension of the range. In fact, it was shown in [**23**, **47**] that the closedness assumption on the range is not necessary, as it automatically follows from the remaining assumptions. Moreover, we would like to point out that if $\mathcal{U}$ and $\mathcal{V}$ are finite-dimensional Banach spaces of the same dimension, then Assumption 4.1 is always true.

Assumption 4.1 describes the basic framework that is convenient for the study of bifurcation problems. In addition, we will only consider possible bifurcation points with a one-dimensional nullspace. This leads to the following second assumption.

ASSUMPTION 4.2 (One Dimensional Nullspace). *Suppose that Assumption 4.1 holds. Assume further that the linearization $L = D_u\mathcal{F}(\lambda_0, u_0)$ has a one-dimensional kernel. Since L has index zero, its range has then codimension one. In this case, we have*

$$N(L) = \operatorname{span}[\varphi_0] \qquad \textit{and} \qquad R(L) = N\left(\psi_0^*\right)$$

for some nonzero elements $\varphi_0 \in \mathcal{U}$ and $\psi_0^* \in \mathcal{V}^*$, where $\mathcal{V}^*$ denotes the dual space of the Banach space $\mathcal{V}$. Finally, let $\tilde{\mathcal{U}} \subset \mathcal{U}$ and $\tilde{\mathcal{V}} \subset \mathcal{V}$ denote closed subspaces such that

$$\mathcal{U} = N(L) \oplus \tilde{\mathcal{U}} \qquad \textit{and} \qquad \mathcal{V} = \tilde{\mathcal{V}} \oplus R(L) \,.$$

The linear projector $P : \mathcal{V} \to \mathcal{V}$ is defined via $R(P) = \tilde{\mathcal{V}}$ and $N(P) = R(L)$, while the projector $Q : \mathcal{U} \to \mathcal{U}$ is defined via $R(Q) = N(L)$ and $N(Q) = \tilde{\mathcal{U}}$. Notice that both P and Q have rank one and are continuous.

In the above assumption, the introduction of an eigenfunction φ_0 which spans the one-dimensional nullspace is natural, and φ_0 will clearly play a prominent role in the sufficient condition for a saddle-node bifurcation point. Note, however, that it is also necessary to have a characterization of the range of L at hand, since in our situation the linearization will no longer be onto at the bifurcation point. The most convenient way to do this is via the element ψ_0^* in Assumption 4.2. In the finite-dimensional case $\mathcal{V} = \mathbb{R}^d$, the dual space $\mathcal{V}^*$ is isomorphic to $\mathcal{V}$, i.e., the element ψ_0^* is just a vector in $\mathbb{R}^d$. Moreover, one can easily see that then the condition $v \in R(L)$ is equivalent to the dot product of ψ_0^* and v being zero. Thus, the vector ψ_0^* has to be orthogonal to the range $R(L)$. One can show that in the general case, we have to have $\psi_0^* \in N(L^*)$, where L^* denotes the dual operator of L.

After these preparations, we now turn our attention to the first and simplest type of bifurcation — the saddle-node bifurcation. As mentioned earlier, this is the only bifurcation point which can be observed in generic systems. For this, assume that we have a solution (λ_0, u_0) of the problem (4.1), and that Assumption 4.2 holds. Then the condition

$$\psi_0^* D_\lambda \mathcal{F}(\lambda_0, u_0) \neq 0 \tag{4.2}$$

is generically satisfied, and in this case one often refers to (λ_0, u_0) as a *simple saddle-node bifurcation point*.

In order to understand the implications of condition (4.2), we briefly return to Theorem 3.7. Since at the moment we assume to have a precise solution (λ_0, u_0) of problem (4.1) at hand, and since we defined φ_0 as an element in the kernel of $D_u\mathcal{F}(\lambda_0, u_0)$, the estimates in (3.25) are satisfied with $\varrho = 0$ and $\sigma = 0$. If, in addition, we choose $\mathcal{H} = I - Q$ and $\mathcal{W} = \tilde{\mathcal{U}}$, with the projection Q and the subspace $\tilde{\mathcal{U}}$ from Assumption 4.2, then $\mathcal{U} = \operatorname{span}[\varphi_0] \oplus R(\mathcal{H})$ is satisfied as well. Moreover, condition (4.2) implies that the vector $D_\lambda\mathcal{F}(\lambda_0, u_0)$ is not contained in the range of $D_u\mathcal{F}(\lambda_0, u_0)$, which in combination with the Fredholm property yields that the linear operator

$$\mathbb{R} \times \tilde{\mathcal{U}} \ni (\bar\lambda, \bar w) \quad \mapsto \quad D_\lambda\mathcal{F}(\lambda_0, u_0)\bar\lambda + D_u\mathcal{F}(\lambda_0, u_0)\left[\mathcal{H}\bar w\right] \in \mathcal{V}$$

is one-to-one and onto, i.e., there exists a constant $K > 0$ such that (3.26) is satisfied. Finally, notice that due to $\varrho = 0$ both inequalities in (3.27) are trivially valid, and therefore we can apply the saddle-node branch verification theorem. This shows that there exists a small branch of solutions of (4.1) which lies in the direction of the line $\alpha \mapsto u_0 + \alpha\varphi_0$ and which is uniquely determined in a neighborhood of the pair (λ_0, u_0).

Drawn in a bifurcation diagram with axes λ and u, the just-established solution branch emanates vertically from the point (λ_0, u_0). Note, however, that this does not automatically imply that the point (λ_0, u_0) is a bifurcation point, as the simple one-dimensional example $\mathcal{F}(\lambda, u) = \lambda - u^3$ shows. For this, we need an additional condition involving the second derivative of $\mathcal{F}$, which is contained in the following *sufficient condition* for a saddle-node bifurcation point, whose proof can be found for example in [**36**].

PROPOSITION 4.3 (Sufficient Condition for Saddle-Node Bifurcation). *Suppose that Assumptions* 4.1 *and* 4.2 *are satisfied, and that* (4.2) *holds. If in addition the generic condition*

$$\psi_0^* D_{uu}\mathcal{F}(\lambda_0, u_0)[\varphi_0, \varphi_0] \neq 0 \tag{4.3}$$

is true, then the nonlinear problem (4.1) *undergoes a saddle-node bifurcation at the point* (λ_0, u_0). *Furthermore, if we have*

$$\frac{\psi_0^* D_{uu}\mathcal{F}(\lambda_0, u_0)[\varphi_0, \varphi_0]}{\psi_0^* D_\lambda\mathcal{F}(\lambda_0, u_0)} > 0 \,, \tag{4.4}$$

then the bifurcating solutions exist for $\lambda < \lambda_0$ *close to the bifurcation point, if the ratio is negative then they exist for* $\lambda > \lambda_0$. *These two cases are usually referred to as a* subcritical *or a* supercritical saddle-node bifurcation, *respectively.*

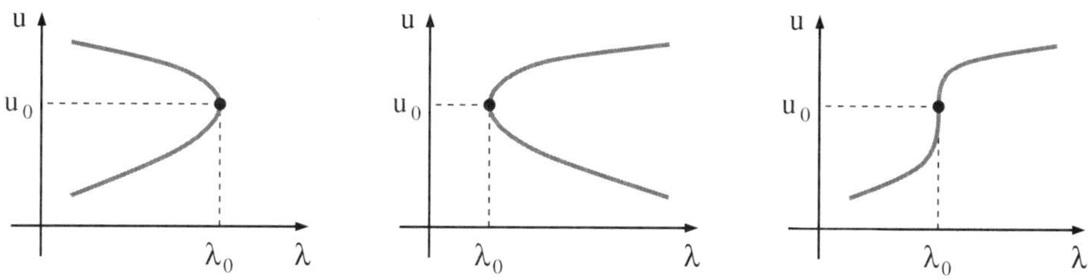

FIGURE 10. Visualization of the sufficient condition for a saddle-node bifurcation given in Proposition 4.3. The three panels show possible shapes of the solution branch of (4.1) near the solution (λ_0, u_0) as long as (4.2) is satisfied. While the first two panels are for the cases of strictly positive and negative values, respectively, of the fraction in (4.4), the third panel shows one of several cases which are possible if $\psi_0^* D_{uu}\mathcal{F}(\lambda_0, u_0)[\varphi_0, \varphi_0] = 0$. In other words, in this inconclusive case (λ_0, u_0) might or might not be a bifurcation point.

The statement of the proposition is illustrated in Figure 10. The left two panels show sub- and supercritical saddle-node bifurcation points, respectively, which are guaranteed as long as (4.3) is satisfied. If the latter condition is violated, the proposition still guarantees a solution branch with vertical tangent at (λ_0, u_0), but its precise shape can not be inferred from second derivative information alone. One possible geometry is shown in the right-most panel of the figure, in which (λ_0, u_0) is not a bifurcation point at all.

While the above result provides generic conditions that guarantee a saddle-node bifurcation, they are not yet amenable to a rigorous computational approach which involves the theory developed so far. For this, we need to reformulate Proposition 4.3 as a nonlinear system in which isolated zeros corresponds to saddle-node bifurcation points. For this, we follow the approach in [**40**] and consider a suitable extended system. More precisely, we supplement the nonlinear parameter-dependent equation (4.1) by a second one which forces the existence of a kernel function v of the appropriate Fréchet derivative, together with a normalizing condition on v. This leads to the extended system

$$\begin{aligned} \mathcal{F}(\lambda, u) &= 0 , \\ D_u\mathcal{F}(\lambda, u)[v] &= 0 , \\ \ell(v) - 1 &= 0 , \end{aligned} \tag{4.5}$$

where $\ell \in \mathcal{U}^*$ is a fixed element of the dual space of $\mathcal{U}$. We abbreviate this system as

$$\mathcal{G}(\lambda, u, v) = (0, 0, 0) ,$$

where

$$\mathcal{G} : \left\{ \begin{array}{rcl} \mathbb{R} \times \mathcal{U} \times \mathcal{U} & \to & \mathbb{R} \times \mathcal{V} \times \mathcal{V} \\ (\lambda, u, v) & \mapsto & (\ell(v) - 1,\ \mathcal{F}(\lambda, u),\ D_u\mathcal{F}(\lambda, u)[v]) . \end{array} \right. \tag{4.6}$$

Then the following result is analogous to [**40, 53**]. Since in these papers only operators acting on one Banach space are considered, we present the straightforward extension to mappings between different Banach spaces. The proof of the result can be found in [**36**].

THEOREM 4.4 (Saddle-Node Bifurcations via Extended Systems). *Suppose that Assumption 4.1 is satisfied. Then the following two statements hold.*

(a) *If the nonlinear operator $\mathcal{F}$ satisfies Assumption 4.2, as well as both conditions (4.2) and (4.3), and if $\ell \in \mathcal{U}^*$ is any functional such that $\ell(\varphi_0) = 1$, then the Fréchet derivative $D_{(\lambda,u,v)}\mathcal{G}(\lambda_0, u_0, \varphi_0)$ is invertible, i.e., the solution $(\lambda_0, u_0, \varphi_0)$ of the extended system (4.5) is an isolated non-degenerate zero of the mapping $\mathcal{G}$.*

(b) *Conversely, if there exists a functional $\ell \in \mathcal{U}^*$ and an element $\varphi_0 \in \mathcal{U}$ such that $\mathcal{G}(\lambda_0, u_0, \varphi_0) = (0,0,0)$ is satisfied, and if the Fréchet derivative $D_{(\lambda,u,v)}\mathcal{G}(\lambda_0, u_0, \varphi_0)$ is invertible, then the nonlinear operator $\mathcal{F}$ satisfies Assumption 4.2, as well as both conditions (4.2) and (4.3).*

In other words, the nonlinear problem (4.1) undergoes a saddle-node bifurcation at (λ_0, u_0) in the sense of Lemma 4.3, if and only if the triple $(\lambda_0, u_0, \varphi_0)$ is a non-degenerate zero of the nonlinear map $\mathcal{G}$ which defines the extended system (4.5).

With Theorem 4.4 we have placed the verification of saddle-node bifurcation points firmly into the framework outlined in Section 3. By applying the parameter-independent version of the constructive implicit function theorem to the extended system (4.5), one can easily establish the existence of a saddle-node bifurcation point. Moreover, if the nonlinear problem under consideration depends on a second parameter, one can even establish branches of saddle-node bifurcation points using Theorem 3.5, or follow such branches around folds using Theorem 3.7. We close this section with a brief application to the discrete Allen-Cahn equation.

EXAMPLE 4.5 (Saddle-Node Bifurcations in the Discrete Allen-Cahn Equation). We again consider the discrete Allen-Cahn equation in the form (3.31), i.e., the nonlinear function $\mathcal{F}$ is given by $\mathcal{F}(\lambda, u) = Au + \lambda f(u)$ for $\lambda \in \mathbb{R}$ and $u \in \mathbb{R}^n$, and we let $f(u) = u - u^3$. Our goal is to apply the parameter-independent version of Theorem 3.1 to the associated extended system (4.5), where throughout the example, we use the maximum norm for vectors, as well as the induced matrix norm for matrices, see again (3.12).

The constructive implicit function theorem can easily be applied. For this, suppose we have found a numerical approximation $(\lambda^*, u^*) \in \mathbb{R} \times \mathbb{R}^n$ to a saddle-node bifurcation point, and assume that $v^* \in \mathbb{R}^n \setminus \{0\}$ is an approximation of a kernel function at the bifurcation point. Let $\varrho > 0$ be a constant with

$$\|\mathcal{F}(\lambda^*, u^*)\| \le \varrho\,, \qquad \|D_u\mathcal{F}(\lambda^*, u^*)[v^*]\| \le \varrho\,, \qquad \text{and} \qquad \left|\hat{v}^t v^* - 1\right| \le \varrho\,,$$

where the vector $\hat{v} \in \mathbb{R}^n$ is a fixed normalization vector. Furthermore, let $d_u > 0$, introduce the abbreviation

$$f_{\max}^{(p)} = \max\left\{\left|f^{(p)}(\xi)\right| \;:\; |\xi| \le \|u^*\| + d_u\right\}, \tag{4.7}$$

and define

$$L = 2f_{\max}^{(1)} + f_{\max}^{(2)}\left(2\,|\lambda^*| + 2\,\|v^*\| + d_u\right) + f_{\max}^{(3)}\,|\lambda^*|\,\|v^*\|\,. \tag{4.8}$$

Finally, let $K > 0$ be such that

$$\left\| \left(\begin{array}{c|c|c} A + \lambda^* \operatorname{diag}(f'(u^*)) & 0 & f(u^*) \\ \hline \lambda^* \operatorname{diag}(f''(u^*)) \operatorname{diag}(v^*) & A + \lambda^* \operatorname{diag}(f'(u^*)) & \operatorname{diag}(f'(u^*))v^* \\ \hline 0 & 2(v^*)^t & 0 \end{array} \right)^{-1} \right\| \le K,$$

and suppose that

$$4K^2 \varrho L < 1 \qquad \text{and} \qquad 2K\varrho < d_u .$$

Then for every constant δ which satisfies $2K\varrho \le \delta \le \min\{1/(2KL), d_u\}$ there exists a unique triple $(\lambda_0, u_0, v_0) \in \mathbb{R} \times \mathbb{R}^n \times \mathbb{R}^n$ which solves the extended system (4.5) and which satisfies the estimates

$$|\lambda_0 - \lambda^*| \le \delta , \qquad \|u_0 - u^*\| \le \delta , \qquad \text{and} \qquad \|v_0 - v^*\| \le \delta .$$

In other words, the maximum norm ball of radius $2K\varrho$ centered at the pair (λ^*, u^*) contains a unique saddle-node bifurcation point for $\mathcal{F}(\lambda, u) = 0$.

The statements of the last paragraph follow immediately from the parameter-independent version of the constructive implicit function theorem. One only has to apply the result to the nonlinear mapping $\mathcal{G} : \mathbb{R}^n \times \mathbb{R}^n \times \mathbb{R} \to \mathbb{R}^n \times \mathbb{R}^n \times \mathbb{R}$ defined by the triple

$$\mathcal{G}(x) = \left(\mathcal{F}(\lambda, u) \, , \, D_u\mathcal{F}(\lambda, u)[v] \, , \, \hat{v}^t v - 1 \right) , \qquad \text{where} \qquad x = (u, v, \lambda) .$$

Then one can easily see that its Jacobian matrix is given by

$$D_x\mathcal{G}(x) = \left(\begin{array}{c|c|c} D_u\mathcal{F}(\lambda, u) & 0 & D_\lambda\mathcal{F}(\lambda, u) \\ \hline D_{uu}\mathcal{F}(\lambda, u)[v, \cdot] & D_u\mathcal{F}(\lambda, u) & D_{\lambda u}\mathcal{F}(\lambda, u)[v] \\ \hline 0 & \hat{v}^t & 0 \end{array} \right) ,$$

which for the discrete Allen-Cahn equation takes the concrete form

$$D_x\mathcal{G}(x) = \left(\begin{array}{c|c|c} A + \lambda \operatorname{diag}(f'(u)) & 0 & f(u) \\ \hline \lambda \operatorname{diag}(f''(u)) \operatorname{diag}(v) & A + \lambda \operatorname{diag}(f'(u)) & \operatorname{diag}(f'(u))v \\ \hline 0 & \hat{v}^t & 0 \end{array} \right) .$$

Standard mean value theorem arguments imply for $x \in \mathbb{R}^{2n+1}$ with $\|x - x^*\| \le d_u$ the estimate

$$\|D_x\mathcal{G}(x) - D_x\mathcal{G}(x^*)\| \;\le\; L\,\|x - x^*\| ,$$

with L as defined in (4.8). In other words, hypothesis (H3) holds with $\ell_\alpha = 0$ and $\ell_x = d_u$, and with Lipschitz constants $L_1 = L$ and $L_2 = 0$. Since we are only interested in the parameter-independent version of Theorem 3.1, hypothesis (H4) does not have to be verified, and the above result follows. For more details, we refer the reader to [**52**].

Using this result, one can easily establish the existence of the saddle-node bifurcation points which were described in Section 2.1. As a numerical example, we return to the mosaic solution close to the sign vector $\bar{u}_m$ defined in (3.34). As we saw in Example 3.8, the associated solution branch is created via a saddle-node bifurcation close to $\lambda^* = 6.8330142962$, and a numerical approximation to the vector u^* can be found in [**52**], see also the left panel in Figure 11. With these approximations, which were produced by AUTO using error tolerances of the order 10^{-8}, the above result can be used to rigorously establish the existence of a saddle-node bifurcation point within a maximum norm ball of radius $\delta_{\min} = 2.95 \cdot 10^{-7}$, and this bifurcation point is unique within a ball of radius $\delta_{\max} = 2.84 \cdot 10^{-4}$. Tighter bounds can be achieved if one first refines the solution approximation through a

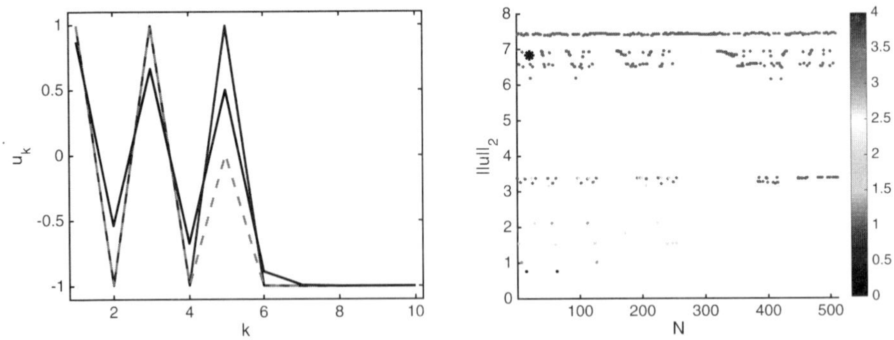

FIGURE 11. Verification of saddle-node bifurcation points in the discrete Allen-Cahn model (2.2) for $n = 10$. The left image shows the numerical approximation u^* of a saddle-node point in black, while the solid blue and dashed red curves depict the equilibrium solutions on the generated solution branches at $\lambda = 300$. The location of this saddle-node bifurcation point is indicated in the right panel as a black star. The horizontal axis in this image depends on the integer N, which encodes the ± 1-pattern of the resulting mosaic solution via the binary representation of N. The bifurcation point in the left panel corresponds to $N = 21$.

few Newton iterations of the extended system (4.5). This leads to an improved bifurcation point approximation less than 10^{-9} away from the pair computed with AUTO, and another application of Theorem 3.1 now furnishes $\delta_{\min} = 3.68 \cdot 10^{-14}$ and $\delta_{\max} = 2.84 \cdot 10^{-4}$. This change is mostly due to the resulting smaller value of the residual ϱ, which drops from about 10^{-8} to 10^{-15}, while the constants $K \approx 11.8$ and $L \approx 148.6$ remain basically unchanged.

This example computation is illustrated in Figure 11. In the left panel of the figure, the saddle-node bifurcation point approximation $u^* \in \mathbb{R}^{10}$ is shown in black, while the solutions on the created branches at $\lambda = 300$ are shown in solid blue and dashed red. The right image shows the location of the bifurcation point as a black star. In this image, the vertical axis denotes the λ-value at which a saddle-node bifurcation occurs, while the integer N on the horizontal axis encodes the ± 1-pattern of the resulting mosaic solution through the binary representation of N. The above $\bar{u}_m$ corresponds to $N = 21$. We would like to point out that all of the remaining dots in the right panel of Figure 11 have been validated using the above approach. For illustration purposes, this panel only contains half of the N-values contained in the right image of Figure 3. Yet, validation was performed on all points.

All of these computations focused on the specific nonlinearity $f(u) = u - u^3$. Notice, however, that the formula for L in (4.8) is based on the general constants in (4.7), and these can easily be adjusted for other nonlinearities f. For more examples, we refer the reader to [**52**]. $\diamondsuit$

Due to time and space constraints, we refrain from detailed applications to the diblock copolymer model in the context of saddle-node bifurcations. These can be found in [**36**], and will briefly be mentioned at the end of the next section.

4.2. Symmetry-Breaking Pitchfork Bifurcations. It was mentioned in the introduction that in general generic systems one would expect only saddle-node bifurcation points. This is due to the fact that in view of Sard's theorem, there always exist arbitrarily small perturbations of a nonlinear function $\mathcal{F}(\lambda, u)$ such that zero becomes a regular value. This implies that at any zero (λ_0, u_0) of $\mathcal{F}$ the total derivative has full rank, and this in turn yields that the implicit function theorem can be applied *in some direction*. In other words, the solution set of $\mathcal{F}(\lambda, u) = 0$ is comprised of smooth curves which do not intersect.

In reality, however, the situation is more complicated. The above argument requires that we allow for *arbitrary perturbations*. But what if the model under consideration has certain internal structures which should be part of any realistic perturbation? In such cases, Sard's theorem would not apply, and it is therefore feasible to assume that for certain models, it might not be possible to break up pitchfork bifurcations via *realistic perturbations*. One situation which is frequently encountered in applications involves *inherent symmetries* in models. Such symmetries can come in a great variety of forms, and we refer the reader to [**13**] for an in-depth account. For the purposes of this lecture, we assume that symmetry occurs in the following simple specific form.

DEFINITION 4.6 (Symmetry in the Form of $\mathbb{Z}_2$-Equivariance). In the situation of Assumptions 4.1 and 4.2, suppose in addition that there exist two bounded linear operators $S_{\mathcal{U}} \in \mathcal{L}(\mathcal{U}, \mathcal{U})$ and $S_{\mathcal{V}} \in \mathcal{L}(\mathcal{V}, \mathcal{V})$ such that

$$S_{\mathcal{U}} \neq I\,, \qquad S_{\mathcal{V}} \neq I\,, \qquad S_{\mathcal{U}}^2 = I\,, \qquad S_{\mathcal{V}}^2 = I\,,$$

as well as

$$\mathcal{F}(\lambda, S_{\mathcal{U}} u) \;=\; S_{\mathcal{V}} \mathcal{F}(\lambda, u) \quad \text{for all} \quad \lambda \in \mathbb{R} \quad \text{and} \quad u \in \mathcal{U}\,. \tag{4.9}$$

Then we say that $\mathcal{F}$ is $\mathbb{Z}_2$ *equivariant*. Based on the symmetry operators $S_{\mathcal{U}}$ and $S_{\mathcal{V}}$ one can also decompose the underlying Banach spaces into the *symmetric elements* and the *antisymmetric elements*. More precisely, for the Banach space $\mathcal{U}$ we define

$$\mathcal{U}_s = \{u \in \mathcal{U} \,:\, S_{\mathcal{U}} u = u\} \qquad \text{and} \qquad \mathcal{U}_a = \{u \in \mathcal{U} \,:\, S_{\mathcal{U}} u = -u\}\,,$$

and analogously one can define the subspaces $\mathcal{V}_s$ and $\mathcal{V}_a$ of $\mathcal{V}$. One can easily see that

$$\mathcal{U} = \mathcal{U}_s \oplus \mathcal{U}_a \qquad \text{as well as} \qquad \mathcal{V} = \mathcal{V}_s \oplus \mathcal{V}_a\,,$$

since $u = (u + S_{\mathcal{U}} u)/2 + (u - S_{\mathcal{U}} u)/2$ yields a decomposition of an arbitrary element u into a symmetric and an antisymmetric one.

For the nonlinear equation (4.1), equivariance has immediate consequences regarding invariance of subspaces, both for the equation and for certain derivatives of $\mathcal{F}$. For example, by differentiating the identity (4.9) with respect to u one immediately obtains

$$D_u \mathcal{F}(\lambda, S_{\mathcal{U}} u)\,[S_{\mathcal{U}} \bar{u}] = S_{\mathcal{V}} D_u \mathcal{F}(\lambda, u)\,[\bar{u}] \tag{4.10}$$

for all $\lambda \in \mathbb{R}$ and arbitrary $u, \bar{u} \in \mathcal{U}$. If one assumes in addition that $u \in \mathcal{U}_s$, then (4.10) implies the $\mathbb{Z}_2$-equivariance of the Fréchet derivative $D_u \mathcal{F}(\lambda, u)$. The following lemma collects a number of similar properties, which shed more light on the effects of $\mathbb{Z}_2$-equivariance. The straightforward proof can be found in [**59**].

LEMMA 4.7 (General Consequences of $\mathbb{Z}_2$-Equivariance). *Suppose that Assumptions* 4.1 *and* 4.2 *hold, and that* (4.1) *is* $\mathbb{Z}_2$*-equivariant as in Definition* 4.6. *Then the following statements are true for all* $\lambda \in \mathbb{R}$ *and* $u \in \mathcal{U}_s$*:*

(a) *We have both* $\mathcal{F}(\lambda, u) \in \mathcal{V}_s$ *and* $D_\lambda \mathcal{F}(\lambda, u) \in \mathcal{V}_s$.
(b) *Both the inclusions* $D_u\mathcal{F}(\lambda, u)[\mathcal{U}_s] \subset \mathcal{V}_s$ *and* $D_u\mathcal{F}(\lambda, u)[\mathcal{U}_a] \subset \mathcal{V}_a$ *are satisfied, as well as* $D_{\lambda u}\mathcal{F}(\lambda, u)[\mathcal{U}_s] \subset \mathcal{V}_s$ *and* $D_{\lambda u}\mathcal{F}(\lambda, u)[\mathcal{U}_a] \subset \mathcal{V}_a$.
(c) *The inclusions* $D_{uu}\mathcal{F}(\lambda, u)[\mathcal{U}_s, \mathcal{U}_s] \subset \mathcal{V}_s$ *and* $D_{uu}\mathcal{F}(\lambda, u)[\mathcal{U}_a, \mathcal{U}_a] \subset \mathcal{V}_s$ *are satisfied, as well as* $D_{uu}\mathcal{F}(\lambda, u)[\mathcal{U}_s, \mathcal{U}_a] \subset \mathcal{V}_a$.

The above lemma applies to the derivatives of $\mathcal{F}$ at any pair (λ, u), as long as $u \in \mathcal{U}_s$ is a symmetric element. If we consider specifically a pair (λ_0, u_0) as in Assumption 4.2, even more can be said. As the following result shows, both the eigenfunction φ_0 and the element ψ_0^* necessarily have to be either symmetric or antisymmetric. In addition, the complementary spaces $\tilde{\mathcal{U}}$ and $\tilde{\mathcal{V}}$ in Assumption 4.2 can always be chosen in such a way that they respect the symmetry operations as well.

LEMMA 4.8 ($\mathbb{Z}_2$-Equivariance and One-Dimensional Kernels). *Suppose that Assumptions* 4.1 *and* 4.2 *hold, that* (4.1) *is* $\mathbb{Z}_2$*-equivariant as in Definition* 4.6, *and that* $u_0 \in \mathcal{U}_s$. *Then the following statements are true:*

(a) *The eigenfunction* φ_0 *which spans the nullspace* $N(L)$ *of* $L = D_u\mathcal{F}(\lambda_0, u_0)$ *is either an element of* $\mathcal{U}_s$ *or of* $\mathcal{U}_a$*, i.e., we have* $S_\mathcal{U}\varphi_0 = \varepsilon_\mathcal{U}\varphi_0$ *for some sign* $\varepsilon_\mathcal{U} \in \{\pm 1\}$.
(b) *The element* ψ_0^* *which characterizes* $R(L)$ *is either symmetric or antisymmetric with respect to the equivariance* $S_\mathcal{V}^*$*, i.e., we have* $S_\mathcal{V}^*\psi_0^* = \varepsilon_\mathcal{V}\psi_0^*$ *for some* $\varepsilon_\mathcal{V} \in \{\pm 1\}$.
(c) *The projections* P *and* Q *in Assumption* 4.2 *can be chosen in such a way that they commute with the symmetry actions, i.e., such that* $S_\mathcal{V}P = PS_\mathcal{V}$ *and* $S_\mathcal{U}Q = QS_\mathcal{U}$.

At first glance, it seems somewhat surprising that the kernel function φ_0 has to be either a symmetric or an antisymmetric element. Notice, however, that due to Lemma 4.7*(b)* we have both $L\mathcal{U}_s \subset \mathcal{V}_s$ and $L\mathcal{U}_a \subset \mathcal{V}_a$, i.e., the splitting into symmetric and antisymmetric elements is respected by L. If we now consider

$$\varphi_0 = \varphi_{0,s} + \varphi_{0,a} \in \mathcal{U}_s \oplus \mathcal{U}_a \quad \text{with} \quad \varphi_{0,s} = \frac{\varphi_0 + S_\mathcal{U}\varphi_0}{2} \quad \text{and} \quad \varphi_{0,a} = \frac{\varphi_0 - S_\mathcal{U}\varphi_0}{2},$$

then the splitting gives $0 = L\varphi_0 = L\varphi_{0,s} + L\varphi_{0,a}$, and therefore $L\varphi_{0,s} = -L\varphi_{0,a}$, which in turn implies that both $L\varphi_{0,s}$ and $L\varphi_{0,a}$ are contained in $\mathcal{U}_s \cap \mathcal{U}_a = \{0\}$. Together, this shows that both $\varphi_{0,s}$ and $\varphi_{0,a}$ are in $N(L)$, hence multiples of φ_0. Since one of these two elements has to be nonzero, this yields that either $\varphi_0 \in \mathcal{U}_s$ or $\varphi_0 \in \mathcal{U}_a$, which is equivalent to $S_\mathcal{U}\varphi_0 = \varphi_0$ or $S_\mathcal{U}\varphi_0 = -\varphi_0$, respectively. In other words, statement *(a)* is true. The remaining parts of Lemma 4.8 can be established using similar arguments, see also [**36**].

After these preparations we now return to the study of pitchfork bifurcations. We will see below that such bifurcation points frequently occur in nonlinear problems which are $\mathbb{Z}_2$-equivariant. Similar to our approach in the last section, we first need to formulate a sufficient condition which guarantees the existence of a pitchfork bifurcation, and then as a second step reformulate this condition as a zero finding problem to make it amenable to the constructive implicit function theorem.

For the first step, we make use of a classical technique in nonlinear analysis, which reduces the solution of a possibly infinite-dimensional algebraic system to the solution of a finite- and usually low-dimensional equation. This method is summarized in the following proposition.

PROPOSITION 4.9 (Lyapunov-Schmidt Reduction). *In the situation of Assumptions 4.1 and 4.2 there exist a neighborhood Λ_0 of λ_0, a neighborhood V_0 of the point $v_0 = Qu_0 \in N(L)$, a smooth function $W : \Lambda_0 \times V_0 \to \tilde{\mathcal{U}}$, as well as a smooth real-valued function b which is defined in a neighborhood of the point $(\lambda_0, 0) \in \mathbb{R}^2$ such that the following hold:*

(a) *If (λ, α) is sufficiently close to the point $(\lambda_0, 0) \in \mathbb{R}^2$ and satisfies the identity $b(\lambda, \alpha) = 0$, then*

$$\mathcal{F}(\lambda, u) = 0 \quad \text{for} \quad u = v_0 + \alpha\varphi_0 + W(\lambda, v_0 + \alpha\varphi_0) \; .$$

(b) *Conversely, if the pair (λ, u) is close enough to (λ_0, u_0) and solves the equation $\mathcal{F}(\lambda, u) = 0$, then for α defined via the identity $\alpha\varphi_0 = Q(u - u_0)$ both $b(\lambda, \alpha) = 0$ and $u = Qu + W(\lambda, Qu)$ are satisfied. Notice that in this case we also have the identity $Qu = v_0 + \alpha\varphi_0$.*

In other words, the solution set of the

$$\text{bifurcation equation} \qquad b(\lambda, \alpha) = 0$$

in a neighborhood of the point $(\lambda_0, 0) \in \mathbb{R}^2$ is in one-to-one correspondence to the solution set of $\mathcal{F}(\lambda, u) = 0$ in a neighborhood of (λ_0, u_0).

Even though we do not prove the result in detail in these lecture notes, the basic idea can easily be conveyed. Using the projections P and Q from Assumption 4.2, one can see that solving the nonlinear problem (4.1) is equivalent to solving the pair of equations

$$P\mathcal{F}(\lambda, v + w) = 0 \qquad \text{and} \qquad (I - P)\mathcal{F}(\lambda, v + w) = 0 \; , \tag{4.11}$$

where $v = Qu$ and $w = (I - Q)u$. Using the abbreviation

$$G(\lambda, v, w) = (I - P)\mathcal{F}(\lambda, v + w) \; ,$$

our assumptions imply that G is a mapping $G : \mathbb{R} \times N(L) \times \tilde{\mathcal{U}} \to R(L)$. Now set $v_0 = Qu_0$ and $w_0 = (I - Q)u_0$. Then we have $G(\lambda_0, v_0, w_0) = 0$, and one can show that $D_w G(\lambda_0, v_0, w_0) \in \mathcal{L}(\tilde{\mathcal{U}}, R(L))$ is a continuous isomorphism. The implicit function theorem can then be used to solve the second equation in (4.11) locally for w as a function of λ and v. This guarantees the function W as in the formulation of the theorem. Plugging W into the first equation (4.11) shows that locally near (λ_0, u_0) a pair (λ, u) solves the nonlinear problem $\mathcal{F}(\lambda, u) = 0$ if and only if the pair $(\lambda, v) = (\lambda, Qu)$ satisfies $P\mathcal{F}(\lambda, v + W(\lambda, v)) = 0$. If we finally set

$$b(\lambda, \alpha) = \psi_0^* \left(P\mathcal{F} \left(\lambda, v_0 + \alpha\varphi_0 + W(\lambda, v_0 + \alpha\varphi_0) \right) \right) \; , \tag{4.12}$$

then Proposition 4.9 follows due to the choices of ψ_0^* and P.

In our setting of a linearization which is a Fredholm operator of index zero and which has a one-dimensional kernel at the solution pair (λ_0, u_0), the bifurcation equation $b(\lambda, \alpha) = 0$ is particularly simple. It is a single equation in two real unknowns. In fact, one can easily derive a Taylor expansion for the bifurcation function $b(\lambda, \alpha)$ near the point $(\lambda_0, 0)$ in the form

$$\begin{aligned} b(\lambda_0 + \nu, \alpha) &= \nu \cdot D_\lambda b(\lambda_0, 0) + \frac{\nu^2}{2} \cdot D_{\lambda\lambda} b(\lambda_0, 0) + \alpha\nu \cdot D_{\lambda\alpha} b(\lambda_0, 0) \\ &+ \frac{\alpha^2}{2} \cdot D_{\alpha\alpha} b(\lambda_0, 0) \frac{\nu^3}{6} \cdot D_{\lambda\lambda\lambda} b(\lambda_0, 0) + \frac{\alpha\nu^2}{2} \cdot D_{\lambda\lambda\alpha} b(\lambda_0, 0) \\ &+ \frac{\alpha^2\nu}{2} \cdot D_{\lambda\alpha\alpha} b(\lambda_0, 0) \frac{\alpha^3}{6} \cdot D_{\alpha\alpha\alpha} b(\lambda_0, 0) + R(\nu, \alpha) , \end{aligned}$$

where $R(\nu, \alpha) = O(\|(\nu, \alpha)\|^4)$. Despite the fact that the function W which appears in Proposition 4.9 usually is not known explicitly, one can explicitly compute the derivatives of b at the pair $(\lambda_0, 0)$, see [**36**] for more details. For example, one can show that $D_\lambda b(\lambda_0, 0) = \psi_0^* D_\lambda F(\lambda_0, u_0)$, and this can immediately be used to give an alternative proof of Proposition 4.3.

For our study of pitchfork bifurcations, we need a refinement of Proposition 4.9 which takes $\mathbb{Z}_2$-equivariance into account. This leads to the following result, whose proof can be found in [**13, 36**].

PROPOSITION 4.10 (Equivariant Lyapunov-Schmidt Reduction). *Suppose that all the assumptions of Proposition* 4.9 *are satisfied, and that $\mathcal{F}$ is $\mathbb{Z}_2$-equivariant as in Definition* 4.6. *Finally, assume that $u_0 \in \mathcal{U}_s$, and suppose that the projections P and Q are chosen as in Lemma* 4.8*(c). Then the following hold:*

(a) *The nullspace $N(L)$ of $L = D_u\mathcal{F}(\lambda_0, u_0)$ is invariant under $S_\mathcal{U}$, and the range $R(L)$ is invariant under $S_\mathcal{V}$.*

(b) *The mapping W appearing in the the Lyapunov-Schmidt reduction in Proposition* 4.9 *is $\mathbb{Z}_2$-equivariant, i.e., we have*

$$W(\lambda, S_\mathcal{U} v) = S_\mathcal{U} W(\lambda, v) \quad \text{for all} \quad \lambda \in \mathbb{R} \ \text{ and } \ v \in N(L) .$$

(c) *The bifurcation function $b(\lambda, \alpha)$ satisfies*

$$b(\lambda, \varepsilon_\mathcal{U} \alpha) = \varepsilon_\mathcal{V} b(\lambda, \alpha) \quad \text{for all} \quad (\lambda, \alpha) \ \text{ close to } \ (\lambda_0, 0) ,$$

where $\varepsilon_\mathcal{U}$ and $\varepsilon_\mathcal{V}$ encode the symmetry properties of φ_0 and ψ_0^* as in Lemma 4.8.

While in general it does not seem to be the case that $\varepsilon_\mathcal{U}$ and $\varepsilon_\mathcal{V}$ have to be related, there are special situations when they have to coincide, see for example the discussion in [**36**]. Of particular interest for us is the case $\varepsilon_\mathcal{U} = \varepsilon_\mathcal{V} = -1$, since then Proposition 4.10*(c)* implies that the bifurcation function b defined in (4.12) is an odd function with respect to α. This in turn automatically guarantees that there is a trivial solution line $(\lambda, \alpha) = (\lambda, 0)$ for the bifurcation equation $b(\lambda, \alpha) = 0$, for all λ close to λ_0. In fact, in this situation one generically can observe pitchfork bifurcations, which are called *symmetry-breaking pitchfork bifurcations*. A sufficient condition for their existence is the subject of the next result.

PROPOSITION 4.11 (Sufficient Condition for Symmetry-Breaking Bifurcation). *Suppose that Assumptions* 4.1 *and* 4.2 *hold, and that* (4.1) *is $\mathbb{Z}_2$-equivariant as in Definition* 4.6. *Furthermore, assume that*

$$S_\mathcal{U} u_0 = u_0 , \qquad S_\mathcal{U} \varphi_0 = -\varphi_0 , \qquad \text{as well as} \qquad S_\mathcal{V}^* \psi_0^* = -\psi_0^* , \tag{4.13}$$

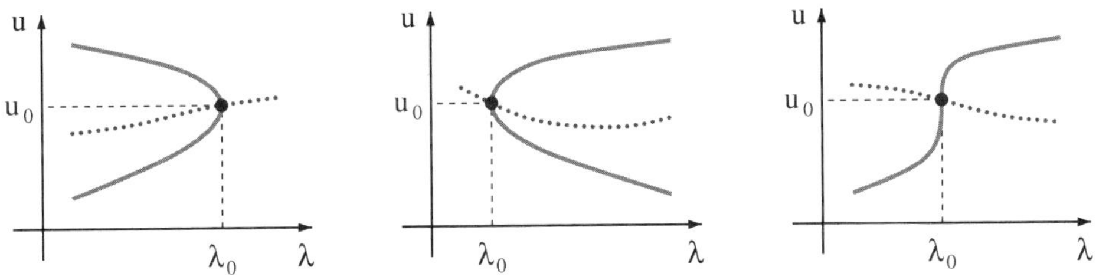

FIGURE 12. Visualization of the sufficient condition for a symmetry-breaking pitchfork bifurcation given in Proposition 4.11. The three panels show possible shapes of the solution branches of (4.1) near the solution (λ_0, u_0). While the first two panels are for the cases $\gamma > 0$ and $\gamma < 0$, respectively, the third panel shows one of several cases which are possible in the final and inconclusive case $\gamma = 0$. In all images, the branch of symmetric solutions is shown in green(dotted line), and the symmetry-breaking branch is shown in red.

that the projections P and Q are chosen as in Lemma 4.8(c), and that

$$\psi_0^* D_{\lambda u}\mathcal{F}(\lambda_0, u_0)[\varphi_0] + \psi_0^* D_{uu}\mathcal{F}(\lambda_0, u_0)[\varphi_0, \xi_0] \neq 0 \,, \tag{4.14}$$

where $\xi_0 \in \mathcal{U}_s$ solves the equation

$$D_u\mathcal{F}(\lambda_0, u_0)[\xi_0] + (I - P)D_\lambda\mathcal{F}(\lambda_0, u_0) = 0 \,. \tag{4.15}$$

Then the nonlinear problem (4.1) undergoes a pitchfork bifurcation at (λ_0, u_0). Locally at this point the solution set of (4.1) consists of a smooth solution curve parameterized by λ, together with a bifurcating curve which is tangent to φ_0 at (λ_0, u_0). Consider the ratio

$$\gamma = \frac{\psi_0^* D_{uuu}\mathcal{F}(\lambda_0, u_0)[\varphi_0, \varphi_0, \varphi_0] + 3\psi_0^* D_{uu}\mathcal{F}(\lambda_0, u_0)[\varphi_0, \zeta_0]}{\psi_0^* D_{\lambda u}\mathcal{F}(\lambda_0, u_0)[\varphi_0] + \psi_0^* D_{uu}\mathcal{F}(\lambda_0, u_0)[\varphi_0, \xi_0]} \,,$$

where ξ_0 was defined in (4.15) and $\zeta_0 \in \mathcal{U}_s$ is defined by

$$D_u\mathcal{F}(\lambda_0, u_0)[\zeta_0] + (I - P)D_{uu}\mathcal{F}(\lambda_0, u_0)[\varphi_0, \varphi_0] = 0 \,.$$

If the ratio γ is positive, then the solutions on the bifurcating branch exist for $\lambda < \lambda_0$ close to the bifurcation point, if γ is negative then they exist for $\lambda > \lambda_0$. If $\gamma = 0$, either half of the bifurcating branch could lie on either side of λ_0.

This sufficient condition is illustrated in Figure 12. From left to right the images show the three cases outlined in the proposition. While the first two panels are for the inequalities $\gamma > 0$ and $\gamma < 0$, respectively, the last panel is for the inconclusive situation $\gamma = 0$. In all images, the green curve represents the primary branch of symmetric solutions, which correspond to the trivial solution of the bifurcation equation $b(\lambda, \alpha) = 0$. In contrast, solutions on the red bifurcating branch break this symmetry, since in a small neighborhood of the bifurcation point (λ_0, u_0) they are close to the line $\alpha \mapsto u_0 + \alpha\varphi_0$, which consists of linear combinations of the symmetric solution u_0 and the antisymmetric eigenfunction φ_0.

The detailed proof of Proposition 4.11 can be found in **[36]**, but its main idea can easily be described. We have already seen earlier that due to (4.13), the bifurcation equation $b(\lambda, \alpha) = 0$ guaranteed by Propositions 4.9 and 4.10 has the trivial solution $b(\lambda, 0) \equiv 0$. If we then define a function r in a neighborhood of $(\lambda_0, 0)$ by setting

$$r(\lambda, \alpha) = \begin{cases} \dfrac{b(\lambda, \alpha)}{\alpha} & \text{for} \quad \alpha \neq 0 \,, \\ D_\alpha b(\lambda, 0) & \text{for} \quad \alpha = 0 \,, \end{cases}$$

one can show that close to the solution pair $(\lambda_0, 0)$ the new mapping r is smooth with $b(\lambda, \alpha) = \alpha \cdot r(\lambda, \alpha)$. While the condition $\alpha = 0$ corresponds to the primary branch of symmetric solutions, the bifurcating branch has to solve the reduced equation $r(\lambda, \alpha) = 0$. From the expansion of the bifurcation function b stated earlier one can see that

$$r(\lambda_0, 0) = D_\alpha b(\lambda_0, 0) = 0 \,, \quad \text{and}$$

$$D_\lambda r(\lambda_0, 0) = D_{\lambda\alpha} b(\lambda_0, 0) = \psi_0^* D_{\lambda u} F(\lambda_0, u_0)[\varphi_0] + \psi_0^* D_{uu} F(\lambda_0, u_0)[\varphi_0, \xi_0] \neq 0 \,,$$

where ξ_0 was defined in equation (4.15), and the inequality in the second line follows from (4.14). An application of the classical implicit function theorem then implies that the equation $r(\lambda, \alpha) = 0$ can be solved locally for λ as a function of α, and this gives rise to the red branch in Figure 12. For the tangency statements of the proposition, we refer the reader to [**36**].

Finally we are in a position to return to computer-assisted proofs. As the last step, we need to reformulate the conditions of Proposition 4.11 in such a way that the constructive implicit function theorem can be used to infer the existence of symmetry-breaking pitchfork bifurcations from a numerical approximation. Unfortunately, however, we can clearly no longer use the extended system (4.5), since an isolated zero of the system implies the existence of a saddle-node bifurcation point. While it is still true that (4.5) has a zero at a pitchfork bifurcation point, the Jacobian matrix of the mapping $\mathcal{G}$ defined in (4.6) at this zero is no longer invertible.

Luckily, the prevalent role of symmetries in the formation of pitchfork bifurcations allows for a straightforward adjustment. For this, we still consider the extended system as defined in (4.5). This time, however, the map $\mathcal{G}$ induced by the system is restricted in domain and range to certain symmetry-induced subspaces. More precisely, consider $\mathcal{G}$ defined as

$$\mathcal{G} \;:\; \begin{cases} \mathbb{R} \times \mathcal{U}_s \times \mathcal{U} & \rightarrow \quad \mathbb{R} \times \mathcal{V}_s \times \mathcal{V} \\ (\lambda, u, v) & \mapsto \quad (\ell(v) - 1, \; \mathcal{F}(\lambda, u), \; D_u \mathcal{F}(\lambda, u)[v]) \end{cases} \tag{4.16}$$

where the nonlinear operator part of the map is restricted to the subspace $\mathcal{U}_s$ of symmetric elements of $\mathcal{U}$. Notice that the restriction to $\mathcal{V}_s$ in the image is justified by Lemma 4.7*(a)*. Then the following result holds, which is a slight extension of an analogous result in [**53**] to the case of different Banach spaces in domain and range. For the proof, see [**36**].

THEOREM 4.12 (Symmetry-Breaking Pitchfork Bifurcations via Extended Systems). *Suppose that Assumption* 4.1 *is satisfied and that $\mathcal{F}$ is $\mathbb{Z}_2$-equivariant in the sense of Definition* 4.6. *Then the following two statements hold.*

(a) *Suppose that all assumptions of Proposition* 4.11 *are satisfied, and consider a functional $\ell \in \mathcal{U}^*$ such that $\ell(\varphi_0) = 1$. Then the Fréchet derivative $D_{(\lambda,u,v)}\mathcal{G}(\lambda_0, u_0, \varphi_0)$ of the mapping defined in* (4.16) *is invertible, i.e.,* *the solution $(\lambda_0, u_0, \varphi_0)$ of the extended system $\mathcal{G}(\lambda, u, \varphi) = (0,0,0)$ is an isolated non-degenerate zero.*

(b) *Conversely, if there exist an $\ell \in \mathcal{U}^*$ and a $\varphi_0 \in \mathcal{U}_a$ such that $(\lambda_0, u_0, \varphi_0)$ is a zero of the equation $\mathcal{G}(\lambda, u, \varphi) = (0,0,0)$, and if the Fréchet derivative $D_{(\lambda,u,v)}\mathcal{G}(\lambda_0, u_0, \varphi_0)$ of the mapping defined in (4.16) is invertible, then the nonlinear operator $\mathcal{F}$ satisfies all assumptions of Proposition 4.11. In other words, the point (λ_0, u_0) is a symmetry-breaking pitchfork bifurcation point for (4.1).*

As in the case of saddle-node bifurcations, Theorem 4.12 allows us to establish the existence of symmetry-breaking pitchfork bifurcations using the framework from Section 3. By applying the parameter-independent version of Theorem 3.1 to the map $\mathcal{G}$, single bifurcation points can be verified, and branches of pitchfork bifurcations can be validated using Theorems 3.5 and 3.7, as long as the problem under consideration depends on an additional parameter. We close this section with a brief application to the diblock copolymer model.

EXAMPLE 4.13 (Bifurcations in the Diblock Copolymer Model). As we saw in Section 2.2, equilibrium solutions of the diblock copolymer model have to satisfy the nonlinear elliptic problem (2.5). Consider now the special case of total mass $\mu = 0$ and $\Omega = (0,1)$. Then finding equilibrium solutions of the evolution equation is equivalent to solving the nonlinear operator equation

$$\mathcal{F}(\lambda, u) \;=\; -\left(u_{xx} + \lambda f(u)\right)_{xx} - \lambda \sigma u \;=\; 0 \,,$$

where $\mathcal{F} : \mathbb{R} \times \mathcal{U} \to \mathcal{V}$ for suitable Banach spaces $\mathcal{U}$ and $\mathcal{V}$. In the interest of space and time, we only mention that these spaces can be defined using Fourier cosine series, where the domain $\mathcal{U}$ incorporates the boundary conditions and the mass constraint $\int_0^1 u\,dx = 0$. See **[36]** for more details.

Now assume that the pair $(\lambda_0, u_0) \in \mathbb{R} \times \mathcal{U}$ is arbitrary. Then the Fréchet derivative of the nonlinear operator $\mathcal{F}$ with respect to u is given by

$$Lv \;=\; D_u\mathcal{F}(\lambda_0, u_0)[v] \;=\; -\left(v_{xx} + \lambda_0 f'(u_0)v\right)_{xx} - \lambda_0 \sigma v \,,$$

and the associated adjoint operator is $L^*w = -w_{xxxx} - \lambda_0 f'(u_0) w_{xx} - \lambda_0 \sigma w$. One can then show that the operator L is a Fredholm operator of index zero. Furthermore, if we assume that $N(L)$ is one-dimensional, and if ψ_0 denotes a solution of the linear elliptic problem $L^*w = 0$ subject to homogeneous Neumann boundary conditions for both w and w_{xx}, then the range $R(L)$ of L can be characterized as

$$R(L) = N(\psi_0^*) \,, \qquad \text{where} \qquad \psi_0^*(w) = \int_0^1 \psi_0(x) w(x)\,dx \,.$$

In other words, Assumptions 4.1 and 4.2 are satisfied.

We can now apply the characterizations given in Theorems 4.4 and 4.12 to rigorously establish bifurcation points for the diblock copolymer model close to numerical approximations. This was done in **[36]** using the radii polynomial approach, which was prominently displayed in most of the other lectures. Rather than going through the specific estimates, we therefore only survey a couple of results:

- In the context of saddle-node bifurcation points, Figure 13 shows two numerical approximations u^* of solutions of the nonlinear elliptic equation $\mathcal{F}(\lambda^*, u) = 0$ at the same parameter value $\lambda^* \approx 262.9$. In both

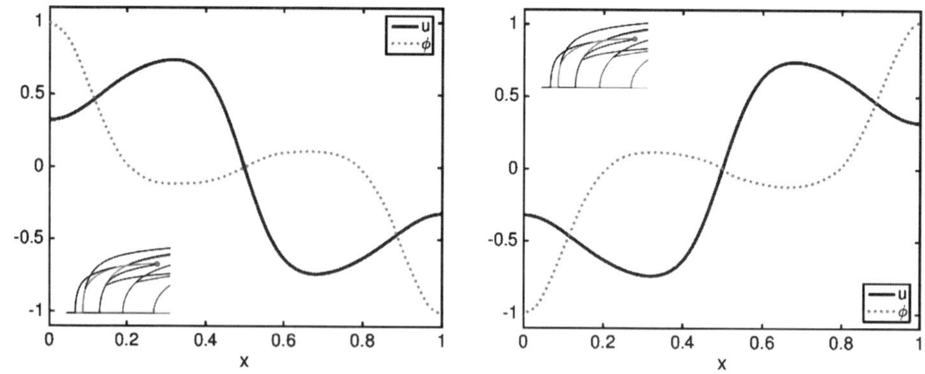

FIGURE 13. Saddle-node bifurcation points for the diblock copolymer model with $\sigma = 6$, total mass $\mu = 0$, and on the one-dimensional domain $\Omega = (0, 1)$. The two blue functions are approximations to saddle-node bifurcation points at the same parameter value $\lambda^* \approx 262.9$, and with the same $L^2(0, 1)$-norm close to 0.562. Using Theorem 4.4 one can prove that actual saddle-node bifurcation points are nearby. The red curves are approximations to kernel functions at the bifurcation points.

of these cases, Theorem 4.4 can be applied successfully, and it furnishes actual saddle-node points in a small neighborhood.

- Similarly, symmetry-breaking pitchfork bifurcation points can be validated using Theorem 4.12. For this, consider Figure 14, which shows four approximations u^* to equilibrium solutions in blue. In each image, the location of the approximating stationary state in the bifurcation diagram is indicated in the overlayed diagram, and an approximation to the normalized kernel function of the Fréchet derivative of $\mathcal{F}$ with respect to u at the point u^* is drawn in red. In order to apply the above result, we need to specify suitable symmetry operations. Consider for example the symmetry operators $S_{\mathcal{U}}$ and $S_{\mathcal{V}}$ defined by the same formula

$$(Su)(x) = u(1 - x) \qquad \text{for} \qquad x \in \Omega = (0, 1) \ .$$

Then $\mathcal{F}$ is $\mathbb{Z}_2$-equivariant, and the solution approximations in the right column of Figure 14 are symmetric with respect to S, while the corresponding kernel functions are antisymmetric. Moreover, one can show that the functions in the nullspace of the adjoint operator are antisymmetric as well. In both cases, Theorem 4.12 can be applied, and this guarantees symmetry-breaking pitchfork bifurcation points which lie on the second and fourth bifurcation branches from the trivial solution curve shown in the lower left image of Figure 5.

But what about the pitchfork bifurcation points on the first and third branches? These cases are depicted in the left column of Figure 14, and the solutions on the branch are no longer symmetric with respect to the above symmetry. Yet, if instead we define a new symmetry operator via

$$(Su)(x) = -u(1 - x) \qquad \text{for} \qquad x \in \Omega = (0, 1) \ ,$$

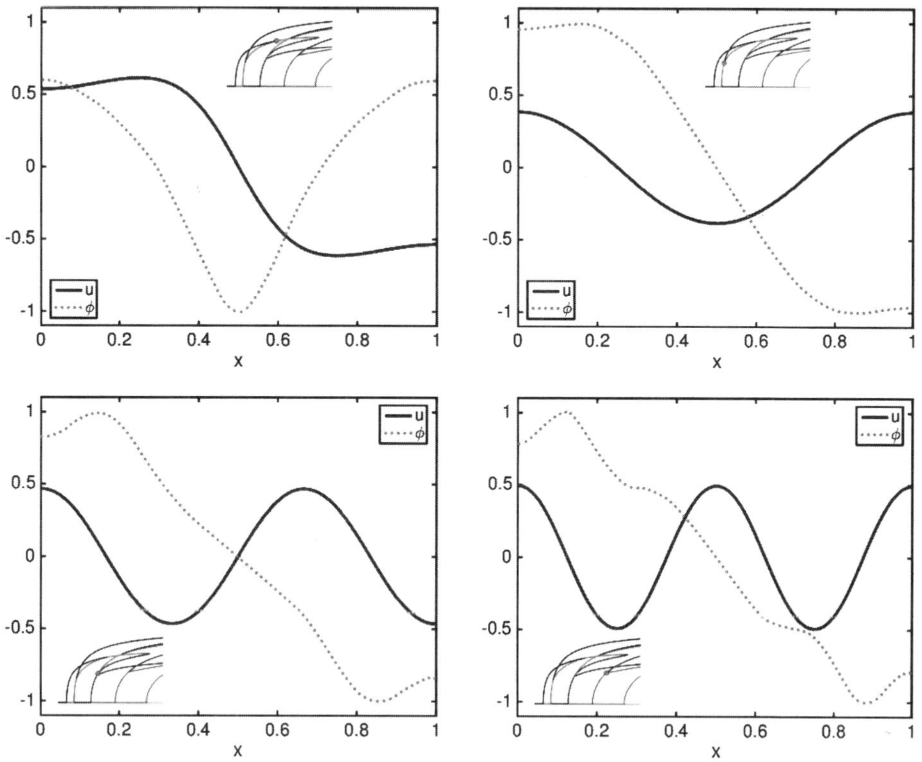

FIGURE 14. Symmetry-breaking pitchfork bifurcation points for the diblock copolymer model with $\sigma = 6$, total mass $\mu = 0$, and on the one-dimensional domain $\Omega = (0, 1)$. In each panel, an approximation to an equilibrium solution is shown in blue (solid line), an approximation to the normalized kernel function of the Fréchet derivative of $\mathcal{F}$ with respect to u at this point is drawn in red (dotted line), and the location of the solution in the bifurcation diagram is indicated in the overlayed diagram. Using Theorem 4.12 one can show that close to the functions shown in the top row, as well as in the bottom right image, there are true pitchfork bifurcation points. Note, however, that the situation shown in the lower left image is not covered by our approach.

then $\mathcal{F}$ remains $\mathbb{Z}_2$-equivariant, and the blue functions in the left column of Figure 14 are again symmetric elements. Since the kernel function shown in the upper left image of the figure is antisymmetric with respect to this new symmetry, one can apply Theorem 4.12, and this guarantees an actual bifurcation point nearby. Note, however, that in the lower left panel of Figure 14 the kernel function is not antisymmetric, so our result no longer applies. In fact, this bifurcation is not a $\mathbb{Z}_2$-symmetry-breaking bifurcation, but rather a symmetry-breaking bifurcation with a different equivariance group.

For more details and explicit bounds we refer the reader to [**36**]. $\Diamond$

References

[1] Robert A. Adams, *Sobolev spaces*, Academic Press [A subsidiary of Harcourt Brace Jovanovich, Publishers], New York-London, 1975. Pure and Applied Mathematics, Vol. 65. MR0450957

[2] Gianni Arioli and Hans Koch, *Computer-assisted methods for the study of stationary solutions in dissipative systems, applied to the Kuramoto-Sivashinski equation*, Arch. Ration. Mech. Anal. **197** (2010), no. 3, 1033–1051, DOI 10.1007/s00205-010-0309-7. MR2679365

[3] M. Bahiana and Y. Oono, *Cell dynamical system approach to block copolymers*, Physical Review A **41** (1990), 6763–6771.

[4] Frank S. Bates, *Block copolymer thermodynamics: Theory and experiment*, Annual Review of Physical Chemistry **41** (1990), 525–557.

[5] Frank S. Bates and G. H. Fredrickson, *Block copolymers–designer soft materials*, Physics Today **52** (1999), 32–39.

[6] Peter W. Bates and Paul C. Fife, *The dynamics of nucleation for the Cahn-Hilliard equation*, SIAM J. Appl. Math. **53** (1993), no. 4, 990–1008, DOI 10.1137/0153049. MR1232163

[7] Dirk Blömker, Bernhard Gawron, and Thomas Wanner, *Nucleation in the one-dimensional stochastic Cahn-Hilliard model*, Discrete Contin. Dyn. Syst. **27** (2010), no. 1, 25–52, DOI 10.3934/dcds.2010.27.25. MR2600760

[8] Dirk Blömker, Stanislaus Maier-Paape, and Thomas Wanner, *Phase separation in stochastic Cahn-Hilliard models*, Mathematical methods and models in phase transitions, Nova Sci. Publ., New York, 2005, pp. 1–41. MR2590943

[9] Dirk Blömker, Evelyn Sander, and Thomas Wanner, *Degenerate nucleation in the Cahn-Hilliard-Cook model*, SIAM J. Appl. Dyn. Syst. **15** (2016), no. 1, 459–494, DOI 10.1137/15M1028844. MR3463690

[10] Robert F. Brown, *A topological introduction to nonlinear analysis*, Birkhäuser Boston, Inc., Boston, MA, 1993. MR1232418

[11] John W. Cahn, Shui-Nee Chow, and Erik S. Van Vleck, *Spatially discrete nonlinear diffusion equations*, Rocky Mountain J. Math. **25** (1995), no. 1, 87–118, DOI 10.1216/rmjm/1181072270. Second Geoffrey J. Butler Memorial Conference in Differential Equations and Mathematical Biology (Edmonton, AB, 1992). MR1339995

[12] John W. Cahn and J. E. Hilliard, *Free energy of a nonuniform system I. Interfacial free energy*, Journal of Chemical Physics **28** (1958), 258–267.

[13] Pascal Chossat and Reiner Lauterbach, *Methods in equivariant bifurcations and dynamical systems*, Advanced Series in Nonlinear Dynamics, vol. 15, World Scientific Publishing Co., Inc., River Edge, NJ, 2000. MR1831950

[14] Shui Nee Chow and Jack K. Hale, *Methods of bifurcation theory*, Grundlehren der Mathematischen Wissenschaften [Fundamental Principles of Mathematical Science], vol. 251, Springer-Verlag, New York-Berlin, 1982. MR660633

[15] Shui-Nee Chow and John Mallet-Paret, *Pattern formation and spatial chaos in lattice dynamical systems. I*, IEEE Transactions on Circuits and Systems. I. Fundamental Theory and Applications **42** (1995), no. 10, 746–751.

[16] Shui-Nee Chow, John Mallet-Paret, and Erik S. Van Vleck, *Dynamics of lattice differential equations*, Proceedings of the Workshop on Discretely-Coupled Dynamical Systems, Part I (Santiago de Compostela, 1995), Internat. J. Bifur. Chaos Appl. Sci. Engrg. **6** (1996), no. 9, 1605–1621, DOI 10.1142/S0218127496000977. MR1434332

[17] Shui-Nee Chow, John Mallet-Paret, and Erik S. Van Vleck, *Pattern formation and spatial chaos in spatially discrete evolution equations*, Random Comput. Dynam. **4** (1996), no. 2-3, 109–178. MR1402415

[18] Sarah Day, Jean-Philippe Lessard, and Konstantin Mischaikow, *Validated continuation for equilibria of PDEs*, SIAM J. Numer. Anal. **45** (2007), no. 4, 1398–1424, DOI 10.1137/050645968. MR2338393

[19] Jonathan P. Desi, Hanein H. Edrees, Joseph J. Price, Evelyn Sander, and Thomas Wanner, *The dynamics of nucleation in stochastic Cahn-Morral systems*, SIAM J. Appl. Dyn. Syst. **10** (2011), no. 2, 707–743, DOI 10.1137/100801378. MR2821252

[20] Jonathan P. Desi, Evelyn Sander, and Thomas Wanner, *Complex transient patterns on the disk*, Discrete Contin. Dyn. Syst. **15** (2006), no. 4, 1049–1078, DOI 10.3934/dcds.2006.15.1049. MR2224497

[21] Paweł Dłotko and Thomas Wanner, *Topological microstructure analysis using persistence landscapes*, Phys. D **334** (2016), 60–81, DOI 10.1016/j.physd.2016.04.015. MR3545970

[22] Eusebius Doedel, *AUTO: a program for the automatic bifurcation analysis of autonomous systems*, Proceedings of the Tenth Manitoba Conference on Numerical Mathematics and Computing, Vol. I (Winnipeg, Man., 1980), Congr. Numer. **30** (1981), 265–284. MR635945

[23] D. E. Edmunds and W. D. Evans, *Spectral theory and differential operators*, Oxford Mathematical Monographs, The Clarendon Press, Oxford University Press, New York, 1987. Oxford Science Publications. MR929030

[24] C. M. Elliott and A. M. Stuart, *The global dynamics of discrete semilinear parabolic equations*, SIAM J. Numer. Anal. **30** (1993), no. 6, 1622–1663, DOI 10.1137/0730084. MR1249036

[25] Marcio Gameiro, Jean-Philippe Lessard, and Konstantin Mischaikow, *Validated continuation over large parameter ranges for equilibria of PDEs*, Math. Comput. Simulation **79** (2008), no. 4, 1368–1382, DOI 10.1016/j.matcom.2008.03.014. MR2487806

[26] Marcio Gameiro, Konstantin Mischaikow, and Thomas Wanner, *Evolution of pattern complexity in the Cahn-Hilliard theory of phase separation*, Acta Materialia **53** (2005), no. 3, 693–704.

[27] Christopher P. Grant, *Grain sizes in the discrete Allen-Cahn and Cahn-Hilliard equations*, Discrete Contin. Dynam. Systems **7** (2001), no. 1, 127–146, DOI 10.3934/dcds.2001.7.127. MR1806377

[28] Christopher P. Grant, *Superabundance of stationary solutions for the discrete Allen-Cahn equation*, Dyn. Contin. Discrete Impuls. Syst. Ser. B Appl. Algorithms **8** (2001), no. 1, 71–91. MR1824286

[29] Christopher P. Grant and Erik S. Van Vleck, *Slowly migrating transition layers for the discrete Allen-Cahn and Cahn-Hilliard equations*, Nonlinearity **8** (1995), no. 5, 861–876. MR1355047

[30] M. Grinfeld and A. Novick-Cohen, *Counting stationary solutions of the Cahn-Hilliard equation by transversality arguments*, Proc. Roy. Soc. Edinburgh Sect. A **125** (1995), no. 2, 351–370, DOI 10.1017/S0308210500028079. MR1331565

[31] Jack K. Hale, *Numerical dynamics*, Chaotic numerics (Geelong, 1993), Contemp. Math., vol. 172, Amer. Math. Soc., Providence, RI, 1994, pp. 1–30, DOI 10.1090/conm/172/01795. MR1294406

[32] Ian Johnson, Evelyn Sander, and Thomas Wanner, *Branch interactions and long-term dynamics for the diblock copolymer model in one dimension*, Discrete Contin. Dyn. Syst. **33** (2013), no. 8, 3671–3705, DOI 10.3934/dcds.2013.33.3671. MR3021375

[33] Tosio Kato, *Perturbation theory for linear operators*, Classics in Mathematics, Springer-Verlag, Berlin, 1995. Reprint of the 1980 edition. MR1335452

[34] Steven G. Krantz and Harold R. Parks, *The implicit function theorem*, Modern Birkhäuser Classics, Birkhäuser/Springer, New York, 2013. History, theory, and applications; Reprint of the 2003 edition. MR2977424

[35] Yuri A. Kuznetsov, *Elements of applied bifurcation theory*, 2nd ed., Applied Mathematical Sciences, vol. 112, Springer-Verlag, New York, 1998. MR1711790

[36] Jean-Philippe Lessard, Evelyn Sander, and Thomas Wanner, *Rigorous continuation of bifurcation points in the diblock copolymer equation*, Journal of Computational Dynamics, to appear, DOI: 10.3934/jcd.2017003

[37] Stanislaus Maier-Paape and Thomas Wanner, *Spinodal decomposition for the Cahn-Hilliard equation in higher dimensions. I. Probability and wavelength estimate*, Comm. Math. Phys. **195** (1998), no. 2, 435–464, DOI 10.1007/s002200050397. MR1637817

[38] Stanislaus Maier-Paape and Thomas Wanner, *Spinodal decomposition for the Cahn-Hilliard equation in higher dimensions: nonlinear dynamics*, Arch. Ration. Mech. Anal. **151** (2000), no. 3, 187–219, DOI 10.1007/s002050050196. MR1753703

[39] John Mallet-Paret and Shui-Nee Chow, *Pattern formation and spatial chaos in lattice dynamical systems. II*, IEEE Transactions on Circuits and Systems. I. Fundamental Theory and Applications **42** (1995), no. 10, 752–756.

[40] G. Moore and A. Spence, *The calculation of turning points of nonlinear equations*, SIAM J. Numer. Anal. **17** (1980), no. 4, 567–576, DOI 10.1137/0717048. MR584731

[41] Ramon E. Moore, R. Baker Kearfott, and Michael J. Cloud, *Introduction to interval analysis*, Society for Industrial and Applied Mathematics (SIAM), Philadelphia, PA, 2009. MR2482682

[42] Yasumasa Nishiura and Isamu Ohnishi, *Some mathematical aspects of the micro-phase separation in diblock copolymers*, Phys. D **84** (1995), no. 1-2, 31–39, DOI 10.1016/0167-2789(95)00005-O. MR1334695

[43] T. Ohta and K. Kawasaki, *Equilibrium morphology of block copolymer melts*, Macromolecules **19** (1986), 2621–2632.

[44] Michael Plum, *Existence and enclosure results for continua of solutions of parameter-dependent nonlinear boundary value problems*, J. Comput. Appl. Math. **60** (1995), no. 1-2, 187–200, DOI 10.1016/0377-0427(94)00091-E. Linear/nonlinear iterative methods and verification of solution (Matsuyama, 1993). MR1354655

[45] Michael Plum, *Enclosures for two-point boundary value problems near bifurcation points*, Scientific computing and validated numerics (Wuppertal, 1995), Math. Res., vol. 90, Akademie Verlag, Berlin, 1996, pp. 265–279. MR1394244

[46] Michael Plum, *Computer-assisted proofs for semilinear elliptic boundary value problems*, Japan J. Indust. Appl. Math. **26** (2009), no. 2-3, 419–442. MR2589483

[47] A. G. Ramm, *A simple proof of the Fredholm alternative and a characterization of the Fredholm operators*, Amer. Math. Monthly **108** (2001), no. 9, 855–860, DOI 10.2307/2695558. MR1864050

[48] Siegfried M. Rump, *INTLAB - INTerval LABoratory*, Developments in Reliable Computing (Tibor Csendes, ed.), Kluwer Academic Publishers, Dordrecht, 1999, http://www.ti3.tuhh.de/rump/, pp. 77–104.

[49] Siegfried M. Rump, *Verification methods: rigorous results using floating-point arithmetic*, Acta Numer. **19** (2010), 287–449, DOI 10.1017/S096249291000005X. MR2652784

[50] Evelyn Sander and Thomas Wanner, *Monte Carlo simulations for spinodal decomposition*, J. Statist. Phys. **95** (1999), no. 5-6, 925–948, DOI 10.1023/A:1004550416829. MR1712442

[51] Evelyn Sander and Thomas Wanner, *Unexpectedly linear behavior for the Cahn-Hilliard equation*, SIAM J. Appl. Math. **60** (2000), no. 6, 2182–2202, DOI 10.1137/S0036139999352225. MR1763320

[52] Evelyn Sander and Thomas Wanner, *Validated saddle-node bifurcations and applications to lattice dynamical systems*, SIAM J. Appl. Dyn. Syst. **15** (2016), no. 3, 1690–1733, DOI 10.1137/16M1061011. MR3546337

[53] A. Spence and B. Werner, *Nonsimple turning points and cusps*, IMA J. Numer. Anal. **2** (1982), no. 4, 413–427, DOI 10.1093/imanum/2.4.413. MR692288

[54] Jan Bouwe van den Berg, Jean-Philippe Lessard, and Konstantin Mischaikow, *Global smooth solution curves using rigorous branch following*, Math. Comp. **79** (2010), no. 271, 1565–1584, DOI 10.1090/S0025-5718-10-02325-2. MR2630003

[55] Thomas Wanner, *Maximum norms of random sums and transient pattern formation*, Trans. Amer. Math. Soc. **356** (2004), no. 6, 2251–2279, DOI 10.1090/S0002-9947-03-03480-9. MR2048517

[56] Thomas Wanner, *Topological analysis of the diblock copolymer equation*, Mathematical challenges in a new phase of materials science, Springer Proc. Math. Stat., vol. 166, Springer, [Tokyo], 2016, pp. 27–51, DOI 10.1007/978-4-431-56104-0_2. MR3557602

[57] Thomas Wanner, *Computer-assisted equilibrium validation for the diblock copolymer model*, Discrete Contin. Dyn. Syst. **37** (2017), no. 2, 1075–1107, DOI 10.3934/dcds.2017045. MR3583512

[58] Yoshitaka Watanabe, Kaori Nagatou, Michael Plum, and Mitsuhiro T. Nakao, *Verified computations of eigenvalue exclosures for eigenvalue problems in Hilbert spaces*, SIAM J. Numer. Anal. **52** (2014), no. 2, 975–992, DOI 10.1137/120894683. MR3196951

[59] B. Werner and A. Spence, *The computation of symmetry-breaking bifurcation points*, SIAM J. Numer. Anal. **21** (1984), no. 2, 388–399, DOI 10.1137/0721029. MR736340

[60] Eberhard Zeidler, *Nonlinear functional analysis and its applications. I*, Springer-Verlag, New York, 1986. Fixed-point theorems; Translated from the German by Peter R. Wadsack. MR816732

Index

Allen-Cahn equation
  discrete, *see also* discrete Allen-Cahn equation
  parabolic partial differential equation, 127

bifurcation diagram, 124, 154
bifurcation point, 125
  direct localization, 154, 167
  necessary condition, 126
  one-dimensional kernel, 155
  pitchfork, 125, 134, 152, 164
  saddle-node, 125, 147, 149, 154, 156, 157
  secondary, 134

Cahn-Hilliard equation, 130
  equilibrium solutions, 132

diblock copolymer model, 130
  branch validation, 145
  equilibrium solutions, 132
  free energy, 130
  multistability, 131
  pitchfork bifurcation, 168
  saddle-node bifurcation, 167
  secondary bifurcation, 133
discrete Allen-Cahn equation, 127, 128
  abundance of equilibria, 128
  branch validation, 151
  mosaic solutions, 129, 139, 153
  saddle-node bifurcation, 129, 158
  unbounded branch validation, 139

equilibrium, 124

Fredholm operator, 155, 167

implicit function theorem
  classical, 126
  constructive, 136–137, 140, 144, 149
interface motion, 128
interval arithmetic, 151
Intlab, 151

Lyapunov-Schmidt reduction, 134, 163
  bifurcation equation, 163
  equivariant, 164

mosaic solutions, *see also* discrete Allen-Cahn equation, mosaic solutions

norm estimate
  for inverse linear operators, 138
  use of interval arithmetic, 141

pinning, 128

saddle-node bifurcation
  subcritical, 156
  sufficient condition, 156
  supercritical, 156
  via extended systems, 158
Sobolev embedding theorem, 146
Sobolev space, 145
stationary solution, 124
symmetry
  antisymmetric element, 161
  in the form of $\mathbb{Z}_2$-equivariance, *see also* $\mathbb{Z}_2$-equivariance
  symmetric element, 161
symmetry-breaking pitchfork bifurcation
  sufficient condition, 164
  via extended systems, 166

verification
  bifurcation points in the diblock copolymer model, 167–169
  branch segments, 144
  branch segments in the diblock copolymer model, 145–147
  branch segments in the discrete Allen-Cahn equation, 151–153
  saddle-node bifurcations in the discrete Allen-Cahn equation, 158–160
  saddle-node branch, 149
  simple matrix eigenvalues, 140–141
  unbounded branches in the discrete Allen-Cahn equation, 139–140

$\mathbb{Z}_2$-equivariance, 161
  general consequences, 162
  one-dimensional kernel, 162

Department of Mathematical Sciences, George Mason University, Fairfax, VA 22030, USA

Email address: `twanner@gmu.edu`

Proceedings of Symposia in Applied Mathematics
Volume **74**, 2018
http://dx.doi.org/10.1090/psapm/074/00640

Dynamics and chaos for maps and the Conley index

Sarah Day

Abstract. Discrete-time dynamical systems modeled by iteration of continuous maps exhibit a wide variety of interesting behaviors. One illustrative example is the one-dimensional logistic model. For the logistic model, chaotic dynamics may be proven via a topological conjugacy onto an appropriate subshift of finite type, a symbolic system that acts as a catalogue of dynamics and for which a proof of chaos is attainable. Analysis and proofs of dynamics for other models, especially in dimensions larger than one, often prove to be more challenging. In these notes, we examine methods for constructing *outer approximations*, finite representations of discrete-time models that are amenable to computational studies and computer-assisted proofs. These methods rely heavily on *Conley index theory*, an algebraic topological generalization of Morse Theory. Both theory and algorithms will be presented with sample results for the Hénon map shown for illustration.

Contents

1. Symbolic Dynamics and Topological Entropy
2. Itineraries and Topological Semi-conjugacy
3. Conley Index Theory and Surjectivity
4. Combinatorial Outer Approximation
5. Computational Conley Index Theory
6. The Hénon Map: Sample Results
References
Index

Discrete-time dynamical systems governed by continuous maps $f : X \to X$ use iteration to describe movement and change. One example is the *logistic map*, $f : [0,1] \to [0,1]$ given by $f(x) = rx(1-x)$. Here, $x \in [0,1]$ gives the size of a population as a fraction of a pre-set, large population size N for the model species and the parameter $r \in [0,4]$ represents the species reproductive rate at small population sizes. This relatively simple unimodal map models a reproducing population that experiences the effects of overcrowding and/or starvation at larger population sizes. For an initial (normalized) population size $x_0 \in [0,1]$, $x_1 := f(x_0)$ gives the size of the population after one generation or time step.

Continuing this process by taking $x_{n+1} = f(x_n)$ leads naturally to attempts at prediction. Will the population go extinct/approach a steady state/do something more complicated? As n tends towards infinity, $x_n \to 0$ describes a population headed towards extinction and $x_n \to x^*$ reflects a population limiting to the steady state x^*. Note that by continuity, $f(x^*) = x^*$ in this case. Another possibility is that the population exhibits periodic behavior with $x_{p-1} = x_0$. In this case, p is the *period* of this periodic orbit. As noted by Robert May in a now famous paper [**May76**], the logistic model may exhibit far more complicated dynamics than these relatively simple cases. In fact, for $r = 4$ one can prove that the logistic map is *topologically conjugate* (i.e. can be shown to be equivalent via a change of coordinates that preserves dynamics) to the *full shift on 2 symbols*, a symbolic discrete-time system that is provably chaotic, contains periodic orbits of all periods and displays sensitive dependence on initial conditions, a defining property of chaotic systems (see [**ASY97**]). Topological conjugacy and the full shift on 2 symbols are defined and discussed in Section 2.

The logistic map example motivates our approach to building symbolic systems that may be used to describe dynamics for a given discrete-time model $f : X \to X$. As systems grow in dimension and complexity, the approach taken for the logistic map example quickly unravels. More specifically, for most systems we lose the ability construct a topological conjugacy that maps the studied system to an appropriate symbolic system. Instead, we seek in this approach to construct a symbolic system that we prove is *topological semi-conjugate* to $f : S \to S$, where S is an appropriate (invariant) subset of X. (See Section 2 for definitions.) The relaxation of the topological conjugacy (used for the logistic map) to a topological semi-conjugacy establishes the constructed symbolic system as a "lower bound" for the dynamics, while acknowledging that we and the methods may have missed some of the dynamics of f on S.

The two-dimensional *Hénon map* [**Hén76**], first established by Michel Hénon as a simplified model of stretching and folding, offers a useful test case for this approach. Here we study a rescaled version $f : \mathbb{R}^2 \to \mathbb{R}^2$ given by

$$\begin{pmatrix} x \\ y \end{pmatrix} \to \begin{pmatrix} 1 - ax^2 + y/5 \\ 5bx \end{pmatrix}. \tag{1}$$

Like the logistic map, the Hénon map is quadratic and exhibits chaos at certain parameter values (e.g. $a = 1.3$ and $b = 0.2$, the parameter values used for the sample results presented in Section 6). Unlike the logistic map, there is no known topological conjugacy linking the Hénon map at these chaotic parameter values to a symbolic system.

In what follows, we outline an approach for extracting symbolic dynamics from discrete-time systems governed by continuous maps $f : X \to X$. These notes cover some basic definitions and ideas from dynamical systems as well as the essential framework for computational Conley index theory for discrete-time systems. Sample computations for the Hénon map will be used for illustration and the reader is encouraged to refer to the figures in Section 6 for concrete examples throughout. The notes also contain additional references including [**LM95**, **Rob95**] for dynamics, [**Con78**, **MM02**] for Conley index theory, and [**KMM04**, **DJM05**, **DJM04**, **Day03**, **DFT08**] for computational Conley index theory.

1. Symbolic Dynamics and Topological Entropy

The computational framework described in these notes may be used in computer-assisted proofs of dynamics ranging from fixed points to chaos for discrete-time systems. In this approach, we aim to construct a symbolic dynamical system that is topologically semi-conjugate to the system under study. The topological semi-conjugacy links the two systems, establishing the constructed symbolic system as a "lower bound" on the dynamics of the original system. That is, dynamics exhibited by the symbolic system represents proven dynamics in the original system. Furthermore, the symbolic system acts as a catalogue of dynamics – fixed points, periodic orbits, connecting orbits, and topological entropy are all readily available from a directed graph representation of the symbolic system as self-loops and cycles, connecting paths, and the log of the spectral radius (of the associated adjacency matrix for the graph) respectively. We give some basic definitions below. The sources [**LM95**, **Rob95**] offer more detailed descriptions of symbolic dynamics and topological entropy.

The symbolic systems we focus on here are *sofic shifts*. These are defined as invariant subsystems of full shifts as follows. Given a set of symbols $\mathcal{A}$, also referred to as an *alphabet*, we define the (one-sided) *full shift* to be the set of all infinite symbol sequences

$$\mathcal{A}^{\mathbb{N}} = \{a_0a_1a_2\ldots | a_i \in \mathcal{A}\}$$

together with the shift map $\sigma : \mathcal{A}^{\mathbb{N}} \to \mathcal{A}^{\mathbb{N}}$

$$\sigma(a_0a_1a_2\ldots) := a_1a_2a_3\ldots.$$

A *subshift* is given by a set $\Sigma \subset \mathcal{A}^{\mathbb{N}}$ that is invariant under σ, that is, $\sigma(\Sigma) \subseteq \Sigma$ so that $\sigma : \Sigma \to \Sigma$ is a well-defined subsystem. There are various presentations for a subshift $\sigma : \Sigma \to \Sigma$. One method for defining a subshift is creating a list of *prohibited words*, or blocks of symbols, and allowing all infinite symbol sequences that do not contain a prohibited word. This list of prohibited words is finite in the case of *subshifts of finite type* and methods described in [**DFT08**] focus on the construction of subshifts of this form. Graphical presentations, including *vertex shifts* and *edge shifts*, are also useful. See [**LM95**] for more details. In what follows we focus on vertex shift presentations.

DEFINITION 1. *Let G be a directed graph with vertex set $V(G)$ and edge set $E(G)$. Given an alphabet $\mathcal{A}$ and vertex labeling $\ell : V(G) \to \mathcal{A}$, we define the corresponding collection of label sequences of infinite walks in G by*

$$\Sigma_G = \{\ell(v_0)\ell(v_1)\ell(v_2)\ldots | \, (v_i, v_{i+1}) \in E(G)\} \subseteq \mathcal{A}^{\mathbb{N}}.$$

We have $\sigma(\Sigma_G) \subset \Sigma_G$ since each $\boldsymbol{a} = \ell(v_0)\ell(v_1)\ell(v_2)\ldots \in \Sigma_G$ has a corresponding walk $v_0v_1v_2\ldots$ in G, and $\sigma(\boldsymbol{a})$ will be given as the label sequence for the walk $v_1v_2v_3\ldots$ in G obtained by removing the first vertex/edge. A graph G is a vertex presentation *of a subshift $\Sigma \subseteq \mathcal{A}^{\mathbb{N}}$ if $\Sigma_G = \Sigma$. If, furthermore, for each node $v \in V(G)$ and pair of edges $(v, u_1), (v, u_2) \in E(G)$ out of v, the labels on u_i satisfy $\ell(u_1) \neq \ell(u_2)$, then we say that G is* right-resolving.

A subshift $\Sigma \subseteq \mathcal{A}^{\mathbb{N}}$ is *sofic* if it has a right-resolving vertex presentation with finitely many vertices. During our construction of sofic subshifts, we also consider when one subshift is contained in another. The language of *admissible blocks* allows us to present an alternative way of checking that $\Sigma \subset \Sigma'$.

DEFINITION 2. *Given a subshift* $\Sigma \subseteq \mathcal{A}^{\mathbb{N}}$, *the* language $\mathcal{B}(\Sigma)$ *of* Σ, *also called the set of* admissible n-blocks, *is the set of finite words appearing in points of* Σ. *Formally, given* $\boldsymbol{a} \in \mathcal{A}^{\mathbb{N}}$, *let* $[\boldsymbol{a}]_n = a_0 a_1 \cdots a_{n-1}$ *and* $\mathcal{B}_n(\Sigma) = \{[\boldsymbol{a}]_n : \boldsymbol{a} \in \Sigma\}$. *Then* $\mathcal{B}(\Sigma) = \bigcup_{n\in\mathbb{N}_+} \mathcal{B}_n(\Sigma) = \{[\boldsymbol{a}]_n : \boldsymbol{a} \in \Sigma, n \in \mathbb{N}_+\}$.

It is important to note that for an appropriate choice of metric on $\mathcal{A}^{\mathbb{N}}$ (and hence on Σ_G), σ is a continuous map and $\sigma : \Sigma_G \to \Sigma_G$ is a dynamical system (see e.g. [**Rob95**]). Sofic subshifts given with a (finite) vertex shift presentation G are particularly nice for extracting dynamics. For example, if one is looking for a period n orbit, then one checks that there is a symbol sequence $\boldsymbol{a}^* = (a_0, a_1, \ldots) \in \Sigma_G$ such that $a_{i+n} = a_i$ for all $i = 0, 1, \ldots$. This periodic symbol sequence corresponds to a cycle in G.

One method for quantifying the complexity of a given dynamical system is to compute its *topological entropy*. The following is based on Bowen's definition of topological entropy in [**Bow71**].

DEFINITION 3. *Let* $f : S \to S$ *be a continuous map. A set* $W \subset S$ *is called* (n, ϵ, f)*-separated if for any two different points* $x, y \in W$ *there is an integer* j *with* $0 \leq j < n$ *so that the distance between* $f^j(x)$ *and* $f^j(y)$ *is greater than* ϵ. *Let* $s(n, \epsilon, f)$ *be the maximum cardinality of any* (n, ϵ, f)*-separated set. The* topological entropy *of* f *is the number*

$$h_{\text{top}}(f) = \lim_{\epsilon\to 0} \limsup_{n\to\infty} \frac{\log(s(n, \epsilon, f))}{n}. \tag{2}$$

As a measurement of chaos, we say that a map f for which $h_{\text{top}}(f) > 0$ is chaotic, and, if $h_{\text{top}}(f) > h_{\text{top}}(g)$, then f is exhibits more complexity than g.

Once again, we can turn to symbolic dynamics in order to perform concrete computations. See [**Rob95**] for more details.

THEOREM 4. *Let* G *be vertex shift presentation of the sofic subshift* $\sigma : \Sigma_G \to \Sigma_G$. *Then*

$$h_{\text{top}}(\sigma|_{\Sigma_G}) = \lim_{N\to\infty} \frac{|\mathcal{B}_N(\Sigma_G)|}{N} = \log(\text{sp}(G))$$

where $sp(G)$ *is the spectral radius of the adjacency matrix* A *with*

$$a_{ij} = \begin{cases} 1 & \text{if } (v_i, v_j) \in E(G) \\ 0 & \text{otherwise} \end{cases}$$

for G.

In essence, (n, ϵ, σ)-separation is encoded in the representation of the system and may be computed directly from the vertex shift presentation G.

2. Itineraries and Topological Semi-conjugacy

Topological conjugacies and topological semi-conjugacies link two systems, preserving information about dynamics.

The *itinerary function* defined below allows us to re-write a system $f : S \to S$ as a subshift. Our methods are designed to ensure that the itinerary function serves as a topological semi-conjugacy between the two systems.

DEFINITION 5. *A continuous map* $\rho : X \to Y$ *is a* topological semi-conjugacy *from* $\psi : Y \to Y$ *to* $\phi : X \to X$ *if* $\rho \circ \phi = \psi \circ \rho$ *and* ρ *is surjective (onto). If, in addition,* ρ *is injective (one-to-one), then* ρ *is a* topological conjugacy.

Topological conjugacies preserve many properties of dynamical systems. One such example is the following theorem. (See also [**Dev89**].)

THEOREM 6. *Let* ρ *be a topological conjugacy between* $\phi : X \to X$ *and* $\psi : Y \to Y$*. Then* $y \in Y$ *is a periodic point of period* n *under* ψ *(i.e.* $\psi^n(y) = y$*) if and only if* $\rho^{-1}(y)$ *is a periodic point of period* n *under* ϕ*. In addition,* $h_{\text{top}}(\phi) = h_{\text{top}}(\psi)$*.*

If $f : S \to S$ is topologically conjugate to a sofic subshift, then we have a convenient list of trajectories of f given by the subshift. Indeed, in this case, the topological conjugacy acts as a coordinate transformation of the original system onto a decipherable (symbolic) system.

EXAMPLE 1. *There is a topological conjugacy between the logistic map* $f(x) = rx(1-x)$ *with* $r = 4$ *and the full shift on two symbols* Σ_G*, where* G *is the complete graph on two vertices. Defining properties of chaos including density of periodic points, sensitive dependence on initial conditions, and topological transitivity may all be proven for* $\sigma : \Sigma_G \to \Sigma_G$ *and, therefore, for the logistic map. We also have that* $h_{\text{top}}(f) = h_{\text{top}}(\sigma|_{\Sigma_G}) = \log(2)$*. (See* [**ASY97**] *for further details.)*

In practice, such a complete description may be beyond our reach and we instead construct sofic subshifts that we prove are topologically semi-conjugate to $f : S' \to S'$ for some appropriately defined subset S'. The topologically semi-conjugate system ($\psi = \sigma$) acts as a lower bound for dynamics under $\phi = f$ resulting in $h_{\text{top}}(f) \geq h_{\text{top}}(\sigma)$.

DEFINITION 7. *Suppose* $N \subset X$ *may be decomposed into* $m < \infty$ *disjoint, closed subsets (*$N = \cup_{i=1,\ldots m} N_i$*,* $N_i \cap N_j = \emptyset$ *for all* $i \neq j$*) and let* $\mathcal{A} = \{1, 2, \ldots, m\}$ *be the associated alphabet of symbols. Let* S *be the maximal invariant set in* N *(i.e.* S *is the largest set such that* $S \subset N$ *and* $f(S) = S$*). Then* $f^j(S) \subset N$ *for all* $j = 0, 1, \ldots$*. The* itinerary function $\rho : S \to \mathcal{A}^{\mathbb{N}}$ *is given by* $\rho(x) = s_0 s_1 \ldots$*, where* $s_j = i$ *for* $f^j(x) \in N_i$*.*

The itinerary function is continuous under the appropriate choice of metrics and naturally satisfies the commutativity condition required for topological semi-conjugacy (that is, $\rho \circ f = \sigma \circ \rho$). (See also [**Dev89**], [**Rob95**].) In what follows, we describe a procedure based on Conley index theory that allows us to construct a sofic subshift $\sigma : \Sigma_G \to \Sigma_G$ with vertex presentation G and $\Sigma_G \subset \mathcal{A}^{\mathbb{N}}$ so that for some $S' \subseteq S$, $\rho : S' \to \Sigma_G$ is surjective. The surjectivity condition completes the proof that ρ is a topological semi-conjugacy from $\sigma : \Sigma_G \to \Sigma_G$ to $f : S' \to S'$.

Since if g is topologically semi-conjugate to f then $h_{top}(f) \geq h_{top}(g)$, the following corollary allows us to use a semi-conjugate sofic subshift to obtain a lower bound for the topological entropy of the system under study. (See also [**LM95**] for further details.)

COROLLARY 8. *Suppose that the itinerary function* ρ *is a semi-conjugacy from* $\sigma : \Sigma_G \to \Sigma_G$ *to* $f : S' \to S'$ *for some* $S' \subset X$ *and sofic subshift with vertex shift presentation* G*. Then*

$$h_{\text{top}}(f) \geq \log(\text{sp}(G))$$

where $sp(G)$ *is the spectral radius of the adjacency matrix for* G*.*

3. Conley Index Theory and Surjectivity

We now present some of the topological tools used to build the sofic subshift and prove surjectivity of the itinerary map ρ. These tools are based on Conley index theory for which we now give definitions, facts, and theorems. (See [**KMM04, DJM05, DJM04, Day03, DFT08**] for more details.) A discussion of the implementation of these ideas in a computational framework follows in Sections 4 and 5.

Let $f : \mathbb{R}^n \to \mathbb{R}^n$ be a continuous map. A *trajectory* through $x \in \mathbb{R}^n$ is a sequence

$$\gamma_x := (\ldots, x_{-1}, x_0, x_1, \ldots) \tag{3}$$

such that $x_0 = x$ and $x_{n+1} = f(x_n)$ for all $n \in \mathbb{Z}$. The *invariant set relative to* $N \subset \mathbb{R}^n$ is

$$\operatorname{Inv}(N, f) := \{x \in N \mid \text{there exists a trajectory } \gamma_x \text{ with } \gamma_x \subset N\}. \tag{4}$$

One example of a relative invariant set is the domain $S = \operatorname{Inv}(N, f)$ on which we define the itinerary function ρ in Definition 7.

We are now ready to present some of the basic structures in Conley index theory.

Definition 9. *A compact set $N \subset \mathbb{R}^n$ is an* isolating neighborhood *if*

$$\operatorname{Inv}(N, f) \subset \operatorname{int}(N) \tag{5}$$

where $\operatorname{int}(N)$ *denotes the interior of N. S is an* isolated invariant set *if $S = \operatorname{Inv}(N, f)$ for some isolating neighborhood N.*

We use the next two definitions to encode the dynamics on an isolating neighborhood.

Definition 10. *Let $P = (P_1, P_0)$ be a pair of compact sets with $P_0 \subset P_1 \subset X$. The map induced on the pointed quotient space $(P_1/P_0, [P_0])$ is*

$$f_P(x) := \begin{cases} f(x) & \text{if } x, f(x) \in P_1 \setminus P_0 \\ [P_0] & \text{otherwise.} \end{cases} \tag{6}$$

Definition 11. *([**RS88**]) The pair of compact sets $P = (P_1, P_0)$ with $P_0 \subset P_1 \subset X$ is an* index pair *for f provided that*

(1) *the induced map, f_P, is continuous,*
(2) *$\overline{P_1 \setminus P_0}$, the closure of $P_1 \setminus P_0$, is an isolating neighborhood.*

In this case, we say that P is an index pair for the isolated invariant set $S = \operatorname{Inv}(\overline{P_1 \setminus P_0}, f)$.

The following definition is required for the definition of the Conley index.

Definition 12. *Two group homomorphisms, $\phi : G \to G$ and $\psi : G' \to G'$ on abelian groups G and G' are* shift equivalent *if there exist group homomorphisms $r : G \to G'$ and $s : G' \to G$ and a constant $m \in \mathbb{N}$ (referred to as the 'lag') such that*

$$r \circ \phi = \psi \circ r, \quad s \circ \psi = \phi \circ s, \quad r \circ s = \psi^m, \quad \text{and} \quad s \circ r = \phi^m.$$

The shift equivalence class *of ϕ, denoted $[\phi]_s$, is the set of all homomorphisms ψ such that ψ is shift equivalent to ϕ.*

DEFINITION 13. *Let $P = (P_1, P_0)$ be an index pair for the isolated invariant set $S = \mathrm{Inv}(\overline{P_1 \setminus P_0}, f)$ and let $f_{P*} : H_*(P_1, P_0) \to H_*(P_1, P_0)$ be the map induced on the relative homology groups $H_*(P_1, P_0)$ from the map f_P. The* Conley index *of S is the shift equivalence class of f_{P*}*

$$\mathrm{Con}(S, f) := [f_{P*}]_s. \tag{7}$$

The Conley index for the isolated invariant set S given in Definition 13 is well-defined. That is every isolated invariant set has an index pair, and the corresponding shift equivalence class remains invariant under different choices for this index pair (see e.g. [**MM02, KMM04**]).

So far we have passed from continuous maps to induced maps on relative homology. Our overall goal, however, is to describe the dynamics of our original map. Here we present measurements based on the map on homology that may give us information about the original map. The first theorem is Ważewski's Principle in the context of Conley index theory.

THEOREM 14. *If* $\mathrm{Con}(S, f) \neq [0]_s$, *then* $S \neq \emptyset$.

The Lefschetz Theorem may be used to prove the existence of a fixed point.

THEOREM 15. *If the* Lefschetz number

$$L(S, f) := \sum_k (-1)^k \operatorname{tr}(f_{Pk}) \tag{8}$$

is nonzero, then S contains a fixed point.

By requiring additional structure in the isolating neighborhood N of S, we can use modifications of Theorems 14 and 15 to study finer structure in S. This follows closely the construction in [**Szy97a**].

COROLLARY 16. *Let $N \subset X$ be the union of pairwise disjoint, compact sets $N_1, \ldots, N_m$ and let $S := \mathrm{Inv}(N, f)$ be the isolated invariant set relative to N. For $B_n = a_0 a_1 \ldots a_{n-1}$, an n-block of symbols from the alphabet $\mathcal{A} = \{1, \ldots, m\}$, set*

$$f^{B_n} := f_{N_{a_{n-1}}} \circ \cdots \circ f_{N_{a_0}}$$

where $f_{N_{a_i}}$ denotes the restriction of the map f to the region N_{a_i}. Then for $S' = \mathrm{Inv}(N, f^{B_n}) \subset S$, if

$$\mathrm{Con}(S', f^{B_n}) \neq [0]_s, \tag{9}$$

then $S' \neq \emptyset$. More specifically, there exists a point in S whose trajectory under f travels through the regions $N_{a_0}, \ldots, N_{a_{n-1}}$ in the prescribed order. Similarly, if

$$L(S', f^{B_n}) \neq 0, \tag{10}$$

then S' contains a periodic point whose trajectory travels through the regions $N_{a_0}, \ldots, N_{a_{n-1}}$ in the prescribed order.

We note here that under the hypotheses of Corollary 16, we may obtain the index of S' from the computed index map f_{P*}, where $P = (P_1, P_0)$ is an index pair with $N = \overline{P_1 \setminus P_0}$. Using an approach developed by Szymczak in [**Szy97b**], we set

$$f_P^{ij}(x) := \begin{cases} f(x) & \text{if } x \in N_i \text{ and } f(x) \in N_j \\ [P_0] & \text{otherwise.} \end{cases} \tag{11}$$

Then $f^{ij}_{P*} : H_*(P_1, P_0 \cup (\cup_{l\neq i} N_l)) \to H_*(P_1, P_0 \cup (\cup_{l\neq j} N_l))$. Given f_{Pk} in matrix form representing the linear map on $H_k(P_1, P_0)$, we may label the columns/rows by location of the associated relative homology generators in the subgroups $H_k(P_1, P_0 \cup (\cup_{l\neq 1} N_l)), \ldots H_k(P_1, P_0 \cup (\cup_{l\neq n} N_l))$. To simplify notation, we say that generator g is in region N_i if $g \in H_k(P_1, P_0 \cup (\cup_{l\neq i} N_l))$. Then f^{ij}_{Pk} is the $n_j \times n_i$ submatrix with n_i columns corresponding to the n_i generators in N_i and n_j rows corresponding to the n_j generators in N_j. Furthermore, for $B_n = a_0 a_1 \cdots a_{n-1}$, $(P_1, P_0 \cup (\cup_{a\neq a_0} N_a))$ is an index pair for the isolated invariant set $S' = \mathrm{Inv}(N_{a_0}, f_{N_{a_{n-1}}} \circ \cdots \circ f_{N_{a_0}})$ with index map $f^{B_n}_{P*} := f^{a_{n-1}a_0}_{P*} \circ \cdots \circ f^{a_0 a_1}_{P*} : H_*(P_1, P_0 \cup (\cup_{l\neq a_0} N_l)) \to H_*(P_1, P_0 \cup (\cup_{l\neq a_0} N_l))$. Therefore,

$$\mathrm{Con}(S', f^{B_n}) = [f^{B_n}_{P*}]_s = [f^{a_{n-1}a_0}_{P*} \circ \cdots \circ f^{a_0 a_1}_{P*}]_s \tag{12}$$

with shift equivalence class representative $f^{a_{n-1}a_0}_{P*} \circ \cdots \circ f^{a_0 a_1}_{P*}$ computed as the product of appropriate submatrices of f_{P*}.

The Lefschetz number (Theorem 15) is computable given a representative $f^{B_n}_{P*}$. However, using Ważewski's Principle (Theorem 14) directly is less immediate. In general, determining whether the linear map $f^{B_n}_{P*}$ is not shift equivalent to 0 may be difficult. We here focus on a computable, sufficient condition. Nilpotency is preserved by shift equivalence, and so if $f^{B_n}_{Pk}$ is not nilpotent for some k then $\mathrm{Con}(S, f^{B_n}) \neq [0]_s$. Algorithms that identify symbol sequences for which no power of the corresponding matrix product may be 0 are presented in [**DFT08, DF**]. These conditions may be checked by hand for the sample results presented in Section 6.

Recall that by construction, the remaining condition to check in order for $\rho : S \to \Sigma_G$ to be a topological semi-conjugacy is surjectivity. For systems Σ_G constructed as the closure of a set of periodic points, we first show that $\mathrm{Con}(S', f^{B_n}) \neq [0]_s$ for every block B_n corresponding to a cycle in G. Since ρ is continuous and S is compact, ρ must then map onto Σ_G, the closure of the set of periodic points. This approach is summarized in the following corollary.

COROLLARY 17. *If $f^{B_n}_{P*}$ is not nilpotent for every block B_n corresponding to a cycle in G and Σ_G is the closure of the set of periodic points in Σ_G, then $\rho : S \to \Sigma_G$ is surjective and is, therefore, a topological semi-conjugacy.*

4. Combinatorial Outer Approximation

Now that we have the relevant tools from Conley index theory, we can begin applying them algorithmically to extract information about the dynamical system $f : X \to X$. In this section, we describe the construction of a *combinatorial representation* of f. This combinatorial representation is an example of a *multivalued map* F that will be used to incorporate error bounds in the representation. See [**KMM04, DJM05, DJM04, Day03, DFT08**] for more details.

DEFINITION 18. *The* multivalued map $F : X \rightrightarrows X$ *is a map from X to its power set, i.e. for all $x \in X$, $F(x) \subset X$. If for a continuous, single-valued map $f : X \to X$, $f(x) \in F(x)$ for all $x \in X$, then f is a* continuous selector *of F and F is an* outer approximation *of f.*

While not strictly necessary (see [**HKMP16**]), the following computations become simpler if we further require that for all $x \in X$, $F(x)$ is acyclic, that is, has the homology of a point. In what follows, we discuss some methods used to construct a *(combinatorial) outer approximation* of the map under study that does contain acyclic images. The purpose of the outer approximation is to incorporate round-off and other errors that occur in computations. This construction requires rigorous, small error bounds in order to create an outer approximation whose images are not so large as to obscure relevant dynamics. Given an appropriate outer approximation, the topological tools from Section 3 may be used to uncover dynamics of the underlying map. Furthermore, there are algorithms for both the construction of the outer approximation and the computation of the Conley index. These algorithms require a further step – discretizing the domain in order to store it in the computer as a finite list of objects.

A finite sublattice of closed regular sets may be used to discretize the domain (see [**KMV16**]). For ease of both presentation and computation, in what follows we use a rectangular grid to discretize a rectangular subset of the domain. The following subdivision procedure defines the grid $\mathcal{G}$ on the specified rectangular region in X. In practice, the region chosen for representation is usually determined either experimentally through non-rigorous numerical simulations or analytically given special structure or symmetry for the system (e.g. a compact attracting region). Although variations exist, the simplest is a *uniformly-subdivided cubical grid* of a rectangular set $W = \prod_{k=1}^{n}[x_k^-, x_k^+] \subset \mathbb{R}^n$ given by

$$\mathcal{G}^{(d)} := \left\{ \prod_{k=1}^{n} \left[x_k^- + \frac{i_k r_k}{2^d}, x_k^- + \frac{(i_k+1) r_k}{2^d} \right] \;\middle|\; i_k \in \{0, \ldots, 2^d - 1\} \right\}$$

where $r_k = x_k^+ - x_k^-$ is the radius of W in the kth coordinate and the depth d is a nonnegative integer. We call an element of the grid,

$$B = \prod_{k=1}^{n} \left[x_k^- + \frac{i_k r_k}{2^d}, x_k^- + \frac{(i_k+1) r_k}{2^d} \right],$$

a *box*. For a collection of boxes, $G \subset \mathcal{G} = \mathcal{G}^{(d)}$, define the *topological realization* of G as $|G| := \cup_{B \in G} B \subset \mathbb{R}^n$.

Constructing a useful combinatorial outer approximation involves bounding all round-off and other errors. In our study of the Hénon map in Section 6, we use interval arithmetic to bound $f(|G|)$. This produces a bounding box, $\tilde{f}(|G|)$, for the image $f(|G|)$, which is then intersected with the grid $\mathcal{G}$ to produce the combinatorial image

$$\mathcal{F}(G) := \{G' \in \mathcal{G} : |G'| \cap \tilde{f}(|G|) \neq \emptyset\}.$$

The combinatorial map, $\mathcal{F} : \mathcal{G} \rightrightarrows \mathcal{G}$, yields an outer approximation $F = |\mathcal{F}|$ of f in the following way: define $|\mathcal{F}| : W \rightrightarrows W$, where $W = \cup_{G \in \mathcal{G}} |G|$,

$$|\mathcal{F}|(x) := \bigcup_{G \in \mathcal{G} \text{ with } x \in |G|} |\mathcal{F}(G)|. \tag{13}$$

Dynamics of a continuous selector f forces structure in $\mathcal{F}$. Viewing $\mathcal{F}$ as the directed graph $G(\mathcal{F}) = (V, E)$ where $V = \mathcal{G} = \{G\}$ and $(G_i, G_j) \in E$ whenever $G_j \in \mathcal{F}(G_i)$,

- $(G, G) \in E$ whenever $f(x) = x$ for some $x \in |G|$,
- periodic points of f must be contained in cycles of $G(\mathcal{F})$,
- recurrent sets under f must be contained in strongly connected components of $G(\mathcal{F})$,
- connecting orbits under f are contained in connecting paths in $G(\mathcal{F})$,

- vertices for which all forward paths terminate in a trapping region ($\mathcal{S}$ such that $\mathcal{F}(\mathcal{S}) \subseteq \mathcal{S}$) correspond to points in the basin of attraction for that trapping region,
- the maximal invariant set under f is contained in the maximal invariant set of $G(\mathcal{F})$.

The above list is helpful for determining candidate regions for dynamics of f. For example, self loops $(G, G) \in E$ yield regions, $|G|$ containing possible fixed points for f. However, a box with a self-loop may not contain a fixed point of f. The extreme example is the combinatorial outer approximation $\mathcal{F} : \mathcal{G} \rightrightarrows \mathcal{G}$ given by $\mathcal{F}(G) = \mathcal{G}$ for every $G \in \mathcal{G}$. Every box $G \in \mathcal{G}$ has a self-loop, but this could just be due to large image bounds that are not able to resolve finer dynamics. We use Conley index theory in order to *prove* that dynamics observed in $\mathcal{F}$ exists for a continuous selector f. In what follows, we focus on an algorithmic approach for computing Conley indices from combinatorial outer approximations.

5. Computational Conley Index Theory

In this section, we list sample algorithms for computing isolating neighborhoods, index pairs, and Conley indices. These algorithms are shown in more detail in [**DJM05**, **DFT08**].

DEFINITION 19. *A* combinatorial trajectory *of a combinatorial outer approximation $\mathcal{F}$ through $G \in \mathcal{G}$ is a bi-infinite sequence $\gamma_G = (\ldots, G_{-1}, G_0, G_1, \ldots)$ with $G_0 = G$, $G_n \in \mathcal{G}$, and $G_{n+1} \in \mathcal{F}(G_n)$ for all $n \in \mathbb{Z}$.*

DEFINITION 20. *The* combinatorial invariant set *in $\mathcal{N} \subset \mathcal{G}$ for a combinatorial outer approximation $\mathcal{F}$ is*

$$\operatorname{Inv}(\mathcal{N}, \mathcal{F}) := \{G \in \mathcal{G} : \text{ there exists a trajectory } \gamma_G \subset \mathcal{N}\}.$$

DEFINITION 21. *The* combinatorial neighborhood *of $\mathcal{B} \subset \mathcal{G}$ is*

$$o(\mathcal{B}) := \{G \in \mathcal{G} : |G| \cap |\mathcal{B}| \neq \emptyset\}.$$

This set, $|o(\mathcal{B})|$, sometimes referred to as a *one box neighborhood of $\mathcal{B}$ in $\mathcal{G}$*, is the smallest representable neighborhood of $|B|$ in the grid $\mathcal{G}$.

While there are different characterizations of isolation in the setting of combinatorial outer approximations, we chose the following for simplicity and illustration purposes.

DEFINITION 22. *If*

$$o(\operatorname{Inv}(\mathcal{N}, \mathcal{F})) \subset \mathcal{N}$$

then $\mathcal{N} \subset \mathcal{G}$ is a combinatorial isolating neighborhood *under $\mathcal{F}$.*

Note that by construction, the topological realization $|\mathcal{N}|$ of a combinatorial isolating neighborhood $\mathcal{N}$ is an isolating neighborhood for any continuous selector $f \in |\mathcal{F}|$. This definition is stronger than what is actually required to guarantee isolation on the topological level. It is, however, the definition that we will use in this work and is computable using the following approach.

Let $\mathcal{S} \subset \mathcal{G}$. Set $\mathcal{N} = \operatorname{Inv}(\mathcal{S})$ and let $o(\mathcal{N})$ be the combinatorial neighborhood of $\mathcal{N}$ in $\mathcal{G}$. If $\operatorname{Inv}(o(\mathcal{N}), \mathcal{F}) = \mathcal{N}$, then $\mathcal{N}$ is isolated under $\mathcal{F}$. If not, set $\mathcal{N} := \operatorname{Inv}(o(\mathcal{N}), \mathcal{F})$ and repeat the above procedure. In this way, we grow the set $\mathcal{N}$ until either the isolation condition is met, or the set grows to intersect the boundary of $\mathcal{G}$ in which case the algorithm fails to locate an isolating neighborhood in $\mathcal{G}$. This procedure is outlined in more detail in the following modified version of the algorithm from [**DJM04**].

Algorithm 1: Grow Isolating Neighborhood

```
INPUT:  grid 𝒢, combinatorial outer approximation ℱ on 𝒢, set 𝒮 ⊂ 𝒢
OUTPUT: a combinatorial isolating neighborhood 𝒩 containing Inv(𝒮)
        or 𝒩 = ∅ if the isolation condition is not met

𝒩 = grow_isolating_neighborhood(𝒢, ℱ, 𝒮)
    𝒢_boundary:= {G ∈ 𝒢 : |G| ∩ ∂|𝒢| ≠ ∅};
    𝒩 := Inv(𝒮);
    while Inv(o(𝒩), ℱ)) ⊄ 𝒩 and 𝒩 ∩ 𝒢_boundary= ∅,
        𝒩 := Inv(o(𝒩), ℱ);
    end
    if 𝒩 ∩ 𝒢_boundary= ∅, return 𝒩;
    else return ∅;
    end
```

Once we have an isolating neighborhood for f, our next goal is to compute a corresponding index pair. The following definition of a *combinatorial index pair* again emphasizes our goal of using the combinatorial outer approximation to compute structures for f.

DEFINITION 23. *A pair* $\mathcal{P} = (\mathcal{P}_1, \mathcal{P}_0)$ *of cubical sets is a* combinatorial index pair *for a combinatorial outer approximation* $\mathcal{F}$ *if the corresponding topological realization* $P = (|\mathcal{P}_1|, |\mathcal{P}_0|)$, *is an index pair for any continuous selector* $f \in |\mathcal{F}|$. *Namely,* $\overline{|\mathcal{P}_1| \setminus |\mathcal{P}_0|} = |\mathcal{P}_1 \setminus \mathcal{P}_0|$ *is an isolating neighborhood under* f *and the map* f_P, *as defined in Definition* 10, *is continuous.*

The following algorithm produces a combinatorial index pair associated to a combinatorial isolating neighborhood produced via Algorithm 1. While there are other algorithms for producing combinatorial index pairs, this algorithm works well with later index computations. For more details, see the description of *modified combinatorial index pairs* in [**Day03**].

We now have an isolating neighborhood $|\mathcal{N}|$ and corresponding index pair $P := (|\mathcal{P}_1|, |\mathcal{P}_0|)$ for f. What remains in computing the Conley index for the associated isolated invariant set, $S := \text{Inv}(|\mathcal{N}|, f)$, is to compute the map $f_{P*} : H_*(|\mathcal{P}_1|, |\mathcal{P}_0|) \to H_*(|\mathcal{P}_1|, |\mathcal{P}_0|)$. Once again, the combinatorial outer approximation offers the appropriate computational framework and we may use a computational homology software program such as *homcubes* in [**Pil98**] to compute f_{P*}. The output is a sequence of matrices for the maps $f_{P0}, f_{P1}, \ldots, f_{Pn}$ where n is the dimension of the phase space X. For $k > n$, $f_{Pk} = 0$. The associated Conley index is $\text{Con}_*(S) = [f_{P*}]_s$, for $S := \text{Inv}(|\mathcal{P}_1 \setminus \mathcal{P}_0|, f)$. The submaps $f_{Pk}^{ij} : H_k(|\mathcal{P}_1|, |\mathcal{P}_0| \cup_{l \neq i} |\mathcal{N}_l|) \to H_k(|\mathcal{P}_1|, |\mathcal{P}_0| \cup_{l \neq j} |\mathcal{N}_l|)$, where $|\mathcal{N}_1|, \ldots |\mathcal{N}_n|$ are the connected components of $|\mathcal{P}_1 \setminus \mathcal{P}_0|$, are given as submatrices of f_{Pk}. These are

Algorithm 2: Build Index Pair

```
INPUT:  grid 𝒢, combinatorial outer approximation ℱ on 𝒢,
        combinatorial isolating neighborhood 𝒩 produced by Algorithm 1
OUTPUT: combinatorial index pair 𝒫 = (𝒫1, 𝒫0) with 𝒫1 \ 𝒫0 = 𝒩

[𝒫1, 𝒫0] = build_index_pair(𝒢, ℱ, 𝒩);
    𝒫0 := ∅;
    New := ℱ(𝒩) ∩ o(𝒩) \ 𝒩;
    while New ≠ ∅
        𝒫0 := 𝒫0 ∪ New;
        New := (ℱ(𝒫0) ∩ o(𝒩)) \ 𝒫0;
    end
    𝒫1 := 𝒩 ∪ 𝒫0;
    return [𝒫1, 𝒫0];
```

the maps required for Corollary 16. In the following section, we present sample computations to illustrate the methods.

6. The Hénon Map: Sample Results

We now apply the approach described in the previous sections to the 2-dimensional Hénon map (1) at the standard parameter values $a = 1.3$ and $b = 0.2$. Results using these methods on the Hénon map are also given in [**Day03**, **DJM05**, **DFT08**]. For the application of these methods to other systems and extensions of the methods to families of systems and infinite-dimensional systems, see e.g. [**Day03**, **AKK+09**, **DJM04**, **DK13**, **BCHM16**, **BGH+12**, **AGG+12**]. For high and infinite-dimensional systems, the construction of the combinatorial outer approximation often requires additional dimension reduction techniques and error bound analysis. Following this construction, however, the computation and processing of Conley index information follows in a similar fashion to what is presented here.

In what follows, we use the software package GAIO [**DFJ01**] and homcubes [**Pil98**] to produce sample results. For the first sample result, we use a uniformly subdivided cubical grid at depth $d = 7$ constructed by subdividing the box $W = [-0.9311, 1.2845]^2$ 14 times (7 times in each of the two directions). Keeping only the boxes covering the maximal invariant set results in 1188 boxes, each of box radius $[0.0087, 0.0087]$. This box covering of the maximal invariant set is shown in Figure 1. Outward rounding interval arithmetic for computing image bounds results in a combinatorial outer approximation $\mathcal{F}$, on these boxes.

As an initial study, we look for a 2-cycle in $G(\mathcal{F})$. We use the algorithms in Section 5 to produce a (combinatorial) index pair shown in Figure 2.

The relative homology of the index pair depicted in Figure 2 is

$$H_*(|\mathcal{P}_1|, |\mathcal{P}_0|) \cong (0,\ \mathbb{Z}^2,\ 0,\ 0,\ \ldots)$$

and the only nontrivial map induced on homology is

$$f_{P1} := \begin{bmatrix} 0 & 1 \\ -1 & 0 \end{bmatrix}.$$

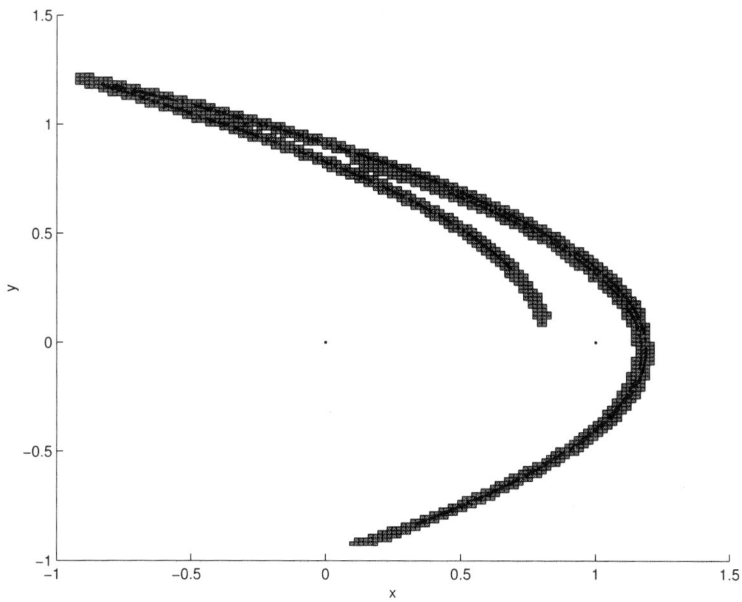

FIGURE 1. An initial simulation of a trajectory (in black) and box covering of the maximal invariant set in this region (in green/grey).

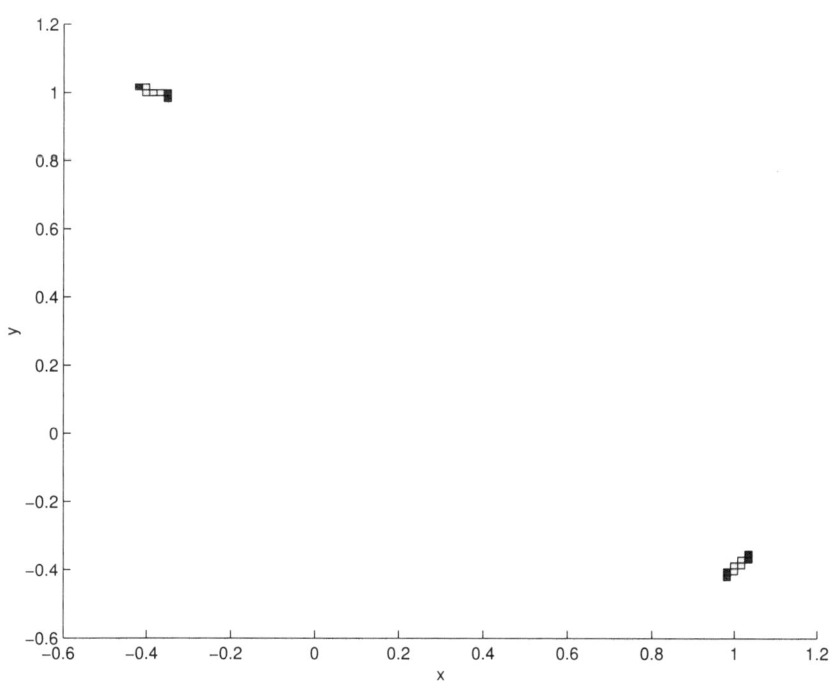

FIGURE 2. A index pair for a 2-cycle containing a period-2 orbit. The isolating neighborhood is shown in yellow (lighter grey) while the exit set, $\mathcal{P}_0$, is shown in red (darker grey).

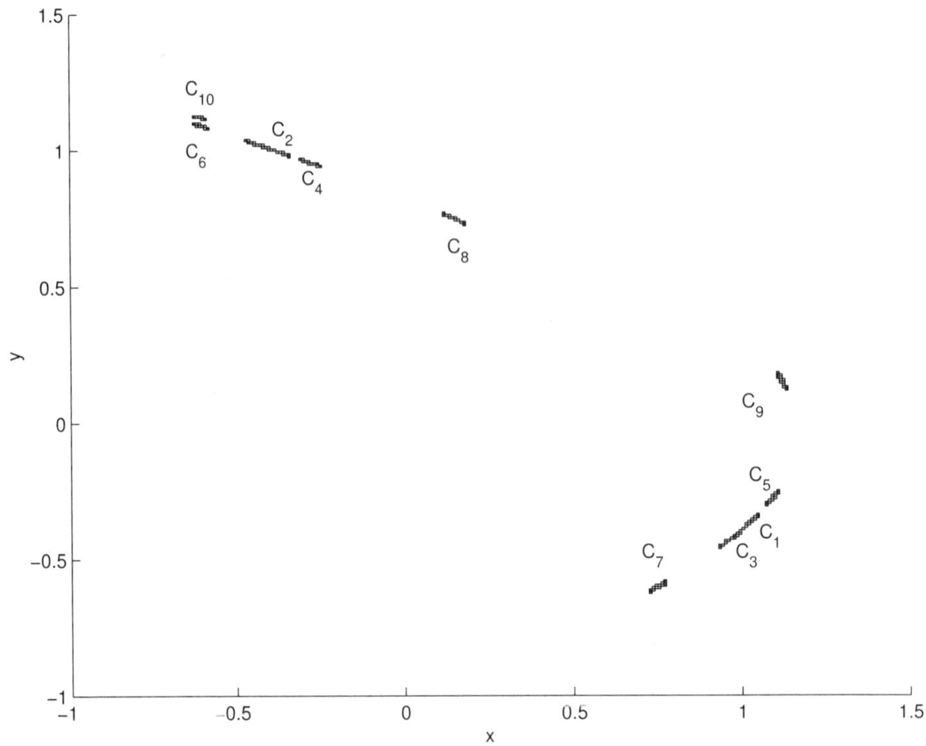

FIGURE 3. An index pair for a 2-cycle, 4-cycle and a connecting path between the two. The isolating neighborhood is shown in yellow (lighter grey) while the exit set, $\mathcal{P}_0$, is shown in red (darker grey). The isolating neighborhood contains a period-2 orbit, and period-4 orbit, and a heteroclinic orbit between neighborhoods of the two periodic orbits. Labels for the disjoint components of the isolating neighborhood are shown as well.

SAMPLE RESULT 1. *There exists a periodic orbit of minimal period two for the Hénon map with one point in each of the disjoint connected components of the isolating neighborhood shown in Figure 2.*

Proof. The Lefschetz number $L(S, f^2) = -\operatorname{tr}(f^2_{P1}) = -2$ is nonzero so $\mathcal{S}$ contains a periodic point of period two. Furthermore, this orbit has minimal period two since $\mathcal{F}$ prohibits there being a fixed point in $\mathcal{S}$. (Equivalently, there are no self-loops in $G(\mathcal{F}|_{\mathcal{S}})$.)

We now search for an orbit connecting a period 2 orbit to a period 4 orbit in $\mathcal{F}$ at depth $d = 9$. The union of a 2-cycle, 4-cycle and connecting path from the 2-cycle to 4-cycle in $G(\mathcal{F})$ serves as the input to the algorithms in Section 5. The resulting index pair is depicted in Figure 3.

The computed relative homology for the index pair in Figure 3 is

$$H_*(|\mathcal{P}_1|, |\mathcal{P}_0|) \cong (0,\ \mathbb{Z}^{10},\ 0,\ 0,\ \ldots)$$

and the map on $H_1(|\mathcal{P}_1|, |\mathcal{P}_0|)$ is given by

$$f_{P1} := \begin{bmatrix} 0 & -1 & 0 & 0 & 0 & 0 & 0 & 0 & 0 & 0 \\ 1 & 0 & 0 & 0 & 0 & 0 & 0 & 0 & 0 & 0 \\ 0 & 1 & 0 & 0 & 0 & 0 & 0 & 0 & 0 & 0 \\ 0 & 0 & -1 & 0 & 0 & 0 & 0 & 0 & 0 & 0 \\ 0 & 0 & 0 & 1 & 0 & 0 & 0 & 0 & 0 & 0 \\ 0 & 0 & 0 & 0 & -1 & 0 & 0 & 0 & 0 & 0 \\ 0 & 0 & 0 & 0 & 0 & 1 & 0 & 0 & 0 & 1 \\ 0 & 0 & 0 & 0 & 0 & 0 & -1 & 0 & 0 & 0 \\ 0 & 0 & 0 & 0 & 0 & 0 & 0 & -1 & 0 & 0 \\ 0 & 0 & 0 & 0 & 0 & 0 & 0 & 0 & -1 & 0 \end{bmatrix}.$$

In this case, there is one generator per region and, through careful labeling, f_{P1}^{ij} is entry (i, j) of f_{P1}.

Sample Result 2. *There exists an orbit for the Hénon map which limits in forward time to a box neighborhood of a period 4 orbit, and in backward time to a box neighborhood containing a period 2 orbit.*

Proof. Since tr $f_{P1}^{12} = -1$ and tr $f_{P1}^{B_4} = -1$ for B_4 giving the 4-cycle through generators $7, 8, 9, 10$, Lefschetz number computations confirm that period 2 and period 4 orbits exist in the given regions.

Next, note that f_{P*} is not shift equivalent to $f_{C_1 \cup C_2 *} \oplus f_{\cup_{i\in\{7,8,9,10\}} C_i *}$ where $f_{C_1\cup C_2 *}$ are the induced maps on $(P_1, P_0 \cup (\cup_{l\neq 1,2} N_l))$ and $(P_1, P_0 \cup (\cup_{l\neq 7,8,9,10} N_l))$ giving the indices of the two periodic regions respectively. Therefore, the Conley indices of $\mathrm{Inv}(S, f)$ and $\mathrm{Inv}(S \cup_{i\in\{1,2,7,8,9,10\}} C_i, f) = \mathrm{Inv}(S \cup_{i\in\{1,2\}} C_i, f) \cup \mathrm{Inv}(S \cup_{i\in\{7,8,9,10\}} C_i, f)$ are different and $\mathrm{Inv}(C, f) \neq \mathrm{Inv}(\cup_{i\in\{1,2,7,8,9,10\}} C_i, f)$

This, in addition to the combinatorial outer approximation only allowing trajectories to move from the neighborhood of the period 2 orbit to the neighborhood of the period 4 orbit, leads to the conclusion that there is the sought connecting orbit.

Finally, we consider the input set from the previous example with the addition of a connecting path from the 4 cycle back to the 2-cycle. The computed isolating neighborhood and index pair are shown in Figure 4.

The map on the relative homology of the index pair is

$$H_*(|\mathcal{P}_1|, |\mathcal{P}_0|) \cong (0,\ \mathbb{Z}^{15},\ 0,\ 0,\ \ldots).$$

while the induced map f_{P1} is shown in Figure 5.

Sample Result 3. [**DJM05**] *There is a set contained in the isolating neighborhood shown in Figure 4, on which f is topologically semi-conjugate to the subshift Σ_G with vertex shift presentation given in Figure 5(a).*

Proof. First, note that Σ_G is the closure of the set of periodic points in Σ_G. In order to use Corollary 17, we need only show that $f_{P1}^{B_n}$ is not nilpotent for any block B_n corresponding to a cycle in Σ_G. The map $f_{P1}^{B_n}$ is the product of matrices listed on edges in B_n in Figure 5(b). It is not difficult to see that for any B_n corresponding to a cycle, $f_{P1}^{B_n} = \pm 1$ and is, therefore, not nilpotent. Corollary 17 completes the proof.

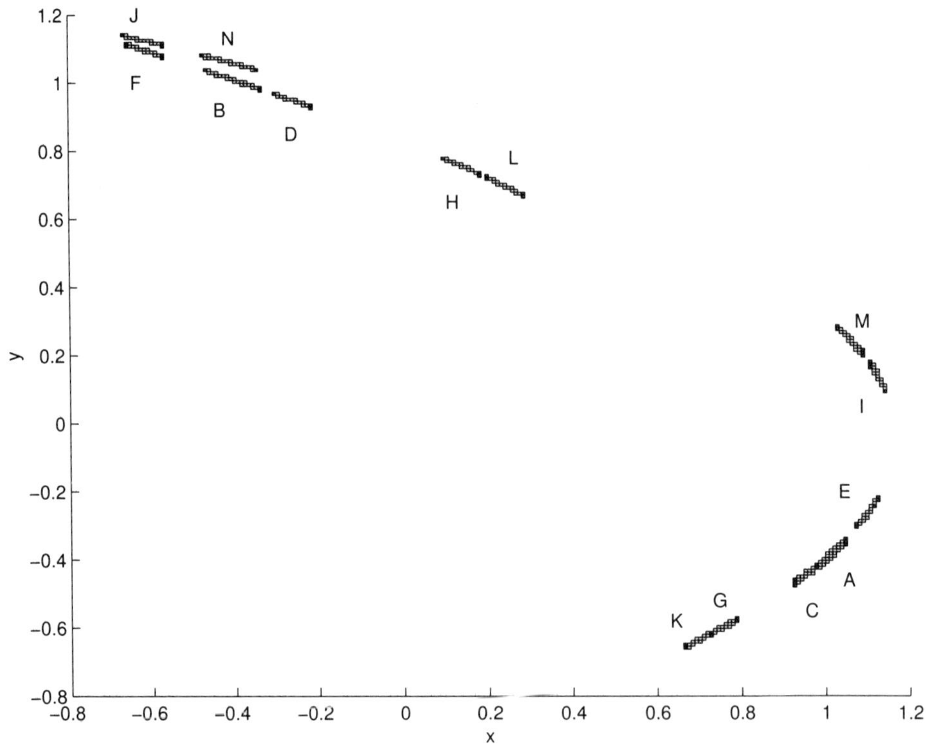

FIGURE 4. An index pair for a 2-cycle, 4-cycle, and connecting paths between the two. The isolating neighborhood is shown in yellow (lighter grey) while the exit set ($\mathcal{P}_0$) is shown in red (darker grey). Labels for the disjoint components of the isolating neighborhood are shown as well. The isolating neighborhood contains infinitely many periodic orbits (corresponding to cycles in Figure 5(a)) and chaotic dynamics.

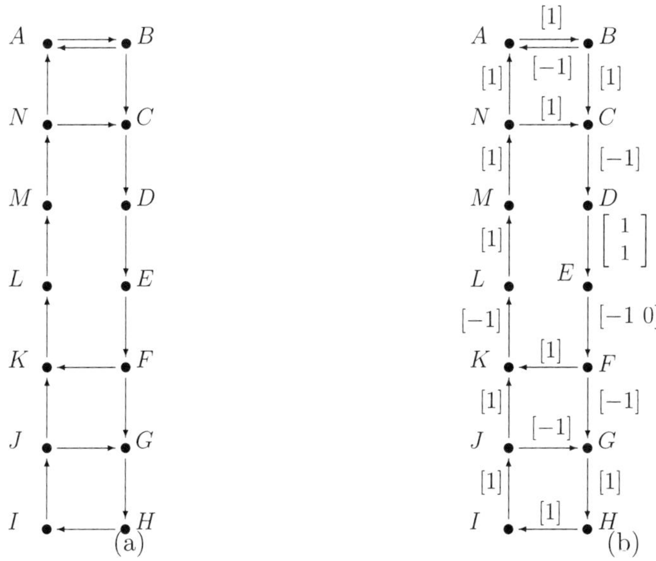

FIGURE 5. (a) Transition graph G on labeled regions. (b) The induced map on homology with nontrivial maps $f_{P1}^{s_i,s_j}$ shown on the edge (s_i, s_j).

References

[AGG+12] Zin Arai, Marcio Gameiro, Tomas Gedeon, Hiroshi Kokubu, Konstantin Mischaikow, and Hiroe Oka, *Graph-based topological approximation of saddle-node bifurcation in maps*, Far-from-equilibrium dynamics, RIMS Kôkyûroku Bessatsu, B31, Res. Inst. Math. Sci. (RIMS), Kyoto, 2012, pp. 225–241. MR3156802

[AKK+09] Zin Arai, William Kalies, Hiroshi Kokubu, Konstantin Mischaikow, Hiroe Oka, and Paweł Pilarczyk, *A database schema for the analysis of global dynamics of multiparameter systems*, SIAM J. Appl. Dyn. Syst. **8** (2009), no. 3, 757–789, DOI 10.1137/080734935. MR2533624

[ASY97] Kathleen T. Alligood, Tim D. Sauer, and James A. Yorke, *Chaos*, Textbooks in Mathematical Sciences, Springer-Verlag, New York, 1997. An introduction to dynamical systems. MR1418166

[BCHM16] Justin Bush, Wes Cowan, Shaun Harker, and Konstantin Mischaikow, *Conley-Morse databases for the angular dynamics of Newton's method on the plane*, SIAM J. Appl. Dyn. Syst. **15** (2016), no. 2, 736–766, DOI 10.1137/15M1017971. MR3484393

[BGH+12] Justin Bush, Marcio Gameiro, Shaun Harker, Hiroshi Kokubu, Konstantin Mischaikow, Ippei Obayashi, and Paweł Pilarczyk, *Combinatorial-topological framework for the analysis of global dynamics*, Chaos **22** (2012), no. 4, 047508, 16, DOI 10.1063/1.4767672. MR3388721

[Bow71] Rufus Bowen, *Periodic points and measures for Axiom A diffeomorphisms*, Trans. Amer. Math. Soc. **154** (1971), 377–397, DOI 10.2307/1995452. MR0282372

[Con78] Charles Conley, *Isolated invariant sets and the Morse index*, CBMS Regional Conference Series in Mathematics, vol. 38, American Mathematical Society, Providence, R.I., 1978. MR511133

[Day03] Sarah Lynn Day, *A rigorous numerical method in infinite dimensions*, ProQuest LLC, Ann Arbor, MI, 2003. Thesis (Ph.D.)–Georgia Institute of Technology. MR2704788

[Dev89] Robert L. Devaney, *An introduction to chaotic dynamical systems*, 2nd ed., Addison-Wesley Studies in Nonlinearity, Addison-Wesley Publishing Company, Advanced Book Program, Redwood City, CA, 1989. MR1046376

[DF] Sarah Day and Rafael Frongillo, *Sofic shifts via Conly index theory: Computing lower bounds on recurrent dynamics for maps.*

[DFJ01] Michael Dellnitz, Gary Froyland, and Oliver Junge, *The algorithms behind GAIO-set oriented numerical methods for dynamical systems*, Ergodic theory, analysis, and efficient simulation of dynamical systems, Springer, Berlin, 2001, pp. 145–174, 805–807. MR1850305

[DFT08] Sarah Day, Rafael Frongillo, and Rodrigo Treviño, *Algorithms for rigorous entropy bounds and symbolic dynamics*, SIAM J. Appl. Dyn. Syst. **7** (2008), no. 4, 1477–1506, DOI 10.1137/070688080. MR2470974

[DJM04] S. Day, O. Junge, and K. Mischaikow, *A rigorous numerical method for the global analysis of infinite-dimensional discrete dynamical systems*, SIAM J. Appl. Dyn. Syst. **3** (2004), no. 2, 117–160, DOI 10.1137/030600210. MR2067140

[DJM05] ———, *Towards automated chaos verification.*, Proceeding of Equadiff 2003 (2005), 157–162.

[DK13] Sarah Day and William D. Kalies, *Rigorous computation of the global dynamics of integrodifference equations with smooth nonlinearities*, SIAM J. Numer. Anal. **51** (2013), no. 6, 2957–2983, DOI 10.1137/120903129. MR3124898

[Hén76] M. Hénon, *A two-dimensional mapping with a strange attractor*, Comm. Math. Phys. **50** (1976), no. 1, 69–77. MR0422932

[HKMP16] Shaun Harker, Hiroshi Kokubu, Konstantin Mischaikow, and Paweł Pilarczyk, *Inducing a map on homology from a correspondence*, Proc. Amer. Math. Soc. **144** (2016), no. 4, 1787–1801, DOI 10.1090/proc/12812. MR3451254

[KMM04] Tomasz Kaczynski, Konstantin Mischaikow, and Marian Mrozek, *Computational homology*, Applied Mathematical Sciences, vol. 157, Springer-Verlag, New York, 2004. MR2028588

[KMV16] William D. Kalies, Konstantin Mischaikow, and Robert C. A. M. Vandervorst, *Lattice structures for attractors II*, Found. Comput. Math. **16** (2016), no. 5, 1151–1191, DOI 10.1007/s10208-015-9272-x. MR3552843

[LM95] Douglas Lind and Brian Marcus, *An introduction to symbolic dynamics and coding*, Cambridge University Press, Cambridge, 1995. MR1369092

[May76] Robert M. May, *Simple mathematical models with very complicated dynamics*, Nature **261** (1976), no. 5560, 459–467.

[MM02] Konstantin Mischaikow and Marian Mrozek, *Conley index*, Handbook of dynamical systems, Vol. 2, North-Holland, Amsterdam, 2002, pp. 393–460, DOI 10.1016/S1874-575X(02)80030-3. MR1901060

[Pil98] P. Pilarczyk, *Homology computation-software and examples*, Jagiellonian University, 1998, (http://www.im.uj.edu.pl/~pilarczy/homology.htm).

[Rob95] Clark Robinson, *Dynamical systems*, Studies in Advanced Mathematics, CRC Press, Boca Raton, FL, 1995. Stability, symbolic dynamics, and chaos. MR1396532

[RS88] Joel W. Robbin and Dietmar Salamon, *Dynamical systems, shape theory and the Conley index*, Ergodic Theory Dynam. Systems **8*** (1988), no. Charles Conley Memorial Issue, 375–393, DOI 10.1017/S0143385700009494. MR967645

[Szy97a] Andrzej Szymczak, *A combinatorial procedure for finding isolating neighbourhoods and index pairs*, Proc. Roy. Soc. Edinburgh Sect. A **127** (1997), no. 5, 1075–1088, DOI 10.1017/S0308210500026901. MR1475647

[Szy97b] Andrzej Szymczak, *A combinatorial procedure for finding isolating neighbourhoods and index pairs*, Proc. Roy. Soc. Edinburgh Sect. A **127** (1997), no. 5, 1075–1088, DOI 10.1017/S0308210500026901. MR1475647

Index

admissible n-block, 178

chaotic dynamics, 190
combinatorial index pair, 185
combinatorial invariant set, 184
combinatorial isolating neighborhood, 184
combinatorial neighborhood, 184
combinatorial outer approximation, 182
combinatorial trajectory, 184
Conley index, 181
continuous selector, 182
cubical grid, 183

Hénon map, 176

index pair, 180, 186–188
isolated invariant set, 180
isolating neighborhood, 180, 187–190
itinerary function, 179

Lefschetz number, 181, 188
logistic map, 175

maximal invariant set, 179
multivalued map, 182

outer approximation, 182

periodic orbit, 188

relative invariant set, 180

shift equivalent, 180
sofic shifts, 177
sofic subshift, 177
subshift, 177

topological conjugacy, 179
topological entropy, 178
topological semi-conjugacy, 179
topologically semi-conjugate, 189
trajectory, 180, 187

vertex presentation, 177
vertex shift presentation, 189

Department of Mathematics, College of William & Mary, Williamsburg, Virginia
Email address: `sday@math.wm.edu`

Proceedings of Symposia in Applied Mathematics
Volume **74**, 2018
http://dx.doi.org/10.1090/psapm/074/00641

Rigorous computational dynamics in the context of unknown nonlinearities

Konstantin Mischaikow

ABSTRACT. Models of multiscale systems, such as those encountered in systems biology, are often characterized by heuristic nonlinearities and poorly defined parameters. Furthermore, it is typically not possible to obtain precise experimental data for these systems. Nevertheless, verification of the models requires the ability to obtain meaningful dynamical structures that can be compared quantitatively with the experimental data.

With this in mind we present an approach to characterizing dynamics that is based on combinatorial/algebraic/topological techniques. Combinatorics is used to model and describe the dynamics. Partitioning of parameter space is done via semi-algebraic sets. Algebraic topology is used to provide rigorous guarantees of the dynamics These ideas are described in the context of models for gene regulatory networks.

1. Introduction

As is made clear in the other articles of this proceedings considerable advances are being made in using the computer to rigorously determine specific solutions and/or dynamics of explicit nonlinear systems arising either from differential equations or maps. The importance of the development of these methods is made clear in [**25**]. However, motivated by challenges associated with multiscale phenomena – the life sciences provide a canonical example – it is equally important to be able to make rigorous mathematical statements about the dynamics of systems for which the nonlinearities are often derived based on heuristic principles. While it appears impossible to give a precise description of the dynamics without precise nonlinearities, one might hope that if the model is based on reasonably accurate heuristics, then it might be possible to give an accurate description of the dynamics. The goal of these notes is to provide a brief introduction to a novel approach to dynamics whose aim is to achieve this hope in a computationally tractable manner. The focus is on readability as opposed to generality or completeness and the reader will have to turn to the original sources for details.

As is made clear in the following sections we characterize dynamics using the language of combinatorics and algebraic topology. A consequence of this is that we give up the ability to directly and precisely describe invariant sets. We feel that

2010 *Mathematics Subject Classification.* Primary 34C60, 37M99.

This work was supported in part by grants NSF-DMS-1125174, 1248071, 1521771 and contracts from DARPA.

this is a necessary first step and in Section 2 try to provide some justification for our coarser approach. We also use this section to recall classical dynamic structures that can be recovered using our techniques.

In Section 3 we introduce a few ideas on the level of combinatorial dynamics and in Section 4 discuss how continuous dynamical systems can be approximated by combinatorial systems. This approximation procedure is discussed in two settings. The first (see Section 4.1), for which the theory is reasonably well understood and for which there is a substantial body of algorithms and code, is based on continuous maps. On a conceptual level such a map can be thought of as the generator of a discrete time dynamical system or as arising from the time one map of a differential equation. However, on a practical, computational level there is a significant difference. Currently there is no clear understanding of an appropriate strategy to compute a useful combinatorial approximation for a general ordinary differential equation. Thus, the second approximation procedure (see Section 4.2) that we consider is developed for a particular class of differential equations that can be associated with piecewise constant nonlinearities. Since the first approach is described in considerable detail in a variety of papers [**3**, **5**, **12**, **14**, **14**, **17**] the presentation is quite terse. The second approach is quite new [**8**] and hence explained in greater, though not complete, detail.

The material of Section 4.1 should be viewed as a combinatorial version of numerical analysis. In Section 5 we turn to the question of how to extract rigorous information about the global dynamics. In the context of discrete dynamics we show that the combinatorial structures naturally lead to the classical notion of a Morse decomposition due to C. Conley [**7**]. In the setting of the differential equations that we consider the best that we can offer is a conjecture.

We conclude in Section 6 with a brief indication of how the Conley index can be incorporated into this approach to rigorously guarantee the existence of nontrivial invariant sets. This set of tools has been successfully applied to a variety of discrete dynamical systems. However, the optimal means of applying the Conley index in the setting of differential equations remains an open problem.

2. Concepts from Dynamical Systems

For the sake of simplicity of exposition we restrict our discussion, in this section, to discrete dynamical systems defined by homeomorphisms. For the analogous results for noninvertible continuous maps see [**12**–**14**]. To be more precise, let $F\colon X \times Z \to X$ be a continuous function where the phase space, X, is a compact metric space and the parameter space, Z, is a locally contractible, connected metric space. To discuss dynamics we need to restrict F to a single parameter value, $z \in Z$, and consider the map

$$F_z := F(\cdot, z)\colon X \to X$$

where we assume that F_z is a homeomorphism.

A set $S \subset X$ is *invariant* under F_z if $F_z(S) = S$. The focus of much of the qualitative theory of nonlinear dynamics is on the existence and structure of invariant sets. If one accepts that the invariant sets are of primary importance, then two dynamical systems are equivalent if their collections of invariant sets are equivalent. This occurs if and only if the dynamics systems $f\colon X \to X$ and

$g\colon Y \to Y$ are *conjugate*, i.e. if there exists a homeomorphism $h\colon X \to Y$ such that

$$\begin{array}{ccc} X & \xrightarrow{f} & X \\ h\big\downarrow & & \big\downarrow h \\ Y & \xrightarrow{g} & Y \end{array}$$

commutes. Recall that F is *structurally stable* at $z_0 \in Z$ if there exists a neighborhood U of z_0 such that F_z and F_{z_0} are conjugate for all $z \in U$. From the perspective of applications one does not expect to have exact knowledge of parameter values. Thus, if one wants to compare the dynamics generated by a theoretical model against experimental data, then in general one hopes that the model dynamics of interest occurs at a structurally stable parameter value. A parameter value z_0 is a *bifurcation point* of F if in any neighborhood U of z_0 there exists $z \in U$ such that F_z is not conjugate to F_{z_0}. One of the profound discoveries of the last half century is that sets of bifurcation points can be extremely complicated, and in particular, it is possible that the set of bifurcation points takes the form of a Cantor set [**21**].

Ideally, we want our models to be both accurate and precise. Invariant sets provide precise information about the qualitative structure of dynamics. Bifurcation theory provides limits to the accuracy of this precise information. Therefore, the potential existence of complex structures of bifurcation points suggests that attempts to extract precise information from heuristically derived or poorly parameterized models can lead to inaccuracies. The mathematical approach being promoted in this paper gives up on precision, with the goal of maintaining accuracy.

As indicated in the introduction we are interested in characterizing the dynamics where explicit knowledge of the nonlinearity is not available. To be more specific, we assume that there exists a continuous map $f\colon X \to X$ which is an acceptable model for the system of interest. However, because we are forced to rely on heuristic arguments to derive a nonlinear expression the best we can do is conclude that we have a model $F\colon X \times Z \to X$ for which there exists an unknown parameter value $z_0 \in Z$ such that $f = F_{z_0}$. It is reasonable to expect that the more heuristic the derivation of the model F, the larger the parameter space Z.

As we hope this brief review of dynamics has made clear, to avoid having to deal with the complexity of bifurcation theory requires that we change the primary focus of our inquiry away from invariant sets. This is not meant to imply that we intend to ignore invariant sets altogether. Instead, our goal is to construct an alternative, much cruder, characterization of dynamics from which some information about the existence or structure of invariant sets can be derived. Keeping this in mind we introduce several by now classical structures that our techniques are capable of extracting.

Recall that a compact set $N \subset X$ is a *trapping region* under $f\colon X \to X$ if $f(N) \subset \mathrm{int}(N)$, where int denotes interior. An *attractor* A of f is the *omega limit set* of a trapping region N, i.e.

$$A = \omega(N, f) := \bigcap_{T>0} \mathrm{cl}\left(\bigcup_{t=T}^{\infty} f^t(N)\right),$$

where cl denotes closure. The set of attractors of f, denoted by $\mathsf{Att}(f)$, is a bounded, distributive lattice [**13**].

Since a trapping region N is compact and f is continuous, $f(N)$ is compact. Thus we obtain the following result which indicates that the ability to compute trapping regions allows us to identify the existence of attractors.

PROPOSITION 2.1. *If N is a trapping region, then the associated attractor $\omega(N, f) \neq \emptyset$.*

Under the assumption that f is a homeomorphism, X is an invariant set of f. A *Morse decomposition* of X under f consists of a finite collection of disjoint compact invariant sets $M(p) \subset X$, called *Morse sets*, indexed by a partially ordered set $(\mathsf{P}, <)$ satisfying the following property. If $x \in X \setminus \bigcup_{p \in \mathsf{P}} M(p)$, then there exists $q, p \in \mathsf{P}$ with $q < p$ such that

$$\alpha(x, f) := \bigcap_{T<0} \mathrm{cl}\left(\bigcup_{t=T}^{-\infty} f^t(N)\right) \subset M(p) \quad \text{and} \quad \omega(x, f) \subset M(q).$$

Attractors are defined in terms of trapping regions. An analogous object for a Morse set is an *isolating neighborhood*, i.e. a compact set $N \subset X$ such that

$$\mathrm{Inv}(N, f) := \{x \in N \mid f^n(x) \in N \text{ for all } n \in \mathbb{Z}\} \subset \mathrm{int}(N).$$

An invariant set S is *isolated* if there exists an isolating neighborhood N such that $S = \mathrm{Inv}(N, f)$. Compactness of N and continuity of f implies that S is compact. A special case of an isolating neighborhood is an *isolating block* N defined by the following condition:

$$f^{-1}(N) \cap N \cap f(N) \subset \mathrm{int}(N).$$

An argument based on the continuity of f and the compactness of Morse sets shows that a Morse set is an isolated invariant set.

3. Combinatorial Dynamics

On the most primitive level we can think of dynamics as taking one state to another state. If we cannot exactly specify the current state, then a deterministic model may require that a current state leads to multiple future states. If we let $\mathcal{X}$ denote a *finite* set of states, then a multivalued map

$$\mathcal{F} \colon \mathcal{X} \rightrightarrows \mathcal{X}$$

where $\mathcal{F}(\xi) \subset \mathcal{X}$, for all $\xi \in \mathcal{X}$, provides a reasonable description of the dynamics. Note, that we can also view $\mathcal{F}$ as a directed graph, in which case $\mathcal{X}$ denotes the set of vertices and (ξ_0, ξ_1) is an edge if and only if $\xi_1 \in \mathcal{F}(\xi_0)$. To discuss the induced dynamics backwards in time, we reverse the direction of the edges, thus making use of the *transpose* $\mathcal{F}'$ of $\mathcal{F}$. We alternate between the two views; treating $\mathcal{F}$ as a map highlights the dynamic aspects, while viewing $\mathcal{F}$ as a directed graph naturally leads to efficient algorithms.

Since $\mathcal{F}$ is a coarse representation of the dynamics we are only interested in extracting coarse information: recurrence and gradient-like dynamics. A *Morse set*[1] of $\mathcal{F}$ (also referred to as a *recurrent component* or *strongly connected path component*) is a maximal set $\mathcal{M} \subset \mathcal{X}$ such that for any $\xi_0, \xi_1 \in \mathcal{M}$ there exit

[1]The purpose behind overloading of the concept of Morse set (we do the same for attractor below) is made clear in Theorem 5.6.

positive integers n_0 and n_1 such that $\xi_1 \in \mathcal{F}^{n_0}(\xi_0)$ and $\xi_0 \in \mathcal{F}^{n_1}(\xi_1)$. The collection of all Morse sets is called the *Morse decomposition* of $\mathcal{F}$ and is denoted by

$$\mathsf{MD}(\mathcal{F}) := \{\mathcal{M}(p) \mid p \in (\mathsf{P}, <)\}.$$

The indexing set P is a partially ordered set where the partial order is defined by $q < p$ if and only there exists a positive integer n such that $\mathcal{M}(q) \cap \mathcal{F}^n(\mathcal{M}(p)) \neq \emptyset$. The *Morse graph* of $\mathcal{F}$, denoted by $\mathsf{MG}(\mathcal{F})$, is the Hasse diagram of the poset $(\mathsf{P}, <)$. The elements of $\mathcal{P}$ are called the *Morse nodes* of the graph.

REMARK 3.1. Tarjan [**23**] provides a linear time algorithm for identifying Morse sets. In most applications the number of Morse sets is significantly smaller than the number of elements of $\mathcal{X}$, and thus determining a Morse decomposition can often be done in linear time.

A set $\mathcal{A} \subset \mathcal{X}$ is an *attractor* of $\mathcal{F}$ if $\mathcal{F}(\mathcal{A}) = \mathcal{A}$. The set of attractors of $\mathcal{F}$ is denoted by $\mathsf{Att}(\mathcal{F})$ and as is shown in [**13**] is a finite bounded distributive lattice with operations

$$\mathcal{A} \vee \mathcal{A}' := \mathcal{A} \cup \mathcal{A}' \quad \text{and} \quad \mathcal{A} \wedge \mathcal{A}' := \max\{\mathcal{A}'' \in \mathsf{Att}(\mathcal{F}) \mid \mathcal{A}'' \subset \mathcal{A} \cap \mathcal{A}'\}.$$

Observe that the minimal attractor is $\emptyset$. Since $\mathsf{Att}(\mathcal{F})$ is finite and $\mathcal{A} \vee \mathcal{A}' \in \mathsf{Att}(\mathcal{F})$ for all $\mathcal{A}, \mathcal{A}' \in \mathsf{Att}(\mathcal{F})$, there exists a maximal element. The following result follows directly from the definition of an attractor.

PROPOSITION 3.2. *If for every $\xi_0 \in \mathcal{X}$ there exists $\xi_1 \in \mathcal{X}$ such that $\xi_0 \in \mathcal{F}(\xi_1)$, then $\mathcal{X}$ is the maximal element in $\mathsf{Att}(\mathcal{F})$.*

A set $\mathcal{R} \subset \mathcal{X}$ is a *repeller* of $\mathcal{F}$ if $\mathcal{F}'(\mathcal{R}) = \mathcal{R}$ and the set of repellers of $\mathcal{F}$ is denoted by $\mathsf{Rep}(\mathcal{F})$. As is shown in [**13**] $\mathsf{Rep}(\mathcal{F})$ is a finite bounded distributive lattice and there exists an anti-lattice isomorphism between $\mathsf{Att}(\mathcal{F})$ and $\mathsf{Rep}(\mathcal{F})$. Let $\mathcal{M}$ be a Morse set of $\mathcal{F}$. Observe that

$$\downarrow(\mathcal{M}) := \bigcup_{n \geq 0} \mathcal{F}^n(\mathcal{M}) \in \mathsf{Att}(\mathcal{F}) \quad \text{and} \quad \uparrow(\mathcal{M}) := \bigcup_{n \geq 0} \mathcal{F}'^n(\mathcal{M}) \in \mathsf{Rep}(\mathcal{F}).$$

The following proposition follows from the definition of a Morse set and indicates that Morse sets can be written as the intersection of attractors and repellers.

PROPOSITION 3.3. *If $\mathcal{M} \subset \mathcal{X}$ is a Morse set of $\mathcal{F} \colon \mathcal{X} \rightrightarrows \mathcal{X}$, then*

$$\mathcal{M} = \downarrow(\mathcal{M}) \cap \uparrow(\mathcal{M}).$$

4. Approximating Dynamics

As indicated in the introduction we provide two approaches to approximating dynamics. The first is rather abstract, but extremely general, and we view it as the theoretical basis for the techniques presented here. The second is much more specific and designed for a particular class of ordinary differential equations.

4.1. Outer Approximations. Our long term goal is to demonstrate that we can extract useful, mathematically rigorous information concerning the global structures of a dynamical system generated by a parameterized family of continuous maps $F \colon X \times Z \to X$ via a combinatorial approximation. Thus the first step is to construct an appropriate discretization of the space X.

Recall that $Y \subset X$ is a *regular closed set* if $Y = \text{cl}(\text{int}(Y))$. Let $\mathscr{R}(X)$ denote the collection of all regular closed subsets of X.

PROPOSITION 4.1. [**26**, Proposition 2.3] *Given a topological space X, $\mathscr{R}(X)$ is a Boolean algebra with the following operations:*

(i) $A \leq B$ *if and only if* $A \subset B$*;*
(ii) $A \vee B := A \cup B$*;*
(iii) $A \wedge B := \mathrm{cl}(\mathrm{int}(A \cap B))$*;*
(iv) $A^c := \mathrm{cl}(X \setminus A)$*;*

where $0 = \varnothing$ *and* $1 = X$.

For the purpose of computation we are only interested in finite collections of regular closed sets.

PROPOSITION 4.2. [**14**, Proposition 3.5] *Let $\mathscr{R}_0 \subset \mathscr{R}(X)$ be a finite subalgebra and let $\mathsf{J}(\mathscr{R}_0)$ denote the set of atoms of $\mathscr{R}_0$. Then*

(i) $X = \bigcup\{A \mid A \in \mathsf{J}(\mathscr{R}_0)\}$.
(ii) *If $A, A' \subset X$ are two different atoms of $\mathscr{R}_0$, then $A \cap \mathrm{int}(A') = \varnothing$.*

Conversely, every finite set $\mathsf{J} = \{A \mid A \subset X\}$ of which satisfies (i) and (ii) generates a subalgebra of $\mathscr{R}(X)$ for which J is the set of atoms.

Given a finite subalgebra $\mathscr{R}_0 \subset \mathscr{R}(X)$ we refer to $\mathsf{J}(\mathscr{R}_0)$ as a *grid* on X (see [**12**], [**20**]). We index this grid by $\mathcal{X}$, where this indexing is expressed explicitly by the *evaluation mapping* $|\cdot| : \mathcal{X} \to \mathsf{J}(\mathscr{R}_0)$.

EXAMPLE 4.3. For many models X is often a reasonably nice space, e.g. $\mathbb{R}^n$ or a triangulable manifold. Natural grids for these spaces consist of a finite collection of top dimensional cells arising from a cubical lattice on $\mathbb{R}^n$ or the highest dimensional simplicies from a triangulation.

For simplicity for the remainder of this subsection we assume that X is a compact metric space. The following result is a special case of [**12**, Theorem 2.2].

THEOREM 4.4. *Let X be a compact metric space and $\epsilon > 0$. Then, there exists a grid on X indexed by $\mathcal{X}$ such that* $\mathrm{diam}(|\xi|) \leq \epsilon$ *for all $\xi \in \mathcal{X}$.*

To provide a combinatorial description of the dynamics generated by F_{z_0} for some $z_0 \in Z$ consider a fixed grid of X parameterized by $\mathcal{X}$. The *minimal combinatorial approximation* of F_{z_0} for $\mathcal{X}$ is the multivalued map $\tilde{\mathcal{F}}_{z_0} : \mathcal{X} \rightrightarrows \mathcal{X}$ defined by

$$\tilde{\mathcal{F}}_{z_0}(\xi) := \{\xi' \in \mathcal{X} \mid F_{z_0}(|\xi|) \cap |\xi'| \neq \emptyset\}.$$

In general, we cannot expect to compute $F_{z_0}(|\xi|)$ exactly. The best we can hope for are rigorous bounds, i.e. $F_{z_0}(|\xi|) \subset B_\eta(F_{z_0}(|\xi|))$ for some $\eta > 0$. Furthermore, and this is especially true in higher dimensional settings, determining whether a given set intersects a particular grid element can be prohibitively expensive computationally. With this in mind we make use of the following concept. Given two multivalued maps $\mathcal{F}, \mathcal{G} \colon \mathcal{X} \rightrightarrows \mathcal{X}$, $\mathcal{G}$ is an *extension* of $\mathcal{F}$ if $\mathcal{F}(\xi) \subset \mathcal{G}(\xi)$ for all $\xi \in \mathcal{X}$.

EXAMPLE 4.5. For any $\eta, \nu > 0$, if $\mathcal{F} \colon \mathcal{X} \rightrightarrows \mathcal{X}$ is defined by

$$\mathcal{F}(\xi) := \{\xi' \in \mathcal{X} \mid B_\eta(F_{z_0}(|\xi|)) \cap B_\nu(|\xi'|) \neq \emptyset\},$$

then $\mathcal{F}$ is an extension of $\tilde{\mathcal{F}}_{z_0}$.

EXAMPLE 4.6. The *maximal extension* of any multivalued map is defined by $\mathcal{F}(\xi) = \mathcal{X}$ for all $\xi \in \mathcal{X}$.

The following is the key concept of approximation to obtain rigorous results. A multivalued map $\mathcal{F}\colon \mathcal{X} \rightrightarrows \mathcal{X}$ is an *outer approximation* of F_{z_0} if

$$F_{z_0}(|\xi|) \subset \operatorname{int} |\mathcal{F}(\xi)| \tag{4.1}$$

for all $\xi \in \mathcal{X}$.

PROPOSITION 4.7. [**12**, Proposition 2.5] *$\tilde{\mathcal{F}}_{z_0}$ is an outer approximation of F_{z_0} and hence any extension of $\tilde{\mathcal{F}}_{z_0}$ is an outer approximation of F_{z_0}.*

The importance of Proposition 4.7 is that it implies that given an explicit nonlinearity standard numerical techniques can be applied to obtain an outer approximation. Another immediate observation, based directly on the continuity of F and (4.1), is that outer approximations represent the dynamics of sets of parameter values.

PROPOSITION 4.8. *If $\mathcal{F}$ is an outer approximation of F_{z_0}, then there exists $\delta > 0$ such that $\mathcal{F}$ is an outer approximation of F_z for all $z \in B_\delta(z_0)$.*

Proposition 4.8 provides a conceptually useful perturbation result, however, our interest is in understanding the dynamics of F over large regions of parameter space. For simplicity, for the remainder of this section we assume that the parameter space Z is compact and that $\mathcal{Z}$ denotes an indexing for a grid on Z. For each $\zeta \in \mathcal{Z}$, it is natural to define the associated minimal multivalued map $\tilde{\mathcal{F}}_\zeta\colon \mathcal{X} \rightrightarrows \mathcal{X}$ by

$$\tilde{\mathcal{F}}_\zeta(\xi) := \{\xi' \in \mathcal{X} \mid F(\xi, \zeta) \cap |\xi'| \neq \emptyset\}.$$

The following is an immediate corollary of this definition and Proposition 4.7.

COROLLARY 4.9. *If $\mathcal{F}_\zeta$ is an extension of $\tilde{\mathcal{F}}_\zeta$, then $\mathcal{F}_\zeta$ is an outer approximation for F_z for all $z \in |\zeta|$.*

Corollary 4.9 motivates refering to $\mathcal{F}_\zeta$ as an *outer approximation of* $F_{|\zeta|}$ if $\mathcal{F}_\zeta$ is an extension of $\tilde{\mathcal{F}}_\zeta$.

As discussed in the introduction and Section 2 one of the goals of our approach is to insure accuracy. In the classical setting accuracy can be lost through bifurcations. The analogous situation in our setting arises if $|\zeta_0| \cap |\zeta_1| \neq \emptyset$, but $\mathsf{MG}(\mathcal{F}_{\zeta_0})$ and $\mathsf{MG}(\mathcal{F}_{\zeta_1})$ differ. There is, however, a fundamental difference in that we can simultaneously characterize the dynamics in a neighborhood of $|\zeta_0| \cap |\zeta_1|$ or over all of $|\zeta_0| \cup |\zeta_1|$. To do the former observe that by assumption $\mathcal{F}_{\zeta_0}$ and $\mathcal{F}_{\zeta_1}$ are outer approximations for all $z \in |\zeta_0|$ and all $z \in |\zeta_1|$. Thus we can obtain an outer approximation over F_z for all $z \in |\zeta_0| \cap |\zeta_1|$, by defining

$$\mathcal{F}_{\zeta_0 \cap \zeta_1}(\xi) := \mathcal{F}_{\zeta_0}(\xi) \cap \mathcal{F}_{\zeta_1}(\xi)$$

from which we can compute a refined Morse graph. Alternatively, observe that

$$\mathcal{F}_{\zeta_0 \cup \zeta_1}(\xi) := \mathcal{F}_{\zeta_0}(\xi) \cup \mathcal{F}_{\zeta_1}(\xi)$$

defines an outer approximation for all F_z, $z \in |\zeta_0| \cup |\zeta_1|$. Again, this can be used to derive a Morse graph

We conclude with the following simple result.

PROPOSITION 4.10. *If $\mathcal{F}_\zeta$ is an extension of $\tilde{\mathcal{F}}_\zeta$, then $\mathcal{X}$ is the maximal element in $\mathsf{Att}(\mathcal{F}_\zeta)$.*

PROOF. By assumption $F_z : X \to X$ is a homeomorphism for all $z \in Z$. Therefore, for all $\xi \in \mathcal{X}$, $\mathcal{F}_\zeta(\xi) \neq \emptyset$. Furthermore, given $\xi \in \mathcal{X}$, let $x \in |\xi|$ and $F_z^{-1}(x) \in |\xi'|$, then $\xi \in \mathcal{F}_\zeta(\xi')$. The result now follows from Proposition 3.2. □

REMARK 4.11. The discussion to this point has been fairly abstract, however, these ideas have been implemented and applied to a variety of different models [**3–6**, **15**, **16**].

4.2. Wall Graphs. The discussion in Section 4.1 is extremely general and the essential algorithms are extremely efficient. The only challenge is the construction of the outer approximation $\mathcal{F}$. If the map $F: X \times Z \to X$ is given explicitly, then as indicated in Remark 4.11, there are a variety of examples in which the approach has been successfully applied. However, identifying a general computational method for determining an appropriate $\mathcal{F}$ in the context of differential equations is much more challenging (for a more detailed discussion see [**19**]). Thus, in this section we restrict our attention to a special class of differential equations that are motivated by the study of gene regulatory networks in biology. The literature on the subject of mathematical modeling of regulatory networks is enormous (see [**1**, **2**, **24**] and references therein). The description that we provide is greatly over-simplified, but structured to emphasize the potential of the crude approach to dynamics presented in these notes.

We model a regulatory network involving N genes by a system of ordinary differential equations of the form

$$\dot{x}_i = -\gamma_i x_i + f_i(x), \quad i = 1, \ldots, N, \tag{4.2}$$

where x_i denotes the concentration level of the protein associated with gene i and $\gamma_i > 0$ is a parameter that represents the rate of degradation and/or dilution due to cell growth of protein i. To understand the choice of nonlinearity f_i, recall that an expressed gene produces a protein that can in turn activate or repress the expression of another gene, thereby increasing or decreasing the rate at which the proteins of the second gene are produced. This relationship between genes is often recorded in the form of an annotated directed graph where nodes represent genes and the directed edges are expressed as $j \to i$ or $j \dashv i$ to indicate activation or repression, respectively.

Hill functions are commonly chosen as analytic expressions to represent how the concentration of protein j impacts the rate of production of protein i. In particular, $j \to i$ and $j \dashv i$ lead to nonlinearities of the form

$$h_i^+(x_j) = u_{i,j} \frac{x_j^{n_{i,j}}}{\theta_{i,j}^{n_{i,j}} + x_j^{n_{i,j}}} \quad \text{and} \quad h_i^-(x_j) = u_{i,j} \frac{\theta_{i,j}^{n_{i,j}}}{\theta_{i,j}^{n_{i,j}} + x_j^{n_{i,j}}}, \tag{4.3}$$

respectively. Note that this implies that each edge in the regulatory network gives rise to three positive parameters: a maximal value, $u_{i,j}$; the concentration $\theta_{i,j}$ at which the function achieves half its maximal value; and an exponent $n_{i,j}$ which governs how steep these sigmoidal functions are. It is possible for multiple genes to regulate a single gene in which case the nonlinearity f_i is taken to be a sum, product, or some combination thereof, of appropriate Hill functions.

Observe that a regulatory network with N nodes and E edges has $N + 3E$ parameters that in practice are either poorly measured or unknown. Furthermore, while mathematical justifications for using Hill functions in chemical reactions can be made, they are based on limits that assume the existence of large numbers of elements. In general this is not an appropriate assumption for protein levels in cells. However, their use is often justified, not unreasonably, by the fact that they provide a simple example of a sigmoidal function. In summary, (4.2) provides an important example of systems of differential equations for which the nonlinearities are chosen based on heuristic principles and for which there is limited information about the associated parameters.

To perform computations for systems of this form we replace the Hill functions of (4.3) with step functions that can be viewed as being obtained in part by taking the limit as the exponent $n_{i,j} \to \infty$:

$$\sigma^+_{i,j}(x_j) = \begin{cases} l_{i,j} & \text{if } x_j < \theta_{i,j} \\ u_{i,j} & \text{if } x_j > \theta_{i,j} \end{cases} \quad \text{and} \quad \sigma^-_{i,j}(x_j) = \begin{cases} u_{i,j} & \text{if } x_j < \theta_{i,j} \\ l_{i,j} & \text{if } x_j > \theta_{i,j}. \end{cases} \tag{4.4}$$

Note, however that we have introduced a new parameter $l_{i,j} \in [0, u_{i,j}]$ that represents a basal level of expression (in the Hill functions this is assumed to be 0).

To summarize to understand the dynamics of (4.2) generated by a regulatory network, we consider the *switching system*

$$\dot{x}_i = -\gamma_i x_i + \Lambda_i(x), \quad i = 1, \ldots, N, \tag{4.5}$$

where Λ_i is defined in terms of step functions $\sigma^+_{i,j}(x_j)$ and $\sigma^-_{i,j}(x_j)$ depending on whether there exists an annotated edge $j \to i$ or $j \dashv i$, respectively. For simplicity of expression we rewrite (4.6) as

$$\dot{x} = -\Gamma x + \Lambda(x), \tag{4.6}$$

i,j where Γ is the obvious diagonal matrix and Λ is the vector with entries Λ_i. We denote the parameter space for this problem by $Z \subset [0, \infty)^{N+3E}$ where the parameters are

$$\{0 < l_{i,j} \le u_{i,j}\}, \quad \{0 \le \theta_{i,j}\}, \quad \text{and} \quad \{0 < \gamma_i\}.$$

REMARK 4.12. The careful reader will note that the switching system (4.6) is not defined at points x where $x_i = \theta_{i,j}$. As is made clear below this does not hinder our ability to construct a combinatorial map. More importantly we do not consider this to be an issue, since our perspective is that the purpose of the switching system is to provide us with a computational model to understand the dynamics of the physically relevant model which has the form of (4.2) where the nonlinearities are sufficiently smooth to guarantee existence and uniqueness of solutions. We return to this point in Section 5.2.

EXAMPLE 4.13. Perhaps the simplest gene regulatory network of biological interest is the toggle switch, one of the first synthetic regulatory networks [**9**]. It consists of two genes, each of which down regulates the other as is indicated by the regulatory network shown in Figure 1. The model equations presented in [**9**] make use of Hill function nonlinearities

$$\begin{aligned} \dot{u} &= -u + \frac{\alpha_1}{1 + v^\beta} \\ \dot{v} &= -v + \frac{\alpha_2}{1 + u^\gamma}. \end{aligned} \tag{4.7}$$

FIGURE 1. Regulatory network for toggle switch [9].

In line with the discussion above we use the associated switching system that takes the form

$$\dot{x}_1 = -\gamma_1 x_1 + \begin{cases} u_{1,2} & \text{if } x_2 < \theta_{1,2} \\ l_{1,2} & \text{if } x_2 > \theta_{1,2} \end{cases}$$
(4.8)
$$\dot{x}_2 = -\gamma_2 x_2 + \begin{cases} u_{2,1} & \text{if } x_1 < \theta_{2,1} \\ l_{2,1} & \text{if } x_1 > \theta_{2,1}. \end{cases}$$

Because of the biological motivation the phase space is $[0,\infty)^2$ and the parameter space is $\bar{Z} \subset [0,\infty)^8$.

We now turn to the question of how, given a parameter value z, to derive a multivalued map $\mathcal{F}_z\colon \mathcal{X} \rightrightarrows \mathcal{X}$ that provides a useful characterization of the dynamics of (4.6). The map $\mathcal{F}_z$ is often called a *state transition diagram* [1]. As will be made clear below for the approach we adopt it makes sense to refer to $\mathcal{F}_z$ as a *wall graph*.

The first remark is that we restrict our attention to a parameter set $Z \subset \bar{Z}$ defined as the complement of the set of solutions to the following equations for $i = 1, \ldots, N$,

$$0 = l_{j,i} - u_{j,i}, \tag{4.9}$$

$$0 = \theta_{j,i} - \theta_{j',i} \tag{4.10}$$

$$0 = \gamma_i \theta_{j,i} - \Lambda_i(\kappa) \quad \text{where } \theta_{j,i} \text{ defines a face of } \kappa, \tag{4.11}$$

which we explain in what follows.

Failure to satisfy (4.9) is a natural assumption in that it implies that activation is different from repression.

Observe that failure to satisfy (4.10) is a generic condition, but allows us to use the threshold values $\theta_{i,j}$ to obtain an N-orthotope or hyperrectangular decomposition of phase space $[0,\infty)^N$ where the number of partitions in the x_i direction equals the number of out edges from node i in the regulatory network.

Consider a parameter value $z \in Z$. Then the threshold values $\theta_{i,j}$ are fixed and hence the N-orthotope decomposition of phase space is fixed. Conceptually, the easiest way to define $\mathcal{X}$ is to declare it to be a set via a bijection to the N-orthotopes and the $N-1$ dimensional faces that separate the N-orthotopes in $(0,\infty)^N$. The multivalued map $\mathcal{F}_z$ is determined locally as follows. Consider a single N-orthotope κ. Observe that Λ is constant on the interior of κ and thus the notation $\Lambda(\kappa)$ is well defined. Consider the affine differential equation $\dot{x} = -\Gamma x + \Lambda(\kappa)$ defined on all of $\mathbb{R}^N$. This has an attracting fixed point $\Gamma^{-1}\Lambda(\kappa)$. Let $\xi \in \mathcal{X}$ be identified with an $N-1$ dimensional face κ' of κ. Let $x \in \kappa'$. By (4.11) the vector $-\Gamma x + \Lambda(x)$ is transverse to κ' and thus it points into or out of κ. If it points into κ, then κ' is an *entrance face* of κ, and hence ξ is labelled as an *entrance node for* κ. If it points out of κ, then κ' is an *absorbing face* of κ, and hence ξ is labelled as an *absorbing node for* κ. Observe that it is possible that $\Gamma^{-1}\Lambda(\kappa) \in \kappa$. In this case define the element

$\xi \in \mathcal{X}$ that is identified with κ to be an *absorbing node for* κ and set $\mathcal{F}_\kappa(\xi) = \xi$. For each N-orthotope define $\mathcal{F}_\kappa$ by the rule that each entrance node for κ maps to all absorbing nodes for κ. The combinatorial map $\mathcal{F}_z$ is obtained by taking the union of $\mathcal{F}_\kappa$ over all N-orthotopes κ.

To understand why we call $\mathcal{F}_z$ a wall graph observe that if $\xi \in \mathcal{X}$ is associated with an N-orthotope κ and $\Gamma^{-1}\Lambda(\kappa) \notin \kappa$, then $\mathcal{F}_z(\xi) = \emptyset$ and $\mathcal{F}_z'(\xi) = \emptyset$. Therefore, ξ plays no role in the determination of $\mathsf{MD}(\mathcal{F}_z)$ or $\mathsf{MG}(\mathcal{F}_z)$ and hence can be ignored. Thus, $\mathcal{F}_z$ captures how faces (walls) of the N-orthotopes are mapped to each other. Since it is only at these walls that the dynamics of (4.6) can change, this combinatorial description of the dynamics characterizes observable changes in the dynamics that is associated with evolution past thresholds.

EXAMPLE 4.14. Returning to Example 4.13 and the associated switching system (4.8), observe that phase space is divided into four 2-orthotopes, κ_i, $i = 1, \dots, 4$ as indicated in Figure 2. There are four faces separating these orthotopes and thus $\mathcal{X}$ consists of eight elements. To determine the combinatorial map $\mathcal{F} \colon \mathcal{X} \rightrightarrows \mathcal{X}$ requires a choice of parameters. This problem is simple enough that we can easily enumerate equations (4.9)-(4.11):

$$
\begin{aligned}
0 &= l_{1,2} - u_{1,2}, \quad 0 = l_{2,1} - u_{2,1} \\
0 &= \theta_{1,2}, \quad 0 = \theta_{2,1} \\
0 &= \gamma_1\theta_{2,1} - \Lambda_1(\kappa), \quad 0 = \gamma_2\theta_{1,2} - \Lambda_2(\kappa).
\end{aligned}
\tag{4.12}
$$

Given the constraints used to define Z, the parameter regions of interest are given by

$$
\begin{aligned}
l_{1,2} &< u_{1,2}, \quad l_{2,1} < u_{2,1} \\
0 &< \theta_{1,2}, \quad 0 < \theta_{2,1} \\
0 &\neq \gamma_1\theta_{2,1} - \Lambda_1(\kappa), \quad 0 \neq \gamma_2\theta_{1,2} - \Lambda_2(\kappa).
\end{aligned}
\tag{4.13}
$$

where in this case $\neq$ represents an explicit choice of $<$ or $>$.

For the moment let us choose a particular region by assuming that

$$
l_{1,2} < \gamma_1\theta_{2,1} < u_{1,2}, \quad \text{and} \quad \gamma_2\theta_{1,2} < l_{2,1}. \tag{4.14}
$$

Simple computations show that this implies that

$$
\Gamma^{-1}\Lambda(\kappa_i) \in \kappa_1, i = 1, 2, 3, \quad \text{and} \quad \Gamma^{-1}\Lambda(\kappa_4) \in \kappa_2.
$$

Thus for this set of parameter values $\mathcal{F} \colon \mathcal{X} \rightrightarrows \mathcal{X}$ is as shown in Figure 2 and the resulting Morse graph consists of a single node.

The inequalities of (4.13) lead to nine unbounded connected regions as shown in Figure 3. Observe that we have presented these regions in the form of a graph, which we call the *parameter graph*. Each node represents one of the regions defined by (4.13). Each edge indicates that the sets of inequalities that define the two nodes are the same except for a single inequality. The Morse graph for region (5) consists of two unrelated nodes. The remainder of the regions have the same Morse graph consisting of a single node.

There are two important observations. First, the parameter graph along with the associated Morse graphs provides an extremely condensed representation of the global dynamics over all of parameter space. Second, we can easily augment the Morse graph information, by including the fact that the Morse nodes correspond

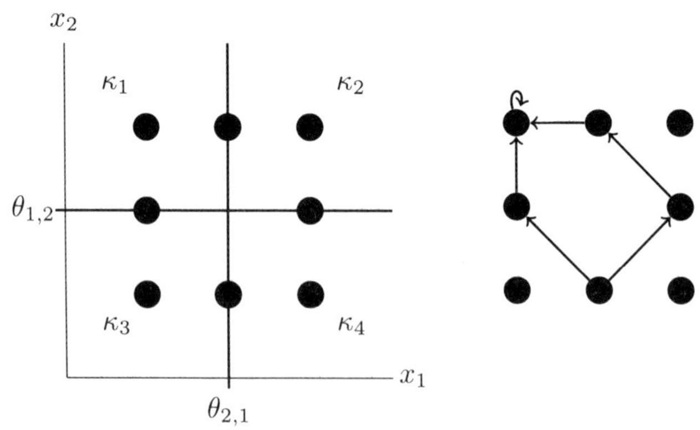

FIGURE 2. (Left) Phase space for Example 4.13, the toggle switch. Black dots indicate the 2-orthotopes and the 1-faces between the 2-orthotopes. (Right) The black dots indicate the elements of $\mathcal{X}$ with the obvious bijection with the 2-orthotopes and 1-faces. The edges indicate the images of $\mathcal{F}$ for the parameter values $l_{1,2} < \gamma_1\theta_{2,1} < u_{1,2}$ and $\gamma_2\theta_{1,2} < l_{2,1}$.

to fixed points in the dynamics. Thus, as is indicated in Figure 3 we label these nodes as FP.

We can go one step further and use the fact that we can label the orthotopes by the thresholds. In particular, we indicate that a point $x \in \kappa_1$ must satisfied the inequalities $0 < x_1 < \theta_{2,1}$ and $\theta_{1,2} < x_2$ by $(0,1)$, i.e. the first coordinate is above no thresholds, while the second coordinate is above the first threshold. Extending this the demarcations for κ_i, $i = 2,3,4$ are $(1,1)$, $(0,0)$, and $(1,0)$, respectively. We can use these demarcations to indicate where the fixed points are, i.e. labeling a Morse set as $\mathsf{FP}(0,1)$ indicates a fixed point that occurs in κ_1. The Morse graphs with this vector annotation are shown in Figure 4.

As indicated above, the toggle switch is one of the first synthetic regulatory networks and in [**9**] it is demonstrated experimentally that, depending upon the choice of parameter values, one obtains a single stable fixed point or two stable fixed points. Furthermore, the stable fixed points are distinguished by the relative values of the two genes. It is worth noting that even though (4.7) and (4.8) are functionally quite different there is an obvious comparison between the stable equilibria reported in [**9**] and the Morse graphs indicated in Figure 4 and furthermore, the desired comparisons occur at the desired relative parameter values.

As indicated in the introduction this is at best a cursory introduction to this approach of identifying dynamics of regulatory networks. For more detail the interested reader is referred to [**8**].

5. Extracting Dynamics from Outer Approximations

Section 4 describes two approaches by which a continuous dynamical system can be reduced to a combinatorial dynamical system. In this section we show that we can use the multivalued map to recover information about the global structure of the dynamics of the original system.

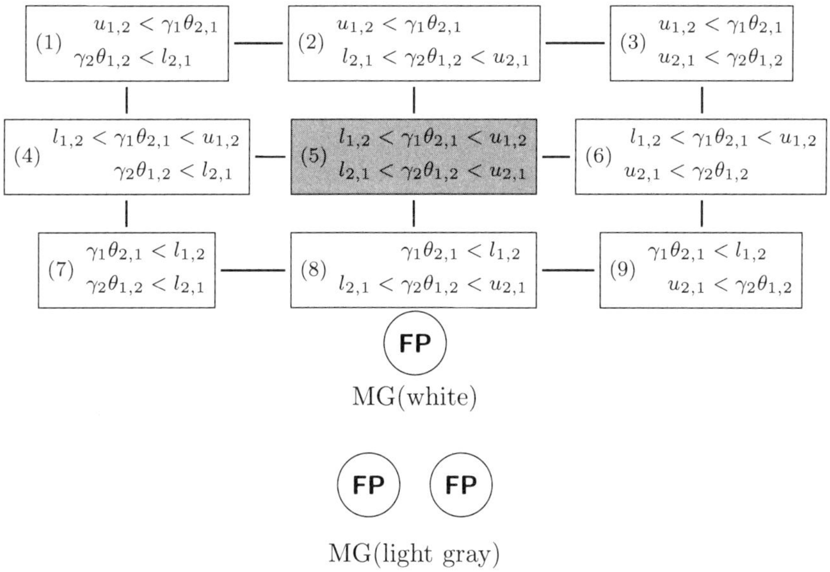

FIGURE 3. (Left) Visualization of parameter graph with explicit bounds on regions in parameter space. Edges indicate difference of one inequality. (Right) Annotated Morse graphs for white and gray parameter regions. FP indicates that the Morse node arose via a fixed point for the switching system.

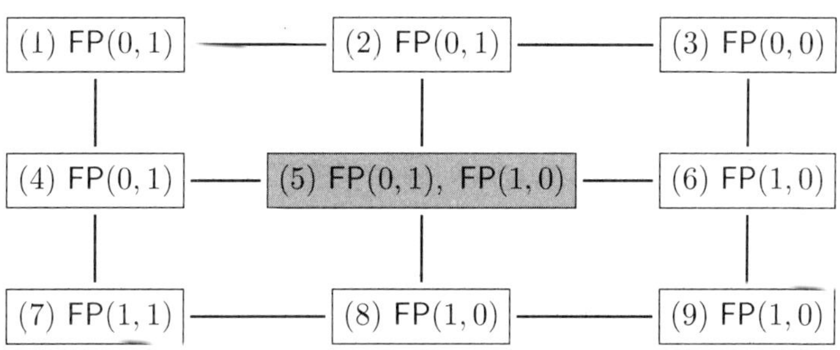

FIGURE 4. Parameter graph with associated Morse graphs for which the Morse nodes have been given a vector annotation.

5.1. From Outer Approximations to Morse Decompositions. For simplicity, throughout this section we assume that $F\colon X \times Z \to X$ is a continuous function where both the phase space, X, and the parameter space, Z, are compact metric spaces, and F_z is a homeomorphism for each $z \in Z$.

THEOREM 5.1. *Let $\mathcal{X}$ and $\mathcal{Z}$ be indexing sets for grids on X and Z, respectively. Given $\zeta \in \mathcal{Z}$, let $\mathcal{F}_\zeta\colon \mathcal{X} \rightrightarrows \mathcal{X}$ be an extension of $\tilde{\mathcal{F}}_\zeta$. If $\mathcal{A} \in \mathsf{Att}(\mathcal{F}_\zeta)$, then $|\mathcal{A}|$ is a trapping region for F_z for all $z \in |\zeta|$. If $\mathcal{R} \in \mathsf{Rep}(\mathcal{F}_\zeta)$, then $|\mathcal{R}|$ is a trapping region for F_z^{-1} for all $z \in |\zeta|$.*

PROOF. Observe that

$$F_z(|\mathcal{A}|) = \bigcup_{\xi\in\mathcal{A}} F_z(|\xi|) \subset \bigcup_{\xi\in\mathcal{A}} \operatorname{int}(\mathcal{F}_\zeta(\xi)) = \operatorname{int}(|\mathcal{F}_\zeta(\mathcal{A})|) \subset \operatorname{int}(|\mathcal{A}|)$$

for all $z \in |\zeta|$. The proof for $\mathcal{R}$ is similar ([**12**, Proposition 2.7] guarantees that $\tilde{\mathcal{F}}'_\zeta$ is an outer approximation of F_z^{-1}). □

The following result is an immediate generalization of Theorem 5.1.

COROLLARY 5.2. *Let $\mathcal{X}$ and $\mathcal{Z}$ be indexing sets for grids on X and Z, respectively. Given $\zeta \in \mathcal{Z}$, let $\mathcal{F}_\zeta \colon \mathcal{X} \rightrightarrows \mathcal{X}$ be an extension of $\tilde{\mathcal{F}}_\zeta$. If $\mathcal{U} \subset \mathcal{X}$ and $\mathcal{F}(\mathcal{U}) \subset \mathcal{U}$ or $\mathcal{F}'(\mathcal{U}) \subset \mathcal{U}$, then $F_z(|\mathcal{U}|) \subset \operatorname{int}(|\mathcal{F}(\mathcal{U})|)$ or $F_z^{-1}(|\mathcal{U}|) \subset \operatorname{int}(|\mathcal{F}'(\mathcal{U})|)$ for all $z \in |\zeta|$.*

An application of Proposition 2.1 guarantees that we can use outer approximations to identify nonempty attractors of F over regions of parameter space.

COROLLARY 5.3. *If $\mathcal{F}_\zeta \colon \mathcal{X} \rightrightarrows \mathcal{X}$ is an outer approximation of $F_{|\zeta|}$ and $\mathcal{A} \neq \emptyset$ is an attractor of $\mathcal{F}_\zeta$, then $\omega(|\mathcal{A}|, F_z) \neq \emptyset$ for all $z \in |\zeta|$.*

There are two important caveats to Corollary 5.3. The first is that $\mathcal{A}, \mathcal{A}' \in \mathsf{Att}(\mathcal{F}_\zeta)$ and $\mathcal{A} \neq \mathcal{A}'$ does not imply that $\omega(|\mathcal{A}|, F_z) \neq \omega(|\mathcal{A}'|, F_z)$. A simple example is the map $f\colon [-1,1] \to [-1,1]$ given by $f(x) = \lambda x$ where $0 < \lambda < 1$. Observe that $\mathsf{Att}(f) = \{\emptyset, \{0\}\}$. However, if one fixes a grid made up of closed intervals of equal length on $[-1,1]$ and chooses λ sufficiently close to one, then $\mathsf{Att}(\tilde{F})$ will have many elements.

The second caveat is that given an outer approximation $\mathcal{F}$ of F_{z_0} and $A \in \mathsf{Att}(F_{z_0})$, we cannot expect that there exists $\mathcal{A} \in \mathsf{Att}(\mathcal{F})$ such that $A = \omega(|\mathcal{A}|, F_{z_0})$. The simplest argument for this caveat is based on the fact that it is possible that $\mathsf{Att}(F_{z_0})$ contains infinitely many elements, while by construction $\mathsf{Att}(\mathcal{F})$ is finite. However, as is shown in [**14**] given any finite bounded sublattice $\mathsf{A} \subset \mathsf{Att}(F_{z_0})$ it is possible to choose a grid such that the lattice $\mathsf{Att}(\tilde{\mathcal{F}}_{z_0})$ for associated minimal multivalued map is isomorphic to A and furthermore the isomorphism is given by the map $\rho\colon \mathsf{Att}(\tilde{\mathcal{F}}_{z_0}) \to \mathsf{A}$ defined by

$$\rho(\mathcal{A}) = \omega(|\mathcal{A}|, F_{z_0}).$$

The importance of this result is that it shows that at any finite level of resolution the lattice structure of attractors of dynamical systems is computable.

The analogue of Theorem 5.1 for Morse sets is the following.

THEOREM 5.4. *Let $\mathcal{X}$ and $\mathcal{Z}$ be indexing sets for grids on X and Z, respectively. Given $\zeta \in \mathcal{Z}$, let $\mathcal{F}_\zeta \colon \mathcal{X} \rightrightarrows \mathcal{X}$ be an extension of $\tilde{\mathcal{F}}_\zeta$. If $\mathcal{M}$ is a Morse set of $\mathcal{F}$, then $|\mathcal{M}|$ is an isolating block for F_z for all $z \in |\zeta|$.*

PROOF. Observe that $|\mathcal{M}(p)|$ is compact, since X is compact and $|\mathcal{M}(p)|$ is the finite union of closed sets. By Proposition 3.3 $\mathcal{M} = {\downarrow}(\mathcal{M}) \cap {\uparrow}(\mathcal{M})$. By Theorem 5.1 $|{\downarrow}(\mathcal{M})|$ is a trapping region for F_z and $|{\uparrow}(\mathcal{M})|$ is a trapping region for F_z^{-1}. Therefore $F_z(|\mathcal{M}|) \cap |\mathcal{M}| \cap F_z^{-1}(|\mathcal{M}|) \subset \operatorname{int}(|\mathcal{M}|)$. □

Theorem 5.4 allows us to show that outer approximations can be used to identify Morse decompositions. We begin with a lemma that follows from Theorem 5.4 and the fact that if $x \in |\xi|$, then $F_z(x) \in |\mathcal{F}(\xi)|$.

LEMMA 5.5. *If $S = \omega(x, F_z)$ or $S = \alpha(x, F_z)$, then there exists $p \subset \mathsf{P}$ such that $S \subset |\mathcal{M}(p)|$, and therefore $S \subset M(p)$.*

THEOREM 5.6. *Let $\mathcal{X}$ and $\mathcal{Z}$ be indexing sets for grids on X and Z, respectively. Given $\zeta \in \mathcal{Z}$, assume that $\mathcal{F}_\zeta : \mathcal{X} \rightrightarrows \mathcal{X}$ is an extension of $\tilde{\mathcal{F}}_\zeta$ with Morse decomposition*

$$\mathsf{MD}(\mathcal{F}) := \{\mathcal{M}(p) \mid p \in (\mathsf{P}, <)\}.$$

For $z \in |\zeta|$, set $M_z(p) := \mathrm{Inv}(|\mathcal{M}(p)|, F_z)$. Then the collection of sets $M(p)$ forms a Morse decomposition of X under F_z with indexing set $(\mathsf{P}, <)$.

PROOF. By Theorem 5.4, $|\mathcal{M}(p)|$ is an isolating block. Therefore $M_z(p) := \mathrm{Inv}(|\mathcal{M}(p)|, F_z)$ is a compact invariant set. Furthermore, $p \neq q$ implies that $\mathcal{M}(p) \cap \mathcal{M}(q) = \emptyset$ and hence $\mathrm{int}(|\mathcal{M}(p)|) \cap \mathrm{int}(|\mathcal{M}(q)|) = \emptyset$. Therefore, the $M_z(p)$ are mutually disjoint compact invariant sets.

Consider $x \in X \setminus \bigcup_{p \in \mathsf{P}} M(p)$. Since F_z is a homeomorphism and X is compact, $\omega(x, F_z) \neq \emptyset$ and $\alpha(x, F_z) \neq \emptyset$. Furthermore, there exists $\xi \in \mathcal{X}$ such that $x \in |\xi|$. We consider two cases: (i) $\xi \notin \bigcup_{p \in \mathsf{P}} \mathcal{M}(p)$, and (ii) $\xi \in \mathcal{M}(p)$ for some $p \in \mathsf{P}$.

Assume $\xi \notin \bigcup_{p \in \mathsf{P}} \mathcal{M}(p)$. Let $\mathcal{U} := \downarrow\xi$ and $\mathcal{V} := \uparrow\xi$. Let $\mathcal{A}$ ($\mathcal{R}$) be the maximal attractor (repeller) in $\mathcal{U}$ ($\mathcal{V}$). Observe that $\mathcal{U} \cap \mathcal{V} = \xi$. Furthermore, $\mathcal{F}(\mathcal{U}) \cap \mathcal{F}'(\mathcal{V}) = \emptyset$, since $\mathcal{F}(\mathcal{U}) \subset \mathcal{U} \setminus \{\xi\}$ and $\mathcal{F}'(\mathcal{V}) \subset \mathcal{V} \setminus \{\xi\}$. Therefore, $\mathcal{A} \cap \mathcal{R} = \emptyset$. Repeated applications of Corollary 5.2 allow us to conclude that $\omega(|\xi|, F_z) \subset \mathrm{int}(|\mathcal{A}|)$ and $\alpha(|\xi|, F_z) \subset \mathrm{int}(|\mathcal{R}|)$. By Lemma 5.5 $\omega(|\xi|, F_z) \subset M(q) \subset \mathrm{int}(|\mathcal{A}|)$ and $\alpha(|\xi|, F_z) \subset M(p) \subset \mathrm{int}(|\mathcal{A}|)$, where $q \neq p$. We leave it to the reader to check that $q < p$.

Assume $\xi \in \mathcal{M}(p)$ *for some* $p \in \mathsf{P}$. Since $x \notin M_z(p)$ there exists $n \in \mathbb{Z}$ such that $F_z^n(x) \notin |\mathcal{M}(p)|$. Let $\bar{\xi} \in \mathcal{X}$ such that $F_z^n(x) \in |\bar{\xi}|$. Since $\omega(x, F_z) = \omega(F_z^n(x), F_z)$ and $\alpha(x, F_z) = \alpha(F_z^n(x), F_z)$, it is sufficient to apply the previous argument to $\bar{\xi}$. □

We can summarize Theorem 5.6 as follows. Given a dynamical system $F: X \times Z \to X$ where X and Z are compact we can compute Morse decompositions of X under F_z for every parameter value $z \in Z$. It is important to note, however, that if $M_z(p)$ is not a minimal Morse set, i.e. not an attractor, then it is possible that $M_z(p) = \emptyset$. We address this issue in Section 6

5.2. From Wall Graphs to Morse Decompositions. Recalling Remark 4.12, it should not be surprising that the general theory presented in Section 5.1 is not directly applicable to switching systems. Switching systems are used to guide computations, but the dynamics of interest are given by a system of the form of (4.2) for which the explicit nonlinearities f_i are unknown. In particular, we have no general direct analogue of Theorem 5.6 that relates the Morse decomposition of the wall graph as constructed in Section 4.2 to a Morse decomposition of an associated system of smooth differential equations given by (4.2). What we can provide is a conjecture.

DEFINITION 5.7. Consider a switching system given by (4.5) where each Λ_i is defined in terms of step functions $\sigma_{i,j}^{\pm}(x_j)$ involving parameters $0 < l_{i,j} < u_{i,j}$ and $0 < \theta_{i,j}$. Fix $\delta > 0$ and $\mu \geq 0$. A function $s_{i,j}^{\pm} : [0, \infty) \to [0, \infty)$ is δ, μ*-close* to $\sigma_{i,j}^{\pm}$ if

$$l_{i,j} \leq s_{i,j}^{\pm}(x_j) \leq u_{i,j} \quad \text{for all } x_j \in [\theta - \delta, \theta + \delta]$$

and

$$|s^{\pm}_{i,j}(x_j) - \sigma^{\pm}_{i,j}(x_j)| \leq \mu \quad \text{for all } x_j \in [0, \theta - \delta) \cup (\theta + \delta, \infty).$$

A *smooth* δ, μ*-approximation* of (4.5) is a system of the form (4.2) where f_i is obtained by replacing each $\sigma^{\pm}_{i,j}(x_j)$ used to define Λ_i by a smooth function $s^{\pm}_{i,j}$ that is δ, μ-close to $\sigma^{\pm}_{i,j}$.

EXAMPLE 5.8. We derived the switching system by starting with a model (4.2) defined in terms of Hill functions and then letting the exponents $n_{i,j} \to \infty$. Observe that for fixed $\delta, \mu > 0$, a switching system can be δ, μ-approximated by choosing Hill functions with sufficiently large exponents.

CONJECTURE 5.9. Consider a switching system given by (4.5) where each Λ_i is defined in terms of step functions $\sigma^{\pm}_{i,j}(x_j)$ involving parameters $0 < l_{i,j} < u_{i,j}$ and $0 < \theta_{i,j}$. Fix a parameter value z and let $(\mathsf{P}, <)$ be the partial ordering for the Morse graph for the associated wall graph $\mathcal{F}$. Define a poset $(\hat{P}, \hat{<})$ by $\hat{P} = P \cup \{\hat{p}\}$ where $\hat{<}$ is the same as $<$ on P and $p \hat{<} \hat{p}$ for all $p \in P$.

There exists $\delta, \mu > 0$ such that if (4.2) is a smooth δ, μ-approximation of (4.5) then there exists a Morse decomposition of the global attractor of (4.2) with partial order given by $(\hat{P}, \hat{<})$.

REMARK 5.10. The necessity of extending P to $\hat{P}$ arises from the simplicity of the construction of the wall graph $\mathcal{F}$, which cannot capture unstable fixed points. This can be seen explicitly by considering the toggle switch, Example 4.13, at parameter values which give rise to the Morse graph consisting of two nodes.

A version of this conjecture has been proven in the context of a rather general two-dimensional switching system where in addition explicit bounds on δ have been given [**10**]. The key element in the proof of this result is the ability to construct a lattice homomorphism from the lattice of attractors of the wall graph $\mathcal{F}$ to a lattice of trapping regions for the associated smooth δ, μ-approximation.

6. Conley Index

As indicated in the introduction combinatorial approximations provide a computationally efficient means of obtaining a description of the global structure of nonrecurrent dynamics. What is missing is information about existence and structure of the recurrent dynamics and more detailed information concerning gradient like invariant sets. A powerful tool, based on algebraic topology, to obtain this type of information is the Conley index. Anything more than a cursory description of this theory is beyond the scope of this paper and in fact we do not even provide a definition of the Conley index here. The interested reader is referred to [**18**] and references therein. We do, however, discuss index pairs since this is of greatest direct relevance to the question of the effectiveness of this approach to the rigorous computations of nonlinear dynamics.

DEFINITION 6.1. A pair of compact sets $P = (P_1, P_0)$ with $P_0 \subset P_1$ is an *index pair* for a continuous function $f \colon X \to X$, if the following two conditions are satisfied.

(1) $\mathrm{cl}(P_1 \setminus P_0)$ is an isolating neighborhood for f.

(2) Let $(P_1/P_0, [P_0])$ denoted the pointed space obtained by quotienting the subset P_0 to a single point $[P_0]$. The *index map* $f_P\colon (P_1/P_0, [P_0]) \to (P_1/P_0, [P_0])$ defined by

$$f_P([x]) := \begin{cases} f(x) & \text{if } x, f(x) \in P_1 \setminus P_0, \\ [P_0] & \text{otherwise.} \end{cases}$$

is continuous.

The following proposition provides one of the simplest characterizations of an index pair (for a proof see [**22**]).

PROPOSITION 6.2. *A pair of compact sets $P = (P_1, P_0)$ is an index pair for f if $P_0 \subset P_1$ and the following conditions are satisfied:*

(1) $\mathrm{cl}(P_1 \setminus P_0)$ *is an isolating neighborhood for f;*
(2) $f(P_1 \setminus P_0) \subset P_1$;
(3) $f(P_0) \cap P_1 \subset P_0$.

The following proposition makes it clear that index pairs can be constructed directly from the information carried by an outer approximation.

PROPOSITION 6.3. *Let $\mathcal{F}_\zeta\colon \mathcal{X} \rightrightarrows \mathcal{X}$ be an outer approximation of $F_{|\zeta|}$. Let $\mathcal{M} \subset \mathcal{X}$ be a Morse set for $\mathcal{F}_\zeta$. If*

$$P_1 := |{\downarrow}(\mathcal{M})| \quad \text{and} \quad P_0 = |{\downarrow}(\mathcal{M}) \setminus \mathcal{M}|,$$

then $P = (P_1, P_0)$ is an index pair for F_z for all $z \in |\zeta|$.

PROOF. The proof is a direct application of Proposition 6.2.

(1) By Theorem 5.4 $|\mathcal{M}| = \mathrm{cl}(P_1 \setminus P_0)$ is an isolating neighborhood for F_z.

(2) By construction ${\downarrow}(\mathcal{M}) \in \mathsf{Att}(\mathcal{F})$ and hence by Theorem 5.1, $F_z(P_1) \subset \mathrm{int}(P_1) \subset P_1$.

(3) Finally, observe that $\mathcal{F}({\downarrow}(\mathcal{M}) \setminus \mathcal{M}) \cap \mathcal{M} = \emptyset$ and hence $\mathcal{F}({\downarrow}(\mathcal{M}) \setminus \mathcal{M}) \subset {\downarrow}(\mathcal{M}) \setminus \mathcal{M}$. The same argument used to prove Theorem 5.1 shows that P_0 is a trapping region for F_z. Therefore, $F_z(P_0) \cap P_1 \subset F_z(P_0) \subset \mathrm{int}(P_0) \subset P_0$. □

A fundamental result related to the Conley index is that if P is an index pair and the induced map on homology of the index map,

$$f_{P*}\colon H_*(P_1/P_0, [P_0]) \to H_*(P_1/P_0, [P_0]),$$

is not nilpotent, then $\mathrm{Inv}(\mathrm{cl}(P_1 \setminus P_0), f) \neq \emptyset$. Proposition 6.3 implies that if one can compute an outer approximation $\mathcal{F}$ of f, then one can obtain an index pair described in terms of the grid elements. Thus, the remaining question is whether one can compute f_{P*} from the information provided by $\mathcal{F}$. This cannot be done in the complete generality of Section 4.1 since in general the topology of a regular closed set can be quite complicated. However, if X is a CW complex whose top cells are given by $\mathsf{J}(\mathscr{R}_0)$ then the algorithms described in [**11**] can be used to compute f_{P*}.

In summary, this shows that, under reasonable conditions, there are techniques for determining that a Morse set $M(p) := \mathrm{Inv}(\mathcal{M}(p), f)$ identified using an outer approximation $\mathcal{F}$ of f is nontrivial. We also remark that, as described in [**18**], one can use information related to the index map to identify structure of the invariant set $\mathrm{Inv}(\mathrm{cl}(P_1 \setminus P_0), f)$, e.g. the existence of fixed points, periodic orbits, heteroclinic orbits, and even chaotic dynamics.

At first glance the Conley index appears simpler for flows since the index map always induces the identity on homology. However, the construction of index pairs is often more difficult. It remains an open question as to what is a computationally optimal means for computing Conley indices in the setting of switching systems.

References

[1] Réka Albert, James J. Collins, and Leon Glass, *Introduction to focus issue: quantitative approaches to genetic networks*, Chaos **23** (2013), no. 2, 025001, 8, DOI 10.1063/1.4810923. MR3389671

[2] Uri Alon, *An introduction to systems biology*, Chapman & Hall/CRC Mathematical and Computational Biology Series, Chapman & Hall/CRC, Boca Raton, FL, 2007. Design principles of biological circuits. MR2259607

[3] Zin Arai, William Kalies, Hiroshi Kokubu, Konstantin Mischaikow, Hiroe Oka, and Paweł Pilarczyk, *A database schema for the analysis of global dynamics of multiparameter systems*, SIAM J. Appl. Dyn. Syst. **8** (2009), no. 3, 757–789, DOI 10.1137/080734935. MR2533624

[4] Justin Bush, Wes Cowan, Shaun Harker, and Konstantin Mischaikow, *Conley-Morse databases for the angular dynamics of Newton's method on the plane*, SIAM J. Appl. Dyn. Syst. **15** (2016), no. 2, 736–766, DOI 10.1137/15M1017971. MR3484393

[5] Justin Bush, Marcio Gameiro, Shaun Harker, Hiroshi Kokubu, Konstantin Mischaikow, Ippei Obayashi, and Paweł Pilarczyk, *Combinatorial-topological framework for the analysis of global dynamics*, Chaos **22** (2012), no. 4, 047508, 16, DOI 10.1063/1.4767672. MR3388721

[6] Justin Bush and Konstantin Mischaikow, *Coarse Dynamics for Coarse Modeling: An Example From Population Biology*, Entropy **16** (2014), no. 6, 3379–3400.

[7] Charles Conley, *Isolated invariant sets and the Morse index*, CBMS Regional Conference Series in Mathematics, vol. 38, American Mathematical Society, Providence, R.I., 1978. MR511133

[8] Bree Cummins, Tomas Gedeon, Shaun Harker, Konstantin Mischaikow, and Kafung Mok, *Combinatorial representation of parameter space for switching networks*, SIAM J. Appl. Dyn. Syst. **15** (2016), no. 4, 2176–2212, DOI 10.1137/15M1052743. MR3572361

[9] Timothy Gardner, Charles Cantor, and James Collins, *Construction of a genetic toggle switch in Escherichia coli*, Nature **403** (2000), no. 6767, 339–342.

[10] Tomáš Gedeon, Shaun Harker, Hiroshi Kokubu, Konstantin Mischaikow, and Hiroe Oka, *Global dynamics for steep nonlinearities in two dimensions*, Phys. D **339** (2017), 18–38, DOI 10.1016/j.physd.2016.08.006. MR3575050

[11] Shaun Harker, Konstantin Mischaikow, Marian Mrozek, and Vidit Nanda, *Discrete Morse theoretic algorithms for computing homology of complexes and maps*, Found. Comput. Math. **14** (2014), no. 1, 151–184, DOI 10.1007/s10208-013-9145-0. MR3160710

[12] W. D. Kalies, K. Mischaikow, and R. C. A. M. VanderVorst, *An algorithmic approach to chain recurrence*, Found. Comput. Math. **5** (2005), no. 4, 409–449, DOI 10.1007/s10208-004-0163-9. MR2189545

[13] William D. Kalies, Konstantin Mischaikow, and Robert C. A. M. Vandervorst, *Lattice structures for attractors I*, J. Comput. Dyn. **1** (2014), no. 2, 307–338. MR3415257

[14] William D. Kalies, Konstantin Mischaikow, and Robert C. A. M. Vandervorst, *Lattice structures for attractors II*, Found. Comput. Math. **16** (2016), no. 5, 1151–1191, DOI 10.1007/s10208-015-9272-x. MR3552843

[15] Diána H. Knipl, Paweł Pilarczyk, and Gergely Röst, *Rich bifurcation structure in a two-patch vaccination model*, SIAM J. Appl. Dyn. Syst. **14** (2015), no. 2, 980–1017, DOI 10.1137/140993934. MR3355763

[16] Eduardo Liz and Paweł Pilarczyk, *Global dynamics in a stage-structured discrete-time population model with harvesting*, J. Theoret. Biol. **297** (2012), 148–165, DOI 10.1016/j.jtbi.2011.12.012. MR2899025

[17] Konstantin Mischaikow, *Topological techniques for efficient rigorous computation in dynamics*, Acta Numer. **11** (2002), 435–477, DOI 10.1017/S0962492902000065. MR2009377

[18] Konstantin Mischaikow and Marian Mrozek, *Conley index*, Handbook of dynamical systems, Vol. 2, North-Holland, Amsterdam, 2002, pp. 393–460, DOI 10.1016/S1874-575X(02)80030-3. MR1901060

[19] Tomoyuki Miyaji, Paweł Pilarczyk, Marcio Gameiro, Hiroshi Kokubu, and Konstantin Mischaikow, *A study of rigorous ODE integrators for multi-scale set-oriented computations*, Appl. Numer. Math. **107** (2016), 34–47, DOI 10.1016/j.apnum.2016.04.005. MR3504856

[20] Marian Mrozek, *An algorithm approach to the Conley index theory*, J. Dynam. Differential Equations **11** (1999), no. 4, 711–734, DOI 10.1023/A:1022615629693. MR1725408

[21] Jacob Palis and Floris Takens, *Hyperbolicity and sensitive chaotic dynamics at homoclinic bifurcations*, Cambridge Studies in Advanced Mathematics, vol. 35, Cambridge University Press, Cambridge, 1993. Fractal dimensions and infinitely many attractors. MR1237641

[22] Joel W. Robbin and Dietmar Salamon, *Dynamical systems, shape theory and the Conley index*, Ergodic Theory Dynam. Systems **8*** (1988), no. Charles Conley Memorial Issue, 375–393, DOI 10.1017/S0143385700009494. MR967645

[23] Robert Tarjan, *Depth-first search and linear graph algorithms*, SIAM J. Comput. **1** (1972), no. 2, 146–160, DOI 10.1137/0201010. MR0304178

[24] John J. Tyson and Bella Novak, *Chapter 14 - irreversible transitions, bistability and checkpoint controls in the eukaryotic cell cycle: A systems-level understanding*, Handbook of Systems Biology (A.J. Marian WalhoutMarc VidalJob Dekker, ed.), Academic Press, San Diego, 2013, pp. 265 – 285.

[25] Jan Bouwe van den Berg and Jean-Philippe Lessard, *Rigorous numerics in dynamics*, Notices Amer. Math. Soc. **62** (2015), no. 9, 1057–1061, DOI 10.1090/noti1276. MR3444942

[26] Russell C. Walker, *The Stone-Čech compactification*, Springer-Verlag, New York-Berlin, 1974. Ergebnisse der Mathematik und ihrer Grenzgebiete, Band 83. MR0380698

Department of Mathematics, Hill Center Busch Campus, Rutgers, The State University of New Jersey, Piscataway, NJ 08854-8019, USA

Email address: mischaik@math.rutgers.edu

SELECTED PUBLISHED TITLES IN THIS SERIES

74 **Jan Bouwe van den Berg and Jean-Philippe Lessard, Editors,** Rigorous Numerics in Dynamics, 2018

73 **Kasso A. Okoudjou, Editor,** Finite Frame Theory, 2016

72 **Van H. Vu, Editor,** Modern Aspects of Random Matrix Theory, 2014

71 **Samson Abramsky and Michael Mislove, Editors,** Mathematical Foundations of Information Flow, 2012

70 **Afra Zomorodian, Editor,** Advances in Applied and Computational Topology, 2012

69 **Karl Sigmund, Editor,** Evolutionary Game Dynamics, 2011

68 **Samuel J. Lomonaco, Jr., Editor,** Quantum Information Science and Its Contributions to Mathematics, 2010

67 **Eitan Tadmor, Jian-Guo Liu, and Athanasios E. Tzavaras, Editors,** Hyperbolic Problems: Theory, Numerics and Applications, 2009

66 **Dorothy Buck and Erica Flapan, Editors,** Applications of Knot Theory, 2009

65 **L. L. Bonilla, A. Carpio, J. M. Vega, and S. Venakides, Editors,** Recent Advances in Nonlinear Partial Differential Equations and Applications, 2007

64 **Reinhard C. Laubenbacher, Editor,** Modeling and Simulation of Biological Networks, 2007

63 **Gestur Ólafsson and Eric Todd Quinto, Editors,** The Radon Transform, Inverse Problems, and Tomography, 2006

62 **Paul Garrett and Daniel Lieman, Editors,** Public-Key Cryptography, 2005

61 **Serkan Hoşten, Jon Lee, and Rekha R. Thomas, Editors,** Trends in Optimization, 2004

60 **Susan G. Williams, Editor,** Symbolic Dynamics and its Applications, 2004

59 **James Sneyd, Editor,** An Introduction to Mathematical Modeling in Physiology, Cell Biology, and Immunology, 2002

58 **Samuel J. Lomonaco, Jr., Editor,** Quantum Computation, 2002

57 **David C. Heath and Glen Swindle, Editors,** Introduction to Mathematical Finance, 1999

56 **Jane Cronin and Robert E. O'Malley, Jr., Editors,** Analyzing Multiscale Phenomena Using Singular Perturbation Methods, 1999

55 **Frederick Hoffman, Editor,** Mathematical Aspects of Artificial Intelligence, 1998

54 **Renato Spigler and Stephanos Venakides, Editors,** Recent Advances in Partial Differential Equations, Venice 1996, 1998

53 **David A. Cox and Bernd Sturmfels, Editors,** Applications of Computational Algebraic Geometry, 1998

52 **V. Mandrekar and P. R.Masani, Editors,** Proceedings of the Norbert Wiener Centenary Congress, 1994, 1997

51 **Louis H. Kauffman, Editor,** The Interface of Knots and Physics, 1996

50 **Robert Calderbank, Editor,** Different Aspects of Coding Theory, 1995

49 **Robert L. Devaney, Editor,** Complex Dynamical Systems: The Mathematics Behind the Mandelbrot and Julia Sets, 1994

48 **Walter Gautschi, Editor,** Mathematics of Computation 1943–1993: A Half-Century of Computational Mathematics, 1995

47 **Ingrid Daubechies, Editor,** Different Perspectives on Wavelets, 1993

46 **Stefan A. Burr, Editor,** The Unreasonable Effectiveness of Number Theory, 1992

45 **De Witt L. Sumners, Editor,** New Scientific Applications of Geometry and Topology, 1992

For a complete list of titles in this series, visit the
AMS Bookstore at **www.ams.org/bookstore/psapmseries/**.

ISBN 978-1-4704-2814-3
9 781470 428143
PSAPM/74